Lecture Notes in Computer Science 15674

Founding Editors

Gerhard Goos
Juris Hartmanis

AF147155

Editorial Board Members

Elisa Bertino, *Purdue University, West Lafayette, IN, USA*
Wen Gao, *Peking University, Beijing, China*
Bernhard Steffen , *TU Dortmund University, Dortmund, Germany*
Moti Yung , *Columbia University, New York, NY, USA*

The series Lecture Notes in Computer Science (LNCS), including its subseries Lecture Notes in Artificial Intelligence (LNAI) and Lecture Notes in Bioinformatics (LNBI), has established itself as a medium for the publication of new developments in computer science and information technology research, teaching, and education.

LNCS enjoys close cooperation with the computer science R & D community, the series counts many renowned academics among its volume editors and paper authors, and collaborates with prestigious societies. Its mission is to serve this international community by providing an invaluable service, mainly focused on the publication of conference and workshop proceedings and postproceedings. LNCS commenced publication in 1973.

Tibor Jager · Jiaxin Pan
Editors

Public-Key Cryptography – PKC 2025

28th IACR International Conference
on Practice and Theory of Public-Key Cryptography
Røros, Norway, May 12–15, 2025
Proceedings, Part I

 Springer

Editors
Tibor Jager 🆔
University of Wuppertal
Wuppertal, Germany

Jiaxin Pan 🆔
University of Kassel
Kassel, Germany

ISSN 0302-9743   ISSN 1611-3349 (electronic)
Lecture Notes in Computer Science
ISBN 978-3-031-91819-3   ISBN 978-3-031-91820-9 (eBook)
https://doi.org/10.1007/978-3-031-91820-9

© International Association for Cryptologic Research 2025

This work is subject to copyright. All rights are solely and exclusively licensed by the Publisher, whether the whole or part of the material is concerned, specifically the rights of translation, reprinting, reuse of illustrations, recitation, broadcasting, reproduction on microfilms or in any other physical way, and transmission or information storage and retrieval, electronic adaptation, computer software, or by similar or dissimilar methodology now known or hereafter developed.
The use of general descriptive names, registered names, trademarks, service marks, etc. in this publication does not imply, even in the absence of a specific statement, that such names are exempt from the relevant protective laws and regulations and therefore free for general use.
The publisher, the authors and the editors are safe to assume that the advice and information in this book are believed to be true and accurate at the date of publication. Neither the publisher nor the authors or the editors give a warranty, expressed or implied, with respect to the material contained herein or for any errors or omissions that may have been made. The publisher remains neutral with regard to jurisdictional claims in published maps and institutional affiliations.

This Springer imprint is published by the registered company Springer Nature Switzerland AG
The registered company address is: Gewerbestrasse 11, 6330 Cham, Switzerland

If disposing of this product, please recycle the paper.

Preface

The 28th International Conference on Practice and Theory of Public-Key Cryptography (PKC 2025) was held in Røros, Norway, on May 12–15, 2025. It was sponsored by the International Association for Cryptologic Research (IACR) and is the main IACR-sponsored conference with an explicit focus on public-key cryptography. PKC 2025 authors from many different countries brought a vibrant international community of cryptography researchers to Norway.

The conference received 199 submissions, reviewed by the program committee of 74 experts (including five area chairs) working with 170 external reviewers. The selection process took about two months for independent reviewing and another two months for discussion. During the discussion phase, the program chairs facilitated interactions between authors and reviewers by contacting authors to address critical questions that arose, ensuring informed decision-making. The program committee selected 60 papers to appear in PKC 2025. Among them four papers were soft-merged, namely, their final proceedings versions were fully included, but they resulted in two longer talks at the conference. Papers were reviewed in the usual double-blind fashion with an average of about three reviews per paper. Program committee members were limited to three submissions (four if two of them are with students), and their submissions were scrutinized more closely. The two program chairs were not allowed to submit any paper.

The Program Committee also selected one best paper: *PRISM: Simple And Compact Identification and Signatures From Large Prime Degree Isogenies* by Andrea Basso, Giacomo Borin, Wouter Castryck, Maria Corte-Real Santos, Riccardo Invernizzi, Antonin Leroux, Luciano Maino, Frederik Vercauteren, and Benjamin Wesolowski.

The Test of Time Award committee (Masayuki Abe, Aggelos Kiayias, Qiang Tang, Jiaxin Pan, and Edoardo Persichetti) chose the winner of the PKC Test of Time Award for 2025.

PKC is a remarkable undertaking, and it can only be possible through the hard work and significant contributions of many individuals:

- We would like to thank Bor de Kock (TNO, the Netherlands), Tjerand Silde (Norwegian University of Science and Technology, Norway) and the team at the Norwegian University of Science and Technology for making the general arrangements such a success.
- We would like to express our sincere gratitude to all the authors for their trust in us and giving us the opportunity to consider their work.
- We also thank the Program Committee, external reviewers, session chairs, invited speaker, and presenters for their enormous work and contributions to the success of PKC 2025.
- Special thanks to the area chairs: Mihir Bellare, Alexander May, Miyako Ohkubo, Claudio Orlandi, and Stefano Tessaro. Their specialist knowledge and good judgement were critical for making good decisions.

We hope that you enjoyed the conference and the warm welcome in Røros.
Takk skal du ha!

May 2025   Tibor Jager
                                                                           Jiaxin Pan

Organization

General Chairs

Bor de Kock   TNO, the Netherlands
Tjerand Silde   Norwegian University of Science and Technology,
                             Norway

Program Committee Chairs

Tibor Jager   University of Wuppertal, Germany
Jiaxin Pan   University of Kassel, Germany & NTNU, Norway

Steering Committee

Masayuki Abe   NTT, Japan
Shi Bai   Florida Atlantic University, USA
Jung Hee Cheon   Seoul National University, South Korea
Yvo Desmedt   University of Texas at Dallas, USA
Goichiro Hanaoka   National Institute of Advanced Industrial Science
                             and Technology, Japan
Tibor Jager   University of Wuppertal, Germany
Aggelos Kiayias   University of Edinburgh, UK
Tanja Lange   Eindhoven University of Technology, the
                             Netherlands
Jiaxin Pan   University of Kassel, Germany & NTNU, Norway
Edoardo Persichetti   Florida Atlantic University, USA
Duong Hieu Phan   Télécom Paris, Institut Polytechnique de Paris,
                             France
Yu Yu   Shanghai Jiao Tong University, China
Moti Yung (Secretary)   Google Inc. and Columbia University, USA
Yuliang Zheng (Chair)   University of Alabama at Birmingham, USA

Program Committee

Navid Alamati	VISA Research, USA
Nuttapong Attrapadung	AIST, Japan
Benedikt Auerbach	PQShield, Austria
Shi Bai	Florida Atlantic University, USA
Mihir Bellare	University of California San Diego, USA
Olivier Blazy	École Polytechnique, France
Wouter Castryck	KU Leuven, Belgium
Sofía Celi	Brave, Portugal
Melissa Chase	Microsoft, USA
Rongmao Chen	National University of Defense Technology, China
Yu Chen	Shandong University, China
Liqun Chen	University of Surrey, UK
Sherman S. M. Chow	Chinese University of Hong Kong, China
Daniel Collins	Purdue University, USA
Gareth T. Davies	NXP Semiconductors Belgium, Belgium
Hannah Davis	Seagate Technology, USA
Thomas Debris-Alazard	Inria and Laboratoire d'Informatique de l'École Polytechnique, France
Benjamin Dowling	King's College London, UK
Rafael Dowsley	Monash University, Australia
Léo Ducas	Centrum Wiskunde & Informatica and Leiden University, Netherlands
Nico Döttling	CISPA, Germany
Nils Fleischhacker	Ruhr University Bochum, Germany
Steven Galbraith	University of Auckland, New Zealand
Kristian Gjøsteen	NTNU - Norwegian University of Science and Technology, Norway
Aurore Guillevic	Centre Inria de l'Université de Rennes, France
Fuchun Guo	University of Wollongong, Australia
Shuai Han	Shanghai Jiao Tong University, China
Lucjan Hanzlik	CISPA Helmholtz Center for Information Security, Germany
Hans Heum	NTNU, Norway
Kathrin Hövelmanns	Eindhoven University of Technology, Netherlands
Miran Kim	Hanyang University, South Korea
Lisa Kohl	CWI, Netherlands
Veronika Kuchta	Florida Atlantic University, USA
Sabrina Kunzweiler	Inria and IMB France, France

Peter Kutas	Eötvös Loránd University, Hungary and University of Birmingham, UK
Russell W. F. Lai	Aalto University, Finland
Tanja Lange	Eindhoven University of Technology, Netherlands
Xiangyu Liu	Purdue University and Georgia Institute of Technology, USA
Eleftheria Makri	Leiden University, Netherlands
Mark Manulis	Universität der Bundeswehr München, Germany
Varun Maram	SandboxAQ, UK
Alexander May	Ruhr University Bochum, Germany
Adam O'Neill	University of Massachusetts Amherst, USA
Miyako Ohkubo	NICT, Japan
Cristina Onete	Université de Limoges/XLIM/CNRS, France
Claudio Orlandi	Aarhus University, Denmark
Omkant Pandey	Stony Brook University, USA
Krzysztof Pietrzak	Institute of Science and Technology Austria, Austria
Bertram Poettering	IBM Research Zurich, Switzerland
Sebastian Ramacher	AIT Austrian Institute of Technology, Austria
Doreen Riepel	UC San Diego, USA
Guilherme Rito	Ruhr-Universität Bochum, Germany
Andy Rupp	University of Luxembourg, Luxembourg and KASTEL Security Research Labs, Germany
Paul Rösler	FAU Erlangen-Nürnberg, Germany
Amin Sakzad	Monash University, Australia
Dominique Schröder	TU Wien, Austria
Jacob Schuldt	AIST, Japan
Rebecca Schwerdt	Karlsruhe Institute of Technology, Germany
Sven Schäge	TU Eindhoven, Netherlands
Yannick Seurin	Ledger, France
Daniel Slamanig	Universität der Bundeswehr München, Germany
Yongsoo Song	Seoul National University, South Korea
Vanessa Teague	Thinking Cybersecurity Pty Ltd., Democracy Developers Ltd., and Australian National University, Australia
Stefano Tessaro	University of Washington, USA
Daniele Venturi	Sapienza University of Rome, Italy
Benedikt Wagner	Ethereum Foundation, Germany
Weiqiang Wen	Télécom Paris, France
Thom Wiggers	PQShield, Netherlands
David Wu	UT Austin, USA
Keita Xagawa	Technology Innovation Institute, United Arab Emirates

Yu Yu	Shanghai Jiao Tong University, China
Runzhi Zeng	University of Kassel, Germany

Additional Reviewers

Eduardo Soria-Vazquez	Jonathan Eriksen
Behzad Abdolmaleki	Sebastian Faller
Ojaswi Acharya	Valerie Fetzer
Amit Agarwal	Mariana Gama
Zhiyuan An	Daniel Gardham
Melissa Azouaoui	Rachit Garg
Renas Bacho	Konstantin Gegier
Ruben Baecker	Paul Gerhart
Mirza Ahad Baig	Suparno Ghoshal
David Balbás	Oskar Goldhahn
Shalini Banerjee	Dov Gordon
Slim Bettaieb	Lénaïck Gouriou
Pedro Branco	Rishab Goyal
Pierre Briaud	Antonio Guimarães
Kevin Carrier	Máté Gyarmati
André Chailloux	Jinguang Han
Suvradip Chakraborty	Keisuke Hara
Jeffrey Champion	Raphael Heitjohann
Rohit Chatterjee	Aymeric Hiltenbrand
Yuanmi Chen	Charlotte Hoffmann
Yuanmi Chen	Janik Huth
Hao Chen	Hansraj Jangir
Jie Chen	Jonas Janneck
Bohang Chen	Mingming Jiang
Mingjie Chen	Andes Y. L. Kei
Wonseok Choi	Paul Kirchner
Arka Rai Choudhuri	Sreehari Kollath
Valerio Cini	Dmitrii Koshelev
Anamaria Costache	Sulani Kottal Baddhe Vidhanalage
Jolijn Cottaar	Stephan Krenn
Miguel Cueto Noval	Mukul Kulkarni
Daniel De Almeida Braga	Naman Kumar
Thomas Decru	Akshaya Kumar
Julien Devevey	Yi-Fu Lai
Minglang Dong	Roman Langrehr
Catalin Dragan	Jason LeGrow
Jesko Dujmovic	Chen Li
Youssef El Housni	Hao Lin
Nada El Kassem	Chen-Da Liu-Zhang

George Lu
Lin Lyu
You Lyu
Jack P. K. Ma
Laurane Marco
Damien Marion
Takahiro Matsuda
Jonas Meers
Matthias Meijers
Long Meng
Omid Mir
Alice Murphy
Anne Müller
Hugo Nartz
Shafik Nassar
Chris Newton
Lucien K. L. Ng
Tran Ngo
Jérôme Nguyen
Khoa Nguyen
Aysan Nishaburi
Kazuma Ohara
Michał Osadnik
Tapas Pal
Ying-yu Pan
Lorenz Panny
Alex Pellegrini
Alice Pellet–Mary
Paola Perthuis (de)
Rafael del Pino
Antigoni Polychroniadou
Thomas Prest
Ludo Pulles
Chen Qian
Rahul Rachuri
Mahesh Rajasree
Rishabh Ranjan
Fabian Regen
Michael Reichle
Pascal Reisert
Krijn Reijnders
Silvia Ritsch
Yusuke Sakai
Caroline Sandsbråten
Rahul Satish
Sina Schaeffler

Markus Schoenauer
Michael Scott
Nicolas Sendrier
Istvan Andras Seres
Sacha Servan-Schreiber
Laura Shea
Yixin Shen
Xuanyu Shi
Mark Simkin
Jaspal Singh
Christopher Smith
Garbiele Spini
Patrick Struck
Shuang Sun
Kaoru Takemure
Yuhao Tang
Lea Thiemt
Yangguang Tian
Marcel Tiepelt
Junichi Tomida
Kazunari Tozawa
Filip Trenkic
Monika Trimoska
Binbin Tu
Marloes Venema
Fernando Virdia
Yu Wang
Yalan Wang
Xiaoyang Wei
Bhagya Wimalasiri
Harry W. H. Wong
Ivy K. Y. Woo
Tiancheng Xie
Anshu Yadav
Shota Yamada
Yingfei Yan
Naoto Yanai
Yang Yang
Hongxu Yi
William Youmans
Min Zhang
Yunxiao Zhou
Yu Zhou
Paola de Perthuis
Aron van Baarsen
Morten Øygarden

Contents – Part I

Proofs and Arguments

MPC and Friends

Non-Interactive Distributed Point Functions

Elette Boyle[1,3] , Lalita Devadas[2] , and Sacha Servan-Schreiber[2(✉)]

[1] Reichman University, Herzliya, Israel
eboyle@alum.mit.edu
[2] Massachusetts Institute of Technology, Cambridge, USA
{lali,3s}@mit.edu
[3] NTT Research, Sunnyvale, USA

Abstract. Distributed point functions (DPFs) are a useful cryptographic primitive enabling a dealer to distribute short keys to two parties, such that the keys encode additive secret shares of a secret point function. However, in many applications of DPFs, no single dealer entity has full knowledge of the secret point function, necessitating the parties to run an interactive protocol to emulate the setup. Prior works have aimed to minimize complexity metrics of such distributed setup protocols, e.g., *round complexity*, while remaining black-box in the underlying cryptography.

We construct *non-interactive* DPFs (NIDPF), which have a one-round (*simultaneous-message*, semi-honest) setup protocol, removing the need for a trusted dealer. Specifically, our construction allows each party to publish a special "public key" to a public channel or bulletin board, where the public key encodes the party's secret function parameters. Using the public key of another party, any pair of parties can *locally* derive a DPF key for the point function described by the two parties' joint parameter choices.

We realize NIDPF from an array of standard assumptions, including DCR, SXDH, QR, and LWE. Each party's public key is of size $O(N^{2/3})$, for point functions with a domain of size N, which leads to a sublinear communication setup protocol. The only prior approach to realizing such a non-interactive setup required using multi-key fully homomorphic encryption or indistinguishability obfuscation.

As immediate applications of our construction, we obtain "public-key setup" protocols for several existing constructions of pseudorandom correlation generators and round-efficient protocols for secure comparisons.

1 Introduction

A point function, denoted by $P_{i,v}$, is a function that evaluates to a message v on input i, and evaluates to zero on all other inputs $j \neq i$ in its domain. A distributed point function (DPF) [17,36] allows a trusted dealer to distribute short keys to two parties, where the keys jointly encode a point function $P_{i,v}$ for parameters (i, v) chosen by the dealer. Individually, a DPF key does not reveal

© International Association for Cryptologic Research 2025
T. Jager and J. Pan (Eds.): PKC 2025, LNCS 15674, pp. 3–35, 2025.
https://doi.org/10.1007/978-3-031-91820-9_1

any information about the secret index i or message v to the party. However, using their key, each party can locally "evaluate" the point function on a public input x, to obtain an additive *secret share* of $y := P_{i,v}(x)$.

DPFs are the backbone of many useful primitives and protocols relating to multi-party computation (MPC). In particular, DPFs enable communication-efficient generation of correlated randomness in MPC protocols [3,5,9–14,45,51], can be used to instantiate distributed oblivious RAM [35,47], privacy-preserving machine learning [38,44,52], private database queries [30,31,46,49] and analytics [7,39,40,42], and mixed-mode secure computation [8,20].

However, in many of these applications, there is no trusted dealer that can generate and distribute the DPF keys to the parties. Instead, the trusted dealer is emulated by the parties via a distributed key generation protocol [21,35,47,48], which the parties invoke to obtain their respective DPF keys. More concretely, in a distributed generation protocol, each party holds a *secret share* of the parameters (i, v). After invoking the protocol, the parties end up with DPF keys that correspond to the point function $P_{i,v}$, such that neither party learns the parameters (i, v) in the process.

Early approaches to distributed key generation simply used generic secure computation, resulting in protocols with at least two rounds of communication, while being non-black-box in the underlying cryptographic primitives. It was shown by Doerner and shelat [35] how to achieve black-box distributed two-party key generation with logarithmically many communication rounds. Later, the DPF construction of Boyle et al. [21] admitted a 5-round black-box protocol. In both approaches, the DPF key size was polylogarithmic in the domain size N. If one instead relaxes the key size, e.g., to $N^{1/2}$, these approaches can yield black-box distributed generation protocols with round complexity as low as two sequential calls to 1-out-of-$N^{1/2}$ oblivious transfer, resulting in a small constant number of rounds (e.g., four rounds when using two-round OT).

At first glance, it is tempting to think that lower-bounds from the MPC literature [37] would set the minimum number of rounds required for a distributed DPF generation protocol to two. However, upon closer inspection, we observe that because the parties obtain a *key* (which in some DPF constructions can even be distributed pseudorandomly [17,21]), a DPF generation protocol is *not* subjected to the two-round lower bound because each key can be efficiently simulated. In particular, we can hope to achieve a *non-interactive* generation protocol mimicking non-interactive key exchange protocols like Diffie–Hellman [32]. Indeed, spooky encryption [34] already gives such a protocol through the use of multi-key fully homomorphic encryption (FHE) or indistinguishability obfuscation ($i\mathcal{O}$). However, to date, this has been the *only* known approach to realizing a "non-interactive" protocol (a protocol where each party only needs to read the other party's public key to locally derive a joint DPF key).

1.1   Our Results

In this paper, we put forth and study the notion of a "non-interactive" DPF, and demonstrate constructions from new assumptions. This is motivated by the search for (round-efficient) protocols for eliminating the dealer, that do not require heavy tools like multi-key FHE, and can be instantiated from an array of standard assumptions.

Non-interactive DPFs. Our definition of a *non-interactive* DPF (NIDPF) enables two parties to locally (non-interactively) derive DPF keys by simply reading each other's public keys from a bulletin board. More generally, this model is captured by a one-round, simultaneous-message semi-honest protocol. A simultaneous-message communication pattern captures the interaction of non-interactive key exchange protocols like Diffie–Hellman: (1) two parties exchange messages simultaneously, then (2) each party can use the other party's message to locally derive a joint output (key). Such a model of communication is highly desirable because the first message can be reused (i.e., the message of the first party can be reused indefinitely with many different parties) and the parties do *not* need to be online at the same time to participate.

The problem of generating DPF keys in a simultaneous-message protocol is much more challenging compared to key exchange. This is due to the fact that a DPF setup requires the *total communication* between parties (i.e., the size of the public keys) to be sublinear in the domain of the point function. This requirement is generally challenging to achieve—indeed, the only way we currently know of achieving such succinctness is via multi-key FHE [34]. Moreover, this connection to "multi-key"-like primitives is inherent, as we remark on later.

Constructing NIDPF. Our primary contribution is to show that, perhaps surprisingly, we can rely on simple cryptography and assumptions to achieve the sublinearity requirements. In particular, inspired by the recent work of Abram, Roy, and Scholl [2], we show that we can realize NIDPF schemes "directly," without going through heavier primitives like multi-key FHE. A NIDPF scheme immediately implies non-interactive key exchange, and thus public-key encryption, which eliminates the possibility of using only lightweight symmetric-key cryptography (e.g., one-way functions). However, we are able to realize NIDPFs from many standard assumptions, including the decisional composite residuosity (DCR) assumption, symmetric external Diffie–Hellman (SXDH) assumption, quadratic residuosity (QR) assumption, the enhanced Diffie–Hellman (EDDH) assumption in class groups, and the learning with errors (LWE) assumption. We summarize our results in Table 1 and Theorem 1.

Theorem 1 (Informal). *Let N be a domain size. There exists a non-interactive DPF (NIDPF) with a key size $O(N^{2/3})$ and evaluation time $O(N^{5/3})$ under either (1) the DCR assumption, (2) the QR assumption, (3) the EDDH assumption and the uniformity assumption in class groups, (4) the SXDH assumption, or (5) the LWE assumption with a superpolynomial-modulus-to-noise ratio. Here, $O(\cdot)$ hides polynomial factors in the security parameter.*

As an independent contribution, we define a new abstraction that we call *non-interactive multiplication*, which captures all existing "non-interactive" primitives from a recent line of work. In particular, we identify a surprising (but

Table 1. Summary of our instantiations of NIDPF with domains of size N. Constants and polynomial factors (in the security parameter) are ignored in the asymptotic key size for readability. See Sect. 3 for details on the cryptographic assumptions used. *The SXDH-based construction only supports random payloads (output messages).

	Assumption	Transparent Setup	Key Size
[34,50]	LWE / $i\mathcal{O}$+DDH	✓	$\log(N)$
	LWE / RLWE	✓	$N^{2/3}$
This Work	DCR / QR	✗	$N^{2/3}$
	SXDH* / Class Groups+EDDH	✓	$N^{2/3}$

rather obvious in retrospect) connection between our abstraction and Homomorphic Secret Sharing (HSS). This connection results in constructions of "succinct *multi-key* HSS" (restricted to a special class of computations) from a variety of assumptions, including DDH, DCR, and the EDDH assumption in class groups. To the best of our knowledge, the only prior approaches for such non-interactive computation required using multi-key FHE techniques [34,50]. More concretely, our abstraction allows us to adapt the recent result of Abram et al. [2] constructing succinct (but not multi-key) HSS for "special RMS" programs into a multi-key (i.e., non-interactive), albeit restricted to a slightly weaker class of functions. Specifically, unlike with standard HSS, our construction does not require a correlated setup between parties and only requires a common reference string. Moreover, the additional succinctness property allows one party to have a large input x while maintaining that the input share is succinct in the size of x. We summarize this generalization of our techniques in Theorem 2 and provide more details in the full version of this work [16].

Theorem 2 (Informal). *Let* HSS *be an HSS scheme for the function class* $\mathcal{F}$ *and let* $\mathcal{P}$ *be the set of constant-degree polynomials. There exists a succinct, multi-key HSS scheme for computing functions of the form* $P(x, f(y))$, *where* $P \in \mathcal{P}$ *and* $f \in \mathcal{F}$, *one party has a (large) input* x, *and the other party has a (short) input* y. *Moreover, the total size of both parties' input shares is* $o(|x|) + O(|y|)$, *ignoring polynomial factors in the security parameter.*

1.2 Applications

We describe two immediate applications of our NIDPF construction. The primary application is replacing multi-round DPF setup protocols with a non-interactive "public key" setup. In particular, many applications of DPFs require two parties, each holding a secret share of an index $t \in [N]$, to generate DPF keys (through a secure setup protocol) that encode a point function parameterized by t. Concretely, Alice and Bob hold shares $t_A, t_B \in [N]$, such that $t_A + t_B = t$ mod N, jointly generate DPF keys for the point function $P_{t,1}$. (We assume additive secret sharing of the index t, following [5,21]; some protocols also consider bit-wise XOR secret shares of t, however, applications typically require working with additive secret sharing, e.g., [5,6,14].)

PCGs with a "Public-Key" Setup. Pseudorandom Correlation Generators (PCGs) [3,5,9–14,45] are a cryptographic primitive enabling parties to generate long pseudorandom correlations given access to short correlated seeds. In particular, to jointly generate long correlations, it suffices for parties to first execute a secure computation protocol to jointly sample the short PCG seeds, and then *locally* expand them into a large number of pseudorandom correlations. PCG constructions exist for a variety of correlations, including oblivious transfer (OT), vector olivious linear evaluation (VOLE), and Beaver triple correlations, and make heavy use of DPFs. Indeed, the dominant cost of the setup protocol for these constructions is jointly generating DPF keys [3,5,14,45].

Interestingly, a recent line of work [23,41] has shown that when it comes to OT/VOLE correlations specifically, the parties do not need to engage in the initial interactive setup protocol. Instead, two parties can non-interactively derive a pair of seeds that enables them to expand their correlations locally. Such PCGs are said to have a "public-key setup" protocol, which follows the same non-interactive communication pattern we motivated in Sect. 1. However, to date, the only such "public-key PCG" constructions that exist are for the OT/VOLE correlation [23,41]. It has remained an open problem to realize public-key PCGs for other correlation types (e.g., Beaver triple correlations), for which we have constructions of PCGs from a variety of standard assumptions but no corresponding public-key setup protocol.

By instantiating the DPF in existing PCG constructions (for further classes of correlations) with an NIDPF, it becomes possible to obtain a semi-honest "public-key setup" protocol for the PCG.

Mixed-Mode Secure Computation in One Round. Recent works on mixed-mode secure computation, beginning with the work of Boyle et al. [8], have demonstrated that the round and communication complexity of MPC protocols can be improved by using DPFs to help directly evaluate complex functions such as comparisons and equality of secret-shared values, without needing to express the computations as Boolean or arithmetic circuits.

For example, consider the case of securely computing secret shares of an equality predicate evaluated between a public threshold t and secret shared input x, in a two-party setting. The idea, at a high level, is to have a trusted dealer distribute DPF keys to two parties for the point function $P_{t+r,1}$ that evaluates to 1 on index $t + r$, where r is uniformly random in the domain. The dealer additionally distributes additive shares of r to the parties. The parties, holding additive shares of a value x (assumed to be in the domain of the point function), can publicly open the value $y := x + r$ by locally masking their shares of x with their shares of r and broadcasting the result. Then, observe that by evaluating the DPF on input y, the parties obtain shares of 1 if and only if $x + r = t + r$, which is the case if and only if $x = t$.

Because the DPF is "one-time-use" due to the masking term r, the efficiency gains obtained by such a protocol depend heavily on the efficiency of the DPF setup protocol used by the parties to emulate the dealer. However, when using a NIDPF to replace the dealer, the parties can *simultaneously*: (1) choose their own share $\langle r \rangle_\sigma$ of the random mask r, (2) broadcast their masked share $\langle x \rangle_\sigma + \langle r \rangle_\sigma$, and (3) generate and send their NIDPF key message for the point function $P_{t+r,1}$. This already enables the parties to locally compute additive shares of the t-equality predicate on x, yielding a *single (simultaneous) round* protocol for the equality predicate computation.

2   Technical Overview

In this section, we provide a detailed technical overview of our NIDPF construction. The main building block we use in our construction is a novel abstraction we call non-interactive multiplication (NIM), which we overview in Sect. 2.1, and which we view as a contribution of independent interest. In Sect. 2.2, we provide an overview of our NIDPF construction.

2.1   Building Block: Non-interactive Multiplication

At a high level, a NIM allows two parties, Alice and Bob, each holding a ring element as input, to obtain secret shares of the multiplication of their inputs by exchanging one message simultaneously (or posting their message to a public bulletin board). The NIM abstraction captures several primitives recently introduced in various contexts. In particular, NIM directly implies *non-interactive* variants of OT [4], VOLE [1,2,23,25,41], and inner-products [28], where parties obtain secret-shares of the computation by exchanging one message simultaneously.

The NIM abstraction also captures the case where Alice and Bob have *matrices* as inputs, and wish to compute secret shares of the matrix product. In particular, a NIM scheme for matrix multiplication allows Alice with a matrix $\mathbf{A}$ and Bob with a matrix $\mathbf{B}$ to compute additive secret shares of $\mathbf{AB}$. Surprisingly, a NIM scheme for matrix multiplication can have *sublinear communication* (in the size of one input matrix), using techniques developed in two recent works that build *succinct* VOLE [2,23]. This succinct NIM variant is the main building block we use in Sect. 5 to construct NIDPFs. We obtain the following instantiations of succinct NIM for matrix multiplication:

Theorem 3 (Informal; Implicit in [2,23]). *Let $\mathcal{R}$ be a ring and N, ℓ, m be integer parameters. For $\ell = N^{2/3}$ and $m = N^{1/3}$, there exists a succinct NIM scheme computing shares of $\mathbf{AB}$ with $O(N^{2/3})$ communication, for all matrices $\mathbf{A} \in \mathcal{R}^{\ell \times m}$ and $\mathbf{B} \in \mathcal{R}^{m \times m}$, if one of the following assumptions hold: (1) DCR, (2) QR, (3) an "enhanced" DDH assumption in class groups, (4) LWE with a superpolynomial modulus-to-noise ratio, or (5) SXDH in bilinear groups when the NIM output sharing is defined multiplicatively. In the above, $O(\cdot)$ hides polynomial factors in the security parameter.*

Our proof of Theorem 3 follows from ideas presented in the recent work of Abram et al. [2] in their construction of "succinct" Homomorphic Secret Sharing (HSS) [18] and a concurrent work of [23] constructing succinct non-interactive

VOLE. In particular, their constructions internally use the ability to multiply a matrix $\mathbf{A}$ by another matrix $\mathbf{B} := \Delta \cdot \mathbf{I}$ (where Δ is a scalar and $\mathbf{I}$ is the identity matrix), with sublinear communication in the size of $\mathbf{A}$. However, in both these works, the primary goal was constructing a non-interactive VOLE scheme. Non-interactive VOLE, in and of itself, neither implies NIDPFs nor succinct NIM for matrix multiplication, and is overall a weaker primitive. In this paper, we show that their constructions not only generalize to *any* matrix $\mathbf{B}$ (of appropriate size)—while still preserving sublinear communication—but also use it as a building block to construct NIDPFs in Sect. 5.

Comparison to HSS. While at first glance, it may appear as though using HSS would be sufficient to construct NIM, there are subtle yet important distinctions between these primitives which make them very different. Concretely, we show in Sect. 4 that our NIM abstraction implies a form of (2-party) *multi-key* HSS, in an analogous sense to multi-key FHE, which is a stronger primitive compared to standard HSS.

In particular, the NIM abstraction has a universal setup that consists of a common reference string used by everyone, which enables us to realize a truly "non-interactive" (or multi-key) primitive, eliminating the requirement for multi-round setup protocols. In contrast, HSS [15,18], including succinct HSS [2], requires a *trusted setup process* to distribute evaluation keys to each party before any computation can be performed, and the setup cannot be used in a computation involving other parties. In a network with many parties, each *pair* of parties needs to generate a unique pair of HSS evaluation keys and can only compute over inputs assigned to them, resulting in quadratic communication overheads. Compare this with *multi-key* HSS [26,50] or spooky encryption [34], where any pair of parties can compute a function "on the fly" over their joint inputs and *without* needing to perform a joint setup process ahead of time to do so. As such, we view our NIM abstraction as a potential stepping-stone to uncovering new constructions for efficient MPC. Indeed, in the full version [16], we generalize the ideas we use to realize our NIDPF constructions to realize a form of multi-key HSS for a restricted class of computations, which may prove to have additional applications.

2.2   Overview of the NIDPF Construction

A NIDPF consists of a generation algorithm Gen and evaluation algorithm Eval. We let $\mathcal{R}$ be a finite ring and the message space of the NIDPF. A party Alice, with point function parameters (t_A, v_A), uses Gen to generate a public key pk_A and a secret key sk_A. Bob does the same with (t_B, v_B). Then, using the public key of the other party in conjunction with their own secret key, Alice and Bob can locally derive a DPF key encoding the point function with parameters $(t_A + t_B, v_A + v_B)$. Importantly, the public keys generated by Alice and Bob need to be *short*—sublinear in the truth-table size of the point function.

Similarly to some other DPF constructions (and all non-generic DPF key generation protocols) [21,24,35], our construction of NIDPF is tailored to the "full-domain evaluation" regime, where the parties obtain the output of the point function evaluated on all inputs in the domain. We let N denote the domain size of the point function, and view the point function evaluation on the entire domain (i.e., for every $x \in [N]$) as being a one-hot vector $\mathbf{u} \in \mathcal{R}^N$, where $\mathbf{u}[t] = 1$ and t is the special index.

For suitable choices of N, we can represent $x \in [N]$ by (i, j) where $i = x$ (mod ℓ) and $j = x$ (mod m) for some coprime integers $\ell, m \in [N]$ such that $N = \ell \cdot m$. Such a mapping (à la Chinese Remainder Theorem) allows us to interpret the length-N vector $\mathbf{u}$ as a $\ell \times m$ matrix, while still preserving arithmetic modulo N via the residue number system. This places a restriction on N, which ideally we would like to avoid. In Sect. 5.1, we sketch an alternative approach that works for arbitrary (non-coprime) integers ℓ, m, but has a 2× cost in efficiency.

At a high level, our approach to realizing our NIDPF construction is the following. Assume that Alice parses her index $t_A \in [N]$ as $t_A = (i_A, j_A) \in [\ell] \times [m]$ and Bob parses his index t_B as $(i_B, j_B) \in [\ell] \times [m]$. The goal is to have Alice and Bob derive secret shares of the $\ell \times m$ matrix, where the $(i_A + i_B, j_A + j_B)$-th entry is non-zero. In particular, note that this matrix will be reinterpreted as the unit vector $\mathbf{u}$ with non-zero coordinate $t = t_A + t_B \in [N]$, where $t = i_A + i_B$ (mod ℓ) and $t = j_A + j_B$ (mod m). This is equivalent to the full-domain evaluation of the point function $P_{t,1}$.[1]

Our construction achieves this in two steps, which we overview next.

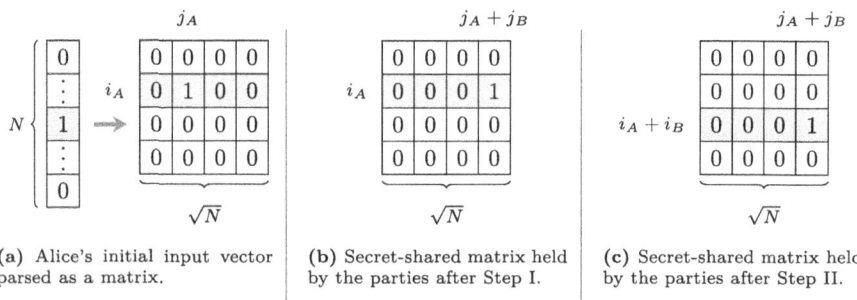

(a) Alice's initial input vector parsed as a matrix.

(b) Secret-shared matrix held by the parties after Step I.

(c) Secret-shared matrix held by the parties after Step II.

Fig. 1. Running example used in the overview of the NIDPF construction. The matrix represents the full evaluation of the point function with a domain of size N, where the parameters ℓ, m (as defined in Definition 9) are $\ell = m = \sqrt{N}$, for simplicity.

Step I: Shifting the Columns Using NIM. Alice begins by defining a $\ell \times m$ matrix $\mathbf{A}$ with 1 at entry (i_A, j_A) and zeros elsewhere. This is illustrated for the case where $\ell = m = \sqrt{N}$ in Fig. 1a. Then, the main idea is to obliviously "shift" this matrix by Bob's input (i_B, j_B).

---

[1] For now, we assume that the point function outputs $v = 1$ at the special index i and later generalize to arbitrary outputs.

First, we observe that we can perform one dimension of this shift using a matrix multiplication: Bob defines the $m \times m$ *cyclic shift* matrix $\mathbf{S}_{j_B}$ that shifts each column of $\mathbf{A}$ cyclically to the right by j_B (wrapping around modulo m). Using NIM, Alice and Bob can non-interactively compute shares of the matrix $\mathbf{A}\mathbf{S}_{j_B}$. Note that $\mathbf{A}\mathbf{S}_{j_B}$ is a matrix where the only non-zero entry is located at row i_A and column $j_A + j_B$. This is illustrated in Fig. 1b for our running example. By applying Theorem 3, we have that the communication between Alice and Bob in this process is *sublinear* in N. Moreover, by the security of the NIM scheme (see Sect. 4), Bob does not learn the value of (i_A, j_A) and Alice does not learn the value of j_B.

Finally, by interpreting the resulting shares back to a vector $\mathbf{y}$, the parties obtain secret shares corresponding to the full-evaluation of the point function $P_{i_A \cdot m + j_A + j_B, 1}$. Unfortunately, this is not quite what we want, since our goal is for the parties to obtain shares of the full-evaluation corresponding to the point function $P_{(i_A + i_B) \cdot m + j_A + j_B, 1} \equiv P_{t_A + t_B, 1}$. In particular, notice that following the cyclic shift, Alice still knows which *row* of the resulting matrix contains the non-zero index, since the row index does not currently depend on Bob's input i_B. To remedy this, we need a way for Bob to cyclically shift the rows of the resulting secret-shared matrix by his secret index i_B, which ideally could be done by multiplying the result with another "shift matrix" parameterized by i_B.

Sadly, multiplying by another shift matrix is not possible, since this would require a "NIM" for the degree-3 computation $\mathbf{S}_{i_B}(\mathbf{A}\mathbf{S}_{j_B})$, where $\mathbf{S}_{j_B}$ cyclically shifts the columns of $\mathbf{A}$ by j_B and $\mathbf{S}_{i_B}$ cyclically shifts the rows by i_B. We do not know how to realize such a primitive for degree-3 computations (*even if we sacrifice the succinctness requirement*) without going through "high-end" tools like multi-key FHE [34].

However, we show that Bob can cyclically shift the rows using degree-2, secret-key HSS (the weakest form of non-trivial HSS [18], which can be instantiated from a wide range of assumptions). In particular, our usage of HSS to let Bob cyclically shift the rows is only possible *after* computing the NIM to cyclically shift the columns, as will become apparent later. We stress that secret-key HSS alone cannot be used to directly build NIDPFs—for one, the NIDPF abstraction directly implies public key encryption, while secret-key HSS (even for higher degree computations) does not [29].

Step II: Shifting the Rows with Degree-2 HSS. Our idea is to compose degree-2 HSS with NIM to allow Bob to obliviously cyclically shift the rows *and* columns of Alice's matrix $\mathbf{A}$. This composition with HSS is inspired by the multi-party DPF construction of Abram et al. [2], where they use HSS to obliviously select an appropriate cyclic shift of a one-hot vector by computing an inner product with all possible shifts. However, to apply this idea to the non-interactive setting, there are several challenges we need to overcome.

The first challenge is that HSS schemes, even for degree-2 functions, require a *trusted setup process*, which would prevent us from getting a non-interactive solution (the parties would need to engage in a multi-round setup protocol).

The second challenge is that HSS does not enable computing degree-2 functions on additive secret shares. Instead, typical HSS schemes (following [18]) require parties to have "memory shares" and "input shares" of the secret values in order to perform computations over them. In particular, degree-2 HSS allows two parties to locally compute an additive sharing of xy from an input share of a value x and memory share of a value y. At a very high level, an input share of a message $x \in \mathcal{R}$ is just an encryption of x; and memory shares of a message $y \in \mathcal{R}$ are additive shares of the tuple $(x, x \cdot \mathsf{sk})$, where $\mathsf{sk} \in \mathcal{R}^k$ is the secret key used to encrypt the input share (see Sect. 3.5 for additional background).

If the parties can somehow obtain memory shares of $\mathbf{AS}_{j_B}$ and input shares of an input provided by Bob, then using HSS for computing degree-2 functions, we have the following solution for cyclically shifting the rows. First, Bob defines the one-hot vector $\mathbf{e}_{i_B}$ representing his row index i_B and sends HSS input shares of $\mathbf{e}_{i_B}$ to Alice. Let $\mathbf{T} := \mathbf{AS}_{j_B}$ which, for now, we assume Alice and Bob hold memory shares of at the end of Step I. Then, the parties locally define the list of ℓ "shifted" matrices $\mathbf{T}_1, \ldots, \mathbf{T}_\ell$, such that $\mathbf{T}_i$ is the matrix $\mathbf{T}$ with the rows cyclically shifted down by i. Finally, using HSS, the parties compute the following degree-2 equation to "obliviously select" $\mathbf{T}_{i_B}$:

$$\langle \mathbf{e}_{i_B}, (\mathbf{T}_1, \ldots, \mathbf{T}_\ell) \rangle = \mathbf{T}_{i_B}. \tag{1}$$

Observe that this allows Alice and Bob to compute shares of the one-hot matrix with a non-zero entry at index $(i_A + i_B, j_A + j_B)$, as required. A similar idea underpins the multi-party DPF construction of Abram et al. [2]. However, their requirement for a trusted setup makes their approach for obtaining the necessary compatible input and memory shares inherently interactive. We make use of the following two ideas to avoid interaction:

Idea I: Bob Generates the HSS Setup. To avoid needing a trusted setup, we exploit the fact that Bob knows the full input $\mathbf{e}_{i_B}$, which means that he can act as the trusted dealer to generate the HSS setup in our case. Moreover, we observe that *secret-key* HSS suffices, since only Bob needs to encrypt his input $\mathbf{e}_{i_B}$. This allows us to use the most basic form of HSS, making it easy to instantiate from many standard assumptions, including a novel instantiation we present in Sect. 5.3.1 from the SXDH assumption in bilinear groups.

Idea II: NIM Outputs Memory Shares. To make the output of the NIM compatible with HSS, we need a way for Alice and Bob to obtain memory shares of the matrix $\mathbf{T}$ rather than additive shares. To achieve this, we use the following trick from prior work [2,27] to generate memory shares. Observe that if Bob multiplies his cyclic shift matrix $\mathbf{S}_{j_B}$ by any scalar $c \in \mathcal{R}$, the output of the NIM will be an additive share of $c \cdot \mathbf{AS}_{j_B}$. This can be generalized to computing $\mathsf{sk} \otimes \mathbf{AS}_{j_B}$ in the natural way. Then, the idea is to have Alice and Bob engage in two copies of the NIM protocol simultaneously. In both cases Alice inputs $\mathbf{A}$. Bob, on the other hand, inputs the cyclic shift matrix $\mathbf{S}_{j_B}$ in one instance, and the scaled matrix $\mathsf{sk} \otimes \mathbf{S}_{j_B}$ in the other. Together, the NIM outputs produce an HSS memory share of $\mathbf{AS}_{j_B}$ under Bob's secret key. In parallel to this, Bob generates an HSS input share for his vector $\mathbf{e}_{i_B}$ and an evaluation key ek_A, which he sends to Alice. Then, using HSS, Alice and Bob compute shares of the inner product from Eq. (1).

Examining the Communication Costs. The communication is dominated by the NIM encodings and the length of $\mathbf{e}_{i_B}$, which is $O(\ell)$ (ignoring $\mathsf{poly}(\lambda)$ factors). Thus, the total communication is $O(\ell + m^2)$, which is sublinear in the domain size N using Theorem 3. Moreover, because this whole protocol only requires one simultaneous exchange of information, Alice and Bob can simply post their messages in the form of a public key, which aligns with our design goals.

Arbitrary Payload. The above overview captures a NIDPF construction where the non-zero output (i.e., the payload) of the point function at the special index is the scalar $1 \in \mathcal{R}$. However, to satisfy a more general definition, we need to allow Alice and Bob to also jointly specify the payload v as the sum of their individual payloads v_A and v_B.

To achieve this, we observe that we can use the same "scaling trick" used by Bob to compute the product with his secret key sk to allow either Alice or Bob to specify v_A or v_B as the output. Specifically, it is enough for one of the parties (say Alice) to simply multiply their input matrix by v_σ before generating the NIM encoding. This enables a "half-chosen" variant of the NIDPF, where only one of the two parties is allowed to specify the (secret) payload.

To generalize this to the case where the output is message $v = v_A + v_B$ jointly defined by the two parties, the parties can engage in two instances of the half-chosen protocol, in parallel, and add the resulting shares together. We explain this further in Sect. 5.

2.2.1 Random-Payload NIDPF from SXDH

In some applications of DPFs, the payload can be *random* and only determined by the random coins of the generation algorithms.[2] Here, we overview a construction of such a NIDPF under the SXDH assumption in bilinear groups. In a nutshell, a bilinear group consists of a triple of cyclic groups: $\mathbb{G}_1$, $\mathbb{G}_2$, and $\mathbb{G}_T$ with an efficient map (pairing) $e : \mathbb{G}_1 \times \mathbb{G}_2 \to \mathbb{G}_T$. Let g_1, g_2, and g_T be generators for $\mathbb{G}_1$, $\mathbb{G}_2$, and $\mathbb{G}_T$, respectively. Then, for all g_1^x and g_2^y, it holds that $e(g_1^x, g_2^y) = g_T^{xy} \in \mathbb{G}_T$. This feature enables computing the multiplication "in the exponent" of the bilinear group.

Idea: Replacing Degree-2 HSS with a Pairing. The main idea behind our NIDPF construction in bilinear groups is to follow the template outlined in Sect. 2.2 but replace Step II with a "multiplication in the exponent" using the pairing. We first construct a special succinct NIM scheme from the DDH assumption (over any suitable cyclic group $\mathbb{G}$), which outputs the result of the matrix product "in the exponent" of the group $\mathbb{G}$, restricting the ring $\mathcal{R}$ to $\mathbb{Z}_p$. This variant of NIM is appealing since it allows us to use *any* DDH group $\mathbb{G}$ to

---

[2] Note that a secret sharing of the random payload can be derived non-interactively by each party summing all entries of its length-N DPF evaluation vector.

compute the matrix multiplication, but is limiting in that we cannot obtain the memory shares required for the HSS computation in Step II of Sect. 2.2. However, we observe that we don't need to do so if we have a pairing! Specifically, we can instead replace the HSS computation in Step II by computing the multiplication using the pairing, as sketched above.

More concretely, in our DDH-based succinct NIM variant, the parties obtain *multiplicative* shares $g^{\mathbf{R}_A}$ and $g^{\mathbf{R}_B}$, respectively, such that $g^{\mathbf{R}_A} \cdot g^{\mathbf{R}_B} = g^{\mathbf{AB}}$ (where the notation $g^{\mathbf{M}}$ denotes the matrix of group elements $g^{m_{ij}}$ for all entries $m_{ij} \in \mathbf{M}$). Therefore, by instantiating this NIM scheme in the group $\mathbb{G}_1$ of a bilinear group, the parties obtain multiplicative shares of $g_1^{\mathbf{T}}$, rather than additive shares of $\mathbf{T}$ (defined in Step II above). Nonetheless, the parties can still define multiplicative shares of the vectors $\mathbf{T}_1, \ldots, \mathbf{T}_\ell$ "in the exponent" of g_1, as before. Then, Bob can encrypt his one-hot vector $\mathbf{e}_{i_B}$ with the aim of selecting the appropriate $\mathbf{T}_{i_B}$. However, instead of using HSS to do so, Bob simply uses ElGamal encryption in the group $\mathbb{G}_2$ to compute:

$$(g_2^{r_j}, g_2^{e_{i_B,j}} h_2^{r_j}), \ \forall j \in [m],$$

where $h_2 := g_2^{\mathsf{sk}}$ is an ElGamal public key for an sk known to Bob, and each r_j is uniformly random. Since now we need DDH to hold in both $\mathbb{G}_1$ and $\mathbb{G}_2$, we must rely on the SXDH assumption.

Given these ciphertexts, Alice and Bob compute the inner product from Eq. (1) "in the exponent" using the pairing and obtain multiplicative shares of the inner product in $\mathbb{G}_T$:

$$g_T^{\langle \mathbf{e}_{i_B}, (\mathbf{T}_1, \ldots, \mathbf{T}_\ell) \rangle} = g_T^{\mathbf{T}_{i_B}}. \tag{2}$$

We can view this as replacing the HSS scheme used by Bob in the overview of Sect. 2.2 with a "multiplicative HSS" scheme from pairings: i.e., where the HSS outputs are multiplicatively, rather than additively, secret shared. However, as with the first scheme, Alice and Bob still need to compute "memory shares" for this multiplicative variant of HSS. Memory shares now take on the form $(g_1^{\mathbf{T}}, g_1^{\mathsf{sk}\cdot\mathbf{T}})$, which can be obtained by having Bob scale his matrix by sk.

Converting from Multiplicative to Additive Shares. Now the issue we face is the following. The result in Eq. (2) is a *multiplicative* sharing of the full-domain evaluation, which does not correspond to the desired additive shares we need for the NIDPF. To solve this problem, we need a way to "bring down" the exponent and convert it to additive shares. One way to achieve this would be using the Distributed Discrete Logarithm (DDLog) procedure [18].

Using the DDLog algorithm, Alice and Bob can derive additive shares of $\mathbf{T}_{i_B}$ by applying DDLog to each entry of $g_T^{\mathbf{T}_{i_B}}$. However, there is now a problem of *correctness* for the resulting output shares of the NIDPF. Specifically, DDLog has a $1/\mathsf{poly}(\lambda)$ error (in which case it outputs a uniformly random value in $\{0, 1, \ldots, M\}$), which would translate to a $1 - 1/\mathsf{poly}(\lambda)$ correctness for the output shares of the NIDPF. Having a (non-negligible) correctness error is undesirable, and prevents applying the resulting NIDPF in many contexts. We show how to sidestep this problem by making an important observation regarding use of the DDLog procedure, which we explain next.

Random Payload. Surprisingly, we show that the error can in fact be avoided entirely when constructing a NIDPF with a random payload (i.e., a NIDPF which outputs a random message at the special index). In particular, we observe that existing constructions of DDLog have *no error* when given multiplicative shares of the identity element g^0 [18,33]. Inspired by this observation, we show that we can obtain a NIDPF with random payloads. We observe that $\mathbf{T}_{i_B}$ is a one-hot matrix, and so has only one non-zero entry. By having the parties set their payload share to a uniformly random scalar, they can further ensure the non-zero value of $\mathbf{T}_{i_B}$ has high (pseudo)entropy to both parties. Thus, we can simply use a PRF F_K with outputs in $\mathbb{Z}_M$ to generate additive shares from the multiplicative shares. To see this, note that:

- for the multiplicative shares g^{x_0}, g^{x_1} of the *non-zero* entry $g^{x_0+x_1}$ of $\mathbf{T}_{i_B}$, $F_K(g^{x_0}) - F_K(g^{-x_1})$ is a pseudorandom value in $\mathbb{Z}_M$ (even given the PRF key K); however,
- for all multiplicative shares g^{x_0}, g^{x_1} such that $g^{x_0} \cdot g^{x_1} = g^0$, we have $F_K(g^{x_0}) - F_K(g^{-x_1}) = 0$.

This means that parties obtain pseudorandom shares of zero on all entries except for the entry with the non-zero value, where they obtain shares of some pseudorandom value. We provide details on the DDLog algorithm and our NIDPF construction from SXDH in Sect. 5.

3 Preliminaries

In this section, we provide the necessary notational and cryptographic preliminaries that we use our construction of NIDPF.

3.1 Notation

We let $\mathbb{N}$ denote the set of natural numbers, $\mathbb{Z}$ denote the set of integers, and $\mathbb{G}$ denote a finite group. We let $\mathcal{R}$ denote a finite ring. We denote by $\mathsf{poly}(\cdot)$ the set of all polynomials and by $\mathsf{negl}(\cdot)$ any negligible function. We occasionally abuse notation and let poly denote a fixed polynomial.

Vectors and Matrices. We denote a vector $\mathbf{u}$ using bold lowercase letters and let $\mathbf{u}[i]$ denote the i-th coordinate of $\mathbf{u}$. We denote matrices $\mathbf{A}$ with bold uppercase letters and let $\mathbf{A}[i,j]$ denote the element of $\mathbf{A}$ located at the i-th row, j-th column.

Sampling and Assignment. We let $x \leftarrow_\$ S$ denote a uniformly random sample drawn from a set S. We let $x \leftarrow \mathcal{A}$ denote assignment from a randomized algorithm $\mathcal{A}$ and $x := y$ denote initialization of x to the value of y (which may be the output of a deterministic algorithm).

Efficiency and Indistinguishability. By an *efficient* algorithm $\mathcal{A}$ we mean that $\mathcal{A}$ is modeled by a (possibly non-uniform) Turing Machine that runs in probabilistic polynomial time. We write $D_0 \approx_c D_1$ to mean that two distributions D_0 and D_1 are *computationally* indistinguishable to all efficient distinguishers $\mathcal{D}$ and $D_0 \approx_s D_1$ to mean that D_0 and D_1 are *statistically* indistinguishable.

Rounding. We let $\lfloor x \rceil$ denote the rounding of a real number x to the nearest integer. For integers $q > p \geq 2$, we define the modular rounding function $\lfloor \cdot \rceil_p : \mathbb{Z}_q \to \mathbb{Z}_p$ as $\lfloor v \rceil_p = \lfloor (p/q) \cdot v \rceil$.

Party Identifiers. We identify parties with letters A and B, and use $\sigma \in \{A, B\}$ to refer to a party. We will slightly abuse notation by letting $1 - \sigma$, for some $\sigma \in \{A, B\}$, refer to the party identifier in the singleton set $\{A, B\} \setminus \{\sigma\}$.

3.2 Additive Secret Sharing

We define the function $\mathsf{Share}_{\mathbb{G}}(\cdot)$ to be the (randomized) function that outputs a tuple of additive shares in $\mathbb{G}$, such that each share is individually uniformly random over $\mathbb{G}$. For simplicity, we will denote the tuple of additive shares of a secret s by $(\langle s \rangle_0, \langle s \rangle_1)$, such that $\langle s \rangle_0 + \langle s \rangle_1 = s \in \mathbb{G}$.

3.3 Cryptographic Assumptions

In this section, we present the cryptographic assumptions we build NIDPFs from, including the DDH assumption, the SXDH assumption, and the NIDLS framework.

Definition 1 (Decisional Diffie–Hellman (DDH) Assumption). *Let λ be a security parameter. Let $\mathbb{G}$ be a cyclic group of prime order $p = p(\lambda) \in \mathsf{poly}(\lambda)$ with generator g. The DDH assumption states that: $(g, g^a, g^b, g^{ab}) \approx_c (g, g^a, g^b, g^c)$, where $a, b, c \leftarrow\!\!\$\, \mathbb{Z}_p$.*

Definition 2 (Symmetric External Diffie–Hellman (SXDH) Assumption). *Let $(\mathbb{G}_1, \mathbb{G}_2, \mathbb{G}_T, e)$ be a bilinear group, where $\mathbb{G}_1, \mathbb{G}_2$, and $\mathbb{G}_T$ are cyclic groups of prime order $p = p(\lambda) \in \mathsf{poly}(\lambda)$, and $e : \mathbb{G}_1 \times \mathbb{G}_2 \to \mathbb{G}_T$ is a non-degenerate bilinear map. Let g_1 and g_2 be generators of $\mathbb{G}_1$ and $\mathbb{G}_2$, respectively. The SXDH assumption states that the DDH assumption (cf. Definition 1) holds in both $\mathbb{G}_1$ and $\mathbb{G}_2$.*

Definition 3 (Learning with Errors Assumption). *Let χ denote a discrete Gaussian noise distribution. Let $n = n(\lambda), m = m(\lambda)$, and $q = q(\lambda)$, all polynomial in λ. The learning with errors (LWE) assumption states that $(\mathbf{A}, \mathbf{A}^\top \mathbf{s} + \mathbf{e}) \approx_c (\mathbf{A}, \mathbf{u})$ where $\mathbf{A} \leftarrow\!\!\$\, \mathbb{Z}_q^{n \times m}, \mathbf{s} \leftarrow\!\!\$\, \mathbb{Z}_q^n, \mathbf{e} \leftarrow\!\!\$\, \chi^m, \mathbf{u} \leftarrow\!\!\$\, \mathbb{Z}_q^m$.*

Definition 4 (Distributed Discrete Logarithm [18]). *Let $\lambda \in \mathbb{N}$ be a security parameter and $\epsilon = \epsilon(\lambda)$. Let $\mathbb{G}$ be an arbitrary cyclic group with generator g and let $1 \leq M \ll |\mathbb{G}|$ be an integer. Let $\mathsf{crs} := (\mathbb{G}, g, M)$ be a common reference string. An efficient algorithm DDLog solves the distributed discrete logarithm in*

$\mathbb{G}$ with ϵ-correctness, if for all $x \in \mathbb{Z}_M$ and every pair of elements $h_A, h_B \in \mathbb{G}$ such that $h_A \cdot h_B = g^x$,

$$\Pr\left[\langle z \rangle_A - \langle z \rangle_B = x \quad : \quad \langle z \rangle_\sigma := \mathsf{DDLog}(\mathsf{crs}, h_\sigma), \ \forall \sigma \in \{A, B\} \right] \geq \epsilon(\lambda).$$

3.4 The NIDLS Framework

The non-interactive discrete log sharing (NIDLS) framework [1] abstracts several HSS constructions [41, 43]. The NIDLS framework defines a finite Abelian group $\mathbb{G} = F \times H$, where the discrete log problem is easy in F and assumed to be computationally intractable in H. Essentially, this allows two parties to non-interactively compute secret shares of a discrete log in F.

Definition 5 (NIDLS Framework [1]). *The NIDLS framework consists of three efficient algorithms* $(\mathsf{GGen}, \mathcal{D}, \mathsf{DDLog})$ *with the following functionality:*

- $\mathsf{GGen}(1^\lambda) \to \mathsf{crs} := (\mathbb{G}, F, H, g, p, t, \mathsf{aux})$. *The randomized group generation algorithm takes as input the security parameter and outputs a common reference string* crs *which consists of:*
  - *finite Abelian group* $\mathbb{G}$,
  - *subgroups* F *and* H *such that* $\mathbb{G} = F \times H$,
  - *generator* g *and order* p *of* F,
  - *positive integer* t,
  - *and auxiliary information* aux.
- $\mathcal{D}(1^\lambda, \mathsf{crs}) \to (h, \rho)$. *The randomized sampling algorithm takes as input the security parameter and common reference string, and outputs a group element* $h \in \mathbb{G}$ *along with some auxiliary information* ρ.
- $\mathsf{DDLog}(\mathsf{crs}, h) \to s$. *The deterministic distributed discrete log algorithm takes as input a common reference string and a group element, and outputs an element* $s \in \mathbb{Z}_p$.

The above functionality needs to satisfy the following properties:

Correctness. *For all security parameters* $\lambda \in \mathbb{N}$ *and efficient adversaries* $\mathcal{A}$, *there exists a negligible function* negl *such that the following probability is lower bounded by* $1 - \mathsf{negl}(\Lambda)$:

$$\Pr\left[\langle s \rangle_A - \langle s \rangle_B = m \pmod{p} \quad : \quad \begin{array}{r} \mathsf{crs} := (\mathbb{G}, F, H, g, p, t, \mathsf{aux}) \leftarrow \mathsf{GGen}(1^\lambda) \\ (h_A, m) \leftarrow \mathcal{A}(1^\lambda, \mathsf{crs}) \\ h_B := g^m \cdot h_A \\ \langle s \rangle_A := \mathsf{DDLog}(\mathsf{crs}, h_A) \\ \langle s \rangle_B := \mathsf{DDLog}(\mathsf{crs}, h_B) \end{array} \right].$$

Security. *For all security parameters* $\lambda \in \mathbb{N}$, *it holds that:*

$$\left\{ (\text{crs}, h, \rho, h^r) \;\middle|\; \begin{array}{c} \text{crs} := (\mathbb{G}, F, H, g, p, t, \text{aux}) \leftarrow \text{GGen}(1^\lambda) \\ (h, \rho) \leftarrow \mathcal{D}(1^\lambda, \text{crs}) \\ r \leftarrow\!\!\$ \, [t] \end{array} \right\}$$

$$\approx_s \left\{ (\text{crs}, h, \rho, h') \;\middle|\; \begin{array}{c} \text{crs} := (\mathbb{G}, F, H, f, p, t, \text{aux}) \leftarrow \text{GGen}(1^\lambda) \\ (h, \rho) \leftarrow \mathcal{D}(1^\lambda, \text{crs}) \\ h' \leftarrow\!\!\$ \, \langle h \rangle \end{array} \right\} .$$

I.e., the group elements h^r and h' are statistically indistinguishable.

Known Instantiations. The NIDLS framework has been instantiated in the Paillier group under the DCR assumption, in class groups under a variant of the DDH assumption (see below), and in the group of elements in $\mathbb{Z}_n^*$ with a Jacobi symbol of 1 (under the quadratic residuosity assumption), where n is the product of two large random safe primes. We refer to [1,2] for formal definitions of these instantiations.

To instantiate "ElGamal-like" encryption in class groups, we will need to use the Enhanced DDH assumption [2]. This assumption states that given the parameters of the NIDLS group and $\ell+1$ group elements $g_0, \ldots, g_\ell$ sampled from $\mathcal{D}$ (along with the corresponding auxiliary information $\rho_0, \ldots, \rho_\ell$), it is hard to distinguish between $(g_0^w, \ldots, g_\ell^w)$ for a random w and $(f^{r_0} \cdot g_0^w, \ldots, f^{r_\ell} \cdot g_\ell^w)$ for random $r_0, \ldots, r_\ell \in \mathbb{Z}_q$.

Definition 6 (The ℓ-ary Enhanced DDH Assumption [2]). *Let* GGen *and* $\mathcal{D}$ *be as defined in Definition 5. The ℓ-ary Enhanced DDH (ℓ-EDDH) assumption in the NIDLS framework states that:*

$$\left\{ \begin{array}{l} \text{crs} \\ h_0, \ldots, h_\ell \\ \rho_0, \ldots, \rho_\ell \\ h_0^w, \ldots, h_\ell^w \end{array} \;\middle|\; \begin{array}{c} (\mathbb{G}, F, H, g, q, t, \text{aux}) \leftarrow \text{GGen}(1^\lambda) \\ (h_j, \rho_j) \leftarrow \mathcal{D}(1^\lambda, \text{crs}), \; \forall j \in \{0, 1, \ldots, \ell\} \\ w \leftarrow\!\!\$ \, [t] \end{array} \right\}$$

$$\approx_c \left\{ \begin{array}{l} \text{crs} \\ h_0, \ldots, h_\ell \\ \rho_0, \ldots, \rho_\ell \\ g^{r_0} \cdot h_0^w, \ldots, g^{r_\ell} \cdot h_\ell^w \end{array} \;\middle|\; \begin{array}{c} (\mathbb{G}, F, H, g, q, t, \text{aux}) \leftarrow \text{GGen}(1^\lambda) \\ (h_j, \rho_j) \leftarrow \mathcal{D}(1^\lambda, \text{crs}), \; \forall j \in \{0, 1, \ldots, \ell\} \\ w \leftarrow\!\!\$ \, [t] \\ r_j \xleftarrow{\$} \mathbb{Z}_q, \forall j \in \{0, 1, \ldots, \ell\} \end{array} \right\} .$$

3.5 Degree-2 Secret-Key HSS

Here, we define the most minimal form of Homomorphic Secret Sharing (HSS), which will be sufficient for our construction of NIDPFs. The definition is adapted from a more general definition of secret-key HSS and is satisfied by existing HSS constructions in the NIDLS framework and from lattice-based assumptions.

Definition 7 (Degree-2 Secret-Key HSS; Adapted from [18,29]). *Let λ be a security parameter and $\mathcal{R}$ be a finite ring. A Degree-2 (secret key) HSS scheme with message space $\mathcal{R}$ consists of four efficient algorithms* HSS = (Setup, Share, Convert, Mult) *with the following syntax:*

– $\mathsf{Setup}(1^\lambda) \to (\mathsf{sk}, (\mathsf{ek}_A, \mathsf{ek}_B))$. *The randomized setup algorithm takes as input the security parameter and outputs a secret key* sk *and a pair of HSS evaluation keys* $(\mathsf{ek}_A, \mathsf{ek}_B)$.
– $\mathsf{Share}(\mathsf{sk}, x) \to (\llbracket x \rrbracket_A, \llbracket x \rrbracket_B)$. *The randomized share algorithm takes as input the secret key* sk *and message* $x \in \mathcal{R}$. *It outputs a pair of input shares of* x.
– $\mathsf{Convert}(\sigma, \mathsf{ek}_\sigma, \llbracket x \rrbracket_\sigma) \to \langle\!\langle x \rangle\!\rangle_\sigma$. *The deterministic conversion algorithm takes as input the party identifier* $\sigma \in \{A, B\}$, *an evaluation key* ek_σ, *and input share of* x. *It outputs a memory share of* x.
– $\mathsf{Mult}(\sigma, \mathsf{ek}_\sigma, \llbracket x \rrbracket_\sigma, \langle\!\langle y \rangle\!\rangle_\sigma) \to \langle z \rangle_\sigma$. *The deterministic multiplication algorithm takes as input the party identifier* $\sigma \in \{A, B\}$, *an evaluation key* ek_σ, *an input share of* x, *and a memory share of* y. *It outputs a share of* z.

When $\mathsf{Alg} \in \{\mathsf{Share}, \mathsf{Convert}, \mathsf{Mult}\}$ *is given as input a vector of input (or memory) shares, it outputs the vector obtained by evaluating* Alg *on each coordinate of the input vector independently.*

The above algorithms must satisfy correctness and security:

Correctness. *For all security parameters* $\lambda \in \mathbb{N}$, *and for all messages* $x, y \in \mathcal{R}$, *we say the HSS scheme is* ϵ-*correct, for some* $0 < \epsilon \leq 1$ *if there exists a negligible function* $\mathsf{negl}(\cdot)$ *such that:*

$$
\Pr \left[\langle z \rangle_A - \langle z \rangle_B = xy \ : \ \begin{array}{l} (\mathsf{sk}, (\mathsf{ek}_A, \mathsf{ek}_B)) \leftarrow \mathsf{Setup}(1^\lambda) \\ (\llbracket x \rrbracket_A, \llbracket x \rrbracket_B) \leftarrow \mathsf{Share}(\mathsf{sk}, x) \\ (\llbracket y \rrbracket_A, \llbracket y \rrbracket_B) \leftarrow \mathsf{Share}(\mathsf{sk}, y) \\ \langle\!\langle y \rangle\!\rangle_\sigma := \mathsf{Convert}(\sigma, \mathsf{ek}_\sigma, \llbracket y \rrbracket_\sigma), \ \forall \sigma \in \{A, B\} \\ \langle z \rangle_\sigma := \mathsf{Mult}(\sigma, \mathsf{ek}_\sigma, \llbracket x \rrbracket_\sigma, \langle\!\langle y \rangle\!\rangle_\sigma) \end{array} \right]
$$
$$
\geq \epsilon - \mathsf{negl}(\lambda).
$$

Security. *For all security parameters* $\lambda \in \mathbb{N}$ *such that, for every* $\sigma \in \{A, B\}$, *and all efficient adversaries* $\mathcal{A}$, *there exists a negligible function* $\mathsf{negl}(\cdot)$,

$$
\Pr \left[b' = b \ : \ \begin{array}{l} (\mathsf{sk}, (\mathsf{ek}_A, \mathsf{ek}_B)) \leftarrow \mathsf{Setup}(1^\lambda) \\ (\mathbf{x}_0, \mathbf{x}_1, \mathsf{st}) \leftarrow \mathcal{A}(1^\lambda, \mathsf{ek}_\sigma) \\ b \leftarrow_\$ \{0, 1\} \\ (\llbracket \mathbf{x}_b \rrbracket_A, \llbracket \mathbf{x}_b \rrbracket_B) \leftarrow \mathsf{Share}(\mathsf{sk}, \mathbf{x}_b) \\ b' \leftarrow \mathcal{A}(\mathsf{st}, \llbracket \mathbf{x}_b \rrbracket_\sigma) \end{array} \right] \leq \frac{1}{2} + \mathsf{negl}(\lambda),
$$

where for all $b \in \{0, 1\}$, $\mathbf{x}_b \in \mathcal{R}^\ell$ *and* $k = k(\lambda) \in \mathsf{poly}(\lambda)$.

3.5.1 Memory Shares in HSS Schemes

All existing HSS constructions in the NIDLS framework [1,2], and direct constructions from DDH [15,18] or lattice-based assumptions [22], are constructed using the following template. The HSS secret key sk is a vector of ring elements from the ring $\mathcal{R}$ and corresponds to the decryption key of some additively-homomorphic encryption scheme with message space $\mathcal{R}$, supporting some form of linear (or nearly-linear) decryption. The evaluation keys $(\mathsf{ek}_A, \mathsf{ek}_B)$ are additive shares of the secret key sk. For degree-2 computations, *input shares* are simply encryptions of the message x under sk, while *memory shares* consist of additive shares of x and $\mathsf{sk} \cdot x$. Multiplication of an input share of x with a memory share of y can then be computed as follows. First, using the homomorphism of the encryption scheme, compute an encryption of the additive share of $z = x \cdot y$ by multiplying the encrypted message with the additive share of y. Second, using the linear decryption property of the encryption scheme, compute the decryption of the resulting ciphertext using the additive share of $y \cdot \mathsf{sk}$ to recover the additive share of z.

We formalize the property of "multiplication by a memory share," which we will use in our NIDPF construction. We note that several prior works (e.g., [2,27]) make use of such "multiplication by memory shares," without explicitly formalizing the property.

Definition 8 (Multiplication by Memory Shares). *Let* $\mathsf{HSS} = (\mathsf{Input}, \mathsf{Share}, \mathsf{Eval})$ *with a finite ring* $\mathcal{R}$ *as the message space. We say an HSS scheme supports* multiplication by a memory share *if the following three properties are simultaneously satisfied:*

(1) The secret key of the HSS scheme is a vector $\mathsf{sk} \in \mathcal{R}^k$, *for some* $k \in \mathbb{N}$.
(2) A memory share $\langle\!\langle y \rangle\!\rangle_\sigma$ *for any message* $y \in \mathcal{R}$ *consists of an additive share of the tuple* $(y, y \cdot \mathsf{sk})$, *defined over* $\mathcal{R}$.
(3) There exists an efficient, deterministic algorithm $\mathsf{MultEval}$ *with the same syntax as* Eval, *such that for all messages* $y \in \mathcal{R}$, *all memory shares* $(\langle\!\langle y \rangle\!\rangle_A, \langle\!\langle y \rangle\!\rangle_B)$ *of* y, *all input shares* $([\![x]\!]_A, [\![x]\!]_B)$ *of* $x \in \mathcal{R}$, *and all functions* f *in the family of functions computable by* HSS, *it holds that:*

$$\Pr\left[\langle z \rangle_A - \langle z \rangle_B = y \cdot f(x) \quad : \quad \begin{array}{c} \langle z \rangle_\sigma := \mathsf{MultEval}(\sigma, \mathsf{ek}_\sigma, f, [\![x]\!]_\sigma, \langle\!\langle y \rangle\!\rangle_\sigma), \\ \forall \sigma \in \{A, B\} \end{array} \right]$$
$$\geq 1 - \mathsf{negl}(\lambda).$$

In words, any computation evaluated by the HSS scheme can be "premultiplied" by a value y *given only a memory share of* y.

We note that Definition 7 explicitly captures property (3) from Definition 8. Importantly to us, Definition 8 is satisfied by all existing HSS constructions, including HSS construction from the DDH [15,18,19], DCR [41,43], QR [1,41] (for degree-2 computations), class groups [1], and LWE [22].

4   Non-interactive Multiplication

In this section, we define the notion of non-interactive multiplication. As mentioned in the technical overview, this definition captures the core ingredient used in several prior works, including the non-interactive OT construction of [4], non-interactive VOLE (e.g., [2,23,41]), and the notion of non-interactive inner-products [28]. We believe that our abstraction is of independent interest and may aid in further studying the applications of these primitives. Indeed, in the full version [16], we show that we can bootstrap the NIM abstraction to compute more expressive functions in a "non-interactive" manner.

Definition 9 (Non-Interactive Multiplication). *Let λ be a security parameter and $\mathcal{R}$ be a finite ring. A Non-Interactive Multiplication (NIM) scheme consists of five efficient algorithms,*

$$\mathsf{NIM} = (\mathsf{Setup}, (\mathsf{Encode}_\sigma, \mathsf{Decode}_\sigma)_{\sigma \in \{A,B\}}),$$

with the following syntax:

- $\mathsf{Setup}(1^\lambda) \to \mathsf{crs}$. *The randomized setup algorithm takes as input the security parameter and outputs a common reference string (CRS) crs.*
- $\mathsf{Encode}_\sigma(\mathsf{crs}, v) \to (\mathsf{pe}_\sigma, \mathsf{st}_\sigma)$. *The randomized encoding algorithm is parameterized by a party identifier $\sigma \in \{A, B\}$. It takes as input the CRS crs and message v. It outputs a public encoding pe_σ and secret state st_σ.*
- $\mathsf{Decode}_\sigma(\mathsf{crs}, \mathsf{pe}_{1-\sigma}, \mathsf{st}_\sigma) \to \langle z \rangle_\sigma$. *The deterministic decoding algorithm is parameterized by a party identifier $\sigma \in \{A, B\}$. It takes as input the CRS crs, public encoding $\mathsf{pe}_{1-\sigma}$ belonging to the other party, and a secret state st_σ belonging to party σ. It outputs a share of z over $\mathcal{R}$.*

The above functionality must satisfy correctness and security:

Correctness. *For all security parameters $\lambda \in \mathbb{N}$ and every pair of elements $x, y \in \mathcal{R}$, a NIM scheme is said to be correct if there exists a negligible function $\mathsf{negl}(\cdot)$ such that:*

$$\Pr\left[\langle z \rangle_A - \langle z \rangle_B = xy \; : \; \begin{array}{r} \mathsf{crs} \leftarrow \mathsf{Setup}(1^\lambda) \\ (\mathsf{pe}_A, \mathsf{st}_A) \leftarrow \mathsf{Encode}_A(\mathsf{crs}, x) \\ (\mathsf{pe}_B, \mathsf{st}_B) \leftarrow \mathsf{Encode}_B(\mathsf{crs}, y) \\ \langle z \rangle_A := \mathsf{Decode}_A(\mathsf{crs}, \mathsf{pe}_B, \mathsf{st}_A) \\ \langle z \rangle_B := \mathsf{Decode}_B(\mathsf{crs}, \mathsf{pe}_A, \mathsf{st}_B) \end{array} \right] \geq 1 - \mathsf{negl}(\lambda).$$

Security. *For all efficient adversaries $\mathcal{A}$, for all $\sigma \in \{A, B\}$, there exists a negligible function $\mathsf{negl}(\cdot)$ such that:*

$$\Pr\left[b = b' \; : \; \begin{array}{r} \mathsf{crs} \leftarrow \mathsf{Setup}(1^\lambda) \\ (v_0, v_1, \mathsf{st}) \leftarrow \mathcal{A}(\mathsf{crs}) \\ b \leftarrow_\$ \{0,1\} \\ (\mathsf{pe}_\sigma, \mathsf{st}_\sigma) \leftarrow \mathsf{Encode}_\sigma(\mathsf{crs}, v_b) \\ b' \leftarrow \mathcal{A}(\mathsf{st}, \mathsf{pe}_\sigma) \end{array} \right] \leq \frac{1}{2} + \mathsf{negl}(\lambda).$$

In words, the public encoding hides the message.

4.1   NIM with Multiplicative Output Reconstruction

We also define *multiplicative* rather than additive reconstruction for NIM, which will serve us in instantiating a NIDPF in bilinear groups. In this case, Decode_σ outputs a group element Z_σ for $\sigma \in \{A, B\}$, such that $Z_A/Z_B = g^{xy}$, where g is a generator of a cyclic group $\mathbb{G}$.

Definition 10 (Multiplicative Reconstruction). *A NIM scheme* NIM *is said to have* multiplicative reconstruction *if the correctness property of Definition 9 is instead stated as follows.*

Multiplicative-Output Correctness. *Let $\mathbb{G}$ be an Abelian group of order p with generator g. For all security parameters $\lambda \in \mathbb{N}$ and every pair of elements $x, y \in \mathbb{Z}_p$, a NIM scheme (instantiated with $\mathcal{R} = \mathbb{Z}_p$) is said to be correct if there exists a negligible function $\mathsf{negl}(\cdot)$ such that:*

$$\Pr \left[Z_A \cdot Z_B = g^{xy} \quad : \quad \begin{array}{r} \mathsf{crs} \leftarrow \mathsf{Setup}(1^\lambda) \\ (\mathsf{pe}_A, \mathsf{st}_A) \leftarrow \mathsf{Encode}_A(\mathsf{crs}, x) \\ (\mathsf{pe}_B, \mathsf{st}_B) \leftarrow \mathsf{Encode}_B(\mathsf{crs}, y) \\ Z_A := \mathsf{Decode}_A(\mathsf{crs}, \mathsf{pe}_B, \mathsf{st}_A) \\ Z_B := \mathsf{Decode}_B(\mathsf{crs}, \mathsf{pe}_A, \mathsf{st}_B) \end{array} \right] \geq 1 - \mathsf{negl}(\lambda).$$

Remark 1 (General reconstruction). We note that we could have defined NIM (Definition 9) to have an arbitrary reconstruction algorithm, that we then instantiate either as being addition or multiplication. However, because for most applications of NIM the additive reconstruction property is more desirable, we choose to instead provide two definitions noting that the more general abstraction is possible.

4.2   Succinct NIM for Matrix Multiplication

When computing non-interactive *matrix* multiplication, we can realize a "batch NIM" scheme that achieves sublinear encoding size relative to the size of the output matrix, which translates to sublinearity with respect to one of the party's inputs (or the size of the joint output). Note that we cannot, in general, require succinctness in *both* of the parties inputs since this would contradict information-theoretic lower bounds [2].

Definition 11 (ϵ-succinct Matrix NIM). *A NIM scheme for matrix multiplication is said to be ϵ-succinct, for some $0 \leq \epsilon < 1$, if for all security parameters $\lambda \in \mathbb{N}$, every CRS* crs, *integers $\ell, m, k \in \mathbb{N}$ such that $\ell > k$, and every pair of matrices $(\mathbf{M}_A, \mathbf{M}_B) \in \mathcal{R}^{\ell \times m} \times \mathcal{R}^{m \times k}$, it holds that for $N := \ell \cdot m$,*

$$|\mathsf{pe}_A| \leq N^\epsilon \cdot \mathsf{poly}(\lambda, \log|\mathcal{R}|),$$

where $(\mathsf{pe}_A, \_) \leftarrow \mathsf{Encode}_A(\mathsf{crs}, \mathbf{M}_A)$. In words, the public encoding generated by the party with the larger matrix is sublinear in the size of its matrix.

Remark 2 (Connection to "Bilinear HSS"). Abram et al. [2] define the notion of Bilinear HSS, which is conceptually related to our formalization of succinct NIM. While the notions share some similarities, succinct NIM is a stronger definition due to the non-interactivity requirement. Bilinear HSS, in contrast, captures an "HSS-like" syntax, where a trusted setup process distributes keys to the parties. Succinct NIM follows straightforwardly from Bilinear HSS with (1) Strong Hasher Privacy, (2) Strong Matrix Privacy, (3) Transparent Hasher Privacy, and (4) Transparent Matrix Privacy, using the terminology and definitions from [2]. However, Property (4) is not defined in [2], even though we believe that it can be easily be inferred as a variant of (3).

5   Non-interactive DPF

In this section, we define and construct Non-Interactive DPFs (NIDPFs). Our construction makes use of the NIM abstraction and constructions from Sect. 4.

Definition 12 (Non-Interactive Distributed Point Function). *Let λ be a security parameter and $\mathbb{G}$ be a cyclic group. A non-interactive distributed point function (NIDPF) with input domain $\mathbb{Z}_N$ consists of four efficient algorithms,*

$$\mathsf{NIDPF} = (\mathsf{Setup}, (\mathsf{Gen}_\sigma, \mathsf{KeyDer}_\sigma, \mathsf{Eval}_\sigma)_{\sigma \in \{A,B\}}),$$

with the following syntax:

- $\mathsf{Setup}(1^\lambda) \to \mathsf{crs}$. *The randomized setup algorithm takes as input the security parameter and outputs a common reference string crs.*
- $\mathsf{Gen}_\sigma(\mathsf{crs}, t_\sigma, v_\sigma) \to (\mathsf{pk}_\sigma, \mathsf{sk}_\sigma)$. *The randomized generation algorithm is parameterized by a party identifier $\sigma \in \{A, B\}$. It takes as input the crs, an index $t_\sigma \in \mathbb{Z}_N$, and a message $v_\sigma \in \mathbb{G}$. It outputs a public key pk_σ and secret key sk_σ.*
- $\mathsf{KeyDer}_\sigma(\mathsf{crs}, \mathsf{pk}_{1-\sigma}, \mathsf{sk}_\sigma) \to \kappa_\sigma$. *The deterministic key derivation algorithm is parameterized by a party identifier $\sigma \in \{A, B\}$. It takes as input the crs, public key $\mathsf{pk}_{1-\sigma}$ belonging to the other party, and a secret key sk_σ belonging to party σ. It outputs a DPF key κ_σ for party σ.*
- $\mathsf{Eval}_\sigma(\mathsf{crs}, \kappa_\sigma, x) \to \langle y \rangle_\sigma$. *The deterministic evaluation algorithm is parameterized by a party identifier $\sigma \in \{A, B\}$. It takes as input the crs, the party's DPF key κ_σ, and an input $x \in \mathbb{Z}_N$. It outputs a share of the evaluation result y.*

Let $P_{i,v} \colon \mathbb{Z}_N \to \mathbb{G}$ be the point function that outputs 0 for all inputs $x \neq i$ and outputs v otherwise. The above functionality must satisfy the following correctness and security properties:

Correctness. *For all security parameters $\lambda \in \mathbb{N}$, every pair of indices $t_A, t_B \in \mathbb{Z}_N$ such that $t = t_A + t_B \in \mathbb{Z}_N$, every pair of messages $v_A, v_B \in \mathbb{G}$ such that*

$v = v_A + v_B \in \mathbb{G}$, and every input $x \in \mathbb{Z}_N$, a NIDPF scheme is correct if there exists a negligible function negl such that:

$$\Pr\left[\langle y\rangle_A - \langle y\rangle_B = P_{t,v}(x) \quad : \quad \begin{array}{r} \mathsf{crs} \leftarrow \mathsf{Setup}(1^\lambda) \\ (\mathsf{pk}_\sigma, \mathsf{sk}_\sigma) \leftarrow \mathsf{Gen}_\sigma(\mathsf{crs}, t_\sigma, v_\sigma), \ \forall \sigma \in \{A, B\} \\ \kappa_A := \mathsf{KeyDer}_A(\mathsf{crs}, \mathsf{pk}_B, \mathsf{sk}_A) \\ \kappa_B := \mathsf{KeyDer}_B(\mathsf{crs}, \mathsf{pk}_A, \mathsf{sk}_B) \\ \langle y\rangle_\sigma := \mathsf{Eval}_\sigma(\mathsf{crs}, \kappa_\sigma, x), \ \forall \sigma \in \{A, B\} \end{array}\right]$$
$$\geq 1 - \mathsf{negl}(\lambda),$$

where the probability is taken over the random coins used by Gen.

Security. For all efficient adversaries $\mathcal{A}$, for all $\sigma \in \{A, B\}$, there exists a negligible function $\mathsf{negl}(\cdot)$ such that:

$$\Pr\left[b = b' \quad : \quad \begin{array}{r} \mathsf{crs} \leftarrow \mathsf{Setup}(1^\lambda) \\ (t_0, v_0, t_1, v_1, \mathsf{st}) \leftarrow \mathcal{A}(\mathsf{crs}) \\ b \leftarrow_\$ \{0, 1\} \\ (\mathsf{pk}_\sigma, \mathsf{sk}_\sigma) \leftarrow \mathsf{Gen}_\sigma(\mathsf{crs}, t_b, v_b) \\ b' \leftarrow \mathcal{A}(\mathsf{st}, \mathsf{pk}_\sigma) \end{array}\right] \leq \frac{1}{2} + \mathsf{negl}(\lambda).$$

In words, the public key computationally hides the encoded index and message.

We now define two variants of NIDPF that we will consider in this paper. The first variant, which we call a *half-chosen* NIDPF, only allows one of the parties to specify the output message, forcing the second party to input $\perp$ to Gen. The second variant, which we call a *random-output* NIDPF, does not allow the parties to specify the output message: the output v is uniformly random and determined solely based on the random coins of Gen_A and Gen_B.

Definition 13 (Half-Chosen NIDPF). *We say that a NIDPF scheme has a* half-chosen payload *if for a fixed $\sigma \in \{A, B\}$, Gen_σ only accepts $v_\sigma = 0$.*

Definition 14 (Random-Payload NIDPF). *We say that a NIDPF scheme has a* random payload *if both Gen_A and Gen_B do not take any message parameter, and the NIDPF correctness property from Definition 12 instead holds with respect to a random payload $v \in \mathbb{G}$ (determined by the random coins of Gen).*

Lemma 1 (Half-Chosen NIDPF $\implies$ NIDPF). *Given a half-chosen NIDPF with (public and secret) encoding size S and evaluation time T, we can obtain a NIDPF with encoding size size $2S$ and evaluation time $2T$.*

The lemma follows directly from the composition theorem of function secret sharing [17, Section 3.2]. In particular, the parties run two instances of the half-chosen NIDPF in parallel, where each party specifies its own payload in turn by reversing roles, then the outputs of the two instances are summed together.

Remark 3 (Full-domain evaluation). Our construction will focus on settings where the evaluation algorithm Eval is applied on all inputs in the domain $\mathbb{Z}_N$ (in which case we need to assume that N is polynomial in the security parameter, for efficiency). That is, given a NIDPF scheme NIDPF = (Setup, $(\text{Gen}_\sigma, \text{KeyDer}_\sigma,$ $\text{Eval}_\sigma)_{\sigma \in \{A,B\}}$), we will denote by EvalAll_σ the algorithm that runs NIDPF.Eval_σ on every input $x \in \mathbb{G}$. As such, EvalAll_σ only takes as input the crs and key κ_σ.

This setting captures a motivated range of applications and implemented systems, including constructions of pseudorandom correlation generators, private "reading" applications such as Private Information Retrieval, and private "writing" applications such as secure distributed storage, voting, and aggregation. (See, e.g., [21] for further discussion.)

We additionally remark that all present black-box distributed DPF setup protocols require domains of feasible size. Indeed, removing this limitation while remaining black-box in the underlying cryptography would seem to pose a significant challenge.

5.1 Emulating Arithmetic Modulo N

Here, we briefly describe two natural approaches for representing arithmetic over the inputs of Alice and Bob. We want our construction to give parties the ability to generate keys for the point function with a non-zero index at $t_A + t_B \mod N$. Unfortunately, our NIDPF construction requires Alice and Bob to parse their inputs $t_A, t_B \in [N]$ as $(i_A, j_A), (i_B, j_B) \in \mathbb{Z}_\ell \times \mathbb{Z}_m$, where $N = \ell \cdot m$ and only allows them to compute a DPF key encoding a point function with special index:

$$(i_A + i_B \mod \ell) \cdot m + (j_A + j_B \mod m). \tag{3}$$

If we parse the indices t_A and t_B of each party in the simplest way, i.e., $t_A = i_A \cdot m + j_A$ and $t_B = i_B \cdot m + j_B$, the above operation does not capture addition of t_A and t_B modulo N. Specifically, it is possible that $j_A + j_B$ has a "carry bit" b in the case when $j_A + j_B \geq m$, which then has to be added to the $i_A + i_B$ component as:

$$(i_A + i_B + b \mod \ell) \cdot m + (j_A + j_B \mod m). \tag{4}$$

Concretely, in our NIDPF construction, this will require shifting the rows of the matrix **T** by $i_B + b$ in the case that the carry bit is set (recall Step II from Sect. 2.2).

Remark 4 (Random point function). We remark that in the case that Alice and Bob need a point function with a *random* non-zero index, they do not need to emulate addition modulo N and can instead simply sample uniformly random (i_σ, j_σ) for their inputs to the NIDPF.

Here, we present two approaches for emulating addition (modulo N) using arithmetic represented over ℓ and m, as in Eq. (3).

Approach I: Emulating Arithmetic via a Residue Number System. As described in Sect. 2, we can let ℓ be coprime to m, which immediately allows us to emulate arithmetic modulo N in a residue number system, using ℓ and m as the coprime moduli. In this case, we no longer need to worry about the carry bit, since we can compute locally modulo $\mathbb{Z}_\ell$ and $\mathbb{Z}_m$ and then map back to $\mathbb{Z}_N$. Alice and Bob represent their indices $t_A, t_B \in [N]$ as (i_A, j_A) and (i_B, j_B) where

$$
\begin{aligned}
t_A &\equiv i_A \pmod{\ell}, & t_B &\equiv i_B \pmod{\ell}, \\
t_A &\equiv j_A \pmod{m}, & t_B &\equiv j_B \pmod{m}.
\end{aligned}
$$

After executing the protocol, they hold secret shares of a matrix that is nonzero in location $(i_A + i_B \pmod{\ell}, j_A + j_B \pmod{m})$. Let α, α' be integers such that $\alpha\ell + \alpha'm = 1$, which exist since ℓ and m are coprime. Alice and Bob can each map location (i, j) of their $\ell \times m$ matrix to location $l \in [N]$ in a vector of length N where $l \equiv i\alpha'm + j\alpha\ell \pmod{N}$. Suppose t is the resulting one-hot index in the vector Alice and Bob now hold shares for. By the Chinese Remainder Theorem, we have that

$$
\left.
\begin{aligned}
t &\equiv i_A + i_B \pmod{\ell} \\
t &\equiv j_A + j_B \pmod{m}
\end{aligned}
\right\} \implies t \equiv t_A + t_B \pmod{N}.
$$

Approach II: Emulating the Carry. For some applications, it may be inconvenient or impossible for ℓ and m to be coprime, such as if $N = \ell \cdot m$ is a power of 2. An alternative strategy we can use in this case is to prevent the "erasure" of the carry bit modulo m. Specifically, we observe that if the cyclic shift is performed modulo $2m$, then we do not lose information on the carry: the non-zero entry of Alice's matrix $\mathbf{A} \in \mathcal{R}^{\ell \times 2m}$ will either contain the non-zero entry in the "left half" or the "right half" of the columns depending on whether or not the carry occurred. At this point, Alice and Bob will hold shares of a matrix $\mathbf{T}$ that can be parsed as $[\mathbf{T}_0 \ \mathbf{T}_1]$, where $\mathbf{T}_0, \mathbf{T}_1 \in \mathcal{R}^{\ell \times m}$ and $\mathbf{T}_{1-b} = \mathbf{0}$ when b is the value of the carry bit. Then, Alice and Bob can cyclically shift their rows of $\mathbf{T}_1$ down by one (this operation is a linear function over their shares of $\mathbf{T}_1$), and compute $\mathbf{T} := \mathbf{T}_0 + \mathsf{ShiftDown}(\mathbf{T}_1, 1)$. Observe that because $\mathbf{T}_{1-b}$ is always zero, they obtain shares of the matrix $\mathbf{T}$ that has exactly one non-zero entry and the rows cyclically shifted down precisely if the carry bit is set. Note that this approach works regardless of the choice of ℓ and m.

5.2   NIDPF Framework

Here, we formalize the NIDPF construction, closely following the technical overview from Sect. 2.2. We present a construction for the "half-chosen payload" (Definition 13) NIDPF in Fig. 2, which can be extended to satisfy the full NIDPF definition via Lemma 1 (however, for the applications described in Sect. 1.2, the payload is public, and so the half-chosen variant sufficient on its own).

Our construction uses the following auxiliary functions as building blocks.

Auxiliary Functions. We define two deterministic functions that simplify the presentation of our NIDPF construction in Fig. 2.

- Shift: $\mathcal{R}^{\ell \times m} \times [\ell] \to \mathcal{R}^{\ell \times m}$. Shift takes as input a $\ell \times m$ matrix (for arbitrary integers ℓ, m) and a shift $i \in [\ell]$. It outputs the matrix with the rows cyclically shifted down by i.
- Mat2Vec: $\mathcal{R}^{\ell \times m} \to \mathcal{R}^{\ell \cdot m}$. Mat2Vec takes as input a $\ell \times m$ matrix (for arbitrary integers ℓ, m) and outputs the vector obtained by concatenating the rows of the matrix together.

Proposition 1. *Let* NIM *be a succinct NIM scheme (Definition 11) and let* HSS *be a (degree-2, secret-key) HSS scheme (Definition 7). The construction presented in Fig. 2 is a half-chosen NIDPF (Definition 13).*

Proof. The proof is deferred to the full version [16]. ∎

Corollary 1. *There exist the following instantiations of Fig. 2 with a $O(N^{2/3})$ public key size, $O(N)$ key generation time, $O(N^{4/3})$ key derivation time, and $O(N^{5/3})$ full domain evaluation time, where $O(\cdot)$ hides a factor of* $\mathsf{poly}(\lambda, \log |\mathcal{R}|)$:

- *under the DCR assumption over the Paillier group $\mathbb{Z}_{n^2}^*$, when $\mathcal{R} \subseteq \mathbb{Z}_n$;*
- *under the QR assumption over the RSA group $\mathbb{Z}_n^*$ where n is the product of two large safe-primes, when $\mathcal{R} = \mathbb{Z}_2$;*
- *under the $N^{1/3}$-ary EDDH assumption and the uniformity assumption in class groups, when $\mathcal{R} = \mathbb{Z}_p$, for any suitable prime $p = \Omega(2^\lambda)$; and*
- *under the LWE/RLWE assumption with a superpolynomial modulus-to-noise ratio, when $\mathcal{R} = \mathbb{Z}_p$, for any integer p.*

The class group and LWE/RLWE instantiations have a transparent setup.

Proof. We set parameters $\ell = N^{2/3}$ and $m = N^{1/3}$. Since the HSS secret key length $k = k(\lambda) = \mathsf{poly}(\lambda)$, we will ignore factors of k in our analysis below.

The size of the public key generated for the larger matrix with dimensions $\ell \times m$ grows with the number of rows, resulting in an asymptotic size of $N^{2/3}$. The size of the public key generated for a smaller matrix with dimensions $m \times m$ grows with the size of the matrix, resulting in an asymptotic size of $N^{1/3} \cdot N^{1/3} = N^{2/3}$. Key generation time is dominated by the NIM encoding algorithm for a matrix of size $\ell \times m$, resulting in an asymptotic runtime of $N^{2/3} \cdot N^{1/3} = N$.

Key derivation time is dominated by the NIM decoding algorithm for matrices with dimensions $\ell \times m$ and $m \times m$, resulting in an asymptotic runtime of $N^{2/3} \cdot N^{1/3} \cdot N^{1/3} = N^{4/3}$. Full domain evaluation time is dominated by running the HSS multiplication algorithm ℓ times for a matrix with dimensions $\ell \times m$, resulting in an asymptotic runtime of $N^{2/3} \cdot N^{2/3} \cdot N^{1/3} = N^{5/3}$. ∎

NIDPF Framework

Public Parameters. Domain size N and matrix dimensions ℓ, m such that $\ell \cdot m = N$. Set of cyclic shift matrices $\mathcal{S}_m = \{\mathbf{S}_j : j \in [m]\}$, where $\mathbf{S}_j$ is the j-th canonical cyclic shift matrix. Succinct NIM scheme NIM = (Setup, (Encode$_\sigma$, Decode$_\sigma$)$_{\sigma \in \{A,B\}}$) and (degree-2, secret-key) HSS scheme HSS = (Setup, Share, Convert, Mult). We instantiate the full-domain evaluation algorithm NIDPF.EvalAll, described in Remark 3.

NIDPF.Setup(1^λ):

1 : crs $\leftarrow$ NIM.Setup(1^λ)

2 : **return** crs

NIDPF.Gen$_A$(crs, t_A, v):

1 : **parse** $t_A = (i_A, j_A) \in [\ell] \times [m]$

2 : $\mathbf{A} := \mathbf{0} \in \mathcal{R}^{\ell \times m}$, $\mathbf{A}[i_A, j_A] := v$

3 : $(\mathsf{pe}_A, \mathsf{st}_A) \leftarrow \mathsf{Encode}_A(\mathsf{crs}, \mathbf{A})$

4 : $(\mathsf{pk}_A, \mathsf{sk}_A) := (\mathsf{pe}_A, \mathsf{st}_A)$

5 : **return** $(\mathsf{pk}_A, \mathsf{sk}_A)$

NIDPF.KeyDer$_\sigma$(crs, $\mathsf{pk}_{1-\sigma}$, sk_σ):

1 : **parse** $(\mathsf{pk}_{1-\sigma}, \mathsf{sk}_\sigma)$
$= (\mathsf{pe}_{1-\sigma}, \mathsf{ek}_\sigma, [\![\mathbf{e}_{i_B}]\!]_\sigma, \mathsf{st}_\sigma)$

2 : $\mathbf{U}_\sigma := \mathsf{Decode}_\sigma(\mathsf{pe}_{1-\sigma}, \mathsf{st}_\sigma)$

3 : **parse** $\mathbf{U}_\sigma = \langle\!\langle \mathbf{T} \rangle\!\rangle_\sigma$

4 : $\kappa_\sigma := (\langle\!\langle \mathbf{T} \rangle\!\rangle_\sigma, \mathsf{ek}_\sigma, [\![\mathbf{e}_{i_B}]\!]_\sigma)$

5 : **return** κ_σ

NIDPF.Gen$_B$(crs, t_B, $\bot$):

1 : **parse** $t_B = (i_B, j_B) \in [\ell] \times [m]$

2 : $(\mathsf{sk}, (\mathsf{ek}_A, \mathsf{ek}_B)) \leftarrow \mathsf{HSS.Setup}(1^\lambda)$

3 : **parse** $\mathsf{sk} = (\mathsf{sk}_B, \ldots, \mathsf{sk}_k) \in \mathcal{R}^k$
// k is determined by the HSS scheme.

4 : $([\![\mathbf{e}_{i_B}]\!]_A, [\![\mathbf{e}_{i_B}]\!]_B) \leftarrow \mathsf{HSS.Share}(\mathsf{sk}, \mathbf{e}_{i_B})$
// $\mathbf{e}_{i_B}$ is the i_B-th canonical unit vector.

5 : $\mathbf{E} := \left[\mathbf{S}_{j_B} \mid \mathsf{sk}_B \cdot \mathbf{S}_{j_B} \mid \cdots \mid \mathsf{sk}_k \cdot \mathbf{S}_{j_B} \right]$

6 : $(\mathsf{pe}_B, \mathsf{st}_B) \leftarrow \mathsf{Encode}_B(\mathsf{crs}, \mathbf{E})$

7 : $\mathsf{pk}_B := (\mathsf{pe}_B, \mathsf{ek}_A, [\![\mathbf{e}_{i_B}]\!]_A)$

8 : $\mathsf{sk}_B := (\mathsf{st}_B, \mathsf{ek}_B, [\![\mathbf{e}_{i_B}]\!]_B)$

9 : **return** $(\mathsf{pk}_B, \mathsf{sk}_B)$

NIDPF.EvalAll$_\sigma$(crs, κ_σ):

1 : **parse** $\kappa_\sigma = (\langle\!\langle \mathbf{T} \rangle\!\rangle_\sigma, \mathsf{ek}_\sigma, [\![\mathbf{e}_{i_B}]\!]_\sigma)$
// $[\![\mathbf{e}_{i_B}]\!]_\sigma = ([\![e_{i_B,1}]\!]_\sigma, \ldots, [\![e_{i_B,k}]\!]_\sigma)$.

2 : **foreach** $j \in [\ell]$:

3 : $\langle\!\langle \mathbf{T}_j \rangle\!\rangle_\sigma := \mathsf{Shift}(\langle\!\langle \mathbf{T} \rangle\!\rangle_\sigma, i)$

4 : $\mathbf{Z}_\sigma^{(j)} := \mathsf{Mult}(\sigma, \mathsf{ek}_\sigma, [\![\mathbf{e}_{i_B,j}]\!]_\sigma, \langle\!\langle \mathbf{T}_j \rangle\!\rangle_\sigma)$

5 : $\mathbf{Z}_\sigma := \sum_{j=1}^\ell \mathbf{Z}_\sigma^{(j)}$

6 : $\langle \mathbf{y} \rangle_\sigma := \mathsf{Mat2Vec}(\mathbf{Z}_\sigma)$

7 : **return** $\langle \mathbf{y} \rangle_\sigma$

Fig. 2. NIDPF framework.

5.3   Random-Payload Instantiation from SXDH

Here, we provide a construction of Fig. 2 with random payload (see Definition 14) from the SXDH assumption over bilinear groups. Our starting point is the observation that if we replace the NIM in Fig. 2 with the multiplicative-output NIM (Definition 10), we can avoid the error introduced from the DDLog procedure converting the multiplicative shares into additive shares. However, by having the output of NIM be multiplicative, we lose the ability to compute the HSS multiplication in EvalAll, since HSS requires additive memory shares.

We overcome this by constructing a new degree-2 HSS scheme satisfying Definition 7 and which has "multiplicative" memory shares (i.e., additive memory shares "in the exponent") that are compatible with the outputs of the multiplicative NIM.

5.3.1   Degree-2 HSS with Multiplicative Memory Shares

In Fig. 3, we construct a (secret-key, degree-2) HSS scheme satisfying Definition 7 under the SXDH assumption in bilinear groups.[3] The construction follows the standard template for realizing HSS in cyclic groups. However, one difference is that we define input shares over the group $\mathbb{G}_1$ and memory shares over the group $\mathbb{G}_2$, which allows us to compute the multiplication using a pairing operations. This slightly complicates the scheme since now we need to convert input shares to memory shares using Convert by "hopping between groups," which necessitates defining two independent encryptions of the message in HSS.Share when generating an input share. Importantly, the encryptions in $\mathbb{G}_1$ need to be generated using an encryption key α that is independent from the encryption key β used to encrypt the messages in $\mathbb{G}_2$ (otherwise the security of the encryption would be trivially broken via the pairing).

Proposition 2. *The construction presented in Fig. 3 satisfies Definition 7 (degree-2, secret-key) HSS with $\epsilon = 1 - 1/\mathsf{poly}(\lambda)$ correctness assuming the SXDH assumption holds in the bilinear group $\mathbb{G} := (p, \mathbb{G}_1, \mathbb{G}_2, \mathbb{G}_T, g_1, g_2, e)$.*

Proof. Deferred to the full version of this work [16]. ∎

5.3.2   Random "DDLog" Procedure

In Fig. 3, correctness of the output shares depends on the correctness of the DDLog procedure. However, in cyclic groups $\mathbb{G}$, the DDLog procedure has an inherent $1/\mathsf{poly}(\lambda)$ error [18,33], which the NIDLS framework overcomes by using specific groups $\mathbb{G}$ (e.g., $\mathbb{Z}_{n^2}^*$) and requiring different assumptions (e.g., DCR). This is why Fig. 3 only achieves $\epsilon = 1 - 1/\mathsf{poly}(\lambda)$ correctness, in general. The crucial observation we make here is that the DDLog procedure has *no error* when given multiplicative shares of $g^0 \in \mathbb{G}$ and, moreover, because we additionally only require uniformly random payloads in the case where the parties hold

---

[3]   The construction can easily be made *public key*, but we present the secret-key variant for consistency with the rest of this paper.

Degree-2 Secret-key HSS from SXDH

Public Parameters. Bilinear group of order p defined by $(p, \mathbb{G}_1, \mathbb{G}_2, \mathbb{G}_T, g_1, g_2, e)$. For convenience, we define $g_T := e(g_1, g_2) \in \mathbb{G}_T$. Additive secret sharing algorithm $\mathsf{Share}_{\mathbb{G}}(\cdot)$ outputting two-out-of-two shares in the group $\mathbb{G}$ (see Section 3.2). Distributed discrete logarithm algorithm DDLog (Definition 4) and an integer $2 \leq M \leq \mathsf{poly}(\lambda)$ defining the message space $\{0, 1, \ldots, M-1\}$.

$\mathsf{HSS.Setup}(1^\lambda)$:

1 : $\alpha, \beta \leftarrow\!\!\$\, \mathbb{Z}_p$, $\gamma := \alpha\beta$, $\mathsf{sk} := (\alpha, \beta, \gamma)$

2 : $(\langle\alpha\rangle_A, \langle\alpha\rangle_B) \leftarrow \mathsf{Share}_{\mathbb{Z}_p}(\alpha)$

3 : $(\langle\beta\rangle_A, \langle\beta\rangle_B) \leftarrow \mathsf{Share}_{\mathbb{Z}_p}(\beta)$

4 : $(\langle\gamma\rangle_A, \langle\gamma\rangle_B) \leftarrow \mathsf{Share}_{\mathbb{Z}_p}(\gamma)$

5 : $\mathbf{foreach}\ \sigma \in \{A, B\}$:

6 : $\mathsf{ek}_\sigma := (\langle\alpha\rangle_\sigma, \langle\beta\rangle_\sigma, \langle\gamma\rangle_\sigma)$

7 : $\mathbf{return}\ (\mathsf{sk}, (\mathsf{ek}_A, \mathsf{ek}_B))$

$\mathsf{HSS.Convert}(\sigma, \mathsf{ek}_\sigma, [\![x]\!]_\sigma)$:

1 : $\mathbf{parse}\ \mathsf{ek}_\sigma = (\langle\alpha\rangle_\sigma, \langle\beta\rangle_\sigma, \langle\gamma\rangle_\sigma)$

2 : $\mathbf{parse}\ [\![x]\!]_\sigma = (\_, \_, E_0, E_1)$

3 : $\langle\!\langle x\rangle\!\rangle_\sigma := (E_1 \cdot E_0^{-\langle\beta\rangle_\sigma}, E_1^{\langle\alpha\rangle_\sigma} \cdot E_0^{-\langle\gamma\rangle_\sigma})$

4 : $\mathbf{return}\ \langle\!\langle x\rangle\!\rangle_\sigma$

$\mathsf{HSS.Share}(\mathsf{sk}, x)$:

1 : $r, r' \leftarrow\!\!\$\, \mathbb{Z}_p$

2 : $\mathbf{foreach}\ \sigma \in \{A, B\}$:

3 : $[\![x]\!]_\sigma := (g_1^r, g_1^{x+\alpha\cdot r}, g_2^{r'}, g_2^{x+\beta\cdot r'})$

4 : $\mathbf{return}\ ([\![x]\!]_A, [\![x]\!]_B)$

$\mathsf{HSS.Mult}(\sigma, \mathsf{ek}_\sigma, [\![x]\!]_\sigma, \langle\!\langle y\rangle\!\rangle_\sigma)$:

1 : $\mathbf{parse}\ [\![x]\!]_\sigma = (D_0, D_1, \_, \_)$

2 : $\mathbf{parse}\ \langle\!\langle y\rangle\!\rangle_\sigma = (S_\sigma^{(0)}, S_\sigma^{(1)})$

3 : $Z_\sigma := e(D_0, S_\sigma^{(1)}) \cdot e(D_1, S_\sigma^{(0)})$

4 : $\tau := 0$ if $\sigma = A$; $\mathbf{else}\ \tau := 1$

5 : $\langle z\rangle_\sigma := \mathsf{DDLog}((\mathbb{G}_T, g_T, M), Z_\sigma^{-1^\tau})$

6 : $\mathbf{return}\ \langle z\rangle_\sigma$

Fig. 3. Degree-2 secret-key HSS from SXDH.

multiplicative shares of g^u, for some $u \neq 0$, we can construct a trivial algorithm "DDLog" procedure using just a PRF, as we show in the following lemma.

Lemma 2 (Random Distributed Discrete Logarithm). *Let $\mathbb{G}$ be an arbitrary cyclic group with generator g and $1 \leq M \ll |\mathbb{G}|$ be an integer. There exists an efficient algorithm DDLog satisfying Definition 4 such that:*

(1) For all elements $h_A, h_B \in \mathbb{G}$ where $h_A \cdot h_B = g^0$,

$$\Pr\left[\ \langle z\rangle_A - \langle z\rangle_B = 0\ :\ \langle z\rangle_\sigma := \mathsf{DDLog}((\mathbb{G}, g, M), h_\sigma), \forall\sigma \in \{A, B\}\right] = 1;$$

(2) For all $h_A, h_B \in \mathbb{G}$ where $h_A \cdot h_B \neq g^0$, it holds that for all $\sigma \in \{A, B\}$:

$$\left\{ \left(\langle z \rangle_\sigma, h_{1-\sigma} \right) \ \middle| \ \langle z \rangle_\sigma := \mathsf{DDLog}((\mathbb{G}, g, M), h_\sigma) \right\}$$
$$\approx_c \left\{ \left(\langle z \rangle_\sigma, h_{1-\sigma} \right) \ \middle| \ \langle z \rangle_\sigma \leftarrow\!\!\$\, \mathbb{Z}_M \right\}.$$

Proof. We construct DDLog satisfying the two required properties using any PRF family $F \colon \{0,1\}^\lambda \times \mathbb{G} \to \mathbb{Z}_M$. Define DDLog as $((\mathbb{G}, g, M), h_\sigma) \mapsto F_K((h_\sigma)^{-1^T}),$[4] where K is a public uniformly random PRF key. Then, (1) the output of DDLog consists of pseudorandom shares of zero whenever $h_A \cdot h_B = g^0$ and (2) the output of DDLog for all non-zero values is uniformly random in $\mathbb{Z}_M$ (thus satisfying the second property).

To see (1), note that if $h_A \cdot h_B = g^0$, then it holds that $h_A = h_B^{-1}$, which in turn implies that $F_K(h_A) - F_K(h_B) = 0$, with probability 1.

To see (2), note that if $h_A \cdot h_B = g^u$, for some non-zero u with high (pseudo)entropy independent of the PRF key K, then DDLog outputs two pseudorandom and independent elements of $\mathbb{Z}_M$, which guarantees computational indistinguishability by the security of the PRF. ∎

Corollary 2. *Under the SXDH assumption over a bilinear group, there exists an instantiation of Fig. 2 with random payloads (cf. Definition 14) in the message space $\mathbb{Z}_M$, for any integer M, with a $O(N^{2/3})$ public key size, $O(N)$ key generation time, $O(N^{4/3})$ key derivation time, and $O(N^{5/3})$ full domain evaluation time, where $O(\cdot)$ hides a factor of $\mathsf{poly}(\lambda, \log |\mathcal{R}|)$.*

Proof. The construction consists of Fig. 2 instantiated with a multiplicative-output NIM (Definition 10) and the degree-2 HSS construction from SXDH (Fig. 3) using the modified DDLog from Lemma 2.

The public key size, key generation time, and evaluation time follows from the proof of Corollary 1. Then, by Lemma 2 we immediately get correctness and a random payload on the non-zero coordinate. However, to additionally ensure pseudorandomness of the payload given the PRF key K, the parties must set their payload to a uniformly random scalar. That is, party σ sets the non-zero coordinate to be Δ_σ (for some uniformly random $\Delta_\sigma \leftarrow\!\!\$\, \mathbb{Z}_p$, where p is the prime order of $\mathbb{G}$). Then, the parties obtain multiplicative shares of a uniformly random value in $\Delta_A \cdot \Delta_B \in \mathbb{Z}_p$ which guarantees the resulting PRF output is pseudorandom. ∎

Remark 5 (Guaranteeing a non-zero output). We remark that because the payload is uniformly random in $\mathbb{Z}_M$, it may be zero with noticeable probability if M is small. To guarantee a negligible probability of the payload being zero, we can choose the $M \geq 2^\lambda$ so as to ensure the output is non-zero with all but negligible probability. In particular, the DDLog procedure of Lemma 2 does not require M to be polynomial in the security parameter.

---

[4] Here, DDLog is implicitly parameterized by the party identifier σ and the global PRF key K. We leave this implicit for readability.

Acknowledgments. We thank Srini Devadas and the anonymous reviewers for helpful comments and suggestions. Elette Boyle's research is supported, in part, by AFOSR Award FA9550-21-1-0046 and ERC Project HSS (852952).

References

1. Abram, D., Damgård, I., Orlandi, C., Scholl, P.: An algebraic framework for silent preprocessing with trustless setup and active security. In: Dodis, Y., Shrimpton, T. (eds.) CRYPTO 2022, Part IV. LNCS, vol. 13510, pp. 421–452. Springer, Cham (2022). https://doi.org/10.1007/978-3-031-15985-5_15
2. Abram, D., Roy, L., Scholl, P.: Succinct homomorphic secret sharing. In: Joye, M., Leander, G. (eds.) EUROCRYPT 2024, Part VI. LNCS, vol. 14656, pp. 301–330. Springer, Cham (2024). https://doi.org/10.1007/978-3-031-58751-1_11
3. Abram, D., Scholl, P.: Low-communication multiparty triple generation for SPDZ from ring-LPN. In: Hanaoka, G., Shikata, J., Watanabe, Y. (eds.) PKC 2022, Part I. LNCS, vol. 13177, pp. 221–251. Springer, Cham (2022). https://doi.org/10.1007/978-3-030-97121-2_9
4. Bellare, M., Micali, S.: Non-interactive oblivious transfer and applications. In: Brassard, G. (ed.) CRYPTO 1989. LNCS, vol. 435, pp. 547–557. Springer, New York (1990). https://doi.org/10.1007/0-387-34805-0_48
5. Bombar, M., Bui, D., Couteau, G., Couvreur, A., Ducros, C., Servan-Schreiber, S.: FOLEAGE: F4OLE-based multi-party computation for boolean circuits. In: Chung, K.M., Sasaki, Y. (eds.) ASIACRYPT 2024, Part VI, LNCS, vol. 15489, pp. 69–101. Springer, Singapore (2024)
6. Bombar, M., Couteau, G., Couvreur, A., Ducros, C.: Correlated pseudorandomness from the hardness of quasi-abelian decoding. In: Handschuh, H., Lysyanskaya, A. (eds.) CRYPTO 2023, Part IV. LNCS, vol. 14084, pp. 567–601. Springer, Cham (2023). https://doi.org/10.1007/978-3-031-38551-3_18
7. Boneh, D., Boyle, E., Corrigan-Gibbs, H., Gilboa, N., Ishai, Y.: Lightweight techniques for private heavy hitters. In: 2021 IEEE Symposium on Security and Privacy, pp. 762–776. IEEE Computer Society Press (2021). https://doi.org/10.1109/SP40001.2021.00048
8. Boyle, E., et al.: Function secret sharing for mixed-mode and fixed-point secure computation. In: Canteaut, A., Standaert, F.X. (eds.) EUROCRYPT 2021, Part II. LNCS, vol. 12697, pp. 871–900. Springer, Cham (2021). https://doi.org/10.1007/978-3-030-77886-6_30
9. Boyle, E., Couteau, G., Gilboa, N., Ishai, Y.: Compressing vector OLE. In: Lie, D., Mannan, M., Backes, M., Wang, X. (eds.) ACM CCS 2018, pp. 896–912. ACM Press (2018). https://doi.org/10.1145/3243734.3243868
10. Boyle, E., et al.: Correlated pseudorandomness from expand-accumulate codes. In: Dodis, Y., Shrimpton, T. (eds.) CRYPTO 2022, Part II. LNCS, vol. 13508, pp. 603–633. Springer, Cham (2022). https://doi.org/10.1007/978-3-031-15979-4_21
11. Boyle, E., et al.: Efficient two-round OT extension and silent non-interactive computation. In: Cavallaro, L., Kinder, J., Wang, X., Katz, J. (eds.) ACM CCS 2019, pp. 291–308. ACM Press (2019). https://doi.org/10.1145/3319535.3354255
12. Boyle, E., Couteau, G., Gilboa, N., Ishai, Y., Kohl, L., Scholl, P.: Efficient pseudorandom correlation generators: silent OT extension and more. In: Boldyreva, A., Micciancio, D. (eds.) CRYPTO 2019, Part III. LNCS, vol. 11694, pp. 489–518. Springer, Cham (2019). https://doi.org/10.1007/978-3-030-26954-8_16

13. Boyle, E., Couteau, G., Gilboa, N., Ishai, Y., Kohl, L., Scholl, P.: Correlated pseudorandom functions from variable-density LPN. In: 61st FOCS, pp. 1069–1080. IEEE Computer Society Press (2020). https://doi.org/10.1109/FOCS46700.2020.00103

14. Boyle, E., Couteau, G., Gilboa, N., Ishai, Y., Kohl, L., Scholl, P.: Efficient pseudorandom correlation generators from ring-LPN. In: Micciancio, D., Ristenpart, T. (eds.) CRYPTO 2020, Part II. LNCS, vol. 12171, pp. 387–416. Springer, Cham (2020). https://doi.org/10.1007/978-3-030-56880-1_14

15. Boyle, E., Couteau, G., Gilboa, N., Ishai, Y., Orrù, M.: Homomorphic secret sharing: optimizations and applications. In: Thuraisingham, B.M., Evans, D., Malkin, T., Xu, D. (eds.) ACM CCS 2017, pp. 2105–2122. ACM Press (2017). https://doi.org/10.1145/3133956.3134107

16. Boyle, E., Devadas, L., Servan-Schreiber, S.: Non-interactive distributed point functions. Cryptology ePrint Archive, Paper 2025/095 (2025). https://eprint.iacr.org/2025/095

17. Boyle, E., Gilboa, N., Ishai, Y.: Function secret sharing. In: Oswald, E., Fischlin, M. (eds.) EUROCRYPT 2015, Part II. LNCS, vol. 9057, pp. 337–367. Springer, Heidelberg (2015). https://doi.org/10.1007/978-3-662-46803-6_12

18. Boyle, E., Gilboa, N., Ishai, Y.: Breaking the circuit size barrier for secure computation under DDH. In: Robshaw, M., Katz, J. (eds.) CRYPTO 2016, Part I. LNCS, vol. 9814, pp. 509–539. Springer, Heidelberg (2016). https://doi.org/10.1007/978-3-662-53018-4_19

19. Boyle, E., Gilboa, N., Ishai, Y.: Group-based secure computation: optimizing rounds, communication, and computation. In: Coron, J.S., Nielsen, J.B. (eds.) EUROCRYPT 2017, Part II. LNCS, vol. 10211, pp. 163–193. Springer, Cham (2017). https://doi.org/10.1007/978-3-319-56614-6_6

20. Boyle, E., Gilboa, N., Ishai, Y.: Secure computation with preprocessing via function secret sharing. In: Hofheinz, D., Rosen, A. (eds.) TCC 2019, Part I. LNCS, vol. 11891, pp. 341–371. Springer, Cham (2019). https://doi.org/10.1007/978-3-030-36030-6_14

21. Boyle, E., Gilboa, N., Ishai, Y., Kolobov, V.I.: Programmable distributed point functions. In: Dodis, Y., Shrimpton, T. (eds.) CRYPTO 2022, Part IV. LNCS, vol. 13510, pp. 121–151. Springer, Cham (2022). https://doi.org/10.1007/978-3-031-15985-5_5

22. Boyle, E., Kohl, L., Scholl, P.: Homomorphic secret sharing from lattices without FHE. In: Ishai, Y., Rijmen, V. (eds.) EUROCRYPT 2019, Part II. LNCS, vol. 11477, pp. 3–33. Springer, Cham (2019). https://doi.org/10.1007/978-3-030-17656-3_1

23. Bui, D., Couteau, G., Meyer, P., Passelègue, A., Riahinia, M.: Fast public-key silent OT and more from constrained Naor-Reingold. In: Joye, M., Leander, G. (eds.) EUROCRYPT 2024, Part VI. LNCS, vol. 14656, pp. 88–118. Springer, Cham (2024). https://doi.org/10.1007/978-3-031-58751-1_4

24. Corrigan-Gibbs, H., Boneh, D., Mazières, D.: Riposte: an anonymous messaging system handling millions of users. In: 2015 IEEE Symposium on Security and Privacy, pp. 321–338. IEEE Computer Society Press (2015). https://doi.org/10.1109/SP.2015.27

25. Couteau, G., Devadas, L., Devadas, S., Koch, A., Servan-Schreiber, S.: QuietOT: lightweight oblivious transfer with a public-key setup. In: Chung, K.M., Sasaki, Y. (eds.) ASIACRYPT 2024, Part II. LNCS, vol. 15485, pp. 197–231. Springer, Singapore (2024). https://doi.org/10.1007/978-981-96-0888-1_7

26. Couteau, G., Devadas, L., Hegde, A., Jain, A., Servan-Schreiber, S.: Multi-key homomorphic secret sharing. Cryptology ePrint Archive, Paper 2025/094 (2025). https://eprint.iacr.org/2025/094

27. Couteau, G., Meyer, P., Passelègue, A., Riahinia, M.: Constrained pseudorandom functions from homomorphic secret sharing. In: Hazay, C., Stam, M. (eds.) EURO-CRYPT 2023, Part III. LNCS, vol. 14006, pp. 194–224. Springer, Cham (2023). https://doi.org/10.1007/978-3-031-30620-4_7

28. Couteau, G., Zarezadeh, M.: Non-interactive secure computation of inner-product from LPN and LWE. In: Agrawal, S., Lin, D. (eds.) ASIACRYPT 2022, Part I. LNCS, vol. 13791, pp. 474–503. Springer, Cham (2022). https://doi.org/10.1007/978-3-031-22963-3_16

29. Dao, Q., Ishai, Y., Jain, A., Lin, H.: Multi-party homomorphic secret sharing and sublinear MPC from sparse LPN. In: Handschuh, H., Lysyanskaya, A. (eds.) CRYPTO 2023, Part II. LNCS, vol. 14082, pp. 315–348. Springer, Cham (2023). https://doi.org/10.1007/978-3-031-38545-2_11

30. Dauterman, E., Feng, E., Luo, E., Popa, R.A., Stoica, I.: DORY: an encrypted search system with distributed trust. In: 14th USENIX Symposium on Operating Systems Design and Implementation (OSDI 2020), pp. 1101–1119 (2020)

31. Dauterman, E., Rathee, M., Popa, R.A., Stoica, I.: Waldo: a private time-series database from function secret sharing. In: 2022 IEEE Symposium on Security and Privacy, pp. 2450–2468. IEEE Computer Society Press (2022). https://doi.org/10.1109/SP46214.2022.9833611

32. Diffie, W., Hellman, M.E.: New directions in cryptography. IEEE Trans. Inf. Theory **22**(6), 644–654 (1976). https://doi.org/10.1109/TIT.1976.1055638

33. Dinur, I., Keller, N., Klein, O.: An optimal distributed discrete log protocol with applications to homomorphic secret sharing. J. Cryptol. **33**(3), 824–873 (2019). https://doi.org/10.1007/s00145-019-09330-2

34. Dodis, Y., Halevi, S., Rothblum, R.D., Wichs, D.: Spooky encryption and its applications. In: Robshaw, M., Katz, J. (eds.) CRYPTO 2016, Part III. LNCS, vol. 9816, pp. 93–122. Springer, Heidelberg (2016). https://doi.org/10.1007/978-3-662-53015-3_4

35. Doerner, J., Shelat, A.: Scaling ORAM for secure computation. In: Thuraisingham, B.M., Evans, D., Malkin, T., Xu, D. (eds.) ACM CCS 2017, pp. 523–535. ACM Press (2017). https://doi.org/10.1145/3133956.3133967

36. Gilboa, N., Ishai, Y.: Distributed point functions and their applications. In: Nguyen, P.Q., Oswald, E. (eds.) EUROCRYPT 2014. LNCS, vol. 8441, pp. 640–658. Springer, Heidelberg (2014). https://doi.org/10.1007/978-3-642-55220-5_35

37. Halevi, S., Lindell, Y., Pinkas, B.: Secure computation on the web: computing without simultaneous interaction. In: Rogaway, P. (ed.) CRYPTO 2011. LNCS, vol. 6841, pp. 132–150. Springer, Heidelberg (2011). https://doi.org/10.1007/978-3-642-22792-9_8

38. Jawalkar, N., Gupta, K., Basu, A., Chandran, N., Gupta, D., Sharma, R.: Orca: FSS-based secure training and inference with GPUs. In: 2024 IEEE Symposium on Security and Privacy, pp. 597–616. IEEE Computer Society Press (2024). https://doi.org/10.1109/SP54263.2024.00063

39. Mouris, D., Patton, C., Davis, H., Sarkar, P., Tsoutsos, N.G.: Mastic: private weighted heavy-hitters and attribute-based metrics. Cryptology ePrint Archive, Report 2024/221 (2024). https://eprint.iacr.org/2024/221

40. Mouris, D., Sarkar, P., Tsoutsos, N.G.: PLASMA: private, lightweight aggregated statistics against malicious adversaries. PoPETs **2024**(3), 4–24 (2024). https://doi.org/10.56553/popets-2024-0064

41. Orlandi, C., Scholl, P., Yakoubov, S.: The rise of Paillier: homomorphic secret sharing and public-key silent OT. In: Canteaut, A., Standaert, F.X. (eds.) EURO-CRYPT 2021, Part I. LNCS, vol. 12696, pp. 678–708. Springer, Cham (2021). https://doi.org/10.1007/978-3-030-77870-5_24

42. Rathee, M., Zhang, Y., Corrigan-Gibbs, H., Popa, R.A.: Private analytics via streaming, sketching, and silently verifiable proofs. Cryptology ePrint Archive (2024)

43. Roy, L., Singh, J.: Large message homomorphic secret sharing from DCR and applications. In: Malkin, T., Peikert, C. (eds.) CRYPTO 2021, Part III. LNCS, vol. 12827, pp. 687–717. Springer, Cham (2021). https://doi.org/10.1007/978-3-030-84252-9_23

44. Ryffel, T., Tholoniat, P., Pointcheval, D., Bach, F.R.: AriaNN: low-interaction privacy-preserving deep learning via function secret sharing. PoPETs **2022**(1), 291–316 (2022). https://doi.org/10.2478/popets-2022-0015

45. Schoppmann, P., Gascón, A., Reichert, L., Raykova, M.: Distributed vector-OLE: improved constructions and implementation. In: Cavallaro, L., Kinder, J., Wang, X., Katz, J. (eds.) ACM CCS 2019, pp. 1055–1072. ACM Press (2019). https://doi.org/10.1145/3319535.3363228

46. Servan-Schreiber, S., Langowski, S., Devadas, S.: Private approximate nearest neighbor search with sublinear communication. In: 2022 IEEE Symposium on Security and Privacy, pp. 911–929. IEEE Computer Society Press (2022). https://doi.org/10.1109/SP46214.2022.9833702

47. Vadapalli, A., Henry, R., Goldberg, I.: DUORAM: a bandwidth-efficient distributed ORAM for 2- and 3-party computation. In: Calandrino, J.A., Troncoso, C. (eds.) USENIX Security 2023, pp. 3907–3924. USENIX Association (2023)

48. Vadapalli, A., Storrier, K., Henry, R.: Sabre: sender-anonymous messaging with fast audits. In: 2022 IEEE Symposium on Security and Privacy, pp. 1953–1970. IEEE Computer Society Press (2022). https://doi.org/10.1109/SP46214.2022.9833601

49. Wang, F., Yun, C., Goldwasser, S., Vaikuntanathan, V., Zaharia, M.: Splinter: practical private queries on public data. In: 14th USENIX Symposium on Networked Systems Design and Implementation (NSDI 2017), pp. 299–313 (2017)

50. Xu, P., Wang, L.P.: Multi-key homomorphic secret sharing from LWE without multi-key HE. In: Simpson, L., Baee, M.A.R. (eds.) ACISP 23. LNCS, vol. 13915, pp. 248–269. Springer, Cham (2023). https://doi.org/10.1007/978-3-031-35486-1_12

51. Yang, K., Weng, C., Lan, X., Zhang, J., Wang, X.: Ferret: fast extension for correlated OT with small communication. In: Ligatti, J., Ou, X., Katz, J., Vigna, G. (eds.) ACM CCS 2020, pp. 1607–1626. ACM Press (2020). https://doi.org/10.1145/3372297.3417276

52. Yang, P., et al.: FssNN: communication-efficient secure neural network training via function secret sharing. Cryptology ePrint Archive, Report 2023/073 (2023). https://eprint.iacr.org/2023/073

Watermarkable and Zero-Knowledge Verifiable Delay Functions from Any Proof of Exponentiation

Charlotte Hoffmann$^{(\boxtimes)}$ ⓘ and Krzysztof Pietrzak

Institute of Science and Technology Austria, Klosterneuburg, Austria
{charlotte.hoffmann,pietrzak}@ist.ac.at

Abstract. A verifiable delay function $\mathtt{VDF}(x,T) \to (y,\pi)$ maps an input x and time parameter T to an output y together with an efficiently verifiable proof π certifying that y was correctly computed. The function runs in T sequential steps, and it should not be possible to compute y much faster than that. The only known practical VDFs use sequential squaring in groups of unknown order as the sequential function, i.e., $y = x^{2^T}$. There are two constructions for the proof of exponentiation (PoE) certifying that $y = x^{2^T}$, with Wesolowski (Eurocrypt'19) having very short proofs, but they are more expensive to compute and the soundness relies on stronger assumptions than the PoE proposed by Pietrzak (ITCS'19).

A recent application of VDFs by Arun, Bonneau and Clark (Asiacrypt'22) are short-lived proofs and signatures, which are proofs and signatures that are only sound for some time t, but after that can be forged by anyone. For this they rely on "watermarkable VDFs", where the proof embeds a prover chosen watermark. To achieve stronger notions of proofs/signatures with reusable forgeability, they rely on "zero-knowledge VDFs", where instead of the output y, one just proves knowledge of this output. The existing proposals for watermarkable and zero-knowledge VDFs all build on Wesolowski's PoE, for the watermarkable VDFs there's currently no security proof.

In this work we give the first constructions that transform any PoEs in hidden order groups into watermarkable VDFs and into zkVDFs, solving an open question by Arun et al. Unlike our watermarkable VDF, the zkVDF (required for reusable forgeability) is not very practical as the number of group elements in the proof is a security parameter. To address this, we introduce the notion of zero-knowledge proofs of sequential work (zkPoSW), a notion that relaxes zkVDFs by not requiring that the output is unique. We show that zkPoSW are sufficient to construct proofs or signatures with reusable forgeability, and construct efficient zkPoSW from any PoE, ultimately achieving short lived proofs and signatures that improve upon Arun et al.'s construction in several dimensions (faster forging times, arguably weaker assumptions).

A key idea underlying our constructions is to not directly construct a (watermarked or zk) proof for $y = x^{2^T}$, but instead give a (watermarked or zk) proof for the more basic statement that x', y' satisfy $x' = x^r, y' = y^r$ for some r, together with a normal PoE for $y' = (x')^{2^T}$.

© International Association for Cryptologic Research 2025
T. Jager and J. Pan (Eds.): PKC 2025, LNCS 15674, pp. 36–66, 2025.
https://doi.org/10.1007/978-3-031-91820-9_2

1   Introduction

Verifiable delay functions (VDFs), introduced by Boneh et al. [6], are functions that take a prescribed amount of T steps to compute and can be verified in time much less than T. They have found a lot of applications including the design of blockchains [14], randomness beacons [41,45], proofs of data replication [6] and computational time-stamping [13,33].

Time-Based Deniability from VDFs. A recent application of VDFs was presented by Arun, Bonneau and Clark in [2]. The authors construct so called *short-lived proofs* and *short-lived signatures* from VDFs that satisfy some additional properties. Short-lived proofs and signatures are only valid for a prescribed amount of time T. After time T they are easy to forge by anyone and hence validity cannot be verified anymore. The authors of [2] achieve this notion for any relation $\mathcal{R}$ by combining a proof system for $\mathcal{R}$ with a VDF computation using a simple OR statement: A short-lived proof is correct if either the proof for $\mathcal{R}$ is correct or a VDF computation has been performed. This way the proof for $\mathcal{R}$ is only valid before time T has passed since after time T anyone can output a valid proof by proving that they have performed the VDF computation. One useful property that short-lived proofs and signatures can have is *reusable forgeability*, which means that one slow computation enables efficient proof forgery for many statements.

Zero-Knowledge VDFs. Zero-Knowledge VDFs are VDFs that can verify that a prover $\mathcal{P}$ knows the result $y = x^{2^T}$ without revealing any other information about y to the verifier $\mathcal{V}$, i.e., instead of sending the result y to $\mathcal{V}$, $\mathcal{P}$ and $\mathcal{V}$ engage in a *zero-knowledge proof of knowledge* of y. Such VDFs were introduced by Arun, Bonneau and Clark in [2], where they use it as a building block to construct short-lived proofs. The zero-knowledge VDF in [2] is a zero-knowledge version of Wesolowski's VDF. Using this VDF in the OR construction described above to obtain a short-lived proof provides some form of reusable forgeability: After performing one slow computation of the delay function, one can forge proofs for multiple statements of the same sender by providing a re-randomized VDF proof for each statement. Using the zero-knowledge VDF in [2] computing a re-randomized proof takes time roughly $T/\log(T)$ since this is the time it takes compute Wesolowski's VDF proof. Since Pietrzak's VDF proof can be computed in time $T/\sqrt{T}$, a zero-knowledge version of Pietrzak's VDF would enable much faster forging times. The authors of [2] leave a construction of a zero-knowledge version of Pietrzak's VDF as an open problem.

Watermarkable VDFs. Watermarkable VDFs are VDFs in which the proof can be watermarked, i.e., tied to a specific prover. They were informally introduced by Wesolowski in [50], where he claims that his VDF can be watermarked by including a unique identifier in the computation of the random challenge. The authors of [2] point out that security of this scheme is not proven since the proof of Wesolowski's VDF reveals the value x^q for a large q which may speed up the computation of $y = x^{2^T}$ and hence the computation of a proof with a different watermark. They propose to watermark the proof of their zero-knowledge VDF construction by including a unique identifier in the computation of the random challenge of the proof. Since the protocol is zero-knowledge, the watermarked proof does not reveal any information that might help computing a proof with a different watermark. However, this also means that the value $y = x^{2^T}$ cannot be revealed, which might be relevant in other applications of watermarkable VDFs.

1.1   Our Contribution

We give the first constructions that transform *any* PoE in hidden order groups into a watermarkable VDF and into a zero-knowledge VDF. We note that this gives the first practical watermarkable VDF with a security proof, and the zkVDF solves the open problem stated in [2] asking for a zkVDF based on Pietrzak's VDF.

Instantiating the watermarkable VDFs with Pietrzak's PoE and using it in the [2] construction of short-lived proofs (without reusable forgeability) we get proofs with significantly faster forging times and under different (arguably weaker) assumptions than the construction in [2].

Our watermarkable VDF is practically efficient and only slightly increases the proof size of the PoE. However, the zero-knowledge VDF increases the proof size by roughly 4λ group elements, where λ is a statistical security parameter. While the proof size is still independent of the time parameter T, a blow-up by 4λ group elements is undesirable in practice.

To address this, we introduce the notion of zero-knowledge proofs of sequential work (zkPoSW). We show that zkPoSW can replace zkVDFs in the construction of short-lived proofs and signatures with reusable forgeability from [2], and also give a construction that transforms any PoE into a zkPoSW which only increases the proof size of the PoE by 3 group elements. As before, using Pietrzak's PoE we get short lived proofs and signatures with shorter forging times and different assumptions than [2].

Watermarkable VDFs. We construct the first general watermarkable VDF scheme from any PoE in hidden order groups. In this construction the proof of the statement $x^{2^T} = y$ is computed as follows:

1. Sample a random $r \leftarrow \pm[2^\lambda]$.
2. Compute $x' := x^r$ and $y' := y^r$.
3. Compute a PoE proof π_{PoE} for the statement $(x')^{2^T} = y'$.
4. Compute a watermarked zero-knowledge proof of knowledge of r, denoted by π_{PoK}.
5. Publish $x, x', y, y', \pi_{\mathsf{PoE}}$ and π_{PoK}.

Watermarking the proof of knowledge is done by including a unique identifier in the computation of the random challenge. Watermark unforgeability holds by soundness of the proof of knowledge, a decisional variant of the discrete log assumption in hidden order groups and a decisional variant of the iterated squaring assumption: If the proof of knowledge is sound, then the only two ways for an adversary to forge a proof with its own watermark are the following:

- Find r such that $x^r = x'$ and $y^r = y'$, copy π_{PoE} and honestly compute π_{PoK}. By finding r, the adversary finds a small discrete log of x' with base x.
- Compute a PoE for a new statement $(x^{r'})^{2^T} = y^{r'}$ faster than time T. If the adversary is able to do this, then in particular it can also recognize that y is indeed the result of x^{2^T} in time faster than T, which breaks the decisional iterated squaring assumption.

The construction in [2] is only slightly more efficient than ours: It increases the proof size of Wesolowski's proof by one group element, whereas our construction increases the proof size of a PoE by four group elements. However, our construction can watermark *any* PoE, while the construction in [2] cannot be generalized to other PoEs than Wesolowski's. Further, the watermarkable VDF in [2] cannot reveal the output of the iterated squaring instance since it is based on a zero knowledge VDF, which may be undesirable for other applications.

Zero-Knowledge VDFs. We construct the first general zero-knowledge VDF from any PoE in hidden order groups. It is similar to the watermarkable VDF construction but instead of publishing the element y, the prover just proves knowledge of y. In this construction the proof of the statement $x^{2^T} = y$ is computed as follows:

1. Sample a random $r \leftarrow \pm[2^\lambda]$.
2. Compute $x' := x^r$ and $y' := y^r$.
3. Compute a PoE proof π_{PoE} for the statement $(x')^{2^T} = y'$.
4. Compute a zero-knowledge proof of knowledge of y and r, denoted by π_{PoK}.
5. Publish $x, x', y', \pi_{\mathsf{PoE}}$ and π_{PoK}.

To prove that this scheme is zero-knowledge, the simulator needs a precomputed pair x^*, y^* and a PoE for the statement $(x^*)^{2^T} = y^*$, which we can include in the public parameters. Then it can output a simulated proof simply by forging the proof of knowledge of y and r. We need to rely on a decisional version of the discrete log assumption in hidden order groups so that the adversary cannot decide if there exists a small discrete log between elements x^* and x or not. The bottleneck of this construction is the zero-knowledge proof of knowledge of y and r. We obtain it by combing Schnorr's protocol with the Guillou-Quisquater protocol for proving knowledge of a s-root in hidden order groups. In our setting we can only prove soundness of this scheme when using challenge space $\{0,1\}$ and running λ many repetitions, which makes the scheme impractical.

Zero-Knowledge Proofs of Sequential Work. We salvage the efficiency of the above scheme by dropping the requirement of a proof of knowledge of y. This means that our construction is not a VDF anymore: The prover might not know the unique result $y = x^{2^T}$ since it can also just compute $y' = (x^r)^{2^T}$ and output a valid proof. However, we assume that computing the proof still requires T steps, which is sufficient for a proof of sequential work. We call the assumption that computing $(x^r)^{2^T}$ for an adversarially chosen $r \neq 0$ takes T sequential steps *generalized iterated squaring assumption*. In this construction, given x, the proof of sequential work is computed as follows:

1. Compute $y = x^{2^T}$ together with advice string α.
2. Sample a random $r \leftarrow \pm[2^\lambda]$.
3. Compute $x' := x^r$ and $y' := y^r$.
4. Compute a PoE proof π_{PoE} for the statement $(x')^{2^T} = y'$ using α.
5. Compute a zero-knowledge proof of knowledge of r, denoted by π_{PoK}.
6. Publish $x, x', y, y', \pi_{\mathsf{PoE}}$ and π_{PoK}.

New Assumptions. As discussed above, we use two assumptions in this work that are natural modifications of well-known assumptions but, to the best of our knowledge, have not already been defined in previous work.

– The *decisional discrete log assumption with small exponents* (defined in Sect. 4) states that given group elements a, b it's hard to decide if there exists a discrete logarithm $w, b = a^w$ even if the discrete logarithm w is guaranteed to be bounded by 2^λ for a security parameter λ (rather than uniform as in the standard discrete log assumption).
  We require this assumption to hold in the groups of unknown order over which the corresponding VDFs are defined. In groups of known order a stronger assumption is sometimes made in Diffie-Hellman key exchange where, for efficiency reasons, the exponents are chosen to be random numbers of only, say 275 bits (https://www.rfc-editor.org/rfc/rfc7919#section-5.2). In [9] Canetti makes an even stronger assumption (DHI Assumption II) in groups of order $2q + 1$ for a large prime q, which implies that discrete log is hard even when the set from which the exponent is chosen is "well spread", which basically means it can be an arbitrary set of only slightly superpolynomial size.
– The *generalized iterated squaring assumption* (defined in Sect. 7.2) states that given x, computing a tuple (r, y) such that $y = (x^r)^{2^T}$ requires T steps. This generalizes the iterated squaring assumption where one requires $r = 1$. Rotem and Segev [44] analyze the delay property of generic ring functions. They show that, based on the hardness of factoring, any generic ring function is a delay function with time parameter determined by the sequentiality depth of the function. While the generalized iterated squaring assumption does not consider a *function* (the correct output is not unique), we believe that the techniques of Rotem and Segev can be applied in a straightforward manner to show that, in the generic ring model, breaking the generalized iterated squaring assumption is equivalent to factoring.

1.2   Related Work

Time-Release Cryptography. VDFs are an example of timed-release cryptographic primitives [39]. The first such primitives were time-lock puzzles (TLPs)

[42] and timed commitments [8]. A TLP can be seen as a delay function that also allows efficient computation (and hence verification) of its output via a trapdoor. The TLP from [42] uses repeated squaring as the delay function, with the factorization of the modulus as the trapdoor. Prior to VDFs the notion of proofs of sequential work (PoSWs) was introduced by Mahmoody, Moran and Vadhan [36]. Unlike TLPs, PoSWs can be constructed from random oracles [35]. The construction from [36] is based on random oracles but is not practical as the prover needs *space* linear in T to compute the PoSW. A construction using just $\log(T)$ space was given in [14]. Constructions with extra properties like being "reversible" [1] or "incremental" [19] were proposed shortly afterwards. The sloth function of Lenstra and Wesolowski [34] is already close to a unique PoSW. However, verification takes time linear in T. Finally, VDFs were introduced by Boneh et al. [6]. Mahmoody, Smith and Wu [37] showed that VDFs cannot be built from hash functions.

Proofs of Exponentiation. One way to obtain practical VDFs is to rely on iterated squaring in a hidden order group as the delay function and then construct a proof of exponentiation (PoE) to make the result verifiable. The first PoEs were introduced concurrently by Wesolowski [50] and Pietrzak [40]. Block et al. [5] presented the first statistically-sound PoE in any group, which they use to build polynomial commitment schemes. The PoE in [25] is built on their protocol and reduces the complexity, whenever the exponent can be chosen in a special way. [27] construct a PoE in an extension field of $\mathbb{Z}_N$ to build a VDF from a potentially weaker assumption than iterated squaring. In [26] a PoE for Proth number groups is given to certify proofs of non-primality. Batching protocols for PoEs can be found in [28,43].

Other Verifiable Delay Functions. There are several candidate VDFs not based on iterated squaring, such as the isogenies-based constructions [11,18,48], the permutation-polynomial based construction [6] and the constructions from lattice problems [12,32]. Freitag, Pass and Sirkin [23] constructed VDFs from any sequentially hard function and polynomial hardness of learning with errors. While some of the above construction possibly provide post quantum security, they are currently not as efficient as the VDFs built from iterated squaring. Other VDF candidates rely on "arithmetization friendly" symmetric primitives and practically efficient SNARKs [6,30,47].

Time-Based Deniability. Baldimtsi et al. [3] build so called *proofs of work or knowledge*, with which a prover can prove that they either know the witness of a statement or it has solved a proof of work puzzle. However, in their work both cases are indistinguishable from the beginning, whereas in short-lived proofs the cases are indistinguishable only after time T has passed. Specter, Park and Green [49] build protocols that prove that either a prover knows the witness of a statement or it has seen a value released at time T. Ferrari, Géraud and Sirkin [20] construct *fading* signatures that also lose validity after a certain amount of time based on the RSW time-lock puzzle. However, they need to rely on a trusted authority that knows a trapdoor and they need that the verifier is more powerful than the prover.

Colburn [15] constructs short-lived proofs and signatures from proofs of work in his master thesis. The proofs of work in his thesis consist of finding preimages of hash functions and are thus parallelizable.

Wesolowski [50] was the first one to use VDFs as a building block for time-based deniability. He presents an identification protocol based on a trapdoor VDF that loses its validity after time T. Finally, Arun, Bonneau and Clark [2] were the first ones to build general short-lived proofs and signatures from VDFs.

2   Preliminaries

In the rest of the paper, we let λ denote a security parameter. We use $[n] := \{1, \dots, n\}$ to denote the set of all positive integers smaller than or equal to n.

2.1   Relations and Interactive Proofs

A *relation* $\mathcal{R} \subset \mathcal{X} \times \mathcal{W}$ is a set of pairs (x, w), where x is called the instance and w is called the witness. The set of all values x for which there exists a witness w such that $(x, w) \in \mathcal{R}$ is called the *language* $L_{\mathcal{R}}$ for $\mathcal{R}$.

Definition 1 (interactive proof). *For a function $\varepsilon : \mathbb{N} \to [0, 1]$, an interactive proof for a relation $\mathcal{R}$ is a pair of interacting PPT algorithms $(\mathcal{P}, \mathcal{V})$, called the* prover *and the* verifier, *where $\mathcal{P}$ takes as input a pair $(x, w) \in \mathcal{R}$ and $\mathcal{V}$ takes as input x. We require the algorithms to satisfy the following properties*

- *Completeness: For every $x \in L_{\mathcal{R}}$, if $\mathcal{V}$ interacts with $\mathcal{P}$ on the common instance x, then $\mathcal{V}$ accepts with probability 1.*
- *Soundness: For every $x \notin L_{\mathcal{R}}$ and every cheating prover strategy $\widetilde{\mathcal{P}}$, the acceptance probability of the verifier $\mathcal{V}$ when interacting with $\widetilde{\mathcal{P}}$ is less than $\varepsilon(|x|)$, where ε is called the* soundness error.

Definition 2 (proof of knowledge). *A* proof of knowledge *is an interactive proof that is* knowledge sound, *i.e., there exists an efficient extractor $\mathcal{E}$ such that for every (potentially malicious) prover $\mathcal{P}^*$ that makes $\mathcal{V}$ accept proof π for instance x of bit-length n with probability δ, the extractor $\mathcal{E}$, which can interact with $\mathcal{P}^*$, outputs a witness w such that $(x, w) \in \mathcal{R}$ with probability at least $(\delta - \varepsilon)/\mathsf{poly}(n)$, where poly is some positive polynomial and $\varepsilon \in [0, 1]$ is called the* soundness error.

Sometimes the knowledge extractor $\mathcal{E}$ only manages to output a witness for a relation that slightly differs to the relation for which completeness holds. In this case we say that the proof of knowledge soundness is *not tight*. This can affect the choice of parameters and assumptions needed for soundness.

To prove knowledge soundness it is often easier to show that the protocol satisfies *special soundness*. It is well known that special soundness implies knowledge soundness for 3-round protocols.

Definition 3 (special soundness). *A 3-round protocol is called* special sound *if there exist a polynomial time extractor that on input an instance x and two accepting transcripts (a, c, z) and (a, c', z') with common first message a and $c \neq c'$ outputs a witness $w \in \mathcal{R}$.*

In this work we consider special honest verifier zero-knowledge which is a special case of honest verifier zero-knowledge. Note that proving zero-knowledge against an honest verifier is sufficient for us because the protocols will be made non-interactive via the Fiat-Shamir transform.

Definition 4 (special honest verifier zero-knowledge proof). *A special honest verifier zero-knowledge proof is an interactive proof that is zero knowledge when the verifier is honest. That means there exists an efficient simulator $\mathcal{S}$ that, given instance $x \in L_{\mathcal{R}}$ and a uniformly random value r from the randomness space of the verifier, can output an accepting transcript for x with verifier's message r which is indistinguishable from a real transcript with an honest verifier.*

It is well known that any constant round interactive proof in which the verifier messages only consist of random elements can be transformed into a non-interactive proof via the Fiat-Shamir heuristic [21] by deriving the verifier's messages via a suitable hash function. If the interactive proof is honest verifier zero-knowledge, the non-interactive version is fully *zero-knowledge* (i.e., no assumption on the behavior of the verifier is needed) in the *random oracle model*. In the random oracle model the hash function is modelled as a publicly available random function $\mathcal{O}$. The simulator $\mathcal{S}$ has *programmable* access to $\mathcal{O}$, which means that it can set the output of $\mathcal{O}$ to a value of its choice as long as the distribution of the output values is uniform.

Definition 5 (proof of exponentiation). *A* proof of exponentiation *(PoE) in a group $\mathbb{G}$ is an interactive proof for the language*

$$L = \{(x, y, e) \in \mathbb{G}^2 \times \mathbb{N} \mid x^{2^e} = y\}.$$

2.2 Verifiable Delay Functions

Verifiable Delay Functions were introduced by Boneh et al. in [6].

Definition 6. *A verifiable delay function (VDF) is a set of algorithms (Setup, Eval, Prove, Verify), where*

Setup$(1^\lambda, T) \to$ pp on input statistical security parameter 1^λ and time parameter T outputs public parameters pp.
Eval(pp, x) $\to (y, \alpha)$ on input (pp, x, T) outputs (y, α), where α is an advice string.
Prove(pp, x, y, α) $\to (y, \pi)$ outputs a proof π for y.
Verify(pp, x, y, π) $\to$ accept/reject checks that $y = $ Eval(pp, x).

The algorithm Eval is deterministic and can compute the output y in T sequential steps. A VDF must additionally satisfy three properties:

Completeness: For all tuples $(\mathbf{pp}, x, y, \pi)$, where $y = \texttt{Eval}(\mathbf{pp}, x)$ and $\pi = \texttt{Prove}(\mathbf{pp}, x, y, \alpha)$, algorithm $\texttt{Verify}(\mathbf{pp}, x, y, \pi)$ outputs accept.

Sequentiality: Any parallel algorithm that uses at most $\mathsf{poly}(\lambda)$ processors and outputs $y = \texttt{Eval}(\mathbf{pp}, x)$ with noticeable probability runs in time at least T.

Soundness: If $\texttt{Verify}(\mathbf{pp}, x, y, \pi)$ outputs accept, then the probability that $y \neq \texttt{Eval}(\mathbf{pp}, x)$ is negligible.

2.3 Assumptions

In this paper we need the following well-known assumptions in hidden-order groups. In Sects. 4 and 7.2 we state the novel assumption that we need.

Definition 7 (strong RSA assumption). *Let $\texttt{GGen}(1^\lambda)$ be a randomized algorithm that outputs the description of a hidden-order group $\mathbb{G}$. We say that the* strong RSA assumption *holds for $\texttt{GGen}$ if, for any probabilistic polynomial-time algorithm $\mathcal{A}$, the probability of winning the following game is negligible in λ:*

1. *$\mathcal{A}$ takes as input the description of a group $\mathbb{G}$ output by $\texttt{GGen}(1^\lambda)$ and an element $a \leftarrow \mathbb{G}$.*
2. *$\mathcal{A}$ outputs a pair $(e, b) \in \mathbb{Z} \times \mathbb{G}$.*
3. *$\mathcal{A}$ wins if and only if $e \neq 1$ and $b^e = a$.*

The following assumption, which was first formalized in [7], states that it is (computationally) hard to find elements of low order. Note that our assumption is a bit stronger than theirs because our upper bound on the order is $2^{3\lambda+2}$, while they assume the upper bound 2^λ. There are groups in which this assumption holds information theoretically because such elements do not exist: The group of signed quadratic residues QR_N^+ of an RSA integer $N = pq$, where p and q are safe primes, i.e., $p = 2p' + 1$ and $q = 2q' + 1$ for some primes p', q' that are larger than $2^{3\lambda+2}$.

Definition 8 (low order assumption). *Let $\texttt{GGen}(1^\lambda)$ be a randomized algorithm that outputs the description of a hidden-order group $\mathbb{G}$. We say that the* low order assumption *holds for $\texttt{GGen}$ if, for any probabilistic polynomial-time algorithm $\mathcal{A}$, the probability of winning the following game is negligible in λ:*

1. *$\mathcal{A}$ takes as input the description of a group $\mathbb{G}$ output by $\texttt{GGen}(1^\lambda)$.*
2. *$\mathcal{A}$ outputs a pair $(d, a) \in [2^{3\lambda+2}] \times \mathbb{G}$.*
3. *$\mathcal{A}$ wins if and only if $a \neq 1$ and $a^d = 1$.*

The following assumption was first stated by Rivest, Shamir and Wagner [42].

Definition 9 (iterated squaring assumption). *Let $\texttt{GGen}(1^\lambda)$ be a randomized algorithm that outputs the description of a hidden-order group $\mathbb{G}$. We say that the* iterated squaring assumption *holds for $\texttt{GGen}$ if, for any probabilistic parallel algorithm $\mathcal{A}$ that uses at most $\mathsf{poly}(\lambda)$ processors and runs in time less than T, the probability of winning the following game is negligible in λ:*

1. $\mathcal{A}$ *takes as input the description of a group* $\mathbb{G}$ *output by* GGen(1^λ), *a random group element* x *and an integer* T.
2. $\mathcal{A}$ *wins if it outputs element* $y = x^{2^T}$.

Remark 1. We note that, strictly speaking, the iterated assumption as stated above does not hold. Bernstein and Sorenson [4] showed that one can reduce the *sequential* time of computing an iterated squaring instance x^{2^T} from T to $T/\log\log(T)$ using at least T^2 processors. While this is a nice theoretical result, it is not practical in our setting. In practice the time parameter T will be at most 2^{32}, so the algorithm by Bernstein and Sorenson can reduce the sequential time by at most a factor of 6, for which it would need at least $T^2 = 2^{64}$ processors. For simplicity we will ignore this $\log\log(T)$ factor in the rest of the paper.

In the decisional version of the iterated squaring assumption we consider an adversary that gets as input a pair of group elements (x, y) and needs to decide whether or not $y = x^{2^T}$. The YES instances are pairs (x, x^{2^T}) for a uniformly random group element x. The NO instances are pairs (x, z^2) for uniformly random group elements x and z. Note that it is necessary to square the element z because x^{2^T} is a square and in RSA groups one can rule out that an element is a square, whenever its (efficiently computable) Jacobi symbol is -1. The assumption was first stated explicitly in [38] and analyzed in the GGM in [44].

Definition 10 (decisional iterated squaring assumption). *Let* GGen(1^λ) *be a randomized algorithm that outputs the description of a hidden-order group* $\mathbb{G}$. *We say that the* decisional iterated squaring assumption *holds for* GGen *if, for any probabilistic parallel algorithm* $\mathcal{A}$ *that uses at most* poly(λ) *processors and runs in time less than* T, *the probability of winning the following game is negligible in* λ:

1. $\mathcal{A}$ *takes as input the description of a group* $\mathbb{G}$ *output by* GGen(1^λ), *a random group element* x, *an integer* T *and a group element* y *which, with probability* $1/2$ *each, takes one of the following two forms: either* $y = z^2$ *for a uniformly random group element* z *or* $y = x^{2^T}$.
2. $\mathcal{A}$ *outputs 0 or 1 indicating whether or not* $y = x^{2^T}$.
3. $\mathcal{A}$ *wins if it outputs the correct bit with probability greater than* $1/2$.

2.4   The Group of Signed Quadratic Residues

One example of a hidden order group that has useful properties is the group of signed quadratic residues [22,29] with a safe prime modulus. We call a prime number p *safe* if $p = 2p' + 1$ for a prime number p'. We say that $N = pq$ is a *safe prime modulus*, if both p and q are safe primes. Let $\mathbb{Z}_N^*$ denote the multiplicative group modulo N. The group of quadratic residues modulo N is defined as $\mathrm{QR}_N := \{a^2 \mod N : a \in \mathbb{Z}_N^*\}$ and the group of signed quadratic residues is defined as

$$\mathrm{QR}_N^+ := \{|\, b\,| : b \in \mathrm{QR}_N\},$$

Instance: $(a_1, a_2, \mathbb{G})$, where $a_1, a_2 \in \mathbb{G}$

Parameters: statistical security parameter λ

Witness: Exponent $w \in \pm[2^\lambda]$ such that $a_1^w = a_2$ in $\mathbb{G}$

Protocol:

1. $\mathcal{P}$ samples $t \leftarrow \pm[2^{3\lambda}]$ uniformly at random, computes $b := a_1^t$ and sends it to $\mathcal{V}$.
2. $\mathcal{V}$ samples $c \leftarrow [2^\lambda]$ uniformly at random and sends it to $\mathcal{P}$.
3. $\mathcal{P}$ computes $s := t + cw$ and sends it to $\mathcal{V}$.
4. $\mathcal{V}$ checks if $s \in \pm[2^{3\lambda+1}]$ and $a_1^s = ba_2^c$ and outputs accept or reject accordingly.

Fig. 1. Proof of Knowledge of Discrete Log [31,46].

where $\mid b \mid$ is the absolute value of b when representing the elements of $\mathbb{Z}_N$ as $\{-(N-1)/2, \ldots, (N-1)/2\}$. QR_N^+ is a cyclic group with group operation $a \circ b := \mid a \cdot b \mod N \mid$. Unlike in QR_N, membership in QR_N^+ can be efficiently tested: We have that $b \in \mathrm{QR}_N^+$ if $0 \le b \le (N-1)/2$ and the Jacobi symbol of b modulo N is $+1$.

3   Three Zero-Knowledge Proofs of Knowledge

We begin by presenting three zero-knowledge proofs of knowledge. We need the first one to construct a zero-knowledge proof of sequential work in Sect. 7, the second one to construct a watermarkable VDF in Sect. 5 and the third one to construct a zero-knowledge VDF in Sect. 6. The proofs of knowledge are not *tight*: while the size of the witness of an honest prover is bounded by 2^λ, the extractor might extract a witness of size up to $2^{3\lambda+2}$. Jumping ahead, this will affect the strength of the low order assumption needed for our VDF constructions: We will need to assume that it is hard to find elements of order up to $23\lambda + 2$.

3.1   Proof of Knowledge of Discrete Log

In Fig. 1 we present Schnorr's protocol [46] in hidden order groups. We use it as a building block to construct the zero knowledge PoSW in Sect. 7. Schnorr originally defined and analyzed the protocol in prime order groups. Later, Kiayias, Tsiounis and Yung [31] proved that it is also secure in hidden order groups, where knowledge soundness is based on the strong RSA assumption. We note that the soundness property only guarantees knowledge of an exponent in $\pm[2^{3\lambda+2}]$ instead of $\pm[2^\lambda]$. This is sufficient for our application. The authors of [16] claim that knowledge soundness of the protocol can be based on the RSA assumption instead of the Strong-RSA assumption but we are not aware of a formal proof.

Theorem 1 ([31]). *Under the strong RSA assumption, the protocol in Fig. 1 is an honest verifier zero-knowledge proof of knowledge with soundness error $1/2^\lambda$. The soundness property guarantees knowledge of an exponent in $\pm[2^{3\lambda+2}]$.*

Theorem 1 is a special case of [31, Theorem 10]. For completeness we restate the proof for this case.

Proof (Proof of Theorem 1). Completeness follows by inspection of the protocol. To prove knowledge soundness we construct an extractor $\mathcal{E}$ that outputs a witness w given two accepting transcripts (a_1, a_2, b_1, c, s) and $(a_1, a_2, b_1, c^*, s^*)$. Since both transcripts are accepting, it holds that $a_1^{s-s^*} = a_2^{c-c^*}$. Let $\gamma = \gcd(s - s^*, c - c^*)$ and α, β be such that $\gamma = \alpha(s - s^*) + \beta(c - c^*)$. With high probability it holds that γ is coprime to the order of $\mathbb{G}$ since otherwise we could factor the group order and in particular break the strong RSA assumption. We thus have

$$a_1^{\frac{s-s^*}{\gamma}} = a_2^{\frac{c-c^*}{\gamma}}$$

and hence

$$a_1 = a_1^{\alpha \frac{s-s^*}{\gamma} + \beta \frac{c-c^*}{\gamma}} = (a_2^\alpha a_1^\beta)^{\frac{c-c^*}{\gamma}}.$$

Now if $c - c^* > \gamma$, we can transform the prover into an algorithm that breaks the strong RSA assumption: $a_2^\alpha a_1^\beta$ is the $((c - c^*)/\gamma)$-root of a_1. We therefore have that $c - c^* = \gamma$ and hence $w = (s - s^*)/(c - c^*)$ is the discrete log of a_2 with base a_1. Since $s, s^* \in \pm[2^{3\lambda+1}]$ we have that $w \in \pm[2^{3\lambda+2}]$.

It remains to prove that the protocol is honest verifier zero knowledge. Consider the simulator $\mathcal{S}$ that takes as input a tuple (a_1, a_2, c^*), samples $s^* \leftarrow \pm[2^{3\lambda}]$ uniformly at random and computes $b^* = a_1^s a_2^{-c}$. To prove that this transcript is indistinguishable from a real transcript, we show that the statistical distance of the random variable $s^* \leftarrow \pm[2^{3\lambda}]$ to the random variable $s = t + cw$ for a fixed $w \in \pm[2^{2\lambda}]$ and uniformly random $t \leftarrow \pm[2^{3\lambda}]$ and $c \leftarrow [2^\lambda]$ is negligible. Since s^* is distributed uniformly over $\pm[2^{3\lambda}]$, it takes each value in this set with probability $1/2^{3\lambda+1}$. Now consider the distribution of s. Any value in the range $[-2^{3\lambda} + 2^{2\lambda}, 2^{3\lambda} - 2^{2\lambda}]$ is selected with probability $2^\lambda/(2^\lambda 2^{3\lambda+1}) = 1/2^{3\lambda+1}$ since for any choice of c we can find a t that yields the respective value. On the rest of the values the distributions might differ. If follows that the statistical distance of the two distributions is at most

$$1 - \frac{2^{3\lambda+1} - 2^{2\lambda+1}}{2^{3\lambda+1}} = \frac{1}{2^\lambda}.$$

$\square$

3.2 Proof of Knowledge of Same Discrete Log

The main tool in our construction of a watermarkable signature scheme is a proof of knowledge of the same discrete log for two different bases. The protocol is a special case of the general proof of knowledge for "discrete-log relations sets" introduced by Kiayias, Tsiounis and Yung in [31]. It was first constructed in prime order groups by Chaum and Pederson [10]. We present it in Fig. 2.

Instance: $(a_1, a_2, a_3, a_4, \mathbb{G})$, where $a_1, a_2, a_3, a_4 \in \mathbb{G}$

Parameters: statistical security parameter λ

Witness: Exponent $w \in \pm[2^\lambda]$ such that $a_1^w = a_2$ and $a_3^w = a_4$ in $\mathbb{G}$

Protocol:

1. $\mathcal{P}$ samples $t \leftarrow [2^{3\lambda}]$ uniformly at random, computes $b_1 := a_1^t$ and $b_2 := a_3^t$ and sends (b_1, b_2) to $\mathcal{V}$.
2. $\mathcal{V}$ samples $c \leftarrow [2^\lambda]$ uniformly at random and sends it to $\mathcal{P}$.
3. $\mathcal{P}$ computes $s := t + cw$ and sends it to $\mathcal{V}$.
4. $\mathcal{V}$ checks if $s \in \pm[2^{3\lambda+1}]$, $a_1^s = b_1 a_2^c$ and $a_3^s = b_2 a_4^c$ holds and outputs **accept** or **reject** accordingly.

Fig. 2. Proof of Knowledge of same discrete log [31]

Theorem 2 ([31, Theorem 10]). *Under the Strong-RSA assumption, the protocol in Fig. 2 is an honest verifier zero-knowledge proof of knowledge with soundness error $1/2^\lambda$. The soundness property guarantees knowledge of an exponent in $\pm[2^{3\lambda+2}]$.*

Theorem 2 is a special case of [31, Theorem 10]. The proof is very similar to the proof of Theorem 1 so we omit it. To make the protocol non-interactive, we apply the Fiat-Shamir heuristic, i.e., we replace the challenge sent by the verifier by a hash of the instance, the first message and an identifier ID of the prover. The protocol can be found in Fig. 3. In our application to watermarkable VDFs, we need this protocol to be watermarked. We achieve this by including an ID of the prover in the input of the hash function that computes the Fiat-Shamir challenge.

3.3 Proof of Knowledge of Same Discrete Log with One Hidden Base

In our zero-knowledge VDF construction we need a proof of knowledge that's similar to the one in the last subsection but without revealing element a_3. The protocol is given in Fig. 4. It is a combination of the protocol in Fig. 2 and the well-known Guillou-Quisquater protocol [24] for proving knowledge of a root.

Theorem 3. *Under the Strong-RSA assumption, the protocol in Fig. 4 is an honest verifier zero-knowledge proof of knowledge with soundness error $1/2^\lambda$. The soundness property guarantees knowledge of an exponent in $\pm[2^{3\lambda+2}]$.*

Proof. Completeness follows by inspection of the protocol. To prove knowledge soundness we consider one of the λ many executions. We construct an extractor $\mathcal{E}$ that outputs a witness (w, a_3) given four accepting transcripts $(b_1, 0, a_6, b_2, b_3, c, s)$, $(b_1, 0, a_6, b_2, b_3, c^*, s^*)$, $(b_1, 1, a_6^*, b_2^*, b_3^*, c^{**}, s^{**})$ and $(b_1, 1, a_6^*, b_2^*, b_3^*, c^{***}, s^{***})$. $\mathcal{E}$ first extracts w and then a_3.

Instance: $(a_1, a_2, a_3, a_4, \text{ID}, \mathbb{G})$, where $a_1, a_2, a_3, a_4 \in \mathbb{G}$ and ID is a unique identifier of $\mathcal{P}$

Parameters: statistical security parameter λ, hash function H

Witness: Exponent $w \in [2^\lambda]$ such that $a_1^w = a_2$ and $a_3^w = a_4$ in $\mathbb{G}$

Protocol:

1. $\mathcal{P}$ samples $t \leftarrow [2^{3\lambda+1}]$ uniformly at random and computes $b_1 := a_1^t$ and $b_2 := a_3^t$.
2. $\mathcal{P}$ computes $c := H(a_1, a_2, a_3, a_4, b_1, b_2, \text{ID})$
3. $\mathcal{P}$ computes $s := t + cw$ and publishes (b_1, b_2, c, s) as the proof.
4. To check the proof (b_1, b_2, c, s), $\mathcal{V}$ checks if $H(a_1, a_2, a_3, a_4, b_1, b_2, \text{ID}) = c$, $s \in \pm[2^{3\lambda+1}]$ and if both $a_1^s = b_1 a_2^c$ and $a_3^s = b_2 a_4^c$ hold and outputs accept or reject accordingly.

Fig. 3. PoKsDL: The watermarked non-interactive Proof of Knowledge of same discrete log

1. Since the first and the second transcripts are accepting, it holds that $a_1^{s-s^*} = a_2^{c-c^*}$. Let $\gamma = \gcd(s-s^*, c-c^*)$ and α, β be such that $\gamma = \alpha(s-s^*) + \beta(c-c^*)$. Then we have

$$a_1^{\frac{s-s^*}{\gamma}} = a_2^{\frac{c-c^*}{\gamma}}$$

and hence

$$a_1 = a_1^{\alpha\frac{s-s^*}{\gamma} + \beta\frac{c-c^*}{\gamma}} = (a_2^\alpha a_1^\beta)^{\frac{c-c^*}{\gamma}}.$$

Now if $c - c^* > \gamma$, we can transform the prover into an algorithm that breaks the strong RSA assumption: $a_2^\alpha a_1^\beta$ is the $(c - c^*/\gamma)$-root of a_1. We therefore have that $c - c^* = \gamma$ and hence $w = (s - s^*/c - c^*)$ is the discrete log of a_2 with base a_1 and the discrete log of b_1 with base a_6. By the same argument we get that $w = (s^{**} - s^{***}/c^{**} - c^{***})$ is the discrete log of $b_1 a_4$ with base a_6^*.
2. Now consider the second and third transcript. We have seen above that $a_6^w = b_1$ and $(a_6^*)^w = b_1 a_4$. This means that a_6^*/a_6 is a w-root of a_4.

It remains to prove honest verifier zero-knowledge. Given (a_1, a_2, a_4, b, c), the simulator $\mathcal{S}$ constructs an accepting transcript $(b_1, b, a_6, b_2, b_3, c, s)$ as follows: It first samples $s \leftarrow \pm[2^{3\lambda}]$ and $a_6 \leftarrow \mathbb{G}$ uniformly at random. If $b = 0$, $\mathcal{S}$ samples $e \leftarrow \pm[2^\lambda]$ uniformly at random and sets $b_1 = a_6^e$. If $b = 1$, it samples $b_1 \leftarrow \mathbb{G}$ uniformly at random. Finally, $\mathcal{S}$ computes $b_2 = a_1^s a_2^{-c}$ and $b_3 = a_6^s b_1^{-c} a_4^{-bc}$. Indistinguishability follows since the distribution of the simulated s has statistical distance $1/2^\lambda$ from the distribution of an honestly computed s as we have seen in the proof of Theorem 1.   □

Instance: $(a_1, a_2, a_4, \mathbb{G})$, where $a_1, a_2, a_4 \in \mathbb{G}$

Parameters: statistical security parameter λ

Witness: Element a_3 and exponent $w \in \pm[2^\lambda]$ such that $a_1^w = a_2$ and $a_3^w = a_4$ in $\mathbb{G}$

Protocol: $\mathcal{P}$ and $\mathcal{V}$ repeat the following procedure λ times:

1. $\mathcal{P}$ samples $a_5 \leftarrow \mathbb{G}$ uniformly at random, computes $b_1 := a_5^w$ and sends b_1 to $\mathcal{V}$.
2. $\mathcal{V}$ samples a bit $b \leftarrow \{0,1\}$ uniformly and random and sends it to $\mathcal{P}$.
3. $\mathcal{P}$ samples $t \leftarrow \pm[2^{3\lambda}]$ uniformly at random, computes $a_6 := a_5 a_3^b$, $b_2 := a_1^t$ and $b_3 := a_6^t$ and sends (a_6, b_2, b_3) to $\mathcal{V}$.
4. $\mathcal{V}$ samples $c \leftarrow [2^\lambda]$ uniformly at random and sends it to $\mathcal{P}$.
5. $\mathcal{P}$ computes $s := t + cw$ and sends it to $\mathcal{V}$.
6. $\mathcal{V}$ checks if $s \in \pm[2^{3\lambda+1}]$, $a_1^s = b_2 a_2^c$ and $a_6^s = b_3(b_1 a_4^b)^c$ hold and outputs accept or reject accordingly.

Fig. 4. Proof of Knowledge of same discrete log with one hidden base

4   Modified Discrete-Log Assumptions

In our constructions we need to rely on the assumption that it is hard to recognize whether there exists a small discrete log between two given elements or not. Note that this is easy in one case: Given two elements $a, b \in \mathbb{G}$, where a is a square and b is a non-square, there exists no discrete log of b to base a since a raised to any power yields a square. We assume that it is hard in all other cases.

Definition 11 (discrete log assumption with small exponents). *Let GGen(1^λ) be a randomized algorithm that outputs the description of a hidden-order group $\mathbb{G}$. We say that the discrete log assumption with small exponents holds for GGen if, for any probabilistic polynomial-time algorithm $\mathcal{A}$, the probability of winning the following game is negligible in λ:*

1. *$\mathcal{A}$ takes as input the description of a group $\mathbb{G}$ output by GGen(1^λ), and two elements $a, b \in \mathbb{G}$, where a is uniformly random and $b = a^w$ for some $w \leftarrow \pm[2^{\lambda-1}]$.*
2. *$\mathcal{A}$ outputs an integer $w' \in \pm[2^{\lambda-1}]$.*
3. *$\mathcal{A}$ wins if and only if $b = a^{w'}$.*

Definition 12 (decisional discrete log assumption with small exponents). *Let GGen(1^λ) be a randomized algorithm that outputs the description of a hidden-order group $\mathbb{G}$. We say that the decisional discrete log assumption with small exponents holds for GGen if, for any probabilistic polynomial-time algorithm $\mathcal{A}$, the probability of winning the following game is negligible in λ:*

1. *$\mathcal{A}$ takes as input the description of a group $\mathbb{G}$ output by GGen(1^λ), and two elements $a, b \in \mathbb{G}$, where a is uniformly random and for b there are two*

possibilities of probability $1/2$ each: Either $b = a^w$ for some $w \leftarrow \pm[2^{\lambda-1}]$ or $b = z^{2^b}$ for a uniformly random group element $z \in \mathbb{G}$, where $b = 1$ if a is a square and $b = 0$ if not.

2. $\mathcal{A}$ outputs 0 or 1 indicating whether or not $b = a^w$ for some $w \in \pm[2^{\lambda-1}]$.
3. $\mathcal{A}$ wins if and only if it outputs the correct bit with probability greater than $1/2$.

Remark 2 (the special case of QR_N^+*).* Note that the decisional discrete log assumption with small exponents holds information theoretically in the group of signed quadratic residues QR_N^+, where N is a safe prime modulus, whenever the group order of QR_N^+ is at least 2^λ. This is because in this group almost all elements are generators and all elements are squares. Hence, if you pick two random group elements, the discrete log of one element to the base the other element exists with high probability so the two cases in the assumption are statistically indistinguishable.

Further, in this case, we have a straightforward reduction from the strong RSA assumption to the discrete log assumption with small exponents: Given a random group element g, one can solve the strong RSA challenge by sampling a random group element h and sending (h, g) to the adversary $\mathcal{A}$ that breaks the discrete log assumption with small exponents. When $\mathcal{A}$ outputs w, the reduction sends (w, h) to the strong RSA challenger.

5 Watermarkable VDFs

In this section we show how to transform any PoE into a watermarkable VDF. We begin by recalling the definition of watermarkable VDFs.

5.1 Definition

Watermarkable verifiable delay functions were informally introduced by Wesolowski [50]. The first formal definition was given by Arun, Bonneau and Clark in [2].

Definition 13. *A watermarkable VDF is a set of algorithms (*Setup*,* Eval*,* WatermarkProve*,* Verify*), where*

Setup$(1^\lambda, T) \to \mathbf{pp}$ *on input statistical security parameter* 1^λ *and time parameter* T *outputs public parameters* $\mathbf{pp}$.

Eval$(\mathbf{pp}, x) \to (y, \alpha)$ *on input* $(\mathbf{pp}, x, T)$ *outputs* (y, α)*, where* α *is an advice string.*

WatermarkProve$(\mathbf{pp}, x, \mu, y, \alpha) \to (y, \pi_\mu)$ *outputs a proof for* y *with embedded watermark* μ.

Verify$(\mathbf{pp}, x, \tilde{\mu}, y, \pi_\mu) \to$ accept/reject *checks that* $y = $ Eval$(\mathbf{pp}, x)$ *and that the watermark* $\tilde{\mu}$ *is embedded in* π_μ.

The algorithm Eval is deterministic and can compute the output y in T sequential steps. A watermarkable VDF must additionally satisfy four properties: The security properties of a basic VDF and watermark unforgeability. We state them informally below. The formal definitions can be found in [2,6].

Setup$(1^\lambda, T) \to \mathbf{pp} = (\mathbb{G}, H)$ outputs a finite abelian group $\mathbb{G}$ of unknown order and an efficiently computable hash function H.

Eval$(\mathbf{pp}, x) \to (y, \alpha)$ on input $(\mathbf{pp}, x, T)$ outputs (y, α), where $y = x^{2^T}$ and α is an advice string for PoE.

WatermarkProve$(\mathbf{pp}, x, \mathtt{ID}, y, \alpha) \to (y, \pi_\mu)$ outputs y and

$$\pi_\mu = (x', y', \mathsf{PoKsDL}(\mathbf{pp}, x, x', y, y', \mathtt{ID}), \mathsf{PoE}(\mathbf{pp}, x', y', T)),$$

where $x' := x^r$ and $y' := y^r$ for some uniformly random $r \leftarrow \pm[2^\lambda]$.

Verify$(\mathbf{pp}, x, \tilde{\mu}, y, \pi_\mu) \to$ accept/reject checks if both $\mathsf{PoKsDL}(\mathbf{pp}, x, x', y, y', \mathtt{ID})$ and $\mathsf{PoE}(\mathbf{pp}, x', y', T))$ verify.

Fig. 5. A Watermarkable VDF from any proof of exponentiation using the proof of knowledge PoKsDL presented in Fig. 3. By $\mathsf{PoE}(\mathbf{pp}, x, y, T)$ we denote the chosen proof of exponentiation with group parameters $\mathbf{pp}$ and statement $x^{2^T} = y$.

Completeness: For all tuples $(\mathbf{pp}, x, \mu, y, \pi_\mu)$, where $y = $ Eval$(\mathbf{pp}, x)$ and $\pi_\mu = $ WatermarkProve$(\mathbf{pp}, x, \mu, y, \alpha)$, algorithm Verify$(\mathbf{pp}, x, \mu, y, \pi_\mu)$ outputs accept.

Sequentiality: Any parallel algorithm that uses at most poly(λ) processors and outputs $y = $ Eval$(\mathbf{pp}, x)$ with noticeable probability runs in time at least T.

Soundness: If Verify$(\mathbf{pp}, x, \tilde{\mu}, y, \pi_\mu)$ outputs accept, then the probability that $y \neq$ Eval$(\mathbf{pp}, x)$ is negligible.

Watermark Unforgeability: For any pair of algorithms $(\mathcal{A}_0, \mathcal{A}_1)$, where $\mathcal{A}_0$ runs in time $O(\mathrm{poly}(T, \lambda))$ and $\mathcal{A}_1$ runs in time less than T, the probability that $(\mathcal{A}_0, \mathcal{A}_1)$ wins the following game is negligible:
1. The challenger C runs Setup$(1^\lambda, T) \to \mathbf{pp}$ and sends $\mathbf{pp}$ to $(\mathcal{A}_0, \mathcal{A}_1)$.
2. Precomputation algorithm $\mathcal{A}_0(\mathbf{pp})$ outputs advice string $\tilde{\alpha}$.
3. Challenger C samples a random input x, runs Eval$(\mathbf{pp}, x) \to (y, \alpha)$ and sends $(x, y, \tilde{\alpha})$ to $\mathcal{A}_1$.
4. Online algorithm $\mathcal{A}_1$ sends q many watermark queries μ_i to C and obtains WatermarkProve$(\mathbf{pp}, x, \mu_i, y, \alpha) \to \pi_{\mu_i}$.
5. Algorithm $\mathcal{A}_1$ outputs a forgery pair (μ_*, π_{μ_*}) and wins if $\mu_* \neq \mu_i$ for all $i \in [q]$ and Verify$(\mathbf{pp}, x, \tilde{\mu}, y, \pi_\mu)$ outputs accept.

5.2 Construction

In Fig. 5 we present our watermarkable VDF. The main idea is to randomize the instance (x, y) to $(x', y') := (x^r, y^r)$ with a secret exponent r and then provide a PoE for the statement $(x')^{2^T} = y'$ and a watermarked proof of knowledge for r using the protocol in Fig. 2. We present the protocol as non-interactive since only non-interactive proofs need to be watermarked.

Theorem 4. *Let PoE be a complete and sound proof of exponentiation. The algorithms in Fig. 5 define a sound and complete VDF, relative to the iterated squaring assumption, the strong RSA assumption and the low order assumption.*

Proof. Sequentiality of the VDF follows immediately from the iterated squaring assumption. Completeness follows by inspection of the protocol from the completeness property of PoE. Soundness follows from the low order assumption, the strong RSA assumption and soundness of PoE. To see this, we show how to transform an adversary $\mathcal{A}$ that outputs an accepting proof

$$\pi_\mu = (x', y', \text{PoKsDL}(\mathbf{pp}, x, x', y, y', \text{ID}), \text{PoE}(\mathbf{pp}, x', y', T))$$

with $x^{2^T} \neq y$ with probability δ into an adversary $\mathcal{B}$ that breaks either the low order assumption, the strong RSA assumption or soundness of PoE with probability δ. The adversary $\mathcal{B}$ does the following:

1. Try to extract the secret exponent r from PoKsDL. If this is not possible, use $\mathcal{A}$ to break the strong RSA assumption similar to the proof of Theorem 2.
2. If r is extractable, compute $\tilde{y} := x^{2^T}$ and $\alpha := \tilde{y}y^{-r}$. If $\alpha \neq 1$, check if $\alpha^r = 1$. If so, then α is an element of low order and r is a multiple of its order. $\mathcal{B}$ outputs (α, r) and breaks the low order assumption.
3. If $\alpha = 1$ or $\alpha^r \neq 1$, then $(x')^{2^T} \neq y'$, so $\text{PoE}(\mathbf{pp}, x', y', T)$ is a proof for a false statement, which is a contradiction to the assumption that PoE is sound.

Whenever the proof output by $\mathcal{A}$ is accepting but $x^{2^T} \neq y$, algorithm $\mathcal{B}$ terminates in one of the steps, which concludes the proof.   □

Remark 3 (On the running time of algorithm $\mathcal{B}$). Note that in the above proof the running time of algorithm $\mathcal{B}$ might be linear in the time parameter T because it needs to solve an iterated squaring instance in the second step. This means that, to break the low order assumption or the soundness of the PoE, it needs at least T steps. Giving an adversary time linear in T to break the soundness of the PoE is necessary for a meaningful soundness definition since an honest prover also needs T steps to compute the result of an instance and the corresponding proof. Giving an adversary against the low order assumption time linear in T to break it, is in line with its usage in the literature (see [40,50], where it is needed for soundness of PoEs). If $\mathcal{B}$ breaks the strong RSA assumption it is much faster since it never gets to step 2. In particular, we have that its running time is independent of T in this case.

Theorem 5. *Let PoE be a complete and sound proof of exponentiation. The VDF defined by the algorithms in Fig. 5 is watermark unforgeable in the random oracle model, relative to the strong RSA assumption, the decisional discrete log assumption with small exponents, the low order assumption and the decisional iterated squaring assumption.*

Proof. We show how to transform an adversary $\mathcal{A}$ that wins the watermark unforgeability game with probability δ into an adversary $\mathcal{B}$ that breaks either the soundness of PoKsDL (and hence the strong RSA assumption), the discrete log assumption or the decisional iterated squaring assumption with probability $\delta/2$.

1. Let q be the number of queries that $\mathcal{A}$ is allowed to make. Upon receiving as input a group $\mathbb{G}$ and a time parameter T, $\mathcal{B}$ precomputes $q' \geq q$ tuples $\{(x_i, y_i, \mathsf{PoE}(\mathbf{pp}, x_i, y_i, T))\}_{i \in [q']}$, where for all $i \in [q']$, $x_i \leftarrow \mathbb{G}$ is a uniformly random group element, $y_i = x_i^{2^T}$ and $\mathsf{PoE}(\mathbf{pp}, x_i, y_i, T)$ is an honestly computed proof of exponentiation. Call L the list of those tuples. $\mathcal{B}$ computes those tuples until L contains q entries in which x_i is a square.
2. $\mathcal{B}$ gets as input a discrete log challenge (g, g^a), where g is a random group element in $\mathbb{G}$ and a is a random number in $\pm[2^{\lambda-1}]$. Note that by the decisional discrete log assumption with small exponents, $\mathcal{B}$ should not be able to find a.
3. $\mathcal{B}$ sends $\mathbb{G}$ to $\mathcal{A}_0$ and obtains advice string $\tilde{a}$.
4. $\mathcal{B}$ gets as input a decisional iterated squaring challenge consisting of two group elements x_d, y_d that are either uniformly random elements in $\mathbb{G}$ or x_d is uniformly random in $\mathbb{G}$ and $y_d = x_d^{2^T}$
5. To simulate the watermark unforgeability game for the statement $x^{2^T} = y$, it chooses one of the following two strategies at random, each with probability $1/2$. Note that $\mathcal{B}$ can always forge a proof of knowledge of same discrete log since PoKsDL is honest verifier zero-knowledge and the random oracle is programmable.

   Strategy 1: Compute $y := g^{2^T}$ and $y' := (g^a)^{2^T}$ and send $(\mathbb{G}, H, g, y, \tilde{a})$ to $\mathcal{A}_1$. When $\mathcal{A}_1$ makes a watermark query ID_i, sample a random $r \leftarrow \pm[2^{\lambda-1}]$, forge $\mathsf{PoKsDL}(\mathbf{pp}, g, g^{ar}, y, (y')^r, \mathsf{ID}_i)$ and compute $\mathsf{PoE}(\mathbf{pp}, g^{ar}, (y')^r, T)$. Send

   $$\pi_i := (g^{a+r}, (y')^r, \mathsf{PoKsDL}(\mathbf{pp}, g, g^{ar}, y, (y')^r, \mathsf{ID}_i), \mathsf{PoE}(\mathbf{pp}, g^{ar}, (y')^r, T))$$

   to $\mathcal{A}_1$. If $\mathcal{A}_1$ wins the game, it outputs

   $$(\mathsf{ID}_*, \pi_* = (x_*, y_*, \mathsf{PoKsDL}(\mathbf{pp}, g, x_*, y, y_*, \mathsf{ID}_*)), \mathsf{PoE}(\mathbf{pp}, x_*, y_*, T)).$$

   If $(x_*, y_*) \neq (x_i, y_i)$ for all $i \in [q]$, abort. Else, let $\ell \in [2^\lambda]$ be such that $(x_*, y_*) = (g^{a\ell}, (y')^\ell)$. $\mathcal{B}$ tries to extract an exponent ω from PoKsDL. If it is successful, it computes $a' := \omega/\ell$ over $\mathbb{Z}$ and checks if $g^{a'} = g^a$. If so, it can output a' and break the discrete log assumption. If it does not hold then $a' \neq a$ but $g^{a'\ell} = g^{a\ell}$ and hence $g^{a'}/g^a$ is an element of low order ℓ. If it is not able to extract, it can use $\mathcal{A}$ to break the strong RSA assumption similar to the proof of Theorem 2.

   Strategy 2: Send $(\mathbf{pp}, x_d, y_d, \tilde{a})$ to $\mathcal{A}_1$. If x_d is a square, remove all tuples $(x_i, y_i, \mathsf{PoE}(\mathbf{pp}, x_i, y_i, T))$, where x_i is not a square, from the list L. When $\mathcal{A}_1$ makes a watermark query ID_i, pick an unused tuple $(x_i, y_i, \mathsf{PoE}(\mathbf{pp}, x_i, y_i, T))$ from L, forge $\mathsf{PoKsDL}(\mathbf{pp}, x_d, x_i, y_d, y_i, \mathsf{ID}_i)$ and send

   $$\pi_i := (x_i, y_i, \mathsf{PoKsDL}(\mathbf{pp}, x_d, x_i, y_d, y_i, \mathsf{ID}_i), \mathsf{PoE}(\mathbf{pp}, x_i, y_i, T))$$

   to $\mathcal{A}_1$. By the decisional discrete log assumption with small exponents and the zero-knowledge property of PoKsDL, π_i is indistinguishable from an honestly computed watermarked proof. If $\mathcal{A}_1$ outputs

   $$(\mathsf{ID}_*, \pi_* = (x_*, y_*, \mathsf{PoKsDL}(\mathbf{pp}, x_d, x_*, y_d, y_*, \mathsf{ID}_*), \mathsf{PoE}(\mathbf{pp}, x_*, y_*, T)),$$

check if $(x_*, y_*) = (x_i, y_i)$ for some $i \in [q]$ and abort if it holds. Otherwise, try to extract the secret r from PoKsDL. If this is not possible, use $\mathcal{A}$ to break the strong RSA assumption as above. If it is possible, we have that the statement $x_d^{2^T} = y_d$ holds since the PoE is sound. In this case $\mathcal{B}$ sends 1 to the decisional iterated squaring challenger. If $\mathcal{A}_1$ does not output a tuple of the form above, $\mathcal{B}$ sends 0 or 1 to the decisional iterated squaring challenger each with probability $1/2$.

If adversary $\mathcal{B}$ does not abort in Strategy 1, it breaks either the strong RSA assumption or the decisional discrete log assumption with small exponents with probability δ. If $\mathcal{B}$ does not abort in Strategy 2, it either breaks the strong RSA assumption with probability δ or it recognizes a true instance in the decisional iterated squaring game with probability $1/2 + \delta/2$. Since aborting in Strategy 1 and aborting in Strategy 2 are mutually exclusive, the claim follows.   □

Remark 4 (On the running time of algorithm $\mathcal{B}$). Note that in the first strategy $\mathcal{B}$ runs in time linear in T to break the strong RSA assumption or the discrete log assumption. We therefore need to assume that these assumptions are secure against adversaries that run in time linear in T, which is at most 2^{32} in practice.

The next corollary follows from the discussion in Remark 2.

Corollary 1. *Let PoE be a complete and sound proof of exponentiation and let $\mathbb{G} = \mathrm{QR}_N^+$, where N is a safe prime modulus. The construction in Fig. 5 is a watermarkable VDF in $\mathbb{G}$ relative to the decisional iterated squaring assumption and the strong RSA assumption.*

Efficiency. Watermarking a PoE with the construction in Fig. 5 increases the complexity of the underlying PoE scheme as follows:

- The proof size grows by 4 group elements and one integer of size at most $2^{3\lambda+1}$.
- The verifier needs to perform 4 additional small group exponentiations (with exponents of size at most $2^{3\lambda+1}$) and 2 group multiplications.
- The prover needs to perform 4 additional small exponentiations (with exponents of size at most $2^{3l\lambda}$).

6   Zero-Knowledge VDFs

6.1   Definition

Zero-knowledge verifiable delay functions were introduced by Arun, Bonneau and Clark in [2].

Definition 14. *A zero-knowledge VDF is a set of algorithms (Setup, Eval, Prove Verify, Sim), where*

$Setup(1^\lambda, T) \to \mathbf{pp}$ *on input statistical security parameter* 1^λ *and time parameter* T *outputs public parameters* $\mathbf{pp}$.

$Eval(\mathbf{pp}, x) \to (y, \alpha)$ *on input* $(\mathbf{pp}, x, T)$ *outputs* (y, α), *where* α *is an advice string*.

$Prove(\mathbf{pp}, x, y, \alpha) \to \pi$ *outputs a proof* π *of knowledge of element* y.

$Verify(\mathbf{pp}, x, \pi) \to \mathtt{accept/reject}$ *checks that* π *is a valid proof of knowledge*.

$Sim(\mathbf{pp}, x, c^*) \to \pi^*$ *outputs a simulated proof of knowledge* π^* *using randomness* c^*.

The algorithm $Eval$ is deterministic and can compute the output y in T sequential steps. A zero-knowledge VDF must additionally satisfy four properties: Completeness, sequentiality, knowledge soundness and zero-knowledge.

Completeness: For all tuples $(\mathbf{pp}, x, y, \pi)$, where $y = Eval(\mathbf{pp}, x)$ and $\pi = Prove(\mathbf{pp}, x, y, \alpha)$, algorithm $Verify(\mathbf{pp}, x, y, \pi)$ outputs $\mathtt{accept}$.

Sequentiality: Any parallel algorithm that uses at most $poly(\lambda)$ processors and outputs $y = Eval(\mathbf{pp}, x)$ with noticeable probability runs in time at least T.

Knowledge Soundness: For any adversary $\mathcal{A}$ that outputs a proof π for instance x of bit-length n, such that $Verify(\mathbf{pp}, x, \pi)$ outputs $\mathtt{accept}$ with probability δ, there exists an extractor $\mathcal{E}$ that with probability at least $(\delta - \varepsilon)/poly(n)$ outputs element $y = Eval(\mathbf{pp}, x)$ in time less than T, where poly is some positive polynomial and $\varepsilon \in [0, 1]$ is called the *soundness error*.

Zero Knowledge: There exists a simulator $\mathcal{S}$ that, given instance x and randomness c^*, outputs a proof π^* in time less than T such that $Verify(\mathbf{pp}, x, \pi^*)$ outputs $\mathtt{accept}$ and π^* is indistinguishable from an honestly computed proof.

6.2   Construction

Our construction of a zero-knowledge VDF can be found in Fig. 6. We note that this construction can be transformed into a watermarkable zero-knowledge VDF by including a unique identifier in the computation of the randomness in the proof of knowledge of same discrete log. Since this extension is a straightforward combination of our two constructions, we refrain from analyzing it formally.

Theorem 6. *Let PoE be a complete and sound proof of exponentiation. The algorithms in Fig. 6 define a zero-knowledge VDF, relative to the iterated squaring assumption, the strong RSA assumption, the low order assumption and the decisional discrete log assumption with small exponents.*

Proof. Sequentiality of the VDF follows immediately from the iterated squaring assumption. Completeness follows by inspection of the protocol and from the completeness property of PoE. Knowledge soundness follows from the low order assumption, the strong RSA assumption and soundness of PoE. To see this, we describe an extractor $\mathcal{E}$ that outputs $y = x^{2^T}$ in time less than T by interacting with an adversary $\mathcal{A}$ that outputs an accepting proof

$$\pi = (x', y', \mathtt{PoKsDLh}(\mathbf{pp}, x, x', y'), \mathtt{PoE}(\mathbf{pp}, x', y', T)).$$

$\texttt{Setup}(1^{\lambda}, T) \to \textbf{pp} = (\mathbb{G}, x_1^*, y_1^*, \texttt{PoE}(\textbf{pp}, x_1^*, y_1^*, T), x_2^*, y_2^*, \texttt{PoE}(\textbf{pp}, x_2^*, y_2^*, T), H)$
  outputs a finite abelian group $\mathbb{G}$ of unknown order, a random square x_1^*,
  a random non-square x_2^* and the corresponding PoEs and an efficiently
  computable hash function H.

$\texttt{Eval}(\textbf{pp}, x, T) \to (y, \alpha)$ outputs (y, α), where $y = x^{2^T}$ and α is an advice string
  for PoE.

$\texttt{Prove}(\textbf{pp}, x, \texttt{ID}, y, \alpha) \to \pi$ outputs

$$\pi = (x', y', \texttt{PoKsDLh}(\textbf{pp}, x, x', y'), \texttt{PoE}(\textbf{pp}, x', y', T)),$$

  where $x' := x^r$ and $y' := y^r$ for a uniformly random $r \leftarrow \pm[2^{\lambda}]$.

$\texttt{Verify}(\textbf{pp}, x, \pi) \to \texttt{accept/reject}$ checks   if $\texttt{PoKsDLh}(\textbf{pp}, x, x', y')$ and
  $\texttt{PoE}(\textbf{pp}, x', y', T)$ verify.

$\texttt{Sim}(\textbf{pp}, x, c^*) \to \pi^*$ on input $\textbf{pp}, x, c^*$, simulates $\texttt{PoKsDLh}(\textbf{pp}, x, x^*, y^*)$ with randomness c^* and outputs

$$\pi^* = (x^*, y^*, \texttt{PoKsDLh}(\textbf{pp}, x, x^*, y^*), \texttt{PoE}(\textbf{pp}, x^*, y^*, T)),$$

  for $x^* := x_1^*$, if x is a square and $x^* \leftarrow \{x_1^*, x_2^*\}$ uniformly random if x is a
  non-square.

Fig. 6. A zero-knowledge VDF from any proof of exponentiation. $\texttt{PoKsDLh}$ is the non-interactive version of the proof of knowledge presented in Fig. 4. By $\texttt{PoE}(\textbf{pp}, x, y, T)$ we denote the chosen proof of exponentiation with group parameters $\textbf{pp}$ and statement $x^{2^T} = y$.

The extractor $\mathcal{E}$ first tries to extract an exponent r and a base element $\tilde{y}$ from $\texttt{PoKsDLh}$ such that $x^r = x'$ and $\tilde{y}^r = y'$. If this is not possible, it can break the strong RSA assumption similar to the proof of Theorem 3. Assume that $\tilde{y} \neq y$. Then we would have that $(\tilde{y}/y)^r = 1$ and hence $\tilde{y}/y$ would be an element of low order. Hence, by the low order assumption $\tilde{y} = y$. Since the running time of the extractor is independent of T, knowledge soundness follows.

It remains to prove zero knowledge. Consider the simulator $\texttt{Sim}$. From the zero-knowledge property of $\texttt{PoKsDLh}$ and the decisional discrete log assumption with small exponents, we follow that the simulated proof π^* is computationally indistinguishable from an honest proof.   □

The next corollary follows from the discussion in Remark 2.

Corollary 2. *Let $\texttt{PoE}$ be a complete and sound proof of exponentiation and let $\mathbb{G} = \texttt{QR}_N^+$, where N is a safe prime modulus. The construction in Fig. 6 is a zero-knowledge VDF in $\mathbb{G}$ relative to the iterated squaring assumption and the strong RSA assumption.*

Efficiency. Transforming a PoE into a zero-knowledge VDF with the construction in Fig. 6 increases the complexity of the underlying PoE scheme as follows:

- The proof size grows by $4\lambda + 2$ group elements and λ many integers of size at most $2^{3\lambda+1}$.
- The verifier needs to perform 4λ additional small group exponentiations (with exponents of size at most $2^{3\lambda+1}$) and 3λ group multiplications.
- The prover needs to perform $3\lambda + 2$ additional small exponentiations (with exponents of size at most $2^{3\lambda}$).

7 Zero-Knowledge Proofs of Sequential Work

Our construction of a general zero-knowledge VDF is not practical, with the proof of knowledge of y being the bottleneck. Without it our construction does not satisfy the definition of a zero-knowledge VDF: If the prover just needed to output x, x', y' and a proof of knowledge of r such that $x^r = x'$, then it could first raise x to a random r and then compute $y' = (x')^{2^T}$. In particular, it would produce the output without ever knowing y. The main observation in this section is that, while this protocol does not satisfy the definition of a zero-knowledge VDF, it is still sufficient for the application to short-lived proofs presented in [2, Section 7] because the prover still needs at least T steps to compute the output. The protocol can be found in Fig. 7 and the application to short-lived proofs in the next section.

7.1 Definition

Definition 15. *A zero-knowledge proof of sequential work is a set of algorithms* (Setup, Prove Verify, Sim), *where*

Setup$(1^\lambda, T) \to$ **pp** *on input statistical security parameter 1^λ and time parameter T outputs public parameters* **pp**.
Prove$(\mathbf{pp}, x, y, \alpha) \to \pi$ *outputs a proof π of sequential work of T steps.*
Verify$(\mathbf{pp}, x, \pi) \to$ accept/reject *checks that π is a valid proof of sequential work.*
Sim$(\mathbf{pp}, x, c^*) \to \pi^*$ *outputs a simulated proof of sequential work π^* using randomness c^*.*

The algorithm Eval is deterministic and can compute the output y in T sequential steps. A zero-knowledge proof of sequential work must additionally satisfy four properties: Completeness, sequentiality, soundness and zero-knowledge.

Completeness: For all tuples $(\mathbf{pp}, x, y, \pi)$, where $y = \mathrm{Eval}(\mathbf{pp}, x)$ and $\pi = \mathrm{Prove}(\mathbf{pp}, x, y, \alpha)$, algorithm Verify$(\mathbf{pp}, x, \pi)$ outputs accept.
Sequentiality: Any parallel algorithm that uses at most poly(λ) processors and outputs a proof π', such that Verify$(\mathbf{pp}, x, \pi')$ outputs accept with noticeable probability runs in time at least T.
Zero Knowledge: There exists a simulator $\mathcal{S}$ that, given instance x and randomness c^*, outputs a proof π^* in time less than T such that Verify$(\mathbf{pp}, x, \pi^*)$ outputs accept and π^* is indistinguishable from an honestly computed proof.

$\texttt{Setup}(1^\lambda, T) \to \mathbf{pp} = (\mathbb{G}, x_1^*, y_1^*, \texttt{PoE}(\mathbf{pp}, x_1^*, y_1^*, T), x_2^*, y_2^*, \texttt{PoE}(\mathbf{pp}, x_2^*, y_2^*, T), H)$
   outputs a finite abelian group $\mathbb{G}$ of unknown order, a random square x_1^*,
   a random non-square x_2^* and the corresponding PoEs and an efficiently
   computable hash function H.

$\texttt{Prove}(\mathbf{pp}, x) \to \pi$ outputs

$$\pi := (x', y', \texttt{PoKDL}(\mathbf{pp}, x, x'), \texttt{PoE}(\mathbf{pp}, x', y', T)),$$

   where $x' := x^r$ and for some uniformly random $r \leftarrow \pm[2^\lambda]$.

$\texttt{Verify}(\mathbf{pp}, x, \pi) \to \texttt{accept/reject}$ checks if both $\texttt{PoKDL}(\mathbf{pp}, x, x')$ and
   $\texttt{PoE}(\mathbf{pp}, x', y', T))$ verify.

$\texttt{Sim}(\mathbf{pp}, x, c^*) \to \pi^*$ on input $\mathbf{pp}, x, c^*$, simulates $\texttt{PoKDL}(\mathbf{pp}, x, x^*)$ with randomness c^* and outputs

$$\pi^* = (x^*, y^*, \texttt{PoKDL}(\mathbf{pp}, x, x^*), \texttt{PoE}(\mathbf{pp}, x^*, y^*, T)),$$

   for $x^* := x_1^*$, if x is a square and $x^* \leftarrow \{x_1^*, x_2^*\}$ uniformly random if x is a
   non-square.

Fig. 7. A Zero-Knowledge Proof of Sequential Work from any proof of exponentiation PoE. PoKDL is the non-interactive version of the proof of knowledge presented in
Fig. 1. By $\texttt{PoE}(\mathbf{pp}, x, y, T)$ we denote the chosen proof of exponentiation with group
parameters $\mathbf{pp}$ and statement $x^{2^T} = y$.

7.2   The Generalized Iterated Squaring Assumption

For the security of our construction we need to make the following assumption.

Definition 16 (generalized iterated squaring assumption) *Let $\mathit{GGen}(1^\lambda)$
be a randomized algorithm that outputs the description of a hidden-order group
$\mathbb{G}$. We say that the generalized iterated squaring assumption holds for GGen if,
for any probabilistic parallel algorithm $\mathcal{A}$ that uses at most $\mathsf{poly}(\lambda)$ processors
and runs in time less than T, the probability of winning the following game is
negligible in λ:*

1. *$\mathcal{A}$ takes as input the description of a group $\mathbb{G}$ output by $\mathit{GGen}(1^\lambda)$, a random
   group element x and an integer T.*
2. *$\mathcal{A}$ outputs a pair $(r, y) \in \mathbb{Z} \times \mathbb{G}$.*
3. *$\mathcal{A}$ wins if and only if $r \neq 0$ and $y = (x^r)^{2^T}$.*

7.3   Construction

Theorem 7. *Let PoE be a complete and sound proof of exponentiation. The
algorithms in Fig. 7 define a zero-knowledge PoSW, relative to the generalized
iterated squaring assumption, the strong RSA assumption and the decisional
discrete log assumption with small exponents.*

Proof. Completeness follows by inspection of the protocol and from the completeness property of PoE. Sequentiality of the PoSW follows from the generalized iterated squaring assumption, the RSA assumption and soundness of PoE: Assume that an adversary $\mathcal{A}$ can output π in time less than T. We construct an adversary $\mathcal{B}$ that breaks either the RSA assumption or the generalized iterated squaring assumption as follows:

1. $\mathcal{B}$ obtains as input a the description of a group $\mathbb{G}$ and a generalized iterated squaring challenge $x \in \mathbb{G}$.
2. $\mathcal{B}$ forwards $\mathbb{G}$ and x to adversary $\mathcal{A}$.
3. If $\mathcal{A}$ is successful, it outputs a valid proof

$$\pi = (x', y', \mathsf{PoKDL}(\mathbf{pp}, x, x'), \mathsf{PoE}(\mathbf{pp}, x', y', T)).$$

4. $\mathcal{B}$ first tries to extract the secret exponent r from PoKDL. If this is not possible, it can use $\mathcal{A}$ to break the RSA assumption similar to the proof of Theorem 1.
5. If it is possible, $\mathcal{B}$ outputs (r, y') to break the generalized iterated squaring assumption.

The running time of $\mathcal{B}$ is independent of T. By soundness of PoE we have that $\mathcal{B}$ breaks one of the two assumptions with the same probability as the winning probability of $\mathcal{A}$. It remains to prove zero knowledge. Consider the simulator Sim. From the zero-knowledge property of PoKDL and the decisional discrete log assumption with small exponents, we follow that the simulated proof π^* is computationally indistinguishable from an honest proof. □

The next corollary follows from the discussion in Remark 2.

Corollary 3. *Let PoE be a complete and sound proof of exponentiation and let $\mathbb{G} = \mathrm{QR}_N^+$, where N is a safe prime modulus. The construction in Fig. 7 is a zero-knowledge PoSW in $\mathbb{G}$ relative to the generalized iterated squaring assumption and the strong RSA assumption.*

Efficiency. Transforming a PoE into a zero-knowledge proof of sequential work with the construction in Fig. 7 increases the complexity of the underlying PoE scheme as follows:

- The proof size grows by 3 group elements and one integer of size at most $2^{3\lambda+1}$.
- The verifier needs to perform 2 additional small group exponentiations (with exponents of size at most $2^{3\lambda+1}$) and 1 group multiplications.
- The prover needs to perform 3 additional small exponentiations (with exponents of size at most $2^{3\lambda}$).

$\texttt{Setup}(1^{\lambda}, T) \to \mathbf{pp} = (\mathbf{pp}_{\texttt{zkPoSW}}, \mathbf{pp}_{\mathcal{R}}) = (\mathbb{G}, b^{*}, y^{*}, \pi_{\texttt{PoE}}^{*}, H, \mathbf{pp}_{\mathcal{R}})$ outputs a finite abelian group $\mathbb{G}$ of unknown order, a uniformly random $b^{*} \leftarrow \mathbb{G}$, $y^{*} = (b^{*})^{2^{T}}$, $\pi_{\texttt{PoE}}^{*} = \texttt{PoE}(\mathbf{pp}_{\texttt{zkPoSW}}, b^{*}, y^{*}, T)$, an efficiently computable hash function H and the public parameters of the proof system for $\mathcal{R}$.

$\texttt{Prove}(\mathbf{pp}, T, x, b, w) \to (\pi_{\texttt{zkPoSW}}, \pi_{\mathcal{R}})$ outputs
- Forged
$$\pi_{\texttt{zkPoSW}} = (b^{*}, y^{*}, \texttt{PoKDL}(\mathbf{pp}_{\texttt{zkPoSW}}, b, b^{*}), \pi_{\texttt{PoE}}),$$
  where $\texttt{PoKDL}(\mathbf{pp}_{\texttt{zkPoSW}}, b, b^{*})$ is forged with challenge c_{1}.
- An honestly computed proof $\pi_{\mathcal{R}}$ with random challenge c_{2} such that $c_{1} + c_{2} = c = H(x, b, a)$, where a is the first element of $\pi_{\mathcal{R}}$.

$\texttt{Forge}(\mathbf{pp}, T, x, b) \to (\tilde{\pi}_{\texttt{zkPoSW}}, \tilde{\pi}_{\mathcal{R}})$ outputs
- Honestly computed
$$\tilde{\pi}_{\texttt{zkPoSW}} = (b', y', \texttt{PoKDL}(\mathbf{pp}_{\texttt{zkPoSW}}, b, b'), \texttt{PoE}(\mathbf{pp}_{\texttt{zkPoSW}}, b', y', T))$$
  with random challenge c_{1}.
- A forged proof $\tilde{\pi}_{\mathcal{R}}$ with challenge c_{2} such that $c_{1} + c_{2} = c = H(x, b, a)$, where a is the first element of $\pi_{\mathcal{R}}$.

$\texttt{Verify}(\mathbf{pp}, x, \pi_{\texttt{zkPoSW}}, \pi_{\mathcal{R}}) \to \texttt{accept/reject}$ checks $\pi_{\texttt{zkPoSW}}$ and $\pi_{\mathcal{R}}$ and outputs $\texttt{accept}$ if and only if both proofs verify.

Fig. 8. A short-lived proof from our zero knowledge PoSW. PoKDL is the non-interactive version of the proof of knowledge presented in Fig. 1. By $\texttt{PoE}(\mathbf{pp}, x, y, T)$ we denote the chosen proof of exponentiation with group parameters $\mathbf{pp}$ and statement $x^{2^{T}} = y$.

8   Short-Lived Proofs from Our Zero-Knowledge PoSW

In this section we discuss how one can use our zero knowledge PoSW in the short-lived proof construction of [2]. The main idea in the construction of [2] is to transform any sigma protocol Σ for a relation $\mathcal{R}$ into a short lived proof for $\mathcal{R}$ by combining Σ with a zero-knowledge VDF (which is also a sigma protocol) via the standard OR combination of sigma protocols. Since anyone can construct a valid VDF proof in T steps, the combined proof loses its validity after time $T \cdot \texttt{poly}(\lambda)$. The zero-knowledge property of the VDF is needed since an honest prover needs to be able to forge a VDF proof in time less than T, which is indistinguishable from an honest proof also after time $T \cdot \texttt{poly}(\lambda)$ has passed. We first recall some facts about sigma protocols before presenting our construction of a short-lived proof.

8.1   Sigma Protocols

Definition 17 (sigma protocol). *A* sigma protocol *(Σ-protocol) is an interactive honest verifier zero-knowledge proof of knowledge consisting of three messages:*

- *a first message by $\mathcal{P}$ denoted by u,*

- a second message by $\mathcal{V}$ denoted by c and
- a third message by $\mathcal{P}$ denoted by z.

Cramer, Damgård and Schoenmakers [17] showed that the set of relations with Σ-protocols is closed under disjunction: Let $\Sigma_1 = (u_1, c_1, z_1)$ be a sigma protocol for relation $\mathcal{R}_1$ and $\Sigma_2 = (u_2, c_2, z_2)$ be a sigma protocol for relation $\mathcal{R}_2$ and let x_1 be an instance of $\mathcal{R}_1$ and x_2 an instance of $\mathcal{R}_2$. The following protocol is an honest verifier zero-knowledge proof of knowledge of either a witness w_1 for x_1 or a witness w_2 for x_2. Assume without loss of generality that $\mathcal{P}$ knows witness w_1.

1. $\mathcal{P}$ picks a random c_2 and simulates $\Sigma_2 = (u_2, c_2, z_2)$.
2. $\mathcal{P}$ computes the message u_1 and sends (u_1, u_2) to $\mathcal{V}$.
3. $\mathcal{V}$ sends a random message c to $\mathcal{P}$.
4. $\mathcal{P}$ computes $c_1 = c \oplus c_2$, computes the honest third message z_1 and sends (z_1, z_2) to $\mathcal{V}$.
5. $\mathcal{V}$ accepts if and only if $c_1 \oplus c_2 = c$ and the transcripts for both Σ_1 and Σ_2 are valid.

8.2   Our Construction

In this section we show how to transform any sigma protocol Σ for a relation $\mathcal{R}$ into a short-lived proof for relation $\mathcal{R}$. The protocol can be found in Fig. 8. It differs from the construction of [2] in three ways:

- We don't work with a zero-knowledge VDF but a zero-knowledge PoSW. This is possible because the protocol does not need the uniqueness property of the VDF.
- We need to include a precomputed PoE in the public parameters because the honest prover simulates the outputs of the zkPoSW and in our construction the simulator needs a precomputed PoE.
- Our zkPoSW is not a sigma protocol but the proof of knowledge PoKDL is. In our construction it is sufficient to combine Σ and PoKDL via the standard disjunction of sigma protocols.

Using Pietrzak's PoE [40] one can not only re-randomize the precomputed PoEs but also the PoEs needed for the forged proofs. Hence, it achieves much faster forging times than the construction based on a zero-knowledge version of Wesolowksi's proof given in [2].

9   Conclusion and Open Problems

In this work we have seen how to efficiently watermark any proof of exponentiation to obtain practical watermarkable VDFs. We also constructed practical zero-knowledge proofs of sequential work that can be used to build short-lived proofs for any NP statement with fast forging times. Our zero-knowledge VDF construction is asymptotically efficient but not practical: The proof size grows by a factor λ because the proof of knowledge that is being used as a building block needs λ repetitions to be sound. One interesting open problem that remains is to construct a *practical* zero-knowledge version of Pietrzak's VDF, by either removing the need for λ repetitions in our general construction or by working directly with Pietrzak's protocol.

References

1. Abusalah, H., Kamath, C., Klein, K., Pietrzak, K., Walter, M.: Reversible proofs of sequential work. In: Ishai, Y., Rijmen, V. (eds.) EUROCRYPT 2019. LNCS, vol. 11477, pp. 277–291. Springer, Cham (2019). https://doi.org/10.1007/978-3-030-17656-3_10

2. Arun, A., Bonneau, J., Clark, J.: Short-lived zero-knowledge proofs and signatures. In: Agrawal, S., Lin, D. (eds.) ASIACRYPT 2022, Part III. LNCS, vol. 13793, pp. 487–516. Springer, Heidelberg (2022). https://doi.org/10.1007/978-3-031-22969-5_17

3. Baldimtsi, F., Kiayias, A., Zacharias, T., Zhang, B.: Indistinguishable proofs of work or knowledge. In: Cheon, J.H., Takagi, T. (eds.) ASIACRYPT 2016. LNCS, vol. 10032, pp. 902–933. Springer, Heidelberg (2016). https://doi.org/10.1007/978-3-662-53890-6_30

4. Bernstein, D., Sorenson, J.: Modular exponentiation via the explicit Chinese remainder theorem. Math. Comput. **76**, 443–454 (2007)

5. Block, A.R., Holmgren, J., Rosen, A., Rothblum, R.D., Soni, P.: Time- and space-efficient arguments from groups of unknown order. In: Malkin, T., Peikert, C. (eds.) CRYPTO 2021. LNCS, vol. 12828, pp. 123–152. Springer, Cham (2021). https://doi.org/10.1007/978-3-030-84259-8_5

6. Boneh, D., Bonneau, J., Bünz, B., Fisch, B.: Verifiable delay functions. In: Shacham, H., Boldyreva, A. (eds.) CRYPTO 2018. LNCS, vol. 10991, pp. 757–788. Springer, Cham (2018). https://doi.org/10.1007/978-3-319-96884-1_25

7. Boneh, D., Bünz, B., Fisch, B.: A survey of two verifiable delay functions. Cryptology ePrint Archive, Report 2018/712 (2018). https://eprint.iacr.org/2018/712

8. Boneh, D., Naor, M.: Timed commitments. In: Bellare, M. (ed.) CRYPTO 2000. LNCS, vol. 1880, pp. 236–254. Springer, Heidelberg (2000). https://doi.org/10.1007/3-540-44598-6_15

9. Canetti, R.: Towards realizing random oracles: hash functions that hide all partial information. In: Kaliski, B.S. (ed.) CRYPTO 1997. LNCS, vol. 1294, pp. 455–469. Springer, Heidelberg (1997). https://doi.org/10.1007/BFb0052255

10. Chaum, D., Pedersen, T.P.: Wallet databases with observers. In: Brickell, E.F. (ed.) CRYPTO 1992. LNCS, vol. 740, pp. 89–105. Springer, Heidelberg (1993). https://doi.org/10.1007/3-540-48071-4_7

11. Chavez-Saab, J., Rodríguez-Henríquez, F., Tibouchi, M.: Verifiable isogeny walks: towards an isogeny-based postquantum VDF. In: AlTawy, R., Hülsing, A. (eds.) Selected Areas in Cryptography, pp. 441–460. Springer, Cham (2022). https://doi.org/10.1007/978-3-030-99277-4_21

12. Cini, V., Lai, R.W.F., Malavolta, G.: Lattice-based succinct arguments from vanishing polynomials - (extended abstract). In: Handschuh, H., Lysyanskaya, A. (eds.) CRYPTO 2023, Part II. LNCS, vol. 14082, pp. 72–105. Springer, Heidelberg (2023). https://doi.org/10.1007/978-3-031-38545-2_3
13. Clark, J., Essex, A.: CommitCoin: carbon dating commitments with bitcoin. In: Keromytis, A.D. (ed.) FC 2012. LNCS, vol. 7397, pp. 390–398. Springer, Heidelberg (2012). https://doi.org/10.1007/978-3-642-32946-3_28
14. Cohen, B., Pietrzak, K.: Simple proofs of sequential work. In: Nielsen, J.B., Rijmen, V. (eds.) EUROCRYPT 2018. LNCS, vol. 10821, pp. 451–467. Springer, Cham (2018). https://doi.org/10.1007/978-3-319-78375-8_15
15. Colburn, M.: Short-lived signatures. Master's thesis, Concordia University (2018)
16. Couteau, G., Peters, T., Pointcheval, D.: Removing the strong RSA assumption from arguments over the integers. In: Coron, J.-S., Nielsen, J.B. (eds.) EUROCRYPT 2017. LNCS, vol. 10211, pp. 321–350. Springer, Cham (2017). https://doi.org/10.1007/978-3-319-56614-6_11
17. Cramer, R., Damgård, I., Schoenmakers, B.: Proofs of partial knowledge and simplified design of witness hiding protocols. In: Desmedt, Y.G. (ed.) CRYPTO 1994. LNCS, vol. 839, pp. 174–187. Springer, Heidelberg (1994). https://doi.org/10.1007/3-540-48658-5_19
18. De Feo, L., Masson, S., Petit, C., Sanso, A.: Verifiable delay functions from supersingular isogenies and pairings. In: Galbraith, S.D., Moriai, S. (eds.) ASIACRYPT 2019. LNCS, vol. 11921, pp. 248–277. Springer, Cham (2019). https://doi.org/10.1007/978-3-030-34578-5_10
19. Döttling, N., Lai, R., Malavolta, G.: Incremental proofs of sequential work. In: Ishai, Y., Rijmen, V. (eds.) EUROCRYPT 2019. LNCS, vol. 11477, pp. 292–323. Springer, Cham (2019). https://doi.org/10.1007/978-3-030-17656-3_11
20. Ferradi, H., Géraud, R., Naccache, D.: Slow motion zero knowledge identifying with colliding commitments. In: Lin, D., Wang, X.F., Yung, M. (eds.) Inscrypt 2015. LNCS, vol. 9589, pp. 381–396. Springer, Cham (2016). https://doi.org/10.1007/978-3-319-38898-4_22
21. Fiat, A., Shamir, A.: How to prove yourself: practical solutions to identification and signature problems. In: Odlyzko, A.M. (ed.) CRYPTO 1986. LNCS, vol. 263, pp. 186–194. Springer, Heidelberg (1987). https://doi.org/10.1007/3-540-47721-7_12
22. Fischlin, R., Schnorr, C.P.: Stronger security proofs for RSA and Rabin bits. J. Cryptol. 13(2), 221–244 (2000)
23. Freitag, C., Pass, R., Sirkin, N.: Parallelizable delegation from LWE. In: Kiltz, E., Vaikuntanathan, V. (eds.) TCC 2022, Part II. LNCS, vol. 13748, pp. 623–652. Springer, Heidelberg (2022). https://doi.org/10.1007/978-3-031-22365-5_22
24. Guillou, L.C., Quisquater, J.-J.: A "Paradoxical" indentity-based signature scheme resulting from zero-knowledge. In: Goldwasser, S. (ed.) CRYPTO 1988. LNCS, vol. 403, pp. 216–231. Springer, New York (1990). https://doi.org/10.1007/0-387-34799-2_16
25. Hoffmann, C., Hubáček, P., Kamath, C., Klein, K., Pietrzak, K.: Practical statistically-sound proofs of exponentiation in any group. In: Dodis, Y., Shrimpton, T. (eds.) CRYPTO 2022, Part II. LNCS, vol. 13508, pp. 370–399. Springer, Heidelberg (2022). https://doi.org/10.1007/978-3-031-15979-4_13
26. Hoffmann, C., Hubáček, P., Kamath, C., Pietrzak, K.: Certifying giant nonprimes. In: Boldyreva, A., Kolesnikov, V. (eds.) PKC 2023, Part I. LNCS, vol. 13940, pp. 530–553. Springer, Heidelberg (2023). https://doi.org/10.1007/978-3-031-31368-4_19

27. Hoffmann, C., Hubáček, P., Kamath, C., Krňák, T.: (Verifiable) delay functions from Lucas sequences. In: Rothblum, G.N., Wee, H. (eds.) TCC 2023, Part IV. LNCS, vol. 14372, pp. 336–362. Springer, Cham (2023). https://doi.org/10.1007/978-3-031-48624-1_13

28. Hoffmann, C., Hubáček, P., Ivanova, S.: Practical batch proofs of exponentiation. Cryptology ePrint Archive, Paper 2024/145 (2024). https://eprint.iacr.org/2024/145

29. Hofheinz, D., Kiltz, E.: The group of signed quadratic residues and applications. In: Halevi, S. (ed.) CRYPTO 2009. LNCS, vol. 5677, pp. 637–653. Springer, Heidelberg (2009). https://doi.org/10.1007/978-3-642-03356-8_37

30. Khovratovich, D., Maller, M., Tiwari, P.R.: MinRoot: candidate sequential function for Ethereum VDF. Cryptology ePrint Archive, Report 2022/1626 (2022). https://eprint.iacr.org/2022/1626

31. Kiayias, A., Tsiounis, Y., Yung, M.: Traceable signatures. In: Cachin, C., Camenisch, J.L. (eds.) EUROCRYPT 2004. LNCS, vol. 3027, pp. 571–589. Springer, Heidelberg (2004). https://doi.org/10.1007/978-3-540-24676-3_34

32. Lai, R.W.F., Malavolta, G.: Lattice-based timed cryptography. In: Handschuh, H., Lysyanskaya, A. (eds.) CRYPTO 2023. LNCS, vol. 14085, pp. 782–804. Springer, Cham (2023). https://doi.org/10.1007/978-3-031-38554-4_25

33. Landerreche, E., Stevens, M., Schaffner, C.: Non-interactive cryptographic timestamping based on verifiable delay functions. In: Bonneau, J., Heninger, N. (eds.) FC 2020. LNCS, vol. 12059, pp. 541–558. Springer, Cham (2020). https://doi.org/10.1007/978-3-030-51280-4_29

34. Lenstra, A.K., Wesolowski, B.: Trustworthy public randomness with sloth, unicorn, and TRX. Int. J. Appl. Cryptogr. **3**(4), 330–343 (2017). https://doi.org/10.1504/IJACT.2017.10010315

35. Mahmoody, M., Moran, T., Vadhan, S.: Time-lock puzzles in the random oracle model. In: Rogaway, P. (ed.) CRYPTO 2011. LNCS, vol. 6841, pp. 39–50. Springer, Heidelberg (2011). https://doi.org/10.1007/978-3-642-22792-9_3

36. Mahmoody, M., Moran, T., Vadhan, S.P.: Publicly verifiable proofs of sequential work. In: Kleinberg, R.D. (ed.) ITCS 2013: 4th Innovations in Theoretical Computer Science, pp. 373–388. Association for Computing Machinery, Berkeley, CA, USA, 9–12 January 2013

37. Mahmoody, M., Smith, C., Wu, D.J.: Can verifiable delay functions be based on random oracles? In: Czumaj, A., Dawar, A., Merelli, E. (eds.) ICALP 2020: 47th International Colloquium on Automata, Languages and Programming. LIPIcs, vol. 168, pp. 83:1–83:17. Schloss Dagstuhl - Leibniz-Zentrum fuer Informatik, Saarbrücken, Germany, 8–11 July 2020

38. Malavolta, G., Thyagarajan, S.: Homomorphic time-lock puzzles and applications. In: Boldyreva, A., Micciancio, D. (eds.) CRYPTO 2019. LNCS, vol. 11692, pp. 620–649. Springer, Cham (2019). https://doi.org/10.1007/978-3-030-26948-7_22

39. May, T.C.: Timed-release crypto (1994)

40. Pietrzak, K.: Simple verifiable delay functions. In: Blum, A. (ed.) ITCS 2019: 10th Innovations in Theoretical Computer Science Conference. vol. 124, pp. 60:1–60:15. LIPIcs, San Diego, CA, USA, 10–12 January 2019

41. Rabin, M.O.: Transaction protection by beacons. J. Comput. Syst. Sci. **27**(2), 256–267 (1983)

42. Rivest, R.L., Shamir, A., Wagner, D.A.: Time-lock puzzles and timed-release crypto. Technical report, Massachusetts Institute of Technology (1996)

43. Rotem, L.: Simple and efficient batch verification techniques for verifiable delay functions. In: Nissim, K., Waters, B. (eds.) TCC 2021. LNCS, vol. 13044, pp. 382–414. Springer, Cham (2021). https://doi.org/10.1007/978-3-030-90456-2_13

44. Rotem, L., Segev, G.: Generically speeding-up repeated squaring is equivalent to factoring: sharp thresholds for all generic-ring delay functions. In: Micciancio, D., Ristenpart, T. (eds.) CRYPTO 2020. LNCS, vol. 12172, pp. 481–509. Springer, Cham (2020). https://doi.org/10.1007/978-3-030-56877-1_17

45. Schindler, P., Judmayer, A., Hittmeir, M., Stifter, N., Weippl, E.R.: RandRunner: distributed randomness from trapdoor VDFs with strong uniqueness. In: ISOC Network and Distributed System Security Symposium – NDSS 2021. The Internet Society, Virtual, 21–25 February 2021

46. Schnorr, C.P.: Efficient signature generation by smart cards. J. Cryptol. **4**(3), 161–174 (1991). https://doi.org/10.1007/BF00196725

47. Segal, K., Brand, T.: Presenting: VeeDo a STARK-based VDF service. Technical report, StarkWare (2019). https://medium.com/starkware/presenting-veedo-e4bbff77c7ae

48. Shani, B.: A note on isogeny-based hybrid verifiable delay functions. Cryptology ePrint Archive, Paper 2019/205 (2019). https://eprint.iacr.org/2019/205

49. Specter, M.A., Park, S., Green, M.: KeyForge: non-attributable email from forward-forgeable signatures. In: Bailey, M., Greenstadt, R. (eds.) USENIX Security 2021: 30th USENIX Security Symposium, pp. 1755–1773. USENIX Association, 11–13 August 2021

50. Wesolowski, B.: Efficient verifiable delay functions. In: Ishai, Y., Rijmen, V. (eds.) EUROCRYPT 2019. LNCS, vol. 11478, pp. 379–407. Springer, Cham (2019). https://doi.org/10.1007/978-3-030-17659-4_13

Higher Residuosity Attacks on Small RSA Subgroup Decision Problems

Xiaopeng Zhao[1]([⊠]) [ID], Zhenfu Cao[2] [ID], Xiaolei Dong[2], and Zhusen Liu[3] [ID]

[1] School of Computer Science and Technology, Donghua University,
Shanghai 201620, China
zxp@dhu.edu.cn

[2] Department of Cryptography and Cyber Security, East China Normal University,
Shanghai 200062, China
{zfcao,dongxiaolei}@sei.ecnu.edu.cn

[3] Hangzhou Innovation Institute of Beihang University, Zhejiang 311121,
Hangzhou, China

Abstract. Secure two-party comparison, known as Yao's millionaires' problem, has been a fundamental challenge in privacy-preserving computation. It enables two parties to compare their inputs without revealing the exact values of those inputs or relying on any trusted third party. One elegant approach to secure computation is based on homomorphic encryption. Recently, building on this approach, Carlton et al. (CT-RSA 2018) and Bourse et al. (CT-RSA 2020) presented novel solutions for the problem of secure integer comparison. These protocols have demonstrated significantly improved performance compared to the well-known and frequently used DGK protocol (ACISP 2007 and Int. J. Appl. Cryptogr. $1(4)$,323-324, 2009). In this paper, we introduce a class of higher residuosity attacks, which can be regarded as an extension of the classical quadratic residuosity attack on the decisional Diffie-Hellman problem. We demonstrate that the small RSA subgroup decision problems, upon which both the CEK and BST protocols are based, are not difficult to solve when the prime base p_0 is small (e.g., $p_0 < 100$). Under these conditions, the protocols achieve optimal overall performance. Furthermore, we offer recommendations for precluding such attacks, including one approach that does not adversely affect performance. We hope that these attacks can be applied to analyze other number-theoretic hardness assumptions.

Keywords: Secure two-party comparison · Small RSA subgroup decision problem · Higher residuosity attacks

1 Introduction

Secure two-party comparison, known as Yao's millionaires' problem [33], has been a fundamental challenge in privacy-preserving computation. The traditional solution to this problem is based on Yao's Garbled Circuit [33]. In Yao's protocol,

ⓒ International Association for Cryptologic Research 2025
T. Jager and J. Pan (Eds.): PKC 2025, LNCS 15674, pp. 67–87, 2025.
https://doi.org/10.1007/978-3-031-91820-9_3

two parties use their bitwise representations of private inputs to securely evaluate a comparison function, which is represented as a Boolean circuit, in the presence of semi-honest adversaries. However, the memory, energy, and communication costs associated with garbled circuit evaluation protocols are substantial.

Another significant approach to secure computation is based on homomorphic encryption. This method is typically less computationally efficient than protocols utilizing garbled circuits; however, it is more straightforward to implement and incurs a lower overall communication cost. Fischlin [13] first constructed a secure comparison of two numbers using a Boolean circuit based on the XOR-homomorphic Goldwasser-Micali cryptosystem [15]. Other notable examples of secure Boolean evaluation of bitwise encryption of integers include the schemes developed by Blake and Kolesnikov [2], Garay et al. [14] and Lin and Tzeng [25]. Later, Damgård, Geisler, and Krøigaard (DGK) enhanced this approach in [11,12]. Drawing inspiration from the strong RSA subgroup assumption (related to high residuosity assumptions) proposed by Groth in [16] as well as the DGK comparison protocol in [11,12], Carlton et al. [8] employed an *RSA quintuple* (see Definition 1) as a public key in their encryption scheme. Notably, they discovered that the encryption possesses a *threshold* (scalar) homomorphic property. Leveraging this property, they constructed a protocol (termed the CEK protocol) that efficiently compares two encrypted integers through the (nearly) direct application of the homomorphism on a single encrypted value. Following a similar approach, Bourse et al. [4] improved the CEK protocol (termed the BST protocol) by avoiding one round induced by the plaintext equality test. Both the CEK and BST protocols have been proven to be secure under the small RSA subgroup decision problems. Performance results indicate that they are several times faster than the DGK protocol.

However, we will demonstrate that the small RSA subgroup decision problems are not difficult to solve when the public prime base p_0 is small (e.g., $p_0 < 100$), in which case both the CEK and BST protocols achieve optimal overall performance. The small RSA subgroup decision problems involve an RSA quintuple that contains an RSA modulus $N = pq$ such that $p = 2p_0^d p_s p_t + 1$ and $q = 2p_0^d q_s q_t + 1$ where p_s, q_s, p_t, q_t are pairwise distinct primes, d is an integer greater than 1. Our attacks on them mainly utilize the leakage of an element of order p_0 in $\mathbb{Z}_N^*$, in which case a partial decomposition of N in the algebraic integer ring $\mathbb{Z}[\zeta_{p_0}]$ can be easily computed. Consequently, higher residuosity attacks that leverage power residue symbols naturally arise from this leakage, even though the classical quadratic residuosity attack[1] does not work. Since both protocols reveal an RSA quintuple as part of the public key, we can similarly present practical higher residuosity attacks against them (see Sect. 5). Furthermore, we provide recommendations for precluding such attacks, including one approach that does not adversely affect their performance.

The rest of this paper is organized as follows. Section 2 introduces the background knowledge on small RSA subgroup decision problems. In Sect. 3, we

---

[1] Because of this attack the decisional Diffie-Hellman problem in the group $\mathbb{Z}_p^*$ is not hard.

provide a detailed quartic residuosity attack on these problems with $p_0 = 2$. Section 4 presents a higher residuosity attack on these problems when p_0 is an odd prime. In Sect. 5, we discuss practical higher residuosity attacks on the CEK and BST protocols and offer recommendations for precluding such attacks. Finally, conclusions are drawn in Sect. 6.

2 Preliminaries

2.1 Notations

For the sake of clarity, Table 1 summarizes the frequently used notations in this paper.

Table 1. Frequently Used Notations

$\mathbb{Z}, \mathbb{Q}$	the integers, the rational numbers
$\mathbb{N}^+$	the set of positive integers
$\mathbb{C}$	the complex numbers
K	a number field
$\mathcal{O}_K$	the ring of integers in a number field K
$\mathfrak{a}, \mathfrak{b}, \ldots$	the ideals in $\mathcal{O}_K$
$\mathbb{Z}_n$	$= \{0, 1, \ldots, n-1\}$ integers mod n
$\mathbb{Z}_n^*$	$= \{b \in \mathbb{Z}_n \mid \gcd(b, N) = 1\}$ multiplicative group mod n
$\mathbb{F}_p$	$= \mathbb{Z}/p\mathbb{Z}$ the field of p elements for a prime p
$R^\times$	the unit group of the multiplicative monoid of a ring R
ζ_n	a primitive n^{th} root of unity, i.e., $\zeta_n = e^{2\pi i/n}$
i	the imaginary unit, i.e., $i = \zeta_4$
$a \mid b$	a divides b
$\langle X \rangle$	the group generated by a set X
$(a, b, \ldots)$	the ideal generated by $a, b, \ldots$
$\gcd(a, b)$	the greatest common divisor of a, b
$a \equiv b \pmod{\mathfrak{D}}$	the relation $a - b \in \mathfrak{D}$, where elements $a, b \in \mathcal{O}_K$
$\varphi(n)$	the number of elements in $\mathbb{Z}_n^*$
$\log$	the binary logarithm
$|A|$	the number of elements of a set A
$\mathcal{N}(\alpha)$	the norm of $\alpha \in \mathbb{Z}[\zeta_n]$ given by $\mathcal{N}(\alpha) = \prod_{k \in \mathbb{Z}_n^*} \sigma_k(\alpha)$ where $\sigma_k : \zeta_n \mapsto \zeta_n^k$
$\mathcal{N}(\mathfrak{a})$	$= \|\mathcal{O}_K/\mathfrak{a}\|$
$\left(\frac{\cdot}{\cdot}\right)$	the Jacobi symbol
$\mathcal{QR}_n$	$= \{x^2 : x \in \mathbb{Z}_n^*\}$ the set of quadratic residues in the group $\mathbb{Z}_n^*$
PPT	probabilistic polynomial time
O	the big-oh notation
$\mathcal{D}$	a distinguisher, possibly a probabilistic one

2.2   Small RSA Subgroup Decision Problems

In this section, we will first briefly review the small RSA subgroup decision problems as defined in [8, Definition 2] and in [4, Definition 2], respectively, and then we will discuss the close relationship between them. The following definition is drawn from [8, Definition 1] and [4, Section 3.1].

Definition 1. *An* RSA quintuple *is a quintuple* (N, p_0, d, g, u) *where:*

1. *u is an integer such that the Discrete Logarithm Problem is computationally infeasible in a subgroup of $\mathbb{Z}_N^*$ whose order is a prime of bit-length u;*
2. *p_0 is a prime of bit-length less than u;*
3. *d is an integer greater than 1;*
4. *$N = pq$ is a composite integer with computationally infeasible factorization, where the primes p and q are constructed as:*

$$p = 2p_0^d p_s p_t + 1 \quad and \quad q = 2p_0^d q_s q_t + 1,$$

   satisfying the following conditions:
   - *p_s and q_s are primes of bit-length u;*
   - *p_t and q_t are primes with bit-length different from u;*
   - *p_s, q_s, p_t, q_t are pairwise distinct;*
5. *g is an element in $\mathbb{Z}_N^*$ which has order p_0^d modulo p and modulo q.*

Remark 1. We slightly modify the condition 5 for security purposes. The original definition only requires g to be of order p_0^d in $\mathbb{Z}_N^*$, whereas this might lead to the leakage of the factorization of N since both g and its order are public: consider the case where g has order p_0^d in $\mathbb{Z}_p^*$ but has order $p_0^{d'}$ for some integer $d' < d$ in $\mathbb{Z}_q^*$, then g would have the correct order p_0^d in $\mathbb{Z}_N^*$, thus $\gcd(g^{p_0^{d-1}} - 1, N)$ would immediately give a factor of N.

The BST and CEK protocols have been proven secure, relying on the hardness of the Small RSA Subgroup Decision Problem SRSDP and $\widetilde{\text{SRSDP}}$, respectively. These two problems are defined as follows.

Definition 2 (Small RSA Subgroup Decision Problem [4] (SRSDP)). *Given an RSA quintuple (N, p_0, d, g, u), distinguish the two uniform distributions over $\mathcal{QR}_N$ and over $\{x^{p_0^d p_t q_t} \mid x \in \mathcal{QR}_N\}$, respectively.*

Definition 3 (Small RSA Subgroup Decision Problem [8] ($\widetilde{\text{SRSDP}}$)). *Given an RSA quintuple (N, p_0, d, g, u), distinguish the two uniform distributions over $\mathcal{QR}_N$ and over $\{x \in \mathcal{QR}_N \mid x \text{ has order } p_s q_s \text{ in } \mathbb{Z}_N^*\}$, respectively.*

Definition 4 (Advantage for Solving the SRSDP). *Given an instance $\mathcal{I} = \{(N, p_0, d, g, u), x\}$ of SRSDP, where x is sampled according to one of the two distributions stated in Definition 2, the advantage of a distinguisher $\mathscr{D}$ for solving the SRSDP (being able to correctly guess the target) is defined as*

$$\mathsf{Adv}_{\mathscr{D},\mathcal{I}}^{SRSDP} = \Pr[\mathscr{D}(\mathcal{I}) \text{ outputs "yes"} \mid x \text{ is of the form } y^{p_0^d p_t q_t} \text{ with } y \in \mathcal{QR}_N] - \frac{1}{2}$$

$$+ \Pr[\mathscr{D}(\mathcal{I}) \text{ outputs "no"} \mid x \in \mathcal{QR}_N] - \frac{1}{2}$$

Remark 2. According to the probabilistic definition of $\mathsf{Adv}_{\mathscr{D},\mathcal{I}}^{\mathsf{SRSDP}}$, a perfect distinguisher would not have an advantage of 1.

The advantage for solving the $\widetilde{\mathsf{SRSDP}}$ can be defined analogously. Theorem 1 is crucial to reveal the close relationship between the SRSDP and the $\widetilde{\mathsf{SRSDP}}$.

Theorem 1. *Given an RSA quintuple (N, p_0, d, g, u) and $x \in \mathcal{QR}_N$, if x has order $p_s q_s$ in $\mathbb{Z}_N^*$, then x can be written in the form $y^{p_0^d p_t q_t}$ for some $y \in \mathcal{QR}_N$.*

Proof. Suppose that x has order $p_s q_s$ in $\mathbb{Z}_N^*$. Then x must have order p_s in $\mathbb{Z}_p^*$ and order q_s in $\mathbb{Z}_q^*$. Let g_p and g_q be primitive roots modulo p and q, respectively. Then x can be written as $x \equiv g_p^{2p_0^d p_t a} \pmod{p}$ and $x \equiv g_q^{2p_0^d q_t b} \pmod{q}$ with $p_s \nmid a$ and $q_s \nmid b$. Let $y \in \mathcal{QR}_N$ be such that $y \equiv g_p^{2\ell} \pmod{p}$ and $y \equiv g_q^{2\ell'} \pmod{q}$ where $q_t \ell \equiv a \pmod{p_s}$ and $p_t \ell' \equiv b \pmod{q_s}$. Thus, x can be written as $x = y^{p_0^d p_t q_t}$ in $\mathbb{Z}_N^*$. $\square$

Remark 3. It follows quite easily that a counterexample to the reverse direction is $y = 1$. Let

$$H = \{x \in \mathcal{QR}_N \mid x \text{ has order } p_s q_s \text{ in } \mathbb{Z}_N^*\},$$
$$G = \{x \in \mathcal{QR}_N \mid x \text{ is of the form } y^{p_0^d p_t q_t} \text{ with } y \in \mathcal{QR}_N\}.$$

By the proof of Theorem 1 we can see that

$$|H| = (p_s - 1)(q_s - 1) \text{ and } |G| = p_s q_s.$$

Remark 4. Let $||n||$ denote the bit-length of the integer n. Since the SRSDP problem operates on the group G whose order is $p_s q_s$ and $u = ||p_s|| = ||q_s||$, u should define a length for which computing the discrete logarithm in a group of prime u-bit order is infeasible. Therefore, working at the 128-bit security level requires $||N|| = 3072$, $u = 256$; The 192-bit security level requires $||N|| = 7680$, $u = 384$ and the 256-bit security level requires $||N|| = 15360$, $u = 512$.

Theorem 2 below shows that if there exists a PPT distinguisher being able to solve the SRSDP with light advantage then one can solve the $\widetilde{\mathsf{SRSDP}}$ in polynomial time with non-negligible advantage. Therefore, we next focus mainly on investigating the hardness of the SRSDP. We remark that all of the attacks described in the following sections have advantages of at least $1/2$.

Theorem 2. *Let $\mathscr{D}$ be a PPT distinguisher being able to solve the SRSDP with*

$$\mathsf{Adv}_{\mathscr{D},\mathcal{I}}^{\mathsf{SRSDP}} - \frac{(p_s + q_s - 1)}{p_s q_s}$$

non-negligible. Then given an RSA quintuple (N, p_0, d, g, u), there exists a PPT distinguisher $\mathscr{D}'$ being able to solve the $\widetilde{\mathsf{SRSDP}}$, i.e., distinguish whether a random element in $\mathcal{QR}_N$ has order $p_s q_s$ in $\mathbb{Z}_N^*$ with non-negligible advantage.

Proof. We construct $\mathscr{D}'$ that takes an RSA quintuple and $x \in \mathcal{QR}_N$ as input, and whose goal is to determine whether x has order $p_s q_s$ in $\mathbb{Z}_N^*$:

Distinguisher $\mathscr{D}'$: $\mathscr{D}'$ is given as input an RSA quintuple (N, p_0, d, g, u) and $x \in \mathcal{QR}_N$.

1: Construct an instance $\mathcal{I} = \{(N, p_0, d, g, u), x\}$ and run $\mathscr{D}(\mathcal{I})$ to obtain an output string w.
2: Output w.

$\mathscr{D}'$ clearly runs in polynomial time because $\mathscr{D}$ does. By Theorem 1 and Remark 3, we see that $H \subset G$ and the advantage of $\mathscr{D}'$ is given by

$$
\mathsf{Adv}_{\mathscr{D}',\mathcal{I}}^{\widetilde{\mathsf{SRSDP}}} = \Pr[\mathscr{D}'(\mathcal{I}) \text{ outputs "yes"} \mid x \in H] + \Pr[\mathscr{D}'(\mathcal{I}) \text{ outputs "no"} \mid x \in \mathcal{QR}_N] - 1
$$

$$
\geq \Pr[\mathscr{D}(\mathcal{I}) \text{ outputs "yes"} \mid x \in G] - \frac{|G| - |H|}{|G|}
$$

$$
+ \Pr[\mathscr{D}(\mathcal{I}) \text{ outputs "no"} \mid x \in \mathcal{QR}_N] - 1
$$

$$
= \mathsf{Adv}_{\mathscr{D},\mathcal{I}}^{\mathsf{SRSDP}} - \frac{p_s + q_s - 1}{p_s q_s},
$$

which is non-negligible under the assumption in the theorem.   □

3   A Quartic Residuosity Attack on the **SRSDP** when $p_0 = 2$

Carlton et al. [8] suggested to take $p_0 = 2$ in the CEK protocol for efficiently computing a discrete logarithm in the cyclic group generated by g. The BST protocol also achieves the best performance in this case. However, in this section, we shall show that the SRSDP with $p_0 = 2$ can be efficiently solved with advantage $1/2$ by using quartic residuosity.

3.1   The Quartic Jacobi Symbol

We start with the elementary results concerning the ring of *Gaussian integers* $\mathbb{Z}[i]$. It is a Euclidean Domain and $\mathbb{Z}[i]^\times = \langle i \rangle$. For every prime element $\pi = a + bi \in \mathbb{Z}[i]$, the norm of π is given by $\mathcal{N}(\pi) = \pi\overline{\pi} = a^2 + b^2$; there is a unique prime $p \in \pi\mathbb{Z}[i]$ such that $\pi\mathbb{Z}[i] \cap \mathbb{Z} = p\mathbb{Z}$, and if $p \equiv 1 \bmod 4$ then $p = \pi\overline{\pi}$. The residue class ring $\mathbb{Z}[i]/\pi\mathbb{Z}[i]$ is a finite field with $\mathcal{N}(\pi)$ elements. In particular, $(\mathbb{Z}[i]/\pi\mathbb{Z}[i])^\times$ is a cyclic group of order $\mathcal{N}(\pi) - 1$. An element $\alpha \in \mathbb{Z}[i]$ is called *primary* if $\alpha \equiv 1 \bmod (1 + i)^3$. If $\alpha \notin (1 + i)\mathbb{Z}[i]$, then there exists a unique $u \in \mathbb{Z}[i]^\times$ such that $u\alpha$ is primary.

Let $\pi \in \mathbb{Z}[i] \setminus (1 + i)\mathbb{Z}[i]$ be a prime element. Then there exists a unique character $\chi_\pi : (\mathbb{Z}[i]/\pi\mathbb{Z}[i])^\times \mapsto \mathbb{C}^\times$ of order 4 such that

$$
\chi_\pi(\xi) + \pi\mathbb{Z}[i] = \xi^{\frac{\mathcal{N}(\pi)-1}{4}} \quad \text{for all} \quad \xi \in (\mathbb{Z}[i]/\pi\mathbb{Z}[i])^\times.
$$

For $\alpha \in \mathbb{Z}[i]$, we define the *quartic residue symbol* of α modulo π by

$$\left(\frac{\alpha}{\pi}\right)_4 = \begin{cases} 0, & \text{if } \pi \mid \alpha \text{ ;} \\ \chi_\pi(\alpha + \pi\mathbb{Z}[i]) \in \{\pm 1, \pm i\}, & \text{if } \pi \nmid \alpha. \end{cases}$$

Suppose that $\beta = \epsilon \pi_1 \cdots \pi_r \in \mathbb{Z}[i] \setminus (1+i)\mathbb{Z}[i]$, where $r \in \mathbb{N}^+$, $\epsilon \in \mathbb{Z}[i]^\times$ and $\pi_1, \ldots, \pi_r \in \mathbb{Z}[i] \setminus (1+i)\mathbb{Z}[i]$ are prime elements. For $\alpha \in \mathbb{Z}[i]$, the *quartic Jacobi symbol* $\left(\frac{\alpha}{\beta}\right)_4$ is defined by

$$\left(\frac{\alpha}{\beta}\right)_4 = \prod_{j=1}^{r} \left(\frac{\alpha}{\pi_j}\right)_4.$$

Theorem 3 below is known as the *general quartic reciprocity law* in $\mathbb{Z}[i]$. Equation (1) was proposed by Gauss and later proved by Jacobi and Eisenstein. This theorem together with its supplement deals with the beautiful relations that exist among quartic Jacobi symbols and gives an efficient method for computation (see Algorithm 1 and Table 3). We refer the reader to [19, Chapter 9] and [17, Chapter 7] for more details.

Theorem 3 (Quartic Reciprocity Law [17, Theorem 7.4.7]). *Let $\alpha, \beta \in \mathbb{Z}[i] \setminus (1+i)\mathbb{Z}[i]$ be such that $\gcd(\alpha, \beta) = 1$, $\alpha = a + bi$ and $\beta = c + di$, where $a, b, c, d \in \mathbb{Z}$.*

1. *(Jacobi, Kaplan) If $a \equiv c \equiv 1 \pmod 4$ and $b \equiv d \equiv 0 \pmod 2$, then*

$$\left(\frac{\alpha}{\beta}\right)_4 = \left(\frac{\beta}{\alpha}\right)_4 (-1)^{bd/4}.$$

2. *(Gauss, Eisenstein) If α and β are both primary, then*

$$\begin{aligned} \left(\frac{\alpha}{\beta}\right)_4 &= \left(\frac{\beta}{\alpha}\right)_4 (-1)^{bd/4} = \left(\frac{\beta}{\alpha}\right)_4 (-1)^{\frac{a-1}{2}\frac{c-1}{2}} \\ &= \left(\frac{\beta}{\alpha}\right)_4 (-1)^{\frac{N(\alpha)-1}{4}\frac{N(\beta)-1}{4}}. \end{aligned} \tag{1}$$

Theorem 4 (Supplement to the Quartic Reciprocity Law [17, Theorem 7.4.8]). *Suppose that $a, b \in \mathbb{Z}$ and $\beta = a + bi \in \mathbb{Z}[i]$. Then*

$$\left(\frac{-1}{\beta}\right)_4 = (-1)^{b/2} \quad \text{if} \quad \beta \equiv 1 \pmod 2,$$

and if β is primary,

$$\left(\frac{i}{\beta}\right)_4 = i^{(1-a)/2} \quad \text{and} \quad \left(\frac{1+i}{\beta}\right)_4 = i^{(a-b-b^2-1)/4}.$$

3.2   Computing the GCD and the Quartic Jacobi Symbol in $\mathbb{Z}[i]$

Since $\mathbb{Z}[i]$ is Euclidean and, by [19, Proposition 1.4.1], it allows a *Euclidean Algorithm* for computing $\gcd(a,b)$ for every $a,b \in \mathbb{Z}[i]$, $b \neq 0$: by successive "divisions" (actually in $\mathbb{Q}(i)$) we can write:

$$a = q_0 b + r_1 \qquad \mathcal{N}(r_1) \leq \frac{1}{2}\mathcal{N}(b),$$

$$b = q_1 r_1 + r_2 \qquad \mathcal{N}(r_2) \leq \frac{1}{2}\mathcal{N}(r_1),$$

$$r_1 = q_2 r_2 + r_3 \qquad \mathcal{N}(r_3) \leq \frac{1}{2}\mathcal{N}(r_2),$$

$$\vdots$$

$$r_{n-1} = q_n r_n + r_{n+1} \qquad \mathcal{N}(r_{n+1}) = 0.$$

Then after a finite number of steps there must exist n such that $r_{n+1} = 0$ and hence $r_n = \gcd(a,b)$. This is because $0 = \mathcal{N}(r_{n+1}) < 1 \leq \mathcal{N}(r_n) \leq 1/2\mathcal{N}(r_{n-1}) \leq \ldots \leq 1/2^n \mathcal{N}(b)$ and $\mathcal{N}(b)$ is finite. As $n \leq \lceil \log \mathcal{N}(b) \rceil$, it follows that $\gcd(a,b)$ can be computed in time $O\left((\log \mathcal{N}(ab))^3\right)$ by means of the Euclidean Algorithm in $\mathbb{Z}[i]$. In [10], Dåmgard et al. presented more efficient algorithms for computing the GCD and cubic (resp. quartic) residuosity in the ring of Eisenstein (resp. Gaussian) integers, which only take time $O\left((\log \mathcal{N}(ab))^2\right)$ and can be seen as generalisations of the binary integer GCD and derived Jacobi symbol algorithms.

Knowing Theorem 3 and Theorem 4, it is easy to obtain Algorithm 1 for computing the quartic Jacobi symbol. Note that β is primary in each iteration. The algorithm terminates since $\mathcal{N}(\beta)$ is strictly decreasing in each iteration of the **while** loop. Upon termination, it is clear that $\beta = 1$, and thus c is the desired result since it is deduced from Theorem 3 and Theorem 4. Using the complexity analysis of the GCD algorithm, it can likewise be shown that Algorithm 1 also takes $O\left((\log \mathcal{N}(\alpha\beta))^3\right)$ time to compute $\left(\frac{\alpha}{\beta}\right)_4$. By virtue of a connection between the quartic residue symbol and the Hilbert symbol, Weilert [31] described a fast algorithm for the computation of the quartic residue symbol, whose running time is $O\left(n(\log n)^2 \log \log n\right)$ for Gaussian integers bounded by 2^n in the norm.

3.3   Attacking the **SRSDP** via the Quartic Jacobi Symbol

With the preparation for the quartic Jacobi symbol in $\mathbb{Z}[i]$, attacks on the SRSDP with $p_0 = 2$ are possible. Given an RSA quintuple $(N, p_0 := 2, d, g, u)$ and a sample $x \in \mathcal{QR}_N$, $\mathcal{D}$ first computes $h = g^{p_0^d/4} \bmod N$, whose order is 4 in both $\mathbb{Z}_p^*$ and $\mathbb{Z}_q^*$. Then it computes $\rho = \gcd(N, h - i)$ by the Euclidean Algorithm in $\mathbb{Z}[i]$. Let $p = \pi\overline{\pi}$, $q = \lambda\overline{\lambda}$ for some prime elements $\pi, \lambda \in \mathbb{Z}[i]$. We see that $h^2 \equiv -1 \bmod N$ and $\pi\overline{\pi} \mid (h+i)(h-i)$, $\lambda\overline{\lambda} \mid (h+i)(h-i)$. Since $\pi, \overline{\pi}, \lambda, \overline{\lambda}$ are

---

Algorithm 1: Compute the quartic Jacobi symbol in $\mathbb{Z}[i]$

Input: $\alpha \in \mathbb{Z}[i]$, $\beta \in \mathbb{Z}[i] \setminus (1+i)\mathbb{Z}[i]$

Output: $c = \left(\frac{\alpha}{\beta}\right)_4$

1 $c = 1$

2 Let primary γ be defined by $\beta = i^{j_1}\gamma$.

3 $\beta \leftarrow \gamma$

4 while $\beta \neq 1$ **do**

5 $\quad$ Let $\alpha = \mu\beta + \nu$ with $\mathcal{N}(\nu) = 0$ or $\mathcal{N}(\nu) \leq \frac{1}{2}\mathcal{N}(\beta)$.

6 $\quad \alpha \leftarrow \nu$

7 $\quad$ **if** α == 0 **then** $\qquad\qquad\qquad\qquad\qquad\qquad$ // $\gcd(\alpha, \beta) \neq 1$

8 $\quad\quad$ | $\quad$ **return** 0

9 $\quad$ **end**

$\quad$ /* remove factors of $1 + i$ in α and apply Theorem 4 $\qquad$ */

10 $\quad$ Let $\beta = a + bi$ and let primary $\delta = e + fi$ be defined by $\alpha = i^{j_1}(1+i)^{j_2}\delta$.

11 $\quad c \leftarrow c \times i^{(a-1)j_1/2} \times i^{(a-b-b^2-1)j_2/4}$.

12 $\quad \alpha \leftarrow \delta$

$\quad$ /* apply Theorem 3 $\qquad\qquad\qquad\qquad\qquad\qquad\qquad\qquad\qquad$ */

13 $\quad$ **if** $a \equiv 3 \bmod 4$ and $e \equiv 3 \bmod 4$ **then**

14 $\quad\quad$ | $\quad c \leftarrow -c$

15 $\quad$ **end**

16 $\quad$ Interchange α, β.

17 end

18 return c

---

prime elements and $p = \pi\overline{\pi} \nmid h + i$, it follows that one of π or $\overline{\pi}$ (resp. one of λ or $\overline{\lambda}$) must divide $h - i$. By renaming π and λ if needed, we may write $\rho = \pi\lambda$. Finally, $\mathscr{D}$ computes $c = \left(\frac{x}{\rho}\right)_4$ by Algorithm 1, it outputs "yes" if $c = 1$ and "no" otherwise. Note that if x is of the form $y^{p_0^d p_t q_t}$ with $y \in \mathcal{QR}_N$ then we must have

$$c = \left(\frac{y^{2^d p_t q_t}}{\rho}\right)_4 = \left(\frac{y}{\rho}\right)_4^{2^d p_t q_t} = 1 \text{ (since } d > 1 \text{ and } \gcd(y, \rho) = \gcd(y, N) = 1).$$

This gives us with an efficient distinguisher $\mathscr{D}$:

Distinguisher $\mathscr{D}$: $\mathscr{D}$ is given as input an RSA quintuple $(N, p_0 := 2, d, g, u)$ and a sample $x \in \mathcal{QR}_N$.

1: Compute $h = g^{p_0^d/4} \bmod N$.

2: Compute $\rho = \gcd(N, h - i)$ by the Euclidean Algorithm in $\mathbb{Z}[i]$.

3: Compute $c = \left(\frac{x}{\rho}\right)_4$ by Algorithm 1.

4: **if** c == 1 **then**

5: $\quad$ Output "yes".

6: **else**

7: $\quad$ Output "no".

8: **end if**

According to the complexity analysis in Sect. 3.2, the overall time complexity of $\mathscr{D}$ will then be

$$O\left(\log\left(\frac{p_0^d}{4}\right)\cdot(\log N)^2\right)+O\left((\log\mathcal{N}(N(h-i)))^3\right)+O\left((\log\mathcal{N}(x\rho))^3\right)=O\left((\log N)^3\right)$$

bit operations, so that $\mathscr{D}$ runs in polynomial time. To show that $\mathscr{D}$ can solve the SRSDP with non-negligible advantage, we need the following two lemmas. To state them, we define the function $\mathbb{I}_\epsilon$ ($\epsilon\in\mathbb{Z}[i]^\times$) by $\mathbb{I}_\epsilon[\epsilon]=1$ and $\mathbb{I}_\epsilon[\delta]=0$ for all $\delta\in\mathbb{Z}[i]^\times\setminus\{\epsilon\}$.

Lemma 1. *Let $p\equiv 1\bmod 4$ be a prime and let $p=\pi\bar{\pi}$ for some prime element $\pi\in\mathbb{Z}[i]$. Then for $\epsilon\in\{\pm1\}$ we have*

$$\sum_{\substack{0\leq r\leq p-1\\ \left(\frac{r}{p}\right)=1}}\mathbb{I}_\epsilon\left[\left(\frac{r}{\pi}\right)_4\right]=\frac{p-1}{4},$$

and for $\delta\in\{\pm i\}$ we have

$$\sum_{\substack{0\leq r\leq p-1\\ \left(\frac{r}{p}\right)=-1}}\mathbb{I}_\delta\left[\left(\frac{r}{\pi}\right)_4\right]=\frac{p-1}{4}.$$

Proof. We calculate

$$\sum_{\substack{0\leq r\leq p-1\\ \left(\frac{r}{p}\right)=1}}\mathbb{I}_\epsilon\left[\left(\frac{r}{\pi}\right)_4\right]=\frac{\epsilon}{4}\sum_{1\leq r\leq p-1}\left[\left(\frac{r}{p}\right)+1\right]\left[\left(\frac{r}{\pi}\right)_4+\epsilon\right]$$

$$=\frac{\epsilon}{4}\left[\sum_{1\leq r\leq p-1}\left(\frac{r}{\pi}\right)_4^3+\sum_{1\leq r\leq p-1}\epsilon\right]$$

$$=\frac{\epsilon}{4}\sum_{1\leq r\leq p-1}\left(\frac{r}{\bar{\pi}}\right)_4+\frac{p-1}{4}$$

$$=\frac{p-1}{4}$$

where the last three lines follow from the three facts:

- If χ is a non-trivial multiplicative character, then $\sum_{t\in\mathbb{F}_p}\chi(t)=0$.
- If $\alpha\in\mathbb{Z}[i]$, $\beta\in\mathbb{Z}[i]^\times$ and $\gcd(2\alpha,\beta)=1$, then $\gcd(\bar{\alpha},\bar{\beta})=1$ and $\overline{\left(\frac{\alpha}{\beta}\right)_4}=\left(\frac{\alpha}{\beta}\right)_4^3=\left(\frac{\bar{\alpha}}{\bar{\beta}}\right)_4$.
- If $a\in\mathbb{Z}$, $\beta\in\mathbb{Z}[i]^\times$ and $\gcd(2a,\beta)=1$, then $\left(\frac{a}{\beta}\right)_4^2=\left(\frac{a}{\mathcal{N}(\beta)}\right)$.

The second formula can be proved similarly.   □

Lemma 2. *Let $p \equiv q \equiv 1 \bmod 4$ be two distinct primes and let $p = \pi\bar{\pi}$, $q = \lambda\bar{\lambda}$ for some prime elements $\pi, \lambda \in \mathbb{Z}[i]$. Set $N = pq$ and $\gamma = \pi\lambda$. Then*

$$\sum_{k \in \mathcal{QR}_N} \mathbb{I}_1\left[\left(\frac{k}{\gamma}\right)_4\right] = \sum_{k \in \mathcal{QR}_N} \mathbb{I}_{-1}\left[\left(\frac{k}{\gamma}\right)_4\right] = \frac{(p-1)(q-1)}{8}. \tag{2}$$

Proof. We calculate

$$\sum_{k \in \mathcal{QR}_N} \mathbb{I}_1\left[\left(\frac{k}{\gamma}\right)_4\right] = \sum_{\substack{1 \leq k \leq N \\ \left(\frac{k}{p}\right)=\left(\frac{k}{q}\right)=1}} \mathbb{I}_1\left[\left(\frac{k}{\gamma}\right)_4\right]$$

$$= \sum_{\substack{0 \leq r \leq p-1, 0 \leq s \leq q-1 \\ k \equiv r \bmod p,\, k \equiv s \bmod q \\ \left(\frac{k}{p}\right)=\left(\frac{k}{q}\right)=1}} \mathbb{I}_1\left[\left(\frac{k}{\pi\lambda}\right)_4\right]$$

$$= \sum_{\substack{0 \leq r \leq p-1, 0 \leq s \leq q-1 \\ \left(\frac{r}{p}\right)=\left(\frac{s}{q}\right)=1}} \mathbb{I}_1\left[\left(\frac{r}{\pi}\right)_4 \left(\frac{s}{\lambda}\right)_4\right].$$

Since $\left(\frac{r}{p}\right) = \left(\frac{s}{q}\right) = 1$ if and only if both $\left(\frac{r}{\pi}\right)_4$ and $\left(\frac{s}{\lambda}\right)_4$ are equal to ± 1, it follows by Lemma 1 that

$$\sum_{\substack{0 \leq r \leq p-1, 0 \leq s \leq q-1 \\ \left(\frac{r}{p}\right)=\left(\frac{s}{q}\right)=1}} \mathbb{I}_1\left[\left(\frac{r}{\pi}\right)_4 \left(\frac{s}{\lambda}\right)_4\right] = \sum_{\substack{0 \leq r \leq p-1 \\ \left(\frac{r}{p}\right)=1}} \mathbb{I}_1\left[\left(\frac{r}{\pi}\right)_4\right] \times \sum_{\substack{0 \leq s \leq q-1 \\ \left(\frac{s}{q}\right)=1}} \mathbb{I}_1\left[\left(\frac{s}{\lambda}\right)_4\right]$$

$$+ \sum_{\substack{0 \leq r \leq p-1 \\ \left(\frac{r}{p}\right)=1}} \mathbb{I}_{-1}\left[\left(\frac{r}{\pi}\right)_4\right] \times \sum_{\substack{0 \leq s \leq q-1 \\ \left(\frac{s}{q}\right)=1}} \mathbb{I}_{-1}\left[\left(\frac{s}{\lambda}\right)_4\right]$$

$$= \frac{(p-1)(q-1)}{8}.$$

The second formula can be proved in a similar way. $\qquad\square$

Theorem 5. *Given an instance $\mathcal{I} = \{(N, p_0 := 2, d, g, u), x\}$ of SRSDP, the advantage of the above distinguisher $\mathscr{D}$ for solving the SRSDP satisfies*

$$\mathrm{Adv}_{\mathscr{D},\mathcal{I}}^{\mathsf{SRSDP}} = \frac{1}{2}.$$

Proof. By Definition 4 and the method explained above, we have

$$\mathrm{Adv}_{\mathscr{D},\mathcal{I}}^{\mathsf{SRSDP}} = \Pr[\mathscr{D}(\mathcal{I}) \text{ outputs "yes"} \mid \underset{\text{with } y \in \mathcal{QR}_N}{x \text{ is of the form } y^{p_0^d p_t q_t}}] - \frac{1}{2}$$

$$+ \Pr[\mathscr{D}(\mathcal{I}) \text{ outputs "no"} \mid x \in \mathcal{QR}_N] - \frac{1}{2}$$

$$= \Pr[\mathscr{D}(\mathcal{I}) \text{ outputs "no"} \mid x \in \mathcal{QR}_N].$$

Note that $\rho = \pi\lambda$ can be computed by $\mathscr{D}$ where $N = pq$ and $p = \pi\bar{\pi}$, $q = \lambda\bar{\lambda}$, then Lemma 2 implies that

$$\Pr[\mathscr{D}(\mathcal{I}) \text{ outputs "no"} \mid x \in \mathcal{QR}_N] = \frac{\dfrac{(p-1)(q-1)}{8}}{\dfrac{(p-1)(q-1)}{4}} = \frac{1}{2}. \qquad (3)$$

This concludes the proof of the theorem.   □

3.4   Examples

To better understand how $\mathscr{D}$ shown in Sect. 3.3 works, we give a toy example as follows.

Example 1. Assume that the parameters of the SRSDP are set as in Table 2. Note that here g is of order $p_0^d = 8$ in both $\mathbb{Z}_p^*$ and $\mathbb{Z}_q^*$, and x is a sample from the uniform distributions over $\mathcal{QR}_N$.

Table 2. Parameters of the SRSDP in Example 1

Parameter	Value	Parameter	Value
p_0	2	d	3
p_s	5	p	$3761 = (56 + 25\mathrm{i})(56 - 25\mathrm{i})$
p_t	47	q	$2129 = (40 + 23\mathrm{i})(40 - 23\mathrm{i})$
q_s	7	N	8007169
q_t	19	g	18315
u	3	x	$200003 \equiv 555183^2 \pmod{N}$

$\mathscr{D}$ first calculates

$$g^{p_0^d/4} \equiv 7145296 \pmod{N}$$

and

$$\gcd(N, 7145296 - \mathrm{i}) = 2815 - 288\mathrm{i}.$$

(indeed, $2815 - 288\mathrm{i} = (40 - 23\mathrm{i})(56 + 25\mathrm{i})$). Next, $\mathscr{D}$ calculates $\left(\frac{200003}{2815-288\mathrm{i}}\right)_4$ as in Table 3 and obtains

$$\left(\frac{200003}{2815 - 288\mathrm{i}}\right)_4 = \mathrm{i} \times -\mathrm{i} \times -1 \times 1 = -1.$$

without knowing the factorization of N or $2815 - 288\mathrm{i}$.

Finally, $\mathscr{D}$ correctly outputs "no" because the above quartic Jacobi symbol is not equal to 1, which means that $x = 200003$ is not a quartic residue and x

Table 3. Procedures for calculating $\left(\frac{200003}{2815 - 288i}\right)_4$

Make the modulus of a quartic residue symbol primary	Calculate the remainder of a primary when divided by an element in $\mathbb{Z}[i]$	Remove factors of $1+i$ and apply the general quartic reciprocity law (Theorem 3) and its supplement (Theorem 4)
$\left(\frac{200003}{2815-288i}\right)_4 = \left(\frac{200003}{-2815+288i}\right)_4$	$200003 = (-2815+288i)(-70-7i)$ $+ (937+455i)$	$\left(\frac{200003}{-2815+288i}\right)_4 = \left(\frac{937+455i}{-2815+288i}\right)_4 = \left(\frac{(1+i)(696-241i)}{-2815+288i}\right)_4$ $= 1 \times \left(\frac{696-241i}{-2815+288i}\right)_4$ $= \left(\frac{-i}{-2815+288i}\right)_4 \left(\frac{241+696i}{-2815+288i}\right)_4$ $= 1 \times \left(\frac{241+696i}{-2815+288i}\right)_4 = \left(\frac{-2815+288i}{241+696i}\right)_4$
$\left(\frac{-2815+288i}{241+696i}\right)_4 = \left(\frac{-2815+288i}{241+696i}\right)_4$	$-2815+288i = (241+696i)(-1+4i)$ $+ (210+20i)$	$\left(\frac{-2815+288i}{241+696i}\right)_4 = \left(\frac{210+20i}{241+696i}\right)_4 = \left(\frac{(1+i)(10-105i)}{241+696i}\right)_4$ $= 1 \times \left(\frac{10-105i}{241+696i}\right)_4$ $= \left(\frac{i}{241+696i}\right)_4 \left(\frac{-105-10i}{241+696i}\right)_4$ $= 1 \times \left(\frac{-105-10i}{241+696i}\right)_4 = \left(\frac{241+696i}{-105-10i}\right)_4$
$\left(\frac{241+696i}{-105-10i}\right)_4 = \left(\frac{241+696i}{-105-10i}\right)_4$	$241+696i = (-105-10i)(-3-6i)$ $+ (-14+36i)$	$\left(\frac{241+696i}{-105-10i}\right)_4 = \left(\frac{-14+36i}{-105-10i}\right)_4 = \left(\frac{(1+i)^2(18+7i)}{-105-10i}\right)_4$ $= -1 \times \left(\frac{18+7i}{-105-10i}\right)_4$ $= -1 \times \left(\frac{i}{-105-10i}\right)_4 \left(\frac{7-18i}{-105-10i}\right)_4$ $= -i \times \left(\frac{7-18i}{-105-10i}\right)_4 = i \times \left(\frac{-105-10i}{7-18i}\right)_4$
$\left(\frac{-105-10i}{7-18i}\right)_4 = \left(\frac{-105-10i}{7-18i}\right)_4$	$-105-10i = (7-18i)(-1-5i)$ $+ (-8+7i)$	$\left(\frac{-105-10i}{7-18i}\right)_4 = \left(\frac{-8+7i}{7-18i}\right)_4 = \left(\frac{(1+i)(-8+7i)}{7-18i}\right)_4$ $= 1 \times \left(\frac{-8+7i}{7-18i}\right)_4 = \left(\frac{-i}{7-18i}\right)_4 \left(\frac{-7-8i}{7-18i}\right)_4$ $= -i \times \left(\frac{-7-8i}{7-18i}\right)_4 = -i \times \left(\frac{7-18i}{-7-8i}\right)_4$
$\left(\frac{7-18i}{-7-8i}\right)_4 = \left(\frac{7-18i}{-7-8i}\right)_4$	$7-18i = (-7-8i)(1+2i)$ $+ (-2+4i)$	$\left(\frac{7-18i}{-7-8i}\right)_4 = \left(\frac{-2+4i}{-7-8i}\right)_4 = \left(\frac{(1+i)^2(2+i)}{-7-8i}\right)_4$ $= 1 \times \left(\frac{2+i}{-7-8i}\right)_4 = \left(\frac{-i}{-7-8i}\right)_4 \left(\frac{-1+2i}{-7-8i}\right)_4$ $= 1 \times \left(\frac{-1+2i}{-7-8i}\right)_4 = \left(\frac{-7-8i}{-1+2i}\right)_4$
$\left(\frac{-7-8i}{-1+2i}\right)_4 = \left(\frac{-7-8i}{-1+2i}\right)_4$	$-7-8i = (-1+2i)(-2+4i)$ $+ (-1)$	$\left(\frac{-7-8i}{-1+2i}\right)_4 = \left(\frac{-1}{-1+2i}\right)_4 = \left(\frac{(1+i)^0(-1)}{-1+2i}\right)_4$ $= 1 \times \left(\frac{-1}{-1+2i}\right)_4 = \left(\frac{-1}{-1+2i}\right)_4 \left(\frac{1}{-1+2i}\right)_4$ $= -1 \times \left(\frac{1}{-1+2i}\right)_4 = -1 \times \left(\frac{-1+2i}{1}\right)_4$
$\left(\frac{-1+2i}{1}\right)_4 = \left(\frac{-1+2i}{1}\right)_4$	$-1+2i = (1)(-1+2i) + (0)$	$\left(\frac{-1+2i}{1}\right)_4 = \left(\frac{0}{1}\right)_4 = 1$

cannot therefore be written as $y^{p_0^d p_t q_t}$ for any $y \in \mathcal{QR}_N$. Further, its order in $\mathbb{Z}_N^*$ is

$$50008 = 2^3 \times 7 \times 19 \times 47$$

not equal to $p_s q_s = 5 \times 7$.

The C++ codes for the above attack can be found at https://github.com/tcet030840zxp/Quartic-Residuosity-Attack-on-the-SRSDP.

4   A Higher Residuosity Attack on the **SRSDP**

In this section, we describe a higher residuosity attack on the SRSDP when p_0 is an odd prime. The success probability of this attack is very high, but computing the p_0^{th} power residue symbol for large p_0 turns out to be its efficiency bottleneck in practical implementations.

4.1   The Power Residue Symbol

Let K be a number field. We say a prime ideal $\mathfrak{p}$ in $\mathcal{O}_K$ is prime to an integer $\ell \geq 1$ if $\mathfrak{p} \nmid \ell \mathcal{O}_K$, this is equivalent to the assertion that $\gcd(\mathcal{N}(\mathfrak{p}), \ell) = 1$, where $\mathcal{N}(\mathfrak{p}) = |\mathcal{O}_K/\mathfrak{p}|$. Since the multiplicative group of $\mathcal{O}_K/\mathfrak{p}$ has $\mathcal{N}(\mathfrak{p}) - 1$ elements, we have

$$\alpha^{\mathcal{N}(\mathfrak{p})-1} \equiv 1 \pmod{\mathfrak{p}} \quad \text{for } \alpha \in \mathcal{O}_K, \ \alpha \notin \mathfrak{p}.$$

Furthermore, if we have an additional condition that $\zeta_\ell \in K$, then the order of the group $\langle \zeta_\ell/\mathfrak{p} \rangle$ generated in $(\mathcal{O}_K/\mathfrak{p})^\times$ is ℓ, and hence $\ell \mid \mathcal{N}(\mathfrak{p}) - 1$. Now, we can define the ℓth *power residue symbol* $\left(\frac{\alpha}{\mathfrak{p}}\right)_\ell$ as follows: if $\alpha \in \mathfrak{p}$, then $\left(\frac{\alpha}{\mathfrak{p}}\right)_\ell = 0$; otherwise, $\left(\frac{\alpha}{\mathfrak{p}}\right)_\ell$ is the unique ℓ^{th} root of unity such that

$$\left(\frac{\alpha}{\mathfrak{p}}\right)_\ell \equiv \alpha^{\frac{\mathcal{N}(\mathfrak{p})-1}{\ell}} \pmod{\mathfrak{p}}.$$

This definition can be naturally extended to the case that $\mathfrak{a} = \prod_i \mathfrak{p}_i$ is prime to ℓ, i.e., $\gcd(\mathcal{N}(\mathfrak{p}_i), \ell) = 1$ for each i. For $\alpha \in \mathcal{O}_K$, define the generalized ℓ^{th} power residue symbol as

$$\left(\frac{\alpha}{\mathfrak{a}}\right)_\ell = \prod_i \left(\frac{\alpha}{\mathfrak{p}_i}\right)_\ell.$$

If $\beta \in \mathcal{O}_K$ and β is prime to ℓ define $\left(\frac{\alpha}{\beta}\right)_\ell = \left(\frac{\alpha}{(\beta)}\right)_\ell$. We suggest interested readers to refer to [19, 23, 28] for more details about the power residue symbol. In the rest of this paper, we shall simply consider the case of $K = \mathbb{Q}(\zeta_\ell)$ for $\ell > 2$. In this case, it is well known that $\mathcal{O}_K = \mathbb{Z}[\zeta_\ell]$ and that $\mathcal{O}_K^\times$ is a finitely generated abelian group of rank $r = \varphi(\ell)/2 - 1$; there exists a *fundamental system of units* $\{u_1, \ldots, u_r\}$ of K such that every element $x \in \mathcal{O}_K^\times$ can be written in a unique way as $x = \zeta u_1^{n_1} \cdots u_r^{n_r}$ where $n_i \in \mathbb{Z}$ and $\zeta \in \langle \pm\zeta_\ell \rangle$ (e.g., $\ell = 5$, $r = 1$, and $u_1 = 1 + \zeta_5$).

We now turn to the case ℓ is an odd prime. Let $\omega = 1 - \zeta_\ell$, we have $(\ell) = (\omega)^{\ell-1}$ and (ω) is a prime ideal of degree 1. An element $\alpha \in \mathbb{Z}[\zeta_\ell]$ is called *primary* if $\alpha \not\equiv 0 \bmod \omega$, $\alpha \equiv B \bmod \omega^2$ and $\alpha\bar{\alpha} \equiv B^2 \bmod \ell$ for some $B \in \mathbb{Z}$. If $\mathbb{Q}(\zeta_\ell)$

is *regular*[2], then each $\alpha \in \mathbb{Z}[\zeta_\ell]$ prime to ℓ can be transformed into a primary number on multiplication by a suitable unit [18, Theorem 157]. More properties of primary elements can be found in [7, Lemma 2.6]. *Kummer's reciprocity law* is crucial to the computation of power residue symbols, especially when $\mathbb{Z}[\zeta_\ell]$ is *norm-Euclidean* (e.g., $\ell \leq 13$ [6,22,24]). The complementary laws for ω, ℓ and units can be found in [7].

Theorem 6 (Kummer's Reciprocity Law [18, Theorem 161]). *Let ℓ be a regular prime number and let α and β be two primary elements in $\mathbb{Z}[\zeta_\ell]$. Then*

$$\left(\frac{\alpha}{\beta}\right)_\ell = \left(\frac{\beta}{\alpha}\right)_\ell .$$

Theorem 6 was established in 1850. It is restricted to so-called "regular" primes, which include the odd primes $p \leq 13$. It is crucial for designing algorithms to compute residue symbols, akin to the quadratic reciprocity law used for evaluating the Jacobi symbol in $\mathbb{Z}$). For $\ell \leq 11$, these results can be integrated with Lenstra's norm-Euclidean algorithm [24] (see also [7, Section 7]) to develop an effective algorithm for computing $\left(\frac{\alpha}{\beta}\right)_\ell$ in $\mathbb{Q}(\zeta_\ell)$. We present a list of references for the relevant fast algorithms in Table 4.

Table 4. Algorithms for Computing the ℓth Power Residue Symbol

ℓ	3	5	7	11	13
References	[10,30,32]	Scheidler et al. [30]	Caranay et al. [7]	Joye et al. [21]	Brier et al. [6]

The general case of computing higher power residue symbols was tackled by de Boer [3] and the resulting algorithms are probabilistic. However, it has not yet been proven to be a polynomial-time algorithm. De Boer's computational results [3, Chapter 5] show that for degrees around 100 the computation of one single power residue symbol might last for several weeks.

4.2   Attacking the **SRSDP** via the Power Residue Symbol

With the preparation for the power residue symbol, attacks on the SRSDP are possible when p_0 is a small odd prime number. Given an RSA quintuple (N, p_0, d, g, u) and a sample $x \in \mathcal{QR}_N$, $\mathscr{D}$ first computes $h = g^{p_0^{d-1}} \bmod N$, whose order is p_0 in $\mathbb{Z}_N^*$. Let $K = \mathbb{Q}(\zeta_{p_0})$. Then the prime decomposition of p in $\mathcal{O}_K$ can be obtained immediately from [9, Theorem 4.8.13] as follows:

$$p\mathcal{O}_K = \prod_{i=1}^{p_0-1} \mathfrak{p}_i$$

---

[2] If the class number of $\mathbb{Q}(\zeta_\ell)$ is not divisible by ℓ, then $\mathbb{Q}(\zeta_\ell)$ is called a *regular cyclotomic field* and ℓ is called a *regular prime number*. The first few *irregular prime numbers* are 37, 59, 67, 101, 103, 149 and 157.

where $\mathfrak{p}_i = p\mathcal{O}_K + (h^i - \zeta_{p_0})\mathcal{O}_K$ and $\mathcal{N}(\mathfrak{p}_i) = p$. Similarly,

$$q\mathcal{O}_K = \prod_{i=1}^{p_0-1} \mathfrak{q}_i$$

where $\mathfrak{q}_i = q\mathcal{O}_K + (h^i - \zeta_{p_0})\mathcal{O}_K$ and $\mathcal{N}(\mathfrak{q}_i) = q$. Next, $\mathcal{D}$ sets

$$\mathfrak{a} = \mathfrak{p}_1\mathfrak{q}_1 = N\mathcal{O}_K + (h - \zeta_{p_0})\mathcal{O}_K.$$

Finally, $\mathcal{D}$ computes $c = \left(\frac{x}{\mathfrak{a}}\right)_{p_0}$ using the algorithms introduced earlier, it outputs "yes" if $c = 1$ and "no" otherwise. Note that if x is of the form $y^{p_0^d p_t q_t}$ with $y \in \mathcal{QR}_N$ then we must have $c = 1$. This gives us a distinguisher $\mathcal{D}$:

Distinguisher $\mathcal{D}$: $\mathcal{D}$ is given as input an RSA quintuple $(N, p_0(> 2), d, g, u)$ and a sample $x \in \mathcal{QR}_N$.

1: Compute $h = g^{p_0^{d-1}} \bmod N$.
2: **if** $p_0 \leq 13$ **then**
3:     Compute $\beta = \gcd(N, h - \zeta_{p_0})$ by Lenstra's norm-Euclidean algorithm [24] for $p_0 \leq 11$ and by McKenzie's norm-Euclidean algorithm [26] for $p_0 = 13$.
4:     Compute $c = \left(\frac{x}{\beta}\right)_{p_0}$ by the algorithms in Table 4.
5: **else**
6:     Set $\mathfrak{a} = N\mathcal{O}_K + (h - \zeta_{p_0})\mathcal{O}_K$.
7:     Compute $c = \left(\frac{x}{\mathfrak{a}}\right)_{p_0}$ by de Boer's Algorithm [3].
8: **end if**
9: **if** $c == 1$ **then**
10:    Output "yes".
11: **else**
12:    Output "no".
13: **end if**

Notice that when $p_0 \leq 13$, $\mathcal{D}$ runs in polynomial time and is efficient. To show that $\mathcal{D}$ can solve the SRSDP with non-negligible advantage, we need the following lemma.

Lemma 3. *With notations as above, let*

$$S_\epsilon = \left\{ k \in \mathcal{QR}_N : \left(\frac{k}{\mathfrak{a}}\right)_{p_0} = \epsilon \right\}, \quad \epsilon \in \langle \zeta_{p_0} \rangle.$$

Then $|S_\epsilon| = \frac{(p-1)(q-1)}{4p_0}$ for every $\epsilon \in \langle \zeta_{p_0} \rangle$.

Proof. It is easy to see that $\sum_{\epsilon \in \langle \zeta_{p_0} \rangle} |S_\epsilon| = |\mathcal{QR}_N| = \frac{(p-1)(q-1)}{4}$, so it suffices to prove that all of the S_ϵ's have identical cardinalities. Let a_p (resp. a_q) be a generator of $\mathcal{QR}_p$ (resp. $\mathcal{QR}_q$). Then the order of $a_p^{\frac{p-1}{p_0}}$ (resp. $a_q^{\frac{q-1}{p_0}}$) is p_0, and therefore $\left(\frac{a_p}{\mathfrak{p}_1}\right)_{p_0} = \zeta_{p_0}^i$ for some $0 < i < p_0$ (resp. $\left(\frac{a_q}{\mathfrak{q}_1}\right)_{p_0} = \zeta_{p_0}^j$ for some $0 < j < p_0$). For every $k \in \mathbb{Z}_{p_0}$, we have $\left(\frac{a}{\mathfrak{a}}\right)_{p_0} = \zeta_{p_0}^k$ if a is chosen so that $a \equiv a_p^{k(i^{-1} \bmod p_0)} \pmod{p}$ and $a \equiv a_q^{p_0} \pmod{q}$, so if $|S_\alpha| < |S_\beta|$ for some $\alpha, \beta \in \langle \zeta_{p_0} \rangle$, then there exists $b \in \mathcal{QR}_N$ such that the coset $bS_\beta \subset S_\alpha$, a contradiction. In fact, S_1 is a subgroup of $\mathbb{Z}_N^*$ and all of the remaining sets S_ϵ ($\epsilon \in \langle \zeta_{p_0} \rangle \setminus \{1\}$) are its cosets. $\qquad\square$

Theorem 7. *Given an instance* $\mathcal{I} = \{(N, p_0(>2), d, g, u), x\}$ *of SRSDP, the advantage of the above distinguisher $\mathcal{D}$ for solving the SRSDP satisfies*

$$\mathsf{Adv}_{\mathcal{D},\mathcal{I}}^{SRSDP} = \frac{p_0 - 1}{p_0}.$$

Proof. By Definition 4 and the method explained above, we have

$$\mathsf{Adv}_{\mathcal{D},\mathcal{I}}^{SRSDP} = \Pr[\mathcal{D}(\mathcal{I}) \text{ outputs "yes"} \mid {\scriptstyle x \text{ is of the form } y^{p_0^d p_\ell q_\ell} \atop \scriptstyle \text{with } y \in \mathcal{QR}_N}] - \frac{1}{2}$$
$$+ \Pr[\mathcal{D}(\mathcal{I}) \text{ outputs "no"} \mid x \in \mathcal{QR}_N] - \frac{1}{2}$$
$$= \Pr[\mathcal{D}(\mathcal{I}) \text{ outputs "no"} \mid x \in \mathcal{QR}_N].$$

Note that $\mathfrak{a} = N\mathcal{O}_K + (h - \zeta_{p_0})\mathcal{O}_K$ can be computed by $\mathcal{D}$, then Lemma 3 implies that

$$\Pr[\mathcal{D}(\mathcal{I}) \text{ outputs "no"} \mid x \in \mathcal{QR}_N] = \frac{\dfrac{(p-1)(q-1)(p_0-1)}{4p_0}}{\dfrac{(p-1)(q-1)}{4}}$$
$$= \frac{p_0 - 1}{p_0}. \qquad (4)$$

This concludes the proof of the theorem. $\qquad\square$

5   Higher Residuosity Attacks on the CEK and BST Protocols

In this section, we present practical higher residuosity attacks on the CEK and BST protocols. Throughout this section, we assume that the prime base p_0 is small enough so that the p_0^{th} power residue symbol can be efficiently computed, e.g., $p_0 < 100$ according to de Boer's computational results [3, Chapter 5].

We first show that the encryption scheme $\Pi = (\mathsf{KGen}, \mathsf{Enc}, \mathsf{Dec})$ proposed in [8, Section 4], which is the principal ingredient in both protocols, is not semantically secure. Except for replacing b with p_0, we use the notations as in [8, Section 4]. Consider the following experiment between a challenger $\mathscr{C}$ and an adversary $\mathscr{A}$:

1. $\mathscr{C}$ runs $\mathsf{KGen}(\tau)$ to obtain keys $\mathcal{PK} = (N, p_0, d(\geq 3), g, u, h)$ and $\mathcal{SK}$, where (N, p_0, d, g, u) is an RSA quintuple, h has order p_s in $\mathbb{Z}_p^*$ and q_s in $\mathbb{Z}_q^*$.
2. $\mathscr{A}$ is given $\mathcal{PK}$, and outputs a pair of messages $m_0 = 0$, $m_1 = 1$.
3. $\mathscr{C}$ chooses a uniform bit $b \in \{0, 1\}$, and then a challenge ciphertext $C \leftarrow \mathsf{Enc}(\mathcal{PK}, m_b) := g^{p_0^{m_b}} h^r \bmod N$ is computed and given to $\mathscr{A}$, where r is chosen uniformly from $\{1, \ldots, 2^u - 1\}$.
4. $\mathscr{A}$ computes[3]

$$
c = \begin{cases}
\left(\dfrac{C}{\gcd\left(N, g^{p_0^{d-3}} - \zeta_8 \right)} \right)_8, & \text{if } p_0 = 2 ; \\[3ex]
\left(\dfrac{C}{\left(N, g^{p_0^{d-1}} - \zeta_{p_0} \right)} \right)_{p_0}, & \text{otherwise.}
\end{cases}
$$

It outputs a bit $b' = 1$ if $c = 1$ and $b' = 0$ otherwise. If $b' = b$ we say that $\mathscr{A}$ correctly guesses the encrypted message.

We claim that the advantage of correctly guessing the encrypted message in the above experiment is 1 when $2p_0 \nmid p_s p_t + q_s q_t$. From the proof of Theorem 1, h is a p_0^{th} power, hence $c = 1$ if $m_b = 1$; otherwise we have

$$
c = \begin{cases}
\left(\dfrac{g}{\gcd\left(N, g^{p_0^{d-3}} - \zeta_8 \right)} \right)_8 = \zeta_4^{p_s p_t + q_s q_t}, & \text{if } p_0 = 2 ; \\[3ex]
\left(\dfrac{g}{\left(N, g^{p_0^{d-1}} - \zeta_{p_0} \right)} \right)_{p_0} = \zeta_{p_0}^{2(p_s p_t + q_s q_t)}, & \text{otherwise.}
\end{cases}
$$

If $2p_0 \nmid p_s p_t + q_s q_t$, then we have $c \neq 1$, thus the claim is established.

From the attack above, we can see that the ciphertext may leak information about whether the corresponding plaintext is 0. Since in the first pass of both the CEK and BST protocols the party P_1 (having private input m_1) sends the encryption of integer multiples of m_1 to the party P_2, then P_2 is able to determine whether m_1 is zero, hence neither of the two protocols protects the privacy of P_1.

Finally, to preclude such attacks, we provide the following suggestions for improvement:

1. use larger p_0, so that it is infeasible to compute the p_0^{th} power residue symbol.
2. choose two distinct large primes p_s and q_s such that $p_s \mid p - 1$ and $q_s \mid q - 1$, and then choose g to be of order $p_0^d p_s q_s$, modify the protocols as in [12].
3. force the RSA quintuple to satisfy $2p_0^d \mid p_s p_t + q_s q_t$ and try to prove the semantic security under some number-theoretic hardness assumptions pertaining to higher residuosity, the protocols' performance is not impacted in this way.

---

[3] See [20] for an algorithm to evaluate octic residue symbols. Lenstra's norm-Euclidean algorithm [24] can be used for GCD computation.

6 Conclusion

Quadratic and higher residuosity are powerful tools that find applications in various cryptographic constructions. For instance, they are used in encryption schemes [1,15,30,32], authentication schemes [5,27], and digital signatures [29]. In this paper, we present higher residuosity attacks against two efficient two-party comparison protocols recently proposed by Carlton et al. [8] and Bourse et al. [4]. For a small public prime base p_0, any adversary with access to an element of order p_0 in $\mathbb{Z}_N^*$ in the two protocols would be able to employ such attacks, leading to privacy leakage. All of these attacks are grounded in higher reciprocity laws. Future work will investigate whether a more efficient algorithm exists for computing power residue symbols modulo a two-element representation ideal. The attacks we propose are currently ineffective against other famous power-residuosity-type assumptions, such as the Gap 2^k-residuosity assumption, which underpins the security of the Joye-Libert cryptosystem proposed in [1]. The Gap 2^k-residuosity assumption in $\mathbb{Z}_N^*$ consists in distinguishing a uniform element of $V_0 = \{x \in \mathcal{J}_N \setminus \mathcal{QR}_N\}$ from a uniform element of $V_1 = \{y^{2^k} \bmod N \mid y \in \mathbb{Z}_N^*\}$, given only $N = pq$. This ineffectiveness arises because the attacker cannot effectively find an element of order 2^k ($k \geq 2$) in $\mathbb{Z}_N^*$ in advance. We hope that this paper will serve as a valuable resource for future protocol designers working with RSA-type problems. Additionally, we believe that the higher residuosity attacks discussed herein can be employed to analyze other number-theoretic hardness assumptions.

Acknowledgments. We would like to thank Professor Jun Shao for his constant encouragement and careful reading of the manuscript. We also extend our appreciation to all anonymous reviewers of PKC 2025 for their thorough reading of our manuscript and for their valuable comments. This work was supported by the Shanghai Science and Technology Commission [grant number 23YF1401000], the National Natural Science Foundation of China [grant number 62132005], the Fundamental Research Funds for the Central Universities [grant number 2232022D-25], and the Natural Science Foundation of Zhejiang Province [grant number LQN25F020030].

Disclosure of Interests. All authors disclosed no relevant relationships.

References

1. Benhamouda, F., Herranz, J., Joye, M., Libert, B.: Efficient cryptosystems from 2^k-th power residue symbols. J. Cryptol. **30**(2), 519–549 (2017). https://doi.org/10.1007/S00145-016-9229-5
2. Blake, I.F., Kolesnikov, V.: Conditional encrypted mapping and comparing encrypted numbers. In: Di Crescenzo, G., Rubin, A. (eds.) FC 2006. LNCS, vol. 4107, pp. 206–220. Springer, Heidelberg (2006). https://doi.org/10.1007/11889663_18
3. de Boer, K.: Computing the power residue symbol. Master's thesis. Nijmegen, Radboud University (2016). www.koendeboer.com

4. Bourse, F., Sanders, O., Traoré, J.: Improved secure integer comparison via homomorphic encryption. In: Jarecki, S. (ed.) CT-RSA 2020. LNCS, vol. 12006, pp. 391–416. Springer, Cham (2020). https://doi.org/10.1007/978-3-030-40186-3_17

5. Brier, É., Ferradi, H., Joye, M., Naccache, D.: New number-theoretic cryptographic primitives. J. Math. Cryptol. **14**(1), 224–235 (2020)

6. Brier, E., Naccache, D.: The thirteenth power residue symbol. IACR Cryptol. ePrint Arch. **2019**, 1176 (2019). https://eprint.iacr.org/2019/1176

7. Caranay, P.C., Scheidler, R.: An efficient seventh power residue symbol algorithm. Int. J. Number Theory **6**(08), 1831–1853 (2010)

8. Carlton, R., Essex, A., Kapulkin, K.: Threshold properties of prime power subgroups with application to secure integer comparisons. In: Topics in Cryptology - CT-RSA 2018 - The Cryptographers' Track at the RSA Conference. LNCS, vol. 10808, pp. 137–156. Springer, Cham (2018). https://doi.org/10.1007/978-3-319-76953-0_8

9. Cohen, H.: A Course in Computational Algebraic Number Theory, vol. 138. Springer Science & Business Media, Heidelberg (2013). https://doi.org/10.1007/978-3-662-02945-9

10. Damgård, I., Frandsen, G.S.: Efficient algorithms for the GCD and cubic residuosity in the ring of eisenstein integers. J. Symb. Comput. **39**(6), 643–652 (2005). https://doi.org/10.1016/j.jsc.2004.02.006

11. Damgård, I., Geisler, M., Krøigaard, M.: Efficient and secure comparison for online auctions. In: Pieprzyk, J., Ghodosi, H., Dawson, E. (eds.) ACISP 2007. LNCS, vol. 4586, pp. 416–430. Springer, Heidelberg (2007). https://doi.org/10.1007/978-3-540-73458-1_30

12. Damgård, I., Geisler, M., Krøigaard, M.: A correction to efficient and secure comparison for on-line auctions. Int. J. Appl. Cryptogr. **1**(4), 323–324 (2009). https://doi.org/10.1504/IJACT.2009.028031

13. Fischlin, M.: A cost-effective pay-per-multiplication comparison method for millionaires. In: Naccache, D. (ed.) CT-RSA 2001. LNCS, vol. 2020, pp. 457–471. Springer, Heidelberg (2001). https://doi.org/10.1007/3-540-45353-9_33

14. Garay, J.A., Schoenmakers, B., Villegas, J.: Practical and secure solutions for integer comparison. In: Okamoto, T., Wang, X. (eds) Proceedings of 10th International Conference on Practice and Theory in Public-Key Cryptography - PKC 2007. LNCS, vol. 4450, pp. 330–342. Springer, Heidelberg (2007). https://doi.org/10.1007/978-3-540-71677-8_22

15. Goldwasser, S., Micali, S.: Probabilistic encryption and how to play mental poker keeping secret all partial information. In: Proceedings of 14th Annual ACM Symposium on Theory of Computing, pp. 365–377. ACM Press (1982). https://doi.org/10.1145/800070.802212

16. Groth, J.: Cryptography in subgroups of $\mathbb{Z}_n^*$. In: Kilian, J. (ed.) TCC 2005. LNCS, vol. 3378, pp. 50–65. Springer, Heidelberg (2005). https://doi.org/10.1007/978-3-540-30576-7_4

17. Halter-Koch, F.: Quadratic Irrationals: An Introduction to Classical Number Theory. CRC Press, New York (2013)

18. Hilbert, D.: The theory of algebraic number fields. Springer Science & Business Media, Heidelberg (1998). https://doi.org/10.1007/978-3-662-03545-0

19. Ireland, K., Rosen, M.: A Classical Introduction to Modern Number Theory. GTM, vol. 84, p. A Classical Introduction to Modern Number Theory. Springer, New York (1990). https://doi.org/10.1007/978-1-4757-2103-4

20. Joye, M.: Evaluating octic residue symbols. IACR Cryptol. ePrint Arch., 1196 (2019). https://eprint.iacr.org/2019/1196

21. Joye, M., Lapiha, O., Nguyen, K., Naccache, D.: The eleventh power residue symbol. J. Math. Cryptol. **15**(1), 111–122 (2021). https://doi.org/10.1515/jmc-2020-0077
22. Lemmermeyer, F.: The Euclidean algorithm in algebraic number fields. Expo. Math. **13**, 385–416 (1995)
23. Lemmermeyer, F.: Reciprocity laws: from Euler to Eisenstein. In: Sasaki, C., Sugiura, M., Dauben, J.W. (eds) The Intersection of History and Mathematics. Science Networks Historical Studies, vol 15. Springer Science & Business Media, Heidelberg (2013). https://doi.org/10.1007/978-3-0348-7521-9_6
24. Lenstra, H.W.: Euclid's algorithm in cyclotomic fields. J. London Math. Soc. **10**, 457–465 (1975)
25. Lin, H., Tzeng, W.: An efficient solution to the millionaires' problem based on homomorphic encryption. In: Ioannidis, J., Keromytis, A., Yung, M. (eds) Proceedings of 3rd International Conference on Applied Cryptography and Network Security - ACNS 2005. LNCS, vol. 3531, pp. 456–466. Springer, Heidelberg (2005). https://doi.org/10.1007/11496137_31
26. McKenzie, R.G.: The ring of cyclotomic integers of modulus thirteen is norm-Euclidean. Ph.D. thesis, Michigan State University (1988)
27. Monnerat, J., Vaudenay, S.: Short undeniable signatures based on group homomorphisms. J. Cryptol. **24**, 545–587 (2011)
28. Neukirch, J.: Algebraic Number Theory, vol. 322. Springer Science & Business Media, Heidelberg (2013). https://doi.org/10.1007/978-3-662-03983-0
29. Rabin, M.O.: Digitalized signatures and public-key functions as intractable as factorization. Technical Report (1979)
30. Scheidler, R., Williams, H.C.: A public-key cryptosystem utilizing cyclotomic fields. Des. Codes Cryptogr. **6**(2), 117–131 (1995). https://doi.org/10.1007/BF01398010
31. Weilert, A.: Fast computation of the biquadratic residue symbol. J. Number Theory **96**(1), 133–151 (2002)
32. Williams, H.C.: An M^3 public-key encryption scheme. In: Williams, H.C. (ed.) CRYPTO 1985. LNCS, vol. 218, pp. 358–368. Springer, Heidelberg (1986). https://doi.org/10.1007/3-540-39799-X_26
33. Yao, A.C.: How to generate and exchange secrets (extended abstract). In: Proceedings of 27th Annual Symposium on Foundations of Computer Science, pp. 162–167 (1986). https://doi.org/10.1109/SFCS.1986.25

Advanced PKE I

Adaptively Secure IBE from Lattices with Asymptotically Better Efficiency

Weidan Ji[1], Zhedong Wang[1(✉)], Lin Lyu[2], and Dawu Gu[1(✉)]

[1] Shanghai Jiao Tong University, Shanghai, China
{jiweidan,wzdstill,dwgu}@sjtu.edu.cn
[2] University of Wuppertal, Wuppertal, Germany
lin.lyu@uni-wuppertal.de

Abstract. Current adaptively secure identity-based encryption (IBE) constructions from lattices are unable to achieve a good balance among the master public key size, secret key size, modulus and reduction loss. All existing lattice-based IBE schemes share a common restriction: the modulus is quadratic in the trapdoor norm.

In this work, we remove this restriction and present a new adaptively secure IBE scheme from lattices in the standard model, which improves the state-of-the-art construction proposed by Abla et al. (TCC 2021) and achieves asymptotically better efficiency. More precisely, we achieve the asymptotically minimal number of public vectors among all the existing schemes, along with a significantly smaller modulus compared to the scheme by Abla et al. (TCC 2021). Furthermore, our scheme enjoys the smallest Gaussian width of the secret key among all existing schemes and has the same tightness as Abla et al.'s scheme.

We propose a novel cross-multiplication design for our IBE scheme, along with several novel tools and techniques, including: (a) a homomorphic computation algorithm that outputs BGG+-style encoding with two distinct-norm trapdoors; (b) a sampling algorithm with hybrid Gaussian outputs; and (c) a partial rerandomization algorithm. These new tools and techniques are general and could find rich applications in lattice-based cryptography.

Keywords: Lattice-based cryptography · Identity-based encryption · GSW-style encryption · BGG+-style encoding · Sampling algorithm

1 Introduction

Identity-based encryption (IBE), proposed by Shamir [33] as a way to simplify public key and certificate management, is a generalization of public key encryption, where the public key can be an arbitrary string, such as a name, a telephone number, or an email address. Since its first realization proposed by Boneh and Franklin [7], various IBEs based on bilinear maps [5,6,18,34,35], quadratic residues modulo composite [9,14], and lattices [1,2,13,16,19,21,24,36,37] have been proposed.

© International Association for Cryptologic Research 2025
T. Jager and J. Pan (Eds.): PKC 2025, LNCS 15674, pp. 91–124, 2025.
https://doi.org/10.1007/978-3-031-91820-9_4

Two major security notions, selective security and adaptive security, have been studied in the literature. The former requires the adversary to choose the challenge identity before seeing the master public key (mpk), while the latter does not have this restriction. Adaptive security offers stronger protection and is more desirable in practical settings. However, realizing this notion is quite challenging, especially when aiming for efficiency comparable to that of selectively secure designs in the plain model.

Prior constructions from bilinear groups have achieved this goal using the powerful dual-system framework [35]. However, it remains uncertain whether the dual-system framework can be instantiated from other assumptions, particularly from post-quantum candidates such as lattices. In the post-quantum context, although there are adaptively secure lattice-based IBEs, the current instantiations are unable to achieve a good balance between mpk size, secret key size, modulus, and reduction loss, i.e., either with large mpk and reduction loss, small modulus and secret key, or with small mpk and (almost) tight reduction, yet large modulus and secret key. (See Table 1 for details.) Achieving a good balance among these aspects is a crucial step toward realizing a practical post-quantum IBE. In this work, we focus on constructing adaptively secure lattice-based IBE with compact mpk, small modulus, small secret key size, and tight reduction simultaneously in the standard model. Below we discuss the challenges faced by current approaches and introduce our new ideas.

Challenges in Current Techniques. In Eurocrypt 2010, Agrawal et al. [2] constructed an efficient adaptively secure IBE in the standard model. However, this construction is not compact in the sense that the public parameter contains $O(\lambda)$ number of basic matrices, where λ is the security parameter. To deal with this issue, Yamada [36] constructed IBE schemes from lattices based on the partitioning technique and reduced the number of the public matrices to $O(\lambda^{1/\tau})$, where $\tau \in \mathbb{N}$ is an arbitrary constant. However, these schemes require a super-polynomial LWE modulus. Subsequently, Katsumata and Yamada [24] proposed a more efficient IBE scheme from the ring LWE (RLWE) assumption with asymptotically the same number of public matrices, but only with polynomial modulus. Later, Yamada [37] proposed two new constructions and reduced the number of the public parameters to $\omega(\log \lambda)$ in his second construction. However, his second construction relies on the Barrington's Theorem [3] to compute an NC1 boolean circuit, which can be done in polynomial time in theory yet would not be expected to be efficient in practice.

Besides, there exists a bootstrapping technique by [12,15] which can transform any selectively secure IBE into an adaptively secure one without blowing up the mpk at all. However, the resulting scheme is not considered (even close to) practical as each ciphertext consists of ℓ garbled circuits (ℓ is the bit length of ID). In a separate line of work, Boyen and Li [11], along with the subsequent work by Lai et al. [26], presented adaptively secure IBE schemes with (almost) tight security from lattices. Their constructions follow the Katz-Wang framework [25] but fail to achieve a compact mpk. Specifically, their constructions require homomorphic computation of a PRF, which leads to the need for encoding the PRF's seed into the mpk. Both constructions use a bit-by-bit encoding that requires $O(\lambda)$ additional random public matrices in the mpk.

Recently, Abla et al. [1] proposed a more compact IBE scheme (ALWW-IBE) with only $\omega(1)$ ring vectors in the public parameters. Moreover, they further improved previous works in two aspects: (1) every component in their construction is explicit, i.e., without relying on Barrington's Theorem [3] and (2) they achieved a tighter security reduction. Despite these theoretical advancements, the construction in [1] still has a distance to practicality. The main drawback of their construction is that it requires a large modulus (about at least $O(n^{13.5})$, where n is the dimension of the underlying ring). This drawback also affects the total size of the mpk[1], the total size of the ciphertext, the running time of the scheme, and the concrete hardness of the underlying RLWE problem. Specifically, their construction is based on the partitioning technique with a subtle design of partition function and homomorphic computation in cyclotomic rings. However, this paradigm involves heavy homomorphic evaluation of the partition function. What's worse, the modulus is at least the quadratic of the norm of the trapdoor after homomorphic evaluation due to the noise re-randomization as described in [24]. It seems that the existing approach, particularly the noise re-randomization, inherently induces the modulus to be quadratic of the trapdoor norm, and thus harshly increases the modulus. This raises a natural question:

Can we remove the quadratic restriction of modulus on the trapdoor norm, and thus design an adaptively secure lattice-based IBE that inherits the compactness and tightness of ALWW-IBE, but with small modulus?

1.1 Our Contributions

In this work, we provide an affirmative answer to this question. Particularly, we remove the quadratic restriction of modulus, and thus obtain an adaptively secure IBE from lattices in the standard model, with the same compactness and tightness of ALWW-IBE, but with significantly smaller modulus. The key innovation lies in a novel cross-multiplication design, supported by several novel tools and techniques. We believe that these tools can find broad applications in other lattice-based primitives and thus are of general interests. Below we summarize our two major contributions, and present our new techniques in Sect. 1.2.

- Our IBE scheme, like [1], achieves the asymptotically minimal number of basic vectors in mpk among all the existing schemes, and as tight as the ALWW-IBE, but with significantly smaller modulus compared to [1]. Furthermore, our scheme enjoys the smallest Gaussian width of the secret key among all existing schemes (including [1]). For a detailed overview and comparison, please refer to Table 1.

---

[1] The number of matrices in mpk is unchanged. But due to a large modulus, the size of each matrix is large and leads to a large mpk.

Table 1. Comparison with previous lattice-based IBE constructions with adaptive security in the standard model.

Scheme	$\|\mathsf{mpk}\|$ # of $\mathcal{R}_q^k$ vec.♯	RLWE param $\frac{1}{\alpha} = \frac{q}{\sigma_{\mathsf{RLWE}}}$	Gaussian width of the $\mathsf{sk_{id}}$	$\|\mathsf{sk_{id}}\|, \|\mathsf{ct}\|$ # of $\mathcal{R}^k, \mathcal{R}_q^k$ vec.	Reduction cost
[2]+[10]	$O(\lambda)$	$\tilde{O}(n^{5.5})$	$\tilde{O}(n^2)$	$O(1)$	$O(\varepsilon^2/qQ)$
[11]	$O(\lambda)$	superpoly(n)	$\tilde{O}(n^3)$	$O(1)$	$O(\epsilon/\lambda)$
[26]	$O(\lambda)$	$O(n^8)$	$O(n^{3.5})$	$O(1)$	$O(\epsilon/\lambda)$
[36]	$O(\lambda^{1/\tau})^\star$	superpoly(n)	superpoly(n)	$O(1)$	$O(\epsilon^{\tau+1}/\ell Q^\tau)$
[24]	$O(\lambda^{1/\tau})$	$O(n^{2.5+2\tau})$	$O(n^\tau)$	$O(1)$	$O(\lambda^{\tau-1}\epsilon^\tau/Q^\tau)^{\tau+1})$
[37] I+[23]	$\omega(\log^2(\lambda))$	$\tilde{O}(n^{5.5})$	$\tilde{O}(n^{2.5})$	$O(1)$	$O(\varepsilon^{v+1}/Q^v)^\Xi$
[37] II	$\omega(\log(\lambda))$	poly(n)†	poly(n)	$O(1)$	$O(\varepsilon^2/\ell^2 Q)$
[1]	$\omega(1)$	$O(n^{11+\frac{4}{\kappa}})$‡,♮	$O(n^{4.5+\frac{2}{\kappa}})$	$O(1)$	$O(\varepsilon^2/Q)^\ast$
Ours	$\omega(1)$	$O(n^{6.5+\frac{2}{\kappa}})^♮$	$O(n^{1.5})$	$O(1)$	$O(\epsilon^2/Q)^\ast$

Notations: $\|\mathsf{mpk}\|$, $\|\mathsf{ct}\|$, and $\|\mathsf{sk_{id}}\|$ denote the size of the master public key, ciphertext, and secret key of the IBE. λ, n, q, σ_{RLWE} denote the security parameter, ring dimension, modulus, and Gaussian parameter of RLWE. Q and ε denote the number of key extraction queries and the advantage in attacking the IBE scheme. All the schemes set the ring dimension $n = \Theta(\lambda)$. To measure the reduction cost, we show the advantage of the RLWE algorithm constructed from the adversary against the corresponding IBE scheme, just like [37]. To be fair, we calculate the reduction cost by employing the technique of Bellare and Ristenpart [4] for all schemes.

♯ $\mathcal{R}_q = \mathbb{Z}_q[x]/(x^n + 1)$ is a polynomial ring, and $k = \lceil \log_b q \rceil$ where b is a small constant (e.g., $b = 2$) or a polynomial in n (e.g., n^v for any real v).

$\star$ $\tau \in \mathbb{N}$ is a constant that can be chosen arbitrarily. Since the reduction cost is exponential in τ, this value is typically set very small (e.g., $\tau = 2$ or 3).

Ξ $v > 1$ is a constant that can be set small, depending on the underlying error correcting code.

† poly(n) denotes some fixed but large polynomial. It is hard to determine an explicit bound for comparison due to the implicit construction of the work.

‡ $\kappa \geq 1$ can be any constant that satisfies $n^{\frac{1}{\kappa}} > 3 + \kappa$, e.g., 2 or 4, depending on the parameters of the underlying error correcting code.

♮ Note that [1, Section 3] does their analysis in both the plain model and the CRS model. A smaller RLWE parameter $(\tilde{O}(n^{7.5+\frac{\kappa}{4}}))$ can be achieved in the CRS model. Here, we only compare the parameters (in [1] and ours) in the plain model. Our analysis in the plain model can be easily adapted to the CRS model, which results in a smaller RLWE parameter. We refer to the full version [22, Appendix E] for the detailed parameter analysis in both models.

$\ast$ In the ALWW-IBE paper [1], the authors obtain $T' = T + \min\{\tilde{O}(\lambda^{1/\kappa}Q/\epsilon), O(\lambda^{1+3/\kappa})Q^{\kappa+3}\}$ and $\epsilon' = O(\epsilon/\lambda^{1/\kappa}Q)$ using the bit-security framework [30]. Here we analyse their reduction cost with the most common technique [4] without relying on the bit-security framework. We note that our IBE could have the same reduction cost as the ALWW-IBE in the bit-security model, as it contains the same partition function as in the ALWW-IBE. The analysis in the bit-security model of our IBE is similar to [1, Lemma 5.4] and we omit it in our paper.

  – Technically, we propose three novel tools and techniques to obtain our IBE scheme. They are (a) homomorphic computation outputting BGG+-style encoding with two distinct-norm trapdoors; (b) sampling algorithm with hybrid Gaussian outputs; and (c) partial re-randomization. These tools and techniques are general, not only restricted to ring settings, but also can be applied to LWE-based IBE as shown in the full version [22, Appendix F]. We believe it could find rich application scenarios in lattice-based cryptography.

1.2 Techniques Overview

Our IBE follows the framework of the ALWW-IBE and we remove the quadratic restriction of modulus by using a novel cross-multiplication design with the help of several novel tools/techniques including a) homomorphic computation outputting BGG+-style encoding with two distinct-norm trapdoors; b) sampling algorithm with (D_r, D_σ)-hybrid outputs; c) partial re-randomization. In this subsection, we recap the ALWW-IBE framework and provide a high level overview of the ideas of our construction.

Recap of ALWW-IBE [1]. For a polynomial ring $\mathcal{R} = \mathbb{Z}[x]/(x^n + 1)$, the ALWW-IBE construction follows the general framework [2] of constructing lattice-based IBE which associates each identity id a vector

$$\mathsf{pk}_{\mathsf{id}}^\top = [\mathbf{b}^\top | F(\mathsf{id})^\top] \in \mathcal{R}_q^{2k}, \tag{1}$$

where $\mathbf{b} \in \mathcal{R}_q^k$ is a vector chosen uniformly at random. One of the main technical contributions of [1] is that they propose a succinct hash function and reduce the size of the public vectors to $\omega(1)$. More concretely, they use the equality test function $\mathsf{Equal}_\beta(x^\alpha)$ that outputs 1 if $\alpha = \beta$ and 0 otherwise, and compute the function $F(\mathsf{id})$ as

$$F(\mathsf{id}) = -\mathbf{c}_\gamma + \sum\nolimits_{i \in [t]} \sum\nolimits_{j \in [L+1]} H\text{-}\mathsf{Equal}_j(\mathbf{c}_i) \cdot x^{f(i,j)}, \tag{2}$$

where $\mathbf{c}_\gamma, \{\mathbf{c}_i\}_{i \in [t]} \in \mathcal{R}_q^k$ are public vectors, $f : [t] \times [L+1] \to [n]$ is a function related to an error correcting code with position index L, and $H\text{-}\mathsf{Equal}_j(\mathbf{c}_i)$ is a homomorphic computation of $\mathsf{Equal}_j(\cdot)$ from the public vectors $\{\mathbf{c}_i\}_{i \in [t]}$. The number of the public vectors is $\omega(1)$, i.e., $t = \omega(1)$. During the security proof, the reduction algorithm first prepares some random monomials $x^\gamma, \{x^i\}_{i \in [t]} \in \mathcal{R}$ and random matrices $\mathbf{R}_\gamma, \{\mathbf{R}_i\}_{i \in [t]} \in \mathcal{R}^{k \times k}$ with a small spectral norm, and sets the public vectors by "BGG+-style encoding" form [8] as

$$\mathbf{c}_\gamma^\top = \mathbf{b}^\top \mathbf{R}_\gamma + x^\gamma \mathbf{g}^\top \in \mathcal{R}_q^k, \quad \mathbf{c}_i^\top = \mathbf{b}^\top \mathbf{R}_i + x^i \mathbf{g}^\top \in \mathcal{R}_q^k, \tag{3}$$

where $\mathbf{g} = [1|b|b^2|\cdots|b^{k-1}] \in \mathcal{R}_q^k$ is the gadget vector with well-known trapdoor $\mathbf{T_g}$ [28]. Then, the equality test function can be homomorphically computed as

$$H\text{-}\mathsf{Equal}_j(\mathbf{c}_i) = \mathbf{b}^\top \mathbf{R}_{i,j} + \mathsf{Equal}_j(x^i) \mathbf{g}^\top.$$

Further, the function $F(\mathsf{id})$ in Eq. (2) can be homomorphically computed as

$$
\begin{aligned}
F(\mathsf{id})^\top &= -\left(\mathbf{b}^\top \mathbf{R}_\gamma + x^\gamma \mathbf{g}^\top\right) + \sum_{i \in [t]} \sum_{j \in [L+1]} \left(\mathbf{b}^\top \mathbf{R}_{i,j} + \mathsf{Equal}_j(x^i)\mathbf{g}^\top\right) \cdot x^{f(i,j)} \\
&= \mathbf{b}^\top \underbrace{\left(\sum_{i,j} \mathbf{R}_{i,j} \cdot x^{f(i,j)} - \mathbf{R}_\gamma\right)}_{:= \mathbf{R}_{\mathsf{id}}} + \underbrace{\left(\sum_{i,j} \mathsf{Equal}_j(x^i) \cdot x^{f(i,j)} - x^\gamma\right)}_{:= H(\mathsf{id}), \text{ invertible}} \mathbf{g}^\top \\
&= \mathbf{b}^\top \mathbf{R}_{\mathsf{id}} + H(\mathsf{id})\mathbf{g}^\top.
\end{aligned}
$$

$$(4)$$

The sampling vector for identity id in Eq. (1) is now converted into

$$
\mathsf{pk}_{\mathsf{id}}^\top = [\mathbf{b}^\top | \mathbf{b}^\top \mathbf{R}_{\mathsf{id}} + H(\mathsf{id})\mathbf{g}^\top] \in \mathcal{R}_q^{2k}. \tag{5}
$$

For any uniformly random $u \in \mathcal{R}_q$, the reduction algorithm can sample a short vector $\mathbf{x}$ satisfying $\mathsf{pk}_{\mathsf{id}}^\top \cdot \mathbf{x} = u$, using the public trapdoor $\mathbf{T_g}$ if and only if $H(\mathsf{id}) \neq 0$. In more detail, we first sample a perturbation[2] $\mathbf{p} \in \mathcal{R}^{2k}$ following the idea of Gaussian convolution by Peikert [31]. Then, by the Gaussian sampling algorithm [28] and public trapdoor $\mathbf{T_g}$, we can obtain a short vector $\tilde{\mathbf{x}}$ such that $\mathbf{g}^\top \cdot \tilde{\mathbf{x}} = H(\mathsf{id})^{-1} \cdot (u - \mathsf{pk}_{\mathsf{id}}^\top \cdot \mathbf{p})$ under the condition that $H(\mathsf{id}) \neq 0$ and $H(\mathsf{id})$ is invertible. Finally, the secret key for identity id is a short vector $\mathbf{x}$ defined as

$$
\underbrace{[\mathbf{b}^\top | \mathbf{b}^\top \mathbf{R}_{\mathsf{id}} + H(\mathsf{id})\mathbf{g}^\top]}_{\mathsf{pk}_{\mathsf{id}}^\top} \cdot \underbrace{\left(\mathbf{p} + \begin{bmatrix} -\mathbf{R}_{\mathsf{id}} \\ \mathbf{I} \end{bmatrix} \cdot \tilde{\mathbf{x}}\right)}_{\mathsf{sk}_{\mathsf{id}}(:=\mathbf{x})} = u.
$$

By the definition of $\mathbf{x}$, the size of $\mathbf{x}$ is *linear* in the norm of the matrix $\mathbf{R}_{\mathsf{id}}$[3]. We also note that $\mathbf{x}$ is close to a spherical Gaussian distribution.

The IBE ciphertext of a message m is akin to a dual Regev ciphertext [19,32] which consists of two parts:

$$
c_0 = u \cdot v + e_0 + \left\lceil \frac{q}{2} \right\rceil \cdot m \in \mathcal{R}_q, \quad \mathbf{c}_1 = \mathsf{pk}_{\mathsf{id}} \cdot v + \mathbf{e}_1 \in \mathcal{R}_q^{2k},
$$

where $v \in \mathcal{R}_q$ is a secret and $e_0 \leftarrow D_{\mathcal{R},\sigma_0}, \mathbf{e}_1 \leftarrow D_{\mathcal{R}^{2k},\sigma_1}$ are some errors. Note that in the security reduction, the challenge ciphertext can be seen as $(\mathbf{c}_1^*)^\top = [\mathbf{b}^\top | \mathbf{b}^\top \mathbf{R}_{\mathsf{id}^*}] \cdot v + \mathbf{e}_1$ because $H(\mathsf{id}^*) = 0$, then the challenge ciphertext

---

[2] We need to take a perturbation, since the output secret key $\mathbf{x}$ should follow a spherical Gaussian distribution to ensure that no information about the trapdoor matrix $\mathbf{R}_{\mathsf{id}}$ is revealed.

[3] The size of the short vector $\tilde{\mathbf{x}}$ depends on the public trapdoor $\mathbf{T_g}$ and has a small norm. The perturbation $\mathbf{p}$ acts as a mask for $\mathbf{R}_{\mathsf{id}}$ and does not have a noticeable impact on the overall size of $\mathbf{x}$. So we don't need to pay attention to them here.

$\mathbf{c}_1^*$ can be simulated by a re-randomization[4] algorithm as follows:

$$(\mathbf{c}_1^*)^\top = \mathsf{ReRand}\left([\mathbf{I}_k|\mathbf{R}_{\mathsf{id}^*}], \mathbf{b}\cdot v + \mathbf{e}_0', \sigma_0, \frac{\sigma_1}{2\sigma_0}\right) = \mathbf{b}^\top[\mathbf{I}_k|\mathbf{R}_{\mathsf{id}^*}]\cdot v + (\mathbf{e}_1')^\top,$$

where $\mathbf{e}_0' \leftarrow D_{\mathcal{R}^k,\sigma_0}$ and the distribution of $\mathbf{e}_1'$ is statistically close to the discrete Gaussian distribution $D_{\mathcal{R}^{2k},\sigma_1}$. For the re-randomization algorithm, it requires $\frac{\sigma_1}{2\sigma_0} \geq \|[\mathbf{I}_k|\mathbf{R}_{\mathsf{id}^*}]\|$, thus the size of the error $\mathbf{e}_1 \leftarrow D_{\mathcal{R}^{2k},\sigma_1}$ is *linear* in the norm of the matrix $\mathbf{R}_{\mathsf{id}^*}$[5]. During the decryption step, the user (who owns the secret key $\mathsf{sk}_{\mathsf{id}} := \mathbf{x}$) can compute

$$c_0 - \mathbf{c}_1^\top \cdot \mathbf{x} = \left\lceil\frac{q}{2}\right\rceil \cdot m + \underbrace{e_0 - \mathbf{e}_1^\top \cdot \mathbf{x}}_{\text{error term}}. \tag{6}$$

To ensure decryption correctness, the modulus q should be larger than the error term.

As mentioned above, the sizes of the error $\mathbf{e}_1$ and the secret key $\mathbf{x}$ are both *linear* in the norm of the matrix $\mathbf{R}_{\mathsf{id}}$, so the size of error term would be at least *quadratic* of the norm of the matrix $\mathbf{R}_{\mathsf{id}}$. Recall that the matrix $\mathbf{R}_{\mathsf{id}}$ is generated by homomorphic computation of the partition function[6] $H(\cdot)$ as in Eq. (4), which itself has a relatively large norm due to the complex circuit of the partition function. Therefore, the restriction, i.e., the modulus q should be at least the *quadratic* of the trapdoor matrix $\mathbf{R}_{\mathsf{id}}$'s norm, leads to large modulus.

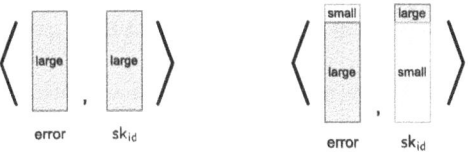

Fig. 1. The error term of ALWW-IBE (left) and ours (right), where $\langle\cdot,\cdot\rangle$ represents vector inner product.

Remove the Quadratic Restriction of Modulus. Our goal is to remove the quadratic restriction of the modulus q on the trapdoor matrix $\mathbf{R}_{\mathsf{id}}$'s norm. At a high level, our idea can be represented by Fig. 1. Specifically, the error term[7]

---

[4] On input a vector $\mathbf{b}+\mathbf{x} \in \mathcal{R}^k$, a matrix $\mathbf{V} \in \mathcal{R}^{k\times l}$, two reals σ_0 and σ_1 such that $\sigma_1 \geq 2\sigma_0 \cdot \|\mathbf{V}\|$ and $\mathbf{x} \leftarrow D_{\mathcal{R},\sigma_0}$, the re-randomization algorithm $\mathsf{ReRand}(\mathbf{V}, \mathbf{b}+\mathbf{x}, \sigma_0, \frac{\sigma_1}{2\sigma_0})$ outputs $\mathbf{b}^\top\mathbf{V} + (\mathbf{x}')^\top$, where the distribution of $\mathbf{x}' \in \mathcal{R}^l$ is statistically close to the discrete Gaussian with width σ_1.

[5] The Gaussian parameter σ_0 is only related to the hardness of the RLWE assumption, not related to $\mathbf{R}_{\mathsf{id}^*}$, so we don't consider it here.

[6] We call $H(\cdot)$ as "partition function" since $H(\mathsf{id}) = 0$ if and only if $\mathsf{id} = \mathsf{id}^*$.

[7] We ignore the term e_0 because it only depends on the hardness of the RLWE problem and it has a small norm.

in ALWW-IBE (Eq. (6)) is the inner product of a large error $\mathbf{e}_1$ (i.e., *linear* in $\mathbf{R}_{\mathsf{id}}$'s norm) and a large secret key $\mathbf{x}$ (i.e., *linear* in $\mathbf{R}_{\mathsf{id}}$'s norm). Our idea is to design the error term to be the inner product of a $(D_{\sigma_0}, D_{\sigma_1})$-hybrid error with $\sigma_1 \gg \sigma_0$ and a (D_r, D_σ)-hybrid secret key with $r \gg \sigma$[8], where D_θ represents a Gaussian distribution with width θ and $(D_{\theta_0}, D_{\theta_1})$-hybrid represents that the first part is sampled according to D_{θ_0} and the second part is sampled according to D_{θ_1}. In our design, the error term is a cross-multiplication, i.e., "small $\times$ large + large $\times$ small", thus removing the quadratic restriction.

We approach our idea in two parts: (1) obtaining a (D_r, D_σ)-hybrid secret key; (2) obtaining a $(D_{\sigma_0}, D_{\sigma_1})$-hybrid error. Below, we provide some details of our techniques.

(1) Obtaining a (D_r, D_σ)-hybrid secret key. To achieve this, we first design a series of homomorphic computation algorithms to output a BGG+-style encoding that encodes the partition function $H(\mathsf{id})$ and has two trapdoors with distinct norms. Using such a BGG+-style encoding as our new sampling vector, we design a new sampling algorithm with (D_r, D_σ)-hybrid outputs.

(1.1) Homomorphic computation outputting BGG+-style encoding with two distinct-norm trapdoors.

Homomorphic Computation of Partition Function in GSW-Style Encryption Form. First, instead of setting the public parameters as in Eq. (3), we use the "GSW-style encryption" form [20] to construct as follows

$$\mathbf{C}_\gamma = \mathbf{AR}_\gamma + x^\gamma \mathbf{G} \in \mathcal{R}_q^{2 \times 2k}, \quad \mathbf{C}_i^\top = \mathbf{AR}_i + x^i \mathbf{G} \in \mathcal{R}_q^{2 \times 2k}, \tag{7}$$

where $\mathbf{R}_\gamma, \mathbf{R}_i \in \mathcal{R}^{2k \times 2k}$ is some random matrices with small spectral norm, $\mathbf{G} = \begin{bmatrix} \mathbf{g}^\top & \mathbf{0}^\top \\ \mathbf{0}^\top & \mathbf{g}^\top \end{bmatrix} \in \mathcal{R}_q^{2 \times 2k}$ is the public gadget matrix, and $\mathbf{A} = \begin{bmatrix} \mathbf{a}^\top \\ \mathbf{a}^\top s + \mathbf{e}^\top \end{bmatrix} \in \mathcal{R}_q^{2 \times 2k}$
is the public key of the GSW-style encryption scheme, consisting of RLWE samples: a uniformly random vector $\mathbf{a} \in \mathcal{R}_q^{2k}$, a secret $s \in \mathcal{R}_q$ and an error vector $\mathbf{e} \in \mathcal{R}^{2k}$. Similar to Eq. (4), the function $F(\mathsf{id})$ can be homomorphically computed by the public parameters in Eq. (7) as

$$F(\mathsf{id}) = \mathbf{AR}_{\mathsf{id}} + H(\mathsf{id})\mathbf{G} \in \mathcal{R}_q^{2 \times 2k}. \tag{8}$$

Note that the function $F(\mathsf{id})$ in Eq. (4) is a BGG+-style *encoding* of the partition function $H(\mathsf{id})$ and cannot be decrypted. In contrast, the function $F(\mathsf{id})$ in Eq. (8) is a GSW-style *encryption* of the partition function $H(\mathsf{id})$ and is decryptable.

Homomorphic Transformation from GSW-Style Encryption to BGG+-Style Encoding. To generate the sampling vector similar to Eq. (5), we first sample a uniform vector $\mathbf{b} \in \mathcal{R}_q^k$, and prepare an additional public vector in the

---

[8] To further shrink the size of the secret key, we only take the D_σ part (small) as the user's secret key in our IBE construction. It does not affect the decryption, since anyone can compute the D_r part (large) after it gets the D_σ part.

"BGG+-style encoding" form [8] (similar to Eq. (3)) as

$$\mathbf{c}_s^\top = \mathbf{b}^\top \mathbf{R}_s + s \cdot \mathbf{g}^\top,$$

where $\mathbf{R}_s \in \mathcal{R}^{k \times k}$ is a random matrix with small spectral norm and $s \in \mathcal{R}_q$ is the secret key of the GSW-style homomorphic encryption scheme. Then, we use the decryptable property of the GSW-style ciphertext and do a homomorphic "incomplete decryption" of the GSW-style ciphertext $F(\text{id})$ in Eq. (8) in two steps: (1) write the last k columns of the matrix $\mathbf{R}_{\text{id}}$ as $\hat{\mathbf{R}}_{\text{id}} \in \mathcal{R}^{2k \times k}$, and take the last k columns of the ciphertext $F(\text{id})$ as $\begin{bmatrix} \hat{\mathbf{c}}_0^\top \\ \hat{\mathbf{c}}_1^\top \end{bmatrix} = \begin{bmatrix} \mathbf{a}^\top \hat{\mathbf{R}}_{\text{id}} \\ (\mathbf{a}^\top s + \mathbf{e}^\top)\hat{\mathbf{R}}_{\text{id}} + H(\text{id})\mathbf{g}^\top \end{bmatrix}$; (2) compute the following equation

$$
\begin{aligned}
\widehat{F(\text{id})}^\top &= \hat{\mathbf{c}}_1^\top - \mathbf{c}_s^\top \cdot \mathbf{g}^{-1}(\hat{\mathbf{c}}_0^\top) = \hat{\mathbf{c}}_1^\top - (\mathbf{b}^\top \mathbf{R}_s + s \cdot \mathbf{g}^\top) \cdot \mathbf{g}^{-1}(\hat{\mathbf{c}}_0^\top) \\
&= \mathbf{b}^\top \cdot -\mathbf{R}_s \cdot \mathbf{g}^{-1}(\hat{\mathbf{c}}_0^\top) + (\hat{\mathbf{c}}_1^\top - s \cdot \hat{\mathbf{c}}_0^\top) \\
&= \mathbf{b}^\top \cdot \underbrace{-\mathbf{R}_s \cdot \mathbf{g}^{-1}(\hat{\mathbf{c}}_0^\top)}_{\mathbf{R}} + H(\text{id})\mathbf{g}^\top + \underbrace{\mathbf{e}^\top \hat{\mathbf{R}}_{\text{id}}}_{\mathbf{e}_{\text{id}}^\top} \quad (9) \\
&= \mathbf{b}^\top \mathbf{R} + H(\text{id})\mathbf{g}^\top + \mathbf{e}_{\text{id}}^\top.
\end{aligned}
$$

Note that the real GSW-style decryption first computes $\hat{\mathbf{c}}_1 - s \cdot \hat{\mathbf{c}}_0$ and then do a rounding for the final element to recover the message. Equation (9) actually does a homomorphic computation of the first step (This is where our "incomplete decryption" comes from). It homomorphically transforms a GSW-style ciphertext (Eq. (8)) into a BGG+-style encoding (Eq. (9)) of the same message $H(\text{id})$.

Now we get the sampling vector $[\mathbf{b}^\top | \widehat{F(\text{id})}^\top]$ for the identity id as follows

$$\text{pk}_{\text{id}}^\top = [\mathbf{b}^\top | \mathbf{b}^\top \mathbf{R} + H(\text{id})\mathbf{g}^\top + \mathbf{e}_{\text{id}}^\top] \in \mathcal{R}_q^{2k}. \qquad (10)$$

Note that $\mathbf{e}_{\text{id}}$ has a large norm (i.e., *linear* in $\mathbf{R}_{\text{id}}$'s norm), while $\mathbf{R}$ is a fresh matrix and thus has a small norm. Compared to Eq. (5), our new sampling vector in Eq. (10) has two trapdoors with distinct norms (i.e., small $\mathbf{R}$ and large $\mathbf{e}_{\text{id}}$), which allows us to sample a (D_r, D_σ)-hybrid secret key in the next step.

(1.2) Sampling algorithm with (D_r, D_σ)-hybrid outputs. Now we can use our new vector pk_{id} in Eq. (10) to sample the secret key. Generally speaking, for a given uniform $u \in \mathcal{R}_q$, we design a new sampling algorithm, to sample a small-norm (i.e., D_σ) vector $\mathbf{x} \in \mathcal{R}^{2k}$ and a large-norm (i.e., D_r, where $r \gg \sigma$) error $w \in \mathcal{R}$ such that $\text{pk}_{\text{id}}^\top \cdot \mathbf{x} = u + w$.

In more detail, we first sample a perturbation $\mathbf{p} \in \mathcal{R}^{2k}$ that masks the trapdoor matrix $\mathbf{R}$ by Gaussian convolution. Using the trapdoor $\mathbf{T_g}$, we obtain a short vector $\widetilde{\mathbf{x}}$ such that $\mathbf{g}^\top \cdot \widetilde{\mathbf{x}} = H(\text{id})^{-1} \cdot (u - \text{pk}_{\text{id}}^\top \cdot \mathbf{p})$ under the condition that $H(\text{id}) \neq 0$ and $H(\text{id})$ is invertible. Then, we get a short vector $\mathbf{x}$ satisfying

$$\underbrace{[\mathbf{b}^\top | \mathbf{b}^\top \mathbf{R} + H(\text{id})\mathbf{g}^\top + \mathbf{e}_{\text{id}}^\top]}_{\text{pk}_{\text{id}}^\top} \cdot \underbrace{\left(\mathbf{p} + \begin{bmatrix} -\mathbf{R} \\ \mathbf{I} \end{bmatrix} \cdot \widetilde{\mathbf{x}} \right)}_{:= \mathbf{x}} = u + \underbrace{\mathbf{e}_{\text{id}}^\top \cdot \widetilde{\mathbf{x}}}_{\text{error}}.$$

Obviously, the error would leak some information about the trapdoor $\mathbf{e}_{\mathsf{id}}$. To solve this problem, a trivial idea is to add a perturbation that masks the trapdoor $\mathbf{e}_{\mathsf{id}}$, just like the perturbation $\mathbf{p}$ masking the trapdoor $\mathbf{R}$. Concretely, we first sample a perturbation $h \in \mathcal{R}$ and compute $u' = u + h$, then follow the same steps as above except for replacing u with u', we get

$$\underbrace{[\mathbf{b}^{\top}|\mathbf{b}^{\top}\mathbf{R} + H(\mathsf{id})\mathbf{g}^{\top} + \mathbf{e}_{\mathsf{id}}^{\top}]}_{\mathsf{pk}_{\mathsf{id}}^{\top}} \cdot \underbrace{\left(\mathbf{p} + \begin{bmatrix} -\mathbf{R} \\ \mathbf{I} \end{bmatrix} \cdot \widetilde{\mathbf{x}}\right)}_{\mathbf{x}} = u + \underbrace{(h + \mathbf{e}_{\mathsf{id}}^{\top} \cdot \widetilde{\mathbf{x}})}_{\text{error}}.$$

It is true that the error would not leak any information about $\mathbf{e}_{\mathsf{id}}$, just as $\mathbf{x}$ does not reveal $\mathbf{R}$. However, both $\mathbf{x}$ and the error use the same source of randomness, i.e., $\widetilde{\mathbf{x}}$, which results in that $\mathbf{x}$ and the error both have the same Gaussian width. This violates our design goal that $\mathbf{x}$ and the error have different widths. Therefore, we introduce a new source of randomness to deal with this issue. Specifically, we additionally sample a perturbation $\bar{\mathbf{p}} \in \mathcal{R}^k$ and compute $u^* = u' + \mathbf{e}_{\mathsf{id}}^{\top} \cdot \bar{\mathbf{p}}$, then follow the previous steps except for replacing u' with u^*, we get

$$\underbrace{[\mathbf{b}^{\top}|\mathbf{b}^{\top}\mathbf{R} + H(\mathsf{id})\mathbf{g}^{\top} + \mathbf{e}_{\mathsf{id}}^{\top}]}_{\mathsf{pk}_{\mathsf{id}}^{\top}} \cdot \underbrace{\left(\mathbf{p} + \begin{bmatrix} -\mathbf{R} \\ \mathbf{I} \end{bmatrix} \cdot \widetilde{\mathbf{x}}\right)}_{\mathbf{x},\ \text{small}} = u + \underbrace{(h + \mathbf{e}_{\mathsf{id}}^{\top} \cdot (\underbrace{\bar{\mathbf{p}} + \widetilde{\mathbf{x}}}_{:=\bar{\mathbf{x}}}))}_{:=w,\ \text{large error}}.$$

Then $\begin{bmatrix} \bar{\mathbf{x}} \\ \mathbf{x} \end{bmatrix} = \begin{bmatrix} \bar{\mathbf{p}} \\ \mathbf{p} \end{bmatrix} + \begin{bmatrix} \mathbf{I} \\ \mathbf{T} \end{bmatrix}\widetilde{\mathbf{x}}$ where $\mathbf{T} = \begin{bmatrix} -\mathbf{R} \\ \mathbf{I} \end{bmatrix}$. Now both $\mathbf{x}$ and $\bar{\mathbf{x}}$ use the same source of randomness $\widetilde{\mathbf{x}}$, allowing us to simultaneously guarantee they have the same width and are independent. Consequently, the source of randomness $\bar{\mathbf{x}}$ in the error w is unrelated to $\mathbf{x}$, and we conclude that the two outputs ($w \in \mathcal{R}, \mathbf{x} \in \mathcal{R}^{2k}$) are independent and have different Gaussian widths.

We combine the large w and the small $\mathbf{x}$ into a (D_r, D_σ)-hybrid secret key.

(2) Obtaining a $(D_{\sigma_0}, D_{\sigma_1})$-hybrid error. To achieve this, we pick an IBE ciphertext with $(D_{\sigma_0}, D_{\sigma_1})$-hybrid errors. To simulate such a ciphertext in the security reduction, we run the re-randomization algorithm to generate partial ciphertext (i.e., the D_{σ_1} part) and incorporate some tricks.

(2.1) IBE ciphertext with $(D_{\sigma_0}, D_{\sigma_1})$-hybrid errors. Our IBE scheme outputs ciphertext $(c_0, \mathbf{c}_1)$ where $\mathbf{c}_1$ has $(D_{\sigma_0}, D_{\sigma_1})$-hybrid errors. We have that $\sigma_1 \gg \sigma_0$ which corresponds to the (D_r, D_σ)-hybrid secret key and follows our idea of "cross-multiplication".

$$c_0 = u \cdot v + e_0 + \left\lceil \frac{q}{2} \right\rceil \cdot m \in \mathcal{R}_q, \quad \mathbf{c}_1 = d \cdot \begin{bmatrix} 1 \\ \mathsf{pk}_{\mathsf{id}} \end{bmatrix} \cdot v + \begin{bmatrix} e_1 \\ \mathbf{e}_2 \end{bmatrix} \in \mathcal{R}_q^{2k+1},$$

where $e_1 \leftarrow D_{\mathcal{R},\sigma_0}$ is a small error and $\mathbf{e}_2 \leftarrow D_{\mathcal{R}^{2k},\sigma_1}$ is a large error. Note that we add an invertible element $d \in \mathcal{R}_q$ to align with the corresponding term in the security reduction in the next step. Similarly, we modify the input of the secret key sampling algorithm (in (1.2)) from u to $d^{-1}u$, thus we have $\mathsf{pk}_{\mathsf{id}}^{\top} \cdot \mathbf{x} = d^{-1}u + w$.

(2.2) Partial re-randomization. In the security reduction, we use the fact that $H(\mathsf{id}^*) = 0$ and $\mathsf{pk}_{\mathsf{id}^*}^\top = [\mathbf{b}^\top | \mathbf{b}^\top \mathbf{R}^* + \mathbf{e}_{\mathsf{id}^*}^\top]$ (defined in Eq. (10)). To simulate the challenge ciphertext $(\mathbf{c}_1^*)^\top = d \cdot [1 | \mathbf{b}^\top | \mathbf{b}^\top \mathbf{R}^* + \mathbf{e}_{\mathsf{id}^*}^\top] \cdot v + [e_1 | \mathbf{e}_2^\top]$, a direct approach is to run the re-randomization algorithm as follows:

$$(\mathbf{c}_1^*) = \mathsf{ReRand}\left(\left[\mathbf{I}_{k+1} \begin{bmatrix} \mathbf{R}^* \\ \mathbf{e}_{\mathsf{id}^*}^\top \end{bmatrix} \right], d \cdot \begin{bmatrix} 1 \\ \mathbf{b} \end{bmatrix} \cdot v + \mathbf{e}_0', \sigma_0, \frac{\sigma_1}{2\sigma_0} \right)$$

$$= d \cdot [1 | \mathbf{b}^\top] \cdot \left[\mathbf{I}_{k+1} \begin{bmatrix} \mathbf{e}_{\mathsf{id}^*}^\top \\ \mathbf{R}^* \end{bmatrix} \right] \cdot v + \mathbf{e}'$$

$$= d \cdot [1 | \mathbf{b}^\top | \mathbf{b}^\top \mathbf{R}^* + \mathbf{e}_{\mathsf{id}^*}^\top] \cdot v + \mathbf{e}'$$

where the distribution $\mathbf{e}'$ is statistically close to the discrete Gaussian $D_{\mathcal{R}^{2k+1}, \sigma_1}$. However, this does not match our desired ciphertext distribution since each component of the $2k + 1$ vector $\mathbf{e}'$ follows the same Gaussian distribution.

To solve this problem, we first use the re-randomization algorithm to generate a partial ciphertext:

$$(\tilde{\mathbf{c}}_1^*)^\top = \mathsf{ReRand}\left(\begin{bmatrix} \mathbf{I}_k & \mathbf{R}^* \\ \mathbf{0}^\top & \mathbf{e}_{\mathsf{id}^*}^\top \end{bmatrix}, d \cdot \begin{bmatrix} \mathbf{b} \\ 1 \end{bmatrix} \cdot v + \mathbf{e}_0', \sigma_0, \frac{\sigma_1}{2\sigma_0} \right)$$

$$= d \cdot [\mathbf{b}^\top | 1] \cdot \begin{bmatrix} \mathbf{I}_k & \mathbf{R}^* \\ \mathbf{0}^\top & \mathbf{e}_{\mathsf{id}^*}^\top \end{bmatrix} \cdot v + (\mathbf{e}_2')^\top$$

$$= d \cdot [\mathbf{b}^\top | \mathbf{b}^\top \mathbf{R}^* + \mathbf{e}_{\mathsf{id}^*}^\top] \cdot v + (\mathbf{e}_2')^\top.$$

Then, we concatenate the last element of $d \cdot \begin{bmatrix} \mathbf{b} \\ 1 \end{bmatrix} \cdot v + \mathbf{e}_0'$ [9] and the partial ciphertext $\tilde{\mathbf{c}}_1^*$, to generate the ciphertext $\mathbf{c}_1^*$ as follows:

$$(\mathbf{c}_1^*)^\top = d \cdot [1 | \mathbf{b}^\top | \mathbf{b}^\top \mathbf{R}^* + \mathbf{e}_{\mathsf{id}^*}^\top] \cdot v + [e_1' | \mathbf{e}_2'],$$

where $e_1' \leftarrow D_{\mathcal{R}, \sigma_0}$ is the last element of the small error $\mathbf{e}_0'$ and the distribution of $\mathbf{e}_2'$ is statistically close to the discrete Gaussian distribution $D_{\mathcal{R}^{2k}, \sigma_1}$. For the re-randomization algorithm, it requires $\frac{\sigma_1}{2\sigma_0} \geq \left\| \begin{bmatrix} \mathbf{I}_k & \mathbf{R}^* \\ \mathbf{0}^\top & \mathbf{e}_{\mathsf{id}^*}^\top \end{bmatrix} \right\|$, thus the error $\mathbf{e}_2 \sim D_{\mathcal{R}^{2k}, \sigma_1}$ is related to the vector $\mathbf{e}_{\mathsf{id}^*}$ and has a large norm.

We obtain a $(D_{\sigma_0}, D_{\sigma_1})$-hybrid error, consisting of small e_1 and large $\mathbf{e}_2$.

Realizing Our Idea. During the decryption step, the user can compute

$$c_0 - \mathbf{c}_1^\top \cdot \begin{bmatrix} -w \\ \mathbf{x} \end{bmatrix} = \begin{bmatrix} q \\ 2 \end{bmatrix} \cdot m + (e_0 + \underbrace{e_1 \cdot w}_{\text{small} \times \text{large}} - \underbrace{\mathbf{e}_2^\top \cdot \mathbf{x}}_{\text{large} \times \text{small}}). \qquad (11)$$

Compared to the error term in Eq. (6), our error term in Eq. (11) has a cross-multiplication characteristic, i.e., "small × large + large × small", thus removing the quadratic restriction of the modulus q on the trapdoor norm.

---

[9] Consider $d \cdot \begin{bmatrix} \mathbf{b} \\ 1 \end{bmatrix} \cdot v + \mathbf{e}_0'$ as RLWE samples. We add $d \in \mathcal{R}_q$ to mask the secret v in the extra "1" term. Thus, we can view the last element as $d \cdot v + e_1'$, which constitutes a single RLWE sample.

2   Preliminaries

Notations. We denote $\mathbb{Z}, \mathbb{N}$ and $\mathbb{R}$ as the set of integers, the set of natural numbers and the set of real numbers, respectively. We use bold uppercase letters (e.g., $\mathbf{A}$) to denote matrices, and bold lowercase letters (e.g., $\mathbf{a}$) for column vectors. We use $\|\mathbf{a}\|$ to denote the Euclidean norm of vector $\mathbf{a}$ and define $\|\mathbf{A}\| := \sup_{\|\mathbf{x}\|=1} \|\mathbf{A}\mathbf{x}\|$. We denote the horizontal concatenation of two vectors $\mathbf{a}, \mathbf{b}$ by $[\mathbf{a}^\top | \mathbf{b}^\top]$. We use $\widetilde{\mathbf{A}}$ to denote the Gram-Schmidt orthogonalization of $\mathbf{A}$. For a (quotient) polynomial ring $\mathcal{R}$ over $\mathbb{Z}$ and a set $S \subset \mathbb{Z}$, we denote $S_\mathcal{R} \subseteq \mathcal{R}$ as the set of elements in $\mathcal{R}$ with all coefficients in S. For a positive integer k, let $[k]$ be the set of integers $\{0, 1, \cdots, k-1\}$ and $[-k, k] := \{-k, \cdots, -1, 0, 1, \cdots, k\}$. We say a function $f : \mathbb{N} \to \mathbb{R}$ is negligible if $\forall c > 0, \exists \lambda_0 \in \mathbb{N}, \forall \lambda > \lambda_0, f(\lambda) < 1/\lambda^c$ and we use $\mathsf{negl}(\lambda)$ to denote any negligible function. We use "PPT" to denote probabilistic polynomial time. For a distribution D, we use $d \leftarrow D$ to denote sampling d according to D and use $d \sim D$ to denote that d follows the distribution D. For a set S, we use $U(S)$ to denote the uniform distribution over S and use $s \xleftarrow{\$} S$ to denote $s \leftarrow U(S)$. For any probabilistic algorithm $\mathcal{A}$, we use $y \xleftarrow{\$} \mathcal{A}(x)$ as running $\mathcal{A}$ with fresh randomness on input x and assigning the output to y. For any two random variables X and Y with support Ω, denote their statistical distance as $\triangle(X, Y) = \frac{1}{2} \sum_{s \in \Omega} |\Pr[X = s] - \Pr[Y = s]|$.

2.1   Identity-Based Encryption (IBE)

Syntax. We recall the standard syntax of IBE [7,33] in the following. An identity-based encryption scheme Π with identity space $\mathcal{ID}$ consists of four PPT algorithms (Setup, KeyGen, Enc, Dec) as follows.

- Setup(1^λ): Given the security parameter λ, it outputs the master public key mpk and the master secret key msk.
- KeyGen(mpk, msk, id): Given (mpk, msk) and an identity id $\in \mathcal{ID}$, it outputs the secret key $\mathsf{sk_{id}}$.
- Enc(mpk, id, m): Given the master public key mpk, an identity id $\in \mathcal{ID}$, and a message m, it outputs a ciphertext ct.
- Dec(mpk, $\mathsf{sk_{id}}$, ct): Given the master public key mpk, the secret key $\mathsf{sk_{id}}$, and a ciphertext ct, it outputs a message m' or $\perp$.

Correctness. We say an IBE scheme Π is correct, if for all id $\in \mathcal{ID}$ and all m in the specified message space, it holds that $\Pr[\mathsf{Dec}(\mathsf{mpk}, \mathsf{sk_{id}}, \mathsf{ct}) \neq m] = \mathsf{negl}(\lambda)$, where the probability is taken over the randomness used in (mpk, msk) $\xleftarrow{\$}$ Setup(1^λ), $\mathsf{sk_{id}} \xleftarrow{\$}$ KeyGen(mpk, msk, id) and ct $\xleftarrow{\$}$ Enc(mpk, id, m).

Adaptive Anonymous Security. We consider the adaptive anonymous security notion for IBE as in [37], which implies the adaptive (non-anonymous) security considered in [1]. This security is defined by the following game between a challenger and an adversary $\mathcal{A}$.

Setup: At the beginning of the game, the challenger runs $\mathsf{Setup}(1^\lambda)$ to get $(\mathsf{mpk}, \mathsf{msk})$ and sends mpk to $\mathcal{A}$.

Phase 1: $\mathcal{A}$ may adaptively make key extraction queries. When $\mathcal{A}$ submits id, the challenger returns $\mathsf{sk_{id}} \xleftarrow{\$} \mathsf{KeyGen}(\mathsf{mpk}, \mathsf{msk}, \mathsf{id})$.

Challenge: At some point, $\mathcal{A}$ outputs a message μ and an identity id^*, on which it wishes to be challenged. Then, the challenger picks a random bit $\mathsf{coin} \xleftarrow{\$} \{0, 1\}$ and a random ciphertext $\mathsf{ct}_1^* \leftarrow \mathcal{C}$ from the ciphertext space. If $\mathsf{coin} = 0$, it runs $\mathsf{ct}_0^* \xleftarrow{\$} \mathsf{Enc}(\mathsf{mpk}, \mathsf{id}^*, \mu)$ and gives the challenge ciphertext ct_0^* to $\mathcal{A}$. If $\mathsf{coin} = 1$, it gives ct_1^* to $\mathcal{A}$.

Phase 2: $\mathcal{A}$ continues to make key queries with a restriction that $\mathsf{id} \neq \mathsf{id}^*$.

Guess: Finally, $\mathcal{A}$ outputs a bit $\widehat{\mathsf{coin}}$ for coin.

The advantage of $\mathcal{A}$ is defined as $|\Pr[\widehat{\mathsf{coin}} = \mathsf{coin}] - \frac{1}{2}|$. We say that the scheme satisfies adaptively-anonymous security if the advantage of any PPT $\mathcal{A}$ is negligible.

2.2   Lattices and Gaussians

Lattices. An n-dimensional (full rank) lattice $\Lambda \subseteq \mathbb{R}^n$ is the set of all integer linear combinations of some set of n linearly independent basis vectors $\mathbf{B} = \{\mathbf{b}_1, \cdots, \mathbf{b}_n\} \subseteq \mathbb{R}^n$, $\Lambda = \{\mathbf{Bx} \mid \mathbf{x} \in \mathbb{Z}^n\}$. We denote the dual lattice of Λ by $\Lambda^* := \{\mathbf{y} \in \mathrm{span}(\Lambda) \mid \langle \mathbf{y}, \mathbf{x} \rangle \in \mathbb{Z}, \forall \mathbf{x} \in \Lambda\}$. For a matrix $\mathbf{A} \in \mathbb{Z}_q^{n \times m}$, define $\Lambda_q^\perp(\mathbf{A}) := \{\mathbf{e} \in \mathbb{Z}^m : \mathbf{Ae} = \mathbf{0} \bmod q\}$, which is a full-rank m-dimensional integer lattice. We omit q when it is clear from the context.

Gaussian Distributions. The Gaussian function $\rho : \mathbb{R}^m \to (0, 1]$ is defined as $\rho(\mathbf{x}) = \exp(-\pi \cdot \langle \mathbf{x}, \mathbf{x} \rangle)$. Applying a linear transformation given by an invertible matrix $\mathbf{B}$ yields $\rho_{\mathbf{B}}(\mathbf{x}) = \rho(\mathbf{B}^{-1}\mathbf{x}) = \exp(-\pi \cdot \mathbf{x}^\top \Sigma^{-1} \mathbf{x})$, where $\Sigma = \mathbf{BB}^\top$. Since $\rho_{\mathbf{B}}$ is exactly determined by Σ, we also write it as $\rho_{\sqrt{\Sigma}}$. For a lattice Λ and $\mathbf{c} \in \mathrm{span}(\Lambda)$, the discrete Gaussian distribution $D_{\Lambda+\mathbf{c}, \sqrt{\Sigma}}$ is defined as: for any $\mathbf{x} \in \Lambda + \mathbf{c}$,

$$D_{\Lambda+\mathbf{c}, \sqrt{\Sigma}}(\mathbf{x}) = \frac{\rho_{\sqrt{\Sigma}}(\mathbf{x})}{\rho_{\sqrt{\Sigma}}(\Lambda + \mathbf{c})}.$$

When $\Sigma = \sigma^2 \mathbf{I}$ for some real $\sigma > 0$, we write $\rho_{\sqrt{\Sigma}}, D_{\Lambda+\mathbf{c}, \sqrt{\Sigma}}$ as $\rho_\sigma, D_{\Lambda+\mathbf{c}, \sigma}$.

We recall the definition of smoothing parameter of lattices as follows.

Definition 1 ([29], smoothing parameter). *For any $\epsilon > 0$, any n-dimensional lattice Λ, the smoothing parameter $\eta_\epsilon(\Lambda)$ is the smallest real $s > 0$ such that $\rho_{1/s}(\Lambda^* \backslash \{\mathbf{0}\}) \leq \epsilon$.*

For the discrete Gaussian over lattices, we have the following tail bounds.

Lemma 1 ([24]). *For $\sigma > \eta_\epsilon(\mathbb{Z}^n)$, $t \geq 0$, $\mathbf{x} \in \mathbb{Z}^n$, $\Pr_{\mathbf{e} \leftarrow D_{\mathbb{Z}^n, \sigma}}[|\mathbf{e}^\top \mathbf{x}| \geq t] \leq 2e^{-\pi \cdot \frac{t^2}{\|\mathbf{x}\|^2 \sigma^2}}$.*

Lemma 2 ([29]). *For n-dimensional lattice Λ, $\epsilon \in (0, \frac{1}{2})$, $s \geq \eta_\epsilon(\Lambda)$, we have* $\mathsf{Pr}_{\mathbf{x} \leftarrow D_{\Lambda,s}} [\|\mathbf{x}\| > s\sqrt{n}] \leq 2^{-n}$.

The following lemma can be used to re-establish the discrete Gaussian distribution after multiplying with a matrix.

Lemma 3 ([24], noise re-randomization). *Let q, l, m be positive integers and σ_1 be a positive real satisfying $\sigma_1 > \max\{\eta_\epsilon(\mathbb{Z}^m), \eta_\epsilon(\mathbb{Z}^l)\}$. Let $\mathbf{b} \in \mathbb{Z}_q^m$ be arbitrary and $\mathbf{x}$ chosen from $D_{\mathbb{Z}^m, \sigma_1}$. Then for any $\mathbf{V} \in \mathbb{Z}^{m \times l}$ and positive real $\sigma_2 > \|\mathbf{V}\|$, there exists a PPT algorithm $\mathsf{ReRand}(\mathbf{V}, \mathbf{b} + \mathbf{x}, \sigma_1, \sigma_2)$ that outputs $\mathbf{b'}^\top = \mathbf{b}^\top \mathbf{V} + \mathbf{x'}^\top \in \mathbb{Z}_q^l$ where the statistical distance of the discrete Gaussian $D_{\mathbb{Z}^l, 2\sigma_1\sigma_2}$ and the distribution of $\mathbf{x'}$ is within 8ϵ.*

2.3 Rings and Ideal Lattices

Rings. In this paper, we consider the polynomial ring $\mathcal{R} := \mathbb{Z}[x]/(x^n + 1)$ where n (the degree of $\mathcal{R}$) is a power of 2. Any element $a \in \mathcal{R}$ can be denoted as $a = \sum_{i=0}^{n-1} a_i x^i$, where $a_i \in \mathbb{Z}$. For any prime integer q, we denote $\mathcal{R}_q$ as $\mathcal{R}/q\mathcal{R} = \mathbb{Z}_q[x]/(x^n + 1)$ and $\mathcal{R}_q^\times$ as the set of invertible elements of $\mathcal{R}_q$.

Coefficient Embedding. We define a coefficient map $\phi : \mathcal{R} \to \mathbb{Z}^n$ that sends a ring element $a = \sum_{i=0}^{n-1} a_i x^i \in \mathcal{R}$ to its coefficient vector $\mathbf{a} = [a_0 | \cdots | a_{n-1}]^\top \in \mathbb{Z}^n$. Furthermore, we can define another map $\mathsf{Rot} : \mathcal{R} \to \mathbb{Z}^{n \times n}$ that sends $a \in \mathcal{R}$ to a matrix in $\mathbb{Z}^{n \times n}$ such that the i-th row is $\phi(a \cdot x^{i-1} \bmod (x^n + 1))^\top \in \mathbb{Z}^n$. We can extend the maps ϕ and Rot to ring vectors and matrices. The norms of ring matrices (or vectors) are defined by their corresponding coefficient embedding matrices (or vectors), i.e., for any $\mathbf{A} \in \mathcal{R}^{s \times t}, \|\mathbf{A}\| := \|\mathsf{Rot}(\mathbf{A})\|$. The Gram-Schmidt orthogonalization of ring matrices is defined analogously, i.e., for any $\mathbf{A} \in \mathcal{R}^{s \times t}, \widetilde{\mathbf{A}} := \widetilde{\mathsf{Rot}(\mathbf{A})}$.

Discrete Gaussian Over Rings. For $\Sigma = \mathbf{B}\mathbf{B}^\top$ where $\mathbf{B}$ is an invertible matrix over $\mathbb{R}$, we denote $D_{\mathcal{R}^k, \sqrt{\Sigma}}$ as the distribution of sampling $\mathbf{x} \leftarrow D_{\mathbb{Z}^{nk}, \sqrt{\Sigma}}$ and output $\phi^{-1}(\mathbf{x}) \in \mathcal{R}^k$. When Σ is a matrix over $\mathbb{R}[x]/(x^n + 1)$, we use the notation $D_{\mathcal{R}^k, \sqrt{\Sigma}}$ to denote $D_{\mathcal{R}^k, \mathsf{Rot}(\sqrt{\Sigma})}$, where Rot can be naturally extended to $\mathbb{R}[x]/(x^n + 1)$.

We extend Lemma 1 to the ring setting via the following lemma.

Corollary 1 (Corollary of Lemma 1). *For positive interger k, $\sigma > \eta_\epsilon(\mathbb{Z}^{nk})$, real number $t \geq 0$, $\mathbf{x} \in \mathcal{R}^k$, we have* $\mathsf{Pr}_{\mathbf{e} \leftarrow D_{\mathcal{R}^k, \sigma}} [|\phi(\mathbf{e}^\top \mathbf{x})_j| \geq t] \leq 2e^{-\pi \cdot \frac{t^2}{\|\mathbf{x}\|^2 \sigma^2}}$.

The proof of Corollary 1 is trivial and we omit it due to space limit.

Lemma 4 ([24], Regularity lemma). *Let n be a power of two, $q \equiv 3 \bmod 8$ be a prime and l, k, ρ be positive integers that $\rho < \frac{1}{2}\sqrt{q/n}$. For $\mathbf{A} \xleftarrow{\$} \mathcal{R}_q^{k' \times k}$ and $\mathbf{R} \xleftarrow{\$} [-\rho, \rho]_{\mathcal{R}}^{k \times l}$, we have $\triangle((\mathbf{A}, \mathbf{A}\mathbf{R}), (\mathbf{A}, U(\mathcal{R}_q^{k' \times l}))) \leq \frac{l}{2} \cdot \left(\frac{q^{k'}}{(2\rho+1)^k} \right)^{n/2}$.*

Ring Learning with Errors. The Learning With Errors (LWE) problem was introduced by Regev [32] and we will use the ring version of it, namely RLWE [27].

Definition 2 ([27], RLWE). *For positive integers $n = n(\lambda), k = k(n)$, a prime integer $q = q(n) > 2$, an error distribution $\chi = \chi(n)$ over $\mathcal{R}$, and an algorithm $\mathcal{B}$, consider the experiment where a secret bit* coin $\xleftarrow{\$} \{0,1\}$ *is chosen and then $\mathcal{B}(\{(u_i, y_i)\}_{i=1}^k)$ is called when* coin $= 0$, $\mathcal{B}(\{(u_i, u_i \cdot v + e_i)\}_{i=1}^k)$ *is called when* coin $= 1$ *where $u_1, \cdots, u_k, y_1, \cdots, y_k, v \xleftarrow{\$} \mathcal{R}_q$ and $e_1, \cdots, e_k \xleftarrow{\$} \chi$. Finally, $\mathcal{B}$ outputs a bit* coin' *and $\mathcal{B}$ wins the experiment if* coin' $=$ coin. *The advantage of $\mathcal{B}$ is defined as $|\Pr[\text{coin}' = \text{coin}] - \frac{1}{2}|$. We say the* RLWE$_{n,k,q,\chi}$ *assumption holds if the advantage of any PPT $\mathcal{B}$ is negligible.*

We note that the RLWE problem is at least as hard as some worst-case lattice problem. We refer to [22, Lemma 23] for details.

2.4   Lattice Trapdoor Over Rings and Gaussian Sampling

We recall the public gadget and its trapdoor defined in [28] and related lemmas.

Definition 3 ([28]). *For positive integers b and $k \geq k' = \lceil \log_b q \rceil$, the public gadget vector is defined as $\mathbf{g} := [1|b|b^2|\cdots|b^{k'-1}|\mathbf{0}^\top]^\top \in \mathcal{R}_q^k$, and there is a publicly known matrix $\mathbf{T_g}$ such that $\mathsf{Rot}(\mathbf{T_g}) \in \mathbb{Z}^{nk \times nk}$ is a basis of the lattice $\Lambda^\perp(\mathsf{Rot}(\mathbf{g}^\top))$ and $\|\widetilde{\mathbf{T_g}}\| \leq \sqrt{b^2 + 1}$.*

Lemma 5 ([1]). *For integers k, q, b satisfying the requirements of Definition 3, on input a vector $\mathbf{u} \in \mathcal{R}_q^k$, there exists a deterministic polynomial-time algorithm $\mathbf{g}^{-1}(\cdot)$ which outputs the matrix $\mathbf{R} = \mathbf{g}^{-1}(\mathbf{u}^\top)$ such that $\mathbf{R} \in [-b, b]_{\mathcal{R}}^{k \times k}$, $\mathbf{g}^\top \cdot \mathbf{R} = \mathbf{u}^\top$ and $\|\mathbf{R}\| \leq nkb$.*

For the $\mathbf{G}$ matrix defined in [28], we have the following corollary of Lemma 5. We note that Lemma 5 and Corollary 2 can also hold in the $\mathbb{Z}_q$ setting, we refer to the full version [22, Appendix A] for details.

Corollary 2. *For the gadget matrix $\mathbf{G} = \begin{bmatrix} \mathbf{g}^\top & \mathbf{0}^\top \\ \mathbf{0}^\top & \mathbf{g}^\top \end{bmatrix} \in \mathcal{R}_q^{2 \times 2k}$, on input a matrix $\mathbf{U} \in \mathcal{R}_q^{2 \times 2k}$, there exists a deterministic polynomial-time algorithm $\mathbf{G}^{-1}(\cdot)$ which outputs the matrix $\mathbf{R} = \mathbf{G}^{-1}(\mathbf{U})$ such that $\mathbf{R} \in [-b, b]_{\mathcal{R}}^{2k \times 2k}$, $\mathbf{G} \cdot \mathbf{R} = \mathbf{U}$ and $\|\mathbf{R}\| \leq 2nkb$.*

Next, we recall a general trapdoor generation method in the ring setting as defined in [1] together with some useful lemmas for the trapdoor pair.

Lemma 6 ([1]). *For positive integers ρ, q such that $\rho < \frac{1}{2}\sqrt{q/n}$, $k \geq 2\log_\rho q$, there exists a polynomial time algorithm $\mathsf{TrapGen}(n, k, \rho, b, q)$ that outputs a vector $\mathbf{b} \in \mathcal{R}_q^k$ and a matrix $\mathbf{T_b} \in \mathcal{R}^{k \times k}$, where $\mathsf{Rot}(\mathbf{b}^\top) \in \mathbb{Z}^{n \times nk}$ is a full-rank matrix and $\mathsf{Rot}(\mathbf{T_b}) \in \mathbb{Z}^{nk \times nk}$ is a basis of $\Lambda^\perp(\mathsf{Rot}(\mathbf{b}^\top))$, such that $\mathbf{b}$ is statistically close to $U(\mathcal{R}_q^k)$ and $\mathsf{Rot}(\mathbf{b}^\top) \in \mathbb{Z}_q^{n \times nk}$ has full (column) rank, and $\|\widetilde{\mathbf{T_b}}\| \leq O(b\rho\sqrt{n \log_\rho q})$.*

Lemma 7 ([19], adapted to the ring setting). *For a trapdoor pair* $(\mathbf{b}, \mathbf{T_b}) \in \mathcal{R}_q^k \times \mathcal{R}^{k \times k}$ *satisfying* $\mathbf{b}^\top \cdot \mathbf{T_b} = \mathbf{0}^\top \bmod q$ *and* $\mathsf{Rot}(\mathbf{b}^\top) \in \mathbb{Z}^{n \times nk}$ *is a full-rank matrix,* $\sigma \geq \eta_\epsilon(\mathbb{Z}^{nk}) \cdot \|\widetilde{\mathbf{T_b}}\|$ *and a given target* $u \xleftarrow{\$} \mathcal{R}_q$, *there exists a preimage sampling algorithm* $\mathsf{SamPre}(\mathbf{b}, \mathbf{T_b}, u, \sigma)$ *that outputs a short vector* $\mathbf{x}$ *such that* $\mathbf{b}^\top \cdot \mathbf{x} = u \bmod q$ *and the distribution of* $\mathbf{x}$ *is statistically close to* $D_{\mathcal{R}^k, \sigma}$.

Lemma 8 ([19], adapted to the ring setting). *For a trapdoor pair* $(\mathbf{b}, \mathbf{T_b}) \in \mathcal{R}_q^k \times \mathcal{R}^{k \times k}$ *satisfying* $\mathbf{b}^\top \cdot \mathbf{T_b} = \mathbf{0}^\top \bmod q$ *and* $\mathsf{Rot}(\mathbf{b}^\top) \in \mathbb{Z}^{n \times nk}$ *is a full-rank matrix, and let* $\epsilon \in (0, \frac{1}{2})$ *and* $\sigma \geq \eta_\epsilon(\mathbb{Z}^{nk}) \cdot \|\widetilde{\mathbf{T_b}}\|$. *Then, for* $\mathbf{x} \leftarrow D_{\mathcal{R}^k, \sigma}$, *the distribution of the syndrome* $u = \mathbf{b}^\top \cdot \mathbf{x} \bmod q$ *is statistically close to uniform distribution over* $\mathcal{R}_q$.

Finally, we recall the following lemma about perturbation of non-spherical Gaussians, which originates from [31].

Lemma 9 ([17,28,38], adapted to the ring setting). *For* $\mathbf{T} \in \mathcal{R}^{m \times k}, \sigma^2 \geq (s^2 + \eta_\epsilon^2(\mathbb{Z}^{nk})) \cdot (\|\mathbf{T}\|^2 + 1)$, $\Sigma_p = \sigma^2 \mathbf{I}_m - s^2 \mathbf{T} \mathbf{T}^\top$, *the following two distributions are statistically close:*

- *sample* $\mathbf{z} \leftarrow D_{\mathcal{R}^k, s}$, $\mathbf{p} \leftarrow D_{\mathcal{R}^m, \sqrt{\Sigma_p}}$, *output* $\mathbf{p} + \mathbf{T}\mathbf{z}$;
- *output* $\mathbf{x} \leftarrow D_{\mathcal{R}^m, \sigma}$.

2.5 Homomorphic Encryption and Homomorphic Computation

Here, we describe the GSW-style [20] homomorphic encryption scheme over ring elements and δ-expanding homomorphic computation.

The Ring-GSW Homomorphic Encryption Scheme. We first recall the Ring-GSW homomorphic encryption scheme in [20], which consists of six algorithms (Setup, KeyGen, Enc, Dec, Add, Mul).

- Setup(1^λ): on input the security parameter λ, do:
  - set the ring dimension $n := n(\lambda)$ which is a power of 2, the modulus $q := q(n)$, the base $b := b(n)$, the positive integer $\rho := \rho(n)$, $k := \lceil \log_b q \rceil$, and the noise distribution χ over $\mathcal{R}$.
  - output the public parameter $pp := (n, q, b, \rho, k, \chi)$. We assume that pp is an input to all the following algorithms.
- KeyGen(pp): on inputs the public parameter pp, do:
  - pick $\mathbf{a} \xleftarrow{\$} \mathcal{R}_q^{2k}$, $s \xleftarrow{\$} \mathcal{R}_q$, $\mathbf{e} \leftarrow \chi^{2k}$.
  - set the encryption key $\mathsf{ek} := \mathbf{A} = \begin{bmatrix} \mathbf{a}^\top \\ \mathbf{a}^\top s + \mathbf{e}^\top \end{bmatrix}$, the decryption key $\mathsf{dk} := s$.
- Enc(ek, m): on input encryption key $\mathsf{ek} := \mathbf{A}$, a message $m \in \{0,1\}_\mathcal{R}$, do:
  - sample a random matrix $\mathbf{R} \xleftarrow{\$} [-\rho, \rho]_\mathcal{R}^{2k \times 2k}$.
  - set the public gadget matrix $\mathbf{G} = \begin{bmatrix} \mathbf{g}^\top & \mathbf{0}^\top \\ \mathbf{0}^\top & \mathbf{g}^\top \end{bmatrix} \in \mathcal{R}_q^{2 \times 2k}$.

- output the ciphertext $\mathbf{C} = \mathbf{AR} + m\mathbf{G} \in \mathcal{R}_q^{2 \times 2k}$.
- Dec(dk, $\mathbf{C}$): on input the decryption key dk and a ciphertext $\mathbf{C}$, takes the last column of ciphertext and split it into two elements (c_0, c_1), do:
  - compute $\left\lfloor \frac{1}{b^{k-1}} \cdot (c_1 - c_0 \cdot s) \right\rceil$.
- Add($\mathbf{C}_1, \mathbf{C}_2$): on input two ciphertexts $\mathbf{C}_1, \mathbf{C}_2$, output:

$$\mathbf{C}_{\mathsf{Add}} = \mathbf{C}_1 + \mathbf{C}_2 = \mathbf{A}(\mathbf{R}_1 + \mathbf{R}_2) + (m_1 + m_2)\mathbf{G}.$$

- Mul($\mathbf{C}_1, \mathbf{C}_2$): on input two ciphertexts $\mathbf{C}_1, \mathbf{C}_2$, output:

$$\mathbf{C}_{\mathsf{Mul}} = \mathbf{C}_1 \cdot \mathbf{G}^{-1}(\mathbf{C}_2) = (\mathbf{AR}_1 + m_1\mathbf{G}) \cdot \mathbf{G}^{-1}(\mathbf{AR}_2 + m_2\mathbf{G})$$
$$= \mathbf{A}\left(\mathbf{R}_1 \cdot \mathbf{G}^{-1}(\mathbf{AR}_2 + m_2\mathbf{G}) + \mathbf{R}_2 m_1\right) + (m_1 m_2)\mathbf{G}.$$

The following definition expresses the quality of the homomorphic evaluation by the factor δ, which is useful in the noise analysis of the IBE scheme.

Definition 4 ([37], δ-expanding evaluation). *Let k be a natural number. We say that the deterministic algorithms (PubEval, TrapEval) as in are δ-expanding for a function family $\mathcal{F} = \{f : \mathcal{X}^t \to \mathcal{Y}\}$ where $\mathcal{X}, \mathcal{Y} \subset \mathcal{R}$ if they are efficient and satisfy the following properties:*

- PubEval($\{\mathbf{C}_i \in \mathcal{R}_q^{2 \times 2k}\}_{i \in [t]}, f \in \mathcal{F}) = \mathbf{C}_f \in \mathcal{R}_q^{2 \times 2k}$
- TrapEval($\mathbf{A} \in \mathcal{R}_q^{2 \times 2k}, \{\mathbf{R}_i \in \mathcal{R}^{2k \times 2k}\}_{i \in [t]}, \{z_i\}_{i \in [t]}\}, f \in \mathcal{F}) = \mathbf{R}_f \in \mathcal{R}^{2k \times 2k}$

for $\mathbf{z} = [z_1|\cdots|z_t]^\top \in \mathcal{X}^t$. We require the following holds:

$$\mathsf{PubEval}(\{\mathbf{AR}_i + z_i\mathbf{G}\}_{i \in [t]}, f) = \mathbf{AR}_f + f(\mathbf{z})\mathbf{G},$$

and we have $\|\mathbf{R}_f\| \leq \delta \cdot \max_{i \in [t]}\{\|\mathbf{R}_i\|\}$.

3   Homomorphic Computation Outputting BGG+-Style Encoding with Two Distinct-Norm Trapdoors

In TCC 2021, Abla et al. [1] proposed a specific equality test function and a succinct partition function (using the equality test function as a sub-function), which can be homomorphically computed using $\omega(1)$ public vectors. In this section, we first homomorphically compute the equality test function and the partition function in the GSW-style encryption form (defined in Sect. 2.5). By the decryptable property of the GSW-style ciphertext, we design an incomplete decryption function to homomorphically transform the GSW-style encryption to a BGG+-style encoding (defined in Definition 9), which has two trapdoors with distinct norms.

3.1 Homomorphic Computation of Equality Test Function in GSW-Style Encryption Form

As the introduction mentions, this work focuses on the cyclotomic rings of power-of-two, which have simpler mathematical structures. Let $\mathcal{R} = \mathbb{Z}[x]/\Phi_m(x)$ be the m-th cyclotomic ring, modulus q be co-prime to m, and $\mathcal{R}_q = \mathcal{R}/q\mathcal{R}$. For this setting, we have $\Phi_m(x) = x^n + 1$ where $n = \varphi(m) = m/2$.

Definition 5 (Equality test function). *Define function* $\mathsf{Equal}_\beta(\cdot)$ *parameterized by* $\beta \in [m]$ *as follows: on input* $x^\alpha \in \mathcal{R}$, *the function* $\mathsf{Equal}_\beta(x^\alpha)$ *outputs* 1 *if* $\alpha \equiv \beta \bmod m$ *and* 0 *otherwise.*

In [1], the authors provide algorithms to homomorphically compute the equality test functions and analyze the expansion factor of their algorithms. We adapt their algorithms to our Ring-GSW homomorphic encryption setting and provide new algorithms ($\mathsf{PubEval}_\mathsf{E}$, $\mathsf{TrapEval}_\mathsf{E}$) in Construction 2 of the full version [22, Appendix B.1]. Due to space limit, we put our algorithms in the full version [22, Appendix B]. We bound the expansion factor of our algorithms with the following theorem.

Theorem 1. *The algorithms* ($\mathsf{PubEval}_\mathsf{E}$, $\mathsf{TrapEval}_\mathsf{E}$) *in Construction 2 of the full version [22, Appendix B.1] are* $2mn(kb)^2$-*expanding with respect to the function family* $\{\mathsf{Equal}_\beta\}_{\beta \in [m]}$.

The proof of this theorem is an adaptation of the proof in [1]. Due to space limit, we put the proof in the full version [22, Appendix B.1].

3.2 Homomorphic Computation of Partition Function in GSW-Style Encryption Form

In this subsection, we first recall the definition of the partition function and the partition function family[10] in [1] that will be used in our IBE construction.

Definition 6 ([1], partition function). *Let* p, t, L, η, m, n *be integers such that* $tp \leq n$, $m = 2n$, $L + 1 \leq m^{\eta 11}$; $\mathsf{ECC} : \mathcal{D} \to \mathbb{Z}_p^L$ *be a function[12], whose image is indexed by* $\{1, \cdots, L\}$ *and* $\mathsf{ECC}(z)[0] = 0$ *for every* $z \in \mathcal{D}$. *For any* $(\alpha, \beta) \in [L+1]^t \times \mathbb{Z}_p^t$, *the partition function* $H_{\alpha,\beta}^{\mathcal{R},t} : \mathcal{D} \to \mathcal{R}$ *as*
$$H_{\alpha,\beta}^{\mathcal{R},t}(z) := \sum_{i \in [t]} \left(x^{ip + \mathsf{ECC}(z)[\alpha_i]} - x^{ip + \beta_i} \right).$$

Abla et al. [1] gave another form of the partition function for homomorphic computation as follows.

---

[10] We provide some supplementary notes about the "partition" property in the full version [22, Appendix B.2].

[11] Note that m, η and the relationship $L + 1 \leq m^\eta$ are actually not used in this definition. We keep them in this definition because they will be used in another form of the partition function as in Definition 7.

[12] In [1], ECC is an error correcting code with relative distance Υ. Here we consider a more general definition for simplicity.

Definition 7 ([1]). *Let p, t, L, η, m, n be integers such that $tp \leq n$, $m = 2n$, $L+1 \leq m^\eta$ where numbers in $[L+1]$ can be represented in m-ary;* $\mathsf{ECC} : \mathcal{D} \to \mathbb{Z}_p^L$ *be a function whose image is indexed by $\{1, \cdots, L\}$ and $\mathsf{ECC}(z)[0] = 0$ for every $z \in \mathcal{D}$. For each $j \in [L+1]$, denote j's m-ary representation as $(j[0], \cdots, j[\eta-1])$. Let $\mathcal{R} := \mathbb{Z}[x]/(x^n + 1)$. For any $z \in \mathcal{D}$, on input $(\{\alpha_{i,i'}\}_{i \in [t], i' \in [\eta]} \in [m]^{t \times \eta}, \widetilde{\beta} \in \mathcal{R}_q)$, the partition function G_z is defined as*

$$G_z(\{\alpha_{i,i'}\}_{i \in [t], i' \in [\eta]}, \widetilde{\beta}) := -\widetilde{\beta} + \sum_{i \in [t], j \in [L+1]} \left(\prod_{i' \in [\eta]} \mathsf{Equal}_{j[i']}(x^{\alpha_{i,i'}}) \right) \cdot x^{ip + \mathsf{ECC}(z)[j]}.$$

Note that the function defined in Definition 6 and Definition 7 can be equal for certain parameters. More precisely, when $\{\alpha_{i,i'}\}_{i' \in [\eta]}$ is the m-ary representation of α_i and $\widetilde{\beta} = \sum_{i \in [t]} x^{ip + \beta_i}$, we have that $H_{\alpha,\beta}^{\mathcal{R},t}(z) = G_z(\{\alpha_{i,i'}\}_{i \in [t], i' \in [\eta]}, \widetilde{\beta})$. We put the full derivation process of this equation into the full version [22, Appendix B.3].

Definition 8 ([1], partition function family). *For any $t' \in [t]$, the class $\mathcal{H}^{\mathcal{R},t,t'}$ is defined as*

$$\mathcal{H}^{\mathcal{R},t,t'} = \left\{ H_{\alpha,\beta}^{\mathcal{R},t} : \alpha' \in ([L+1]\backslash\{0\})^{t'}, \beta' \in \mathbb{Z}_p^{t'}, \alpha^\top = (\alpha'^\top, \mathbf{0}^\top), \beta^\top = (\beta'^\top, \mathbf{0}^\top) \right\},$$

where $\mathbf{0}^\top = (0, \cdots, 0) \in \mathbb{Z}_p^{t-t'}$, i.e., padding 0's to match the dimension t. Furthermore, define $\mathcal{H}^{\mathcal{R},t} = \cup_{t' \in [t]} \mathcal{H}^{\mathcal{R},t,t'}$.

In [1], the authors provide algorithms to homomorphically compute this partition function and analyze the expansion factor of their algorithms. We adapt their algorithms to our Ring-GSW homomorphic encryption setting and provide new algorithms $(\mathsf{PubEval}_G, \mathsf{TrapEval}_G)$ in Construction 3 of the full version [22, Appendix B.1]. Due to space limit, we put our algorithms in the full version [22, Appendix A]. We bound the expansion factor of our algorithms with the following theorem.

Theorem 2. *For parameters as stated in Definition 6, and assuming the underlying algorithms $(\mathsf{PubEval}_E, \mathsf{TrapEval}_E)$ are δ-expanding for $\{\mathsf{Equal}_j\}_{j \in [m]}$, the algorithms $(\mathsf{PubEval}_G, \mathsf{TrapEval}_G)$ in Construction 3 of the full version [22, Appendix B.1] are $(L+1)t \cdot \eta \cdot 2nkb \cdot \delta$-expanding with respect to the function family $\{G_z\}_{z \in \mathcal{D}}$.*

The proof of this theorem is an adaptation of the proof in [1]. Due to space limit, we put the proof in the full version [22, Appendix B.4].

3.3 Homomorphic Transformation from GSW-Style Encryption to BGG+-Style Encoding

In this subsection, we first recall the BGG+-style encoding in [8]. Then, we design an incomplete decryption function for a GSW-style ciphertext and its homomorphic computation algorithm. Specifically, this homomorphic computation algorithm takes in a GSW-style ciphertext for some message m and transforms it into a BGG+-style encoding of m with some additional errors (with the help of a BGG+-style encoding for the decryption key s).

First, we recall the BGG+-style encoding over ring elements.

Definition 9 ([8], **BGG+-style encoding**). *Given a public vector* $\mathbf{b} \in \mathcal{R}_q^k$ *and a positive integer* ρ, *to encode* $\alpha \in \mathcal{R}$, *we choose a random small-norm matrix* $\mathbf{R}_\alpha \xleftarrow{\$} [-\rho, \rho]_{\mathcal{R}}^{k \times k}$, *and define the encoding as* $\mathbf{c}^\top := \mathbf{b}^\top \cdot \mathbf{R}_\alpha + \alpha \cdot \mathbf{g}^\top$.

Then, we give our new definition of the incomplete decryption function.

Definition 10 (Incomplete decryption function). *On input a GSW-style ciphertext (as in Sect. 2.5)* $\mathbf{C} \in \mathcal{R}_q^{2 \times 2k}$ *with* $\begin{bmatrix} \mathbf{c}_0^\top \\ \mathbf{c}_1^\top \end{bmatrix}$ *as the last k-columns and the corresponding decryption key $s \in \mathcal{R}_q$, the incomplete decryption function is defined as* $\widetilde{\mathsf{Dec}}(\mathbf{C}, s) := \mathbf{c}_1 - s \cdot \mathbf{c}_0$.

Next, we provide homomorphic computation algorithms for $\widetilde{\mathsf{Dec}}$ and analyze the expansion bound.

Construction 1. *On input a GSW-style ciphertext (as in Sect. 2.5)* $\mathbf{C}_m = \begin{bmatrix} \mathbf{a}^\top \\ \mathbf{a}^\top s + \mathbf{e}^\top \end{bmatrix} \cdot \mathbf{R}_m + m \cdot \mathbf{G}$ *for* $m \in \mathcal{R}$ *for* $m \in \mathcal{R}$ *and a BGG+-style encoding (as in Definition 9)* $\mathbf{c}_s^\top = \mathbf{b}^\top \cdot \mathbf{R}_s + s \cdot \mathbf{g}^\top$ *for* $s \in \mathcal{R}$, *we construct* $(\mathsf{Eval}^{\mathsf{Pub}}, \mathsf{Eval}^{\mathsf{Trap}}, \mathsf{Eval}^{\mathsf{Error}})$ *for the incomplete decryption function* $\widetilde{\mathsf{Dec}}$ *as follows.*

$\mathsf{Eval}^{\mathsf{Pub}}(\mathbf{C}_m, \mathbf{c}_s)$: *output* $\mathbf{c}_1^\top - \mathbf{c}_s^\top \cdot \mathbf{g}^{-1}(\mathbf{c}_0^\top)$, *where* $\begin{bmatrix} \mathbf{c}_0^\top \\ \mathbf{c}_1^\top \end{bmatrix}$ *is* $\mathbf{C}_m$'s *last k-columns.*

$\mathsf{Eval}^{\mathsf{Trap}}(\mathbf{R}_s, \mathbf{C}_m)$: *output* $-\mathbf{R}_s \cdot \mathbf{g}^{-1}(\mathbf{c}_0^\top)$, *where* $\mathbf{c}_0$ *is the vector defined in* $\mathsf{Eval}^{\mathsf{Pub}}$.

$\mathsf{Eval}^{\mathsf{Error}}(\mathbf{e}, \mathbf{R}_m)$: *output* $\mathbf{e}^\top \cdot \hat{\mathbf{R}}_m$, *where* $\hat{\mathbf{R}}_m$ *is the last k-columns of* $\mathbf{R}_m$.

Theorem 3. *In the algorithms* $(\mathsf{Eval}^{\mathsf{Pub}}, \mathsf{Eval}^{\mathsf{Trap}}, \mathsf{Eval}^{\mathsf{Error}})$ *for the incomplete decryption function* $\widetilde{\mathsf{Dec}}$, *the 2-norm of the output of the* $\mathsf{Eval}^{\mathsf{Trap}}$ *is bounded by* $nkb \cdot \|\mathbf{R}_s\|$, *the 2-norm of the output of the* $\mathsf{Eval}^{\mathsf{Error}}$ *is bounded by* $\|\mathbf{e}\| \cdot \|\mathbf{R}_m\|$.

Proof. It is easy to see that

$$
\begin{aligned}
\mathbf{c}_1^\top - \mathbf{c}_s^\top \cdot \mathbf{g}^{-1}(\mathbf{c}_0^\top) &= \mathbf{c}_1^\top - (\mathbf{b}^\top \cdot \mathbf{R}_s + s \cdot \mathbf{g}^\top) \cdot \mathbf{g}^{-1}(\mathbf{c}_0^\top) \\
&= \mathbf{b}^\top \cdot (-\mathbf{R}_s) \cdot \mathbf{g}^{-1}(\mathbf{c}_0^\top) + (\mathbf{c}_1^\top - s \cdot \mathbf{c}_0^\top) \\
&= \underbrace{\mathbf{b}^\top \cdot (-\mathbf{R}_s) \cdot \mathbf{g}^{-1}(\mathbf{c}_0^\top)}_{\mathsf{Eval}^{\mathsf{Trap}}} + m \cdot \mathbf{g}^\top + \underbrace{\mathbf{e}^\top \cdot \hat{\mathbf{R}}_m}_{\mathsf{Eval}^{\mathsf{Error}}}.
\end{aligned}
$$

By Lemma 5, we have $\| -\mathbf{R}_s \cdot \mathbf{g}^{-1}(\mathbf{c}_0^\top) \| \leq nkb \cdot \|\mathbf{R}_s\|$. By the definition of $\hat{\mathbf{R}}_m$ as in $\mathsf{Eval}^{\mathsf{Error}}$ algorithm, we have $\|\mathbf{e}^\top \cdot \hat{\mathbf{R}}_m\| \leq \|\mathbf{e}\| \cdot \|\hat{\mathbf{R}}_m\| \leq \|\mathbf{e}\| \cdot \|\mathbf{R}_m\|$.

4   Sampling Algorithms with (D_r, D_σ)-Hybrid Outputs

In this section, we follow the idea of the sampling algorithms in [2] and design new sampling algorithms with (D_r, D_σ)-hybrid outputs. Due to space limitation, we recall the sampling algorithms from [2] in the full version [22, Appendix C.1].

Our sampling algorithm would like to obtain $(w, \mathbf{x})$ which is a (D_r, D_σ)-hybrid pair where $r \gg \sigma$, satisfying

$$\mathbf{f}^\top \mathbf{x} = u + w \bmod q, \tag{12}$$

for any given uniformly random $u \in \mathcal{R}_q$. The vector $\mathbf{f}$ is

$$\mathbf{f}^\top = [\mathbf{b}^\top | \mathbf{b}^\top \mathbf{R} + y\mathbf{g}^\top + \mathbf{e}^\top] \in \mathcal{R}_q^{2k} \tag{13}$$

where $\mathbf{b} \in \mathcal{R}_q^k$, $\mathbf{R} \in \mathcal{R}^{k \times k}$ is a matrix with small entries, $\mathbf{e} \in \mathcal{R}^k$ is a vector with (relatively) large entries, $y \in \mathcal{R}_q^\times$ is an invertible element, and $\mathbf{g} = [1|b|\cdots|b^{k-1}]^\top \in \mathcal{R}_q^k$ is the specific gadget vector as defined in Definition 3, whose trapdoor $\mathbf{T_g}$ is publicly known.

4.1   Our New Sampling Algorithms

Our sampling algorithms with (D_r, D_σ)-hybrid outputs consist of two parts: $\mathsf{SampleLeft}_{\mathsf{hybrid}}$ and $\mathsf{SampleRight}_{\mathsf{hybrid}}$.

Let $(\mathbf{b}, \mathbf{T_b}) \in \mathcal{R}_q^k \times \mathcal{R}^{k \times k}$ be a trapdoor pair satisfying the requirements of Lemma 6 and SamPre be the algorithm in Lemma 7. Consider the following two algorithms.

$\mathsf{SampleLeft}_{\mathsf{hybrid}}(\mathbf{b}, \mathbf{c} \in \mathcal{R}_q^k, \mathbf{T_b} \in \mathcal{R}^{k \times k}, u \in \mathcal{R}_q, \sigma, r \in \mathbb{R})$

– sample $w \leftarrow D_{\mathcal{R}, r}, \mathbf{x}_2 \leftarrow D_{\mathcal{R}^k, \sigma}$, set $\tilde{u} = u + w$.
– run $\mathbf{x}_1 \leftarrow \mathsf{SamPre}(\mathbf{b}, \mathbf{T_b}, u', \sigma)$ where $u' = \tilde{u} - \mathbf{c}^\top \mathbf{x}_2$.
– output $(w, \mathbf{x} = [\begin{smallmatrix} \mathbf{x}_1 \\ \mathbf{x}_2 \end{smallmatrix}])$.

$\mathsf{SampleRight}_{\mathsf{hybrid}}(\mathbf{b}, \mathbf{g} \in \mathcal{R}_q^k, \mathbf{e} \in \mathcal{R}^k, \mathbf{T_g}, \mathbf{R} \in \mathcal{R}^{k \times k}, y \in \mathcal{R}_q^\times, u \in \mathcal{R}_q, \sigma, s, r \in \mathbb{R})$

– sample $h \leftarrow D_{\mathcal{R}, \sqrt{\Sigma_h}}$ where $\Sigma_h := r^2 - \sigma^2 \mathbf{e}^\top \mathbf{e}$.
– sample $\mathbf{p}' = [\begin{smallmatrix} \bar{\mathbf{p}} \\ \mathbf{p} \end{smallmatrix}] \leftarrow D_{\mathcal{R}^{3k}, \sqrt{\Sigma_p}}$ where $\bar{\mathbf{p}} \in \mathcal{R}^k, \mathbf{p} \in \mathcal{R}^{2k}$, and $\Sigma_p := \sigma^2 \mathbf{I}_{3k} - s^2 \mathbf{T}' \mathbf{T}'^\top$ for $\mathbf{T} = [\begin{smallmatrix} -\mathbf{R} \\ \mathbf{I}_k \end{smallmatrix}] \in \mathcal{R}^{2k \times k}$ and $\mathbf{T}' = [\begin{smallmatrix} \mathbf{I}_k \\ \mathbf{T} \end{smallmatrix}] \in \mathcal{R}^{3k \times k}$.
– set $u^\star = u + h + \mathbf{e}^\top \bar{\mathbf{p}}$.
– compute $v = y^{-1}(u^\star - \mathbf{f}^\top \mathbf{p})$ where $\mathbf{f}$ is defined in Eq. (13).
– run $\mathbf{z} \leftarrow \mathsf{SamPre}(\mathbf{g}, \mathbf{T_g}, v, s)$.
– compute $w = h + \mathbf{e}^\top (\bar{\mathbf{p}} + \mathbf{z})$ and $\mathbf{x} = \mathbf{p} + \mathbf{T}\mathbf{z}$.
– output $(w, \mathbf{x})$.

4.2 Analysis of Our New Sampling Algorithms

In this subsection, we analyze our new sampling algorithms and prove the output distributions of these two algorithms are statistically close.

Theorem 4. *For any trapdoor pair* $(\mathbf{b}, \mathbf{T_b}) \in \mathcal{R}_q^k \times \mathcal{R}^{k \times k}$ *satisfying* $\mathbf{b}^\top \cdot \mathbf{T_b} = \mathbf{0}^\top \bmod q$ *and* $\mathsf{Rot}(\mathbf{b}^\top) \in \mathbb{Z}^{n \times nk}$ *is a full-rank matrix, any* $\mathbf{c} \in \mathcal{R}_q^k$, $\sigma \geq \eta_\epsilon(\mathbb{Z}^{nk}) \cdot \|\widetilde{\mathbf{T_b}}\|$ *and any real* $r > 0$, *define* $\mathbf{f}^\top = [\mathbf{b}^\top | \mathbf{c}^\top]$, *then the following two distributions are statistically close*

- $\{(\mathbf{f}, w, \mathbf{x}, u) : u \xleftarrow{\$} \mathcal{R}_q, (w, \mathbf{x}) \leftarrow \mathsf{SampleLeft}_{\mathsf{hybrid}}(\mathbf{b}, \mathbf{c}, \mathbf{T_b}, u, \sigma, r)\}$.
- $\{(\mathbf{f}, w, \mathbf{x}, u) : w \leftarrow D_{\mathcal{R}, r}, \mathbf{x} \leftarrow D_{\mathcal{R}^{2k}, \sigma}, u = \mathbf{f}^\top \mathbf{x} - w\}$.

Proof. Consider the first distribution $(\mathbf{f}, w, \mathbf{x}, u)$. We omit $\mathbf{f}$ since it is fixed in this distribution and we only consider the $(w, \mathbf{x} = [\begin{smallmatrix} \mathbf{x}_1 \\ \mathbf{x}_2 \end{smallmatrix}], u)$ part where $u \xleftarrow{\$} \mathcal{R}_q$, $(w, \mathbf{x})$ are sampled using the algorithm $\mathsf{SampleLeft}_{\mathsf{hybrid}}(\mathbf{b}, \mathbf{c}, \mathbf{T_b}, u, \sigma, r)$ Note that the $\mathsf{SampleLeft}_{\mathsf{hybrid}}$ algorithm samples $w \leftarrow D_{\mathcal{R}, r}, \mathbf{x}_2 \leftarrow D_{\mathcal{R}^k, \sigma}$ and $\mathbf{x}_1 \leftarrow \mathsf{SamPre}(\mathbf{b}, \mathbf{T_b}, u + w - \mathbf{c}^\top \mathbf{x}_2, \sigma)$.

Hybrid 1. Now we consider a hybrid distribution $(w, \mathbf{x} = [\begin{smallmatrix} \mathbf{x}_1 \\ \mathbf{x}_2 \end{smallmatrix}], u)$ where $w, \mathbf{x}_2$ are sampled as above, $\mathbf{x}_1 \leftarrow D_{\mathcal{R}^k, \sigma}, u' = \mathbf{b}^\top \mathbf{x}_1$ and finally compute $u = u' - w + \mathbf{c}^\top \mathbf{x}_2$. We note that Hybrid 1 and the first distribution are statistically close due to the following claim.

Claim. For any trapdoor pair $(\mathbf{b}, \mathbf{T_b}) \in \mathcal{R}_q^k \times \mathcal{R}^{k \times k}$ satisfying $\mathbf{b}^\top \cdot \mathbf{T_b} = \mathbf{0}^\top \bmod q$ and $\mathsf{Rot}(\mathbf{b}^\top) \in \mathbb{Z}^{n \times nk}$ is a full-rank matrix, $\sigma \geq \eta_\epsilon(\mathbb{Z}^{nk}) \cdot \|\widetilde{\mathbf{T_b}}\|$, the following two distributions are statistically close:

- sample $u' \xleftarrow{\$} \mathcal{R}_q$, then sample $\mathbf{x}_1 \leftarrow \mathsf{SamPre}(\mathbf{b}, \mathbf{T_b}, u', \sigma)$, output $(\mathbf{x}_1, u')$;
- sample $\mathbf{x}_1 \leftarrow D_{\mathcal{R}^k, \sigma}$, then compute $u' = \mathbf{b}^\top \mathbf{x}_1$, output $(\mathbf{x}_1, u')$.

It is obvious that this claim follows from Lemma 7 and Lemma 8.

Note that Hybrid 1 is exactly the second distribution in Theorem 4. This completes the proof. □

Theorem 5. *For a vector* $\mathbf{b} \in \mathcal{R}_q^k$, *the public gadget trapdoor pair* $(\mathbf{g}, \mathbf{T_g}) \in \mathcal{R}_q^k \times \mathcal{R}^{k \times k}$ *satisfying* $\mathbf{g}^\top \cdot \mathbf{T_g} = \mathbf{0}^\top \bmod q$ *and* $\mathsf{Rot}(\mathbf{g}^\top) \in \mathbb{Z}^{n \times nk}$ *is a full-rank matrix, any matrix* $\mathbf{R} \in \mathcal{R}^{k \times k}$ *and vector* $\mathbf{e} \in \mathcal{R}^k$, *any invertible element* $y \in \mathcal{R}_q^\times$, $s \geq \eta_\epsilon(\mathbb{Z}^{nk}) \cdot \|\widetilde{\mathbf{T_g}}\|$, $\sigma^2 \geq (s^2 + \eta_\epsilon^2(\mathbb{Z}^{nk})) \cdot (\|\mathbf{T}'\|^2 + 1)$ *where* $\mathbf{T}' = [\begin{smallmatrix} \mathbf{I}_k \\ \mathbf{T} \end{smallmatrix}]$ *and* $\mathbf{T} = [\begin{smallmatrix} -\mathbf{R} \\ \mathbf{I}_k \end{smallmatrix}]$, $r^2 \geq (\sigma^2 + \eta_\epsilon^2(\mathbb{Z}^{nk})) \cdot (\|\mathbf{e}\|^2 + 1)$, *define* $\mathbf{f}^\top = [\mathbf{b}^\top | \mathbf{b}^\top \mathbf{R} + y\mathbf{g}^\top + \mathbf{e}^\top]$, *then the following two distributions are statistically close*

- $\{(\mathbf{f}, w, \mathbf{x}, u) : u \xleftarrow{\$} \mathcal{R}_q, (w, \mathbf{x}) \leftarrow \mathsf{SampleRight}_{\mathsf{hybrid}}(\mathbf{b}, \mathbf{g}, \mathbf{e}, \mathbf{T_g}, \mathbf{R}, y, u, \sigma, s, r)\}$;
- $\{(\mathbf{f}, w, \mathbf{x}, u) : w \leftarrow D_{\mathcal{R}, r}, \mathbf{x} \leftarrow D_{\mathcal{R}^{2k}, \sigma}, u = \mathbf{f}^\top \mathbf{x} - w\}$.

Proof. Consider the first distribution $(\mathbf{f}, w, \mathbf{x}, u)$. We omit $\mathbf{f}$ since it is fixed in this distribution and we only consider the $(w, \mathbf{x}, u)$ part where $u \xleftarrow{\$} \mathcal{R}_q$, $(w, \mathbf{x})$ are sampled using the algorithm $\mathsf{SampleRight}_{\mathsf{hybrid}}(\mathbf{b}, \mathbf{g}, \mathbf{e}, \mathbf{T_g}, \mathbf{R}, y, u, \sigma, s, r)$.

Hybrid 1. Now we consider a hybrid distribution $(w, \mathbf{x}, u)$ where $w, \mathbf{x}$ are sampled as above. We swap the sampling order of u and $u^\star$ where $u^\star$ is used in $\mathsf{SampleRight}_{\mathsf{hybrid}}$, i.e., we first sample $u^\star \xleftarrow{\$} \mathcal{R}_q$, $h \leftarrow D_{\mathcal{R}, \sqrt{\Sigma_h}}$, $\mathbf{p}' = \begin{bmatrix} \bar{\mathbf{p}} \\ \mathbf{p} \end{bmatrix} \leftarrow D_{\mathcal{R}^{3k}, \sqrt{\Sigma_p}}$ and then compute $u = u^\star - h - \mathbf{e}^\top \bar{\mathbf{p}}$. Clearly, the first distribution and Hybrid 1 are identically distributed.

Hybrid 2. Now we consider the second hybrid distribution $(w, \mathbf{x}, u)$ where $w, \mathbf{x}$ are sampled as above. We swap the order of sampling $u^\star$ and v where v is used in $\mathsf{SampleRight}_{\mathsf{hybrid}}$, i.e., we first sample $v \xleftarrow{\$} \mathcal{R}_q$, set $u^\star = yv + \mathbf{f}^\top \mathbf{p}$ and set u as above. We claim that Hybrid 1 and Hybrid 2 are identically distributed. Since $y \in \mathcal{R}_q^\times$ is invertible and $v \xleftarrow{\$} \mathcal{R}_q$, the term yv follows a uniform distribution over $\mathcal{R}_q$, then $u^\star = yv + \mathbf{f}^\top \mathbf{p}$ as well.

Hybrid 3. Now we consider the third hybrid distribution $(w, \mathbf{x}, u)$ where $w, \mathbf{x}$ are sampled as above. We swap the order of sampling v and $\mathbf{z}$, i.e., we first sample $\mathbf{z} \leftarrow D_{\mathcal{R}^k, s}$, then compute $v = \mathbf{g}^\top \mathbf{z}$ and set u as above. We note that Hybrid 3 and Hybrid 2 are statistically close due to the following claim.

Claim. For the gadget trapdoor pair $(\mathbf{g}, \mathbf{T_g}) \in \mathcal{R}_q^k \times \mathcal{R}^{k \times k}$ satisfying $\mathbf{g}^\top \cdot \mathbf{T_g} = \mathbf{0}^\top \bmod$ and $\mathsf{Rot}(\mathbf{g}^\top) \in \mathbb{Z}^{n \times nk}$ is a full-rank matrix, $s \geq \eta_\epsilon(\mathbb{Z}^{nk}) \cdot \|\widetilde{\mathbf{T_g}}\|$, the following two distribution are statistically close:

- sample $v \xleftarrow{\$} \mathcal{R}_q$, then sample $\mathbf{z} \leftarrow \mathsf{SamPre}(\mathbf{g}, \mathbf{T_g}, v, s)$, output $(\mathbf{z}, v)$;
- sample $\mathbf{z} \leftarrow D_{\mathcal{R}^k, s}$, then compute $v = \mathbf{g}^\top \mathbf{z}$, output $(\mathbf{z}, v)$.

It is obvious that this claim follows from Lemma 7 and Lemma 8.

Note that in Hybrid 3, w is computed by $h + \mathbf{e}^\top (\bar{\mathbf{p}} + \mathbf{z})$ and $\mathbf{x}$ is computed by $\mathbf{x} = \mathbf{p} + \mathbf{T}\mathbf{z}$ where $\mathbf{p}' = \begin{bmatrix} \bar{\mathbf{p}} \\ \mathbf{p} \end{bmatrix} \leftarrow D_{\mathcal{R}^{3k}, \sqrt{\Sigma_p}}$, $\mathbf{z} \leftarrow D_{\mathcal{R}^k, s}$, $h \leftarrow D_{\mathcal{R}, \sqrt{\Sigma_h}}$. We define $\bar{\mathbf{x}} := \bar{\mathbf{p}} + \mathbf{I}_k \cdot \mathbf{z}$, then $w = h + \mathbf{e}^\top \bar{\mathbf{x}}$. We further define $\mathbf{x}' := \begin{bmatrix} \bar{\mathbf{x}} \\ \mathbf{x} \end{bmatrix}$, then $\mathbf{x}' = \begin{bmatrix} \bar{\mathbf{p}} + \mathbf{I}_k \mathbf{z} \\ \mathbf{p} + \mathbf{T}\mathbf{z} \end{bmatrix} = \mathbf{p}' + \mathbf{T}'\mathbf{z}$ in Hybrid 3.

By routine computation, we have that

$$u = u^\star - h - \mathbf{e}^\top \bar{\mathbf{p}} = \mathbf{f}^\top \mathbf{x} - w. \tag{14}$$

We put the full derivation process of Eq. (14) in the full version [22, Appendix C.2]. Then we compute $u = \mathbf{f}^\top \mathbf{x} - w$ in the following hybrids.

Hybrid 4. Now we consider the fourth hybrid distribution $(w, \mathbf{x}, u)$ where u is sampled as above, $\mathbf{x}' = \begin{bmatrix} \bar{\mathbf{x}} \\ \mathbf{x} \end{bmatrix} \leftarrow D_{\mathcal{R}^{3k}, \sigma}$ and w is computed as above. Note that Hybrid 4 is statistically close to Hybrid 3 due to the following claim.

Claim. For a matrix $\mathbf{T}' \in \mathcal{R}^{3k \times k}$, $\sigma^2 \geq (s^2 + \eta_\epsilon^2(\mathbb{Z}^{nk})) \cdot (\|\mathbf{T}'\|^2 + 1)$, $\Sigma_p = \sigma^2 \mathbf{I}_{3k} - s^2 \mathbf{T}'\mathbf{T}'^\top$, the following two distributions are statistically close:

- sample $\mathbf{z} \leftarrow D_{\mathcal{R}^k,s}$, $\mathbf{p}' \leftarrow D_{\mathcal{R}^{3k},\sqrt{\Sigma_p}}$, output $\mathbf{p}' + \mathbf{T}'\mathbf{z}$;
- output $\mathbf{x}' \leftarrow D_{\mathcal{R}^{3k},\sigma}$.

Directly, it comes from Lemma 9.

Hybrid 5. Now we consider the last hybrid distribution $(w, \mathbf{x}, u)$ where $\mathbf{x}, u$ are sampled as above and $w \leftarrow D_{\mathcal{R},r}$. Note that Hybrid 5 is statistically close to Hybrid 4 due to the following claim.

Claim. For a matrix $\mathbf{e} \in \mathcal{R}^{1 \times k}$, $r^2 \geq (\sigma^2 + \eta_\epsilon^2(\mathbb{Z}^{nk})) \cdot (\|\mathbf{e}\|^2 + 1)$, $\Sigma_h = r^2 - \sigma^2 \mathbf{e}^\top \mathbf{e}$, the following two distributions are statistically close:

- sample $\bar{\mathbf{x}} \leftarrow D_{\mathcal{R}^k,\sigma}$, $h \leftarrow D_{\mathcal{R},\sqrt{\Sigma_h}}$, output $h + \mathbf{e}^\top \bar{\mathbf{x}}$;
- output $w \leftarrow D_{\mathcal{R},r}$.

Directly, it comes from Lemma 9.

Note that in Hybrid 5, $\mathbf{x}' = \begin{bmatrix} \bar{\mathbf{x}} \\ \mathbf{x} \end{bmatrix} \leftarrow D_{\mathcal{R}^{3k},\sigma}$ which means that $\mathbf{x}$ follows the distribution of $D_{\mathcal{R}^{2k},\sigma}$, $u = \mathbf{f}^\top \mathbf{x} - w$ from Hybrid 3 and w follows the distribution of $D_{\mathcal{R},r}$. This means that the distribution in Hybrid 5 is exactly the same as the second distribution in Theorem 5. This completes the proof.   □

Theorem 6. *For any trapdoor pair $(\mathbf{b}, \mathbf{T_b}) \in \mathcal{R}_q^k \times \mathcal{R}^{k \times k}$ satisfying $\mathbf{b}^\top \cdot \mathbf{T_b} = \mathbf{0}^\top \bmod q$ and $\mathrm{Rot}(\mathbf{b}^\top) \in \mathbb{Z}^{n \times nk}$ is a full-rank matrix, the gadget trapdoor pair $(\mathbf{g}, \mathbf{T_g}) \in \mathcal{R}_q^k \times \mathcal{R}^{k \times k}$ satisfying $\mathbf{g}^\top \cdot \mathbf{T_g} = \mathbf{0}^\top \bmod q$ and $\mathrm{Rot}(\mathbf{g}^\top) \in \mathbb{Z}^{n \times nk}$ is a full-rank matrix, any matrix $\mathbf{R} \in \mathcal{R}^{k \times k}$ and vector $\mathbf{e} \in \mathcal{R}^k$, any invertible element $y \in \mathcal{R}_q^\times$, $s \geq \eta_\epsilon(\mathbb{Z}^{nk}) \cdot \|\mathbf{T_g}\|$, $\sigma^2 \geq (s^2 + \eta_\epsilon^2(\mathbb{Z}^{nk})) \cdot (\|\mathbf{T}'\|^2 + 1)$ for $\mathbf{T} = \begin{bmatrix} -\mathbf{R} \\ \mathbf{I}_k \end{bmatrix} \in \mathcal{R}^{2k \times k}$ and $\mathbf{T}' = \begin{bmatrix} \mathbf{I}_k \\ \mathbf{T} \end{bmatrix} \in \mathcal{R}^{3k \times k}$, $r^2 \geq (\sigma^2 + \eta_\epsilon^2(\mathbb{Z}^{nk})) \cdot (\|\mathbf{e}\|^2 + 1)$, $\sigma \geq \eta_\epsilon(\mathbb{Z}^{nk}) \cdot \|\widetilde{\mathbf{T_b}}\|$, define $\mathbf{f}^\top = [\mathbf{b}^\top | \mathbf{c}^\top] = [\mathbf{b}^\top | \mathbf{b}^\top \mathbf{R} + y\mathbf{g}^\top + \mathbf{e}^\top]$, then the distributions of outputs from $\mathsf{SampleLeft}_{\mathrm{hybrid}}$ and $\mathsf{SampleRight}_{\mathrm{hybrid}}$ are statistically close. More precisely, the following two distributions are statistically close*

- $\{(\mathbf{f}, w, \mathbf{x}, u) : u \xleftarrow{\$} \mathcal{R}_q, (w, \mathbf{x}) \leftarrow \mathsf{SampleLeft}_{\mathrm{hybrid}}(\mathbf{b}, \mathbf{c}, \mathbf{T_b}, u, \sigma, r)\}$;

- $\{(\mathbf{f}, w, \mathbf{x}, u) : u \xleftarrow{\$} \mathcal{R}_q, (w, \mathbf{x}) \leftarrow \mathsf{SampleRight}_{\mathrm{hybrid}}(\mathbf{b}, \mathbf{g}, \mathbf{e}, \mathbf{T_g}, \mathbf{R}, y, u, \sigma, s, r)\}$.

Proof. Directly from Theorem 4 and Theorem 5.   □

5   IBE Scheme

In this section, combining the homomorphic computation of the partition function in the GSW-style encryption form and the homomorphic transformation from GSW-style encryption to BGG+-style encoding (Sect. 3), our new sampling algorithms with (D_r, D_σ)-hybrid outputs (Sect. 4), we provide an adaptively secure lattice-based IBE scheme with smaller modulus, smaller secret key size than ALWW-IBE [1]. Particularly, we provide the construction in Sect. 5.1, the security proof in Sect. 5.2 and parameter analysis in Sect. 5.3.

5.1 Construction

Let $n := n(\lambda)$, $q := q(n)$, $b := b(n)$, $\rho := \rho(n)$, $k := k(n)$, $s := s(n)$, $\sigma_0 := \sigma_0(n)$, $\sigma_0' := \sigma_0'(n)$, $\sigma_1 := \sigma_1(n)$, $\sigma := \sigma(n)$, $r := r(n)$ be parameters that are specified later. Let $\mathcal{R} = \mathbb{Z}[x]/(x^n + 1)$, $\mathcal{R}_q = \mathcal{R}/q\mathcal{R}$ and $\chi := D_{\mathcal{R},\sigma_0'}$.

Let the identity space of the scheme be $\mathcal{ID} = \{0,1\}^l$ for some $l \in \mathbb{N}$ and the message space be $\mathcal{M} = \{0,1\}^n \subset \mathcal{R}$. Let GSW be the Ring-GSW homomorphic encryption scheme in Sect. 2.5. We define the IBE scheme (Setup, KeyGen, Enc, Dec) in the following.

Setup(1^λ). On input a security parameter λ, do:
1. $pp := (n, q, b, \rho, k, \chi) \leftarrow$ GSW.Setup(1^λ) .
2. $(\mathsf{ek} := \mathbf{A} = \begin{bmatrix} \mathbf{a}^\top \\ \mathbf{a}^\top s + \mathbf{e}^\top \end{bmatrix}, \mathsf{dk} := s) \leftarrow$ GSW.KeyGen(pp).
3. $(\mathbf{b} \in \mathcal{R}_q^k, \mathbf{T_b} \in \mathcal{R}^{k \times k}) \leftarrow$ TrapGen(pp).
4. $\left\{ \{\mathbf{C}_{\boldsymbol{\alpha}_{i,i'}}\}_{i\in[t],i'\in[\eta]}, \mathbf{C}_{\widetilde{\beta}} \right\} \leftarrow$ GSW.Enc$(\mathsf{ek}, 0)$.
5. $\widehat{\mathbf{c}} \xleftarrow{\$} \mathcal{R}_q^k$, $\mathbf{c}_s \xleftarrow{\$} \mathcal{R}_q^k$, $d \xleftarrow{\$} \mathcal{R}_q^\times$, $u \xleftarrow{\$} \mathcal{R}_q$.
6. output $\mathsf{mpk} := (\mathbf{b}, \{\mathbf{C}_{\boldsymbol{\alpha}_{i,i'}}\}_{i\in[t],i'\in[\eta]}, \mathbf{C}_{\widetilde{\beta}}, \widehat{\mathbf{c}}, \mathbf{c}_s, \mathbf{A}, d, u)$, $\mathsf{msk} := (\mathbf{T_b}, s)$.

KeyGen$(\mathsf{mpk}, \mathsf{msk}, \mathsf{id})$. On inputs the master public key mpk, the master secret key msk, and an identity $\mathsf{id} \in \mathcal{ID}$, do:
1. define G_id as the function as in Definition 7 with index id.
2. compute $\mathbf{C}_G = \mathsf{PubEval}_G(\left\{ \{\mathbf{C}_{\boldsymbol{\alpha}_{i,i'}}\}_{i\in[t],i'\in[\eta]}, \mathbf{C}_{\widetilde{\beta}} \right\}, G_\mathsf{id}) \in \mathcal{R}_q^{2\times 2k}$.
3. compute $F(\mathsf{id}) = \mathsf{Eval}^\mathsf{Pub}(\mathbf{C}_G, \mathbf{c}_s) \in \mathcal{R}_q^k$.
4. sample $(w, \mathbf{x}) \leftarrow \mathsf{SampleLeft}_\mathsf{hybrid}(\mathbf{b}, \widehat{\mathbf{c}} + F(\mathsf{id}), \mathbf{T_b}, d^{-1}u, \sigma, r)$, satisfying

$$[\mathbf{b}^\top | \widehat{\mathbf{c}}^\top + F(\mathsf{id})^\top] \cdot \mathbf{x} = d^{-1}u + w.$$

5. output $\mathsf{sk}_\mathsf{id} := \mathbf{x} \in \mathcal{R}^{2k}$.

Enc$(\mathsf{mpk}, \mathsf{id}, m)$. On inputs the master public key mpk, an identity id, and a message m, do:
1. set $\mu = m_0 + m_1 x + \cdots m_{n-1} x^{n-1} \in \mathcal{R}_q$.
2. compute $\mathbf{C}_G = \mathsf{PubEval}_G(\left\{ \{\mathbf{C}_{\boldsymbol{\alpha}_{i,i'}}\}_{i\in[t],i'\in[\eta]}, \mathbf{C}_{\widetilde{\beta}} \right\}, G_\mathsf{id}) \in \mathcal{R}_q^{2\times 2k}$.
3. compute $F(\mathsf{id}) = \mathsf{Eval}^\mathsf{Pub}(\mathbf{C}_G, \mathbf{c}_s) \in \mathcal{R}_q^k$.
4. sample $v \xleftarrow{\$} \mathcal{R}_q$, $e_0, e_1 \leftarrow D_{\mathcal{R},\sigma_0}$, $\mathbf{e}_2 \leftarrow D_{\mathcal{R}^{2k},\sigma_1}$.
5. compute $c_0 = u \cdot v + e_0 + \lceil \frac{q}{2} \rceil \cdot \mu$, $\mathbf{c}_1 = d \cdot \begin{bmatrix} 1 \\ \mathbf{b} \\ \widehat{\mathbf{c}} + F(\mathsf{id}) \end{bmatrix} \cdot v + \begin{bmatrix} e_1 \\ \mathbf{e}_2 \end{bmatrix}$.
6. output the ciphertext $\mathsf{ct} := (c_0, \mathbf{c}_1) \in \mathcal{R}_q \times \mathcal{R}_q^{2k+1}$.

Dec$(\mathsf{mpk}, \mathsf{sk}_\mathsf{id} = \mathbf{x}, \mathsf{ct} = (c_0, \mathbf{c}_1))$. on inputs the master public key mpk, the user secret key sk_id, and the ciphertext ct, do:
1. compute $\mathbf{C}_G = \mathsf{PubEval}_G(\left\{ \{\mathbf{C}_{\boldsymbol{\alpha}_{i,i'}}\}_{i\in[t],i'\in[\eta]}, \mathbf{C}_{\widetilde{\beta}} \right\}, G_\mathsf{id}) \in \mathcal{R}_q^{2\times 2k}$.
2. compute $F(\mathsf{id}) = \mathsf{Eval}^\mathsf{Pub}(\mathbf{C}_G, \mathbf{c}_s) \in \mathcal{R}_q^k$.
3. compute $w = [\mathbf{b}^\top | \widehat{\mathbf{c}}^\top + F(\mathsf{id})^\top] \cdot \mathbf{x} - d^{-1}u$.

4. output $m = \lfloor \frac{2}{q} \cdot \phi(c_0 - \mathbf{c}_1^\top \cdot [\begin{smallmatrix} -w \\ \mathbf{x} \end{smallmatrix}]) \rceil \bmod 2$, where the rounding function $\lfloor \cdot \rceil$ is applied component-wise.

Remark 1. In the KeyGen step, we use our new algorithm SampleLeft$_{\text{hybrid}}$ to sample $(w, \mathbf{x})$ (which are (D_r, D_σ)-hybrid outputs where $r \gg \sigma$). To shrink the size of the secret key, we only take $\mathbf{x}$ (i.e., D_σ part) as the user's secret key. Note that w can be deterministically computed from $\mathbf{x}, \mathsf{mpk}$ and id, i.e., steps 1–3 of the decryption algorithm. This means that during the key query phase of the IBE security game, an adversary is able to compute w itself after obtaining $\mathbf{x}$ from the challenger.

Lemma 10 (Correctness). *For any positive number w, if $q \geq 5w(\sigma_0 + r\sigma_0\sqrt{n} + \sigma_1\sigma\sqrt{2nk})$, then the above IBE scheme has a decryption error at most $6e^{-\pi w^2} + 2^{-2nk} + 2^{-n}$.*

Proof. For the Dec algorithm, we show that the error term in decryption would not exceed $q/5$. Specifically, the decryption algorithm calculates

$$c_0 - \mathbf{c}_1^\top \cdot \begin{bmatrix} -w \\ \mathbf{x} \end{bmatrix} = u \cdot v + e_0 + \lceil \frac{q}{2} \rceil \cdot \mu - (d \cdot [1|\mathbf{b}^\top|\hat{\mathbf{c}}^\top + F(\text{id})^\top] \cdot v + [e_1|e_2^\top]) \cdot \begin{bmatrix} -w \\ \mathbf{x} \end{bmatrix}$$

$$= \lceil \frac{q}{2} \rceil \cdot \mu + \underbrace{(e_0 + w \cdot e_1 - e_2^\top \cdot \mathbf{x})}_{\text{error term}}.$$

Then, the following inequalities hold[13]:

- by [22, Lemma 20] and $e_0 \sim D_{\mathcal{R},\sigma_0}$, we have $\Pr[|\phi(e_0)_j| \geq t_1] \leq 2e^{-\pi \frac{t_1^2}{\sigma_0^2}}$.
- by Theorem 4, we have $\mathbf{x} \sim D_{\mathcal{R}^{2k},\sigma}$[14], $w \sim D_{\mathcal{R},r}$.

- by Corollary 1 and $w \sim D_{\mathcal{R},r}$, we have $\Pr[|\phi(w \cdot e_1)_j| \geq t_2] \leq 2e^{-\pi \frac{t_2^2}{\|e_1\|^2 r^2}}$.
- by Lemma 2 and $e_1 \sim D_{\mathcal{R},\sigma_0}$, $\Pr[\|e_1\| \geq \sigma_0\sqrt{n}] \leq 2^{-n}$.

- by Corollary 1 and $\mathbf{e}_2 \sim D_{\mathcal{R}^{2k},\sigma_1}$, we have $\Pr[|\phi(e_2^\top \cdot \mathbf{x})_j| \geq t_3] \leq 2e^{-\pi \cdot \frac{t_3^2}{\|\mathbf{x}\|^2 \sigma_1^2}}$.
- by Lemma 2 and $\mathbf{x} \sim D_{\mathcal{R}^{2k},\sigma}$, we have $\Pr[\|\mathbf{x}\| \geq \sigma\sqrt{2nk}] \leq 2^{-2nk}$.

Taking $t_1 = w\sigma_0$, $t_2 = wr\sigma_0\sqrt{n}$, $t_3 = w\sigma_1\sigma\sqrt{2nk}$, by union bound, we have

$$\Pr[|\phi(e_0 + w \cdot e_1 - e_2^\top \cdot \mathbf{x})_j| \geq t_1 + t_2 + t_3] \leq 6e^{-\pi w^2} + 2^{-2nk} + 2^{-n}.$$

Therefore, if $w(\sigma_0 + r\sigma_0\sqrt{n} + \sigma_1\sigma\sqrt{2nk}) \leq q/5$, then the decryption error occurs with probability at most $6e^{-\pi w^2} + 2^{-2nk} + 2^{-n}$. □

---

[13] In this correctness analysis, we use multiple lemmas and theorems without explicitly specifying the parameters. We note that all the requirements of these lemmas and theorems are met for the parameters in Sect. 5.3.

[14] Actually, Theorem 4 guarantees that $\mathbf{x}$ is statistically close to $D_{\mathcal{R}^{2k},\sigma}$. Since the statistical distance is negligible, we omit the statistical distance and do the correctness analysis without it.

5.2 Security Proof

In this section, we analyze the security of our IBE scheme. Due to space limitations, we put the proofs of all the lemmas involved in Theorem 7 (Lemmas 11 to 14 and 16 to 18) in the full version [22, Appendix D], except for Lemma 15, because the proof of Lemma 15 shows how we run the re-randomization algorithm to simulate a partial ciphertext.

Theorem 7. *The above IBE scheme is adaptively-anonymous security assuming the assumptions* $\mathsf{RLWE}_{n,2k,q,D_{\mathcal{R},\sigma_0'}}$ *and* $\mathsf{RLWE}_{n,k+2,q,D_{\mathcal{R},\sigma_0}}$ *hold.*

Proof. Let $\mathcal{A}$ be a PPT adversary that breaks the adaptive security of the IBE scheme. Let $\epsilon = \epsilon(\lambda)$ and $Q = Q(\lambda)$ be its advantage and the number of the key queries. In each game, a value $\mathsf{coin}' \in \{0,1\}$ is defined. While it is set $\mathsf{coin}' = \widehat{\mathsf{coin}}$ in the first game, these values might be different in the later games. In the following, we define E_i to be the event that $\mathsf{coin}' = \mathsf{coin}$.

Game 0. This is the real security game. Recall that since the ciphertext space is $\mathcal{C} = \mathcal{R}_q \times \mathcal{R}_q^{2k+1}$, in the challenge phase, the challenge ciphertext is set as $\mathsf{ct}^* = (c_0, \mathbf{c}_1^*) \xleftarrow{\$} \mathcal{R}_q \times \mathcal{R}_q^{2k+1}$ if $\mathsf{coin} = 1$. At the end of the game, $\mathcal{A}$ outputs a guess $\widehat{\mathsf{coin}}$ for coin. Finally, the challenger sets $\mathsf{coin}' = \widehat{\mathsf{coin}}$. By definition, we have $\left|\Pr[E_0] - \frac{1}{2}\right| = \left|\Pr[\mathsf{coin}' = \mathsf{coin}] - \frac{1}{2}\right| = \left|\Pr[\widehat{\mathsf{coin}} = \mathsf{coin}] - \frac{1}{2}\right| = \epsilon$.

Game 1. In this game, the challenger performs an additional abort check at the end of the game. First, the challenger chooses a random partitioning function $H \xleftarrow{\$} \mathcal{H}^{\mathcal{R},t,t'}$ as Definition 8, where $t' = \lceil \log_c \frac{3Q}{\epsilon} \rceil$[15]. Specifically, the challenger picks random vectors $\boldsymbol{\alpha}' \in [L+1]^{t'}$, $\boldsymbol{\beta}' \in \mathbb{Z}_p^{t'}$, denotes $\boldsymbol{\alpha} = (\boldsymbol{\alpha}', \mathbf{0}) \in [L+1]^t$, $\boldsymbol{\beta} = (\boldsymbol{\beta}', \mathbf{0}) \in \mathbb{Z}_p^t$, and sets and keeps the partition function:

$$H(\mathsf{id}) := G_{\mathsf{id}}(\boldsymbol{\alpha}, \boldsymbol{\beta}) = H_{\boldsymbol{\alpha}, \boldsymbol{\beta}}^{\mathcal{R},t}(\mathsf{id}) = \sum_{i \in [t]} \left(x^{ip + \mathsf{ECC}(\mathsf{id})[\alpha_i]} - x^{ip + \beta_i} \right).$$

Then, the challenger checks whether the following condition holds:

$$H(\mathsf{id}^*) = 0 \quad \wedge \quad H(\mathsf{id}^{(1)}) = \cdots H(\mathsf{id}^{(Q)}) = 1,$$

where id^* is the challenge identity, $\mathsf{id}^{(1)}, \cdots, \mathsf{id}^{(Q)}$ are identities for which $\mathcal{A}$ has made key extraction queries. If it does not hold, the challenger ignores the output $\widehat{\mathsf{coin}}$ of $\mathcal{A}$, and sets $\mathsf{coin}' \xleftarrow{\$} \{0,1\}$. If it holds, the challenger sets $\mathsf{coin}' = \widehat{\mathsf{coin}}$.

Lemma 11. $\left|\Pr[E_1] - \frac{1}{2}\right| \geq \frac{2}{3} \cdot \frac{1}{p^{t'}} \cdot \epsilon.$

Game 2. In this game, we change the way $\left\{\{\mathbf{C}_{\alpha_{i,i'}}\}_{i \in [t], i' \in [\eta]}, \mathbf{C}_{\tilde{\beta}}\right\}$ are chosen.

---

[15] $c := \frac{1}{1-\Upsilon}$ where Υ is the relative distance of the error correcting code ECC.

- in Game 1, $\mathbf{C}_{\boldsymbol{\alpha}_{i,i'}} \leftarrow \mathsf{GSW.Enc}(\mathsf{ek}, 0)$, $\mathbf{C}_{\widetilde{\beta}} \leftarrow \mathsf{GSW.Enc}(\mathsf{ek}, 0)$.
- in Game 2, the challenger first picks $\boldsymbol{\alpha} \in [L+1]^t, \boldsymbol{\beta} \in \mathbb{Z}_p^t$ as Game 1, and generates $\mathbf{C}_{\boldsymbol{\alpha}_{i,i'}} \leftarrow \mathsf{GSW.Enc}(\mathsf{ek}, x^{\alpha_{i,i'}})$, $\mathbf{C}_{\widetilde{\beta}} \leftarrow \mathsf{GSW.Enc}(\mathsf{ek}, \sum_{i \in [t]} x^{ip+\beta_i})$ with randomness $\mathbf{R}_{\boldsymbol{\alpha}_{i,i'}}, \mathbf{R}_{\widetilde{\beta}}$, respectively.

Lemma 12. *By the* $\mathsf{RLWE}_{n,2k,q,D_{\mathcal{R},\sigma'_0}}$ *assumption (Definition 2) and the regularity lemma (Lemma 4), we have* $|\Pr[E_1] - \Pr[E_2]| = \mathsf{negl}(n)$.

Game 3. In this game, we change the way $\widehat{\mathbf{c}}, \mathbf{c}_s$ are chosen.
- in Game 2, $\widehat{\mathbf{c}}, \mathbf{c}_s \xleftarrow{\$} \mathcal{R}_q^k$.
- in Game 3, the challenger chooses $\mathbf{R}_0, \mathbf{R}_s \xleftarrow{\$} [-\rho, \rho]_{\mathcal{R}}^{k \times k}$, and sets $\widehat{\mathbf{c}} = \mathbf{b}^\top \mathbf{R}_0$, $\mathbf{c}_s = \mathbf{b}^\top \mathbf{R}_s + s \cdot \mathbf{g}^\top$.

Lemma 13. *By the* $\mathsf{TrapGen}$ *algorithm (Lemma 6), and the regularity lemma (Lemma 4), we have* $|\Pr[E_2] - \Pr[E_3]| = \mathsf{negl}(n)$.

Note. Before entering the next game, we first define the matrix $\mathbf{R}_G \in \mathcal{R}^{2k \times 2k}$ for an identity $\mathsf{id} \in \mathcal{ID}$ as

$$\mathbf{R}_G = \mathsf{TrapEval}_G \left(\mathbf{A}, \left\{ \{\mathbf{R}_{\boldsymbol{\alpha}_{i,i'}}\}, \mathbf{R}_{\widetilde{\beta}} \right\}, (\boldsymbol{\alpha}, \boldsymbol{\beta}), G_{\mathsf{id}} \right) \in \mathcal{R}^{2k \times 2k}.$$

By Theorem 2 and Construction 3 in the full version [22, Appendix B.4],

$$\mathbf{C}_G = \mathsf{PubEval}_G \left(\left\{ \{\mathbf{C}_{\boldsymbol{\alpha}_{i,i'}}\}, \mathbf{C}_{\widetilde{\beta}} \right\}, G_{\mathsf{id}} \right) = \mathbf{A}\mathbf{R}_G + G_{\mathsf{id}}(\boldsymbol{\alpha}, \boldsymbol{\beta}) \cdot \mathbf{G} \in \mathcal{R}_q^{2 \times 2k}.$$

Then, we define the matrix $\mathbf{R}_{\mathsf{id}} \in \mathcal{R}^{k \times k}$ and the vector $\mathbf{e}_{\mathsf{id}} \in \mathcal{R}^k$ as

$$\mathbf{R}_{\mathsf{id}} = \mathsf{Eval}^{\mathsf{Trap}}(\mathbf{R}_s, \mathbf{C}_G) \in \mathcal{R}^{k \times k}, \quad \mathbf{e}_{\mathsf{id}} = \mathsf{Eval}^{\mathsf{Error}}(\mathbf{e}, \mathbf{R}_G) \in \mathcal{R}^k.$$

By Construction 1 and Theorem 3, we have

$$F(\mathsf{id}) = \mathsf{Eval}^{\mathsf{Pub}}(\mathbf{C}_G, \mathbf{c}_s) = \mathbf{b}^\top \mathbf{R}_{\mathsf{id}} + G_{\mathsf{id}}(\boldsymbol{\alpha}, \boldsymbol{\beta}) \cdot \mathbf{g}^\top + \mathbf{e}_{\mathsf{id}}^\top \in \mathcal{R}_q^k.$$

Game 4. In this game, we change the way to generate the public vector $\mathbf{b}$ and to respond to the secret key queries.
- in Game 3, the challenger generates $(\mathbf{b}, \mathbf{T_b}) \leftarrow \mathsf{TrapGen}(pp)$, and answers each of the secret key queries using this trapdoor $\mathbf{T_b}$, i.e., $(w, \mathbf{x}) \leftarrow \mathsf{SampleLeft}_{\mathsf{hybrid}}(\mathbf{b}, \widehat{\mathbf{c}} + F(\mathsf{id}), \mathbf{T_b}, u, \sigma, r)$.
- in Game 4, $\mathcal{C}$ samples $\mathbf{b} \xleftarrow{\$} \mathcal{R}_q^k$ uniformly at random instead of running TrapGen algorithm, and answers each of the secret key queries using the newly defined trapdoors $\mathbf{R}_{\mathsf{id}}, \mathbf{e}_{\mathsf{id}}$, i.e., $(w, \mathbf{x}) \leftarrow \mathsf{SampleRight}_{\mathsf{hybrid}}(\mathbf{b}, \mathbf{g}, \mathbf{e}_{\mathsf{id}}, \mathbf{T_g}, \mathbf{R}_0 + \mathbf{R}_{\mathsf{id}}, G_{\mathsf{id}}(\boldsymbol{\alpha}, \boldsymbol{\beta}), u, \sigma, s, r)$.

Lemma 14. *By the* TrapGen *algorithm (Lemma 6) and the sampling algorithms (Theorem 6), we have* $|\Pr[E_3] - \Pr[E_4]| = \mathsf{negl}(n)$.

Game 5. In this game, we change the way challenge ciphertext $\mathbf{c}_1^*$ is created when coin = 0.

- in Game 4, $\mathbf{c}_1^* = d \cdot \begin{bmatrix} 1 \\ \mathbf{b} \\ F(\mathsf{id}^*) \end{bmatrix} \cdot v + \begin{bmatrix} e_1 \\ \mathbf{e}_2 \end{bmatrix}$ for $e_1 \leftarrow D_{\mathcal{R},\sigma_0}$ and $\mathbf{e}_2 \leftarrow D_{\mathcal{R}^{2k},\sigma_1}$.

- in Game 5, the challenger samples $\mathbf{y} = d \cdot \begin{bmatrix} \mathbf{b} \\ 1 \end{bmatrix} \cdot v + \mathbf{e}_0'$ for $\mathbf{e}_0' \leftarrow D_{\mathcal{R}^{k+1},\sigma_0}$, calls the last element of the vector $\mathbf{y}$ as $\bar{y}$, and constructs $\mathbf{c}_1^* = \begin{bmatrix} \bar{y} \\ \bar{\mathbf{c}}_1^* \end{bmatrix}$, where $\bar{\mathbf{c}}_1^* = \mathsf{ReRand}\left(\begin{bmatrix} \mathbf{I}_k & \mathbf{R}_0 + \mathbf{R}_{\mathsf{id}^*} \\ \mathbf{0}^\top & \mathbf{e}_{\mathsf{id}^*}^\top \end{bmatrix}, \mathbf{y}, \sigma_0, \frac{\sigma_1}{2\sigma_0} \right)$.

Lemma 15. *By Lemma 3, we have* $|\Pr[E_4] - \Pr[E_5]| = \mathsf{negl}(n)$.

Proof. In Game 4, we use the fact that when $\mathsf{id} = \mathsf{id}^*$, $G_{\mathsf{id}}(\boldsymbol{\alpha},\boldsymbol{\beta}) = 0$, i.e., $F(\mathsf{id}^*)^\top = \mathbf{b}^\top(\mathbf{R}_0 + \mathbf{R}_{\mathsf{id}^*}) + \mathbf{e}_{\mathsf{id}^*}^\top$, then $\mathbf{c}_1^*$ can be re-written as

$$\mathbf{c}_1^* = d \cdot \begin{bmatrix} 1 \\ \mathbf{b} \\ F(\mathsf{id}^*) \end{bmatrix} \cdot v + \begin{bmatrix} e_1 \\ \mathbf{e}_2 \end{bmatrix} = \begin{bmatrix} d \cdot v + e_1 \\ d \cdot \begin{bmatrix} \mathbf{b} \\ F(\mathsf{id}^*) \end{bmatrix} \cdot v + \mathbf{e}_2 \end{bmatrix}. \tag{15}$$

In Game 5, by the re-randomization algorithm ReRand, we have $(\bar{\mathbf{c}}_1^*)^\top = d \cdot [\mathbf{b}^\top|1] \cdot \begin{bmatrix} \mathbf{I}_k & \mathbf{R}_0 + \mathbf{R}_{\mathsf{id}^*} \\ \mathbf{0}^\top & \mathbf{e}_{\mathsf{id}^*}^\top \end{bmatrix} \cdot v + (\mathbf{e}_2')^\top = d \cdot [\mathbf{b}^\top|\mathbf{b}^\top(\mathbf{R}_0 + \mathbf{R}_{\mathsf{id}^*}) + \mathbf{e}_{\mathsf{id}^*}^\top] \cdot v + (\mathbf{e}_2')^\top = d \cdot [\mathbf{b}^\top|F(\mathsf{id}^*)^\top] \cdot v + (\mathbf{e}_2')^\top$ where the distribution of $\mathbf{e}_2'$ is statistically close to the discrete Gaussian distribution $D_{\mathcal{R}^{2k},\sigma_1}$. By the construction of $\mathbf{c}_1^*$ in Game 5, we have

$$\mathbf{c}_1^* = \begin{bmatrix} \bar{y} \\ \bar{\mathbf{c}}_1^* \end{bmatrix} = \begin{bmatrix} d \cdot v + e_1' \\ d \cdot \begin{bmatrix} \mathbf{b} \\ F(\mathsf{id}^*) \end{bmatrix} \cdot v + \mathbf{e}_2' \end{bmatrix}, \tag{16}$$

where e_1' is the last element of $\mathbf{e}_0'$, i.e., $e_1' \leftarrow D_{\mathcal{R},\sigma_0}$. Comparing Eq. (15) and Eq. (16), Game 4 and Game 5 are statistically indistinguishable.

Game 6. In this game, we further change the way challenge ciphertext $(c_0^*, \mathbf{c}_1^*)$ is created when coin = 0.

- in Game 5, the challenger picks $\mathbf{y} = d \cdot \begin{bmatrix} \mathbf{b} \\ 1 \end{bmatrix} \cdot v + \mathbf{e}_0'$ and sets $c_0^* = u \cdot v + e_0 + \lceil \frac{q}{2} \rceil \cdot \mu$, $\mathbf{c}_1^* = \begin{bmatrix} \bar{y} \\ \bar{\mathbf{c}}_1^* \end{bmatrix}$, where $\bar{\mathbf{c}}_1^* = \mathsf{ReRand}\left(\begin{bmatrix} \mathbf{I}_k & \mathbf{R}_0 + \mathbf{R}_{\mathsf{id}^*} \\ \mathbf{0}^\top & \mathbf{e}_{\mathsf{id}^*}^\top \end{bmatrix}, \mathbf{y}, \sigma_0, \frac{\sigma_1}{2\sigma_0} \right)$.

- in Game 6, the challenger picks $y_0' \xleftarrow{\$} \mathcal{R}_q$, $\mathbf{y}' \xleftarrow{\$} \mathcal{R}_q^{k+1}$, $c_0^* = y_0' + e_0 + \lceil \frac{q}{2} \rceil \cdot \mu$, $\mathbf{c}_1^* = \begin{bmatrix} \bar{y} \\ \bar{\mathbf{c}}_1^* \end{bmatrix}$, where $\bar{\mathbf{c}}_1^* = \mathsf{ReRand}\left(\begin{bmatrix} \mathbf{I}_k & \mathbf{R}_0 + \mathbf{R}_{\mathsf{id}^*} \\ \mathbf{0}^\top & \mathbf{e}_{\mathsf{id}^*}^\top \end{bmatrix}, \mathbf{y}' + \mathbf{e}_0', \sigma_0, \frac{\sigma_1}{2\sigma_0} \right)$.

Lemma 16. *By the* $\mathsf{RLWE}_{n,k+2,q,D_{\mathcal{R}.\sigma_0}}$ *assumption (Definition 2), then we have that* $|\Pr[E_5] - \Pr[E_6]| = \mathsf{negl}(n)$.

Game 7. In this game, we further change the way challenge ciphertext $\mathbf{c}_1^*$ is created when coin = 0. Specifically, the challenger picks $\mathbf{y}_1 \xleftarrow{\$} \mathcal{R}_q^k$, $y_2 \xleftarrow{\$} \mathcal{R}_q$, $\mathbf{e}_2' \leftarrow D_{\mathcal{R}^{2k},\sigma_1}$, and sets $\bar{\mathbf{c}}_1^* = [\mathbf{y}_1^\top|\mathbf{y}_1^\top(\mathbf{R}_0 + \mathbf{R}_{\mathsf{id}^*}) + y_2 \cdot \mathbf{e}_{\mathsf{id}^*}^\top] + (\mathbf{e}_2')^\top$.

Lemma 17. *By Lemma 3, we have* $|\Pr[E_6] - \Pr[E_7]| = \mathsf{negl}(n)$.

Game 8. In this game, we change the challenge ciphertext to be a random vector, regardless of whether $\mathsf{coin} = 0$ or 1. It is obvious that $\Pr[E_8] = \frac{1}{2}$.

Lemma 18. *By Lemma 4, we have* $|\Pr[E_7] - \Pr[E_8]| = \mathsf{negl}(n)$.

Analysis. Combining Lemmas 11 to 18, we have

$$
\left| \Pr[E_8] - \frac{1}{2} \right| = \left| \Pr[E_1] - \frac{1}{2} + \sum_{i=1}^{7} (\Pr[E_{i+1}] - \Pr[E_i]) \right|
$$

$$
\geq \left| \Pr[E_1] - \frac{1}{2} \right| - \sum_{i=1}^{7} |\Pr[E_{i+1}] - \Pr[E_i]| \geq \frac{2}{3} \cdot \frac{1}{p^{t'}} \cdot \epsilon - \mathsf{negl}(\lambda).
$$

Table 2. Asymptotic and concrete parameters of our IBE scheme[*].

Definition	Params	(Set I) $b = 2, \rho = 1$		(Set II) $b = \rho = n^{\nu}$[♮]	
		Asymptotic	**Concrete**	**Asymptotic**	**Concrete**
security parameter	λ		λ		λ
identity length	l	$O(\lambda)$	$\leq 4\lambda$	$O(\lambda)$	$\leq 4\lambda$
bound on the number of key queries	Q	$\mathsf{poly}(\lambda)$	Q	$\mathsf{poly}(\lambda)$	Q
ring dimension	n	$\Theta(\lambda)$	n	$\Theta(\lambda)$	n
length of the gadget vector	k	$O(\log(\lambda))$	$2\log q$	$O(1)$	$2\log_b q$
repetition number in partition function	t	$\omega(1)$	$\log_c(3Q)$[‡]	$\omega(1)$	$\log_c(3Q)$
small positive real regarding smoothing parameter	ϵ	$\lambda^{-\omega(1)}$	$2^{-3\lambda}$	$\lambda^{-\omega(1)}$	$2^{-3\lambda}$
ECC parameters[*]	L	$O(\lambda^{1+\frac{2}{\kappa}})$[†]	$\frac{(\sqrt[\kappa]{n})^2 l}{\log(\lambda)}$	$O(\lambda^{1+\frac{2}{\kappa}})$	$\frac{(\sqrt[\kappa]{n})^2 l}{\log(\lambda)}$
	p	$O(\lambda^{\frac{1}{\kappa}})$	$n^{\frac{1}{\kappa}}$	$O(\lambda^{\frac{1}{\kappa}})$	$n^{\frac{1}{\kappa}}$
	Υ	$1 - O(\lambda^{-\frac{1}{\kappa}})$	$1 - \frac{\kappa+3}{\sqrt[\kappa]{n}}$	$1 - O(\lambda^{-\frac{1}{\kappa}})$	$1 - \frac{\kappa+3}{\sqrt[\kappa]{n}}$
Gaussian parameter of $\mathbf{e}$ in GSW public matrix $\mathbf{A}$	σ_0'	$O(\lambda^{1.5})$	σ_0'	$O(\lambda^{1.5})$	σ_0'
Gaussian parameter of e_0, e_1 in IBE ciphertext c_0, c_1	σ_0	$O(\lambda^{1.5})$	σ_0	$O(\lambda^{1.5})$	σ_0
Gaussian parameter of $\mathbf{x}$ in sampling algorithms	σ	$O(\lambda^{1.5})$	$n^{2.5}$	$O(\lambda^{1.5}b^2)$	$n^{2.5}b^2$
Gaussian parameter of w in sampling algorithms	r	$O(\lambda^{6+\frac{2}{\kappa}})$	$n^{7.5+\frac{2}{\kappa}}\lambda$	$O(\lambda^{6+\frac{2}{\kappa}}b^4)$	$n^{7.5+\frac{2}{\kappa}}\lambda b^4$
Gaussian parameter of e_2 in IBE ciphertext c_1	σ_1	$O(\lambda^{6+\frac{2}{\kappa}})$	$n^{5.5+\frac{2}{\kappa}} \cdot \sigma_0$	$O(\lambda^{6+\frac{2}{\kappa}}b^4)$	$n^{5.5+\frac{2}{\kappa}}b^4 \cdot \sigma_0$
system modulus	q	$O(\lambda^{8+\frac{2}{\kappa}})$	$n^{9.5+\frac{2}{\kappa}} \cdot \sigma_0$	$O(\lambda^{8+\frac{2}{\kappa}}b^6)$	$n^{9.5+\frac{2}{\kappa}}b^6 \cdot \sigma_0$

⋆ we note that we present the parameters in the *plain model* here. As said in the full version [22, Appendix E], we can simply calculate the corresponding parameters in the *CRS model*, only the parameters r, σ_1, q would be changed.

∗ we set the parameter in error correcting code L, p, Υ refer to ALWW-IBE [1].

† $\kappa > 1$ can be any constant that satisfies $n^{\frac{1}{\kappa}} > 3 + \kappa$, depending on how we set parameters of the error correcting code.

‡ $c > 1$ is a parameter defined by the relative distance as $c := \frac{1}{1-\Upsilon}$.

♮ $\nu > 0$ is any positive real.

Since ϵ is noticeable and Q is polynomially bounded, the value $p^{t'}$ is polynomially bounded, and thus $\left|\Pr[E_8] - \frac{1}{2}\right|$ is noticeable, which is contradicts to the fact that $\Pr[E_8] = \frac{1}{2}$. This completes the proof. $\square$

5.3   Asymptotic and Concrete Parameters

Due to space limit, we present the constraints on our IBE scheme's parameters in the full version [22, Appendix E]. In this section, we present two possible sets of the parameters for our IBE construction in Table 2, concretely and asymptotically.

Acknowledgments. We thank the anonymous reviewers of PKC 2025 for their insightful comments and constructive suggestions. This work was supported by National Natural Science Foundation of China (Grant No. 62202305), Young Elite Scientists Sponsorship Program by China Association for Science and Technology (YESS20220150), National Cryptologic Science Fund of China (No. 2025NCSF02036), and supported by the European Research Council (ERC) under the European Union's Horizon 2020 research and innovation programme, grant agreement 802823.

References

1. Abla, P., Liu, F.-H., Wang, H., Wang, Z.: Ring-based identity based encryption – asymptotically shorter MPK and tighter security. In: Nissim, K., Waters, B. (eds.) TCC 2021. LNCS, vol. 13044, pp. 157–187. Springer, Cham (2021). https://doi.org/10.1007/978-3-030-90456-2_6

2. Agrawal, S., Boneh, D., Boyen, X.: Efficient lattice (H)IBE in the standard model. In: Gilbert, H. (ed.) EUROCRYPT 2010. LNCS, vol. 6110, pp. 553–572. Springer, Heidelberg (2010). https://doi.org/10.1007/978-3-642-13190-5_28

3. Barrington, D.A.M.: Bounded-width polynomial-size branching programs recognize exactly those languages in NC^1. J. Comput. Syst. Sci. **38**(1), 150–164 (1989). https://doi.org/10.1016/0022-0000(89)90037-8

4. Bellare, M., Ristenpart, T.: Simulation without the artificial abort: simplified proof and improved concrete security for waters' IBE scheme. In: Joux, A. (ed.) EUROCRYPT 2009. LNCS, vol. 5479, pp. 407–424. Springer, Heidelberg (2009). https://doi.org/10.1007/978-3-642-01001-9_24

5. Boneh, D., Boyen, X.: Efficient selective-ID secure identity-based encryption without random oracles. In: Cachin, C., Camenisch, J.L. (eds.) EUROCRYPT 2004. LNCS, vol. 3027, pp. 223–238. Springer, Heidelberg (2004). https://doi.org/10.1007/978-3-540-24676-3_14

6. Boneh, D., Boyen, X.: Secure identity based encryption without random oracles. In: Franklin, M. (ed.) CRYPTO 2004. LNCS, vol. 3152, pp. 443–459. Springer, Heidelberg (2004). https://doi.org/10.1007/978-3-540-28628-8_27

7. Boneh, D., Franklin, M.: Identity-based encryption from the weil pairing. In: Kilian, J. (ed.) CRYPTO 2001. LNCS, vol. 2139, pp. 213–229. Springer, Heidelberg (2001). https://doi.org/10.1007/3-540-44647-8_13

8. Boneh, D., et al.: Fully key-homomorphic encryption, arithmetic circuit ABE and compact garbled circuits. In: Nguyen, P.Q., Oswald, E. (eds.) EUROCRYPT 2014. LNCS, vol. 8441, pp. 533–556. Springer, Heidelberg (2014). https://doi.org/10.1007/978-3-642-55220-5_30

9. Boneh, D., Gentry, C., Hamburg, M.: Space-efficient identity based encryption without pairings. In: FOCS 2007, pp. 647–657. IEEE Computer Society (2007). https://doi.org/10.1109/FOCS.2007.64

10. Boyen, X.: Lattice mixing and vanishing trapdoors: a framework for fully secure short signatures and more. In: Nguyen, P.Q., Pointcheval, D. (eds.) PKC 2010. LNCS, vol. 6056, pp. 499–517. Springer, Heidelberg (2010). https://doi.org/10.1007/978-3-642-13013-7_29

11. Boyen, X., Li, Q.: Towards tightly secure lattice short signature and id-based encryption. In: Cheon, J.H., Takagi, T. (eds.) ASIACRYPT 2016. LNCS, vol. 10032, pp. 404–434. Springer, Heidelberg (2016). https://doi.org/10.1007/978-3-662-53890-6_14

12. Brakerski, Z., Lombardi, A., Segev, G., Vaikuntanathan, V.: Anonymous IBE, leakage resilience and circular security from new assumptions. In: Nielsen, J.B., Rijmen, V. (eds.) EUROCRYPT 2018. LNCS, vol. 10820, pp. 535–564. Springer, Cham (2018). https://doi.org/10.1007/978-3-319-78381-9_20

13. Cash, D., Hofheinz, D., Kiltz, E., Peikert, C.: Bonsai trees, or how to delegate a lattice basis. In: Gilbert, H. (ed.) EUROCRYPT 2010. LNCS, vol. 6110, pp. 523–552. Springer, Heidelberg (2010). https://doi.org/10.1007/978-3-642-13190-5_27

14. Cocks, C.: An identity based encryption scheme based on quadratic residues. In: Honary, B. (ed.) Cryptography and Coding 2001. LNCS, vol. 2260, pp. 360–363. Springer, Heidelberg (2001). https://doi.org/10.1007/3-540-45325-3_32

15. Döttling, N., Garg, S.: From selective IBE to full IBE and selective HIBE. In: Kalai, Y., Reyzin, L. (eds.) TCC 2017. LNCS, vol. 10677, pp. 372–408. Springer, Cham (2017). https://doi.org/10.1007/978-3-319-70500-2_13

16. Ducas, L., Lyubashevsky, V., Prest, T.: Efficient identity-based encryption over NTRU lattices. In: Sarkar, P., Iwata, T. (eds.) ASIACRYPT 2014. LNCS, vol. 8874, pp. 22–41. Springer, Heidelberg (2014). https://doi.org/10.1007/978-3-662-45608-8_2

17. Genise, N., Micciancio, D., Peikert, C., Walter, M.: Improved discrete gaussian and subgaussian analysis for lattice cryptography. In: Kiayias, A., Kohlweiss, M., Wallden, P., Zikas, V. (eds.) PKC 2020. LNCS, vol. 12110, pp. 623–651. Springer, Cham (2020). https://doi.org/10.1007/978-3-030-45374-9_21

18. Gentry, C.: Practical identity-based encryption without random oracles. In: Vaudenay, S. (ed.) EUROCRYPT 2006. LNCS, vol. 4004, pp. 445–464. Springer, Heidelberg (2006). https://doi.org/10.1007/11761679_27

19. Gentry, C., Peikert, C., Vaikuntanathan, V.: Trapdoors for hard lattices and new cryptographic constructions. In: Dwork, C. (ed.) STOC 2008, pp. 197–206. ACM (2008). https://doi.org/10.1145/1374376.1374407

20. Gentry, C., Sahai, A., Waters, B.: Homomorphic encryption from learning with errors: conceptually-simpler, asymptotically-faster, attribute-based. In: Canetti, R., Garay, J.A. (eds.) CRYPTO 2013. LNCS, vol. 8042, pp. 75–92. Springer, Heidelberg (2013). https://doi.org/10.1007/978-3-642-40041-4_5

21. Ji, W., Wang, Z., Jin, H., Wang, Q., Wang, G., Gu, D.: Identity-based encryption from lattices with more compactness in the standard model. Cryptology ePrint Archive, Paper 2024/1295 (2024). https://eprint.iacr.org/2024/1295

22. Ji, W., Wang, Z., Lyu, L., Gu, D.: Adaptively secure IBE from lattices with asymptotically better efficiency. Cryptology ePrint Archive, Paper 2025/253 (2025). https://eprint.iacr.org/2025/253

23. Katsumata, S.: On the untapped potential of encoding predicates by arithmetic circuits and their applications. In: Takagi, T., Peyrin, T. (eds.) ASIACRYPT 2017. LNCS, vol. 10626, pp. 95–125. Springer, Cham (2017). https://doi.org/10.1007/978-3-319-70700-6_4

24. Katsumata, S., Yamada, S.: Partitioning via non-linear polynomial functions: more compact IBEs from ideal lattices and bilinear maps. In: Cheon, J.H., Takagi, T. (eds.) ASIACRYPT 2016. LNCS, vol. 10032, pp. 682–712. Springer, Heidelberg (2016). https://doi.org/10.1007/978-3-662-53890-6_23

25. Katz, J., Wang, N.: Efficiency improvements for signature schemes with tight security reductions. In: Jajodia, S., Atluri, V., Jaeger, T. (eds.) CCS 2003, pp. 155–164. ACM (2003). https://doi.org/10.1145/948109.948132

26. Lai, Q., Liu, F.-H., Wang, Z.: Almost tight security in lattices with polynomial moduli – PRF, IBE, all-but-many LTF, and more. In: Kiayias, A., Kohlweiss, M., Wallden, P., Zikas, V. (eds.) PKC 2020. LNCS, vol. 12110, pp. 652–681. Springer, Cham (2020). https://doi.org/10.1007/978-3-030-45374-9_22

27. Lyubashevsky, V., Peikert, C., Regev, O.: On ideal lattices and learning with errors over rings. In: Gilbert, H. (ed.) EUROCRYPT 2010. LNCS, vol. 6110, pp. 1–23. Springer, Heidelberg (2010). https://doi.org/10.1007/978-3-642-13190-5_1

28. Micciancio, D., Peikert, C.: Trapdoors for lattices: simpler, tighter, faster, smaller. In: Pointcheval, D., Johansson, T. (eds.) EUROCRYPT 2012. LNCS, vol. 7237, pp. 700–718. Springer, Heidelberg (2012). https://doi.org/10.1007/978-3-642-29011-4_41

29. Micciancio, D., Regev, O.: Worst-case to average-case reductions based on gaussian measures. SIAM J. Comput. **37**(1), 267–302 (2007). https://doi.org/10.1137/S0097539705447360

30. Micciancio, D., Walter, M.: On the bit security of cryptographic primitives. In: Nielsen, J.B., Rijmen, V. (eds.) EUROCRYPT 2018. LNCS, vol. 10820, pp. 3–28. Springer, Cham (2018). https://doi.org/10.1007/978-3-319-78381-9_1

31. Peikert, C.: An efficient and parallel gaussian sampler for lattices. In: Rabin, T. (ed.) CRYPTO 2010. LNCS, vol. 6223, pp. 80–97. Springer, Heidelberg (2010). https://doi.org/10.1007/978-3-642-14623-7_5

32. Regev, O.: On lattices, learning with errors, random linear codes, and cryptography. In: Gabow, H.N., Fagin, R. (eds.) STOC 2005, pp. 84–93. ACM (2005). https://doi.org/10.1145/1060590.1060603

33. Shamir, A.: Identity-based cryptosystems and signature schemes. In: Blakley, G.R., Chaum, D. (eds.) CRYPTO 1984. LNCS, vol. 196, pp. 47–53. Springer, Heidelberg (1985). https://doi.org/10.1007/3-540-39568-7_5

34. Waters, B.: Efficient identity-based encryption without random oracles. In: Cramer, R. (ed.) EUROCRYPT 2005. LNCS, vol. 3494, pp. 114–127. Springer, Heidelberg (2005). https://doi.org/10.1007/11426639_7

35. Waters, B.: Dual system encryption: realizing fully secure IBE and HIBE under simple assumptions. In: Halevi, S. (ed.) CRYPTO 2009. LNCS, vol. 5677, pp. 619–636. Springer, Heidelberg (2009). https://doi.org/10.1007/978-3-642-03356-8_36

36. Yamada, S.: Adaptively secure identity-based encryption from lattices with asymptotically shorter public parameters. In: Fischlin, M., Coron, J.-S. (eds.) EUROCRYPT 2016. LNCS, vol. 9666, pp. 32–62. Springer, Heidelberg (2016). https://doi.org/10.1007/978-3-662-49896-5_2

37. Yamada, S.: Asymptotically compact adaptively secure lattice IBEs and verifiable random functions via generalized partitioning techniques. In: Katz, J., Shacham, H. (eds.) CRYPTO 2017. LNCS, vol. 10403, pp. 161–193. Springer, Cham (2017). https://doi.org/10.1007/978-3-319-63697-9_6
38. Yu, Y., Jia, H., Wang, X.: Compact lattice gadget and its applications to hash-and-sign signatures. In: Handschuh, H., Lysyanskaya, A. (eds.) CRYPTO 2023. LNCS, vol. 14085, pp. 390–420. Springer, Cham (2023). https://doi.org/10.1007/978-3-031-38554-4_13

Adaptively-Secure Big-Key Identity-Based Encryption

Jeffrey Champion[1]($\boxtimes$), Brent Waters[1,2], and David J. Wu[1]

[1] University of Texas at Austin, Austin, TX, USA
jchampion@utexas.edu
[2] NTT Research, Sunnyvale, CA, USA

Abstract. Key-exfiltration attacks on cryptographic keys represent a significant threat to computer security. One proposed defense against such attacks is big-key cryptography which seeks to make cryptographic secrets so large that it is infeasible for an adversary to exfiltrate the key (without being detected). However, this also introduces an inconvenience to the user who must now store the large key on all of their different devices. The work of Döttling, Garg, Sekar and Wang (TCC 2022) introduces an elegant solution to this problem in the form of big-key *identity-based* encryption (IBE). Here, there is a large master secret key, but very short identity keys. The user can now store the large master secret key as her long-term key, and can provision each of her devices with short ephemeral identity keys (say, corresponding to the current date). In this way, the long-term secret key is protected by conventional big-key cryptography, while the user only needs to distribute short ephemeral keys to their different devices. Döttling et al. introduce and construct big-key IBE from standard pairing-based assumptions. However, their scheme only satisfies *selective* security where the adversary has to declare its challenge set of identities at the beginning of the security game. The more natural notion of security is *adaptive* security where the user can adaptively choose which identities it wants to challenge *after* seeing the public parameters (and part of the master secret key).

In this work, we give the first adaptively-secure construction of big-key IBE from standard cryptographic assumptions. Our first construction relies on indistinguishability obfuscation (and one-way functions), while our second construction relies on witness encryption for NP together with standard pairing-based assumptions. To prove adaptive security, we rely on the dual-system methodology.

1 Introduction

Security breaches are increasingly common today, and one of the highest-value targets in a security breach are the cryptographic keys residing on a user's system. Once an adversary successfully recovers a user's secret cryptographic key, they gain the ability to decrypt all of the user's potentially sensitive data and can even impersonate the user to other clients. This problem is further aggravated

© International Association for Cryptologic Research 2025
T. Jager and J. Pan (Eds.): PKC 2025, LNCS 15674, pp. 125–157, 2025.
https://doi.org/10.1007/978-3-031-91820-9_5

when using more advanced encryption systems such as identity-based encryption (IBE) [BF01, Coc01] where a central authority holds on to a long-term secret key. Such systems introduce a single point of failure and if the central authority's single long-term secret key is compromised, then the adversary breaks security for *all* of the users in the system.

Cryptography in the Bounded Retrieval Model. One proposal to mitigate the threat of a key-exfiltration attack is to make it difficult or infeasible for the adversary to exfiltrate the secret key. This has motivated the "bounded-storage model" and the concept of "big-key" cryptography [Dzi06, CLW06, CDD+07, ADW09, ADN+10, BKR16, MW20, DGSW22]. Here, the idea is to make the cryptographic keys sufficiently large that key exfiltration becomes infeasible to an adversary that only has a bounded amount of storage. In practice, the bounded storage might translate to an adversary being able to retrieve a bounded number of bits from a compromised system before the adversary is detected and its access removed.

A number of works have studied constructions of big-key public-key encryption in the bounded storage model [ADN+10, MW20]. In these settings, the goal is to have a large secret key (which is hard to exfiltrate) and a *short* public key. Moreover, the honest user should not incur the penalty of having to manipulate a large cryptographic key. In particular, encryption and decryption should both be fast; in the case of decryption, the idea is that the decryption algorithm only needs random access to a few *ciphertext-dependent* bits of the secret key to decrypt. The main security requirement is semantic security (for a fresh ciphertext) should hold even if the adversary gets arbitrary *bounded* leakage on the large secret key. As discussed in [DGSW22], a major disadvantage of this model is the fact that the large secret key has to replicated to each of the user's devices. This can impose significant storage burdens for each device that needs a copy of the secret key.

IBE with Incompressible Master Secret Key. Döttling, Garg, Sekar, and Wang [DGSW22] propose an elegant solution to the problem of needing to replicate the large secret key to each device owned by the user. They introduce the notion of a big-key IBE scheme where there is a long incompressible master secret key, but *short* identity keys. Recall first that in an IBE scheme, both secret keys and ciphertexts are associated with an identity id and decryption succeeds (i.e., recovers the plaintext associated with the ciphertext) if the identities associated with the ciphertext matches that of the decryption key. In the setting envisioned by [DGSW22], the long-term key would be the large master secret key for the IBE scheme. Each ciphertext in the system would be encrypted to an identity that identifies a particular time window (e.g., the current date). Users would provision each of their devices with the identity keys for the time intervals of interest. These ephemeral keys are identity keys and thus, are short. Moreover, if an identity key is compromised, it only compromises the security of messages tagged with that particular time window. In a sense, the individual identity keys in the system are viewed as short ephemeral keys while the long-term key is the *large* master secret key for the IBE scheme. Importantly, in this model, the user only needs to store one copy of the long-term master secret key; each of the user's devices would only need to store ephemeral identity keys.

The Challenge: Adaptive Security. In the same work, Döttling et al. [DGSW22] showed how to construct a big-key IBE scheme from standard assumptions on groups with bilinear maps. One limitation of their system is it only provides *selective* security. Namely, the adversary in the IBE security game must pre-declare the set of identities it wants to target at the beginning of the security game (before it sees the public key of the scheme or makes key-generation queries). This is in contrast to the more natural notion of adaptive (or full) security where the adversary can adaptively choose which identities it wants to target *after* it sees the public parameters as well as its choice of leakage on the master secret key. Their work leaves open the question of constructing a big-key IBE scheme with adaptive security.

This Work. In this work, we give two constructions of adaptively-secure big-key IBE schemes from standard assumptions. Our first construction relies on indistinguishability obfuscation [BGI+01, GGH+13] (and one-way functions) while our second construction relies on witness encryption [GGSW13] for NP in conjunction with standard pairing-based assumptions. To prove adaptive security of our scheme, we rely on a dual-system proof [Wat09, LW10]. The intricacies of carrying out this dual system proof strategy (see Sect. 1.1) is a key reason why our approach relies on considerably stronger machinery (either indistinguishability obfuscation or witness encryption) compared to the previous selectively-secure construction. Along the way, we also highlight some issues in the previous definitions and analysis of big-key IBE; we provide a more detailed discussion of these definitional issues in Sect. 3.

1.1 Technical Overview

In this section, we provide a general overview of our main constructions of adaptively-secure big-key IBE from indistinguishability obfuscation and from witness encryption.

Identity-Based Encryption. We start by recalling the syntax of a standard identity-based encryption (IBE) scheme [BF01, Coc01]:

– **Setup:** The setup algorithm in an IBE scheme generates the public parameters pp and the master secret key msk for the scheme.
– **Key generation:** The key-generation algorithm takes the master secret key msk and an identity id, and outputs a secret key $\mathsf{sk_{id}}$ for the particular identity.
– **Encryption:** The encryption algorithm takes the public parameters pp, an identity id, and a message m, and outputs a ciphertext ct.
– **Decryption:** The decryption algorithm takes a ciphertext ct (associated with an identity id and message m) together with a secret key $\mathsf{sk_{id'}}$ (associated with an identity id') and either outputs the message m if id = id' or $\perp$ if id $\neq$ id'.

The semantic security requirement for an IBE scheme states that the adversary should not be able to distinguish between an encryption of m_0 from an encryption of m_1 for any challenge identity id for which it does not have the corresponding secret key.

Big-Key IBE. In a big-key IBE scheme [DGSW22], the correctness requirement is the same as for vanilla IBE. However, the security requirement is modified to give the adversary (bounded) leakage on the master secret key:

- In the big-key security game, the adversary can specify any efficiently-computable leakage function f (with output length at most ℓ) and learn $f(\mathsf{msk})$. The output length $\ell \geq 0$ is the leakage parameter for the scheme.
- Next, instead of a single challenge identity, the adversary specifies a set of k challenge identities $\mathcal{J}$. To win, the adversary must break semantic security for *all* identities within the challenge set $\mathcal{J}$. Here, the parameter k is a function of the security parameter λ and the leakage length ℓ. In the adaptive security game, we allow the adversary to choose the set of identities $\mathcal{J}$ after it receives the public parameters, the leakage on msk, and after it makes key-generation queries on identities of its choosing (with the stipulation that the adversary does not make a key-generation query on any identity in the challenge set $\mathcal{J}$).

The adversary's task is *necessarily* harder in the big-key IBE security game compared to the vanilla IBE security game because the adversary must break semantic security of k identities rather than 1. This is inherent because the leakage function the adversary chooses can allow it to learn the secret keys for a handful of identities. The work of [DGSW22] consider the setting where $k = \ell+1$; namely, if the adversary gets ℓ bits of leakage about the master secret key, then it wins only if it breaks semantic security on at least $k = \ell + 1$ identities.

In addition, for big-key IBE, we require that the running times of the key-generation, encryption, and decryption algorithms to be efficient and run in time that is $\mathsf{poly}(\lambda, \log \ell)$. Notably, while the length of the master secret key msk can (and necessarily) must grow with the leakage parameter ℓ, the key-generation algorithm only needs to read a few bits of msk to generate an identity key.

In this work, we will focus on the simpler setting where the length of the public parameters can grow with the leakage size ℓ. However, we will still require that encryption and decryption only need to read $\mathsf{poly}(\lambda, \log \ell)$ bits of the (possibly long) public key. Döttling et al. [DGSW22] showed how to use a non-interactive secure computation (NISC) scheme to generically transform a big-key IBE scheme with large public parameters (but fast encryption and decryption) into one with short public parameters. As we show in the full version of this paper, this transformation still preserves adaptive security. Thus, for the remainder of this overview (and throughout this work), we can focus on the simpler setting of big-key IBE with long public keys.

The [DGSW22] *Approach.* We begin with a brief description of the approach from [DGSW22]. Their scheme relies on a puncturable pseudo-entropy function

(PEF). A PEF [BHK11] is a function whose outputs at certain inputs are statistically unpredictable even given leakage on the key to the PEF. The work of [DGSW22] show how to construct a PEF where the key consists of a large number of blocks $k = (k_1, \ldots, k_N)$ and moreover, the PEF supports *local* evaluation where the value of the PEF at an input x only depends on a small (and random-looking) subset of blocks of the secret key. Their construction then operates as follows:

- The master secret key consists of the PEF key $k = (k_1, \ldots, k_N)$ and the public parameters consist of commitments $\mathsf{pp} = (c_1, \ldots, c_N)$ to the blocks of the secret key.
- The secret key $\mathsf{sk_{id}}$ for an identity id consists of the evaluation of the $y = \mathsf{PEF}(k, \mathsf{id})$ together with a non-interactive zero-knowledge (NIZK) proof that y was correctly computed with respect to the committed key $\mathsf{pp} = (c_1, \ldots, c_N)$. For this to be succinct, it is critical that the PEF is locally-computable (i.e., the output of $\mathsf{PEF}(k, \mathsf{id})$ only depend on k_i for some $i \in I_{\mathsf{id}} \subset [N]$, where $|I_{\mathsf{id}}| \ll N$).
- An encryption of a message to an identity id is essentially a witness encryption[1] of the message m for the relation that essentially checks that the decrypter possesses a valid NIZK proof that $y = \mathsf{PEF}(k, \mathsf{id})$ with respect to the (subset of) committed keys c_i for $i \in I_{\mathsf{id}}$. Here, the work of [DGSW22] show that a special witness encryption scheme tailored for NIZK proofs on committed values [BL20] suffices, which can in turn be instantiated by standard pairing-based assumptions.

The proof of selective security then proceeds along the following lines:

- First, the identity keys consist of zero-knowledge proofs of openings to the commitments c_i. Thus, they hide the values of the actual bits k_i in the master secret key. The only leakage on the PEF key k is through the leakage function (applied to the master secret key $\mathsf{msk} = k$).
- Next, [DGSW22] rely on *puncturing*. Namely, they show how to puncture the PEF key at a set of identities $\mathcal{J}$ to obtain a punctured key $k_{\mathcal{J}}$. The property is that the punctured key $k_{\mathcal{J}}$ can be used to evaluate the PEF on all inputs $i \notin \mathcal{J}$ while the values on $\mathcal{J}$ retain high statistical min-entropy. The idea in the *selective* security proof is that the reduction algorithm will first puncture the PEF key on the challenge set $\mathcal{J}$. In this case, they can show that for every challenge set $\mathcal{J}$, there will exist at least one identity $\mathsf{id}^* \in \mathcal{J}$ such that the value of $y_{\mathsf{id}^*} = \mathsf{PEF}(k, \mathsf{id}^*)$ is statistically unpredictable to the adversary (even given the leakage on the PEF key). In combination with the security of the witness encryption, they can argue that such an adversary cannot have non-negligible advantage breaking semantic security with respect to id^*.

---

[1] In a witness encryption scheme [GGSW13], one can encrypt a message m to an arbitrary NP statement x. To decrypt, one provides a witness w for the statement x. If the witness is valid, then decryption recovers the message m. If the statement x is false (i.e., no witness exists), then the ciphertext computationally hides the message m.

The use of partitioning means the reduction algorithm needs to know the challenge identities ahead of time in order to program them into the scheme parameters. It is unclear how to extend this approach to the adaptive setting where the reduction algorithm does not know in advance which identities the adversary might query.

While we can envision some type of partitioning strategy [BF01, Wat05] that has been successful for arguing adaptive security in the setting of plain IBE, it is less clear how to execute such a strategy in this setting. In plain IBE, there is just a single challenge identity, so the idea in the partitioning proof is to partition the identity space into two sets S, T, with the property that the reduction algorithm is able to generate secret keys for identities id $\in S$ but not for identities id $\in T$. The hope then is that the adversary's key-generation queries fall into set S while its challenge query falls into set T. If the adversary only makes a single challenge query, the reduction can choose S, T such that with inverse polynomial probability, all of the key-generation queries land in S while the single challenge query lands in T. In the big-key setting, the challenge is that the adversary now specifies a *set* $\mathcal{J}$ of challenge identities. For the adversary to be useful, we need to set up the reduction so that an adversary that succeeds in breaking semantic security for any identity id $\in \mathcal{J}$ in the challenge set can be used to break the computational assumption. In this setting, we do not see a way to partition the identity space into sets S, T such that with good probability, all of the adversary's key-generation queries fall into S while all of the challenge queries fall into T. Thus, proving adaptive security will require a different proof technique.

Our Approach. To prove adaptive security, we take a dual-system approach [Wat09, LW10]. Implementing a dual-system proof strategy will require additional machinery and as a result, our constructions either rely on indistinguishability obfuscation or general-purpose witness encryption. We begin by describing our basic template, which is a slimmed-down version of the construction from [DGSW22], where we no longer have a PEF:

- The master secret key is a random bit-string of length $N = \mathsf{poly}(\lambda, \ell)$: $\mathsf{msk} = (r_1, \ldots, r_N)$. The public parameters are commitments to the bits of the master secret key: $\mathsf{pp} = (c_1, \ldots, c_N)$.
- A secret key $\mathsf{sk}_{\mathsf{id}}$ for an identity id is a NIZK proof of the openings to the commitments c_i for $i \in I_{\mathsf{id}}$ where the subset I_{id} is derived from a hash function $I_{\mathsf{id}} = \mathcal{H}(\mathsf{id})$ on the identity. Note that the set of indices I_{id} is substantially smaller than N.
- To encrypt to an identity id, the encrypter prepares a program that takes as input a proof π and checks whether π is a NIZK proof of openings to the commitments c_i for all $i \in I_{\mathsf{id}} = \mathcal{H}(\mathsf{id})$. If so then, the program outputs the message, and otherwise, it outputs $\perp$. Decryption just corresponds to evaluating the obfuscated program on the secret key. As we elaborate more below, the obfuscated program that checks the NIZK proof can be implemented using either indistinguishability obfuscation or using witness encryption.

Correctness follows immediately. Moreover, if the size of each set I_{id} is bounded by $\mathsf{poly}(\lambda, \log \ell)$, then the scheme also supports fast key-generation, encryption, and decryption. The high-level idea underlying security is similar to [DGSW22]. First, the identity keys consist of NIZK proofs of openings to the commitments c_i, so they hide the values of the actual bits r_i. Second, the only information the adversary gets on the master secret key then is its ℓ bits of leakage. Next, if the hash function $\mathcal{H}$ that maps identities id to indices I_{id} is "well-spread," then we can hope to argue that there is at least one identity id^* in the challenge set $\mathcal{J}$ for which the adversary does *not* know most of the bits of r_i for $i \in \mathcal{H}(id^*)$. In this case, the adversary will not be able to construct a NIZK proof that it knows the openings to c_i for $i \in \mathcal{H}(id^*)$. We can then hope to rely on security of the obfuscation scheme (or witness encryption scheme) to conclude that the message is hidden. We now show how to instantiate this basic template from indistinguishability obfuscation as well as from witness encryption in a way that allows us to prove *adaptive* security.

Big-Key IBE from iO. We first describe how to instantiate the above template using indistinguishability obfuscation in conjunction with the following primitives: (1) a plain (adaptively-secure) identity-based encryption scheme; (2) a NIZK proof system for NP; and (3) a (one-time) dual-mode bit commitment scheme [Nao89] (i.e., a commitment scheme where the common reference string can be sampled in one of two computationally indistinguishable modes: one mode is statistically binding while the other is statistically hiding). We then instantiate our template as follows:

- The master secret key $\mathsf{msk} = (r_1, \ldots, r_N)$ is a random bit string: $r_i \xleftarrow{\text{R}} \{0,1\}$. The public parameters $\mathsf{pp} = (\mathsf{crs}_{\mathsf{Com}}, \mathsf{crs}_{\mathsf{NIZK}}, \mathsf{pp}_{\mathsf{IBE}}, c_1, \ldots, c_N)$ for the scheme contains the common reference string $\mathsf{crs}_{\mathsf{Com}}$ for the bit commitment scheme (in binding mode), the common reference string $\mathsf{crs}_{\mathsf{NIZK}}$ for the NIZK, the public parameters $\mathsf{pp}_{\mathsf{IBE}}$ for the plain IBE scheme, and commitments c_i to the bits r_i. The master secret key msk also contains the openings to the commitments $\sigma_1, \ldots, \sigma_N$.
- The secret key for an identity id is $\mathsf{sk}_{id} = (\mathsf{ct}_{\mathsf{IBE}}, \pi)$. Here,

$$\mathsf{ct}_{\mathsf{IBE}} = \mathsf{IBE}.\mathsf{Encrypt}(\mathsf{pp}_{\mathsf{IBE}}, id, \vec{r}_{id}; \rho_{\mathsf{enc}}) \qquad (1.1)$$

is an IBE ciphertext that encrypts the tuple of bits $\vec{r}_{id} = (r_i)_{i \in I_{id}}$ of the secret key indexed by $I_{id} = \mathcal{H}(id)$, where $\mathcal{H}$ is a (fixed) hash function that maps identities onto a set of indices. We let ρ_{enc} denote the encryption randomness. In addition, the secret key contains a NIZK proof π that the commitments $\vec{c}_{id} = (c_i)_{i \in I_{id}}$ in pp is a valid commitment to $\vec{r}_{id}$ and that ct is an encryption of $\vec{r}_{id}$ with randomness ρ_{enc}. Here, the statement in the NIZK proof is $(id, \vec{c}_{id}, \mathsf{ct}_{\mathsf{IBE}})$ and the witness is $(\vec{r}_{id}, \rho_{\mathsf{enc}}, \vec{\sigma}_{id})$, where $\vec{\sigma}_{id} = (\sigma_i)_{i \in I_{id}}$.
- To encrypt a message m to an identity id^*, the encrypter computes an obfuscation of a program P that has the identity id^*, the message m, the common reference string $\mathsf{crs}_{\mathsf{NIZK}}$, and the commitments $\vec{c}_{id^*}$ hard-wired inside. The program takes as input a secret key $\mathsf{sk}_{id} = (\mathsf{ct}_{\mathsf{IBE}}, \pi)$ and outputs the message if

π is a valid proof for the statement $(\mathsf{id}^*, \vec{c}_{\mathsf{id}^*}, \mathsf{ct}_{\mathsf{IBE}})$. Otherwise, the program outputs $\perp$.

Proving Adaptive Security via a Dual-System Approach. As mentioned before, we leverage a dual-system strategy [Wat09, LW10] to prove that the above scheme is *adaptively* secure. In a dual-system proof, we define a sequence of hybrid experiments where we gradually replace the normal ciphertexts and secret keys (given out in the security game) with "semi-functional" analogs. The invariant we enforce is that normal keys can decrypt semi-functional ciphertexts and semi-functional keys can decrypt normal ciphertexts. However, semi-functional keys are unable to decrypt semi-functional ciphertexts, and moreover, the adversary is unable to tell whether a key or ciphertext is normal or semi-functional. In particular, this means that it should be hard for an adversary to generate semi-functional ciphertexts on its own (if it could, then it could trivially distinguish semi-functional keys for normal keys). In the final hybrid, all of the keys and ciphertexts the adversary receives from the challenger are semi-functional. At this point, we can rely on a simple statistical argument to argue that the adversary's distinguishing advantage is negligible. We now describe the structure of the semi-functional ciphertexts and keys in the proof:

- **Semi-functional ciphertexts:** The semi-functional ciphertext ct for a message m and identity id^* contains an obfuscation of a modified program P^*. The program P^* additionally contains a secret key $\mathsf{sk}_{\mathsf{id}^*}$ and a bit string $t = \mathsf{PRG}(h(\vec{r}_{\mathsf{id}^*}))$, where PRG is a length-doubling pseudorandom generator (PRG) and h is a universal hash function. The program P^* takes $(\mathsf{ct}_{\mathsf{IBE}}, \pi)$ as input, but outputs m only if π is a valid proof (on the statement $(\mathsf{id}^*, \vec{c}_{\mathsf{id}^*}, \mathsf{ct}_{\mathsf{IBE}})$) *and* $\mathsf{PRG}(h(\mathsf{IBE.Decrypt}(\mathsf{sk}_{\mathsf{id}^*}, \mathsf{id}^*, \mathsf{ct}_{\mathsf{IBE}}))) = t$.
- **Semi-functional keys:** The semi-functional key $\mathsf{sk}_{\mathsf{id}} = (\mathsf{ct}_{\mathsf{IBE}}, \pi)$ has a simulated proof π and moreover, the ciphertext $\mathsf{ct}_{\mathsf{IBE}}$ is an encryption of the all-zeroes string $\mathsf{ct}_{\mathsf{IBE}} = \mathsf{IBE.Encrypt}(\mathsf{pp}_{\mathsf{IBE}}, \mathsf{id}, 0; \rho_{\mathsf{enc}})$.

To show security, we first switch the challenge ciphertexts to be semi-functional. Then we switch each of the keys to be semi-functional. Once all of the challenge ciphertexts and keys are semi-functional, semantic security follows by a simple statistical argument together with security of the obfuscation scheme. We give a sketch below:

- **Switching ciphertexts to be semi-functional:** To switch ciphertexts into semi-functional mode, we appeal to $i\mathcal{O}$ security. Specifically, it suffices to show that the original program P and the modified program P^* are functionally equivalent. This follows immediately by (statistical) soundness of the NIZK and correctness of the IBE scheme. Specifically, statistical soundness of the NIZK means that if the proof π verifies, then

$$\mathsf{ct}_{\mathsf{IBE}} = \mathsf{IBE.Encrypt}(\mathsf{pp}_{\mathsf{IBE}}, \mathsf{id}^*, \vec{r}_{\mathsf{id}^*}).$$

Correctness of IBE now implies that the

$$\mathsf{IBE.Decrypt}(\mathsf{sk}_{\mathsf{id}^*}, \mathsf{id}^*, \mathsf{ct}_{\mathsf{IBE}}) = \vec{r}_{\mathsf{id}^*}.$$

In this case, the additional PRG check that P^* performs always succeeds.

- **Switching keys to semi-functional.** We now switch the keys $\mathsf{sk}_{\mathsf{id}} = (\mathsf{ct}_{\mathsf{IBE}}, \pi)$ to semi-functional. To do so, we first appeal to simulation security of the NIZK (to switch from real proofs to simulated proofs). We then leverage semantic security of the IBE scheme to switch $\mathsf{ct}_{\mathsf{IBE}}$ from an encryption of $\vec{r}_{\mathsf{id}}$ to an encryption of the all-zeroes string. Note that at this point in the proof, the challenge ciphertexts are semi-functional, and thus, simulating a challenge ciphertext for an identity id^* requires knowledge of $\mathsf{sk}_{\mathsf{id}^*}$. However, the reduction algorithm can obtain these keys from the IBE challenger. Note that this is admissible because the adversary in the big-key IBE game is not allowed to query for a key for an identity $\mathsf{id}^* \in \mathcal{J}$ that appears in the challenge set $\mathcal{J}$.

- **Completing the proof:** To finish the proof, we switch the commitments to hiding mode. This essentially "erases" the bits $r_1, \ldots, r_N$ from the public parameters. At this point in the proof, the only information on the bits r_i is contained in the leakage function on msk aside from the ℓ bits of leakage. When the challenge set $\mathcal{J}$ is sufficiently large, there must exist some identity $\mathsf{id}^* \in \mathcal{J}$ such that $\vec{r}_{\mathsf{id}^*}$ has high min-entropy given the leakage. For this to work, we require that the mapping $\mathcal{H}$ from identities to the indices of the master secret key has good "spread." That is, it should be the case that the set $\{\vec{r}_{\mathsf{id}}\}_{\mathsf{id} \in \mathcal{J}}$ contains many distinct indices of msk. Then, there exists some $\mathsf{id}^* \in \mathcal{J}$ such that $\vec{r}_{\mathsf{id}^*}$ has high min-entropy. At this point, we can appeal to the leftover hash lemma [HILL99] to argue that $t = \mathsf{PRG}(h(\vec{r}_{\mathsf{id}^*}))$ is statistically close to $t = \mathsf{PRG}(u)$, where u is a random seed. By PRG security, the string t is computationally indistinguishable from a uniform string. Since the PRG is length-doubling, with overwhelming probability over the choice of t, it is no longer in the image of the PRG. At this point, the additional check that P^* performs (i.e., that $\mathsf{PRG}(h(\mathsf{IBE.Decrypt}(\mathsf{sk}_{\mathsf{id}^*}, \mathsf{id}^*, \mathsf{ct}_{\mathsf{IBE}}))) = t$) is unsatisfiable. Correspondingly, the program P^* outputs $\bot$ on all inputs, so by $i\mathcal{O}$ security, it is computationally indistinguishable from the program that always outputs $\bot$. Since this program is independent of the message m, semantic security holds trivially.

We provide the full construction and analysis in Sect. 4. Thus, we obtain a simple construction of an adaptively-secure big-key IBE scheme from indistinguishability obfuscation and one-way functions; specifically, all of the underlying building blocks can be built from $i\mathcal{O}$ and one-way functions [SW14, ABSV15].

Using Witness Encryption in Place of Obfuscation. If we inspect our above template for constructing big-key IBE, we observe that the ciphertext is essentially an obfuscated program that takes as input a proof and checks whether the proof is valid or not. Thus, similar to the approach in [DGSW22], it seems plausible that we could also replace the obfuscated program with a witness encryption scheme [GGSW13]. In this work, we show that this is indeed possible, but will require a more involved construction. Specifically, in witness encryption, a user can encrypt a message m to an NP statement x; the decryption algorithm takes an NP witness w for x and outputs the statement. The security requirement then says that if x is not in the language, then the ciphertext computationally hides the associated message. Witness encryption provide no guarantees if the statement x is in the language, even if the witness is computationally hard to find. In our basic template above, the ciphertext always encodes a *true* instance (since decryption is possible), and we rely on $i\mathcal{O}$ security to (gradually) replace it with an instance that is unsatisfiable (in the final hybrid experiment). Such a proof strategy does not work in the setting of witness encryption since it provides no hiding properties for the underlying NP relation. Thus, substituting witness encryption in place of indistinguishability obfuscation will require some additional tools.

Specifically, in the $i\mathcal{O}$ construction, the semi-functional ciphertexts introduces an *additional* check that the provided secret key $\mathsf{sk}_{\mathsf{id}^*} = (\mathsf{ct}_{\mathsf{IBE}}, \pi)$ satisfies $\mathsf{PRG}(h(\mathsf{IBE.Decrypt}(\mathsf{sk}_{\mathsf{id}^*}, \mathsf{id}^*, \mathsf{ct}_{\mathsf{IBE}}))) = t$. Since this check always passes, security of $i\mathcal{O}$ ensures that the resulting program remains functionally equivalent to a normal program. In the case of witness encryption, we do not have the flexibility to change the NP relation associated with a challenge ciphertext, so we will have to augment the NP relation in the *normal* ciphertexts to also perform this additional check. We now give an outline of our approach, focusing on the places that differ from our $i\mathcal{O}$ construction:

– The master secret key still consists of a random string $r_1, \ldots, r_N \xleftarrow{\mathsf{R}} \{0,1\}$. As before, the public parameters include commitments $c_1, \ldots, c_N$ to $r_1, \ldots, r_N$, and the master secret key contains the corresponding openings.
– The secret key for an identity id will contain a testing key $\mathsf{sk}_{\mathsf{out}}$ for $\vec{r}_{\mathsf{id}}$ (where $\vec{r}_{\mathsf{id}} = (r_i)_{i \in I_{\mathsf{id}}}$ and $I_{\mathsf{id}} = \mathcal{H}(\mathsf{id})$ as before). The testing key $\mathsf{sk}_{\mathsf{out}}$ plays the role of the IBE ciphertext in the $i\mathcal{O}$ construction. In addition, the secret key also contains a NIZK proof (like in the $i\mathcal{O}$ construction) which affirms that $\mathsf{sk}_{\mathsf{out}}$ is an encoding of $\vec{r}_{\mathsf{id}}$ and that $\vec{r}_{\mathsf{id}}$ are the bits associated with the commitment $\vec{c}_{\mathsf{id}}$.
– To encrypt a message m to an identity id^*, the user first samples a random encoding $\mathsf{ct}_{\mathsf{out}}$, and prepares a witness encryption ciphertext for the statement $(\mathsf{id}^*, \vec{c}_{\mathsf{id}^*}, \mathsf{ct}_{\mathsf{out}})$; for simplicity of exposition, we omit the common reference strings for the NIZK and the bit commitments in this sketch. The witness for the witness encryption scheme is a secret key $\mathsf{sk}_{\mathsf{id}} = (\mathsf{sk}_{\mathsf{out}}, \pi)$, and the associated NP relation first checks the proof π is valid, and moreover, that the encoding $\mathsf{ct}_{\mathsf{out}}$ is valid with respect to the testing key $\mathsf{sk}_{\mathsf{out}}$.

The additional validity check between $\mathsf{sk}_{\mathsf{out}}$ and $\mathsf{ct}_{\mathsf{out}}$ is the analog of the additional check that the semi-functional ciphertexts performs in the earlier $i\mathcal{O}$ construction. Specifically, we require the encodings satisfy the following properties:

– There is a public algorithm that allows one to sample a fresh encoding. This is used during encryption to sample $\mathsf{ct}_{\mathsf{out}}$. The first requirement is that the testing key $\mathsf{sk}_{\mathsf{out}}$ always accepts a normal encoding (this ensures correctness).

– Next, we define the notion of a semi-functional encoding. Using a trapdoor, it is possible to sample a semi-functional encoding $\mathsf{ct}_{\mathsf{out}}$ of a vector $\vec{r}_{\mathsf{id}}$. Here, the requirement is that a (normal) testing key $\mathsf{sk}_{\mathsf{out}}$ for $\vec{r}_{\mathsf{id}}$ will always *reject* a semi-functional encoding of $\vec{r}_{\mathsf{id}}$.

We refer to these encodings as a privately-testable encoding since given a trapdoor, it is possible to generate a (semi-functional) key to test whether an encoding is of a particular target value or not. In the security proof, we will switch the encodings in the challenge ciphertexts (for an identity id) from normal encodings (which can be decrypted normally) into semi-functional encodings of $\vec{r}_{\mathsf{id}}$. Consider now a candidate witness $(\mathsf{sk}_{\mathsf{out}}, \pi)$ for a challenge ciphertext:

– If the NIZK proof π verifies, then by statistical binding of the commitment scheme and statistical soundness of the NIZK proof system, it must be the case that $\mathsf{sk}_{\mathsf{out}}$ is an encoding of $\vec{r}_{\mathsf{id}}$.
– However, if the encoding $\mathsf{ct}_{\mathsf{out}}$ in the challenge ciphertext is a semi-functional encoding of $\vec{r}_{\mathsf{id}}$, then $\mathsf{sk}_{\mathsf{out}}$ will always reject $\mathsf{ct}_{\mathsf{out}}$.

Thus, for all candidate witnesses for the statement associated with a challenge ciphertext, either the NIZK proof fails to verify or the encoding check fails. In both cases, the relation is not satisfied, and so the statement is false. We can now appeal to semantic security of the witness encryption scheme.

Simulating NIZK Proofs. The above proof strategy critically requires on statistical soundness of the NIZK (to ensure that if the adversary produces a valid proof π, then the associated testing key is bound to the vector $\vec{r}_{\mathsf{id}}$). However, in the reduction, we still require a way to simulate proofs *without* knowledge of $r_1, \ldots, r_N$ (to ensure that the only leakage on the bits $r_1, \ldots, r_N$ is from the leakage function). Essentially, the reduction needs a way to simulate secret key without knowledge of the randomness $r_1, \ldots, r_N$ and still retain statistical soundness. We achieve this using an or-proof construction. Specifically, we introduce an additional branch into the NIZK proof system so the proof either asserts validity of the testing key $\mathsf{sk}_{\mathsf{out}}$ (with respect to the commitments $\vec{c}_{\mathsf{id}}$) as above, or alternatively, the prover knows a trapdoor embedded within the CRS. In the real scheme, only the first branch will be used while in the security proof, the reduction algorithm will simulate proofs using the simulation trapdoor.

At this point, we still need to ensure that the simulated proofs do not help the adversary break semantic security. In particular, by switching to the or-proof, we can no longer argue that a valid proof π means that the testing key $\vec{r}_{\mathsf{id}}$ is correctly constructed. To get around this problem, we introduce the concept of a split encoding. At a very high level, we include an auxiliary encoding $\mathsf{sk}_{\mathsf{aux}}$ and $\mathsf{ct}_{\mathsf{aux}}$ with each secret key and ciphertext, respectively. The ciphertext component $\mathsf{ct}_{\mathsf{aux}}$ would be embedded as part of the statement in witness encryption while the secret key component $\mathsf{sk}_{\mathsf{aux}}$ would be part of the witness. The NP relation associated with the witness encryption scheme would then check that $\mathsf{ct}_{\mathsf{aux}}$ is valid with respect to $\mathsf{sk}_{\mathsf{aux}}$. To preserve correctness, we require that for normally-generated encodings, the check always passes. However, the check rejects when both $\mathsf{ct}_{\mathsf{aux}}$ and $\mathsf{sk}_{\mathsf{aux}}$ are switched to *semi-functional* encodings. We now modify the trapdoor branch of the or-language in the NIZK proof system to also check that the key encoding $\mathsf{sk}_{\mathsf{aux}}$ is a semi-functional encoding. In the proof, the semi-functional ciphertexts have semi-functional encodings $\mathsf{ct}_{\mathsf{aux}}$. This way, whenever the NIZK proof verifies, one of two properties must hold:

- The provided encoding $\mathsf{sk}_{\mathsf{out}}$ is a testing key for $\vec{r}_{\mathsf{id}}$, which would reject the encoding $\mathsf{ct}_{\mathsf{out}}$ in the challenge ciphertext. Thus, the witness encryption relation is not satisfied.
- The auxiliary encoding $\mathsf{sk}_{\mathsf{aux}}$ is a semi-functional encoding, which would reject the semi-functional $\mathsf{ct}_{\mathsf{aux}}$ in the challenge ciphertext. Once again, the witness encryption relation is not satisfied.

With these two encodings, we now have a way for the reduction algorithm to simulate key-generation queries (without knowledge of $r_1, \ldots, r_N$). Moreover, once all of the secret keys and challenge ciphertexts are semi-functional, the associated relation is false. Semantic security then follows from security of the witness encryption scheme. We provide the formal description of our privately-testable and split encodings as well as our construction of big-key IBE from witness encryption in the full version of this paper.

Constructing Privately-Testable and Split Encodings. In the full version of this paper, we show how to construct the encoding schemes we use from standard assumptions over groups. Specifically, privately-testable encodings follow from the SXDH assumption in pairing groups while split encodings can be built from the DDH assumption in pairing-free groups.

Shortening Public Parameters. As described so far, our big-key IBE scheme has long public parameters. Critically, the encryption algorithm only requires local access to the long public parameters. Previously, the authors of [DGSW22] showed a generic approach based on non-interactive secure computation to compile any big-key IBE scheme with long public parameters (but where the underlying algorithm only require local access to the public parameters) into a scheme with short public parameters. This transformation also applies to our constructions. For completeness, we show that this transformation still preserves adaptive security in the full version of this paper.

Comparison with [WW24]. The recent work of Waters and Wichs [WW24] shows how to construct adaptively-secure attribute-based encryption from witness encryption. As part of their proof strategy, they introduce the notion of a "functional tag system." A functional tag system consists of function tags and input tags, each of which has a semi-functional mode that is indistinguishable from the normal mode. Our notion of split encoding is conceptually similar to a functional tag system, but specialized to the case of an equality function (since we aim for IBE rather than ABE). However, for our application, we rely on a stronger notion of mode indistinguishability. In particular, mode indistinguishability needs to hold with respect to multiple functions and multiple input tags. The Waters-Wichs notion considers many functions, but a single input tag. The need to simulate many input tags comes from the fact that in the big-key IBE security game, the reduction algorithm needs to simulate multiple challenge ciphertexts (to estimate the adversary's success probability and determine whether it is successful or not). We do not see a way to generically amplify a scheme that supports a single input tag (and many functions) into one that supports multiple input tags.

2   Preliminaries

We write λ to denote the security parameter. For an integer $n \in \mathbb{N}$, we write $[n]$ to denote the set $\{1, 2, \ldots, a\}$. For integers $a < b$, we use $[a, b]$ to denote the set of integers $\{a, a+1, \ldots, b\}$. When $\vec{x} = (x_1, \ldots, x_N)$ is a vector of elements and $S \subseteq [N]$ is a set of indices, we will write $\vec{x}_S$ to denote the ordered sub-vector $(x_i)_{i \in S}$. For a distribution $\mathcal{D}$ we write $x \leftarrow \mathcal{D}$ to denote that x is a random draw from $\mathcal{D}$. For a finite set S, we write $x \xleftarrow{\text{R}} S$ to denote a uniform random draw from S. When indexing a set S, we write $S[i]$ to denote the ith element of S (in lexicographic order). For distributions $\mathcal{D}_0, \mathcal{D}_1$, we denote the statistical distance between them by $\Delta(\mathcal{D}_0, \mathcal{D}_1)$. We use boldface letters (e.g., $\mathbf{x}$) to denote vectors. We write $\mathsf{poly}(\lambda)$ to denote a fixed function that is $O(\lambda^c)$ for some $c \in \mathbb{N}$ and $\mathsf{negl}(\lambda)$ to denote a function that is $o(\lambda^{-c})$ for all $c \in \mathbb{N}$. We say an event occurs with overwhelming probability if its complement occurs with negligible probability. We say an algorithm is efficient if it runs in probabilistic polynomial time (in the length of its input).

Hoeffding's Inequality. We will use Hoeffding's bound on the sum of independent random variables [Hoe63]:

Fact 2.1 (Hoeffding's Inequality [Hoe63]). *Let* $X_1, \ldots, X_T$ *be independent random variables where* $0 \leq X_i \leq 1$ *for all* $i \in [T]$. *Let* $S = \sum_{i \in [T]} X_i$ *and let* $\mathbb{E}[S]$ *denote the expected value of* S. *Then, for any* $k \geq 0$,

$$\Pr[|S - \mathbb{E}[S]| \geq Tk] \leq 2^{-\Omega(Tk^2)}.$$

Min-Entropy. We recall some basic definitions on min-entropy. Our definitions are adapted from those in [DORS08]. For a (discrete) random variable X, we write $\mathbf{H}_\infty(X) = -\log(\max_x \Pr[X = x])$ to denote its min-entropy. For two (possibly correlated) discrete random variables X and Y, we define the average min-entropy of X given Y to be $\mathbf{H}_\infty(X \mid Y) = -\log(\mathbb{E}_{y \leftarrow Y} \max_x \Pr[X = x \mid Y = y])$. The optimal probability of an unbounded adversary guessing X given the correlated value Y is $2^{-\mathbf{H}_\infty(X|Y)}$. We now state some useful properties on the conditional min-entropy:

Lemma 2.2 (Conditional Min-Entropy [DORS08, Lemma 2.2]). *Let* A, B, C *be random variables and suppose there are at most* 2^λ *elements in the support of* B. *Then* $\mathbf{H}_\infty(A \mid (B, C)) \geq \mathbf{H}_\infty(A, B \mid C) - \lambda \geq \mathbf{H}_\infty(A \mid C) - \lambda$. *Additionally, for any* $\delta > 0$, *with probability at least* $1 - \delta$ *over the choice of* $b \leftarrow B$, *we have* $\mathbf{H}_\infty(A \mid B = b) \geq \mathbf{H}_\infty(A \mid B) - \log(1/\delta)$.

Lemma 2.3 (Min-Entropy Splitting Lemma [DFR+07, DGSW22]**).** *Let* $X_1, \ldots, X_\ell$ *be a sequence of random variables such that* $\mathbf{H}_\infty(X_1, \ldots X_\ell) \geq \alpha$. *Then there exists a random variable* C *over* $[\ell]$ *such that* $\mathbf{H}_\infty(X_C \mid C) \geq \alpha/\ell - \log \ell$.

Dispersers. Our construction will rely on a disperser (also known as a "one-sided extractor"). At a high level, a disperser can be modeled as a bipartite graph with the property that every subset of nodes of a certain (minimal) size on the left is guaranteed to have a large number of neighbors on the right. We recall the formal definition from [TUZ07]. First, a bipartite graph $G = (L, R, E)$ consists of two sets of vertices L and R together with a set of edges E, where each edge $e \in E$ is a pair of nodes $(u, v) \in L \times R$. For a set $S \subseteq L$, we write $N(S) \subseteq R$ to denote the neighborhood of S: $N(S) = \{v \in R : \exists (u, v) \in E \wedge u \in S\}$. We say G is D-left-regular if every node $u \in L$ has exactly D neighbors: $|N(\{u\})| = d$ for all $u \in L$.

Definition 2.4 (Disperser [TUZ07, **Definition 1.3]).** *Let* $G = (L, R, E)$ *be a bipartite graph. Then,* G *is a degree-D (T, ε)-disperser if* G *is D-left-regular and for all subsets* $S \subseteq L$ *of size at least* T, *the neighborhood* $N(S)$ *has size at least* $(1 - \varepsilon) \cdot |R|$. *A disperser is explicit if the index of the* i^{th} *neighbor of a vertex* $v \in L$ *can be computed in* $\mathsf{poly}(\log N, \log D)$ *time.*

Fact 2.5 (Disperser [Par19, **Theorem 3]).** Let c be a universal constant, $\varepsilon > 0$ be any constant, and n be a set size parameter. Let $k = k(n)$, $D = D(n)$, $k_1 = k_1(n)$ be polynomials such that $c \log(n/\varepsilon) < k < n$ and $k_1 \geq k + O(\log^3(k/\varepsilon))$. Then, there exists an explicit degree-D $(2^{k_1}, \varepsilon)$-disperser $G = (L, R, E)$ where $D = \mathsf{poly}(n/\varepsilon)$, $|L| = 2^n$, and $|R| = 2^{k_1 + \Omega(\log(n/\varepsilon))}$.

Randomness Extractors. We now recall the definition of randomness extractors (from the leftover hash lemma).

Definition 2.6 (Strong Randomness Extractor). *A function* $\mathsf{Ext} \colon \{0,1\}^n \times \{0,1\}^d \to \{0,1\}^m$ *is a (k, ε)-strong randomness extractor if for all distributions* X *over* $\{0,1\}^n$ *such that* $\mathbf{H}_\infty(X) \geq k$, *it holds that*

$$\Delta\Big((s, \mathsf{Ext}(X, s)), (U_d, U_m)\Big) \leq \varepsilon,$$

where $s \xleftarrow{\text{R}} \{0,1\}^d$, *and* U_d, U_s *are the uniform distributions on* $\{0,1\}^d$, *and* $\{0,1\}^m$, *respectively. An extractor is explicit if it is efficiently-computable.*

Lemma 2.7 (Leftover Hash Lemma [ILL89, HILL99]**).** *Let* X *be a random variable with support* U *and suppose* $\mathbf{H}_\infty(X) \geq k$. *Take any* $\varepsilon > 0$ *and let* $\mathcal{H}$ *be a universal hash family of size* 2^d *and output length* $m = k - 2\log(1/\varepsilon)$. *Define* $\mathsf{Ext}(x, h) := h(x)$. *Then* Ext *is a $(k, \varepsilon/2)$-strong extractor with seed length d and output length m.*

Corollary 2.8 (Explicit Strong Extractor). *Take any $\lambda \in \mathbb{N}$. Then, there exists an explicit $(\lambda + \omega(\log \lambda), \mathsf{negl}(\lambda))$-strong randomness extractor* $\mathsf{Ext} \colon \{0,1\}^{\mathsf{poly}(\lambda)} \times \{0,1\}^{\mathsf{poly}(\lambda)} \to \{0,1\}^{\lambda}$.

Corollary 2.9 (Inner Product Extractor). *Let $\mathbb{F}$ be a finite field and let X be a random variable with support $U = \mathbb{F}^n$. Take any $\varepsilon > 0$ and suppose $\mathbf{H}_{\infty}(X) \geq k = 2\log(1/\varepsilon) + \log|\mathbb{F}|$. Let $S = \mathbb{F}^n$ be a seed space and define* $\mathsf{Ext}(\boldsymbol{x}, \mathbf{s}) := \mathbf{s}^{\mathsf{T}}\boldsymbol{x}$. *Then Ext is a $(k, \varepsilon/2)$-strong extractor with seed length $n\log|\mathbb{F}|$ and output length $\log|\mathbb{F}|$.*

2.1 Cryptographic Primitives

In this section, we recall the main cryptographic notions we use in this work.

Definition 2.10 (Pseudorandom Generator). *Let λ be a security parameter. A pseudorandom generator with output length $m = m(\lambda)$ is an efficiently-computable function family* $\mathsf{PRG} = \{\mathsf{PRG}_{\lambda}\}_{\lambda \in \mathbb{N}}$ *where* $\mathsf{PRG}_{\lambda} \colon \{0,1\}^{\lambda} \to \{0,1\}^{m(\lambda)}$. *We say that PRG is secure if for all efficient adversaries $\mathcal{A}$ there exists a negligible function $\mathsf{negl}(\cdot)$ such that for all $\lambda \in \mathbb{N}$:*

$$\left| \Pr[\mathcal{A}(1^{\lambda}, \mathsf{PRG}_{\lambda}(x)) = 1 : x \xleftarrow{\text{R}} \{0,1\}^{\lambda}] - \Pr[\mathcal{A}(1^{\lambda}, y) = 1 : y \xleftarrow{\text{R}} \{0,1\}^{m(\lambda)}] \right| = \mathsf{negl}(\lambda).$$

Definition 2.11 (Pseudorandom Function). *Let $\mathcal{K} = \{\mathcal{K}_{\lambda}\}_{\lambda \in \mathbb{N}}$, $\mathcal{X} = \{\mathcal{X}_{\lambda}\}_{\lambda \in \mathbb{N}}$, and $\mathcal{Y} = \{\mathcal{Y}_{\lambda}\}_{\lambda \in \mathbb{N}}$ be ensembles of finite sets indexed by a security parameter λ. Let $\mathsf{PRF} = \{\mathsf{PRF}_{\lambda}\}_{\lambda \in \mathbb{N}}$ be an efficiently-computable collection of functions $\mathsf{PRF}_{\lambda} \colon \mathcal{K}_{\lambda} \times \mathcal{X}_{\lambda} \to \mathcal{Y}_{\lambda}$. We say that PRF is secure if for all efficient adversaries $\mathcal{A}$ there exists a negligible function $\mathsf{negl}(\cdot)$ such that for all $\lambda \in \mathbb{N}$:*

$$\left| \Pr[\mathcal{A}^{\mathsf{PRF}_{\lambda}(k, \cdot)}(1^{\lambda}) = 1 : k \xleftarrow{\text{R}} \mathcal{K}_{\lambda}] - \Pr[\mathcal{A}^{f_{\lambda}(\cdot)}(1^{\lambda}) = 1 : f_{\lambda} \xleftarrow{\text{R}} \mathsf{Funs}[\mathcal{X}_{\lambda}, \mathcal{Y}_{\lambda}]] \right| = \mathsf{negl}(\lambda),$$

where $\mathsf{Funs}[\mathcal{X}_{\lambda}, \mathcal{Y}_{\lambda}]$ is the set of all functions from $\mathcal{X}_{\lambda}$ to $\mathcal{Y}_{\lambda}$.

Definition 2.12 (Identity-Based Encryption [Sha84, BF01, Coc01]). *An identity-based encryption (IBE) scheme with identity space $\mathcal{ID} = \{\mathcal{ID}_{\lambda}\}_{\lambda \in \mathbb{N}}$ and message space $\mathcal{M} = \{\mathcal{M}_{\lambda}\}_{\lambda \in \mathbb{N}}$ is a tuple of efficient algorithms $\Pi_{\mathsf{IBE}} = (\mathsf{Setup}, \mathsf{KeyGen}, \mathsf{Encrypt}, \mathsf{Decrypt})$ with the following syntax:*

- $\mathsf{Setup}(1^{\lambda}) \to (\mathsf{pp}, \mathsf{msk})$: *On input the security parameter λ, the setup algorithm outputs the set of public parameters pp and a master secret key msk. We assume that pp and msk include the security parameter 1^{λ}.*
- $\mathsf{KeyGen}(\mathsf{msk}, \mathsf{id}) \to \mathsf{sk}_{\mathsf{id}}$: *On input the master secret key msk and an identity $\mathsf{id} \in \mathcal{ID}_{\lambda}$, the key-generation algorithm outputs an identity key $\mathsf{sk}_{\mathsf{id}}$. We assume the secret key $\mathsf{sk}_{\mathsf{id}}$ contains the security parameter 1^{λ} (from msk).*
- $\mathsf{Encrypt}(\mathsf{pp}, \mathsf{id}, m) \to \mathsf{ct}$: *On input the public parameters pp, an identity $\mathsf{id} \in \mathcal{ID}_{\lambda}$, and a message $m \in \mathcal{M}_{\lambda}$, the encryption algorithm outputs a ciphertext ct.*

- Decrypt($\mathsf{sk_{id}}$, id, ct) → m: *On input an identity secret key $\mathsf{sk_{id}}$, an identity* id ∈ $\mathcal{ID}_\lambda$, *and a ciphertext* ct, *the decryption algorithm outputs a message* $m \in \mathcal{M}_\lambda$.

Moreover, Π_{IBE} should satisfy the following properties:

- **Correctness:** *For all security parameters* $\lambda \in \mathbb{N}$, *all identities* id ∈ $\mathcal{ID}_\lambda$, *all* (pp, msk) *in the support of* $\mathsf{Setup}(1^\lambda)$, *and all messages* $m \in \mathcal{M}_\lambda$,

$$\Pr\left[\mathsf{Decrypt}(\mathsf{sk_{id}}, \mathsf{ct}) = m : \begin{array}{l} \mathsf{sk_{id}} \leftarrow \mathsf{KeyGen}(\mathsf{msk}, \mathsf{id}) \\ \mathsf{ct} \leftarrow \mathsf{Encrypt}(\mathsf{pp}, \mathsf{id}, m) \end{array}\right] = 1.$$

- **Semantic security:** *For a security parameter* λ *and a bit* $b \in \{0,1\}$, *we define the (adaptive) semantic security game between an adversary $\mathcal{A}$ and a challenger as follows:*
  - **Setup:** *The challenger starts by sampling* (pp, msk) ← $\mathsf{Setup}(1^\lambda)$ *and gives* pp *to $\mathcal{A}$.*
  - **Pre-challenge queries:** *Algorithm $\mathcal{A}$ can now issue key-generation queries to the challenger. On each key-generation query, adversary $\mathcal{A}$ specifies an identity* id ∈ $\mathcal{ID}_\lambda$, *and the challenger replies with* $\mathsf{sk_{id}}$ ← $\mathsf{KeyGen}(\mathsf{msk}, \mathsf{id})$.
  - **Challenge:** *Algorithm $\mathcal{A}$ outputs a challenge identity* id^* *and two messages* $m_0, m_1 \in \mathcal{M}_\lambda$. *The challenger replies with* ct_b ← $\mathsf{Encrypt}(\mathsf{pp}, \mathsf{id}^*, m_b)$.
  - **Post-challenge queries:** *Algorithm $\mathcal{A}$ can continue to make key-generation queries as in the pre-challenge phase.*
  - **Output:** *At the end of the game, algorithm $\mathcal{A}$ outputs a bit* $b' \in \{0,1\}$, *which is the output of the experiment.*

  An adversary $\mathcal{A}$ is admissible for the semantic security game if it does not issue a key-generation query on the challenge identity id^*. *We say Π_{IBE} satisfies adaptive security if for all efficient and admissible adversaries $\mathcal{A}$, there exists a negligible function* negl(·) *such that for all* $\lambda \in \mathbb{N}$,

$$|\Pr[b' = 1 \mid b = 1] - \Pr[b' = 1 \mid b = 0]| = \mathsf{negl}(\lambda)$$

  in the semantic security game.

Definition 2.13 (Indistinguishability Obfuscation [BGI+12, GGH+13]).
Let $\mathcal{C} = \{\mathcal{C}_\lambda\}_{\lambda \in \mathbb{N}}$ *be a family of polynomial-size circuits and* $\ell_\mathcal{C}(\lambda)$ *be a size parameter, such that every circuit* $C \in \mathcal{C}_\lambda$ *has size exactly* $\ell_\mathcal{C}(\lambda)$. *An indistinguishability obfuscator* $i\mathcal{O}$ *is an efficient algorithm that takes as input the security parameter* 1^λ, *a circuit* $C \in \mathcal{C}_\lambda$, *and outputs a circuit* C'. *An* $i\mathcal{O}$ *scheme should satisfy the following properties:*

- **Functionality-preserving:** *For all security parameters* $\lambda \in \mathbb{N}$, *all* $C \in \mathcal{C}_\lambda$, *and all inputs* x, *we have that* $C'(x) = C(x)$ *where* $C' \leftarrow i\mathcal{O}(1^\lambda, C)$.

– **Security:** *For all efficient adversaries* $\mathcal{A} = (\mathsf{Samp}, \mathcal{A}')$, *there exists a negligible function* $\mathsf{negl}(\cdot)$ *such that the following holds: if for all security parameters* $\lambda \in \mathbb{N}$,

$$\Pr[\forall x, C_0(x) = C_1(x) : (C_0, C_1, \mathsf{st}) \leftarrow \mathsf{Samp}(1^\lambda)] = 1 - \mathsf{negl}(\lambda)$$

then

$$\left| \Pr[\mathcal{A}'(\mathsf{st}, i\mathcal{O}(1^\lambda, C_0)) = 1] - \Pr[\mathcal{A}'(\mathsf{st}, i\mathcal{O}(1^\lambda, C_1)) = 1] \right| = \mathsf{negl}(\lambda),$$

where $(C_0, C_1, \mathsf{st}) \leftarrow \mathsf{Samp}(1^\lambda)$.

Definition 2.14 (Witness Encryption [GGSW13, adapted]). *Let* $\mathcal{M} = \{\mathcal{M}_\lambda\}_{\lambda \in \mathbb{N}}$ *be a message space. A witness encryption scheme for an* NP *language* $\mathcal{L}$ *with witness relation* $\mathcal{R}_\mathcal{L}$ *is a tuple of efficient algorithms* $\Pi_{\mathsf{WE}} = (\mathsf{Encrypt}, \mathsf{Decrypt})$ *with the following syntax:*

– $\mathsf{Encrypt}(1^\lambda, m, x) \to \mathsf{ct}$: *On input the security parameter* λ, *a message* $m \in \mathcal{M}_\lambda$, *and an instance* x *for the language* $\mathcal{L}$, *the encryption algorithm outputs a ciphertext* ct. *We assume* ct *includes* 1^λ *and* x.
– $\mathsf{Decrypt}(\mathsf{ct}, w) \to m$: *On input a ciphertext* ct *and a witness* w, *the decryption algorithm outputs a message* $m \in \mathcal{M}_\lambda$.

Moreover, Π_{WE} *should satisfy the following properties:*

– **Correctness:** *For all* $\lambda \in \mathbb{N}$, *messages* $m \in \mathcal{M}_\lambda$, *and tuples* $(x, w) \in \mathcal{R}_\mathcal{L}$, *it holds that*

$$\Pr[\mathsf{Decrypt}(\mathsf{ct}, w) = m : \mathsf{ct} \leftarrow \mathsf{Encrypt}(1^\lambda, m, x)] = 1.$$

– **Semantic security:** *For a security parameter* λ *and a bit* $b \in \{0, 1\}$, *we define the semantic security game between an adversary* $\mathcal{A}$ *and a challenger as follows:*
  - *On input the security parameter* 1^λ, *algorithm* $\mathcal{A}$ *outputs a statement* x *and two messages* $m_0, m_1 \in \mathcal{M}_\lambda$.
  - *The challenger replies with* $\mathsf{ct} \leftarrow \mathsf{Encrypt}(1^\lambda, m_b, x)$.
  - *Algorithm* $\mathcal{A}$ *outputs a bit* $b' \in \{0, 1\}$, *which is the output of the experiment.*

  The scheme Π_{WE} *satisfies semantic security if for all efficient adversaries* $\mathcal{A}$, *there exists a negligible function* $\mathsf{negl}(\cdot)$ *such that for all* $\lambda \in \mathbb{N}$,

$$|\Pr[b' = 1 \wedge x \notin \mathcal{L} \mid b = 1] - \Pr[b' = 1 \wedge x \notin \mathcal{L} \mid b = 0]| = \mathsf{negl}(\lambda)$$

  in the semantic security game.

One-Time Dual-Mode Commitment. We recall the notion of a one-time dual-mode commitment, which can be constructed from one way functions [Nao89].

Definition 2.15 (One-Time Dual-Mode Commitment [DN02]). *A one-time dual-mode commitment scheme with input space* $\mathcal{X} = \{\mathcal{X}_\lambda\}_{\lambda \in \mathbb{N}}$ *is a tuple of efficient algorithms* $\Pi_{\mathsf{Com}} = (\mathsf{Setup}, \mathsf{Commit}, \mathsf{Verify})$ *with the following syntax:*

- $\mathsf{Setup}(1^\lambda, \mathsf{mode}) \to (\mathsf{crs}, \mathsf{td}, c)$: *On input the security parameter* λ *and* $\mathsf{mode} \in \{\mathsf{bind}, \mathsf{hide}\}$, *the setup algorithm outputs a common reference string* crs. *When* $\mathsf{mode} = \mathsf{hide}$, *it also outputs a trapdoor* td *and commitment* c. *We assume* crs *and* td *(implicitly) contain the security parameter* 1^λ.
- $\mathsf{Commit}(\mathsf{crs}, x) \to (c, \sigma)$: *On input the common reference string* crs *and an input* $x \in \mathcal{X}_\lambda$, *the commit algorithm outputs a commitment* c *and an opening* σ.
- $\mathsf{Verify}(\mathsf{crs}, c, x, \sigma) \to \{0, 1\}$: *On input the common reference string* crs, *a commitment* c, *a value* $x \in \mathcal{X}_\lambda$, *and an opening* σ, *the verification algorithm outputs a bit* $b \in \{0, 1\}$.

Moreover, Π_{Com} *should satisfy the following properties:*

- **Correctness:** *For all security parameters* $\lambda \in \mathbb{N}$, *all inputs* $x \in \mathcal{X}_\lambda$, *all modes* $\mathsf{mode} \in \{\mathsf{bind}, \mathsf{hide}\}$,

$$\Pr\left[\mathsf{Verify}(\mathsf{crs}, c, x, \sigma) = 1 : \begin{array}{l} (\mathsf{crs}, \mathsf{td}, c') \leftarrow \mathsf{Setup}(1^\lambda, \mathsf{mode}); \\ (c, \sigma) \leftarrow \mathsf{Commit}(\mathsf{crs}, x) \end{array}\right] = 1.$$

- **Statistically binding in binding mode:** *For all adversaries* $\mathcal{A}$, *there exists a negligible function* $\mathsf{negl}(\cdot)$ *such that for all* $\lambda \in \mathbb{N}$,

$$\Pr\left[\mathsf{Verify}(\mathsf{crs}, c, x_0, \sigma_0) = \mathsf{Verify}(\mathsf{crs}, c, x_1, \sigma_1) = 1 \wedge x_0 \neq x_1\right] = \mathsf{negl}(\lambda),$$

where $\mathsf{crs} \leftarrow \mathsf{Setup}(1^\lambda, \mathsf{bind})$ *and* $(c, x_0, x_1, \sigma_0, \sigma_1) \leftarrow \mathcal{A}(\mathsf{crs})$.
- **Mode indistinguishability:** *For a security parameter* λ, *a bit* $b \in \{0, 1\}$, *and a simulator* $\mathcal{S}_{\mathsf{open}}$, *we define the mode indistinguishability game between an adversary* $\mathcal{A}$ *and a challenger as follows:*
  1. *The challenger samples* $\mathsf{crs} \leftarrow \mathsf{Setup}(1^\lambda, \mathsf{bind})$ *if* $b = 0$ *or* $(\mathsf{crs}, \mathsf{td}, c_1) \leftarrow \mathsf{Setup}(1^\lambda, \mathsf{hide})$ *if* $b = 1$ *and gives* crs *to* $\mathcal{A}$.
  2. *Algorithm* $\mathcal{A}$ *outputs a value* $x \in \mathcal{X}_\lambda$.
  3. *If* $b = 0$ *the challenger computes* $(c_0, \sigma_0) \leftarrow \mathsf{Commit}(\mathsf{crs}, x)$. *If* $b = 1$, *the challenger computes a simulated opening* $\sigma_1 \leftarrow \mathcal{S}_{\mathsf{open}}(\mathsf{td}, x)$. *The challenger sends* (c_b, σ_b) *to* $\mathcal{A}$.
  4. *Algorithm* $\mathcal{A}$ *outputs a bit* $b' \in \{0, 1\}$, *which is the output of the experiment.*

The scheme Π_{Com} *satisfies mode indistinguishability if there exists an efficient simulator* $\mathcal{S}_{\mathsf{open}}$ *such that for all efficient adversaries* $\mathcal{A}$, *there exists a negligible function* $\mathsf{negl}(\cdot)$ *such that for all* $\lambda \in \mathbb{N}$,

$$|\Pr[b' = 1 \mid \beta = 0] - \Pr[b' = 1 \mid \beta = 1]| = \mathsf{negl}(\lambda)$$

in the mode indistinguishability game.

Non-interactive Zero-Knowledge. Next, we recall the notion of a non-interactive zero-knowledge (NIZK) proof for NP [GMR85, BFM88]. Specifically, we consider NIZKs for the language of Boolean circuit satisfiability which we define below. We also recall the weaker notion of *witness indistinguishability*, which is more convenient to use in some of our proofs. It is easy to see that zero-knowledge implies witness indistinguishability.

Definition 2.16 (Boolean Circuit Satisfiability). *The language* $\mathcal{L}$ *of Boolean circuit satisfiability consists of pairs* (C, x) *of circuits* $C \colon \{0,1\}^n \times \{0,1\}^h \to \{0,1\}$ *and inputs* $x \in \{0,1\}^n$ *such that there exists* $w \in \{0,1\}^h$ *where* $C(x, w) = 1$:

$$\mathcal{L} = \left\{ (C, x) : \begin{array}{c} C \colon \{0,1\}^n \times \{0,1\}^h \to \{0,1\}, x \in \{0,1\}^n \\ \exists w \in \{0,1\}^h : C(x, w) = 1 \end{array} \right\}.$$

Definition 2.17 (NIZK for NP [GMR85, BFM88]). *A non-interactive zero-knowledge (NIZK) proof for Boolean circuit satisfiability is a tuple of efficient algorithms* $\Pi_{\mathsf{NIZK}} = (\mathsf{Setup}, \mathsf{Prove}, \mathsf{Verify})$ *with the following syntax:*

- $\mathsf{Setup}(1^\lambda) \to \mathsf{crs}$: *On input the security parameter* $\lambda \in \mathbb{N}$, *the setup algorithm outputs a common reference string* crs. *We assume* crs *implicitly contains a description of the security parameter* 1^λ.
- $\mathsf{Prove}(\mathsf{crs}, C, x, w) \to \pi$: *On input the common reference string* crs, *a Boolean circuit* $C \colon \{0,1\}^n \times \{0,1\}^h \to \{0,1\}$, *a statement* $x \in \{0,1\}^n$, *and a witness* $w \in \{0,1\}^h$, *the prove algorithm outputs a proof* π.
- $\mathsf{Verify}(\mathsf{crs}, C, x, \pi) \to b$: *On input the common reference string* crs, *the Boolean circuit* $C \colon \{0,1\}^n \times \{0,1\}^h \to \{0,1\}$, *a statement* $x \in \{0,1\}^n$, *and a proof* π, *the verification algorithm outputs a bit* $b \in \{0,1\}$.

Moreover, Π_{NIZK} *should satisfy the following properties:*

- **Completeness:** *For all* $\lambda \in \mathbb{N}$, *all Boolean circuits* $C \colon \{0,1\}^n \times \{0,1\}^h \to \{0,1\}$, *all statements* $x \in \{0,1\}^n$, *and all witnesses* $w \in \{0,1\}^h$ *where* $C(x, w) = 1$,

$$\Pr\left[\mathsf{Verify}(\mathsf{crs}, C, x, \pi) = 1 : \begin{array}{c} \mathsf{crs} \leftarrow \mathsf{Setup}(1^\lambda) \\ \pi \leftarrow \mathsf{Prove}(\mathsf{crs}, C, x, w) \end{array} \right] = 1.$$

- **Statistical soundness:** *For all adversaries* $\mathcal{A}$, *there exists a negligible function* $\mathsf{negl}(\cdot)$ *such that for all* $\lambda \in \mathbb{N}$,

$$\Pr\left[(C, x) \notin \mathcal{L} \wedge \mathsf{Verify}(\mathsf{crs}, C, x, \pi) = 1 : \begin{array}{c} \mathsf{crs} \leftarrow \mathsf{Setup}(1^\lambda) \\ (C, x, \pi) \leftarrow \mathcal{A}(\mathsf{crs}) \end{array} \right] = \mathsf{negl}(\lambda).$$

- **Computational zero-knowledge:** *For every efficient adversary* $\mathcal{A}$, *there exists an efficient simulator* $\mathcal{S} = (\mathcal{S}_1, \mathcal{S}_2)$ *and a negligible function* $\mathsf{negl}(\cdot)$ *such that for all* $\lambda \in \mathbb{N}$,

$$\left| \Pr\left[\mathcal{A}^{\mathcal{O}_0(\mathsf{crs}, \cdot, \cdot, \cdot)}(1^\lambda, \mathsf{crs}) = 1 \right] - \Pr\left[\mathcal{A}^{\mathcal{O}_1(\mathsf{st}_\mathcal{S}, \cdot, \cdot, \cdot)}(1^\lambda, \widetilde{\mathsf{crs}}) = 1 \right] \right| = \mathsf{negl}(\lambda),$$

where $\mathsf{crs} \leftarrow \mathsf{Setup}(1^\lambda)$, $(\widetilde{\mathsf{crs}}, \mathsf{st}_\mathcal{S}) \leftarrow \mathcal{S}_1(1^\lambda)$, *and the oracles* $\mathcal{O}_0$ *and* $\mathcal{O}_1$ *are defined as follows:*

- $\mathcal{O}_0(\mathsf{crs}, C, x, w)$: *On input* crs, *a circuit* $C\colon \{0,1\}^n \times \{0,1\}^h \to \{0,1\}$, *a statement* $x \in \{0,1\}^n$, *and a witness* $w \in \{0,1\}^h$, *the oracle outputs* $\perp$ *if* $C(x,w) = 0$. *If* $C(x,w) = 1$, *it outputs* $\mathsf{Prove}(\mathsf{crs}, C, x, w)$.
- $\mathcal{O}_1(\mathsf{st}_\mathcal{S}, C, x, w)$: *On input the simulator state* $\mathsf{st}_\mathcal{S}$, *a circuit* $C\colon \{0,1\}^n \times \{0,1\}^h \to \{0,1\}$, *a statement* $x \in \{0,1\}^n$, *and a witness* $w \in \{0,1\}^h$, *the oracle outputs* $\perp$ *if* $C(x,w) = 0$. *If* $C(x,w) = 1$, *it outputs* $\mathcal{S}_2(\mathsf{st}_\mathcal{S}, C, x)$.

Definition 2.18 (Computational Witness Indistinguishability). *Let* $\Pi_{\mathsf{NIZK}} = (\mathsf{Setup}, \mathsf{Prove}, \mathsf{Verify})$ *be a NIZK proof for Boolean circuit satisfiability. We say that* Π_{NIZK} *satisfies computational witness indistinguishability if for every efficient adversary* $\mathcal{A}$, *there exists a negligible function* negl *such that for all* $\lambda \in \mathbb{N}$,

$$\left| \Pr\left[\mathcal{A}^{\mathcal{O}_0(\mathsf{crs},\cdot,\cdot,\cdot,\cdot)}(1^\lambda, \mathsf{crs}) = 1 \right] - \Pr\left[\mathcal{A}^{\mathcal{O}_1(\mathsf{crs},\cdot,\cdot,\cdot,\cdot)}(1^\lambda, \mathsf{crs}) = 1 \right] \right| = \mathsf{negl}(\lambda),$$

where $\mathsf{crs} \leftarrow \mathsf{Setup}(1^\lambda)$ *and for* $b \in \{0,1\}$, *the oracle* $\mathcal{O}_b$ *is defined as follows:*

- $\mathcal{O}_b(\mathsf{crs}, C, x, w_0, w_1)$: *On input* crs, *a circuit* $C\colon \{0,1\}^n \times \{0,1\}^h \to \{0,1\}$, *a statement* $x \in \{0,1\}^n$, *and witnesses* $w_0, w_1 \in \{0,1\}^h$, *the oracle outputs* $\mathsf{Prove}(\mathsf{crs}, C, x, w_b)$ *if* $C(x, w_0) = 1 = C(x, w_1)$. *Otherwise, it outputs* $\perp$.

3   Big-Key Identity-Based Encryption

In this section, we give a formal definition of big-key IBE. Our definition is based on the corresponding definition from [DGSW22], but has an important difference where we only consider inverse-polynomial advantage thresholds rather than all non-negligible advantage thresholds. This is an important distinction as the previous notion from [DGSW22] is unsatisfiable (see Remark 3.2). We begin by highlighting the main difference between big-key IBE and vanilla IBE (Definition 2.12):

- In big-key IBE, we allow the adversary to specify any efficiently-computable leakage function f that outputs at most ℓ bits, where ℓ is a leakage parameter. The challenger then replies with $f(\mathsf{msk})$. In the adaptive security experiment, the adversary chooses the challenge identities after it observes the (arbitrary) leakage on the master secret key.
- Since the adversary is given *arbitrary* leakage on the master secret key, its leakage may simply encode a secret key for the challenge identity. Thus, the usual notion of semantic security is not meaningful in this model. Instead, the adversary must declare a set of challenge identities $\mathcal{J}$. To win the game, the adversary must be able to break semantic security for all identities $\mathsf{id} \in \mathcal{J}$ with advantage greater than some threshold ε.

We now provide the formal definition and then discuss how it compares with the previous definition from [DGSW22].

Definition 3.1 (Big-Key Identity-Based Encryption [DGSW22, adapted]**).** *A big-key identity-based encryption scheme with identity space* $\mathcal{ID} = \{\mathcal{ID}_\lambda\}_{\lambda \in \mathbb{N}}$ *and message space* $\mathcal{M} = \{\mathcal{M}_\lambda\}_{\lambda \in \mathbb{N}}$ *is a tuple of efficient algorithms* $\Pi_{\mathsf{bkIBE}} = (\mathsf{Setup}, \mathsf{KeyGen}, \mathsf{Encrypt}, \mathsf{Decrypt})$ *with the following syntax:*

- $\mathsf{Setup}(1^\lambda, 1^\ell) \to (\mathsf{pp}, \mathsf{msk})$*: On input the security parameter* λ *and the leakage parameter* ℓ*, the setup algorithm outputs public parameters* pp *and a master secret key* msk*. We assume that* pp *and* msk *include the security parameter* 1^λ*.*
- $\mathsf{KeyGen}(\mathsf{msk}, \mathsf{id}) \to \mathsf{sk}_{\mathsf{id}}$*: On input the master secret key* msk *and an identity* $\mathsf{id} \in \mathcal{ID}_\lambda$*, the key-generation algorithm outputs an identity secret key* $\mathsf{sk}_{\mathsf{id}}$*. We assume the secret key* $\mathsf{sk}_{\mathsf{id}}$ *contains the security parameter* 1^λ *(from* msk*).*
- $\mathsf{Encrypt}(\mathsf{pp}, \mathsf{id}, m) \to \mathsf{ct}$*: On input the public parameters* pp*, an identity* $\mathsf{id} \in \mathcal{ID}_\lambda$*, and a message* $m \in \mathcal{M}_\lambda$*, the encryption algorithm outputs a ciphertext* ct*.*
- $\mathsf{Decrypt}(\mathsf{sk}_{\mathsf{id}}, \mathsf{id}, \mathsf{ct}) \to m$*: On input an identity secret key* $\mathsf{sk}_{\mathsf{id}}$*, an identity* $\mathsf{id} \in \mathcal{ID}_\lambda$*, and a ciphertext* ct*, the decryption algorithm outputs a message* $m \in \mathcal{M}_\lambda$*.*

Moreover, Π_{bkIBE} *should satisfy the following properties:*

- **Correctness:** *For all security parameters* $\lambda \in \mathbb{N}$*, all leakage parameters* $\ell \in \mathbb{N}$*, all identities* $\mathsf{id} \in \mathcal{ID}_\lambda$*, all* $(\mathsf{pp}, \mathsf{msk})$ *in the support of* $\mathsf{Setup}(1^\lambda, 1^\ell)$*, and all messages* $m \in \mathcal{M}_\lambda$*,*

$$\Pr\left[\mathsf{Decrypt}(\mathsf{sk}_{\mathsf{id}}, \mathsf{id}, \mathsf{ct}) = m : \begin{matrix} \mathsf{sk}_{\mathsf{id}} \leftarrow \mathsf{KeyGen}(\mathsf{msk}, \mathsf{id}) \\ \mathsf{ct} \leftarrow \mathsf{Encrypt}(\mathsf{pp}, \mathsf{id}, m) \end{matrix}\right] = 1.$$

- **Efficiency:** *We impose the following efficiency requirements on the scheme parameters:*
  - **Public key size:** *We say that a big-key IBE scheme has short public parameters if the public parameters* pp *output by* $\mathsf{Setup}(1^\lambda, 1^\ell)$ *satisfies* $|\mathsf{pp}| = \mathsf{poly}(\lambda, \log \ell)$*. We say the scheme has long public parameters if* $|\mathsf{pp}| = \mathsf{poly}(\lambda, \ell)$*.*
  - **Secret key size:** *We require that the identity secret keys* $\mathsf{sk}_{\mathsf{id}}$ *output by* KeyGen *to satisfy* $|\mathsf{sk}_{\mathsf{id}}| = \mathsf{poly}(\lambda, \log \ell)$*.*
  - **Key-generation and encryption time:** *We require that* KeyGen *and* $\mathsf{Encrypt}$ *run in time* $\mathsf{poly}(\lambda, \log \ell)$ *given random access to the master secret key* msk *and the public parameters* pp*, respectively. In other words,* KeyGen *only needs to read* $\mathsf{poly}(\lambda, \log \ell)$ *bits of* msk *and* $\mathsf{Encrypt}$ *only needs to read* $\mathsf{poly}(\lambda, \log \ell)$ *bits of* pp*. Note that if the scheme has short public parameters (i.e., if* $|\mathsf{pp}| = \mathsf{poly}(\lambda, \log \ell)$*), then the encryption requirement is trivially satisfied.*
- **Adaptive security under bounded leakage:** *For a security parameter* λ*, a challenge parameter* $k = k(\lambda, \ell)$*, and an advantage function* $\varepsilon = \varepsilon(\lambda)$*, we define the adaptive security game between an adversary* $\mathcal{A} = (\mathcal{A}_1, \mathcal{A}_2)$ *and a challenger as follows:*

- **Setup:** *On input the security parameter, algorithm $\mathcal{A}_1$ starts by outputting a leakage parameter 1^ℓ, which it gives to the challenger. The challenger samples $(\mathsf{pp}, \mathsf{msk}) \leftarrow \mathsf{Setup}(1^\lambda, 1^\ell)$ and gives pp to $\mathcal{A}_1$.*
- **Pre-leakage queries:** *Algorithm $\mathcal{A}_1$ can now issue key-generation queries to the challenger. On each key-generation query, algorithm $\mathcal{A}_1$ specifies an identity $\mathsf{id} \in \mathcal{ID}_\lambda$ and the challenger replies with $\mathsf{sk}_{\mathsf{id}} \leftarrow \mathsf{KeyGen}(\mathsf{msk}, \mathsf{id})$.*
- **Leakage:** *Algorithm $\mathcal{A}_1$ outputs the description of an efficiently-computable function f with output length at most ℓ. The challenger replies with $\mathsf{leak} := f(\mathsf{msk})$.*
- **Post-leakage queries:** *Algorithm $\mathcal{A}_1$ can continue to make key-generation queries to the challenger.*
- **Challenge:** *Algorithm $\mathcal{A}_1$ outputs a set $\mathcal{J} \subseteq \mathcal{ID}_\lambda$ of size at least $k = k(\lambda, \ell)$, two messages $m_0, m_1 \in \mathcal{M}_\lambda$, and a state st.*
- **Output:** *The output of the adaptive security game is $b' = 1$ if*

$$\forall \mathsf{id} \in \mathcal{J} : \mathsf{Adv}^{\mathsf{id}}(\mathsf{msk}, \mathsf{pp}, \mathsf{st}, \mathsf{leak}) \geq \varepsilon(\lambda) \tag{3.1}$$

and $b' = 0$ otherwise. The distinguishing advantage $\mathsf{Adv}^{\mathsf{id}}(\mathsf{msk}, \mathsf{pp}, \mathsf{st}, \mathsf{leak})$ is defined as follows:

For an identity $\mathsf{id} \in \mathcal{ID}_\lambda$, define the experiment $\mathsf{Exp}^{\mathsf{id}}(\mathsf{msk}, \mathsf{pp}, \mathsf{st}, \mathsf{leak})$ as follows:

- * *The challenger samples $b \xleftarrow{\mathsf{R}} \{0,1\}, \mathsf{ct} \leftarrow \mathsf{Encrypt}(\mathsf{pp}, \mathsf{id}, m_b)$ and gives $(\mathsf{st}, \mathsf{id}, \mathsf{ct})$ to $\mathcal{A}_2$.*
- * *Algorithm $\mathcal{A}_2$ can now issue key-generation queries to the challenger. On each key-generation query, algorithm $\mathcal{A}_2$ specifies an identity $\mathsf{id} \in \mathcal{ID}_\lambda$ and the challenger replies with $\mathsf{sk}_{\mathsf{id}} \leftarrow \mathsf{KeyGen}(\mathsf{msk}, \mathsf{id})$.*
- * *After $\mathcal{A}_2$ has finished making key-generation queries, it outputs a bit $\beta \in \{0,1\}$, which is used to compute the output of the experiment as 1 if $b = \beta$ and 0 otherwise.*

The advantage $\mathsf{Adv}^{\mathsf{id}}(\mathsf{msk}, \mathsf{pp}, \mathsf{st}, \mathsf{leak})$ is then defined as

$$\mathsf{Adv}^{\mathsf{id}}(\mathsf{msk}, \mathsf{pp}, \mathsf{st}, \mathsf{leak}) = \left| \Pr[\mathsf{Exp}^{\mathsf{id}}(\mathsf{msk}, \mathsf{pp}, \mathsf{st}, \mathsf{leak}) = b] - 1/2 \right|.$$

We say that an algorithm $\mathcal{A} = (\mathcal{A}_1, \mathcal{A}_2)$ is admissible for the adaptive security game if neither $\mathcal{A}_1$ nor $\mathcal{A}_2$ makes a key-generation query on any identity $\mathsf{id} \in \mathcal{J}$. We say Π_{bkIBE} satisfies adaptive security under bounded leakage with challenge parameter $k = k(\lambda, \ell)$ if for all efficient adversaries $\mathcal{A} = (\mathcal{A}_1, \mathcal{A}_2)$ and every inverse polynomial advantage function $\varepsilon = 1/\mathsf{poly}(\lambda)$, there exists a negligible function $\mathsf{negl}(\cdot)$ such that for all $\lambda \in \mathbb{N}$, $\Pr[b' = 1] = \mathsf{negl}(\lambda)$ in the adaptive security game.

Remark 3.2 (Comparison with [DGSW22]). Beyond the extension from selective security to adaptive security, Definition 3.1 differs from the notion in [DGSW22,

Definition 3] in an important manner. The definition in [DGSW22] says that a big-key IBE scheme satisfies (selective) security under bounded leakage if for all efficient adversaries $\mathcal{A} = (\mathcal{A}_1, \mathcal{A}_2)$ and all *non-negligible* functions ε, there exists a negligible function $\mathsf{negl}(\cdot)$ such that for all $\lambda \in \mathbb{N}$,

$$\Pr[\forall \mathsf{id} \in \mathcal{J} : \mathsf{Adv}^{\mathsf{id}}(\mathsf{msk}, \mathsf{pp}, \mathsf{st}, \mathsf{leak}) \geq \varepsilon(\lambda)] = \mathsf{negl}(\lambda). \qquad (3.2)$$

In contrast, our definition (Definition 3.1) requires the advantage threshold ε to be *inverse polynomial*. While "non-negligible" and "inverse-polynomial" may seem like a small distinction, it is an important one. Indeed, we can show that the definition is unsatisfiable if we require Eq. (3.2) to hold for all non-negligible functions ε. To wit, suppose ε is the following piecewise function:

$$\varepsilon(\lambda) = \begin{cases} 1 & \lambda \text{ is odd} \\ 0 & \lambda \text{ is even.} \end{cases}$$

Observe that $\varepsilon(\lambda)$ is non-negligible by construction. However, Eq. (3.2) cannot hold for any scheme with respect to ε. This is because for every adversary $\mathcal{A}$, and every even value of $\lambda \in \mathbb{N}$, it holds that

$$\mathsf{Adv}^{\mathsf{id}}(\mathsf{msk}, \mathsf{pp}, \mathsf{st}, \mathsf{leak}) \geq 0 = \varepsilon(\lambda).$$

This means that whenever λ is even, it follows that

$$\Pr[\forall \mathsf{id} \in \mathcal{J} : \mathsf{Adv}^{\mathsf{id}}(\mathsf{msk}, \mathsf{pp}, \mathsf{st}, \mathsf{leak}) \geq \varepsilon(\lambda)] = 1.$$

As such, we cannot bound the probability in Eq. (3.2) by a negligible function, and Eq. (3.2) does not hold. For this reason, the original definition from [DGSW22] is unsatisfiable. In this work, we require ε to be an inverse polynomial function $1/\mathsf{poly}(\lambda)$, where $\mathsf{poly}(\lambda)$ is a *fixed* polynomial. This rules out such pathological functions.

Advantage Checking. In Definition 3.1, the output of the experiment requires checking whether Eq. (3.1) holds or not:

$$\forall \mathsf{id} \in \mathcal{J} : \mathsf{Adv}^{\mathsf{id}}(\mathsf{msk}, \mathsf{pp}, \mathsf{st}, \mathsf{leak}) \geq \varepsilon(\lambda),$$

where $\varepsilon(\lambda)$ is some advantage threshold. We note that in general, the exact advantage of an adversary is *not* efficiently-computable. As such, the challenger in Definition 3.1 cannot necessarily efficiently determine whether the adversary $\mathcal{A}$ is successful or not. While having an inefficient challenger is perfectly acceptable from a definitional standpoint, it introduces new challenges in the security analysis. Namely, given a candidate adversary $\mathcal{A}$, a reduction algorithm that uses $\mathcal{A}$ to solve some computational problem may not be able to determine whether $\mathcal{A}$ was successful or not. To address this problem, we define an alternative version of the adaptive security game where we replace the win condition (Eq. (3.1)) with an efficiently-checkable variant based on *estimating* the success probability of the adversary (Definition 3.3).[2] We then show in Theorem 3.4 that a scheme satisfying our alternative security game implies a scheme that is secure under our main definition (Definition 3.1). Then, in the remainder of this paper, we only consider Definition 3.3 where the output of the game is efficiently-computable (Fig. 1).

Inputs: *security parameter* λ, *advantage threshold* $\varepsilon \in (0,1)$, *identity* id $\in \mathcal{ID}_\lambda$, *master secret key* msk, *public parameters* pp, *state* st, *string* leak, *and (oracle) access to an algorithm* $\mathcal{A}$

- *Let* $T = \lambda/\varepsilon^2$ *and initialize a counter* WINS $\leftarrow 0$.
- *The advantage-checker algorithm now simulates* T *independent executions of experiment* $\mathsf{Exp}^{\mathsf{id}}(\mathsf{msk}, \mathsf{pp}, \mathsf{st}, \mathsf{leak})$ *for algorithm* $\mathcal{A}$.
  1. *Sample* $\beta \xleftarrow{R} \{0,1\}$.
  2. *Compute* ct $\leftarrow \mathsf{Encrypt}(\mathsf{pp}, \mathsf{id}, m_\beta)$, *and start running algorithm* $\mathcal{A}$ *on input* $(\mathsf{st}, \mathsf{id}, \mathsf{ct})$.
  3. *Whenever algorithm* $\mathcal{A}$ *makes a key-generation query on an identity* id $\in \mathcal{ID}_\lambda$, *compute* $\mathsf{sk}_{\mathsf{id}} \leftarrow \mathsf{KeyGen}(\mathsf{msk}, \mathsf{id})$ *and reply to* $\mathcal{A}$ *with the identity key* $\mathsf{sk}_{\mathsf{id}}$.
  4. *After* $\mathcal{A}$ *has finished making key-generation queries, it outputs a bit* $\beta' \in \{0,1\}$.
  5. *If* $\beta = \beta'$, *then increment* WINS $\leftarrow$ WINS $+ 1$.
- *Output 1 if* $\left|\mathsf{WINS} - \frac{T}{2}\right| \geq \frac{\varepsilon T}{2}$ *and 0 otherwise*.

Fig. 1. Function $\mathsf{AdvCheck}^{\mathcal{A}}\left(1^\lambda, 1^{1/\varepsilon}, \mathsf{id}, \mathsf{msk}, \mathsf{pp}, \mathsf{st}, \mathsf{leak}\right)$

Definition 3.3 (Adaptive Advantage-Checker Security). *Let* Π_{bkIBE} *be a big-key IBE scheme as in Definition 3.1. We define the following property:*

- *Adaptive advantage-checker security under bounded leakage: This security game is identical to the adaptive security game in Definition 3.1 except the output of the game is* $b' = 1$ *if*

$$\forall \mathsf{id} \in \mathcal{J} : \mathsf{AdvCheck}^{\mathcal{A}_2}\left(1^\lambda, 1^{1/\varepsilon}, \mathsf{id}, \mathsf{msk}, \mathsf{pp}, \mathsf{st}, \mathsf{leak}\right) = 1$$

and $b' = 0$ *otherwise. The algorithm* $\mathsf{AdvCheck}$ *is defined as follows: We say that an algorithm* $\mathcal{A} = (\mathcal{A}_1, \mathcal{A}_2)$ *is admissible for the* k-*adaptive advantage-checker security game if neither* $\mathcal{A}_1$ *nor* $\mathcal{A}_2$ *makes a key-generation*

---

[2] We note here that this issue appears to have been glossed over in the previous work of [DGSW22] as their security proofs do not describe how the reduction algorithm uses the adversary's output to solve the underlying computational problem. We believe that their analysis can be repaired by formally defining a similar intermediary game with an efficiently-computable challenger.

query on any identity id $\in \mathcal{J}$. *The scheme* Π_{bkIBE} *satisfies adaptive advantage-checker security under bounded leakage with challenge parameter* $k = k(\lambda, \ell)$ *if for all efficient adversaries* $\mathcal{A} = (\mathcal{A}_1, \mathcal{A}_2)$ *and every inverse polynomial advantage function* $\varepsilon = 1/\mathsf{poly}(\lambda)$, *there exists a negligible function* $\mathsf{negl}(\cdot)$ *such that for all* $\lambda \in \mathbb{N}$, $\Pr[b' = 1] = \mathsf{negl}(\lambda)$ *in the adaptive advantage-checker security game.*

Theorem 3.4 (Adaptive Security from Adaptive Advantage-Checker Security). *Suppose* Π_{bkIBE} *is a big-key IBE scheme that satisfies adaptive advantage-checker security under bounded leakage with challenge parameter* $k = k(\lambda, \ell)$. *Then,* Π_{bkIBE} *satisfies adaptive security under bounded leakage with the same challenge parameter* k.

Proof. Let Hyb_0 be the adaptive security experiment from Definition 3.1 and Hyb_1 be the advantage checker security experiment from Definition 3.3. For an adversary $\mathcal{A} = (\mathcal{A}_1, \mathcal{A}_2)$ and an advantage function ε, we write $\mathsf{Hyb}_i(\mathcal{A}, \varepsilon)$ to denote the output of Hyb_i with adversary $\mathcal{A}$ and advantage function ε. We now show that for all efficient adversaries $\mathcal{A}$ and all inverse polynomial advantage functions $\varepsilon = 1/\mathsf{poly}(\lambda)$, there exists a negligible function negl such that for all $\lambda \in \mathbb{N}$,

$$\Pr[\mathsf{Hyb}_0(\mathcal{A}, \varepsilon) = 1] \leq \Pr[\mathsf{Hyb}_1(\mathcal{A}, \varepsilon) = 1] + \mathsf{negl}(\lambda),$$

which proves the claim. By construction, the only difference between Hyb_0 and Hyb_1 is how the output bit $b' \in \{0, 1\}$ is computed. Suppose in an execution of Hyb_0 that the output bit is 1. This means that for all id $\in \mathcal{J}$,

$$\mathsf{Adv}^{\mathsf{id}}(\mathsf{msk}, \mathsf{pp}, \mathsf{st}, \mathsf{leak}) \geq \varepsilon. \tag{3.3}$$

Consider the output computed according to the specification of Hyb_1. The $\mathsf{AdvCheck}$ algorithm perfectly simulates T executions of $\mathsf{Exp}^{\mathsf{id}}$. For each $i \in [T]$, let $X_i \in \{0, 1\}$ be the random variable for whether algorithm $\mathcal{A}_2$'s output is correct (i.e., if $\beta' = \beta$) on the ith iteration. If Eq. (3.3) holds, then

$$|\mathbb{E}[X_i] - 1/2| = |\Pr[X_i = 1] - 1/2| \geq \varepsilon$$

In Hyb_1, we have $\mathsf{WINS} = \sum_{i \in [T]} X_i$ and since each X_i is identically distributed, it follows that

$$|\mathbb{E}[\mathsf{WINS}] - T/2| \geq \varepsilon T.$$

By Hoeffding's inequality (Fact 2.1),

$$\Pr[|\mathsf{WINS} - T/2| < \varepsilon T/2] \leq \Pr[|\mathsf{WINS} - \mathbb{E}[\mathsf{WINS}]| > \varepsilon T/2] \leq 2^{-\Omega(T\varepsilon^2/4)} = \mathsf{negl}(\lambda),$$

since $T = \lambda/\varepsilon^2$. Thus, if Eq. (3.3) holds, then with probability $1 - \mathsf{negl}(\lambda)$, $|\mathsf{WINS} - T/2| \geq \varepsilon T/2$ in an execution of $\mathsf{AdvCheck}^{\mathcal{A}_2}(1^\lambda, 1^{1/\varepsilon}, \mathsf{id}, \mathsf{msk}, \mathsf{pp}, \mathsf{st}, \mathsf{leak})$. In this case, $\mathsf{AdvCheck}$ outputs 1. By a union bound, if Eq. (3.3) holds for all id $\in \mathcal{J}$, then $\mathsf{AdvCheck}$ also outputs 1 for all id $\in \mathcal{J}$ with probability $1 - |\mathcal{J}| \cdot \mathsf{negl}(\lambda)$. If $\mathcal{A}$ is efficient, then the size of the challenge set $\mathcal{J}$ is polynomially-bounded, so we conclude that whenever experiment $\mathsf{Hyb}_0(\mathcal{A}, \varepsilon)$ outputs 1, then with probability $1 - \mathsf{negl}(\lambda)$, experiment $\mathsf{Hyb}_1(\mathcal{A}, \varepsilon)$ also outputs 1, and the claim follows.

Remark 3.5 (Challenge Parameter k). The challenge parameter k in Definitions 3.1 and 3.3 determines the minimum size of the challenge set $\mathcal{J}$ as a function of the security parameter λ and the leakage parameter ℓ. A larger value of k increases the difficulty for the adversary while a small value of k makes the adversary's job simpler. In [DGSW22], the parameter k was set to be $\ell + 1$; namely, given ℓ bits of leakage, the adversary has to compromise at least $\ell + 1$ identities. In this work, we show multiple bits of leakage are necessary to compromise any single identity key. Namely, we show how to achieve challenge parameter $k = \ell/\mathsf{poly}(\lambda)$.

4   Adaptively Secure Big-Key IBE from Indistinguishability Obfuscation

In this section, we describe how to construct an adaptively-secure big-key IBE scheme using indistinguishability obfuscation (Definition 2.13), an adaptively-secure IBE scheme (Definition 2.12), a NIZK proof for NP (Definition 2.17), a one-time dual-mode commitment scheme (Definition 2.15), and a pseudorandom generator (Definition 2.10).

Expanding Hash Function. First, we define the notion of an "expanding" hash function, which will be a useful building block in our constructions. At a high-level, an expanding hashing function $\mathcal{H}\colon \{0,1\}^\lambda \to [N]^d$ maps a string $x \in \{0,1\}^\lambda$ onto a set of elements $S \subseteq [N]$ of size $|S| = d$ with the property that for every collection of inputs $x_1, \ldots, x_k \in \{0,1\}^\lambda$, the set $\bigcup_{i \in [k]} \mathcal{H}(x_i)$ covers almost dk indices of the set $[N]$. In the context of our big-key IBE schemes, we will subdivide the master secret key into N blocks, and the secret key for an identity id will contain the blocks indexed by $\mathcal{H}(\mathsf{id})$. The security analysis will rely on the fact that for any set of k identities that the adversary can possibly corrupt, there will always exist at least one block of the master secret key that the adversary does not know. Namely, the number of blocks of the master secret key covered by every set of k identities is always *greater* than the amount of leakage the adversary is allowed on the master secret key. We now define the property formally, and show that such a hash function can be built from a disperser (Definition 2.4 and Fact 2.5).

Definition 4.1 (Expanding Hash Function). *We say a hash function $\mathcal{H}\colon \{0,1\}^\lambda \to [N]^d$ is (k, α)-expanding if there exists an explicit and efficient algorithm for computing $\mathcal{H}(x)$ in $\mathsf{poly}(\lambda, d, \log N)$ time, and moreover, for every collection of exactly k inputs $x_1, \ldots x_k \in \{0,1\}^\lambda$, it holds that $|\bigcup_{i \in [k]} \mathcal{H}(x_i)| \geq \alpha k$.*

Lemma 4.2 (Expanding Hash Function). *There exists a constant $c \in \mathbb{N}$ such that for every $\lambda \in \mathbb{N}$, every constant $\delta \in (0,1)$, and every polynomially-bounded function $t(\lambda) > \lambda^c$ where $t(\lambda)$ is a power of 4, there exists functions $\alpha = \omega(\log \lambda)$, $d = \mathsf{poly}(\lambda)$, and a (t, α)-expanding hash function $\mathcal{H}\colon \{0,1\}^\lambda \to [N]^d$, where $\alpha t = (1 - \delta)N$.*

Proof. This follows immediately from Fact 2.5. Specifically, let $G = (L, R, E)$ be the construction from Fact 2.5 instantiated with parameters $n = \lambda$, $\varepsilon = \delta$, $k = (\log t)/2$, and $k_1 = 2k = \log t$. Then, G is a degree-D (t, ε)-disperser where $D = \mathsf{poly}(\lambda)$, $|L| = 2^\lambda$ and $|R| = t \cdot 2^{\Omega(\log \lambda)}$. We now construct the expanding hash function $\mathcal{H} \colon \{0,1\}^\lambda \to [N]^d$ as follows:

- Set $N = |R| = t \cdot 2^{\Omega(\log \lambda)}$, $\alpha = (1 - \delta) \cdot 2^{\Omega(\log \lambda)}$, and $d = D = \mathsf{poly}(\lambda)$.
- For an input $x \in \{0,1\}^\lambda$, define $\mathcal{H}(x)$ to be the indices of the nodes in the neighborhood of node $x \in G$ (here, we index the 2^λ nodes in L with a bit-string in $\{0,1\}^\lambda$). Note that computing $\mathcal{H}(x)$ requires time $\mathsf{poly}(\lambda, d, \log N)$ since the disperser is explicit. Thus, $\mathcal{H}$ is efficiently-computable.

We now show the expanding property. This follows immediately from the fact that G is a disperser. Consider any set of t inputs $x_1, \ldots, x_t$. Let $S = \{x_1, \ldots, x_t\}$. Since G is a (t, ε)-disperser, and by construction of $\mathcal{H}$, it follows that

$$\left| \bigcup_{i \in [t]} \mathcal{H}(x_i) \right| = |N(S)| \geq (1 - \varepsilon) \cdot |R| = (1 - \delta)N = \alpha t,$$

where $N(S)$ denotes the neighborhood of S in G. To finish the proof we show the constraint on α and that t is a valid choice in Fact 2.5. Clearly $\alpha = (1 - \delta) \cdot 2^{\Omega(\log \lambda)} = \omega(\log \lambda)$ holds. It is also immediate that choosing $k_1 = 2k \geq k + O(\log^3 k)$ is sufficient.

Big-Key IBE Construction. We now give our first construction of an adaptively-secure big-key IBE scheme.

Construction 4.3 (Big-Key IBE from $i\mathcal{O}$). Let $\lambda \in \mathbb{N}$ be a security parameter, $\mathcal{ID} = \{\mathcal{ID}_\lambda\}_{\lambda \in \mathbb{N}}$ be the identity space, $\mathcal{M} = \{\mathcal{M}_\lambda\}_{\lambda \in \mathbb{N}}$ be the message space, ℓ be the leakage parameter, $N = N(\lambda, \ell)$ be a key-size parameter, and $d = d(\lambda)$ be an output-size parameter. Our construction relies on the following primitives (Fig. 2):

- Let $i\mathcal{O}$ be an indistinguishability obfuscation scheme. We will assume that all programs described here (and in the proof of Theorem 4.6) are padded to the size $\ell_C(\lambda)$ of the largest program among them.
- Let $\mathsf{PRG} \colon \{0,1\}^\lambda \to \{0,1\}^{2\lambda}$ be a pseudorandom generator. Note that the PRG is only used in the security analysis and does not appear in the main construction.
- Let $\mathcal{H} \colon \mathcal{ID}_\lambda \to [N]^d$ be a hash function. We interpret the output elements $[N]^d$ as an ordered list of d indices in $[N]$.
- Let $\Pi_{\mathsf{NIZK}} = (\mathsf{NIZK.Setup}, \mathsf{NIZK.Prove}, \mathsf{NIZK.Verify})$ be a NIZK proof for NP.
- Let $\Pi_{\mathsf{Com}} = (\mathsf{Com.Setup}, \mathsf{Com.Commit}, \mathsf{Com.Verify})$ be a one-time dual-mode commitment scheme (Definition 2.15) with input space $\mathcal{X} = \{\mathcal{X}_\lambda\}_{\lambda \in \mathbb{N}}$, and let $\ell_x = \ell_x(\lambda)$ be the bit-length of an input.
- Let $\Pi_{\mathsf{IBE}} = (\mathsf{IBE.Setup}, \mathsf{IBE.KeyGen}, \mathsf{IBE.Encrypt}, \mathsf{IBE.Decrypt})$ be an IBE scheme with identity space $\mathcal{ID}$ and message space $\mathcal{X}^d$.
- For public parameters $\mathsf{pp}_{\mathsf{IBE}}$, define the NP relation $\mathcal{R}[\mathsf{pp}_{\mathsf{IBE}}]$ as follows: Let $C_{\mathcal{R}}[\mathsf{pp}_{\mathsf{IBE}}]$ be the circuit computing the NP relation $\mathcal{R}[\mathsf{pp}_{\mathsf{IBE}}]$.

Hard-wired: public parameters pp_{IBE}

Statement: a vector of common reference strings $crs_{Com}^{(I)}$ indexed by a set $I \subset \mathbb{N}$, a tuple of commitments $\vec{c}_I$, ciphertext ct, identity id

Witness: strings $\vec{r}_I$, randomness ρ_{enc}, openings $\vec{\sigma}_I$

Output 1 if all of the following conditions hold:

- For each $i \in I$, $Com.Verify(crs_{Com}^{(i)}, c_i, r_i, \sigma_i) = 1$;
- $IBE.Encrypt(pp_{IBE}, id, \vec{r}_I; \rho_{enc}) = ct$

Otherwise, output 0.

Fig. 2. Relation $\mathcal{R}[pp_{IBE}]$.

We now construct our big-key IBE scheme $\Pi_{bkIBE} = (Setup, KeyGen, Encrypt, Decrypt)$ as follows:

- $Setup(1^\lambda, 1^\ell)$: On input the security parameter λ and the leakage parameter ℓ, the setup algorithm proceeds as follows:
  1. Sample $(pp_{IBE}, msk_{IBE}) \leftarrow IBE.Setup(1^\lambda)$ and $crs_{NIZK} \leftarrow NIZK.Setup(1^\lambda)$.
  2. For each $i \in [N]$, sample a random string $r_i \xleftarrow{R} \{0,1\}^{\ell_\pi}$. Then, sample a common reference string $crs_{Com}^{(i)} \leftarrow Com.Setup(1^\lambda, bind)$ and compute $(c_i, \sigma_i) \leftarrow Com.Commit(crs_{Com}^{(i)}, r_i)$.

  Let $\vec{c} = (c_1, \ldots, c_N)$, $\vec{r} = (r_1, \ldots, r_N)$, and $\vec{\sigma} = (\sigma_1, \ldots, \sigma_N)$. For a set $I \subseteq [N]$, we write $\vec{c}_I$, $\vec{r}_I$, and $\vec{\sigma}_I$ to be the respective sub-vector of indices in I. Similarly, we define $crs_{Com}^{(I)} := (crs_{Com}^{(i)})_{i \in I}$. Output

  $$pp = \left(\{crs_{Com}^{(i)}\}_{i \in [N]}, \vec{c}, crs_{NIZK}, pp_{IBE} \right) \quad \text{and} \quad msk = (pp, \vec{r}, \vec{\sigma}). \quad (4.1)$$

- $KeyGen(msk, id)$: On input the master secret key msk (with components as in Eq. (4.1)) and an identity $id \in \mathcal{ID}_\lambda$, the key generation algorithm proceeds as follows:
  1. Compute $I \leftarrow \mathcal{H}(id)$.
  2. Compute $ct \leftarrow IBE.Encrypt(pp_{IBE}, id, \vec{r}_I; \rho_{enc})$ where ρ_{enc} is the encryption randomness and $\vec{r}_I$ is as defined in Eq. (4.1).
  3. Compute $\pi \leftarrow NIZK.Prove(crs_{NIZK}, C_{\mathcal{R}}[pp_{IBE}], (crs_{Com}^{(I)}, \vec{c}_I, ct, id), (\vec{r}_I, \rho_{enc}, \vec{\sigma}_I))$, where $crs_{Com}^{(I)}$, $\vec{c}_I$, $\vec{r}_I$, and $\vec{\sigma}_I$ are as defined in Eq. (4.1).

  Output the identity secret key $sk_{id} = (ct, \pi)$.

- $Encrypt(pp, id, m)$: On input the public parameters pp, an identity $id \in \mathcal{ID}_\lambda$ and a message $m \in \mathcal{M}_\lambda$, the encryption algorithm defines the following program:

  The encryption algorithm then computes $I \leftarrow \mathcal{H}(id)$ and the obfuscated program (Fig. 3)

  $$\tilde{C} \leftarrow i\mathcal{O}(Check\text{-}Bits[crs_{NIZK}, C_{\mathcal{R}}[pp_{IBE}], crs_{Com}^{(I)}, \vec{c}_I, m, id]).$$

It outputs the ciphertext $\mathsf{ct} = \widetilde{C}$.

- $\mathsf{Decrypt}(\mathsf{sk}_{\mathsf{id}}, \mathsf{id}, \mathsf{ct})$: On input an identity secret key $\mathsf{sk}_{\mathsf{id}}$, an identity $\mathsf{id} \in \mathcal{ID}_\lambda$, and a ciphertext $\mathsf{ct} = \widetilde{C}$, the decryption algorithm outputs $\widetilde{C}(\mathsf{sk}_{\mathsf{id}})$.

Hard-wired: common reference string $\mathsf{crs}_{\mathsf{NIZK}}$, a vector of common reference strings $\mathsf{crs}_{\mathsf{Com}}^{(I)}$ indexed by a set $I \subset \mathbb{N}$, a circuit C, a tuple of commitments $\vec{c}_I$, message m, identity id
Inputs: ciphertext ct, proof π

1. If $\mathsf{NIZK.Verify}\left(\mathsf{crs}_{\mathsf{NIZK}}, C, \left(\mathsf{crs}_{\mathsf{Com}}^{(I)}, \vec{c}_I, \mathsf{ct}, \mathsf{id}\right), \pi\right) = 1$, output m.
2. Otherwise, output $\perp$.

Fig. 3. Program $\mathsf{Check\text{-}Bits}\left[\mathsf{crs}_{\mathsf{NIZK}}, C, \mathsf{crs}_{\mathsf{Com}}^{(I)}, \vec{c}_I, m, \mathsf{id}\right]$.

Theorem 4.4 (Correctness). *Suppose Π_{Com} is correct, $i\mathcal{O}$ is correct, and Π_{NIZK} is complete. Then, Construction 4.3 is correct.*

Proof. Take any security parameter λ, identity $\mathsf{id} \in \mathcal{ID}_\lambda$, and message m. Let $(\mathsf{pp}, \mathsf{msk}) \leftarrow \mathsf{Setup}(1^\lambda, 1^\ell)$, where $\mathsf{pp} = \left(\left\{\mathsf{crs}_{\mathsf{Com}}^{(i)}\right\}_{i \in [N]}, \vec{c}, \mathsf{crs}_{\mathsf{NIZK}}, \mathsf{pp}_{\mathsf{IBE}}\right)$, $\mathsf{msk} = (\mathsf{pp}, \vec{r}, \vec{\sigma})$. Let $\mathsf{sk}_{\mathsf{id}} = (\mathsf{ct}, \pi) \leftarrow \mathsf{KeyGen}(\mathsf{msk}, \mathsf{id})$ and $\widetilde{C} \leftarrow \mathsf{Encrypt}(\mathsf{pp}, \mathsf{id}, m)$. Consider the output of $\mathsf{Decrypt}(\mathsf{sk}_{\mathsf{id}}, \mathsf{id}, \widetilde{C})$:

- By construction of KeyGen and correctness of Π_{Com}, we have

$$((\mathsf{crs}_{\mathsf{Com}}^{(I)}, \vec{c}_I, \mathsf{ct}, \mathsf{id}), (\vec{r}_I, \rho_{\mathsf{enc}}, \vec{\sigma}_I)) \in \mathcal{R}[\mathsf{pp}_{\mathsf{IBE}}],$$

  and $\pi \leftarrow \mathsf{NIZK.Prove}(\mathsf{crs}_{\mathsf{NIZK}}, C_{\mathcal{R}}[\mathsf{pp}_{\mathsf{IBE}}], (\mathsf{crs}_{\mathsf{Com}}^{(I)}, \vec{c}_I, \mathsf{ct}, \mathsf{id}), (\vec{r}_I, \rho_{\mathsf{enc}}, \vec{\sigma}_I))$.
- By construction of $\mathsf{Encrypt}$ and $i\mathcal{O}$ correctness, $\widetilde{C}$ is a program which outputs the message m when the NIZK proof verifies on statement $(\mathsf{crs}_{\mathsf{Com}}^{(I)}, \vec{c}_I, \mathsf{ct}, \mathsf{id})$ where ct is an input.
- By completeness of Π_{NIZK}, the proof π from KeyGen verifies and thus $\widetilde{C}(\mathsf{sk}_{\mathsf{id}}) = m$, as required. $\qquad\square$

Theorem 4.5 (Efficiency). *If $\mathcal{H}$ runs in $\mathsf{poly}(\lambda, \log N)$-time, then Construction 4.3 is efficient.*

Proof. This holds by inspection and assumption on $\mathcal{H}$, since our other primitives run in $\mathsf{poly}(\lambda)$-time by definition. Furthermore, the KeyGen and $\mathsf{Encrypt}$ algorithms only needs to read $\mathsf{poly}(\lambda) \cdot d(\lambda)$ bits of the master secret key msk and/or the public parameters pp. The size of these quantities are independent of the leakage parameter ℓ.

Theorem 4.6 (Adaptive Advantage-Checker Security under Bounded Leakage). *Suppose the following conditions hold:*

- *The obfuscator $i\mathcal{O}$ is secure.*
- *The hash function $\mathcal{H}$ is (k, α)-expanding, where $(1 - \eta)\alpha(\lambda)\ell_x(\lambda) \geq \lambda + \omega(\log \lambda)$ for some constant $\eta \in (0, 1)$.*
- *The IBE scheme Π_{IBE} satisfies correctness and adaptive semantic security.*
- *The NIZK Π_{NIZK} satisfies statistical soundness and computational zero-knowledge.*
- *The one-time dual-mode commitment scheme Π_{Com} satisfies mode indistinguishability and statistical binding in binding mode.*
- *The pseudorandom generator PRG is secure.*
- *There exists an explicit universal hash family $\mathcal{H}_{\mathsf{fam}}$ of size at most $2^{\mathsf{poly}(\lambda)}$, where each function $h\colon \mathcal{X}_\lambda^d \to \{0,1\}^\lambda$ has domain $\mathcal{X}_\lambda^d$ and range $\{0,1\}^\lambda$. Moreover, the extractor $\mathsf{Ext}(x, h) = h(x)$ is a $(\lambda + \omega(\log \lambda), \mathsf{negl}(\lambda))$-strong randomness extractor.*

Then for all polynomially-bounded and sufficiently large $\ell = \ell(\lambda)$, Construction 4.3 is adaptively advantage-checker secure under bounded leakage with challenge parameter $k \geq \frac{\ell}{\eta\alpha\ell_x}$.

Proof. We give the proof in the full version of this paper.

Corollary 4.7 (Adaptive Security under Bounded Leakage). *Suppose the conditions in Theorem 4.6 hold. Then, Construction 4.3 is adaptively secure under bounded leakage for the same k as in Theorem 4.6.*

Proof. Follows directly from Theorem 3.4.

Remark 4.8 (Leakage Rate). By the condition on k in Theorem 4.6, we have $\eta \cdot k\alpha\ell_x \geq \ell$ for $\eta \in (0, 1)$. By construction, the number of bits in $\vec{r} = (r_1, \dots, r_N)$ is $\ell_x \cdot N$. By using the hash function from Corollary 4.2, we have that $\alpha k = (1 - \delta)N$ for any $\delta \in (0, 1)$. Thus, $\eta \cdot (1 - \delta)N\ell_x = \eta' \cdot N\ell_x \geq \ell$ for any $\eta' \in (0, 1)$. Since the only private components in msk are $\vec{r}$ and $\vec{\sigma}$, the leakage rate is then dependent on the number of bits in $\vec{\sigma}$ compared to $\vec{r}$. With the Naor commitment scheme based on one-way functions [Nao89], we obtain leakage rate $1/O(\lambda)$ since an opening to a single bit is $O(\lambda)$ bits. However, by substituting an algebraic dual-mode commitment where the size of the opening is at most $2\times$ the bit-length of the underlying message (e.g., [GS08, BL20]), we can achieve leakage rate approaching $1/3$, matching [DGSW22].

References

[ABSV15] Ananth, P., Brakerski, Z., Segev, G., Vaikuntanathan, V.: From selective to adaptive security in functional encryption. In: Gennaro, R., Robshaw, M. (eds.) CRYPTO 2015. LNCS, vol. 9216, pp. 657–677. Springer, Heidelberg (2015). https://doi.org/10.1007/978-3-662-48000-7_32

[ADN+10] Alwen, J., Dodis, Y., Naor, M., Segev, G., Walfish, S., Wichs, D.: Public-key encryption in the bounded-retrieval model. In: Gilbert, H. (ed.) EURO-CRYPT 2010. LNCS, vol. 6110, pp. 113–134. Springer, Heidelberg (2010). https://doi.org/10.1007/978-3-642-13190-5_6

[ADW09] Alwen, J., Dodis, Y., Wichs, D.: Leakage-resilient public-key cryptography in the bounded-retrieval model. In: Halevi, S. (ed.) CRYPTO 2009. LNCS, vol. 5677, pp. 36–54. Springer, Heidelberg (2009). https://doi.org/10.1007/978-3-642-03356-8_3

[BF01] Boneh, D., Franklin, M.: Identity-based encryption from the weil pairing. In: Kilian, J. (ed.) CRYPTO 2001. LNCS, vol. 2139, pp. 213–229. Springer, Heidelberg (2001). https://doi.org/10.1007/3-540-44647-8_13

[BFM88] Blum, M., Feldman, P., Micali, S.: Non-interactive zero-knowledge and its applications (extended abstract). In: STOC, pp. 103–112 (1988)

[BGI+01] Barak, B., et al.: On the (im)possibility of obfuscating programs. In: Kilian, J. (ed.) CRYPTO 2001. LNCS, vol. 2139, pp. 1–18. Springer, Heidelberg (2001). https://doi.org/10.1007/3-540-44647-8_1

[BGI+12] Barak, B., et al.: On the (im)possibility of obfuscating programs. J. ACM **59**(2), 1–48 (2012)

[BHK11] Braverman, M., Hassidim, A., Kalai, Y.T.: Leaky pseudo-entropy functions. Innov. Comput. Sci. 353–366 (2011)

[BKR16] Bellare, M., Kane, D., Rogaway, P.: Big-key symmetric encryption: resisting key exfiltration. In: Robshaw, M., Katz, J. (eds.) CRYPTO 2016. LNCS, vol. 9814, pp. 373–402. Springer, Heidelberg (2016). https://doi.org/10.1007/978-3-662-53018-4_14

[BL20] Benhamouda, F., Lin, H.: Mr NISC: multiparty reusable non-interactive secure computation. In: Pass, R., Pietrzak, K. (eds.) TCC 2020. LNCS, vol. 12551, pp. 349–378. Springer, Cham (2020). https://doi.org/10.1007/978-3-030-64378-2_13

[CDD+07] Cash, D., Ding, Y.Z., Dodis, Y., Lee, W., Lipton, R., Walfish, S.: Intrusion-resilient key exchange in the bounded retrieval model. In: Vadhan, S.P. (ed.) TCC 2007. LNCS, vol. 4392, pp. 479–498. Springer, Heidelberg (2007). https://doi.org/10.1007/978-3-540-70936-7_26

[CLW06] Di Crescenzo, G., Lipton, R., Walfish, S.: Perfectly secure password protocols in the bounded retrieval model. In: Halevi, S., Rabin, T. (eds.) TCC 2006. LNCS, vol. 3876, pp. 225–244. Springer, Heidelberg (2006). https://doi.org/10.1007/11681878_12

[Coc01] Cocks, C.: An identity based encryption scheme based on quadratic residues. In: Honary, B. (ed.) Cryptography and Coding 2001. LNCS, vol. 2260, pp. 360–363. Springer, Heidelberg (2001). https://doi.org/10.1007/3-540-45325-3_32

[DFR+07] Damgård, I.B., Fehr, S., Renner, R., Salvail, L., Schaffner, C.: A tight high-order entropic quantum uncertainty relation with applications. In: Menezes, A. (ed.) CRYPTO 2007. LNCS, vol. 4622, pp. 360–378. Springer, Heidelberg (2007). https://doi.org/10.1007/978-3-540-74143-5_20

[DGSW22] Döttling, N., Garg, S., Sekar, S., Wang, M.: IBE with incompressible master secret and small identity secrets. In: Kiltz, E., Vaikuntanathan, V. (eds.) Theory of Cryptography. TCC 2022. Lecture Notes in Computer Science, vol. 13747, pp. 588–617. Springer, Cham (2022). https://doi.org/10.1007/978-3-031-22318-1_21

[DN02] Damgård, I., Nielsen, J.B.: Perfect hiding and perfect binding universally composable commitment schemes with constant expansion factor. In: Yung, M. (ed.) CRYPTO 2002. LNCS, vol. 2442, pp. 581–596. Springer, Heidelberg (2002). https://doi.org/10.1007/3-540-45708-9_37

[DORS08] Dodis, Y., Ostrovsky, R., Reyzin, L., Smith, A.D.: Fuzzy extractors: how to generate strong keys from biometrics and other noisy data. SIAM J. Comput. **38**(1), 97–139 (2008)

[Dzi06] Dziembowski, S.: Intrusion-resilience via the bounded-storage model. In: Halevi, S., Rabin, T. (eds.) TCC 2006. LNCS, vol. 3876, pp. 207–224. Springer, Heidelberg (2006). https://doi.org/10.1007/11681878_11

[GGH+13] Garg, S., Gentry, C., Halevi, S., Raykova, M., Sahai, A., Waters, B.: Candidate indistinguishability obfuscation and functional encryption for all circuits. In: FOCS, pp. 40–49 (2013)

[GGSW13] Garg, S., Gentry, C., Sahai, A., Waters, B.: Witness encryption and its applications. In: STOC, pp. 467–476 (2013)

[GMR85] Goldwasser, S., Micali, S., Rackoff, C.: The knowledge complexity of interactive proof-systems (extended abstract). In: STOC, pp. 291–304 (1985)

[GS08] Groth, J., Sahai, A.: Efficient non-interactive proof systems for bilinear groups. In: Smart, N. (ed.) EUROCRYPT 2008. LNCS, vol. 4965, pp. 415–432. Springer, Heidelberg (2008). https://doi.org/10.1007/978-3-540-78967-3_24

[HILL99] Håstad, J., Impagliazzo, R., Levin, L.A., Luby, M.: A pseudorandom generator from any one-way function. SIAM J. Comput. **28**(4), 1364–1396 (1999)

[Hoe63] Hoeffding, W.: Probability inequalities for sums of bounded random variables. J. Am. Stat. Assoc. **58**(301) (1963)

[ILL89] Impagliazzo, R., Levin, L.A., Luby, M.: Pseudo-random generation from one-way functions (extended abstracts). In: STOC, pp. 12–24 (1989)

[LW10] Lewko, A., Waters, B.: New techniques for dual system encryption and fully secure HIBE with short ciphertexts. In: Micciancio, D. (ed.) TCC 2010. LNCS, vol. 5978, pp. 455–479. Springer, Heidelberg (2010). https://doi.org/10.1007/978-3-642-11799-2_27

[MW20] Moran, T., Wichs, D.: Incompressible encodings. In: Micciancio, D., Ristenpart, T. (eds.) CRYPTO 2020. LNCS, vol. 12170, pp. 494–523. Springer, Cham (2020). https://doi.org/10.1007/978-3-030-56784-2_17

[Nao89] Naor, M.: Bit commitment using pseudo-randomness. In: Brassard, G. (ed.) CRYPTO 1989. LNCS, vol. 435, pp. 128–136. Springer, New York (1990). https://doi.org/10.1007/0-387-34805-0_13

[Par19] Parzanchevski, N.: Dispersers with logarithmic entropy loss. M.Sc thesis, Tel-Aviv University (2019)

[Sha84] Shamir, A.: Identity-based cryptosystems and signature schemes. In: Blakley, G.R., Chaum, D. (eds.) CRYPTO 1984. LNCS, vol. 196, pp. 47–53. Springer, Heidelberg (1985). https://doi.org/10.1007/3-540-39568-7_5

[SW14] Sahai, A., Waters, B.: How to use indistinguishability obfuscation: deniable encryption, and more. In: STOC, pp. 475–484 (2014)

[TUZ07] Ta-Shma, A., Umans, C., Zuckerman, D.: Lossless condensers, unbalanced expanders, and extractors. Combinatorica **27**(2), 213–240 (2007). https://doi.org/10.1007/s00493-007-0053-2

[Wat05] Waters, B.: Efficient identity-based encryption without random oracles. In: Cramer, R. (ed.) EUROCRYPT 2005. LNCS, vol. 3494, pp. 114–127. Springer, Heidelberg (2005). https://doi.org/10.1007/11426639_7

[Wat09] Waters, B.: Dual system encryption: realizing fully secure IBE and HIBE under simple assumptions. In: Halevi, S. (ed.) CRYPTO 2009. LNCS, vol. 5677, pp. 619–636. Springer, Heidelberg (2009). https://doi.org/10.1007/978-3-642-03356-8_36

[WW24] Waters, B., Wichs, D.: Adaptively secure attribute-based encryption from witness encryption. In: Boyle, E., Mahmoody, M. (eds.) Theory of Cryptography. TCC 2024. Lecture Notes in Computer Science, vol. 15366, pp. 65–90. Springer, Cham (2024). https://doi.org/10.1007/978-3-031-78020-2_3

Non-committing Identity Based Encryption: Constructions and Applications

Rishab Goyal[2], Fuyuki Kitagawa[1], Venkata Koppula[3], Ryo Nishimaki[1], Mahesh Sreekumar Rajasree[4(✉)], and Takashi Yamakawa[1]

[1] NTT Social Informatics Laboratories, Tokyo, Japan
`{fuyuki.kitagawa,ryo.nishimaki,takashi.yamakawa}@ntt.com`
[2] UW-Madison, Madison, USA
`rishab@cs.wisc.edu`
[3] IIT Delhi, New Delhi, India
`kvenkata@iitd.ac.in`
[4] CISPA Helmholtz, Saarbrücken, Germany
`srmahesh1994@gmail.com`

Abstract. A receiver non-committing encryption (RNCE) scheme [Canetti *et al.*, STOC 1996; Canetti *et al.*, TCC 2005] allows one to sample a public key pk and (dummy) ciphertext ct without knowing the message m. Later, when the message is known, one can sample a secret key sk that looks like the secret key corresponding to pk, and decryption of ct produces m. In this work, we study receiver non-committing identity-based encryption (RNC-IBE). We give constructions based on standard assumptions on bilinear groups (prior works [Hiroka *et al.*, ASIACRYPT 2021] require indistinguishability obfuscation).

Our RNC-IBE constructions have important implications for incompressible identity based encryption. This notion was recently introduced by Goyal *et al.*, ITCS 2025. However, there were no constructions for the strongest security definitions in Goyal *et al.*, ITCS 2025. Our RNC-IBE scheme also leads to the first incompressible IBE scheme with optimal ciphertext size, which was another open question in Goyal *et al.*, ITCS 2025.

We also give constructions for relaxed RNC-IBE (where the identity space is polynomial in the security parameter, but the public key is compact) that are based on DDH, LWE. This leads to a relaxed incompressible IBE scheme with strong security from the same assumptions.

Keywords: non-committing · identity-based encryption · incompressible encryption

M. S. Rajasree—Funded by the European Union (ERC, LACONIC, 101041207). Views and opinions expressed are however those of the author(s) only and do not necessarily reflect those of the European Union or the European Research Council. Neither the European Union nor the granting authority can be held responsible for them.
M. S. Rajasree—This work is done while the author was a Post-Doctoral Fellow at IIT Delhi, India.

© International Association for Cryptologic Research 2025
T. Jager and J. Pan (Eds.): PKC 2025, LNCS 15674, pp. 158–193, 2025.
https://doi.org/10.1007/978-3-031-91820-9_6

1   Introduction

Non-committing Encryption. Non-committing public-key encryption (NCE), introduced by Canetti, Feige, Goldreich and Naor [17], is a crucial cryptographic tool in the design of adaptively secure multiparty computation protocols [17,20]. An NCE scheme consists of the following algorithms - Setup, Enc, Dec and $\mathsf{Sim} = (\mathsf{Sim}_1, \mathsf{Sim}_2)$. The syntax for Setup, Enc and Dec mirrors that of (standard) public key encryption (PKE) schemes. Additionally, the simulator Sim enables the sampling of ciphertext without knowledge of the underlying message. Once the message is revealed, the simulator can generate the necessary randomness to reconcile the public key and the ciphertext. More formally, security is captured using the real and ideal world framework. In the real-world, the adversary first receives the public key. It then sends a message m, and receives an encryption of m, together with the randomness r_{enc} used for encryption, and the randomness r_{setup} used for sampling the public key. In the ideal world, the simulator Sim_1 produces the public key pk and ciphertext ct^* (together with internal state st which is passed to Sim_2). After the adversary receives the public key, it sends the message m^*. The second-stage simulator Sim_2 receives the message m^* (and the internal state st) samples randomness r_{setup} that can explain pk, and randomness r_{enc} to explain ct^*. The adversary receives $\mathsf{ct}^*, r_{\mathsf{enc}}$ and r_{setup}, and must distinguish between the real-world and ideal-world. Today, we have several constructions of NCE, from a wide range of assumptions [14,21,26,51,71] as well a good understanding of the barriers [60].

Prior works have also explored weaker notions of non-committing encryption. Receiver NCE (RNCE)[1] is one such relaxation which has garnered significant attention. Here, the simulator Sim_2 only needs to output the secret key corresponding to pk (but does not need to produce the randomness r_{enc} and r_{setup}). Receiver NCE has been used for applications such as designing secure multiparty computation protocols [17,20], adaptive secure attribute-based encryption for Turing Machines [45], selective opening secure schemes [50] and more. In this work, we will focus on RNCE, with the aim to go beyond public key encryption.

Receiver Non-committing Identity Based Encryption (and Beyond). Identity based encryption (IBE) [64] is a powerful generalization of public key encryption, where users can encrypt messages for any identity using a master public key. The master public key, together with a corresponding master secret key, is sampled by the master authority using a Setup algorithm. The master secret key can be used to issue secret keys for every identity using a Keygen algorithm. Using a secret key for identity id, one can decrypt a ciphertext for identity id. Intuitively, security says that even if an adversary has polynomially many secret keys corresponding to identities of its choice, if it does not have a secret key for id^*, then the adversary cannot decrypt an encryption for id^*.

In the non-commmitting setting, identity-based encryption (and more generally, attribute-based encryption) was introduced by Hiroka, Morimae, Nishimaki and Yamakawa [53] in the context of attribute-based quantum encryption

---

[1] Also referred to as weak NCE [45].

with certified deletion. In a receiver non-committing identity-based encryption (RNC-IBE) scheme, in addition to (Setup, Keygen, Enc, Dec), we have a simulator Sim = (Sim$_1$, Sim$_2$) that can produce the master public key, secret keys and challenge ciphertext without knowing the challenge message. Later, when the message is revealed, the simulator can sample a master secret key that is consistent with the master public key, secret keys and the challenge ciphertext. More formally, in the real world, the adversary receives the master public key mpk. Then, it can send polynomially many identities, and receives the secret keys corresponding to these identities. The adversary then sends the challenge identity id*, together with challenge messages m^*, and receives ct$^* \leftarrow$ Enc(mpk, id*, m^*) together with the master secret key msk. In the ideal world, the adversary interacts with a simulator. The simulator first sends the master public key mpk. Then, the adversary receives secret keys for identities of its choice. Finally, in the challenge phase, when the adversary sends the challenge identity id* and the challenge message m^*, the simulator must first produce ct* using just id*. Later, when it receives m^*, it must produce a master secret key msk. The adversary finally receives ct* and msk, and must distinguish the real and ideal worlds.

While we have several constructions for IBE [1–3, 9–13, 15, 18, 22, 23, 27, 30, 31, 38–40, 43, 49, 55, 57, 65, 66, 70] (and even ABE [4, 5, 7, 41, 42, 45, 46, 62, 68]), our understanding with respect to RNC-IBE and RNC-ABE is very limited. Hiroka *et al.* [53] gave a construction for RNC-ABE using indistinguishability obfuscation. This brings us to the first central question of our work.

Q1. Can we construct RNC-IBE from the same assumptions that give us (regular) IBE?

Besides being a natural question in itself, this would resolve interesting open questions in the landscape of incompressible cryptography, which we discuss next.

Incompressible (Identity-Based) Encryption. The concept of incompressible public key encryption was introduced by Guan, Wichs and Zhandry [47] to address scenarios where the adversary eventually receives the entire secret decryption key, but has limited long-term storage, and as a result, cannot store the entire ciphertext. For S-incompressible security, we require that no adversary should win the following game (with non-negligible probability): the adversary, after receiving the public key pk, sends two challenge messages m_0, m_1, and receives the challenge ciphertext ct*. It must then compress the ciphertext into a short state st of size at most S bits. After it computes the compressed state st, it receives the secret key sk, and must guess whether m_0 was encrypted or m_1. Guan *et al.* gave two constructions of incompressible PKE: one based on general PKE (with ciphertext size being $(S + |m|) \cdot \mathrm{poly}(\lambda)$), and another based on indistinguishability obfuscation (with ciphertext size $\max(S, |m|) + \mathrm{poly}(\lambda)$).

Later works [44, 48] observed that any RNCE scheme can be used to build an incompressible PKE scheme with ciphertext size $S + |m| + \mathrm{poly}(\lambda)$ as follows. Consider an RNCE scheme and an incompressible SKE scheme with a secret key size of $\mathrm{poly}(\lambda)$ and a ciphertext size $(|m| + S + \mathrm{poly}(\lambda))$ (Dziembowzki [32] gave a construction of such incompressible SKE scheme, based on one-way functions). In the incompressible PKE scheme, the public and secret keys are identical to those of the RNCE scheme. To encrypt a message m, first generate a fresh secret key inc.sk for the incompressible SKE scheme. Using this key, encrypt the message to produce an incompressible ciphertext inc.ct. Next, encrypt inc.sk using the RNCE to obtain nce.ct, and the final ciphertext becomes ct := (nce.ct, inc.ct). Note that this scheme is ciphertext-rate preserving, as the size of nce.ct is $|nce.ct| = S + |m| + \text{poly}'(\lambda)$.

To argue security, we begin by switching the RNCE to simulation mode, which allows us to freely program the secret key so that nce.ct can decrypt to any desired value. At this point, the scheme's security relies on the incompressibility of the SKE scheme.

In this work, we focus on incompressible identity based encryption schemes. This primitive, introduced in a recent work by Goyal, Koppula, Rajasree and Verma [44], is a natural generalization of incompressible PKE to the IBE setting. Here again, the syntax is same as that of (regular) IBE. For incompressibility security, however, note that there can be multiple flavors of security. Goyal *et al.* defined two notions of security for incompressible IBE:

- (regular) incompressible security: in this case, the adversary first receives the master public key. Then it can send polynomially many identities, and receives secret keys for these identities. During the challenge phase, the adversary sends a challenge identity id^* together with challenge messages m_0, m_1, and receives the challenge ciphertext, followed by post-challenge secret key queries (similar to the pre-challenge secret key queries). Finally, the adversary must compress the ciphertext into a short state st of size at most S bits. After this, it receives the secret key corresponding to id^*, and must guess whether m_0 was encrypted or m_1.
- strong incompressible security: this game is similar to that of regular incompressible IBE. However, instead of receiving the secret key for id^* at the end, the adversary receives the entire master secret key.

Goyal *et al.* gave constructions for (regular) incompressible IBE, however there were no constructions achieving strong incompressibility! Our first observation is that the connection between incompressible PKE and RNCE also extends to IBE, and as a result, if we construct an RNC-IBE scheme, then that also resolves the following question (left open in [44]).

Q2. Can we construct strongly secure incompressible IBE?

Ciphertext Rate of Incompressible Encryption Schemes. An important parameter in the design of incompressible encryption schemes is the size of the ciphertext, as a function of the message size and the adversary's long-term storage bound S. The optimal ciphertext size (ignoring dependence on λ) is $\max(S, |m|)$. Guan *et al.* [47] showed how to construct incompressible PKE schemes with optimal ciphertext size, using indistinguishability obfuscation. Later, Branco, Döttling and Dujmovic [16] showed how to construct incompressible PKE schemes with optimal ciphertext size using standard assumptions (that is, without using obfuscation). A natural question is whether we can achieve incompressible IBE schemes with optimal ciphertext size. This was also left as an open question by Goyal *et al.* [44].

> *Q3. Can we construct incompressible IBE schemes*
> *with optimal ciphertext size?*

1.1   Our Results

In this work, we introduce new constructions for RNC-IBE and receiver non-committing identity-based key encapsulation mechanism, based on various standard assumptions. These construction, in turn, give us the first strong incompressible IBE scheme *with* optimal ciphertext size.

Main Results: The first construction is based on the bilinear DDH assumption, utilizing the dual system technique of Waters [67]. Notably, this construction achieves a robust security notion where the adversary obtains the entire randomness used by the setup algorithm (see Remark 1 for further details). Also, the size of the ciphertext is independent of the size of the session key.

Theorem 1. *Assuming the hardness of* SXDH *problem, there exists an adaptively secure RNC-IB-KEM. Additionally, the adversary is allowed to learn the entire randomness of setup, and the size of the ciphertext is independent of the size of the session key.*

Note that Theorem 1 addresses Q1 from above. Additionally, it also resolves questions Q2 and Q3 simultaneously! In fact, the resulting incompressible IBE scheme achieves the strongest possible security, where even the randomness used during setup can be revealed to the adversary. This is obtained by combining the RNC-IB-KEM with the incompressible secret key encryption scheme of [16] (based on the LWE or DCR assumptions). In this incompressible encryption scheme, the size of the ciphertext is $\max(S, |m|) + \text{poly}(\lambda)$. The size of the secret key grows with $|S|$, but since the size of the RNC-IB-KEM's ciphertext is independent of the session-key size, this does not affect the final ciphertext size.

Theorem 2. *Assuming the existence of RNC-IB-KEM such that the size of the ciphertext is independent of the size of the session key, there exists an adaptively secure strongly incompressible IBE scheme with optimal ciphertext size* $(\max(S, |m|) + \text{poly}(\lambda))$. *In particular, we get adaptively secure strongly incompressible IBE with optimal ciphertext size, assuming the hardness of* SXDH *and* LWE *(or* DCR*).*

RNC-IBE and Incompressible IBE Constructions for Polynomially Bounded Identity Space: The second RNC-IBE construction supports polynomially many identities with compact master public key. It can be instantiated from a broader class of assumptions such as {DDH, LWE}. This construction introduces an additional feature where non-committing ciphertext can be generated together with the master public key, i.e., it does not require knowledge of the target identity id*. This is the first construction to offer such capability which may be of independent interest. Similar to the first construction, this scheme remains secure when the randomness used by the setup algorithm is provided to the adversary.

Theorem 3. *Assuming the hardness of $\mathcal{X}$ where $\mathcal{X} \in \{\mathsf{DDH}, \mathsf{LWE}\}$, there exists an adaptively secure NC-IBE that supports polynomially many identities.*

By combining these results with an incompressible secret key encryption scheme in a hybrid encryption framework, we obtain the first strongly incompressible IBE schemes from $\mathsf{DDH}/\mathsf{LWE}$. The incompressible IBE scheme supports polynomially many identities with compact master public key. Finally, it remains secure even if the adversary receives the randomness used during the setup.

Theorem 4. *Assuming the hardness of $\mathcal{X}$ where $\mathcal{X} \in \{\mathsf{DDH}, \mathsf{LWE}\}$, there exists an adaptively secure (super) strongly incompressible IBE schemes that supports polynomially many identities.*

Constructions from Indistinguishability Obfuscation: We additionally present an RNC-IBE scheme using indistinguishability obfuscation (iO) and one-way functions. While [53] also gave a construction of RNC-ABE using iO and one way functions, our approach differs substantially.

Theorem 5. *Assuming the existence of iO and one-way functions, there exists selective secure RNC-IBE.*

The construction and the proof for the above theorem is provided in the full version. In this construction, the ciphertext rate is poor because the size of the ciphertext depends on both the length of the identity and $|m| \cdot \mathsf{poly}(\lambda)$. However, by employing Dziembowzki's incompressible SKE scheme (with secret key size of $\mathsf{poly}(\lambda)$), we can obtain rate-$\frac{1}{2}$ strongly incompressible IBE schemes (see Theorem 10).

Theorem 6. *Assuming the existence of iO and one-way functions, there exists a rate-$\frac{1}{2}$ selectively secure strongly incompressible IBE schemes.*

1.2   Related Works

In the field of incompressible encryption, Dziembowski [32] introduced the first constructions for incompressible symmetric key encryption (SKE). He presented an information-theoretic scheme with a rate of $\frac{1}{3}$, as well as a construction achieving a rate of $\frac{1}{2}$ based on one-way functions. After a decade, Guan et al. [47] introduced two incompressible public key encryption (PKE) schemes – the first, although based on standard PKE, had poor compression efficiency, while the second employed indistinguishability obfuscators [36,37,63] to realize a rate-1 scheme. Branco *et al.* [16] followed up by designing a rate-1 incompressible PKE scheme that offers chosen ciphertext attack (CCA) security, combining a rate-1 incompressible SKE with programmable hash proof systems. More recently, Guan *et al.* [48] advanced the notion by developing multi-user incompressible encryption. Here, the adversary is given multiple ciphertexts encrypted with different secret keys.

Goyal *et al.* [44] extended the concept to functional and attribute-based encryption (ABE), introducing a variety of incompressible security notions for functional encryption, attribute-based encryption, and identity-based encryption. Their work also provided constructions for incompressible functional encryption that achieves optimal trade-off between ciphertext-size and secret key size.

In another direction, Bhushan *et al.* [8] explored incompressible encryption in the context of leakage resilience. They presented a range of leakage-resilient incompressible encryption schemes tailored to various leakage functions. Their work also examined the challenges of constructing rate-1 schemes with short ciphertexts or schemes that can withstand significant leakage.

In addition to encryption, Guan *et al.* [47] also proposed incompressible signature schemes, which guarantee that an adversary cannot forge or reconstruct a signature from a compressed version. A related area is incompressible encodings [28,34,59], where it is computationally hard to reconstruct a codeword from a compressed version, even with access to the original message. Prior research [28,34,59] has shown positive results for incompressible encodings within the random oracle and common reference string (CRS) models.

The area of non-committing encryption (NCE) has also seen significant work focusing on building NCE schemes where the adversary gains access to the randomness used during the setup and encryption phases. These works developed schemes under various assumptions with the goal of achieving high ciphertext-rate [6,14,17,21,26,29,51,52,71,72].

Another direction explores optimizing parameters for weaker forms of NCE, where the adversary is restricted to gain access to the randomness used in either the setup (receiver) or encryption (sender). Jarecki and Lysyanskaya [56] introduced a scheme that is non-committing only for the receiver, whereas Canetti, Halevi and Katz [19] constructed a constant-rate NCE with erasures, where the adversary only receives the secret key and the ciphertext. Hiroka *et al.* [53] introduced non-committing attribute-based encryption (NC-ABE) using indistinguishable obfuscators, focusing on achieving ABE with certified deletion in quantum settings, where the adversary receives the master secret key along with the ciphertext.

2   Technical Overview

RNC-IBE from Bilinear Groups

Dual system encryption is a versatile framework employed in the construction of numerous IBE [25,35,54,57,67] and ABE [4,5,23,24,33,41,58,61,69] schemes.

In our construction, we utilize a pairing group $e : \mathbb{G}_1 \times \mathbb{G}_2 \to \mathbb{G}_T$, where $\mathbb{G}_1, \mathbb{G}_2, \mathbb{G}_T$ are all cyclic groups of prime order p, generated respectively by g_1, g_2, and $e(g_1, g_2)$, where e is a non-degenerate bilinear map, that is, for all $a, b \in \mathbb{Z}_p, e(g_1^a, g_2^b) = e(g_1, g_2)^{ab}$. We use bracket notations, where for all exponents $a \in \mathbb{Z}_p$ and all groups $s \in \{1, 2, T\}$, we denote by $[a]_s$ the group element g_s^a. This notation extends to vectors and matrices as well.

We describe our construction, which produces a session key in $\mathbb{G}_T$. The setup algorithm generates $\mathbf{a}, \mathbf{b} \leftarrow \mathbb{Z}_p^2$ and $\mathbf{W}_1, \mathbf{W}_2 \leftarrow \mathbb{Z}_p^{2 \times 2}$ and sets the public parameters

$$\mathsf{pp} := ([\mathbf{a}]_1, [\mathbf{b}]_2, [\mathbf{W}_1 \mathbf{a}]_1, [\mathbf{W}_2 \mathbf{a}]_1, [\mathbf{W}_1^\top \mathbf{b}]_2, [\mathbf{W}_2^\top \mathbf{b}]_2)$$

.

It then generates a secret vector $\mathbf{k} \leftarrow \mathbb{Z}_p^2$, setting the master public key as $\mathsf{mpk} := [\mathbf{a}^\top \mathbf{k}]_T$ and the master secret key as $\mathsf{msk} := \mathbf{k}$.

To generate a secret key for a specific identity $\mathsf{id} \in \mathbb{Z}_p$, the algorithm sample a random element $s \leftarrow \mathbb{Z}_p$ and output $\mathsf{sk}_{\mathsf{id}} := ([s\mathbf{b}]_2, [\mathbf{k} + s(\mathbf{W}_1 + \mathsf{id} \cdot \mathbf{W}_2)^\top \mathbf{b}]_2)$. To generate a session key and its corresponding ciphertext for a target identity id^*, the algorithm generates a random element $r \leftarrow \mathbb{Z}_p$ and produces the ciphertext $\mathsf{ct} := ([r\mathbf{a}]_1, [r(\mathbf{W}_1 + \mathsf{id} \cdot \mathbf{W}_2)\mathbf{a}]_1)$ and the session key $\mathsf{seskey} := [r\mathbf{a}^\top \mathbf{k}]_T$. For decapsulation, given the secret key $\mathsf{sk}_{\mathsf{id}} = ([\mathbf{d}]_2, [\mathbf{d}']_2)$ and a ciphertext $\mathsf{ct} = ([\mathbf{c}]_1, [\mathbf{c}']_1)$, the algorithm outputs $e([\mathbf{c}]_1^\top, [\mathbf{d}']_2)/e([\mathbf{c}']_1^\top, [\mathbf{d}]_2)$.

We will demonstrate that the experiment can be indistinguishably changed into non-committing experiment where the session key seskey^* is set to $[x]_T$ for randomly chosen $x \leftarrow \mathbb{Z}_p$ and the master secret key is computed so that it in fact maps the challenge KEM ciphertext ct^* to $\mathsf{seskey}^* = [x]_T$. For simplicity, we assume that the adversary has queried a single identity, denoted by id, and that the adversary's target identity is denoted as id^*. We begin with the following:

$$\mathsf{sk}_{\mathsf{id}} := ([s\mathbf{b}]_2, [\mathbf{k} + s(\mathbf{W}_1 + \mathsf{id} \cdot \mathbf{W}_2)^\top \mathbf{b}]_2)$$

$$\mathsf{ct} := ([r^*\mathbf{a}]_1, [r^*(\mathbf{W}_1 + \mathsf{id}^* \cdot \mathbf{W}_2)\mathbf{a}]_1) \quad \text{and} \quad \mathsf{seskey} := [r^*\mathbf{a}^\top \mathbf{k}]_T$$

By applying the SXDH assumption, we can replace $r^*\mathbf{a}$ and $s\mathbf{b}$ with a truly random elements $\mathbf{u}, \mathbf{v} \leftarrow \mathbb{Z}_p$.

$$\mathsf{sk}_{\mathsf{id}} := ([\mathbf{v}]_2, [\mathbf{k} + (\mathbf{W}_1 + \mathsf{id} \cdot \mathbf{W}_2)^\top \mathbf{v}]_2)$$

$$\mathsf{ct}^* := ([\mathbf{u}]_1, [(\mathbf{W}_1 + \mathsf{id}^* \cdot \mathbf{W}_2)\mathbf{u}]_1) \quad \text{and} \quad \mathsf{seskey} := [\mathbf{u}]_T$$

Next, we change the sampling method by sampling $\mathbf{W}_1 := \hat{\mathbf{W}}_1 + w_1 \mathbf{W}_0$ and $\mathbf{W}_2 := \hat{\mathbf{W}}_2 + w_2 \mathbf{W}_0$ where $\hat{\mathbf{W}}_1, \hat{\mathbf{W}}_2 \leftarrow \mathbb{Z}_p^{2 \times 2}$ and $\mathbf{W}_0 := \mathbf{b}^\perp (\mathbf{a}^\perp)^\top / (\mathbf{b}^\perp)^\top \mathbf{a}^\perp$. This maintains the same distribution, but now the secret key and ciphertext involve w_1, w_2 as follows.

$$\mathsf{sk}_{\mathsf{id}} := ([\mathbf{v}]_2, [\mathbf{k} + (\hat{\mathbf{W}}_1 + \mathsf{id} \cdot \hat{\mathbf{W}}_2)^\top \mathbf{v} + t(w_1 + \mathsf{id}w_2)\mathbf{a}^\perp]_2)$$

$$\mathsf{ct}^* := ([\mathbf{u}]_1, [(\hat{\mathbf{W}}_1 + \mathsf{id}^* \cdot \hat{\mathbf{W}}_2)\mathbf{u} + r(w_1 + \mathsf{id}^* w_2)]_1) \quad \text{and} \quad \mathsf{seskey} := [\mathbf{u}]_T$$

where $\mathbf{u} = r'\mathbf{a} + r\mathbf{b}^{\perp}$ and $\mathbf{v} = t'\mathbf{a} + t\mathbf{b}^{\perp}$ such that $r', r, t', t \in \mathbb{Z}_p$, i.e., we can express $\mathbf{u}, \mathbf{v}$ in terms of $\mathbf{a}, \mathbf{b}^{\perp}$ because they are linearly independent with high probability. Since, $\mathsf{id} \neq \mathsf{id}^*$, the following holds.

$$\{w_1 + \mathsf{id}^* w_2, w_1 + \mathsf{id} w_2\} \equiv \{w_1 + \mathsf{id}^* w_2, w\}$$

where w is chosen uniformly at random. Therefore, we can change to

$$\mathsf{sk}_{\mathsf{id}} := ([\mathbf{v}]_2, [\mathbf{k} + (\hat{\mathbf{W}}_1 + \mathsf{id} \cdot \hat{\mathbf{W}}_2)^{\top} \mathbf{v} + w\mathbf{a}^{\perp}]_2)$$

$$\mathsf{ct}^* := ([\mathbf{u}]_1, [(\hat{\mathbf{W}}_1 + \mathsf{id}^* \cdot \hat{\mathbf{W}}_2)\mathbf{u} + r(w_1 + \mathsf{id}^* w_2)]_1) \quad \text{and} \quad \mathsf{seskey} := [\mathbf{u}]_T$$

In the actual proof, multiple secret keys are involved, and this modification cannot be made if all the secret keys contain information about w_1 and w_2. However, by introducing additional hybrid steps and ensuring that at any moment only one secret key retains information about w_1 and w_2, we will carefully modify the secret keys one by one.

Now, we revert back to the original $\mathbf{W}_1, \mathbf{W}_2$ and use DDH assumption to reach

$$\mathsf{sk}_{\mathsf{id}} := ([s\mathbf{b}]_2, [\mathbf{k} + s(\mathbf{W}_1 + \mathsf{id} \cdot \mathbf{W}_2)^{\top} \mathbf{b} + w\mathbf{a}^{\perp}]_2)$$

$$\mathsf{ct}^* := ([\mathbf{u}]_1, [(\mathbf{W}_1 + \mathsf{id}^* \cdot \mathbf{W}_2)\mathbf{u}]_1) \quad \text{and} \quad \mathsf{seskey} := [\mathbf{u}]_T$$

We now sample $k_1, k_2 \leftarrow \mathbb{Z}_p$ and set $\mathbf{k} := \frac{k_1}{|\mathbf{a}|^2} \cdot \mathbf{a} + \frac{k_2}{|\mathbf{a}^{\perp}|^2} \cdot \mathbf{a}^{\perp}$. This modification results in $\mathsf{mpk} = [k_1]_T$. Note that this is merely a conceptual change. We now modify the secret key as follows:

$$\mathsf{sk}_{\mathsf{id}} := ([s\mathbf{b}]_2, [\frac{k_1}{|\mathbf{a}|^2} \cdot \mathbf{a} + s(\mathbf{W}_1 + \mathsf{id} \cdot \mathbf{W}_2)^{\top} \mathbf{b} + w\mathbf{a}^{\perp}]_2)$$

$$\mathsf{ct}^* := ([\mathbf{u}]_1, [(\mathbf{W}_1 + \mathsf{id}^* \cdot \mathbf{W}_2)\mathbf{u}]_1) \quad \text{and} \quad \mathsf{seskey} := [\mathbf{u}]_T$$

This change is indistinguishable because w is chosen uniformly at random. We can express $\mathbf{u} = u_1 \mathbf{a} + u_2 \mathbf{a}^{\perp}$ where $u_1, u_2 \leftarrow \mathbb{Z}_p$ because $\mathbf{u}$ is chosen uniformly at random. Now, given a uniformly random $x \leftarrow \mathbb{Z}_p$, we can program the master secret key as $k_2 = \dfrac{x - u_1 k_1}{u_2}$. For verification, let us check that generating a secret key for id^* and decrypting ct^* would yield $[x]_T$. A secret key for id^* would be

$$\mathsf{sk}_{\mathsf{id}^*} := ([s^*\mathbf{b}]_2, [\mathbf{k} + s^*(\mathbf{W}_1 + \mathsf{id}^* \cdot \mathbf{W}_2)^{\top}\mathbf{b}]_2)$$

and decryption would result in

$$\frac{e([\mathbf{u}^{\top}]_1, [\mathbf{k} + s^*(\mathbf{W}_1 + \mathsf{id}^* \cdot \mathbf{W}_2)^{\top}\mathbf{b}]_2)}{e([((\mathbf{W}_1 + \mathsf{id}^* \cdot \mathbf{W}_2)\mathbf{u})^{\top}]_1, [s^*\mathbf{b}]_2)} = \frac{e([\mathbf{u}^{\top}]_1, [\mathbf{k}]_2) \cdot e([\mathbf{u}^{\top}]_1, [s^*(\mathbf{W}_1 + \mathsf{id}^* \cdot \mathbf{W}_2)^{\top}\mathbf{b}]_2)}{e([((\mathbf{W}_1 + \mathsf{id}^* \cdot \mathbf{W}_2)\mathbf{u})^{\top}]_1, [s^*\mathbf{b}]_2)}$$

$$= e([\mathbf{u}^{\top}]_1, [\mathbf{k}]_2) = [\mathbf{u}^{\top}\mathbf{k}]_T$$

$$= [(u_1\mathbf{a} + u_2\mathbf{a}^{\perp})^{\top}(k_1\mathbf{a} + k_2\mathbf{a}^{\perp})]_T$$

$$= [u_1 k_1 + u_2 k_2]_T = [x]_T$$

RNC-IBE from Batch Encryption

Let us start by reviewing the concept of batch encryption. A batch encryption scheme is a form of public key encryption where the key generation process is a projection-this means that the secret key is used to produce a shorter public key. When the secret key has a length of n, the scheme allows the simultaneous encryption of $n \times 2$ messages. During decryption, only one message from each pair can be recovered, and this is determined by the corresponding bit in the secret key.

To elaborate, the setup algorithm BE.Setup takes as input a secret key $\mathsf{sk} \in \{0,1\}^n$ and outputs a public key pk. The encryption algorithm encrypts a matrix $M \in \mathcal{M}^{n \times 2}$ using the public key to generate a ciphertext ct. Here, $\mathcal{M}$ is an appropriate message space. The decryption algorithm takes as input the secret key sk and the ciphertext ct and outputs a vector $m \in \mathcal{M}^n$ such that $m_i = M_{i,\mathsf{sk}[i]}$, for all $i \in [n]$.

The RNC-IBE scheme uses the batch encryption and garbling scheme as follows. Let $d = \log(\mathrm{poly}(\lambda))$ be an integer and $T = 2^d$ be a polynomial in the security parameter that denotes the number of identities the scheme supports. The setup algorithm generates T pairs of NCE public and secret keys, denoted as $\{\mathsf{nce.pk}_j, \mathsf{nce.sk}_j\}_{j \in [T]}$, where each pair corresponds to a different identity. These keys together form the master secret key of the RNC-IBE scheme. The master public key is a public key of the batch encryption scheme generated by $\mathsf{be.pk} \leftarrow \mathsf{BE.Setup}(\{\mathsf{nce.pk}_j\}_{j \in [T]})$, i.e., $\{\mathsf{nce.pk}_j\}_{j \in [T]}$ is the secret key associated with $\mathsf{be.pk}$.

The secret key for the ith identity consists of all the NCE public keys $\{\mathsf{nce.pk}_j\}_{j \in [T]}$ along with the ith secret key $\mathsf{nce.sk}_i$. To encrypt a message m for the ith identity, the encryption algorithm generates T garbled circuit labels as follows:

- For the ith identity, it generates $(\tilde{\mathcal{C}}^{(i)}, \{\mathsf{lab}_{j,b}^{(i)}\}) \leftarrow \mathsf{GC.Grbl}(\mathsf{NCE.Enc}(\cdot, m))$.
- For the remaining identity, it generates $(\tilde{\mathcal{C}}^{(k)}, \{\mathsf{lab}_{j,b}^{(k)}\}) \leftarrow \mathsf{GC.Grbl}(\mathsf{NCE.Enc}(\cdot, m^{(k)}))$ where $m^{(k)}$ is randomly generated.

A matrix $M \in \{0,1\}^{nT \times 2}$ is then constructed such that $M[k \cdot n + j, b] = \mathsf{lab}_{j,b}^{(k)}$. The batch encryption scheme is then used to produce $\mathsf{be.ct} \leftarrow \mathsf{BE.Enc}(\mathsf{be.pk}, M)$. The final ciphertext is $\mathsf{ct} := (\{\tilde{\mathcal{C}}^{(k)}\}_k, \mathsf{be.ct})$.

The simulation works as follows. First, the simulator generates the NCE public keys and corresponding ciphertexts using the NCE simulators and constructs the master public key. The simulator then produces the non-committing ciphertext by simulating all garbled circuit labels, i.e., $(\tilde{\mathcal{C}}^{(k)}, \{\mathsf{lab}_j^{(k)}\}) \leftarrow \mathsf{GC.Sim}(\mathsf{nce.ct}^{(k)})$.

Upon receiving the target identity i and target message m, the simulator uses the NCE simulator to simulate $\mathsf{nce.sk}_i$ such that the ciphertext $\mathsf{nce.ct}_i$ will decrypt to m using $\mathsf{nce.sk}_i$. For the other identities, the simulator uses the NCE simulators to simulate $\mathsf{nce.sk}_k$ on random messages $m^{(k)}$. For more details, refer Sect. 6.

3   Preliminaries

Let PPT denote probabilistic polynomial time. We denote the set of all positive integers up to n as $[n] := \{1, \ldots, n\}$ and $[n]_0 := \{0, 1, \ldots, n\}$. In addition, we use $[i, j]$ to denote the set of all non-negative integers between i and j including i, j, i.e., $[i, j] := \{i, i+1, \ldots, j\}$. For any two binary string x, y, we use the notation $x \preceq y$ (or $x \in \mathsf{prefix}(y)$) to imply that x is a prefix of y and $x \| y$ to denote x concatenated with y. And $x[i, j]$ denotes the substring $x[i] \| x[i+1] \| \ldots \| x[j]$ when $i \leq j$ and $x[i, j] = \epsilon$ where $i > j$. Throughout this paper, unless specified, all polynomials we consider are positive polynomials. For any finite set S, $x \leftarrow S$ denotes a uniformly random element x from the set S. Suppose, S is an ordered set of n element, i.e., $S = (a_1, \ldots, a_n)$, then we use the notation $(b_1, \ldots, b_n) \leftarrow S$ to denote that b_i is assigned the value a_i, for all $i \in [n]$.

We use a pairing group $e : \mathbb{G}_1 \times \mathbb{G}_2 \to \mathbb{G}_T$, where $\mathbb{G}_1, \mathbb{G}_2, \mathbb{G}_T$ are all cyclic groups of prime order p, generated respectively by g_1, g_2, and $e(g_1, g_2)$, where e is a non-degenerate bilinear map, that is, for all $a, b \in \mathbb{Z}_p, e(g_1^a, g_2^b) = e(g_1, g_2)^{ab}$.

We use bracket notations, where for all exponents $a \in \mathbb{Z}_p$ and all groups $s \in \{1, 2, T\}$, we denote by $[a]_s$ the group element g_s^a. We generalize this notation for vectors and matrices as follows. For any $\mathbf{A} \in \mathbb{Z}_p^{n \times m}$, $[\mathbf{A}]_s := g_s^{\mathbf{A}}$ denotes an $n \times m$ matrix with elements from $\mathbb{G}_s$ such that (i, j)-th element is $[\mathbf{A}_{i,j}]_s$. Since, $[\cdot]_s$ is a linear functions, we can $[\mathbf{AB}]_s$ from $[\mathbf{A}]_s$ and $[\mathbf{B}]_s$ for any matrices $\mathbf{A}, \mathbf{B}$ over $\mathbb{Z}_p$. Also, given $[\mathbf{A}]_1$ and $[\mathbf{B}]_2$, we define $[\mathbf{AB}]_T = e([\mathbf{A}]_1, [\mathbf{B}]_2)$.

3.1   Hardness Assumptions

Decisional Diffie-Hellman: The Decisional Diffie-Hellman (DDH) assumption with respect to a group $\mathbb{G}$, is that for every PPT adversary $\mathcal{A}$ it holds that

$$\left| \Pr_{\substack{(\mathbb{G},g,q) \leftarrow \mathcal{G}(1^\lambda) \\ a,b \leftarrow \mathbb{Z}_q}} [\mathcal{A}(1^\lambda, (\mathbb{G}, g, q), g^a, g^b, g^{a \cdot b}) = 1] - \right.$$

$$\left. \Pr_{\substack{(\mathbb{G},g,q) \leftarrow \mathcal{G}(1^\lambda) \\ a,b,u \leftarrow \mathbb{Z}_q}} [\mathcal{A}(1^\lambda, (\mathbb{G}, g, q), g^a, g^b, g^u) = 1] \right| = \mathsf{negl}(\lambda)$$

Computational Diffie-Hellman: The Computational Diffie-Hellman (CDH) assumption with respect to a group generator $\mathcal{G}$, is that for every PPT adversary $\mathcal{A}$ it holds that

$$\Pr_{\substack{(\mathbb{G},g,q) \leftarrow \mathcal{G}(1^\lambda) \\ a,b \leftarrow \mathbb{Z}_q}} [\mathcal{A}(1^\lambda, (\mathbb{G}, g, q), g^a, g^b) = g^{a \cdot b}] = \mathsf{negl}(\lambda)$$

Symmetric eXternal Diffie-Hellman: The Symmetric eXternal Diffie-Hellman (SXDH) assumption holds for a pairing group $(\mathbb{G}_1, \mathbb{G}_2, \mathbb{G}_T, p, g_1, g_2, g_T, e) \leftarrow \mathcal{G}(1^\lambda)$ if DDH holds for $\mathbb{G}_1$ and $\mathbb{G}_2$.

Learning with Error: The Learning with Error assumption holds if for all PPT adversary $\mathcal{A}$, there exists a negligible function $\mathsf{negl}(\cdot)$ such that for all $\lambda \in \mathbb{N}$, $k = k(\lambda), q = q(\lambda)$ and D_σ being an error distribution,

$$|\Pr[\mathcal{A}(\mathbf{A}, \mathbf{s}\mathbf{A} + \mathbf{e}) = 1] - \Pr[\mathcal{A}(\mathbf{A}, \mathbf{u}) = 1]| = \mathsf{negl}(\lambda)$$

for all $n \in \mathbb{N}$ such that $\mathbf{A} \leftarrow \mathbb{Z}_q^{k \times n}, \mathbf{s} \leftarrow \mathbb{Z}_q^k, \mathbf{e} \leftarrow D_\sigma^n$ and $\mathbf{u} \leftarrow \mathbb{Z}_q^n$.

3.2 Batch Encryption

Let $B = B(\lambda, n)$ be a global parameter. A batch encryption (BE) scheme consists of the following four algorithms.

$\mathsf{Params}(1^\lambda, 1^n)$: The algorithm takes as input the security parameter 1^λ and a parameter 1^n and outputs a public parameter pp.

$\mathsf{Setup}(\mathsf{pp}, \mathsf{sk})$: The setup algorithm takes as input a public parameter pp and a secret key $\mathsf{sk} \in [B]^n$ and outputs a public key pk.

$\mathsf{Enc}(\mathsf{pk}, M)$: The encryption algorithm takes as input a public key pk and a matrix $M \in \{0, 1\}^{n \times B}$ and outputs a ciphertext ct.

$\mathsf{Dec}(\mathsf{sk}, \mathsf{ct})$: The decryption algorithm takes as input a secret key sk and a ciphertext ct and outputs either outputs $\bot$ or a vector $m \in \{0, 1\}^n$.

Correctness. For correctness, we require that for all $\lambda \in \mathbb{N}, n, B \in \mathbb{N}, \mathsf{sk} \in [B]^n, M \in \{0, 1\}^{n \times B}$,

$$\Pr\left[\mathsf{Dec}(\mathsf{sk}, \mathsf{ct}) = m \mid \mathsf{ct} \leftarrow \mathsf{Enc}(\mathsf{pk}, M), \mathsf{pk} \leftarrow \mathsf{Setup}(\mathsf{pp}, \mathsf{sk}), \mathsf{pp} \leftarrow \mathsf{Params}(1^\lambda, 1^n)\right] = 1$$

where the probability is over the random bits used in the $\mathsf{Params}, \mathsf{Setup}, \mathsf{Enc}$ algorithm and $m[i] = M[i, \mathsf{sk}[i]], \forall i \in [n]$.

IND-based Security. Consider the following experiment with an adversary $\mathcal{A}$.

– **Initialization Phase:** The adversary takes 1^λ as input, and sends $1^n, x \in [B]^n$ to the challenger. The challenger runs $\mathsf{pp} \leftarrow \mathsf{Params}(1^\lambda, 1^n)$ and sends pk to $\mathcal{A}$.
– **Challenge Phase:** $\mathcal{A}$ outputs two message $M_0, M_1 \in \{0, 1\}^{n \times B}$ to the challenger. The challenger computes $\mathsf{pk} \leftarrow \mathsf{Setup}(\mathsf{pp}, \mathsf{sk})$ and randomly chooses $b \in \{0, 1\}$. It computes a ciphertext $\mathsf{ct}^* = \mathsf{Enc}(\mathsf{pk}, M_b)$ and sends $(\mathsf{pk}, \mathsf{ct}^*)$ to $\mathcal{A}$.
– **Response Phase:** $\mathcal{A}$ outputs b'. $\mathcal{A}$ wins the experiment if $b = b'$.

Definition 1. *An BE scheme satisfies indistinguishability-based security if for all PPT adversaries $\mathcal{A}$, there exists a negligible function $\mathsf{negl}(\cdot)$ such that for all $\lambda \in \mathbb{N}$,*

$$\Pr[\mathcal{A} \text{ wins in the above experiment}] \leq \frac{1}{2} + \mathsf{negl}(\lambda)$$

In this work, we will require an *oblivious* batch encryption which has the following properties.

1. Params outputs pp without using any randomness other than pp itself.
2. Setup is a deterministic algorithm.

In other words, the randomness used in Params and Setup is pp only. We emphasis that the constructions given in [15] for blind batch encryptions are oblivious.

Theorem 7 ([15]). *Assuming the hardness of $\mathcal{C}$ where $\mathcal{C} \in \{\mathsf{CDH}, \mathsf{LWE}\}$, there exists a secure oblivious BE scheme such that the size of the public key is a polynomial in λ, i.e., $|\mathsf{pk}| = \mathrm{poly}(\lambda)$.*

3.3 Non-committing Encryption

A non-committing encryption (NCE) scheme consists of the following algorithms.

$\mathsf{Setup}(1^\lambda; r_{\mathsf{Setup}})$: The setup algorithm takes as input the security parameter 1^λ. Using the random coins r_{Setup}, it outputs the public key pk and secret key sk.

$\mathsf{Enc}(\mathsf{pk}, m; r_{\mathsf{Enc}})$: The encryption algorithm takes as input a master public key pk, a message m and using random coins r_{Enc} outputs a ciphertext ct.

$\mathsf{Dec}(\mathsf{sk}, \mathsf{ct})$: The decryption algorithm takes as input a secret key sk and a ciphertext ct and outputs either a message m or $\bot$.

$\mathsf{Sim}_1(1^\lambda)$: The first simulator takes as input the security parameter 1^λ and outputs a public key pk, a ciphertext ct^* and a state st_1.

$\mathsf{Sim}_2(\mathsf{st}_1, m)$: The second simulator takes as input a state st_1 and a message m and outputs $(r_{\mathsf{Enc}}, r_{\mathsf{Setup}})$.

Correctness. For correctness, we require that there exists a negligible function $\mathsf{negl}(\cdot)$ such that for all $\lambda \in \mathbb{N}, T \in \mathbb{N}$ and $(\mathsf{pk}, \mathsf{sk})$ output by $\mathsf{Setup}(1^\lambda)$, any message m,

$$\Pr_r[\mathsf{Dec}(\mathsf{sk}, \mathsf{ct}) = m \mid \mathsf{ct} = \mathsf{Enc}(\mathsf{pk}, m; r))] = 1 - \mathsf{negl}(\lambda)$$

where r is sampled uniformly at random.

Non-committing Security. Consider the following two experiments with an adversary $\mathcal{A}$.

Real World:

– **Initialization Phase:** The challenger computes $(\mathsf{pk}, \mathsf{sk}) \leftarrow \mathsf{Setup}(1^\lambda; r_{\mathsf{Setup}})$ and sends pk to $\mathcal{A}$.
– **Challenge Phase:** The adversary $\mathcal{A}$ sends m^* to the challenger. The challenger computes $\mathsf{ct}^* \leftarrow \mathsf{Enc}(\mathsf{pk}, m^*; r_{\mathsf{Enc}})$ and returns $(\mathsf{ct}^*, r_{\mathsf{Enc}}, r_{\mathsf{Setup}})$ to $\mathcal{A}$.

– **Response Phase:** $\mathcal{A}$ outputs b.

Simulated World:

– **Initialization Phase:** The challenger computes $(\mathsf{pk}, \mathsf{ct}^*, \mathsf{st}_1) \leftarrow \mathsf{Sim}_1(1^\lambda)$ and sends mpk to $\mathcal{A}$.
– **Challenge Phase:** The adversary $\mathcal{A}$ sends m^* to the challenger. The challenger computes $(r_{\mathsf{Enc}}, r_{\mathsf{Setup}}) \leftarrow \mathsf{Sim}_2(\mathsf{st}_1, m^*)$ and returns $(\mathsf{ct}^*, r_{\mathsf{Enc}}, r_{\mathsf{Setup}})$ to $\mathcal{A}$.
– **Response Phase:** $\mathcal{A}$ outputs b.

Let p_{real} and p_{sim} be the probabilities with which $\mathcal{A}$ outputs 0 in the real world and simulated world, respectively.

Definition 2. *An NCE scheme is said to be secure if for all PPT adversaries $\mathcal{A}$, there exists a negligible function $\mathsf{negl}(\cdot)$ such that, for all $\lambda \in \mathbb{N}$,*

$$|p_{\mathsf{real}} - p_{\mathsf{sim}}| = \mathsf{negl}(\lambda)$$

Theorem 8 ([14,72]). *Assuming the hardness of LWE and DDH, there exists a secure non-committing encryption scheme.*

3.4 Incompressible Secret Key Encryption

An incompressible secret key encryption scheme $\mathsf{IncSKE} = (\mathsf{Setup}, \mathsf{Enc}, \mathsf{Dec})$ with message space $\{\mathcal{M}_\lambda\}_\lambda$ consists of the following PPT algorithms.

– $\mathsf{Setup}(1^\lambda, 1^S)$: The setup algorithm is a randomized algorithm that takes as input the security parameter 1^λ, a parameter 1^S and outputs a secret key sk.
– $\mathsf{Enc}(\mathsf{sk}, m)$: The encryption algorithm is a randomized algorithm that takes as input a secret key sk and a message $m \in \mathcal{M}_\lambda$ and outputs a ciphertext ct.
– $\mathsf{Dec}(\mathsf{sk}, \mathsf{ct})$: The decryption algorithm takes as input a secret key sk and a ciphertext ct and outputs either a message $m \in \mathcal{M}_\lambda$ or $\bot$.

Correctness. For correctness, we require that for all $\lambda \in \mathbb{N}, S \in \mathbb{N}, m \in \mathcal{M}_\lambda$ and $\mathsf{sk} \leftarrow \mathsf{Setup}(1^\lambda, 1^S)$,

$$\Pr[\mathsf{Dec}(\mathsf{sk}, \mathsf{Enc}(\mathsf{sk}, m)) = m] = 1$$

where the probability is over the random bits used in the encryption algorithm.

Definition 3 (Incompressible SKE Security). *Consider the following experiment with an adversary $\mathcal{A} = (\mathcal{A}_1, \mathcal{A}_2)$.*

– **Initialization Phase:** *$\mathcal{A}_1$ on input 1^λ, outputs an upper bound on the state size 1^S. The challenger runs $\mathsf{sk} \leftarrow \mathsf{Setup}(1^\lambda, 1^S)$.*

- **Challenge Phase:** $\mathcal{A}_1$ *outputs a message* (m_0, m_1), *along with an auxiliary information* aux. *The challenger randomly chooses* $b \in \{0, 1\}$. *It computes a ciphertext* $\mathsf{ct}^* = \mathsf{Enc}(\mathsf{sk}, m_b)$ *and sends it to* $\mathcal{A}_1$.
- **First Response Phase:** $\mathcal{A}_1$ *computes a state* st *such that* $|\mathsf{st}| \leq S$.
- **Second Response Phase:** $\mathcal{A}_2$ *receives* $(\mathsf{sk}, \mathsf{aux}, \mathsf{st})$ *and outputs* b'. $\mathcal{A}$ *wins the experiment if* $b = b'$.

An SKE scheme is said to be incompressible secure if for all **PPT** *adversaries* $\mathcal{A}$, *there exists a negligible function* $\mathsf{negl}(\cdot)$ *such that for all* $\lambda \in \mathbb{N}$,

$$\Pr[\mathcal{A} \text{ wins in the above experiment}] \leq \frac{1}{2} + \mathsf{negl}(\lambda)$$

The rate of a scheme is defined as the ratio between the size of a message and the size of a ciphertext, i.e., $\frac{|m|}{|\mathsf{ct}|}$. We say a scheme has rate-1 if $\frac{|m|}{|\mathsf{ct}|} = |m| - o(|m|)$.

Theorem 9 ([16]). *Assume the hardness of* **LWE** *or* **DCR**, *there exists a rate-1 incompressible SKE whose secret key size is* $|\mathsf{sk}| = n(1 + o(1)) + \mathrm{poly}(\lambda)$ *where* n *is the size of the message.*

Theorem 10 ([32]). *There exists a rate-$\frac{1}{2}$ incompressible SKE from one-way functions whose secret key size is* $|\mathsf{sk}| = \mathrm{poly}(\lambda)$.

3.5 Incompressible IBE

In this section, we define the strong version of the incompressible security game for IBE scheme[2] where Setup takes an additional input 1^S and the second adversary obtains the *master secret key*. The game is played against two adversaries $\mathcal{A}_1, \mathcal{A}_2$. The first adversary $\mathcal{A}_1$ will be provided with the complete challenge ciphertext and produce a compressed version of it. The second adversary $\mathcal{A}_2$ is provided with the master public key, compressed challenge ciphertext which was created by $\mathcal{A}_1$ and certain secret keys.

Definition 4. *(Incompressible IBE Security). Let* IBE $=$ (Setup, KeyGen, Enc, Dec) *be an IBE scheme in which the setup algorithm takes an additional parameter* 1^S *as input. Consider the following experiment with an adversary* $\mathcal{A} = (\mathcal{A}_1, \mathcal{A}_2)$.

Initialization Phase: $\mathcal{A}_1$ *on input* 1^λ, *outputs an upper bound on the state size* 1^S. *The challenger runs* $(\mathsf{msk}, \mathsf{mpk}) \leftarrow \mathsf{Setup}(1^\lambda, 1^S; r_{\mathsf{Setup}})$ *and sends* mpk *to* $\mathcal{A}_1$.
Pre-Challenge Query Phase: *In this phase,* $\mathcal{A}_1$ *is allowed to make polynomially many key queries. For each query* id *sent to the challenger, the challenger computes* $\mathsf{sk}_{\mathsf{id}} \leftarrow \mathsf{KeyGen}(\mathsf{msk}, \mathsf{id})$ *and returns* $\mathsf{sk}_{\mathsf{id}}$ *to* $\mathcal{A}_1$.

---

[2] The only difference between a standard IBE scheme and an incompressible IBE scheme is that the setup algorithm takes an additional parameter 1^S that specifies the compression size.

Challenge Phase: $\mathcal{A}_1$ *outputs two messages* m_0, m_1, *an identity* id* *along with an auxiliary information* aux. *If there exists a query for* id* *made by* $\mathcal{A}_1$, *the challenger aborts the game. Else, it randomly chooses* $b \in \{0, 1\}$ *and computes a ciphertext* ct* = Enc(mpk, id*, m_b) *and sends it to* $\mathcal{A}_1$.

Post-Challenge Query Phase: *This is similar to the pre-challenge query phase. The adversary* $\mathcal{A}_1$ *is allowed to send polynomially many key queries. For each query* id, *if* id* = id, *the challenger sends* $\perp$. *Else, computes* $\mathsf{sk}_{\mathsf{id}} \leftarrow$ KeyGen(msk, id) *and returns* $\mathsf{sk}_{\mathsf{id}}$ *to* $\mathcal{A}_1$.

First Response Phase: $\mathcal{A}_1$ *computes a state* st *such that* $|st| \le S$.

Second Response Phase: $\mathcal{A}_2$ *receives* (mpk, msk, aux, st). *Finally,* $\mathcal{A}_2$ *outputs* b'. $\mathcal{A}$ *wins the experiment if* $b = b'$.

An IBE scheme is said to be **strong** *incompressible secure if for all PPT adversaries* $\mathcal{A} = (\mathcal{A}_1, \mathcal{A}_2)$, *there exists a negligible function* negl$(\cdot)$ *such that for all* $\lambda \in \mathbb{N}$,

$$\Pr[\mathcal{A} \text{ wins in the above experiment}] \le \frac{1}{2} + \mathsf{negl}(\lambda)$$

Definition 5. *An IBE scheme is said to be* **super-strong** *incompressible secure if for all PPT adversaries* $\mathcal{A} = (\mathcal{A}_1, \mathcal{A}_2)$, *there exists a negligible function* negl$(\cdot)$ *such that for all* $\lambda \in \mathbb{N}$,

$$\Pr[\mathcal{A} \text{ wins in the above experiment}] \le \frac{1}{2} + \mathsf{negl}(\lambda)$$

provided the second adversary $\mathcal{A}_2$ *receives the random coins* r_{Setup} *used in the setup algorithm instead of* mpk, msk.

4   Receiver Non-Committing Identity-Based Primitives: Definitions

In this section, we will present the definitions of a receiver non-committing identity-based encryption (RNC-IBE) scheme and receiver non-committing identity-based key-encapsulation mechanism (RNC-IB-KEM) where in the challenge phase, the challenger returns the master secret key msk instead of the random coins used in the Setup and Enc algorithms.

4.1   Receiver Non-Committing Identity-Based Encryption

A receiver non-committing identity-based encryption (RNC-IBE) scheme consists of the following algorithms.

Setup$(1^\lambda, 1^n)$: The setup algorithm takes as input the security parameter 1^λ and the length of the identities 1^n (in some cases the number of identities 1^T). It outputs the master public key mpk and master secret key msk.

Keygen(msk, id) : The key generation algorithm takes as input a master secret key msk and an identity id and outputs a secret key $\mathsf{sk}_{\mathsf{id}}$.

Enc(mpk, id, m) : The encryption algorithm takes as input a master public key mpk, an identity id and a message m and outputs a ciphertext ct.

Dec(sk, ct) : The decryption algorithm takes as input a secret key sk and a ciphertext ct and outputs either a message m or $\perp$.

$\mathsf{Sim}_1(1^\lambda, 1^n)$: The first simulator takes as input the security parameter 1^λ and the length of the identities 1^n (in some cases the number of identities 1^T) and outputs a master public key mpk and a state st_1.

$\mathsf{Sim}_2(\mathsf{st}_1, \mathsf{id})$: The second simulator is a stateful algorithm with an internal state st_2 that takes as input a state st_1 and an identity id and outputs a secret key $\mathsf{sk}_{\mathsf{id}}$ and updates st_2.

$\mathsf{Sim}_3(\mathsf{st}_2, \mathsf{id}^*)$: The third simulator takes as input a state st_2 and an identity id^* and outputs a ciphertext ct^* and a state st_3.

$\mathsf{Sim}_4(\mathsf{st}_3, m^*)$: The fourth simulator takes as input a state st_3 and a message m^* and outputs a master secret key msk.

Correctness. For correctness, we require that there exists a negligible function $\mathsf{negl}(\cdot)$ such that for all $\lambda \in \mathbb{N}, n \in \mathbb{N}$ and $(\mathsf{mpk}, \mathsf{msk}) \leftarrow \mathsf{Setup}(1^\lambda, 1^n)$, any identity id and message m,

$$\Pr_{r_1, r_2}\left[\mathsf{Dec}(\mathsf{sk}_{\mathsf{id}}, \mathsf{ct}) = m \mid \begin{array}{l} \mathsf{ct} = \mathsf{Enc}(\mathsf{mpk}, \mathsf{id}, m; r_1) \\ \mathsf{sk}_{\mathsf{id}} = \mathsf{Keygen}(\mathsf{msk}, \mathsf{id}; r_2) \end{array}\right] = 1 - \mathsf{negl}(\lambda)$$

Security. Consider the following two experiments with an adversary $\mathcal{A}$.

Real World:

- **Initialization Phase:** $\mathcal{A}$ on input 1^λ, outputs 1^T. The challenger computes $(\mathsf{mpk}, \mathsf{msk}) \leftarrow \mathsf{Setup}(1^\lambda, 1^T)$ and sends mpk to $\mathcal{A}$.
- **Pre-Challenge Query Phase:** In this phase, $\mathcal{A}$ is allowed to make multiple queries id. For each id, the challenger returns $\mathsf{sk}_{\mathsf{id}} \leftarrow \mathsf{Keygen}(\mathsf{msk}, \mathsf{id})$ to $\mathcal{A}$.
- **Challenge Phase:** The adversary $\mathcal{A}$ sends m^*, id^* to the challenger where id^* was never queried in the pre-challenge query phase. The challenger computes $\mathsf{ct}^* \leftarrow \mathsf{Enc}(\mathsf{mpk}, \mathsf{id}^*, m^*)$ and returns $(\mathsf{msk}, \mathsf{ct}^*)$ to $\mathcal{A}$.
- **Response Phase:** $\mathcal{A}$ outputs b.

Simulated World:

- **Initialization Phase:** $\mathcal{A}$ on input 1^λ, outputs 1^T. The challenger computes $(\mathsf{mpk}, \mathsf{st}_1) \leftarrow \mathsf{Sim}_1(1^\lambda, 1^T)$ and sends mpk to $\mathcal{A}$.
- **Pre-Challenge Query Phase:** In this phase, $\mathcal{A}$ is allowed to make multiple queries id. For each id, the challenger returns $\mathsf{sk}_{\mathsf{id}} \leftarrow \mathsf{Sim}_2(\mathsf{st}_1, \mathsf{id})$ to $\mathcal{A}$.
- **Challenge Phase:** The adversary $\mathcal{A}$ sends m^*, id^* to the challenger where id^* was never queried in the pre-challenge query phase. The challenger computes $(\mathsf{ct}^*, \mathsf{st}_3) \leftarrow \mathsf{Sim}_3(\mathsf{st}_2, \mathsf{id}^*)$ and $\mathsf{msk} \leftarrow \mathsf{Sim}_4(\mathsf{st}_3, m^*)$. It returns $(\mathsf{msk}, \mathsf{ct}^*)$ to $\mathcal{A}$.
- **Response Phase:** $\mathcal{A}$ outputs b.

It is important to note that in the challenge phase, the adversary obtains only the master secret key and the challenge ciphertext, and not the randomness used by the Setup algorithm or Enc algorithm to generate the challenge ciphertext. Let p_{real} and p_{sim} be the probabilities with which $\mathcal{A}$ outputs 0 in the real world and simulated world, respectively.

Definition 6. *An RNC-IBE scheme is said to be **adaptive** secure if for all PPT adversaries $\mathcal{A}$, there exists a negligible function $\mathsf{negl}(\cdot)$ such that, for all $\lambda \in \mathbb{N}$,*

$$|p_{\text{real}} - p_{\text{sim}}| = \mathsf{negl}(\lambda)$$

Definition 7. *An RNC-IBE scheme is said to be **selectively** secure if for all PPT adversaries $\mathcal{A}$, there exists a negligible function $\mathsf{negl}(\cdot)$ such that, for all $\lambda \in \mathbb{N}$,*

$$|p_{\text{real}} - p_{\text{sim}}| = \mathsf{negl}(\lambda)$$

provided the adversary commits to the challenge identity id* *at the beginning of the game and* Sim_1 *addition takes* id* *also as an additional input.*

4.2   Receiver Non-Committing Identity-Based Key-Encapsulation Mechanism

A receiver non-committing identity-based key-encapsulation mechanism (RNC-IB-KEM) consists of the following algorithms.

$\mathsf{Setup}(1^\lambda, 1^n)$: The setup algorithm takes as input the security parameter 1^λ and the length of the identities 1^n (in some cases the number of identities 1^T). It outputs the master public key mpk and master secret key msk.

$\mathsf{Keygen}(\mathsf{msk}, \mathsf{id})$: The key generation algorithm takes as input a master secret key msk and an identity id and outputs a secret key $\mathsf{sk}_{\mathsf{id}}$.

$\mathsf{Encap}(\mathsf{mpk}, \mathsf{id})$: The encryption algorithm takes as input a master public key mpk and an identity id and outputs a ciphertext ct and a session key seskey.

$\mathsf{Decap}(\mathsf{sk}, \mathsf{ct})$: The decryption algorithm takes as input a secret key sk and a ciphertext ct and outputs either a session key seskey or $\perp$.

$\mathsf{Sim}_1(1^\lambda, 1^n)$: The first simulator takes as input the security parameter 1^λ and the length of the identities 1^n (in some cases the number of identities 1^T) and outputs a master public key mpk and a state st_1.

$\mathsf{Sim}_2(\mathsf{st}_1, \mathsf{id})$: The second simulator is a stateful algorithm with an internal state st_2 that takes as input a state st_1 and an identity id and outputs a secret key $\mathsf{sk}_{\mathsf{id}}$ and updates st_2.

$\mathsf{Sim}_3(\mathsf{st}_2, \mathsf{id}^*)$: The third simulator takes as input a state st_2, an identity id* and outputs a ciphertext ct* and a state st_3.

$\mathsf{Sim}_4(\mathsf{st}_3, \mathsf{seskey})$: The third simulator takes as input a state st_3, a session key seskey and outputs a ciphertext msk.

Correctness. For correctness, we require that there exists a negligible function $\mathsf{negl}(\cdot)$ such that for all $\lambda \in \mathbb{N}, n \in \mathbb{N}$ and $(\mathsf{mpk}, \mathsf{msk}) \leftarrow \mathsf{Setup}(1^\lambda, 1^n)$, any identity id,

$$\Pr_{r_1, r_2} \left[\mathsf{Decap}(\mathsf{sk}_{\mathsf{id}}, \mathsf{ct}) = \mathsf{seskey} : \begin{array}{l} (\mathsf{ct}, \mathsf{seskey}) = \mathsf{Encap}(\mathsf{mpk}, \mathsf{id}; r_1) \\ \mathsf{sk}_{\mathsf{id}} \leftarrow \mathsf{Keygen}(\mathsf{msk}, \mathsf{id}; r_2) \end{array} \right] = 1 - \mathsf{negl}(\lambda)$$

Security. Consider the following two experiments with an adversary $\mathcal{A}$.

Real World:

- **Initialization Phase:** $\mathcal{A}$ on input 1^λ, outputs 1^T. The challenger computes $(\mathsf{mpk}, \mathsf{msk}) \leftarrow \mathsf{Setup}(1^\lambda, 1^T)$ and sends mpk to $\mathcal{A}$.
- **Pre-Challenge Query Phase:** In this phase, $\mathcal{A}$ is allowed to make multiple queries id. For each id, the challenger returns $\mathsf{sk}_{\mathsf{id}} \leftarrow \mathsf{Keygen}(\mathsf{msk}, \mathsf{id})$ to $\mathcal{A}$.
- **Challenge Phase:** The adversary $\mathcal{A}$ sends id^* to the challenger where id^* was never queried in the pre-challenge query phase. The challenger computes $(\mathsf{ct}^*, \mathsf{seskey}) \leftarrow \mathsf{Enc}(\mathsf{mpk}, \mathsf{id}^*)$ and returns $(\mathsf{msk}, \mathsf{ct}^*, \mathsf{seskey})$ to $\mathcal{A}$.
- **Response Phase:** $\mathcal{A}$ outputs b.

Simulated World:

- **Initialization Phase:** $\mathcal{A}$ on input 1^λ, outputs 1^T. The challenger computes $(\mathsf{mpk}, \mathsf{st}_1) \leftarrow \mathsf{Sim}_1(1^\lambda, 1^T)$ and sends mpk to $\mathcal{A}$.
- **Pre-Challenge Query Phase:** In this phase, $\mathcal{A}$ is allowed to make multiple queries id. For each id, the challenger returns $\mathsf{sk}_{\mathsf{id}} \leftarrow \mathsf{Sim}_2(\mathsf{st}_1, \mathsf{id})$ to $\mathcal{A}$.
- **Challenge Phase:** The adversary $\mathcal{A}$ sends id^* to the challenger where id^* was never queried in the pre-challenge query phase. The challenger computes $(\mathsf{ct}^*, \mathsf{st}_3) \leftarrow \mathsf{Sim}_3(\mathsf{st}_2, \mathsf{id}^*)$ and $\mathsf{msk} \leftarrow \mathsf{Sim}_4(\mathsf{st}_3, \mathsf{seskey})$ where seskey is randomly generated. It returns $(\mathsf{msk}, \mathsf{ct}^*, \mathsf{seskey})$ to $\mathcal{A}$.
- **Response Phase:** $\mathcal{A}$ outputs b.

It is important to note that in the challenge phase, the adversary obtains only the master secret key, the challenge ciphertext and the session key, and not the randomness used by the Setup algorithm or Encap algorithm to generate the challenge ciphertext and the session key. Let p_{real} and p_{sim} be the probabilities with which $\mathcal{A}$ outputs 0 in the real world and simulated world, respectively.

Definition 8. *An RNC-IB-KEM scheme is said to be secure if for all PPT adversaries $\mathcal{A}$, there exists a negligible function $\mathsf{negl}(\cdot)$ such that, for all $\lambda \in \mathbb{N}$,*

$$|p_{\mathrm{real}} - p_{\mathrm{sim}}| = \mathsf{negl}(\lambda)$$

By combining an RNC-IB-KEM with *one-time pad* encryption in a hybrid encryption approach, we can obtain an RNC-IBE scheme. This is possible because the RNC-IB-KEM (and RNC-IBE) requires the disclosure of the master secret key and not the randomness used by the Setup and/or Enc algorithms. However, the ciphertext-size will be the sum of the RNC-IB-KEM ciphertext-size and the size of the session-key.

Theorem 11. *Assuming the existence of secure RNC-IB-KEM, there exists secure RNC-IBE schemes.*

5   Receiver Non-Committing IB-KEM and IBE from Bilinear Groups

In this section, we present an adaptive secure receiver non-committing identity based key encapsulation mechanism (RNC-IB-KEM) using the concepts of dual system encryption [67].

5.1   Construction

Our construction is as follows. Let $\mathsf{HC} : \mathbb{G}_T \times \{0,1\}^{\log(p)} \to \{0,1\}$ denote a 1-bit randomness extractor over a group element and $\ell := \ell(\lambda)$ be a polynomial in λ.

$\mathsf{Gen}(1^\lambda)$:
- Generate a bilinear group $(\mathbb{G}_1, \mathbb{G}_2, \mathbb{G}_T, e, p, g_1, g_2)$.
- Generate $\mathbf{a}, \mathbf{b} \leftarrow \mathbb{Z}_p^2$ and $\mathbf{W}_1, \mathbf{W}_2 \leftarrow \mathbb{Z}_p^{2\times 2}$.
- Output $\mathsf{pp} := ([\mathbf{a}]_1, [\mathbf{b}]_2, [\mathbf{W}_1\mathbf{a}]_1, [\mathbf{W}_2\mathbf{a}]_1, [\mathbf{W}_1^\top\mathbf{b}]_2, [\mathbf{W}_2^\top\mathbf{b}]_2)$. We assume that $(\mathbb{G}_1, \mathbb{G}_2, \mathbb{G}_T, e, p, g_1, g_2)$ is included in pp and omit to write it.

$\mathsf{Setup}(\mathsf{pp})$:
- Parse $([\mathbf{a}]_1, [\mathbf{b}]_2, [\mathbf{W}_1\mathbf{a}]_1, [\mathbf{W}_2\mathbf{a}]_1, [\mathbf{W}_1^\top\mathbf{b}]_2, [\mathbf{W}_2^\top\mathbf{b}]_2) \leftarrow \mathsf{pp}$.
- Generate $h \leftarrow \{0,1\}^{\log(p)}$.
- Generate $\mathbf{k}_i \leftarrow \mathbb{Z}_p^2, \forall i \in [\ell]$.
- Output $\mathsf{mpk} := (\{[\mathbf{a}^\top\mathbf{k}_i]_T\}_{i\in[\ell]}, h)$ and $\mathsf{msk} := \{\mathbf{k}_i\}_{i\in[\ell]}$.

$\mathsf{Keygen}(\mathsf{pp}, \mathsf{msk}, \mathsf{id} \in \mathbb{Z}_p)$:
- Parse $([\mathbf{a}]_1, [\mathbf{b}]_2, [\mathbf{W}_1\mathbf{a}]_1, [\mathbf{W}_2\mathbf{a}]_1, [\mathbf{W}_1^\top\mathbf{b}]_2, [\mathbf{W}_2^\top\mathbf{b}]_2) \leftarrow \mathsf{pp}$ and $\{\mathbf{k}_i\} \leftarrow \mathsf{msk}$.
- Generate $s_i \leftarrow \mathbb{Z}_p, \forall i \in [\ell]$.
- Output $\mathsf{sk}_{\mathsf{id}} := \{([s_i\mathbf{b}]_2, [\mathbf{k}_i + s_i(\mathbf{W}_1 + \mathsf{id}\cdot\mathbf{W}_2)^\top\mathbf{b}]_2)\}_{i\in[\ell]}$.

$\mathsf{Encap}(\mathsf{pp}, \mathsf{mpk}, \mathsf{id})$:
- Parse $([\mathbf{a}]_1, [\mathbf{b}]_2, [\mathbf{W}_1\mathbf{a}]_1, [\mathbf{W}_2\mathbf{a}]_1, [\mathbf{W}_1^\top\mathbf{b}]_2, [\mathbf{W}_2^\top\mathbf{b}]_2) \leftarrow \mathsf{pp}$ and $(\{[\mathbf{a}^\top\mathbf{k}_i]_T\}_{i\in[\ell]}, h) \leftarrow \mathsf{mpk}$.
- Generate $r \leftarrow \mathbb{Z}_p$.
- Output $\mathsf{ct} := ([r\mathbf{a}]_1, [r(\mathbf{W}_1 + \mathsf{id}\cdot\mathbf{W}_2)\mathbf{a}]_1)$ and $\mathsf{seskey} := \{\mathsf{HC}([r\mathbf{a}^\top\mathbf{k}_i]_T, h)\}_{i\in[\ell]}$.

$\mathsf{Decap}(\mathsf{pp}, \mathsf{sk}_{\mathsf{id}}, \mathsf{ct})$:
- Parse $\{([\mathbf{d}_i]_2, [\mathbf{d}_i']_2)\}_{i\in[\ell]} \leftarrow \mathsf{sk}_{\mathsf{id}}$ and $([\mathbf{c}]_1, [\mathbf{c}']_1) \leftarrow \mathsf{ct}$.
- Output $\mathsf{seskey} := \{\mathsf{HC}(e([\mathbf{c}]_1^\top, [\mathbf{d}_i']_2)/e([\mathbf{c}']_1^\top, [\mathbf{d}_i]_2), h)\}_{i\in[\ell]}$.

$\mathsf{Sim}_1(1^\lambda, 1^p)$:
- Generate a bilinear group $(\mathbb{G}_1, \mathbb{G}_2, \mathbb{G}_T, e, p, g_1, g_2)$.
- Generate $\mathbf{a}, \mathbf{b} \leftarrow \mathbb{Z}_q$ and $\mathbf{W}_1, \mathbf{W}_2 \leftarrow \mathbb{Z}_p^{2\times 2}$.
- Generate $k_{i,1} \leftarrow \mathbb{Z}_p, \forall i \in [\ell]$ and $h \leftarrow \{0,1\}^{\log(p)}$.
- Output $\mathsf{pp} := ([\mathbf{a}]_1, [\mathbf{b}]_2, [\mathbf{W}_1\mathbf{a}]_1, [\mathbf{W}_2\mathbf{a}]_1, [\mathbf{W}_1^\top\mathbf{b}]_2, [\mathbf{W}_2^\top\mathbf{b}]_2)$ and $\mathsf{mpk} := (\{[k_{i,1}]_T\}_{i\in[\ell]}, h)$ and $\mathsf{st}_1 = (\{k_{i,1}\}_{i\in[\ell]}, \mathbf{a})$.

$\mathsf{Sim}_2(\mathsf{st}_1, \mathsf{id})$:
- Generate $s_i, w_i \leftarrow \mathbb{Z}_p, \forall i \in [\ell]$.

- Output $\mathsf{sk_{id}} := \{([s_i\mathbf{b}]_2, [\frac{k_1}{|\mathbf{a}|^2} \cdot \mathbf{a} + s_i(\mathbf{W}_1 + \mathsf{id} \cdot \mathbf{W}_2)^\top \mathbf{b} + w_i\mathbf{a}^\perp]_2)\}_{i\in[\ell]}$ and $\mathsf{st}_2 := \mathsf{st}_1$.

$\mathsf{Sim}_3(\mathsf{st}_2, \mathsf{id}^*)$:
- Generate $u_1, u_2 \leftarrow \mathbb{Z}_p$ and set $\mathbf{u} = u_1\mathbf{a} + u_2\mathbf{a}^\perp$.
- Outputs $\mathsf{ct}^* := ([\mathbf{u}]_1, [(\mathbf{W}_1 + \mathsf{id}^* \cdot \mathbf{W}_2)\mathbf{u}]_1)$ and $\mathsf{st}_3 := (\mathsf{st}_2, u_1, u_2)$.

$\mathsf{Sim}_4(\mathsf{st}_3, \mathsf{seskey} \in \{0,1\}^\ell)$:
- Generate $x_i \in \mathbb{Z}_p$ such that $\mathsf{seskey}_i = \mathsf{HC}([x_i]_T, h)$ via rejection sampling.
- Set $k_{i,2} := \frac{x_i - u_1 k_{i,1}}{u_2}$.
- Output $\mathsf{msk} := \{\frac{k_{i,1}}{|\mathbf{a}|^2} \cdot \mathbf{a} + \frac{k_{i,2}}{|\mathbf{a}^\perp|^2} \cdot \mathbf{a}^\perp\}_{i\in[\ell]}$.

Remark 1. The randomness used in the setup algorithm includes h, which is part of the master public key and the set $\{k_i\}$, which constitutes the entire master secret key. Since, the challenger outputs h in the initialization phase and provides the master secret key in the challenge, the adversary effectively gains access to all the randomness used in the setup algorithm during the challenge phase.

Parameters. The size of a ciphertext is $\mathsf{poly}(\lambda)$, i.e., it is independent of ℓ. Whereas, the size of the master public key, master secret key and secret keys depend on ℓ.

Correctness. For correctly generated $\mathsf{sk_{id}} := (\{[s_i\mathbf{b}]_2, [\mathbf{k}_i + s_i(\mathbf{W}_1 + \mathsf{id} \cdot \mathbf{W}_2)^\top \mathbf{b}]_2)\}_{i\in[\ell]}$ and $\mathsf{ct} := ([r\mathbf{a}]_1, [r(\mathbf{W}_1 + \mathsf{id} \cdot \mathbf{W}_2)\mathbf{a}]_1)$, we have

$$\frac{e([r\mathbf{a}]_1^\top, [\mathbf{k}_i + s_i(\mathbf{W}_1 + \mathsf{id} \cdot \mathbf{W}_2)^\top \mathbf{b}]_2)}{e([r(\mathbf{W}_1 + \mathsf{id} \cdot \mathbf{W}_2)\mathbf{a}]_1^\top, [s_i\mathbf{b}]_2)} = \frac{[r\mathbf{a}^\top\mathbf{k}_i + rs_i\mathbf{a}^\top(\mathbf{W}_1 + \mathsf{id} \cdot \mathbf{W}_2)^\top \mathbf{b}]_T}{[rs_i\mathbf{a}^\top(\mathbf{W}_1 + \mathsf{id} \cdot \mathbf{W}_2)^\top \mathbf{b}]_T}$$
$$= [r\mathbf{a}^\top\mathbf{k}_i]_T$$

for all $i \in [\ell]$. Since, $\mathsf{HC}(\cdot, \cdot)$ is a deterministic function, the correctness follows immediately.

Theorem 12. *Assuming the hardness of* SXDH, *the above scheme is a secure receiver non-committing identity-based key encapsulation mechanism.*

Proof. Consider the following experiment for an adversary $\mathcal{A}$ that makes q queries to $O_{\mathsf{UserKeyGen}}$.

Hyb_0: This corresponds to the real experiment of non-committing security.
1. The challenger generates $\mathsf{pp}, \mathsf{mpk}, \mathsf{msk}$ as follows.
    - Generate a bilinear group $(\mathbb{G}_1, \mathbb{G}_2, \mathbb{G}_T, e, p, g_1, g_2)$.
    - Generate $\mathbf{a}, \mathbf{b} \leftarrow \mathbb{Z}_p^2$ and $\mathbf{W}_1, \mathbf{W}_2 \leftarrow \mathbb{Z}_p^{2\times 2}$.
    - Generate $\mathbf{k}_i \leftarrow \mathbb{Z}_p^2, \forall i \in [\ell]$ and $h \leftarrow \{0,1\}^{\log(p)}$.
    - Set $\mathsf{pp} := ([\mathbf{a}]_1, [\mathbf{b}]_2, [\mathbf{W}_1\mathbf{a}]_1, [\mathbf{W}_2\mathbf{a}]_1, [\mathbf{W}_1^\top\mathbf{b}]_2, [\mathbf{W}_2^\top\mathbf{b}]_2)$, $\mathsf{mpk} := (\{[\mathbf{a}^\top\mathbf{k}_i]_T\}_i, h)$, and $\mathsf{msk} := \{\mathbf{k}_i\}_i$.
    The challenger sends pp and mpk to $\mathcal{A}$.

2. $\mathcal{A}$ can get access to the following oracle that provides access to Keygen$(\mathsf{pp}, \mathsf{msk}, \cdot)$.

$O_{\mathsf{UserKeyGen}}(\mathsf{id}^j)$: Given the j-query $\mathsf{id}^j \in \mathbb{Z}_p$ as an input, it returns $\mathsf{sk}_{\mathsf{id}^j}$ generated as follows.

- Generate $s_i^j \leftarrow \mathbb{Z}_p, \forall i \in [\ell]$.
- Set $\mathsf{sk}_{\mathsf{id}^j} := \{([s_i^j \mathbf{b}]_2, [\mathbf{k}_i + s_i^j (\mathbf{W}_1 + \mathsf{id}^j \cdot \mathbf{W}_2)^\top \mathbf{b}]_2)\}_i$.

3. $\mathcal{A}$ outputs $\mathsf{id}^* \in \mathbb{Z}_p$. The challenger generates $(\mathsf{ct}^*, \mathsf{seskey}^*)$ as follows.

- Generate $r \leftarrow \mathbb{Z}_p$.
- Set $\mathsf{ct}^* := ([r\mathbf{a}]_1, [r(\mathbf{W}_1 + \mathsf{id}^* \cdot \mathbf{W}_2)\mathbf{a}]_1)$ and $\mathsf{seskey}^* := \{\mathsf{HC}([r\mathbf{a}^\top \mathbf{k}_i]_T, h)\}_i$.

The challenger sends $(\mathsf{msk}, \mathsf{ct}^*, \mathsf{seskey}^*)$ to $\mathcal{A}$.

4. $\mathcal{A}$ outputs $\mathsf{coin}' \in \{0, 1\}$.

Using a sequence of hybrid experiments, we will prove that the experiment can be indistinguishably changed into non-committing experiment. We will denote the probability that $\mathcal{A}$ outputs 0 in the hybrid Hyb_i using $p_{\mathcal{A}, H_i}$.

Below, we assume that $\mathbf{a}$ and $\mathbf{b}^\perp$ are linearly independent and $\mathbf{a}^\perp$ and $\mathbf{b}$ are also linearly independent, which hold with overwhelming probability over the choice of $\mathbf{a}$ and $\mathbf{b}$.

Changing the Challenge Ciphertext into Semi-functional Mode.

Hybrid Hyb_1: This is the same as Hyb_0 except $(\mathsf{ct}^*, \mathsf{seskey}^*)$ is generated as $\mathsf{ct}^* := ([\mathbf{u}]_1, [(\mathbf{W}_1 + \mathsf{id}^* \cdot \mathbf{W}_2)\mathbf{u}]_1)$ and $\mathsf{seskey}^* := \{\mathsf{HC}([\mathbf{u}^\top \mathbf{k}_i]_T, h)\}_i$, where $\mathbf{u} \leftarrow \mathbb{Z}_p^2$.

We have $|p_{\mathcal{A}, H_1} - p_{\mathcal{A}, H_0}| = \mathsf{negl}(\lambda)$ from the DDH assumption on $\mathbb{G}_1$.

Lemma 1. *For all PPT adversaries $\mathcal{A}$, there exists a PPT adversary $\mathcal{B}$ such that, $|p_{\mathcal{A}, H_1} - p_{\mathcal{A}, H_0}| \leq p_{\mathcal{B}, \mathsf{DDH}}$.*

We define $\mathsf{Hyb}_{1,0,5}$ as Hyb_1.

Changing the user secret keys into semi-functional mode. We change the user secret keys into semi-functional mode using $\mathsf{Hyb}_{1,i,1}, \cdots, \mathsf{Hyb}_{1,i,5}$ for $i \in [q]$. Below, we define $\mathbf{W}_0 := \mathbf{b}^\perp (\mathbf{a}^\perp)^\top / (\mathbf{b}^\perp)^\top \mathbf{a}^\perp$.

Hybrid $\mathsf{Hyb}_{1,i,1}$: This is the same as $\mathsf{Hyb}_{1,i-1,5}$ except that $O_{\mathsf{UserKeyGen}}$ behaves as follows.

$O_{\mathsf{UserKeyGen}}(\mathsf{id})$: Given the j-th query $\mathsf{id}^j \in \mathbb{Z}_p$ as an input, it behaves as follows.

- If $j < i$, return $\mathsf{sk}_{\mathsf{id}^j}$ generated as follows.
  • Generate $s_d^j, w_d^j \leftarrow \mathbb{Z}_p, \forall d \in [\ell]$.
  • Set $\mathsf{sk}_{\mathsf{id}^j} := \{([s_d^j \mathbf{b}]_2, [\mathbf{k}_d + s_d^j (\mathbf{W}_1 + \mathsf{id}^j \cdot \mathbf{W}_2)^\top \mathbf{b} + w_d^j \mathbf{a}^\perp]_2)\}_d$.
- If $j = i$, return $\mathsf{sk}_{\mathsf{id}^i}$ generated as follows.
  • Generate $\mathsf{v}_d^i \leftarrow \mathbb{Z}_p^2, \forall d \in [\ell]$.

- Set $\mathsf{sk}_{\mathsf{id}^i} := \{([\mathsf{v}_d^i]_2, [\mathbf{k}_d + (\mathbf{W}_1 + \mathsf{id}^i \cdot \mathbf{W}_2)^\top \mathsf{v}_d^i]_2)\}_d$.
  - If $j > i$, return $\mathsf{sk}_{\mathsf{id}^j}$ generated as follows.
    - Generate $s_d^j \leftarrow \mathbb{Z}_p, \forall d \in [\ell]$.
    - Set $\mathsf{sk}_{\mathsf{id}^j} := \{([s_d^j \mathbf{b}]_2, [\mathbf{k}_d + s_d^j (\mathbf{W}_1 + \mathsf{id}^j \cdot \mathbf{W}_2)^\top \mathbf{b}]_2)\}_d$.

We have $|p_{\mathcal{A}, H_{1,1,1}} - p_{\mathcal{A}, H_1}| = \mathsf{negl}(\lambda)$ from the DDH assumption on $\mathbb{G}_2$.

Lemma 2. *For all PPT adversaries $\mathcal{A}$, there exists a PPT adversary $\mathcal{B}$ such that, $|p_{\mathcal{A}, H_{1,1,1}} - p_{\mathcal{A}, H_1}| \le \ell \cdot p_{\mathcal{B}, \mathsf{DDH}}$.*

Hybrid $\mathsf{Hyb}_{1,i,2}$: This is the same as $\mathsf{Hyb}_{1,i,1}$ except that we generate $\hat{\mathbf{W}}_1, \hat{\mathbf{W}}_2 \leftarrow \mathbb{Z}_p^{2\times2}$ and $w_1, w_2 \leftarrow \mathbb{Z}_p$, and set $\mathbf{W}_1 := \hat{\mathbf{W}}_1 + w_1 \mathbf{W}_0$ and $\mathbf{W}_2 := \hat{\mathbf{W}}_2 + w_2 \mathbf{W}_0$.

We have $|p_{\mathcal{A}, H_{1,i,2}} - p_{\mathcal{A}, H_{1,i,1}}| = 0$ since the distribution of $\mathbf{W}_1, \mathbf{W}_2$ do not change.

Lemma 3. *For all PPT adversaries $\mathcal{A}$ and all $\lambda \in \mathbb{N}$, $|p_{\mathcal{A}, H_{1,i,2}} - p_{\mathcal{A}, H_{1,i,1}}| = 0$.*

We prove that w_1 and w_2 appears only in ct^* in the form of $w_1 + \mathsf{id}^* \cdot w_2$ and in $\mathsf{sk}_{\mathsf{id}^i}$ in the form of $w_1 + \mathsf{id}^i \cdot w_2$. First, we have $[\mathbf{W}_\alpha \mathbf{a}]_1 = [\hat{\mathbf{W}}_\alpha \mathbf{a}]_1$ and $[\mathbf{W}_\alpha^\top \mathbf{b}]_2 = [\hat{\mathbf{W}}_\alpha^\top \mathbf{b}]_2$ for $\alpha \in \{1, 2\}$. For ct^*, we can write $\mathbf{u} = r\mathbf{a} + r'\mathbf{b}^\perp$, and thus we have

$$\mathsf{ct}^* = ([\mathbf{u}]_1, [(\mathbf{W}_1 + \mathsf{id}^* \cdot \mathbf{W}_2)\mathbf{u}]_1)$$
$$= ([\mathbf{u}]_1, [(\hat{\mathbf{W}}_1 + \mathsf{id}^* \cdot \hat{\mathbf{W}}_2)\mathbf{u} + r'(w_1 + \mathsf{id}^* \cdot w_2)\mathbf{b}^\perp]_1).$$

Also, for $\mathsf{sk}_{\mathsf{id}^i}$, we can write $\mathbf{v}_d^i = s_d^i \mathbf{b} + t_d^i \mathbf{a}^\perp$ and thus we have

$$\mathsf{sk}_{\mathsf{id}^i} = \{([\mathbf{v}_d^i]_2, [\mathbf{k}_d + (\mathbf{W}_1 + \mathsf{id}^i \cdot \mathbf{W}_2)^\top \mathbf{v}_d^i]_2)\}_d$$
$$= \{([\mathbf{v}_d^i]_2, [\mathbf{k}_d + (\hat{\mathbf{W}}_2 + \mathsf{id}^i \cdot \hat{\mathbf{W}}_2)^\top \mathbf{v}_d^i + t_d^i(w_1 + \mathsf{id}^i \cdot w_2)\mathbf{a}^\perp]_2)\}_d.$$

Moreover, for $j \ne i$, we can write $\mathsf{sk}_{\mathsf{id}^j}$ as

$$\mathsf{sk}_{\mathsf{id}^j} = \begin{cases} \{([s_d^j \mathbf{b}]_2, [\mathbf{k}_d + s_d^j(\hat{\mathbf{W}}_1 + \mathsf{id}^j \cdot \hat{\mathbf{W}}_2)^\top \mathbf{b} + w_d^j \mathbf{a}^\perp]_2)\}_d & \text{for } j < i \\ \{([s_d^j \mathbf{b}]_2, [\mathbf{k}_d + s_d^j(\hat{\mathbf{W}}_1 + \mathsf{id}^j \cdot \hat{\mathbf{W}}_2)^\top \mathbf{b}]_2)\}_d & \text{for } j > i \end{cases}$$

Hybrid $\mathsf{Hyb}_{1,i,3}$: This is the same as $\mathsf{Hyb}_{1,i,2}$ except that for the i-th query id^i, $O_{\mathsf{UserKeyGen}}$ returns $\mathsf{sk}_{\mathsf{id}^i} := \{([\mathbf{v}_d^i]_2, [\mathbf{k}_d + (\mathbf{W}_1 + \mathsf{id}^i \cdot \mathbf{W}_2)^\top \mathbf{v}_d^i + w_d^i \mathbf{a}^\perp]_2)\}_d$, where $w_d^i \leftarrow \mathbb{Z}_p$.

It is important to note that only the secret key $\mathsf{sk}_{\mathsf{id}^i}$ contains information about w_1 and w_2, while the remaining secret keys do not. Therefore, we have $|p_{\mathcal{A}, H_{1,i,3}} - p_{\mathcal{A}, H_{1,i,2}}| = \mathsf{negl}(\lambda)$, since $\mathsf{id}^* \ne \mathsf{id}^i$, which implies

$$\{w_1 + \mathsf{id}^* \cdot w_2, w_1 + \mathsf{id}^i \cdot w_2\}_{w_1, w_2} \equiv \{w_1 + \mathsf{id}^* \cdot w_2, u\}_{w_1, w_2, u}$$

and with probability $\frac{p-1}{p}$, a randomly chosen t_d^i is invertible.

Lemma 4. *For all PPT adversaries* $\mathcal{A}$ *and* $\lambda \in \mathbb{N}$, $|p_{\mathcal{A}, H_{1,i,3}} - p_{\mathcal{A}, H_{1,i,2}}| =$ $\mathsf{negl}(\lambda)$.

Hybrid $\mathsf{Hyb}_{1,i,4}$: This is the same as $\mathsf{Hyb}_{1,i,3}$ except that we undo the change between $\mathsf{Hyb}_{1,i,1}$ and $\mathsf{Hyb}_{1,i,2}$. Namely, we generate $\mathbf{W}_1, \mathbf{W}_2 \leftarrow \mathbb{Z}_p^{2\times 2}$.

Lemma 5. *For all PPT adversaries* $\mathcal{A}$, $|p_{\mathcal{A}, H_{1,i,4}} - p_{\mathcal{A}, H_{1,i,3}}| = 0$.

Hybrid $\mathsf{Hyb}_{1,i,5}$: This is the same as $\mathsf{Hyb}_{1,i,4}$ except that for the i-th query id^i, $O_{\mathsf{UserKeyGen}}$ returns $\mathsf{sk}_{\mathsf{id}^i} := \{([s_d^i \mathbf{b}]_2, [\mathbf{k}_d + s_d^i(\mathbf{W}_1 + \mathsf{id}^i \cdot \mathbf{W}_2)^\top \mathbf{b} + w_d^i \mathbf{a}^\perp]_2)\}_d$, where $s_d^i, w_d^i \leftarrow \mathbb{Z}_p$.

We have $|p_{\mathcal{A}, H_{1,i,5}} - p_{\mathcal{A}, H_{1,i,4}}| = \mathsf{negl}(\lambda)$ from the DDH assumption on $\mathbb{G}_2$.

Lemma 6. *For all PPT adversaries* $\mathcal{A}$, *there exists a PPT adversary* $\mathcal{B}$ *such that,* $|p_{\mathcal{A}, H_{1,i,5}} - p_{\mathcal{A}, H_{1,i,4}}| \leq \ell \cdot p_{\mathcal{B}, \mathsf{DDH}}$.

We also have $|p_{\mathcal{A}, H_{1,i+1,1}} - p_{\mathcal{A}, H_{1,i,5}}| = \mathsf{negl}(\lambda)$ from DDH assumption on $\mathbb{G}_2$.

Lemma 7. *For all PPT adversaries* $\mathcal{A}$, *there exists a PPT adversary* $\mathcal{B}$ *such that,* $|p_{\mathcal{A}, H_{1,i+1,1}} - p_{\mathcal{A}, H_{1,i,5}}| \leq \ell \cdot p_{\mathcal{B}, \mathsf{DDH}}$.

Final Steps Towards Non-committing Mode.

Hybrid Hyb_2: We define Hyb_2 as the same game as $\mathsf{Hyb}_{1,q,5}$. The detailed description is as follows.
1. The challenger generates $\mathsf{pp}, \mathsf{mpk}, \mathsf{msk}$ as follows.
   - Generate a bilinear group $(\mathbb{G}_1, \mathbb{G}_2, \mathbb{G}_T, e, p, g_1, g_2)$.
   - Generate $\mathbf{a}, \mathbf{b} \leftarrow \mathbb{Z}_q$ and $\mathbf{W}_1, \mathbf{W}_2 \leftarrow \mathbb{Z}_p^{2\times 2}$.
   - Generate $\mathbf{k}_i \leftarrow \mathbb{Z}_p^2$, $\forall i \in [\ell]$ and $h \leftarrow \{0,1\}^{\log(p)}$.
   - Set $\mathsf{pp} := ([\mathbf{a}]_1, [\mathbf{b}]_2, [\mathbf{W}_1 \mathbf{a}]_1, [\mathbf{W}_2 \mathbf{a}]_1, [\mathbf{W}_1^\top \mathbf{b}]_2, [\mathbf{W}_2^\top \mathbf{b}]_2)$ and $\mathsf{mpk} :=$ $(\{[\mathbf{a}^\top \mathbf{k}_i]_T\}_i, h)$ and $\mathsf{msk} := \{\mathbf{k}_i\}_i$.
   The challenger sends pp and mpk to $\mathcal{A}$.
2. $\mathcal{A}$ can get access to the following oracle.
   $O_{\mathsf{UserKeyGen}}(\mathsf{id}^j)$: Given the j-query $\mathsf{id}^j \in \mathbb{Z}_p$ as an input, it returns $\mathsf{sk}_{\mathsf{id}^j}$ generated as follows.
      - Generate $s_d^j, w_d^j \leftarrow \mathbb{Z}_p$, $\forall d \in [\ell]$.
      - Set $\mathsf{sk}_{\mathsf{id}^j} := \{([s_d^j \mathbf{b}]_2, [\mathbf{k}_d + s_d^j(\mathbf{W}_1 + \mathsf{id}^j \cdot \mathbf{W}_2)^\top \mathbf{b} + w_d^j \mathbf{a}^\perp]_2)\}_d$.
3. $\mathcal{A}$ outputs $\mathsf{id}^* \in \mathbb{Z}_p$. The challenger generates $(\mathsf{ct}^*, \mathsf{seskey}^*)$ as follows.
   - Generate $\mathbf{u} \leftarrow \mathbb{Z}^2$.
   - Set $\mathsf{ct}^* := ([\mathbf{u}]_1, [(\mathbf{W}_1 + \mathsf{id}^* \cdot \mathbf{W}_2)\mathbf{u}]_1)$ and $\mathsf{seskey}^* :=$ $\{\mathsf{HC}([\mathbf{u}^\top \mathbf{k}_i]_T, h)\}_i$.
   The challenger sends $(\mathsf{msk}, \mathsf{ct}^*, \mathsf{seskey}^*)$ to $\mathcal{A}$.
4. $\mathcal{A}$ outputs $\mathsf{coin}' \in \{0,1\}$.

Hybrid Hyb_3: This is the same as Hyb_2 except that we generate $k_{i,1}, k_{i,2} \leftarrow \mathbb{Z}_p$ and set $\mathbf{k}_i \leftarrow \frac{k_{i,1}}{|\mathbf{a}|^2} \cdot \mathbf{a} + \frac{k_{i,2}}{|\mathbf{a}^\perp|^2} \cdot \mathbf{a}^\perp$. By this change, we have $\mathsf{mpk} = \{[k_{i,1}]_T\}_i$.

This is just conceptual change and we have $|p_{\mathcal{A},H_3} - p_{\mathcal{A},H_2}| = 0$.

Lemma 8. *For all PPT adversaries $\mathcal{A}$ and all $\lambda \in \mathbb{N}$, $|p_{\mathcal{A},H_3} - p_{\mathcal{A},H_2}| = 0$.*

Hybrid Hyb_4: This is the same as Hyb_3 except that for the j-th query id^j, $\mathcal{O}_{\mathsf{UserKeyGen}}$ returns $\mathsf{sk}_{\mathsf{id}^j} := \{([s_d^j \mathbf{b}]_2, [\frac{k_1}{|\mathbf{a}|^2} \cdot \mathbf{a} + s_d^j (\mathbf{W}_1 + \mathsf{id}^j \cdot \mathbf{W}_2)^\top \mathbf{b} + w_d^j \mathbf{a}^\perp]_2)\}_d$, where $s_d^j, w_d^j \leftarrow \mathbb{Z}_p$.

We have $|p_{\mathcal{A},H_4} - p_{\mathcal{A},3}| = 0$ since $\frac{k_2}{|\mathbf{a}^\perp|^2} + w_d^j$ and w_d^j identically distributes for every $j \in [q], d \in [\ell]$ when w_d^j is chosen uniformly at random.

Lemma 9. *For all PPT adversaries $\mathcal{A}$ and for all $\lambda \in \mathbb{N}$, $|p_{\mathcal{A},H_4} - p_{\mathcal{A},3}| = 0$.*

Hybrid Hyb_5: This is the same as Hyb_4 except that we generate $u_1, u_2 \leftarrow \mathbb{Z}_p$ and set $\mathbf{u} \leftarrow u_1 \mathbf{a} + u_2 \mathbf{a}^\perp$.

This is just conceptual change and we have $|p_{\mathcal{A},H_5} - p_{\mathcal{A},4}| = 0$.

Lemma 10. *For all PPT adversaries $\mathcal{A}$ and for all $\lambda \in \mathbb{N}$, $|p_{\mathcal{A},H_5} - p_{\mathcal{A},4}| = 0$.*

Hybrid Hyb_6: This is the same as Hyb_5 except that we generate $x_i \leftarrow \mathbb{Z}_p$ and we set $k_{i,2} = \frac{x_i - u_1 k_{i,1}}{u_2}$. By this change, we have $\mathsf{seskey}^* = \{\mathsf{HC}([x_i]_T, h)\}_i$.

We have $|p_{\mathcal{A},H_6} - p_{\mathcal{A},5}| \leq \mathsf{negl}(\lambda)$ since k_2 still distributes uniformly at random when u_2 is invertible which occurs with high probability.

Lemma 11. *For all PPT adversaries $\mathcal{A}$ and $\lambda \in \mathbb{N}$, $|p_{\mathcal{A},H_6} - p_{\mathcal{A},5}| \leq \mathsf{negl}(\lambda)$.*

Hybrid Hyb_7: This is the same as Hyb_6 except that we defer the generation of k_2 until the challenge phase. The detailed description is as follows.

1. The challenger generates $\mathsf{pp}, \mathsf{mpk}, \mathsf{msk}$ as follows.
   - Generate a bilinear group $(\mathbb{G}_1, \mathbb{G}_2, \mathbb{G}_T, e, p, g_1, g_2)$.
   - Generate $\mathbf{a}, \mathbf{b} \leftarrow \mathbb{Z}_q$ and $\mathbf{W}_1, \mathbf{W}_2 \leftarrow \mathbb{Z}_p^{2 \times 2}$.
   - Generate $k_{i,1} \leftarrow \mathbb{Z}_p, \forall i \in [\ell]$ and $h \leftarrow \{0,1\}^{\log(p)}$.
   - Set $\mathsf{pp} := ([\mathbf{a}]_1, [\mathbf{b}]_2, [\mathbf{W}_1 \mathbf{a}]_1, [\mathbf{W}_2 \mathbf{a}]_1, [\mathbf{W}_1^\top \mathbf{b}]_2, [\mathbf{W}_2^\top \mathbf{b}]_2)$ and $\mathsf{mpk} := (\{[k_{i,1}]_T\}_i, h)$.

   The challenger sends pp and mpk to $\mathcal{A}$.
2. $\mathcal{A}$ can get access to the following oracle.
   $\mathcal{O}_{\mathsf{UserKeyGen}}(\mathsf{id}^j)$: Given the j-query $\mathsf{id}^j \in \mathbb{Z}_p$ as an input, it returns $\mathsf{sk}_{\mathsf{id}^j}$ generated as follows.
      - Generate $s_d^j, w_d^j \leftarrow \mathbb{Z}_p, \forall d \in [\ell]$.
      - Set $\mathsf{sk}_{\mathsf{id}^j} := \{([s_d^j \mathbf{b}]_2, [\frac{k_1}{|\mathbf{a}|^2} \cdot \mathbf{a} + s_d^j (\mathbf{W}_1 + \mathsf{id}^j \cdot \mathbf{W}_2)^\top \mathbf{b} + w_d^j \mathbf{a}^\perp]_2)\}_d$.
3. $\mathcal{A}$ outputs $\mathsf{id}^* \in \mathbb{Z}_p$. The challenger generates $(\mathsf{ct}^*, \mathsf{seskey}^*)$ as follows.
      - Generate $u_1, u_2 \leftarrow \mathbb{Z}_p$ and set $\mathbf{u} = u_1 \mathbf{a} + u_2 \mathbf{a}^\perp$.

- Generate $x_i \leftarrow \mathbb{Z}_p, \forall i \in [\ell]$
- Set $\mathsf{ct}^* := ([\mathbf{u}]_1, [(\mathbf{W}_1 + \mathsf{id}^* \cdot \mathbf{W}_2)\mathbf{u}]_1)$ and $\mathsf{seskey}^* := \{\mathsf{HC}([x_i]_T, h)\}_i$.
- Set $k_{i,2} = \frac{x_i - u_1 k_{i,1}}{u_2}$ and $\mathsf{msk} := \{\frac{k_{i,1}}{|\mathbf{a}|^2} \cdot \mathbf{a} + \frac{k_{i,2}}{|\mathbf{a}^\perp|^2} \cdot \mathbf{a}^\perp\}_i$.

  The challenger sends $(\mathsf{msk}, \mathsf{ct}^*, \mathsf{seskey}^*)$ to $\mathcal{A}$.
4. $\mathcal{A}$ outputs $\mathsf{coin}' \in \{0,1\}$.

It is easy to see that Hyb_7 can be simulated using the RNC-IB-KEM simulators. Using the above lemma along with triangular inequality, the theorem follows. $\square$

Combining Theorem 11 and Theorem 12, we obtain the following.

Theorem 13. *Assuming hardness of* SXDH, *there exists secure RNC-IBE schemes.*

6   Receiver Non-Committing IBE from Batch Encryption

In this section, we construct an adaptive secure RNC-IBE scheme which supports polynomially many identities. Let

- BE = (BE.Params, BE.Setup, BE.Enc, BE.Dec) be oblivious batch encryption.
- GC = (GC.Grbl, GC.Eval, GC.Sim) be a garbling scheme.
- NCE = (NCE.Setup, NCE.Enc, NCE.Dec) be a NCE scheme.

Let d be the length of the identities such that $T = 2^d = \mathsf{poly}(\lambda)$ and n be the length of the public keys of NCE.

$\mathsf{Setup}(1^\lambda, 1^T)$:
- Generate $\mathsf{be.pp} \leftarrow \mathsf{BE.Params}(1^\lambda, 1^{nT})$.
- Generate $(\mathsf{nce.pk}_i, \mathsf{nce.sk}_i) \leftarrow \mathsf{NCE.Setup}(1^\lambda; r^{(i)}_{\mathsf{NCE.Setup}})$ for $i \in \{0,1\}^d$.
- Generate $\mathsf{be.pk} = \mathsf{BE.Setup}(\mathsf{be.pp}, \{\mathsf{nce.pk}_i\}_{i \in \{0,1\}^d})$.
- Output $\mathsf{msk} := \{\mathsf{nce.pk}_i, \mathsf{nce.sk}_i\}_{i \in \{0,1\}^d}$ and $\mathsf{mpk} := (\mathsf{be.pp}, \mathsf{be.pk})$.

$\mathsf{Keygen}(\mathsf{msk}, \mathsf{id} \in \{0,1\}^d)$:
- Output $\mathsf{sk}_{\mathsf{id}} := (\{\mathsf{nce.pk}_i\}_{i \in \{0,1\}^d}, \mathsf{nce.sk}_{\mathsf{id}})$.

$\mathsf{Enc}(\mathsf{mpk}, \mathsf{id}, m)$:
- Generate r uniformly at random.
- Generate $(\tilde{C}^{(\mathsf{id})}, \{\mathsf{lab}^{(\mathsf{id})}_{i,b}\}) \leftarrow \mathsf{GC.Grbl}(1^\lambda, \mathsf{NCE.Enc}(\cdot, m; r))$.
- Generate $(\tilde{C}^{(k)}, \{\mathsf{lab}^{(k)}_{i,b}\}) \leftarrow \mathsf{GC.Grbl}(1^\lambda, \mathsf{NCE.Enc}(\cdot, m^k; r^k))$ where m^k, r^k are randomly generated for all $k \in \{0,1\}^d \setminus \{\mathsf{id}\}$.
- Generate a matrix $M \in [\{0,1\}^\lambda]^{nT \times 2}$ such that $M[int(k) \cdot n + j, b] = \mathsf{lab}^{(k)}_{j,b}$ for all $k \in \{0,1\}^d, b \in \{0,1\}, j \in [n]$ where $int : \{0,1\}^d \rightarrow [T]_0$ is a lexicographical mapping from the set of binary string to integers.
- Compute $\mathsf{be.ct} \leftarrow \mathsf{BE.Enc}(\mathsf{mpk}, M)$.
- Output $\mathsf{ct} := (\{\tilde{C}^{(k)}\}_{k \in \{0,1\}^d}, \mathsf{be.ct})$.

$\mathsf{Dec}(\mathsf{sk}_{\mathsf{id}}, \mathsf{ct})$:
- Compute $d \leftarrow \mathsf{BE.Dec}(\mathsf{be.pp}, \{\mathsf{nce.pk}_i\}_{i \in \{0,1\}^d}, \mathsf{be.ct})$.
- Set $\mathsf{lab}_i := d[int(\mathsf{id}) \cdot n + i]$ for all $i \in [n]$.

- Compute $\mathsf{nce.ct_{id}} \leftarrow \mathsf{GC.Eval}(\tilde{\mathcal{C}}^{(id)}, \{\mathsf{lab}_i\}_{i \in [n]})$.
- Output $m \leftarrow \mathsf{NCE.Dec}(\mathsf{nce.sk_{id}}, \mathsf{nce.ct_{id}})$.

$\mathsf{Sim}_1(1^\lambda, 1^T)$:

- Compute $\mathsf{be.pp} \leftarrow \mathsf{BE.Params}(1^\lambda, 1^{nT})$
- Generate $(\mathsf{nce.pk}_i, \mathsf{nce.ct}_i, \mathsf{nce.st}_i) \leftarrow \mathsf{NCE.Sim}_1(1^\lambda)$ for $i \in \{0,1\}^d$.
- Compute $\mathsf{be.pk} := \mathsf{BE.Setup}(\mathsf{be.pp}, \{\mathsf{nce.pk}_i\}_{i \in \{0,1\}^d})$.
- Set $\mathsf{mpk} := (\mathsf{be.pp}, \mathsf{be.pk})$.
- Generate $(\tilde{\mathcal{C}}^{(k)}, \{\mathsf{lab}_i^{(k)}\}) \leftarrow \mathsf{GC.Sim}(1^\lambda, \mathsf{nce.ct}_k)$ for all $k \in \{0,1\}^d$.
- Generate a matrix $M \in [\{0,1\}^\lambda]^{nT \times 2}$ and sets $M[int(k) \cdot n + j, b] = \mathsf{lab}_j^{(k)}$ for all $k \in \{0,1\}^d, j \in [n]$.
- Compute $\mathsf{be.ct} \leftarrow \mathsf{BE.Enc}(\mathsf{mpk}, M)$.
- Set $\mathsf{ct} := (\{\tilde{\mathcal{C}}^{(k)}\}_{k \in \{0,1\}^d}, \mathsf{be.ct})$ and $\mathsf{st}^{(1)} := \{\mathsf{be.pp}, \{\mathsf{nce.ct}_i, \mathsf{nce.pk}_i, \mathsf{nce.st}_i\}_i\}$.
- Output $(\mathsf{mpk}, \mathsf{ct}, \mathsf{st}^{(1)})$.

$\mathsf{Sim}_2(\mathsf{st}^{(1)}, \mathsf{id})$:

- If $(\mathsf{id}, \cdot) \notin \mathsf{st}^{(2)}$, it computes $(\cdot, r_{\mathsf{NCE.Setup}}^{\mathsf{id}}) \leftarrow \mathsf{NCE.Sim}_2(\mathsf{nce.st_{id}}, m)$ where m is randomly generated and updates $\mathsf{st}^{(2)} = \mathsf{st}^{(2)} \cup \{\mathsf{id}, r_{\mathsf{NCE.Setup}}^{\mathsf{id}}\}$.
- Compute $(\cdot, \mathsf{nce.sk_{id}}) \leftarrow \mathsf{NCE.Setup}(1^\lambda; r_{\mathsf{NCE.Setup}}^{(\mathsf{id})})$.
- Output $\mathsf{sk_{id}} := (\{\mathsf{nce.pk}_i\}_{i \in \{0,1\}^d}, \mathsf{nce.sk_{id}})$.

$\mathsf{Sim}_3(\mathsf{st}^{(1)}, \mathsf{st}^{(2)}, \mathsf{id}, m)$:

- Compute $(\cdot, r_{\mathsf{NCE.Setup}}^{\mathsf{id}}) \leftarrow \mathsf{NCE.Sim}_2(\mathsf{nce.st_{id}}, m)$.
- For all $\mathsf{id}' \notin \{\mathsf{st}^{(2)}[0] \cup \{\mathsf{id}\}\}$, it computes $(\cdot, r_{\mathsf{NCE.Setup}}^{\mathsf{id}'}) \leftarrow \mathsf{NCE.Sim}_2(\mathsf{nce.st_{id'}}, m_{\mathsf{id}'})$ where $m_{\mathsf{id}'}$'s are randomly generated.
- Output $r_{\mathsf{Setup}} := \{\mathsf{be.pp}, \{r_{\mathsf{NCE.Setup}}^i\}_{i \in \{0,1\}^d}\}$.

Remark 2. From the oblivious property of BE, the randomness used in the setup algorithm is $r_{\mathsf{Setup}} = \{\mathsf{be.pp}, \{r_{\mathsf{NCE.Setup}}^{(i)}\}_{i \in \{0,1\}^d}\}$

Parameters. The size of a ciphertext is $\mathsf{poly}(2^d, |m|, \lambda)$, whereas the size of the master public key, master secret key and secret keys are of the form $\mathsf{poly}(2^d, \lambda)$.

Correctness. For a correctly generated secret key $\mathsf{sk_{id}} := (\{\mathsf{nce.pk}_i\}_{i \in \{0,1\}^d}, \mathsf{nce.sk_{id}})$ and a ciphertext $\mathsf{ct} := (\{\tilde{\mathcal{C}}^{(k)}\}_{k \in \{0,1\}^d}, \mathsf{be.ct})$, after performing the BE decryption $d \leftarrow \mathsf{BE.Dec}(\mathsf{be.pp}, \{\mathsf{nce.pk}_i\}_{i \in \{0,1\}^d}, \mathsf{be.ct})$, we have $d[int(\mathsf{id}) \cdot n + i] = \mathsf{lab}_{i,\mathsf{nce.pk_{id}}[i]}$. This is due to the correctness of the BE scheme. From the correctness of GC scheme, we have $\mathsf{nce.ct_{id}} \leftarrow \mathsf{GC.Eval}(\tilde{\mathcal{C}}^{(id)}, \{\mathsf{lab}_i\}_{i \in [n]})$ where $\mathsf{nce.ct_{id}} = \mathsf{NCE.Enc}(\mathsf{nce.pk_{id}}, m^*)$. Finally, by the decryption correctness of the NCE, we have $m \leftarrow \mathsf{NCE.Dec}(\mathsf{nce.sk_{id}}, \mathsf{nce.ct_{id}})$.

Theorem 14. *Assuming* BE *is a secure oblivious batch encryption,* GC *is a secure garbling scheme and* NCE *is a secure non-committing encryption scheme, the above scheme is an adaptively secure RNC-IBE that support polynomially many identities.*

Proof. We will show that the above scheme is an adaptive secure RNC-IBE using a sequence of hybrid arguments.

Hybrid Hyb_0 : This is the original adaptive NC-IBE game.
1. The challenger generates $\mathsf{mpk}, \mathsf{msk}$ as follows.
   - Generate $\mathsf{be.pp} \leftarrow \mathsf{BE.Params}(1^\lambda, 1^{nT})$.
   - Generate $(\mathsf{nce.pk}_i, \mathsf{nce.sk}_i) \leftarrow \mathsf{NCE.Setup}(1^\lambda; r^{(i)}_{\mathsf{NCE.Setup}})$ for $i \in \{0,1\}^d$.
   - Generate $\mathsf{be.pk} = \mathsf{BE.Setup}(\mathsf{be.pp}, \{\mathsf{nce.pk}_i\}_{i \in \{0,1\}^d})$.
   - Set $\mathsf{msk} := \{\mathsf{nce.pk}_i, \mathsf{nce.sk}_i\}_{i \in \{0,1\}^d}$ and $\mathsf{mpk} := (\mathsf{be.pp}, \mathsf{be.pk})$.
   The challenger sends mpk to $\mathcal{A}$.
2. $\mathcal{A}$ can get access to the following oracle.
   $O_{\mathsf{UserKeyGen}}(\mathsf{id}^j)$: Given the j-query id^j as an input, it returns $\mathsf{sk}_{\mathsf{id}^j} = (\{\mathsf{nce.pk}_i\}_{i \in \{0,1\}^d}, \mathsf{nce.sk}_{\mathsf{id}^j})$.
3. $\mathcal{A}$ outputs id^*, m^*. The challenger generates ct^* as follows.
   - Generate r uniformly at random.
   - Generate $(\tilde{C}^{(\mathsf{id})}, \{\mathsf{lab}^{(\mathsf{id})}_{i,b}\}) \leftarrow \mathsf{GC.Grbl}(1^\lambda, \mathsf{NCE.Enc}(\cdot, m; r))$.
   - Generate $(\tilde{C}^{(k)}, \{\mathsf{lab}^{(k)}_{i,b}\}) \leftarrow \mathsf{GC.Grbl}(1^\lambda, \mathsf{NCE.Enc}(\cdot, m^k; r^k))$ where m^k, r^k are randomly generated for all $k \in \{0,1\}^d \setminus \{\mathsf{id}\}$.
   - Generate a matrix $M \in [\{0,1\}^\lambda]^{nT \times 2}$ such that $M[int(k) \cdot n + j, b] = \mathsf{lab}^{(k)}_{j,b}$ for all $k \in \{0,1\}^d, b \in \{0,1\}, j \in [n]$.
   - Set $\mathsf{ct} := (\{\tilde{C}^{(k)}\}_{k \in \{0,1\}^d}, \mathsf{be.ct})$.
   The challenger sends $(\mathsf{ct}^*, \{r^{(i)}_{\mathsf{NCE.Setup}}\})$ to $\mathcal{A}$.
4. $\mathcal{A}$ outputs $\mathsf{coin}' \in \{0,1\}$.

Hybrid Hyb_1 : In this game, the matrix M during the challenge phase is computed as $M[int(\mathsf{id}) \cdot n + j, b] = \mathsf{lab}^{(\mathsf{id})}_{j, \mathsf{nce.pk}_{\mathsf{id}}[j]}$ for all $j \in [n-1], b \in \{0,1\}, \mathsf{id} \in \{0,1\}^d$.

Lemma 12. *Assume that* BE *is a secure batch encryption scheme, then for all PPT adversaries* $\mathcal{A}$ *there exists a negligible function* $\mathsf{negl}(\cdot)$ *such that for all* $\lambda \in \mathbb{N}, |p_{\mathcal{A},\mathsf{Hyb}_1} - p_{\mathcal{A},\mathsf{Hyb}_0}| \leq \mathsf{negl}(\lambda).$

Proof. This follows from the security of batch encryption. The reduction can generate $\{\mathsf{nce.pk}_i\}$ and sends it to the challenger who replies with $\mathsf{be.pp}$ (which is also the randomness used during $\mathsf{BE.Params}$). It can use $\mathsf{be.pp}$ to generates the master public key mpk. The reduction can generate the two matrices used in Hyb_0 and Hyb_1 and sends it to the challenger. Note that these matrices differ only at indices $(int(k) \cdot n + j, 1 - \mathsf{nce.pk}_k[j])$. It will receive $\mathsf{be.ct}$ from the challenger and then simulate the entire game using these values. Observe that the reduction generates all the keys $(\mathsf{nce.pk}_{\mathsf{id}}, \mathsf{nce.sk}_{\mathsf{id}})$, so it has $r^{\mathsf{id}}_{\mathsf{NCE.Setup}}$ and $\mathsf{be.pp}$. $\square$

Hybrid Hyb_2 : In this game, the garbled circuit $\tilde{\mathcal{C}}^{(k)}$ and labels are simulated, i.e., $(\tilde{\mathcal{C}}^{(k)}, \{\mathsf{lab}_i^{(k)}\}) \leftarrow \mathsf{GC.Sim}(1^\lambda, \mathsf{nce.ct}^{(k)})$ where $\mathsf{nce.ct}^{(k)} \leftarrow \mathsf{NCE.Enc}_1(\mathsf{nce.pk}_k, m^{(k)}; r^{(k)})$ for all $k \in \{0,1\}^d \setminus \{\mathsf{id}^*\}$. And, $\mathsf{nce.ct}^{(\mathsf{id}^*)} \leftarrow \mathsf{NCE.Enc}(\mathsf{nce.pk}_{\mathsf{id}^*}, m^*)$.

Lemma 13. *Assume that* GC *is a secure garbling scheme, then for all* PPT *adversaries* $\mathcal{A}$ *there exists a negligible function* $\mathsf{negl}(\cdot)$ *such that for all* $\lambda \in \mathbb{N}$,, $|p_{\mathcal{A},\mathsf{Hyb}_2} - p_{\mathcal{A},\mathsf{Hyb}_1}| \leq \mathsf{negl}(\lambda)$.

Proof. This directly follows from the security of GC because the matrix M requires only $\mathsf{lab}_{i,\mathsf{nce.pk}_{\mathsf{id}}[i]}^{(\mathsf{id})}$ labels for all $\mathsf{id} \in \{0,1\}$. $\qquad\square$

Hybrid Hyb_3 : In this game, $\mathsf{nce.ct}^{(\mathsf{id})}$ and $\mathsf{nce.sk}_{\mathsf{id}}$ are all simulated using the NCE simulators.

Lemma 14. *Assume that* NCE *is a secure NCE scheme, then for all* PPT *adversaries* $\mathcal{A}$ *there exists a negligible function* $\mathsf{negl}(\cdot)$ *such that for all* $\lambda \in \mathbb{N}$,, $|p_{\mathcal{A},\mathsf{Hyb}_3} - p_{\mathcal{A},\mathsf{Hyb}_2}| \leq \mathsf{negl}(\lambda)$.

Proof. We will show that an adversary $\mathcal{A}$ that can distinguish Hyb_3 from Hyb_2 can be transformed into an adversary $\mathcal{B}$ that breaks the NCE security. We achieve this by considering $T+1$ many intermediate hybrids $\mathsf{Hyb}_{2,i}$ where $\mathsf{Hyb}_{2,0} = \mathsf{Hyb}_2$ and $\mathsf{Hyb}_{2,T+1} = \mathsf{Hyb}_3$. The description of $\mathsf{Hyb}_{2,i}$ is as follows.

- The challenger generates the first i public keys using the first NCE simulator. Recall that the simulator will also generate fake ciphertexts. The remaining public-secret keys are generated honestly.
- To respond to a key query, if $\mathsf{id} > i$, it returns $\mathsf{sk}_{\mathsf{id}} = (\{\mathsf{nce.pk}_i\}_{i\in\{0,1\}^d}, \mathsf{nce.sk}_{\mathsf{id}})$. Whereas, if $\mathsf{id} \leq i$, it first checks whether $(\mathsf{id}, r_{\mathsf{NCE.Setup}}^{\mathsf{id}}) \in \mathsf{st}^{(2)}$. If it exists, then it computes $(\cdot, \mathsf{nce.sk}_{\mathsf{id}}) \leftarrow \mathsf{NCE.Setup}(1^\lambda; r_{\mathsf{Setup}}^{\mathsf{id}})$ and then returns $\mathsf{sk}_{\mathsf{id}}$ accordingly. If not, it calls the second simulator of the NCE on a random message m which returns $(\cdot, r_{\mathsf{Setup}}^{(\mathsf{id})})$. It computes $(\cdot, \mathsf{nce.sk}_{\mathsf{id}}) \leftarrow \mathsf{NCE.Setup}(1^\lambda; r_{\mathsf{Setup}}^{\mathsf{id}})$ and then returns $\mathsf{sk}_{\mathsf{id}}$ accordingly. It also updates $\mathsf{st}^{(2)} = \mathsf{st}^{(2)} \cup (\mathsf{id}, r_{\mathsf{Setup}}^{(\mathsf{id})})$.
- In the challenge phase, when it receives the challenger identity id^* and message m^*, it will generate $\mathsf{nce.ct}^{(k)}$ for all $k > i$ honestly, i.e., using $\mathsf{NCE.Enc}$ algorithm. The remaining $\mathsf{nce.ct}^{(k)}$ for $k \leq i$ will be the ciphertext simulated by the first simulator in the initialization phase. Then, it produces to generate $(\tilde{\mathcal{C}}^{(k)}, \{\mathsf{lab}_i^{(k)}\})$ for all k and sets up M appropriate to generate $\mathsf{be.ct}$. Finally,
  - if $\mathsf{id}^* \leq i$, it will use the NCE simulator on m^* to obtain $r_{\mathsf{Setup}}^{\mathsf{id}^*}$.
  - For all $\mathsf{id} \leq i$ that was not queried and not equal to id^*, it will use the NCE simulator on a random m to obtain $r_{\mathsf{Setup}}^{\mathsf{id}}$.
  Finally, it will output $(\tilde{\mathcal{C}}^{(k)}, \mathsf{be.ct})$ and $\{r_{\mathsf{Setup}}^{\mathsf{id}}\}_{\mathsf{id}}$.

It is easy to show that an $\mathcal{A}$ that can distinguish $\mathsf{Hyb}_{2,i}$ from $\mathsf{Hyb}_{2,i+1}$ can be transformed into an adversary $\mathcal{B}$ that breaks the NCE security.   □

Using the above lemmas and triangular inequality, for all PPT adversaries $\mathcal{A}$, there exists a negligible function $\mathsf{negl}(\cdot)$ such that for all $\lambda \in \mathbb{N}$, $|p_{\mathcal{A},\mathsf{Hyb}_0} - p_{\mathcal{A},\mathsf{Hyb}_3}| \leq \mathsf{negl}(\lambda)$.   □

Using Theorem 8 and Theorem 7, we have Theorem 3.

7   Rate-1 Strongly Incompressible IBE from RNC-IB-KEM

In this section, we show a construction for strongly incompressible IBE using an RNC-IB-KEM and an incompressible SKE scheme. Let IBKEM = (IBKEM.Setup, IBKEM.KeyGen, IBKEM.Encap, IBKEM.Decap) be an RNC-IB-KEM and IncSKE = (IncSKE.Setup, IncSKE.Enc, IncSKE.Dec) be an incompressible SKE scheme such that IncSKE.Setup outputs a truly random string.

$\mathsf{Setup}(1^\lambda, 1^S)$: The setup algorithm takes as input the security parameter λ and the upper bound for the state bound S. It computes $(\mathsf{ibkem.mpk}, \mathsf{ibkem.msk}) \leftarrow \mathsf{IBKEM.Setup}(1^\lambda, 1^{|\mathsf{inc.sk}|})$ and outputs $\mathsf{mpk} := \mathsf{ibkem.mpk}$ and $\mathsf{msk} := \mathsf{ibkem.msk}$.

$\mathsf{KeyGen}(\mathsf{msk}, \mathsf{id})$: The key generation algorithm takes as input a master secret key $\mathsf{msk} = \mathsf{ibkem.msk}$ and an identity id and computes $\mathsf{ibkem.sk_{id}} \leftarrow \mathsf{IBKEM.KeyGen}(\mathsf{ibkem.msk}, \mathsf{id})$. It outputs $\mathsf{ibkem.sk_{id}}$.

$\mathsf{Enc}(\mathsf{mpk}, \mathsf{id}, m)$: The encryption algorithm takes as input a master public key $\mathsf{mpk} = \mathsf{ibkem.mpk}$, an identity id and message m. It generates $(\mathsf{ibkem.ct}, \mathsf{seskey}) \leftarrow \mathsf{IBKEM.Encap}(\mathsf{ibkem.mpk}, \mathsf{id})$ and sets $\mathsf{inc.sk} := \mathsf{seskey}$. It then computes $\mathsf{inc.ct} \leftarrow \mathsf{IncSKE.Enc}(\mathsf{inc.sk}, m)$ and returns $\mathsf{ct} := (\mathsf{ibkem.ct}, \mathsf{inc.ct})$.

$\mathsf{Dec}(\mathsf{sk}, \mathsf{ct})$: The decryption algorithm takes as input a secret key $\mathsf{sk} = \mathsf{ibkem.sk}$ and a ciphertext $\mathsf{ct} = (\mathsf{ibkem.ct}, \mathsf{inc.ct})$. It first computes $\mathsf{inc.sk} \leftarrow \mathsf{IBKEM.Decap}(\mathsf{ibkem.sk}, \mathsf{ibkem.ct})$. Then, it computes $m \leftarrow \mathsf{IncSKE.Dec}(\mathsf{inc.sk}, \mathsf{inc.ct})$. It returns m.

Correctness. The correctness is straight-forward from the correctness of NC-IBE scheme and incompressible SKE scheme.

Parameters. The size of a ciphertext for a message m is $|\mathsf{ibkem.ct}| + |\mathsf{inc.ct}|$. If the incompressible SKE scheme has rate-1 (see Theorem 9), then $|\mathsf{inc.ct}| = |m|(1 + o(1)) + \mathrm{poly}(\lambda)$. If the NC-IBE scheme generates ciphertext whose size is independent of the session key, we have $|\mathsf{ibkem.ct}| = \mathrm{poly}(\lambda)$. Therefore, the rate of the incompressible IBE scheme is $1 - o(1)$.

Theorem 15. *Assuming that* IBKEM *is a secure RNC-IB-KEM scheme and* IncSKE *is a incompressible SKE scheme, the above construction is a secure strongly incompressible IBE scheme.*

Proof Sketch. We will show that the construction is secure using a sequence of hybrid arguments.

Hybrid H_0: This is the original strongly incompressible IBE security game.

Hybrid H_1: In this game, the IBKEM scheme is changed to simulation mode. To be precise, the first simulator is used generate the master public key ibkem.mpk. The second simulator will be used to handle the key queries. The third simulator will be invoked on id^* to produce the simulated ciphertext ibkem.ct. Finally, for a randomly generated inc.sk, the fourth simulator on input inc.sk will produce the master secret key ibkem.msk. The indistinguishability of H_0 from H_1 follows directly from the security of the RNC-IBE.

We now argue that there is no PPT adversary that can win in H_1 with non-negligible probability. This follows from the security of the incompressible SKE scheme. This is because an adversary $\mathcal{A} = (\mathcal{A}_1, \mathcal{A}_2)$ that wins in H_1 can be used to build an adversary $\mathcal{B} = (\mathcal{B}_1, \mathcal{B}_2)$ that breaks the security of the underlying incompressible SKE as follows. $\mathcal{B}$ can simulate H_1 using the first two IBKEM simulators upto the challenge phase. On receiving (m_0, m_1) from $\mathcal{A}_1$, it will forward it to the SKE challenger and receives inc.ct*. It will relay (ibkem.ct, inc.ct*) where ibkem.ct is generated by the third IBKEM simulator. In the second phase, it will receive inc.sk from the SKE challenger and will use the fourth IBKEM simulator will generate ibkem.msk.   □

Combining Theorem 15, Theorem 9, Theorem 12, we obtain Theorem 2.

Remark 3. We highlight that a similar approach can be employed to construct incompressible IBE from RNC-IBE and incompressible SKE. In this approach, during the encryption process with inputs m and identity id, a secret key inc.sk of the incompressible SKE is freshly generated and encrypted, producing ibe.ct $\leftarrow$ IBE.Enc(mpk, id, inc.sk). Then, the message m is encrypted as inc.ct $\leftarrow$ IncSKE.Enc(inc.sk, m), and the final ciphertext is ct := (ibe.ct, inc.ct). Note that the size of the ciphertext ct depends on both |inc.sk| and |inc.ct| because ibe.ct is an encryption of inc.sk. Therefore, combining Theorem 3 and Theorem 10, we get Theorem 4.

References

1. Agrawal, S., Boneh, D., Boyen, X.: Efficient lattice (h) IBE in the standard model. In: Advances in Cryptology–EUROCRYPT 2010: 29th Annual International Conference on the Theory and Applications of Cryptographic Techniques, French Riviera, 30 May–3 June 2010. Proceedings 29, pp. 553–572. Springer, Cham (2010)
2. Agrawal, S., Boneh, D., Boyen, X.: Lattice basis delegation in fixed dimension and shorter-ciphertext hierarchical IBE. In: Rabin, T. (ed.) CRYPTO 2010. LNCS, vol. 6223, pp. 98–115. Springer, Heidelberg (2010). https://doi.org/10.1007/978-3-642-14623-7_6
3. Agrawal, S., Boyen, X.: Identity-based encryption from lattices in the standard model. Manuscript, July 3 (2009)

4. Attrapadung, N.: Dual system encryption via doubly selective security: framework, fully secure functional encryption for regular languages, and more. In: Nguyen, P.Q., Oswald, E. (eds.) EUROCRYPT 2014. LNCS, vol. 8441, pp. 557–577. Springer, Heidelberg (2014). https://doi.org/10.1007/978-3-642-55220-5_31

5. Attrapadung, N.: Dual system encryption framework in prime-order groups via computational pair encodings. In: Cheon, J.H., Takagi, T. (eds.) ASIACRYPT 2016. LNCS, vol. 10032, pp. 591–623. Springer, Heidelberg (2016). https://doi.org/10.1007/978-3-662-53890-6_20

6. Beaver, D.: Plug and play encryption. In: Kaliski, B.S. (ed.) CRYPTO 1997. LNCS, vol. 1294, pp. 75–89. Springer, Heidelberg (1997). https://doi.org/10.1007/BFb0052228

7. Bethencourt, J., Sahai, A., Waters, B.: Ciphertext-policy attribute-based encryption. In: 2007 IEEE Symposium on Security and Privacy (SP'07), pp. 321–334. IEEE (2007)

8. Bhushan, K., Goyal, R., Koppula, V., Narayanan, V., Prabhakaran, M., Rajasree, M.S.: Leakage-resilient incompressible cryptography: constructions and barriers. Cryptology ePrint Archive (2024)

9. Boneh, D., Boyen, X.: Efficient selective-ID secure identity-based encryption without random oracles. In: Cachin, C., Camenisch, J.L. (eds.) EUROCRYPT 2004. LNCS, vol. 3027, pp. 223–238. Springer, Heidelberg (2004). https://doi.org/10.1007/978-3-540-24676-3_14

10. Boneh, D., Boyen, X.: Secure identity based encryption without random oracles. In: Annual International Cryptology Conference, pp. 443–459. Springer, Cham (2004)

11. Boneh, D., Boyen, X., Goh, E.J.: Hierarchical identity based encryption with constant size ciphertext. In: Annual International Conference on the Theory and Applications of Cryptographic Techniques, pp. 440–456. Springer, Cham (2005)

12. Boneh, D., Franklin, M.: Identity-based encryption from the weil pairing. In: Annual International Cryptology Conference, pp. 213–229. Springer, Cham (2001)

13. Boneh, D., Gentry, C., Hamburg, M.: Space-efficient identity based encryption without pairings. In: 48th Annual IEEE Symposium on Foundations of Computer Science (FOCS'07), pp. 647–657. IEEE (2007)

14. Brakerski, Z., Branco, P., Döttling, N., Garg, S., Malavolta, G.: Constant ciphertext-rate non-committing encryption from standard assumptions. In: Pass, R., Pietrzak, K. (eds.) TCC 2020. LNCS, vol. 12550, pp. 58–87. Springer, Cham (2020). https://doi.org/10.1007/978-3-030-64375-1_3

15. Brakerski, Z., Lombardi, A., Segev, G., Vaikuntanathan, V.: Anonymous IBE, leakage resilience and circular security from new assumptions. In: Annual International Conference on the Theory and Applications of Cryptographic Techniques, pp. 535–564. Springer, Cham (2018)

16. Branco, P., Döttling, N., Dujmović, J.: Rate-1 incompressible encryption from standard assumptions. In: Theory of Cryptography Conference, pp. 33–69. Springer, Cham (2022)

17. Canetti, R., Feige, U., Goldreich, O., Naor, M.: Adaptively secure multi-party computation. In: Proceedings of the Twenty-Eighth Annual ACM Symposium on Theory of Computing, pp. 639–648 (1996)

18. Canetti, R., Halevi, S., Katz, J.: A forward-secure public-key encryption scheme. In: Biham, E. (ed.) EUROCRYPT 2003. LNCS, vol. 2656, pp. 255–271. Springer, Heidelberg (2003). https://doi.org/10.1007/3-540-39200-9_16

19. Canetti, R., Halevi, S., Katz, J.: Adaptively-secure, non-interactive public-key encryption. In: Theory of Cryptography Conference, pp. 150–168. Springer, Cham (2005)

20. Canetti, R., Lindell, Y., Ostrovsky, R., Sahai, A.: Universally composable two-party and multi-party secure computation. In: Proceedings of the Thiry-Fourth Annual ACM Symposium on Theory of Computing, pp. 494–503 (2002)
21. Canetti, R., Poburinnaya, O., Raykova, M.: Optimal-rate non-committing encryption. In: International Conference on the Theory and Application of Cryptology and Information Security, pp. 212–241. Springer, Cham (2017)
22. Cash, D., Hofheinz, D., Kiltz, E., Peikert, C.: Bonsai trees, or how to delegate a lattice basis. J. Cryptol. **25**, 601–639 (2012)
23. Chen, J., Gay, R., Wee, H.: Improved dual system ABE in prime-order groups via predicate encodings. In: Annual International Conference on the Theory and Applications of Cryptographic Techniques. pp. 595–624. Springer, Cham (2015)
24. Chen, J., Gong, J., Kowalczyk, L., Wee, H.: Unbounded ABE via bilinear entropy expansion, revisited. In: Annual International Conference on the Theory and Applications of Cryptographic Techniques, pp. 503–534. Springer, Cham (2018)
25. Chen, J., Wee, H.: Fully, (almost) tightly secure IBE and dual system groups. In: Annual Cryptology Conference, pp. 435–460. Springer, Cham (2013)
26. Choi, S.G., Dachman-Soled, D., Malkin, T., Wee, H.: Improved non-committing encryption with applications to adaptively secure protocols. In: Matsui, M. (ed.) ASIACRYPT 2009. LNCS, vol. 5912, pp. 287–302. Springer, Heidelberg (2009). https://doi.org/10.1007/978-3-642-10366-7_17
27. Cocks, C.: An identity based encryption scheme based on quadratic residues. In: Cryptography and Coding: 8th IMA International Conference Cirencester, UK, 17–19 December 2001 Proceedings 8, pp. 360–363. Springer, Cham (2001)
28. Damgård, I., Ganesh, C., Orlandi, C.: Proofs of replicated storage without timing assumptions. In: Boldyreva, A., Micciancio, D. (eds.) CRYPTO 2019. LNCS, vol. 11692, pp. 355–380. Springer, Cham (2019). https://doi.org/10.1007/978-3-030-26948-7_13
29. Damgård, I., Nielsen, J.B.: Improved Non-committing encryption schemes based on a general complexity assumption. In: Bellare, M. (ed.) CRYPTO 2000. LNCS, vol. 1880, pp. 432–450. Springer, Heidelberg (2000). https://doi.org/10.1007/3-540-44598-6_27
30. Döttling, N., Garg, S.: Identity-based encryption from the Diffie-Hellman assumption. In: Annual International Cryptology Conference, pp. 537–569. Springer, Cham (2017)
31. Döttling, N., Garg, S.: From selective IBE to full IBE and selective HIBE. In: Theory of Cryptography Conference, pp. 372–408 (2017)
32. Dziembowski, S.: On forward-secure storage. In: Dwork, C. (ed.) CRYPTO 2006. LNCS, vol. 4117, pp. 251–270. Springer, Heidelberg (2006). https://doi.org/10.1007/11818175_15
33. Feng, S., Gong, J., Chen, J.: Master-key KDM-secure ABE via predicate encoding. In: IACR International Conference on Public-Key Cryptography, pp. 543–572. Springer, Cham (2021)
34. Garg, R., Lu, G., Waters, B.: New techniques in replica encodings with client setup. In: Theory of Cryptography Conference, pp. 550–583. Springer, Cham (2020)
35. Garg, S., Gay, R., Hajiabadi, M.: Master-key KDM-secure IBE from pairings. In: IACR International Conference on Public-Key Cryptography, pp. 123–152. Springer, Cham (2020)
36. Garg, S., Gentry, C., Halevi, S., Raykova, M., Sahai, A., Waters, B.: Candidate indistinguishability obfuscation and functional encryption for all circuits. In: FOCS (2013)

37. Garg, S., Gentry, C., Halevi, S., Raykova, M., Sahai, A., Waters, B.: Candidate indistinguishability obfuscation and functional encryption for all circuits. SIAM J. Comput. **45**(3), 882–929 (2016)
38. Gentry, C., Halevi, S.: Hierarchical identity based encryption with polynomially many levels. In: Theory of Cryptography Conference, pp. 437–456. Springer, Cham (2009)
39. Gentry, C., Peikert, C., Vaikuntanathan, V.: Trapdoors for hard lattices and new cryptographic constructions. In: Proceedings of the Fortieth Annual ACM Symposium on Theory of Computing, pp. 197–206 (2008)
40. Gentry, C., Silverberg, A.: Hierarchical ID-based cryptography. In: Zheng, Y. (ed.) ASIACRYPT 2002. LNCS, vol. 2501, pp. 548–566. Springer, Heidelberg (2002). https://doi.org/10.1007/3-540-36178-2_34
41. Gong, J., Waters, B., Wee, H.: ABE for DFA from k-Lin. In: Boldyreva, A., Micciancio, D. (eds.) CRYPTO 2019. LNCS, vol. 11693, pp. 732–764. Springer, Cham (2019). https://doi.org/10.1007/978-3-030-26951-7_25
42. Gong, J., Wee, H.: Adaptively secure ABE for DFA from k-lin and more. In: Annual International Conference on the Theory and Applications of Cryptographic Techniques, pp. 278–308. Springer, Cham (2020)
43. Goyal, R., Koppula, V., Rajasree, M.S.: A note on adaptive security in hierarchical identity-based encryption. Cryptology ePrint Archive, Paper 2025/291 (2025)
44. Goyal, R., Koppula, V., Rajasree, M.S., Verma, A.: Incompressible functional encryption. In: Meka, R. (ed.) 16th Innovations in Theoretical Computer Science Conference (ITCS 2025). Leibniz International Proceedings in Informatics (LIPIcs), vol. 325, pp. 56:1–56:22. Schloss Dagstuhl – Leibniz-Zentrum für Informatik, Dagstuhl, Germany (2025)
45. Goyal, R., Syed, R., Waters, B.: Bounded collusion ABE for TMS from IBE. In: International Conference on the Theory and Application of Cryptology and Information Security, pp. 371–402. Springer, Cham (2021)
46. Goyal, V., Pandey, O., Sahai, A., Waters, B.: Attribute-based encryption for fine-grained access control of encrypted data. In: Juels, A., Wright, R.N., di Vimercati, S.D.C. (eds.) Proceedings of the 13th ACM Conference on Computer and Communications Security, CCS 2006, Alexandria, VA, USA, 30 October–3 November 2006, pp. 89–98. ACM (2006)
47. Guan, J., Wichs, D., Zhandry, M.: Incompressible Cryptography. In: Dunkelman, O., Dziembowski, S. (eds.) Advances in Cryptology - EUROCRYPT 2022, pp. 700–730. Lecture Notes in Computer Science, Springer, Cham (2022). https://doi.org/10.1007/978-3-031-06944-4_24
48. Guan, J., Wichs, D., Zhandry, M.: Multi-instance randomness extraction and security against bounded-storage mass surveillance. In: Theory of Cryptography Conference, pp. 93–122. Springer, Cham (2023)
49. Hanaoka, G., Katsumata, S., Kimura, K., Takemure, K., Yamada, S.: Tighter adaptive IBEs and VRFs: revisiting waters' artificial abort. In: Theory of Cryptography Conference, pp. 124–155. Springer, Cham (2024)
50. Hazay, C., Patra, A., Warinschi, B.: Selective opening security for receivers. In: Advances in Cryptology–ASIACRYPT 2015: 21st International Conference on the Theory and Application of Cryptology and Information Security, Auckland, New Zealand, 29November–3 December 2015, Proceedings, Part I 21, pp. 443–469. Springer, Cham (2015)
51. Hemenway, B., Ostrovsky, R., Richelson, S., Rosen, A.: Adaptive security with quasi-optimal rate. In: Theory of Cryptography Conference, pp. 525–541. Springer, Cham (2015)

52. Hemenway, B., Ostrovsky, R., Rosen, A.: Non-committing encryption from ϕ-hiding. In: Theory of Cryptography Conference, pp. 591–608. Springer, Cham (2015)

53. Hiroka, T., Morimae, T., Nishimaki, R., Yamakawa, T.: Quantum encryption with certified deletion, revisited: public key, attribute-based, and classical communication. In: Advances in Cryptology–ASIACRYPT 2021: 27th International Conference on the Theory and Application of Cryptology and Information Security, Singapore, 6–10 December 2021, Proceedings, Part I 27, pp. 606–636. Springer, Cham (2021)

54. Hofheinz, D., Koch, J., Striecks, C.: Identity-based encryption with (almost) tight security in the multi-instance, multi-ciphertext setting. In: IACR International Workshop on Public Key Cryptography, pp. 799–822. Springer, Cham (2015)

55. Horwitz, J., Lynn, B.: Toward hierarchical identity-based encryption. In: International Conference on the Theory and Applications of Cryptographic Techniques, pp. 466–481. Springer, Cham (2002)

56. Jarecki, S., Lysyanskaya, A.: Adaptively secure threshold cryptography: introducing concurrency, removing erasures. In: Preneel, B. (ed.) EUROCRYPT 2000. LNCS, vol. 1807, pp. 221–242. Springer, Heidelberg (2000). https://doi.org/10.1007/3-540-45539-6_16

57. Lewko, A., Waters, B.: New techniques for dual system encryption and fully secure HIBE with short ciphertexts. In: Theory of Cryptography Conference, pp. 455–479. Springer, Cham (2010)

58. Lewko, A., Waters, B.: Unbounded HIBE and attribute-based encryption. In: Annual International Conference on the Theory and Applications of Cryptographic Techniques, pp. 547–567. Springer, Cham (2011)

59. Moran, T., Wichs, D.: Incompressible encodings. In: Micciancio, D., Ristenpart, T. (eds.) CRYPTO 2020. LNCS, vol. 12170, pp. 494–523. Springer, Cham (2020). https://doi.org/10.1007/978-3-030-56784-2_17

60. Nielsen, J.B.: Separating random oracle proofs from complexity theoretic proofs: the non-committing encryption case. In: Annual International Cryptology Conference, pp. 111–126. Springer, Cham (2002)

61. Okamoto, T., Takashima, K.: Fully secure unbounded inner-product and attribute-based encryption. In: International Conference on the Theory and Application of Cryptology and Information Security, pp. 349–366. Springer, Cham (2012)

62. Sahai, A., Waters, B.: Fuzzy identity-based encryption. In: EUROCRYPT, pp. 457–473 (2005)

63. Sahai, A., Waters, B.: How to use indistinguishability obfuscation: deniable encryption, and more. In: STOC, pp. 475–484 (2014)

64. Shamir, A.: Identity-based cryptosystems and signature schemes. In: Advances in Cryptology: Proceedings of CRYPTO 84 4, pp. 47–53. Springer, Cham (1985)

65. Shi, E., Waters, B.: Delegating capabilities in predicate encryption systems. In: International Colloquium on Automata, Languages, and Programming, pp. 560–578. Springer, Cham (2008)

66. Waters, B.: Efficient identity-based encryption without random oracles. In: Cramer, R. (ed.) EUROCRYPT 2005. LNCS, vol. 3494, pp. 114–127. Springer, Heidelberg (2005). https://doi.org/10.1007/11426639_7

67. Waters, B.: Dual system encryption: realizing fully secure IBE and HIBE under simple assumptions. In: Annual International Cryptology Conference, pp. 619–636. Springer, Cham (2009)

68. Waters, B.: Functional encryption for regular languages. In: Annual Cryptology Conference, pp. 218–235. Springer, Cham (2012)

69. Wee, H.: Dual system encryption via predicate encodings. In: Theory of Cryptography Conference, pp. 616–637. Springer, Cham (2014)
70. Wu, H., Chow, S.S.: Anonymous (hierarchical) identity-based encryption from broader assumptions. In: International Conference on Applied Cryptography and Network Security, pp. 366–395. Springer, Cham (2023)
71. Yoshida, Y., Kitagawa, F., Tanaka, K.: Non-committing encryption with quasi-optimal ciphertext-rate based on the DDH problem. In: Advances in Cryptology–ASIACRYPT 2019: 25th International Conference on the Theory and Application of Cryptology and Information Security, Kobe, Japan, 8–12 December 2019, Proceedings, Part III 25, pp. 128–158. Springer, Cham (2019)
72. Yoshida, Y., Kitagawa, F., Xagawa, K., Tanaka, K.: Non-committing encryption with constant ciphertext expansion from standard assumptions. In: Moriai, S., Wang, H. (eds.) ASIACRYPT 2020. LNCS, vol. 12492, pp. 36–65. Springer, Cham (2020). https://doi.org/10.1007/978-3-030-64834-3_2

Registration-Based Encryption in the Plain Model

Jesko Dujmovic[1,2(✉)], Giulio Malavolta[3], and Wei Qi[3]

[1] CISPA Helmholtz Center for Information Security, Saarbrücken, Germany
jesko.dujmovic@cispa.de
[2] Saarland University, Saarbruecken, Germany
[3] Bocconi University, Milan, Italy
giulio.malavolta@hotmail.it, wei.qi@unibocconi.it

Abstract. Registration-based encryption (RBE) is a recently developed alternative to identity-based encryption, that mitigates the well-known key-escrow problem by letting each user sample its own key pair. In RBE, the key authority is substituted by a key curator, a completely transparent entity whose only job is to reliably aggregate users' keys. However, one limitation of all known RBE scheme is that they all rely on one-time trusted setup, that must be computed honestly.

In this work, we ask whether this limitation is indeed inherent and we initiate the systematic study of RBE in the *plain model*, without any common reference string. We present the following main results:

– (Definitions) We show that the standard security definition of RBE is unachievable without a trusted setup and we propose a slight weakening, where one honest user is required to be registered in the system.
– (Constructions) We present constructions of RBE in the plain model, based on standard cryptographic assumptions. Along the way, we introduce the notions of non-interactive witness indistinguishable (NIWI) proofs secure against chosen statements attack and re-randomizable RBE, which may be of independent interest. A major limitation of our constructions, is that users must be updated upon every new registration.
– (Lower Bounds) We show that this limitation is in some sense inherent. We prove that any RBE in the plain model that satisfies a certain structural requirement, which holds for all known RBE constructions, must update all but a vanishing fraction of the users, upon each new registration. This is in contrast with the standard RBE settings, where users receive a logarithmic amount of updates throughout the lifetime of the system.

Keywords: Registration Based Encryption · Plain Model · Lower Bound

1 Introduction

Not long after the introduction of public-key encryption [9], Shamir envisioned a cryptographic primitive that would allow one to encrypt a message by just knowing the identity of the receiver. In an identity-based encryption (IBE), Alice can encrypt her messages to Bob knowing just Bob's identity, along with some additional public parameters. Bob can then decrypt Alice's ciphertexts using an identity-specific secret key that

© International Association for Cryptologic Research 2025
T. Jager and J. Pan (Eds.): PKC 2025, LNCS 15674, pp. 194–226, 2025.
https://doi.org/10.1007/978-3-031-91820-9_7

he obtains from the key authority. The work of Boneh and Franklin [5], which proposed the first cryptographic construction of IBE, started a fruitful line of investigation in cryptography that lead to new schemes [8, 10, 17, 18, 31] and new cryptographic primitives generalizing IBE [6, 21, 30]. However, IBE also comes with important limitations. Most prominently, it suffers from the well-known *key escrow problem*: In an IBE system, the key authority that generates the public parameters and the decryption keys can also decrypt any message ever encrypted. In many cases, this is not an acceptable compromise, and IBE has received strong criticism [29] because of this problem.

A series of recent works [12, 15, 16, 19] proposes a new notion of encryption aimed at solving this problem. In registration-based encryption (RBE) the trusted authority of IBE is substituted by a completely transparent party, called the key curator (KC). The KC is responsible to aggregate the public keys of the users in a *small digest*, that can be later on used to encrypt with respect to an identity, thus mimicking the functionality of IBE. Differently from IBE however, the public keys are sampled locally by the users themselves, and the role of the KC is limited to reliably store and aggregate the users' keys, similarly to what a public key infrastructure would do. Thus, RBE can be seen as combining the best-of-both-worlds between public-key encryption and IBE. RBE has recently seen a surge of interest, with constructions getting closer and closer to practicality [12, 19] and works achieving more and more general functionalities [13, 23].

Despite these promising properties, one shortcoming shared by *all constructions* of RBE, is that they rely on a one-time trusted setup, needed to sample a common reference string (CRS). Granted, this is a one-time operation that can be realized using various techniques (such as running an MPC between mutually distrustful parties), and thus it does not detract substantial value from this notion. Nevertheless, a trusted setup goes against the transparent spirit of RBE, and it would be desirable to avoid it, if possible. Motivated by this concern, in this work we put forward the following question:

Is a trusted setup necessary for RBE?

Before stating the results of this work, we shall make an important distinction between existing RBE schemes. The trusted setup of an RBE can be either *structured* [19] or *transparent* [12, 15, 16], where the latter means that it can be sampled using public random coins. In practice, the latter setup is much more desirable, since it is easy and efficient to *heuristically* sample it by, e.g., hashing the current date and time. While these are important considerations, we do not think that the existence of RBE schemes with a transparent setup makes our question easy or uninteresting, since we are interested in constructions that we can prove secure in the standard model. Similarly, the existence of non-interactive zero-knowledge (NIZK) proofs with a transparent setup, does not solve the problem of constructing non-interactive proofs in the plain model, without a trusted setup, such as [2, 22].

1.1 Our Results

In this work we initiate the systematic study of RBE in the plain model, without any trusted setup. The aim of this work is to develop a formal study of RBE in these settings, and to characterize the efficiency/security tradeoffs of this notion. Overall, our main contributions can be summarized as follows.

- **Definitions:** We extend the definition of RBE to handle the absence of a trusted setup. In contrast with previous definitions [15], our security experiment requires the existence of *at least one honest user* registered in the system, which results in slightly weaker security. We show that this limitation is necessary in the trustless setting, by presenting a generic attack against any RBE without setup.
- **Constructions:** We present two constructions of RBE without setup. Our first construction is in a relaxed model where the key registration is interactive (in fact, a two-message protocol) and it is based on the combination of re-randomizable RBE and non-interactive witness indistinguishable (NIWI) proofs secure against *chosen statement* attacks, two primitives that we introduce in this work and that may be of independent interest. We show how to construct the former from the computational Diffie-Hellman assumption, and the latter from a combination of regular NIWIs and CCA-secure commitments.

  Our second construction is in the standard communication model of RBE, where the key registration consists of a single message from the user to the KC. This construction additionally assumes the existence of indistinguishability obfuscation [1].
- **Lower Bounds:** Both of our constructions have an important limitation, namely that upon every registration *all* users' keys must be updated. Thus the constructions are qualitatively closer to the weaker notion of laconic encryption, as proposed in [12]. We show that this is not a coincidence, by proving any RBE in the plain model that satisfies a certain structural requirement (which holds for all known RBE construction) must update all but a vanishing fraction of the users, upon each new registration. It can be shown that any scheme in the plain model must have $\Omega(n)$ number of updates where n is the number of registered users. This shall be contrasted with the standard RBE in the CRS model, where each user receives at most $O(\log n)$ updates.

1.2 Technical Overview

In the following we present a high-level overview of our techniques, focusing more on clarity than precision. For more rigorous statements, we refer the reader to the technical sections.

A Primer on RBE. To establish some notation, let us first recall in somewhat more details the notion of RBE. In an RBE system, user sample their own key locally, via the KeyGen algorithm, and they then send their public key to the KC, who is responsible for maintaining the public parameters pp of the scheme. This is done via the Reg algorithm, that the KC uses to determine the new public parameters. Since the public parameters must change upon each user registration, it might be the case that a set of other users have to update their decryption key, which the KC computes using the Upd algorithm. The relevant set of users is then notified by the KC of the update. Recall that the update information u is necessary for decryption, but it is not a substitute of the secret key, and in fact u can be published without affecting the security of the scheme. For efficiency reasons, it is important to keep the number of per-user updates at a minimum, and a lot of ingenuity in RBE constructions goes into designing schemes that require as few updates as possible (more on this later). Given the current public parameters pp and an identity id, anyone can encrypt (Enc) a message for the user identified with id. Provided that such users have registered some keys, they can indeed decrypt (Dec) the message, possibly after receiving some update from the KC.

Security is defined via an experiment, where the attacker is allowed to ask honest users to register keys and to register (possibly corrupted) keys itself. At some point of the execution, the attacker submits two messages m_0 and m_1 and an identity id, then the challenger flips a coin $b \in \{0,1\}$ and encrypts m_b with respect to id using the current public parameter. The attacker wins the experiment if it can guess the encrypted message with probability non-negligibly better than $1/2$. Furthermore, the attacker is considered to be admissible if id does not correspond to a corrupted key, at the time of encryption.

Plain Model Impossibility. At a very high-level, the reason why known constructions of RBE require a common reference string crs, is the fact that the (deterministic) registration algorithm can be thought of as a *hash* function of the public keys and identities of the n registered users. In fact, we can think of the public parameter pp as the output of this hash function. By the compactness and efficiency requirement of RBE, the size of pp is $o(n)$, which means there must be two different sets of n users with the same keys that will result in the exact same hash pp. Note that even thought such a collision always exists, it could depend on crs. But, if there is no crs, a non-uniform adversary can simply hard-wire such a collision and register one set of the users and decrypt successfully with overwhelming probability any message encrypted to any identity in the other set using the common public parameter pp, due to the completeness of RBE, and break the security of RBE.

In more detail, the non-uniform adversary will get as advice a collision for an $i \in [n]$: A list of public and secret keys $(\mathsf{pk}_1, \mathsf{sk}_1), \cdots, (\mathsf{pk}_n, \mathsf{sk}_n)$, and two lists of identities $\mathsf{id}_1, \cdots, \mathsf{id}_n$ and $\mathsf{id}'_1, \cdots, \mathsf{id}'_n$ such that: (i) Registering $(\mathsf{id}_1, \mathsf{pk}_1), \cdots (\mathsf{id}_n, \mathsf{pk}_n)$ and registering $(\mathsf{id}'_1, \mathsf{pk}_1), \cdots, (\mathsf{id}'_n, \mathsf{pk}_n)$ will generate the same public parameter pp and (ii) the identity id'_i is not in the first list of identities. One can show that such an advice must exist using the compactness requirement $|\mathsf{pp}| < o(n)$. The adversary can ask the challenger to register $(\mathsf{id}_1, \mathsf{pk}_1), \cdots (\mathsf{id}_n, \mathsf{pk}_n)$, which should produce pp. Now, the adversary can simply ask the challenger to encrypt to id'_i using pp and decrypt successfully with overwhelming probability, due to the completeness of the RBE scheme. Note that if an update is needed for decryption, the adversary has all the information it needed to locally compute the correct update u'_i. Since id'_i is not even registered by the challenger, this constitutes a legitimate attack against the security of RBE.

Weakening the Security Model. As explained above, in normal RBE the attacker can ask the challenger to encrypt the challenge ciphertext with respect to any non-corrupted identity id. Because the attack above particularly uses the fact that the challenge can be with respect to non-registered party an obvious weakening of the security requirement is to not allow encryptions to non-registered users.

One might argue that this is a realistic security model because a user could check whether an identity is registered before they encrypt with respect to that identity. We believe this goes against the purpose of RBE because this check would require storing information that scales linearly with the number of registered users, which is exactly what RBE is trying to avoid.

Therefore, our positive results are in a security model that sits in between the two. We require at least one honest party being registered. This is clearly a weaker security notion than not allowing challenges with respect to non-registered users because the only non-corrupted but registered users are honest one, so clearly an honest party has to be registered.

RBE in the Plain Model. Once we have established the definition that we are aiming for, it is natural to ask whether we can actually build an RBE without a trusted setup. Since we have seen that an RBE inherently is a collision resistant hash function one would hope to just take a construction of an RBE and replace the implied hash function by a keyless hash function. This, however, first require to build RBE from unstructured collision resistant hash functions, which is an interesting open problem in itself. In this work, we propose a construction using the following cryptographic ingredients:

1. A one-way permutation f.
2. A non-interactive witness indistinguishable (NIWI) proof.
3. An RBE with re-randomizable CRS. Loosely speaking, this is an RBE where anyone can take the current CRS and "re-randomize" it, to produce a new CRS that is indistinguishable from a freshly sampled one.

We defer the discussion on how to instantiate these cryptographic building blocks to a later point in this overview, and for now we proceed to explain our general recipe to construct RBE in the plain model. Our starting point is the RBE with re-randomizable CRS, which we refer to as our *base RBE*. Our first modification to the base scheme is that, before registering their key, each honest user re-randomizes the current CRS and submits the new crs' to the KC. Additionally, it samples a random x_i and submits $y_i = f(x_i)$ along with the updated CRS. To ensure that each user re-randomizes the CRS appropriately, we also ask them to include a NIWI proof for the following statement:

– (Regular branch) I updated correctly the CRS, OR
– (Trapdoor branch) I know a valid pre-image x_i such that $f(x_i) = y_i$, AND for *all previous* CRSs sent by the j-th party ($1 \leq j < i$):
  • The j-th update was performed correctly, OR
  • I know the corresponding pre-image x_j.

Clearly, the honest user will always compute the NIWI using the witness for the regular branch, whereas the trapdoor branch will become useful later, during the security proof. Once the new CRS is received, the KC re-registers all existing users against the new CRS (more discussion on this later) and sends out the corresponding updates. At this point, we have a well-formed RBE system, that can be used to encrypt/decrypt messages using the algorithms provided by the base RBE scheme.

We prove security of this construction with a reduction against the base RBE. Since we know that there exists at least one honest user, our objective will be to *plant* the challenge common reference string crs* as the CRS for such user. However, in order to do so, the reduction cannot compute the honest branch of the NIWI, since it does not know the witness for the correct update. Instead, the reduction will *extract* the witness of *all previous NIWIs* (this procedure is potentially inefficient, but we will deal with this aspect later), which allows us to compute the new NIWI using the trapdoor branch. This allows us to plant crs* as the CRS after the honest user registration. However, we still have to deal with updates of the CRS that may happen *after* the honest user is registered. Once again, the reduction extracts the update information from the NIWI supplied by the adversary: This allows us to *translate* the challenge ciphertext computed against crs* into a ciphertext computed against the current (possibly updated) CRS. At this point, we can reduce the security to that of the base RBE.

Finally, to deal with the fact that the reduction is not efficient (since it requires extracting witnesses from adversarial NIWI proofs), we use a technique commonly referred to as *complexity leveraging*: In brief, we set the security parameter of the base RBE to be large enough so that even an adversary that has enough power to break NIWIs, still cannot break the security of the base RBE scheme.

We conclude this discussion by highlighting the fact that, in the construction as described above, the key generation algorithm depends on the current CRS, which is not standard for RBE, where the key generation only takes as input the security parameter. Concretely, this means that the key generation is a two-message protocol, instead of being completely non-interactive. We can overcome this limitation by additionally assuming the existence of indistinguishability obfuscation: Instead of sending directly the output of the KeyGen algorithm, each user sends an obfuscated circuit that, on input the current CRS, outputs a freshly sampled key (along with the appropriate NIWI proof). The security of this variant can be reduced to the security of the interactive scheme, via a standard puncturing argument.

NIWIs Secure Against Chosen-Statement Attacks. Next, we discuss how to instantiate the necessary cryptographic building blocks. A subtle aspect of the above security argument is that, at some point of the proof, we have to simultaneously extract the witness from adversarial NIWI proofs, while at the same time appeal to the witness indistinguishability of an honestly computed NIWI. We formalize this property as *security against chosen statement attacks (CSA)*, where we require that witness indistinguishability holds, even in the presence of an oracle that (inefficiently) extracts a witness from any input NIWI. Importantly, the oracle only extracts NIWIs for statements that are not equal to the challenge statement (this is akin to the standard notion of CCA-security for encryption/commitments). To complete the picture, we show that CSA-secure NIWI can be constructed from regular NIWIs, combined with non-interactive CCA-secure commitments, which in turn can be built from a variety of computational assumptions [3, 24–26, 28].

RBE with Re-randomizable CRS. Our starting point is the RBE construction of [15], where users' keys are hashed in a Merkle tree, and the witness needed to decrypt is the root-to-leaf path for the corresponding identity. The crucial building block is the notion of *hash encryption* [11], which allows one to encrypt a message with respect to an index i and a bit b: If the i-th bit of the hash pre-image equals b, then decryption is possible. The entire RBE construction reduces to building hash encryption, and therefore for us it will suffice to construct hash encryption with re-randomizable keys. We observe that the CDH chameleon encryption of [10] when interpreted as a hash encryption, indeed, has a re-randomizable key. In more details, the hash key corresponds to a matrix

$$\left(g, \begin{pmatrix} g_{1,0} & g_{2,0} & \cdots & g_{n,0} \\ g_{1,1} & g_{2,1} & \cdots & g_{n,1} \end{pmatrix}\right)$$

and to encrypt with respect to a hash h, an index i, and a bit b, one computes a ciphertext

$$\left(h^\rho, \begin{pmatrix} g_{1,0}^\rho & g_{2,0}^\rho & \cdots & g_{i-1,0}^\rho & g_{i+1,0}^\rho & \cdots & g_{n,0}^\rho \\ g_{1,1}^\rho & g_{2,1}^\rho & \cdots & g_{i-1,1}^\rho & g_{i+1,1}^\rho & \cdots & g_{n,1}^\rho \end{pmatrix}\right)$$

and the message is masked with $m \oplus \mathrm{GL}(g_{i,b}^\rho)$, where GL is the Goldreich-Levin hardcore predicate. Our re-randomization process will select uniform $\{\beta_{i,b}\}$ and re-randomize the CRS by computing

$$\left(g, \begin{pmatrix} g_{1,0}^{\beta_{1,0}} & g_{2,0}^{\beta_{2,0}} & \cdots & g_{n,0}^{\beta_{n,0}} \\ g_{1,1}^{\beta_{1,1}} & g_{2,1}^{\beta_{2,1}} & \cdots & g_{n,1}^{\beta_{n,1}} \end{pmatrix}\right)$$

which is easy to see that it is identically distributed as a freshly sampled CRS. For the security proof, it will be useful also to "update" a ciphertext according to a particular re-randomization factor, which can be easily done by computing

$$\left(\left(\frac{h^\rho}{\prod_{j\neq i} g_{j,x_j}^\rho}\right)^{\beta_{i,x_i}} \cdot \prod_{j\neq i} g_{j,x_j}^{\rho\cdot\beta_{j,x_j}}, \begin{pmatrix} g_{1,0}^{\rho\cdot\beta_{1,0}} & g_{2,0}^{\rho\cdot\beta_{2,0}} & \cdots & g_{i-1,0}^{\rho\cdot\beta_{i-1,0}} & g_{i+1,0}^{\rho\cdot\beta_{i+1,0}} & \cdots & g_{n,0}^{\rho\cdot\beta_{n,0}} \\ g_{1,1}^{\rho\cdot\beta_{1,1}} & g_{2,1}^{\rho\cdot\beta_{2,1}} & \cdots & g_{i-1,1}^{\rho\cdot\beta_{i-1,1}} & g_{i+1,1}^{\rho\cdot\beta_{i+1,1}} & \cdots & g_{n,1}^{\rho\cdot\beta_{n,1}} \end{pmatrix}\right)$$

where $x = (x_1, \ldots, x_n)$ is the pre-image of h. Once again, it is easy to see that such ciphertext is indeed a well-formed ciphertext under the updated key. In the technical sections, we will actually use a slightly different strategy to prove that security is preserved in the presence of a re-randomized keys, with a direct reduction against the CDH problem. However, the property outlined here provides a good intuition on what enables re-randomization.

Lower Bounds on the Number of Updates. The savvy reader may have noticed that in our construction each user needs to receive an update every time that a new public key is registered. This is in contrast with the standard notion of RBE, where each user receives at most a logarithmic number of updates throughout the lifetime of the system. We argue this disadvantage is necessary unless we find a completely new way to build registration based encryption by showing a lower bound on the number of updates.

All known constructions follow the same structure: the public parameters consist of one (or more) succinct commitments of the public keys of the users. Then, to decrypt a ciphertext the user knows the opening for his public key, along with the corresponding secret key. We then assume this structure and prove that any plain-model RBE that follows this structure[1] has to update a constant fraction of users.

---

[1] This assumption is simplified for exposition purposes. In the actual prove we assume that there exist two deterministic (not necessarily efficient) algorithms Ext₁ and Ext₂ such that

Intuitively, the argument says if a dishonest user does not get an update when the first honest party joins, then this means the succinct commitment where its identity and public key are did not change. Therefore, these commitments only contain adversarially chosen identities and public keys. Just like in Sect. 1.2 these commitments define a collision resistant hash function on the identities. Similarly, we can use non-uniform advice to make sure that the part of the collision we don't register contains the challenge identity but under a malicious public key.

Notice, this attack chooses the challenge ciphertext to be with respect to an honest party. Therefore, this lower bound also applies in the weaker security notion, where the challenge can not be with respect to a non-registered user.

1.3 Open Problems

We view our work as a starting point for a promising avenue of research, and there is a number of problems that remain open. On the theoretical side, it is interesting to understand what are the minimal assumptions needed to build RBE in the plain model. Regular RBE can be constructed just assuming the hardness of the CDH problem, whereas our construction in the plain model requires much stronger cryptographic tools, such as NIWI proofs and, in some of the settings, indistinguishability obfuscation. Another interesting question is to design an RBE in the plain model with *non-interactive* key generation, where there is no upper bound on the total number of registered users (our *interactive* construction achieves that, but we lose this property once we apply our compiler). Finally, from a more practical standpoint, it would be interesting to design RBE schemes with better concrete efficiency.

2   Cryptographic Preliminaries

Throughout this work, we write λ to denote the security parameter. We say a function $f : \mathbb{N} \to \mathbb{R}^+$ is negligible if for every $c > 0$ there exists $n_c \in \mathbb{N}$ such that $f(n) < \frac{1}{n^c}$ for $n > n_c$. We denote by $\mathrm{negl}(\lambda)$ a negligible function of λ. We say an algorithm is efficient if it runs in probabilistic polynomial time (PPT) in the length of its input. For a randomized algorithm A, the notation $y \leftarrow \mathsf{A}(x)$ means y is sampled by running A on input x and the notation $y \leftarrow \mathsf{A}(x; r)$ means y is computed by running A on input x with explicit randomness r. Furthermore, the notation $y \in \mathsf{A}(x)$ means there is a randomness r such that $y \leftarrow \mathsf{A}(x; r)$.

We recall the computational Diffie-Hellman (CDH) assumption [9].

Definition 1 (CDH Assumption). *Let* $(p, g, \mathbb{G})$ *be a group* $\mathbb{G}$ *of prime order* $p \in O(\lambda)$ *with generator* g. *We say that such group is CDH-hard if there exists a negligible function* negl *such that for all PPT adversaries* $\mathcal{A}$ *it holds that*

$$\Pr\left[g^{x \cdot y} = \mathsf{Adv}\left(g, g^x, g^y\right)\right] = \mathrm{negl}(\lambda).$$

$\mathsf{Ext}_1(\mathsf{id}_i, i, \mathsf{pk}_i, \mathsf{u}_i) = \mathsf{Ext}_2(\mathsf{pp}, i)$ if and only if a user with the corresponding sk_i and u_i can successfully decrypt message encrypted with respect to id_i using pp. Think of Ext_1 as extracting the commitments from the update and Ext_2 them from the public parameters.

2.1 CCA-Secure Commitments

In this work we consider the notion of tag-based commitment scheme Com, where we say that the commitment is binding if for all tags t, all messages m_0 and m_1, and all randomnesses r_0 and r_1 it holds that

$$\mathsf{Com}(t, m_0; r_0) \neq \mathsf{Com}(t, m_1; r_1).$$

We additionally require that the commitment satisfies the strong notion of CCA-security [7], which we recall in the following.

Definition 2 (CCA-Security). *A tag-based commitment* Com *is CCA-secure if there exists a negligible function* negl *such that for all PPT adversaries* $\mathcal{A}$, *all tags* t, *and all pairs of messages* (m_0, m_1) *it holds that*

$$\left| \Pr[1 = \mathsf{Adv}^{\mathcal{O}}(t, \mathsf{Com}(t, m_0))] - \Pr[1 = \mathsf{Adv}^{\mathcal{O}}(t, \mathsf{Com}(t, m_1))] \right| \leq \mathrm{negl}(\lambda)$$

where the oracle $\mathcal{O}$ *takes as input a tag* t^* *and a commitment* c^*. *If* $t^* \neq t$, *it (inefficiently) computes the message committed in* c^* *and returns it as an output. If no such message exists, the oracle returns* $\perp$.

CCA commitments can be constructed from adaptively secure one-way functions [28], time-lock puzzles [26], obfuscation [25], sub-exponentially hard injective one-way functions [3], or quantum-easy commitments [24].

2.2 Indistinguishability Obfuscation

We recall the definition of indistinguishability obfuscation (iO) for circuits from the articles [1, 14].

Definition 3 (iO for Circuits). *A PPT machine* Obf *is an indistinguishable obfuscator for circuit class* $\{\mathcal{C}_\lambda\}$, *if the following are satisfied:*

- *(Functional Equivalence) For all* $\lambda \in \mathbb{N}$, *all* $C \in \mathcal{C}_\lambda$, *all inputs* x, *we have*

$$\Pr\left[C'(x) = C(x) : C' \leftarrow \mathsf{Obf}(C)\right] = 1$$

- *(Indistinguishability) For all* $\lambda \in \mathbb{N}$, *all pairs of circuit* $(C_0, C_1) \in \mathcal{C}_\lambda$ *such that* $|C_0| = |C_1|$ *and* $C_0(x) = C_1(x)$ *on all inputs* x, *it holds that the following distributions are computationally indistinguishable*

$$\mathsf{Obf}(C_0) \approx \mathsf{Obf}(C_1).$$

2.3 Puncturable Pseudorandom Functions

A puncturable pseudorandom function (PRF) is an augmented PRF that has an additional puncturing algorithm. Such an algorithm produces a punctured version of the key that can evaluate the PRF at all points except for the punctured one. It is required that the PRF value at that specific point is pseudorandom even given the punctured key. A puncturable PRF can be constructed from any one-way function [20].

Definition 4 (Puncturable PRFs). *A puncturable family of PRFs is a tuple of PPT algorithms* $(PRF, \mathsf{Puncture})$ *defined as follows.*

- $PRF(K, i) \rightarrow y$: *A deterministic algorithm that takes as input a key* $K \in \mathcal{K}$ *and a point* $i \in \mathcal{X}$ *and returns a value* $y \in \mathcal{Y}$.
- $\mathsf{Puncture}(K, i) \rightarrow K_i$: *A deterministic algorithm that takes as input a key* $K \in \mathcal{K}$ *and a point* $i \in \mathcal{X}$ *and returns a punctured key* K_i.

We require that a puncturable PRF satisfies the following properties.

- *(Correctness) For all* $\lambda \in \mathbb{N}$, *for all keys* $K \leftarrow \{0,1\}^\lambda$, *for all* $i \in \mathcal{X}$ *and* $x \in \mathcal{X} \setminus i$, *and for all* $K_i \leftarrow \mathsf{Puncture}(K, i)$, *we have that*

$$PRF(K_i, x) = PRF(K, x).$$

- *(Pseudorandomness) For all* $\lambda \in \mathbb{N}$ *and for all* $i \in \mathcal{X}$ *the following distributions are computationally indistinguishable*

$$\{i, K_i, PRF(K, i)\} \approx \{i, K_i, u\}$$

where $K_i \leftarrow \mathsf{Puncture}(K, i)$ *and* $u \leftarrow \mathcal{Y}$ *is uniformly sampled.*

3 NIWI Proofs Secure Against Chosen Statement Attacks

We recall the notion of non-interactive witness-indistinguishable (NIWI) proof for NP from [2].

Definition 5 (NIWI Proof for NP). *A NIWI proof* (NIWI.Prove, NIWI.Verify) *for an NP-language* $\mathcal{L}$ *with relation* $\mathcal{R}$ *consists of the following efficient algorithms.*

- NIWI.Prove$(1^\lambda, w, x) \rightarrow \pi$: *On input the security parameter* 1^λ, *a witness* w, *and a statement* x, *the proving algorithm returns a proof* π.
- NIWI.Verify$(\pi, x) \rightarrow b$: *On input a proof* π, *and a statement* x, *the verification algorithm returns a bit* $b \in \{0, 1\}$.

We define the properties of interest below, including correctness, soundness and computational witness indistinguishability.

Definition 6 (Correctness). *A NIWI proof* (NIWI.Prove, NIWI.Verify) *is correct if for all* $\lambda \in \mathbb{N}$, *all* $x \in \mathcal{L}$, *and all* $w \in \mathcal{R}(x)$ *it holds that*

$$\Pr\left[\mathsf{NIWI.Verify}(\mathsf{NIWI.Prove}(1^\lambda, w, x), x) = 1\right] = 1.$$

Definition 7 (Soundness). *A NIWI proof* (NIWI.Prove, NIWI.Verify) *is sound if for all* $x^* \notin \mathcal{L}$ *and all proofs* π^* *it holds that*

$$\Pr[\text{NIWI.Verify}(\pi^*, x^*) = 1] = 0.$$

Definition 8 (Computational Witness Indistinguishability). *A NIWI proof* NIWI = (Prove, Verify) *is witness indistinguishable if for all* $x \in \mathcal{L}$, *and all pairs of witnesses* $w_0, w_1 \in \mathcal{R}(x)$ *it holds that the following distributions are computationally indistinguishable*

$$\text{NIWI.Prove}(1^\lambda, w_0, x) \approx \text{NIWI.Prove}(1^\lambda, w_1, x).$$

NIWI proofs are known to exist under a variety of assumptions, such as trapdoor permutations [2], bilinear pairings [22], and obfuscation and one-way permutations [4].

CSA-Security. In the following we present our construction of *chosen statement attack* (CSA) secure NIWI. Informally, a NIWI is CSA-secure if the witness-indistinguishability property holds, even in the presence of an oracle that extracts a witness from NIWIs for different statements. Before defining this property, we define the notion of *witness extractable* NIWI.

Definition 9 (Witness Extractability). *A NIWI proof* (NIWI.Prove, NIWI.Verify) *is witness extractable if there exists an inefficient algorithm* NIWI.Extract *such that for all* $x \in \mathcal{L}$ *and all proofs* π *it holds that*

$$\text{NIWI.Verify}(\pi, x) = 1 \implies w \in \mathcal{R}(x)$$

where $w \leftarrow \text{NIWI.Extract}(\pi, x)$.

Note that this definition does not contradict witness indistinguishability, since the extractor is not efficient. We are now ready to define the notion of CSA-security for NIWIs.

Definition 10 (CSA-Security). *A witness extractable NIWI proof* (NIWI.Prove, NIWI.Verify, NIWI.Extract) *is CSA-secure if there exists a negligible function* negl *such that for all PPT adversaries* $\mathcal{A}$, *all statements* x, *and all pairs of witnesses* $(w_0, w_1) \in \mathcal{R}(x)$ *it holds that*

$$\left| \Pr[1 = \text{Adv}^{\mathcal{O}}(x, \text{NIWI.Prove}(1^\lambda, w_0, x))] - \Pr[1 = \text{Adv}^{\mathcal{O}}(x, \text{NIWI.Prove}(1^\lambda, w_1, x))] \right|$$
$$\leq \text{negl}(\lambda)$$

where the oracle $\mathcal{O}$ *takes as input a statement* x^* *and a proof* π^*. *If* $x^* \neq x$ *and* NIWI.Verify$(\pi^*, x^*) = 1$, *it returns* $w^* \leftarrow \text{NIWI.Extract}(\pi^*, x^*)$.

Construction of CSA-Secure NIWI. We show that a simple combination of CCA-secure commitments and (standard) NIWIs with sub-exponential security already suffices to construct CSA-secure NIWI. More in details, on input a statement x and a witness w, the prover algorithm computes

$$c_0 \leftarrow \text{Com}(x, w) \quad \text{and} \quad c_1 \leftarrow \text{Com}(x, 0)$$

and furthermore it computes a (regular) NIWI proof π for the statement:

$$(x, c_0, c_1) = \{\exists(w, b) : c_b \in \mathsf{Com}(x, w) \quad \& \quad w \in \mathcal{R}(x)\}.$$

(Recall that $c_b \in \mathsf{Com}(x, w)$ means there is a randomness r with $c_b \leftarrow \mathsf{Com}(x, w; r)$.)

We denote by λ_{Com} the security parameter of the commitment and we set λ (the security parameter of the NIWI) so that

$$\lambda = (\lambda_{\mathsf{Com}})^C$$

for some constant $C > 1$, and we require that witness indistinguishability holds against all attackers running in time polynomial in $2^{\lambda_{\mathsf{Com}}}$ (sub-exponential security).

By the soundness of the NIWI, it is clear that the above construction is witness extractable, since an inefficient extractor can simply brute-force both commitments and recover a valid witness from at least one of them. The following theorem shows that this NIWI is also CSA-secure.

Theorem 1. *Let* (NIWI.Prove, NIWI.Verify) *be a sub-exponentially secure NIWI proof and let* Com *be a CCA-secure commitment scheme. Then the construction as described above is a CSA-secure NIWI.*

Proof. Let us fix the bit of the experiment to 0, in which case the view of the adversary includes the variables

$$\mathsf{Com}(x, w_0) \quad \text{and} \quad \mathsf{Com}(x, 0) \quad \text{and} \quad \mathsf{NIWI.Prove}(1^\lambda, (0, w_0), (x, c_0, c_1))$$

along with the queries to the oracle $\mathcal{O}$ as defined in Definition 10. We then argue that the following distributions ensembles are computationally indistinguishable, even in the presence of such an oracle:

$$\{\mathsf{Com}(x, w_0), \mathsf{Com}(x, 0), \mathsf{NIWI.Prove}(1^\lambda, (0, w_0), (x, c_0, c_1))\}$$
$$\approx \{\mathsf{Com}(x, w_0), \mathsf{Com}(x, w_1), \mathsf{NIWI.Prove}(1^\lambda, (0, w_0), (x, c_0, c_1))\}$$
$$\approx \{\mathsf{Com}(x, w_0), \mathsf{Com}(x, w_1), \mathsf{NIWI.Prove}(1^\lambda, (1, w_1), (x, c_0, c_1))\}$$
$$\approx \{\mathsf{Com}(x, w_1), \mathsf{Com}(x, w_1), \mathsf{NIWI.Prove}(1^\lambda, (1, w_1), (x, c_0, c_1))\}$$
$$\approx \{\mathsf{Com}(x, w_1), \mathsf{Com}(x, w_1), \mathsf{NIWI.Prove}(1^\lambda, (0, w_1), (x, c_0, c_1))\}$$
$$\approx \{\mathsf{Com}(x, w_1), \mathsf{Com}(x, 0), \mathsf{NIWI.Prove}(1^\lambda, (0, w_1), (x, c_0, c_1))\}$$

which suffices to conclude the proof, since the last distribution is precisely identical to the experiment with the bit fixed to 1. We only discuss indistinguishability for the first two hybrid distributions, and the further ones follow along the same lines. For the first hybrid, note that the only difference is that c_1 is computed as a commitment to 0 or a commitment to w_1. Note that the NIWI is computed using the random coins of c_0, and therefore indistinguishability follows by the CCA-security of the commitment: The reduction can simulate the witness extraction oracle using the oracle provided by the security of the commitment scheme. Note that the witness extraction oracle always returns $\bot$ if the statement equals x, which in particular means that the tag of the commitment must be different, in order for the oracle to return an answer.

As for the second hybrid, the only change here is the witness that we use in the NIWI proof. We can prove indistinguishability by appealing to the sub-exponential witness indistinguishability of the NIWI: The reduction simply simulates the extraction oracle by brute-forcing the commitments, thus running in time polynomial in $2^{\lambda_{\mathsf{Com}}}$. By our choice of parameters, the reduction runtime is still low enough to derive a contradiction against the witness indistinguishability of the NIWI proof. The indistinguishability of the remaining hybrids is argued along the same lines as the ones above.

4 Model and Definitions

We recall the standard definitions of RBE.

4.1 Standard RBE Definitions

In more detail, a registration-based encryption has the following algorithms as defined in [15]:

$\mathsf{Setup}(1^{\lambda}) \rightarrow \mathsf{crs}$: The setup algorithm takes as input the security parameter 1^{λ} and outputs a common reference string crs.

$\mathsf{KeyGen}(1^{\lambda}) \rightarrow (\mathsf{pk}, \mathsf{sk})$: The key generation algorithm takes as input the security parameter and outputs a public key pk and a secret key sk. This algorithm should be run by any party who wishes to register.

$\mathsf{Reg}^{[\mathsf{aux}]}(\mathsf{crs}, \mathsf{pp}, \mathsf{id}, \mathsf{pk}) \rightarrow \mathsf{pp}'$: The deterministic registration algorithm takes as input a common reference string crs, public parameters pp, identity id, and public key pk and outputs new public parameters pp'. In this process Reg has read-write access to aux. This algorithm should be run by the key curator.

$\mathsf{Enc}(\mathsf{crs}, \mathsf{pp}, \mathsf{id}, \mathsf{m}) \rightarrow \mathsf{ct}$: The encryption algorithm takes as input the common reference string crs, the public parameters pp, an identity id, and a message m and outputs a ciphertext ct.

$\mathsf{Upd}^{\mathsf{aux}}(\mathsf{pp}, \mathsf{id}) \rightarrow \mathsf{u}$: The deterministic update algorithm Upd takes public parameters pp and identity id as input and outputs an update u. This algorithm has read access to aux. This algorithm should also be run by the key curator.

$\mathsf{Dec}(\mathsf{sk}, \mathsf{u}, \mathsf{ct}) \rightarrow \mathsf{m}$: The deterministic decryption algorithm takes as input a secret key sk, an update u, and ciphertext ct and outputs a message m.

Definition 11 (Completeness, compactness, and efficiency of RBE). *Consider the following game for a computationally unbounded adversary* Adv *which still has only polynomially many rounds of interaction with a challenger* Chal.

1. *Initialization:* Chal *sets* $\mathsf{pp} \leftarrow \bot$, $\mathsf{aux} \leftarrow \bot$, $u \leftarrow \bot$, $\mathsf{ID} \leftarrow \emptyset$, $\mathsf{id}^* \leftarrow \bot$, $t \leftarrow 0$, $\mathsf{crs} \leftarrow \mathsf{Setup}(1^{\lambda})$ *and send* crs *to* Adv.
2. *Every round* Adv *does one of these actions:*
   (a) *Registering a new (non-target) identity:* Adv *sends a new identity* $\mathsf{id} \notin \mathsf{ID}$ *and a public key* pk *to* Chal, *which registers and updates* $\mathsf{pp} = \mathsf{Reg}^{[\mathsf{aux}]}(\mathsf{crs}, \mathsf{pp}, \mathsf{id}, \mathsf{pk})$. *The challenger* Chal *also updates* $\mathsf{ID} \leftarrow \mathsf{ID} \cup \{\mathsf{id}\}$.

(b) *Registering the target identity: If the target identity* id* *is already chosen then do nothing. Otherwise* Adv *sends a target identity* id* *to* Chal. *If* id* ∉ ID *then* Chal *samples an honest public-key-secret-key pair* (pk*, sk*) ← KeyGen(λ) *and registers and updates* pp ← Reg$^{[aux]}$(crs, pp, id*, pk*), ID ← ID ∪ {id*}, *and sends* pk* *to* Adv.

(c) *Encrypting to the target identity: If the target identity* id* *is not yet chosen then do nothing. Otherwise,* Chal *sets* $t \leftarrow t + 1$ *and receives a message* m_t *from* Adv. Chal *sends a ciphertext* ct$_t$ ← Enc(crs, pp, id*, m_t) *to* Adv.

(d) *Decrypting for target identity: The adversary* Adv *sends* $i \in [t]$ *to* Chal, *which computes the plaintext* m'_i ← Dec(sk, u, ct$_i$). *If* m'_i = GetUpd, *then* Chal *computes the update* u ← Upd^{aux}(pp, id*) *and computes the plaintext* m'_i ← Dec(sk, u, ct$_i$).

The Adv *wins if* $m_i \neq m'_i$ *at some point in the game.*

We require the following requirements to be met, where $n = |ID|$:

- *Completeness:* Adv *wins with probability* ≤ negl(λ).
- *Compactness of public parameters and updates:* |pp| *and* |u| *are both at most* poly(λ, log n).
- *Efficiency of Registration and Updates:* Reg *and* Upd *run both in time at most* poly(λ, log n).
- *Number of Updates: The total number* Upd *calls for identity* id* *in step 2d is* ≤ O(log n).

The security is defined similarly using an experiment.

Definition 12 (RBE Security). *Consider the following game between an interactive PPT adversary* Adv *and a challenger* Chal:

1. *Initialization:* Chal *sets* pp ← ⊥, aux ← ⊥, u ← ⊥, ID ← ∅, id* ← ⊥, t ← 0, crs ← Setup(1^λ) *and send* crs *to* Adv.
2. *Every round* Adv *does one of these actions:*
   (a) *Registering a new (non-target) identity: The adversary* Adv *sends a new identity* id ∉ ID *and a public key* pk *to* Chal, *which registers and updates* pp = Reg$^{[aux]}$(crs, pp, id, pk). *The challenger* Chal *also updates* ID ← ID ∪ {id}.
   (b) *Registering the target identity: If the target identity* id* *is already chosen then do nothing. Otherwise* Adv *sends a target identity* id* ∉ ID *to* Chal, *which samples an honest public-key-secret-key pair* (pk*, sk*) ← KeyGen(1^λ) *and registers and updates* pp ← Reg$^{[aux]}$(crs, pp, id*, pk*), ID ← ID ∪ {id*}, *and sends* pk* *to* Adv.
3. *Encrypting for target identity: If no target identity* id* *is chosen* Adv *sends* id* *to* Chal. *Then, the challenger* Chal *samples a random bit* b ← {0, 1} *and generates an encryption to the target identity* ct* ← Enc(crs, pp, id*, b) *and sends* ct *to* Adv.
4. Adv *outputs a bit* b' *and wins the game if* b = b'.

We call an RBE secure if the adversary wins with probability $1/2$ + negl(λ).

Remark 1 (Interactive RBE). In this work, we consider also a variant of the standard RBE, as an intermediate abstraction, where the registration process requires one round of interaction between the key curator and the clients. This is modeled by allowing the key generation algorithm to have read-only access to the auxiliary information. Namely, an interactive RBE is obtained from standard RBE by replacing $\mathsf{KeyGen}(1^\lambda) \to (\mathsf{pk}, \mathsf{sk})$ by $\mathsf{KeyGen}^{\mathsf{aux}}(1^\lambda) \to (\mathsf{pk}, \mathsf{sk})$.

4.2 Necessity of One Honest User

Now we show that without a CRS no RBE scheme can satisfy both Definition 11 and Definition 12 against non-uniform PPT adversary. The proof is very reminiscent of proof that there can not be collision resistant hash functions without setup.

Proposition 1. *Let* Π = $(\mathsf{Setup}, \mathsf{KeyGen}, \mathsf{Gen}, \mathsf{Enc}, \mathsf{Upd}, \mathsf{Dec})$ *be an RBE scheme without CRS satisfying Definition 11. Then, there exists a non-uniform PPT adversary* $\mathcal{A}$ *that breaks the security of* Π *defined in Definition 12.*

Proof. Fix a list of n pairs of public and secret keys $(\mathsf{pk}_1, \mathsf{sk}_1), \cdots, (\mathsf{pk}_n, \mathsf{sk}_n)$ where $(\mathsf{pk}_i, \mathsf{sk}_i) \leftarrow \Pi.\mathsf{KeyGen}(1^\lambda)$. Define $H_n(\mathsf{id}_1, \cdots, \mathsf{id}_n)$ recursively by

$$H_{i+1}(\mathsf{id}_1, \cdots, \mathsf{id}_{i+1}) := \mathsf{Reg}^{[\mathsf{aux}]}(H_i(\mathsf{id}_1, \cdots, \mathsf{id}_i), \mathsf{id}_{i+1}, \mathsf{pk}_{i+1})$$

for $i = 0, \cdots, n-1$ and $H_0 = \bot$.

By definition, we know $|\mathsf{pp}| \leq \mathsf{poly}(\lambda, \log n) \leq \lambda^{c_1} \cdot (\log n)^{c_2}$ for some constants $c_1, c_2 > 0$. Without loss of generality, assume the length of identities is $|\mathsf{id}| = \lambda$. There are $\binom{2^\lambda}{n}$ different sets of n identities. We identify each set as a list of n identities. By the well known lower bound for binomial coefficients, we have $\log \binom{2^\lambda}{n} \geq n \cdot (\lambda - \log n)$. Take $n = \lambda^{c_1}$. One can easily check that $n \cdot (\lambda - \log n) > \lambda^{c_1} \cdot (\log n)^{c_2}$ for sufficiently large λ.

This implies there exist $(\mathsf{id}_1, \cdots, \mathsf{id}_n)$ and $(\mathsf{id}'_1, \cdots, \mathsf{id}'_n)$ where there exists $i \in [n]$ such that $\mathsf{id}'_i \neq \mathsf{id}_j$ for every $j \in [n]$ and $H_n(\mathsf{id}_1, \cdots, \mathsf{id}_n) = H_n(\mathsf{id}'_1, \cdots, \mathsf{id}'_n)$. Consider the following adversary Adv given the two lists of identities, the list of keys and the index i as advice.

1. Send $(\mathsf{id}_j, \mathsf{pk}_j)$ to the challenger Chal to register for $j = 1, \cdots, n$.
2. Locally register $((\mathsf{id}'_j, \mathsf{pk}_j))$ for $j = 1, \cdots, n$.
3. Ask Chal to encrypt to id'_i.
4. Locally compute update u'_i for id'_i.
5. Use $(\mathsf{sk}_i, \mathsf{u}'_i)$ to decrypt and output the bit.

Efficiency and Legitimacy. The adversary Adv is clearly efficient. The attack is legitimate because id'_i has not been registered by the challenger.

Advantage. By construction, registering $(\mathsf{id}_j, \mathsf{pk}_j)$ for $j = 1, \cdots, n$ and registering $(\mathsf{id}'_j, \mathsf{pk}_j)$ for $j = 1, \cdots, n$ produces the exact same public parameter pp. Then, decryption will succeed with overwhelming probability, due to completeness.

5   RBE in the Plain Model

In this section, we show despite the impossibility results how to construct RBE in the plain model.

5.1   One Honest User Security

In the following, we define a variant of registration-based encryption that only has any security if one of the users is honest. We believe this is still meaningful. We mark the difference from the previous definition in grey.

Definition 13 (One Honest User Security). *Consider the following game between an interactive PPT adversary* Adv *and a challenger* Chal:

1. *Initialization:* Chal *sets* $\mathsf{pp} \leftarrow \bot$, $\mathsf{aux} \leftarrow \bot$, $u \leftarrow \bot$, $\mathsf{ID} \leftarrow \emptyset$, $\mathsf{HID} \leftarrow \emptyset$, $\mathsf{id}^* \leftarrow \bot$, $t \leftarrow 0$, $\mathsf{crs} \leftarrow \mathsf{Setup}(1^\lambda)$ *and send* crs *to* Adv.
2. *Every round* Adv *does one of these actions:*
   (a) *Registering a new (non-target) identity: The adversary* Adv *sends a new identity* id $\notin$ ID *and public key* pk *to* Chal, *which updates the public parameter* $\mathsf{pp} = \mathsf{Reg}^{[\mathsf{aux}]}(\mathsf{crs}, \mathsf{pp}, \mathsf{id}, \mathsf{pk})$ *and updates* ID $\leftarrow$ ID $\cup \{\mathsf{id}\}$.
   (b) *Registering an honest identity: The adversary* Adv *sends a new identity* id $\notin$ ID *then* Chal *samples an honest public-key-secret-key pair* $(\mathsf{pk}, \mathsf{sk}) \leftarrow \mathsf{KeyGen}(1^\lambda)$. *Then, the challenger* Chal *updates* $\mathsf{pp} \leftarrow \mathsf{Reg}^{[\mathsf{aux}]}(\mathsf{crs}, \mathsf{pp}, \mathsf{id}, \mathsf{pk})$, ID $\leftarrow$ ID $\cup \{\mathsf{id}\}$ *and* HID $\leftarrow$ HID $\cup \{\mathsf{id}\}$, *and then sends* pk *to* Adv.
3. *Encrypting for target identity:* Adv *sends a target identity* $\mathsf{id}^* \in \mathsf{HID}$ *or* $\mathsf{id}^* \notin \mathsf{ID}$ *to* Chal, *which samples a random bit* $b \leftarrow \{0, 1\}$ *and computes the encryption* $\mathsf{ct}^* \leftarrow \mathsf{Enc}(\mathsf{crs}, \mathsf{pp}, \mathsf{id}^*, b)$ *with respect to* id^* *and send* ct *to* Adv
4. Adv *outputs a bit* b' *and wins the game if* $b = b'$ *and* HID $\neq \emptyset$.

We call an RBE one honest user secure if the adversary wins with probability $1/2 + \mathrm{negl}(\lambda)$.

All that really changes is that we keep track of the honestly registered identities. We track those in HID and we require that HID $\neq \emptyset$ for the adversary to win. The major differences are highlighted.

Interactive Registration Based Encryption. We start by constructing an interactive RBE and showing that the construction satisfies the above one honest user security. Please see Remark 1 for the syntax of an interactive RBE.

Construction 2 (Interactive Registration Based Encryption) *Let* NIWI = (Prove, Verify, Extract) *be a CSA-secure NIWI,* RRRBE = (Setup, SampleRand, ReRand, KeyGen, Reg, Upd, Enc, Dec) *be a re-randomizable RBE scheme, and* f *be an one-way permutation defined on* $\mathcal{X} = \{0, 1\}^\lambda$. *We construct the algorithms of an interactive RBE. (In the following, part of* aux *is identified as the auxiliary information* $\mathsf{aux}_{\mathsf{RRRBE}}$ *for the underlying re-randomizable RBE* RRRBE.)

- $\mathsf{KeyGen}^{\mathsf{aux}}(1^\lambda) \rightarrow (\mathsf{pk},\mathsf{sk})$: *First compute* $(\mathsf{pk}',\mathsf{sk}') \leftarrow \mathsf{RRRBE.KeyGen}(1^\lambda)$. *If* $\mathsf{aux} = \bot$, *which means no user has been registered yet, compute* $\mathsf{crs}_0 = \mathsf{RRRBE.Setup}(1^\lambda, 0; r_0)$ *with fixed randomness* $r_0 = 0$. *Otherwise, read from* aux *a list* $(\mathsf{crs}_0, \cdots, \mathsf{crs}_i)$ *and a list* $(y_1, \cdots, y_i)$. *(Here the index* i *is the number of users already registered. In the previous case where* $\mathsf{aux} = \bot$, *we let* $i = 0$.) *Then do the following.*

  1. *Sample* $r_{i+1} \leftarrow \mathsf{RRRBE.SampleRand}(1^\lambda)$ *and compute* $\mathsf{crs}_{i+1} = \mathsf{RRRBE.ReRand}(\mathsf{crs}_i; r_{i+1})$.
  2. *Sample* $x_{i+1} \leftarrow \mathcal{X}$ *and compute* $y_{i+1} = f(x_{i+1})$.
  3. *Compute* $\pi = \mathsf{NIWI.Prove}(1^{\lambda_{\mathrm{NIWI}}}, r_{i+1}, \mathsf{stm})$ *where* $\lambda_{\mathrm{NIWI}} = \lambda^C$, *for some constant* $C < 1$, $\mathsf{stm} = ((\mathsf{crs}_0, \cdots, \mathsf{crs}_{i+1}), (y_1, \cdots, y_{i+1}))$ *and* $\mathcal{R}(\mathsf{stm})$ *is defined to be:*
     - r *such that* $\mathsf{crs}_{i+1} = \mathsf{RRRBE.ReRand}(\mathsf{crs}_i; r)$, *or*
     - x *such that* $y_{i+1} = f(x)$, *and for all* $j \in [i]$
       * r_j *such that* $\mathsf{crs}_j = \mathsf{RRRBE.ReRand}(\mathsf{crs}_{j-1}; r_j)$, *or*
       * x_j *such that* $y_j = f(x_j)$.
  4. *Output* $(\mathsf{pk} = (\mathsf{crs}_{i+1}, y_{i+1}, \pi, \mathsf{pk}'), \mathsf{sk} = \mathsf{sk}')$.

- $\mathsf{Reg}^{[\mathsf{aux}]}(1^\lambda, \mathsf{pp}, \mathsf{id}, \mathsf{pk}) \rightarrow \mathsf{pp}'$: *If* $\mathsf{aux} = \bot$, *which means no user has been registered yet, compute* $\mathsf{crs}_0 = \mathsf{RRRBE.Setup}(1^\lambda, 0; r_0)$ *with fixed randomness* $r_0 = 0$. *Add* crs_0 *to* aux. *Otherwise, read from* aux *a list* $(\mathsf{crs}_0, \cdots, \mathsf{crs}_i)$ *and a list* $(y_1, \cdots, y_i)$, *where* i *is the number of registered users. Parse* $\mathsf{pk} = (\mathsf{crs}_{i+1}, y_{i+1}, \pi, \mathsf{pk}')$. *Reconstruct* stm *and run* $\mathsf{NIWI.Verify}(\pi, \mathsf{stm})$. *If verification fails, halt and output nothing. Otherwise, add* $\mathsf{crs}_{i+1}, y_{i+1}$ *to* aux. *Then, perform re-registration of previous users and the registration of new user in the following way. Compute* $\mathsf{pp}_1 \leftarrow \mathsf{Reg}^{[\mathsf{aux}]}(\mathsf{crs}_{i+1}, \bot, \mathsf{id}_1, \mathsf{pk}_1)$. *Then, for each* $j = 2, \cdots, i+1$, *compute* $\mathsf{pp}_j \leftarrow \mathsf{Reg}^{[\mathsf{aux}]}(\mathsf{crs}_{i+1}, \mathsf{pp}_{j-1}, \mathsf{id}_j, \mathsf{pk}_j)$. *Finally, output* $\mathsf{pp}' = \mathsf{pp}_{i+1}$.

- $\mathsf{Enc}(\mathsf{pp}, \mathsf{id}, \mathsf{m}) \rightarrow \mathsf{ct}$:
  - *Parse* pp *as* $(\mathsf{crs}', \mathsf{pp}')$.
  - *Compute* $\mathsf{ct}' \leftarrow \mathsf{RRRBE.Enc}(\mathsf{crs}', \mathsf{pp}', \mathsf{id}, \mathsf{m})$.
  - *Output* $\mathsf{ct} = (\mathsf{crs}', \mathsf{ct}')$.

- $\mathsf{Upd}^{\mathsf{aux}}(\mathsf{pp}, \mathsf{id}) \rightarrow \mathsf{u}$:
  - *Parse* pp *as* $(\mathsf{crs}', \mathsf{pp}')$.
  - *Output the update* $\mathsf{u} = \mathsf{RRRBE.Upd}^{\mathsf{aux}_{\mathrm{RRRBE}}}(\mathsf{pp}', \mathsf{id})$.

- $\mathsf{Dec}(\mathsf{sk}, \mathsf{u}, \mathsf{ct}) \rightarrow \mathsf{m}$:
  - *Parse* ct *as* $(\mathsf{crs}', \mathsf{ct}')$.
  - *Output* $\mathsf{m} = \mathsf{RRRBE.Dec}(\mathsf{crs}', \mathsf{sk}, \mathsf{u}, \mathsf{ct}')$.

Correctness, compactness, and efficiency directly follow from the underlying re-randomizable RBE, one-way permutation and NIWI. In the following, we show that the construction is secure.

Proposition 2. *The RBE of Construction 2 is secure as defined in Definition 13.*

Proof. The proof proceeds by defining a series of hybrid experiments, where we modify the challenger's behaviour. We define the following series of hybrids.

- Hyb_0: This is the original experiment.
- Hyb_1: Let i be the index of the first registered honest identity. Extract the witnesses from the NIWIs from all identities previous to i. Call these witnesses $w_1, \ldots, w_{i-1}$. This can be done because of witness extractability of the NIWI.
- Hyb_2: Introduce a condition that if the extracted witnesses $w_1, \ldots, w_{i-1}$ do not for each $j \in [i-1]$ contain
  - an r_j such that $crs_j = RRRBE.ReRand(crs_{j-1}; r_j)$, or
  - an x_j such that $y_j = f(x_j)$

  the adversary wins automatically. This condition does not happen by the soundness of the NIWI.
- Hyb_3: In this hybrid, we change how the challenger proves the NIWI for the first honestly registered use π_i. It uses the extracted witnesses $w_1, \ldots, w_{i-1}$ and input to the one-way permutation x_i to switch to the second branch. By CSA-Security this change stays unnoticed with all but negligible probability.
- Hyb_4: In this hybrid, we change how the crs_i is computed. Instead of re-randomizing crs_{i-1} we generate a fresh $crs_i \leftarrow RRRBE.Setup(1^\lambda, i)$. An adversary can not detect this change because a freshly generated crs is identically distributed to a re-randomized one as it fulfills Definition 17.
- Hyb_5: Extract the witnesses from the NIWIs from all identities after i. Call these witnesses $w_{i+1}, \ldots, w_m$, where m is the number of registered parties at the end.
- Hyb_6: In this hybrid, we introduce a condition that if the extracted witnesses $w_{i+1}, \ldots, w_m$ contain x_i, the input to the one-way permutation of the first honest user, the adversary wins automatically. This condition does not happen with all but negligible probability by the one-wayness of f.
- Hyb_7: In this hybrid, we introduce a condition that if the extracted witnesses $w_{i+1}, \ldots, w_m$ contain r_i, randomness with the property that if crs_i matches the re-randomized crs $RRRBE.ReRand(crs_{i-1}; r_i)$, the adversary wins automatically. This condition does not happen with all but negligible probability by the one-wayness of the re-randomization of the RBE.
- Hyb_8: In this hybrid, we introduce a condition, that checks, whether $w_{i+1}, \ldots, w_m$ contain randomnesses $r_{i+1}, \ldots, r_m$ such that $crs_j = RRRBE.ReRand(crs_{j-1}; r_j)$ for all $j \in [i+1, m]$. This condition does happen by the soundness of the NIWI.

Hyb_8 reduces to re-randomizable RBE because every registered user after i can at most modify the CRS by re-randomizing it.

5.2 From Interactive To Non-interactive Registration

In the following we present a generic method to turn an RBE scheme with interactive registration (i.e., where the key generation takes as input the public parameters pp instead of the common reference string crs) into a standard RBE, with non-interactive registration. Given an RBE scheme (Setup, KeyGen, Reg, Enc, Upd, Dec) with interactive registration, our new RBE will only modify the key generation, registration, and decryption algorithms, which we describe below. Let PKEnc be the encryption algorithm for a semantically secure public-key encryption scheme.

$\mathsf{KeyGen}^*(1^\lambda) \to (\mathsf{pk}, \mathsf{sk})$: Sample a regular public-key encryption pair $(\mathsf{pk}^*, \mathsf{sk}^*)$. Sample $K \leftarrow \{0,1\}^\lambda$ to be the key of a puncturable PRF. Then compute $\tilde{C} \leftarrow \mathsf{Obf}(C_{K,\mathsf{pk}^*})$ and return $\tilde{C}$ as the public key and sk^* as the secret key. The circuit C_{K,pk^*} is defined to take as input some public parameters pp and it behaves as follows:

- Evaluate $(r_0, r_1) \leftarrow \mathsf{PRF}(K, \mathsf{pp})$.
- Compute $(\mathsf{pk}, \mathsf{sk}) \leftarrow \mathsf{KeyGen}(\mathsf{pp}; r_0)$.
- Return pk and $c \leftarrow \mathsf{PKEnc}(\mathsf{pk}^*, \mathsf{sk}; r_1)$.

$\mathsf{Reg}^{*[\mathsf{aux}]}(\mathsf{crs}, \mathsf{pp}, \mathsf{id}, \mathsf{pk}) \to \mathsf{pp}'$: The new registration algorithm evaluates $(\mathsf{pk}, c) \leftarrow \tilde{C}(\mathsf{pp})$ and proceeds as the old Reg, recording c as part of the auxiliary information.

$\mathsf{Dec}^*(\mathsf{sk}, u, \mathsf{ct}) \to m$: We assume without loss of generality that the ciphertext c is part of the update u. Then the decryption algorithm uses sk^* to decrypt c and recover sk, which is then used as input to run the old Dec algorithm.

The correctness of the new scheme follows easily from the correctness of the old RBE. The following theorem summarizes the result of this section.

Theorem 3. *Let* $(\mathsf{Setup}, \mathsf{KeyGen}, \mathsf{Reg}, \mathsf{Enc}, \mathsf{Upd}, \mathsf{Dec})$ *be an RBE with interactive registration. Then the construction as described above is a secure RBE.*

Proof. The proof proceeds by defining a series of hybrid experiments, where we modify the way we compute the output of the key generation algorithm KeyGen^* for all honest parties in the experiment. For the i-th party, we define the following series of hybrids.

- $\mathsf{Hyb}_{i,0}$: This is the original experiment.
- $\mathsf{Hyb}_{i,1}$: In this hybrid, we modify the way the obfuscated circuit is computed. Let pp^* be the current version of the public parameters of the scheme, we define $K\{\mathsf{pp}^*\} \leftarrow \mathsf{Puncture}(K, \mathsf{pp}^*)$ and $(r_0^*, r_1^*) \leftarrow \mathsf{PRF}(K, \mathsf{pp}^*)$. We then obfuscate the circuit $C_{K\{\mathsf{pp}^*\},\mathsf{pk}^*,r_0^*,r_1^*}$ defined as follows:
  - If $\mathsf{pp} = \mathsf{pp}^*$ set $(r_0, r_1) = (r_0^*, r_1^*)$. Else evaluate $(r_0, r_1) \leftarrow \mathsf{PRF}(K\{\mathsf{pp}^*\}, \mathsf{pp})$.
  - Compute $(\mathsf{pk}, \mathsf{sk}) \leftarrow \mathsf{KeyGen}(\mathsf{pp}; r_0)$.
  - Return pk and $c \leftarrow \mathsf{PKEnc}(\mathsf{pk}^*, \mathsf{sk}; r_1)$.
  It is easy to see that the two circuits are functionally equivalent, and therefore computational indistinguishability follows from the security of Obf.
- $\mathsf{Hyb}_{i,2}$: In this hybrid, we proceed as before except that we substitute (r_0^*, r_1^*) with two uniformly random values. Indistinguishability follows by the security of the puncturable pseudorandom function.
- $\mathsf{Hyb}_{i,3}$: In this hybrid, we hardwire the outputs of key generation $\mathsf{KeyGen}(\mathsf{pp}^*; r_0^*)$ and encryption $\mathsf{PKEnc}(\mathsf{pk}^*, \mathsf{sk}; r_1^*)$ in the obfuscated circuit, instead of computing them on-the-fly. Indistinguishability follows once again by appealing to the security of the obfuscation scheme.
- $\mathsf{Hyb}_{i,4}$: We substitute the hardwired c with an encryption of 0. Indistinguishability follows by the semantic security of the public-key encryption scheme.

After we have switched all distributions for all calls to the honest key generation algorithm, we can see that the security of the modified scheme follows by a simple reduction to the security of the underlying RBE. For calls to the honest key generation algorithm, the reduction hardwires the public keys sampled by the old KeyGen algorithm in the obfuscated circuit, as shown above. Since the key curator is acting honestly, the public parameters are always kept consistent across the experiment. Thus, the adversarial advantage in breaking the new scheme is bounded by that against the old scheme, up to some negligible factors lost in the above hybrid transitions.

We remark that, because of the programming argument in the proof, we have to scale up the size of the obfuscated circuit to be able to contain the largest key. Since the size of the key potentially depends on the current number of users, this means that we need to set an upper-bound on the total number of users, that one needs to be aware when running the key generation algorithm.

6   CRS Re-randomizable RBE

We construct a CRS re-randomizable RBE. We start by constructing a re-randomizable hash encryption and then compile it into a re-randomizable RBE.

6.1   Key Re-randomizable Hash Encryption

We construct a hash encryption according to the definition of [11]. The construction is heavily inspired by the chameleon encryption from CDH by [10] for a p (prime)-order group $\mathbb{G}$ and detailed in Proposition 5.

Construction 4. *We construct the algorithms of the hash encryption scheme.*

$\mathsf{Gen}(1^\lambda, n) \to k$: *For each $j \in [n]$, sample $\alpha_{j,0}, \alpha_{j,1} \xleftarrow{\$} \mathbb{Z}_p^*$ uniformly at random and compute $g_{j,0} \leftarrow g^{\alpha_{j,0}}$ and $g_{j,1} \leftarrow g^{\alpha_{j,1}}$.*

$$\text{Output } k := \left(g, \begin{pmatrix} g_{1,0} \; g_{2,0} \; \cdots \; g_{n,0} \\ g_{1,1} \; g_{2,1} \; \cdots \; g_{n,1} \end{pmatrix} \right)$$

$\mathsf{H}(k, x) \to h$:
  - *Parse k as above and $x \in \{0,1\}^n$.*
  - *Output $h := \prod_{j=1}^n g_{j,x_j}$.*

$\mathsf{Enc}(k, (h, i, b), \mathsf{m}) \to \mathsf{ct}$:
  - *Parse k as above, $(h, i, b) \in \mathbb{G} \times [n] \times \{0,1\}$, and $\mathsf{m} \in \{0,1\}$.*
  - *Sample $\rho \xleftarrow{\$} \mathbb{Z}_p$ uniformly at random.*
  - *Let $c \leftarrow h^\rho$.*
  - *For every $j \in [n] \setminus \{i\}$, set $c_{j,0} \leftarrow g_{j,0}^\rho$ and $c_{j,1} \leftarrow g_{j,1}^\rho$.*
  - *Let $c_{i,0} \leftarrow \bot$ and $c_{i,1} \leftarrow \bot$.*
  - *Let $e := \mathsf{m} \oplus GL(g_{i,b}^\rho)$.*
  - *Output $\mathsf{ct} := \left(e, c, \begin{pmatrix} c_{1,0} \; c_{2,0} \; \cdots \; c_{n,0} \\ c_{1,1} \; c_{2,1} \; \cdots \; c_{n,1} \end{pmatrix} \right)$.*

$\mathsf{Dec}(k, x, \mathsf{ct}) \to \mathsf{m}$:
  - *Parse k as above, $x \in \{0,1\}^n$, and ct as above.*
  - *Output $\mathsf{m} = e \oplus GL\left(\frac{c}{\prod_{j \in [n] \setminus \{i\}} c_{j,x_j}} \right)$.*

We show that it is a hash encryption according to the definition of [11] even with a semi-honestly re-randomized key. Formally, we prove the following two properties:

Perfect Correctness. For all $i \in [n]$, $x \in \{0,1\}^n$, $m \in \{0,1\}$, and $k \in \mathbb{G} \times \mathbb{G}^{2 \times n}$, we have

$$\mathsf{Dec}(k, x, \mathsf{Enc}(k, (\mathsf{H}(k, x), i, x_i), m)) = m.$$

Proof. We have $\mathsf{H}(k, x) = \prod_{j=1}^n g_{j,x_j} = h$. Then, we have

$$\mathsf{Enc}(k, (h, i, x_i), m)$$

$$= \left(e = \mathsf{GL}(g_{i,x_i}^\rho) \oplus m, c = \prod_{j=1}^n g_{j,x_j}^\rho, (c_{j,0}, c_{j,1}) = (g_{j,0}^\rho, g_{j,1}^\rho)_{j \in [n] \setminus \{i\}} \right)$$

$$= ct$$

and

$$\mathsf{Dec}(k, x, ct) = e \oplus \mathsf{GL} \left(\frac{\prod_{j=1}^n g_{j,x_j}^\rho}{\prod_{j \in [n] \setminus \{i\}} g_{j,x_j}^\rho} \right) = \mathsf{GL}(g_{i,x_i}^\rho) \oplus \mathsf{GL}(g_{i,x_i}^\rho) \oplus m = m.$$

Re-randomizable Key. We add two new algorithms to the construction: SampleRand and ReRand. SampleRand samples randomness for the re-randomization and ReRand re-randomizes the key. More specifically, the syntax of these algorithms is as follows:

SampleRand$(1^\lambda, n) \rightarrow$ rand: Takes as input the security parameter λ and integer n and outputs randomness rand.

ReRand$(k, \mathsf{rand}) \rightarrow k'$: Takes as input a key k and randomness rand and outputs a new key k'.

We then want the following properties to hold:

Definition 14 (Re-Randomizable Key). *For all keys k, we have that a re-randomized key $k' \leftarrow \mathsf{ReRand}(k, \mathsf{SampleRand}(1^\lambda, n))$ is identically distributed to $\mathsf{Gen}(1^\lambda, n)$.*

Definition 15 (Re-Randomizing One-Wayness). *For all keys k and $k' \leftarrow \mathsf{Gen}(1^\lambda, n)$ we have that any PPT adversary $\mathsf{Adv}(k, k')$ only has a negligible probability of computing an r such that $k' = \mathsf{ReRand}(k, r)$.*

Definition 16 (Security with Re-Randomized Key). *A hash encryption is secure with re-randomized key if for all PPT adversaries Adv_1 and Adv_2, $n \in \mathbb{N}$, $x \in \{0,1\}^n$ there exists a negligible function negl such that for all $\lambda \in \mathbb{N}$ the adversary's probability of winning the following experiment is $1/2 + \mathsf{negl}(\lambda)$:*

1. *Let $k_0 \leftarrow \mathsf{Gen}(1^\lambda, n)$.*
2. *Let $(i, m_0, m_1, l, (\mathsf{rand}_j)_{j \in [l]}, st) \leftarrow \mathsf{Adv}_1(k_0)$.*
3. *For $j \in [l]$ let $k_j \leftarrow \mathsf{ReRand}(k_{j-1}, \mathsf{rand}_j)$.*
4. *Sample $b \xleftarrow{\$} \{0,1\}$ uniformly at random.*
5. *Let $ct \leftarrow \mathsf{Enc}(k_l, (\mathsf{H}(k_l, x), i, 1 - x_i), m_b)$.*
6. *Let $b' \leftarrow \mathsf{Adv}_2(st, k_l, ct)$.*
7. *The adversary wins if $b' = b$.*

Extending DGHM. For Construction 4 we define the algorithms SampleRand and ReRand as follows:

SampleRand($1^\lambda, n$): For each $j \in [n]$, sample $\beta_{j,0}, \beta_{j,1} \xleftarrow{\$} \mathbb{Z}_p^*$ uniformly at random.

$$\text{Output rand} := \begin{pmatrix} \beta_{1,0} \ \beta_{2,0} \ \cdots \ \beta_{n,0} \\ \beta_{1,1} \ \beta_{2,1} \ \cdots \ \beta_{n,1} \end{pmatrix}.$$

ReRand(k, rand):
  - Parse k as above and rand $= (\beta_{i,j})_{i \in [n], j \in \{0,1\}}$.
  - Output $k' := \left(g, \begin{pmatrix} g_{1,0}^{\beta_{1,0}} \ g_{2,0}^{\beta_{2,0}} \ \cdots \ g_{n,0}^{\beta_{n,0}} \\ g_{1,1}^{\beta_{1,1}} \ g_{2,1}^{\beta_{2,1}} \ \cdots \ g_{n,1}^{\beta_{n,1}} \end{pmatrix} \right).$

Proposition 3 (Re-Randomizable Key). *Construction 4 has a re-randomizable key according to Definition 14.*

Proof. For all $k \in (\mathbb{G} \setminus \{1\})^{2 \times n}$, we have that

$$k' \leftarrow \text{ReRand}(k, \text{SampleRand}(1^\lambda, n))$$

and Gen($1^\lambda, n$) are uniform distributions over $(\mathbb{G} \setminus \{1\})^{2 \times n}$.

Proposition 4. *In Construction 4 re-randomizion is one-way according to Definition 15.*

Proof. The key of the hash function has $2n$ elements but for this argument we only need to look at a single fixed one, say the position $(1, 1)$. Because the adversary Adv can depend on the key k there also exists an adversary Adv' that has non-uniform advice of the discrete logarithm of the $(1, 1)$-th element of k and can break the discrete logarithm.

  Adv'$(h)[\alpha]$:
  - Has non-uniform advise α such that $g^\alpha = k_{1,1}$.
  - Sample $k' \xleftarrow{\$} (\mathbb{G} \setminus \{1\})^{2 \times n}$ uniformly at random.
  - Replace $k'_{1,1}$ by h^α.
  - Get $(d_{i,j})_{i \in \{0,1\}, j \in [n]} \leftarrow \text{Adv}_k(k')$.
  - Output $d_{1,1}$.

The modified k' that Adv receives has the correct distribution as all elements are uniform over $\mathbb{G} \setminus \{1\}$, so Adv behave like it does on a real challenge with respect to k. If Adv has an output that breaks one-wayness of the re-randomization then $h^\alpha = k'_{1,1} = k_{1,1}^{d_{1,1}} = g^{\alpha d_{1,1}}$. Therefore, $g^{d_{1,1}} = h$ and Adv' wins as well.

Proposition 5 (Security with Re-Randomized Key). *The hash encryption of Construction 4 is secure with re-randomizable key according to Definition 16.*

Proof. This proof follows the security proof of the chameleon encryption of [10] up to the details of the re-randomized key. We prove via reduction to CDH. Given an adversary Adv that can win the security with re-randomizable key game with non-negligible advantage we construct an adversary Adv' that can win the CDH game over group $(\mathbb{G}, p, g)$ with non-negligible advantage.

$\mathsf{Adv}'(g, U, V)$:

- For $j \in [n]$:
  - Sample $\alpha_{j,0}, \alpha_{j,1} \xleftarrow{\$} \mathbb{Z}_p^*$ uniformly at random.
  - Let $g_{j,0} = g^{\alpha_{j,0}}$ and $g_{j,1} = g^{\alpha_{j,1}}$.
- Sample $x^* \xleftarrow{\$} \{0,1\}$ and $i^* \xleftarrow{\$} [n]$ uniformly at random.
- Replace $g_{i^*, 1-x_i}$ by U.
- Let $k := \left(g, \begin{pmatrix} g_{1,0} & g_{2,0} & \cdots & g_{n,0} \\ g_{1,1} & g_{2,1} & \cdots & g_{n,1} \end{pmatrix} \right)$.
- Let $(i, m_0, m_1, l, (\text{rand}_j)_{j \in [l]}, st) \leftarrow \mathsf{Adv}_1(k)$ where

$$\text{rand}_j = \begin{pmatrix} \beta_{1,0}^{(j)} & \beta_{2,0}^{(j)} & \cdots & \beta_{n,0}^{(j)} \\ \beta_{1,1}^{(j)} & \beta_{2,1}^{(j)} & \cdots & \beta_{n,1}^{(j)} \end{pmatrix}$$

- Let $\beta := \begin{pmatrix} \beta_{1,0} := \prod_{i \in [l]} \beta_{1,0}^{(i)} & \beta_{2,0} := \prod_{i \in [l]} \beta_{2,0}^{(i)} & \cdots & \beta_{n,0} := \prod_{i \in [l]} \beta_{n,0}^{(i)} \\ \beta_{1,1} := \prod_{i \in [l]} \beta_{1,1}^{(i)} & \beta_{2,1} := \prod_{i \in [l]} \beta_{2,1}^{(i)} & \cdots & \beta_{n,1} := \prod_{i \in [l]} \beta_{n,1}^{(i)} \end{pmatrix}$

- Let $k' := \left(g, \begin{pmatrix} g_{1,0}^{\beta_{1,0}} & g_{2,0}^{\beta_{2,0}} & \cdots & g_{n,0}^{\beta_{n,0}} \\ g_{1,1}^{\beta_{1,1}} & g_{2,1}^{\beta_{2,1}} & \cdots & g_{n,1}^{\beta_{n,1}} \end{pmatrix} \right)$.

- If $i \neq i^*$ or $x^* \neq x_i$ output a uniformly random bit $b \xleftarrow{\$} \{0,1\}$.
- Otherwise:
  - Let $V' := V^{\beta_{i^*, 1-x^*}^{-1}}$.
  - Let $ct := \left(e, c, \begin{pmatrix} c_{1,0}, c_{2,0}, \ldots, c_{n,0} \\ c_{1,1}, c_{2,1}, \ldots, c_{n,1} \end{pmatrix} \right)$ where

    $c := V', e \xleftarrow{\$} \{0,1\}$, for all $j \in [n] \setminus \{i\}$ we have $c_{j,0} := V'^{\alpha_{j,0} \cdot \beta_{j,0}}, c_{j,1} := V'^{\alpha_{j,1} \cdot \beta_{j,1}}$

  - $b \leftarrow \mathsf{Adv}_2(st, k', ct)$.
  - Output $b \oplus e$.

Observe that the distribution of k is identical to that of Gen. This implies that the view of Adv_1 is identical to the one in the experiment. We call the event that $i = i^*$ and $x = x^*$ event E. The event E happens with probability $\frac{1}{2n}$. Conditioned on E we have that the view of Adv_2 is identically distributed to the view in the experiment where ct is an encryption of $e \oplus \mathsf{GL}(g^{u \cdot v})$, where $U = g^u$ and $V = g^v$. Now if Adv_2 correctly predicts $e \oplus \mathsf{GL}(g^{u \cdot v})$ with non-negligible probability then Adv' predicts $\mathsf{GL}(g^{u \cdot v})$ with non-negligible probability.

6.2 Compiling to CRS Re-randomizable RBE

We compile a key re-randomizable hash encryption into a CRS re-randomizable RBE. A CRS re-randomizable RBE is an RBE with two extra algorithms SampleRand that samples randomness for the re-randomization and ReRand that re-randomizes the CRS. These algorithms have the following syntax:

SampleRand(1^λ) $\rightarrow$ rand: Takes as input the security parameter λ and outputs randomness rand.

ReRand$^{[\text{aux}]}$(crs, rand) $\rightarrow$ crs': Takes as input a crs and rand and outputs a new crs'.

further, we amend the syntax for Setup slightly.

Setup$(1^\lambda, i) \rightarrow$ crs: Takes as input the security parameter λ an index i and outputs a common reference string crs.

In addition to previous RBE properties, we need the following three properties to hold.

Definition 17 (Re-Randomizable CRS). *For all* $i \in [2^\lambda]$ *and* crs *from the range of* Setup$(1^\lambda, i - 1)$, *we have* ReRand(crs, SampleRand(1^λ)) *is identically distributed as* Setup$(1^\lambda, i)$.

Definition 18 (Re-Randomizing One-Wayness). *For all* $i \in [2^\lambda]$ *and CRS* crs *from the range of* Setup$(1^\lambda, i - 1)$ *and* crs$'$ $\leftarrow$ Setup$(1^\lambda, i)$ *we have that any randomized sub-exponential time adversary* Adv(crs, crs$'$) *only has a negligible probability of computing an* r *such that* crs$'$ $=$ ReRand(crs, r).

Definition 19 (CRS Re-Randomizable RBE Security). *Consider the following game between an interactive PPT adversary* Adv *and a challenger* Chal*:*

1. *Initialization:* Chal *sets* pp $\leftarrow \bot$, aux $\leftarrow \bot$, $u \leftarrow \bot$, ID $\leftarrow \emptyset$, id$^* \leftarrow \bot$, $t \leftarrow 0$, crs $\leftarrow$ Setup$(1^\lambda, 0)$ *and sends* crs *to* Adv.
2. *Every round* Adv *does one of these actions:*
   (a) *Registering a new (non-target) identity:* Adv *sends a new identity* id $\notin$ ID *and its corresponding public key* pk *to* Chal. Chal *registers the public key* pk *on identity* id *and obtains an update* $u =$ Reg$^{[\text{aux}]}$(crs, pp, id, pk) *and updated (non-target) list* ID $\leftarrow$ ID $\cup$ {id}.
   (b) *Registering the target identity: If the target identity* id* *is already chosen then do nothing. Otherwise,* Adv *sends a target identity* id* *to* Chal. *If* id$^* \notin$ ID *then* Chal *samples an honest public key and secret key pair* (pk*, sk*) $\leftarrow$ KeyGen(1^λ) *and update the public parameter* pp $\leftarrow$ Reg$^{[\text{aux}]}$(crs, pp, id*, pk*), ID $\leftarrow$ ID $\cup$ {id*}, *and sends* pk* *to* Adv.
   (c) *Re-randomizing the CRS: The challenger* Chal *receives* rand *from* Adv *and re-randomizes the CRS* crs $\leftarrow$ ReRand(crs, rand). *Then, the challenger* Chal *re-registers all users using the new* crs *in the following way. Let* n *be the number of users that have already been registered and* (id$_i$, pk$_i$) *be the identity and public key pair of the* $i-$th *registered user. (This information can be read from the auxiliary information* aux.*) First, clear the auxiliary information* aux. *Then, compute* pp$_1 \leftarrow$ Reg$^{[\text{aux}]}$(crs, $\bot$, id$_1$, pk$_1$) *and then for each* $i = 2, \cdots, n$, *compute* pp$_i \leftarrow$ Reg$^{[\text{aux}]}$(crs, pp$_{i-1}$, id$_i$, pk$_i$). *Finally, set* pp $\leftarrow$ pp$_n$ *and send* crs *to the adversary* Adv.
3. *Encrypting for target identity: If no target identity* id* *is chosen* Adv *sends* id* *to the challenger* Chal *first. Then the challenger* Chal *samples a random bit* $b \leftarrow \{0, 1\}$, *compute its encryption to the target identity* ct$^* \leftarrow$ Enc(crs, pp, id*, b) *and sends* ct* *to* Adv.
4. Adv *outputs a bit* b' *and wins the game if* $b = b'$.

We call a CRS Re-Randomizable RBE secure if the probability of any sub-exponential adversary Adv*'s winning in the above game is* $< 1/2 + \text{negl}(\lambda)$.

The completeness definition of registration-based encryption can be similarly adapted to CRS re-randomizable RBE by adding a re-randomization query. Since the modification is mainly syntactic and not fundamental, we omit it here.

We now show that with minor modifications the registration-based encryption of [16] based on hash encryption is a CRS re-randomizable RBE. The only changes we need to make are specific to re-randomizing and keeping track of the number of re-randomizations.

Construction 5. *Let* RBE′ = (Setup, KeyGen, Reg, Upd, Enc, Dec) *be the RBE of [16] and* HashEnc = (Gen, H, Enc, Dec, SampleRand, ReRand) *be the key re-randomizable hash encryption used to instantiate the hash encryption of* RBE′. *We define the CRS re-randomizable RBE* RBE *as follows:*

Setup($1^\lambda, i$):
- Let $k \leftarrow$ HashEnc.Gen($1^\lambda, n$) *for some n as determined by the RBE construction in [16].*
- *Output* crs $\leftarrow$ (crs′ := k, i), *where* crs′ *is exactly the CRS of* RBE′.

KeyGen(λ): *Output* (pk, sk) $\leftarrow$ RBE′.KeyGen(λ).

Reg$^{[\text{aux}]}$((crs′, t), pp, id, pk):
- *Split* aux *into* aux′ *and* aux*, *where* aux′ *is the auxiliary information for* RBE′.
- *Store* (id, pk) *in* aux*.
- *Output* pp′ $\leftarrow$ RBE′.Reg$^{[\text{aux}']}$(crs′, pp, id, pk).

Upd^{aux}(pp, id):
- *Split* aux *into* aux′ *and* aux*, *where* aux′ *is the auxiliary information for* RBE′.
- *Output* $u \leftarrow$ RBE′.Upd$^{\text{aux}'}$(pp, id).

Enc((crs′, t), pp, id, b):
- *Let* ct′ $\leftarrow$ RBE′.Enc(crs′, pp, id, b).
- *Output* (ct′, t).

Dec((crs′, t), sk, u, ct = (ct′, t^*)):
- *If* $t^* = t$ *then output* RBE′.Dec(crs′, sk, u, ct′).
- *Else output* GetUpd.

We add the following two algorithms to the construction, in which we crucially use the fact that the CRS is exactly the key of the hash encryption and that the hash encryption is re-randomizable.

SampleRand(1^λ): *Output rand* $\leftarrow$ HashEnc.SampleRand($1^\lambda, n$).

ReRand((crs′, t), *rand*):
- *Parse* crs′ *as* k.
- *Let* $k' \leftarrow$ HashEnc.ReRand(k, *rand*).
- *Output* crs = (crs′ = $k', t+1$).

Correctness, compactness, and efficiency directly follows from the correctness, compactness, and efficiency of the RBE of [16].

CRS re-randomizability and one-wayness of the re-randomization follow directly from the fact that the CRS is only a key of a re-randomizeable hash encryption with these properties and a counter.

CRS re-randomizable security follows from the property of the RBE of [16] that the CRS is only used for hash encryptions and Proposition 5, which tells us that the hash encryption stays secure, even if the CRS is re-randomized. They only make black-box use of the security property in the reduction, therefore, the re-randomizable RBE security follows from their proof straightforwardly.

7   Lower Bound on Number of Updates

In this section, we show that $\Omega(n)$ number of updates is necessary for RBE without CRS under two mild assumptions that are satisfied by known constructions.

Assumptions

The first assumption is about fixed update times, as in Definition 2.4 in [27]. Conceptually, this assumption states that the time when a registered user requires an update is fixed and known. We capture this using a DAG, where the i−th user is represented by vertex i and an edge from i to j means that the i−th registered user needs an update immediately after the registration of the j−th user. Since an user can receive updates only after it has already been registered, it is clear that in such graphs edges can only go from smaller vertices to larger vertices, which we refer to as *Forward DAGs*.

Definition 20 (Forward DAGs). *Let $G = (\mathcal{V}_G, \mathcal{E}_G)$ be a directed acyclic graph (DAG) with vertices $\mathcal{V}_G = [n]$ (in case of being finite) or $\mathcal{V}_G = \mathbb{N}$ (in case of being infinite). We write $(i,j) \in G$ if $(i,j) \in \mathcal{E}_G$ (i.e., there is an edge from i to j in G). We call G a forward DAG, if for all $(i,j) \in G$, we have $i \leq j$.*

With the use of Forward DAGs, we state our first assumption. Conceptually, we say that an RBE scheme has fixed update times according to a forward DAG G if completeness of the scheme holds when user i receives an update at time j for every edge $(i,j) \in G$. In particular, we demand each decryption query to return a message. This is in contrast with the original completeness of RBE where a decryption query can return the special symbol GetUpd, upon seeing which an user can request decryption update. Since we are assuming a user only needs updates at times specified in the forward DAG and every user is indeed given the required update at the right time, decryption query should never output GetUpd.

Definition 21 (Completeness of RBE with fixed update times). *Let G be an infinite forward DAG. For an RBE scheme and any interactive computationally unbounded adversary Adv that still has a limited $\text{poly}(\lambda)$ round complexity, consider the game $\text{UpdTimes}^G_{\text{Adv}}(\lambda)$ between Adv and a challenger Chal as follows.*

1. *Initialization.* Chal *sets* pp $= \perp$, aux $= \perp$, u $= \perp$, $\mathcal{D} = \emptyset$, $\mathcal{S} = \emptyset$, $t = 0$, *and* crs $\leftarrow U_{\text{poly}(\lambda)}$, *and sends the sampled* crs *to* Adv.
2. *Till* Adv *continues (which is at most* $\text{poly}(\lambda)$ *steps), proceed as follows. At every iteration,* Adv *chooses exactly one of the actions below to perform.*

(a) **Registering identities.** Adv *performs exactly one out of Step 2(a)i and Step 2(a)ii below, but regardless of this choice,* Chal *will continue to send the updates as described next.*

   i. **Registering a corrupted non-target identity.** Adv *sends some* id $\notin \mathcal{D}$ *and* pk *to* Chal. Chal *registers* (id, pk) *by letting* pp := $\mathsf{Reg}^{[\mathsf{aux}]}$(crs, pp, id, pk) *and* $\mathcal{D} := \mathcal{D} \cup \{\mathsf{id}\}$.

   ii. **Registering the target uncorrupted identity.** *This step is allowed only if* id* = $\bot$. *In that case,* Adv *sends some* id* $\notin \mathcal{D}$ *to* Chal. Chal *then samples* (pk*, sk*) $\leftarrow$ KeyGen(1^λ), *runs* pp := $\mathsf{Reg}^{[\mathsf{aux}]}$(crs, pp, id*, pk*), $\mathcal{D}$:= $\mathcal{D} \cup \{\mathsf{id}^*\}$, *and sends* pk* *to* Adv.

   Immediately updating the target identity, if required by G. *This step is allowed only if* id* $\neq \bot$ *(otherwise this step is skipped). Suppose* id* *was the ith registered identity, and let the identity registered in either of Step 2(a)i Step or 2(a)ii be the jth identity. If* $(i, j) \in G$ *(i.e., there is an edge from i to j), then we update the decryption information* u = $\mathsf{Upd}^{\mathsf{aux}}$(pp, id*) *for the target identity.*

(b) **Encrypting for the target identity.** *This step is allowed only if* id* $\neq \bot$. *In that case,* Chal *sets* $t = t + 1$. Adv *sends* $m_t \in \{0, 1\}^*$ *to* Chal *who then sets* $m'_t := m_t$ *and sends back a corresponding ciphertext* $ct_t \leftarrow$ Enc(crs, pp, id*, m_t) *to* Adv.

(c) **Decryption for the target identity.** Adv *sends* $j \in [t]$ *to* Chal *who lets* $m'_j =$ Dec(sk*, u, ct_j).

The adversary Adv *wins above, if there is some* $j \in [t]$ *for which* $m'_j \neq m_j$. *This particularly holds, e.g., if* $m'_j =$ GetUpd. *We say that* G *is an update graph for the RBE scheme, if* Pr[Adv *wins*] = negl(λ). *In this case, we also say that the completeness holds with fixed update graph* G.

The second assumption states that encryption and decryption succeed if and only if one can recover part of the public parameters from the update witness. This is motivated by known constructions, where the update witness is the opening of a succinct commitment and the decryption recomputes some public information depending on the index. As an example, it is useful to keep in mind the example of Merkle-tree based schemes, where the witness is just a root-to-leaf path, which in particular allows one to recompute the root of the tree.

Definition 22 (PP-recoverability). *Let* Π = (Setup, KeyGen, Reg, Upd, Enc, Dec) *be an RBE scheme with completeness probability* ρ. *We say* Π *is* pp-recoverable *if there exist two deterministic algorithms* Ext$_1$ *and* Ext$_2$ *such that for all* pp, crs, id, u, *and any* (pk, sk) $\in$ KeyGen(1^λ), *there exists an index* i *such that*

$$\mathsf{Ext}_1(\mathsf{crs}, (\mathsf{id}, \mathsf{pk}), \mathsf{u}) = \mathsf{Ext}_2(\mathsf{crs}, \mathsf{pp}, i)$$

if and only if

$$\Pr[\mathsf{Dec}(\mathsf{sk}, \mathsf{u}, \mathsf{Enc}(\mathsf{crs}, \mathsf{pp}, \mathsf{id}, \mathsf{m})) = \mathsf{m}] \geq \rho$$

for any message m.

Justification for the Two Assumptions. We use the construction in the first RBE paper [15] as a concrete example to illustrate and justify the assumptions since follow-up works all follow the same paradigm of accumulating identity and key pairs into succinct commitments and encrypting with respect to the commitments. The construction works in the following way: KC maintains a list of Merkle trees where the leaves are the identity and key pairs and publish roots as public parameters. An update for a user is an opening for the corresponding identity and key leaf in the tree. Encryption is an obfuscated program which first checks that the identity and key provided by whoever wishes to decrypt are consistent with one of the roots in the public parameter and then outputs an encryption of the message using the provided key. To justify fixed update times assumption, note that an update is needed if and only if two trees are merged and the times when two trees are merged only depend on the number of registered users. To justify PP-recoverability, note that to verify an identity and key pair, one uses the pair and an opening to re-compute a root and check it against the published roots. If there is a valid opening for some identity and key pair that results in one of the roots, then the obfuscated program will accept the public key and use it to generate an encryption, which can be decrypted using the corresponding secret key. Some papers use other scheme than Merkle trees, such as vector commitment scheme [19]. However, since the underlying ideas are the same, the assumptions still hold.

Proof of Main Result

Theorem 6 (Main Result). *Let Π be an RBE scheme without CRS satisfying (1) completeness with fixed update times in Definition 21, (2) one honest user security in Definition 13, and (3) pp-recoverability in Definition 22. Then, the number of decryption updates cannot be $o(n)$.*

The proof takes the following main steps.

1. Define the concept of a good tuple (i, n) for an RBE scheme Π.
2. Show that if (i, n) is a good tuple then the ith identity requires a decryption update at time $n + 1$.
3. Show that there are $\Omega(n)$ many good tuples of the form (i, n) for every n. Then, by a simple counting argument, the result follows.

Definition 23 (Good Tuple). *Let $\Pi =$ (Setup, KeyGen, Reg, Upd, Enc, Dec) be an RBE scheme without CRS. We say (i, n), where $1 \leq i \leq n$, is a good tuple for Π if there exist*

1. *$((\mathsf{pk}_1, \mathsf{sk}_1), \cdots, (\mathsf{pk}_n, \mathsf{sk}_n))$ where $(\mathsf{pk}_j, \mathsf{sk}_j) \leftarrow \mathsf{KeyGen}(1^\lambda)$, and*
2. *$(\mathsf{id}_1, \cdots, \mathsf{id}_n)$ and $(\mathsf{id}'_1, \cdots, \mathsf{id}'_n)$ where $\mathsf{id}'_i \notin (\mathsf{id}_1, \cdots, \mathsf{id}_n)$*

satisfying $H^n_{n,\mathsf{pk}_1,\cdots,\mathsf{pk}_n}(\mathsf{id}_1, \cdots, \mathsf{id}_n) = H^n_{\mathsf{pk}_1,\cdots,\mathsf{pk}_n}(\mathsf{id}'_1, \cdots, \mathsf{id}'_n)$, where

$$H^{i+1}_{\mathsf{pk}_1,\cdots,\mathsf{pk}_n}(\mathsf{id}_1, \cdots, \mathsf{id}_{i+1}) := \mathsf{Reg}^{[\mathsf{aux}]}(H^i_{\mathsf{pk}_1,\cdots,\mathsf{pk}_n}(\mathsf{id}_1, \cdots, \mathsf{id}_i), \mathsf{id}_{i+1}, \mathsf{pk}_{i+1})$$

for $i = 0, \cdots, n-1$ and $H^0_{\mathsf{pk}_1,\cdots,\mathsf{pk}_n} = \bot$.

Lemma 1. *Let $\Pi = (\mathsf{Setup}, \mathsf{KeyGen}, \mathsf{Reg}, \mathsf{Upd}, \mathsf{Enc}, \mathsf{Dec})$ be an RBE scheme without CRS satisfying (1) completeness with fixed update times, (2) one honest user security, and (3) pp-recoverability. Let G be the update graph for Π. If (i, n) is a good tuple for Π, then $(i, n + 1)$ is an edge in G.*

Proof. For contradiction, assume $(i, n + 1)$ is not an edge in G. We will show that there exists a non-uniform adversary breaking the security of Π.

First of all, since (i, n) is a good tuple for Π, the following advice must exist.

Advice:

- i, n.
- $(\mathsf{pk}_1, \mathsf{sk}_1), \cdots, (\mathsf{pk}_n, \mathsf{sk}_n))$ where each $(\mathsf{pk}_j, \mathsf{sk}_j) \leftarrow \mathsf{KeyGen}(1^\lambda)$.
- $(\mathsf{id}_1, \cdots, \mathsf{id}_n)$ and $(\mathsf{id}'_1, \cdots, \mathsf{id}'_n)$ satisfying $id'_i \notin (\mathsf{id}_1, \cdots, \mathsf{id}_n)$ and

$$H^n_{\mathsf{pk}_1, \cdots, \mathsf{pk}_n}(\mathsf{id}_1, \cdots, \mathsf{id}_n) = H^n_{\mathsf{pk}_1, \cdots, \mathsf{pk}_n}(\mathsf{id}'_1, \cdots, \mathsf{id}'_n).$$

Given the above advice, we construct the following non-uniform adversary.

Adversary:

1. Send each $(\mathsf{id}_j, \mathsf{pk}_j)$ for $j = 1, \ldots, n$ to Chal to register. (After this step, Chal will update the public parameter to pp_n.)
2. Send id'_i to Chal to register as the honest user. Note that this is legitimate since $id'_i \notin (\mathsf{id}_1, \cdots, \mathsf{id}_n)$. (In the view of Chal, id'_i is the identity of the $(n + 1)$th user id_{n+1}. After this step, Chal will update the public parameter to pp_{n+1}.)
3. Locally register $(\mathsf{id}'_j, \mathsf{pk}_j)$ for $j = 1, \ldots, n$ and generate decryption update u'_i for id'_i.
4. Ask Chal to send $\mathsf{ct} \leftarrow \mathsf{Enc}(\mathsf{pp}_{n+1}, \mathsf{id}_{n+1} = \mathsf{id}'_i, b)$.
5. Output $\mathsf{Dec}(\mathsf{sk}_i, \mathsf{u}'_i, \mathsf{ct})$.

Legitimacy. Clearly, the adversary is efficient. Also, the attack is legitimate since there is one honest user $\mathsf{id}_{n+1} = \mathsf{id}'_i \notin (\mathsf{id}_1, \cdots, \mathsf{id}_n)$.

Noticeable Advantage. Let u_i be the decryption update generated for id_i after registering $(\mathsf{id}_j, \mathsf{pk}_j)$ for $j = 1, \ldots, n$ and recall that in the attack u'_i is the decryption update generated for id'_i after registering $(\mathsf{id}'_j, \mathsf{pk}_j)$ for $j = 1, \ldots, n$.

We first show that $\mathsf{Ext}_1((\mathsf{id}_i, \mathsf{pk}_i), \mathsf{u}_i) = \mathsf{Ext}_1((\mathsf{id}'_i, \mathsf{pk}_i), \mathsf{u}'_i)$. Note that by construction, we must have $\mathsf{Ext}_1((\mathsf{id}_i, \mathsf{pk}_i), \mathsf{u}_i) = \mathsf{Ext}_2(\mathsf{pp}_n, i)$ due to completeness and pp-recoverability. Similarly, we must have $\mathsf{Ext}_1((\mathsf{id}'_i, \mathsf{pk}_i), \mathsf{u}'_i) = \mathsf{Ext}_2(\mathsf{pp}_n, i)$.

We then show that $\mathsf{Ext}_1((\mathsf{id}_i, \mathsf{pk}_i), \mathsf{u}_i) = \mathsf{Ext}_2(\mathsf{pp}_{n+1}, i)$. Since $(i, n + 1) \notin G$, we have

$$\Pr[\mathsf{Dec}(\mathsf{sk}_i, \mathsf{u}_i, \mathsf{Enc}(\mathsf{pp}_{n+1}, \mathsf{id}_i, \mathsf{m})) = \mathsf{m}] \geq \rho$$

for any message m, by completeness. By pp-recoverability, we must have that

$$\mathsf{Ext}_1((\mathsf{id}_i, \mathsf{pk}_i), \mathsf{u}_i) = \mathsf{Ext}_2(\mathsf{pp}_{n+1}, i)$$

We thus have $\mathsf{Ext}_1((\mathsf{id}'_i, \mathsf{pk}_i), u'_i) = \mathsf{Ext}_2(\mathsf{pp}_{n+1}, i)$. Then, by pp-recoverability, we must have

$$\Pr[\mathsf{Dec}(\mathsf{sk}_i, u'_i, \mathsf{Enc}(\mathsf{pp}_{n+1}, \mathsf{id}'_i, m)) = m] \geq \rho$$

for any message m.

In the following, let α be the length of the public parameter, β be the length of the identity and γ be the upper bound for number of decryption updates.

Proposition 6. *Let $\Pi = (\mathsf{Setup}, \mathsf{KeyGen}, \mathsf{Reg}, \mathsf{Upd}, \mathsf{Enc}, \mathsf{Dec})$ be an RBE scheme. Let n be a positive integer. Then there are at least $(1 - \frac{\log n}{\beta}) \cdot n - \frac{\alpha}{\beta}$ good tuples of the form (i, n).*

Proof. Fix n pairs of keys $(\mathsf{pk}_1, \mathsf{sk}_1), \cdots, (\mathsf{pk}_n, \mathsf{sk}_n)$. There are $\binom{2^\beta}{n}$ distinct sets of n identities. We identify each of them as an ordered list of identities. Note that there are 2^α different public parameters.

- Suppose $\binom{2^\beta}{n} \leq 2^\alpha$. Since $0 \geq \log(\frac{\binom{2^\beta}{n}}{2^\alpha}) > (\beta - \log n) \cdot n - \alpha$, we know $(1 - \frac{\log n}{\beta}) \cdot n - \frac{\alpha}{\beta}$ is a lower bound for number of good tuples.
- Suppose $\binom{2^\beta}{n} > 2^\alpha$. Consider a public parameter pp such that $|(H^n_{\mathsf{pk}_1, \cdots, \mathsf{pk}_n})^{-1}(\mathsf{pp})| = \max_{\mathsf{pp}'} |(H^n_{\mathsf{pk}_1, \cdots, \mathsf{pk}_n})^{-1}(\mathsf{pp}')|$. Since $\binom{2^\beta}{n} > 2^\alpha$, we know $|(H^n_{\mathsf{pk}_1, \cdots, \mathsf{pk}_n})^{-1}(\mathsf{pp})| \geq 2$. Take two different lists of identities from $(H^n_{\mathsf{pk}_1, \cdots, \mathsf{pk}_n})^{-1}(\mathsf{pp})$. There must exist $i_1 \in [n]$ where the i_1th identity of one list does not belong to the other list. This means (i_1, n) is a good tuple.

  • Suppose $\frac{\binom{2^\beta}{n}}{2^\alpha} \leq 2^\beta$. Since $\beta \geq \log(\frac{\binom{2^\beta}{n}}{2^\alpha}) \geq (\beta - \log n) \cdot n - \alpha$, which implies $1 \geq (1 - \frac{\log n}{\beta}) \cdot n - \frac{\alpha}{\beta}$, we again have $(1 - \frac{\log n}{\beta}) \cdot n - \frac{\alpha}{\beta}$ as a lower bound for number of good tuples.

  • Suppose $\frac{\binom{2^\beta}{n}}{2^\alpha} > 2^\beta$. Let m be the largest positive integer such that $\frac{\binom{2^\beta}{n}}{2^\alpha} > (2^\beta)^m$. Consider the i_1th identity of every list in $(H^n_{\mathsf{pk}_1, \cdots, \mathsf{pk}_n})^{-1}(\mathsf{pp})$. Since there are only 2^β different values for identity and $\frac{\binom{2^\beta}{n}}{2^\alpha} > 2^\beta$, there must be two different lists of identities from $(H^n_{\mathsf{pk}_1, \cdots, \mathsf{pk}_n})^{-1}(\mathsf{pp})$ whose i_1th identities are the same. This means there must exist $i_2 \neq i_1$ such that (i_2, n) is a good tuple. Moreover, we know there must exist a value id_{i_1} such that there are at least $\frac{\binom{2^\beta}{n}}{2^\alpha \cdot 2^\beta}$ lists of identities in $(H^n_{\mathsf{pk}_1, \cdots, \mathsf{pk}_n})^{-1}(\mathsf{pp})$ whose i_1th identities have value id_{i_1}. One can proceed similarly again and show that there are at least $m + 1$ good tuples. By definition, we know $2^{(m+1) \cdot \beta} \geq \frac{\binom{2^\beta}{n}}{2^\alpha} \geq \frac{(2^\beta)^n}{2^\alpha}$. Equivalently, we have $(m + 1) \cdot \beta \geq (\beta - \log n) \cdot n - \alpha$. This means $(1 - \frac{\log n}{\beta}) \cdot n - \frac{\alpha}{\beta}$ is a lower bound for number of good tuples.

Proposition 7. *Let $\Pi = (\mathsf{Setup}, \mathsf{KeyGen}, \mathsf{Reg}, \mathsf{Upd}, \mathsf{Enc}, \mathsf{Dec})$ be an RBE scheme without CRS satisfying (1) completeness with fixed update times, (2) one honest user security, and (3) pp-recoverability. Let G be the update graph for Π. Let n be a positive integer. There exists an $i \in [n]$ with at least $(1 - \frac{\log n}{\beta}) \cdot \frac{n}{2} - \frac{\alpha}{\beta}$ out degrees in G_n, the graph G restricted to the first n vertices.*

Proof. For every $i \in [n-1]$, there are $(1 - \frac{\log i}{\beta}) \cdot i - \frac{\alpha}{\beta}$ good tuples of the form (j, i). This means $i + 1$ has at least $(1 - \frac{\log i}{\beta}) \cdot i - \frac{\alpha}{\beta}$ in degree. We thus know there are at least

$$\sum_{i=1}^{n-1} (1 - \frac{\log i}{\beta}) \cdot i - \frac{\alpha}{\beta} \geq \sum_{i=1}^{n-1} (1 - \frac{\log n}{\beta}) \cdot i - \frac{\alpha}{\beta} = (1 - \frac{\log n}{\beta}) \cdot \frac{n \cdot (n-1)}{2} - (n-1) \cdot \frac{\alpha}{\beta}$$

edges in G_n. Therefore, there exists an $i \in [n-1]$ with at least $(1 - \frac{\log n}{\beta}) \cdot \frac{n}{2} - \frac{\alpha}{\beta}$ out degrees in G_n.

Proof (Proof of Theorem 6). It remains to find a polynomial $n = \mathrm{poly}(\lambda)$, which can depend on α, β, and show that $(1 - \frac{\log n}{\beta}) \cdot \frac{n}{2} - \frac{\alpha}{\beta} > c \cdot n$ for some $c > 0$ and sufficiently large λ.

Note that $\alpha \leq \mathrm{poly}(\lambda, \log n)$ and $\beta = \mathrm{poly}(\lambda)$. Thus, we have $\frac{\alpha}{\beta} \leq \mathrm{poly}(\lambda, \log n) \leq \lambda^{c_1} \cdot (\log n)^{c_2}$ for sufficiently large λ. Take $n = \lambda^{2c_1}$. For sufficiently large λ, we have $1 - \frac{\log n}{\beta} > \frac{1}{2}$. We thus have $(1 - \frac{\log n}{\beta}) \cdot \frac{n}{2} - \frac{\alpha}{\beta} > \frac{n}{4} - \frac{\alpha}{\beta}$.

It is also obvious that

$$\frac{1}{8} \cdot n = \frac{1}{8} \cdot \lambda^{2c_1} > \lambda^{c_1} \cdot (2c_1 \cdot \log \lambda)^{c_2} = \lambda^{c_1} \cdot (\log n)^{c_2} \geq \frac{\alpha}{\beta}$$

for sufficiently large λ. We then have $\frac{1}{4} \cdot n - \frac{\alpha}{\beta} > \frac{1}{8} \cdot n$.

Acknowledgement. G.M. is supported by the European Research Council through an ERC Starting Grant (Grant agreement No. 101077455, ObfusQation). G.M. is also funded by the Deutsche Forschungsgemeinschaft (DFG, German Research Foundation) under Germanys Excellence Strategy - EXC 2092 CASA 390781972. J.D. is supported by the European Research Council through an ERC Starting Grant (Grant agreement No. 101041207, LACONIC). W.Q. is supported by the European Research Council (ERC) under the European Unions Horizon 2020 research and innovation programme (Grant agreement No. 101019547).

References

1. Barak, B., Goldreich, O., Impagliazzo, R., Rudich, S., Sahai, A., Vadhan, S.P., Yang, K.: On the (im)possibility of obfuscating programs. In: Kilian, J. (ed.) CRYPTO 2001. LNCS, vol. 2139, pp. 1–18. Springer, Heidelberg (2001). https://doi.org/10.1007/3-540-44647-8_1
2. Barak, B., Ong, S.J., Vadhan, S.: Derandomization in cryptography. In: Boneh, D. (ed.) CRYPTO 2003. LNCS, vol. 2729, pp. 299–315. Springer, Heidelberg (2003). https://doi.org/10.1007/978-3-540-45146-4_18
3. Bitansky, N., Lin, H.: One-message zero knowledge and non-malleable commitments. In: Beimel, A., Dziembowski, S. (eds.) TCC 2018. LNCS, vol. 11239, pp. 209–234. Springer, Cham (2018). https://doi.org/10.1007/978-3-030-03807-6_8
4. Bitansky, N., Paneth, O.: ZAPs and non-interactive witness indistinguishability from indistinguishability obfuscation. In: Dodis, Y., Nielsen, J.B. (eds.) TCC 2015. LNCS, vol. 9015, pp. 401–427. Springer, Heidelberg (2015). https://doi.org/10.1007/978-3-662-46497-7_16
5. Boneh, D., Franklin, M.: Identity-based encryption from the weil pairing. In: Kilian, J. (ed.) CRYPTO 2001. LNCS, vol. 2139, pp. 213–229. Springer, Heidelberg (2001). https://doi.org/10.1007/3-540-44647-8_13

6. Boneh, D., Sahai, A., Waters, B.: Functional encryption: definitions and challenges. In: Ishai, Y. (ed.) TCC 2011. LNCS, vol. 6597, pp. 253–273. Springer, Heidelberg (2011). https://doi.org/10.1007/978-3-642-19571-6_16

7. Canetti, R., Lin, H., Pass, R.: Adaptive hardness and composable security in the plain model from standard assumptions. In: 51st FOCS, pp. 541–550. IEEE Computer Society Press, October 2010. https://doi.org/10.1109/FOCS.2010.86

8. Cocks, C.: An identity based encryption scheme based on quadratic residues. In: Honary, B. (ed.) Cryptography and Coding 2001. LNCS, vol. 2260, pp. 360–363. Springer, Heidelberg (2001). https://doi.org/10.1007/3-540-45325-3_32

9. Diffie, W., Hellman, M.E.: New directions in cryptography. IEEE Trans. Inf. Theory (1976)

10. Döttling, N., Garg, S.: Identity-based encryption from the Diffie-Hellman assumption. In: Katz, J., Shacham, H. (eds.) CRYPTO 2017. LNCS, vol. 10401, pp. 537–569. Springer, Cham (2017). https://doi.org/10.1007/978-3-319-63688-7_18

11. Döttling, N., Garg, S., Hajiabadi, M., Masny, D.: New constructions of identity-based and key-dependent message secure encryption schemes. In: Abdalla, M., Dahab, R. (eds.) PKC 2018. LNCS, vol. 10769, pp. 3–31. Springer, Cham (2018). https://doi.org/10.1007/978-3-319-76578-5_1

12. Döttling, N., Kolonelos, D., Lai, R.W., Lin, C., Malavolta, G., Rahimi, A.: Efficient laconic cryptography from learning with errors. In: In: Hazay, C., Stam, M. (eds) EUROCRYPT 2023. LNCS, vol. 14006, pp. 417–446. Springer, Cham (2023). https://doi.org/10.1007/978-3-031-30620-4_14

13. Francati, D., Friolo, D., Maitra, M., Malavolta, G., Rahimi, A., Venturi, D.: Registered (inner-product) functional encryption. Cryptology ePrint Archive (2023)

14. Garg, S., Gentry, C., Halevi, S., Raykova, M., Sahai, A., Waters, B.: Candidate indistinguishability obfuscation and functional encryption for all circuits. In: 54th FOCS, pp. 40–49. IEEE Computer Society Press, October 2013. https://doi.org/10.1109/FOCS.2013.13

15. Garg, S., Hajiabadi, M., Mahmoody, M., Rahimi, A.: Registration-based encryption: removing private-key generator from IBE. In: Beimel, A., Dziembowski, S. (eds.) TCC 2018. LNCS, vol. 11239, pp. 689–718. Springer, Cham (2018). https://doi.org/10.1007/978-3-030-03807-6_25

16. Garg, S., Hajiabadi, M., Mahmoody, M., Rahimi, A., Sekar, S.: Registration-based encryption from standard assumptions. In: Lin, D., Sako, K. (eds.) PKC 2019. LNCS, vol. 11443, pp. 63–93. Springer, Cham (2019). https://doi.org/10.1007/978-3-030-17259-6_3

17. Gentry, C.: Practical identity-based encryption without random oracles. In: Vaudenay, S. (ed.) EUROCRYPT 2006. LNCS, vol. 4004, pp. 445–464. Springer, Heidelberg (2006). https://doi.org/10.1007/11761679_27

18. Gentry, C., Peikert, C., Vaikuntanathan, V.: Trapdoors for hard lattices and new cryptographic constructions. In: Ladner, R.E., Dwork, C. (eds.) 40th ACM STOC, pp. 197–206. ACM Press, May 2008. https://doi.org/10.1145/1374376.1374407

19. Glaeser, N., Kolonelos, D., Malavolta, G., Rahimi, A.: Efficient registration-based encryption. In: Proceedings of the 2023 ACM SIGSAC Conference on Computer and Communications Security, pp. 1065–1079 (2023)

20. Goldreich, O., Goldwasser, S., Micali, S.: How to construct random functions (extended abstract). In: 25th FOCS, pp. 464–479. IEEE Computer Society Press, October 1984. https://doi.org/10.1109/SFCS.1984.715949

21. Goyal, V., Pandey, O., Sahai, A., Waters, B.: Attribute-based encryption for fine-grained access control of encrypted data. In: Juels, A., Wright, R.N., De Capitani di Vimercati, S. (eds.) ACM CCS 2006, pp. 89–98. ACM Press, October/November 2006. https://doi.org/10.1145/1180405.1180418, available as Cryptology ePrint Archive Report 2006/309

22. Groth, J., Ostrovsky, R., Sahai, A.: Non-interactive zaps and new techniques for NIZK. In: Dwork, C. (ed.) CRYPTO 2006. LNCS, vol. 4117, pp. 97–111. Springer, Heidelberg (2006). https://doi.org/10.1007/11818175_6
23. Hohenberger, S., Lu, G., Waters, B., Wu, D.J.: Registered attribute-based encryption. In: Hazay, C., Stam, M. (eds.) EUROCRYPT 2023. LNCS, vol. 14006, pp. 511–542. Springer, Cham (2023). https://doi.org/10.1007/978-3-031-30620-4_17
24. Kalai, Y.T., Khurana, D.: Non-interactive non-malleability from quantum supremacy. In: Boldyreva, A., Micciancio, D. (eds.) CRYPTO 2019, Part III. LNCS, vol. 11694, pp. 552–582. Springer, Cham (2019). https://doi.org/10.1007/978-3-030-26954-8_18
25. Khurana, D.: Non-interactive Distributional Indistinguishability (NIDI) and non-malleable commitments. In: Canteaut, A., Standaert, F.-X. (eds.) EUROCRYPT 2021, Part III. LNCS, vol. 12698, pp. 186–215. Springer, Cham (2021). https://doi.org/10.1007/978-3-030-77883-5_7
26. Lin, H., Pass, R., Soni, P.: Two-round and non-interactive concurrent non-malleable commitments from time-lock puzzles. In: Umans, C. (ed.) 58th FOCS, pp. 576–587. IEEE Computer Society Press, October 2017. https://doi.org/10.1109/FOCS.2017.59
27. Mahmoody, M., Qi, W., Rahimi, A.: Lower bounds for the number of decryption updates in registration-based encryption. In: Kiltz, E., Vaikuntanathan, V. (eds.) Theory of Cryptography, pp. 559–587. Springer Nature Switzerland, Cham (2022)
28. Pandey, O., Pass, R., Vaikuntanathan, V.: Adaptive one-way functions and applications. In: Wagner, D. (ed.) CRYPTO 2008. LNCS, vol. 5157, pp. 57–74. Springer, Heidelberg (Aug 2008). https://doi.org/10.1007/978-3-540-85174-5_4
29. Rogaway, P.: The moral character of cryptographic work. Cryptology ePrint Archive (2015)
30. Sahai, A., Waters, B.R.: Fuzzy identity-based encryption. In: Cramer, R. (ed.) EUROCRYPT 2005. LNCS, vol. 3494, pp. 457–473. Springer, Heidelberg (May 2005). https://doi.org/10.1007/11426639_27
31. Waters, B.R.: Efficient identity-based encryption without random oracles. In: Cramer, R. (ed.) EUROCRYPT 2005. LNCS, vol. 3494, pp. 114–127. Springer, Heidelberg (May 2005). https://doi.org/10.1007/11426639_7

Security of Post-quantum Signatures

Thorough Power Analysis on Falcon Gaussian Samplers and Practical Countermeasure

Xiuhan Lin[1] , Shiduo Zhang[2] , Yang Yu[2,3,4(✉)] , Weijia Wang[1,4] ,
Qidi You[5,6], Ximing Xu[7], and Xiaoyun Wang[1,2,3,4]

[1] School of Cyber Science and Technology, Shandong University, Qingdao, China
xhlin@mail.sdu.edu.cn
[2] Institute for Advanced Study, Tsinghua University, Beijing, China
{zsd,yu-yang,xiaoyunwang}@mail.tsinghua.edu.cn
[3] Zhongguancun Laboratory, Beijing, China
[4] State Key Laboratory of Cryptography and Digital Economy Security,
Beijing, China
wjwang@sdu.edu.cn
[5] State Key Laboratory of Space-Ground Integrated Information Technology,
Beijing, China
[6] Space Star Technology Co., Ltd., Beijing, China
youqd@spacestar.com.cn
[7] China Mobile Internet, Guangzhou, China
xuximing@chinamobile.com

Abstract. Falcon is one of post-quantum signature schemes selected by NIST for standardization. With the deployment underway, its implementation security is of great importance. In this work, we focus on the side-channel security of Falcon and our contributions are threefold.

First, by exploiting the symplecticity of NTRU and a recent decoding technique, we dramatically improve the key recovery using power leakages within Falcon Gaussian samplers. Compared to the state of the art (Zhang, Lin, Yu and Wang, EUROCRYPT 2023), the amount of traces required by our attack for a full key recovery is reduced by at least 85%.

Secondly, we present a complete power analysis for two exposed power leakages within Falcon's integer Gaussian sampler. We identify new sources of these leakages, which have not been identified by previous works, and conduct detailed security evaluations within the reference implementation of Falcon on Chipwhisperer.

Thirdly, we propose effective and easy-to-implement countermeasures against both two leakages to protect the whole Falcon's integer Gaussian sampler. Configured with our countermeasures, we provide security evaluations on Chipwhisperer and report performance of protected implementation. Experimental results highlight that our countermeasures admit a practical trade-off between efficiency and side-channel security.

Keywords: Lattice-Based Cryptography · Side-Channel Analysis · Falcon Signature Scheme · Gaussian Sampler · NTRU

© International Association for Cryptologic Research 2025
T. Jager and J. Pan (Eds.): PKC 2025, LNCS 15674, pp. 229–258, 2025.
https://doi.org/10.1007/978-3-031-91820-9_8

1 Introduction

In 2022, the US NIST announced the first batch of PQC algorithms to be standardized: Kyber [SAB+22] for public-key encryption and key establishment and Dilithium [LDK+22], Falcon [PFH+22] and SPHINCS+ [HBD+22] for digital signatures. Among three signature standards, Falcon has competitive overall performance in particular the smallest communication cost (added sizes of a public key and a signature). This makes Falcon an attractive option for quantum-safe embedded systems.

For real-world deployment in embedded systems, implementation security is of great importance. Adversaries can exploit additional information given through side-channels, e.g. execution time, power consumption and electromagnetic radiations of the chips, to assist cryptanalysis and to mount possibly devastating attacks. Such physical attacks are nowadays the major threat to cryptographic embedded devices. For this, the latest NIST status report on PQC standardization process makes particular mention of side-channel analysis and notes that *"It is NIST's hope and expectation that more such work will continue, especially with regard to protecting the implementations of the algorithms announced for standardization"*.

The side-channel security of Falcon is considered as a notably challenging topic. Falcon is a lattice signature scheme based on the GPV hash-and-sign framework [GPV08]. Its signing procedure relies on sophisticated lattice Gaussian sampling and the way the secret key is used in signing is rather opaque. This complicates *identifying*, *exploiting* and *sealing* side-channel leakages. In addition, Falcon signing algorithm requires extensive floating-point operations that are notorious targets for side-channel attacks. While the reference implementation of Falcon can provably resist against timing attacks [HPRR20], the implementation does not come with protection against other types of side-channel attacks, e.g. power analysis. Some recent works [KA21, GMRR22, ZLYW23] have demonstrated side-channel vulnerabilities of Falcon implementations. Nevertheless, many operations of Falcon's algorithms still require closer scrutiny and systematic countermeasures are not well studied.

1.1 Related Works

Earlier side-channel attacks against lattice signatures targeted the Fiat-Shamir type constructions [BHLY16, EFGT17, PBY17, BDE+18]. This spurred the developments of constant-time Gaussian sampling [ZSS20, KRR+18] and masking [BBE+18, BBE+19, MGTF19, GR19].

Side-channel security of hash-and-sign lattice signatures, especially Falcon, greatly lags the Fiat-Shamir case in both attacks and protections. Fouque et al. presented a theoretical timing attack against the round-1 implementation of Falcon in [FKT+20]. The identified leakage has been provably patched [HPRR20]. The signing procedure of Falcon has two operations that leak secret information: pre-image computation and integer Gaussian sampling. Karabulut and Aysu demonstrated an electromagnetic analysis attack targeting the multiplication between two floating-point numbers on Falcon's pre-image computation [KA21]. With regard to Gaussian samplers, Guerreau et al. proposed the first power analysis attacks against Falcon [GMRR22] using the leakage in the base sampler. Later, Zhang et al. [ZLYW23] improved this attack and identified another power leakage with respect to the sign flip in Falcon's integer Gaussian sampler.

Regarding to side-channel protections of Falcon, very few works are in the literature to our knowledge. Besides the isochronous implementation [HPRR20], a very recent work [CC24] provided the first masking floating-point multiplication and addition, which protects Falcon's pre-image computation against the attack of [KA21]. For power analysis on Gaussian samplers, only initial countermeasures were discussed along with corresponding attacks [GMRR22, ZLYW23] and a thorough treatment remains largely unexplored.

1.2   Contributions

The goal of this work is to give a better understanding of the side-channel security of Falcon from the aspects of both attack and defense. Our contributions are mainly threefold.

1. In Sect. 4, we improve the key recovery in the power analysis attack of [ZLYW23]. We make use of the symplecticity of NTRU to combine leakages at multiple positions, which refines the accuracy of statistical learning. Then a recent decoding technique [Pre23, LSZ+24] is applied to correct approximation errors. By this, we gain a substantial improvement: the number of required traces for successful key recovery is reduced by $\geq 85\%$.
2. Section 5 gives a complete analysis of the half Gaussian leakage and the sign leakage that are two crucial power leakages involved in Falcon's integer Gaussian samplers. We scrutinize each correlative component and identify some new sources of power leakages in the reference implementation of Falcon. Furthermore, quantitative side-channel evaluations are carried out on Chipwhisperer.
3. In Sect. 6, we propose practically effective and easy-to-implement countermeasures against both half Gaussian leakage and sign leakage. We implement the countermeasures in portable C and then perform side-channel evaluations on Chipwhisperer. Our countermeasures lower the classification accuracy of the template attack [CRR03] from 100% down to $\lesssim 58\%$ (resp. $\lesssim 62\%$) for the half Gaussian leakage (resp. sign leakage), which makes key recovery impractical. We evaluate the performance of the protected implementation on an Intel Core i5-1135G7 CPU. The overhead on the signing speed of our countermeasures is around $3.5\times$. To the best of our knowledge, our countermeasures are the first one protecting the whole Falcon Gaussian sampler from both half Gaussian leakage and sign leakage.

The source code is available at https://github.com/lxhcrypto/FalconAnalysis for sanity check and reproduction.

2   Preliminaries

Notations. We use bold lowercase letters for (row) vectors and denote by b_i the i-th entry of the vector $\mathbf{b}$. Let $\|\mathbf{b}\|$ (resp. $\|\mathbf{b}\|_1$ and $\|\mathbf{b}\|_\infty$) denote the Euclidean norm (resp. ℓ_1-norm and ℓ_∞-norm) of $\mathbf{b} \in \mathbb{R}^n$. We use bold uppercase letters for matrices and denote by $\mathbf{b}_i$ the i-th row of the matrix $\mathbf{B}$. Let $\lfloor u \rceil$ be the operation rounding the real number u to the closest integer. This is naturally extended to $\mathbf{u} \in \mathbb{R}^n$ by taking rounding coefficient-wisely. We write $y \leftarrow D$ when the random variable y is drawn from the distribution D. Let $y \sim D$ denote the random variable y distributed over D and $D(x)$ denote the probability of $y = x$.

Lattices. Given $\mathbf{B} = (\mathbf{b}_1, \cdots, \mathbf{b}_n) \in \mathbb{R}^{n \times m}$ of full rank, the lattice generated by $\mathbf{B}$ is $\mathcal{L}(\mathbf{B}) = \{\sum_{i=1}^n x_i \mathbf{b}_i \mid x_i \in \mathbb{Z}\}$ and $\mathbf{B}$ is called a basis.

Gaussians. Let $\rho_{\sigma,\mathbf{c}}(\mathbf{x}) = \exp\left(-\frac{\|\mathbf{x}-\mathbf{c}\|^2}{2\sigma^2}\right)$ be the Gaussian function over $\mathbb{R}^n$ with standard deviation $\sigma > 0$ and center $\mathbf{c} \in \mathbb{R}^n$. Let $D_{\mathcal{L},\sigma,\mathbf{c}}$ be the discrete Gaussian over a lattice $\mathcal{L}$ defined by $D_{\mathcal{L},\sigma,\mathbf{c}}(\mathbf{u}) = \frac{\rho_{\sigma,\mathbf{c}}(\mathbf{u})}{\sum_{\mathbf{v} \in \mathcal{L}} \rho_{\sigma,\mathbf{c}}(\mathbf{v})}$ for any $\mathbf{u} \in \mathcal{L}$. When $\mathcal{L} = \mathbb{Z}$, $D_{\mathbb{Z},\sigma,c}$ is called integer Gaussian that is of particular interest. The half integer Gaussian is defined by $D^+_{\mathbb{Z},\sigma,c}(u) = \frac{\rho_{\sigma,c}(u)}{\sum_{v \in \mathbb{N}} \rho_{\sigma,c}(v)}$ for any $u \in \mathbb{N}$.

NTRU. Let $\mathcal{R} = \mathbb{Z}[x]/(x^n + 1)$ with n a power of 2. In a typical NTRU scheme, the secret is a pair of short $(f, g) \in \mathcal{R}^2$ and the public key is $h = g/f \bmod q$. The NTRU lattice defined by h is $\mathcal{L}_{NTRU} = \{(u, v) \in \mathcal{R}^2 \mid u + vh = 0 \bmod q\}$. One special basis of $\mathcal{L}_{NTRU}$, called NTRU trapdoor, is $\mathbf{B}_{f,g} = \begin{pmatrix} g & -f \\ G & -F \end{pmatrix}$ where $F, G \in \mathcal{R}$ such that $fG - gF = q$. We write $\mathbf{B}_{f,g}$ as $\mathbf{B}$ when the context is clear.

2.1   Falcon Signature Scheme

Falcon is an efficient instantiation of the GPV hash-and-sign framework [GPV08] over NTRU lattices. Specifically, the key pair of Falcon consists in the NTRU trapdoor basis $\mathbf{B}_{f,g}$ and public key $h = g/f \bmod q$. For compactness, Falcon chooses (f, g) such that $\|(f, g)\| \approx 1.17\sqrt{q}$ as per [DLP14]. In this paper, we mainly focus on the parameter set of Falcon-512 for the security level NIST-I, in which $n = 512$ and $q = 12289$.

The signing procedure of Falcon is described in Algorithm 1. Its signing is essentially to compute short $(s_1, s_2) \sim D_{(c,0)+\mathcal{L}(\mathbf{B}),\sigma}$ such that $s_1 + s_2 h = c \bmod q$ where $c = \mathsf{H}(r\|msg)$ and r is the salt. Falcon samples it by the fast Fourier sampler ffSampling [DP16]. The ffSampling sampler works on the FFT domain and takes the so-called Falcon tree T, i.e. the Gram-Schmidt Orthogonalization (GSO) of $\mathbf{B}$, as the input. We omit the details of FFT and Falcon tree as they are not necessary for understanding our work. The acceptance bound of signatures is $\lfloor \beta^2 \rfloor$ such that $\beta = 1.1 \cdot \sigma\sqrt{2n}$ where $\sigma = 1.17\sqrt{q} \cdot \eta_\epsilon(\mathcal{R}^2)$ and $\eta_\epsilon(\mathcal{R}^2)$ is the smoothing parameter.

─────────────── Algorithm 1: Sign ───────────────

Input: Message msg, NTRU basis $\mathbf{B}_{f,g}$ and acceptance bound $\lfloor \beta^2 \rfloor$
Output: A valid signature (r, s) of msg

1 $r \xleftarrow{\$} \{0,1\}^{320}$, $c \leftarrow \mathsf{H}(r\|msg)$
2 $\mathbf{t} \leftarrow (\mathsf{FFT}(c), \mathsf{FFT}(0)) \cdot \mathsf{FFT}(\mathbf{B}_{f,g})^{-1}$ ▷ pre-image computation
3 **do**
4 | **do**
5 | $\mathbf{z} \leftarrow \mathsf{ffSampling}(\mathbf{t}, \mathbf{T})$ ▷ trapdoor sampling
6 | $\mathbf{s} \leftarrow (\mathbf{t} - \mathbf{z}) \cdot \mathsf{FFT}(\mathbf{B}_{f,g})$ ▷ $\mathbf{s} \sim D_{(c,0) + \mathcal{L}(\mathbf{B}), \sigma}$
7 | **while** $\|\mathbf{s}\|^2 > \lfloor \beta^2 \rfloor$
8 | $(s_1, s_2) \leftarrow \mathsf{invFFT}(\mathbf{s})$
9 | $s \leftarrow \mathsf{Compress}(s_2)$
10 **while** $s = \perp$
11 **return** (r, s)

Floating-Point Representation. In the generation of Falcon signature and Falcon tree, involved polynomials are represented in the FFT domain, whose coefficients are complex numbers. The real and imaginary part of complex numbers are floating-point values in "double precision" (also called "binary64" format). As per the reference implementation of Falcon, it follows the IEEE-754 standard and uses unsigned 64-bit integer type to encode floating-point values with 53-bit precision. The full 64-bit is divided into three parts: the sign s is specified by the first most significant bit, the following 11 most significant bits represent the exponent e and the remaining 52 least significant bits denote the mantissa m. However, the mantissa m in effect takes 53-bit where 53rd bit remains 1 omitted in the storage. These three parts (s, e, m) assemble into the floating-point value which is given as follows:

$$x = (-1)^s \cdot 2^{e-1023} \cdot (1 + m \cdot 2^{-52}).$$

In the 64-bit floating-point number, the exponent e contains 2046 values from 1 to 2046. More precisely, when $e = 2047$, the value x is either infinity or the erroneous value (also known as NaN). Similarly, when $e = 0$, the value x is either a zero or subnormal. In this format, the mantissa m is an integer such that $m \in [2^{52}, 2^{53})$. In latter discussion, we write the floating-point representation as FPR and Hamming weight as HW for simplicity.

3 Falcon's Integer Gaussian Samplers and Their Leakages

This work focuses on the side-channel security with respect to Falcon's integer Gaussian samplers. Let us first briefly introduce the Gaussian samplers and existing power leakages.

3.1 Algorithmic Descriptions

Falcon uses the ring-efficient Klein-GPV algorithm [DP16] converting lattice
Gaussian sampling into a series of integer Gaussian samplings. To deal with
variable Gaussian parameters, Falcon implements the integer Gaussian sampler
based on rejection sampling and a fixed base sampler. To recap, there are three
levels of samplers in Falcon as illustrated in Fig. 1. Our work targets the integer
sampler SamplerZ and the base sampler BaseSampler.

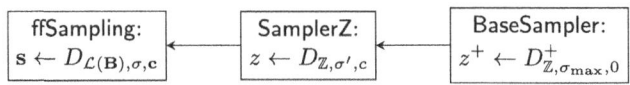

Fig. 1. Flowchart of Falcon's Gaussian samplers.

SamplerZ. To sample from $D_{\mathbb{Z},\sigma',c}$ with different (σ', c), SamplerZ first draws
$z^+ \sim D^+_{\mathbb{Z},\sigma_{max},0}$ using the base sampler, then computes a bimodal Gaussian
$z \leftarrow b + (2b - 1)z^+$ via a random bit b, and finally applies rejection sampling
to guarantee the correct output distribution. The full algorithmic description is
presented in Algorithm 2. In Falcon-512, $\sigma_{min} = 1.2778$ and $\sigma_{max} = 1.8205$. In
addition, the reference implementation of SamplerZ is provably resistant against
timing attacks [HPRR20].

Algorithm 2: SamplerZ

Input: Center c and standard deviation $\sigma' \in [\sigma_{min}, \sigma_{max}]$ that are in FPR
Output: An integer $z \in \mathbb{Z}$ such that $z \sim D_{\mathbb{Z},\sigma',c}$

1 $r \leftarrow c - \lfloor c \rfloor$ ▷ $r \in [0,1)$
2 $ccs \leftarrow \sigma_{min}/\sigma'$
3 **while** *(1)* **do**
4      $z^+ \leftarrow$ BaseSampler()
5      $b \xleftarrow{\$} \{0,1\}$
6      $z \leftarrow b + (2b - 1)z^+$
7      $x \leftarrow \frac{(z-r)^2}{2\sigma'^2} - \frac{(z^+)^2}{2\sigma_{max}^2}$ ▷ With the arithmetics of FPR
8   **if** BerExp$(x, ccs) = 1$ **then**   ▷ reject sampling
9   **return** $z + \lfloor c \rfloor$
10   **end if**
11 **end while**

Algorithm 3: BerExp

Input: x and $ccs \geq 0$ that are in FPR
Output: 1 with probability $\approx ccs \cdot \exp(-x)$

1   $s' \leftarrow \lfloor x/\ln(2) \rfloor$ $\triangleright \ s' \in \mathbb{Z}^+$
2   $r' \leftarrow x - s' \cdot \ln(2)$ $\triangleright \ r' \in [0, \ln(2))$
3   $s' \leftarrow \min(s', 63)$
4   $z' \leftarrow ((\mathsf{ApproxExp}(r', ccs) \ll 1) - 1) \gg s'$ $\triangleright \ z' \approx 2^{64-s'} \cdot ccs \cdot \exp(-r')$
5   $i \leftarrow 64$
6   **do** $\triangleright$ This loop is not constant-time
7        $i \leftarrow i - 8, \ y \xleftarrow{\$} \{0,1\}^8$
8        $w \leftarrow y - ((z' \gg i) \ \& \ \mathsf{0xFF})$
9   **while** $((w = 0) \ and \ (i > 0))$
10 **return** $[\![w < 0]\!]$

In Algorithm 3, given inputs $x = s' \cdot \ln(2) + r'$ and $ccs \geq 0$, BerExp first decomposes x into s' and r', then computes $z' \approx 2^{64} \cdot ccs \cdot \exp(-x)$ and performs lazy Bernoulli sampling to accept z with probability $2^{-64} \cdot z' \approx ccs \cdot \exp(-x)$. The subroutine ApproxExp computes approximate $\exp(-x)$ by polynomial approximation [ZSS20].

Algorithm 4: BaseSampler

Input: -
Output: An integer $z^+ \sim D^+_{\mathbb{Z}, \sigma_{\max}, 0}$

1   $u \xleftarrow{\$} \{0,1\}^{72}$
2   $z^+ \leftarrow 0$
3   **for** $i = 0, \cdots, 17$ **do**
4      $z^+ \leftarrow z^+ + [\![u < \mathsf{RCDT}[i]]\!]$
5   **end for**
6   **return** z^+ $\triangleright \ z^+ \in \{0, \cdots, 18\}$

BaseSampler. The base sampler BaseSampler is implemented with table-based approach. More concretely, it uses the reverse cumulative distribution table (RCDT) that consists of 18 items computed in 72-bit precision. To sample from $D^+_{\mathbb{Z}, \sigma_{\max}, 0}$, BaseSampler draws a 72-bit random value u and determines the output via successively comparing u and each table item $\mathsf{RCDT}[i]$. Algorithm 4 shows the algorithmic description.

3.2   Power Leakages

In context of power analysis, Falcon's integer Gaussian samplers currently exist two kind of leakages, known as half Gaussian leakage and sign leakage. Two leakages can be exploited to mount key recovery attacks [GMRR22, ZLYW23]. Next, we briefly recall these two leakages.

Half Gaussian Leakage. Within the Falcon reference implementation, Guerreau et al. [GMRR22] first observed the visible differences in power consumption by practical simple power analysis in BaseSampler. More concretely, the different Hamming weight of the comparison $[\![u < \mathsf{RCDT}[i]]\!]$ (line 4, Algorithm 4) leads to significant power consumption, which involves at least 8-bit power leakage. This allows to accurately distinguish $z^+ = 0$ or not. The leakage of z^+, thus called half Gaussian leakage, can be combined with statistical learning techniques to recover the signing key as shown in [GMRR22, ZLYW23]. Besides BaseSampler, the half Gaussian leakage spreads to sign flip of z, calculation of x, BerExp and operation "return" in SamplerZ. A complete analysis of this leakage is given in Sect. 5.1.

Sign Leakage. The sign leakage was first identified and exploited in [ZLYW23] within Falcon implementation. To be specific, the sign leakage has been shown to exist in the generation of sign b, sign flip $[\![z \leftarrow b + (2b - 1)z^+]\!]$ (line 6, Algorithm 2) and computation $[\![x \leftarrow \frac{(z-r)^2}{2\sigma'^2} - \frac{(z^+)^2}{2\sigma_{\max}^2}]\!]$ (line 7, Algorithm 2). In this work, we further identify this leakage within the rejection sampling BerExp and the operation "return" in SamplerZ. Detailed analysis is provided in Sect. 5.2.

4   Improvements on the Key Recovery of [ZLYW23]

In [ZLYW23], Zhang et al. presented a side-channel assisted key recovery attack on Falcon. They exploited the half Gaussian leakage and sign leakage to filter signatures in specific domains, and then extract an approximate signing key via statistical learning. For a full key recovery, they resorted to exhaustive enumeration to correct approximate errors. This is only applicable to very small errors, thus requires a large number of power traces.

In this section, we further make use of the symplecticity of NTRU to refine the statistical learning accuracy and combine some recent decoding technique [Pre23, LSZ+24] to refine the key recovery. We dramatically reduced the number of required traces by at least 85%. Detailed results are shown in Table 1, which compares the required traces with success rate at least 25%.

Table 1. Number of required traces by [ZLYW23] and our attack for key recovery against Falcon-512.

	Half Gaussian leakage	Sign leakage	Both two leakages
[ZLYW23]	220,000	170,000	45,000
This work	27,500	25,000	6,500
Vs.	↓ 88%	↓ 85%	↓ 86%

4.1   Refining the Learning Accuracy with NTRU Symplecticity

In [ZLYW23], the attack starts with using power leakages of the $(2n - 1)$-th integer sample z_{2n-1} to filter the signature $\mathbf{s} = \sum_{i=1}^{2n} y_i \cdot \mathbf{b}_i^*$ with y_1 in the specific range, where $\mathbf{b}_i^*$ is i-th row of the GSO of the Falcon trapdoor $\mathbf{B}$. Then the attack computes an approximate $\mathbf{b}_1$ by statistical learning. We observe that the signatures filtered by the samples z_{2n}, z_1 and z_2 can be directly used to refine the approximation of $\mathbf{b}_1$ due to the algebraic properties of the Falcon basis.

Falcon uses a Gaussian sampler based on fast Fourier orthogonalization [DP16], which is a ring-efficient Klein-GPV sampler performed on the NTRU trapdoor basis in the FFT order. Hence, the samples z_{2n-1}, z_{2n}, z_1 and z_2 respectively correspond to $\mathbf{b}_1^*$, $\mathbf{b}_{n/2+1}^*$, $\mathbf{b}_{3n/2}^*$ and $\mathbf{b}_{2n}^*$. According to the symplecticity of NTRU bases [GHN06], we have

$$\frac{\mathbf{b}_1^*}{\|\mathbf{b}_1^*\|} = \frac{\mathbf{b}_{n/2+1}^*}{\|\mathbf{b}_{n/2+1}^*\|} \cdot \mathbf{P} = -\frac{\mathbf{b}_{3n/2}^*}{\|\mathbf{b}_{3n/2}^*\|} \cdot \mathbf{P} \cdot \mathbf{J} \cdot \mathbf{Q} = \frac{\mathbf{b}_{2n}^*}{\|\mathbf{b}_{2n}^*\|} \cdot \mathbf{J} \cdot \mathbf{Q}$$

where $\mathbf{P} = \begin{pmatrix} & -\mathbf{I}_{n/2} \\ \mathbf{I}_{n/2} & \\ & & -\mathbf{I}_{n/2} \\ \mathbf{I}_{n/2} & \end{pmatrix}$, $\mathbf{J}$ is a $2n \times 2n$ reversed identity matrix

and $\mathbf{Q} = \begin{pmatrix} -\mathbf{I}_n & \\ & \mathbf{I}_n \end{pmatrix}$. The power leakage analysis of z_{2n}, z_1 and z_2 is essentially the same with that of z_{2n-1}. Therefore, the signatures filtered by z_{2n-1}, z_{2n}, z_1 and z_2 can be used to learn a more accurate direction of $\mathbf{b}_1$, while other z_i's cannot refine the learning straightforwardly.

Basically, compared with [ZLYW23], one trace can contribute three additional leakages carrying the information of $\mathbf{b}_1$. As a consequence, nearly 4 times samples yields a better learning accuracy. Then we present how to transform the signatures with filtered z_{2n}, z_1 and z_2 into equivalent ones with filtered z_{2n-1}. Let $\mathcal{S} = \varnothing$ be the initialized filtered signature set. We assume that every signature $\mathbf{s} = (s_1, s_2)$ is determined by the exploitable power leakage, i.e. half Gaussian leakage, sign leakage or both. The transformation proceeds as follows:

- For z_{2n-1}, $\mathcal{S} = \mathcal{S} \cup \{\mathbf{s}\}$,
- For z_{2n}, $\mathcal{S} = \mathcal{S} \cup \{\mathbf{s} \cdot \mathbf{P}\}$,
- For z_1, $\mathcal{S} = \mathcal{S} \cup \{-\mathbf{s} \cdot \mathbf{P} \cdot \mathbf{Q} \cdot \mathbf{J}\}$,
- For z_2, $\mathcal{S} = \mathcal{S} \cup \{\mathbf{s} \cdot \mathbf{Q} \cdot \mathbf{J}\}$.

4.2   Correcting Errors with Decoding Technique

By refined learning, one can obtain a noisy vector $\mathbf{b}' = ((b')^{(1)}, (b')^{(2)})$ of the secret basis vector $\mathbf{b} = (b^{(1)}, b^{(2)})$ i.e. $\mathbf{b}_1 = (g, -f) \in \mathcal{R}^2$. Let $\mathbf{b}' = \mathbf{b} + \mathbf{e}$. As per experimental results, $\|\mathbf{e}\|_\infty < 1$ when a moderate number of traces are used. For this case, $\mathbf{v} = \lfloor \mathbf{b}' \rceil - \mathbf{b} = (v^{(1)}, v^{(2)}) \in \{-1, 0, 1\}^{2n}$. The error $\mathbf{v}$ can be eliminated by exhaustive search or lattice reduction, however these methods are costly unless $\mathbf{v}$ is well-bounded, say $\|\mathbf{v}\|_1 < 10$.

To improve the practicality of attacks, we make use of the decoding technique introduced by Prest [Pre23]. This method turns out to be applicable to $\mathbf{v}$ of much larger size, say $\|\mathbf{v}\|_1 > 50$, thus leads to a great reduction on the number of required traces. Specifically, Prest's decoding technique is based on a simple observation that if the half coefficients of $\mathbf{b}'$ are exactly determined, then one can recover the entire NTRU secret by solving linear equations. To this end, it suffices to recover n secret coefficients of $\mathbf{b}$.

Slightly different from Prest's technique [Pre23], we employ the probability-based method of [LSZ+24] to select the half coefficients of $\mathbf{b}'$. In this setting, we simply model $\mathbf{e} = \mathbf{b}' - \mathbf{b}$ as a $2n$-dimensional spherical Gaussian vector of standard deviation σ and center 0. For simplistic hypothesis, it's a simple model that is sufficient to further improve our above refined results. With regard to σ, it is inversely proportional to the number of signatures S used in the recovering of $\mathbf{v}$. In our setting, we can approximate $\sigma \approx K/\sqrt{S}$ with some fixed constants K, which can be experimentally obtained by curve fitting (see Fig. 2).

As illustrated above, we can guess the best half coefficients of $\mathbf{b}'$ according to the fractional part of b_i'. It can be verified that the probability of $v_i = \lfloor b_i' \rfloor - b_i = 0$ is $\varphi_\sigma(x_i) = \frac{\rho_\sigma(x_i)}{\rho_\sigma(x_i + \mathbb{Z})}$ (see Lemma 4 of [LSZ+24]) where known value $x_i = b_i' - \lfloor b_i' \rfloor$. By exploiting such probability-based strategy, for noisy vector $\mathbf{b}'$, we can in effect select n coefficients with the smallest fractional part of b_i', i.e. correctly rounded with the highest probability. Thus, we have the probability p_i that is computed by $\varphi_\sigma(x_i)$ for i-th coefficient of the vector $\mathbf{x} = (x_1, \cdots, x_{2n}) = \mathbf{b}' - \lfloor \mathbf{b}' \rfloor$. We further sort the probability p_i in decreasing order as follows:

$$0 \le p_1 \le p_2 \le \cdots \le p_{2n-1} \le p_{2n} \le 1.$$

As shown above, the best half of coefficients with highest probability can be effectively guessed. Then, we have the equation $b^{(1)} + b^{(2)} \cdot h = 0 \bmod q$ and then $\lfloor (b')^{(1)} \rceil + \lfloor (b')^{(2)} \rceil \cdot h = v^{(1)} + v^{(2)} \cdot h \bmod q$. It means that we can obtain $\mathbf{v}$ by solving the linear system and recover $\mathbf{b}$ entirely.

4.3 Experimental Results

Then, we experimentally verify the effectiveness of aforementioned approach on Falcon-512 instances. We use the same power leakages as in [ZLYW23], refine the statistical learning with the algebraic properties of Falcon trapdoor and finally mount a key recovery using the decoding technique. We greatly reduce the measurement cost compared to [ZLYW23]. For the attack using solely half Gaussian leakage, one can fully recover the signing key with $27,500$ traces on 14 out of 40 instances. For the attack using solely sign leakage, one can completely recover the secret with $25,000$ on 24 out of 40 instances. When the attack simultaneously uses both two leakages, one can launch a full key recovery by decoding with $6,500$ traces on 15 out of 40 instances. Figure 2 shows more detailed experimental results.

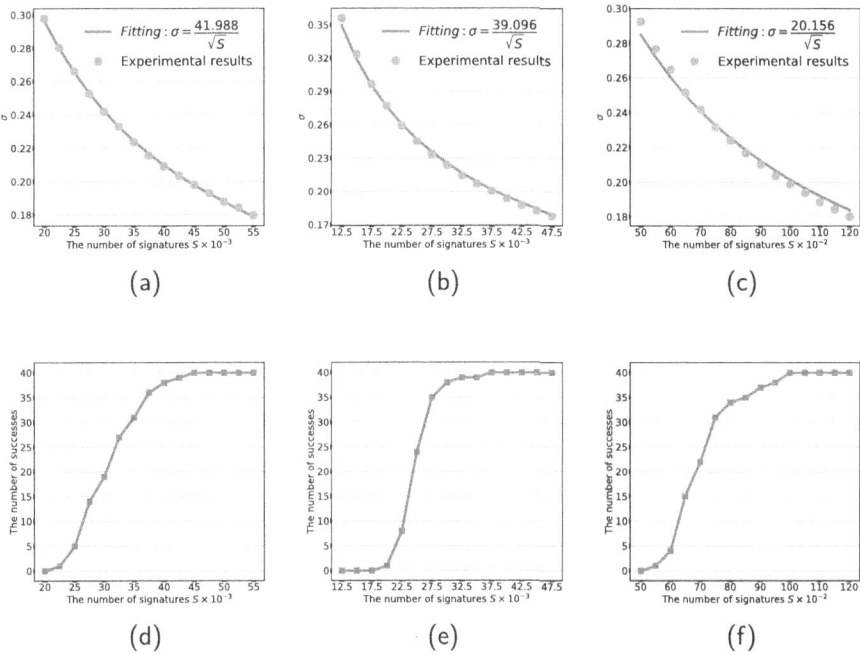

Fig. 2. Experimental results of refined key recovery attacks against Falcon-512 respectively using half Gaussian leakage (left), sign leakage (middle) and both two leakages (right). Figures (a),(b),(c) are for the measures of some constants K through curve fitting and (d),(e),(f) are for the number of successes by refined attacks. Experimental measures are over 40 instances.

5 Complete Analysis of Half Gaussian and Sign Leakages

In [GMRR22, ZLYW23], they identified some sources of half Gaussian leakage and sign leakage and gave empirical countermeasures. Unfortunately, even with their countermeasures, one can still learn the sensitive values with high probability (see Sect. 6.1 for more details). In this section, we further discover some new sources of two leakages by a complete power analysis on the Falcon integer Gaussian sampler SamplerZ. With our new identified leakage sources, one can also learn the sensitive values with high accuracy.

5.1 Power Analysis on Half Gaussian Leakage

The half Gaussian leakage is used to classify whether the output of BaseSampler $z^+ = 0$ or not. Besides BaseSampler, this leakage also exists in the following operations of SamplerZ including the sign flip of z, the computation of x, the rejection sampling BerExp and the operation "return". We next analyze the half Gaussian leakage throughout SamplerZ.

Half Gaussian Leakage in BaseSampler. In BaseSampler, the comparison $[\![u < \mathsf{RCDT}[i]]\!]$ (line 4, Algorithm 4) is the significant source of half Gaussian leakage first identified in [GMRR22]. More specifically, $[\![u < \mathsf{RCDT}[i]]\!]$ is completed by three successive subtractions with a carry bit. The entries of RCDT and u are split into three 24-bit limbs stored in 32-bit registers. For 32-bit two's complement, the first 8 most significant bits are regarded as "sign bits" which enhances power leakages. When $[\![u < \mathsf{RCDT}[i]]\!]$ returns true, 8 most significant bits of 32-bit register are all set 1. Otherwise, 8 most significant bits remain 0. The Hamming distance is 8 for the "sign bits". In addition, the increments of z^+ also produce half Gaussian leakage, but this part is minor compared to the leakage from $[\![u < \mathsf{RCDT}[i]]\!]$.

Half Gaussian Leakage in the Sign Flip of z. The sign flip $[\![z \leftarrow b + (2b - 1)z^+]\!]$ (line 6, Algorithm 2) also leaks the information of z^+. When $z^+ = 0$, the sign flip returns $z \in \{0, 1\}$. The dominating power leakage of the sign flip stems from $[\![(2b - 1)z^+]\!]$. Regardless of the random bit b, the Hamming weight differences exist between $z^+ = 0$ and $z^+ \in \{1, \cdots, 18\}$. Thus, the largest Hamming weight gap is between $z^+ = 0$ and $z^+ = 15$, which happens rarely. In addition, $(2b - 1) = -1$ further enlarges the Hamming weight difference by 32-bit two's complement, since z and z^+ are both stored in the 32-bit registers.

Half Gaussian Leakage in the Computation of x. Concretely, $[\![x \leftarrow \frac{(z-r)^2}{2\sigma'^2} - \frac{(z^+)^2}{2\sigma_{\max}^2}]\!]$ (line 7, Algorithm 2) is first derived by using a series of FPR arithmetics. It is split into three parts: $[\![x_1 \leftarrow \frac{(z-r)^2}{2\sigma'^2}]\!]$, $[\![x_2 \leftarrow \frac{(z^+)^2}{2\sigma_{\max}^2}]\!]$ and $[\![x \leftarrow x_1 - x_2]\!]$. We mainly focus on the analysis of $[\![x_2 \leftarrow \frac{(z^+)^2}{2\sigma_{\max}^2}]\!]$ which is the most relevant to the half Gaussian leakage. To compute x_2, z^+ is first transformed into a floating-point number with FPR for compatibility. The maximal difference in Hamming weight is 10 when $z^+ = 0$ and $z^+ \neq 0$ for $[\![(z^+)^2]\!]$. Then x_2 is fulfilled and further enlarges the gap of Hamming weight. As shown in Table 2, the difference in Hamming weight of x_2 is up to 39, which makes power consumption more significant. The computation of x_1 is indirectly related to half Gaussian leakage and takes the information of z^+ yet. It's noted that $[\![x \leftarrow x_1 - x_2]\!]$ also amplifies the half Gaussian leakage. On the whole, the computation of x involves many FPR arithmetics, including subtraction, multiplication and square, which extensively increases the Hamming weight gap and power consumption for half Gaussian leakage.

Half Gaussian Leakage in BerExp. The subroutine BerExp takes x as one of inputs and its computations are also relevant to half Gaussian leakage. More precisely, the decompositions $[\![s' \leftarrow \lfloor x / \ln(2) \rfloor]\!]$ and $[\![r' \leftarrow x - s' \cdot \ln(2)]\!]$, and the computation of z', can also cause the half Gaussian leakage. However, this leakage is relatively weak in BerExp.

Half Gaussian Leakage in "return". At the end of SamplerZ, it returns $[\![z + \lfloor c \rfloor]\!]$. It's clear that the "return" operation also exposes half Gaussian leakage, since z carries the information of z^+. For each sampling, the center c can be seen

Table 2. The FPR and HW of $[\![(z^+)^2]\!]$ and $[\![x_2 \leftarrow \frac{(z^+)^2}{2\sigma_{\max}^2}]\!]$ from $z^+ = 0$ to $z^+ = 6$

z^+	FPR of $[\![(z^+)^2]\!]$	HW of $[\![(z^+)^2]\!]$	FPR of x_2	HW of x_2
0	0X0000000000000000	0	0X0000000000000000	0
1	0X3FF0000000000000	10	0X3FC34F8BC183BBC2	34
2	0X4010000000000000	2	0X3FE34F8BC183BBC2	35
3	0X4022000000000000	3	0X3FF5B97D39B4333A	39
4	0X4030000000000000	3	0X40034F8BC183BBC2	27
5	0X4039000000000000	5	0X400E2C4A5E5DD55F	31
6	0X4042000000000000	3	0X4015B97D39B4333A	31

as random and thus masks partial information of z^+. Interestingly, one can still detect the half Gaussian leakage within the operation "return" on more precise devices.

5.2 Power Analysis on Sign Leakage

The sign leakage is used to distinguish $z \leq 0$ or $z \geq 1$, first exploited in [ZLYW23]. For this leakage, [ZLYW23] only gave detailed side-channel analysis towards the generation of b, the sign flip of z and the calculation of x. However, in SamplerZ, the rejection sampling BerExp and the operation "return" also reveal the sign information.

Sign Leakage in the Generation of b. In SamplerZ, the sign of z is determined by the random bit b. The step $[\![b \xleftarrow{\$} \{0, 1\}]\!]$ (line 5, Algorithm 2) is original source of the sign leakage (discussed in [ZLYW23]). The Hamming distance is only 1 between $b = 0$ and $b = 1$. Even considering transfer on the bus or storage in the register, the magnitude of power consumption is approximately 1-bit during the generation of b.

Sign Leakage in the Sign Flip of z. For $[\![z \leftarrow b + (2b - 1)z^+]\!]$ (line 6, Algorithm 2), when $b = 0$, the sign is flipped and it outputs $[\![z \leftarrow -z^+]\!]$. Otherwise, it returns $[\![z \leftarrow 1 + z^+]\!]$. The significant power consumption and large Hamming distance exist in these two cases, which are shown in the Table 3. For 32-bit two's complement, the negative values take large Hamming weight. On the contrary, the positive ones have small Hamming weight. In particular, the maximal Hamming distance is 31 for the case $z = 1$ and the case $z = -1$. As shown in [ZLYW23], the sign leakage can be easily identified in the sign flip of z.

Sign Leakage in the Computation of x. The sign leakage also involves in the computation of $[\![x \leftarrow \frac{(z-r)^2}{2\sigma'^2} - \frac{(z^+)^2}{2\sigma_{\max}^2}]\!]$ (line 7, Algorithm 2). The computation of $[\![x_2 \leftarrow \frac{(z^+)^2}{2\sigma_{\max}^2}]\!]$ is irrelevant to the sign leakage, thus we mainly analyze $[\![x_1 \leftarrow \frac{(z-r)^2}{2\sigma'^2}]\!]$. Specifically, the 32-bit integer z is first converted into FPR, then

Table 3. The two's complement numbers and HW of z from $z = -3$ to $z = 4$

z	32-bit two's complement	HW
-3	b'11111111 11111111 11111111 11111101'	31
-2	b'11111111 11111111 11111111 11111110'	31
-1	b'11111111 11111111 11111111 11111111'	32
0	b'00000000 00000000 00000000 00000000'	0
1	b'00000000 00000000 00000000 00000001'	1
2	b'00000000 00000000 00000000 00000010'	1
3	b'00000000 00000000 00000000 00000011'	2
4	b'00000000 00000000 00000000 00000100'	1

minus center r, and finally the following square and multiplication are performed. Table 4 exhibits the Hamming weights of some example cases. From $z = -3$ to $z = 4$, the maximal difference in Hamming weight of $[\![(z - r)^2]\!]$ is 25 for $z = 0$ and $z = 1$, and the minimal one is 0 for $z = -1$ and $z = 3$. With respect to the results of x_1, the corresponding maximal difference in Hamming weight is 29 for $z = -1$ and $z = 3$, and the minimal one is 0 for $z = -2$ and $z = 4$. In practice, the average difference in Hamming weight is not very large between the cases $z \leq 0$ and $z \geq 1$.

Table 4. The FPR and HW of $[\![(z - r)^2]\!]$ and $[\![x_1 \leftarrow \frac{(z-r)^2}{2\sigma'^2}]\!]$ from $z = -3$ to $z = 4$

(z, r)	FPR of $[\![(z - r)^2]\!]$	HW of $[\![(z - r)^2]\!]$	FPR of x_1	HW of x_1
$(-3, 0.9)$	0X402E6B851EB851EB	30	0X40050D4985C1FE3B	27
$(-2, 0.8)$	0X401F5C28F5C28F5B	31	0X3FF5B3D1F00E2C4A	34
$(-1, 0.7)$	0X40071EB851EB851E	28	0X3FE0000000000000	9
$(0, 0.6)$	0X3FD70A3D70A3D70A	34	0X3FAFE3A76B2EF2B7	42
$(1, 0.5)$	0X3FD0000000000000	9	0X3FA6253443526171	29
$(2, 0.4)$	0X40047AE147AE147C	27	0X3FDC5894D10D4988	29
$(3, 0.3)$	0X401D28F5C28F5C2A	28	0X3FF42E0FF1D3B599	38
$(4, 0.2)$	0X402CE147AE147AE1	28	0X4003FC74ED65DE57	34

Sign Leakage in BerExp. As discussed above, the input x of BerExp carries the sign leakage. Similar to the half Gaussian leakage, the sign leakage also spreads to the decomposition of x, including $[\![s' \leftarrow \lfloor x/\ln(2) \rfloor]\!]$ and $[\![r' \leftarrow x - s' \cdot \ln(2)]\!]$, the polynomial approximation ApproxExp and the right shift operation. However, BerExp exposes less information of the sign b, as the sign leakage might be weaken in the computation of x.

Sign Leakage in "return". For $[\![z + \lfloor c \rceil]\!]$, the randomly generated center c cannot entirely conceal the information of the sign b. Therefore, the operation "return" in SamplerZ can also identify the sign leakage as expected.

5.3   Practical Evaluations

Experimental Setup. We perform power analysis and run the reference implementation of Falcon (with the irrelevant delay operation used to separate different parts of leakages) on a Chipwhisperer-Lite, along with STM32F415 UFO target board (ARM Cortex-M4). The power traces of SamplerZ (see Algorithm 2) are collected by Picoscope 3206D at a real-time sampling rate of 1GSa/s, attached with a Mini-Circuits 1.9 MHz low-pass filter. In order to align the power traces, we ignore the traces in which a restart occurs, i.e. we collect the traces of SamplerZ with the acceptance rate $\approx \frac{\sigma_{\min}}{\sigma_{\max}+0.4}$ for all following power analysis experiments.

To roughly predict the existence of both two leakages, we severally collect 10,000 traces with random centers c, standard deviation $\sigma' = 1.7$ and random seeds, then compute the Signal-to-Noise Ratio (SNR) for SamplerZ using the binary information of b and z^+, which are shown in Fig. 3 and Fig. 4.

Furthermore, we exploit different parts of power leakages to perform the Gaussian template attack [CRR03], which displays the magnitude of power leakage. During the profiling phase, we select the training sets where the number of traces is from 70 to 110,000, to obtain different multivariate probability models. In the next attack phase, we collect 5659 traces (filtered in 10,000 traces, evaluation set) and respectively perform the single-trace attack to calculate the classification accuracy for half Gaussian leakage (see Fig. 5) and sign leakage (see Fig. 6). In order to economize computational resources and measures, for every part of power leakages, we first choose the points (with the SNR values ≥ 0.001) of traces, then perform principal components analysis (PCA) before the first profiling and following attack phase, and then empirically select the first 65 principal components as points of interest (POIs) to launch Gaussian template attack.

Evaluation for Half Gaussian Leakage. Figure 3 illustrates the full SNR curve of SamplerZ and it is roughly divided into five sub-graphs for clarity. Clearly, the SNR values from x are much larger than that of other four parts, which is due to the FPR arithmetics. The zoomed-in graphs show that z and BerExp own comparably close SNR values for half Gaussian leakage. Similar cases hold for BaseSampler and "return". Figure 5 exhibits the classification accuracy with respect to the half Gaussian leakage. By consuming few traces for profiling, the leakages in x allow a perfect classification, i.e. 100% accuracy. Using the leakages in BaseSampler, the classification accuracy can achieve $\approx 98\%$ ($\approx 94\%$ accuracy in [GMRR22] with Chipwhisperer-Lite capture board). Moreover, solely using the leakages in z, the percentage of traces, which are correctly classified, is up to $\approx 83\%$. The leakages of BerExp result in the accuracy $\approx 86\%$. We finally evaluate the operation "return" and the corresponding classification accuracy is

$\approx 72\%$. To summarize, for the single-trace attack phase, the leakages in x are more significant than that of other four parts.

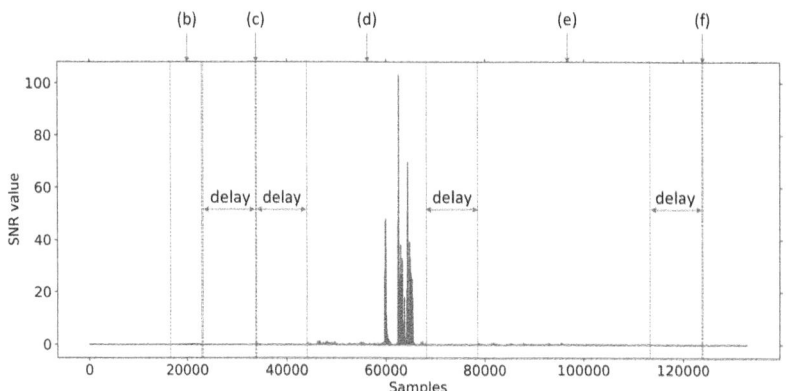

(a) The total SNR curve of SamplerZ for half Gaussian leakage.

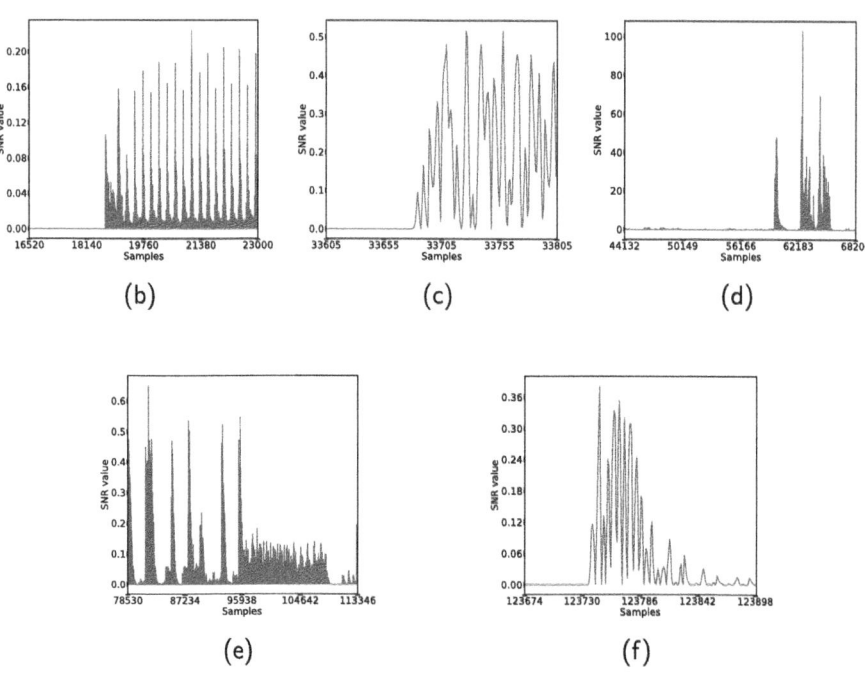

Fig. 3. SNR values of SamplerZ (see Algorithm 2) for half Gaussian leakage. The first graph (a) is the full curve and roughly split into the following five sub-graphs (b), (c), (d), (e), (f), which are respectively for BaseSampler, the sign flip of z, the computation of x, the rejection sampling BerExp, the operation "return" (line 4, 6, 7, 8, 9 of Algorithm 2).

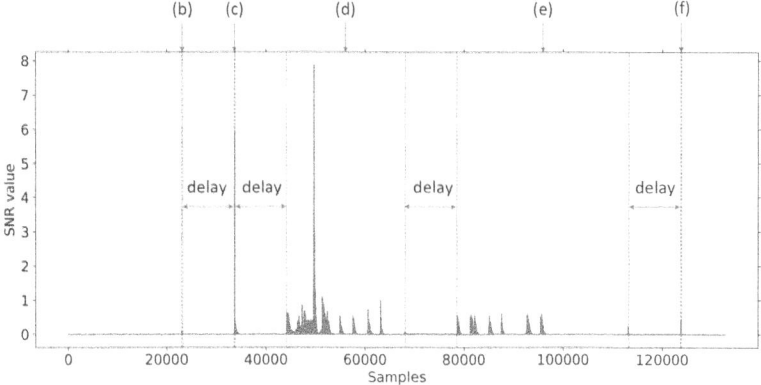

(a) The total SNR curve of SamplerZ for sign leakage.

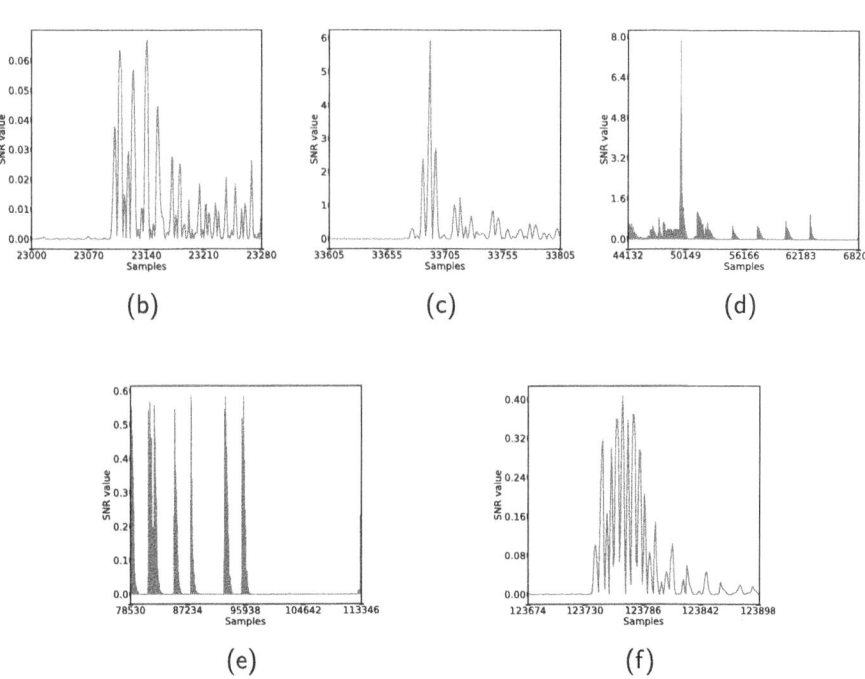

Fig. 4. SNR values of SamplerZ (see Algorithm 2) for sign leakage. The first graph (a) is the full curve and roughly split into the following sub-five graphs (b), (c), (d), (e), (f), which are respectively for the generation of b, the sign flip of z, the computation of x, the rejection sampling BerExp, the operation "return" (line 5, 6, 7, 8, 9 of Algorithm 2).

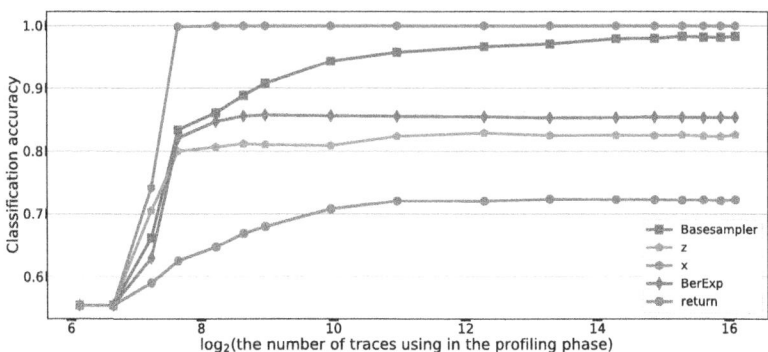

Fig. 5. The classification accuracy for SamplerZ's half Gaussian leakage.

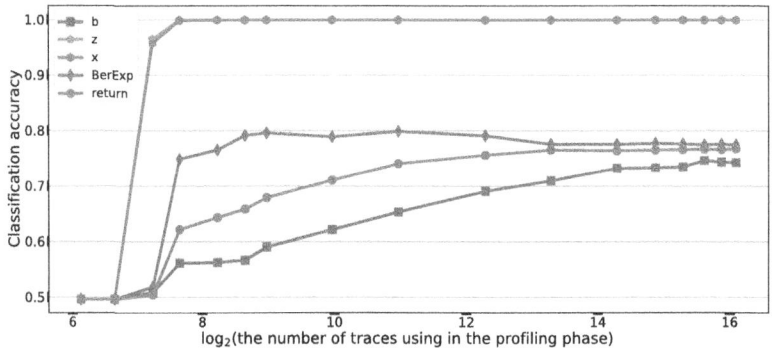

Fig. 6. The classification accuracy for SamplerZ's sign leakage.

Evaluation for Sign Leakage. The sign leakage was first identified and evaluated on an ARM Cortex-M4 STM32F407IGT6 microprocessor in [ZLYW23]. They also used Picoscope 3206D, equipped with 1.9 MHz filter, to collect traces. For similar template attacks, the accuracies are around 52%, 90% and 100% by respectively using these leakages in the generation of b, the sign flip of z and the computation of x. In our work, we choose a more precise and universal platform which is Chipwhisperer-Lite attached with STM32F415 UFO target board, to evaluate the sign leakage. We also compute the full SNR curve of SamplerZ with respect to the random bit b and then split it into five sub-graphs (see Fig. 4). For the sign leakage, the SNR values of x are significantly smaller than that for half Gaussian leakage (see Fig. 3). The sign flip of z and the computation of x have roughly close SNR values. Similar cases hold for BerExp and operation "return". By contrast, the generation of b admits the smallest SNR values by peak clusters, due to the only 1-bit Hamming weight difference. We also evaluate the classification accuracy for sign leakage by performing template attack. As shown in Fig. 6, spending few traces in profiling phase, the leakages in z or x can contribute to perfect classification (100% accuracy). Solely using the leakages in BerExp, the corresponding accuracy is around 78% for correctly determining b. Similarly, the leakages in operation "return" give almost 77% classification accuracy. By contrast, for the generation of b, the classification accuracy is at most $\approx 75\%$.

6   Countermeasures Against Two Leakages

In this section, we propose effective and easy-to-implement countermeasures against both half Gaussian leakage and sign leakage on SamplerZ. Side-channel evaluations on Chipwhisperer show that our countermeasures reduce the classification accuracy of template attacks down to $\lesssim 58\%$ for the half Gaussian leakage and $\lesssim 62\%$ for the sign leakage (see comparison in Table 5). For such low accuracy, even 10 million traces is still far insufficient for practical key recovery as illustrated in [ZLYW23]. In addition, we evaluate the performance of our countermeasures on an Intel Core i5-1135G7 CPU. For the protected implementation, the overhead on signing is around 3.5× compared to the reference implementation of Falcon-512 (see more details in Table 6 and 7).

6.1   Countermeasures

Countermeasures Against Half Gaussian Leakage. As shown in Sect. 5.3, the half Gaussian leakage is more prominent than the sign leakage and is too indelible to mitigate by merely adding random noise. In [GMRR22], Guerreau et al. only proposed a countermeasure to reduce half Gaussian leakage in BaseSampler and validated the effectiveness on their experimental environment. However, to systematically mitigate the half Gaussian leakage, all sources of the leakage in SamplerZ should be taken into account, which complicates the protection.

Countermeasure for BaseSampler. While the countermeasure of [GMRR22] is claimed to have at most 1-bit leakage, advanced acquisitions and classification methods can still achieve a relatively high accuracy. We evaluate their countermeasure on Chipwhisperer-Lite along with STM32F415 UFO target board, use template attacks for classification, and finally achieve $\approx 97\%$ accuracy. Note that the leakage concentrates on the last subtraction of $[\![u < \mathsf{RCDT}[i]]\!]$. To this end, we propose a new countermeasure for this (see Algorithm 5) by using a simple trick to nearly eliminate the difference in Hamming weight. More specifically, $u_{\langle 2 \rangle}$ and $\mathsf{RCDT}[i]_{\langle 2 \rangle}$ are the 24 most significant bits of 72-bit random value u and entry $\mathsf{RCDT}[i]$, which are stored in 32-bit registers. In addition, the carry bit cc is related to the first two subtractions of $[\![u < \mathsf{RCDT}[i]]\!]$.

Similar to the countermeasure of [GMRR22], Algorithm 5 uses a different and well-selected constant value 0X1FFFFFFF to let "overflow" happen when the last subtraction is negative. Thanks to this setting, the 8 most significant bits of 32-bit register are merely set to 2 when $u_{\langle 2 \rangle} < \mathsf{RCDT}[i]_{\langle 2 \rangle} + cc$ and 1 when $u_{\langle 2 \rangle} \geq \mathsf{RCDT}[i]_{\langle 2 \rangle} + cc$. Namely, our countermeasure encodes the "sign bits" with $\{1, 2\}$ instead of $\{0, 255\}$ (for Falcon's reference implementation) or $\{0, 1\}$ (for the countermeasure in [GMRR22]). This simple trick removes the difference in Hamming weight and thus makes the classification of z^+ more difficult.

Algorithm 5: Protected BaseSampler at the last subtraction of $[\![u < \text{RCDT}[i]]\!]$

Input: Two 24-bit integers $u_{\langle 2 \rangle}$ and $\text{RCDT}[i]_{\langle 2 \rangle}$, carry bit cc
Output: 2 if $u_{\langle 2 \rangle} < \text{RCDT}[i]_{\langle 2 \rangle} + cc$ and 1 if $u_{\langle 2 \rangle} \geq \text{RCDT}[i]_{\langle 2 \rangle} + cc$

1 $bb \leftarrow \text{0X1FFFFFF}$
2 $\tilde{z}_j^+[i] \leftarrow ((bb - u_{\langle 2 \rangle} + \text{RCDT}[i]_{\langle 2 \rangle} + cc) \gg 24) \,\&\, \text{0X3}$
3 **return** $\tilde{z}_j^+[i]$ ▷ Table $\tilde{z}_j^+$ with $j \in \{0, 1, 2, 3\}$

Algorithm 6: Protected SamplerZ

Input: Center c and standard deviation $\sigma' \in [\sigma_{\min}, \sigma_{\max}]$ that are in FPR
Output: An integer $z \in \mathbb{Z}$ such that $z \sim D_{\mathbb{Z}, \sigma', c}$

1 $(\tilde{t}[0], \cdots, \tilde{t}[15]) \leftarrow (2, 1, 1, 2, 2, 1, 1, 2, 2, 1, 1, 2, 2, 1, 1, 2)$
2 $c' \leftarrow c - \lfloor c \rfloor$, $ccs \leftarrow \sigma_{\min}/\sigma'$
3 $(\tilde{r}[0], \tilde{r}[1], \tilde{r}[2]) \leftarrow (0, c', 1 - c')$
4 **while** *(1)* **do**
5 $\quad t_{(4)} \xleftarrow{\$} \{0, 1\}^4$, $b' \leftarrow \tilde{t}[t_{(4)}]$
6 $\quad \tilde{z}_0^+ \leftarrow \text{BaseSampler}()$, $\tilde{z}_1^+ \leftarrow \text{BaseSampler}()$
7 $\quad \tilde{z}_2^+ \leftarrow \text{BaseSampler}()$, $\tilde{z}_3^+ \leftarrow \text{BaseSampler}()$
$\qquad\qquad$ ▷ New BaseSampler with countermeasure of Algorithm 5
8 $\quad$ **for** $i = 0, \cdots, 3$ **do**
9 $\quad\quad \tilde{z}^+[i] \leftarrow \lfloor c \rfloor + ((\tilde{z}_i^+[17] \,\&\, 1) + \cdots + (\tilde{z}_i^+[0] \,\&\, 1))$
10 $\quad\quad \tilde{z}^+[i] \leftarrow 18 + 2 * \lfloor c \rfloor - \tilde{z}^+[i]$
11 $\quad$ **end for**
12 $\quad t_{(2)} \xleftarrow{\$} \{0, 1\}^2$
13 $\quad$ **for** $i = 0, \cdots, 18$ **do**
14 $\quad\quad (\tilde{z}[0][i], \tilde{z}[1][i], \tilde{z}[2][i]) \leftarrow (0, \lfloor c \rfloor - i, 1 + \lfloor c \rfloor + i)$
15 $\quad$ **end for**
16 $\quad$ **for** $i = 0, \cdots, 18$ **do**
17 $\quad\quad \tilde{x}[0][i] \leftarrow 0$, $\tilde{x}[1][i] \leftarrow \frac{(\tilde{z}_t^+[i] + \tilde{r}[1])^2}{2\sigma'^2} - \tilde{x}_2[i]$
18 $\quad\quad \tilde{x}[2][i] \leftarrow \frac{(\tilde{z}_t^+[i] + \tilde{r}[2])^2}{2\sigma'^2} - \tilde{x}_2[i]$
$\qquad\qquad$ ▷ Precomputed entries $\tilde{z}_t^+[i] = i$ and $\tilde{x}_2[i] = \frac{i^2}{2\sigma_{\max}^2}$
19 $\quad$ **end for**
20 $\quad$ **if** $\text{BerExp}(\tilde{x}, ccs, \tilde{z}^+, t_{(2)}, \lfloor c \rfloor, b') = 1$ **then**
$\qquad\qquad$ ▷ Protected BerExp in Algorithm 7
21 $\quad\quad$ **return** $\tilde{z}[b'][\tilde{z}^+[t_{(2)}] - \lfloor c \rfloor]$
22 $\quad$ **end if**
23 **end while**

Countermeasure for SamplerZ. We present a practical countermeasure for SamplerZ in Algorithm 6 that greatly mitigates the half Gaussian leakage. In Algorithm 6, we continuously sample 4 half Gaussian tables ($\tilde{z}_0^+$, $\tilde{z}_1^+$, $\tilde{z}_2^+$, $\tilde{z}_3^+$)

by calling protected BaseSampler. This roughly averages the leakage in this BaseSampler and thus lowers the classification accuracy. Less calls of this new BaseSampler with the countermeasure of Algorithm 5 could lead to higher SNR values and classification accuracy. As per Algorithm 5, the entries of $\tilde{z}_i^+$ are all encoded into $\{1,2\}$, then we compute the increments of z^+, add the integer center $\lfloor c \rfloor$ and store them in $\tilde{z}^+$. For each sampling, we use different random integers $\lfloor c \rfloor$ to mask partial information of z^+, instead of generating new randomness. Similarly, we randomly generate 2-bit $t_{(2)}$ as the index for choosing one out of four values in table $\tilde{z}^+$.

During the sign flip of z and computation of x, we traverse all possible $(z^+, b') \in \{0, 1, \cdots, 18\} \times \{1, 2\}$ and store the intermediate results in $\tilde{z}[b']$ and $\tilde{x}[b']$. In the computation of $\tilde{x}$, both $\tilde{z}_t^+$ and $\tilde{x}_2$ involve the transformation from integer to FPR, and can be precomputed to improve performance. As for the rejection sampling BerExp, we apply similar tricks to avoid the half Gaussian leakage. More concretely, we compute all 19 possible values of z^+ in the protected BerExp (see Algorithm 7), including the decomposition of x and computation of z', and severally store them to table $\tilde{s}'[b']$, $\tilde{r}'[b']$ and $\tilde{z}'[b']$. We retrieve the proper item in table $\tilde{z}'$ as per b' and the value $[\![z^+ \leftarrow \tilde{z}^+[t_{(2)}] - \lfloor c \rfloor]\!]$, and perform lazy Bernoulli sampling. At the end of Algorithm 6, we use the same method to obtain the value $z + \lfloor c \rfloor$ in table $\tilde{z}$. Similarly, adding the random integer $\lfloor c \rfloor$ also reduces the half Gaussian leakage in operation "return". To sum up, we transfer the dominating half Gaussian leakage to the end of Algorithm 6 and Algorithm 7, which carries less information of z^+.

Algorithm 7: Protected BerExp

Input: Table $\tilde{x}$ and value $ccs \geq 0$ in FPR, table $\tilde{z}^+$, index $t_{(2)}$, integer $\lfloor c \rfloor$ and b'

Output: 1 with probability $\approx ccs \cdot \exp(-\tilde{x}[b'][\tilde{z}^+[t_{(2)}] - \lfloor c \rfloor])$

1 **for** $i = 1, \cdots, 2$ **do**   ▷ The traversal for sign $b' \in \{1, 2\}$
2   **for** $j = 0, \cdots, 18$ **do**   ▷ For $z^+ \in \{0, \cdots, 18\}$
3        $\tilde{s}'[i][j] \leftarrow \lfloor \tilde{x}[i][j] / \ln(2) \rfloor$
4        $\tilde{r}'[i][j] \leftarrow \tilde{x}[i][j] - \tilde{s}'[i][j] \cdot \ln(2)$
5        $\tilde{s}'[i][j] \leftarrow \min(\tilde{s}'[i][j], 63)$
6        $\tilde{z}'[i-1][j] \leftarrow ((\mathsf{ApproxExp}(\tilde{r}'[i][j], ccs) \ll 1) - 1) \gg \tilde{s}'[i][j]$
7   **end for**
8 **end for**
9 $i \leftarrow 64$, $z'' \leftarrow \tilde{z}'[b' \gg 1][\tilde{z}^+[t_{(2)}] - \lfloor c \rfloor]$
10 **do**
11     $i \leftarrow i - 8$, $y \xleftarrow{\$} \{0,1\}^8$
12     $w \leftarrow y - ((z'' \gg i) \ \& \ \mathsf{0xFF})$
13 **while** $((w = 0) \ and \ (i > 0))$
14 **return** $[\![w < 0]\!]$

Countermeasures Against Sign Leakage. In [ZLYW23], Zhang et al. presented a countermeasure to mitigate the sign leakage from the generation of b, the sign flip of z and the computation of x in SamplerZ. Their countermeasure achieves the classification accuracy $\approx 52\%$ (evaluated on ARM Cortex-M4 STM32F407IGT6 board). We present a more complete countermeasure taking the leakage sources of BerExp and "return" operation into account.

Countermeasure for SamplerZ. Our protected SamplerZ is described in Algorithm 6. It adopts the similar idea of the sign leakage countermeasure in [ZLYW23], i.e. encoding $b \in \{0,1\}$ into $b' \in \{1,2\}$ to eliminate the Hamming weight gap. Furthermore, our countermeasure can simultaneously mitigate both sign leakage and half Gaussian leakage. More precisely, for the generation of b', we use 4-bit random value $t_{(4)}$, as an index, to read the empirically selected look-up table $\tilde{t}$ with $2^4 = 16$ entries in $\{1,2\}$ and then uniformly map the sign from $b \in \{0,1\}$ to $b' \in \{1,2\}$. With regard to the sign flip of z, we apply a similar trick to sample the value of z. Specifically, the table $\tilde{z}[b']$ is computed by $[\![-z^+ + \lfloor c \rfloor]\!]$ when $b' = 1$ or $[\![1 + z^+ + \lfloor c \rfloor]\!]$ when $b' = 2$, and the entry is selected as per $b' \in \{1,2\}$. Moreover, the sign information of z can also be reduced by adding integer $\lfloor c \rfloor$.

In the computation of x, the main source of the sign leakage is $[\![(z-r)^2]\!]$. As shown in [ZLYW23], the leakage in this part can be reduced by computing $[\![(z-c')^2 = (z^+ + \tilde{r}[b'])^2]\!]$ for all two cases of $b' = 1$ and $b' = 2$. However, we observe that $[\![\tilde{x}[i] \leftarrow \frac{(i+\tilde{r}[b'])^2}{2\sigma'^2} - \frac{i^2}{2\sigma_{\max}^2}]\!]$ with $i \in \{0, \cdots, 18\}$ still exists significant sign leakage accumulated by the traversal of z^+. The classification accuracy using these leakages (evaluated on Chipwhisperer) can be up to $\approx 75\%$. To this end, we also traverse all possible $b' \in \{1,2\}$ to compute $\tilde{x}[b']$ and strip the sign leakage in computing x. Similarly, for BerExp, we perform the decomposition of x and the computation of z' by using all possible values of b' and store in table $\tilde{s}'[b']$, $\tilde{r}'[b']$ and $\tilde{z}'[b']$ (see Algorithm 7). As a result, we confine the major sign leakage to the mapping based on b', lazy Bernoulli sampling in Algorithm 7, and operation "return" of Algorithm 6, which yields a low classification accuracy.

6.2 Practical Evaluations

Based on the reference implementation of Falcon, we implement our countermeasures in portable C. This section reports on the practical evaluations on our countermeasures, including side-channel security (Table 5 for accuracy comparison) performance evaluations (Table 6 and 7 for performance comparison).

Security Evaluations Experimental Setup. Our side-channel security evaluations are also performed on Chipwhisperer-Lite with STM32F415 UFO target board (ARM Cortex-M4) and experimental configuration is almost the same with that in Sect. 5.3. We collect $10,000$ traces to compute SNR values of protected SamplerZ (see Algorithm 6), which are shown in Fig. 7 (for half Gaussian leakage) and Fig. 8 (for sign leakage). Furthermore, we also demonstrate the Gaussian

Table 5. Accuracy comparison with protected SamplerZ. The item "A/B" notes the accuracy for unprotected / protected operation

Operation	Half Gaussian leakage
BaseSampler / protected BaseSampler	98% / 57%
sign flip of z / $\tilde{z}$	83% / 50%
computation x / $\tilde{x}$	100% / 51%
BerExp / protected BerExp	86% / 54%
operation "return"	72% / 58%
Operation	Sign leakage
sign b / b'	75% / 62%
sign flip of z / $\tilde{z}$	100% / 51%
computation x / $\tilde{x}$	100% / 57%
BerExp / protected BerExp	78% / 57%
operation "return"	77% / 54%

template attack [CRR03] against the protected SamplerZ, by empirically choosing the first 65 principal components. More precisely, we collect traces (from 70 to 110,000) for profiling and then use 5767 traces (filtered in 10,000 traces) to repeat single-trace attack to obtain the classification accuracy of protected SamplerZ for half Gaussian leakage (see Fig. 9) and sign leakage (see Fig. 10).

Evaluations for Half Gaussian Leakage. As shown in Fig. 7, it still exists significant peak clusters at the begin and end of the SNR values curve. Namely, the protected BaseSampler (line 6–12, Algorithm 6) and operation "return" (line 21, Algorithm 6) can be slightly detected by half Gaussian leakage on Chipwhisperer. In addition, the rest of components in protected BaseSampler are hardly identified in the context of our experimental setup. However, the SNR value of Algorithm 6 for half Gaussian leakage is much lower than that of SamplerZ (see Fig. 3). Since the true value of z should be returned, this part of leakages are difficult to experimentally remove. Therefore, by using the growing number of profiling traces, the classification accuracy for half Gaussian leakage is at most $\approx 58\%$ with different sources of leakages, as depicted by Fig. 9. As per the experimental results of [ZLYW23], such imperfect accuracy for classifying $z^+ = 0$ or not leads to the dramatically increasing number of required traces. A practical key recovery can still be performed with 10 million signatures when the accuracy is 65% (see Fig. 5 of [ZLYW23]). Therefore, equipped with our countermeasures, the required traces leading to full key recovery with half Gaussian leakage are much more than 10 million, which can be considered as infeasible for many real-world applications. As mentioned in [ZLYW23], one can set a counter for the maximum time of signing.

Evaluations for Sign Leakage. For the SNR values curve in Fig. 8, it still exists one single distinct peak clusters in the beginning and implies the sign

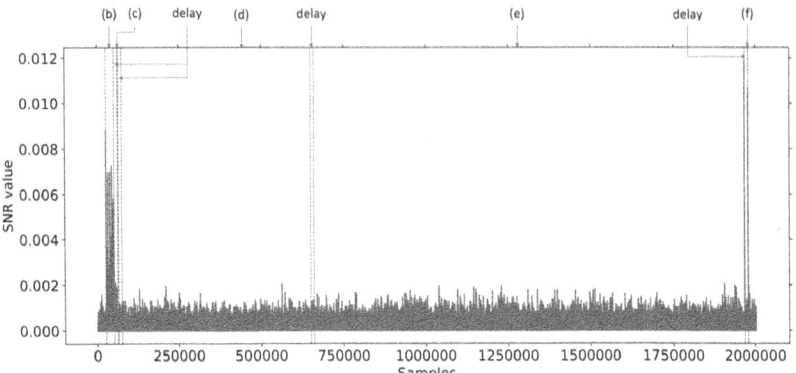

(a) The total SNR curve of protected SamplerZ for half Gaussian leakage.

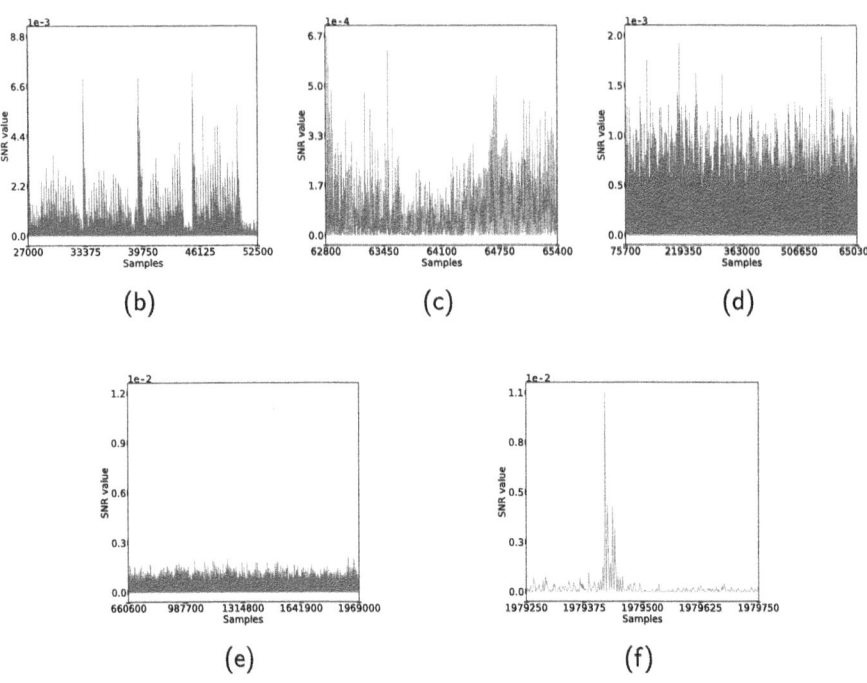

Fig. 7. SNR values of protected SamplerZ (see Algorithm 6) for half Gaussian leakage. The first graph (a) is the full curve and roughly split into the following five subgraphs (b), (c), (d), (e), (f), which are respectively for SNR values include protected BaseSampler, the sign flip of $\tilde{z}$, the computation of $\tilde{x}$, the rejection sampling protected BerExp, the operation "return" (line 6–12, 13–15, 16–19, 20, 21 of Algorithm 6).

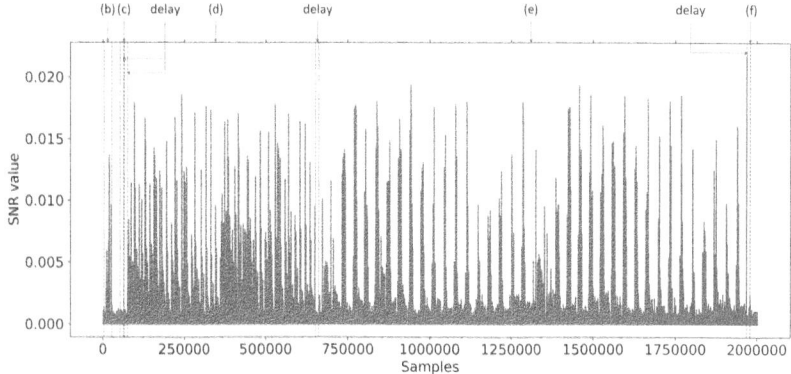

(a) The total SNR curve of protected SamplerZ for sign leakage.

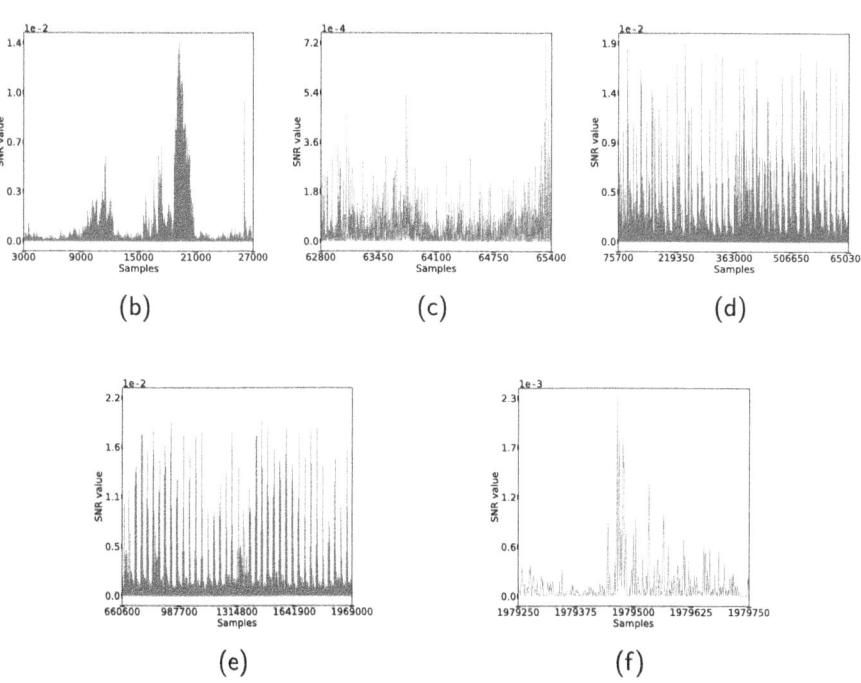

(b)   (c)   (d)

(e)   (f)

Fig. 8. SNR values of protected SamplerZ (see Algorithm 6) for sign leakage. The first graph (a) is the full curve and roughly split into the following five sub-graphs (b), (c), (d), (e), (f), which are respectively for SNR values include the sampling of b', the sign flip of $\tilde{z}$, the computation of $\tilde{x}$, the rejection sampling protected BerExp, the operation "return" (line 5, 13–15, 16–19, 20, 21 of Algorithm 6).

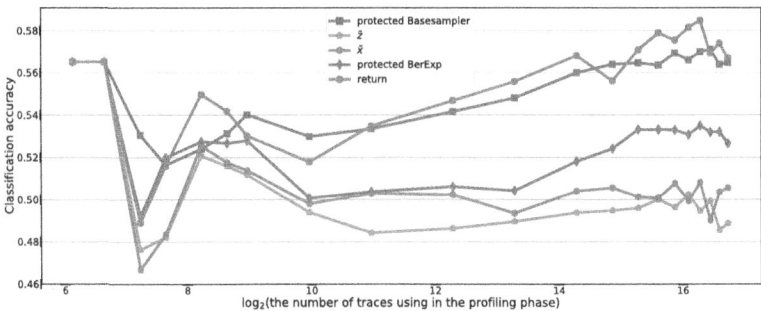

Fig. 9. The classification accuracy of protected SamplerZ for half Gaussian leakage.

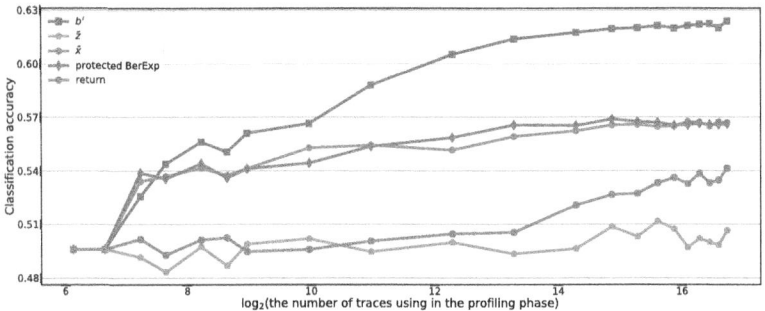

Fig. 10. The classification accuracy of protected SamplerZ for sign leakage.

leakage still persists in the generation of b' in the protected SamplerZ (line 5, Algorithm 6) even if there is no difference in Hamming weight. Based on our setup, the sign leakage in the computation of $\tilde{x}$ (line 16–19, Algorithm 6) and the rejection sampling protected BerExp (line 20, Algorithm 6) can be weakly detected as shown in the Fig. 8. For operation "return" (line 21, Algorithm 6), this leakage still exists in spite of smaller SNR values. In addition, the rest of parts in Algorithm 6 are not strongly related to the sign leakage. By contrast, the SNR values of Algorithm 6 are much lower than that of SamplerZ (see Fig. 4). Furthermore, we calculate the classification accuracy of the sign leakage as illustrated in Fig. 10. More specifically, we can control the accuracy is increasing up to $\approx 62\%$ by using different sources of sign leakages and number of required traces for profiling. As evaluated in [ZLYW23], the inaccurate classification for the sign leakage also results in sharply increasing the number of required traces when the accuracy is $< 65\%$ (see Fig. 12 of [ZLYW23]). Therefore, configured with our countermeasures, the number of required signatures to fully recover the secret with sign leakage is much more than 10 million, which is infeasible for many real-world usecases.

Performance Evaluations. The performance comparison is evaluated on an Intel Core i5-1135G7 CPU clocked at 2.4 GHz with hyper-threading disable. Compilation is executed by `Clang-10.0.0` with optimization cflags `-O0`. We employ the Falcon's benchmarking tool to measure clock time and access system counter to provide cycle counts.

We first test the performance of protected SamplerZ (Algorithm 6) and compare with the reference implementation of Falcon. As shown in Table 6, the bottlenecks stem from the calculations of $\tilde{x}$ and the protected BerExp. Our protected SamplerZ comes with about 6.0× overhead measured by clock time and 19.0× overhead for cycle counts.

Table 6. Performance comparison between SamplerZ and protected SamplerZ

	Algorithm	Clock Time (ns)	Cycles
	Total	2400	1299
	BaseSampler in the line 4	292	287
	generation of b in the line 5	142	18
SamplerZ	sign flip of z in the line 6	138	25
	calculation of x in the line 7	494	306
	BerExp in the line 8	573	428
	"return" in the line 9	138	21
	Total	14428	24744
	sampling of b' in the line 5	146	25
	new BaseSampler in the line 6-12	745	1186
Protected SamplerZ	sign flip of $\tilde{z}$ in the line 13-15	167	76
	computation of $\tilde{x}$ in the line 16-19	4132	7376
	protected BerExp in the line 20	8228	15731
	"return" in the line 21	142	26

Furthermore, in Table 7, we provide benchmarks for signing in the dynamic mode and the tree mode. We apply our countermeasures on Gaussian samplers to apportion the overheads on the whole signing process of Falcon. For Falcon-512 (Falcon-1024), dynamic signing has about 3.7× (3.3×) overhead measured by clock time and 3.5× (3.4×) overhead measured by cycle counts.

Table 7. Performance comparison with the signing dynamic (SD) and signing tree (ST) of Falcon's reference implementation

Claimed Security	Falcon-512		Falcon-1024	
	SD	ST	SD	ST
Unprotected (ms)	6.7	3.1	14.8	6.5
Protected (ms)	24.5	20.5	49.4	41.0
Vs.	3.7×	6.6×	3.3×	6.3×
Unprotected (Mcycles)	16.6	7.3	35.6	15.7
Protected (Mcycles)	58.7	49.9	119.6	99.4
Vs.	3.5×	6.8×	3.4×	6.3×

Acknowledgments. We would like to thank the anonymous reviewers for their useful suggestions and comments. Xiuhan Lin, Yang Yu and Shiduo Zhang are supported by the National Key R&D Program of China (2023YFA1009500) and the National Natural Science Foundation of China (12441104). Weijia Wang's work has been supported by the National Natural Science Foundation of China (Grant No. 62372273) and the Key Research and Development Program of Shandong Province, China (Grant No. 2024ZLGX05).

References

[BBE+18] Barthe, G., et al.: Masking the GLP lattice-based signature scheme at any order. In: Nielsen, J.B., Rijmen, V., (eds) EUROCRYPT 2018, Part II, volume 10821 of LNCS, pp. 354–384, Tel Aviv, Israel. Springer, Cham, Switzerland (2018). https://doi.org/10.1007/s00145-023-09485-z

[BBE+19] Barthe, G., Belaïd, S., Espitau, T., Fouque, P.-A., Rossi, M., Tibouchi, M.: GALACTICS: Gaussian sampling for lattice-based constant- time implementation of cryptographic signatures, revisited. In: Cavallaro, L., Kinder, J., Wang, X., Katz, J., (eds) ACM CCS 2019, pp. 2147–2164, London, UK. ACM Press (2019)

[BDE+18] Bootle, J., Delaplace, C., Espitau, T., Fouque, P.-A., Tibouchi, M.: LWE without modular reduction and improved side-channel attacks against BLISS. In: Peyrin, T., Galbraith, S. (eds.) ASIACRYPT 2018. LNCS, vol. 11272, pp. 494–524. Springer, Cham (2018). https://doi.org/10.1007/978-3-030-03326-2_17

[BHLY16] Groot Bruinderink, L., Hülsing, A., Lange, T., Yarom, Y.: Flush, Gauss, and Reload – a cache attack on the bliss lattice-based signature scheme. In: Gierlichs, B., Poschmann, A.Y. (eds.) CHES 2016. LNCS, vol. 9813, pp. 323–345. Springer, Heidelberg (2016). https://doi.org/10.1007/978-3-662-53140-2_16

[CRR03] Chari, S., Rao, J.R., Rohatgi, P.: Template attacks. In: Kaliski, B.S., Koç, K., Paar, C. (eds.) CHES 2002. LNCS, vol. 2523, pp. 13–28. Springer, Heidelberg (2003). https://doi.org/10.1007/3-540-36400-5_3

[CC24]   Chen, K.-Y., Chen, J.-P.: Masking floating-point number multiplication and addition of falcon first- and higher-order implementations and evaluations. IACR TCHES **2024**(2), 276–303 (2024)

[DLP14]   Ducas, L., Lyubashevsky, V., Prest, T.: Efficient identity-based encryption over NTRU lattices. In: Sarkar, P., Iwata, T. (eds.) ASIACRYPT 2014. LNCS, vol. 8874, pp. 22–41. Springer, Heidelberg (2014). https://doi.org/10.1007/978-3-662-45608-8_2

[DP16]   Ducas, L., Prest, T.: Fast fourier orthogonalization. In: Abramov, S.A., Zima, E.V., Gao, X.-S., (eds) Proceedings of the ACM on International Symposium on Symbolic and Algebraic Computation, ISSAC 2016, Waterloo, ON, Canada, July 19-22, 2016, pp. 191–198. ACM (2016)

[EFGT17] Espitau, T., Fouque, P.-A., Gérard, B., Tibouchi, M.: Side-channel attacks on BLISS lattice-based signatures: exploiting branch tracing against strongSwan and electromagnetic emanations in microcontrollers. In: Thuraisingham, B.M., Evans, D., Malkin, T., Xu, D., (eds) ACM CCS 2017, pp. 1857–1874, Dallas, TX, USA. ACM Press (2017)

[FKT+20] Fouque, P.-A., Kirchner, P., Tibouchi, M., Wallet, A., Yu, Y.: Key recovery from Gram–Schmidt norm leakage in hash-and-sign signatures over NTRU lattices. In: Canteaut, A., Ishai, Y. (eds.) EUROCRYPT 2020. LNCS, vol. 12107, pp. 34–63. Springer, Cham (2020). https://doi.org/10.1007/978-3-030-45727-3_2

[GHN06]   Gama, N., Howgrave-Graham, N., Nguyen, P.Q.: Symplectic lattice reduction and NTRU. In: Vaudenay, S. (ed.) EUROCRYPT 2006. LNCS, vol. 4004, pp. 233–253. Springer, Heidelberg (2006). https://doi.org/10.1007/11761679_15

[GPV08]   Gentry, C., Peikert, C., Vaikuntanathan, V.: Trapdoors for hard lattices and new cryptographic constructions. In: Ladner, R.E., Dwork, C., (eds) 40th ACM STOC, pp. 197–206, Victoria, BC, Canada. ACM Press (2008)

[GR19]   Gérard, F., Rossi, M.: An efficient and provable masked implementation of qTESLA. In: Belaïd, S., Güneysu, T. (eds.) CARDIS 2019. LNCS, vol. 11833, pp. 74–91. Springer, Cham (2020). https://doi.org/10.1007/978-3-030-42068-0_5

[GMRR22] Guerreau, M., Martinelli, A., Ricosset, T., Rossi, M.: The hidden parallelepiped is back again: power analysis attacks on falcon. IACR TCHES **2022**(3), 141–164 (2022)

[HPRR20] Howe, J., Prest, T., Ricosset, T., Rossi, M.: Isochronous Gaussian Sampling: from inception to implementation. In: Ding, J., Tillich, J.-P. (eds.) PQCrypto 2020. LNCS, vol. 12100, pp. 53–71. Springer, Cham (2020). https://doi.org/10.1007/978-3-030-44223-1_4

[HBD+22] Hülsing, A., et al.: SPHINCS+. Technical report, National Institute of Standards and Technology (2022). https://csrc.nist.gov/Projects/post-quantum-cryptography/selected-algorithms-2022

[KA21]   Karabulut, E., Aysu, A.: FALCON down: breaking FALCON post-quantum signature scheme through side-channel attacks. In: 58th ACM/IEEE Design Automation Conference, DAC 2021, San Francisco, CA, USA, December 5-9, 2021, pp. 691–696. IEEE (2021)

[KRR+18] Karmakar, A., Roy, S.S., Reparaz, O., Vercauteren, F., Verbauwhede, I.: Constant-time discrete gaussian sampling. IEEE Trans. Comput. **67**(11), 1561–1571 (2018)

[LSZ+24] Lin, X., et al.: Cryptanalysis of the Peregrine lattice-based signature scheme. In: Tang, Q., Teague, V., (eds) PKC 2024, Part I, volume 14601 of LNCS, pp. 387–412, Sydney, NSW, Australia, April 15–17, 2024. Springer, Cham, Switzerland (2024). https://doi.org/10.1007/978-3-031-57718-5_13

[LDK+22] Lyubashevsky, V., et al.: CRYSTALS-DILITHIUM. Technical report, National Institute of Standards and Technology (2022). https://csrc.nist.gov/Projects/post-quantum-cryptography/selected-algorithms-2022

[MGTF19] Migliore, V., Gérard, B., Tibouchi, M., Fouque, P.-A.: Masking Dilithium - efficient implementation and side-channel evaluation. In: Deng, R.H., Gauthier-Umaña, V., Ochoa, M., Yung, M., (eds) ACNS 19International Conference on Applied Cryptography and Network Security, volume 11464 of LNCS, pp. 344–362, Bogota, Colombia. Springer, Cham, Switzerland (2019). https://doi.org/10.1007/978-3-030-21568-2_17

[PBY17] Pessl, P., Bruinderink, L.G., Yarom, Y.: To BLISS-B or not to be: attacking strongSwan's implementation of post-quantum signatures. In: Thuraisingham, B.M., Evans, D., Malkin, T., Xu, D., (eds) ACM CCS 2017, pp. 1843–1855, Dallas, TX, USA. ACM Press (2017)

[Pre23] Prest, T.: A key-recovery attack against Mitaka in the t-probing model. In: Boldyreva, A., Kolesnikov, V., (eds) PKC 2023, Part I, volume 13940 of LNCS, pp. 205–220, Atlanta, GA, USA. Springer, Cham, Switzerland (2023). https://doi.org/10.1007/978-3-031-31368-4_8

[PFH+22] Prest, T., et al.: FALCON. Technical report, National Institute of Standards and Technology (2022). https://csrc.nist.gov/Projects/post-quantum-cryptography/selected-algorithms-2022

[SAB+22] Schwabe, P., et al.: CRYSTALS-KYBER. Technical report, National Institute of Standards and Technology (2022). https://csrc.nist.gov/Projects/post-quantum-cryptography/selected-algorithms-2022

[ZLYW23] Zhang, S., Lin, X., Yu, Y., Wang, W.: Improved power analysis attacks on falcon. In: Hazay, C., Stam, M. (eds.) Advances in Cryptology – EUROCRYPT 2023: 42nd Annual International Conference on the Theory and Applications of Cryptographic Techniques, Lyon, France, April 23-27, 2023, Proceedings, Part IV, pp. 565–595. Springer Nature Switzerland, Cham (2023). https://doi.org/10.1007/978-3-031-30634-1_19

[ZSS20] Zhao, R.K., Steinfeld, R., Sakzad, A.: FACCT: fast, compact, and constant-time discrete gaussian sampler over integers. IEEE Trans. Comput. **69**(1), 126–137 (2020)

Finding a Polytope: A Practical Fault Attack Against Dilithium

Paco Azevedo-Oliveira[1,2(✉)], Andersson Calle Viera[1,3], Benoît Cogliati[1], and Louis Goubin[2]

[1] Thales DIS, Meudon, France
{paco.azevedo-oliveira,andersson.calle-viera,
benoit-michel.cogliati}@thalesgroup.com
[2] Laboratoire de Mathématiques de Versailles, UVSQ, CNRS,
Université Paris-Saclay, 78035 Versailles, France
louis.goubin@uvsq.fr
[3] Sorbonne Université, CNRS, Inria, LIP6, 75005 Paris, France

Abstract. In Dilithium, the rejection sampling step is crucial for the proof of security and correctness of the scheme. However, to our knowledge, there is no attack in the literature that takes advantage of an attacker knowing rejected signatures. The aim of this paper is to create a practical black-box attack against Dilithium with a weakened rejection sampling. We succeed in showing that an adversary with enough rejected signatures can recover Dilithium's secret key in less than half an hour on a desktop computer. There is one possible application for this result: by physically preventing one of the rejection sampling tests from happening, we obtain two fault attacks against Dilithium.

1 Introduction

In July 2022, the National Institute of Standards and Technology (NIST) selected CRYSTALS-Dilithium, also known as Dilithium, as a new post-quantum digital signature scheme. It is being standardized under the name ML-DSA [NIS23], and the National Security Agency (NSA) has included it in the Commercial National Security Algorithm (CNSA 2.0) suite for national security systems [NSA22]. Moreover, due to its relative efficiency compared to other post-quantum schemes, Dilithium is recommended for computing quantum-secure signatures in most use cases.

From a theoretical point of view, Dilithium benefits from security proofs supporting its Strong existential Unforgeability under Chosen Message Attack (SUF-CMA) in the classical and quantum random oracle models [BDK+21]. To complement this cryptanalytic approach, it is necessary to investigate the security of embedded implementations. The security of Dilithium against Side-Channel Attacks (SCA) and Fault Attacks (FA) thus needs to be carefully assessed.

© International Association for Cryptologic Research 2025
T. Jager and J. Pan (Eds.): PKC 2025, LNCS 15674, pp. 259–283, 2025.
https://doi.org/10.1007/978-3-031-91820-9_9

Following this direction, many papers have already been published about physical attacks [BBK16, BVC+23, BP18, CKA+21, KLH+20, MUTS22, RJH+18, EAB+23, BAE+24, WNGD23, KPLG24] against Dilithium, see also this survey [RCDB22].

In the present paper, we use Linear Programming (LP) [NW88] in several attack scenarios. This kind of technique has already been used in [MUTS22, UMB+23] to mount a fault attack and recover the s_1 value of Dilithium from noisy values, and hence the whole secret key. Note that, in the (very) rare papers using linear programming, this technique has, up to now, been seen as a complement to a computationally heavy profiling phase.

Our LP-based technique is first applied to fault attacks against Dilithium. Up to now, all the developed strategies have consisted of faulting either the NTT-based computations, the nonce $\mathbf{y}$ used to sign, or additions/multiplications with secret polynomials. However, none of the previous attacks have targeted the tests used in the rejection sampling mechanism. This is the core of the fault attack we elaborate in the present paper.

For each attack described here, we consider two versions of the Dilithium signature algorithm. The first is the official specification published in the FIPS (draft) standard [NIS23]. The second one corresponds to the alternative way (described in Sect. 5.1 of [BDK+21]) to perform the validity checks on $\mathbf{r}_0$ and to compute $\mathbf{h}$, which corresponds to the reference implementation [DKL+].

It is essential to analyze the impact of the attacks on these two versions of Dilithium. Indeed, even if they are functionally equivalent, this is no longer true when we consider perturbations of the tests involved in the rejection sampling mechanism or when we have access to internal values in the context of multi-party computation.

In all the attacks we describe in the present paper, the parameter $\mathbf{t}_0$ of Dilithium plays a particular role that has been debated in the literature. In the draft of the FIPS ML-DSA standard [NIS23], $\mathbf{t}_0$ is officially considered as part of the secret key. However, as indicated in the same document: "The vector $\mathbf{t}$ is compressed in the actual public key by dropping the d least significant bits from each coefficient, thus producing the polynomial vector $\mathbf{t}_1$. This compression is an optimization for performance, not security. The low order bits of t can be reconstructed from a small number of signatures and, therefore, need not be regarded as secret." Note that the EUF-CMA security proof provided by the authors of Dilithium [BDK+21] makes the same assumption and considers that $\mathbf{t}$ is public. In the same spirit, Schwabe writes [Sch19]: "$\mathbf{t}_0$ is not part of the secret key, but actually a public value (taken into account in the security analysis). The reason not to make it part of the public key is that it's not needed for verification so we can have smaller public keys." Furthermore, a recent eprint paper [AOCVCG24], would seem to show that $\mathbf{t}_0$ can be reconstructed with 500 000 Dilithium signatures signed under the same secret key. Therefore, in the rest of the paper, we will assume –as in most of the literature about the security of Dilithium– that $\mathbf{t}_0$ is a public parameter.

Our Contributions. In this paper, we describe several kinds of attacks that take advantage of potential weaknesses in the implementations of the tests involved in the rejection sampling mechanism. Our attacks require from 1 million to 4 millions signatures, depending on the security level of Dilithium that is targeted.

The first kind of attack depends on fault injections that allow the attacker to skip the *second* test (on r_0) involved in the rejection sampling mechanism. Two scenarios are considered:

- If the target is the official specification of Dilithium [LDK+22], knowing that the faulty signatures are not valid (they are not accepted by the verification algorithm) allows to recover the secret value s_2. It is well known that s_1 can then be deduced, assuming the attacker knows the t_0 parameter.
- If the target is the official reference implementation of Dilithium [DKL+22], based on an alternative way of performing the validity checks on r_0 and computing h, this time the obtained (faulty) signatures *do* pass the verification phase, as well as normal (non-faulty) signatures. However, the knowledge of t_0 enables to detect the faulty signatures, leading to a recovery of s_2, then s_1.

In both cases, the attack uses Linear Programming (LP) tools, and experiments show that it is very efficient on usual Dilithium parameters (typically less than 30 min).

The second kind of attack is also based on fault injections that are used to skip the *first* test (on z) in the rejection sampling mechanism. We describe a method that is similar to the previous attacks and also makes use of (LP) tools. This attack (which remains the same for all versions of Dilithium) allows to recover s_1 (and thus enables to forge arbitrary many signatures). It is very efficient and does not even require the knowledge of the t_0 parameter.

All these attacks illustrate the power of LP-based methods to recover secret information from faulty/rejected signatures. This can be applied in several attack models (fault attacks, side-channels, white-box, multi-party computation) and bring new arguments supporting the need for protecting not only the values manipulated during the Dilithium signature computation but also the very execution of the tests during the rejection sampling phase.

Outline. This paper is organized as follows. In Sect. 2, we review the necessary knowledge on Dilithium and linear programming. In Sect. 3, we define an attack scenario and an associated problem, then show how this problem can be reformulated in terms of integer optimization. In Sect. 4, we discuss the difference between the algorithm specification, proposed as a standard implementation, and the reference implementation, which does not follow this specification. We explain how to adapt the attack on the reference implementation. In Sect. 5, we propose a method for solving the problem defined in Sect. 3. In Sect. 6, we present our practical results obtained by attacking Dilithium-2, Dilithium-3, and Dilithium-5. Finally, in Sect. 7 we discuss the results obtained, their limitations and their implications in our opinion.

2   Background and Notations

This section recalls the definitions and results already known, which will be useful throughout the rest of the paper. To pose the problem, we recall the notations used in Dilithium and briefly explain how the algorithm works. To reformulate the problem, we give the basic definitions of polytope theory, and finally, to solve the problem, we provide the main linear programming results.

2.1   Lattices

Definition 1 *(Modular Reductions)*
Let α an even integer (resp. odd), we define $r' := r \bmod^{\pm}(\alpha)$ the unique - $\frac{\alpha}{2} < r' \leq \frac{\alpha}{2}$ (resp. $-\frac{\alpha-1}{2} \leq r' \leq \frac{\alpha-1}{2}$) such that $r' = r \mod (\alpha)$. We will speak of centered reduction modulo α. We define $r'' := r \bmod^{+}(\alpha)$ the unique $0 \leq r'' < \alpha$ such that $r'' = r \mod (\alpha)$.

Definition 2 *(Cyclotomic Ring)*
We define $\phi_n = x^n + 1$ with n a power of 2. This is a cyclotomic polynomial (One can show that ϕ_n is the 2n-th cyclotomic polynomial.) In particular, it is irreducible over $\mathbb{Q}$.

For q a prime, we define:

$$\mathcal{Q} := \mathbb{Q}[x]/(\phi_n) \ , \ \mathcal{R} := \mathbb{Z}[x]/(\phi_n) \ and \ \mathcal{R}_q := \mathbb{Z}_q[x]/(\phi_n).$$

Definition 3. *For $w \in \mathbb{Z}_q$:*

$$||w||_\infty := |w \bmod^{\pm} (q)|.$$

For $\boldsymbol{w} = \sum w_i x^i \in \mathcal{R}$:

$$||\boldsymbol{w}||_\infty := \max ||w_i \bmod^{\pm}(q)||_\infty \ and \ ||\boldsymbol{w}|| := \left(\sum ||w_i||_\infty^2 \right)^{1/2}$$

and for $\mathbf{w} = (\mathbf{w}^{[1]}, ..., \mathbf{w}^{[k]}) \in \mathcal{R}^k$,

$$||\mathbf{w}||_\infty := \max ||\mathbf{w}^{[i]}||_\infty \ and \ ||\mathbf{w}|| := \left(\sum ||\mathbf{w}^{[i]}||^2 \right)^{1/2}.$$

Finally, we define two sets $S_\eta, \tilde{S}_\eta \subset \mathcal{R}$:

$$S_\eta := \{\boldsymbol{w} \in \mathcal{R} \mid ||\boldsymbol{w}||_\infty \leq \eta\} \ and \ \tilde{S}_\eta := \{\boldsymbol{w} \bmod^{\pm} (2\eta) \mid \boldsymbol{w} \in \mathcal{R}\}.$$

Notation 1. *For an element $\mathbf{w}_1 \in \mathcal{R}^l$ we will note $\mathbf{w}_1 = (\mathbf{w}_1^{[1]}, ..., \mathbf{w}_1^{[l]}) \in \mathcal{R}^l$ and $\mathbf{w}_{1,i}^{[j]}$ will be the $i-th$ coefficient of the polynomial $\mathbf{w}_1^{[j]}$.*

Notation 2. *We will note $[\![\ statement \ ]\!]$ the boolean operator wich evaluates to 1 if statement is true, and to 0 otherwise.*

2.2 Dilithium, Hints and Inequalities

Dilithium uses $\mathcal{R}_q^{k \times l}$ with k, l varying according to the level of security required and with n and q chosen as:

$$n = 256, \quad q = 2^{23} - 2^{13} + 1 = 8\,380\,417$$

Dilithium uses algorithms that split elements in $\mathbb{Z}_q$. Informally speaking, for an even α divisor of $q - 1$, $r \in \mathbb{Z}_q$ one can define $r = r_1 \alpha + r_0$ with $r_0 = r \bmod^{\pm}(\alpha)$ and $r_1 = (r - r_0)/\alpha$. We will call r_1 the most significant bits of r and r_0 the least significant bits of r. As shown in Fig. 1, for $z \in \mathbb{Z}_q$ such that $|z| \leq \alpha/2$, adding z to r can increase or decrease the most significant bits of r by ± 1. The aim is to be able to calculate the most significant bits of an addition between $r \in \mathbb{Z}_q$ and a small element $z \in \mathbb{Z}_q$, without having to store z. To do this, an algorithm which generates a one bit hint h is used. In Algorithm 1 we give the description of the algorithms and recall in Lemma 1 the main property used.

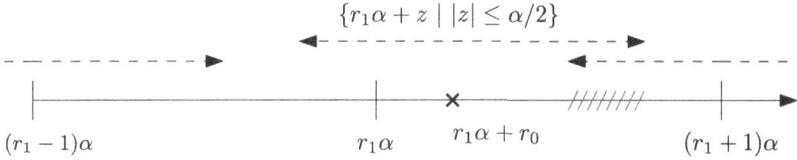

Fig. 1. carry caused by z

Algorithm 1. Supporting algorithms for Dilithium

$\mathsf{Decompose}_q(r, \alpha)$:

1: $r = r \bmod^+ q$
2: $r_0 = r \bmod^{\pm} \alpha$
3: **if** $r - r_0 = q - 1$ **then** $r_1 = 0\ r_0 = r_0 - 1$
4: **else** $r_1 = (r - r_0)/\alpha$
5: **return** (r_1, r_0)

$\mathsf{HighBits}_q(r, \alpha)$:

1: $(r_1, r_0) = \mathsf{Decompose}_q(r, \alpha)$
2: **return** r_1

$\mathsf{LowBits}_q(r, \alpha)$:

1: $(r_1, r_0) = \mathsf{Decompose}_q(r, \alpha)$
2: **return** r_0

$\mathsf{MakeHint}_q(z, r, \alpha)$:

1: $r_1 = \mathsf{HighBits}_q(r, \alpha)$
2: $v_1 = \mathsf{HighBits}_q(r + z, \alpha)$
3: **return** $[\![r_1 \neq v_1]\!]$

$\mathsf{UseHint}_q(h, r, \alpha)$:

1: $m = (q - 1)/\alpha$
2: $(r_1, r_0) = \mathsf{Decompose}_q(r, \alpha)$
3: **if** $h = 1$ and $r_0 > 0$ **then return** $(r_1 + 1) \bmod^+ m$
4: **if** $h = 1$ and $r_0 \leq 0$ **then return** $(r_1 - 1) \bmod^+ m$
5: **return** r_1

Lemma 1 *[LDK+22]. Let q and α be two positive integers such that $q > 2\alpha$, $q \equiv 1 \mod (\alpha)$ and α even. Let $\mathbf{r}$ and $\mathbf{z}$ be two vectors of $\mathcal{R}_q$ such that $\|\mathbf{z}\|_\infty \leq \alpha/2$ and let $\mathbf{h}, \mathbf{h}'$ be bit vectors. So the algorithms* $\mathtt{HighBits}_q$, $\mathtt{MakeHint}_q$, $\mathtt{UseHint}_q$ *satisfy the properties:*

$$\mathtt{UseHint}_q(\mathtt{MakeHint}_q(\mathbf{z}, \mathbf{r}, \alpha), \mathbf{r}, \alpha) = \mathtt{HighBits}_q(\mathbf{r} + \mathbf{z}, \alpha).$$

Remark 1. *Dilithium uses these algorithms to reduce the size of the public key: it splits a part of the public key $\mathbf{t}$ into two using an algorithm named* $\mathtt{Power2Round}$ *defined in the specification of Dilithium [BDK+21] and makes public only $\mathbf{t}_1$, the most significant bits of $\mathbf{t}$. In return, the signer adds a few hint bits to the signature to enable the signature to be verified without knowledge of the least significant bits of $\mathbf{t}$.*

2.3   Algorithm Description

The remainder of this section gives a quick overview of Dilithium, for an exhaustive description of the functions used see [BDK+21].

Key Generation: The key generation consists of sampling two short vectors of polynomials s_1 and s_2 with a public matrix $\mathbf{A}$. We then calculate $\mathbf{t} = \mathbf{A}s_1 + s_2$, which will also become public. To reduce the size of the public key, only the most significant bits of $\mathbf{t}$, $\mathbf{t}_1$, are part of the public key. For the same reason, we keep only the seed ρ used to generate $\mathbf{A}$. The vectors of small polynomials s_1 and s_2 remain secret. The key generation algorithm is described in Algorithm 2.

Algorithm 2. KeyGen

Ensure: (pk, sk)
1: $\zeta \leftarrow \{0, 1\}^{256}$
2: $(\rho, \rho', K) \in \{0, 1\}^{256} \times \{0, 1\}^{512} \times \{0, 1\}^{256} := \mathrm{H}(\zeta)$
3: $\mathbf{A} \in \mathcal{R}_q^{k \times l} := \mathtt{ExpandA}(\rho)$ ▷ $\mathbf{A}$ is generated and stored in NTT as $\hat{\mathbf{A}}$
4: $(s_1, s_2) \in S_\eta^l \times S_\eta^k := \mathtt{ExpandS}(\rho')$
5: $\mathbf{t} := \mathbf{A}s_1 + s_2$ ▷ Compute $\mathbf{A}s_1$ as $\mathtt{NTT}^{-1}(\hat{\mathbf{A}} \cdot \mathtt{NTT}(s_1))$
6: $(\mathbf{t}_1, \mathbf{t}_0) := \mathtt{Power2Round}_q(\mathbf{t}, d)$
7: $tr \in \{0, 1\}^{256} := \mathrm{H}(\rho \,\|\, \mathbf{t}_1)$
8: **return** $pk = (\rho, \mathbf{t}_1)$, $sk = (\rho, K, tr, s_1, s_2, \mathbf{t}_0)$

Signature: Dilithium is based on the"Fiat-Shamir with aborts" framework: a signature is generated and accepted if it meets certain conditions; if it does not, the process is repeated until a valid signature is obtained. The signer draws a random polynomial vector $\mathbf{y} \in \tilde{S}_{\gamma_1}^l$. Then from $\mathtt{HighBits}_q(\mathbf{A}\mathbf{y}, 2\gamma_2)$ using a hash function, it creates a challenge c. Then, it calculates $\mathbf{z} := \mathbf{y} + c\mathbf{s}_1$ the definition of $\mathbf{z}$ and $\mathbf{t}$ gives:

$$\texttt{HighBits}_q(\mathbf{Az} - c\mathbf{t}, 2\gamma_2) = \texttt{HighBits}_q(\mathbf{Ay} - c\mathbf{s}_2, 2\gamma_2).$$

Furthermore, $\mathbf{y}$ is chosen such that:

$$\texttt{HighBits}_q(\mathbf{Ay} - c\mathbf{s}_2, 2\gamma_2) = \texttt{HighBits}_q(\mathbf{Ay}, 2\gamma_2)$$

As $\mathbf{t}_0$ is not public, the signer adds a vector of hint $\mathbf{h} = \texttt{MakeHint}_q(-c\mathbf{t}_0, \mathbf{Ay} - c\mathbf{s}_2 + c\mathbf{t}_0, 2\gamma_2)$ to enable the verifier to calculate $\texttt{HighBits}_q(\mathbf{Az} - c\mathbf{t}, 2\gamma_2)$ and then recalculate c without knowledge of $\mathbf{t}_0$. The signature algorithm is described in Algorithm 3.

Algorithm 3. Sig

Require: sk, M
Ensure: $\sigma = (\tilde{c}, \mathbf{z}, \mathbf{h})$
  1: $\mathbf{A} \in \mathcal{R}_q^{k \times l} := \texttt{ExpandA}(\rho)$ $\triangleright$ $\mathbf{A}$ is generated and stored in NTT as $\hat{\mathbf{A}}$
  2: $\mu \in \{0,1\}^{512} := \text{H}(tr \,\|\, M)$
  3: $\kappa := 0, (\mathbf{z}, \mathbf{h}) := \bot$
  4: $\rho' \in \{0,1\}^{512} := \text{H}(K \,\|\, \mu)$
  5: **while** $(\mathbf{z}, \mathbf{h}) = \bot$ **do** $\triangleright$ Pre-compute $\hat{s}_1 := \texttt{NTT}(\mathbf{s}_1)$, $\hat{s}_2 := \texttt{NTT}(\mathbf{s}_2)$ and $\hat{t}_0 := \texttt{NTT}(\mathbf{t}_0)$
  6:     $\mathbf{y} \in \tilde{S}_{\gamma_1}^l := \texttt{ExpandMask}(\rho', \kappa)$
  7:     $\mathbf{w} := \mathbf{A}\,\mathbf{y}$ $\triangleright$ $\mathbf{w} := \texttt{NTT}^{-1}(\hat{\mathbf{A}} \cdot \texttt{NTT}(\mathbf{y}))$
  8:     $\mathbf{w}_1 = \texttt{HighBits}_q(\mathbf{w}, 2\gamma_2)$
  9:     $\tilde{c} \in \{0,1\}^{256} := \text{H}(\mu \,\|\, \mathbf{w}_1)$
 10:     $c \in B_\tau := \texttt{SampleInBall}(\tilde{c})$ $\triangleright$ Store c in NTT representation as $\hat{c} = \texttt{NTT}(c)$
 11:     $\mathbf{z} := \mathbf{y} + c\mathbf{s}_1$ $\triangleright$ Compute $c\mathbf{s}_1$ as $\texttt{NTT}^{-1}(\hat{c} \cdot \hat{s}_1)$
 12:     $\mathbf{r}_0 := \texttt{LowBits}_q(\mathbf{w} - c\mathbf{s}_2, 2\gamma_2)$ $\triangleright$ Compute $c\mathbf{s}_2$ as $\texttt{NTT}^{-1}(\hat{c} \cdot \hat{s}_2)$
 13:     **if** $\|\mathbf{z}\|_\infty \geq \gamma_1 - \beta$ or $\|\mathbf{r}_0\|_\infty \geq \gamma_2 - \beta$ **then**
 14:         $(\mathbf{z}, \mathbf{h}) := \bot$
 15:     **else**
 16:         $\mathbf{h} := \texttt{MakeHint}_q(-c\mathbf{t}_0, \mathbf{w} - c\mathbf{s}_2 + c\mathbf{t}_0, 2\gamma_2)$ $\triangleright$ Compute $c\mathbf{t}_0$ as $\texttt{NTT}^{-1}(\hat{c} \cdot \hat{t}_0)$
 17:         **if** $\|c\mathbf{t}_0\|_\infty \geq \gamma_2$ or $|\mathbf{h}|_{\mathbf{h}_j=1} > \omega$ **then**
 18:             $(\mathbf{z}, \mathbf{h}) := \bot$
 19:     $\kappa := \kappa + l$
 20: **return** $\sigma = (\tilde{c}, \mathbf{z}, \mathbf{h})$

Verification: From the signature, c is recalculated. The verifier then uses the hints to recalculate $\mathbf{w}_1'$ the value to which the signer has committed. If the commitment is correct and $\mathbf{z}$ meets other conditions, the signature is accepted. Otherwise it is rejected. The verification algorithm is described in Algorithm 4.

Algorithm 4. Ver

Require: pk, σ

1: $\mathbf{A} \in \mathcal{R}_q^{k \times l} := \texttt{ExpandA}(\rho)$

2: $\mu \in \{0,1\}^{512} := \mathrm{H}(\mathrm{H}(\rho \,\|\, \mathbf{t}_1) \,\|\, M)$

3: $c := \texttt{SampleInBall}(\tilde{c})$

4: $\mathbf{w}_1' := \texttt{UseHint}_q(\mathbf{h}, \mathbf{Az} - c\mathbf{t}_1 \cdot 2^d, 2\gamma_2)$

5: **return** $[\![\|\mathbf{z}\|_\infty < \gamma_1 - \beta]\!]$ and $[\![\tilde{c} = \mathrm{H}(\mu \,\|\, \mathbf{w}_1')]\!]$ and $[\![|\mathbf{h}|_{\mathbf{h}_j = 1} \leq \omega]\!]$

2.4   The Basis of Polyhedral Theory

In the rest of the paper, we will show that some rejected signatures of Dilithium provide inequalities on the coefficients of $\mathbf{s}_2$. Therefore $\mathbf{s}_2$ is one of the solutions to a set of inequalities. We are going to show that this type of set has certain properties, and we will need to define a natural notion of dimension. As this dimension is linked to the number of points in the set, we will need a practical way of estimating it. We would like to point out that the general definitions and unproven propositions come from [NW88].

Definition 4. *A set of points $x_1, ..., x_k \in \mathbb{R}^n$ is affinely independent if the unique solution of $\sum_{i=1}^k \alpha_i x_i = 0$, $\sum_{i=1}^k \alpha_i = 0$ is $\alpha_i = 0$ for $i = 1, ..., k$.*

Remark 2. *When dealing with linear inequalities it is often more appropriate to use the concept of affine independence, linear independence implies affine independence, but the converse is not true.*

Definition 5. *A polyhedron $P \subset \mathbb{R}^n$ is the set of points that satisfy a finite number of linear inequalities, $P = \{x \in \mathbb{R}^n : Ax \leq b\}$ where (A, b) is a $m \times (n+1)$ matrix.*

Definition 6. *A polyhedron $P \subset \mathbb{R}^n$ is bounded if there exists an $w \in \mathbb{R}_+$ such that $P \subset \{x \in \mathbb{R}^n : -w \leq x_j \leq w \text{ for } j = 1, ..., n\}$. A bounded polyhedron is called a polytope.*

Definition 7. *A polyhedron P is of dimension k, denoted by $dim(P) = k$, if the maximum number of affinely independent points in P is $k + 1$.*

Remark 3. *It is essential to calculate the dimension of a polytope formed by a set of inequalities efficiently, as the dimension of the polytope gives us a upper-bound on the number of its elements. More importantly, if we collect enough inequalities so that the dimension of the associated polytope becomes 0, we know that $\mathbf{s}_2$ will be the only solution to this set of inequalities.*

Definition 8. *We note a^i the $i-th$ row of A. Let $M = \{1, 2, ..., m\}$, $M^= = \{i \in M : a^i x = b_i$ for all $x \in P\}$ and let $M^{\leq} = M \backslash M^=$. Let $(A^=, b^=)$ and $(A^{\leq}, b^{\leq})$ be the corresponding rows of (A, b). We refer to the equality and inequality sets of representation (A, b) of P, that is:*

$$P = \{x \in \mathbb{R}^n : A^= = b^=, A^{\leq} x \leq b^{\leq}\}.$$

Proposition 1. *If $P \subset \mathbb{R}^n$, then $dim(P) + rank(A^=, b^=) = n$.*

Remark 4. *Unfortunately, finding the matrix $(A^=, b^=)$ corresponding to a polyhedron P can be computationally expensive. Instead, we will use the following proposition, which is more appropriate in our case.*

Proposition 2. *Let $P \subset \mathbb{R}^n$ be a polyhedron, let $I = \{i \in M : \exists w_i \in \mathbb{R}, \forall x \in P, x_i = w_i\}$ then:*

$$dim(P) \leq n - card(I).$$

Proof. There exist real numbers $(w_i)_{i \in I}$ such that $P \subset \tilde{P} = \{x \in \mathbb{R}^n : \forall i \in I, x_i = w_i\}$ and according to the previous proposition: $dim(\tilde{P}) = n - card(I)$.

2.5   The Basis of Integer Programming

In the previous section we looked at the properties of polytopes, which represent sets of solutions to inequalities. Even if we collect enough inequalities for s_2 to be the only solution, we still need to find s_2 efficiently. The aim of this section is to study the basics of integer linear programming, this will enable us to efficiently find a solution to a set of inequalities, in other words: To find a point on the polytope containing s_2. The general linear programming problem is to find:

$$z_{LP} = \max\{cx : Ax \leq b, x \in \mathbb{R}_+\}$$

where A is a $m \times n$ matrix and c, b are $m \times 1$ matrices. This problem is well defined is the sense that if it is feasible and does not have unbounded optimal values, then it has an optimal solution. In the rest of this paper, we will note (LP) and write it in the following form:

$$\begin{array}{l} \text{maximize } cx \\ \text{subject to } Ax \leq b \\ \qquad\qquad x \in \mathbb{R} \end{array}$$

One can also define the integer programming problem, noted (IP):

$$\begin{array}{l} \text{maximize } cx \\ \text{subject to } Ax \leq b \\ \qquad\qquad x \in \mathbb{Z} \end{array}$$

Integer programming is a harder problem than linear programming, linear programming algorithms are very often used as a subroutine in integer programming algorithms to obtain upper bounds on the value of the integer program. Exact resolution algorithms exist and we believe it is important from a theoretical point of view to recall the following theorems:

Theorem 1. *[NW88] For a fixed n there is a polynomial algorithm for the integer programming problem (IP).*

Theorem 2. *[NW88] For a fixed m there is a polynomial algorithm for the integer programming problem (IP).*

For a fixed m, the degree of the polynomial by which the running time of the algorithm in [NW88] is bounded as an exponential function of n. Therefore it does not achieve the performance required to solve certain problems. Instead, a wide range of approximate solvers have been developed which provide much more efficient results. In this paper, we use a free solver called lpsolve [MB04], which uses heuristic methods that are very efficient in practice.

Remark 5. *In our case, we are trying to find s_2 from a number of inequalities on its coefficients. If we collect enough inequalities on the coefficients of s_2, solving an (IP) or (LP) problem will give the same result because s_2 will be the only solution (integer or not). Since solving a (LP) problem is much more efficient, in the rest of the document we will focus on (LP) problems related to s_2.*

3   Problem Definition and Reformulation

We study the case of an attacker who retrieves rejected signatures. More precisely, we want to mount a practical attack against Dilithium without the first or second condition from the line 13. The attack methodology we used is independent of the condition.

However, attacking Dilithium without the second condition in line 13 of Algorithm 3 is less straightforward because we first need to retrieve $\mathbf{w}_1$ to exploit such signatures. In this paper, we have chosen to focus on this attack. Nonetheless, sub-section 6.4 briefly explains how to transpose the attack on Dilithium without the first condition and gives the obtained experimental results. Formally, we define another signature algorithm called F-Sig in Algorithm 5, and we demonstrate the existence of a practical attack against it.

Remark 6. *As Dilithium's proof of security does not use the knowledge of $\mathbf{t}_0$, most of the literature considers it public data. Recently, a paper published on eprint [AOCVCG24] appears to prove that $\mathbf{t}_0$ can indeed be reconstructed from a reasonable amount of Dilithium signatures. From now on and in the rest of the paper, we will assume that $\mathbf{t}_0$ is public.*

Remark 7. *The verification algorithm will not always accept the signature generated by F-Sig. Moreover, we know in advance that the Dilithium security proof does not apply here, as we have deliberately removed a security check. In the event of a physical attack that would skip this condition, the security of Dilithium would fall back to F-Sig.*

Algorithm 5. F-Sig

Require: sk, M

Ensure: $\sigma = (\tilde{c}, \mathbf{z}, \mathbf{h})$

1:   $\mathbf{A} \in \mathcal{R}_q^{k \times l} := \texttt{ExpandA}(\rho)$ ▷ $\mathbf{A}$ is generated and stored in NTT as $\hat{\mathbf{A}}$

2:   $\mu \in \{0,1\}^{512} := \mathrm{H}(tr \, || \, M)$

3:   $\kappa := 0$, $(\mathbf{z}, \mathbf{h}) := \bot$

4:   $\rho' \in \{0,1\}^{512} := \mathrm{H}(K \, || \, \mu)$

5:   **while** $(\mathbf{z}, \mathbf{h}) = \bot$ **do** ▷ Pre-compute $\hat{s}_1 := \texttt{NTT}(\mathbf{s}_1)$, $\hat{s}_2 := \texttt{NTT}(\mathbf{s}_2)$ and $\hat{\mathbf{t}}_0 := \texttt{NTT}(\mathbf{t}_0)$

6:       $\mathbf{y} \in \tilde{S}_{\gamma_1}^l := \texttt{ExpandMask}(\rho', \kappa)$

7:       $\mathbf{w} := \mathbf{A}\,\mathbf{y}$ ▷ $\mathbf{w} := \texttt{NTT}^{-1}(\hat{\mathbf{A}} \cdot \texttt{NTT}(\mathbf{y}))$

8:       $\mathbf{w}_1 = \texttt{HighBits}_q(\mathbf{w}, 2\gamma_2)$

9:       $\tilde{c} \in \{0,1\}^{256} := \mathrm{H}(\mu \, || \, \mathbf{w}_1)$

10:     $c \in B_\tau := \texttt{SampleInBall}(\tilde{c})$ ▷ Store c in NTT representation as $\hat{c} = \texttt{NTT}(c)$

11:     $\mathbf{z} := \mathbf{y} + c\mathbf{s}_1$ ▷ Compute $c\mathbf{s}_1$ as $\texttt{NTT}^{-1}(\hat{c} \cdot \hat{s}_1)$

12:     $\mathbf{r}_0 := \texttt{LowBits}_q(\mathbf{w} - c\mathbf{s}_2, 2\gamma_2)$ ▷ Compute $c\mathbf{s}_2$ as $\texttt{NTT}^{-1}(\hat{c} \cdot \hat{s}_2)$

13:     **if** $\|\mathbf{z}\|_\infty \geq \gamma_1 - \beta$ **then**

14:         $(\mathbf{z}, \mathbf{h}) := \bot$

15:     **else**

16:         $\mathbf{h} := \texttt{MakeHint}_q(-c\mathbf{t}_0, \mathbf{w} - c\mathbf{s}_2 + c\mathbf{t}_0, 2\gamma_2)$ ▷ Compute $c\mathbf{t}_0$ as $\texttt{NTT}^{-1}(\hat{c} \cdot \hat{\mathbf{t}}_0)$

17:         **if** $\|c\mathbf{t}_0\|_\infty \geq \gamma_2$ or $|\mathbf{h}|_{\mathbf{h}_j = 1} > \omega$ **then**

18:            $(\mathbf{z}, \mathbf{h}) := \bot$

19:     $\kappa := \kappa + l$

20: **return** $\sigma = (\tilde{c}, \mathbf{z}, \mathbf{h})$

3.1 Turning it into a Linear Programming Problem

The aim of this part is to prove (under hypotheses verified in practice) that a non-negligible proportion of signatures of F-Sig provide inequalities on the coefficients of $\mathbf{s}_2$. Thus, finding $\mathbf{s}_2$ from a set of signatures of F-Sig is equivalent to finding $\mathbf{s}_2$ among the points of a polytope defined by a set of inequalities. If we collect enough inequations so that the dimension of the polytope containing $\mathbf{s}_2$ is 0, we can find it using linear programming. The first step is to show the following: from a signature $\sigma = (\tilde{c}, \mathbf{z}, \mathbf{h})$ of F-Sig we can find the polynomial vector $\mathbf{w}_1$ used in the signature. To do this, we need a hypothesis that will be verified in practice, through simulations.

Assumption 1. *With overwhelming probability, for a signature of* F-Sig *the polynomial vector* $\mathbf{w}_1 - \mathbf{w}_1'$ *has at most one non-zero coefficient, which will be 1 or −1.*

Proposition 3. *Under Assumption 1, if σ is a signature of* F-Sig, *with overwhelming probability we can find* $\mathbf{w}_1$ *by knowing* $\mathbf{w}_1'$.

Proof. If the signature is accepted by the verification, we get directly $\mathbf{w}_1 = \mathbf{w}_1'$. If the signature is rejected, we carry out an exhaustive search on the coefficients of $\mathbf{w}_1$ (because we know that $c = \mathrm{H}(\mu \,\|\, \mathbf{w}_1)$). According to Assumption 1, we will have at most $2 \times k \times 256$ values to test.

Proposition 4. *For any* $\sigma = (\tilde{c}, \mathbf{z}, \mathbf{h})$ *signature of* F-Sig *that is not accepted by the verification algorithm, there exists a unique* $j \in \{1, ..., k\}$ *and a unique* $i \in \{0, ..., 255\}$ *such that:*

- *if* $(\mathbf{w}_1 - \mathbf{w}_1')_i^{[j]} = 1$:

$$(cs_2)_i^{[j]} \geq \gamma_2 - \mathbf{r}_{0,i}^{[j]} \geq 0,$$

- *if* $(\mathbf{w}_1 - \mathbf{w}_1')_i^{[j]} = -1$:

$$(cs_2)_i^{[j]} \leq -\gamma_2 - \mathbf{r}_{0,i}^{[j]} \leq 0.$$

Proof. Let $\sigma = (\tilde{c}, \mathbf{z}, \mathbf{h})$ be a rejected signature. We have $\mathbf{w}_1 \neq \mathbf{w}_1'$. If we assume that the non-zero coefficient of $\mathbf{w}_1 - \mathbf{w}_1'$ is 1, according to Assumption 1, there exists a unique $j \in \{1, ..., k\}$ and a unique $i \in \{0, ..., 255\}$ such that:

$$\mathtt{HighBits}_q((\mathbf{w})_i^{[j]}, 2\,\gamma_2) = \mathtt{HighBits}_q((\mathbf{w}')_i^{[j]}, 2\,\gamma_2) + 1.$$

Thus, one has

$$\mathtt{HighBits}_q(\mathbf{Ay}, 2\,\gamma_2)_i^{[j]} = \mathtt{HighBits}_q(\mathbf{Ay} - cs_2, 2\,\gamma_2)_i^{[j]} + 1,$$

since $\mathbf{r}_0 = \mathtt{LowBits}_q(\mathbf{Ay} - cs_2, 2\,\gamma_2)_i^{[j]}$, we have:

$$(cs_2)_i^{[j]} \geq \gamma_2 - \mathbf{r}_{0,i}^{[j]} \geq 0.$$

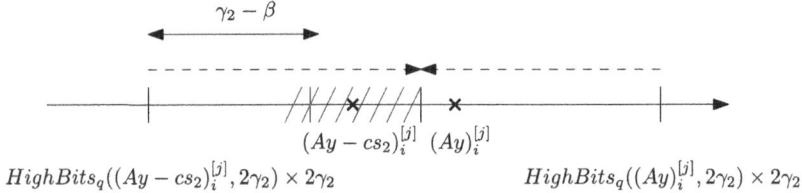

Fig. 2. In red, impossible values for $(cs_2)_i^{[j]}$ (Color figure online)

The same arguments can be used to show the second inequality when the non-zero coefficient of $\mathbf{w}_1 - \mathbf{w}_1'$ is -1. A graphical representation of the proof can be found in Fig. 2.

Remark 8. *Since $\sigma = (\tilde{c}, \mathbf{z}, \mathbf{h})$, $\mathbf{A}$ and $\mathbf{t}_0$ are known, $\mathbf{r}_0$ can be calculated, using the relation $\mathbf{Az} - c\mathbf{t} = \mathbf{Ay} - c\mathbf{s}_2$. Therefore, each signature not accepted by the verification algorithm* Ver *will provide an inequality verified by certain coefficients of the polynomial vector $\mathbf{s}_2$. We are going to use the linear programming theory, firstly to estimate how many inequalities it would take for $\mathbf{s}_2$ to be the only solution, and secondly to find this solution efficiently. As [BP18, RJH+18] shows, recovering $\mathbf{t}_0$ and $\mathbf{s}_2$ allows to forge arbitrary signatures, and to an equivalent key recovery.*

Building the (LP) System. After collecting enough signatures, we will have multiple inequalities on the k polynomials of $\mathbf{s}_2$ independently, so we can split the problem into k smaller ones, one for each polynomial of the vector $\mathbf{s}_2$. For the sake of clarity, let us explain the methodology for a single polynomial of the vector $\mathbf{s}_2 = (\mathbf{s}_2^{[1]}, ..., \mathbf{s}_2^{[k]})$. We select a signature that gives an inequation on $\mathbf{s}_2^{[1]}$. Let $\sigma = (\tilde{c}, \mathbf{z}, \mathbf{h})$ be such a signature, we have:

If $(\mathbf{w}_1 - \mathbf{w}_1')_i^{[1]} = 1$:

$$(c\mathbf{s}_2)_i^{[1]} \geq \gamma_2 - \mathbf{r}_{0,i}^{[1]} \tag{1}$$

$$\sum_{j=0}^{n-1} s_{2,j}^{[1]}(cx^j)_i \geq \gamma_2 - \mathbf{r}_{0,i}^{[1]} \tag{2}$$

Since the polynomial c is known, σ gives us an inequality on the coefficients of $\mathbf{s}_2^{[1]}$. The case of $(\mathbf{w}_1 - \mathbf{w}_1')_i^{[1]} = -1$ is treated in the same way. Thus, with its rejected signatures, we can construct two matrices A_+ and A_- and two vectors b_+ and b_- such that $\mathbf{s}_2^{[1]} \in \{x \in [-\eta, \eta]^n \mid A_+x \geq b_+ \text{ and } A_-x \leq b_-\}$. Each row of one of these matrices representing an inequality collected on $\mathbf{s}_2^{[1]}$. In particular, if we collect enough inequalities for $\mathbf{s}_2^{[1]}$ to be the only solution, we can find $\mathbf{s}_2^{[1]}$ by solving the following (LP) problem of dimension $n = 256$:

$$\begin{aligned} &\text{maximize } 0 \\ &\text{subject to } A_+x \geq b_+ \\ &\qquad\qquad A_-x \leq b_- \\ &\qquad\qquad x \in [-\eta, \eta]^n \end{aligned}$$

Fig. 3. The (LP) problem related to $\mathbf{s}_2^{[1]}$.

4 Differences Between Specification Algorithm and Reference Implementation

For Dilithium, the reference implementation noted Sig_{Ref} uses an alternative way of decomposing and calculating hints, to avoid calling the Decompose_q function three times. This method, which we will note $\texttt{MakeHint\_ref}_q$, is detailed in the Dilithium specification [DKL+22], in Section 5.1. Remark that this alternative method to compute the hints is no longer equivalent if we remove the condition on $\tilde{r}_0$. Rather than re-describing an attack by detailing the entire procedure, we explain only the main ideas for transforming our attack into an attack against $\texttt{Sig}_{\texttt{Ref}}$. Algorithm 6 gives the pseudo code of $\texttt{Sig}_{\texttt{Ref}}$.

Remark 9. *To avoid copying the* $\texttt{Sig}_{\texttt{Ref}}$ *and* $\texttt{F-Sig}_{\texttt{Ref}}$ *algorithms, which are similar, we only write* $\texttt{Sig}_{\texttt{Ref}}$. $\texttt{F-Sig}_{\texttt{Ref}}$ *is obtained by removing the condition* $\|\tilde{r}_0\|_\infty \geq \gamma_2 - \beta$ *on line 13. Even if* $\texttt{Sig}_{\texttt{Ref}}$ *and* $\texttt{Sig}$ *work in the same way, our attack on* $\texttt{F-Sig}_{\texttt{Ref}}$ *will be more difficult to detect, as all the signatures produced will be accepted by the verification algorithm.*

Algorithm 6. $\texttt{Sig}_{\texttt{Ref}}$

Require: sk, M
Ensure: $\sigma = (\tilde{c}, \mathbf{z}, \mathbf{h})$
1: $\mathbf{A} \in R_q^{k \times l} := \texttt{ExpandA}(\rho)$ ▷ $\mathbf{A}$ is generated and stored in NTT as $\hat{\mathbf{A}}$
2: $\mu \in \{0,1\}^{512} := \mathrm{H}(tr \,\|\, M)$
3: $\kappa := 0, (\mathbf{z}, \mathbf{h}) := \bot$
4: $\rho' \in \{0,1\}^{512} := \mathrm{H}(K \,\|\, \mu)$
5: **while** $(\mathbf{z}, \mathbf{h}) = \bot$ **do** ▷ Pre-compute $\hat{s}_1 := \texttt{NTT}(\mathbf{s}_1)$, $\hat{s}_2 := \texttt{NTT}(\mathbf{s}_2)$ and $\hat{\mathbf{t}}_0 := \texttt{NTT}(\mathbf{t}_0)$
6:      $\mathbf{y} \in \tilde{S}_{\gamma_1}^l := \texttt{ExpandMask}(\rho', \kappa)$
7:      $\mathbf{w} := \mathbf{A}\mathbf{y}$ ▷ $\mathbf{w} := \texttt{NTT}^{-1}(\hat{\mathbf{A}} \cdot \texttt{NTT}(\mathbf{y}))$
8:      $(\mathbf{w}_1, \mathbf{w}_0) = \texttt{Decompose}_q(\mathbf{w}, 2\gamma_2)$
9:      $\tilde{c} \in \{0,1\}^{256} := \mathrm{H}(\mu \,\|\, \mathbf{w}_1)$
10:      $c \in B_\tau := \texttt{SampleInBall}(\tilde{c})$ ▷ Store c in NTT representation as $\hat{c} = \texttt{NTT}(c)$
11:      $\mathbf{z} := \mathbf{y} + c\mathbf{s}_1$ ▷ Compute $c\mathbf{s}_1$ as $\texttt{NTT}^{-1}(\hat{c} \cdot \hat{s}_1)$
12:      $\tilde{r}_0 := \mathbf{w}_0 - c\mathbf{s}_2$ ▷ Compute $c\mathbf{s}_2$ as $\texttt{NTT}^{-1}(\hat{c} \cdot \hat{s}_2)$
13:      **if** $\|\mathbf{z}\|_\infty \geq \gamma_1 - \beta$ or $\|\tilde{r}_0\|_\infty \geq \gamma_2 - \beta$ **then**
14:          $(\mathbf{z}, \mathbf{h}) := \bot$
15:      **else**
16:          $\mathbf{h} := \texttt{MakeHint\_ref}_q(\mathbf{w}_1, \mathbf{w}_0 - c\mathbf{s}_2 + c\mathbf{t}_0, 2\gamma_2)$
17:          **if** $\|c\mathbf{t}_0\|_\infty \geq \gamma_2$ or $|\mathbf{h}|_{\mathbf{h}_j=1} > \omega$ **then**
18:              $(\mathbf{z}, \mathbf{h}) := \bot$
19:      $\kappa := \kappa + l$
20: **return** $\sigma = (\tilde{c}, \mathbf{z}, \mathbf{h})$

Assumption 2. *The signature made by* $\texttt{F-Sig}_{\texttt{Ref}}$ *will always be accepted by the Dilithium verification algorithm* $\texttt{Ver}$.

Proposition 5. *Under Assumption 2, let* $\sigma = (\tilde{c}, \mathbf{z}, \mathbf{h})$ *be a signature of* F-Sig$_{\text{Ref}}$, *then either* $\mathbf{w}_1 = \text{HighBits}_q(\mathbf{Az} - ct, 2\gamma_2)$ *or there exists at least one* $j \in \{1, ..., k\}$ *and at least one* $i \in \{0, ..., 255\}$ *such that:*

- *if* $(\mathbf{w}'_1 - \text{HighBits}_q(\mathbf{Az} - ct, 2\gamma_2))_i^{[j]}$ *is positive:*

$$(cs_2)_i^{[j]} \geq \gamma_2 - r_{0,i}^{[j]} \geq 0,$$

- *if* $(\mathbf{w}'_1 - \text{HighBits}_q(\mathbf{Az} - ct, 2\gamma_2))_i^{[j]}$ *is negative:*

$$(cs_2)_i^{[j]} \leq -\gamma_2 - r_{0,i}^{[j]} \leq 0.$$

Proof. Let $\sigma = (\tilde{c}, \mathbf{z}, \mathbf{h})$ be a signature of F-Sig$_{\text{Ref}}$ which verifies Assumption 2. Since the signature is validated by the verification algorithm, $\mathbf{w}_1 = \mathbf{w}'_1$. Lets assume that for this σ, $\mathbf{w}_1 \neq \text{HighBits}_q(\mathbf{Az} - ct, 2\gamma_2)$. We have $\mathbf{Az} - ct = \mathbf{Ay} - cs_2$ so $\mathbf{w}_1 \neq \text{HighBits}_q(\mathbf{Ay} - cs_2, 2\gamma_2)$. There exists a $j \in \{1, ..., k\}$ and a $i \in \{0, ..., 255\}$ such that:

$$\text{HighBits}_q((\mathbf{Ay})_i^{[j]}, 2\gamma_2) \neq \text{HighBits}_q((\mathbf{Ay} - cs_2)_i^{[j]}, 2\gamma_2).$$

If $(\mathbf{w}'_1 - \text{HighBits}_q(\mathbf{Az} - ct, 2\gamma_2))_i^{[j]}$ is positive, then because $\|cs_2\|_\infty \leq \beta$:

$$\text{HighBits}_q((\mathbf{Ay})_i^{[j]}, 2\gamma_2) = \text{HighBits}_q((\mathbf{Ay} - cs_2)_i^{[j]}, 2\gamma_2) + 1,$$

and:
$$(cs_2)_i^{[j]} \geq \gamma_2 - \text{LowBits}_q((\mathbf{Ay} - cs_2)_i^{[j]}, 2\gamma_2) \geq 0.$$

But by definition, $\mathbf{r}_0 := \text{LowBits}_q(\mathbf{Ay} - cs_2, 2\gamma_2)$, finally:

$$(cs_2)_i^{[j]} \geq \gamma_2 - \mathbf{r}_{0,i}^{[j]} \geq 0.$$

The same arguments can be used to show the second inequality when $(\mathbf{w}'_1 - \text{HighBits}_q(\mathbf{Az} - ct, 2\gamma_2))_i^{[j]}$ is negative.

5   Finding a Polytope

The aim is to find the $k \times 256$ coefficients of the polynomial vector $\mathbf{s}_2$. But as explained in Sect. 3, we can find the coefficients of each polynomial of $\mathbf{s}_2$ separately. In the following, we will only study how to find the first polynomial of $\mathbf{s}_2$. By signing messages, we will obtain inequalities verified by $\mathbf{s}_2^{[1]}$. Once we have obtained enough inequalities, $\mathbf{s}_2^{[1]}$ is the only solution, and we can find it by solving a (LP) problem with a arbitrary objective function, such as the null function. In other words, we want enough inequalities so that the dimension of the associated polytope $P \subset [-\eta, \ldots, \eta]^{256}$ is 0. By the same procedure, we will find all the polynomials in $\mathbf{s}_2$, in practice in Sect. 6. To estimate the dimension of the polytope P, we will use proposition 2 proved in Sect. 2. For $i \in \{1, \ldots, n\}$, by solving the following two (LP) problems (Fig. 4):

$$\begin{array}{ll}\text{minimize } x_i & \text{maximize } x_i \\ \text{subject to } A_+ x \geq b_+ & \text{subject to } A_+ x \geq b_+ \\ \quad A_- x \leq b_- & \quad A_- x \leq b_- \\ \quad x \in [-\eta, \eta]^n & \quad x \in [-\eta, \eta]^n \end{array}$$

Fig. 4. The 2×256 (LP) problems related to $s_2^{[1]}$.

We can calculate $\text{card}(\{i \in \{1, \dots, n\} : \exists w_i \in \mathbb{R}, \forall x \in P, x_i = w_i\})$ and therefore upper-bound the dimension of the polytope containing $s_2^{[1]}$.

Remark 10. *To estimate $dim(P)$ we need to solve 2×256 (LP) problems (2 for each coordinate function). Some of these problems were costly because the solution time depends on the function chosen and can soar when the number of inequations is insufficient. Despite efforts, we were unable to produce statistics using exactly this method. In the following section, we described a slightly modified method to estimate the number of inequalities required for the dimension of the polytope containing $s_2^{[1]}$ to become 0.*

5.1 Evolution of Polytopes Dimensions

Our goal is to provide an empirical justification for the number of inequalities required to find $s_2^{[1]}$. We will do what an attacker might do: we choose random keys and simulate not having access to the j first coefficients of $s_2^{[1]}$. By collecting rejected signatures, we will obtain inequalities on the "missing" $s_2^{[1]}$ coefficients. By doing this, we reduce ourselves to a polytope of lower maximum dimension (of maximum dimension j). The corresponding $2 \times j$ (LP) problems will be less costly to solve. By solving these problems for increasing values of j, we can try to guess the number of inequalities required when no coefficients are known. In this subsection only, we assume that some coefficients of $s_2^{[1]}$ are known. We sign messages with F-Sig to obtain inequalities on the missing coefficients of $s_2^{[1]}$. Table 1 summarizes the obtained results, for Dilithium-2[1]

Table 1. Evolution of the dimension as a function of the unknowns

Unknown coefficients	32	64	128	256
Nb tests	100	100	100	-
Inequalities	323	1306	3917	10 445 (predicted)
Polytopes dimensions	0	0	0	-
Attack time	1.36 s	17.4 s	227.3 s	-

The number of inequations appears to be linear on the number of unknowns. Based on the results, we conjecture that on average 10 000 inequalities will be

[1] For each time and probability of success, this is an average over 100 randoms keys.

sufficient to guarantee that $s_2^{[1]}$ is the unique solution to the associated (LP) problem. Hence an opponent who does not know any coefficient of $s_2^{[1]}$ will need 10 000 inequalities on average to find it.

Remark 11. *Note that even if the theory remains unchanged, these practical results are highly dependent on the size of the secret coefficients s_2, and therefore on the security level of Dilithium. So, the expected number of inequalities needed to recover the 256 coefficients is likely to change with the security level.*

6   Experimental Results

The purpose of this section is to evaluate the usability of Proposition 4 and 5 in practice. We tested the key recovery methodology for both versions of Dilithium, Sig and Sig_{Ref}, as well as the three different security levels, Dilithium-2, Dilithium-3, and Dilithium-5.

Experimental Setup. We use the C reference implementation of Dilithium from [DKL+22] as well as a modified version that follows the specification [LDK+22]. We adapt both of them to get implementations of F-Sig and F-Sig$_{\text{Ref}}$, as stated in Algorithm 5 and Algorithm 6. We use the resulting signatures in a Sage script that allows us to formulate the (LP) problems for a given secret key. The (LP) solving is done using the lpsolve library from Python. The tests were done on a laptop equipped with an Intel(R) Core(TM) i7-10850H 2.70GHz CPU. All the materials used to collect the signatures and perform the attack are available at https://github.com/anders1901/Polytope_attack. For our study, we focus on finding all polynomials of s_2. In our evaluations attack time means the time taken to find s_2 once the inequations have been extracted from the signatures generated.

Remark 12. *In a fault attack scenario, various fault injection techniques, such as clock and voltage glitches, laser, and electromagnetic pulse injection can lead to the skipping of an instruction [DRPR19, MDP+20, CPHR21]. In the context of our attack, we are interested in skipping the call to the* polyveck_checknorm *function, which allows us to output signatures without checking the norm of* z *or* r_0*. Our attack applies to both the deterministic and randomized versions of Dilithium. However, targeting the randomized version may require a more powerful attacker model. Indeed, injecting faults into the randomized version generally involves taking into account the rejection sampling step of the signature algorithm without prior analysis of the signature execution trace.*

Remark 13. *For both the specification and implementation of Dilithium we focus on retrieving the 100 keys produced by the KAT from [DKL+22].*

6.1   Attack on Dilithium's Specification

In the previous section, we conjectured that approximately 10 445 inequalities per polynomial of s_2 are needed to determine its $k \times 256$ coefficients. Therefore, the primary goal is to determine the number of signatures of F-Sig required to collect the given number of inequalities.

Assumption 1 in Practice. To measure the frequency with which Assumption 1 was verified, we collected 1 250 000 signatures for an equal number of random messages for each of the 100 keys obtained from the KAT files. Of the total 1 250 000 signatures for each key, more than half have at least one coefficient among the $k \times n$ exceeding the bound $\gamma_2 - \beta$. On average within this subset of 717 448 signatures, 46 459 do not pass signature verification, indicating potential exploitability under Assumption 1. This assumption states that the vast majority of these 46 459 signatures are likely to have no more than one coefficient where $\mathbf{w}_1$ and $\mathbf{w}_1'$ differ by a magnitude of 1 or -1. We tested for this on the set of 46 459 signatures and the experimental results are summarized in Table 2.

Table 2. Average Inequalities collected for 46 459 signatures over 100 keys

signatures	1 coefficient changed	2 or more coefficients changed	inequalities/polynomial
1 250 000	45 584	874	11 085

From these results we conclude that around 3.6% of the 1 250 000 signatures can be exploited. The vast majority of rejected signatures will provide an inequation on one of the coefficients of a polynomial of s_2, and can be used in the formulation of the (LP) problem. In the worst case, if the hypothesis is not verified, in other words if $\mathbf{w}_1 - \mathbf{w}_1' \neq \pm 1$, the attacker will be unable to exploit the signature produced by F-Sig, as he cannot find the inequation verified by s_2. He simply discards this signature and proceeds with the next one.

Attack Results. After collecting enough inequalities for each of the k polynomials, we expect to recover the entirety of the s_2 vector based on the analysis in Sect. 5. For this, we formulated the k (LP) problem for s_2, as depicted in Fig. 3. In order to be able to produce statistics in a reasonable amount of time, we set the solver resolution time to 30 minutes maximum. Table 3 summarizes the results obtained.

Table 3. Average results of the attack on F-Sig

Signatures	Average inequalities	Success probability	Average time	Median Time
1 250 000	11 085	0.99	277.53 s	180.00 s

We conclude that our attack is very efficient. Moreover, when the key is not found, it is systematically because the solver was unable to solve the system of inequalities in the given time. By increasing the limit we have set to more than 30 minutes, in about 2 and a half hours of calculation we were able to find the missing key.

6.2   Attack on Dilithium's Implementation

As stated in Sect. 4, the attack can easily be mounted for signatures produced by the reference implementation, by using Proposition 5. For completeness, we detail the results obtained for the reference implementation of Dilithium-2.

Assumption 2 in Practice. Just like in the previous sub-section, we collected 1 250 000 signatures for random messages for each of the 100 keys obtained from the KAT files. Among the 1 250 000 signatures collected for each key, in average 717 448 have at least one coefficient among the $k \times n$ exceeding the bound $\gamma_2 - \beta$. But, this time, all the signatures of the algorithm F-Sig$_{Ref}$ are accepted by the verification algorithm Ver, as stated in Assumption 2 (Table 4).

Table 4. Average Inequalities collected over 100 keys

signatures	1 coefficient changed	2 or more coefficients changed	inequalities/polynomial
1 250 000	45 578	875	11 083

Attack Results. Here also we formulate the (LP) problem as in Fig. 3 but with the inequalities from Proposition 5. Using the same methodology as for sub-section 6.1, we tried to recover the 100 keys from the KAT files. The results are summarized in Table 5.

Table 5. Average results of the attack on F-Sig$_{Ref}$

Signatures	Average inequalities	Sucess probability	Average time	Median time
1 250 000	11 083	0.98	261.79 s	148.79 s

Once again, we can see that the attack is very effective and works as the attack described for Dilithium's specification. Note also that when the keys are not recovered, it is always due to solver timeouts. Therefore, we can assume that increasing the solver's limit to more than 30 minutes would allow us to recover the missed keys.

6.3   Attack on Dilithium-3 and Dilithium-5

Since the theory presented above does not change according to the security level of Dilithium, we give the results obtained for the same attack against Dilithium-3 and Dilithium-5. The relevant parameters are summarized in Table 6. Note that the Dilithium specification and its reference implementation are also functionally equivalent. The only change in the attack is the condition to collect the inequality, not the inequality itself. Therefore, as a proof of concept, we decided to focus on evaluating the sensitivity of Dilithium's reference implementation. For this subsection, the evaluation is done only on the first 10 of KAT files. Finally, to confirm that we could eventually have a success rate of 100%, we decided not to set a timeout for the solver.

Table 6. Settings for different security levels of Dilithium

Security level	2	3	5
(k, l)	$(4, 4)$	$(6, 5)$	$(8, 7)$
γ_1	2^{17}	2^{19}	2^{19}
γ_2	$(q-1)/88$	$(q-1)/32$	$(q-1)/32$
η	2	4	2
τ	39	49	60

The primary difference between the different security levels is the dimension of the module, parameterized by k and l. Specifically, for s_2, the relevant dimension is $k = 6$ for Dilithium-3 and $k = 8$ for Dilithium-5. Consequently, due to the increased size of the vector, a larger number of signatures is required to ensure the minimum number of inequalities needed to initiate the attack. Additionally, another difference is the size of η, which is larger for Dilithium-3 compared to both Dilithium-2 and Dilithium-5. This change requires either a greater number of inequalities or an extended solver runtime to recover the coefficients of s_2 for Dilithium-3.

For Dilithium-3: Based on the statistics we ran on the dimension of the polytope for the parameters in Table 6, we estimated that we could run our attack with 3 000 000 signatures collected (i.e., about 18 000 inequalities). In practice, since no timeout was set, and to keep the solver's runtime to no more than twice that of Dilithium-2, we set the number of signatures to 3 500 000 (i.e., about

22 000 of inequalities). It provided a balanced trade-off between the number of signatures to collect and the solver's runtime. Table 7 summarizes the results obtained.

Table 7. Average results of the attack for Dilithium-3

Signatures	Average inequalities	Success probability	Average time	Median time
3 500 000	22 020	1	1 239.36 s	767.69 s

For Dilithium-5: Once again, using the statistics made on the dimension of the polytope, we estimate that the same number of inequalities as for Dilithium-2 will need to be collected. However, because there is twice as much polynomials in the vector $\mathbf{s}_2$, we will need to acquire at least twice more signatures. To be conservative, we collected 4 000 000 signatures. The results obtained are summarized in Table 8.

Table 8. Average results of the attack for Dilithium-5

Signatures	Average inequalities	Success probability	Average time	Median time
4 000 000	15 348	1	186.78 s	177.59 s

6.4   Impact on the Norm Check of Z

If we remove the condition on $\mathbf{z}$ line 13 of the algorithm Sig, we can obtain vectors of polynomials $\mathbf{z}$ which satisfy $\|\mathbf{z}\|_\infty \geq \gamma_1$. According to the definition of $\mathbf{y}$, such a $\mathbf{z}$ provides an inequality on one of the coefficients of $\mathbf{s}_1$. We can exploit these inequalities in the same way as in Sect. 3 to find $\mathbf{s}_1$. We believe that it is easy for an attentive reader to use these inequalities to find $\mathbf{s}_1$ using the same method as described in this paper. Nevertheless, we explicit the proposition that allows us to obtain the inequalities:

Proposition 6. *Let* $\sigma = (\tilde{c}, \mathbf{z}, \mathbf{h})$ *be a rejected signature of* Sig *such that* $\|\mathbf{z}\|_\infty \geq \gamma_1$, *then there exists* $j \in \{1, ..., l\}$ *and* $i \in \{0, ..., 255\}$ *such that:*

 – *if* $\mathbf{z}_i^{[j]} \geq \gamma_1$:

$$(c\mathbf{s}_1)_i^{[j]} \geq \mathbf{z}_i^{[j]} - \gamma_1 \geq 0,$$

 – *if* $\mathbf{z}_i^{[j]} \leq -\gamma_1$:

$$(c\mathbf{s}_1)_i^{[j]} \leq \mathbf{z}_i^{[j]} + \gamma_1 \leq 0.$$

Proof. If $\|\mathbf{z}\|_\infty \geq \gamma_1$, then there exists $j \in \{1, ..., l\}$ and $i \in \{0, ..., 255\}$ such that $|\mathbf{z}_i^{[j]}| \geq \gamma_1$. Lets assume that $\mathbf{z}_i^{[j]} \geq \gamma_1$. We have $\mathbf{z}_i^{[j]} = \mathbf{y}_i^{[j]} + (c\mathbf{s}_1)_i^{[j]}$ and by definition of $\mathbf{y}$, $|\mathbf{y}_i^{[j]}| \leq \gamma_1$. Thus,

$$(c\mathbf{s}_1)_i^{[j]} \geq \mathbf{z}_i^{[j]} - \gamma_1 \geq 0.$$

The same arguments can be used to show the second inequality when $\mathbf{z}_i^{[j]} \leq -\gamma_1$.

As a proof of concept, we ran this attack on $\mathbf{s}_1$ for the first 10 keys in the KAT files, for Dilithium-2. Table 9 summarizes the results obtained.

Table 9. Average results of the attack for Dilithium-2

Signatures	Average inequalities	Success probability	Average time	Median time
2 000 000	13 584	1	51.94 s	49.76 s

Remark 14. *In the Dilithium implementation, the way the signature is packed does not allow us to apply the attack directly, as we have to invert the* `polyz_pack` *function in order to find the coefficient of* $\mathbf{z}$ *which provides an inequality on the coefficients of* $\mathbf{s}_1$. *For our proof of concept, we simply attacked the Dilithium specification, without trying to invert this function.*

7   Conclusion and Discussion

In this paper, we created an attack on Dilithium with weakened rejection sampling, using linear programming tools. Since Dilithium's rejection sampling ensures that the scheme is zero knowledge, the existence of such an attack is not surprising. On the other hand, we think it is surprising that this attack is so effective, requiring just a few million signatures and a few minutes of computation on a modern computer. The main use of this result is that it reformulates as a fault-based attack against Dilithium. We have tested this attack against the official Dilithium implementation with simulated faults, as well as another modified version that strictly follows the main specification, for the three security levels of each implementation.

With regard to the feasibility of the attack, it requires between 1 and 4 million signatures, this amount is considered significant but realistic in the side-channel literature. Regarding the solving method, any lp solver can solve the systems provided by the obtained signatures. In this work we have chosen to use lpsolve, a MILP solver, even though in reality it is only used to solve (LP) problems. The main reason being the solver's performance, we tested the same key recovery with a more generic (and less optimised) lp solver (the one provided by scipy in python) and the solution times were up to 16 times slower. However, as the installation of lp solve can be rather complex, in the artifact we propose a solving with scipy and with lp solve. Finally, to be conservative we have reformulated the problems in the (IP) form for the Dilithium-2 reference implementation, and unsurprisingly we kept the same results with roughly identical computation times.

There are two main consequences of our results. Firstly, we show that rejection sampling is essential for the practical safety of Dilithium: the tests must be protected and not just the values manipulated during the test. Secondly, and perhaps more importantly, the reference implementation behaves differently. Faulty signatures will be accepted by the verification algorithm, which makes fault detection more delicate in restricted environments (for example, verifying signatures before outputting them will not be sufficient).

Acknowledgments. This research was funded in part by the France 2030 program under grant agreement No. ANR-22-PETQ-0008 PQ-TLS and by the ANRT (Association nationale de la recherche et de la technologie).

References

AOCVCG24. Oliveira, P.A., Viera, A.C., Cogliati, B., Goubin, L.: Uncompressing dilithium's public key. Cryptology ePrint Archive, Paper 2024/1373 (2024)

BAE+24. Bronchain, O., Azouaoui, M., ElGhamrawy, M., Renes, J., Schneider, T.: Exploiting small-norm polynomial multiplication with physical attacks: Application to crystals-dilithium. IACR Trans. Cryptographic Hardware Embed. Syst. **2024**(2), 359–383 (2024)

BBK16. Bindel, N., Buchmann, J., Krämer, J.: Lattice-based signature schemes and their sensitivity to fault attacks. In: 2016 Workshop on Fault Diagnosis and Tolerance in Cryptography, FDTC 2016, Santa Barbara, CA, USA, 16 August 2016, pp. 63–77. IEEE Computer Society (2016)

BDK+21. Shi Bai, S., et al.: Algorithm specifications and supporting documentation (version 3.1) (2021). https://pq-crystals.org/dilithium/data/dilithium-specification-round3-20210208.pdf

BP18. Bruinderink, L.G., Pessl, P.: Differential fault attacks on deterministic lattice signatures. IACR TCHES **2018**(3), 21–43 (2018). https://tches.iacr.org/index.php/TCHES/article/view/7267

BVC+23. Berzati, A., Viera, A.C., Chartouny, M., Madec, S., Vergnaud, D., Vigilant, D.: Exploiting intermediate value leakage in dilithium: a template-based approach. IACR TCHES **2023**(4), 188–210 (2023)

CKA+21. Chen, Z., Karabulut, E., Aysu, A., Ma, Y., Jing, J.: An efficient non-profiled side-channel attack on the crystals-dilithium post-quantum signature. In: 2021 IEEE 39th International Conference on Computer Design (ICCD), pp. 583–590 (2021)

CPHR21. Claudepierre, L., Péneau, P.Y., Hardy, D., Rohou, E.: Traitor: a low-cost evaluation platform for multifault injection. In: Proceedings of the 2021 International Symposium on Advanced Security on Software and Systems, ASSS 2021, pp. 51–56, New York, NY, USA, 2021. Association for Computing Machinery

DKL+.   Ducas, L., et al.: Official reference implementation of the dilithium signature scheme. https://github.com/pq-crystals/dilithium/

DKL+22.   Ducas, L., et al.:. PQ-CRYSTALS, Dilithium. https://github.com/pq-crystals/dilithium (2022). GitHub repository. Accessed 15 Dec 2022

DRPR19.   Dutertre, J.-M., Riom, T., Potin, O., Rigaud, J.-B.: Experimental analysis of the laser-induced instruction skip fault model. In: Askarov, A., Hansen, R.R., Rafnsson, W. (eds.) NordSec 2019. LNCS, vol. 11875, pp. 221–237. Springer, Cham (2019). https://doi.org/10.1007/978-3-030-35055-0_14

EAB+23.   ElGhamrawy, M., et al.: From MLWE to RLWE: a differential fault attack on randomized & deterministic dilithium. Cryptology ePrint Archive, Paper 2023/1074 (2023). https://eprint.iacr.org/2023/1074

KLH+20.   Kim, I.J., Lee, T.H., Han, J., Sim, B.Y., Han, D.G.: Novel single-trace ML profiling attacks on NIST 3 round candidate dilithium. Cryptology ePrint Archive, Report 2020/1383 (2020). https://eprint.iacr.org/2020/1383

KPLG24.   Krahmer, E., Pessl, P., Land, G., Güneysu, T.: Correction fault attacks on randomized crystals-dilithium. Cryptology ePrint Archive, Paper 2024/138 (2024). https://eprint.iacr.org/2024/138

LDK+22.   Lyubashevsky, V., et al.: CRYSTALS-DILITHIUM. Technical report, National Institute of Standards and Technology (2022). https://csrc.nist.gov/Projects/post-quantum-cryptography/selected-algorithms-2022

MB04.   Michel Berkelaar, P.N., Eikland, K.: LP solve. https://lpsolve.sourceforge.net/5.5 (2004). Open source (Mixed-Integer) Linear Programming system

MDP+20.   Menu, A., Dutertre, J.M., Potin, O., Rigaud, J.B., Danger, J.L.: Experimental analysis of the electromagnetic instruction skip fault model. In: 2020 15th Design & Technology of Integrated Systems in Nanoscale Era (DTIS), pp. 1–7 (2020)

MUTS22.   Marzougui, S., Ulitzsch, V., Tibouchi, M., Seifert, J.-P.: Profiling side-channel attacks on dilithium: a small bit-fiddling leak breaks it all. Cryptology ePrint Archive, Report 2022/106 (2022). https://eprint.iacr.org/2022/106

NIS23.   NIST: FIPS 204 (draft): module-lattice-based digital signature standard. Federal Inf. Process. Stds. (NIST FIPS), National Institute of Standards and Technology, Gaithersburg, MD (2023). https://nvlpubs.nist.gov/nistpubs/FIPS/NIST.FIPS.204.ipd.pdf

NSA22.   NSA: Announcing the commercial national security algorithm suite 2.0. National Security Agency, U.S Department of Defense (2022). https://media.defense.gov/2022/Sep/07/2003071834/-1/-1/0/CSA_CNSA_2.0_ALGORITHMS_.PDF

NW88.   Wolsey, L.A., Nemhauser, G.L.: Integer and combinatorial optimization. In: Wiley Interscience Series in Discrete Mathematics and Optimization (1988)

RCDB22.   Ravi, P., Chattopadhyay, A., D'Anvers, J.P., Baksi, A.: Side-channel and fault-injection attacks over lattice-based post-quantum schemes (kyber, dilithium): survey and new results. Cryptology ePrint Archive, Paper 2022/737 (2022). https://eprint.iacr.org/2022/737

RJH+18. Ravi, P., Jhanwar, M.P., Howe, J., Chattopadhyay, A., Bhasin, S.: Side-channel assisted existential forgery attack on Dilithium - A NIST PQC candidate. Cryptology ePrint Archive, Report 2018/821 (2018). https://eprint.iacr.org/2018/821

Sch19. Schwabe, P.: Twitter (2019). https://twitter.com/cryptojedi/status/1192375176438128641

UMB+23. Ulitzsch, V.Q., Marzougui, S., Bagia, A., Tibouchi, M., Seifert, J.P.: Loop aborts strike back: defeating fault countermeasures in lattice signatures with ILP. IACR TCHES, **2023**(4), 367–392 (2023)

WNGD23. Wang, R., Ngo, K., Gärtner, J., Dubrova, E.: Single-trace side-channel attacks on crystals-dilithium: myth or reality? Cryptology ePrint Archive, Paper 2023/1931 (2023). https://eprint.iacr.org/2023/1931

One Bit to Rule Them All – Imperfect Randomness Harms Lattice Signatures

Simon Damm$^{(\boxtimes)}$ (ID), Nicolai Kraus$^{(\boxtimes)}$ (ID), Alexander May$^{(\boxtimes)}$ (ID),
Julian Nowakowski$^{(\boxtimes)}$ (ID), and Jonas Thietke$^{(\boxtimes)}$ (ID)

Ruhr-University Bochum, Bochum, Germany
{simon.damm,nicolai.kraus,alex.may,julian.nowakowski,
jonas.thietke}@rub.de

Abstract. The Fiat-Shamir transform is one of the most widely applied methods for secure signature construction. Fiat-Shamir starts with an interactive zero-knowledge identification protocol and transforms this via a hash function into a non-interactive signature. The protocol's zero-knowledge property ensures that a signature does not leak information on its secret key $\mathbf{s}$, which is achieved by blinding $\mathbf{s}$ via proper randomness $\mathbf{y}$. Most prominent Fiat-Shamir examples are DSA signatures and the new post-quantum standard Dilithium.

In practice, DSA signatures have experienced fatal attacks via leakage of a few bits of the randomness $\mathbf{y}$ per signature. Similar attacks now emerge for lattice-based signatures, such as Dilithium.

We build on, improve and generalize the pioneering leakage attack on Dilithium by Liu, Zhou, Sun, Wang, Zhang, and Ming. In theory, their original attack can recover a 256-dimensional subkey of Dilithium-II (aka ML-DSA-44) from leakage in a single bit of $\mathbf{y}$ per signature, in any bit position $j \geq 6$. However, the memory requirement of their attack grows exponentially in the bit position j of the leak. As a consequence, if the bit leak is in a high-order position, then their attack is infeasible.

In our improved attack, we introduce a novel transformation, that allows us to get rid of the exponential memory requirement. Thereby, we make the attack feasible for *all* bit positions $j \geq 6$. Furthermore, our novel transformation significantly reduces the number of required signatures in the attack.

The attack applies more generally to all Fiat-Shamir-type lattice-based signatures. For a signature scheme based on module LWE over an ℓ-dimensional module, the attack uses a 1-bit leak per signature to efficiently recover a $\frac{1}{\ell}$-fraction of the secret key. In the ring LWE setting, which can be seen as module LWE with $\ell = 1$, the attack thus recovers the whole key. For Dilithium-II, which uses $\ell = 4$, knowledge of a $\frac{1}{4}$-fraction of the 1024-dimensional secret key lets its security estimate drop significantly from 128 to 84 bits.

1 Introduction

DSA Attacks as a Warning. DSA signatures are one of the most important cornerstones for securing authenticity in our digital society. The origin of DSA lies in Schnorr's identification protocol [Sch90] that proves knowledge of a secret

© International Association for Cryptologic Research 2025
T. Jager and J. Pan (Eds.): PKC 2025, LNCS 15674, pp. 284–316, 2025.
https://doi.org/10.1007/978-3-031-91820-9_10

discrete logarithm s via revealing some value $z = c \cdot s + y \bmod q$, where c is a known challenge and y an unknown randomness. It is easy to see that for y chosen uniformly at random from $\mathbb{Z}_q$, z is also uniformly random over $\mathbb{Z}_q$. Hence, the value of $c \cdot s$ is information theoretically hidden, thereby perfectly blinding the secret s.

On the attack side, it was soon realized [HGS01, NS02, NS03] that the Boneh-Venkatesan lattice-based algorithm for the *hidden number problem* [BV96] can be utilized to tackle DSA signatures via leakage of y's bits. While the original theoretical bound required $\mathcal{O}(\sqrt{\log q})$ leaked bits of y per signature, this was quickly improved to a few bits of y in practical DSA settings. Ever since then, the cryptographic community has been on a chase for further reducing the required amount of leaked bits per signature [Aka09, DHMP13, ANT+20, AH21, XSWH22, HR23].

A series of devastating real-world attacks [HR07, Rya18, MBA+21, HR23, CVE] demonstrated that *randomness leakage* is not only a theoretical threat. Interestingly, these real-world attacks usually do not require invasive side-channel techniques. Instead, they often simply exploit a slight bias in the choice of y, e.g., when some bits of y are (unintentionally) set to a fixed value. Moreover, the Dual EC disaster [CNE+14] showed that randomness selection may also be biased maliciously. This warns us to carefully secure Fiat-Shamir based post quantum signatures against similar randomness leakage attacks.

History of Code and Lattice-Based Signatures. When looking at post-quantum cryptography in general, the construction of efficient and secure signatures has been a more delicate process than the construction of encryption. While initial constructions for encryption from codes [McE78] and lattices [GGH97, HPS98] basically resisted cryptanalytic efforts and just underwent some modernizations [ABC+22, HRSS17], the story of their signature counterparts [CFS01, HPS01, HHP+03] has seen a series of breaks and improvements.

For codes, the well-known McEliece-type CFS signature [CFS01] suffered from slow signing, initial parameters were broken by a Generalized Birthday attack due to Bleichenbacher (see [FS09]), and later a key distinguishing attack was found [FGUO+13].

For lattices, the NTRU NSS scheme [HPS01] and its successor NTRUSign [HHP+03] have faced effective cryptanalytic attacks [GJSS01, GS02]. Nguyen and Regev [NR09] showed that the inherently leaked information of GGH and NTRU signatures [GGH97, HHP+03] can be exploited to recover the secret key via gradient descent on a multivariate optimization problem. The result of [NR09] already demonstrated that even a small leakage is a serious threat to lattice signing schemes, resulting in full key recovery.

In two breakthrough results on the constructive side, Gentry, Peikert, Vaikuntanathan [GPV08] and Lyubashevsky [Lyu09] demonstrated how to build lattice-based signatures, provably without secret key leakage. While [GPV08] utilizes the hash-and-sign paradigm, Lyubashevsky [Lyu09] uses the Fiat-Shamir transform. Lyubashevsky provides a method called *Fiat-Shamir with Aborts* for achieving a zero-knowledge proof of an LWE secret key $\mathbf{s}$, heavily inspired by Schnorr's protocol [Sch90]. The novel post-quantum standard Dilithium is essentially a highly optimized variant of Lyubashevsky's signature scheme.

Fiat-Shamir with Aborts. Let us dive a little deeper into the details of Lyubashevsky's Fiat-Shamir with Aborts [Lyu09, DFPS23] in various LWE settings. Let $R = \mathbb{Z}[X]/(X^n + 1)$, and let $\mathbf{s} \in R^\ell$ be an LWE secret key having ℓn (small) polynomial coefficients. The reader should think of ℓn as the security parameter. For a challenge $c \in R$ derived from a signed message, Lyubashevsky's scheme blinds the value $c\mathbf{s}$ via some randomness $\mathbf{y} \in R^\ell$ as $\mathbf{z} := c\mathbf{s} + \mathbf{y}$, analogous to [Sch90].

Importantly, while Schnorr's scheme is defined over the *finite* ring $\mathbb{Z}_q$, Lyubashevsky uses the *infinite* ring $R = \mathbb{Z}[X]/(X^n + 1)$. Using an infinite ring comes with the disadvantage that $\mathbf{z}$ can no longer be uniformly random over R. Thereby, $\mathbf{z}$ may leak information on $\mathbf{s}$. To prevent this, Lyubashevsky introduces a clever rejection sampling technique, which reruns the underlying identification protocol, until the resulting $\mathbf{z}$ becomes independent of $\mathbf{s}$. However, this zero-knowledge argument crucially requires that $\mathbf{y}$ is chosen *perfectly secret and uniformly at random*.

Randomness Bit Leakage Model. For simplicity, in the remainder, we call $(c, \mathbf{z})$ a signature, although a Lyubashevsky signature contains more information (that we do not use in our attack).

Notice that the randomness $\mathbf{y} \in R^\ell$ is represented as ℓn polynomial coefficients, denoted $y_1, \ldots, y_{\ell n} \in \mathbb{Z}$. As a running example, let us use Dilithium-II parameters (aka ML-DSA-44) with

$$\ell n = 1024, \text{ and } y_1, \ldots, y_{\ell n} \in (-2^{17}, 2^{17}),$$

resulting in a randomness $\mathbf{y}$ having $1024 \cdot 18 = 18{,}432$ bits. Let us write an 18-bit polynomial coefficient y_i in binary representation as

$$y_i = \sum_{j=0}^{17} y_{i,j} 2^j \text{ with } y_{i,j} \in \{0, 1\},$$

e.g., in the standard *binary two's complement* form. Out of the 18,432 bits for representing $\mathbf{y}$, we assume leakage of *a single fixed bit* $y_{i,j} \in \{0, 1\}$ in a position $j \geq 6$. Our goal is to reconstruct $\mathbf{s}$ from many *leaky signatures* $(c, \mathbf{z}, y_{i,j})$, for $\mathbf{z} = c\mathbf{s} + \mathbf{y}$ (with proper rejection sampling) and leakage bit $y_{i,j}$ of y.

Integer LWE (ILWE). It was observed in [HM17] that *Integer LWE* (ILWE) – i.e., an LWE instance without modular reduction, such as Galbraith's binary matrix LWE [Gal13] – leads to efficient cryptanalysis using methods from linear optimization. In [EFGT17], Espitau, Fouque, Gérard and Tibouchi described a side-channel attack on BLISS signatures that via leakage also leads to ILWE equations. Afterwards, the ILWE problem was systematically studied by Bootle, Delaplace, Espitau, Fouque and Tibouchi [BDE+18], who showed that ILWE can in general be solved by linear regression. More precisely, given an LWE instance $t = As + e$ over the integers, one can use linear regression to efficiently compute an approximation $\hat{s}$ of s over the reals. The authors of [BDE+18] showed that, if the LWE instance has enough *samples* (i.e., A provides sufficiently many rows), then rounding $\hat{s}$ coordinate-wise reveals s.

Liu-Zhou-Sun-Wang-Zhang-Ming Attack [LZS+20]. By construction, a Dilithium signature (c, z) already defines an ILWE instance $z = cs + y$, where y plays the role of an LWE error. However, by Lyubashevsky's zero knowledge result [Lyu09] those equations perfectly protect s, resulting in an unsolvable ILWE instance.

The situation changes if we leak some bit $y_{i,j}$ of y for many signatures (c, z), as first observed in the attack of Liu, Zhou, Sun, Wang, Zhang and Ming [LZS+20]. For Dilithium-II, using knowledge of a single leaked bit $y_{i,j}$ in position $j \geq 6$, the work of [LZS+20] shows how to transform the unsolvable ILWE instance $z = cs + y$ into a solvable ILWE instance, whose solution is a 256-dimensional subkey $\bar{s}$ of Dilithium-II's 1024-dimensional secret s. The authors of [LZS+20] apply the ILWE framework of [BDE+18] to solve via linear regression for the subkey $\bar{s}$. For bit position $j = 6$, the regression successfully recovers all 256 coordinates of $\bar{s}$ using roughly half a million signatures, that in turn lead to half a million ILWE relations. Given the efficiency of linear regression, carrying out such an attack can be done in less than 1 min for recovery of $\bar{s}$.

However, for bit positions $j > 6$, the attack is significantly less efficient. The reason is that, in the [LZS+20] attack, increasing j by 1 increases the number of required signatures by a factor roughly 4. This exponential increase in *signatures and ILWE relations* quickly makes the [LZS+20] attack impractical. As an example, if the bit leak is in the most significant bit $j = 17$, the attack would require solving an ILWE instance with roughly 2^{41} relations, which – due to the large memory consumption – is currently out of reach.

For $j = 6$, the work of Qiao, Liu, Zhou, Ming, Jin and Li [QLZ+22] demonstrated the real-world relevance of the [LZS+20] attack, by realizing randomness bit leakage via a Public Template Attack on a masked Dilithium implementation.

1.1   Our Results

Our starting point is the [LZS+20] attack within the ILWE framework of [BDE+18]. However, we strongly deviate from the original description of [LZS+20].

Understanding Leakage and Zero-Knowledge. The original analysis shows that leakage in y allows generation of new ILWE relations that, seemingly *by chance*, fall into a regime where linear regression can recover the subkey $\bar{s}$. A significant drawback of this approach is, however, that it can not explain *why* leakage in $\mathbf{y}$ actually undermines the zero-knowledge property of the signature scheme. This makes building upon the attack quite challenging. Therefore, we develop a completely new approach towards the attack. We formally analyze the distribution of leaky LWE signatures in detail, allowing us to fully explain how leakage in $\mathbf{y}$ undermines zero-knowledge. This, in turn, allows us to significantly improve the attack in various ways.

Informative Relations. Our novel analysis shows that for increasing bit positions j, most of the resulting ILWE relations actually do not provide *any* information on $\mathbf{s}$. We call such relations *non-informative*. Those relations that actually provide information are called *informative*.

Using again Dilithium-II as an example, [LZS+20] feeds for $j > 6$ a mixture of *many* non-informative and *few* informative relations as input to linear regression. The use of non-informative relations does not only unnecessarily slow down linear regression, but also requires a larger amount of relations in total, since the non-informative relations dilute our input data. If we instead feed only informative relations as input to linear regression, then the amount of required signatures already drops significantly. As a numerical example, while the [LZS+20] attack requires for $j = 9$ around 30 million signatures, we improve to around 3 million.

In the original attack of [LZS+20], the number of required signatures roughly grows by a factor of 4 for every increase in bit position j. In ours, the growth per bit position drops to roughly a factor of 2. Notice that such a (still) exponential growth in j is inherent. The reason is that the amount of non-informative relations roughly doubles per increase in j.

Constant Memory. While obtaining a large number of signatures is generally not problematic in practice, the main bottleneck in [LZS+20] lies in the fact that all the collected signatures must be stored and subsequently used as input for linear regression.

We significantly improve on this state of affairs, by processing the signatures *as a stream*, and storing only those that yield informative relations. After that, we employ a novel transformation to our informative relations. We formally prove that our transformation makes the error term in the underlying ILWE instance independent of the bit position j. Thereby, we require for any bit position j the same number of informative relations for linear regression to succeed. In particular, we achieve *constant memory* and thus make the attack feasible for all bit positions $j \geq 6$.

Power of the Ring. In a Lyubashevsky-type signature scheme based on module LWE over an ℓ-dimensional module, each signature coefficient is a function of only a subkey, an $\frac{1}{\ell}$-fraction of the complete secret key $\mathbf{s}$. In the ring LWE setting with $\ell = 1$, the subkey is in fact the whole secret key $\mathbf{s}$. For Dilithium-II with $\ell = 4$ each signature coefficient depends on a 256-coordinate subkey, a $\frac{1}{4}$-fraction of the full 1024-coordinate $\mathbf{s}$. Thus, assuming only a single bit leak our attack can naturally only recover the corresponding subkey on which the signature coefficient depends. If multiple bits are leaked – one for each of the ℓ rings in module LWE – the attack recovers all subkeys, and thus the complete secret key.

However, throughout the paper we assume only a single bit leak. Thus, our main goal is efficient subkey recovery. For completeness, we also briefly analyze the complexity of recovering the whole key from a $\frac{1}{\ell}$-fraction subkey using standard lattice based methods [DDGR20].

Analysis of Required Relations. The work of [BDE+18] describes a very general framework for solving ILWE via linear regression. By an application of the [BDE+18] framework, [LZS+20] achieve a lower bound for the number of required linear relations to successfully recover a secret key $\mathbf{s}$ via rounding that is quite inaccurate in practice. We provide an improved bound, by fine-tuning the analysis to our attack setting, that accurately matches our experimental results.

Organization of the Paper. In Sect. 2, we recall Lyubashevsky's identification protocol, that together with the Fiat-Shamir transform results in Lyubashevsky's signature scheme. After defining our attack model with leaky LWE signatures in Sect. 3, we describe our improvements to the [LZS+20] attack in Sect. 4. Correctness and run time of our attack are analyzed in Sect. 5, and experimental results are provided in Sect. 6. Eventually, we discuss in Sect. 7 methods to save on the required amount of signatures by combining linear regression with lattice reduction.

2   Lyubashevsky ID Protocol, Fiat-Shamir with Aborts

In this section, we recall Lyubashevsky's identification protocol [Lyu09, Lyu24] (ID protocol), and introduce useful notations.

Notations. Lyubashevsky's ID protocol is defined over the *cyclotomic ring* $R := \mathbb{Z}[X]/(X^n + 1)$, where n is a power of two. Some operations are performed over the ring $R_q := \mathbb{Z}_q[X]/(X^n + 1)$, for some prime q. Every ring element $r \in R$ is represented by a degree-$(n - 1)$ polynomial $r = \sum_{i=0}^{n-1} r_i X^i$, where $r_i \in \mathbb{Z}$. For a ring element $r \in R$, we define $[r]_q := r \mod q$, i.e., applying $[\cdot]_q$ to r reduces the coefficients r_i modulo q. We extend $[\cdot]_q$ to vectors $\mathbf{v} \in R^\ell$ by applying it coordinate-wise. We stress that throughout our paper, *all* operations are performed over R and $\mathbb{Z} \subseteq R$, unless we explicitly indicate modular reduction by the $[\cdot]_m$ operator, for some modulus $m \in \mathbb{N}$.

For $\gamma \in \mathbb{N}$, we write $[\pm\gamma]^n \subset R$ to denote the set of all ring elements $r \in R$ with coefficients $|r_i| \leq \gamma$. If $n = 1$, then we drop the n-superscript from $[\pm\gamma]^n$. Moreover, for $0 \leq \tau \leq n$, we define $[\pm1]^n_\tau \subseteq [\pm1]^n \subset R$ as the set of all ring elements $r \in [\pm1]^n \subset R$ having exactly τ non-zero coefficients.

Prover $P(\mathbf{A}, \mathbf{t}, \mathbf{s}_1, \mathbf{s}_2)$	Verifier $V(\mathbf{A}, \mathbf{t})$
$\mathbf{y}_1 \leftarrow ([\pm\gamma]^n)^\ell, \mathbf{y}_2 \leftarrow ([\pm\gamma]^n)^k,$	
$\mathbf{w} := [\mathbf{A}\mathbf{y}_1 + \mathbf{y}_2]_q$	

$$\xrightarrow{\quad \mathbf{w} \quad}$$

$$c \in [\pm 1]^n_\tau$$

$$\xleftarrow{\quad c \quad}$$

$\mathbf{z}_1 := c\mathbf{s}_1 + \mathbf{y}_1$
$\mathbf{z}_2 := c\mathbf{s}_2 + \mathbf{y}_2$
if $\mathbf{z}_1 \notin ([\pm(\gamma - \beta)]^n)^\ell$ or $\mathbf{z}_2 \notin [\pm(\gamma - \beta)]^{n \cdot k}$
then **restart**.

$$\xrightarrow{\quad (\mathbf{z}_1, \mathbf{z}_2) \quad}$$

Accept iff
$\mathbf{z}_1 \in ([\pm(\gamma - \beta)]^n)^\ell,$
$\mathbf{z}_2 \in [\pm(\gamma - \beta)]^{n \cdot k}$, and
$[\mathbf{A}\mathbf{z}_1 + \mathbf{z}_2 - c\mathbf{t}]_q = \mathbf{w}.$

Fig. 1. Lyubashevsky's ID protocol.

Lyubashevsky's Protocol. The ID protocol is parametrized by

- the ring dimension n,
- the modulus q,
- the LWE-secret dimension ℓ,
- the LWE-error dimension k,
- the LWE-distribution width η,
- the commitment-distribution width γ,
- the randomness-distribution width γ, and
- the challenge weight τ.

For notational convenience, we further define $\beta := \eta \cdot \tau$.

Public keys are of the form $(\mathbf{A}, \mathbf{t}) \in R_q^{k \times \ell} \times R_q^k$, where $\mathbf{A} \in_R R_q^{k \times \ell}$ and $\mathbf{t} = [\mathbf{A}\mathbf{s}_1 + \mathbf{s}_2]_q$, for some $\mathbf{s}_1 \in_R ([\pm\eta]^n)^\ell$ and $\mathbf{s}_2 \in_R ([\pm\eta]^n)^k$. (Throughout the paper, for a set A, we denote by $a \in_R A$ that a is sampled uniformly at random from A.) The secret key corresponding to $(\mathbf{A}, \mathbf{t})$ is $(\mathbf{s}_1, \mathbf{s}_2)$. Hence, a key pair defines a (module) LWE instance. The goal of the ID protocol is to create a zero-knowledge proof of knowledge of the secret key.

Following the notation of Lyubashevsky's recent survey [Lyu24, Figure 5], we formally describe the ID Protocol in Fig. 1. It follows the usual three-step ID structure of the prover P sending a *commitment* $\mathbf{w}$ (depending on some randomness $(\mathbf{y}_1, \mathbf{y_2})$), the verifier V sending a *challenge* c, and the prover sending a *response* $(\mathbf{z}_1, \mathbf{z}_2)$.

Notably, the prover P restarts the protocol, if the coefficients of $\mathbf{z}_1$ and $\mathbf{z}_2$ do not fall into the range $[\pm(\gamma - \beta)]$. This *rejection sampling* of *Fiat-Shamir with Aborts* is crucial for zero-knowledge. To information-theoretically hide the secret key, the coefficients of the response have to be uniformly distributed over the range $[\pm(\gamma - \beta)]$.

Typical parameters for the ID protocol are shown in Table 1. The *ML-DSA* columns show the three standardized Dilithium parameter sets. We provide an additional parameter set, labelled *Ring-LWE-1024*, which is supposed to have the same security level as the ML-DSA-44 parameters. Indeed, in ML-DSA-44 and Ring-LWE-1024, we have $k \cdot n = \ell \cdot n = 1024$, and all remaining parameters are identical. The complexity of all known attacks does not depend on the values of n and ℓ themselves, but only on the product $\ell \cdot n$. However, as we will discuss in the subsequent sections, in the presence of leakage, the values of ℓ and n are very important for security. That is, the smaller ℓ, the more dangerous leakage becomes.

Table 1. Various parameter sets for Lyubashevsky's ID protocol.

	ML-DSA-44	Ring-LWE-1024	ML-DSA-65	ML-DSA-87
n	256	1024	256	256
k	4	1	6	8
ℓ	4	1	5	7
q	8380417	8380417	8380417	8380417
η	2	2	4	2
γ	2^{17}	2^{17}	2^{19}	2^{19}
τ	39	39	49	60
β	78	78	196	120

Differences with Dilithium. For efficiency purposes, Dilithium uses an optimized variant of the ID protocol. Most importantly, it incorporates various clever techniques, that allow to drop $\mathbf{z}_2$ from the response, and to drop the low bits of $\mathbf{t}$ from the public key. We refer the reader to Lyubashevsky's survey [Lyu24, Sections 5.4 and 5.5] for an in-depth explanation of these optimizations.

For ease of notation, throughout the paper we mostly consider the non-optimized version of the ID protocol, as depicted in Fig. 1. We stress, however, that all our results apply to the optimized variant used in Dilithium as well. In particular, dropping $\mathbf{z}_2$ from the response does not affect our attack, since we attack only the $\mathbf{z}_1$-component of the response. Dropping the low bits of $\mathbf{t}$ from the public key also has no effect on our attack, since they can efficiently be recovered via linear programming [OVCG24].

3   Attack Model

We now formally describe our attack model. Consider a Lyubashevsky-type signature scheme based on the ID protocol from Fig. 1. In a nutshell, we assume that there is a flaw in the random number generator for sampling $\mathbf{y}_1 \in R^\ell = (\mathbb{Z}[X]/(X^n + 1))^\ell$. More precisely, we consider the following scenario: Implementations typically identify $\mathbf{y}_1$ with its $(n \cdot \ell)$-dimensional coefficient vector over $\mathbb{Z}^{n \cdot \ell}$. The entries of the coefficient vector are stored in binary two's complement. We assume that *one* fixed bit in this binary two's complement is revealed to the attacker. One possible scenario might be, e.g., that in every signature this bit is stuck at 0. Of course, more general scenarios are also possible.

Binary Two's Complement. For a word width w, the binary two's complement stores signed integers x with $-2^{w-1} \leq x < 2^{w-1}$ as a binary string $(x_{w-1}, x_{w-2}, \ldots, x_1, x_0) \in \{0,1\}^w$, such that

$$x = \left[\sum_{j=0}^{w-1} x_j 2^j \right]_{2^w} \,,$$

where $[\cdot]_{2^w}$ denotes the modulo-2^w operator, that maps any $a \in \mathbb{Z}$ to the unique centered around 0 value $[a]_{2^w}$ with $[a]_{2^w} \equiv a \mod 2^w$ and $-2^{w-1} \leq [a]_{2^w} < 2^{w-1}$. See Table 2 for an example of the binary two's complement representations with word width $w = 3$. For a given j, $0 \leq j < w$, we call x_j the *j-th bit in the binary two's complement representation of x.*

Table 2. Binary two's complement representations with word width $w = 3$.

integer x	3	2	1	0	−1	−2	−3	−4
binary two's complement	011	010	001	000	111	110	101	100

Formalizing Our Problem. In Lyubashevsky's signature scheme, a signature contains (among other values) a ring element $c \in R$ and a vector $\mathbf{z}_1 \in R^\ell$. Recall that $\mathbf{z}_1$ is computed as

$$\mathbf{z}_1 = c\mathbf{s}_1 + \mathbf{y}_1,$$

where $\mathbf{s}_1$ is the LWE secret, coming from the secret key $(\mathbf{s}_1, \mathbf{s}_2) \in R^\ell \times R^k$. It is easy to see that each of the $n \cdot \ell$ coefficients of $\mathbf{z}_1$ yields one linear relation in the LWE secret $\mathbf{s}_1$. Importantly, since $\mathbf{s}_1 = (s_{1,1}, s_{1,2}, \ldots, s_{1,\ell})$ is an ℓ-dimensional vector over the ring R, the first n coefficients of $\mathbf{z}_1$ depend only on the first component $s_{1,1}$, the next n-coefficients depend only on the second component $s_{1,2}$, and so forth. Hence, in our attack model, we are tasked with solving the following problem:

Definition 1 (Leaky-Signature-LWE). *Fix some public parameters j, τ, η, γ, and define $\beta := \eta \cdot \tau$. Let $(\mathbf{A}, \mathbf{t}) \in R_q^{k \times \ell} \times R_q^\ell$ be an LWE public key with corresponding secret key $(\mathbf{s}_1, \mathbf{s}_2) \in ([\pm\eta]^n)^\ell \times ([\pm\eta]^n)^k$. Let $\mathbf{x} \in \mathbb{Z}^n$ be the coefficient vector of one component of $\mathbf{s}_1$. In the Leaky-Signature-LWE problem one is given the public key $(\mathbf{A}, \mathbf{t})$, along with arbitrarily many relations of the form $(\mathbf{c}, z, y_j) \in [\pm 1]_\tau^n \times \mathbb{Z} \times \{0,1\}$, where z*

$$z = \langle \mathbf{c}, \mathbf{x} \rangle + y,$$

for some $y \in [\pm\gamma]$, such that

1. *z follows the uniform distribution over $[\pm(\gamma - \beta)]$, and*
2. *y_j is the j-th bit in the binary two's complement representation of y.*

The goal is to recover the LWE secret $\mathbf{s}_1$.

4   An Improved Algorithm for Leaky-Signature-LWE

Let us now describe our algorithm for solving the Leaky-Signature-LWE problem from Definition 1. In their seminal work [LZS+20], Liu, Zhou, Sun, Wang, Zhang, and Ming, already gave an algorithm for recovering the partial LWE secret $\mathbf{x}$ in the Leaky-Signature-LWE problem. However, as discussed in the introduction, for high-order bit leakage positions j their algorithm becomes impractical.

In this section, we present a novel and significantly simplified view on their algorithm. By that, we obtain new insights, that allow us to make the algorithm practical for all j.

4.1   Breaking Zero-Knowledge via y_j

We begin by rephrasing the main idea behind the attack of [LZS+20]. We strongly deviate from the original description of [LZS+20], and instead follow a more information theoretic approach. We believe that this helps to gain a deeper understanding of the attack.

In the Leaky-Signature-LWE problem, we obtain relations $(\mathbf{c}, z, y_j)$, where z is defined as

$$z = \langle \mathbf{c}, \mathbf{x} \rangle + y$$

and y_j is is the j-th bit in the binary two's complement representation of y. Recall that z is a coefficient of the value $\mathbf{z}_1$ computed in the ID protocol from Fig. 1. By rejection sampling, z follows the uniform distribution over $[\pm(\gamma - \beta)]$, for some parameters β and γ. As a reminder, we note that γ satisfies $|y| \leq \gamma$, and that β satisfies $|\langle \mathbf{c}, \mathbf{x} \rangle| \leq \beta$.[1]

In his original work [Lyu09], Lyubashevsky essentially showed that conditioning the distribution of z to the range $[\pm(\gamma - \beta)]$ makes it independent of the secret key. Thereby, the protocol becomes zero-knowledge. For attack purposes, it is convenient to not only consider the range, where the protocol is zero-knowledge, but to specifically consider, where it is *not*. To this end, we need the following lemma.

Lemma 2. *Let $\langle \mathbf{c}, \mathbf{x} \rangle \in \mathbb{Z}$ be a random inner product drawn from some probability distribution. Suppose we sample $y \in \mathbb{Z}$ uniformly at random from $[\pm\gamma]$, independently from $\langle \mathbf{c}, \mathbf{x} \rangle$. Then for $z := \langle \mathbf{c}, \mathbf{x} \rangle + y$ and any $x \in \mathbb{Z}$ it holds that*

$$\Pr[z = x] \propto \Pr[x - \gamma \leq \langle \mathbf{c}, \mathbf{x} \rangle \leq x + \gamma],$$

i.e., the probabilities $\Pr[z = x]$ and $\Pr[x - \gamma \leq \langle \mathbf{c}, \mathbf{x} \rangle \leq x + \gamma]$ are proportional.

---

[1] By Definition 1, we have $\beta := \eta \cdot \tau$, for some parameters η and τ, such that $\mathbf{x} \in [\pm\eta]^n$ and $\mathbf{c} \in [\pm1]^n_\tau$. Hence, $|\langle \mathbf{c}, \mathbf{x} \rangle| \leq \eta \cdot \tau = \beta$..

Proof. By definition of z, we have

$$\Pr[z = x] = \Pr[y = x - \langle \mathbf{c}, \mathbf{x} \rangle]$$

$$= \sum_{i=-\infty}^{\infty} \Pr[y = x - i \mid \langle \mathbf{c}, \mathbf{x} \rangle = i] \cdot \Pr[\langle \mathbf{c}, \mathbf{x} \rangle = i].$$

Since y is uniformly random over $[\pm\gamma]$ and independent from $\langle \mathbf{c}, \mathbf{x} \rangle$, the above becomes

$$\Pr[z = x] = (2\gamma + 1)^{-1} \sum_{i=x-\gamma}^{x+\gamma} \Pr[\langle \mathbf{c}, \mathbf{x} \rangle = i]$$

$$= (2\gamma + 1)^{-1} \cdot \Pr[x - \gamma \leq \langle \mathbf{c}, \mathbf{x} \rangle \leq x + \gamma],$$

which concludes the proof. □

In the ID protocol from Fig. 1, any coefficient z of $\mathbf{z}_1$ is computed as $z = \langle \mathbf{c}, \mathbf{x} \rangle + y$. Before applying rejection sampling, y is uniformly random over $[\pm\gamma]$. Hence, from Lemma 2 and the fact that $|\langle \mathbf{c}, \mathbf{x} \rangle| \leq \beta$, it follows that the distribution of z before rejection sampling is

$$\Pr[z = x] = \alpha \cdot \begin{cases} 1, & \text{if } -\gamma + \beta \leq x \leq \gamma - \beta, \\ \Pr[\langle \mathbf{c}, \mathbf{x} \rangle \geq x - \gamma], & \text{if } \gamma - \beta < x \leq \gamma + \beta, \\ \Pr[\langle \mathbf{c}, \mathbf{x} \rangle \leq x + \gamma], & \text{if } -\gamma - \beta \leq x < -\gamma + \beta, \\ 0, & \text{else,} \end{cases} \quad (1)$$

for some properly chosen scaling factor α.

By the central limit theorem, the inner product $\langle \mathbf{c}, \mathbf{x} \rangle$ is close to a Gaussian distribution. (Since $\mathbf{c} \in [\pm 1]_\tau^n$ and $\mathbf{x} \in [\pm\eta]$, the inner product $\langle \mathbf{c}, \mathbf{x} \rangle$ is a random sum of τ uniformly random integers from $[\pm\eta]$.) Thus, we may approximate the probability $\Pr[\langle \mathbf{c}, \mathbf{x} \rangle \leq x + \gamma]$ in Eq. (1) by an (appropriately parameterized) cumulative distribution function $\Phi(x + \gamma)$ of the Gaussian distribution. Analogously, we may approximate $\Pr[\langle \mathbf{c}, \mathbf{x} \rangle \geq x - \gamma]$ by $1 - \Phi(x - \gamma)$. The resulting distribution is shown in Fig. 2.

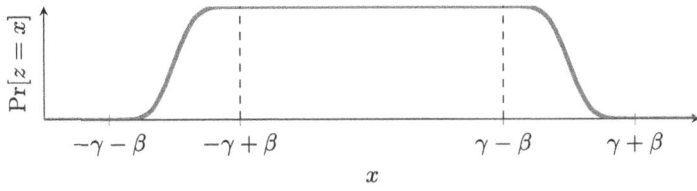

Fig. 2. Distribution of z before rejection sampling.

In Fig. 2, the area between $-\gamma + \beta$ and $\gamma - \beta$ (where z follows the uniform distribution) is exactly the area, in which z does not reveal any information about $\mathbf{s}$. In Lyubashevsky's signature scheme, rejection sampling ensures that we obtain only those z's, that lie inside this exact area.

For *attacking* the signature scheme, however, we would like to have access to z's that lie outside $[\pm(\gamma - \beta)]$. While in our attack scenario, we can not hope to obtain such z's, we show below that by leveraging knowledge of our leaked bit y_j, we can transform our z's, that lie *inside* of $[\pm(\gamma - \beta)]$, into new values $\overline{z}$, that provide as much information about $\mathbf{s}$, as z's *outside* of $[\pm(\gamma - \beta)]$ do.

Leveraging y_j. The authors of [LZS+20] introduce a clever relation extraction technique, that, for all $j \geq \log_2(\beta) + 1$, uses the leaked bit y_j to transform z into a new value $\overline{z}$ of the form

$$\overline{z} = \langle \mathbf{c}, \mathbf{x} \rangle + [y]_{2^j}. \tag{2}$$

We provide a detailed description of a refined variant of this relation extraction in Sect. 4.4. For the moment, let us treat the relation extraction in a black box fashion.

Multi-bit Leakage. One might wonder why we consider for the Leaky-Signature-LWE problem in Definition 1 only a single bit leakage, and how a multi bit leak influences the problem's complexity.

First, single bit leakage is opposed to multi bit leakage a weaker attack model. Thus, obtaining $\mathbf{x}$-recovery from a single bit is a stronger cryptanalytic attack. Second, we show in the following that a multiple bit leak for y does not help an attacker, since only the leak bit y_j in lowest position j matters.

Relation extraction enables us to compute from a relation $z = \langle \mathbf{c}, \mathbf{x} \rangle + y$ the value $\overline{z} = \langle \mathbf{c}, \mathbf{x} \rangle + [y]_{2^j}$, where $[y]_{2^j}$ represents the (unknown) j low order bits of y. It follows that the computation of $z - \overline{z} = y - [y]_{2^j}$ reveals all most significant bits of y from position j onwards.

Information Extraction Provides Information. Recall that the initial value z lies inside $[\pm(\gamma - \beta)]$, and thus does not provide any information about $\mathbf{x}$. Importantly, the new value $\overline{z}$, on the other hand, *does* reveal information about $\mathbf{x}$. Indeed, after reducing y modulo 2^j, the value $[y]_{2^j}$ is essentially uniformly distributed over $[\pm 2^{j-1}]$.[2] Hence, we may apply Lemma 2 to $\overline{z}$, and conclude that the distribution of $\overline{z}$ is the distribution shown in Fig. 3. From Fig. 3 it then easily follows that all $\overline{z}$'s outside the range $[\pm(2^{j-1} - \beta)]$ reveal information about $\mathbf{s}$. In fact, those $\overline{z}'s$ reveal exactly as much information, as the initially rejected z's outside the range $[\pm(\gamma - \beta)]$.

Notice that the $\overline{z}$'s now essentially form an instance of the *Integer LWE* problem with solution $\mathbf{x}$ and error drawn uniformly from $[\pm 2^{j-1}]$. As shown in [LZS+20], when given sufficiently many relations, one can solve this problem

---

[2] The original analysis of [LZS+20, Section 3, Step 4] falsely assumes that not $[y]_{2^j}$, but $\overline{z}$ follows the uniform distribution modulo 2^j. We note that $[y]_{2^j}$ is not *perfectly* uniformly random over $[\pm 2^{j-1}]$, but rather over $\{-2^{j-1}, -2^{j-1} + 1, \ldots, 2^{j-1} - 2, 2^{j-1} - 1\}$. To simplify notation, we ignore this benign technical detail.

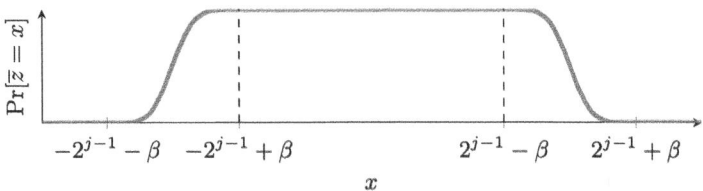

Fig. 3. Distribution of $\overline{z} = \langle \mathbf{c}, \mathbf{s} \rangle + [y]_{2^j}$.

in polynomial time via linear regression. We provide in Sect. 5 improved methods for estimating the number of relations.

Importantly, *polynomial time* does not always mean *feasible* in practice: When trying to solve Integer LWE via linear regression, the required number of relations strongly depends on the error size. Unfortunately, when the error size (and thereby the number of relations) becomes too large, then current state-of-the-art implementations of linear regression become infeasible. In our scenario, the size of the error $[y]_{2^j}$ is directly related to the value of j. That is, the higher j, the larger the error. As a consequence, the original attack of [LZS+20] becomes infeasible for too large j.

As we show in the following Sect. 4.2, we can make the error size independent of j. This implies that the required amount of relations for linear regression no longer increases with j, thereby making our attack feasible for all leakage bit positions.

4.2   Our Novel Transformation: Achieving Independence of j

As discussed above, only $\overline{z}'s$ outside the range $[\pm(2^{j-1} - \beta)]$ reveal information about $\mathbf{s}$, let us call relations with these $\overline{z}'s$ *informative*. Analogous, we call relations with $\overline{z}'s$ inside the range $[\pm(2^{j-1} - \beta)]$ *non-informative*. As a first improvement, we should not feed any *non-informative* relations as input to linear regression.

By including only *informative* relations, we obtain a somewhat odd-looking distribution, as shown in the top half of Fig. 4. To alter the shape of this distribution, we propose as our second improvement to transform $\overline{z}$ as

$$\widetilde{z} := \begin{cases} \overline{z} - 2^{j-1} + \beta, & \text{if } \overline{z} \geq 2^{j-1} - \beta, \\ \overline{z} + 2^{j-1} - \beta, & \text{if } \overline{z} \leq -2^{j-1} + \beta. \end{cases} \tag{3}$$

The resulting distribution of $\widetilde{z}$ is shown in the bottom half of Fig. 4.

By Eqs. (2) and (3), we can write our *(transformed) informative* relations as

$$\widetilde{z} = \langle \mathbf{c}, \mathbf{x} \rangle + \widetilde{y},$$

for some $\widetilde{y}$, that is either $\widetilde{y} = [y]_{2^j} - 2^{j-1} + \beta$ or $\widetilde{y} = [y]_{2^j} + 2^{j-1} - \beta$. As the following theorem shows, $\widetilde{y}$ follows the uniform distribution over $[\pm\beta]$, thereby achieving independence of j.

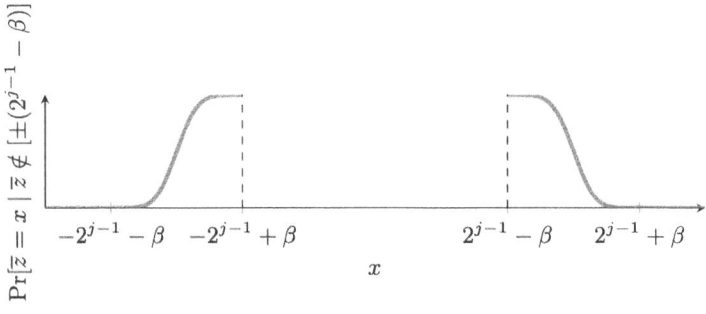

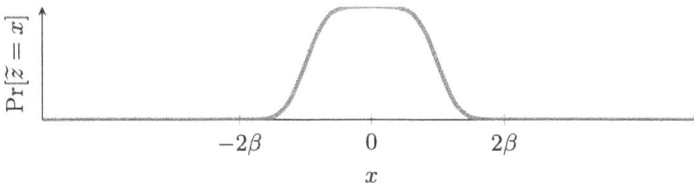

Fig. 4. The top graph shows the distribution of $\bar{z} = \langle \mathbf{c}, \mathbf{s} \rangle + [y]_{2^j}$, conditioned on $\bar{z} \notin [\pm(2^{j-1} - \beta)]$. The bottom graph shows the distribution of $\tilde{z}$.

Theorem 3. *Let $\mathcal{D}$ be a probability distribution over $\mathbb{Z}$ that produces random inner products $\langle \mathbf{c}, \mathbf{x} \rangle$ such that $|\langle \mathbf{c}, \mathbf{x} \rangle| \leq \beta$ with probability 1. Consider the following probability distribution:*

1. *Sample $\langle \mathbf{c}, \mathbf{x} \rangle$ from $\mathcal{D}$ and $\bar{y}$ uniformly at random from $[\pm 2^{j-1}]$.*
2. *Set $\bar{z} := \langle \mathbf{c}, \mathbf{x} \rangle + \bar{y}$.*
3. *If $-2^{j-1} + \beta < \bar{z} < 2^{j-1} - \beta$, go back to Step 1. Otherwise, compute $\tilde{z}$ as in Eq. (3) and output $\tilde{y} := \tilde{z} - \langle \mathbf{c}, \mathbf{x} \rangle$.*

Then $\tilde{y}$ follows the uniform distribution over $[\pm\beta]$.

Proof. As Fig. 4 illustrates, we have

$$\Pr[\tilde{z} = x] = \alpha \cdot \begin{cases} \Pr[\langle \mathbf{c}, \mathbf{x} \rangle \geq x - \beta], & \text{if } 0 \leq x \leq 2\beta, \\ \Pr[\langle \mathbf{c}, \mathbf{x} \rangle \leq x + \beta], & \text{if } -2\beta \leq x < 0, \\ 0, & \text{else}, \end{cases}$$

for some properly chosen scaling factor α. We can write this more compactly as

$$\Pr[\tilde{z} = x] \propto \Pr[x - \beta \leq \langle \mathbf{c}, \mathbf{x} \rangle \leq x + \beta].$$

Suppose we sample an integer u uniformly at random from $[\pm\beta]$. Using u, we define $v := \langle \mathbf{c}, \mathbf{s} \rangle + u$. By Lemma 2, we have

$$\Pr[v = x] \propto \Pr[x - \beta \leq \langle \mathbf{c}, \mathbf{x} \rangle \leq x + \beta],$$

for every $x \in \mathbb{Z}$. In particular, $\Pr[\tilde{z} = x] = \Pr[v = x]$, i.e., $\tilde{z}$ and v follow the same distribution. It follows that the distribution of the random variables $\tilde{z} - \langle \mathbf{c}, \mathbf{x} \rangle$ and $v - \langle \mathbf{c}, \mathbf{x} \rangle$ is also identical. Since $\tilde{z} - \langle \mathbf{c}, \mathbf{x} \rangle = \tilde{y}$ and $v - \langle \mathbf{c}, \mathbf{x} \rangle = u$, this shows that $\tilde{y}$ follows the uniform distribution over $[\pm\beta]$, and thus concludes the proof.
□

Summarizing the above, by excluding all $\bar{z}$'s inside the range $[\pm(2^{j-1}-\beta)]$ and then transforming the remaining $\bar{z}$'s as in Eq. (3), we obtain new Integer LWE relations

$$\tilde{z} = \langle \mathbf{c}, \mathbf{x} \rangle + \tilde{y}, \tag{4}$$

where the error $\tilde{y}$ follows the uniform distribution over $[\pm\beta]$. This significantly improves over [LZS+20], since now

1. all relations reveal information about $\mathbf{x}$, and
2. the error size decreases from 2^{j-1} to β.[3]

In particular, by our transformation, the error size becomes independent of j, i.e., the bit-index, at which we obtain the leak. By that, the attack becomes feasible also for large j.

4.3   Recovering s_1 from x

If we now apply linear regression to our modified Integer LWE relations from Eq. (4), then we efficiently recover the partial key $\mathbf{x} \in \mathbb{Z}^n$. However, to *completely* solve our Leaky-Signature-LWE problem from Definition 1, we have to recover the whole LWE secret $\mathbf{s}_1 \in (\mathbb{Z}[X]/(X^n + 1))^\ell$.

The best known attack strategy for recovering $\mathbf{s}_1$ from $\mathbf{x}$ is based on the *LWE with side information* framework of [DDGR20, DGHK23, MN23]. Here, each of the n-coordinates of $\mathbf{x}$ gives rise to a *perfect hint* on the LWE secret $\mathbf{s}_1$. Given such perfect hints, the framework transforms the lattice problem, that underlies our LWE instance, into a simpler one.

The work of Dachman-Soled, Ducas, Gong and Rossi [DDGR20] provides an estimator, that determines the complexity of the resulting lattice problem within the *Core-SVP model*. In this model, one estimates the smallest *BKZ blocksize* β, at which the BKZ algorithm [Sch87] successfully solves the problem. For a given blocksize β, the bit complexity of BKZ is then estimated as $2^{0.292 \cdot \beta}$.

Dilithium Parameter Sets. We ran the estimator of [DDGR20] on the standardized Dilithium parameter sets (see Table 1), to determine the required BKZ blocksize β for recovering the whole LWE secret key from κ known coordinates (for all $\kappa = 0, 1, 2, \dots, \ell \cdot n$). The results are shown in Fig. 5.

For of our leakage attack, where $\mathbf{x}$ reveals $\kappa = n = 256$ coordinates, we obtain blocksizes $\beta = 287$, $\beta = 469$ and $\beta = 712$ for the parameter sets ML-DSA-44,

---

[3] As noted above, [LZS+20] require $j \geq \log_2(\beta) + 1$. Thus, going from 2^{j-1} to β is indeed a reduction in error size.

ML-DSA-65 and ML-DSA-87, respectively. The corresponding bit complexities are 84, 136 and 208. We conclude that in all three parameter sets, recovering s_1 from x still requires significant computational effort. However, knowledge of x brings security *significantly* below the desired levels of 128, 192 and 256 bits.

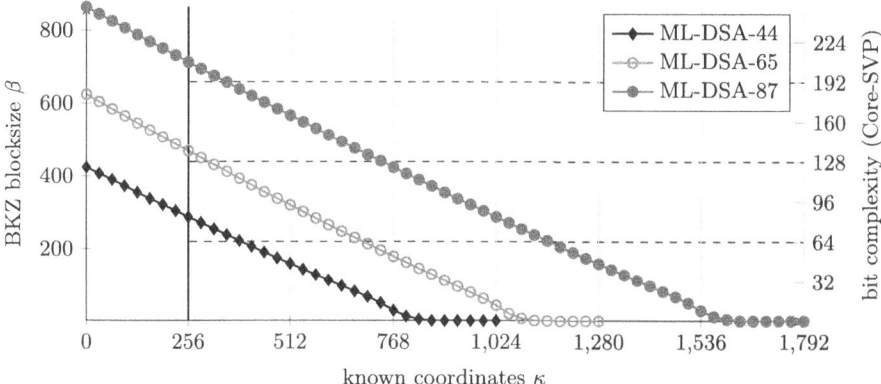

Fig. 5. Required BKZ blocksize to break Dilithium with known coordinates.

Comparison with Ring LWE. The hardness of recovering s_1 from x strongly depends on the value of ℓ, since the n coordinates of $x \in \mathbb{Z}^n$ reveal a $\frac{1}{\ell}$-fraction of the LWE secret $s_1 \in (\mathbb{Z}[X]/(X^n + 1))^\ell$. Naturally, the larger ℓ, the harder recovering s_1 from x becomes.

In the ring LWE setting, where $\ell = 1$, x fully reveals s_1. Hence, we conclude that instantiating Lyubashevsky's signature scheme with ring LWE makes it particularly vulnerable against the leakage attack.

We like to stress, however, that this only applies to the setting, where leakage occurs in one *fixed* component of $y \in (\mathbb{Z}[X]/(X^n + 1))^\ell$. If we would obtain leakage in all ℓ components of y, then module LWE would be as vulnerable as ring LWE, since our attack would recover all ℓ subkeys of s_1.

4.4 Revisiting the LZS$^+$ Relation Extraction

As discussed in Sect. 4.1, at the heart of the attack on the Leaky-Signature-LWE problem lies a clever relation extraction from [LZS+20], that, for all $j \geq \log_2(\beta) + 1$, uses the leaked bit y_j to transform z of the form

$$z = \langle c, x \rangle + y \in_R [\pm(\gamma - \beta)]$$

into Integer LWE relations $\overline{z}$ of the form

$$\overline{z} = \langle c, x \rangle + [y]_{2^j}. \tag{5}$$

In Sect. 4.2, we built our transformation on top of this extraction to obtain relations

$$\widetilde{z} = \langle \mathbf{c}, \mathbf{x} \rangle + \widetilde{y},$$

with small error $\widetilde{y} \in_R [\pm\beta]$.

So far, we treated the relation extraction to produce $\overline{z}$ as in Eq. (5) in a black box fashion. In this section, we provide a detailed description of a refined variant of this relation extraction. While the original analysis of [LZS+20] required intricate arguments on the bit-level, we can instead resort to simple geometric arguments. Additionally, our variant works for the standard binary two's complement, whereas [LZS+20] considered the less standard *sign-and-magnitude* representation, where one bit is reserved for storing the sign.

Partitioning $\mathbb{Z}_{2^{j+1}}$. Before we can describe our relation extraction, we have to make some simple, yet important, observations about the ring $\mathbb{Z}_{2^{j+1}}$. Throughout this section, we identify $\mathbb{Z}_{2^{j+1}}$ with the set

$$\mathbb{Z}_{2^{j+1}} = \{-2^j, -2^j + 1, \dots, 2^j - 1\}.$$

We consider two partitions $\mathbb{Z}_{2^{j+1}} = \mathbb{Z}_{2^{j+1}}^{\leftarrow} \cup \mathbb{Z}_{2^{j+1}}^{\rightarrow}$ and $\mathbb{Z}_{2^{j+1}} = \mathbb{Z}_{2^{j+1}}^{\uparrow} \cup \mathbb{Z}_{2^{j+1}}^{\downarrow}$, where

$$\mathbb{Z}_{2^{j+1}}^{\leftarrow} := \{-2^j, -2^j + 1, \dots, -1\},$$
$$\mathbb{Z}_{2^{j+1}}^{\rightarrow} := \mathbb{Z} \setminus \mathbb{Z}_{2^{j+1}}^{\leftarrow},$$
$$\mathbb{Z}_{2^{j+1}}^{\uparrow} := \{-2^{j-1}, -2^{j-1} + 1, \dots, 2^{j-1} - 1\},$$
$$\mathbb{Z}_{2^{j+1}}^{\downarrow} := \mathbb{Z} \setminus \mathbb{Z}_{2^{j+1}}^{\uparrow}.$$

We also define

$$\mathbb{Z}_{2^{j+1}}^{\nwarrow} := \mathbb{Z}_{2^{j+1}}^{\leftarrow} \cap \mathbb{Z}_{2^{j+1}}^{\uparrow},$$
$$\mathbb{Z}_{2^{j+1}}^{\nearrow} := \mathbb{Z}_{2^{j+1}}^{\rightarrow} \cap \mathbb{Z}_{2^{j+1}}^{\uparrow},$$
$$\mathbb{Z}_{2^{j+1}}^{\searrow} := \mathbb{Z}_{2^{j+1}}^{\rightarrow} \cap \mathbb{Z}_{2^{j+1}}^{\downarrow},$$
$$\mathbb{Z}_{2^{j+1}}^{\swarrow} := \mathbb{Z}_{2^{j+1}}^{\leftarrow} \cap \mathbb{Z}_{2^{j+1}}^{\downarrow}.$$

It is convenient to think of $\mathbb{Z}_{2^{j+1}}$ as a circle, as depicted in Fig. 6. As the figure shows, $\mathbb{Z}_{2^{j+1}} = \mathbb{Z}_{2^{j+1}}^{\leftarrow} \cup \mathbb{Z}_{2^{j+1}}^{\rightarrow}$ partitions our circle into a left and a right half. Similarly, $\mathbb{Z}_{2^{j+1}} = \mathbb{Z}_{2^{j+1}}^{\uparrow} \cup \mathbb{Z}_{2^{j+1}}^{\downarrow}$ partitions it into a top and bottom half, and $\mathbb{Z}_{2^{j+1}} = \mathbb{Z}_{2^{j+1}}^{\nwarrow} \cup \mathbb{Z}_{2^{j+1}}^{\nearrow} \cup \mathbb{Z}_{2^{j+1}}^{\searrow} \cup \mathbb{Z}_{2^{j+1}}^{\swarrow}$ partitions it into four quarters.

We now use Fig. 6, to prove two technical lemmas.

Lemma 4. *For every* $x \in \mathbb{Z}_{2^{j+1}}$, *it holds that*

$$[x]_{2^j} = \begin{cases} x, & \text{if } x \in \mathbb{Z}_{2^{j+1}}^{\uparrow}, \\ x + 2^j, & \text{if } x \in \mathbb{Z}_{2^{j+1}}^{\nearrow}, \\ x - 2^j, & \text{if } x \in \mathbb{Z}_{2^{j+1}}^{\searrow}. \end{cases}$$

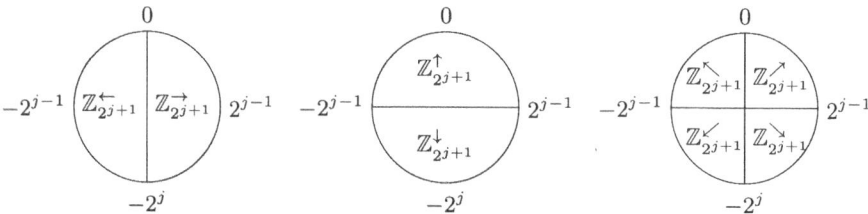

Fig. 6. Intuition for our partitions of $\mathbb{Z}_{2^{j+1}}$.

Proof. Looking at Fig. 6, we obtain

$$\mathbb{Z}_{2^{j+1}}^{\uparrow} = \mathbb{Z}_{2^j},$$

$$\mathbb{Z}_{2^{j+1}}^{\swarrow} = -2^j + \{0, 1, \ldots, 2^{j-1} - 2, 2^{j-1} - 1\},$$

$$\mathbb{Z}_{2^{j+1}}^{\searrow} = 2^j + \{-1, -2, \ldots, -2^{j-1} + 1, -2^{j-1}\},$$

which already proves the lemma. □

Lemma 5. *Let $x \in \mathbb{Z}$ be a signed integer with binary two's complement representation $(x_{w-1}, x_{w-2}, \ldots, x_1, x_0) \in \{0, 1\}^w$, for some word width w. For any $j < w$ we have*

$$x_j = 1 \iff [x]_{2^{j+1}} \in \mathbb{Z}_{2^{j+1}}^{\leftarrow}.$$

Proof. By definition of the binary two's complement, we have $x = \left[\sum_{i=0}^{w-1} x_i 2^i\right]_{2^w}$. Together with Fig. 6, this proves the lemma. □

With the lemmas above, we are now ready to describe the relation extraction for producing $\bar{z}$ as in Eq. (5).

Normal-Form Relations. Recall that in the Leaky-Signature-LWE problem, we obtain relations $(\mathbf{c}, z, y_j)$, where z is defined as

$$z = \langle \mathbf{c}, \mathbf{x} \rangle + y,$$

and y_j is the j-th bit in the binary two's complement representation of y. Before doing the actual relation extraction, we apply some pre-processing to our relations. This brings our relations into a special shape, which we call *normal form*. Dealing only with normal form relations allows us to greatly simplify the relation extraction and its analysis.

Our pre-processing transforms a relation $(\mathbf{c}, z, y_j)$, by replacing z and y_j with

$$z^{\uparrow} := \begin{cases} z + 2^{j-1}, & \text{if } [z]_{2^{j+1}} \in \mathbb{Z}_{2^{j+1}}^{\leftarrow}, \\ z - 2^{j-1}, & \text{if } [z]_{2^{j+1}} \in \mathbb{Z}_{2^{j+1}}^{\rightarrow}, \end{cases} \tag{6}$$

and

$$b_j := \begin{cases} y_j, & \text{if } [z]_{2^{j+1}} \in \mathbb{Z}_{2^{j+1}}^{\leftarrow}, \\ y_j \oplus 1, & \text{if } [z]_{2^{j+1}} \in \mathbb{Z}_{2^{j+1}}^{\rightarrow}, \end{cases} \tag{7}$$

respectively.

Let us explain the effect of our pre-processing. In modulo-2^{j+1} arithmetic, adding 2^{j-1} corresponds to rotating the circles from Fig. 6 by $90°$ clockwise. Similarly, subtracting 2^{j-1} corresponds to rotating the circle by $90°$ counter clockwise. Hence, Eq. (6) ensures that

$$[z^\uparrow]_{2^{j+1}} \in \mathbb{Z}^\uparrow_{2^{j+1}}. \tag{8}$$

Let us write $z^\uparrow = \langle \mathbf{c}, \mathbf{x} \rangle + y^\uparrow$, for some unknown $y^\uparrow$, which (by Eq. (6)) is defined as

$$y^\uparrow := \begin{cases} y + 2^{j-1}, & \text{if } [z]_{2^{j+1}} \in \mathbb{Z}^\leftarrow_{2^{j+1}} \\ y - 2^{j-1}, & \text{if } [z]_{2^{j+1}} \in \mathbb{Z}^\rightarrow_{2^{j+1}} \end{cases}.$$

Assume for a moment that $y^\uparrow = y + 2^{j-1}$, i.e., $[z]_{2^{j+1}} \in \mathbb{Z}^\leftarrow_{2^{j+1}}$. Then by Eq. (7), Lemma 5 and the fact that adding 2^{j-1} rotates the circles Fig. 6 by 90 degrees clockwise, we have the following equivalence:

$$b_j = 1 \iff y_j = 1 \iff [y]_{2^{j+1}} \in \mathbb{Z}^\leftarrow_{2^{j+1}} \iff [y^\uparrow]_{2^{j+1}} \in \mathbb{Z}^\uparrow_{2^{j+1}}.$$

Analogously, if instead $y^\uparrow = y - 2^{j-1}$, we have the following equivalence:

$$b_j = 1 \iff y_j = 0 \iff [y]_{2^{j+1}} \in \mathbb{Z}^\rightarrow_{2^{j+1}} \iff [y^\uparrow]_{2^{j+1}} \in \mathbb{Z}^\uparrow_{2^{j+1}}.$$

Thus, in any case, it holds that

$$b_j = 1 \iff [y^\uparrow]_{2^{j+1}} \in \mathbb{Z}^\uparrow_{2^{j+1}}. \tag{9}$$

Relations $(\mathbf{c}, z^\uparrow, b_j)$ with $z^\uparrow = \langle \mathbf{c}, \mathbf{x} \rangle + y^\uparrow$, for which both Eqs. (8) and (9) and hold, are called *normal form relations*.

A Simplified LZS$^+$ Relation Extraction. With the normal form relations available after pre-processing, we can now describe our simplified relation extraction for constructing $\bar{z}$. Given a normal form relation $(\mathbf{c}, z^\uparrow, b_j)$ with $z^\uparrow = \langle \mathbf{c}, \mathbf{x} \rangle + y^\uparrow$, our relation extraction computes

$$\bar{z} := \begin{cases} [z^\uparrow]_{2^{j+1}}, & \text{if } b_j = 1, \\ [z^\uparrow]_{2^{j+1}} + 2^j, & \text{if } b_j = 0 \text{ and } [z^\uparrow]_{2^{j+1}} \in \mathbb{Z}^\leftarrow_{2^{j+1}}, \\ [z^\uparrow]_{2^{j+1}} - 2^j, & \text{if } b_j = 0 \text{ and } [z^\uparrow]_{2^{j+1}} \in \mathbb{Z}^\rightarrow_{2^{j+1}}. \end{cases} \tag{10}$$

As we show in Theorem 6 below, the resulting $\bar{z}$ has the desired shape. Worth noting, as in the original relation extraction of [LZS+20], we also *crucially* require j to be sufficiently large, such that $j \geq \log_2(\beta) + 1$.

Theorem 6. *Let $(\mathbf{c}, z^\uparrow, b_j)$ be a normal form relation with $z^\uparrow = \langle \mathbf{c}, \mathbf{x} \rangle + y^\uparrow$, where $|\langle \mathbf{c}, \mathbf{x} \rangle| \leq \beta$. If $j \geq \log_2(\beta) + 1$, then for $\bar{z}$ as defined in Eq. (10) it holds that*

$$\bar{z} = \langle \mathbf{c}, \mathbf{x} \rangle + [y^\uparrow]_{2^j}.$$

Proof. Let us define $u := [z^\uparrow]_{2^{j+1}} - \langle \mathbf{c}, \mathbf{x} \rangle$. Then it holds that

$$u \equiv y^\uparrow \mod 2^{j+1}, \tag{11}$$

and, in particular, $[u]_{2^j} = [y^\uparrow]_{2^j}$. To prove the theorem, we show that

$$\bar{z} = \langle \mathbf{c}, \mathbf{x} \rangle + [u]_{2^j}. \tag{12}$$

Since $(\mathbf{c}, z^\uparrow, b_j)$ is a normal form relation, we have by Eq. (8) that $[z^\uparrow]_{2^{j+1}} \in \mathbb{Z}^\uparrow_{2^{j+1}}$. Let us distinguish the two cases

$$[z^\uparrow]_{2^{j+1}} \in \mathbb{Z}^\nwarrow_{2^{j+1}}, \tag{13}$$

and

$$[z^\uparrow]_{2^{j+1}} \in \mathbb{Z}^\nearrow_{2^{j+1}}. \tag{14}$$

Suppose we are in the case of Eq. (13). Then $[z^\uparrow]_{2^{j+1}}$ lies in the upper left quarter of the circles from Fig. 7, i.e., $-2^{j-1} \leq [z^\uparrow]_{2^{j+1}} < 0$. Moreover, since $j \geq \log_2(\beta) + 1$ and $|\langle \mathbf{c}, \mathbf{x} \rangle| \leq \beta$, we have $|\langle \mathbf{c}, \mathbf{x} \rangle| \leq 2^{j-1}$. It follows that $u = [z^\uparrow]_{2^{j+1}} - \langle \mathbf{c}, \mathbf{x} \rangle$ satisfies

$$-2^j \leq u < 2^{j-1}. \tag{15}$$

In other words, u either lies in the upper left quarter, the upper right quarter, or the lower left quarter of the circles from Fig. 7, i.e.,

$$u \notin \mathbb{Z}^\searrow_{2^{j+1}}. \tag{16}$$

Combining Eqs. (11) and (15), we obtain $u = [u]_{2^{j+1}} = [y^\uparrow]_{2^{j+1}}$. Since $(\mathbf{c}, z^\uparrow, b_j)$ is a normal form relation, this implies together with Eq. (9) that

$$u \notin \mathbb{Z}^\downarrow_{2^{j+1}} \iff u \in \mathbb{Z}^\uparrow_{2^{j+1}} \iff [y^\uparrow]_{2^{j+1}} \in \mathbb{Z}^\uparrow_{2^{j+1}} \iff b_j = 1.$$

Hence, by Lemma 4 and Eq. (16),

$$[u]_{2^j} = \begin{cases} u, & \text{if } b_j = 1, \\ u + 2^j, & \text{else.} \end{cases}$$

If we are instead in the case of Eq. (14), one can show completely analogous that

$$[u]_{2^j} = \begin{cases} u, & \text{if } b_j = 1, \\ u - 2^j, & \text{else.} \end{cases}$$

Combining both cases, we obtain

$$[u]_{2^j} = \begin{cases} u, & \text{if } b_j = 1 \\ u + 2^j, & \text{if } b_j = 0 \text{ and } [z^\uparrow]_{2^{j+1}} \in \mathbb{Z}^\leftarrow_{2^{j+1}}, \\ u - 2^j, & \text{if } b_j = 0 \text{ and } [z^\uparrow]_{2^{j+1}} \in \mathbb{Z}^\rightarrow_{2^{j+1}}. \end{cases}$$

Together with Eq. (10) and the fact that $[z^\uparrow]_{2^{j+1}} = \langle \mathbf{c}, \mathbf{x} \rangle + u$, this implies Eq. (12) and thus concludes the proof of the theorem. $\qquad \square$

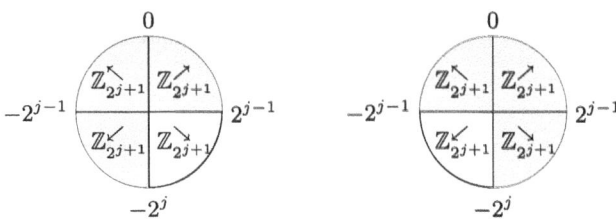

Fig. 7. Intuition for the proof of Theorem 6. The colored area is the range for $u :=$ $[z^\dagger]_{2^j+1} - \langle \mathbf{c}, \mathbf{x} \rangle$, depending on whether $[z^\dagger]_{2^j+1} \in \mathbb{Z}^\searrow_{2^j+1}$ (left) or $[z^\dagger]_{2^j+1} \in \mathbb{Z}^\nearrow_{2^j+1}$ (right).

The Constraint $j \geq \log_2(\beta) + 1$. In the proof of Theorem 6, we crucially require $j \geq \log_2(\beta) + 1$, where β is an upper bound on $|\langle \mathbf{c}, \mathbf{x} \rangle|$. For the ML-DSA-44 parameter set, which has $\beta = 78 \approx 2^{6.3}$ (see Table 1), Theorem 6 thus suggests that our attack requires $j \geq \lceil 6.3 + 1 \rceil = 8$ to work.

However, as we will show in n Sect. 6, our attack works in practice for j as small as $j = 6$. This is due to the fact that, in Dilithium with ML-DSA-44 parameters, the inequality $|\langle \mathbf{c}, \mathbf{x} \rangle| \leq \beta = 78$ is a rather coarse *worst case* bound. Yet, in practice, most $|\langle \mathbf{c}, \mathbf{x} \rangle|$ are significantly smaller than 78: Since $\langle \mathbf{c}, \mathbf{x} \rangle$ is the sum of $\tau = 39$ uniformly random integers from $[\pm\eta] = [\pm 2]$, it follows from the central limit theorem that $\langle \mathbf{c}, \mathbf{x} \rangle$ is close to a Gaussian distribution with mean 0 and variance $\sigma^2 = \frac{(2\eta+1)^2-1}{12} \cdot \tau = 2 \cdot 39 = 78$. (Recall that $\frac{(2\eta+1)^2-1}{12}$ is the variance of the discrete uniform distribution over $[\pm\eta]$.) It is well-known that a Gaussian random variable with variance σ^2 almost never exceeds $3 \cdot \sigma$ in absolute value. Hence, almost all inner products $\langle \mathbf{c}, \mathbf{x} \rangle$ in ML-DSA-44 are bounded by $|\langle \mathbf{c}, \mathbf{x} \rangle| \leq 3 \cdot \sqrt{78} \approx 2^{4.7}$, showing that our attack indeed works for all $j \geq \lceil 4.7 + 1 \rceil = 6$.

For the parameter sets ML-DSA-65 and -87, one can show completely analogously that $\langle \mathbf{c}, \mathbf{x} \rangle$ is close to a Gaussian distribution with standard deviation $\sigma \approx 2^{5.8}$ and $\sigma \approx 2^{5.0}$, respectively. Hence, for these parameter sets, our attack works for all $j \geq 7$ and $j \geq 6$, respectively.

Putting Things Together: Our Leaky-Signature-LWE Attack. Summarizing the previous sections, we finally obtain our full algorithm, as depicted in Algorithm 1.

Algorithm 1: Leaky-Signature-LWE Attack

Input : List L relations $(\mathbf{c}, z, y_j)$ with
     challenge vector $\mathbf{c} \in [\pm 1]_\tau^n$,
     signature coefficient $z \in [\pm(\gamma - \beta)]$,
     knowledge of a bit of the randomness $y_j \in [0, 1]$,
     leakage index j,
     public key $(\mathbf{A}, \mathbf{t})$.
Output: LWE secret $\mathbf{s}_1 \in ([\pm\eta]^n)^\ell$.

1   Initialize empty list $\widetilde{L}$.
2   **for** $(\mathbf{c}, z, y_j) \in L$ **do**
3   **if** $[z]_{2^{j+1}} \in \mathbb{Z}_{2^{j+1}}^{\leftarrow}$ **then**   ▷ Normal form computation, Eq. (6)&(7).
4        $z^\uparrow := z + 2^{j-1}$
5        $b_j := y_j$
6   **else**
7        $z^\uparrow := z - 2^{j-1}$
8        $b_j := y_j \oplus 1$
9   **if** $b_j = 1$ **then**   ▷ Relation extraction $\overline{z} = \langle \mathbf{c}, \mathbf{x} \rangle + [y^\uparrow]_{2^j}$, Eq. (10).
10       $\overline{z} := [z^\uparrow]_{2^{j+1}}$
11   **else if** $[z^\uparrow]_{2^{j+1}} \in \mathbb{Z}_{2^{j+1}}^{\leftarrow}$ **then**
12       $\overline{z} := [z^\uparrow]_{2^{j+1}} + 2^j$
13   **else**
14       $\overline{z} := [z^\uparrow]_{2^{j+1}} - 2^j$
15   **if** $\overline{z} \geq 2^{j-1} - \beta$ or $\overline{z} \leq -2^{j-1} + \beta$ **then** ▷ Only informative relations.
16   **if** $\overline{z} \geq 2^{j-1} - \beta$ **then**   ▷ j-independence Transformation, Eq. (3).
17        $\widetilde{z} := \overline{z} - 2^{j-1} + \beta$
18   **else**
19        $\widetilde{z} := \overline{z} + 2^{j-1} - \beta$
20   Store $(\mathbf{c}, \widetilde{z})$ in $\widetilde{L}$.
21   Let $m := |\widetilde{L}|$. Create an $(m \times n)$-matrix $\mathbf{C}$ with rows $\mathbf{c} \in [\pm 1]_\tau^n$ from $\widetilde{L}$.
22   Create vector $\mathbf{z}$, whose entries are the $\widetilde{z}$'s from $\widetilde{L}$.
23   Apply ordinary least squares regression to $(\mathbf{C}, \mathbf{z})$, to obtain an estimate
   $\hat{\mathbf{x}} = (\mathbf{C}^T \mathbf{C})^{-1} \mathbf{C}^T \mathbf{z} \in \mathbb{Q}^n$ for the partial key $\mathbf{x}$.
24   Compute the subkey $\mathbf{x} := \lfloor \hat{\mathbf{x}} \rceil \in \mathbb{Z}^n$ of $\mathbf{s}_1$ via coordinate-wise rounding.
25   Recover the full LWE secret $\mathbf{s}_1$ via lattice reduction.   ▷ See n Section 4.3.
26   **return** $\mathbf{s}_1$.

---

5   Analysis of Ordinary Least Squares Regression

In this section, we provide a useful lower bound for the required amount m of informative relations such that Algorithm 1 succeeds in line 24 to recover the correct subkey $\mathbf{x}$ of $\mathbf{s}_1$. For estimating $\mathbf{x}$, we use a so-called ordinary least squares regression (OLS), the most commonly used form of a linear regression[4].

---

[4] For further information about OLS in general, we refer to the text book [SL03].

Recall that Algorithm 1 computes in line 23 the estimate $\hat{\mathbf{x}} = (\mathbf{C}^T\mathbf{C})^{-1}\mathbf{C}^T\mathbf{z}$. The following Lemma 7 states the expectation of $\mathbf{C}^T\mathbf{C}$ and shows that we can actually compute the inverse $(\mathbf{C}^T\mathbf{C})^{-1}$.

Lemma 7. *Let $\mathbf{C}$ be an $(m \times n)$ matrix with rows independently sampled from $[\pm 1]^n_\tau$. For $m > n$, it holds that*

$$\mathbb{E}\left[\mathbf{C}^T\mathbf{C}\right] = \frac{m\tau}{n}\mathbf{I}_n. \tag{17}$$

Each entry of $\mathbf{C}^T\mathbf{C}$ converges to its expected value 0 (off-diagonal) or $\frac{m\tau}{n}$ (on-diagonal) exponentially fast in m. For $m > 2n\ln(n)$, it holds that

$$\Pr[\mathbf{C}^T\mathbf{C} \text{ is invertible }] > 1 - ne^{-\frac{m}{2n}}. \tag{18}$$

Proof. See the full version of this paper.

The following estimate provides us a lower bound for the amount of required informative relations.

Estimate 8. *Let $(\mathbf{c}, z, y_i)$ with $\mathbf{c} \in [\pm 1]^n_\tau$ be leaky signatures, where the corresponding LWE secret key $\mathbf{s}_1$ has coordinates from $[\pm \eta]$. Let $\beta = \eta \cdot \tau$.*
    Then the Leaky-Signature-LWE Attack (Algorithm 1) succeeds on input $(\mathbf{c}, z, y_i)$ to recover the correct subkey $\mathbf{x}$ of $\mathbf{s}_1$ in line 24 with probability at least $1 - \delta$ provided that we have at least

$$m := |\tilde{L}| > \frac{2n}{3\tau}((2\beta + 1)^2 - 1)\ln\left(\frac{2n}{\delta}\right) \tag{19}$$

informative relations.

Justification. Algorithm 1 computes in $\tilde{L}$ relations of the form $(\mathbf{C}, \mathbf{z})$ with $\mathbf{C}$ an $(m \times n)$ matrix, where the rows are independent samples of $\mathbf{c} \in [\pm 1]^n_\tau$, and

$$\mathbf{z} = \mathbf{C}^T\mathbf{x} + \mathbf{y}.$$

In Line 23 we compute an OLS estimate

$$\begin{aligned}\hat{\mathbf{x}} &= (\mathbf{C}^T\mathbf{C})^{-1}\mathbf{C}^T\mathbf{z} \\ &= (\mathbf{C}^T\mathbf{C})^{-1}\mathbf{C}^T(\mathbf{C}\mathbf{x} + \mathbf{y}) \\ &= \mathbf{x} + (\mathbf{C}^T\mathbf{C})^{-1}\mathbf{C}^T\mathbf{y}.\end{aligned}$$

According to Theorem 3, the coordinates of $\mathbf{y}$ are i.i.d. samples from a uniform distribution over $[\pm \beta]$. Therefore, the LWE error $\mathbf{y}$ is zero on expectation (i.e. $\mathbb{E}[\mathbf{y}] = 0$), is uncorrelated to $\mathbf{C}$ (i.e. $\mathbb{E}[\mathbf{y}|\mathbf{C}] = 0$), and its covariance matrix is $\mathbb{E}[\mathbf{y}\mathbf{y}^T] = \sigma_y^2\mathbf{I}$ with σ_y^2 the variance of a discrete uniform distribution, i.e., $\sigma_y^2 = \frac{(2\beta+1)^2-1}{12}$.
    It is a well established fact [SL03] that the OLS estimate is unbiased under these three properties, which means that $\mathbb{E}[\hat{\mathbf{x}}] = \mathbf{x}$. That is, on expectation the computed estimate $\hat{\mathbf{x}}$ is indeed the desired subkey $\mathbf{x}$.

Now, we have to show that the estimate $\hat{\mathbf{x}}$ converges with increasing m coordinate-wise to the subkey $\mathbf{x}$.

Using $\mathbb{E}[\mathbf{y}\mathbf{y}^T] = \sigma_y^2 \mathbf{I}_m$, the covariance of the estimation error $\hat{\mathbf{x}} - \mathbf{x}$ can therefore be characterized as

$$
\begin{aligned}
\text{Cov}[\hat{\mathbf{x}} - \mathbf{x}] &= \mathbb{E}[(\hat{\mathbf{x}} - \mathbf{x})(\hat{\mathbf{x}} - \mathbf{x})^T] \\
&= \mathbb{E}\left[((\mathbf{C}^T\mathbf{C})^{-1}\mathbf{C}^T\mathbf{y})((\mathbf{C}^T\mathbf{C})^{-1}\mathbf{C}^T\mathbf{y})^T\right] \\
&= \mathbb{E}_{\mathbf{C},\mathbf{y}}(\mathbf{C}^T\mathbf{C})^{-1}\mathbf{C}^T\mathbf{y}\mathbf{y}^T\mathbf{C}(\mathbf{C}^T\mathbf{C})^{-1}. \\
&= \sigma_y^2 \mathbb{E}_{\mathbf{C}}\left[(\mathbf{C}^T\mathbf{C})^{-1}\mathbf{C}^T\mathbf{C}(\mathbf{C}^T\mathbf{C})^{-1}\right] \\
&= \sigma_y^2 \mathbb{E}[(\mathbf{C}^T\mathbf{C})^{-1}] \\
&\approx \frac{n\sigma_y^2}{m\tau}\mathbf{I}_n.
\end{aligned}
\tag{20}
$$

Note, that the last step follows from Lemma 7: Each entry in $\mathbf{C}^T\mathbf{C}$ converges exponentially fast to those of a scaled identity matrix, and as a consequence the same rate of convergence applies to the entries of the inverse, i.e., $(\mathbf{C}^T\mathbf{C})^{-1} \to \frac{n}{m\tau}\mathbf{I}_n$. We conclude that independently the variance for each coordinate of $\hat{\mathbf{x}} - \mathbf{x}$ is bounded by approximately $\frac{n\sigma_y^2}{m\tau}$.

We proceed by investigating each coordinate j separately and observe that each component of the estimation error $(\mathbf{x} - \hat{\mathbf{x}})_j$ satisfies

$$
(\mathbf{x} - \hat{\mathbf{x}})_j = \sum_{i=1}^{m}((\mathbf{C}^T\mathbf{C})^{-1}\mathbf{C}^T)_{ji}\, \mathbf{y}_i,
$$

which is a sum of independent random variables $\mathbf{y}_i$ weighted by some entry of $(\mathbf{C}^T\mathbf{C})^{-1}\mathbf{C}^T$. We can apply the Lindeberg-Feller central limit theorem [Fel91] which states that the sum of independent random variables with finite variance satisfying the Lindeberg condition converges to a Gaussian distribution.

In our case, the random variables of interest are $Y_i := ((\mathbf{C}^T\mathbf{C})^{-1}\mathbf{C}^T)_{ji}\, \mathbf{y}_i$ with $\mathbb{E}[Y_i] = 0$ and variance $\text{Var}[Y_i] = \sigma_i^2 > 0$. With $\tilde{\sigma}_m^2 := \sum_{i=1}^{m} \sigma_i^2$, the Lindeberg condition reads

$$
\forall \epsilon > 0 : \lim_{m\to\infty} \frac{1}{\tilde{\sigma}_m^2}\sum_{i=1}^{m} \mathbb{E}\left[Y_i^2 \mathbb{1}_{\{|Y_i|>\epsilon\tilde{\sigma}_m\}}\right] \to 0.
\tag{21}
$$

As $|Y_i| = |((\mathbf{C}^T\mathbf{C})^T\mathbf{C}^T)_{ji}\mathbf{y}_i| \in \mathcal{O}(1/m)$ (recall that $(\mathbf{C}^T\mathbf{C})^{-1} \to \frac{n}{m\tau}\mathbf{I}$, which follows from Lemma 7 and entries in $\mathbf{C}^T$ and $\mathbf{y}_i$ are bounded), but $\tilde{\sigma}_m \in \mathcal{O}(1/\sqrt{m})$ (which follows from Eq. (20), where $\tilde{\sigma}_m^2 \approx \frac{n\sigma_y^2}{m\tau}$ is established), we conclude that for any $\epsilon > 0$ there exists $m_0 \in \mathbb{N}$ such that $|Y_i| < \epsilon\tilde{\sigma}_m$, and, thus, the indicator function in Eq. (21) will almost always evaluate to 0 for m large enough. Thus, Lindeberg's condition holds and the Lindeberg-Feller version of the central limit theorem applies, i.e., the estimation error converges to a normal distribution with

$$
\hat{\mathbf{x}} - \mathbf{x} \sim \mathcal{N}\left(0, \frac{n\sigma_y^2}{m\tau}\mathbf{I}_n\right) .
$$

This enables us to apply a Gaussian tail bound for each component

$$\Pr[|\hat{\mathbf{x}}_i - \mathbf{x}_i| > \delta_1] \le 2 \exp\left(-\frac{\delta_1^2 m \tau}{2n\sigma_y^2}\right),$$

and utilize the union bound to cover all n dimensions

$$\Pr[\exists i : |\hat{\mathbf{x}}_i - \mathbf{x}_i| > \delta_1] \le 2n \exp\left(-\frac{\delta_1^2 m \tau}{2n\sigma_y^2}\right).$$

In order to round $\hat{\mathbf{x}}$ successfully to $\mathbf{x}$, we need to establish that no coordinate of $\hat{\mathbf{x}}$ has an error of more than $\delta_1 = \frac{1}{2}$, therefore bounding the ℓ_∞-norm. If we want to succeed with a probability of δ, we can rearrange for the sample complexity:

$$\Pr\left[\|\hat{\mathbf{x}}_i - \mathbf{x}_i\|_\infty > \frac{1}{2}\right] \le 2n \exp\left(-\frac{m\tau}{8n\sigma_y^2}\right) \le \delta$$

$$\implies m \ge \frac{8n\sigma_y^2}{\tau} \ln\left(\frac{2n}{\delta}\right).$$

Plugging in $\sigma_y^2 = \frac{(2\beta+1)^2 - 1}{12}$ gives the desired estimate. $\qquad\diamond$

Table 3. Average run time for ordinary least squares regression, experimentally required number m of informative relations in Algorithm 1 (compare with Fig. 8), our estimate Eq. (19) from Theorem 8, and the estimate Eq. (22) from [LZS+20].

Scheme	regression [seconds]	exp. m [million]	Eq. (19) [million]	Eq. (22) [million]
ML-DSA-44	4	0.50	0.60	11
ML-DSA-87	7	0.75	0.92	17
ML-DSA-65	40	2.4	3.0	54
Ring-LWE-1024	140	2.6	3.4	52

Tightness of Our Bound and Comparison with [LZS+20]. In Table 3, we compare our bound m for the required number of informative relations from Eq. (19) in Theorem 8 to our experimental data from Sect. 6, and to the bound in [LZS+20]. The bound in [LZS+20] was derived from the work in [BDE+18]. For a fair comparison, we instantiate both bounds with success probability $\frac{1}{2}$, which gives for [LZS+20] the formula

$$m \ge \frac{32}{3}\frac{n}{\tau}((2\beta+1)^2 - 1)\ln(2n). \tag{22}$$

From Table 3, we see that our bound from Eq. (19) accurately matches the experimentally required amount of informative relations from column exp. m, and that we significantly improve over Eq. (22). Our improvement comes from tailoring our analysis in Theorem 8 to leaky LWE signatures, whilst the analysis in [LZS+20] relies on simple sub-Gaussian tail bounds.

Reframing Subkey Recovery as a Lattice Problem. Following the framework of [BDE+18], we applied least squares regression with rounding to solve for the secret subkey **x**. As pointed out in [BDE+18], the regression approach may also be phrased in lattice language as follows.

Consider the lattice L spanned by the columns of the basis $\mathbf{C}^T\mathbf{C}$. Then, given the target $\mathbf{C}^T\mathbf{z}$, one may solve a close lattice vector problem as

$$\mathbf{C}^T\mathbf{C}\mathbf{x} = \mathbf{C}^T\mathbf{z} - \mathbf{C}^T\mathbf{y}, \tag{23}$$

i.e., the lattice vector $\mathbf{C}^T\mathbf{C}\mathbf{x}$ is $\mathbf{C}^T\mathbf{y}$-close to the target $\mathbf{C}^T\mathbf{z}$. However, as we showed in Lemma 7, L is almost orthogonal, since it asymptotically converges to a scaled unit matrix. Therefore, multiplying $\mathbf{C}^T\mathbf{z}$ by $(\mathbf{C}^T\mathbf{C})^{-1}$ from the left and rounding to the nearest integer vector provides a close vector solution. This approach is known as *Babai's rounding algorithm*, and the approach is in fact identically to our ordinary least squares regression, see lines 23 & 24 in Algorithm 1.

[BDE+18] also shows that asymptotically no other close vector problem algorithm performs better, including *Babai's nearest plane algorithm*. We experimentally tried to reduce the number of required samples m for subkey reconstruction using Babai's nearest plane algorithm instead of rounding. Our experiments indicate that nearest plane does not help to decrease m.

6 Experimental Results

We implemented our Leaky-Signature-LWE attack (Algorithm 1), and ran it on an AMD EPYC 7763 with 1 TB of RAM, as well as on an AMD EPYC 7742 with 2TB of RAM. Each EPYC was equipped with 128 cores.

We attacked a Lyubashevsky ring LWE signature with $n = 1024$ for full secret key recovery, and all three Dilithium parameter sets ML-DSA-44, ML-DSA-65, and ML-DSA-87, each for a 256-dimensional subkey recovery. In our experiments, we generated sufficiently many leaky signatures $(\mathbf{c}, z, y_j)$ with a single constantly stuck randomness leakage bit $y_j = 0$.

Our results are depicted in Figs. 8, 9 and 10.

Amount of Informative Relations. Figure 8 nicely illustrates the effect of our relation transformation (Sect. 4.2), which makes our attack independent from the leakage position j. Therefore, the required amount of informative relations for successful subkey recovery essentially remains constant. By Theorem 3, informative relations have an error distributed uniformly in $[\pm\beta]$. A smaller error is easier to correct for linear regression. Thus, the smaller β, the fewer relations should be required.

This observation is in line with the results in Fig. 8. ML-DSA-44 with its small $\beta = 78$ (see Table 1) requires the smallest amount of 0.5 million informative relations. For ML-DSA-87 with $\beta = 120$, we require 0.8 million informative relations. For ML-DSA-65 with the largest $\beta = 198$ the number of informative relations increases to 2.4 million.

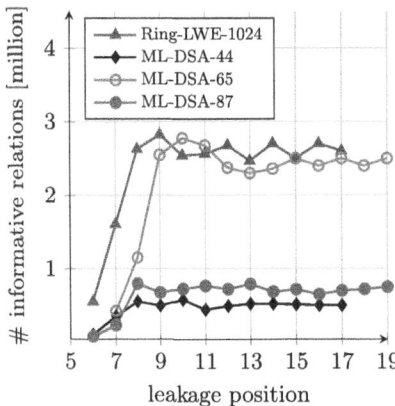
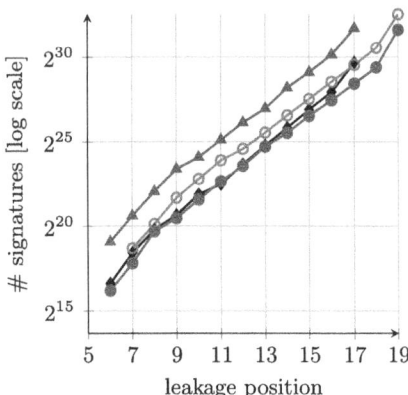

Fig. 8. Required informative relations to recover the secret key in Ring-LWE-1024 or the subkey in Dilithium.

Fig. 9. Required leaky signatures to recover the secret key in Ring-LWE-1024 or the subkey in Dilithium.

Although Ring-LWE-1024 has $\beta = 78$, it still requires 2.6 million relations, because linear regression has to recover $n = 1024$ coordinates of the secret key.

Amount of Signatures. Figure 9 illustrates the total amount of signatures that we require for (sub-)key recovery. We observe from Fig. 9 that for all four attacked schemes the number of signatures roughly doubles with each increase of the leakage position j by 1. This is expected, since the number of *non-informative* relations, that we sort out in n Algorithm 1, also roughly doubles.

Interestingly, the amount of signatures that we require is almost alike for ML-DSA-44 and ML-DSA-87, although by Fig. 8 we need significantly more informative relations for ML-DSA-87. As can be seen by Fig. 4, the larger β, the larger the proportion of *informative relations* among all signatures. This implies that we generate for ML-DSA-87 (with $\beta = 120$) more informative relations than for ML-DSA-44 (with $\beta = 78$) from the same amount of signatures.

The same effect can be observed when comparing the required amount of signatures of Ring-LWE-1024 (with $\beta = 78$) and ML-DSA-65 (with $\beta = 198$). Although both require roughly the same amount of informative relations, we obtain this amount with less ML-DSA-65 signatures.

Comparison with [LZS+20]. Although in absolute numbers we still require for high-order leakage positions j a huge amount of leaky signatures, we would like to stress again that our attack processes all leaky signatures *on the fly*, and stores only informative relations. This is in contrast to the [LZS+20] attack, which produces for every signature a relation that has to be stored for feeding it to linear regression, making [LZS+20]'s attack infeasible for large j.

Figure 10 shows that we do not only improve in run time and memory, but also in the total number of required signatures. While the [LZS+20] attack

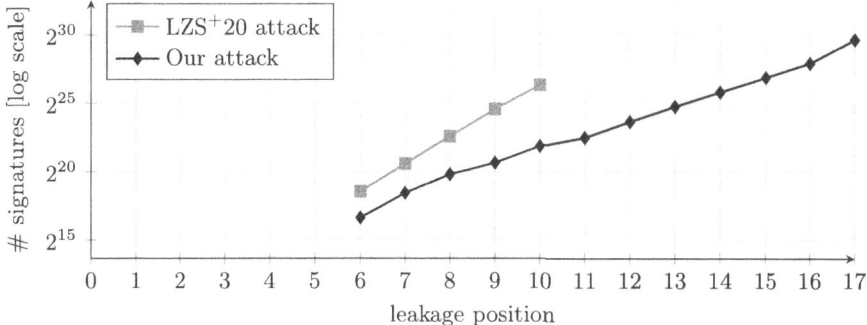

Fig. 10. Required amount of leaky signatures to recover the secret subkey in Dilithium-II (ML-DSA-44).

roughly has a factor 4 increase of required leaky signatures per position, our increase is only by a factor 2, as can be observed by the smaller slope of our attack in Fig. 10. The smaller slope is a result of two improvements in our attack. First, we sort out *non-informative* relations, and second we reduce via our novel transformation the size of the error in the relations.

7   Further Reducing the Amount of Signatures

We know from Sect. 6 that a 256-dimensional subkey $\mathbf{x}$ recovery for ML-DSA-44 requires roughly 500.000 signatures. In this section, we explore what happens if we do not obtain the required amount of ML-DSA-44 signatures to fully recover the subkey via linear regression. Let us say, we receive only 450.000 or 250.000 signatures. Does that mean that we simply cannot run our Algorithm 1?

We will see in the following that we still obtain useful information that helps us to reduce the complexity of a lattice attack on ML-DSA-44.

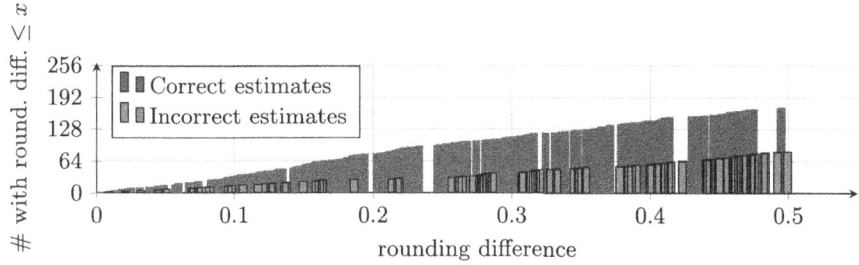

Fig. 11. ML-DSA-44, rounding differences for 50.000 informative relations.

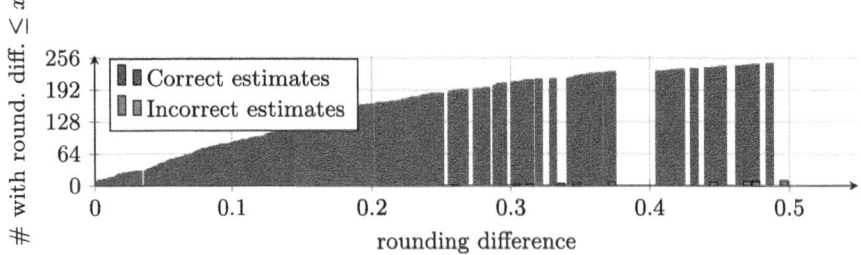

Fig. 12. ML-DSA-44, rounding differences for 250.000 informative relations.

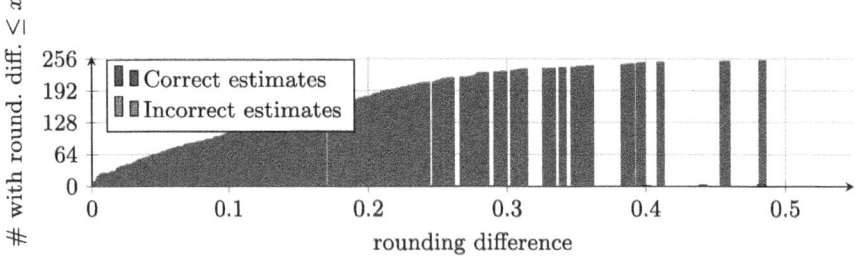

Fig. 13. ML-DSA-44, rounding differences for 450.000 informative relations.

Linear Regression and Rounding. In principle, Algorithm 1 may run linear regression with any available number of relations for ML-DSA-44. Linear regression will always output an estimate $\hat{x} \in \mathbb{Q}^{256}$ of the desired subkey. Our Theorem 8 only guarantees that rounding $\hat{x}$ coordinate-wise to the nearest integer indeed yields the desired subkey x when we use a sufficient amount of relations. This in turn does not imply that for an insufficient amount of relations the estimate $\hat{x} \in \mathbb{Q}^{256}$ is completely off.

We ran Algorithm 1 on ML-DSA-44 with 50.000, 250.000, and 450.000 informative relations, and depicted the results in Figs. 11, 12 and 13, respectively.

Let us have a closer look at Fig. 11 with only 50.000 relations. We see that after rounding already 170 out of the 256 coefficients of x are correctly determined by linear regression. If we use 250.000 relations, then we obtain 240 correctly determined coefficients, and for 450.000 relations we even obtain 250 correct coordinates of x.

Thus, linear regression has the remarkable property that it correctly identifies already a large fraction of all coordinates of the secret x with significantly less relations than required to fully determine x. In other words, the number of correctly identified coordinates quite quickly convergences to n.

Scoring Coordinates. While the property that linear regression identifies a large fraction of coordinates correctly looks promising, it is unclear how to exploit this algorithmically. Enumerating the incorrect coordinates still seems infeasible, since we do not know the positions of the errors.

Instead, we propose the following *scoring* of coordinates. For every coordinate in the estimate $\hat{\mathbf{x}} \in \mathbb{Q}^n$ we determine its remainder $r_i = \hat{\mathbf{x}}_i - \lfloor \hat{\mathbf{x}}_i \rceil$, i.e., r_i is the difference to the next integer. Intuitively, the smaller the score r_i, the more likely is the rounded value $\lfloor \hat{\mathbf{x}}_i \rceil$ indeed the correct coordinate $\mathbf{x}_i$.

We see in Fig. 12 that such a scoring is a useful measure. Among the incorrectly identified coordinates a remainder of $r_i = 0.26$ is the minimal score. So we can identify all coordinates with score smaller than the threshold $r_i = 0.26$ as correct. These would still be an amount of 192 coordinates from $\mathbf{x}$.

Now, we may apply the *LWE with side information framework* from Sect. 4.3. From Fig. 5 we see that by using 192 known coordinates of the secret key, the lattice complexity of ML-DSA-44 drops to below 100 bit.

Acknowledgments. We thank Phong Nguyen for helpful discussions.

Nicolai Kraus is funded by the German Federal Ministry of Education and Research (BMBF) project PQ-CCA. Julian Nowakowski is funded by the Deutsche Forschungsgemeinschaft (DFG, German Research Foundation) grant 465120249. Alexander May is supported by DFG under Germany's Excellence Strategy - EXC 2092 CASA - 390781972.

Disclosure of Interests. The authors have no competing interests.

References

[ABC+22] Albrecht, M.R., et al.: Classic mceliece: conservative code-based cryptography (2022)

[AH21] Albrecht, M.R., Heninger, N.: On bounded distance decoding with predicate: breaking the "lattice barrier" for the hidden number problem. In: Canteaut, A., Standaert, F.-X. (eds.) EUROCRYPT 2021. LNCS, vol. 12696, pp. 528–558. Springer, Cham (2021). https://doi.org/10.1007/978-3-030-77870-5_19

[Aka09] Akavia, A.: Solving hidden number problem with one bit oracle and advice. In: Halevi, S. (ed.) CRYPTO 2009. LNCS, vol. 5677, pp. 337–354. Springer, Heidelberg (2009). https://doi.org/10.1007/978-3-642-03356-8_20

[ANT+20] Aranha, D.F., Novaes, F.R., Takahashi, A., Tibouchi, M., Yarom, Y.: LadderLeak: breaking ECDSA with less than one bit of nonce leakage. In: Ligatti, J., Ou, X., Katz, J., Vigna, G. (eds.) ACM CCS 2020, pp. 225–242. ACM Press (2020)

[BDE+18] Bootle, J., Delaplace, C., Espitau, T., Fouque, P.-A., Tibouchi, M.: LWE without modular reduction and improved side-channel attacks against BLISS. In: Peyrin, T., Galbraith, S. (eds.) ASIACRYPT 2018, Part I. LNCS, vol. 11272, pp. 494–524. Springer, Cham (2018). https://doi.org/10.1007/978-3-030-03326-2_17

[BV96] Boneh, D., Venkatesan, R.: Hardness of computing the most significant bits of secret keys in Diffie-Hellman and related schemes. In: Koblitz, N. (ed.) CRYPTO 1996. LNCS, vol. 1109, pp. 129–142. Springer, Heidelberg (1996). https://doi.org/10.1007/3-540-68697-5_11

[CFS01] Courtois, N.T., Finiasz, M., Sendrier, N.: How to achieve a McEliece-based digital signature scheme. In: Boyd, C. (ed.) ASIACRYPT 2001. LNCS, vol. 2248, pp. 157–174. Springer, Heidelberg (2001). https://doi.org/10.1007/3-540-45682-1_10

[CNE+14] Checkoway, S., et al.: On the practical exploitability of dual EC in TLS implementations. In: Fu, K., Jung, J. (eds.) USENIX Security 2014, pp. 319–335. USENIX Association (2014)

[CVE] CVE-2024-31497. https://nvd.nist.gov/vuln/detail/CVE-2024-31497. Accessed 30 Apr 2024

[DDGR20] Dachman-Soled, D., Ducas, L., Gong, H., Rossi, M.: LWE with side information: attacks and concrete security estimation. In: Micciancio, D., Ristenpart, T. (eds.) CRYPTO 2020, Part II. LNCS, vol. 12171, pp. 329–358. Springer, Cham (2020). https://doi.org/10.1007/978-3-030-56880-1_12

[DFPS23] Devevey, J., Fallahpour, P., Passelègue, A., Stehlé, D.: A detailed analysis of Fiat-Shamir with aborts. In: Handschuh, H., Lysyanskaya, A. (eds.) CRYPTO 2023, Part V. LNCS, vol. 14085, pp. 327–357. Springer, Cham (2023)

[DGHK23] Dachman-Soled, D., Gong, H., Hanson, T., Kippen, H.: Revisiting security estimation for LWE with hints from a geometric perspective. In: Handschuh, H., Lysyanskaya, A. (eds.) CRYPTO 2023, Part V. LNCS, vol. 14085, pp. 748–781. Springer, Cham (2023)

[DHMP13] De Mulder, E., Hutter, M., Marson, M.E., Pearson, P.: Using Bleichenbacher's solution to the hidden number problem to attack nonce leaks in 384-bit ECDSA. In: Bertoni, G., Coron, J.-S. (eds.) CHES 2013. LNCS, vol. 8086, pp. 435–452. Springer, Heidelberg (2013). https://doi.org/10.1007/978-3-642-40349-1_25

[EFGT17] Espitau, T., Fouque, P.A., Gérard, B., Tibouchi, M.: Side-channel attacks on BLISS lattice-based signatures: exploiting branch tracing against strongSwan and electromagnetic emanations in microcontrollers. In: Thuraisingham, B.M., Evans, D., Malkin, T., Xu, D. (eds.) ACM CCS 2017, pp. 1857–1874. ACM Press (2017)

[Fel91] Feller, W.: An introduction to probability theory and its applications, Volume 2, vol. 81. Wiley (1991)

[FGUO+13] Faugere, J.-C., Gauthier-Umana, V., Otmani, A., Perret, L., Tillich, J.-P.: A distinguisher for high-rate mceliece cryptosystems. IEEE Trans. Inf. Theory **59**(10), 6830–6844 (2013)

[FS09] Finiasz, M., Sendrier, N.: Security bounds for the design of code-based cryptosystems. In: Matsui, M. (ed.) ASIACRYPT 2009. LNCS, vol. 5912, pp. 88–105. Springer, Heidelberg (2009). https://doi.org/10.1007/978-3-642-10366-7_6

[Gal13] Galbraith, S.D.: Space-efficient variants of cryptosystems based on learning with errors (2013). https://wwwmath.auckland.ac.nz/~sgal018/compact-LWE.pdf

[GGH97] Goldreich, O., Goldwasser, S., Halevi, S.: Public-key cryptosystems from lattice reduction problems. In: Kaliski, B.S. (ed.) CRYPTO 1997. LNCS, vol. 1294, pp. 112–131. Springer, Heidelberg (1997). https://doi.org/10.1007/BFb0052231

[GJSS01] Gentry, C., Jonsson, J., Stern, J., Szydlo, M.: Cryptanalysis of the NTRU signature scheme (NSS) from Eurocrypt 2001. In: Boyd, C. (ed.) ASIACRYPT 2001. LNCS, vol. 2248, pp. 1–20. Springer, Heidelberg (2001). https://doi.org/10.1007/3-540-45682-1_1

[GPV08] Gentry, C., Peikert, C., Vaikuntanathan, V.: Trapdoors for hard lattices and new cryptographic constructions. In: Ladner, R.E., Dwork, C. (eds.) 40th ACM STOC, pp. 197–206. ACM Press (2008)

[GS02] Gentry, C., Szydlo, M.: Cryptanalysis of the revised NTRU signature scheme. In: Knudsen, L.R. (ed.) EUROCRYPT 2002. LNCS, vol. 2332, pp. 299–320. Springer, Heidelberg (2002). https://doi.org/10.1007/3-540-46035-7_20

[HGS01] Howgrave-Graham, N.A., Smart, N.P.: Lattice attacks on digital signature schemes. Des. Codes Cryptogr. **23**, 283–290 (2001)

[HHP+03] Hoffstein, J., Howgrave-Graham, N., Pipher, J., Silverman, J.H., Whyte, W.: NTRUSIGN: digital signatures using the NTRU lattice. In: Joye, M. (ed.) CT-RSA 2003. LNCS, vol. 2612, pp. 122–140. Springer, Heidelberg (2003)

[HM17] Herold, G., May, A.: LP solutions of vectorial integer subset sums – cryptanalysis of galbraith's binary matrix LWE. In: Fehr, S. (ed.) PKC 2017. LNCS, vol. 10174, pp. 3–15. Springer, Heidelberg (2017). https://doi.org/10.1007/978-3-662-54365-8_1

[HPS98] Hoffstein, J., Pipher, J., Silverman, J.H.: NTRU: a ring-based public key cryptosystem. In: Buhler, J.P. (ed.) ANTS 1998. LNCS, vol. 1423, pp. 267–288. Springer, Heidelberg (1998). https://doi.org/10.1007/BFb0054868

[HPS01] Hoffstein, J., Pipher, J., Silverman, J.H.: NSS: an NTRU lattice-based signature scheme. In: Pfitzmann, B. (ed.) EUROCRYPT 2001. LNCS, vol. 2045, pp. 211–228. Springer, Heidelberg (2001). https://doi.org/10.1007/3-540-44987-6_14

[HR07] Hlaváč, M., Rosa, T.: Extended hidden number problem and its cryptanalytic applications. In: Biham, E., Youssef, A.M. (eds.) SAC 2006. LNCS, vol. 4356, pp. 114–133. Springer, Heidelberg (2007). https://doi.org/10.1007/978-3-540-74462-7_9

[HR23] Heninger, N., Ryan, K.: The hidden number problem with small unknown multipliers: cryptanalyzing MEGA in six queries and other applications. In: Boldyreva, A., Kolesnikov, V. (eds.) PKC 2023, Part I. LNCS, vol. 13940, pp. 147–176. Springer, Cham (2023)

[HRSS17] Hülsing, A., Rijneveld, J., Schanck, J.M., Schwabe, P.: NTRU-HRSS-KEM-submission to the NIST post-quantum cryptography project (2017)

[Lyu09] Lyubashevsky, V.: Fiat-Shamir with aborts: applications to lattice and factoring-based signatures. In: Matsui, M. (ed.) ASIACRYPT 2009. LNCS, vol. 5912, pp. 598–616. Springer, Heidelberg (2009). https://doi.org/10.1007/978-3-642-10366-7_35

[Lyu24] Lyubashevsky, V.: Basic lattice cryptography: the concepts behind kyber (ML-KEM) and dilithium (ML-DSA). Cryptology ePrint Archive, Report 2024/1287 (2024)

[LZS+20] Liu, Y., Zhou, Y., Sun, S., Wang, T., Zhang, R., Ming, J.: On the security of lattice-based Fiat-Shamir signatures in the presence of randomness leakage. IEEE Trans. Inf. Forensics Secur. **16**, 1868–1879 (2020)

[MBA+21] Merget, R., Brinkmann, M., Aviram, N., Somorovsky, J., Mittmann, J., Schwenk, J.: Raccoon attack: finding and exploiting most-significant-bit-oracles in TLS-DH(E). In: Bailey, M., Greenstadt, R. (eds.) USENIX Security 2021, pp. 213–230. USENIX Association (2021)

[McE78] McEliece, R.J.: A public-key cryptosystem based on algebraic. Coding Thv **4244**, 114–116 (1978)

[MN23]   May, A., Nowakowski, J.: Too many hints - when LLL breaks LWE. In: Guo, J., Steinfeld, R. (eds.) ASIACRYPT 2023, Part IV. LNCS, vol. 14441, pp. 106–137. Springer, Singapore (2023)

[NR09]   Nguyen, P.Q., Regev, O.: Learning a parallelepiped: cryptanalysis of GGH and NTRU signatures. J. Cryptol. 22(2), 139–160 (2009)

[NS02]   Nguyen and Shparlinski: The insecurity of the digital signature algorithm with partially known nonces. J. Cryptol. 15, 151–176 (2002)

[NS03]   Nguyen, P.Q., Shparlinski, I.E.: The insecurity of the elliptic curve digital signature algorithm with partially known nonces. Des. Codes Cryptogr. 30, 201–217 (2003)

[OVCG24]   Oliveira, P.A., Viera, A.C., Cogliati, B., Goubin, L.: Uncompressing dilithium's public key. IACR Cryptol. ePrint Arch. 1373 (2024)

[QLZ+22]   Qiao, Z., Liu, Y., Zhou, Y., Ming, J., Jin, C., Li, H.: Practical public template attacks on crystals-dilithium with randomness leakages. IEEE Trans. Inf. Forensics Secur. 18, 1–14 (2022)

[Rya18]   Ryan, K.: Return of the hidden number problem. IACR TCHES 2019(1), 146–168 (2018)

[Sch87]   Schnorr, C.-P.: A hierarchy of polynomial time lattice basis reduction algorithms. Theoret. Comput. Sci. 53(2–3), 201–224 (1987)

[Sch90]   Schnorr, C.P.: Efficient identification and signatures for smart cards. In: Brassard, G. (ed.) CRYPTO 1989. LNCS, vol. 435, pp. 239–252. Springer, New York (1990). https://doi.org/10.1007/0-387-34805-0_22

[SL03]   Seber, G.A.F., Lee, A.J.: Linear regression analysis. Wiley series in probability and statistics, 2nd edn. Wiley-Interscience, Hoboken (2003)

[XSWH22]   Jun, X., Sarkar, S., Wang, H., Lei, H.: Improving bounds on elliptic curve hidden number problem for ECDH key exchange. In: Agrawal, S., Lin, D. (eds.) ASIACRYPT 2022, Part III. LNCS, vol. 13793, pp. 771–799. Springer, Cham (2022)

The Security of Hash-and-Sign with Retry Against Superposition Attacks

Haruhisa Kosuge[1](✉) and Keita Xagawa[2]

[1] NTT Social Informatics Laboratories, Tokyo, Japan
hrhs.kosuge@ntt.com
[2] Technology Innovation Institute, Abu Dhabi, UAE
keita.xagawa@tii.ae

Abstract. Considering security against quantum adversaries, while it is important to consider the traditional existential unforgeability (EUF-CMA security), it is desirable to consider security against adversaries making quantum queries to the signing oracle: Plus-one security (PO security) and blind unforgeability (BU security) proposed by Boneh and Zhandry (Crypto 2013) and Alagic et al. (EUROCRYPT 2020), respectively. Hash-and-sign is one of the most common paradigms for constructing EUF-CMA-secure signature schemes in the quantum random oracle model, employing a trapdoor function and a hash function. It is known that its derandomized version is PO- and BU-secure. A variant of hash-and-sign, known as hash-and-sign with retry (HSwR), formulated by Kosuge and Xagawa (PKC 2024), is widespread since it allows for weakening the security assumptions of a trapdoor function. Unfortunately, it has not been known whether HSwR can achieve PO- and BU-secure even with derandomization.

In this paper, we apply a derandomization with bounded loops to HSwR. We demonstrate that HSwR can achieve PO and BU security through this approach. Since derandomization with bounded loops offers advantages in some implementations, our results support its wider adoption, including in NIST PQC candidates.

Keywords: Post-quantum cryptography · Quantum random oracle model · Superposition attack · Digital signature · Hash-and-sign

1 Introduction

Security Models of Digital Signatures against Quantum Adversaries: Digital signatures are crucial for ensuring the integrity and authenticity of digital communications. The standard and traditional security notion for digital signatures is existential unforgeability against a chosen-message attack (EUF-CMA) [13]. Roughly speaking, we say a signature scheme is EUF-CMA-secure if no efficient adversary can forge a signature even if the adversary has access to a signing oracle, thereby capturing both non-repudiation and authentication.

© International Association for Cryptologic Research 2025
T. Jager and J. Pan (Eds.): PKC 2025, LNCS 15674, pp. 317–349, 2025.
https://doi.org/10.1007/978-3-031-91820-9_11

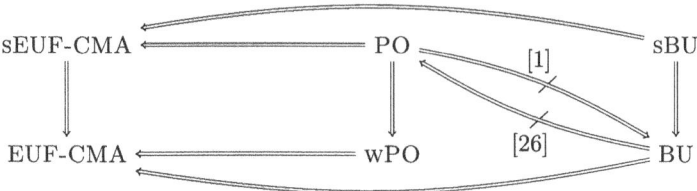

Fig. 1. Relationship between different security notions

The advent of quantum computers has raised concerns about the security of digital signatures due to Shor's algorithm [24]. Consequently, there has been growing interest in post-quantum cryptography (PQC). In 2022, NIST selected three candidates of digital signatures, namely Falcon, Dilithium (ML-DSA), and SPHINCS+ (SLH-DSA), for standardization [22]. Furthermore, NIST initiated an additional call for digital signatures [21].

Given that post-quantum signatures must withstand attacks from quantum computers, their security proofs must be conducted in the quantum random oracle model (QROM) [5], rather than in the random oracle model (ROM), since the QROM models quantum adversaries having offline access to the hash function. The EUF-CMA security in the QROM allows an adversary to make quantum queries to the random oracle and *classical* queries to the signing oracle.

If quantum computing becomes ubiquitous, EUF-CMA might not adequately capture the necessary security requirements for signatures, as end-users may use personal quantum computers for signing. In that case, the adversary may carry out superposition attacks, which force the generation of quantum superpositions of signatures. Even in such a future, the security model of Boneh and Zhandry [6] remains valid, as it assumes *quantum* queries to the signing oracle. This model is called plus-one unforgeability (PO security, in short) [1] since the adversary needs to generate $q+1$ pairs of message/signature with q quantum queries to the signing oracle. Another model, proposed by Alagic et al. [1], is called blind unforgeability (BU security, in short). In this model, certain messages are *blinded*, meaning that the signing oracle is designed not to return signatures for these messages, and the adversary must forge signatures corresponding to the blinded messages. Note that there are strong (PO, sBU, and sEUF-CMA) and weak (wPO, BU, and EUF-CMA) security notions[1]. Since a weak variant of PO is not defined, we introduce a new definition: weak PO (wPO).

Regarding the relationship between security models, a MAC scheme that is PO-secure but BU-insecure has been demonstrated [1, ePrint], as well as a MAC/signature scheme that is BU-secure but PO-insecure [26, Appendix C,

---

[1] The distinction between *strong* and *weak* security is determined by whether an adversary's forgery is considered successful if it targets messages for which the attacker has already obtained information about the corresponding signatures through signing queries (strong) or targets completely new messages (weak).

ePrint]. We illustrate the relationship between these security notions in Fig. 1. As shown in the diagram, the relationship between these security models remains partially understood, necessitating independent evaluation of both PO and BU security.

Hash-and-Sign with Retry: Two paradigms are typically employed to construct EUF-CMA-secure signatures: Hash-and-sign (also known as full domain hash (FDH)) [3,4] and Fiat-Shamir [10]. This paper focuses on hash-and-sign. Hash-and-sign constructs digital signatures from a trapdoor function (TDF) and a hash function. For provable security, hash-and-sign requires a special TDF called preimage-sampleable function (PSF) [12]. Since PSFs are generally hard to build, *hash-and-sign with retry* (HSwR) [19,23], which can construct signatures using non-PSF TDFs, has been widely adopted among multivariate and code-based signatures, including new NIST PQC candidates, QR-UOV [11] and PROV [14]. In the signature generation, the paradigm repeatedly performs loop iterations until certain conditions are met. Kosuge and Xagawa [19] have provided a reduction from the non-invertibility and preimage-simulatability of the underlying TDF to the EUF-CMA security in the QROM.[2]

Current Status of PO *and* BU *Security Proofs:* Boneh and Zhandry [6] and Chatterjee, Chung, Liang, and Malavolta [7] showed that the derandomized version of hash-and-sign (without retry) is PO- and BU-secure, respectively. Also, Xagawa [26] demonstrated PO and BU security proofs of the derandomized version of Fiat-Shamir with aborts [20] that has a similar structure as HSwR. However, whether HSwR achieves PO/BU security even with derandomization remains unclear. Thus, it is natural to pose the following question:

Can HSwR achieve PO *and* BU *security (with derandomization)?*

1.1 Contribution

We affirmatively answer the question. Applying the derandomization and bounding the number of retries to HSwR, we show that the variant is PO- and BU- secure.[3] We refer to this version of HSwR as *derandomized hash-and-sign with bounded retry* (DHSwBR). Additionally, we demonstrate that DHSwBR is EUF-CMA-secure under the same assumption as the existing proof for the original HSwR [19], along with the pseudorandomness of the PRF used for the derandomization.

Note that we evaluate both strong and weak security notions for PO, BU, and EUF-CMA. Additionally, our proofs are reductions from the EUF-NMA

---

[2] In general, *non-invertibility* of TDFs is called *one-wayness*. We make a distinction between them depending on the way to choose challenges (non-invertibility follows [16] and one-wayness follows [3]).

[3] Derandomized HSwR (with unbounded retry) is available as an option in PROV [14], and its security has been evaluated in the ROM by Cogliati et al. [8]. (Unfortunately, their proof contains an error).

Table 1. Summary of the existing and our security proofs in the QROM. In "Paradigm", HS, DHS, PHS, DPHS denote original, derandomized, probabilistic, and derandomized probabilistic hash-and-sign, respectively, and +RF denotes that it replaces PRFs with random functions. In "Assumptions", PSF indicates that the TDF is PSF, while INJ, CR, SPR, and PS represent, in decreasing order of strength, the injection, collision resistance, second-preimage resistance, and preimage-simulatability of the TDF, respectively. Here, "(C-)" denotes that a computational bound may be used for the preimage-simulatability. (q)PRF denotes (quantum) pseudo-randomness of PRFs.

Proof	Paradigm	Security	Assumptions
[5]	HS +RF	sEUF-CMA	CR
[19]	PHS	EUF-CMA	EUF-NMA, (C-)PS
[19]	HSwR	EUF-CMA	EUF-NMA, (C-)PS
[19]	HSwR	sEUF-CMA	EUF-NMA, INJ, (C-)PS
[6]	DHS	PO	PSF, CR, qPRF
[26]	DHS	PO	PSF, CR, qPRF
[26]	DHS +RF	PO	PSF, CR
[7]	DHS	BU	PSF, CR, qPRF
[26]	DHS	sBU	PSF, CR, qPRF
Sect. 4.1	DHSwBR/DPHS	PO	EUF-NMA, CR, PS, qPRF
Sect. 4.1	DHSwBR/DPHS	wPO	EUF-NMA, PS, qPRF
Sect. 4.2	DHSwBR/DPHS	sBU	EUF-NMA, CR, PS, qPRF
Sect. 4.2	DHSwBR/DPHS	BU	EUF-NMA, PS, qPRF
Sect. 4.3	DHSwBR/DPHS	sEUF-CMA	EUF-NMA, SPR, (C-)PS, PRF
Sect. 4.3	DHSwBR/DPHS	EUF-CMA	EUF-NMA, (C-)PS, PRF

security of the original HSwR, where NMA stands for No Message Attack. Kosuge and Xagawa [19] have shown a reduction from non-invertibility of TDF to EUF-NMA. By demonstrating reductions from the EUF-NMA security, we not only establish reductions from non-invertibility but also enable adaptation to new security properties that have yet to be discovered. We summarize the results and their comparison to the existing proofs in Table 1. By setting the number of retries as one, our proof can be applied to the security proof of the derandomized probabilistic hash-and-sign.

Implications of Our Results: Since DHSwBR is interoperable with the original HSwR, it can be considered an option for signature schemes adopting HSwR. In addition to the security advantage of provable security against superposition attacks, the option also offers advantages in certain implementations. When signature generation depends on the entropy of randomness, security is inherently tied to the quality of the implementation. By the derandomization, security can be maintained without relying on the random number generation. This is particularly beneficial for platforms where sufficient entropy in random number generation is not guaranteed. Due to the security and implementation advantages, derandomization with bounded loops should be recognized as a major option for HSwR signatures.

1.2 Technical Overview

Before presenting the technical overview of our proof for (w)PO and (s)BU security, we briefly explain HSwR, its variant DHSwBR, and preimage-simulatability. HSwR uses a TDF that consists of $(\mathsf{Gen}, \mathsf{F}, \mathsf{Inv})$. Gen generates a public/secret key pair (vk, sk) that is also a key pair of the signature scheme. Taking vk and $x \in \mathcal{X}$ as inputs, a hard-to-invert function F deterministicaly outputs $y \in \mathcal{Y}$. The function Inv is a probabilistic function that, given sk and y as input, returns an x such that $\mathsf{F}(vk, x) = y$ with high probability, or outputs $\bot$ (indicating inversion failure). For a message m and a uniformly chosen salt r, the signing algorithm computes $\mathsf{Inv}(sk, \mathsf{H}(r, m))$, where H is a random function. If $\mathsf{Inv}(sk, \mathsf{H}(r, m))$ fails in inversion, a new r is chosen, and this process is repeated until the inversion succeeds. Then, (r, x) is output as the signature. A signature (r, x) is verified if $\mathsf{F}(vk, x) = \mathsf{H}(r, m)$ holds. As for DHSwBR, in addition to sk, the signing key includes keys s and s' for PRFs PRF and PRF'. We use a counter k, which increments by 1 with each loop iteration, to derive a salt as $r := \mathsf{PRF}(s, m, k)$ and a random coin $r' := \mathsf{PRF}'(s', m, k)$ for Inv. Also, the number of retries is bounded by a parameter B. Aside from the above derandomization in the signature generation, DHSwBR is identical to HSwR. An important property of HSwR/DHSwBR is the preimage-simulatability, which assumes that the following two are statistically or computationally indistinguishable [19]:

- x obtained after retrying y until y becomes invertible by $\mathsf{Inv}(sk, y)$.
- x obtained by a simulator that does not use the secret key sk.

Let us now proceed with the technical overview of our proof. In the reduction, the EUF-NMA adversary, which does not possess the signing key, must simulate the signing oracle. To achieve this, the following two steps are required:

- First, it must modify the output of the random function H to make simulated signatures generated in the signing oracle valid.
- Second, the message/signature pair output by the (w)PO or (s)BU adversary must be verified using the original random function. This condition is essential for the EUF-NMA adversary to win its own game.

For the second step, this can be achieved by utilizing the techniques used by Xagawa [26] in proving the PO and sBU security of Fiat-Shamir with aborts taking derandomization with bounded loops. Let (m^*, r^*, x^*) be one of the message/signature pairs output by a (w)PO or (s)BU adversary, and let (r_m, x_m) be a signature generated by the signing oracle taking m. The random function H is modified such that $\mathsf{H}(r_m, m) = \mathsf{F}(vk, x_m)$ holds for any m to accept signatures generated by the signing oracle. We can modify the game so that the adversary can win if and only if $r^* \neq r_{m^*}$ holds[4]. Since the values of $H(r, m)$ for $r \neq r_m$ remain unchanged from the original, the signature (m^*, r^*, x^*) can be verified using the original random function if $r^* \neq r_{m^*}$.

However, modifying outputs of H to accept simulated signatures in the first step cannot be achieved using the techniques from [9, 26]; they rely on the strong assumption of statistical or divergence honest-verifier zero-knowledge (HVZK), which requires simulation of *succeeding and failing attempts*, while preimage-simulatability only requires that of succeeding attempt. We explain the difficulty in simulating the signing oracle. In the real experiment, for a message m, when inversion first succeeds at the k-th iteration, $H(r_i, m) = y_i$ holds for each $\{(r_i, y_i)\}_{i=1,\dots,k}$, where r_i and y_i are generated sequentially from $i = 1$. To simulate this signing oracle, the EUF-NMA adversary must simulate $\{y_i\}_{i=1,\dots,k}$ without using sk; however, preimage-simulatability only assures that the last y_k is simulated by $F(vk, x)$ for some x.

To address this problem, we employ the one-way-to-hiding (O2H) lemma [2, 25]. Assuming that the guessing probability of $\{r_i\}_{i=1,\dots,k-1}$ is negligible, we can eliminate the need for simulation of $\{y_i\}_{i=1,\dots,k-1}$, allowing the EUF-NMA adversary to simulate signatures under the assumption of preimage-simulatability. Note that we can only use statistical preimage-simulatability since we cannot perform adaptive reprogramming [15] in the quantum signing oracle setting, while it is a common technique for establishing computational bound for simulating signatures in the classical signing oracle [9, 15, 19].

1.3 Open Problems

In our proofs of (w)PO/(s)BU security, a computational bound for the preimage-simulatability cannot be used. Since there are cryptographic schemes for which statistical properties cannot be achieved, the relaxation from the statistical bound to the computational one would expand the applicability of our security proofs. One possible way is assuming *quantum* preimage-simulatability as in the case of the Fiat-Shamir signatures [27]; however, this is a strong assumption.

1.4 Organization

Section 2 gives notations and definitions. Section 3 introduces the QROM and its existing proof techniques used for our proofs. Section 4 presents the new security proofs of DHSwBR.

2 Preliminaries

2.1 Notations and Terminology

For $n \in \mathbb{N}$, we let $[n] := \{1, \dots, n\}$. We write any symbol for sets in calligraphic font. For a finite set $\mathcal{X}$, $|\mathcal{X}|$ is the cardinality of $\mathcal{X}$ and $U(\mathcal{X})$ is the uniform

---

[4] In the PO/sBU security proofs, collision-resistance of the TDF is required.

GAME (s)EUF-CMA/EUF-NMA		SIGN(m)	
1 $Q := \emptyset$		10 $\sigma \leftarrow$ Sign(sk, m)	
2 $(vk, sk) \leftarrow$ KeyGen(1^λ)		11 $Q := Q \cup \{m\}$	//EUF-CMA
3 $(m^*, \sigma^*) \leftarrow \mathcal{A}^{\text{SIGN}}(vk)$	//(s)EUF-CMA	12 $Q := Q \cup \{(m, \sigma)\}$	//sEUF-CMA
4 $(m^*, \sigma^*) \leftarrow \mathcal{A}(vk)$	//EUF-NMA	13 **return** σ	
5 **if** $m^* \in Q$ **then**	//EUF-CMA		
6 | **return** $\bot$	//EUF-CMA		
7 **if** $(m^*, \sigma^*) \in Q$ **then**	//sEUF-CMA		
8 | **return** $\bot$	//sEUF-CMA		
9 **return** Vrfy(vk, m^*, σ^*)			

Fig. 2. (S)EUF-CMA and EUF-NMA games

distribution over $\mathcal{X}$. By $x \leftarrow_\$ \mathcal{X}$ and $x \leftarrow \mathcal{D}_\mathcal{X}$, we denote the sampling of an element from $\mathsf{U}(\mathcal{X})$ and $\mathcal{D}_\mathcal{X}$ (distribution on $\mathcal{X}$). We denote a set of functions having a domain $\mathcal{X}$ and a range $\mathcal{Y}$ by $\mathsf{Func}(\mathcal{X}, \mathcal{Y})$. For a set of distributions over $\mathcal{Y}$ indexed by $\mathcal{D} = \{\mathcal{D}_x : x \in \mathcal{X}\}$, we define $\mathsf{Func}_{\mathcal{X}, \mathcal{Y}}(\mathcal{D})$ as a distribution of f in $\mathsf{Func}(\mathcal{X}, \mathcal{Y})$ such that, for each $x \in \mathcal{X}$, $f(x)$ is independently drawn from $\mathcal{D}_x$.

We write any symbol for functions in sans-serif font, oracles in small capitals, and adversaries in calligraphic font. If a function F is deterministic (resp., probabilistic), we write $y := \mathsf{F}(x)$ (resp., $y \leftarrow \mathsf{F}(x)$). We denote by $y \leftarrow \mathcal{A}^{\text{ORCL}}(x)$ (resp., $y \leftarrow \mathcal{A}^{|\text{ORCL}\rangle}(x)$) probabilistic computations of $\mathcal{A}$ on input x with a classical (resp., quantum) oracle access to an oracle ORCL. For a random function H, we denote by $\mathsf{H}^{x^* \mapsto y^*}$ a function such that $\mathsf{H}^{x^* \mapsto y^*}(x) = \mathsf{H}(x)$ for $x \neq x^*$ and $\mathsf{H}^{x^* \mapsto y^*}(x^*) = y^*$. The notation $G^{\mathcal{A}} = y$ denotes an event in which a game G played by $\mathcal{A}$ returns y. For i-th game G_i, we denote W_i as an event $G_i^{\mathcal{A}} = 1$.

We denote 1 if the Boolean statement is true ($\top$) and 0 if the statement is false ($\bot$). For a statement P, $[\![P]\!]$ denotes the truth value of P.

2.2 Digital Signature

We define the syntax of digital signature schemes as follows.

Definition 1 (Digital Signature). *A digital signature scheme* Sig *consists of three algorithms:*

KeyGen(1^λ): *This algorithm takes* 1^λ, *where* λ *is the security parameter, as input and outputs a verification key* vk *and a signing key* sk.

Sign(sk, m): *This algorithm takes a signing key* sk *and a message* m *as input and outputs a signature* σ.

Vrfy(vk, m, σ): *This algorithm takes a verification key* vk, *a message* m, *and a signature* σ *as input, and outputs* $\top$ *(acceptance) or* $\bot$ *(rejection).*

Traditionally, the security of digital signatures is analyzed under EUF-CMA (Existential UnForgeability against Chosen-Message Attack) or its stronger variant, sEUF-CMA (strong EUF-CMA), both of which consider an adversary with access to a signing oracle attempting to forge a signature. Additionally, EUF-NMA (No Message Attack) is used, where the adversary does not have access to the signing oracle.

GAME wPO/PO		$\textsc{Sign}(m)$
1 $\mathcal{Q} := \emptyset$		/* generate r on each query. */
2 $(vk, sk) \leftarrow \mathsf{KeyGen}(1^\lambda)$		/* for m queried in superposition,
3 **run** $\mathcal{A}^{\mid\textsc{Sign})\,,\textsc{Forge}}(vk)$		r is fixed. */
4 **return** $[\![|\mathcal{Q}| > q_S]\!]$		10 $\sigma := \mathsf{Sign}(sk, m; r)$
		11 **return** σ
$\textsc{Forge}(m, \sigma)$		
5 **if** $\mathsf{Vrfy}(vk, m, \sigma) = \top$ **then**		
6 $\quad$ **if** $m \notin \mathcal{Q}$ **then**	//wPO	
7 $\quad\quad \mathcal{Q} := \mathcal{Q} \cup \{m\}$	//wPO	
8 $\quad$ **if** $(m, \sigma) \notin \mathcal{Q}$ **then**	//PO	
9 $\quad\quad \mathcal{Q} := \mathcal{Q} \cup \{(m, \sigma)\}$	//PO	

Fig. 3. PO and wPO games

Definition 2 (Traditional Security of Signature). *Let* Sig *be a signature scheme. Using games given in Fig. 2, we define advantage functions of adversaries playing* EUF-CMA, sEUF-CMA *and* EUF-NMA *games against* Sig *as* $\mathrm{Adv}_{\mathsf{Sig}}^{\mathrm{EUF\text{-}CMA}}(\mathcal{A}) = \Pr[\mathrm{EUF\text{-}CMA}^{\mathcal{A}} = 1]$, $\mathrm{Adv}_{\mathsf{Sig}}^{\mathrm{sEUF\text{-}CMA}}(\mathcal{A}) = \Pr[\mathrm{sEUF\text{-}CMA}^{\mathcal{A}} = 1]$, *and* $\mathrm{Adv}_{\mathsf{Sig}}^{\mathrm{EUF\text{-}NMA}}(\mathcal{A}) = \Pr[\mathrm{EUF\text{-}NMA}^{\mathcal{A}} = 1]$, *respectively. We say* Sig *is* EUF-CMA-*secure,* sEUF-CMA-*secure, or* EUF-NMA-*secure if its corresponding advantage is negligible in the security parameter for any efficient adversary.*

Security models that allow *quantum* queries to the signing oracle, which are prohibited in traditional security models, have been actively studied in recent years. Boneh and Zhandry [6] defined the security notion called EUF-qCMA. We call the security notion as plus-one (PO) security following [1]. Also, we define its weakened version as wPO (weak PO) security.

Definition 3 (Plus-One Unforgeability). *Let* Sig *be a signature scheme. Using games given in Fig. 3, we define advantage functions of adversary playing* PO *and* wPO *games against* Sig *as* $\mathrm{Adv}_{\mathsf{Sig}}^{\mathrm{PO}}(\mathcal{A}) = \Pr\left[\mathrm{PO}^{\mathcal{A}} = 1\right]$ *and* $\mathrm{Adv}_{\mathsf{Sig}}^{\mathrm{wPO}}(\mathcal{A}) = \Pr\left[\mathrm{wPO}^{\mathcal{A}} = 1\right]$. *We say* Sig *is* PO-*secure or* wPO-*secure if its corresponding advantage is negligible in the security parameter for any efficient adversary.*

In the PO game, the adversary must output $q_S + 1$ distinct pairs of message/signature from q_S signing queries. In contrast, in the wPO game, the messages in the $q_S + 1$ pairs must be distinct. Since the condition for a successful attack becomes more stringent, the security definition becomes weaker.

Alagic et al. [1] defined another security notion called blind unforgeability (BU security) and its stronger version sBU (strong BU).

Definition 4 (Blind Unforgeability). *Let* Sig *be a signature scheme. Using games given in Fig. 4, we define advantage functions of adversary playing* BU *(Blind Unforgeability) and* sBU *(strong BU) games against* Sig *as* $\mathrm{Adv}_{\mathsf{Sig}}^{\mathrm{BU}}(\mathcal{A}) =$

GAME BU/sBU		$B_\epsilon\mathrm{SIGN}(m)$	
1 $B_\epsilon \leftarrow \mathrm{Func}_{\mathcal{M},\{0,1\}}(\mathrm{Ber}_\epsilon)$	//BU	/* generate r on each query. */	
2 $B_\epsilon \leftarrow \mathrm{Func}_{\mathcal{M}\times\Sigma,\{0,1\}}(\mathrm{Ber}_\epsilon)$	//sBU	/* for m queried in superposition,	
3 $\mathbf{win} := \bot$		r is fixed. */	
4 $(vk, sk) \leftarrow \mathrm{Sig.KeyGen}(1^\lambda)$		12 if $m \in B_\epsilon$ then	//BU
5 $\mathbf{run}\ \mathcal{A}^{\|B_\epsilon\mathrm{SIGN}),\mathrm{FORGE}}(vk)$		13 $\mid$ return $\bot$	//BU
6 return win		14 $\sigma := \mathrm{Sig.Sign}(sk, m; r)$	
		15 if $(m, \sigma) \in B_\epsilon$ then	//sBU
$\mathrm{FORGE}(m, \sigma)$		16 $\mid$ return $\bot$	//sBU
7 if $\mathrm{Sig.Vrfy}(vk, m, \sigma) = \top$ then		17 return σ	
8 $\mid$ if $m \in B_\epsilon$ then	//BU		
9 $\mid\mid$ win $:= \top$	//BU		
10 $\mid$ if $(m, \sigma) \in B_\epsilon$ then	//sBU		
11 $\mid\mid$ win $:= \top$	//sBU		

Fig. 4. BU and BU games. Ber_ϵ is Berouulli distribution parameterized by ϵ.

GAME PRF_b	GAME $q\mathrm{PRF}_b$
1 if $b = 0$ then	1 if $b = 0$ then
2 $\mid$ $k \leftarrow_\$ \mathcal{K}$	2 $\mid$ $k \leftarrow_\$ \mathcal{K}$
3 $\mid$ $f :=_\$ \mathrm{PRF}(k, \cdot)$	3 $\mid$ $f :=_\$ \mathrm{PRF}(k, \cdot)$
4 else	4 else
5 $\mid$ $f \leftarrow_\$ \mathrm{Func}(\mathcal{X}, \mathcal{Y})$	5 $\mid$ $f \leftarrow_\$ \mathrm{Func}(\mathcal{X}, \mathcal{Y})$
6 $b^* \leftarrow \mathcal{A}^f()$	6 $b^* \leftarrow \mathcal{A}^{\|f\rangle}()$
7 return b^*	7 return b^*

Fig. 5. PRF and $q\mathrm{PRF}$ games

$\Pr\left[\mathrm{BU}^{\mathcal{A}} = 1\right]$ and $\mathrm{Adv}_{\mathrm{Sig}}^{\mathrm{sBU}}(\mathcal{A}) = \Pr\left[\mathrm{sBU}^{\mathcal{A}} = 1\right]$. We say Sig is BU-secure or sBU-secure if its corresponding advantage is negligible in the security parameter for any efficient adversary.

Let $\epsilon \in \{0, \frac{1}{2^p}, ..., \frac{2^p-1}{2^p}\}$ for some parameter p. In the BU game, B_ϵ is a random subset of $\mathcal{M}$, where each $m \in B_\epsilon$ is independently selected with probability ϵ. The BU adversary attempts to find a valid pair (m, σ) such that $m \notin B_\epsilon$, given access to the signing oracle blinded by B_ϵ. In the sBU game, B_ϵ is a random subset of $\mathcal{M} \times \Sigma$, where Σ represents the signature space. Thus, messages are not blinded independently in the sBU game.

2.3 Pseudorandom Function

Definition 5 ((Quantum) Pseudorandom Function). Let $\mathrm{PRF}: \mathcal{K} \times \mathcal{X} \to \mathcal{Y}$ be a deterministic function. Using games given in Fig. 5, we define advantage functions of adversaries playing the PRF and $q\mathrm{PRF}$ games against PRF as $\mathrm{Adv}_{\mathrm{PRF}}^{\mathrm{PRF}}(\mathcal{A}) = |\Pr[\mathrm{PRF}_0^{\mathcal{A}} = 1] - \Pr[\mathrm{PRF}_1^{\mathcal{A}} = 1]|$ and $\mathrm{Adv}_{\mathrm{PRF}}^{q\mathrm{PRF}}(\mathcal{A}) = |\Pr[q\mathrm{PRF}_0^{\mathcal{A}} = 1] - \Pr[q\mathrm{PRF}_1^{\mathcal{A}} = 1]|$. We say PRF is pseudorandom or quantum pseudorandom if its corresponding advantage is negligible in the security parameter for any efficient adversary.

GAME SPR	GAME CR
1 $(vk, sk) \leftarrow \mathsf{Gen}(1^\lambda)$	1 $(vk, sk) \leftarrow \mathsf{Gen}(1^\lambda)$
2 $\hat{x} \leftarrow \mathcal{D}_\mathcal{X}$	2 $(x_1^*, x_2^*) \leftarrow \mathcal{A}(vk)$
3 $x^* \leftarrow \mathcal{A}(vk, \hat{x})$	3 **return**
4 **return**	$[\![x_1^* \neq x_2^* \wedge \mathsf{F}(vk, x_1^*) = \mathsf{F}(vk, x_2^*)]\!]$
$[\![x^* \neq \hat{x} \wedge \mathsf{F}(vk, x^*) = \mathsf{F}(vk, \hat{x})]\!]$	

Fig. 6. SPR and CR games

2.4 Hash-and-Sign with Retry

We define the syntax of the trapdoor function (TDF) as follows.

Definition 6 (Trapdoor Function). *A TDF* T *consists of three algorithms:*

$\mathsf{Gen}(1^\lambda)$*: This algorithm takes* 1^λ*, where* λ *is the security parameter, as input and a public key* vk *and a secret key* sk*.*

$\mathsf{F}(vk, x)$*: This algorithm takes a public key* vk *and* $x \in \mathcal{X}$ *as input and deterministically outputs* $y \in \mathcal{Y}$*.*

$\mathsf{Inv}(sk, y)$*: This algorithm takes a secret key* sk *and* $y \in \mathcal{Y}$ *and outputs* $x \in \mathcal{X}$ *or* $\perp$*.*

T *is* (γ, β)*-correct if for every* $(vk, sk) \leftarrow \mathsf{Gen}(1^\lambda)$*, the following holds:*

$$\Pr[y \leftarrow_\$ \mathcal{Y}, x \leftarrow \mathsf{Inv}(sk, y) : \mathsf{F}(vk, x) = y | x \neq \perp] \geq \gamma,$$

$$\text{and } \Pr[y \leftarrow_\$ \mathcal{Y}, x \leftarrow \mathsf{Inv}(sk, y) : x = \perp] \leq \beta.$$

There are some security notions for TDFs. In this paper, we use the following:

Definition 7 (Second-Preimage Resistance and Collision Resistance).
Let T *be a TDF. Using games given in Fig. 6, we define advantage functions of adversaries playing the* SPR *(Second-Preimage-Resistance) and* CR *(Collision-Resistance) games against* T *as* $\mathrm{Adv}_\mathsf{T}^{\mathrm{SPR}}(\mathcal{A}) = \Pr[\mathrm{SPR}^\mathcal{A} = 1]$ *and* $\mathrm{Adv}_\mathsf{T}^{\mathrm{CR}}(\mathcal{A}) = \Pr[\mathrm{CR}^\mathcal{A} = 1]$*, respectively. We say* T *is second-preimage-resistant or collision-resistant if its corresponding advantage is negligible in the security parameter for any efficient adversary.*

Let $\mathsf{SampDom}$ be a function to output $x \leftarrow \mathsf{SampDom}(vk)$ that simulates Inv. By adding $\mathsf{SampDom}$ to the function set of Definition 6, we can define a preimage sampleable function (PSF) [12]. In this paper, we consider preimage-simulatability [19], which relaxes the conditions of a PSF.

Definition 8 (Preimage Simulatablity [19, Definition 7]). *Let* T *be a TDF with* $\mathsf{SampDom}$*. Using a game defined in Fig. 7, we define an advantage function of an adversary playing the* PS *(Preimage Sampling) game against* T *as* $\mathrm{Adv}_\mathsf{T}^{\mathrm{PS}}(\mathcal{A}) = |\Pr[\mathrm{PS}_0^\mathcal{A} = 1] - \Pr[\mathrm{PS}_1^\mathcal{A} = 1]|$*. We say* T *is preimage-simulatable if its advantage is negligible for any efficient adversary. Also, if* SAMPLE_0 *and* SAMPLE_1 *are* δ*-close[5], we say* T *is* δ*-PS.*

---

[5] For distributions $\mathcal{D}$ and $\mathcal{D}'$ over $y \in \mathcal{Y}$, we say $\mathcal{D}$ is δ-close to $\mathcal{D}'$ if $\sum_{y \in \mathcal{Y}} |\mathcal{D}(y) - \mathcal{D}'(y)| \leq \delta$.

GAME PS_b	SAMPLE$_0$()	SAMPLE$_1$()
1 $(vk, sk) \leftarrow \mathsf{Gen}(1^\lambda)$	4 **repeat**	9 $x \leftarrow \mathsf{SampDom}(vk)$
2 $b^* \leftarrow \mathcal{A}^{\mathrm{SAMPLE}_b}(vk)$	5 $\quad y \leftarrow_\$ \mathcal{Y}$	10 **return** x
3 **return** b^*	6 $\quad x \leftarrow \mathsf{Inv}(sk, y)$	
	7 **until** $x \neq \bot$	
	8 **return** x	

Fig. 7. PS game

KeyGen(1^λ)	KeyGen(1^λ)
1 $(vk, sk) \leftarrow \mathsf{Gen}(1^\lambda)$	1 $(vk, sk) \leftarrow \mathsf{Gen}(1^\lambda)$
2 **return** (vk, sk)	2 $(s, s') \leftarrow_\$ \mathcal{K} \times \mathcal{K}$
	3 **return** $(vk, (sk, s, s'))$
Sign(sk, m)	
3 $k := 0$	Sign$((sk, s, s'), m)$
4 **repeat**	4 $k := 0$
5 $\quad k := k + 1$	5 **repeat**
6 $\quad r_k \leftarrow_\$ \mathcal{R}$	6 $\quad k := k + 1$
7 $\quad y_k := \mathsf{H}(r_k, m)$	7 $\quad r_k := \mathsf{PRF}(s, (m, k))$
8 $\quad x_k \leftarrow \mathsf{Inv}(sk, y_k)$	8 $\quad y_k := \mathsf{H}(r_k, m)$
9 **until** $x_k \neq \bot$	9 $\quad x_k := \mathsf{Inv}(sk, y_k; \mathsf{PRF}'(s', (m, k)))$
10 **return** (r_k, x_k)	10 **until** $x_k \neq \bot \lor k \geq B$
	11 **return** (r_k, x_k)
Vrfy$(vk, m, (r, x))$	
11 **return** $[\![\mathsf{F}(vk, x) = \mathsf{H}(r, m)]\!]$	Vrfy$(vk, m, (r, x))$
	12 **return** $[\![\mathsf{F}(vk, x) = \mathsf{H}(r, m)]\!]$

Fig. 8. Algorithms of hash-and-sign with retry (HSwR) and derandomized hash-and-sign with bounded retry (DHSwBR)

Note that PSF is always preimage-simulatable since it can statistically simulate an honestly generated preimage without retry.

Kosuge and Xagawa [19] formulated a paradigm used in signature schemes proposed by Sakumoto et al. [23] as probabilistic hash-and-sign with retry, which we refer to in this paper as hash-and-sign with retry (HSwR). In this paper, we propose a variant referred to as derandomized hash-and-sign with bounded retry (DHSwBR), as shown in Fig. 8. Let $\mathsf{HSR}[\mathsf{T}, \mathsf{H}]$ and $\mathsf{DHSR}_B[\mathsf{T}, \mathsf{H}, \mathsf{PRF}, \mathsf{PRF}']$ be HSwR and DHSwBR composing of a TDF T, a hash function $\mathsf{H} \colon \mathcal{R} \times \mathcal{M} \to \mathcal{Y}$, and PRFs $\mathsf{PRF} \colon \mathcal{K} \times \mathcal{M} \times [B] \to \mathcal{R}$ and $\mathsf{PRF}' \colon \mathcal{K} \times \mathcal{M} \times [B] \to \mathcal{R}'$, where B denotes the maximum number of retries. PRF generates a salt $r \in \mathcal{R}$ for H and PRF' generates a random coin used for derandomizing Inv.

3 Quantum Random Oracle Model (QROM) and Proof Techniques

In the ROM/QROM, a hash function $\mathsf{H} \colon \mathcal{X} \to \mathcal{Y}$ is modeled as a random function $\mathsf{H} \leftarrow_\$ \mathsf{Func}(\mathcal{X}, \mathcal{Y})$. The random function is under the control of the challenger, and the adversary makes queries to the random oracle (random oracle queries) to compute the hash values. In the ROM, the challenger can choose

```
GAME GSPB_λ
1  {λ(x)}_{x∈𝒳} ← 𝒜_1
2  if ∃x ∈ 𝒳, λ(x) > λ then
3  |  return ⊥
4  for x ∈ 𝒳 do
5  |  g(x) ← Ber_{λ(x)}
6  x* ← 𝒜_2^{|g⟩}
7  return g(x*)
```

Fig. 9. Generic search problem with bounded probabilities (GSPB)

```
GAME AR_b                              Repro(x)
1  H_0 ←$ Func(ℛ × 𝒳, 𝒴)              5  r ←$ ℛ
2  H_1 := H_0                           6  y ←$ 𝒴
3  b* ← 𝒜^{|H_b⟩,Repro}()              7  H_1 := H_1^{(r,x)↦y}
4  return b*                            8  return r
```

Fig. 10. AR (Adaptive Reprogramming) game

$y \leftarrow_\$ \mathcal{Y}$ and program $\mathsf{H} := \mathsf{H}^{x \mapsto y}$ for queried x on-the-fly instead of choosing $\mathsf{H} \leftarrow_\$ \mathsf{Func}(\mathcal{X}, \mathcal{Y})$ at the beginning (lazy sampling technique). In the QROM, the adversary makes queries to H in a superposition of many different values, e.g., $\sum_x \alpha_x |x\rangle |y\rangle$. The challenger computes H and gives a superposition of the results to the adversary, $\sum_x \alpha_x |x\rangle |y \oplus \mathsf{H}(x)\rangle$. Due to the nature of superposition queries and other constraints of quantum computation, traditional techniques in the ROM cannot be directly applied to the QROM. However, recent advancements in QROM research have led to the discovery of many proof techniques. This section introduces the techniques used in this paper.

Generic Quantum Search [17,18,28]: Let $\mathcal{X}$ be a finite set. The generic search problem (GSP, in short) is finding $x \in \mathcal{X}$ satisfying $g(x) = 1$ given access to an oracle $g \colon \mathcal{X} \to \{0,1\}$, where for each $x \in \mathcal{X}$, $g(x)$ is drawn independently according to Ber_λ (Bernoulli distribution parameterized by λ).

Lemma 1. *Let* $\lambda \in [0,1]$. *For any quantum algorithm* $\mathcal{A} = (\mathcal{A}_1, \mathcal{A}_2)$ *making at most q queries to* $|g\rangle$, *we have*

$$\Pr[\mathsf{GSPB}_\lambda^{\mathcal{A}} = 1] \le 8(q+1)^2 \lambda,$$

where GSPB_λ *is defined in Fig. 9.*

Tight Adaptive Reprogramming [15]: Let $\mathsf{H}_0, \mathsf{H}_1 \colon \mathcal{R} \times \mathcal{X} \to \mathcal{Y}$ be random functions. Figure 10 shows a game called AR (Adaptive Reprogramming) game, in which the adversary $\mathcal{A}_{\mathsf{ar}}$ attempts to distinguish H_0 (no reprogramming) from H_1 (reprogrammed by Repro). For a reprogramming query, the challenger reprograms H_1 for $r \leftarrow_\$ \mathcal{R}$ and $y \leftarrow_\$ \mathcal{Y}$, and gives r to $\mathcal{A}$. A distinguishing advantage of the AR game is defined by $\mathsf{Adv}_{\mathsf{H}}^{\mathrm{AR}}(\mathcal{A}_{\mathsf{ar}}) = \left| \Pr[\mathsf{AR}_0^{\mathcal{A}} = 1] - \Pr[\mathsf{AR}_1^{\mathcal{A}} = 1] \right|$.

Lemma 2 (Tight Adaptive Reprogramming [15, Proposition 2]). *For any quantum* AR *adversary* $\mathcal{A}$ *issuing at most* q_R *classical reprogramming queries and* q_H *(quantum) random oracle queries to* H_b, *the distinguishing advantage of the* AR *game is bounded by*

$$\mathrm{Adv}_H^{AR}(\mathcal{A}) \leq \frac{3}{2}q_R\sqrt{\frac{q_H}{|\mathcal{R}|}}.$$

One-Way to Hiding (O2H) [2,25]: We consider two functions H_0 and H_1 such that $H_0(x) = H_1(x)$ for $x \notin S$. We can show the indistinguishability of H_0 and H_1 using the following lemma.

Lemma 3 (Original O2H [2, Theorem 3]). *Let* $H_0, H_1 : \mathcal{X} \to \mathcal{Y}$ *be functions. Assume that* $H_0(x) = H_1(x)$ *for all* $x \notin S$. *Let* z *be a random bitstring.* $(S, H_0, H_1, z$ *may have arbitrary joint distribution.) Let* $\mathcal{A}$ *be a quantum algorithm with* q *quantum queries to* H_0 *or* H_1. *Then, there exists a quantum algorithm* $\mathcal{B}$ *that, given access to the oracle* H_0 *and* $\mathcal{A}$, *finds an element in* S *such that*

$$\left| \Pr\left[\mathcal{A}^{|H_0\rangle}(z) = 1\right] - \Pr\left[\mathcal{A}^{|H_1\rangle}(z) = 1\right] \right| \leq 2q\sqrt{\Pr\left[x \leftarrow \mathcal{B}^{|H_0\rangle,\mathcal{A}}(z) : x \in S\right]}.$$

When using the tight adaptive reprogramming shown in Lemma 2, Lemma 3 cannot be directly applied because it does not assume reprogrammed random functions. Therefore, we extend the original O2H as follows.

Lemma 4 (O2H with Adaptive Reprogramming). *Let* $H_0, H_1 : \mathcal{X} \to \mathcal{Y}$ *be functions that are reprogrammed depending on classical queries to an oracle* O *(H_0 and H_1 may be reprogrammed differently). Assume that* $H_0(x) = H_1(x)$ *for all* $x \notin S$ *when* O *is queried the same number of times with the same inputs. Let* z *be a random bitstring.* $(S, H_0, H_1, z$ *may have arbitrary joint distribution.) Let* $\mathcal{A}$ *be a quantum algorithm with* q *quantum queries to* H_0 *or* H_1 *and some classical queries to* O. *Then, there exists a quantum algorithm* $\mathcal{B}$ *that, given access to the oracle* H_0 *and* $\mathcal{A}$, *finds an element in* S *such that*

$$\left| \Pr\left[\mathcal{A}^{|H_0\rangle,O}(z) = 1\right] - \Pr\left[\mathcal{A}^{|H_1\rangle,O}(z) = 1\right] \right| \leq 2q\sqrt{\Pr[x \leftarrow \mathcal{B}^{|H_0\rangle,O,\mathcal{A}}(z) : x \in S_i]}.$$

See the full version for the proof. We can use the semi-classical O2H [2, Theorems 1 and 2] for the same purpose. Since the multiplicative factor of the technique is $4q$, Lemma 4 is tighter by a factor of 2.

Other Techniques: We introduce two lemmas proven by Boneh and Zhandry [6].

Lemma 5 (Oracle Indistinguishability [6, Lemma 2.5, ePrint]). *Let* $\mathcal{X}$ *and* $\mathcal{Y}$ *be two finite sets. Let* $\mathcal{D} = \{\mathcal{D}_x\}$ *and* $\mathcal{D}' = \{\mathcal{D}'_x\}$ *be two sets of efficiently sampleable distributions over* $\mathcal{X}$ *indexed by* $x \in \mathcal{X}$. *Let* $\mathcal{A}$ *be a quantum adversary making* q *(quantum) queries to an oracle* $f: \mathcal{X} \to \mathcal{Y}$. *If for each* $x \in \mathcal{X}$, $\mathcal{D}_x$ *and* $\mathcal{D}'_x$ *are* ϵ-*close, then*

$$\left| \Pr\left[f \leftarrow \mathsf{Func}_{\mathcal{X},\mathcal{Y}}(\mathcal{D}) : \mathcal{A}^{|f\rangle} = 1\right] - \Pr\left[f \leftarrow \mathsf{Func}_{\mathcal{X},\mathcal{Y}}(\mathcal{D}') : \mathcal{A}^{|f\rangle} = 1\right] \right| \leq \sqrt{(6q)^3\epsilon}.$$

Lemma 6 ([6, Lemma 2.6, ePrint]). *Let $\mathcal{X}$ and $\mathcal{Y}$ be two finite sets. Fix a set $\mathcal{D}$ of distributions $\mathcal{D}_x$ over $\mathcal{Y}$ indexed by $x \in \mathcal{X}$. Let α be the minimum over all $x \in \mathcal{X}$ of the min-entropy of the distribution $\mathcal{D}_x$ and $f \colon \mathcal{X} \to \mathcal{Y}$ be a function chosen according to $\mathsf{Func}_{\mathcal{X},\mathcal{Y}}(\mathcal{D})$. Then, any q-query quantum algorithm can only produce $(q+1)$ input/output pairs of f with probability at most $\frac{q+1}{\lceil 2^\alpha \rceil}$.*

4   Security Proofs for Derandomized Hash-and-Sign with Bounded Retry

In this section, we show reductions from the EUF-NMA security of HSwR to the (w)PO, (s)BU, and (s)EUF-CMA security of DHSwBR. As Kosuge and Xagawa [19] have shown reductions from the non-invertibility of the underlying TDF to the EUF-NMA security of HSwR, these reductions are extended to the reduction from the non-invertibility. Note that our proofs are applied to derandomized probabilistic hash-and-sign by setting $B = 1$, where we can remove terms only related to DHSwBR from the bounds.

4.1   (Weak) Plus-One Unforgeability

We show that $\mathsf{DHSR}_B[\mathsf{T}, \mathsf{H}, \mathsf{PRF}, \mathsf{PRF}']$ shown in Fig. 8 is PO-secure.

Theorem 1 (EUF-NMA + CR + qPRF $\Rightarrow$ PO). *For any quantum PO adversary $\mathcal{A}_{\mathsf{po}}$ of $\mathsf{DHSR}_B[\mathsf{T}, \mathsf{H}, \mathsf{PRF}, \mathsf{PRF}']$ issuing at most q_H quantum queries to H, q_S quantum queries to SIGN, and q_F classical queries to FORGE, there exist an EUF-NMA adversary $\mathcal{A}_{\mathsf{nma}}$ of $\mathsf{HSR}[\mathsf{T}, \mathsf{H}]$, a CR adversary $\mathcal{A}_{\mathsf{cr}}$ of T, and qPRF adversaries $\mathcal{A}_{\mathsf{prf}}$ of PRF and $\mathcal{A}'_{\mathsf{prf}}$ of PRF' issuing at most Bq_S queries such that*

$$
\begin{aligned}
\mathrm{Adv}^{\mathrm{PO}}_{\mathsf{DHSR}}(\mathcal{A}_{\mathsf{po}}) \leq{}& \mathrm{Adv}^{\mathrm{EUF\text{-}NMA}}_{\mathsf{HSR}}(\mathcal{A}_{\mathsf{nma}}) + \mathrm{Adv}^{\mathrm{CR}}_{\mathsf{T}}(\mathcal{A}_{\mathsf{cr}}) + \mathrm{Adv}^{q\mathrm{PRF}}_{\mathsf{PRF}}(\mathcal{A}_{\mathsf{prf}}) \\
&+ \mathrm{Adv}^{q\mathrm{PRF}}_{\mathsf{PRF}'}(\mathcal{A}'_{\mathsf{prf}}) + 8(q_\mathsf{H} + q_\mathsf{S} + q_\mathsf{F} + 1)^2 \left(1 - \gamma\left(1 - \beta^B\right)\right) \\
&+ \frac{q_\mathsf{S}+1}{\lfloor |\mathcal{R}|/B \rfloor} + 2(q_\mathsf{H} + q_\mathsf{F})\sqrt{\frac{B-1}{|\mathcal{R}|}} + 2(q_\mathsf{H} + q_\mathsf{S} + q_\mathsf{F})\sqrt{\frac{2B(B-1)}{|\mathcal{R}|}} \\
&+ \sqrt{6\left(q_\mathsf{H} + 2q_\mathsf{F}\right)^3 \left(\delta + 2\left(1 - \gamma\left(1 - \beta^B\right)\right)\right)},
\end{aligned}
$$

where T is (γ, β)-correct and δ-PS, and the running times of $\mathcal{A}_{\mathsf{nma}}$, $\mathcal{A}_{\mathsf{cr}}$, $\mathcal{A}_{\mathsf{prf}}$, and $\mathcal{A}'_{\mathsf{prf}}$ are about that of $\mathcal{A}_{\mathsf{po}}$.

Proof. We use the sequence of games shown in Fig. 11. Note that adversaries who simulate the games employ $2q$-wise independent functions [29] to simulate random functions, and this applies to all the proofs in this paper as well.

GAME G_0: This is the original PO game, where we execute GetLogs for SIGN, and H is defined as RF_H. We have $\Pr[W_0] = \mathrm{Adv}^{\mathrm{PO}}_{\mathsf{DHSR}}(\mathcal{A}_{\mathsf{po}})$.

GAMES G_0-G_{11}	SIGN(m)

GAMES G_0-G_{11}

1 $\mathsf{RF_H} \leftarrow_\$ \mathsf{Func}(\mathcal{R} \times \mathcal{M}, \mathcal{Y})$
2 $\mathsf{RF_{salt}} \leftarrow_\$ \mathsf{Func}(\mathcal{M} \times [B{+}1], \mathcal{R})$ // G_1-G_{11}
3 $\mathsf{RF_{inv}} \leftarrow_\$ \mathsf{Func}(\mathcal{M} \times [B], \mathcal{R}')$ // G_1-$G_{10.0}$
4 $\mathsf{RF'_H} \leftarrow_\$ \mathsf{Func}(\mathcal{M} \times [B], \mathcal{Y})$ // G_7-$G_{10.0}$
5 $\mathsf{RF_{sd}} \leftarrow_\$ \mathsf{Func}(\mathcal{M}, \mathcal{R}'')$ // $G_{10.1}$-G_{11}
6 $\mathcal{Q} := \emptyset$
7 $\mathbf{win} := \bot$ // $G_{5.0}$-G_{11}
8 $(vk, sk) \leftarrow \mathsf{Gen}(1^\lambda)$
9 $(s, s') \leftarrow_\$ \mathcal{K} \times \mathcal{K}$ // G_0
10 run $\mathcal{A}_{\mathsf{po}}^{|\mathsf{H}\rangle, |\mathsf{SIGN}\rangle, \mathsf{FORGE}}(vk)$
11 return $[\![|\mathcal{Q}| > q_s]\!]$ // G_0-G_4
12 return $[\![|\mathcal{Q}| > q_s]\!] \wedge \mathbf{win}$ // $G_{5.0}$
13 return $\mathbf{win}$ // $G_{5.1}$-G_{11}

$\mathsf{H}(r, m)$

14 if $\mathsf{GetLogs}(m) = \daleth$ then // G_3-G_8
15 | return $\bot$ // G_3-G_8
16 $(r_k, y_k, x_k) := \mathsf{GetLogs}(m)$ // G_2-$G_{5.1}$ · G_8-G_{11}
17 if $r = r_k$ then // G_2-$G_{5.1}$ · G_8-G_{11}
18 | return y_k // G_2-$G_{5.1}$ · G_8-G_{11}
19 $\{(r_i, y_i, x_i)\}_{i \in [k]} := \mathsf{GetLogs}(m)$ // G_6-G_7
20 if $\exists i, r = r_i$ then // G_6-G_7
21 | return y_i // G_6-G_7
22 return $\mathsf{RF_H}(r, m)$

SIGN(m)

23 if $\mathsf{GetLogs}(m) = \daleth$ then // G_3-G_8
24 | return $\bot$ // G_3-G_8
25 $(r_k, y_k, x_k) := \mathsf{GetLogs}(m)$ // G_0-$G_{5.1}$ · G_8-G_{11}
26 $\{(r_i, y_i, x_i)\}_{i \in [k]} := \mathsf{GetLogs}(m)$ // G_6-G_7
27 if $x_k = \bot$ then
28 | return $\bot$
29 return (r_k, x_k)

FORGE$(m, (r, x))$

30 if $\mathsf{GetLogs}(m) = \daleth$ then // G_3-G_8
31 | return $\bot$ // G_3-G_8
32 $(r_k, y_k, x_k) := \mathsf{GetLogs}(m)$ // G_2-$G_{5.1}$ · G_8-G_{11}
33 $\{(r_i, y_i, x_i)\}_{i \in [k]} := \mathsf{GetLogs}(m)$ // G_6-G_7
34 if $\mathsf{F}(vk, x_k) \neq \mathsf{H}(r_k, m)$ then // G_4-G_{11}
35 | return $\daleth$ // G_4-G_{11}
36 if $\mathsf{F}(vk, x) = \mathsf{H}(r, m)$ then
37 | if $(m, (r, x)) \notin \mathcal{Q}$ then
38 | | $\mathcal{Q} := \mathcal{Q} \cup \{(m, (r, x))\}$
39 | if $(r, x) \neq (r_k, x_k)$ then // $G_{5.0}$-$G_{10.1}$
40 | | $\mathbf{win} := \top$ // $G_{5.0}$-$G_{10.1}$
41 | if $r \neq r_k$ then // G_{11}
42 | | $\mathbf{win} := \top$ // G_{11}

$\mathsf{GetLogs}(m)$ for G_0

43 $k := 0$
44 repeat
45 | $k := k + 1$
46 | $r_k := \mathsf{PRF}(s, (m, k))$
47 | $y_k := \mathsf{RF_H}(r_k, m)$
48 | $x_k := \mathsf{Inv}(sk, y_k; \mathsf{PRF'}(s', (m, k)))$
49 until $x_k \neq \bot \vee k \geq B$
50 return (r_k, y_k, x_k)

$\mathsf{GetLogs}(m)$ for $G_{10.1}$-G_{11}

51 $r_k := \mathsf{RF_{salt}}(m, B + 1)$
52 $x_k := \mathsf{SampDom}(vk; \mathsf{RF_{sd}}(m))$
53 $y_k := \mathsf{F}(vk, x_k)$
54 return (r_k, y_k, x_k)

$\mathsf{GetLogs}(m)$ for G_1-$G_{10.0}$

55 $k := 0$
56 repeat
57 | $k := k + 1$
58 | $r_k := \mathsf{RF_{salt}}(m, k)$ // G_1-G_9
59 | $y_k := \mathsf{RF_H}(r_k, m)$ // G_1-G_6
60 | $y_k := \mathsf{RF'_H}(m, k)$ // G_7-$G_{10.0}$
61 | $x_k := \mathsf{Inv}(sk, y_k; \mathsf{RF_{inv}}(m, k))$
62 until $x_k \neq \bot \vee k \geq B$
63 $r_k := \mathsf{RF_{salt}}(m, B + 1)$ // $G_{10.0}$
64 if $\exists (i, j), r_i = r_j$ then // G_3-G_8
65 | return $\daleth$ // G_3-G_8
66 return (r_k, y_k, x_k) // G_1-$G_{5.1}$ · G_8-$G_{10.0}$
67 return $\{(r_i, y_i, x_i)\}_{i \in [k]}$ // G_6-G_7

Fig. 11. Games for EUF-NMA $\Rightarrow$ PO

GAME G_1: We replace PRFs with random functions $\mathsf{RF_{salt}}$ (salt generation) and $\mathsf{RF_{inv}}$ (randomization of Inv).

Lemma 7. *There exist* qPRF *adversaries* $\mathcal{A}_{\mathsf{prf}}$ *of* PRF *and* $\mathcal{A}'_{\mathsf{prf}}$ *of* PRF' *such that*
$$|\Pr[W_0] - \Pr[W_1]| \leq \mathrm{Adv}_{\mathsf{PRF}}^{q\mathrm{PRF}}(\mathcal{A}_{\mathsf{prf}}) + \mathrm{Adv}_{\mathsf{PRF'}}^{q\mathrm{PRF}}(\mathcal{A}'_{\mathsf{prf}}).$$

Proof. Since different keys are used for PRF and PRF', each can be replaced by a random function. The qPRF adversaries $\mathcal{A}_{\mathsf{prf}}$ and $\mathcal{A}'_{\mathsf{prf}}$ can simulate the outputs of PRF or PRF' using the outputs of their oracles. Thus, the advantage gap due to the above transformation is bounded by the qPRF advantages.

GAME G_2: The random function $\mathsf{H}(r, m)$ computes $(r_k, y_k, x_k) := \mathsf{GetLogs}(m)$ and returns y_k if $r = r_k$. Otherwise, $\mathsf{H}(r, m)$ returns $\mathsf{RF}_\mathsf{H}(r, m)$. Also, FORGE computes $\mathsf{GetLogs}$. Since $\mathsf{H}(r_k, m)$ is still computed by $\mathsf{RF}_\mathsf{H}(r_k, m)$, this modification changes nothing. Therefore, $\Pr[W_1] = \Pr[W_2]$ holds.

This is the first step in programming H to ensure that simulated signatures are accepted. Note that the game hops of G_2-G_3 and G_6-$G_{10.1}$ are dedicated to this purpose.

GAME G_3: We modify $\mathsf{GetLogs}$ to check if there is a collision among $\{r_i\}_{i \in [k]}$. If a collision is detected, $\mathsf{GetLogs}$ returns a special symbol $\dashv$. When $\mathsf{GetLogs}$ returns $\dashv$, H, SIGN, and FORGE will return $\perp$, where we add $\perp$ to the range of H. This step is required for G_8, where we replace RF_H with RF'_H, which takes only (m, k) as input. This replacement becomes infeasible if a salt collision occurs. Additionally, in the next game hop, excluding salt collisions simplifies the bound.

Lemma 8. *We have*

$$|\Pr[W_2] - \Pr[W_3]| \le (q_\mathsf{H} + q_\mathsf{S} + q_\mathsf{F})\sqrt{\frac{2B(B-1)}{|\mathcal{R}|}}.$$

Proof. The difference between G_2 and G_3 lies solely in the outputs of $\mathsf{GetLogs}$ when there is a collision among $\{r_i\}_{i \in [k]}$. Hence, we apply the original O2H (see Lemma 3) to $\mathsf{GetLogs}$ in G_2 and G_3. The outputs of $\mathsf{GetLogs}$ differ only in $\mathcal{S} = \{m | \exists (i, j) \in [k] \times [k], r_i = r_j\}$, where $\{(r_i, y_i, x_i)\}_{i \in [k]}$ represents all intermediate and final results inside $\mathsf{GetLogs}(m)$. Let $\mathcal{B}_{\mathsf{o2h}}$ be an adversary that finds $m \in \mathcal{S}$ by running $\mathcal{A}_{\mathsf{cma}}$ in G_3. Since each r_i is generated by the random function $\mathsf{RF}_{\mathsf{salt}}$ with distinct inputs, each r_i is uniformly distributed. Tightening the bound of [9, Lemma 11] slightly, the probability that $\{r_i\}_{i \in [k]}$ contains a collision is bounded by $\frac{B(B-1)}{2|\mathcal{R}|}$. Given that $\mathcal{B}_{\mathsf{o2h}}$ has no information about $\mathcal{S}$, the bound in this lemma follows from Lemma 3.

GAME G_4: We modify FORGE such that it returns $\dashv$ if $\mathsf{F}(vk, x_k) \ne \mathsf{H}(r_k, m)$ holds for $(r_k, y_k, x_k) := \mathsf{GetLogs}(m)$ before checking the validity of the submitted query. This step is necessary for the simulation by the CR adversary in bounding the advantage gap between $G_{10.1}$ and G_{11}. Note that G_4-$G_{5.1}$ and G_{11} are dedicated to ensuring that the EUF-NMA adversary simulating G_{11} can obtain a winning message/signature pair from those in $\mathcal{Q}$.

Lemma 9. *Suppose that* T *is* (γ, β)-*correct. We have*

$$|\Pr[W_3] - \Pr[W_4]| \le 8(q_\mathsf{H} + q_\mathsf{S} + q_\mathsf{F} + 1)^2 \left(1 - \gamma\left(1 - \beta^B\right)\right).$$

Proof. If FORGE does not return $\dashv$, then G_3 and G_4 are indistinguishable. Let $\mathbf{bad}_4$ be an event where $\mathsf{F}(vk, x_k) \ne \mathsf{H}(r_k, m)$ holds (see Line 34 in Fig. 11) and FORGE returns $\dashv$ in G_4. Let $\mathcal{B}_{\mathsf{gspb}} = (\mathcal{B}_1, \mathcal{B}_2)$ be a GSPB adversary shown

$\mathcal{B}_1$	$\mathsf{RF}_{\mathsf{salt}}(m, k)$
1 $(vk, sk) \leftarrow \mathsf{Gen}(1^\lambda)$	15 $\{(r_i, y_i, r'_i)\}_{i \in [B]} := \mathsf{Samp}(m)$
2 compute $\mathcal{S}_{\mathsf{all}}$ and $\mathcal{S}_{\mathsf{bad}}$	16 return r_k
3 $\forall m \in \mathcal{M}, \lambda_{sk}(m) := \frac{|\mathcal{S}_{\mathsf{bad}}|}{|\mathcal{S}_{\mathsf{all}}|}$	
4 return $\{\lambda_{sk}(m)\}_{m \in \mathcal{M}}, (vk, sk)$	$\mathsf{RF}_{\mathsf{H}}(r, m)$
	17 $\{(r_i, y_i, r'_i)\}_{i \in [B]} := \mathsf{Samp}(m)$
$\mathcal{B}_2^{\|g\rangle}$	18 if $\exists i, r = r_i$ then
5 $\mathsf{RF}_{\mathsf{U}} \leftarrow_\$ \mathsf{Func}(\mathcal{M}, \mathcal{R}_{\mathsf{U}})$	19 $\mid$ return y_i
6 $\mathsf{RF}''_{\mathsf{H}} \leftarrow_\$ \mathsf{Func}(\mathcal{R} \times \mathcal{M}, \mathcal{Y})$	20 return $\mathsf{RF}''_{\mathsf{H}}(r, m)$
7 $\hat{m} := \emptyset$	
8 run $\mathcal{A}^{\|H\rangle, \|Sign\rangle, \mathsf{Forge}}(vk)$	$\mathsf{RF}_{\mathsf{inv}}(m, k)$
9 return $\hat{m}$	21 $\{(r_i, y_i, r'_i)\}_{i \in [B]} := \mathsf{Samp}(m)$
	22 return r'_k
$\mathsf{Samp}(m)$	$\mathsf{Forge}(m, (r, x))$
10 if $g(m) = 0$ then	23 $\{(r_i, y_i, x_i)\}_{i \in [k]} := \mathsf{GetLogs}(m)$
11 $\mid \{(r_i, y_i, r'_i)\}_{i \in [B]} := \mathsf{U}(\mathcal{S}_{\mathsf{all}}; \mathsf{RF}_{\mathsf{U}}(m))$	24 if $\mathsf{F}(vk, x_k) \neq \mathsf{H}(r_k, m)$ then
12 if $g(m) = 1$ then	25 $\mid \hat{m} := m$
13 $\mid \{(r_i, y_i, r'_i)\}_{i \in [B]} := \mathsf{U}(\mathcal{S}_{\mathsf{bad}}; \mathsf{RF}_{\mathsf{U}}(m))$	
14 return $\{(r_i, y_i, r'_i)\}_{i \in [B]}$	

Fig. 12. Simulation by GSPB adversary

in Fig. 12, where the target function g outputs 1 if and only if the output of $\mathsf{GetLogs}(m)$ is invalid, that is, $x_i = \bot$ for all $i \in [B]$ or there exist i such that $x_i \neq \bot \wedge \mathsf{F}(vk, x_i) \neq y_i$. We define $\mathcal{S}_{\mathsf{all}} \subset (\mathcal{R} \times \mathcal{Y} \times \mathcal{R}')^B$ as:

$$\mathcal{S}_{\mathsf{all}} = \{\{(r_i, y_i, r'_i)\}_{i \in [B]} \mid \forall i, j \in [B], \ r_i = r_j \Rightarrow y_i = y_j\}.$$

Note that $\mathcal{S}_{\mathsf{all}}$ is consistent between r_i and y_i. Such consistency is required to simulate RF_{H} since $\mathsf{RF}_{\mathsf{H}}(r_i, m) = \mathsf{RF}_{\mathsf{H}}(r_j, m)$ must hold if $r_i = r_j$. Then, we define $\mathcal{S}_{\mathsf{bad}}$ as:

$$\mathcal{S}_{\mathsf{bad}} = \left\{ \{(r_i, y_i, r'_i)\}_{i \in [B]} \in \mathcal{S}_{\mathsf{all}} \ \middle| \ \begin{array}{l} x_i := \mathsf{Inv}(sk, y_i; r'_i) : (\forall i \in [B], x_i = \bot) \\ \vee (\exists i \in [B], \ x_i \neq \bot \wedge \mathsf{F}(vk, x_i) \neq y_i) \end{array} \right\}.$$

$\mathcal{B}_1$ sets $\lambda_{sk}(m) = \lambda_{sk} = \frac{|\mathcal{S}_{\mathsf{bad}}|}{|\mathcal{S}_{\mathsf{all}}|}$ for all m. Using the oracle access to g, $\mathcal{B}_2$ defines a function Samp which outputs $\{(r_i, y_i, r'_i)\}_{i \in [B]}$ according to the value of $g(m)$. Samp uniformly chooses $\{(r_i, y_i, r'_i)\}_{i \in [B]}$ from $\mathcal{S}_{\mathsf{all}}$ or $\mathcal{S}_{\mathsf{bad}}$, where the uniformity is ensured by a random function RF_{U}. Since Samp is used to simulate the random functions, $\mathsf{RF}_{\mathsf{salt}}$, RF_{H}, and $\mathsf{RF}_{\mathsf{inv}}$, $\mathcal{B}_2$ can simulate G_4. $\mathcal{B}_2$ outputs $\hat{m}$ that stores m satisfying $\mathsf{F}(pk, x_k) \neq \mathsf{H}(r_k, m)$ in Line 25 of Fig. 12.

If $\mathbf{bad}_4$ occurs, $\mathsf{GetLogs}$ does not output $\sqcup$ (see Lines 30 and 31 in Fig. 11); therefore, the salts $\{r_i\}_{i \in [B]}$ do not collide in $\mathsf{GetLogs}$. Hence, we can assume that each element of $\{y_i\}_{i \in [B]}$ is randomly generated and we have $\mathrm{Exp}[\lambda_{sk}] \leq 1 - \gamma(1 - \beta^B)^6$. From Lemma 1, fixing (vk, sk), we have $\Pr[\mathbf{bad}_4|(vk, sk)] \leq$

---

[6] In [26, Lemma 5.2], which this proof is based on, a difference lies in consideration of potential collisions among $\{r_i\}_{i \in [B]}$. By not considering collisions, we remove the need to add an extra term related to collisions to the bound on $\mathrm{Exp}[\lambda_{sk}]$.

$8(q_H + q_S + q_F + 1)^2 \lambda_{sk}$. Averaging over keys, we have $\Pr[\mathbf{bad}_4] \leq 8(q_H + q_S + q_F + 1)^2 \left(1 - \gamma \left(1 - \beta^B\right)\right)$, and complete the proof.

GAME $G_{5.0}$: Let **win** be an event that $(r, x) \neq (r_k, x_k)$ holds for queried (r, x) and $(r_k, y_k, x_k) := \mathsf{GetLogs}(m)$ in FORGE. In $G_{5.0}$, **win** $= \top$ is necessary to win. With this modification, the adversary must forge at least one signature that is not derived from the message m in order to achieve **win** $= \top$.

Lemma 10. *We have*

$$|\Pr[W_4] - \Pr[W_{5.0}]| \leq \frac{q_S + 1}{\lfloor |\mathcal{R}|/B \rfloor}.$$

Proof. G_4 and $G_{5.0}$ differ when $|\mathcal{Q}| > q_S$ and **win** $= \bot$ hold simultaneously (i.e., $(r, x) = (r_k, x_k)$ holds for at least $q_S + 1$ queries). We define this event as $\mathbf{bad}_5$. The event $\mathbf{bad}_5$ implies that the adversary obtains at least $q_S + 1$ input/output pairs of $\mathsf{RF}_{\mathsf{salt}}$. The outputs of $\mathsf{RF}_{\mathsf{salt}}$ are obtained only through SIGN queries. Therefore, the adversary produces $q_S + 1$ input/output pairs from q_S queries to $\mathsf{RF}_{\mathsf{salt}}$ when $\mathbf{bad}_5$ occurs. From [26, Proposition 4.1], we have $\max_{r \in \mathcal{R}} \Pr[r_k := \mathsf{RF}_{\mathsf{salt}}(m, k) : r_k = r | H] \leq \frac{B}{|\mathcal{R}|}$ for any m, where H in the condition denotes that the adversary knows the whole table of H. Therefore, the probability of $\mathbf{bad}_5$ is bounded by $\frac{q_S + 1}{\lfloor |\mathcal{R}|/B \rfloor}$ from Lemma 6.

GAME $G_{5.1}$: We eliminate $[\![|\mathcal{Q}| > q_S]\!]$ from the winning condition. Since the winning condition is relaxed, we have $\Pr[W_{5.0}] \leq \Pr[W_{5.1}]$. Then, the adversary can win the game without submitting $q_S + 1$ valid message/signature pairs.

GAME G_6: $\mathsf{GetLogs}$ outputs intermediate/final results $\{(r_i, y_i, x_i)\}_{i \in [k]}$ generated during loop iteration instead of outputting only the final result. Moreover, $H(r, m)$ outputs y_i if there exists i such that $r = r_i$. This modification does not affect the adversary's view, and we have $\Pr[W_{5.1}] = \Pr[W_6]$. This step is necessary for replacing RF_H in $\mathsf{GetLogs}$ in the next step.

GAME G_7: We change the way of generating y_k in $\mathsf{GetLogs}$ from $\mathsf{RF}_H(r_k, m)$ to $\mathsf{RF}'_H(m, k)$. Since there are no collisions among $\{r_i\}_{i \in [k]}$, both $\mathsf{RF}_H(r_k, m)$ and $\mathsf{RF}'_H(m, k)$ follow the uniform distribution. Therefore, the view of the adversary does not change, and $\Pr[W_6] = \Pr[W_7]$ holds. Due to this modification, the value of y_k is independently chosen for each (m, k), satisfying one of the necessary conditions for signature simulation using δ-PS.

GAME G_8: We modify $\mathsf{GetLogs}$ so that it outputs only the final result (r_k, y_k, x_k). Then, only the outputs for which simulation is possible using δ-PS have been programmed for H; thus, the preparation for simulation is complete.

Lemma 11. *We have*

$$|\Pr[W_7] - \Pr[W_8]| \leq 2(q_H + q_F)\sqrt{\frac{B - 1}{|\mathcal{R}|}}.$$

Proof. This modification only affects the outputs of H. For $\{(r_i, y_i, x_i)\}_{i\in[k]}$ generated inside GetLogs(m), we define $\mathcal{S} = \{(r,m)|\exists i \in [k-1], r = r_i\}$. As the outputs of H($r, m$) are different between G_7 and G_8 if and only if $(r,m) \in \mathcal{S}$, we apply the original O2H shown in Lemma 3. Let $\mathcal{B}'_{o2h}$ be an adversary that executes $\mathcal{A}_{cma}$ in G_8 and identifies an element in $\mathcal{S}$. Since $\mathcal{B}'_{o2h}$ has no prior information about $\mathcal{S}$, the probability that $\mathcal{B}'_{o2h}$ outputs $(r,m) \in \mathcal{S}$ is at most $\frac{B-1}{|\mathcal{R}|}$. Following Lemma 3, we obtain the bound $2(q_H + q_F)\sqrt{\frac{B-1}{|\mathcal{R}|}}$. Note that H is called twice in FORGE in Lines 34 and 36. However, $(r_k, m) \notin \mathcal{S}$ is always true since it is guaranteed that there are no collisions among $\{r_i\}_{i\in[k]}$. At the time when GetLogs is executed, it is known that there are no collisions among $\{r_i\}_{i\in[k]}$. Therefore, the H-query in Line 34 can be excluded from consideration.

GAME G_9: We remove the collision check among $\{r_i\}_{i\in[k]}$ from GetLogs since, from the next hop, GetLogs is modified not to perform loop iterations. From Lemma 8, we have

$$|\Pr[W_8] - \Pr[W_9]| \leq (q_H + q_S + q_F)\sqrt{\frac{2B(B-1)}{|\mathcal{R}|}}.$$

GAME $G_{10.0}$: In GetLogs, $r_k := \mathsf{RF}_{salt}(m, k)$ is generated by $\mathsf{RF}_{salt}(m, B+1)$. Note that we modify GetLogs to be performed without using sk in $G_{10.0}$ and $G_{10.1}$.

Lemma 12. *We have* $\Pr[W_9] = \Pr[W_{10.0}]$.

Proof. Since both $\mathsf{RF}_{salt}(m, k)$ and $\mathsf{RF}_{salt}(m, B+1)$ are uniformly distributed, and the adversary obtains only $\mathsf{RF}_{salt}(m, k)$ (resp., $\mathsf{RF}_{salt}(m, B+1)$) in G_9 (resp., $G_{10.0}$), the adversary's view remains unchanged.

GAME $G_{10.1}$: We simulate GetLogs using SampDom, where $\mathsf{RF}_{sd} \leftarrow_\$ \mathsf{Func}(\mathcal{M}, \mathcal{R}'')$ is used for generating a random coin for SampDom.

Lemma 13. *Suppose that* T *is* (γ, β)-*correct and* δ-PS. *We have*

$$|\Pr[W_{10.0}] - \Pr[W_{10.1}]| \leq \sqrt{6(q_H + 2q_F)^3 (\delta + 2(1 - \gamma(1 - \beta^B)))}.$$

Proof. We consider the oracle-indistinguishability of GetLogs in $G_{10.0}$ and $G_{10.1}$ by considering the difference in distributions of $(x,y) \in \mathcal{X}' \times \mathcal{Y}$ output from GetLogs, where $\mathcal{X}' = \mathcal{X} \cup \{\bot\}$. Let $\mathcal{D}_m$ and $\mathcal{D}'_m$ be distributions of $(x,y) \in \mathcal{X}' \times \mathcal{Y}$ output from GetLogs(m) in $G_{10.0}$ and $G_{10.1}$, respectively. Since T is δ-PS (see Definition 8), the distance between x generated by Inv after unbounded retries and $x \leftarrow$ SampDom(vk) is bounded by δ. We define $\mathcal{D}_m^\infty$ as the distribution of $(x, y, k) \in \mathcal{X} \times \mathcal{Y} \times \mathbb{Z}_{>0}$, where GetLogs($m$) retries without any limit, and an additional variable k denotes the number of retries within GetLogs(m). By marginalizing $\mathcal{D}_m^\infty$ and $\mathcal{D}'_m$ over $y \in \mathcal{Y}$, we have

$$\sum_{x \in \mathcal{X}} \left| \sum_{y \in \mathcal{Y}} \left(\sum_{k \in \mathbb{Z}_{>0}} \mathcal{D}_m^\infty(x, y, k) - \mathcal{D}_m'(x, y) \right) \right| \leq \delta. \tag{1}$$

If GetLogs in $G_{10.0}$ outputs $x \neq \perp$, then the number of retries will be less than or equal to B; therefore, for any $(x, y) \in \mathcal{X} \times \mathcal{Y}$, we have

$$\mathcal{D}_m(x, y) = \sum_{k \in [B]} \mathcal{D}_m^\infty(x, y, k). \tag{2}$$

In addition, the probability of outputting $x \neq \perp$ such that $\mathsf{F}(vk, x) = y$ is at least $\gamma(1 - \beta^B)$ due to the (γ, β)-correctness. Therefore, we have

$$\sum_{x \in \mathcal{X}} \mathcal{D}_m(x, \mathsf{F}(vk, x)) \geq \gamma \left(1 - \beta^B \right). \tag{3}$$

Then, we can derive a bound on $\delta' = \sum_{(x,y) \in \mathcal{X}' \times \mathcal{Y}} |\mathcal{D}_m(x, y) - \mathcal{D}_m'(x, y)|$ as follows.

$$\delta' = \sum_{\substack{(x,y) \in \mathcal{X}' \times \mathcal{Y} \\ :x \neq \perp \wedge \mathsf{F}(vk,x)=y}} |\mathcal{D}_m(x, y) - \mathcal{D}_m'(x, y)| + \sum_{\substack{(x,y) \in \mathcal{X}' \times \mathcal{Y} \\ :x=\perp \vee \mathsf{F}(vk,x) \neq y}} \mathcal{D}_m(x, y)$$

$$= \sum_{x \in \mathcal{X}} |\mathcal{D}_m(x, \mathsf{F}(vk, x)) - \mathcal{D}_m'(x, \mathsf{F}(vk, x))| + 1 - \sum_{x \in \mathcal{X}} \mathcal{D}_m(x, \mathsf{F}(vk, x))$$

$$\stackrel{(2)}{=} \sum_{x \in \mathcal{X}} \left| \sum_{k \in [B]} \mathcal{D}_m^\infty(x, \mathsf{F}(vk, x), k) - \mathcal{D}_m'(x, \mathsf{F}(vk, x)) \right| + 1 - \sum_{x \in \mathcal{X}} \mathcal{D}_m(x, \mathsf{F}(vk, x))$$

$$\stackrel{(*)}{\leq} \sum_{x \in \mathcal{X}} \left| \sum_{y \in \mathcal{Y}} \left(\sum_{k \in \mathbb{Z}_{>0}} \mathcal{D}_m^\infty(x, y, k) - \mathcal{D}_m'(x, y) \right) \right| + 1 - \sum_{x \in \mathcal{X}} \mathcal{D}_m(x, \mathsf{F}(vk, x))$$

$$+ \sum_{x \in \mathcal{X}} \left(\sum_{y \in \mathcal{Y}} \sum_{k \in \mathbb{Z}_{>0}} \mathcal{D}_m^\infty(x, y, k) - \sum_{k \in [B]} \mathcal{D}_m^\infty(x, \mathsf{F}(vk, x), k) \right)$$

$$\stackrel{(1)(2)}{\leq} \delta + 2 \left(1 - \sum_{x \in \mathcal{X}} \mathcal{D}_m(x, \mathsf{F}(vk, x)) \right) \stackrel{(3)}{\leq} \delta + 2 \left(1 - \gamma \left(1 - \beta^B \right) \right)$$

Here, $(*)$ follows from $\mathcal{D}_m'(x, \mathsf{F}(vk, x)) = \sum_{y \in \mathcal{Y}} \mathcal{D}_m'(x, y)$ and the triangle inequality, where we do not take the absolute value for the last term because $\sum_{y \in \mathcal{Y}} \sum_{k \in \mathbb{Z}_{>0}} \mathcal{D}_m^\infty(x, y, k)$ includes all the terms of $\sum_{k \in [B]} \mathcal{D}_m^\infty(x, \mathsf{F}(vk, x), k)$. Using Lemma 5, we can derive the bound on $|\Pr[W_{10.0}] - \Pr[W_{10.1}]|$.

GAME G_{11}: We change the condition of $\mathbf{win} = \top$ from $(r, x) \neq (r_k, x_k)$ to $r \neq r_k$ in FORGE. Though the condition $(r, x) \neq (r_k, x_k)$ allows for the possibility that H may not match $\mathsf{RF_H}$ for a queried pair (r, m) in FORGE, this modification ensures that they do. Then, all the necessary conditions for the simulation by the EUF-NMA adversary are now complete.

$\mathcal{A}_{\mathsf{nma}}^{\hat{\mathsf{H}}}(vk)$

1 $\mathsf{RF}_{\mathsf{salt}} \leftarrow_{\$} \mathsf{Func}(\mathcal{M} \times [B+1], \mathcal{R})$
2 $\mathsf{RF}_{\mathsf{sd}} \leftarrow_{\$} \mathsf{Func}(\mathcal{M}, \mathcal{R}'')$
3 $\mathbf{win} = \perp$
4 $\mathbf{run}\ \mathcal{A}_{\mathsf{po}}^{|\mathsf{H}\rangle, |\mathrm{SIGN}\rangle, \mathrm{FORGE}}(vk)$
5 $\mathbf{if\ win\ then}$
6 $|\ \mathbf{return}\ (m^*, (r^*, x^*))$
7 $\mathbf{return}\ \perp$

$\mathsf{H}(r, m)$

8   $(r_k, y_k, x_k) := \mathrm{GetLogs}(m)$
9   $\mathbf{if}\ r = r_k\ \mathbf{then}$
10 $|\ \mathbf{return}\ y_k$
11 $\mathbf{return}\ \hat{\mathsf{H}}(r, m)$

$\mathrm{SIGN}(m)$

12 $(r_k, y_k, x_k) := \mathrm{GetLogs}(m)$
13 $\mathbf{if}\ x_k = \perp\ \mathbf{then}$
14 $|\ \mathbf{return}\ \perp$
15 $\mathbf{return}\ (r_k, x_k)$

$\mathrm{FORGE}(m, (r, x))$

16 $(r_k, y_k, x_k) := \mathrm{GetLogs}(m)$
17 $\mathbf{if}\ \mathsf{F}(vk, x_k) \neq \mathsf{H}(r_k, m)\ \mathbf{then}$
18 $|\ \mathbf{return}\ \lrcorner$
19 $\mathbf{if}\ \mathsf{F}(vk, x) = \mathsf{H}(r, m) \wedge r \neq r_k\ \mathbf{then}$
20 $|\ \mathbf{win} = \top$
21 $|\ (m^*, (r^*, x^*)) := (m, (r, x))$

$\mathrm{GetLogs}(m)$

22 $r_k := \mathsf{RF}_{\mathsf{salt}}(m, B+1)$
23 $x_k := \mathsf{SampDom}(vk; \mathsf{RF}_{\mathsf{sd}}(m))$
24 $y_k := \mathsf{F}(vk, x_k)$
25 $\mathbf{return}\ (r_k, y_k, x_k)$

Fig. 13. Simulation of the modified PO game by EUF-NMA adversary

Lemma 14. *There exists a* CR *adversary* $\mathcal{A}_{\mathsf{cr}}$ *of* T *such that*

$$|\Pr[W_{10.1}] - \Pr[W_{11}]| \leq \mathrm{Adv}_{\mathsf{T}}^{\mathrm{CR}}(\mathcal{A}_{\mathsf{cr}}).$$

Proof. $G_{10.1}$ and G_{11} differ only if the adversary submits (r, x) such that $r = r_k$ and $x \neq x_k$ (i.e., $\mathbf{win} = \top$ holds only in $G_{10.1}$). Let $\mathbf{bad}_{11}$ denote this event, and note that $|\Pr[W_{10.1}] - \Pr[W_{11}]| \leq \Pr[\mathbf{bad}_{11}]$ holds.

We now bound $\Pr[\mathbf{bad}_{11}]$. Due to the modification introduced in G_4, we have $\mathsf{H}(r_k, m) = \mathsf{F}(vk, x_k)$ when FORGE does not return $\lrcorner$. Therefore, when $\mathbf{bad}_{11}$ occurs, a collision pair (x, x_k) satisfying $\mathsf{F}(vk, x) = \mathsf{F}(vk, x_k) = \mathsf{H}(r, m)$ is found. If $\mathbf{bad}_{11}$ occurs during the CR adversary's simulation, the adversary can obtain the colliding pair (x, x_k). Thus, we conclude that $\Pr[\mathbf{bad}_{11}] \leq \mathrm{Adv}_{\mathsf{T}}^{\mathrm{CR}}(\mathcal{A}_{\mathsf{cr}})$.

We conclude the proof by the EUF-NMA adversary's simulation.

Lemma 15. *There exists an* EUF-NMA *adversary* $\mathcal{A}_{\mathsf{nma}}$ *of* $\mathsf{HSR}[\mathsf{T}, \mathsf{H}]$ *such that*

$$\Pr[W_{11}] \leq \mathrm{Adv}_{\mathsf{HSR}}^{\mathrm{EUF\text{-}NMA}}(\mathcal{A}_{\mathsf{nma}}).$$

Proof. To avoid a confusion, we consider $\mathsf{HSR}[\mathsf{T}, \hat{\mathsf{H}}]$ instead of $\mathsf{HSR}[\mathsf{T}, \mathsf{H}]$, where $\hat{\mathsf{H}}: \mathcal{R} \times \mathcal{M} \to \mathcal{Y}$ is a random oracle. The EUF-NMA adversary $\mathcal{A}_{\mathsf{nma}}$ against $\mathsf{HSR}[\mathsf{T}, \hat{\mathsf{H}}]$ with oracle access to $\hat{\mathsf{H}}$ can simulate G_{11} since it can simulate all the oracles by using $\mathsf{SampDom}$ as in Fig. 13. The EUF-NMA adversary outputs $(m^*, (r^*, x^*))$ such that $\mathsf{F}(vk, x^*) = \mathsf{H}(r^*, m^*)$ and $r^* \neq r_k = \mathsf{RF}_{\mathsf{salt}}(m^*, B+1)$ hold in FORGE. Note that $\mathsf{H}(r^*, m^*) = \hat{\mathsf{H}}(r^*, m^*)$ holds since $r^* \neq r_k$. Therefore, $\mathcal{A}_{\mathsf{nma}}$ can win the game and $\Pr[W_{11}]$ is bounded by the EUF-NMA advantage. Since $\mathsf{HSR}[\mathsf{T}, \hat{\mathsf{H}}]$ is equivalent to $\mathsf{HSR}[\mathsf{T}, \mathsf{H}]$, this shows the lemma.

$\square$

The wPO-security does not require the collision-resistance of T as follows.

Corollary 1 (EUF-NMA + qPRF ⇒ wPO). *For any quantum* wPO *adversary* $\mathcal{A}_{\mathsf{po}}$ *of* $\mathsf{DHSR}_B[\mathsf{T},\mathsf{H},\mathsf{PRF},\mathsf{PRF}']$ *issuing at most* q_H *quantum queries to* H, q_S *quantum queries to* SIGN, *and* q_F *classical queries to* FORGE, *there exist an* EUF-NMA *adversary* $\mathcal{A}_{\mathsf{nma}}$ *of* $\mathsf{HSR}[\mathsf{T},\mathsf{H}]$ *and* qPRF *adversaries* $\mathcal{A}_{\mathsf{prf}}$ *of* PRF *and* $\mathcal{A}'_{\mathsf{prf}}$ *of* PRF' *issuing at most* Bq_S *queries such that*

$$
\begin{aligned}
\mathrm{Adv}_{\mathsf{DHSR}}^{\mathrm{WPO}}(\mathcal{A}_{\mathsf{po}}) \le\ & \mathrm{Adv}_{\mathsf{HSR}}^{\mathrm{EUF\text{-}NMA}}(\mathcal{A}_{\mathsf{nma}}) + \mathrm{Adv}_{\mathsf{PRF}}^{q\mathrm{PRF}}(\mathcal{A}_{\mathsf{prf}}) + \mathrm{Adv}_{\mathsf{PRF}'}^{q\mathrm{PRF}}(\mathcal{A}'_{\mathsf{prf}}) \\
& + 8(q_\mathsf{H} + q_\mathsf{S} + q_\mathsf{F} + 1)^2 \left(1 - \gamma\left(1 - \beta^B\right)\right) + \frac{q_\mathsf{S} + 1}{\lfloor |\mathcal{R}|/B \rfloor} \\
& + 2(q_\mathsf{H} + q_\mathsf{F})\sqrt{\frac{B-1}{|\mathcal{R}|}} + 2(q_\mathsf{H} + q_\mathsf{S} + q_\mathsf{F})\sqrt{\frac{2B(B-1)}{|\mathcal{R}|}} \\
& + \sqrt{6\left(q_\mathsf{H} + 2q_\mathsf{F}\right)^3 \left(\delta + 2\left(1 - \gamma\left(1 - \beta^B\right)\right)\right)},
\end{aligned}
$$

where T *is* (γ, β)-correct *and* δ-PS, *and the running times of* $\mathcal{A}_{\mathsf{nma}}$, $\mathcal{A}_{\mathsf{prf}}$, *and* $\mathcal{A}'_{\mathsf{prf}}$ *are about that of* $\mathcal{A}_{\mathsf{po}}$.

Proof. In the proof of Theorem 1, we can modify $G_{5.0}$ by changing the winning condition from $(r, x) \neq (r_k, x_k)$ to $r \neq r_k$ (see Line 39 in Fig. 11) and remove G_{11}. Note that G_{11} is unnecessary for the simulation by the EUF-NMA adversary since the condition of **win** = ⊤ has already been $\mathsf{F}(vk, x) = \mathsf{H}(r, m)$ and $r \neq r_k$ in FORGE. Hence, the collision-resistance of T is not necessary. □

Remark 1. By assuming *quantum* preimage-simulatability, we can use a computational bound. This is an adaptation of the quantum special HVZK used in the BU security proof of Fiat-Shamir [27] to the HSwR context. We define quantum preimage-simulatability by allowing quantum queries in the PS game. We modify the oracles in the PS game to take a message as input and perform preimage sampling corresponding to the message. The advantage of the quantum version of the PS game can be used to bound $|\Pr[W_{10.0}] - \Pr[W_{10.1}]|$ in Theorem 1. See the full version for details.

4.2   (Strong) Blind Unforgeability

We show that $\mathsf{DHSR}_B[\mathsf{T},\mathsf{H},\mathsf{PRF},\mathsf{PRF}']$ is also sBU-secure.

Theorem 2 (EUF-NMA + CR + qPRF ⇒ sBU). *For any quantum* sBU *adversary* $\mathcal{A}_{\mathsf{bu}}$ *of* $\mathsf{DHSR}_B[\mathsf{T},\mathsf{H},\mathsf{PRF},\mathsf{PRF}']$ *issuing at most* q_H *quantum queries to* H, q_S *quantum queries to* SIGN, *and* q_F *classical queries to* FORGE, *there exist an* EUF-NMA *adversary* $\mathcal{A}_{\mathsf{nma}}$ *of* $\mathsf{HSR}[\mathsf{T},\mathsf{H}]$, *a* CR *adversary* $\mathcal{A}_{\mathsf{cr}}$ *of* T, *and* qPRF *adversaries* $\mathcal{A}_{\mathsf{prf}}$ *of* PRF *and* $\mathcal{A}'_{\mathsf{prf}}$ *of* PRF' *issuing at most* Bq_S *queries such that*

$$\mathrm{Adv}^{\mathrm{sBU}}_{\mathsf{DHSR}}(\mathcal{A}_{\mathsf{bu}}) \leq \mathrm{Adv}^{\mathrm{EUF\text{-}NMA}}_{\mathsf{HSR}}(\mathcal{A}_{\mathsf{nma}}) + \mathrm{Adv}^{\mathrm{CR}}_{\mathsf{T}}(\mathcal{A}_{\mathsf{cr}}) + \mathrm{Adv}^{q\mathrm{PRF}}_{\mathsf{PRF}}(\mathcal{A}_{\mathsf{prf}})$$

$$+ \mathrm{Adv}^{q\mathrm{PRF}}_{\mathsf{PRF}'}(\mathcal{A}'_{\mathsf{prf}}) + 8(q_{\mathsf{H}} + q_{\mathsf{S}} + q_{\mathsf{F}} + 1)^2 \left(1 - \gamma\left(1 - \beta^B\right)\right)$$

$$+ \frac{Bq_{\mathsf{F}}}{|\mathcal{R}|} + 2(q_{\mathsf{H}} + q_{\mathsf{F}})\sqrt{\frac{B - 1}{|\mathcal{R}|}} + 2(q_{\mathsf{H}} + q_{\mathsf{S}} + q_{\mathsf{F}})\sqrt{\frac{2B(B - 1)}{|\mathcal{R}|}}$$

$$+ \sqrt{6\left(q_{\mathsf{H}} + 2q_{\mathsf{F}}\right)^3 \left(\delta + 2\left(1 - \gamma\left(1 - \beta^B\right)\right)\right)},$$

where T *is* (γ, β)-*correct and* δ-*PS, and the running times of* $\mathcal{A}_{\mathsf{nma}}$, $\mathcal{A}_{\mathsf{cr}}$, $\mathcal{A}_{\mathsf{prf}}$, *and* $\mathcal{A}'_{\mathsf{prf}}$ *are about that of* $\mathcal{A}_{\mathsf{bu}}$.

Proof. We use the sequence of games shown in Fig. 14. Note that this proof is almost identical to Theorem 1, with the only difference lying in G_5. Here, the effect of introducing G_5 in Theorem 2 is the same as that of $G_{5.0}$ and $G_{5.1}$ in Theorem 1. However, the method for bounding $|\Pr[W_4] - \Pr[W_5]|$ differs due to the distinctions between the PO and sBU games.

GAME G_0: This is the original sBU game: $\Pr[W_0] = \mathrm{Adv}^{\mathrm{sBU}}_{\mathsf{DHSR}}(\mathcal{A}_{\mathsf{bu}})$.

GAME G_1: We replace PRFs with random functions $\mathsf{RF}_{\mathsf{salt}}$ and $\mathsf{RF}_{\mathsf{inv}}$. From Lemma 7, we have $|\Pr[W_0] - \Pr[W_1]| \leq \mathrm{Adv}^{q\mathrm{PRF}}_{\mathsf{PRF}}(\mathcal{A}_{\mathsf{prf}}) + \mathrm{Adv}^{q\mathrm{PRF}}_{\mathsf{PRF}'}(\mathcal{A}'_{\mathsf{prf}})$.

GAME G_2: The oracles H and FORGE compute GetLogs. Since this is a conceptual change, we have $\Pr[W_1] = \Pr[W_2]$.

GAME G_3: We check if a collision occurs among $\{r_i\}_{i \in [k]}$ in GetLogs. If a collision occurs, GetLogs returns $\perp$. From Lemma 8, we have

$$|\Pr[W_2] - \Pr[W_3]| \leq (q_{\mathsf{H}} + q_{\mathsf{S}} + q_{\mathsf{F}})\sqrt{\frac{2B(B - 1)}{|\mathcal{R}|}}.$$

GAME G_4: FORGE returns $\perp$ if $\mathsf{F}(vk, x_k) \neq \mathsf{H}(r_k, m)$ holds, where (r_k, x_k) is a signature generated by GetLogs(m). From Lemma 9, we have $|\Pr[W_2] - \Pr[W_3]| \leq 8(q_{\mathsf{H}} + q_{\mathsf{S}} + q_{\mathsf{F}} + 1)^2 \left(1 - \gamma\left(1 - \beta^B\right)\right)$.

GAME G_5: We add an additional condition to let **win** $= \top$, that is, $(r, x) \neq (r_k, x_k)$ holds.

Lemma 16. *We have*

$$|\Pr[W_4] - \Pr[W_5]| \leq \frac{Bq_{\mathsf{F}}}{|\mathcal{R}|}.$$

Proof. G_4 and G_5 differ only when the adversary submits a query $(m, (r, x))$ such that $\mathsf{F}(vk, x) = \mathsf{H}(r, m)$, $(m, (r, x)) \in B_{\epsilon}$, and $(r, x) = (r_k, x_k)$ holds, because **win** becomes $\top$ in G_4 but remains $\perp$ in G_5. Let $\mathbf{bad}_{11}$ denote this event. We have $|\Pr[W_4] - \Pr[W_5]| \leq \Pr[\mathbf{bad}_{11}]$. Since $(m, (r_k, x_k)) \in B_{\epsilon}$, the adversary cannot obtain $r_k := \mathsf{RF}_{\mathsf{salt}}(m, k)$ from the queries to $B_{\epsilon}\mathrm{SIGN}$. Therefore, the adversary needs to guess $r = r_k$ without knowing r_k. As shown in Lemma 10, $\max_{r \in \mathcal{R}} \Pr[r_k := \mathsf{RF}_{\mathsf{salt}}(m, k) : r_k = r | \mathsf{H}] \leq \frac{B}{|\mathcal{R}|}$ holds. Since the adversary makes q_{F} queries to FORGE, $\Pr[\mathbf{bad}_{11}] \leq \frac{Bq_{\mathsf{F}}}{|\mathcal{R}|}$ holds.

GAMES G_0-G_{11}

1 $\mathsf{RF_H} \leftarrow_\$ \mathsf{Func}(\mathcal{R} \times \mathcal{M}, \mathcal{Y})$
2 $\mathsf{RF_{salt}} \leftarrow_\$ \mathsf{Func}(\mathcal{M} \times [B+1], \mathcal{R})$ // G_1-G_{11}
3 $\mathsf{RF_{inv}} \leftarrow_\$ \mathsf{Func}(\mathcal{M} \times [B], \mathcal{R}')$ // G_1-$G_{10.0}$
4 $\mathsf{RF'_H} \leftarrow_\$ \mathsf{Func}(\mathcal{M} \times [B], \mathcal{Y})$ // G_7-$G_{10.0}$
5 $\mathsf{RF_{sd}} \leftarrow_\$ \mathsf{Func}(\mathcal{M}, \mathcal{R}'')$ // $G_{10.1}$-G_{11}
6 $B_\epsilon \leftarrow \mathsf{Func}_{\mathcal{M} \times (\mathcal{R} \times \mathcal{X}), \{0,1\}}(\mathrm{Ber}_\epsilon)$
7 $\mathbf{win} := \bot$
8 $(vk, sk) \leftarrow \mathsf{Gen}(1^\lambda)$
9 $(s, s') \leftarrow_\$ \mathcal{K} \times \mathcal{K}$ // G_0
10 **run** $\mathcal{A}_{\mathrm{bu}}^{|\mathrm{H}\rangle, |B_\epsilon \mathrm{SIGN}\rangle, \mathrm{FORGE}}(vk)$
11 **return win**

$\mathsf{H}(r, m)$

12 **if** $\mathsf{GetLogs}(m) = \lrcorner$ **then**   // G_3-G_8
13 | **return** $\bot$ // G_3-G_8
14 $(r_k, y_k, x_k) := \mathsf{GetLogs}(m)$
     // G_2-$G_5 \cdot G_8$-G_{11}
15 **if** $r = r_k$ **then**   // G_2-$G_5 \cdot G_8$-G_{11}
16 | **return** y_k // G_2-$G_5 \cdot G_8$-G_{11}
17 $\{(r_i, y_i, x_i)\}_{i \in [k]} := \mathsf{GetLogs}(m)$ // G_6-G_7
18 **if** $\exists i, r = r_i$ **then**   // G_6-G_7
19 | **return** y_i // G_6-G_7
20 **return** $\mathsf{RF_H}(r, m)$

$B_\epsilon \mathrm{SIGN}(m)$

21 **if** $\mathsf{GetLogs}(m) = \lrcorner$ **then**   // G_3-G_8
22 | **return** $\bot$ // G_3-G_8
23 $(r_k, y_k, x_k) := \mathsf{GetLogs}(m)$
     // G_0-$G_5 \cdot G_8$-G_{11}
24 $\{(r_i, y_i, x_i)\}_{i \in [k]} := \mathsf{GetLogs}(m)$ // G_6-G_7
25 **if** $x_k = \bot \vee (m, (r_k, x_k)) \in B_\epsilon$ **then**
26 | **return** $\bot$
27 **return** (r_k, x_k)

$\mathrm{FORGE}(m, (r, x))$

28 **if** $\mathsf{GetLogs}(m) = \lrcorner$ **then**   // G_3-G_8
29 | **return** $\bot$ // G_3-G_8
30 $(r_k, y_k, x_k) := \mathsf{GetLogs}(m)$
     // G_2-$G_5 \cdot G_8$-G_{11}
31 $\{(r_i, y_i, x_i)\}_{i \in [k]} := \mathsf{GetLogs}(m)$ // G_6-G_7
32 **if** $\mathsf{F}(vk, x_k) \neq \mathsf{H}(r_k, m)$ **then**   // G_4-G_{11}
33 | **return** $\lrcorner$ // G_4-G_{11}
34 **if** $\mathsf{F}(vk, x) = \mathsf{H}(r, m) \wedge (m, (r, x)) \in B_\epsilon$
     then
35 | **win** $= \top$ // G_0-G_4
36 | **if** $(r, x) \neq (r_k, x_k)$ **then**   // G_5-$G_{10.1}$
37 | | **win** $= \top$ // G_5-$G_{10.1}$
38 | | **if** $r \neq r_k$ **then**   // G_{11}
39 | | | **win** $= \top$ // G_{11}

$\mathsf{GetLogs}(m)$ for G_0

40 $k := 0$
41 **repeat**
42 | $k := k + 1$
43 | $r_k := \mathsf{PRF}(s, (m, k))$
44 | $y_k := \mathsf{RF_H}(r_k, m)$
45 | $x_k := \mathsf{Inv}(sk, y_k; \mathsf{PRF}'(s', (m, k)))$
46 **until** $x_k \neq \bot \vee k \geq B$
47 **return** (r_k, y_k, x_k)

$\mathsf{GetLogs}(m)$ for $G_{10.1}$-G_{11}

48 $r_k := \mathsf{RF_{salt}}(m, B + 1)$
49 $x_k := \mathsf{SampDom}(vk; \mathsf{RF_{sd}}(m))$
50 $y_k := \mathsf{F}(vk, x_k)$
51 **return** (r_k, y_k, x_k)

$\mathsf{GetLogs}(m)$ for G_1-$G_{10.0}$

52 $k := 0$
53 **repeat**
54 | $k := k + 1$
55 | $r_k := \mathsf{RF_{salt}}(m, k)$ // G_1-G_8
56 | $y_k := \mathsf{RF_H}(r_k, m)$ // G_1-G_2
57 | $y_k := \mathsf{RF'_H}(m, k)$ // G_7-$G_{10.0}$
58 | $x_k := \mathsf{Inv}(sk, y_k; \mathsf{RF_{inv}}(m, k))$
59 **until** $x_k \neq \bot \vee k \geq B$
60 $r_k := \mathsf{RF_{salt}}(m, B + 1)$ // $G_{10.0}$
61 **if** $\exists (i, j), r_i = r_j$ **then**   // G_3-G_8
62 | **return** $\lrcorner$ // G_3-G_8
63 **return** (r_k, y_k, x_k) // G_1-$G_5 \cdot G_8$-$G_{10.0}$
64 **return** $\{(r_i, y_i, x_i)\}_{i \in [k]}$ // G_6-G_7

Fig. 14. Games for EUF-NMA $\Rightarrow$ sBU

GAME G_6: GetLogs outputs $\{(r_i, y_i, x_i)\}_{i \in [k]}$ generated during loop iteration instead of outputting the final result, and $\mathsf{H}(r, m)$ outputs y_i if there exists r_i such that $r = r_i$. This modification does not affect the adversary's view, and we have $\Pr[W_5] = \Pr[W_6]$.

GAME G_7: Instead of $\mathsf{RF_H}(r_k, m)$, $\mathsf{RF'_H}(m, k)$ generates y_k in GetLogs. Since there are no collisions among $\{r_i\}_{i \in [k]}$, the adversary's view does not change; therefore, we have $\Pr[W_6] = \Pr[W_7]$.

GAME G_8: GetLogs only outputs the final result after retries. From Lemma 11, we have

$$|\Pr[W_7] - \Pr[W_8]| \leq 2(q_\mathsf{H} + q_\mathsf{F}) \sqrt{\frac{B - 1}{|\mathcal{R}|}}.$$

GAME G_9: GetLogs does not check collisions among $\{r_i\}_{i \in [k]}$. From Lemma 8, we have

$$|\Pr[W_8] - \Pr[W_9]| \le (q_{\mathsf{H}} + q_{\mathsf{S}} + q_{\mathsf{F}}) \sqrt{\frac{2B(B-1)}{|\mathcal{R}|}}.$$

GAME $G_{10.0}$: In GetLogs, we change the salt generation from $r_k := \mathsf{RF}_{\mathsf{salt}}(m, k)$ to $r_k := \mathsf{RF}_{\mathsf{salt}}(m, B+1)$ for k such that $x_k \neq \bot$. Since the view of the adversary does not change, we have $\Pr[W_9] = \Pr[W_{10}]$.

GAME $G_{10.1}$: We simulate GetLogs using SampDom. From Lemma 13, we have

$$|\Pr[W_9] - \Pr[W_{10}]| \le \sqrt{6 \left(q_{\mathsf{H}} + 2q_{\mathsf{F}}\right)^3 \left(\delta + 2\left(1 - \gamma\left(1 - \beta^B\right)\right)\right)}.$$

GAME G_{11}: We change the condition of $\mathbf{win} = \top$ from $(r, x) \neq (r_k, x_k)$ to $r \neq r_k$ in FORGE. From Lemma 14, we have $|\Pr[W_{10}] - \Pr[W_{11}]| \le \mathrm{Adv}_{\mathsf{T}}^{\mathrm{CR}}(\mathcal{A}_{\mathsf{cr}})$.

The EUF-NMA adversary $\mathcal{A}_{\mathsf{nma}}$ against $\mathsf{HSR}[\mathsf{T}, \hat{\mathsf{H}}]$ with oracle access to $\hat{\mathsf{H}}$ can simulate G_{11} since it can simulate all the oracles by using SampDom. Similar to Lemma 15, the EUF-NMA adversary outputs $(m^*, (r^*, x^*))$ that was queried in FORGE and caused $\mathbf{win}$ to become $\top$. Since $\mathsf{F}(vk, x^*) = \hat{\mathsf{H}}(r^*, m^*)$ holds, the EUF-NMA adversary can win its game if $\mathbf{win} = \top$ in G_{11}. Hence, there exists an EUF-NMA adversary $\mathcal{A}_{\mathsf{nma}}$ such that $\Pr[W_{11}] \le \mathrm{Adv}_{\mathsf{HSR}}^{\mathrm{EUF\text{-}NMA}}(\mathcal{A}_{\mathsf{nma}})$. Since $\mathsf{HSR}[\mathsf{T}, \hat{\mathsf{H}}]$ is equivalent to $\mathsf{HSR}[\mathsf{T}, \mathsf{H}]$, this completes the proof. □

The BU security does not require the collision-resistance of T; therefore, we can eliminate the CR assumption in the BU security as follows:

Corollary 2 (EUF-NMA + qPRF ⇒ BU). *For any quantum* BU *adversary* $\mathcal{A}_{\mathsf{bu}}$ *of* $\mathsf{DHSR}_B[\mathsf{T}, \mathsf{H}, \mathsf{PRF}, \mathsf{PRF}']$ *issuing at most* q_{H} *quantum queries to* H, q_{S} *quantum queries to* SIGN, *and* q_{F} *classical queries to* FORGE, *there exist an* EUF-NMA *adversary* $\mathcal{A}_{\mathsf{nma}}$ *of* $\mathsf{HSR}[\mathsf{T}, \mathsf{H}]$ *and* qPRF *adversaries* $\mathcal{A}_{\mathsf{prf}}$ *of* PRF *and* $\mathcal{A}'_{\mathsf{prf}}$ *of* PRF' *issuing at most* Bq_{S} *queries such that*

$$\mathrm{Adv}_{\mathsf{DHSR}}^{\mathrm{BU}}(\mathcal{A}_{\mathsf{bu}}) \le \mathrm{Adv}_{\mathsf{HSR}}^{\mathrm{EUF\text{-}NMA}}(\mathcal{A}_{\mathsf{nma}}) + \mathrm{Adv}_{\mathsf{PRF}}^{\mathrm{qPRF}}(\mathcal{A}_{\mathsf{prf}}) + \mathrm{Adv}_{\mathsf{PRF}'}^{\mathrm{qPRF}}(\mathcal{A}'_{\mathsf{prf}})$$
$$+ 8(q_{\mathsf{H}} + q_{\mathsf{S}} + q_{\mathsf{F}} + 1)^2 \left(1 - \gamma\left(1 - \beta^B\right)\right)$$
$$+ \frac{Bq_{\mathsf{F}}}{|\mathcal{R}|} + 2(q_{\mathsf{H}} + q_{\mathsf{F}}) \sqrt{\frac{B-1}{|\mathcal{R}|}} + 2(q_{\mathsf{H}} + q_{\mathsf{S}} + q_{\mathsf{F}}) \sqrt{\frac{2B(B-1)}{|\mathcal{R}|}}$$
$$+ \sqrt{6 \left(q_{\mathsf{H}} + 2q_{\mathsf{F}}\right)^3 \left(\delta + 2\left(1 - \gamma\left(1 - \beta^B\right)\right)\right)},$$

where T *is* (γ, β)*-correct and* δ*-PS, and the running times of* $\mathcal{A}_{\mathsf{nma}}$, $\mathcal{A}_{\mathsf{prf}}$, *and* $\mathcal{A}'_{\mathsf{prf}}$ *are about that of* $\mathcal{A}_{\mathsf{po}}$.

Proof. In Theorem 2, we can change the winning condition in G_5 from $(r, x) \neq (r_k, x_k)$ to $r \neq r_k$ (see Line 36 in Fig. 14). Therefore, we can remove G_{11} and the collision-resistance of T is unnecessary for the BU security. □

4.3   (Strong) Existential Unforgeability

We can prove $\mathsf{DHSR}_B[\mathsf{T}, \mathsf{H}, \mathsf{PRF}, \mathsf{PRF}']$ is sEUF-CMA-secure.

Theorem 3 (EUF-NMA + PS + SPR + PRF $\Rightarrow$ sEUF-CMA). *For any quantum* sEUF-CMA *adversary* $\mathcal{A}_{\mathsf{cma}}$ *of* $\mathsf{DHSR}_B[\mathsf{T}, \mathsf{H}, \mathsf{PRF}, \mathsf{PRF}']$ *issuing at most* q_H *quantum queries to* H *and* q_S *quantum queries to* SIGN, *there exist an* EUF-NMA *adversary* $\mathcal{A}_{\mathsf{nma}}$ *of* $\mathsf{HSR}[\mathsf{T}, \mathsf{H}]$, *a* PS *adversary* $\mathcal{A}_{\mathsf{ps}}$ *issuing at most* q_S *queries,* SPR *adversary* $\mathcal{A}_{\mathsf{spr}}$ *of* T, *and* PRF *adversaries* $\mathcal{A}_{\mathsf{prf}}$ *of* PRF *and* $\mathcal{A}'_{\mathsf{prf}}$ *of* PRF' *issuing at most* Bq_S *queries such that*

$$\mathrm{Adv}_{\mathsf{DHSR}}^{\mathrm{sEUF\text{-}CMA}}(\mathcal{A}_{\mathsf{cma}}) \leq \mathrm{Adv}_{\mathsf{HSR}}^{\mathrm{EUF\text{-}NMA}}(\mathcal{A}_{\mathsf{nma}}) + \mathrm{Adv}_\mathsf{T}^{\mathrm{PS}}(\mathcal{A}_{\mathsf{ps}}) + q_\mathsf{S}\mathrm{Adv}_\mathsf{T}^{\mathrm{SPR}}(\mathcal{A}_{\mathsf{spr}})$$
$$+ \mathrm{Adv}_{\mathsf{PRF}}^{\mathrm{PRF}}(\mathcal{A}_{\mathsf{prf}}) + \mathrm{Adv}_{\mathsf{PRF}'}^{\mathrm{PRF}}(\mathcal{A}'_{\mathsf{prf}}) + q_\mathsf{S}\left(1 - \gamma\left(1 - \beta^B\right)\right)$$
$$+ \frac{3}{2}Bq_\mathsf{S}\sqrt{\frac{q_\mathsf{H} + Bq_\mathsf{S} + 1}{|\mathcal{R}|}} + 2(q_\mathsf{H} + 1)\sqrt{\frac{B-1}{|\mathcal{R}|}},$$

where T *is* (γ, β)-*correct and the running times of* $\mathcal{A}_{\mathsf{nma}}$, $\mathcal{A}_{\mathsf{ps}}$, $\mathcal{A}_{\mathsf{spr}}$, $\mathcal{A}_{\mathsf{prf}}$, *and* $\mathcal{A}'_{\mathsf{prf}}$ *are about that of* $\mathcal{A}_{\mathsf{cma}}$.

Proof. We use the sequence of games shown in Fig. 15.

GAME G_0: This is the original sEUF-CMA game: $\Pr[W_0] = \mathrm{Adv}_{\mathsf{DHSR}}^{\mathrm{sEUF\text{-}CMA}}$ $(\mathcal{A}_{\mathsf{cma}})$.

GAME G_1: We replace PRF and PRF' with random functions $\mathsf{RF}_{\mathsf{salt}}$ and $\mathsf{RF}_{\mathsf{inv}}$, respectively.

Lemma 17. *There exist* PRF *adversaries* $\mathcal{A}_{\mathsf{prf}}$ *of* PRF *and* $\mathcal{A}'_{\mathsf{prf}}$ *of* PRF' *such that*

$$|\Pr[W_0] - \Pr[W_1]| \leq \mathrm{Adv}_{\mathsf{PRF}}^{\mathrm{PRF}}(\mathcal{A}_{\mathsf{prf}}) + \mathrm{Adv}_{\mathsf{PRF}'}^{\mathrm{PRF}}(\mathcal{A}'_{\mathsf{prf}}).$$

Proof. As in Lemma 7, we can replace $\mathsf{PRF}(s, \cdot)$ and $\mathsf{PRF}'(s', \cdot)$ separately. Since the PRFs are classically executed, the (classical) PRF adversaries $\mathcal{A}_{\mathsf{prf}}$ and $\mathcal{A}'_{\mathsf{prf}}$ can simulate the outputs of PRF and PRF' using the outputs of their oracles. Thus, the advantage gap due to the above transformation can be bounded by the PRF advantages.

GAME G_2: Let σ be a database of signatures indexed by messages, where each signature $\sigma[m]$ corresponds to a message m used in generating the signature. The signing oracle SIGN returns $\sigma[m]$ if m has been queried previously ($\sigma[m] \neq \emptyset$). Since this is a conceptual change, we have $\Pr[W_1] = \Pr[W_2]$.

Storing σ ensures that, in the subsequent game hops, when randomness is generated without using the random function, the same randomness is used for the same m.

GAME G_3: The signing oracle SIGN uniformly chooses y_k and reprograms $\mathsf{H} := \mathsf{H}^{(r_k, m) \mapsto y_k}$ for the chosen y_k. This step is crucial in the simulation of the signing oracle, as it requires generating y_k independently of (r_k, m) and treating y_k as the output of H when (r_k, m) is given as input.

GAMES G_0-G_6

1    $\mathsf{RF_H} \leftarrow_\$ \mathsf{Func}(\mathcal{R} \times \mathcal{M}, \mathcal{Y})$
2    $\mathsf{RF_{salt}} \leftarrow_\$ \mathsf{Func}(\mathcal{M} \times [B{+}1], \mathcal{R})$ $/\!/ G_1$-$G_{5.1}$
3    $\mathsf{RF_{inv}} \leftarrow_\$ \mathsf{Func}(\mathcal{M} \times [B], \mathcal{R}')$ $/\!/ G_1$-$G_{5.1}$
4    $\mathcal{Q} := \emptyset$
5    $(vk, sk) \leftarrow \mathsf{Gen}(1^\lambda)$
6    $(s, s') \leftarrow_\$ \mathcal{K} \times \mathcal{K}$ $/\!/ G_0$
7    $(m^*, (r^*, x^*)) \leftarrow \mathcal{A}_{\mathsf{cma}}^{\mathsf{SIGN}, |\mathsf{H}\rangle}(vk)$
8   **if** $(m^*, (r^*, x^*)) \in \mathcal{Q}$ **then** $/\!/ G_0$-$G_{5.1}$
9 | **return** $\bot$ $/\!/ G_0$-$G_{5.1}$
10   **if** $(m^*, r^*) \in \mathcal{Q}$ **then** $/\!/ G_6$
11 | **return** $\bot$ $/\!/ G_6$
12   **return** $[\![\mathsf{F}(vk, x^*) = \mathsf{H}(r^*, m^*)]\!]$

$\mathsf{H}(r, m)$

13   **return** $\mathsf{RF_H}(r, m)$

$\mathsf{SIGN}(m)$

14   **if** $\sigma[m] \neq \emptyset$ **then** $/\!/ G_2$-G_6
15 | **return** $\sigma[m]$ $/\!/ G_2$-G_6
16   $(r_k, y_k, x_k) := \mathsf{GetLogs}(m)$
17   **if** $x_k = \bot$ **then**
18 | $\sigma[m] := \bot$ $/\!/ G_2$-G_6
19 | **return** $\bot$
20   $\sigma[m] := (r_k, x_k)$ $/\!/ G_2$-G_6
21   $\mathcal{Q} := \mathcal{Q} \cup \{(m, (r_k, x_k))\}$ $/\!/ G_2$-$G_{5.1}$
22   $\mathcal{Q} := \mathcal{Q} \cup \{(m, r_k)\}$ $/\!/ G_6$
23   **return** (r_k, x_k)

$\mathsf{GetLogs}(m)$ for G_0

24   $k := 0$
25   **repeat**
26 | $k := k + 1$
27 | $r_k := \mathsf{PRF}(s, (m, k))$
28 | $y_k := \mathsf{RF_H}(r_k, m)$
29 | $x_k := \mathsf{Inv}(sk, y_k; \mathsf{PRF}'(s', (m, k)))$
30   **until** $x_k \neq \bot \vee k \geq B$
31   **return** (r_k, y_k, x_k)

$\mathsf{GetLogs}(m)$ for $G_{5.1}$-G_6

32   $r_k := \mathsf{RF_{salt}}(m, B+1)$
33   $x_k \leftarrow \mathsf{SampDom}(vk)$
34   $y_k := \mathsf{F}(vk, x_k)$
35   $\mathsf{RF_H} := \mathsf{RF_H}^{(r_k, m) \mapsto y_k}$
36   **return** (r_k, y_k, x_k)

$\mathsf{GetLogs}(m)$ for G_1-$G_{5.0}$

37   $k := 0$
38   **repeat**
39 | $k := k + 1$
40 | $r_k := \mathsf{RF_{salt}}(m, k)$
41 | $y_k := \mathsf{RF_H}(r_k, m)$ $/\!/ G_1$-G_2
42 | $y_k \leftarrow_\$ \mathcal{Y}$ $/\!/ G_3$-$G_{5.0}$
43 | $x_k := \mathsf{Inv}(sk, y_k; \mathsf{RF_{inv}}(m, k))$
44 | $\mathsf{RF_H} := \mathsf{RF_H}^{(r_k, m) \mapsto y_k}$ $/\!/ G_3$
45   **until** $x_k \neq \bot \vee k \geq B$
46   $r_k := \mathsf{RF_{salt}}(m, B+1)$ $/\!/ G_{5.0}$
47   $\mathsf{RF_H} := \mathsf{RF_H}^{(r_k, m) \mapsto y_k}$ $/\!/ G_4$-$G_{5.0}$
48   **return** (r_k, y_k, x_k)

Fig. 15. Games for EUF-NMA $\Rightarrow$ sEUF-CMA

Lemma 18. *We have*

$$|\Pr[W_2] - \Pr[W_3]| \leq \frac{3}{2} B q_S \sqrt{\frac{q_H + B q_S + 1}{|\mathcal{R}|}}.$$

Proof. The AR adversary $\mathcal{B}_{\mathsf{ar}}$ (see Fig. 10) can simulate G_2 and G_3, where $\mathsf{RF_H}$ is a random function reprogrammed in the AR game. To simulate $\mathsf{GetLogs}$, given m, $\mathcal{B}_{\mathsf{ar}}$ submits m to its oracle REPRO and obtains random $r_k \leftarrow_\$ \mathcal{R}$ until $(x_k \neq \bot) \vee (k \geq B)$. Note that $r_k = \mathsf{RF_{salt}}(m, k)$ is uniformly distributed over $\mathcal{R}$ in both games. Note also that $\mathcal{B}_{\mathsf{ar}}$ can return $\sigma[m]$ without using REPRO if the same m is queried again. Hence, $\mathcal{B}_{\mathsf{ar}}$ can use the oracle's output as the salts in $\mathsf{GetLogs}$. If $\mathcal{B}_{\mathsf{ar}}$ plays AR_0, $\mathsf{RF_H}$ is not reprogrammed; therefore, it can simulate G_2; otherwise $\mathsf{RF_H}$ is reprogrammed for random y and $\mathcal{B}_{\mathsf{ar}}$ can simulates G_3. Therefore, there exists an AR adversary $\mathcal{B}_{\mathsf{ar}}$ such that $|\Pr[W_2] - \Pr[W_3]| \leq \mathsf{Adv}_H^{\mathsf{AR}}(\mathcal{B}_{\mathsf{ar}})$. Since $\mathsf{RF_H}$ is reprogrammed at most $B q_S$ times, we have the bound in this lemma from Lemma 2.

GAME G_4: We cancel the reprogramming executed for intermediate results, and $\mathsf{RF_H}$ is reprogrammed only for the final (r_k, y_k) (see Line 47). By eliminating the need to simulate intermediate results, we are now ready to simulate the signing oracle.

Lemma 19. *We have*

$$|\Pr[W_3] - \Pr[W_4]| \leq 2(q_{\mathsf{H}} + 1)\sqrt{\frac{B-1}{|\mathcal{R}|}}.$$

Proof. The reprogrammings during retries are canceled in G_4. The random function H in G_3 is reprogrammed for each retry attempt, while H in G_4 is reprogrammed only for the final result; therefore, differences of these random functions are all in $\mathcal{S} := \{(r, m) | \exists i \in [k-1], r = r_i\}$ for $\{(r_i, y_i, x_i)\}_{i \in [k]}$ generated inside GetLogs(m). Since the random function is reprogrammed, we use Lemma 4 (O2H with adaptive reprogramming), where we set O as SIGN. Let $\mathcal{B}_{\mathsf{o2h}}$ be an adversary who runs $\mathcal{A}_{\mathsf{cma}}$ in G_4 and finds an element in $\mathcal{S}$. Choosing $i \leftarrow_{\$} [q_{\mathsf{H}}]$, $\mathcal{B}_{\mathsf{o2h}}$ measures the query input register of $\mathcal{A}_{\mathsf{cma}}$ and returns the result. $\mathcal{B}_{\mathsf{o2h}}$ has no information on $\mathcal{S}$ and $\frac{|\mathcal{S}|}{|\mathcal{R} \times \mathcal{M}|} \leq \frac{(B-1)|\mathcal{M}|}{|\mathcal{R}||\mathcal{M}|} = \frac{B-1}{|\mathcal{R}|}$ holds. From Lemma 4, we have this lemma.

GAME $G_{5.0}$: We modify GetLogs in two steps to make it simulatable. Firstly, the value $r_k := \mathsf{RF}_{\mathsf{salt}}(m, k)$ is generated by $\mathsf{RF}_{\mathsf{salt}}(m, B+1)$ in GetLogs. Since both $\mathsf{RF}_{\mathsf{salt}}(m, k)$ and $\mathsf{RF}_{\mathsf{salt}}(m, B+1)$ are uniformly distributed and the adversary can only access outputs of $\mathsf{RF}_{\mathsf{salt}}$ via SIGN, the adversary's view remains unchanged. Consequently, we have $\Pr[W_4] = \Pr[W_{5.0}]$.

GAME $G_{5.1}$: Secondly, we simulate SIGN using SampDom.

Lemma 20. *Suppose that* T *is* (γ, β)-*correct. There exists a PS adversary* $\mathcal{A}_{\mathsf{ps}}$ *of* T *such that*

$$|\Pr[W_{5.0}] - \Pr[W_{5.1}]| \leq \mathsf{Adv}_{\mathsf{T}}^{\mathsf{PS}}(\mathcal{A}_{\mathsf{ps}}) + q_{\mathsf{S}}\left(1 - \gamma\left(1 - \beta^B\right)\right).$$

Proof. We consider the simulation by the PS adversary $\mathcal{A}_{\mathsf{ps}}$. For the signing query, $\mathcal{A}_{\mathsf{ps}}$ returns $r_k := \mathsf{RF}_{\mathsf{salt}}(m, B+1)$ and x_k, which is output by its oracle SAMPLE$_b$. If $\mathcal{A}_{\mathsf{ps}}$ plays PS_1, x_k is generated by SampDom, allowing us to simulate $G_{5.1}$. If $\mathcal{A}_{\mathsf{ps}}$ plays PS_0, we need to account for the possibility that the number of retries exceeds B or that inversion fails ($\mathsf{F}(vk, x_k) \neq y_k$), which we define as $\mathbf{bad}_5$. When $\mathbf{bad}_5$ does not occur, $\mathcal{A}_{\mathsf{ps}}$ simulates $G_{5.1}$. Since $\mathbf{bad}_5$ happens with a probability of at most $q_{\mathsf{S}}(1 - \gamma(1 - \beta^B))$, we have this lemma.

GAME G_6: We change the condition to output $\perp$ from $(m^*, (r^*, x^*)) \in \mathcal{Q}$ to $(m^*, r^*) \in \mathcal{Q}$. As the condition $(m^*, (r^*, x^*)) \notin \mathcal{Q}$ allows for the possibility that H may be reprogrammed on (r^*, m^*), the new condition $(m^*, r^*) \notin \mathcal{Q}$ eliminates that possibility. Then, the EUF-NMA adversary can win its game by submitting $\mathcal{A}_{\mathsf{cma}}$'s output if $\mathcal{A}_{\mathsf{cma}}$ wins G_6.

Lemma 21. *There exists an SPR adversary* $\mathcal{A}_{\mathsf{spr}}$ *of* T *such that*

$$|\Pr[W_{5.1}] - \Pr[W_6]| \leq q_{\mathsf{S}}\mathsf{Adv}_{\mathsf{T}}^{\mathsf{SPR}}(\mathcal{A}_{\mathsf{spr}}).$$

```
𝒜_nma^Ĥ(vk)                                    SIGN(m)
 1  RF_salt ←$ Func(ℳ × [B+1], ℛ)              12  if σ[m] ≠ ∅ then
 2  𝒬 := ∅                                      13  |  return σ[m]
                                                14  (r_k, y_k, x_k) := GetLogs(m)
 3  (m*, (r*, x*)) ← 𝒜_cma^SIGN,|H⟩(vk)         15  if x_k = ⊥ then
 4  if (m*, r*) ∈ 𝒬 then                        16  |  σ[m] := ⊥
 5  |  return ⊥                                  17  |  return ⊥
 6  return (m*, (r*, x*))                        18  σ[m] := (r_k, x_k)
                                                19  𝒬 := 𝒬 ∪ {(m, r_k)}
H(r, m)                                         20  return (r_k, x_k)
 7  if σ[m] ≠ ∅ ∧ σ[m] ≠ ⊥ then
 8  |  (r_k, x_k) := σ[m]                        GetLogs(m)
 9  |  if r = r_k then                           21  r_k := RF_salt(m, B + 1)
10  |  |  return F(vk, x_k)                      22  x_k := SampDom(vk)
11  return Ĥ(r, m)                               23  y_k := F(vk, x_k)
                                                24  return (r_k, y_k, x_k)
```

Fig. 16. Simulation of the modified sEUF-CMA game by EUF-NMA adversary

Proof. $G_{5.1}$ and G_6 differ only if the adversary submits $(m^*, (r^*, x^*))$ such that $(m^*, (r^*, x^*)) \notin \mathcal{Q}$ in $G_{5.1}$, $(m^*, r^*) \in \mathcal{Q}$ in G_6, and $F(vk, x^*) = H(r^*, m^*)$ holds in both games. That is, $r^* = r_k$ and $x^* \neq x_k$, where (r_k, x_k) is generated by SIGN(m^*); therefore, $F(vk, x^*) = F(vk, x_k) = H(r_k, m^*)$ holds. Let $\mathbf{bad}_6$ be such an event and $|\Pr[W_{5.1}] - \Pr[W_6]| \leq \Pr[\mathbf{bad}_6]$ holds.

We show a bound on $\mathbf{bad}_6$ using the SPR game shown in Definition 7. Note that we assume that the distribution of the challenge $\hat{x}$ follows the one of SampDom(vk) in the SPR game. The SPR adversary $\mathcal{A}_{spr}$ simulates G_6 by setting its challenge $\hat{x}$ as the output of SampDom in i-th query to SIGN, where $i \leftarrow_\$ [q_S]$. When $\mathbf{bad}_6$ occurs for $(m^*, (r^*, x^*))$ and m^* is i-th query, $F(vk, x^*) = F(vk, \hat{x}) = H(r^*, m^*)$ holds. Hence, $\mathcal{A}_{spr}$ can win the SPR game by submitting x^* as a second preimage of $\hat{x}$. Since $\mathcal{A}_{spr}$ correctly guesses i with $\frac{1}{q_S}$, $\Pr[\mathbf{bad}_6] \leq q_S \mathrm{Adv}_T^{SPR}(\mathcal{A}_{spr})$ holds.

Then, we can conclude this theorem by bounding $\Pr[W_6]$.

Lemma 22. *There exists an EUF-NMA adversary* $\mathcal{A}_{nma}$ *of* HSR[T, H] *such that*
$$\Pr[W_6] \leq \mathrm{Adv}_{HSR}^{EUF\text{-}NMA}(\mathcal{A}_{nma}).$$

Proof. The EUF-NMA adversary $\mathcal{A}_{nma}$ with oracle access to Ĥ can simulate G_6 as in Fig. 16. Note that $\mathcal{A}_{nma}$ sets $H = \hat{H}$ and outputs of H and $\hat{H}$ differ for reprogrammed points. To simulate the reprogramming in the execution of SIGN, $H(r, m)$ outputs $F(vk, x_k)$ for $(r_k, x_k) = \sigma[m]$ if $r = r_k$ holds (see Lines 7 to 10). When $\mathcal{A}_{cma}$ wins the game by submitting $(m^*, (r^*, x^*))$, $H(r^*, m^*)$ is not reprogrammed from $(m^*, r^*) \notin \mathcal{Q}$. Therefore, $F(vk, x^*) = \hat{H}(r^*, m^*)$ holds and $\mathcal{A}_{nma}$ can win the game by submitting $(m^*, (r^*, x^*))$.

□

The EUF-CMA security does not require second-preimage resistance of T as follows:

Corollary 3 (EUF-NMA + PS + PRF ⇒ EUF-CMA). *For any quantum EUF-CMA adversary $\mathcal{A}_{\mathsf{cma}}$ of* $\mathsf{DHSR}_B[\mathsf{T}, \mathsf{H}, \mathsf{PRF}, \mathsf{PRF}']$ *issuing at most q_{H} quantum queries to* H *and q_{S} quantum queries to* SIGN, *there exist an EUF-NMA adversary $\mathcal{A}_{\mathsf{nma}}$ of* $\mathsf{HSR}[\mathsf{T}, \mathsf{H}]$, *a PS adversary $\mathcal{A}_{\mathsf{ps}}$ issuing at most q_{S} queries, and PRF adversaries $\mathcal{A}_{\mathsf{prf}}$ of* PRF *and $\mathcal{A}'_{\mathsf{prf}}$ of* PRF' *issuing at most Bq_{S} queries such that*

$$\mathrm{Adv}_{\mathsf{DHSR}}^{\mathrm{EUF\text{-}CMA}}(\mathcal{A}_{\mathsf{cma}}) \leq \mathrm{Adv}_{\mathsf{HSR}}^{\mathrm{EUF\text{-}NMA}}(\mathcal{A}_{\mathsf{nma}}) + \mathrm{Adv}_{\mathsf{T}}^{\mathrm{PS}}(\mathcal{A}_{\mathsf{ps}}) + \mathrm{Adv}_{\mathsf{PRF}}^{\mathrm{PRF}}(\mathcal{A}_{\mathsf{prf}})$$
$$+ \mathrm{Adv}_{\mathsf{PRF}'}^{\mathrm{PRF}}(\mathcal{A}'_{\mathsf{prf}}) + q_{\mathsf{S}}\left(1 - \gamma\left(1 - \beta^B\right)\right)$$
$$+ \frac{3}{2}Bq_{\mathsf{S}}\sqrt{\frac{q_{\mathsf{H}} + Bq_{\mathsf{S}} + 1}{|\mathcal{R}|}} + 2(q_{\mathsf{H}} + 1)\sqrt{\frac{B-1}{|\mathcal{R}|}},$$

where T *is (γ, β)-correct and the running times of $\mathcal{A}_{\mathsf{nma}}$, $\mathcal{A}_{\mathsf{ps}}$, $\mathcal{A}_{\mathsf{prf}}$, and $\mathcal{A}'_{\mathsf{prf}}$ are about that of $\mathcal{A}_{\mathsf{cma}}$.*

Proof. Since $\mathcal{Q}$ stores only messages, if $m^* \notin \mathcal{Q}$, then $\mathsf{RF}_{\mathsf{H}}(r^*, m^*)$ is not reprogrammed in the proof of Theorem 3. Therefore, we can skip the last game G_6 and the second-preimage resistance of T is not required for EUF-CMA security. □

Remark 2. We compare the result with the existing proof for the original HSwR by Kosuge and Xagawa [19]. First, we improve the tightness utilizing the derandomization with bounded loop. The security bound of the original HSwR shown in [19] is as follows.

$$\mathrm{Adv}_{\mathsf{HSwR}}^{\mathrm{(s)EUF\text{-}CMA}}(\mathcal{A}_{\mathsf{cma}}) \leq \mathrm{Adv}_{\mathsf{HSwR}}^{\mathrm{EUF\text{-}NMA}}(\mathcal{A}_{\mathsf{nma}}) + \mathrm{Adv}_{\mathsf{T}}^{\mathrm{PS}}(\mathcal{A}_{\mathsf{ps}})$$
$$+ \frac{3}{2}q'_{\mathsf{S}}\sqrt{\frac{q_{\mathsf{H}} + q'_{\mathsf{S}} + 1}{|\mathcal{R}|}} + 2(q_{\mathsf{H}} + 2)\sqrt{\frac{q'_{\mathsf{S}} - q_{\mathsf{S}}}{|\mathcal{R}|}},$$

where q'_{S} is a bound on the total number of retries during q_{S} signing queries ($q'_{\mathsf{S}} \leq Bq_{\mathsf{S}}$ holds in DHSwBR). The last term is replaced with $2(q_{\mathsf{H}}+1)\sqrt{\frac{B-1}{|\mathcal{R}|}}$ in Theorem 3 and Corollary 3. However, as a drawback, the PRF advantage (due to the derandomization) and the probability that no valid signature is generated in signing queries (due to the bounded loop) are added to the security bound. These terms become negligible when well-evaluated PRFs are used and B is set appropriately based on the failing probability β.

Second, we relax the condition of T required for the sEUF-CMA security from *injection* to second-preimage-resistance, where this relaxation is also applied to the original HSwR.

References

1. Alagic, G., Majenz, C., Russell, A., Song, F.: Quantum-access-secure message authentication via blind-unforgeability. In: Canteaut, A., Ishai, Y. (eds.) EURO-CRYPT 2020, Part III. LNCS, vol. 12107, pp. 788–817. Springer, Cham (2020). https://doi.org/10.1007/978-3-030-45727-3_27

2. Ambainis, A., Hamburg, M., Unruh, D.: Quantum security proofs using semi-classical oracles. In: Boldyreva, A., Micciancio, D. (eds.) CRYPTO 2019, Part II. LNCS, vol. 11693, pp. 269–295. Springer, Cham (2019). https://doi.org/10.1007/978-3-030-26951-7_10

3. Bellare, M., Rogaway, P.: Random oracles are practical: a paradigm for designing efficient protocols. In: Denning, D.E., Pyle, R., Ganesan, R., Sandhu, R.S., Ashby, V. (eds.) ACM CCS 1993, pp. 62–73. ACM Press (1993). https://doi.org/10.1145/168588.168596

4. Bellare, M., Rogaway, P.: The exact security of digital signatures-how to sign with RSA and Rabin. In: Maurer, U. (ed.) EUROCRYPT 1996. LNCS, vol. 1070, pp. 399–416. Springer, Heidelberg (1996). https://doi.org/10.1007/3-540-68339-9_34

5. Boneh, D., Dagdelen, Ö., Fischlin, M., Lehmann, A., Schaffner, C., Zhandry, M.: Random oracles in a quantum world. In: Lee, D.H., Wang, X. (eds.) ASIACRYPT 2011. LNCS, vol. 7073, pp. 41–69. Springer, Heidelberg (2011). https://doi.org/10.1007/978-3-642-25385-0_3

6. Boneh, D., Zhandry, M.: Secure signatures and chosen ciphertext security in a quantum computing world. In: Canetti, R., Garay, J.A. (eds.) CRYPTO 2013, Part II. LNCS, vol. 8043, pp. 361–379. Springer, Heidelberg (2013). https://doi.org/10.1007/978-3-642-40084-1_21

7. Chatterjee, R., Chung, K.M., Liang, X., Malavolta, G.: A note on the post-quantum security of (ring) signatures. In: Hanaoka, G., Shikata, J., Watanabe, Y. (eds.) PKC 2022, Part II. LNCS, vol. 13178, pp. 407–436. Springer, Cham (2022). https://doi.org/10.1007/978-3-030-97131-1_14

8. Cogliati, B., Fouque, P.A., Goubin, L., Minaud, B.: New security proofs and techniques for hash-and-sign with retry signature schemes. Cryptology ePrint Archive, Report 2024/609 (2024). https://eprint.iacr.org/2024/609

9. Devevey, J., Fallahpour, P., Passelègue, A., Stehlé, D.: A detailed analysis of Fiat-Shamir with aborts. In: Handschuh, H., Lysyanskaya, A. (eds.) CRYPTO 2023, Part V. LNCS, vol. 14085, pp. 327–357. Springer, Cham (2023). https://doi.org/10.1007/978-3-031-38554-4_11

10. Fiat, A., Shamir, A.: How to prove yourself: practical solutions to identification and signature problems. In: Odlyzko, A.M. (ed.) CRYPTO 1986. LNCS, vol. 263, pp. 186–194. Springer, Heidelberg (1987). https://doi.org/10.1007/3-540-47721-7_12

11. Furue, H., et al.: QR-UOV. Technical report, National Institute of Standards and Technology (2023). https://csrc.nist.gov/Projects/pqc-dig-sig/round-1-additional-signatures

12. Gentry, C., Peikert, C., Vaikuntanathan, V.: Trapdoors for hard lattices and new cryptographic constructions. In: Ladner, R.E., Dwork, C. (eds.) 40th ACM STOC, pp. 197–206. ACM Press (2008). https://doi.org/10.1145/1374376.1374407

13. Goldwasser, S., Micali, S., Rivest, R.L.: A digital signature scheme secure against adaptive chosen-message attacks. SIAM J. Comput. **17**(2), 281–308 (1988). https://doi.org/10.1137/0217017

14. Goubin, L., et al.: PROV — PRovable unbalanced Oil and Vinegar. Technical report, National Institute of Standards and Technology (2023). https://csrc.nist.gov/Projects/pqc-dig-sig/round-1-additional-signatures

15. Grilo, A.B., Hövelmanns, K., Hülsing, A., Majenz, C.: Tight adaptive reprogramming in the QROM. In: Tibouchi, M., Wang, H. (eds.) ASIACRYPT 2021. LNCS, vol. 13090, pp. 637–667. Springer, Cham (2021). https://doi.org/10.1007/978-3-030-92062-3_22

16. Hosoyamada, A., Yasuda, K.: Building quantum-one-way functions from block ciphers: Davies-Meyer and Merkle-Damgård constructions. In: Peyrin, T., Galbraith, S. (eds.) ASIACRYPT 2018, Part I. LNCS, vol. 11272, pp. 275–304. Springer, Cham (2018). https://doi.org/10.1007/978-3-030-03326-2_10

17. Hülsing, A., Rijneveld, J., Song, F.: Mitigating multi-target attacks in hash-based signatures. In: Cheng, C.-M., Chung, K.-M., Persiano, G., Yang, B.-Y. (eds.) PKC 2016, Part I. LNCS, vol. 9614, pp. 387–416. Springer, Heidelberg (2016). https://doi.org/10.1007/978-3-662-49384-7_15

18. Kiltz, E., Lyubashevsky, V., Schaffner, C.: A concrete treatment of Fiat-Shamir signatures in the quantum random-oracle model. In: Nielsen, J.B., Rijmen, V. (eds.) EUROCRYPT 2018. LNCS, vol. 10822, pp. 552–586. Springer, Cham (2018). https://doi.org/10.1007/978-3-319-78372-7_18

19. Kosuge, H., Xagawa, K.: Probabilistic hash-and-sign with retry in the quantum random oracle model. In: Tang, Q., Teague, V. (eds.) PKC 2024, Part I. LNCS, vol. 14601, pp. 259–288. Springer, Cham (2024). https://doi.org/10.1007/978-3-031-57718-5_9

20. Lyubashevsky, V.: Fiat-Shamir with aborts: applications to lattice and factoring-based signatures. In: Matsui, M. (ed.) ASIACRYPT 2009. LNCS, vol. 5912, pp. 598–616. Springer, Heidelberg (2009). https://doi.org/10.1007/978-3-642-10366-7_35

21. NIST: Call for additional digital signature schemes for the post-quantum cryptography standardization process (2022). https://csrc.nist.gov/csrc/media/Projects/pqc-dig-sig/documents/call-for-proposals-dig-sig-sept-2022.pdf

22. NIST: Status report on the third round of the NIST post-quantum cryptography standardization process (2022). https://csrc.nist.gov/publications/detail/nistir/8413/final

23. Sakumoto, K., Shirai, T., Hiwatari, H.: On provable security of UOV and HFE signature schemes against chosen-message attack. In: Yang, B.-Y. (ed.) PQCrypto 2011. LNCS, vol. 7071, pp. 68–82. Springer, Heidelberg (2011). https://doi.org/10.1007/978-3-642-25405-5_5

24. Shor, P.W.: Algorithms for quantum computation: discrete logarithms and factoring. In: 35th FOCS, pp. 124–134. IEEE Computer Society Press (1994). https://doi.org/10.1109/SFCS.1994.365700

25. Unruh, D.: Revocable quantum timed-release encryption. In: Nguyen, P.Q., Oswald, E. (eds.) EUROCRYPT 2014. LNCS, vol. 8441, pp. 129–146. Springer, Heidelberg (2014). https://doi.org/10.1007/978-3-642-55220-5_8

26. Xagawa, K.: Signatures with memory-tight security in the quantum random oracle model. In: Joye, M., Leander, G. (eds.) EUROCRYPT 2024, Part VII. LNCS, vol. 14657, pp. 30–58. Springer, Cham (2024). https://doi.org/10.1007/978-3-031-58754-2_2

27. Yuan, Q., Sun, C., Takagi, T.: Revisiting the security of Fiat-Shamir signature schemes under superposition attacks. In: Zhu, T., Li, Y. (eds.) ACISP 2024, Part II. LNCS, vol. 14896, pp. 164–184. Springer, Heidelberg (2024). https://doi.org/10.1007/978-981-97-5028-3_9

28. Zhandry, M.: How to construct quantum random functions. In: 53rd FOCS. pp. 679–687. IEEE Computer Society Press (Oct 2012). https://doi.org/10.1109/FOCS.2012.37

29. Zhandry, M.: Secure identity-based encryption in the quantum random oracle model. In: Safavi-Naini, R., Canetti, R. (eds.) CRYPTO 2012. LNCS, vol. 7417, pp. 758–775. Springer, Berlin, Heidelberg (Aug 2012). https://doi.org/10.1007/978-3-642-32009-5_44

Proofs and Arguments

Split Prover Zero-Knowledge SNARKs

Sanjam Garg[1], Aarushi Goel[2], Dimitris Kolonelos[1(✉)], Sina Shiehian[3],
and Rohit Sinha[4]

[1] UC Berkeley, Berkeley, USA
{sanjamg,dimitris.kolonelos}@berkeley.edu
[2] Purdue University, West Lafayette, USA
[3] Snap Inc., Santa Monica, USA
shiayan@umich.edu
[4] Swirlds Labs, Dallas, USA

Abstract. We initiate the study of *split prover zkSNARKs*, which allow
Alice to offload part of the zkSNARK computation to her assistant, Bob.
In scenarios like online transactions (e.g., zCash), a significant portion
of the witness (e.g., membership proofs of input coins) is often available
to the prover (Alice) before the transaction begins. This setup offers an
opportunity to Alice to initiate the proof computation early, even before
the entire witness is available. The remaining computation can then be
delegated to Bob, who can complete it once the final witness (e.g., the
transaction amount) is known.

To prevent Bob from generating proofs independently (e.g., initiating
unauthorized transactions), it is essential that the data provided to him
for the second phase of computation does not reveal the witness used
in the first phase. Additionally, the verifier of the zkSNARK should be
unable to determine whether the proof was generated solely by Alice
or through this two-step process. To achieve this efficiently, we require
this two-phase proof generation to only use cryptography in a black-box
manner.

We propose a split prover zkSNARK based on the Groth16 zkSNARKs
[Groth, EUROCRYPT 2016], meeting all these requirements. Our solution is also *asymptotically tight*, meaning it achieves the optimal second
phase proof generation time for Groth16. Importantly, our split prover
zkSNARK preserves the verification algorithm of the original Groth16
zkSNARK, enabling seamless integration into existing deployments of
Groth16.

1 Introduction

Zero-knowledge succinct non-interactive arguments of knowledge (zkSNARKs)
[5,29] are cryptographic tools that allow a prover to generate a compact certificate validating the correctness of a potentially complex computation. These
certificates are efficient to verify and protect any secrets used by the prover
during the computation. zkSNARKs have found utility in various modern cryptographic applications. Investigating the feasibility of zkSNARKs in different

© International Association for Cryptologic Research 2025
T. Jager and J. Pan (Eds.): PKC 2025, LNCS 15674, pp. 353–380, 2025.
https://doi.org/10.1007/978-3-031-91820-9_12

models, under diverse security assumptions, and realizing them efficiently has been an active area of research in recent years.

In this work, we explore a new *prover model* for generating zkSNARKs. Consider a scenario where Alice wants to perform an online transaction (e.g., in zCash [3]). She knows part of the witness (e.g., her private key, membership proof of input coins, upper bound on the transaction amount) needed to generate a zkSNARK for the transaction, but the exact transaction amount is not yet known. Additionally, Alice might be unavailable when the transaction amount becomes known. We ask whether Alice can initiate the zkSNARK computation using the available information and delegate the remaining computation to her assistant, Bob, who can complete it once the transaction amount is determined.

A similar application involves anonymous credentials. For instance, Alice needs electronic authorization for international travel and must prove, using a zkSNARK, that she holds a valid US passport. Can she start the zkSNARK computation using her passport and delegate the remaining computation to Bob, who can finalize it once the travel dates are confirmed?

In these applications, it is crucial to ensure that Bob cannot independently generate unauthorized proofs. The data sent to Bob for the second phase of proof computation must not disclose any part of the witness used in the first phase. Moreover, for seamless integration into existing systems, the verifier receiving the final zkSNARK should not be able to tell whether the proof was generated solely by Alice or through a delegated two-step process. Finally, for efficiency, we require the final proof to be succinct and the two-phase proof generation to only use cryptographic operations in a black-box manner.[1]

In other words, we aim to determine the following:

Is it possible to generate zkSNARKs in two-phases using cryptography in a black-box way, while ensuring that the output of the first phase preserves privacy?

1.1   Our Contributions

In this work, we answer the above question in the affirmative and present the following contributions.

Defining Split Prover zkSNARKs. We introduce the notion of split prover zkSNARKs which enable proof generation to be divided into two phases. Simply put, this means that the secret witness w associated with the statement being proven, can be divided into two segments – one for each phase. By utilizing the first segment to commence proof generation, the remaining zkSNARK computation can be delegated to an external entity, who only needs the second segment of the witness to finalize the proof.

A key requirement here is that even with this two-phase prover setup, the zkSNARK verifier algorithm should remain unchanged. We further require that

---

[1] We defer the reader to Sect. 1.3, for discussion on the disadvantages of a non-black box approach.

the state that is generated in the first phase (and given as input to the external entity for delegation of the second phase) should reveal no information beyond the output of the relation circuit when partially evaluated using the first segment of the witness.

Split Prover zkSNARK Based on Groth16. Next, we present a split prover zkSNARK based on the widely used Groth16 zkSNARK [21] (henceforth referred to as Groth16). More concretely, let C to be any circuit defining an NP relation $\mathcal{R}$ and let C_1 and C_2 be the subcircuits of C corresponding to the two segments of the witness. Then, for a witness $w = (w_\mathrm{I}, w_\mathrm{II})$ and statement $x = (x_\mathrm{I}, x_\mathrm{II})$ split into two segments, we can write $C = C_\mathrm{II}(x_\mathrm{II}, w_\mathrm{II}, C_\mathrm{I}(x_\mathrm{I}, w_\mathrm{I}))$. We obtain the following result:

Informal Theorem 1. *Groth16 admits a split prover, where,*

- *the first phase of proof generation runs in time $O(|C_I| \cdot |C| \log |C|)$,[2]*
- *the second phase of proof generation runs in time $O(\mathsf{Min}\{|C_{II}|^2, |C| \log |C|\})$,[3] and*
- *the verifier algorithm is identical[4] to the Groth16 proof system.*

In the above theorem, if $|C_\mathrm{II}| \in o(\sqrt{|C|})$, then the second phase of proof generation runs in time $O(|C_\mathrm{II}|^2)$. Else, if $|C_\mathrm{II}| \in \Omega(\sqrt{|C|})$, then the second phase of proof generation runs in time $O(|C| \log |C|)$.

Lower Bound for Split Prover Groth16. Since group operations are the main bottleneck in the generation of Groth16 SNARKs, we characterize the number of group operations that must be performed during the second phase of proof generation in any split prover variant of Groth16.

Informal Theorem 2. *In any split prover variant for Groth16, the second phase of proof generation must involve $\Omega(\mathsf{Min}\{|C_{II}|^2, |C|\})$ group operations.*

This shows that the number of group operations performed in the second phase of proof generation in our protocol from Theorem 1 is asymptotically tight.

---

[2] This includes both group and field operations. The total number of group operations performed by the prover in the first phase are $O(|C_\mathrm{I}| \cdot |C|)$ and in the second phase are $O(\mathsf{Min}\{|C_\mathrm{II}|^2, |C|\})$.

[3] This includes both group and field operations. The total number of group operations performed by the prover in the first phase are $O(|C_\mathrm{I}| \cdot |C|)$ and in the second phase are $O(\mathsf{Min}\{|C_\mathrm{II}|^2, |C|\})$.

[4] In Groth16, the common reference string (CRS) can be split into two parts – one for the prover and one for the verifier. While the verifier's part remains unchanged, our split prover adaptation of Groth16 requires the inclusion of some extra terms in the prover's section of the CRS.

1.2   Application to Delegatable Payments and Beyond

As discussed earlier, our work is motivated by applications of zkSNARKs, where the witness can be partitioned into two segments – one accessible to the prover apriori, and the other disclosed later when the prover may be unavailable. This situation presents an opportunity for the prover to initiate the zkSNARK computation using available information and delegate the remaining tasks to an external entity. Now, we delve into how this witness division applies specifically to Zerocash [3] proofs for anonymous payments, enabling a prover to leverage our split prover zkSNARK to delegate a portion of the computation to an external entity.

Consider a simplified version of the zCash[5] [23] JoinSplit transaction. A JoinSplit transaction lets a payer consume two coins and create two new coins – typically, one output coin is issued to the payee, while the other output coin has the left-over change and is issued back to the payer. In Zerocash, a coin is spent (or nullified) by revealing its serial number, while a new coin is created by publishing a (randomized) commitment to a data structure containing the coin's value and the owner's public key. The payment is settled on-chain by submitting a transaction containing $(\mathsf{sn}_1, \mathsf{sn}_2, \mathsf{cm}_1', \mathsf{cm}_2', \pi)$; here, sn_1 and sn_2 denote serial numbers for spent coins, while commitments cm_1' and cm_2' denote the new output coins. Finally, a zero-knowledge proof π attests to the transaction's validity, and it has the following basic form (using the notation and naming in [3]):

- **public variables**: root, sn_1, sn_2, cm_1', cm_2'
- **secret witness**:
  $\mathsf{cm}_1, \mathsf{v}_1, \mathsf{r}_1, \mathsf{s}_1, \rho_1, \mathsf{apk}_1, \mathsf{ask}_1, \mathsf{h}_1^1, \ldots, \mathsf{h}_1^{31}$
  $\mathsf{cm}_2, \mathsf{v}_2, \mathsf{r}_2, \mathsf{s}_2, \rho_2, \mathsf{apk}_2, \mathsf{ask}_2, \mathsf{h}_2^1, \ldots, \mathsf{h}_2^{31}$
  $\mathsf{v}_1', \mathsf{r}_1', \mathsf{s}_1', \rho_1', \mathsf{apk}_1'$
  $\mathsf{v}_2', \mathsf{r}_2', \mathsf{s}_2', \rho_2', \mathsf{apk}_2'$
- **relation**: conjunction of the following five predicates:
  - membership proof that the spent coins were created previously on ledger:
    $\mathsf{MerkleVerify}(\mathsf{root}, \mathsf{cm}_1, \mathsf{h}_1^1, \ldots, \mathsf{h}_1^{31}) \land \mathsf{MerkleVerify}(\mathsf{root}, \mathsf{cm}_2, \mathsf{h}_2^1, \ldots, \mathsf{h}_2^{31})$
  - well-formedness of the data structures encoding the spent coins:
    $\mathsf{cm}_1 = \mathsf{Com}(\mathsf{v}_1, \mathsf{Com}(\mathsf{apk}_1, \rho_1; \mathsf{s}_1); \mathsf{r}_1) \land \mathsf{cm}_2 = \mathsf{Com}(\mathsf{v}_2, \mathsf{Com}(\mathsf{apk}_2, \rho_2; \mathsf{s}_2); \mathsf{r}_2)$
  - ownership of spent coins (via knowledge of openings to commitments):
    $\mathsf{sn}_1 = \mathsf{PRF}(\rho_1; \mathsf{ask}_1) \land \mathsf{apk}_1 = \mathsf{PRF}(0; \mathsf{ask}_1) \land$
    $\mathsf{sn}_2 = \mathsf{PRF}(\rho_2; \mathsf{ask}_2) \land \mathsf{apk}_2 = \mathsf{PRF}(0; \mathsf{ask}_2)$
  - well-formedness of the data structures encoding the new output coins:
    $\mathsf{cm}_1' = \mathsf{Com}(\mathsf{v}_1', \mathsf{Com}(\mathsf{apk}_1', \rho_1'; \mathsf{s}_1'); \mathsf{r}_1') \land$
    $\mathsf{cm}_2' = \mathsf{Com}(\mathsf{v}_2', \mathsf{Com}(\mathsf{apk}_2', \rho_2'; \mathsf{s}_2'); \mathsf{r}_2')$
  - conservation of value: $\mathsf{v}_1 + \mathsf{v}_2 = \mathsf{v}_1' + \mathsf{v}_2'$

---

[5] zCash [23] is a cryptocurrency that deploys the academic work Zerocash [3]. Although, prior versions of zCash were instantiating the zkSNARK component with Groth16 its current implementation has switched to a different SNARK [37]. Our work is still compatible with the cryptographic framework of Zerocash for anonymous transactions.

For simplicity, we hide details such as range checks, viewership keys, etc. Above, we use blue to indicate values available and constraints that can be evaluated by the prover (i.e., delegator) before the transaction amount is known. We let the payer's device choose two of her coins to join for the transaction before she engages in a payment; in practice, this could be the two coins whose cumulative value is the largest, or at least exceeds some expected payment amount. Therefore, the delegator is able to evaluate the arithmetic circuit wires corresponding to the two Merkle verifications; the delegator can also perform the computation necesssary for proving well-formedness and ownership of those spent coins. The commitments to the new coins are determined in later, as are the constraints enforcing the value conservation. As a result, the computation needed for enforcing these constraints and for proving well-formedness of the data structures encoding the new output coins can be delegated to someone else.

Other Applications. In addition to anonymous transaction, we observe this witness split in other classes of applications. In anonymous credentials, the user can prove validity of an issued credential on his own, before delegating the commputation necessary for proving additional properties about the credential to an external entity – we find [31] to be a system which can use the split prover Groth16 construction in this paper. Additionally, applications that need validity proofs for ciphertexts (e.g. [22]), encrypted under a hybrid encryption scheme, can also benefit from our split prover zkSNARK, since the component of the circuit encoding the key encapsulation mechanism can be evaluated long before the message to be encrypted is determined.

1.3   Additional Discussion

Comparison with Recursive SNARKs. An astute reader might wonder how our notion of split prover zkSNARKs relates to the well-studied notion of incrementally verifiable computation (IVC) [34] and, whether recursive zkSNARKs [4,6, 25] – which are used to construct IVCs – could also be utilized to design split prover zkSNARKs. We note that while the IVCs and split prover zkSNARKs bear some similarities, these are distinct notions.

Compared to our split prover zkSNARKs, IVCs have two advantages. First, IVCs allow the proof to be computed in any number of phases (potentially even greater than two). Second, in each phase of IVC, the prover's runtime is proportional to the portion of the computation being proven in that phase, whereas in our construction of split prover zkSNARK, the second phase of proof generation scales with the entire computation.[6]

However, these advantages come at the cost of providing only a theoretically questionable heuristic soundness guarantee, due to the use of idealized oracles such as the random oracle or the generic group model in a non-black-box manner. Such non-black-box use of the random oracle, in general, has recently been shown

---

[6] Unless the the second segment of the witness is small, $|C_{II}| = o(\sqrt{|C|})$, as indicated in Informal Theorem 1.

to be insecure [2]. In contrast, our split prover zkSNARK inherits the same soundness guarantees that Groth16 provides, which can be established in well studied idealized models [16,33]. In contrast, our construction is black-box in the use of cryptography. Another advantage of our split prover zkSNARK is that the verifier algorithm does not depend on how the computation is split into the two phases. In comparison, in IVCs, verification depends on the specific splitting of the computation. Therefore, it is unclear how to use recursive proofs to design a zkSNARK that meets all the requirements of a split prover zkSNARK.

Comparison with Other zkSNARK Delegation Frameworks. An orthogonal problem to ours involves delegating zkSNARK computation to third-party cloud servers to ease the burden of proof computation on provers. This topic has been explored in several prior works [11,13,18,19,27,35]. Unlike our model, in these works, the delegator possesses the entire witness at the time of delegating the computation. While some of these works [11,35] do not focus on privacy-preserving delegation, others either [13,18,27] use MPC for privacy-preserving distributed delegation to multiple servers or rely [19] on the heavy-hammer of fully-homomorphic encryptio (FHE) to ensure privacy.

Barriers for zkSNARKs in the Random Oracle Model. Given our construction for Groth16, a natural question arises as to whether we can extend our techniques to construct split prover versions of other zkSNARKs, namely those in the random oracle model [7–10,12,14,17,24,26,32,36,38]. These zkSNARKs are popular because they have a universal setup and some of them (e.g. [17]) also provide support for flexible gates. Most of these zkSNARKs are obtained by transforming an interactive public-coin protocol into its non-interactive counterpart using the Fiat-Shamir [15] transform. Unfortunately, this incorporation of the Fiat-Shamir transform in these zkSNARKs appears to present an obstacle for us, when it comes to applying our techniques.

Roughly speaking, the main problem is that when the delegator computes a part of the proof apriori, it is unclear how the verifier's challenge messages can be derived. In particular, when applying the Fiat-Shamir transform, the verifier's challenges are derived by querying the random oracle at inputs that depend on the "entire computation" and not just a part of the witness. As such it is unclear what parts of the proof can be pre-computed, without knowledge of these challenge messages. We leave the exploration of new techniques to design split provers for such zkSNARKs as exciting future work.

2   Preliminaries

Notation. Throughout this work, we use $\lambda \in \mathbb{N}$ to denote the security parameter and we assume that each algorithm implicitly takes the security parameter as input. poly and $\mathsf{negl}(\lambda)$ will be used to denote polynomial and negligible functions respectively. We use "PPT" to refer to Probabilistic Polynomial-time Algorithms, and unless otherwise stated all the algorithms of our schemes are such. For any positive integer $n \in \mathbb{Z}$ $[n]$ denotes the set of integers $\{1, \ldots, n\}$ and, more generally, for any $A, B \in \mathbb{Z}$, $A \leq B$, $[A, B]$ denotes the set $\{A, \ldots, B\}$. $x \leftarrow_{\$} X$ is used to imply that x is being uniformly sampled from a finite set X.

We write vectors with bold small letters, e.g. $\boldsymbol{v}$ and with bold capital letters matrices, e.g. $\boldsymbol{A}$. We treat vectors as column matrices, e.g. $\boldsymbol{v} = (v_1 \ v_2 \ \ldots \ v_n)^\top$. We also sometimes write concisely $\boldsymbol{v} = (v_i)_{i \in [n]}$ for vectors or $\boldsymbol{A} = (a_{i,j})_{i \in [n], j \in [m]}$ for matrices.

By $\left\lfloor \frac{f(X)}{g(X)} \right\rfloor$ we denote the quotient polynomial of the division $f(X)/g(X)$. We denote the i-th coefficient of a polynomial $f(X)$ as $\tilde{f}_i$, e.g. $\kappa_5(X) = \tilde{\kappa}_{5,0} + \tilde{\kappa}_{5,1} X + \ldots + \tilde{\kappa}_{5,n} X^n$. By $\boldsymbol{f}(X)$ we denote a vector of polynomials, $\boldsymbol{f}(X) = (f_1(X), f_2(X), \ldots, f_n(X))^\top$. $\tilde{\boldsymbol{f}}_i$ denotes the vector of the corresponding i-th coefficients, i.e. $\tilde{\boldsymbol{f}}_i = (\tilde{f}_{1,i}, \tilde{f}_{2,i}, \ldots, \tilde{f}_{n,i})^\top$. Similarly with $\boldsymbol{F}(X)$ a matrix of polynomials. $L_i(X) = \prod_{j \in [n], j \neq i} \frac{X - \omega^j}{\omega^i - \omega^j}$ will be the lagrange polynomial over a group $\{\omega, \omega^2, \ldots, \omega^n\}$ and $V(x) = \prod_{i=1}^{\ell}(x - \omega^i)$ the vanishing polynomial.

2.1 Bilinear Groups

A bilinear group generator $\mathcal{BG}$ takes as input a security parameter 1^λ and outputs a description $\mathsf{bg} := (p, \mathbb{G}_1, \mathbb{G}_2, \mathbb{G}_T, g_1, g_2, e)$, where p is a prime of $\Theta(\lambda)$ bits, $\mathbb{G}_1$, $\mathbb{G}_2$ and $\mathbb{G}_T$ are cyclic groups of order p, and $e : \mathbb{G}_1 \times \mathbb{G}_2 \to \mathbb{G}_T$ is a non-degenerate bilinear map. We require that the group operations in $\mathbb{G}_1$, $\mathbb{G}_2$, $\mathbb{G}_T$ and the bilinear map e are computable in deterministic polynomial time in λ. Let $g_1 \in \mathbb{G}_1$, $g_2 \in \mathbb{G}_2$ and $g_T = e(g_1, g_2) \in \mathbb{G}_T$ be the respective generators. We employ the *implicit representation* of group elements: for a matrix $\boldsymbol{M}$ over $\mathbb{Z}_p$, we define $[\boldsymbol{M}]_1 := g_1^{\boldsymbol{M}}, [\boldsymbol{M}]_2 := g_2^{\boldsymbol{M}}, [\boldsymbol{M}]_T := g_T^{\boldsymbol{M}}$, where exponentiation is carried out component-wise.

2.2 Zero-Knowledge Succinct Non-interactive Arguments of Knowledge

Here we recall the definition of zkSNARKs.

Definition 1 (zkSNARKs). *A SNARK for a family of relations R_λ consists of three algorithms* (Setup, P, V):

Setup($\mathcal{R}$) → (srs) : *On input a relation $\mathcal{R} \in R_\lambda$ the setup algorithm outputs a structured reference string* srs.

P(srs, x, w) → π : *On input the structured reference string* srs, *a statement x and a witness w the prover algorithm outputs a proof π.*

V(srs, x, π) → 0/1 : *On input the structured reference string* srs, *a statement x and a proof π the verifier algorithm outputs either 1 for accept or 0 for reject.*

It is further required that the following properties hold.

Correctness. *For each $\lambda \in \mathbb{N}$, each relation $\mathcal{R} \in R_\lambda$, and every statement-witness pair $(x, w) \in \mathcal{R}$:*

$$\Pr\left[V(\text{srs}, x, \pi) = 1 : \begin{array}{l} \text{srs} \leftarrow \text{Setup}(\mathcal{R}) \\ \pi \leftarrow P(\text{srs}, x, w) \end{array} \right] = 1$$

Knowledge Soundness. *For every PPT adversarial prover P^*, there exists a PPT extractor $\mathcal{E}_{P^*}$ such that for every security parameter $\lambda \in \mathbb{N}$, every auxiliary input $\text{aux} \in \{0,1\}^{poly}$, and every relation $\mathcal{R} \in R_\lambda$:*

$$\Pr\left[\begin{array}{l} V(\text{srs}, x, \pi) = 1 \\ \wedge (x, w) \notin \mathcal{R} \end{array} : \begin{array}{l} \text{srs} \leftarrow \text{Setup}(\mathcal{R}) \\ (x, \pi)^* \leftarrow P^*(\text{srs}, \text{aux}) \\ w \leftarrow \mathcal{E}_{P^*}(\text{srs}, \text{aux}) \end{array} \right] = negl(\lambda)$$

Succinctness. *There exists a universal polynomial $p(\cdot)$ such that, for every security parameter $\lambda \in \mathbb{N}$, every relation $\mathcal{R} \in R_\lambda$, and every statement-witness pair (x, w):*

- *An honestly generated proof π has size $p(\lambda + \log |w|)$.*
- *The verifier algorithm $V(\text{srs}, x, \pi)$ runs in time $p(\lambda + |x| + \log |w|)$.*

(Perfect) Zero-Knowledge. *For every security parameter $\lambda \in \mathbb{N}$ and every relation $(\mathcal{R}, \text{aux}_R) \leftarrow R_\lambda$, there exists a simulator $\mathcal{S}$ such that, for every statement-witness pair $(x, w) \in \mathcal{R}$ and for every computationally unbounded adversary $\mathcal{A}$:*

$$\Pr\left[\mathcal{A}(R, \text{aux}_R, \text{srs}, \pi) = 1 : \begin{array}{l} \text{srs} \leftarrow \text{Setup}(\mathcal{R}) \\ \pi \leftarrow P(\text{srs}, x, w) \end{array} \right]$$
$$= \Pr\left[\mathcal{A}(R, \text{aux}_R, \text{srs}, \pi) = 1 : (\text{srs}, \pi) \leftarrow \mathcal{S}(x, \mathcal{R}) \right]$$

If the Zero-Knowledge property is not satisfied we call the proof system a SNARK (without zk).

2.3 The Groth16 ZkSNARK

We recall the Groth16 proof system [21].

Rank-1 Constraint Satisfiability (R1CS). Groth16 works for relations encoded with the rank-1 constraint satisfiability (R1CS). Assume that we have n constraints and m variables. The constraint system consists of:

$$\begin{pmatrix} a_{1,1} & a_{2,1} & \cdots & a_{m,1} \\ a_{1,2} & a_{2,2} & \cdots & a_{m,2} \\ \vdots & \vdots & \ddots & \vdots \\ a_{1,n} & a_{2,n} & \cdots & a_{m,n} \end{pmatrix} \begin{pmatrix} z_1 \\ z_2 \\ \vdots \\ z_m \end{pmatrix} \circ \begin{pmatrix} b_{1,1} & b_{2,1} & \cdots & b_{m,1} \\ b_{1,2} & b_{2,2} & \cdots & b_{m,2} \\ \vdots & \vdots & \ddots & \vdots \\ b_{1,n} & b_{2,n} & \cdots & b_{m,n} \end{pmatrix} \begin{pmatrix} z_1 \\ z_2 \\ \vdots \\ z_m \end{pmatrix} = \begin{pmatrix} c_{1,1} & c_{2,1} & \cdots & c_{m,1} \\ c_{1,2} & c_{2,2} & \cdots & c_{m,2} \\ \vdots & \vdots & \ddots & \vdots \\ c_{1,n} & c_{2,n} & \cdots & c_{m,n} \end{pmatrix} \begin{pmatrix} z_1 \\ z_2 \\ \vdots \\ z_m \end{pmatrix}$$

where the matrices A, B, C are fixed and z is what we call the 'extended witness', consisting of the witness and the statement. Informally speaking, a translation to arithmetic circuits would be that the n constraints are the multiplication gates, the m variables the wires and z the actual values of the wires. Of course, R1CS generalizes arithmetic circuits and shall not necessarily be regarded as a translation of such.

Formally an R1CS relation is of the form:

$$\mathcal{R} = \left\{ (x; w) : Az \circ Bz = Cz \wedge z = (x \| w) \right\}$$

where the relation is characterized by the matrices $A, B, C \in \mathbb{Z}_p^{n \times m}$ and $z \in \mathbb{Z}_p^m$.

The Groth16 SNARK. For the proof system first each column of A, B, C is interpolated into polynomials as:

$$a_i(X) = \sum_{j=1}^{n} a_{i,j} L_j(X), \quad b_i(X) = \sum_{j=1}^{n} b_{i,j} L_j(X), \quad c_i(X) = \sum_{j=1}^{n} c_{i,j} L_j(X),$$

for each $i \in [m]$, where $L_j(x)$ the corresponding Lagrange polynomial. Then the prover should convince the verifier that

$$\left(\sum_{i=1}^{m} z_i a_i(X) \right) \cdot \left(\sum_{i=1}^{m} z_i b_i(X) \right) - \sum_{i=1}^{m} z_i c_i(X) = q(X) V(X)$$

where $V(X) = \prod_{i=1}^{n}(X - \omega^i)$ is the vanishing polynomial. This polynomial relation is essentially equivalent to the R1CS satisfiability (we refer to [20, 21, 30] for more details).

The actual Groth16 SNARK is described below. Without loss of generality we assume that $x = (z_1, \dots, z_\ell)$ corresponds to the public statement.

Setup($\mathcal{R}$) $\rightarrow$ srs : Samples uniformly $\tau, \alpha, \beta, \gamma, \delta \leftarrow\!\!\$\, \mathbb{Z}_p$ and outputs:[7]

$$
\text{srs} = \left\{ \{[\alpha]_1, [\beta]_2, [\gamma]_2, [\delta]_1, [\delta]_2, \left\{ \left[\tau^i\right]_1, \left[\tau^i\right]_2 \right\}_{i=0}^{n-1}, \left\{ \left[\frac{V(\tau)\tau^i}{\delta} \right]_1 \right\}_{i=0}^{n-2}, \right.
$$

$$
\left\{ [a_i(\tau)]_1, [b_i(\tau)]_1, [b_i(\tau)]_2 \right\}_{i=1}^{m}, \left\{ \left[\frac{\beta a_i(\tau) + \alpha b_i(\tau) + c_i(\tau)}{\gamma} \right]_1 \right\}_{i=1}^{\ell},
$$

$$
\left. \left\{ \left[\frac{\beta a_i(\tau) + \alpha b_i(\tau) + c_i(\tau)}{\delta} \right]_1 \right\}_{i=\ell+1}^{m} \right\}
$$

---

[7] As noted in [21], a_i, b_i, c_i are public polynomials and thus $\{[a_i(\tau)]_1, [b_i(\tau)]_1, [b_i(\tau)]_2\}_{i=1}^{m}$ can be publicly computed given $\{[\tau^i]_1, [\tau^i]_2\}_{i=0}^{n-1}$ without needing the trapdoor. Nevertheless, they are included in the srs for efficiency purposes.

$\mathsf{P}(\mathsf{srs}, \boldsymbol{x}, \boldsymbol{w}, \pi) \rightarrow \pi$: Sets $\boldsymbol{z} = (\boldsymbol{x} \| \boldsymbol{w})$. Computes the quotient polynomial

$$q(X) = \left\lfloor \frac{(\sum_{i=1}^{m} z_i a_i(X)) \cdot (\sum_{i=1}^{m} z_i b_i(X)) - \sum_{i=1}^{m} z_i c_i(X)}{V(X)} \right\rfloor.$$ Then samples $r, s \leftarrow^{\$} \mathbb{Z}_p$

and computes the group elements:

$$\pi_1 = [\alpha]_1 + \sum_{i=1}^{m} z_i [a_i(\tau)]_1 + r[\delta]_1$$

$$\pi_2 = [\beta]_2 + \sum_{i=1}^{m} z_i [b_i(\tau)]_2 + s[\delta]_2$$

$$\pi_3 = \sum_{i=\ell+1}^{m} z_i \left[\frac{\beta a_i(\tau) + \alpha b_i(\tau) + c_i(\tau)}{\delta} \right]_1 + s \sum_{i=1}^{m} z_i [a_i(\tau)]_1 + r \sum_{i=1}^{m} z_i [b_i(\tau)]_1$$

$$+ \sum_{i=0}^{n-2} \tilde{q}_i \left[\frac{V(\tau)\tau^i}{\delta} \right]_1 + s[\alpha]_1 + r[\beta]_1 + rs[\delta]_1$$

Outputs $\pi = (\pi_1, \pi_2, \pi_3)$
$\mathsf{V}(\mathsf{srs}, \boldsymbol{x}, \pi) \rightarrow 0/1$: Outputs 1 iff:

$$e(\pi_1, \pi_2) = e([\alpha]_1, [\beta]_2) \cdot e \left(\sum_{i=1}^{\ell} z_i \left[\frac{\beta a_i(\tau) + \alpha b_i(\tau) + c_i(\tau)}{\gamma} \right]_1, [\gamma]_2 \right) \cdot e(\pi_3, [\delta]_2)$$

The proof system has knowledge soundness in the generic group model [28,33] and perfect zero-knowledge.

The prover's complexity is dominated by 7 Fast Fourier Transforms (FFTs) for polynomials of degree n over $\mathbb{Z}_p$, a Multi-Scalar Multiplication (MSM) of size m in $\mathbb{G}_1$, a Multi-Scalar Multiplication (MSM) of size m in $\mathbb{G}_2$ and another Multi-Scalar Multiplication (MSM) of size $3m - \ell + n$ in $\mathbb{G}_1$, overall $O(n \log n + m)$. Notably, in practice the dominant cost comes from the group operations (the MSMs) even when $n \log n > m$.

3   Defining Split Prover ZkSNARKs

Here we formally define the notion of Split Prover zkSNARKs. The idea is that in an already well-defined SNARK one can replace the prover P with two phase provers P_I, P_II. For this we further allow for a new setup to possibly run, to generate a split common reference string. The verifier V should, nevertheless, remain the same.

Apart from the functionality, for the primitive to be meaningful we also define a zero-knowledge property for the outcome of the first-phase prover that is passed to the second-phase prover. We formalize this in the Split Zero-Knowledge property.

Definition 2. *Let $\Pi = (\mathsf{Setup}, \mathsf{P}, \mathsf{V})$ be (zk)SNARK, we say that Π admits a split prover if there exist algorithms $\Pi_{\mathsf{split}} = (\mathsf{Setup}_{\mathsf{split}}, \mathsf{P}_I, \mathsf{P}_{II})$ such that for any relation $\mathcal{R} \in R_\lambda$:*

- $\mathsf{Setup}_{\mathsf{split}}(\mathcal{R}, \mathcal{X}_{II}, \mathcal{W}_{II}) \to \widetilde{\mathsf{srs}}$: *On input a relation $\mathcal{R}$ and sets of indices $\mathcal{X}_{II}$ and $\mathcal{W}_{II}$ specifying the portions of the statement and the witness of the second phase respectively, the split prover setup outputs a split prover structured reference string $\widetilde{\mathsf{srs}}$.*
- $\mathsf{P}_I(\widetilde{\mathsf{srs}}, x_I, w_I) \to \mathsf{aux}$: *is a PPT algorithm that on input the split prover structure reference string $\widetilde{\mathsf{srs}}$, the part of the statement that is available in the first phase x_I and the part of the witness that is available in the first phase w_I outputs an auxiliary information for the prover of the second phase, aux.*
- $\mathsf{P}_{II}(\widetilde{\mathsf{srs}}, x_{II}, w_{II}, \mathsf{aux}) \to \pi$: *is a PPT algorithm that on input the split prover structure reference string $\widetilde{\mathsf{srs}}$, the part of the statement that is available in the second phase x_{II}, the part of the witness that is available in the second phase w_{II} and the auxiliary information from P_I, aux, outputs the proof π.*

We further consider the following properties:

Split Correctness. *We say that Π with Π_{split} has (perfect) split correctness if,*

$$
\Pr\left[\mathsf{V}(\mathsf{srs}, x, \pi) = \mathsf{V}(\widetilde{\mathsf{srs}}, x, \pi') \;\middle|\;
\begin{array}{c}
x := (x_I \| x_{II}); \; w := (w_I \| w_{II}) \\
\mathsf{srs} \leftarrow \mathsf{Setup}(\mathcal{R}); \; \pi \leftarrow \mathsf{P}(\mathsf{srs}, x, w); \\
\widetilde{\mathsf{srs}} \leftarrow \mathsf{Setup}_{\mathsf{split}}(\mathcal{R}, \mathcal{X}_{II}, \mathcal{W}_{II}); \\
\mathsf{aux} \leftarrow \mathsf{P}_I(\widetilde{\mathsf{srs}}, x_I, w_I); \\
\pi' \leftarrow \mathsf{P}_{II}(\widetilde{\mathsf{srs}}, x_{II}, w_{II}, \mathsf{aux})
\end{array}
\right] = 1,
$$

for every set of possible indices $\mathcal{X}_{II}$ and $\mathcal{W}_{II}$, every statement x, and every witness w.

Split Zero-Knowledge. We now define the notion of split zero-knowledge. Formally, fix a relation $\mathcal{R}$ decided by a circuit C. Let $\mathcal{X}_{II}$ and $\mathcal{W}_{II}$ be sets of indices specifying the parts of the statement and the witness of phase II. Let C_I be the (maximal) subcircuit of C where all wires can be determined by the parts of the statement and the witness of phase I. We say Π_{split} is perfect split zero-knowledge for $\mathcal{R}$ with respect to $\mathcal{X}_{II}$ and $\mathcal{W}_{II}$, if there exists a simulator $\mathcal{S}$ such that for every security parameter $\lambda \in \mathbb{N}$, every statement-witness pair $(x = (x_I, x_{II}), w = (w_I, w_{II})) \in \mathcal{R}$, and for every computationally unbounded adversary $\mathcal{A}$:

$$
\Pr\left[\mathcal{A}(\mathsf{aux}, \widetilde{\mathsf{srs}}) = 1 \;\middle|\;
\begin{array}{c}
\widetilde{\mathsf{srs}} \leftarrow \mathsf{Setup}_{\mathsf{split}}(\mathcal{R}, \mathcal{X}_{II}, \mathcal{W}_{II}); \\
\mathsf{aux} \leftarrow \mathsf{P}_I(\widetilde{\mathsf{srs}}, x_I, w_I)
\end{array}
\right]
$$
$$
= \Pr\left[\mathcal{A}(\mathsf{aux}, \widetilde{\mathsf{srs}}) = 1 \;\middle|\; (\widetilde{\mathsf{srs}}, \mathsf{aux}) \leftarrow \mathcal{S}(\mathcal{R}, x, \mathcal{X}_{II}, \mathcal{W}_{II}, C_I(x_I, w_I)) \right]
$$

To give an intuition of why $C_I(x_I, w_I)$ cannot be avoided to be leaked, we elaborate on how an arithmetic circuit could be split into two parts. Assume that we have available some inputs of the circuit. We execute the circuit and obtain all the wires that can be possibly obtained, forming the first-phase extended witness z_I. Then at the second phase the P_{II} gets the rest of the input of the circuit. In order to even execute the circuit and compute the rest of the wires, forming the second-phase extended witness z_{II} they need the 'output' wires of the first phase, that we call $C_I(x_I, w_I)$.

Remark 1. $\widetilde{srs}$ in fact consists of $\widetilde{srs}_I$ that is inputed to the first-phase prover P_I and $\widetilde{srs}_{II}$ taken as input by the second-phase prover P_{II}. In order to avoid overwhelming the notation we write both as $\widetilde{srs}$.

Remark 2. We highlight that Split Zero-Knowledge does not imply 'conventional' Zero-Knowledge. Intuitively, Split Zero-Knoweledge is for aux, the information passed from P_I to P_{II} and 'conventional' Zero-Knowledge is for the final proof π. The final proof of a Split Prover (zk)SNARK may or may not satisfy 'conventional' zero-knowledge, following the initial (zk)SNARK and is orthogonal to our Split Prover definition.

4   Split Prover for Groth16

Fix a relation $\mathcal{R}$ decided by a circuit C. Let $\mathcal{X}_{II}$ and $\mathcal{W}_{II}$ be sets of indices specifying the parts of the statement and the witness of the second prover, P_{II}. Let C_I be the (maximal) subcircuit of C where all wires can be determined by the parts of the statement and the witness of the first prover, P_I. We can write $C = C_{II}(x_{II}, w_{II}, C_I(x_I, w_I))$ for some circuit C_{II}. In this section we show that Groth16, as it is, admits a split prover which in addition to satisfying the split correctness notion it also satisfies split zero-knowledge.

For the rest of this section, instead of considering circuits we focus on R1CS instances. In this representation, the first and second components of the circuits correspond to the parts of the extended witness that can be computed from the phase I and phase II witnesses correspondingly and also the parts of the matrices A, B and C that depend on the two parts of the circuit. Furthermore, when the sets of indices are implicit in the context we do not include them as an input to the algorithms.

4.1   Overview of the Protocol

W.l.o.g. let $z_I = (z_1, \ldots, z_{m_1})$ be the part of the extended witness that is known to the prover during the first phase, i.e., z_I contains the known part of the statement and the witness.[8] We assume that the first ℓ_1 positions of the extended witness contain the part of the statement that is known in the phase I, $x_I = (x_1, \ldots, x_{\ell_1})$, i.e. $z_i = x_i$ for each $i \in \{1, \ldots, \ell_1\}$. Similarly $z_{II} = (z_{m_1+1}, \ldots, z_m)$ is the extended witness that cannot be initially computed and the positions

---

[8] In terms of arithmetic circuit, this can be thought of as all the wires that can be computed without the unknown part.

$m_1 + 1, \ldots, m_1 + \ell_2$ contain x_{II}. We use $m_2 := m - m_1$ to denote the size of z_{II}. Precisely, we write:

$$z = (z_{\mathrm{I}}, z_{\mathrm{II}}) = (\overbrace{\underbrace{x_1, \ldots, x_{\ell_1}}_{x_{\mathrm{I}}}, z_{\ell_1+1}, \ldots, z_{m_1}}^{z_{\mathrm{I}}}, \overbrace{\underbrace{x_{m_1+1}, \ldots, x_{m_1+\ell_2}}_{x_{\mathrm{II}}}, z_{m_1+\ell_2+1}, \ldots, z_m}^{z_{\mathrm{II}}})$$

and we define the corresponding sets of indices:

$$\begin{array}{lll}
\mathcal{Z}_{\mathrm{I}} = [1, m_1], & \mathcal{X}_{\mathrm{I}} = [1, \ell_1], & \mathcal{W}_{\mathrm{I}} = [\ell_1 + 1, m_1] \\
\mathcal{Z}_{\mathrm{II}} = [m_1 + 1, m], & \mathcal{X}_{\mathrm{II}} = [m_1 + 1, m_1 + \ell_2], & \mathcal{W}_{\mathrm{II}} = [m_1 + \ell_2 + 1, m]
\end{array}$$

Intuitively the first row is the set of indices of the phase I and the second row the set of indices of the phase II.

Split-R1CS. Assume a rank-1-constraint-satisfiability system $Az \circ Bz = Cz$. The R1CS can be written accordingly:

$$\begin{pmatrix} A_{11} & 0 \\ 0 & A_{22} \\ A_{31} & A_{32} \end{pmatrix} \begin{pmatrix} z_{\mathrm{I}} \\ z_{\mathrm{II}} \end{pmatrix} \circ \begin{pmatrix} B_{11} & 0 \\ 0 & B_{22} \\ B_{31} & B_{32} \end{pmatrix} \begin{pmatrix} z_{\mathrm{I}} \\ z_{\mathrm{II}} \end{pmatrix} = \begin{pmatrix} C_{11} & 0 \\ 0 & C_{22} \\ C_{31} & C_{32} \end{pmatrix} \begin{pmatrix} z_{\mathrm{I}} \\ z_{\mathrm{II}} \end{pmatrix}$$

where $A_{11} \in \mathbb{Z}_p^{n_1 \times m_1}$ are the constraints on z_{I} but not on z_{II}, conversely $A_{22} \in \mathbb{Z}_p^{n_2 \times m_2}$ are the constraints on z_{II} but not on z_{I} and $A_{31} \in \mathbb{Z}_p^{n_3 \times m_1}$, $A_{32} \in \mathbb{Z}_p^{n_3 \times m_2}$ involve both. Similarly, for $B_{11} \in \mathbb{Z}_p^{n_1' \times m_1}$, $B_{22} \in \mathbb{Z}_p^{n_2' \times m_2}$, $B_{31} \in \mathbb{Z}_p^{n_3' \times m_1}$, $B_{32} \in \mathbb{Z}_p^{n_3' \times m_2}$ and $C_{11} \in \mathbb{Z}_p^{n_1'' \times m_1}$, $C_{22} \in \mathbb{Z}_p^{n_2'' \times m_2}$, $C_{31} \in \mathbb{Z}_p^{n_3'' \times m_1}$, $C_{32} \in \mathbb{Z}_p^{n_3'' \times m_2}$. We note that n_i, n_i', n_i'' may not necessarily be the same.

We can re-write the above system as:

$$\left[\overbrace{\begin{pmatrix} A_{11} \\ 0 \\ A_{31} \end{pmatrix}}^{A_{\mathrm{I}}} z_{\mathrm{I}} + \overbrace{\begin{pmatrix} 0 \\ A_{22} \\ A_{32} \end{pmatrix}}^{A_{\mathrm{II}}} z_{\mathrm{II}} \right] \circ \left[\overbrace{\begin{pmatrix} B_{11} \\ 0 \\ B_{31} \end{pmatrix}}^{B_{\mathrm{I}}} z_{\mathrm{I}} + \overbrace{\begin{pmatrix} 0 \\ B_{22} \\ B_{32} \end{pmatrix}}^{B_{\mathrm{II}}} z_{\mathrm{II}} \right] =$$

$$= \left[\overbrace{\begin{pmatrix} C_{11} \\ 0 \\ C_{31} \end{pmatrix}}^{C_{\mathrm{I}}} z_{\mathrm{I}} + \overbrace{\begin{pmatrix} 0 \\ C_{22} \\ C_{32} \end{pmatrix}}^{C_{\mathrm{II}}} z_{\mathrm{II}} \right]$$

or equivalently

$$(C_{\mathrm{I}} \cdot z_{\mathrm{I}}) + (C_{\mathrm{II}} \cdot z_{\mathrm{II}}) = (A_{\mathrm{I}} \cdot z_{\mathrm{I}}) \circ (B_{\mathrm{I}} \cdot z_{\mathrm{I}}) + (A_{\mathrm{I}} \cdot z_{\mathrm{I}}) \circ (B_{\mathrm{II}} \cdot z_{\mathrm{II}})$$
$$+ (A_{\mathrm{II}} \cdot z_{\mathrm{II}}) \circ (B_{\mathrm{II}} \cdot z_{\mathrm{I}}) + (A_{\mathrm{II}} \cdot z_{\mathrm{II}}) \circ (B_{\mathrm{II}} \cdot z_{\mathrm{II}})$$

We refer to this form as the 'Split-R1CS'.

Split Proof Computation. To begin with, from the available statement x_I and witness w_I the first prover can compute their extended witness z_I by computing all the wires of the circuit that are possible with x_I and w_I. Then the second prover having x_{II} and w_{II} can compute their extended witness, i.e. the rest of the wires of the circuit, given $C_I(x_I, w_I)$ which corresponds to the output wires of the subcircuit that was computed by P_I (see the discussion at the beginning of the section). Therefore, the first part of the auxiliary information that needs to be passed from P_I to P_{II} is $\mathsf{aux}_0 = C_I(x_I, w_I)$.

As discussed in Sect. 2.3, a Groth16 proof consists of three group elements π_1, π_2, π_3.

The first group element of the proof, π_1, can be written as:

$$\pi_1 = [\alpha]_1 + \overbrace{\sum_{i \in \mathcal{Z}_I} z_i[a_i(\tau)]_1}^{\mathsf{aux}_1} + \sum_{i \in \mathcal{Z}_{II}} z_i[a_i(\tau)]_1 + r[\delta]_1.$$

Therefore the value $\mathsf{aux}_1 := \sum_{i \in \mathcal{Z}_I} z_i[a_i(\tau)]_1$ can be fully computed in the phase I, as it depends only on z_I. Given this, the final π_1 can be computed in phase II as $\pi_1 = \mathsf{aux}_1 + [\alpha]_1 + \sum_{i \in \mathcal{Z}_{II}} z_i[a_i(\tau)]_1 + r[\delta]_1$, once z_{II} becomes available.

The same argument holds for π_2:

$$\pi_2 = [\beta]_2 + \overbrace{\sum_{i \in \mathcal{Z}_I} z_i[b_i(\tau)]_2}^{\mathsf{aux}_2} + \sum_{i \in \mathcal{Z}_{II}} z_i[b_i(\tau)]_2 + s[\delta]_2.$$

where $\mathsf{aux}_2 := \sum_{i \in \mathcal{Z}_I} z_i[b_i(\tau)]_2$

For the third group element π_3 in the proof, we have:

$$\pi_3 = \overbrace{\sum_{i \in \mathcal{W}_I} z_i \left[\frac{\beta a_i(\tau) + \alpha b_i(\tau) + c_i(\tau)}{\delta}\right]_1}^{\mathsf{aux}_3} + \sum_{i \in \mathcal{W}_{II}} z_i \left[\frac{\beta a_i(\tau) + \alpha b_i(\tau) + c_i(\tau)}{\delta}\right]_1$$

$$+ s \left(\overbrace{\sum_{i \in \mathcal{Z}_I} z_i[a_i(\tau)]_1}^{\mathsf{aux}_1} + \sum_{i \in \mathcal{Z}_{II}} z_i[a_i(\tau)]_1\right) + r \left(\overbrace{\sum_{i \in \mathcal{Z}_I} z_i[b_i(\tau)]_1}^{\mathsf{aux}_4} + \sum_{i \in \mathcal{Z}_{II}} z_i[b_i(\tau)]_1\right)$$

$$+ \sum_{i=0}^{n-2} \tilde{q}_i \left[\frac{V(\tau)\tau^i}{\delta}\right]_1 + s[\alpha]_1 + r[\beta]_1 + rs[\delta]_1.$$

For this, we need to compute the quotient polynomial $q(X) :=$ $\left[\frac{\left(\sum_{i=1}^m z_i a_i(X)\right) \cdot \left(\sum_{i=1}^m z_i b_i(X)\right) - \sum_{i=1}^m z_i c_i(X)}{V(X)}\right]$ that depends on both z_I and z_{II}.

To this end, our first observation is that, following the split R1CS described above, the quotient polynomial can be re-written as:

$$q(X) = \left[\frac{\left(\sum_{i \in \mathcal{Z}_{\mathrm{I}}} z_i a_i(X) \right) \cdot \left(\sum_{i \in \mathcal{Z}_{\mathrm{I}}} z_i b_i(X) \right)}{V(X)} + \right.$$

$$+ \frac{\left(\sum_{i \in \mathcal{Z}_{\mathrm{I}}} z_i a_i(X) \right) \cdot \left(\sum_{i \in \mathcal{Z}_{\mathrm{II}}} z_i b_i(X) \right)}{V(X)} +$$

$$+ \frac{\left(\sum_{i \in \mathcal{Z}_{\mathrm{II}}} z_i a_i(X) \right) \cdot \left(\sum_{i \in \mathcal{Z}_{\mathrm{I}}} z_i b_i(X) \right)}{V(X)} +$$

$$+ \frac{\left(\sum_{i \in \mathcal{Z}_{\mathrm{II}}} z_i a_i(X) \right) \cdot \left(\sum_{i \in \mathcal{Z}_{\mathrm{II}}} z_i b_i(X) \right)}{V(X)} +$$

$$\left. - \frac{\sum_{i \in \mathcal{Z}_{\mathrm{I}}} z_i c_i(X)}{V(X)} - \frac{\sum_{i \in \mathcal{Z}_{\mathrm{II}}} z_i c_i(X)}{V(X)} \right]$$

Our second observation is that the quotient polynomial q is equal to the sum of the six partial quotients (i.e., we can ignore the partial remainders in the above six terms). We formally present this claim in the following lemma.

Lemma 1. *Let $f_1(X), \ldots, f_t(X), g(X)$ be univariate polynomials in $\mathbb{Z}_p[X]$ and $k_1, \ldots, k_t$ be field elements in $\mathbb{Z}_p$. Then $\left\lfloor \frac{\sum_{i=1}^{t} k_i f_i(X)}{g(X)} \right\rfloor = \sum_{i=1}^{t} k_i \left\lfloor \frac{f_i(X)}{g(X)} \right\rfloor$.*

Proof. Let the euclidean division of f_i by g be $f_i(X) = q_i(X)g(X) + r_i(X)$, where $\deg(r_i) < \deg(g)$, for each $i \in [t]$. Similarly $f(X) = q(X)g(X) + r(X)$, where $\deg(r) < \deg(g)$. Then,

$$\sum_{i=1}^{t} k_i f_i(X) = \sum_{i=1}^{t} [k_i q_i(X)g(X) + k_i r_i(X)]$$

$$= \left[\sum_{i=1}^{t} k_i q_i(X) \right] g(X) + \left[\sum_{i=1}^{t} k_i r_i(X) \right]$$

where, $\deg(\sum_{i=1}^{t} k_i r_i) < \deg(g)$, since $\deg(r_i) < \deg(g)$ for each $i \in [t]$ and k_i's are constants (degree 0). Therefore, $q(X) = \sum_{i=1}^{t} k_i q_i(X)$. $\qquad \square$

Finally, notice that $\deg(c_i) < \deg(V)$ for each $i \in [m]$, hence $\left\lfloor \frac{\sum_{i \in \mathcal{Z}_\mathrm{I}} z_i c_i(X)}{V(X)} \right\rfloor =$
$\left\lfloor \frac{\sum_{i \in \mathcal{Z}_\mathrm{II}} z_i c_i(X)}{V(X)} \right\rfloor = 0$. Therefore, the quotient polynomial is actually a sum of four terms:

$$q(X) = \left\lfloor \frac{\left(\sum_{i \in \mathcal{Z}_\mathrm{I}} z_i a_i(X) \right) \cdot \left(\sum_{i \in \mathcal{Z}_\mathrm{I}} z_i b_i(X) \right)}{V(X)} \right\rfloor +$$

$$+ \left\lfloor \frac{\left(\sum_{i \in \mathcal{Z}_\mathrm{I}} z_i a_i(X) \right) \cdot \left(\sum_{i \in \mathcal{Z}_\mathrm{II}} z_i b_i(X) \right)}{V(X)} \right\rfloor +$$

$$+ \left\lfloor \frac{\left(\sum_{i \in \mathcal{Z}_\mathrm{II}} z_i a_i(X) \right) \cdot \left(\sum_{i \in \mathcal{Z}_\mathrm{I}} z_i b_i(X) \right)}{V(X)} \right\rfloor +$$

$$+ \left\lfloor \frac{\left(\sum_{i \in \mathcal{Z}_\mathrm{II}} z_i a_i(X) \right) \cdot \left(\sum_{i \in \mathcal{Z}_\mathrm{II}} z_i b_i(X) \right)}{V(X)} \right\rfloor$$

$$:= q_1(X) + q_2(X) + q_3(X) + q_4(X)$$

For notational convenience and to make the dependence on $\mathbf{z}_\mathrm{I}$ and $\mathbf{z}_\mathrm{II}$ clear we re-write the sums in the above as inner products:

$$q(X) = \left\lfloor \frac{\langle \mathbf{z}_\mathrm{I}, \mathbf{a}_\mathrm{I}(X) \rangle \cdot \langle \mathbf{z}_\mathrm{I}, \mathbf{b}_\mathrm{I}(X) \rangle}{V(X)} \right\rfloor + \left\lfloor \frac{\langle \mathbf{z}_\mathrm{I}, \mathbf{a}_\mathrm{I}(X) \rangle \cdot \langle \mathbf{z}_\mathrm{II}, \mathbf{b}_\mathrm{II}(X) \rangle}{V(X)} \right\rfloor +$$

$$+ \left\lfloor \frac{\langle \mathbf{z}_\mathrm{II}, \mathbf{a}_\mathrm{II}(X) \rangle \cdot \langle \mathbf{z}_\mathrm{I}, \mathbf{b}_\mathrm{I}(X) \rangle}{V(X)} \right\rfloor + \left\lfloor \frac{\langle \mathbf{z}_\mathrm{II}, \mathbf{a}_\mathrm{II}(X) \rangle \cdot \langle \mathbf{z}_\mathrm{II}, \mathbf{b}_\mathrm{II}(X) \rangle}{V(X)} \right\rfloor$$

where $\mathbf{a}(X) = (\mathbf{a}_\mathrm{I}(X) \| \mathbf{a}_\mathrm{II}(X))^\top = (a_1(X), \ldots, a_{m_1}(X), a_{m_1+1}(X), \ldots,$ $a_m(X))^\top$ and $\mathbf{b}(X) = (\mathbf{b}_\mathrm{I}(X) \| \mathbf{b}_\mathrm{II}(X))^\top = (b_1(X), \ldots, b_{m_1}(X), b_{m_1+1}(X), \ldots,$ $b_m(X))^\top$.

Now, notice that since the first term is entirely computable in phase I, the first prover P_I computes the first quotient polynomial $q_1(X)$ and sets $\mathsf{aux}_5 = \sum_{i=0}^{n-2} \tilde{q}_{1,i} \left[\frac{V(\tau)\tau^i}{\delta} \right]$. The second and third terms depend on both $\mathbf{z}_\mathrm{I}$ and $\mathbf{z}_\mathrm{II}$. We re-write these terms as:

$$q_2(X) = \left\lfloor \frac{\langle z_I, a_I(X) \rangle \cdot \langle z_{II}, b_{II}(X) \rangle}{V(X)} \right\rfloor = \left\lfloor \frac{\left\langle z_{II}, \langle z_I, a_I(X) \rangle \cdot b_{II}(X) \right\rangle}{V(X)} \right\rfloor$$

$$\overset{\text{Lemma 1}}{=} \left\langle z_{II}, \overbrace{\left\lfloor \frac{\langle z_I, a_I(X) \rangle \cdot b_{II}(X)}{V(X)} \right\rfloor}^{\mu_2(X)} \right\rangle := \langle z_{II}, \mu_2(X) \rangle$$

$$q_3(X) = \left\lfloor \frac{\langle z_{II}, a_{II}(X) \rangle \cdot \langle z_I, b_I(X) \rangle}{V(X)} \right\rfloor = \left\lfloor \frac{\left\langle z_{II}, a_{II}(X) \cdot \langle z_I, b_I(X) \rangle \right\rangle}{V(X)} \right\rfloor$$

$$\overset{\text{Lemma 1}}{=} \left\langle z_{II}, \overbrace{\left\lfloor \frac{a_{II}(X) \cdot \langle z_I, b_I(X) \rangle}{V(X)} \right\rfloor}^{\mu_3(X)} \right\rangle := \langle z_{II}, \mu_3(X) \rangle.$$

Now prover I proceeds as follows: Computes the vectors of m_2 polynomials $\mu_2(X) = \left\lfloor \frac{\langle z_I, a_I(X) \rangle \cdot b_{II}(X)}{V(X)} \right\rfloor$ and $\mu_3(X) = \left\lfloor \frac{a_{II}(X) \cdot \langle z_I, b_I(X) \rangle}{V(X)} \right\rfloor$ and sets $\mathsf{aux}_6 = \sum_{i=0}^{n-2} \tilde{\mu}_{2,i} \left[\frac{V(\tau)\tau^i}{\delta} \right]_1$ and $\mathsf{aux}_7 = \sum_{i=0}^{n-2} \tilde{\mu}_{3,i} \left[\frac{V(\tau)\tau^i}{\delta} \right]_1$, each consisting of m_2 group elements. In the second phase P_{II} computes the multi-exponentiations $\langle z_{II}, \mathsf{aux}_6 \rangle$ and $\langle z_{II}, \mathsf{aux}_7 \rangle$ to reconstruct $\left[\frac{q_2(\tau)V(\tau)}{\delta} \right]_1$ and $\left[\frac{q_3(\tau)V(\tau)}{\delta} \right]_1$, respectively.

The fourth term of $q_4(X)$ can be fully computed in the second phase by P_{II}. In conclusion the final π_3 can be computed in the phase II as follows:[9]

$$\pi_3 = \left(\mathsf{aux}_3 + \sum_{i \in \mathcal{W}_{II}} z_i \left[\frac{\beta a_i(\tau) + \alpha b_i(\tau) + c_i(\tau)}{\delta} \right]_1 \right)$$

$$+ s \left(\mathsf{aux}_1 + \sum_{i \in \mathcal{Z}_{II}} z_i [a_i(\tau)]_1 \right) + r \left(\mathsf{aux}_4 + \sum_{i \in \mathcal{Z}_{II}} z_i [b_i(\tau)]_1 \right)$$

$$+ \left(\mathsf{aux}_5 + \langle z_{II}, \mathsf{aux}_6 \rangle + \langle z_{II}, \mathsf{aux}_7 \rangle + \sum_{i=0}^{n-2} \tilde{q}_{4,i} \left[\frac{V(\tau)\tau^i}{\delta} \right]_1 \right) + s[\alpha]_1 + r[\beta]_1 + rs[\delta]_1.$$

Optimizing P_{II} for small witnesses, $m_2 = o(\sqrt{n \log n + m})$. P_{II}'s running time, as described above, is dominated by the computation of $q_4(X)$ which, being a polynomial division of degree n, requires $O(n \log n)$ time.

We observe that if the most significant portion of the witness is in the first phase, i.e. the phase II extended witness is small, then there is a more efficient

---

[9] Note that a for a concrete improvement on the size of aux we can merge aux_6 and aux_7 into $\mathsf{aux}_6 + \mathsf{aux}_7$. For more intuitive presentation of our protocol we stick to separate aux_6 and aux_7.

mechanism for P_{II}. In concrete, if $m_2 = o(\sqrt{n \log n + m})$, then we preprocess the polynomials as follows:

$$q_4(X) = \left[\frac{\langle z_{II}, a_{II}(X) \rangle \cdot \langle z_{II}, b_{II}(X) \rangle}{V(X)} \right] = \left[\frac{z_{II} \cdot (a_{II}^\top(X) \otimes b_{II}(X)) \cdot z_{II}^\top}{V(X)} \right]$$

$$\overset{\text{Lemma 1}}{=} z_{II} \cdot \left[\frac{a_{II}^\top(X) \otimes b_{II}(X)}{V(X)} \right] \cdot z_{II}^\top.$$

Let $T(X) = \left[\frac{a_{II}^\top(X) \otimes b_{II}(X)}{V(X)} \right]$ be a $(m_2 \times m_2)$-size matrix of polynomials. In the split setup phase we compute the matrix containing $(m_2 \times m_2)$ group elements $H = \sum_{i=0}^{n-2} \tilde{T}_i \left[\frac{V(\tau)\tau^i}{\delta} \right]_1$ and publish it in $\widetilde{\text{srs}}$. Thereafter, in the second phase the prover II computes $z_{II} H z_{II}^\top$ to reconstruct $\left[\frac{q_4(\tau)V(\tau)}{\delta} \right]_1$.

The the final π_3 can be alternatively computed by P_{II} as:

$$\pi_3 = \left(\text{aux}_3 + \sum_{i \in \mathcal{W}_{II}} z_i \left[\frac{\beta a_i(\tau) + \alpha b_i(\tau) + c_i(\tau)}{\delta} \right]_1 \right)$$

$$+ s \left(\text{aux}_1 + \sum_{i \in \mathcal{Z}_{II}} z_i [a_i(\tau)]_1 \right) + r \left(\text{aux}_4 + \sum_{i \in \mathcal{Z}_{II}} z_i [b_i(\tau)]_1 \right)$$

$$+ \left(\text{aux}_5 + \langle z_{II}, \text{aux}_6 \rangle + \langle z_{II}, \text{aux}_7 \rangle + z_{II} H z_{II}^\top \right) + s[\alpha]_1 + r[\beta]_1 + rs[\delta]_1,$$

taking time $O(m_2^2)$, which is less than $O(n \log n)$.

Split Zero-Knowledge. Until now we have seen how to obtain a split prover for Groth16 that satisfies correctness, ignoring the split zero-knowledge property. In order to add split zero-knowledge to the above we proceed as follows: Assume that we want to build a split prover for the R1CS relation

$$\mathcal{R} = \{(x; w) : Az \circ Bz = Cz \wedge z = (x \| w)\},$$

then, we show a construction with split zero-knowledge for the relation

$$\mathcal{R}' = \{(x; (w, r)) : A'z \circ B'z = C'z \wedge z = (x \| w \| r)\},$$

where $\mathcal{R}'$ defined as follows:

$$\forall x, w, r : (x; (w, r)) \in \mathcal{R}' \iff (x; w) \in \mathcal{R}.$$

Therefore, the two relations are functionally equivalent as for any x, w, r can be seen as a dummy witness that is present solely to achieve the zero-knowledge property.

The idea is to carefully add some extra constraints in the R1CS and wires in the extended witness. Then the extra wires are going to be sampled uniformly at random from P_I in order to 'mask' the auxiliary information. Similar approaches for achieving zero-knowledge can be found in the literature (e.g. [1]).

In more detail, the new R1CS matrices will be:

$$
\overbrace{\begin{pmatrix} A_{11} & \mathbf{0} & 0\,0\,0\,0 \\ \mathbf{0} & A_{22} & \vdots\,\vdots\,\vdots\,\vdots \\ A_{31} & A_{32} & 0\,0\,0\,0 \\ 0\ldots0 & 0\ldots0 & 1\,0\,0\,0 \\ 0\ldots0 & 0\ldots0 & 0\,0\,0\,0 \\ 0\ldots0 & 0\ldots0 & 0\,0\,1\,0 \end{pmatrix}}^{A'} \begin{pmatrix} z_I \\ z_{II} \\ r_1 \\ r_2 \\ r_3 \\ r_4 \end{pmatrix} \circ \overbrace{\begin{pmatrix} B_{11} & \mathbf{0} & 0\,0\,0\,0 \\ \mathbf{0} & B_{22} & \vdots\,\vdots\,\vdots\,\vdots \\ B_{31} & B_{32} & 0\,0\,0\,0 \\ 0\ldots0 & 0\ldots0 & 0\,0\,0\,0 \\ 0\ldots0 & 0\ldots0 & 0\,1\,0\,0 \\ 0\ldots0 & 0\ldots0 & 0\,0\,1\,0 \end{pmatrix}}^{B'} \begin{pmatrix} z_I \\ z_{II} \\ r_1 \\ r_2 \\ r_3 \\ r_4 \end{pmatrix}
$$

$$
= \overbrace{\begin{pmatrix} C_{11} & \mathbf{0} & 0\,0\,0\,0 \\ \mathbf{0} & C_{22} & \vdots\,\vdots\,\vdots\,\vdots \\ C_{31} & C_{32} & 0\,0\,0\,0 \\ 0\ldots0 & 0\ldots0 & 0\,0\,0\,0 \\ 0\ldots0 & 0\ldots0 & 0\,0\,0\,0 \\ 0\ldots0 & 0\ldots0 & 0\,0\,0\,1 \end{pmatrix}}^{C'} \begin{pmatrix} z_I \\ z_{II} \\ r_1 \\ r_2 \\ r_3 \\ r_4 \end{pmatrix}
$$

Equivalently for the corresponding polynomials we get:

- $a_I'(X) = \big(a_1(X), \ldots, a_{m_1}(X), L_{n+1}(X), 0, L_{n+3}(X), 0\big)^\top, \quad a_{II}'(X) = a_{II}$
- $b_I'(X) = \big(b_1(X), \ldots, b_{m_1}(X), 0, L_{n+2}(X), L_{n+3}(X), 0\big)^\top, \quad b_{II}'(X) = b_{II}$

In the modfied R1CS $n' = n+3$ and $m' = m+4$.

We note that this approach is not compatible with an already existing Groth16 srs for $\mathcal{R}$ and one should run a new setup, $\mathsf{Setup}(\mathcal{R}')$ for $\mathcal{R}'$, where $\mathcal{R}'$ is characterized by the above R1CS. The latter is in fact happening in $\mathsf{Setup}_{\mathsf{split}}$.

4.2 The Protocol

Here we describe our protocol formally. We recall the notation:

- $a_i(X), b_i(X), c(X)$ are (publicly) known polynomial that interpolate the i-th column of the A, B, C R1CS matrices respectively.
- $a(X) := (a_I(X) \| a_{II}(X))^\top = (a_1(X), \ldots, a_{m_1}(X), a_{m_1+1}(X), \ldots, a_m(X))^\top$
- $b(X) := (b_I(X) \| b_{II}(X))^\top = (b_1(X), \ldots, b_{m_1}(X), b_{m_1+1}(X), \ldots, b_m(X))^\top$
- $a_I'(X) = \big(a_1(X), \ldots, a_{m_1}(X), L_{n+1}(X), 0, L_{n+3}(X), 0\big)^\top, \quad a_{II}'(X) = a_{II}$
- $b_I'(X) = \big(b_1(X), \ldots, b_{m_1}(X), 0, L_{n+2}(X), L_{n+3}(X), 0\big)^\top, \quad b_{II}'(X) = b_{II}$
- $n' = n+3$ and $m' = m+4$.

$\mathsf{Setup}_{\mathsf{split}}(\mathcal{R}, \mathcal{X}_{\mathrm{II}}, \mathcal{W}_{\mathrm{II}}) \to \mathsf{srs}$: First it runs Groth16's setup for the relation $\mathcal{R}'$. That is, samples uniformly $\tau, \alpha, \beta, \gamma, \delta \leftarrow\!\!{\scriptstyle\$}\, \mathbb{Z}_p$ and outputs:

$$\widetilde{\mathsf{srs}} = \left\{ \{[\alpha]_1, [\beta]_2, [\gamma]_2, [\delta]_1, [\delta]_2, \left\{[\tau^i]_1, [\tau^i]_2\right\}_{i=0}^{n'-1}, \left\{\left[\frac{V(\tau)\tau^i}{\delta}\right]_1\right\}_{i=0}^{n'-2}, \right.$$
$$\left\{[a_i(\tau)]_1, [b_i(\tau)]_1, [b_i(\tau)]_2\right\}_{i=1}^{m'}, \left\{\left[\frac{\beta a_i(\tau) + \alpha b_i(\tau) + c_i(\tau)}{\gamma}\right]_1\right\}_{i\in\mathcal{X}_{\mathrm{I}}\cup\mathcal{X}_{\mathrm{II}}},$$
$$\left.\left\{\left[\frac{\beta a_i(\tau) + \alpha b_i(\tau) + c_i(\tau)}{\delta}\right]_1\right\}_{i\in\mathcal{W}_{\mathrm{I}}\cup\mathcal{W}_{\mathrm{II}}} \right\}$$

Then if $m_2 = o(\sqrt{n\log n} + m)$: First computes the matrix of polynomials:

$$\boldsymbol{T}(X) = \left\lfloor \frac{\boldsymbol{a}_{\mathrm{II}}^{\top}(X) \otimes \boldsymbol{b}_{\mathrm{II}}(X)}{V(X)} \right\rfloor := (t_{i,j}(X))_{i,j\in\mathcal{Z}_{\mathrm{II}}}$$

and using the $\left\{\left[\frac{V(\tau)\tau^i}{\delta}\right]_1\right\}_{i=0}^{n-2}$ of the srs outputs the corresponding matrix of group elements:

$$\boldsymbol{H} = \left(\sum_{k=0}^{n-2} \tilde{t}_{i,j,k}\left[\frac{V(\tau)\tau^i}{\delta}\right]_1\right)_{i,j\in\mathcal{Z}_{\mathrm{II}}}$$

and appends it to the structured reference string, i.e. $\widetilde{\mathsf{srs}} \leftarrow \widetilde{\mathsf{srs}} \cup \boldsymbol{H}$.

$\mathsf{P}_{\mathrm{I}}(\widetilde{\mathsf{srs}}, \boldsymbol{x}_{\mathrm{I}}, \boldsymbol{w}_{\mathrm{I}}) \to \mathsf{aux}$: The prover I samples $r_1, r_2, r_3 \leftarrow\!\!{\scriptstyle\$}\, \mathbb{Z}_p$, sets $r_4 = r_3^2$ and computes:

0. $\mathsf{aux}_0 = C_{\mathrm{I}}(x_{\mathrm{I}}, w_{\mathrm{I}})$,
1. $\mathsf{aux}_1 = \sum_{i\in\mathcal{Z}_{\mathrm{I}}} z_i[a_i(\tau)]_1 + r_1[a_{m+1}(\tau)]_1 + r_3[a_{m+3}(\tau)]_1$,
2. $\mathsf{aux}_2 = \sum_{i\in\mathcal{Z}_{\mathrm{I}}} z_i[b_i(\tau)]_2 + r_2[b_{m+2}(\tau)]_2 + r_3[b_{m+3}(\tau)]_1$,
3.

$$\mathsf{aux}_3 = \sum_{i\in\mathcal{W}_{\mathrm{I}}} z_i\left[\frac{\beta a_i(\tau) + \alpha b_i(\tau) + c_i(\tau)}{\delta}\right]_1 + r_1\left[\frac{\beta a_{m+1}(\tau)}{\delta}\right]_1 + r_3\left[\frac{\beta a_{m+3}(\tau)}{\delta}\right]_1$$
$$+ r_2\left[\frac{\alpha b_{m+2}(\tau)}{\delta}\right]_1 + r_3\left[\frac{\alpha b_{m+3}(\tau)}{\delta}\right]_1 + r_4\left[\frac{c_{m+3}(\tau)}{\delta}\right]_1,$$

4. $\mathsf{aux}_4 = \sum_{i\in\mathcal{Z}_{\mathrm{I}}} z_i[b_i(\tau)]_1 + r_2[b_{m+2}(\tau)]_1 + r_3[b_{m+3}(\tau)]_1$,
5. $\mathsf{aux}_5 = \sum_{i=0}^{n-2} \tilde{q}_{1,i}\left[\frac{V(\tau)\tau^i}{\delta}\right]_1$, where $q_1(X) = \left\lfloor\frac{\langle z_{\mathrm{I}}, a_{\mathrm{I}}'(X)\rangle \cdot \langle z_{\mathrm{I}}, b_{\mathrm{I}}'(X)\rangle}{V(X)}\right\rfloor$,
6. $\mathbf{aux}_6 = \sum_{i=0}^{n-2} \tilde{\mu}_{2,i}\left[\frac{V(\tau)\tau^i}{\delta}\right]_1$, where $\boldsymbol{\mu}_2(X) = \left\lfloor\frac{\langle z_{\mathrm{I}}, a_{\mathrm{I}}'(X)\rangle b_{\mathrm{II}}(X)}{V(X)}\right\rfloor$,
7. $\mathbf{aux}_7 = \sum_{i=0}^{n-2} \tilde{\mu}_{3,i}\left[\frac{V(\tau)\tau^i}{\delta}\right]_1$, where $\boldsymbol{\mu}_3(X) = \left\lfloor\frac{\langle z_{\mathrm{I}}, b_{\mathrm{I}}'(X)\rangle a_{\mathrm{II}}(X)}{V(X)}\right\rfloor$

and outputs $\mathsf{aux} := \{\mathsf{aux}_1, \mathsf{aux}_2, \mathsf{aux}_3, \mathsf{aux}_4, \mathsf{aux}_5, \mathbf{aux}_6, \mathbf{aux}_7\}$

$\mathsf{P}_{\mathrm{II}}(\widetilde{\mathsf{srs}}, \boldsymbol{x}_{\mathrm{II}}, \boldsymbol{w}_{\mathrm{II}}, \mathsf{aux}) \to \pi$: The prover II first computes z_{II} given $\boldsymbol{x}_{\mathrm{II}}$, $\boldsymbol{w}_{\mathrm{II}}$ and aux_0. Then uniformly samples $r, s \leftarrow\!\!{\scriptstyle\$}\, \mathbb{Z}_p$ and computes:

1. $\pi_1 = [\alpha]_1 + \mathsf{aux}_1 + \sum_{i\in\mathcal{Z}_{\mathrm{II}}} z_i[a_i(\tau)]_1 + r[\delta]_1$,
2. $\pi_2 = [\beta]_2 + \mathsf{aux}_2 + \sum_{i\in\mathcal{Z}_{\mathrm{II}}} z_i[b_i(\tau)]_2 + s[\delta]_2$,

3.

$$\pi_3 = \left(\mathsf{aux}_3 + \sum_{i \in \mathcal{W}_{\mathrm{II}}} z_i \left[\frac{\beta a_i(\tau) + \alpha b_i(\tau) + c_i(\tau)}{\delta} \right]_1 \right)$$

$$+ s \left(\mathsf{aux}_1 + \sum_{i \in \mathcal{Z}_{\mathrm{II}}} z_i [a_i(\tau)]_1 \right) + r \left(\mathsf{aux}_4 + \sum_{i \in \mathcal{Z}_{\mathrm{II}}} z_i [b_i(\tau)]_1 \right)$$

$$+ \left(\mathsf{aux}_5 + \langle \mathbf{z}_{\mathrm{II}}, \mathbf{aux}_6 \rangle + \langle \mathbf{z}_{\mathrm{II}}, \mathbf{aux}_7 \rangle + K \right) + s[\alpha]_1 + r[\beta]_1 + rs[\delta]_1,$$

where $K = \mathbf{z}_{\mathrm{II}} \mathbf{H} \mathbf{z}_{\mathrm{II}}^{\top}$ if $m_2 = o(\sqrt{n \log n + m})$ otherwise $K = \sum_{i=0}^{n-2} \tilde{q}_{4,i} \left[\frac{V(\tau)\tau^i}{\delta} \right]_1$.

Finally, outputs $\pi := \{\pi_1, \pi_2, \pi_3\}$

Theorem 1. *The above scheme has perfect split correctness and perfect split zero-knowledge.*

Proof. Split Correctness follows by construction. To avoid repetition we point to Sect. 4.1 where we extensively unveiled the protocol details.

We now show that our construction achieves perfect split zero knowledge. The simulator $\mathcal{S}$ works as follows: It samples $\hat{x}, \hat{y}, \hat{\omega} \leftarrow_\$ \mathbb{Z}_p$ and sets $\mathsf{a\hat{u}x}_1 = [\hat{x}]_1$, $\mathsf{a\hat{u}x}_2 = [\hat{y}]_2$, $\mathsf{a\hat{u}x}_3 = \left[\frac{\beta \hat{x} - \sum_{i \in \mathcal{X}_{\mathrm{I}}} z_i \beta a_i(\tau) + \alpha \hat{y} - \sum_{i \in \mathcal{X}_{\mathrm{I}}} z_i \alpha b_i(\tau)}{\delta} + \hat{\omega} \right]_1$, $\mathsf{a\hat{u}x}_4 = [\hat{y}]_1$, $\mathsf{a\hat{u}x}_5 = \left[\frac{\hat{x}\hat{y}}{\delta} \right]_1$, $\mathsf{a\hat{u}x}_6 = \left[\frac{\hat{x}b_{\mathrm{II}}(\tau)}{\delta} \right]_1$, and $\mathsf{a\hat{u}x}_7 = \left[\frac{\hat{y}a_{\mathrm{II}}(\tau)}{\delta} \right]_1$. Recall that $\mathcal{S}$ samples itself the $\widetilde{\mathsf{srs}}$ so has access to the trapdoors $\alpha, \beta, \delta, \tau$. Finally aux_0 is trivially simulated, since $C_{\mathrm{I}}(x_{\mathrm{I}}, w_{\mathrm{I}})$ is part of its input.

Regarding correctness of the simulation, the distribution of the simulated $\mathsf{a\hat{u}x}$ is identical to the one generated by the protocol. aux_1, $\mathsf{a\hat{u}x}_1$, aux_2, $\mathsf{a\hat{u}x}_2$, aux_3, $\mathsf{a\hat{u}x}_3$ are all uniformly distributed, since the groups $\mathbb{G}_1, \mathbb{G}_2$ are cyclic and $r_1, r_2, r_3, \hat{x}, \hat{y}, \hat{\omega}$ are uniformly random (r_4 is implicitly r_3^2). The rest of the auxiliary values are uniquely determined based on the $\widetilde{\mathsf{srs}}$ and aux_1, aux_2 in the real world. In the simulated world also, they are chosen accordingly using the $\widetilde{\mathsf{srs}}$ trapdoors and $\mathsf{a\hat{u}x}_1$, $\mathsf{a\hat{u}x}_2$. Hence, these are also identically distributed. □

4.3 Efficiency

Here we provide a concrete analysis of the efficiency of our scheme, namely the computational and communication complexities.

Computational Complexity of the Algorithms. First, we define metrics for the two operations that are dominant, Fast Fourier Transforms (FFTs) and Multi-Scalar-Multiplications (MSMs).[10] $\mathsf{MSM}_i(n)$ and $\mathsf{FFT}(n)$ denote an MSM in $\mathbb{G}_i$ and FFT of n elements respectively. For ease of presentation, in MSM and

---

[10] MSMs are also referred to as multi-exponentiations.

FFT we ignore the additive constants that have insignificant contribution, for example for $\sum_{i=1}^{m} d_i[x_i]_1 + e[y]$ we would write $\mathsf{MSM}(m)$ instead of $\mathsf{MSM}(m+1)$.

Our first prover, $\mathsf{P_I}$ requires $O(1)\mathsf{FFT}(n)$, $O(m_2)\mathsf{FFT}(n)$ and $O(m_2)\mathsf{FFT}(n)$ to compute the corresponding quotient polynomials $q_1(X)$, $\boldsymbol{\mu}_2(X)$, $\boldsymbol{\mu}_3(X)$ and then $(2m_2 + 1)\mathsf{MSM}(n)$ to compute aux_5, aux_6, aux_7 respectively. Additionally, $2\mathsf{MSM}_1(m_1) + \mathsf{MSM}_1(m_1 - \ell_1) + \mathsf{MSM}_2(m_1)$ to compute $\mathsf{aux}_1, \mathsf{aux}_2, \mathsf{aux}_3, \mathsf{aux}_4$. Then our second prover is performing as follows: If $m_2 = o(\sqrt{n \log n} + m)$ then $(m_2 + 1)\mathsf{MSM}_1(m_2) + \mathsf{MSM}_1(5m_2 - \ell_2) + \mathsf{MSM}_2(m_2)$ to compute π_1, π_2 and π_3, the dominant cost being the computation of $\boldsymbol{z}_{\mathrm{II}} \boldsymbol{H} \boldsymbol{z}_{\mathrm{II}}^{\top}$, otherwise $5\mathsf{FFT}(n) + \mathsf{MSM}_1(5m_2 - \ell_2) + \mathsf{MSM}_2(m_2)$ to compute π_1, π_2 and π_3, the dominant cost being the FFTs to compute polynomial division for $q_4(X)$.

Communication Complexity in Group Elements. The sizes of the elements of our protocol in group elements precisely are: the size of the auxiliary information (ignoring $\mathsf{aux}_0 = C_I(x_I, w_I)$) passed to the second prover $|\mathsf{aux}| = (2m_2 + 4) |\mathbb{G}_1| + 1 |\mathbb{G}_2|$. For srs and π, they are, again, the same as in Groth16: $|\mathsf{srs}| = (2n + 3m + 1) |\mathbb{G}_1| + (n + m + 3) |\mathbb{G}_2| = O(n + m)$ and $|\pi| = 2 |\mathbb{G}_1| + 1 |\mathbb{G}_2| = O(1)$.

Remark 3. In fact, we can consider an optimization where the second prover time and $\boldsymbol{H}$-size are both $O(\mathsf{rank}(\boldsymbol{A}_{\mathrm{II}}) \times \mathsf{rank}(\boldsymbol{B}_{\mathrm{II}}))$ instead of $O(m_2^2)$, where rank denotes the column rank. For simplicity we describe our protocols assuming that $\boldsymbol{A}_{\mathrm{II}}$ and $\boldsymbol{B}_{\mathrm{II}}$ are both full rank.

5   Lower Bound on the Second Prover Time in Groth16

In this section, we sketch a lower bound on the best achievable phase II prover time in any split prover scheme for the Groth16 [21] proof system, thereby demonstrating that our constructions from Sect. 4 is asymptotically tight. Let $\mathsf{rank}(\boldsymbol{M})$ denote the column rank of matrix $\boldsymbol{M}$. At a high-level, we show that $\mathsf{P_{II}}$ in any split prover variant of Groth16 must receive $\Omega\left(\mathsf{Min}\{n - 1, (\mathsf{rank}(\boldsymbol{A}_{\mathrm{II}}) \times \mathsf{rank}(\boldsymbol{B}_{\mathrm{II}}))\}\right)$ group elements as auxiliary information from the split structured reference string and the first prover. This also implicitly puts a bound on the smallest possible runtime for $\mathsf{P_{II}}$ in Groth16. In particular, it shows that the second prover must perform $\Omega\left(\mathsf{Min}\{n - 1, (\mathsf{rank}(\boldsymbol{A}_{\mathrm{II}}) \times \mathsf{rank}(\boldsymbol{B}_{\mathrm{II}}))\}\right)$ group operations. Before proving our main impossibility result, we find it useful to prove the following helper lemma.

Lemma 2. *Let* $m_1, m_2, \ell_1, \ell_2, n \in \mathbb{N}$ *and let* $(\boldsymbol{A}_I \| \boldsymbol{A}_{II}, \boldsymbol{B}_I \| \boldsymbol{B}_{II}, \boldsymbol{C}_I \| \boldsymbol{C}_{II})$ *be any split RICS instance (as described in Sect. 4.1) for these parameters. For any phase I extended witness* $\boldsymbol{z}_I$ *and any k-sized set of phase II witnesses* $\{\boldsymbol{z}_{II,i}\}_{i \in [k]}$, *let* $\{\pi_{1,i}, \pi_{2,i}, \pi_{3,i}\}_{i \in [k]}$ *be the honestly computed Groth16 proofs for* $\{\boldsymbol{z}_I \| \boldsymbol{z}_{II,i}\}_{i \in [k]}$. *If* $k \geq m_2^2 + 3m_2 + 4$, *and vectors* $\{[\boldsymbol{z}_{II,i}, (\boldsymbol{z}_{II,i}^{\top} \otimes \boldsymbol{z}_{II,i})]\}_{i \in [k]}$ *are* *linearly independent, then there exists a polynomial time algorithm* $\mathcal{M}$ *such that with high probability*

$$\mathcal{M}\left(\{z_{II,i}, \pi_{1,i}, \pi_{2,i}, \pi_{3,i}\}_{i\in[k]}\right) \rightarrow \sum_{i=0}^{n-2} \tilde{\boldsymbol{T}}_i \left[\frac{V(\tau)\tau^i}{\delta}\right]_1,$$

where $\boldsymbol{T}(X)$ *is the vector of* m_2^2 *polynomials computed as* $\left\lfloor \frac{\boldsymbol{a}_{II}^\top(X)\otimes\boldsymbol{b}_{II}(X)}{V(X)} \right\rfloor$.

Proof. Recall that the third group element π_3 in Groth16 is of the form

$$\pi_3 = \sum_{i\in\mathcal{W}_I} z_i \overbrace{\left[\frac{\beta a_i(\tau) + \alpha b_i(\tau) + c_i(\tau)}{\delta}\right]_1}^{\text{var}_1} + \sum_{i\in\mathcal{W}_{II}} z_i \overbrace{\left[\frac{\beta a_i(\tau) + \alpha b_i(\tau) + c_i(\tau)}{\delta}\right]_1}^{\text{var}_{2,i}}$$

$$+ s\left(\sum_{i\in\mathcal{Z}_I} z_i\overbrace{[a_i(\tau)]_1}^{\text{var}_3} + \sum_{i\in\mathcal{Z}_{II}} z_i\overbrace{[a_i(\tau)]_1}^{\text{var}_{4,i}}\right) + r\left(\sum_{i\in\mathcal{Z}_I} z_i\overbrace{[b_i(\tau)]_1}^{\text{var}_5} + \sum_{i\in\mathcal{Z}_{II}} z_i\overbrace{[b_i(\tau)]_1}^{\text{var}_{6,i}}\right)$$

$$+ \sum_{i=0}^{n-2} \tilde{q}_i\overbrace{[\frac{V(\tau)\tau^i}{\delta}]_1}^{\text{var}_7} + s\overbrace{[\alpha]_1}^{\text{var}_8} + r\overbrace{[\beta]_1}^{\text{var}_9} + rs\,[\delta]_1.$$

Here the group elements colored in blue remain constant across all $\pi_{3,j}$. Furthermore, $\sum_{i=0}^{n-2} \tilde{q}_i \left[\frac{V(\tau)\tau^i}{\delta}\right]_1 = \sum_{u\in[4]} \sum_{i=0}^{n-2} \tilde{q}_{u,i} \left[\frac{V(\tau)\tau^i}{\delta}\right]_1$, where

1. $\tilde{q}_{1,i}$'s   are

  the coefficients in the quotient polynomial $\left\lfloor \frac{\left(\sum_{i\in\mathcal{Z}_I} z_i a_i(X)\right)\cdot\left(\sum_{i\in\mathcal{Z}_I} z_i b_i(X)\right)}{V(X)} \right\rfloor$.

  Therefore, $\text{var}_{10} = \sum_{i=0}^{n-2} \tilde{q}_{1,i} \left[\frac{V(\tau)\tau^i}{\delta}\right]_1$ also remains constant across all $\pi_{3,j}$.

2. $\tilde{q}_{2,i}$'s   are   the   coefficients   in   the   quotient   poly-

  nomial $\left\lfloor \frac{\left(\sum_{i\in\mathcal{Z}_I} z_i a_i(X)\right)\cdot\left(\sum_{i\in\mathcal{Z}_{II}} z_i b_i(X)\right)}{V(X)} \right\rfloor = \left\langle z_{II}, \overbrace{\left\lfloor \frac{\langle z_I, \boldsymbol{a}_I(X)\rangle \cdot \boldsymbol{b}_{II}(X)}{V(X)} \right\rfloor}^{\mu_2(X)} \right\rangle$.

  The following m_2 group elements also remain constant across all $\pi_{3,j}$'s:
  $\text{var}_{11} = \sum_{i=0}^{n-2} \tilde{\boldsymbol{\mu}}_{2,i}[\frac{V(\tau)\tau^i}{\delta}]_1$.

3. $\tilde{q}_{3,i}$'s   are   the   coefficients   in   the   quotient   poly-

  nomial $\left\lfloor \frac{\left(\sum_{i\in\mathcal{Z}_{II}} z_i a_i(X)\right)\cdot\left(\sum_{i\in\mathcal{Z}_I} z_i b_i(X)\right)}{V(X)} \right\rfloor = \left\langle z_{II}, \overbrace{\left\lfloor \frac{\boldsymbol{a}_{II}(X) \cdot \langle z_I, \boldsymbol{b}_I(X)\rangle}{V(X)} \right\rfloor}^{\mu_3(X)} \right\rangle$.

  The following m_2 group elements also remain constant across all $\pi_{3,j}$'s:
  $\text{var}_{12} = \sum_{i=0}^{n-2} \tilde{\boldsymbol{\mu}}_{3,i}[\frac{V(\tau)\tau^i}{\delta}]_1$.

4. $\tilde{q}_{4,i}$'s   are   the

  coefficients in the quotient polynomial $\left\lfloor \frac{\left(\sum_{i\in\mathcal{Z}_{II}} z_i a_i(X)\right)\cdot\left(\sum_{i\in\mathcal{Z}_{II}} z_i b_i(X)\right)}{V(X)} \right\rfloor =$

$$\left\langle \overbrace{\begin{bmatrix} \dfrac{\boldsymbol{a}_{\mathrm{II}}^{\top}(X) \otimes \boldsymbol{b}_{\mathrm{II}}(X)}{V(X)} \end{bmatrix}}^{\boldsymbol{T}(X)}, \boldsymbol{z}_{\mathrm{II}}^{\top} \otimes \boldsymbol{z}_{\mathrm{II}} \right\rangle. \text{ The following } m_2^2 \text{ group elements also}$$

remain constant across all $\pi_{3,j}$'s: $\mathbf{var_{13}} = \sum_{i=0}^{n-2} \tilde{\boldsymbol{T}}_i [\frac{V(\tau)\tau^i}{\delta}]_1$

In other words, for each $j \in [k]$, we can re-write $\pi_{3,j}$ as

$$\begin{aligned}
\pi_{3,j} =& \mathbf{var_1} + \langle \boldsymbol{z}_{\mathrm{II},j}, \mathbf{var_2} \rangle + s_j \left(\mathbf{var_3} + \langle \boldsymbol{z}_{\mathrm{II},j}, \mathbf{var_4} \rangle + \mathbf{var_7} \right) \\
&+ r_j \left(\mathbf{var_5} + \langle \boldsymbol{z}_{\mathrm{II},j}, \mathbf{var_6} \rangle + \mathbf{var_8} \right) + r_j s_j \mathbf{var_9} + \mathbf{var_{10}} + \langle \boldsymbol{z}_{\mathrm{II},j}, \mathbf{var_{11}} \rangle \\
&+ \langle \boldsymbol{z}_{\mathrm{II},j}, \mathbf{var_{12}} \rangle + \langle \boldsymbol{z}_{\mathrm{II},j}^{\top} \otimes \boldsymbol{z}_{\mathrm{II},j}, \mathbf{var_{13}} \rangle
\end{aligned}$$

After rearranging we get,

$$\begin{aligned}
\pi_{3,j} =& \mathbf{var_1} + \mathbf{var_{10}} \\
&+ s_j (\mathbf{var_3} + \mathbf{var_7}) \\
&+ r_j (\mathbf{var_5} + \mathbf{var_8}) \\
&+ r_j s_j \mathbf{var_9} \\
&+ \langle \boldsymbol{z}_{\mathrm{II},j}, \mathbf{var_2} + \mathbf{var_{11}} + \mathbf{var_{12}} \rangle \\
&+ \langle s_j \boldsymbol{z}_{\mathrm{II},j}, \mathbf{var_4} \rangle \\
&+ \langle r_j \boldsymbol{z}_{\mathrm{II},j}, \mathbf{var_6} \rangle \\
&+ \langle \boldsymbol{z}_{\mathrm{II},j}^{\top} \otimes \boldsymbol{z}_{\mathrm{II},j}, \mathbf{var_{13}} \rangle
\end{aligned}$$

As a result, $\{\boldsymbol{z}_{\mathrm{II},j}, \pi_{3,j}\}_{j \in [k]}$ can be used to obtain a system of k linear equations in $m_2^2 + 3m_2 + 4$ unknown group elements. If $k \geq m_2^2 + 3m_2 + 4$, then this system of equations can be solved in polynomial time, to learn all the unknown group elements. This includes $\mathbf{var_{13}}$ which is the m_2^2-length vector of group elements $\sum_{i=0}^{n-2} \tilde{\boldsymbol{T}}_i [\frac{V(\tau)\tau^i}{\delta}]_1$. This completes the proof of this lemma.   □

We now present a formal proof for our main impossibility result.

Theorem 2 (Main Lower-Bound). *Let $m_1, m_2, \ell_1, \ell_2, n \in \mathbb{N}$ and let $(\boldsymbol{A}_I \| \boldsymbol{A}_{II}, \boldsymbol{B}_I \| \boldsymbol{B}_{II}, \boldsymbol{C}_I \| \boldsymbol{C}_{II})$ be any split RICS instance (as described in Sect. 4.1) for these parameters. There does not exist a split prover (see Definition 2) for Groth16 [21] in the generic group model, where the phase I prover outputs a group element that has the same form as π_3 in Groth16 and where $\widetilde{\mathrm{srs}}_{II}, \mathrm{aux}$ contain $o\left(\mathrm{Min}\{n-1, (\mathrm{rank}(\boldsymbol{A}_{II}) \times \mathrm{rank}(\boldsymbol{B}_{II}))\}\right)$ group elements.*

Proof. Let $\boldsymbol{K}$ be an $(n-1) \times m_2^2$ sized matrix defined by the evaluation representation of the following m_2^2 quotient polynomials of degree $(n-1)$ each

$$\boldsymbol{T}(X) = \begin{bmatrix} \dfrac{\boldsymbol{a}_{\mathrm{II}}^{\top}(X) \otimes \boldsymbol{b}_{\mathrm{II}}(X)}{V(X)} \end{bmatrix},$$

i.e., the columns in $\boldsymbol{K}$ correspond to the evaluations of the polynomials in $\boldsymbol{T}(X)$ on the nth roots of unity. It is easy to see that the maximum column rank of this matrix is $\mathsf{rank}(\boldsymbol{K}) = \mathsf{Min}\{n-1,(\mathsf{rank}(\boldsymbol{A}_{\mathrm{II}}) \times \mathsf{rank}(\boldsymbol{B}_{\mathrm{II}}))\}$, where $\boldsymbol{A}_{\mathrm{II}}$ and $\boldsymbol{B}_{\mathrm{II}}$ are $n \times m_2$ sized matrices defined by the vector of polynomials $\boldsymbol{a}_{\mathrm{II}}(X)$ and $\boldsymbol{b}_{\mathrm{II}}(X)$ respectively.

Let us now assume for the sake of contradiction that there exists a split prover for Groth16, where $\widetilde{\mathsf{srs}}_{\mathrm{II}}$, aux contain $o\left(\mathsf{Min}\{n-1,(\mathsf{rank}(\boldsymbol{A}_{\mathrm{II}}) \times \mathsf{rank}(\boldsymbol{B}_{\mathrm{II}}))\}\right)$ group elements.

Claim 1. An adversarial P_{II} in this split prover variant for Groth16 can recover the following m_2^2 group elements

$$\sum_{i=0}^{n-2} \tilde{\boldsymbol{T}}_i \left[\frac{V(\tau)\tau^i}{\delta}\right]_1,$$

Proof. The adversary samples $k = m_2^2 + 3m_2 + 4$ random phase II extended-witness $\{z_{\mathrm{II},j}\}_{j \in [k]}$, such that the vectors $\{[z_{\mathrm{II},i},(z_{\mathrm{II},i}^{\top} \otimes z_{\mathrm{II},i})]\}_{i \in [k]}$ are linearly independent. It then uses the given $\widetilde{\mathsf{srs}}_{\mathrm{II}}$, aux on these phase II extended witness to generate a Groth16 proof for each of them, i.e., it computes $\{\pi_{1,j}, \pi_{2,j}, \pi_{3,j}\}_{j \in [k]}$. Observe that each of these Groth16 proofs rely on the same *phase I extended-witness* (this follows from Definition 2). Given these Groth16 proofs and the corresponding set of phase I extended-witnesses, the adversary can then use Lemma 2 to recover the desired m_2^2 group elements. □

Proof. We know that out of the m_2^2 group elements $\sum_{i=0}^{n-2} \tilde{\boldsymbol{T}}_i \left[\frac{V(\tau)\tau^i}{\delta}\right]_1$, $\mathsf{rank}(\boldsymbol{K})$ of them are linearly independent. However, since the generic group model only allows linear operations of the group elements, $|\widetilde{\mathsf{srs}}_{\mathrm{II}}| + |\mathsf{aux}| \in o(\mathsf{rank}(\boldsymbol{K}))$ group elements should not have sufficed to compute all of the m_2^2 group elements $\sum_{i=0}^{n-2} \tilde{\boldsymbol{T}}_i \left[\frac{V(\tau)\tau^i}{\delta}\right]_1$. Hence, our assumption was incorrect and no such split prover for Groth16 exists, where $\widetilde{\mathsf{srs}}_{\mathrm{II}}$, aux contain $o\left(\mathsf{Min}\{n-1,(\mathsf{rank}(\boldsymbol{A}_{\mathrm{II}}) \times \mathsf{rank}(\boldsymbol{B}_{\mathrm{II}}))\}\right)$ group elements. This completes the proof of this theorem. □

As discussed in Remark 3, the phase II proof generation time in our protocols from Sect. 4 can be optimized to have the second prover perform only $O\left(\mathsf{Min}\{n-1,(\mathsf{rank}(\boldsymbol{A}_{\mathrm{II}}) \times \mathsf{rank}(\boldsymbol{B}_{\mathrm{II}}))\}\right)$ group operations. Therefore, our lower bound from Theorem 2 helps demonstrate that the number of group operations performed by the second prover in our protocols is asymptotically tight.

Acknowledgements. This work is supported in part by the AFOSR Award FA9550-24-1-0156 and research grants from the Bakar Fund, J. P. Morgan Faculty Research Award, Supra Inc., Sui Foundation, and the Stellar Development Foundation. Dimitris Kolonelos is also supported in part by a Berkeley Center for Responsible, Decentralized Intelligence (RDI) Fellowship. Part of this work was done while the second author was a postdoc at NTT Research.

References

1. Ames, S., Hazay, C., Ishai, Y., Venkitasubramaniam, M.: Ligero: lightweight sublinear arguments without a trusted setup. In: Thuraisingham, B.M., Evans, D., Malkin, T., Xu, D. (eds.) ACM CCS 2017, pp. 2087–2104. ACM Press (2017). https://doi.org/10.1145/3133956.3134104

2. Barbara, A., Chiesa, A., Guan, Z.: Relativized succinct arguments in the rom do not exist. Cryptology ePrint Archive, Paper 2024/728 (2024). https://eprint.iacr.org/2024/728

3. Ben Sasson, E., et al.: Zerocash: decentralized anonymous payments from bitcoin. In: 2014 IEEE Symposium on Security and Privacy, pp. 459–474 (2014). https://doi.org/10.1109/SP.2014.36

4. Ben-Sasson, E., Chiesa, A., Tromer, E., Virza, M.: Scalable zero knowledge via cycles of elliptic curves. In: Garay, J.A., Gennaro, R. (eds.) CRYPTO 2014. LNCS, vol. 8617, pp. 276–294. Springer, Heidelberg (2014). https://doi.org/10.1007/978-3-662-44381-1_16

5. Bitansky, N., et al.: The hunting of the SNARK. J. Cryptol. **30**(4), 989–1066 (2017). https://doi.org/10.1007/s00145-016-9241-9

6. Bitansky, N., Canetti, R., Chiesa, A., Tromer, E.: Recursive composition and bootstrapping for SNARKS and proof-carrying data. In: Boneh, D., Roughgarden, T., Feigenbaum, J. (eds.) 45th ACM STOC, pp. 111–120. ACM Press (2013). https://doi.org/10.1145/2488608.2488623

7. Bootle, J., Cerulli, A., Ghadafi, E., Groth, J., Hajiabadi, M., Jakobsen, S.K.: Linear-time zero-knowledge proofs for arithmetic circuit satisfiability. In: Takagi, T., Peyrin, T. (eds.) ASIACRYPT 2017. LNCS, vol. 10626, pp. 336–365. Springer, Cham (2017). https://doi.org/10.1007/978-3-319-70700-6_12

8. Bootle, J., Cerulli, A., Groth, J., Jakobsen, S., Maller, M.: Arya: nearly linear-time zero-knowledge proofs for correct program execution. In: Peyrin, T., Galbraith, S. (eds.) ASIACRYPT 2018. LNCS, vol. 11272, pp. 595–626. Springer, Cham (2018). https://doi.org/10.1007/978-3-030-03326-2_20

9. Bootle, J., Chiesa, A., Groth, J.: Linear-time arguments with sublinear verification from tensor codes. In: Pass, R., Pietrzak, K. (eds.) TCC 2020. LNCS, vol. 12551, pp. 19–46. Springer, Cham (2020). https://doi.org/10.1007/978-3-030-64378-2_2

10. Bootle, J., Chiesa, A., Liu, S.: Zero-knowledge IOPs with linear-time prover and polylogarithmic-time verifier. In: Dunkelman, O., Dziembowski, S. (eds.) EUROCRYPT 2022, Part II. LNCS, vol. 13276, pp. 275–304. Springer, Heidelberg (202). https://doi.org/10.1007/978-3-031-07085-3_10

11. Bowe, S., Chiesa, A., Green, M., Miers, I., Mishra, P., Wu, H.: ZEXE: enabling decentralized private computation. In: 2020 IEEE Symposium on Security and Privacy, pp. 947–964. IEEE Computer Society Press (2020). https://doi.org/10.1109/SP40000.2020.00050

12. Chiesa, A., Hu, Y., Maller, M., Mishra, P., Vesely, N., Ward, N.: Marlin: preprocessing zkSNARKs with universal and updatable SRS. In: Canteaut, A., Ishai, Y. (eds.) EUROCRYPT 2020. LNCS, vol. 12105, pp. 738–768. Springer, Cham (2020). https://doi.org/10.1007/978-3-030-45721-1_26

13. Chiesa, A., Lehmkuhl, R., Mishra, P., Zhang, Y.: Eos: efficient private delegation of zksnark provers. In: Calandrino, J.A., Troncoso, C. (eds.) 32nd USENIX Security Symposium, USENIX Security 2023, Anaheim, CA, USA, 9–11 August 2023, pp. 6453–6469. USENIX Association (2023). https://www.usenix.org/conference/usenixsecurity23/presentation/chiesa

14. Chiesa, A., Ojha, D., Spooner, N.: FRACTAL: post-quantum and transparent recursive proofs from holography. In: Canteaut, A., Ishai, Y. (eds.) EUROCRYPT 2020. LNCS, vol. 12105, pp. 769–793. Springer, Cham (2020). https://doi.org/10.1007/978-3-030-45721-1_27

15. Fiat, A., Shamir, A.: How to prove yourself: practical solutions to identification and signature problems. In: Odlyzko, A.M. (ed.) CRYPTO 1986. LNCS, vol. 263, pp. 186–194. Springer, Heidelberg (1987). https://doi.org/10.1007/3-540-47721-7_12

16. Fuchsbauer, G., Kiltz, E., Loss, J.: The algebraic group model and its applications. In: Shacham, H., Boldyreva, A. (eds.) CRYPTO 2018. LNCS, vol. 10992, pp. 33–62. Springer, Cham (2018). https://doi.org/10.1007/978-3-319-96881-0_2

17. Gabizon, A., Williamson, Z.J., Ciobotaru, O.: PLONK: permutations over lagrange-bases for oecumenical noninteractive arguments of knowledge. Cryptology ePrint Archive, Report 2019/953 (2019). https://eprint.iacr.org/2019/953

18. Garg, S., Goel, A., Jain, A., Policharla, G., Sekar, S.: zksaas: zero-knowledge snarks as a service. In: Calandrino, J.A., Troncoso, C. (eds.) 32nd USENIX Security Symposium, USENIX Security 2023, Anaheim, CA, USA, 9–11 August 2023, pp. 4427–4444. USENIX Association (2023). https://www.usenix.org/conference/usenixsecurity23/presentation/garg

19. Garg, S., Goel, A., Wang, M.: How to prove statements obliviously? IACR Cryptol. ePrint Arch. p. 1609 (2023). https://eprint.iacr.org/2023/1609

20. Gennaro, R., Gentry, C., Parno, B., Raykova, M.: Quadratic span programs and succinct NIZKs without PCPs. In: Johansson, T., Nguyen, P.Q. (eds.) EURO-CRYPT 2013. LNCS, vol. 7881, pp. 626–645. Springer, Heidelberg (2013). https://doi.org/10.1007/978-3-642-38348-9_37

21. Groth, J.: On the size of pairing-based non-interactive arguments. In: Fischlin, M., Coron, J.-S. (eds.) EUROCRYPT 2016. LNCS, vol. 9666, pp. 305–326. Springer, Heidelberg (2016). https://doi.org/10.1007/978-3-662-49896-5_11

22. Grubbs, P., Arun, A., Zhang, Y., Bonneau, J., Walfish, M.: Zero-knowledge middleboxes. In: USENIX Security Symposium, pp. 4255–4272. USENIX Association (2022)

23. Hopwood, D., Bowe, S., Hornby, T., Wilcox, N.: Zcash protocol specification (2022). https://zips.z.cash/protocol/protocol.pdf

24. Kothapalli, A., Masserova, E., Parno, B.: A direct construction for asymptotically optimal zksnarks. IACR Cryptol. ePrint Arch. p. 1318 (2020). https://eprint.iacr.org/2020/1318

25. Kothapalli, A., Setty, S., Tzialla, I.: Nova: recursive zero-knowledge arguments from folding schemes. In: Dodis, Y., Shrimpton, T. (eds.) CRYPTO 2022, Part IV. LNCS, vol. 13510, pp. 359–388. Springer, Heidelberg (2022). https://doi.org/10.1007/978-3-031-15985-5_13

26. Lee, J.: Dory: efficient, transparent arguments for generalised inner products and polynomial commitments. In: Nissim, K., Waters, B. (eds.) TCC 2021. LNCS, vol. 13043, pp. 1–34. Springer, Cham (2021). https://doi.org/10.1007/978-3-030-90453-1_1

27. Liu, X., Zhou, Z., Wang, Y., Zhang, B., Yang, X.: Scalable collaborative zk-snark: Fully distributed proof generation and malicious security. IACR Cryptol. ePrint Arch. p. 143 (2024). https://eprint.iacr.org/2024/143

28. Maurer, U.: Abstract models of computation in cryptography. In: Smart, N.P. (ed.) Cryptography and Coding 2005. LNCS, vol. 3796, pp. 1–12. Springer, Heidelberg (2005). https://doi.org/10.1007/11586821_1

29. Micali, S.: CS proofs (extended abstracts). In: 35th FOCS, pp. 436–453. IEEE Computer Society Press (1994). https://doi.org/10.1109/SFCS.1994.365746

30. Parno, B., Howell, J., Gentry, C., Raykova, M.: Pinocchio: nearly practical verifiable computation. In: 2013 IEEE Symposium on Security and Privacy, pp. 238–252. IEEE Computer Society Press (2013). https://doi.org/10.1109/SP.2013.47
31. Rathee, D., Policharla, G.V., Xie, T., Cottone, R., Song, D.: Zebra: snark-based anonymous credentials for practical, private and accountable on-chain access control. Cryptology ePrint Archive, Paper 2022/1286 (2022). https://eprint.iacr.org/2022/1286
32. Setty, S.: Spartan: efficient and general-purpose zkSNARKs without trusted setup. In: Micciancio, D., Ristenpart, T. (eds.) CRYPTO 2020. LNCS, vol. 12172, pp. 704–737. Springer, Cham (2020). https://doi.org/10.1007/978-3-030-56877-1_25
33. Shoup, V.: Lower bounds for discrete logarithms and related problems. In: Fumy, W. (ed.) EUROCRYPT'97. LNCS, vol. 1233, pp. 256–266. Springer, Heidelberg (1997). https://doi.org/10.1007/3-540-69053-0_18
34. Valiant, P.: Incrementally verifiable computation or proofs of knowledge imply time/space efficiency. In: Canetti, R. (ed.) TCC 2008. LNCS, vol. 4948, pp. 1–18. Springer, Heidelberg (2008). https://doi.org/10.1007/978-3-540-78524-8_1
35. Wu, H., Zheng, W., Chiesa, A., Popa, R.A., Stoica, I.: DIZK: a distributed zero knowledge proof system. In: Enck, W., Felt, A.P. (eds.) USENIX Security 2018, pp. 675–692. USENIX Association (2018)
36. Xie, T., Zhang, J., Zhang, Y., Papamanthou, C., Song, D.: Libra: succinct zero-knowledge proofs with optimal prover computation. In: Boldyreva, A., Micciancio, D. (eds.) CRYPTO 2019. LNCS, vol. 11694, pp. 733–764. Springer, Cham (2019). https://doi.org/10.1007/978-3-030-26954-8_24
37. Zcash: The halo2 book. https://zcash.github.io/halo2/index.html
38. Zhang, J., et al.: Doubly efficient interactive proofs for general arithmetic circuits with linear prover time. In: Vigna, G., Shi, E. (eds.) ACM CCS 2021, pp. 159–177. ACM Press (2021). https://doi.org/10.1145/3460120.3484767

Universally Composable Non-interactive Zero-Knowledge from Sigma Protocols via a New Straight-Line Compiler

Megan Chen[1]([✉]), Pousali Dey[2], Chaya Ganesh[3], Pratyay Mukherjee[4], Pratik Sarkar[4], and Swagata Sasmal[2]

[1] Boston University, Boston, USA
megchen@bu.edu
[2] Indian Statistical Institute, Kolkata, India
[3] Indian Institute of Science, Kolkata, India
chaya@iisc.ac.in
[4] Supra Research, San Jose, USA

Abstract. Non-interactive zero-knowledge proofs (NIZK) are essential building blocks in threshold cryptosystems like multiparty signatures, distributed key generation, and verifiable secret sharing, allowing parties to prove correct behavior without revealing secrets. Furthermore, universally composable (UC) NIZKs enable seamless composition in larger cryptosystems. A popular way to construct NIZKs is to compile interactive protocols using the Fiat-Shamir transform. Unfortunately, a Fiat-Shamir transformed NIZK requires rewinding the adversary and is not *straight-line extractable*, making it at odds with UC. Using Fischlin's transform gives straight-line extractability, but at the expense of many repetitions of the underlying protocol leading to poor concrete efficiency and difficulty in setting parameters.

In this work, we propose a simple new transform that compiles a Sigma protocol for an algebraic relation into a UC-NIZK protocol *without any overheads of repetition*.

- Given a Sigma protocol for proving m algebraic statements over n witnesses, we construct a compiler to transform it into a *straight-line extractable* protocol using an additively homomorphic encryption scheme (AHE). Our prover executes the Sigma protocol's prover once and computes $2n$ encryptions. The verification process involves running the Sigma protocol verifier once and then computing n encryptions, which are homomorphically verified against the prover generated encryptions.
- We apply the Fiat-Shamir transform to the above straight-line extractable Sigma protocol to obtain a UC-NIZK. We instantiate AHE using class group based encryption where the public key of the encryption scheme is obliviously sampled using a suitable hash function. This yields a UC-NIZK protocol in the random oracle model.

M. Chen—Supported by DARPA under Agreement No. HR00112020023.
C. Ganesh—Supported in part by Rising Star Award, Intel Corporation.

© International Association for Cryptologic Research 2025
T. Jager and J. Pan (Eds.): PKC 2025, LNCS 15674, pp. 381–417, 2025.
https://doi.org/10.1007/978-3-031-91820-9_13

Keywords: Zero Knowledge Proofs · Universal Composability · Sigma
Protocols

1   Introduction

Non-interactive zero-knowledge proofs (NIZK) [BFM90, BSMP91, FLS99] are
used to enforce honest behavior and are an important building block in the design
of cryptographic protocols like anonymous credentials [RWGM23], threshold signatures [BLS01, KG20, Lin22], distributed key generation [GJKR99, CS04, CD24,
KMM+23], and multi-party computation in general. Typically, NIZKs are analyzed in the standalone setting, where the security is proven by showing individual properties separately such as completeness, zero-knowledge, and (knowledge)
soundness under a setup assumption (like a common reference string (CRS) or
the Random Oracle Model (ROM)). This standalone security guarantee often
does not suffice in applications that run NIZKs concurrently in arbitrarily many
sessions. The Universal Composability (UC) framework [Can01] allows for the
modular analysis of cryptographic protocols guaranteeing security in the presence of arbitrarily many sessions running concurrently, thereby facilitating easy
composability.

NIZKs in the ROM. A common design methodology for constructing NIZKs
is to construct a public-coin interactive argument, prove zero-knowledge and
knowledge-soundness, and then compile this interactive argument into a NIZK
in the ROM. A large class of protocols that render themselves to such compilation
into NIZKs are *Sigma protocols*.

A Sigma protocol is a three-round interactive proof between a prover and
a verifier, both possessing a statement x, and additionally, the prover has a
secret witness w. A Sigma protocol proceeds in three rounds, where the prover
sends a first message (commitment) a to the verifier, the verifier sends a random string c (the challenge), and finally the prover responds with a last message
z (the response). The verifier accepts or rejects the claim using the transcript
(x, a, c, z). Sigma protocols satisfy two main properties: (i) special soundness,
a form of knowledge soundness that guarantees that an extractor can output a
valid witness for x given two accepting proofs with the same initial message a
but distinct challenges, that is, (x, a, c, z) and $(x, a, c', z'), c \neq c'$ and, (ii) honest-
verifier zero knowledge (HVZK), a weak form of the zero-knowledge property
that guarantees simulatability of the transcript given randomly sampled challenge c. Additionally, since the verifier's message is a uniformly random string,
this is public-coin, making Sigma protocols amenable to compilation into NIZKs.

A popular compilation method is the Fiat-Shamir (FS) transform [FS87]: the
prover non-interactively computes the challenge $c = \mathcal{H}(x, a)$ by applying a hash
function $\mathcal{H}$ (modeled as a random oracle [CJS14]) on (x, a). The NIZK proof
sent to the verifier is (x, a, c, z) who checks if $\mathcal{H}(x, a) \overset{?}{=} c$, and then runs the
Sigma protocol verifier. Knowledge-soundness of the transformed NIZK relies on
the special-soundness of the Sigma protocol and therefore requires an extractor

to rewind the malicious prover in order to obtain two transcripts with a shared prefix by programming the RO to $\mathcal{H}(x, a) = c'$ after rewinding. Zero-knowledge of the NIZK follows from HVZK of the Sigma protocol and programming the RO.

Applications of Sigma protocols are plenty [FS87, CDS94, DG03, Mau09, SV12, FKMV12, ORV14] as many algebraic languages admit very efficient Sigma protocols, such as Schnorr [Sch91], Chaum-Pederson [CP93] etc. Moreover, compilers are known for expressive languages [Mau09, CDS94]. FS-transformed Sigma protocols are widely used in practice in signature generation [Sch91], signature aggregation [KS22, CGKN21], proof of correct decryption in threshold cryptosystems, and distributed key generation [GJKR99, CS04, KMM+23] – many of these achieve UC security, assuming that the underlying NIZK is UC secure. A natural and pertinent question, then, is whether this large and useful class of Sigma protocols can be compiled into NIZKs that can be shown to be UC-secure?

Proving Sigma-Compiled NIZK UC-Secure. We now discuss the technical challenges in compiling Sigma protocols to UC-secure NIZKs.

CHALLENGE 1: STRAIGHT-LINE EXTRACTION. In the UC framework, the environment $\mathcal{Z}$, representing all that is external to the execution of the concerned protocol, interacts with the protocol, and outputs a decision bit in the end, indicating its guess of whether it interacted with a "real" adversary $\mathcal{A}$ and parties in the protocol, or with an "ideal" adversary (or simulator) Sim and parties accessing the ideal functionality $\mathcal{F}$ that specifies the ideal outcome of the protocol. NIZKs that rely on rewinding or non-black-box access to the adversary in the proof (either for ZK or for extraction) are at odds with UC. This is because in the UC definition, the environment $\mathcal{Z}$ is an interactive distinguisher between the real protocol and the ideal process, and therefore a simulator Sim in the security proof cannot rewind $\mathcal{Z}$, and does not have the concrete code of $\mathcal{Z}$. Thus, a crucial property that NIZKs must have in order to be compatible with a proof of UC is *black-box straight-line simulation and extraction.*

At a high level, a NIZK in the ROM is straight-line extractable if an extractor succeeds given only the transcript that includes the RO queries made by the prover (and crucially without interacting with any successful prover). This immediately precludes FS-compiled Sigma protocols from being shown UC-secure. There exist alternatives to Fiat-Shamir that provide compilers [Pas03, Fis05] in the ROM, which output a NIZK that is straight-line extractable. Intuitively, the extractor can succeed by observing RO queries made by the prover in the resulting NIZK, even though not all of the query/responses make it to the proof (this does away with the overhead in proof size). However, there is at a cost in efficiency and complexity of the design:[1] Pass's compiler [Pas03] requires repeating the underlying Sigma protocol for security parameter (κ) number of times where

---

[1] For example, since the soundness error is related to the number of repetition, one has to be careful in choosing the parameters, such as the number of repetitions.

κ is the computational security parameter and is as high as $\kappa = 128$, leading to a 128× overhead over the FS-compiled NIZK (that relies on rewinding). Fischlin's compiler [Fis05] partially addresses this overhead using a *proof-of-work* paradigm: the prover is forced to compute several valid proofs, which forces the prover to query many "good" values to the random oracle in order to find a pre-image that hashes to a zero string. Fischlin's transform is known to improve over the Pass transform as shown in [CL24, KS22]. However, choosing the optimal proof-of-work parameters is challenging in practice since it depends on the prover's computation power. Additionally, Fischlin transform also requires repetition of the underlying Sigma protocol and when applied to the Schnorr protocol incurs a 15× overhead as shown by [CL24]. Thus, FS is the most efficient transform, since it incurs essentially no overhead in computation or communication, though the extractor is rewinding. This motivates the question:

Can we construct a generic compiler that transforms a Sigma protocol into a NIZK with straight-line extraction (without incurring communication overhead of repetition or prover overhead of proof-of-work)?

We answer the above question in the affirmative and show a transform that compiles Sigma protocols for algebraic relations into straight-line extractable NIZKs without incurring a repetition overhead or prover overhead.

CHALLENGE 2: SIMULATION EXTRACTABILITY. Another important property crucial for getting UC security is *non-malleability (NM)* [DDN91]. In a malleability attack, an adversary can maul existing proofs observed during the protocol execution, and forge a proof on some statement for which they do not know the corresponding witness. Since $\mathcal{Z}$ may ask uncorrupted provers to produce proofs on arbitrary statement-witness pairs, the ability to maul proofs causes Sim to fail in extracting a witness, leading to $\mathcal{Z}$ successfully distinguishing between real execution and ideal process. Non-malleability is captured by *simulation-extractability* in the context of UC-NIZK [Sah99, DDO+01, PR05, GMY06, JP14, FKMV12], and [Gro06] proved that simulation-extractability is necessary for UC.

FS-transformed Sigma protocols are proven to be simulation-extractable [FKMV12], but are not straight-line and hence not UC-compatible. Among the transformations that yield straight-line extractable NIZKs, a randomized version of Fischlin's transform [KS22] has been shown to be simulation-extractable, and thus UC-secure [LR22b]. In sum, among existing transformations of Sigma protocols to NIZKs: FS transform gives simulation-extractability but not straight-line extraction; Fischlin and Pass transforms give straight-line simulation extraction, but incur the overhead of repetition penalizing proof sizes in practical applications.

Can we transform a Sigma protocol into a UC-NIZK that incurs no overhead compared to FS-transformed NIZK?

We answer the above questions by showing that applying the FS transform on our *straight-line compiled* protocol yields a NIZK that is simulation-extractable, which we then prove is UC-secure.

1.1   Our Contributions

- Primarily we construct a compiler that compiles a Sigma protocol for an algebraic relation into a protocol with *straight-line extraction* using an additively homomorphic encryption (AHE) scheme in the CRS model. For proof of m algebraic statements with n witnesses, the overhead incurred by our compiler is $2n$ encryptions for the prover, and an overhead of $2n$ ciphertexts in the proof size. For proving instances where $m > n$, as it is indeed the case in practical applications of Chaum-Pedersen [CP93], this overhead is amortized away. We discuss such applications at the end of this section.

  Our transformation to a straight-line extractable protocol is independently interesting since the extraction avoids "forking" the adversary [PS96], which in practice leads to a slack in tightness of the security reduction [JT20].
- Applying the Fiat-Shamir transform on this compiled Sigma protocol, we obtain a NIZK that is *straight-line extractable*, showing the first property needed for UC. We show that the Fiat-Shamir compiled NIZK of the transformed Sigma protocol satisfies *simulation-extractability*. Towards this, we show that our compiled NIZK satisfies a property called weak-unique response, that says that no adversary can generate two distinct accepting transcripts that share a common prefix. This notion has been used to prove simulation-extractability of Sigma protocols [FKMV12] and other multi-round protocols [GOP+22], and is also necessary for Fischlin's transform. While this is a natural notion towards non-malleability, not all Sigma protocols satisfy this.[2] Nevertheless, we prove that our straight-line transformed Sigma protocol does satisfy unique response, *even when* the underlying Sigma protocol does not enjoy this property. This is a distinct feature of our transform.
- Finally, we show that the resulting NIZK is UC-secure. Our analysis is in the local ROM. As elaborated next, this has a substantial application in several cryptographic protocols, that rely on random oracle based NIZKs.

Instantiation. We provide a concrete instantiation of the compiler by instantiating the encryption scheme using the additive homomorphic encryption scheme based on class groups [CL15, CLR24]. En route, we show two new properties of the class-group based encryption scheme, namely (i) homomorphic well-formedness, which ensures that if a random linear homomorphic computation of two strings in the ciphertext space is well-formed (that is decryptable), then the strings themselves are well-formed; (ii) oblivious sampleability of the public key, which allows sampling of the public key obliviously, without knowing the corresponding secret-key. We show that the class group encryption scheme satisfies these properties from rough order assumption [BDO23] and a variant of

---

[2] Examples are Okamoto's protocol [Oka93], Sigma protocol for OR composition [CDS94] – our straight-line extractable transform convert these to satisfy unique response. A closer look reveals that when $m < n$, this may not be satisfied, as witnesses are hidden information theoretically by simple algebraic argument.

hard subgroup membership (HSM) assumption respectively.[3] This enables us to remove the uniform CRS from our straightline-extractable protocol by obliviously sampling the public key as part of the proof, yielding a NIZK only in the ROM (without CRS). The public key consists of two class-group elements. We obliviously sample them by hashing into class groups of unknown order using recently proposed hashing algorithms [CLR24, SBK24], compatible with random oracle.

Applications. All applications of Schnorr and Chaum-Pedersen [CP93] benefit from our compiler and achieve UC security without repetition of the underlying Sigma protocol. We outline some applications of Sigma protocols for algebraic relations where UC security is desired and our UC-NIZK can be used as a drop-in replacement.

- *Signature Protocols:* The works of [Lin22, KG20] consider multiparty threshold signatures based on Schnorr. These protocols are UC-secure to permit composition in larger systems. As building blocks they need proofs of knowledge for discrete logarithms which are instantiated using the Fischlin transform. Our UC-NIZK can replace the Fishclin-transformed Schnorr and result in a simpler and potentially more efficient protocol.
- *Public Key Infrastructure (PKI):* Many protocols, defined in the UC framework, rely on a verified public key setup (or PKI) for encryptions with keys of the form $\mathsf{pk} = g^{\mathsf{sk}}$ – establishing this requires a NIZK proof of knowledge of sk in the exponent (a.k.a. Schnorr's proof) of g, a cyclic group element. Proving knowledge soundness of the standard Schnorr would require rewinding, thus leaving a gap between the security argument and the desired UC security of the protocol. Using a UC-compatible NIZK, like ours, one instead get the UC security of the full protocol.
- *Distributed Verifiable Random Functions:* The work of [GLOW21] introduced distributed verifiable random functions (DVRF) based on BLS signatures and it required the proof of knowledge variant of Chaum-Pedersen's proof of equal discrete log for proving that the partial evaluations of the DVRF is correct. The recent work of [KMMM23] introduced output private DVRF, formalized in UC, and they also require the proof of knowledge variant of Chaum-Pedersen's proof for the same purpose. In addition, they need Schnorr's proof of discrete log as part of their input blinding. Currently, these protocols rely on rewinding the adversary to extract the witness. Our compiler can be used to make those proofs UC-secure.
- *Secure Content Moderation and Traceability:* The work of [TGL+19] constructs a secure content moderation protocol over encrypted messaging platforms like Signal. Under the hood, they require a Chaum-Pedersen proof and

---

[3] We note that, assuming a hash function, which behaves as a random oracle and maps to the public-key space of the encryption scheme, then oblivious sampleability holds unconditionally. However, the existing class-group based hash functions [CLR24, SBK24] maps to the entire class group, whereas the public key lies on a cyclic subgroup. Therefore, the need for the variant of HSM assumption arises.

security relies on knowledge-of-exponent assumption. This is not composable due to the non-blackbox nature of the reduction. Using our UC-NIZK will result in a UC-secure content moderation protocol. Our UC-NIZK is also a candidate to be used in the end-to-end secure messaging protocol of [BGJP23] that only traces illegal content.

Our compiler is general enough to work with AND/OR compositions [CDS94, FHJ20] which yields better signature schemes [FHJ20]. We discuss this in the full version [CDG+24].

1.2   Related Work

In this section, we describe the existing approaches to obtain straight line extraction in Sigma protocols and UC-NIZKs.

Fischlin Transform. The work of [KS22] improved upon the original Fischlin transform by rerandomizing the prover's transcript in the transform. The recent works of [LR22b,LR22a] study necessary properties for UC-NIZK in the global ROM and show that randomized Fischlin transforms Sigma protocols into UC-NIZKs. The work of [GKO+23] constructs a compiler to lift any witness-succinct simulation-extractable NIZK into a witness-succinct UC-secure one in the global random oracle model using a Fischlin-like transform. However, all these protocols inherit the downside of Fischlin: they inherently require repetition of the underlying Sigma protocol and the number of repetitions increases to achieve stronger soundness. In contrast, our UC-NIZK protocol is statistically soundness by the correctness guarantee of the decryption procedure in the AHE scheme.

NIZKs in the CRS Model. The work of [FLS99] constructed a NIZK protocol in the CRS model assuming trapdoor permutations. The initial work of [CGH98] proposed to instantiate the hash function in the Fiat-Shamir transform using Correlation intractable (CI) hash functions. Subsequent works [PS19,CCH+19] construct such CI hash functions for sparse relations from LWE in the CRS model. The work of [BKM20] construct CI hash for approximable relations from LPN+DDH assumptions and then construct NIZKs from it, which was improved to using only sub-exponential DDH in [JJ21]. The work of [CSW22] explored NIZKs that satisfy adaptive zero-knowledge, adaptive soundness and security against adaptive corruptions. Our NIZK protocol can also work in this paradigm by replacing the random oracle in the Fiat-Shamir transform with a CI-hash function and embedding the secret key of the encryption inside the CI-hash. However, this would heavily affect the performance and it would be of theoretical interest as computing the CI-hash function to generate the challenge string is an expensive task.

Non-black-Box Extractable NIZKs. Another line of work [GOS12,AF07, KNYY19,KNYY20] uses pairing-based techniques in bilinear groups to construct NIZKs, and NIZKs in [DDO+01,GOS06,Gro06] are UC-secure. These constructions either use specific assumptions over bilinear groups, where DDH is easy and popular protocols like Chaum-Pedersen cannot be instantiated; or are in idealized models (like AGM/GGM) [Sho97,FKL18], or use knowledge-type assumptions [Dam91]. These are incompatible with UC security, since knowledge assumptions are non-black-box and hence the extractor depends on the code of the adversary; or are limited in the class of adversaries considered (generic/algebraic). The UC-AGM framework [ABK+21] models composability in the AGM for algebraic adversaries, but incompatible with standard UC; and [KKK21] enable knowledge assumptions in larger protocols, but in a composition framework [Mau11] different from UC. [BFKT24] demonstrates that one can still prove UC security if one is willing to have a weaker NIZK functionality, in which proofs are re-randomizable (and are malleable in this specific way) but otherwise are non-malleable, and carefully limit the power of the adversary. They show that [Gro16] is UC-realizes the weak NIZK functionality in a the global observable generic bilinear group oracle model, rather than UC-AGM.

NIZK in the CRS+ROM. [Lin15] proposed a transform using a dual-mode commitment and a non-programmable random oracle to obtain zero-knowledge via using the secret trapdoor of the setup string, which was subsequently improved upon in [CPSV16]. However, both protocols do not consider proof of knowledge and hence fail to provide a UC-NIZK.

UC NIZK in the ROM. An approach for designing UC NIZKs in the ROM is identify a protocol which is straightline-extractable in the ROM, then proving that it is UC-secure. Two classes of protocols which are used in this design paradigm include (1) Sigma protocols, which are made straightline extractable via the compilers in the ROM, such as that of Pass [Pas03] and Fischlin [Fis05] (see discussion in *Fischlin Transform* paragraph); and (2) those which are already straightline-extractable in the ROM.

Protocols that are straightline-extractable in the random oracle model include the Kilian-Micali SNARK in the ROM [Kil92,Mic00] and its extension to IOPs [BCS16]. The recent work of [CF24] prove that the Kilian-Micali SNARK UC-realizes $\mathcal{F}_{\mathsf{NIZK}}$ in the global restricted programmable ROM unconditionally, i.e. the adversary is only restricted by the number of random oracle queries but is otherwise computationally unbounded. A concurrent work [Ano] to the present work builds upon [CF24], by giving a modular proof that the Kilian-Micali SNARK UC-realizes $\mathcal{F}_{\mathsf{NIZK}}$; [Ano] formulate non-interactive ideal functionalities for commitment and vector commitment which have access to a global (restricted programmable) random oracle, then show the UC security of the Kilian-Micali protocol realized using a ideal vector commitment plus a PCP in the global (restricted programmable) random oracle model.

Unlike [CF24,Ano], which use the observability property of the global random oracle to get straightline-extractability, our UC NIZK gets straightline-extractability due to additively homomorphic encryption AHE. Another difference is that this work uses a local (i.e., non-global) programmable random oracle, meaning that different protocol instances access independent random oracles. As such, the local ROM is a stronger security assumption compared to the global ROM, in which query responses must be consistent across all protocol instances and the adversary can set the value of certain locations, via programming.

Other Compilers for Straightline-Extractability. Omega protocols [GMY03] use a technique similar to ours – of using PKE and having the corresponding decryption key as a trapdoor – to achieve straightline-extractability. In a nutshell, they are a class of sigma protocols with two additional properties: (i) they need a CRS; (ii) they support straightline-extractability. So, from another perspective, our interactive protocol (Fig 1) is indeed an Omega protocol. Nevertheless, our generic approach to construct such protocols from Sigma-protocols differs significantly from [GMY03], in that an explicit proof of knowledge was used, whereas we exploit the homomorphism of the encryption scheme over both witness and randomness. Moreover, our protocol also has a dense CRS (so it can also be called a dense Omega protocol a la [DSW08]), which is particularly useful for obtaining a simulation-sound non-interactive protocol without CRS via Fiat-Shamir, whereas [GMY03] needs to use a signature additionally (associated PoK of signature augmented in the proof).

The work of [Kat21] constructs a straightline extractable NIZK for proving the possession of a short vector $e \in \mathbf{R}_q^m$ such that $Ae = u$ for a given random matrix $A \in \mathbf{R}_q^{n \times m}$ and vector $u \in \mathbf{R}_q^n$ for appropriate parameters n, m and q. Similar to our compiler, they also utilize an (extractable) lattice commitment scheme that is linearly homomorphic over polynomial ring $\mathbf{R}_q$ to transform Lyubashevsky's [Lyu12] Sigma protocol for the above lattice relation to a straightline extractable one. Then they apply the Fiat Shamir transform in the quantum random oracle model to make it a quantum-secure NIZK. They construct candidates for the commitment scheme based on the hardness of lattice problems: one based on the module learning with errors (MLWE) problem, and the other based on the MLWE and the decisional small matrix ratio (DSMR) problem. However, their compiler is specific to proving lattice relations (of the form $Ae = u$), and their commitment scheme only works over polynomial rings. It is unclear how to make it work for group-based NP statements without reducing the statement to one that is compatible with lattice relations. Converting the group-based NP statement to a corresponding lattice relation may not always be possible, or incur additional overheads. Our NIZK works "directly" for group-based statements, that is, it is designed for group-based statements and works with the native operations of the computation for the statement.

2   Technical Overview

The goal of this work is to construct UC-NIZKs from Sigma protocols for arbitrary algebraic relations (in the exponent), without repetitions. For well-known Sigma protocols (e.g. the Schnorr, Okamoto, and Chaum-Pedersen protocols), compiling these protocols to be non-interactive is straightforward, via applying the Fiat-Shamir transform. However, a remaining technical difficulty is proving that these protocols are also straight-line extractable. Prior compilers include those of [Pas03,Fis05]. We take a totally new approach to design a straight-line compiler.

We proceed in two main steps, which we detail in the coming sections.

Step 1: Construct a non-interactive straight-line extractable NIZK protocol Π_{GenLin} for arbitrary linear relations, in the ROM, using additively-homomorphic encryption (AHE). Notably, this construction *does not* require access to a common reference/random string.

Step 2: Prove that Π_{GenLin} UC-realizes the non-interactive zero knowledge functionality $\mathcal{F}_{\mathsf{NIZK}}$.

For simplicity of exposition, we focus the technical overview on Schnorr's protocol, which is an example of an algebraic Sigma protocol, i.e. 3-move interactive argument between a prover $\mathcal{P}$ and a verifier $\mathcal{V}$, that checks a single linear relation. We remark that all discussion presented here generalizes to protocols with n witnesses and for checking m linear relations, but we refer the reader to Sect. 4 for full details.

2.1 Schnorr's Proof of Discrete Log

Schnorr's Protocol. We begin by recalling Schnorr's protocol for the discrete log relation $\mathcal{R}_{\mathsf{DLog}}$. Specifically the relation is defined as:

$$\mathcal{R}_{\mathsf{DLog}} := \{ (g^w, w) \mid g \in \mathbb{G} \wedge w \in \mathbb{Z}_q \} \ ,$$

where $\mathrm{x} = (g, g^w)$, $\mathrm{w} = w$, $\mathbb{G}$ is a group of prime order q and g is a (fixed, public) generator for $\mathbb{G}$. Schnorr's protocol is the following:

- **Move 1 (commit):** $\mathcal{P}_1(\mathrm{x}, \mathrm{w}) \rightarrow a$:
  1. Sample $s \leftarrow \mathbb{Z}_q$ and compute $S := g^s$ and send $a := S$ to $\mathcal{V}$.
- **Move 2 (challenge):** $\mathcal{V}_1(\mathrm{x}, a) \rightarrow c$:
  1. Sample a random challenge $c \in \mathbb{Z}_q$, and send c to $\mathcal{V}$.
- **Move 3 (response):** $\mathcal{P}_2(\mathrm{x}, \mathrm{w}, (a, c)) \rightarrow z$:
  1. Compute $z := s + c \cdot w \in \mathbb{Z}_q$, and send z to $\mathcal{V}$.
- **Verification:** $\mathcal{V}_2(\mathrm{x}, (a, c, z)) \rightarrow b$:
  1. Parse x as a group element $W \in \mathbb{G}$ and w as $w \in \mathbb{Z}_q$.
  2. If $g^z = S \cdot W^c \in \mathbb{G}$, output 1. Otherwise, output 0.

In other words, the verifier accepts if $z = s + c \cdot w$ in the exponent. (This check is linear in w.)

Proving Knowledge Soundness of Schnorr's Protocol. The standard proof of knowledge soundness for Schnorr's protocol relies on *rewinding* the prover and rerunning it on a different challenge c', generating two protocol transcripts that share the same first message: (a, c, z) and (a, c', z'). Then, the (knowledge soundness) extractor recovers the witness w, via computing $\mathrm{w} := \frac{z' - z}{c' - c} \in \mathbb{Z}_q$.

Furthermore, knowledge extraction fails only when $c = c'$, which occurs with probability $\frac{1}{q}$ since c, c' are sampled uniformly from $\mathbb{Z}_q$.

Unfortunately, this extractor does not satisfy *straight-line* knowledge soundness, i.e. the ability to extract the witness w without rewinding the adversary. This is problematic for proving that Schnorr's protocol is UC-secure: the environment $\mathcal{Z}$ can distinguish that in the ideal world, the adversarial prover algorithm was rewound whereas in the real-world execution, there was no rewinding. Without extracting the correct witness in the ideal world, the simulator cannot complete the simulation.

Given this conundrum, other techniques like the Pass and Fischlin transforms [Pas03, Fis05] were proposed in the random oracle model. However, these approaches require repetitions of the base Sigma protocol (for soundness) and incur at least a 15× overhead [CL24]. Alternatively, one can consider using a knowledge assumption, i.e. given an accepting transcript knowledge of the witness is assumed. However, this approach also violates [KZM+15] UC-security as the simulator needs non-blackbox access to the adversary.

2.2 A New Straight-Line Extractable Schnorr's Proof of Discrete Log from Additively Homomorphic Encryptions (AHE)

We avoid the need for repetition and introduce a new simple compiler for making Schnorr's protocol straight-line extractable in the ROM. The key ingredient is using an additively-homomorphic encryption scheme, denoted $\mathsf{AHE} = (\mathsf{Gen}, \mathsf{Enc}, \mathsf{Dec})$ to encrypt the witness. Note that it is not sufficient to use a commitment scheme, unless it is an extractable commitment; this is equivalent to using encryption.

Compiled Protocol. We briefly describe the compiled scheme. The common reference string includes an encryption key ek for AHE and a (secret) trapdoor, which is the decryption key dk associated with ek. Then, the prover, given AHE, encrypts the NP witness $\mathrm{w} = w$ as ciphertext C_w and the randomness s as C_s. The prover sends the first message $S = g^s$ of the Schnorr's protocol and the two encryptions. The verifier runs the usual Schnorr's verification protocol and in addition, it runs the same check over the encryptions. The additively homomorphic property of AHE allows the verifier to check the linear relation over the encryptions. The protocol is as follows (with differences from baseline Schnorr noted in blue):

- **Setup:** A key pair $(\mathsf{ek}, \mathsf{dk})$ for AHE.
- **Move 1 (commit):** $\mathcal{P}(\mathsf{ek}, \mathrm{x}, \mathrm{w}) \to a$:
    1. Sample $s \leftarrow \mathbb{Z}_q$ and compute $S := g^s$.
    2. Sample encryption randomnesses r_s, r_w.
    3. Compute $C_s := \mathsf{Enc}(\mathsf{ek}, s; r_s)$ and $C_w := \mathsf{Enc}(\mathsf{ek}, w; r_w)$.
    4. Send $a := (S, C_s, C_w)$ to $\mathcal{V}$.
- **Move 2 (challenge):** $\mathcal{V}(\mathsf{ek}, \mathrm{x}, a) \to c$:
    1. Sample a random challenge $c \in \mathbb{Z}_q$, and send c to $\mathcal{P}$.

- **Move 3 (response):** $\mathcal{P}(\mathrm{x}, \mathrm{w}, (a, c)) \to z$:
  1. Compute $z := s + c \cdot w \in \mathbb{Z}_q$, and send z to $\mathcal{V}$.
  2. Compute $r_z := r_s + c \cdot r_w \in \mathbb{Z}_q$, and send (z, r_z) to $\mathcal{V}$.
- **Verification:** $\mathcal{V}(\mathsf{ek}, \mathrm{x}, (a, c, (z, r_z))) \to b$:
  1. Parse x as a group element $W \in \mathbb{G}$ and w as $w \in \mathbb{Z}_q$.
  2. Check that:
     - $g^z = S \cdot W^c \in \mathbb{G}$; and
     - C_s, C_w are valid AHE ciphertexts; and
     - $\mathsf{Enc}(\mathsf{ek}, z; r_z) = C_s + c \cdot C_w$.
  3. If all checks pass, output 1. Otherwise, output 0.

The above protocol satisfies straight-line extraction as follows: the extractor is given access to the secret decryption key dk and simply decrypts C_w. And this holds even for a statistical prover. Furthermore, the honest verifier zero-knowledge (HVZK) property follows from the honest verifier zero-knowledge property of Schnorr and the semantic security of AHE. The ZK simulator samples a random challenge and simulates the Schnorr proof (a, c, z) by running the HVZK simulator of the original Schnorr proof. To simulate the encryptions, the HVZK simulator computes $C_s = \mathsf{Enc}(\mathsf{ek}, 0; r')$ for a random r' and sets $C_w = (\mathsf{Enc}(\mathsf{ek}, z; r) - C_s) \cdot c^{-1}$ for a random r. The simulated encryptions are indistinguishable from the encryptions in a real proof due to the semantic security of AHE.

While the above protocol achieves straight-line knowledge soundness, it has two drawbacks: it (1) is interactive and (2) requires a trusted structured setup with secret values. Fortunately, both of these can be mitigated in the ROM.

2.3   NIZK in ROM Using Fiat-Shamir

As mentioned in Sect. 2.2, we use the random oracle to achieve two goals, achieving non-interactivity and removing the common reference string.

Non-interactivity. Achieving non-interactivity for Schnorr's protocol is straightforward via the Fiat-Shamir transform [FS87].[4] As a result of applying Fiat-Shamir, the security proofs change as follows:

- Straight-line extraction: assuming Q is the number of random oracle queries made by the malicious prover, applying Fiat-Shamir incurs a Q-factor security loss, since the malicious prover may sample at most Q possible first message a values, which generates at most Q possible values of c.
- Zero knowledge: the zero-knowledge simulator must program the random oracle so that $c := \mathsf{RO}(\mathrm{x}, a)$. However, there is no change in distinguishing advantage between the real and simulated proofs.

---

[4] $\mathcal{P}$ and $\mathcal{V}$ have query access to a random oracle $\mathsf{RO} \colon \{0, 1\}^* \to \mathbb{Z}_q$. $\mathcal{P}$ samples the random challenge by itself as $c := \mathsf{RO}(\mathrm{x}, a)$ and sends c to $\mathcal{V}$. $\mathcal{V}$ additionally checks that the received transcript $(a, c, \cdot)$ satisfies $c = \mathsf{RO}(\mathrm{x}, a)$.

Minimizing Setup Assumptions. The above protocol relies on a trusted party to run the AHE key generation algorithm and output the (public) encryption key ek and the (secret) decryption key dk. One way to side-step having a common reference string is via instantiating AHE with a scheme in which public keys are *obliviously sampleable using a hash function*, i.e. the following distributions are indistinguishable

$$\{\, \mathsf{ek} : (\mathsf{ek}, \mathsf{dk}) \leftarrow \mathsf{Gen}(1^\kappa) \,\} \text{ and } \{\, \mathsf{ek} \leftarrow \mathcal{H}_{\mathsf{ek}}(1^\kappa, \cdot) \,\} \quad.$$

Then, both $\mathcal{P}$ and $\mathcal{V}$ can derive an instance-specific encryption key: $\mathsf{ek} := \mathcal{H}_{\mathsf{ek}}(1^\kappa, \mathrm{x})$. Then, in the analysis of knowledge soundness, an additional hybrid is required, so that the knowledge extractor can recover the decryption key dk. Moreover, zero-knowledge is preserved, assuming that it is inefficient to recover a valid decryption key with respect to $\mathsf{ek} \leftarrow \mathcal{H}_{\mathsf{ek}}(1^\kappa, \cdot)$.

We note that the random oracles for the two tasks are distinct. First, they must be domain-separated, so that soundness is preserved (we need the outputs of both invocations to be independently sampled). Second, the output spaces of the hashes are different too. For non-interactivity, the random oracle simulates the verifier's random challenge, i.e. outputs a value in $\mathbb{Z}_q$. For removing the common reference string, the random oracle samples an AHE encryption key, which simulates the distribution of ek output by the AHE key generation algorithm. For the rest of the technical overview, we denote our straightline-extractable protocol in the ROM as Π_{GenLin}.

2.4 Extending Our Straight-Line Extractable NIZK to the UC Setting

In general, stand-alone NIZK constructions are not universally composable because standard security definitions do not consider adversarial behavior in the presence of concurrent protocol executions. In particular, an adversary, after observing polynomially-many proof strings, should not be able to forge a proof for an instance x, for which it doesn't know a corresponding witness w, i.e. if the adversary produces a valid proof, the (UC) simulator should be able to extract a valid witness w for x. This notion is called *non-malleability* or *simulation-extractability* (more common in the UC ZK literature) [FKMV12, Gro06, KZM+15].

Towards proving UC security, we show that Π_{GenLin} satisfies simulation-extractability. This is done by following the paradigm [FKMV12] of reducing simulation-extractability to *weak unique response* (WUR) knowledge soundness, and zero-knowledge. We first show that Π_{GenLin} satisfies WUR, i.e. the probability that an adversary can find two accepting proofs $(a, c, z), (a, c, z')$ for instance x, such that $z \neq z'$, is negligible. Simulation-extractability follows via combining our proof of WUR and the knowledge extractor for Π_{GenLin}. While this is standard, we note that, interestingly, our proof of WUR *does not* rely on WUR of the underlying Sigma protocol. Thus, our compiled protocol is WUR even when the underlying protocol is not. Consider a Sigma protocol resulting from OR composition that does not satisfy WUR. This is because the third message can be computed from one of the many witnesses. In our straight-line compiled protocol, however, the first message consists of a ciphertext encrypting the witness which forces the prover to use the same witness in the response, thus recovering the WUR property. Finally, we conclude UC-security by arguing that the following is a (UC) simulator for Π_{GenLin}: (1) the zero-knowledge simulator of Π_{GenLin} simulates proofs output by Π_{GenLin}; and (2) the simulation extractor (constructed above) extracts witnesses from adversarially generated proof strings.

Extensions. While we focus on linear relations in the exponent, we note that our transform can also work for arbitrary algebraic relation with proper representation[5]. Furthermore, it also works for the OR composition of $\mathcal{R}_{\mathsf{DLog}}$. At a high level, this works by (1) running our UC-NIZK for the NP statement, for which the witness is known; then (2) using the HVZK simulator to generate proofs for all other statements. The straightforward construction is provided in the full version [CDG+24].

3   Preliminaries

We denote by $a \leftarrow \mathcal{D}$ a uniform sampling of an element a from a distribution $\mathcal{D}$. The set of elements $\{1, \ldots, n\}$ is represented by $[n]$. We denote the computational security parameter by κ and statistical security parameter by λ_{st}, respectively.

Vectors and Matrices. We use boldface to denote matrices and vectors. Sometimes we use notations $\boldsymbol{A}_{m \times n}$ to a matrix of dimension $m \times n$. The element in the i-th row and j-th column is denoted by $\boldsymbol{A}_{ij}$, and the j-th column vector (of dimension m) of $\boldsymbol{A}$ is denoted $\boldsymbol{A}_j$. Analogously, for a vector $\boldsymbol{v}$, $\boldsymbol{v}_i$ denotes the i-th element.

   We use standard notion of programmable random oracles, and rely on Universal composability framework. More details are deferred to the full version [CDG+24].

3.1   Definition: Additively Homomorphic Encryption

An *additively-homomorphic encryption scheme* is a tuple of algorithms $\mathsf{AHE} = (\mathsf{Gen}, \mathsf{Enc}, \mathsf{Dec})$ that works as follows.

– $\mathsf{Gen}(1^{\kappa}) \rightarrow (\mathsf{ek}, \mathsf{dk})$. On input a security parameter κ (in unary), outputs a (public) encryption key $\mathsf{ek} \in \mathcal{K}_{\mathsf{ek}}$ and a (secret) decryption key $\mathsf{dk} \in \mathcal{K}_{\mathsf{dk}}$ in the respective key spaces.
– $\mathsf{Enc}(\mathsf{ek}, m, r) \rightarrow c$. On input an encryption key $\mathsf{ek} \in \mathcal{K}_{\mathsf{ek}}$, a message m in message space $\mathcal{M}$ and encryption randomness r in randomness space $\mathcal{R}$, outputs a ciphertext c in ciphertext space $\mathcal{C}$.

---

[5] Note that a polynomial $p(x)$ of degree d is linear in powers of x, $1, x, x^2, \ldots, x^d$. So our protocols work for proving relations $p(x) = y$ over a field as well.

– $\mathsf{Dec}(\mathsf{dk}, c) \rightarrow m$. On input a decryption key $\mathsf{dk} \in \mathcal{K}_{\mathsf{dk}}$ and a ciphertext c, deterministically outputs a message $m \in \mathcal{M}$.

We require the AHE scheme to satisfy standard semantic (CPA) security and correctness, formalizations of which are deferred to the full version [CDG+24]. We also require the scheme to satisfy additive homomorphism

– **Additive homomorphism.** Let $\kappa \in \mathbb{N}$ be a security parameter. Let $(\mathsf{ek}, \mathsf{dk}) \leftarrow \mathsf{Gen}(1^\kappa)$, then there are polynomial time deterministic algorithms Add and ScMult such that:
  - For any $c_1, c_2 \in \mathcal{C}$ define homomorphic addition $c_{(+)} := \mathsf{Add}(c_1, c_2)$ such that if $c_1 := \mathsf{Enc}(\mathsf{ek}, m_1; r_1)$ and $c_2 := \mathsf{Enc}(\mathsf{ek}, m_2; r_2)$, then $c_{(+)} = \mathsf{Enc}(\mathsf{ek}, m_0 + m_1; r_0 + r_1)$. Similarly, we define homomorphic subtraction as $c_{(-)} := \mathsf{Add}(c_1, -c_2)$ such that $c_{(-)} = \mathsf{Enc}(\mathsf{ek}, m_0 - m_1; r_0 - r_1)$. Here we assume the addition/subtraction operations $+/-$ are defined in both $\mathcal{M}$ and $\mathcal{R}$.
  - For any $c \in \mathcal{C}$, and any scalar s which is in $\mathcal{M}$ and $\mathcal{R}$, define scalar multiplication $c_{(\cdot)} := \mathsf{ScMult}(s, c)$ such that if $c := \mathsf{Enc}(\mathsf{ek}, m; r)$, then $c_{(\cdot)} = \mathsf{Enc}(\mathsf{ek}, sm; sr)$.

Finally we need a couple of crucial additional properties from the encryption scheme.

– **Homomorphic well-formedness.** Let $c_1, c_2 \in \mathcal{C}$ be two arbitrary strings in the ciphertext space. Suppose, for any uniformly random scalar $s \in \mathcal{M}$, $c^* := \mathsf{Add}(c_1, \mathsf{ScMult}(s, c_2))$. Also, let $m^* \leftarrow \mathsf{Dec}(\mathsf{dk}, c^*)$, then we have that $m_1 \leftarrow \mathsf{Dec}(\mathsf{dk}, c_1)$ and $m_2 \leftarrow \mathsf{Dec}(\mathsf{dk}, c_2)$ such that $m^* = m_1 + s \cdot m_2$.
– **Oblivious sampleability of public key.** There exists a polynomial time hash function $\mathcal{H}_{\mathsf{ek}}$ such that the public-key can be sampled obliviously as $\mathsf{ek} := \mathcal{H}_{\mathsf{ek}}(1^\kappa, x)$ on an uniform random input x and the following distributions are computationally indistinguishable:

$$\{\, \mathsf{ek} : (\mathsf{ek}, \mathsf{dk}) \leftarrow \mathsf{Gen}(1^\kappa) \,\} \text{ and } \{\, \mathsf{ek} \leftarrow \mathcal{H}_{\mathsf{ek}}(1^\kappa, \cdot) \,\} \ .$$

Looking ahead, $\mathcal{H}_{\mathsf{ek}}$ is to be modeled as a programmable random oracle in security proof. Obliviousness implies that, this can be done without explicit knowledge of the corresponding secret key, and therefore, given x anyone can check whether ek is generated correctly.

Matrix Encryption. We can extend the above notation to compactly capture encrypting a matrix $m \in \mathcal{M}_{k \times n}$ using $\mathsf{MatEnc}(\mathsf{ek}, m)$ which returns a ciphertext matrix $c \in \mathcal{C}_{k \times n}$, in that each element $c_{ij} = \mathsf{Enc}(\mathsf{ek}, m_{ij})$ for $i \in [k], j \in [n]$. Matrix decryption is similarly denoted by $\mathsf{MatDec}(\mathsf{dk}, c)$. The addition and scalar multiplication defined above naturally extends for matrices.

3.2   Definition: Sigma Protocols

We define Sigma protocols for an NP relation $\mathcal{R}$ in the common reference string (CRS) model. It works as follows: A 3-move public coin Sigma protocol [CPV20] for a relation $\mathcal{R}$ is a tuple of algorithms $\Sigma = (\mathsf{Setup}, \mathcal{P} = (\mathcal{P}_1, \mathcal{P}_2), \mathcal{V} = (\mathcal{V}_1, \mathcal{V}_2))$. The prover $\mathcal{P}$ receives an instance $\mathbb{x}$ and witness $\mathbb{w}$ as input. The verifier $\mathcal{V}$ receives $\mathbb{x}$ as input. Σ proceeds in the following format:

- $\mathsf{Setup}(1^\kappa) \to (\mathsf{crs}, \mathsf{td})$: The Setup algorithm runs on (unary) security parameter κ and generates a CRS crs and a trapdoor td. All algorithms receive crs as inputs, and td is only used in extraction/simulation.
- $\mathcal{P}_1(\mathsf{crs}, \mathbb{x}, \mathbb{w}; \rho) \to a$: $\mathcal{P}$ runs (randomized) algorithm $\mathcal{P}_1$ on the (public) instance $\mathbb{x}$, (private) witness $\mathbb{w}$ to obtain the first message a – this is also called a **commitment**. $\mathcal{P}$ sends a to $\mathcal{V}$. Here ρ is the prover's randomness, which is stored to be used later in $\mathcal{P}_2$.
- $\mathcal{V}_1(\mathsf{crs}, a) \to c$: $\mathcal{V}$ samples random **challenge** $c \xleftarrow{\$} \mathcal{C}$ and sends c to $\mathcal{P}$.
- $\mathcal{P}_2(\mathsf{crs}, \mathbb{x}, \mathbb{w}, a, c, \rho) \to z$: $\mathcal{P}$ runs algorithm $\mathcal{P}_2$ with $\mathbb{x}, \mathbb{w}, a, c, \rho$ to output z. It sends **response** z to $\mathcal{V}$.
- $\mathcal{V}_2(\mathsf{crs}, \mathbb{x}, (a, c, z)) \to 1/0$: $\mathcal{V}$, on input the instance and the **transcript** (a, c, z), which together constitutes the proof π, outputs 1 if it accepts and 0 if it rejects.

Let us now define the security properties of a Sigma protocol.

- **Perfect completeness.** If $(\mathbb{x}, \mathbb{w}) \in \mathcal{R}$, then $\mathcal{V}$ accepts all honest 3-move transcripts as long as $\mathcal{P}_1$ and $\mathcal{P}_2$ uses the same ρ.
- **Special soundness.** There exists an efficient extractor Ext that, on input a CRS crs, an instance $\mathbb{x} \in \mathcal{L}$, and two accepting transcripts (a, c, z) and (a, c', z') such that $c \neq c' \in \mathcal{C}$, outputs a witness $\mathbb{w}$ such that $(\mathbb{x}, \mathbb{w}) \in \mathcal{R}$ with probability $1 - \mathsf{negl}(\kappa)$. We call the loss the **special soundness error**.
- **Straight-line knowledge soundness.** There exists an efficient deterministic algorithm called **straight-line Knowledge Extractor** $\mathcal{E}$ that, on input the public information crs, the trapdoor td, instance $\mathbb{x} \in \mathcal{L}$, and a single accepting transcript (a, c, z) outputs an accepting witness $\mathbb{w}$ for which $(\mathbb{x}, \mathbb{w}) \in \mathcal{R}$ with probability $1 - \mathsf{negl}(\kappa)$.
- **Honest-verifier zero knowledge (HVZK).** There exists a PPT simulator algorithm Sim that, on input the setup string crs, trapdoor td for crs, instance $\mathbb{x} \in \mathcal{L}$, and a uniform random challenge $c \xleftarrow{\$} \mathcal{C}$, outputs (a, z) such that $\mathcal{V}_2(\mathsf{crs}, \mathbb{x}, (a, c, z)) = 1$. Further, for every PPT adversary $\mathcal{A}$, the following distributions are indistinguishable:

$$\left\{ \mathcal{A}(\mathbb{x}, (a, c, z)) = 1 \;\middle|\; \begin{array}{c} (\mathsf{crs}, \mathsf{td}) \leftarrow \mathsf{Setup}(1^\kappa) \\ \rho \xleftarrow{\$} \mathcal{R}; a \leftarrow \mathcal{P}_1(\mathsf{crs}, \mathbb{x}, \mathbb{w}, \rho) \\ c \xleftarrow{\$} \mathcal{C}; z \leftarrow \mathcal{P}_2(\mathsf{crs}, \mathbb{x}, \mathbb{w}, c, \rho) \end{array} \right\}$$

$$\text{and} \quad \left\{ \mathcal{A}(\mathbb{x}, (a, c, z)) = 1 \;\middle|\; \begin{array}{c} (\mathsf{crs}, \mathsf{td}) \leftarrow \mathsf{Setup}(1^\kappa) \\ c \xleftarrow{\$} \mathcal{C}; (a, z) \leftarrow \mathsf{Sim}(\mathsf{crs}, \mathsf{td}, \mathbb{x}, c) \end{array} \right\} .$$

3.3   Definition: Straight-Line Extractable NIZKs

We define straight-line-extractable non-interactive zero-knowledge proofs in the random oracle model (ROM) for an NP relation $\mathcal{R}$. The proof system Π consists of a tuple of algorithms $(\mathsf{Setup}, \mathcal{P}^{\mathrm{RO}}, \mathcal{V}^{\mathrm{RO}})$ defined as follows:

- $\mathsf{Setup}(1^\kappa) \to \mathrm{RO}$. On input a security parameter κ, Setup samples a function RO uniformly from the set of all functions mapping $\{0,1\}^* \to \mathcal{C}$.
- $\mathcal{P}^{\mathrm{RO}}(\mathrm{x}, \mathrm{w}) \to \pi$. On input an instance x, and a corresponding witness w, the prover $\mathcal{P}$ computes a proof π.
- $\mathcal{V}^{\mathrm{RO}}(\mathrm{x}, \pi) \to 1/0$. On input an instance x, and a corresponding proof π, the verifier $\mathcal{V}$ computes a decision bit.

We require Π to satisfy the following completeness, (computational) zero-knowledge and (statistical) straight-line knowledge soundness properties in the ROM:

- **Perfect Completeness.** For any adversary (possibly unbounded) $\mathcal{A}$

$$
\Pr\left[
\begin{array}{c}
(\mathrm{x}, \mathrm{w}) \notin \mathcal{R} \\
\wedge \\
(\mathcal{V}^{\mathrm{RO}}(\mathrm{x}, \pi) = 1)
\end{array}
\;\middle|\;
\begin{array}{c}
\mathrm{RO} \leftarrow \mathsf{Setup}(1^\kappa) \\
(\mathrm{x}, \mathrm{w}) \leftarrow \mathcal{A}^{\mathrm{RO}} \\
\pi \leftarrow \mathcal{P}^{\mathrm{RO}}(\mathrm{x}, \mathrm{w})
\end{array}
\right] = 1
$$

The above formulation of completeness allows (x, w) to depend on the oracle RO. Here $\mathcal{A}$ can make unbounded many queries to RO.

- **(Computational) Zero Knowledge.** Before defining zero-knowledge we define **NIZK simulator** (in the random oracle model) and associated **wrapper oracles** for an NP relation $\mathcal{R}$. A NIZK simulator $\mathcal{S}$ in the random oracle model is a stateful PPT algorithm that can operate in two modes. The first mode $(h_i, st) \leftarrow \mathcal{S}(1, st, q_i)$ handles RO queries whereas the second mode $(\mathrm{x}, \pi, st) \leftarrow \mathcal{S}(2, st, \mathrm{x})$ returns a simulated proof for x. Let $\mathcal{S}_1$, $\mathcal{S}_2$ and $\mathcal{S}_2'$ be wrapper oracles that share state. $\mathcal{S}_1(q_i)$ is a wrapper around $\mathcal{S}(1, st, q_i)$ returning only h_i while internally updating st. Similarly, $\mathcal{S}_2(\mathrm{x}, \mathrm{w})$ and $\mathcal{S}_2'(\mathrm{x})$ be wrappers around $\mathcal{S}(2, st, \mathrm{x})$ returning only (x, π) and internally updating st, except that $\mathcal{S}_2(\mathrm{x}, \mathrm{w})$ aborts if $(\mathrm{x}, \mathrm{w}) \notin \mathcal{R}$. We say that Π has *computational zero knowledge* if there exists a simulator $\mathcal{S}$ such that for any PPT adversary $\mathcal{A}$, the following is negligible in κ.

$$
\Pr\left[\mathcal{A}^{\mathrm{RO}, \mathcal{P}(\cdot, \cdot)}(1^\kappa) = 1 \mid \mathrm{RO} \leftarrow \mathsf{Setup}(1^\kappa)\right] - \Pr\left[\mathcal{A}^{\mathcal{S}_1, \mathcal{S}_2}(1^\kappa) = 1 \mid \mathrm{RO} \leftarrow \mathsf{Setup}(1^\kappa)\right]
$$

Above, $\mathcal{P}$ and $\mathcal{S}_2$ both return $\bot$ when queried on $(\mathrm{x}, \mathrm{w}) \notin \mathcal{R}$.

- **(Computational) Straight-line Knowledge Soundness.** We first define a straight-line extractor $\mathcal{E}$ as a stateful PPT algorithm which works in two modes: $(h_i, st) \leftarrow \mathcal{E}(1, q_i, st)$ handles the RO queries using lazy sampling, whereas $(\mathrm{w}, st) \leftarrow \mathcal{E}(2, \mathrm{x}, \pi, st)$ returns a witness. Let $\mathcal{E}_1$ and $\mathcal{E}_2$ be the wrappers around $\mathcal{E}$ such that each outputs the first part of the respective outputs (without the state, which is kept secret). Importantly, $\mathcal{E}$ is straight-line, that is it does not rewind or use forking [JT20]. Π has *straight-line knowledge soundness* if there exists a PPT stateful extractor $\mathcal{E}$ such that for any PPT adversary $\mathcal{A}$, we have that:

$$\Pr\left[\begin{matrix} \mathcal{V}^{\text{RO}}(\mathbb{x}, \pi) = 1 \wedge \\ (\mathbb{x}, \mathbb{w}) \notin \mathcal{R} \end{matrix} \middle| \begin{matrix} \text{RO} \leftarrow \text{Setup}(1^\kappa); (\mathbb{x}, \pi) \leftarrow \mathcal{A}^{\mathcal{E}_1} \\ \mathbb{w} \leftarrow \mathcal{E}_2(\mathbb{x}, \pi) \end{matrix}\right] \le \text{negl}(\kappa)$$

We need a few more definitions for showing a stronger simulation extractability property for Π.

- **Weak Unique Response** [GOP+23]. Π is said to satisfy *weak unique response* with respect to the zero-knowledge simulator $\mathcal{S}$ with wrapper oracles $(\mathcal{S}_1, \mathcal{S}_2')$ (as defined above), if given a simulated transcript $(\mathbb{x}, c, z) \leftarrow \mathcal{S}_2'(\mathbb{x})$, for all PPT adversaries $\mathcal{A}$ the following probability is at most $\text{negl}(\kappa)$.

$$\Pr\left[\begin{matrix} \mathcal{V}^{\mathcal{S}_1}(\mathbb{x}, a, c, z') = 1 \\ \wedge \\ z' \neq z \end{matrix} \middle| \begin{matrix} (\mathbb{x}, a, c, z) \leftarrow \mathcal{S}_2'(\mathbb{x}) \\ (\mathbb{x}, a, c, z') \leftarrow \mathcal{A}^{\mathcal{S}_1}(\mathbb{x}, a, c, z) \end{matrix}\right]$$

- **Simulation Extractability,** [FKMV12] Π is said to satisfy *simulation extractability* with respect to a stateful PPT simulator $\mathcal{S}$ with wrapper oracles $(\mathcal{S}_1, \mathcal{S}_2')$ (as defined above) if there exists a (straight-line) PPT extractor $\hat{\mathcal{E}}$ such that for all PPT adversaries $\mathcal{A}$ the following holds:

$$\Pr\left[\begin{matrix} \mathcal{V}^{\mathcal{S}_1}(\mathbb{x}^*, \pi^*) = 1 \\ \wedge\ (\mathbb{x}^*, \mathbb{w}^*) \notin \mathcal{R}\ \wedge\ (\mathbb{x}^*, \pi^*) \notin \mathcal{T} \end{matrix} \middle| \begin{matrix} (\mathbb{x}^*, \pi^*) \leftarrow \mathcal{A}^{(\mathcal{S}_1, \mathcal{S}_2')} \\ \mathbb{w}^* \leftarrow \hat{\mathcal{E}}(\mathbb{x}^*, \pi^*) \end{matrix}\right] \le \text{negl}(\kappa) \ .$$

Here $\mathcal{T}$ is the list of transcripts received by $\mathcal{A}$ on querying $\mathcal{S}_2'$.

4   Straight-Line Extractable Proof Systems for Arbitrary Linear Relations

4.1   Notations

We assume a cyclic group $\mathbb{G}$ of prime order q with g as a generator, and a corresponding finite field $\mathbb{Z}_q$. Now we define:

- For each matrix $\boldsymbol{a} \in \mathbb{Z}_q^{m \times n}$, we denote the **matrix exponentiation** $\boldsymbol{A} := g^{\boldsymbol{a}} \in \mathbb{G}^{m \times n}$ where each element $A_{ij} = g^{a_{ij}}$. Below we assume $\boldsymbol{A} = g^{\boldsymbol{a}}$.
- The **scalar power** of $\boldsymbol{A} \in \mathbb{G}^{m \times n}$ with respect to a scalar $s \in \mathbb{Z}_q$ is denoted by $\boldsymbol{A}^s \in \mathbb{G}^{m \times n}$, each entry of which is given by $\boldsymbol{A}_{ij}^s := (\boldsymbol{A}_{ij})^s$. Notice that, $\boldsymbol{A}^s = g^{s\boldsymbol{a}}$, where $s\boldsymbol{a}$ is a standard scalar multiplication.
- Given a vector $\boldsymbol{v} \in \mathbb{Z}_q^m$, the **vector power** of $\boldsymbol{A}$ is denoted by $\boldsymbol{A}^{\boldsymbol{v}} = g^{\boldsymbol{v} \cdot \boldsymbol{a}}$, where $\boldsymbol{v} \cdot \boldsymbol{a}$ is a vector-matrix multiplication resulting into a vector of dimension n. Alternatively, the j-th entry of $\boldsymbol{A}^{\boldsymbol{v}}$ is given by a multi-exponentiation $\prod_{i=1}^m A_{ij}^{b_i}$. For example, let $\boldsymbol{A} = \begin{pmatrix} A_{11} & A_{12} & A_{1,3} \\ A_{21} & A_{22} & A_{23} \end{pmatrix}$ and $\boldsymbol{v} = (v_1\ v_2)$ then $\boldsymbol{A}^{\boldsymbol{v}} = \left(A_{11}^{v_1} \cdot A_{21}^{v_2} \mid A_{12}^{v_1} \cdot A_{22}^{v_2} \mid A_{13}^{v_1} \cdot A_{23}^{v_2}\right)$. Also note that, if $\boldsymbol{V} = \boldsymbol{A}^{\boldsymbol{v}}$, then for a scalar $s \in \mathbb{Z}_q$ $\boldsymbol{V}^s = \boldsymbol{A}^{s\boldsymbol{v}}$.

- Given a matrix $a \in \mathbb{Z}_q^{m \times n}$, the **element-wise inverse** of a denoted as $(a^{-1}$, each element of which is the inverse (in $\mathbb{Z}_q$) of each element of the vector a in the same position. For a matrix $A \in \mathbb{G}^{m \times n}$, the element-wise inverse A^{-1} is defined as the matrix, in that each element is equal to A_{ij}^{-1} a multiplicative inverse in $\mathbb{G}$ of an element A_{ij} in A in the same position.

- The **Hadamard product** of two arbitrary matrices of same dimensions $A_{m \times n}$ and $B_{m \times n}$, denoted by $A \bullet B$, defines a matrix $C_{m \times n}$ whose entries are element-wise product of the entries of A and B. That is, $C_{i,j} = A_{i,j} \cdot B_{i,j}$ for $1 \le i \le m$ and $1 \le j \le n$. When $A = g^a$ and $B = g^b$, $A \bullet B = g^{a+b}$, where '$+$' denotes the standard matrix addition over $\mathbb{Z}_q$. Furthermore, if $V = A^v$ and $W = A^w$, then $V \bullet W = A^{v+w}$.

Now, for a vector $w \in \mathbb{Z}_q^n$, and a matrix $y \in \mathbb{Z}_q^{n \times m}$ consider the following linear relation: $U = Y^w \in \mathbb{G}^m$, where $Y = g^y \in \mathbb{G}^{n \times m}$. (Alternatively, we can write $U = g^{w \cdot y}$.) To summarize, define the following relation:

$$\mathcal{R}_{\mathsf{GenLin}} := \left\{ \left((Y \in \mathbb{G}^{n \times m}, U \in \mathbb{G}^m), w \right) : w \in \mathbb{Z}_q^n \text{ and } U = Y^w \right\} . \quad (1)$$

Note that $\mathcal{R}_{\mathsf{GenLin}}$ checks the following in the exponent, with respect to a fixed generator $g \in \mathbb{G}$: for $y \in \mathbb{Z}_q^{n \times m}$ and $u \in \mathbb{Z}_q^m$, there exists $w \in \mathbb{Z}_q^n$ such that $u = wy$.

4.2 Straight-Line Extractable Protocol for $\mathcal{R}_{\mathsf{GenLin}}$

We present our interactive three-move Sigma protocol for any linear relation $\mathcal{R}_{\mathsf{GenLin}}$ that is straight-line extractable in the crs model. An additional ingredient we use here is an additively homomorphic public-key encryption scheme $\mathsf{AHE} = (\mathsf{Gen}, \mathsf{Enc}, \mathsf{Dec})$, which has message space $\mathbb{Z}_q$ and the property that the encryption key is obliviously sampleable. The crs consists of the encryption key ek. Further, recall the extended matrix encryption/decryption notations MatEnc and MatDec (see Sect. 3.1).

In Fig. 1, we present a Sigma protocol $\Sigma = (\mathsf{Setup}, \mathcal{P} = (\mathcal{P}_1, \mathcal{P}_2), \mathcal{V} = (\mathcal{V}_1, \mathcal{V}_2))$ for $\mathcal{R}_{\mathsf{GenLin}}$ (Eq. (1)) – recall that this relation consists of instances $Y \in \mathbb{G}^{n \times m}, U \in \mathbb{G}^m$ and witnesses $w \in \mathbb{Z}_q^n$ satisfying $U = Y^w$.

Theorem 1. *Suppose $\mathbb{G}$ is a group of prime order q. Suppose $\mathsf{AHE} = (\mathsf{Gen}, \mathsf{Enc}, \mathsf{Dec})$ is an additively homomorphic encryption scheme satisfying the perfect correctness, semantic security with distinguishing advantage at most δ_{sem}, and homomorphic well-formedness properties with distinguishing advantage at most $\delta_{\mathsf{st-ks}}$ (defined in Sect. 3.1).[6]*

Then, the Sigma protocol described in Fig. 1 satisfies the following properties in the crs model:

- **Perfect Completeness**, *due to the additive homomorphism of* AHE;

---

[6] We believe that, our reductions are tight, as they are direct reductions to the respective primitives. Same applies for the non-interactive case as there is no loss due to guessing in the random oracle.

Inputs: Both prover and verifier know the public instance $\mathbb{x} := (\boldsymbol{Y} \in \mathbb{G}^{n \times m}, \boldsymbol{U} \in \mathbb{G}^m)$, and the prover exclusively has witness $\mathbb{w} := \boldsymbol{w} \in \mathbb{Z}_q^n$. The $\mathsf{Setup}(1^\lambda)$ samples key pairs $(\mathsf{ek}, \mathsf{dk}) \leftarrow \mathsf{Gen}(1^\lambda)$; set public $\mathsf{crs} := \mathsf{ek}$ and trapdoor $\mathsf{td} := \mathsf{dk}$.

Round-1 (Commit): The prover $\mathcal{P}$ runs algorithm $\mathcal{P}_1(\mathsf{crs}, \mathbb{x}, \mathbb{w})$, which works as follows:
- Sample $\boldsymbol{s} \xleftarrow{\$} \mathbb{Z}_q^n$ and compute $\boldsymbol{S} := \boldsymbol{Y}^{\boldsymbol{s}} \in \mathbb{G}^m$.
- Sample encryption randomness $\boldsymbol{r_s}, \boldsymbol{r_w} \xleftarrow{\$} \mathcal{R}^n$.
- Compute encryptions $\boldsymbol{C_s} := \mathsf{MatEnc}(\mathsf{ek}, \boldsymbol{s}; \boldsymbol{r_s})$ and $\boldsymbol{C_w} := \mathsf{MatEnc}(\mathsf{ek}, \boldsymbol{w}; \boldsymbol{r_w})$ where $\mathsf{ek} = \mathsf{crs}$.
- Set $a := (\boldsymbol{S}, \boldsymbol{C_s}, \boldsymbol{C_w})$ and $\rho := (\boldsymbol{s}, \boldsymbol{r_w}, \boldsymbol{r_s})$.

Send a to the verifier.

Round-2 (Challenge): The verifier $\mathcal{V}$ runs algorithm $\mathcal{V}_1(\mathsf{crs}, a)$, which, on receiving $a = (\boldsymbol{S}, \boldsymbol{C_s}, \boldsymbol{C_w})$ samples challenge $c \xleftarrow{\$} \mathbb{Z}_q$ and send that to the prover.

Round-3 (Response): The prover $\mathcal{P}$, on receiving the challenge c, runs algorithm $\mathcal{P}_2(\mathsf{crs}, \mathbb{x}, \mathbb{w}, a, c, \rho)$, which works as:
- Parse ρ as $(\boldsymbol{s}, \boldsymbol{r_w}, \boldsymbol{r_s})$.
- Compute $\boldsymbol{z} := \boldsymbol{s} + c\boldsymbol{w} \in \mathbb{Z}_q^n$.
- Compute $\boldsymbol{r_z} := \boldsymbol{r_s} + c\boldsymbol{r_w}$.
- Define $z := (\boldsymbol{z}, \boldsymbol{r_z})$.

Send z to the verifier.

Check: The verifier $\mathcal{V}$, on receiving $z = (\boldsymbol{z}, \boldsymbol{r_z})$ outputs whatever is returned by the algorithm $\mathcal{V}_2(\mathsf{crs}, \mathbb{x}, a, c, z)$ which returns 1 if and only if:
- $\boldsymbol{Y}^{\boldsymbol{z}} = \boldsymbol{S} \bullet \boldsymbol{U}^c$.
- $\boldsymbol{C_s}, \boldsymbol{C_w} \in \mathcal{C}$.
- $\mathsf{MatEnc}(\mathsf{ek}, \boldsymbol{z}; \boldsymbol{r_z}) = \mathsf{Add}(\boldsymbol{C_s}, \mathsf{ScMult}(c, \boldsymbol{C_w}))$ where $\mathsf{ek} = \mathsf{crs}$.

Fig. 1. Our straight-line-extractable Sigma protocol for $\mathcal{R}_{\mathsf{GenLin}}$. We highlight the changes from the standard Sigma protocol (detailed in the full version [CDG+24] for completeness)in blue.

- **(Computational) Straight-line Knowledge Soundness** with soundness error $(\delta_{\mathsf{st\text{-}ks}} + 1/q)$, due to the correctness and homomorphic well-formedness of AHE.
- **(Computational) Honest Verifier Zero-Knowledge** with simulation error δ_{sem}, due to the additive homomorphism and the semantic security of AHE.

Proof. **Perfect Completeness.** From the verifier's computation, we have that $\boldsymbol{Y}^{\boldsymbol{z}} = \boldsymbol{Y}^{\boldsymbol{s}+c\boldsymbol{w}} = \boldsymbol{Y}^{\boldsymbol{s}} \bullet \boldsymbol{Y}^{c\boldsymbol{w}} = \boldsymbol{S} \bullet \boldsymbol{U}^c$ and

$$\mathsf{MatEnc}(\mathsf{ek}, \boldsymbol{z} = \boldsymbol{s} + c\boldsymbol{w}, r_z = r_s + c r_w)$$
$$= \mathsf{Add}(\mathsf{MatEnc}(\mathsf{ek}, \boldsymbol{s}; r_s), \mathsf{MatEnc}(\mathsf{ek}, c\boldsymbol{w}; c r_w)$$
$$= \mathsf{Add}(\boldsymbol{C_s}, \mathsf{ScMult}(c, \boldsymbol{C_w})) \ .$$

The second equation holds from the *correctness of the homomorphism* of the encryption scheme. Therefore, the verifier outputs 1 and our protocol is complete.

(Computational) Straight-line Knowledge Soundness. We construct a straight-line knowledge extractor $\mathcal{E}_\Sigma$ which works as follows:

$\mathcal{E}_\Sigma(\mathsf{crs}, \mathsf{td}, \mathbb{x}, \pi)$:

- On input $(\mathsf{crs}, \mathsf{td}, \mathbb{x}, \pi)$ parse $\mathsf{ek} = \mathsf{crs}$, the trapdoor $\mathsf{dk} = \mathsf{td}$, instance $(\boldsymbol{U}, \boldsymbol{Y}) = \mathbb{x}$, and a single accepting transcript $(a, c, z) = \pi$ where:
    - $a = (\boldsymbol{S}, \boldsymbol{C_s})$; $c \in \mathbb{Z}_q$; $z = (\boldsymbol{z}, \boldsymbol{r_z})$
    - $\boldsymbol{Y}^{\boldsymbol{z}} = \boldsymbol{S} \bullet \boldsymbol{U}^c$
    - $\boldsymbol{C_s}, \boldsymbol{C_w} \in \mathcal{C}$.
    - $\mathsf{MatEnc}(\mathsf{ek}, \boldsymbol{z}; \boldsymbol{r_z}) = \mathsf{Add}(\boldsymbol{C_s}, \mathsf{ScMult}(c, \boldsymbol{C_w}))$.
- Use dk to decrypt $\boldsymbol{w} \leftarrow \mathsf{MatDec}(\mathsf{dk}, \boldsymbol{C_w})$ and $\boldsymbol{s} \leftarrow \mathsf{MatDec}(\mathsf{dk}, \boldsymbol{C_s})$.
- Output $\boldsymbol{w}$ if $\boldsymbol{z} = \boldsymbol{s} + c\boldsymbol{w}$.

Now, we argue why the extractor works. First note that, since (a, c, z) is an accepting transcript, both the verification equations satisfy:

- $\boldsymbol{Y}^{\boldsymbol{z}} = \boldsymbol{S} \bullet \boldsymbol{U}^c$.
- $\mathsf{MatEnc}(\mathsf{ek}, \boldsymbol{z}; \boldsymbol{r_z}) = \mathsf{Add}(\boldsymbol{C_s}, \mathsf{ScMult}(c, \boldsymbol{C_w}))$.

Then, combining the *homomorphic well-formedness* property with *correctness of the encryption*, we get that since $\mathsf{Add}(\boldsymbol{C_s}, \mathsf{ScMult}(c, \boldsymbol{C_w}))$ equals $\mathsf{MatEnc}(\mathsf{ek}, \boldsymbol{z}; \boldsymbol{r_z})$ which correctly decrypts to $\boldsymbol{z}$, and c is uniformly at random, each ciphertext $\boldsymbol{C_w}$ and $\boldsymbol{C_s}$ would decrypt successfully except with probability $\delta_{\mathsf{st\text{-}ks}}$. So the extractor $\mathcal{E}$ never fails while decrypting these ciphertexts except with probability $\delta_{\mathsf{st\text{-}ks}}$. Conditioned on extractor's success, we have $\boldsymbol{z} = \boldsymbol{s} + c\boldsymbol{w}$, where $\boldsymbol{s} \leftarrow \mathsf{MatDec}(\mathsf{dk}, \boldsymbol{C_s})$ and $\boldsymbol{w} \leftarrow \mathsf{MatDec}(\mathsf{dk}, \boldsymbol{C_w})$. Since $\mathbb{G}$ is a cyclic group, we can write $\boldsymbol{S} = \boldsymbol{Y}^{\boldsymbol{s}'}$ and $\boldsymbol{U} = \boldsymbol{Y}^{\boldsymbol{w}'}$. The first verification equation is $\boldsymbol{z} = \boldsymbol{s}' + c\boldsymbol{w}'$. If $\boldsymbol{s} \neq \boldsymbol{s}'$ and $\boldsymbol{w} \neq \boldsymbol{w}'$, then c is uniquely defined as $c = (\boldsymbol{s}' - \boldsymbol{s})(\boldsymbol{w} - \boldsymbol{w}')^{-1}$, where the second term is an element-wise inverse of the vector $(\boldsymbol{w} - \boldsymbol{w}')$ – this fixes c in the commitment phase, which happens with probability $1/q$ as c is randomly chosen by verifier later in the challenge phase once $\boldsymbol{s}, \boldsymbol{s}', \boldsymbol{w}, \boldsymbol{w}'$ are fixed in the commitment phase. So, with probability $1 - 1/q$, $\boldsymbol{s} = \boldsymbol{s}'$ and $\boldsymbol{w} = \boldsymbol{w}'$. Hence the soundness holds except with probability $\leq (\delta_{\mathsf{st\text{-}ks}} + 1/q)$. This completes the proof.

(Computational) Honest Verifier Zero Knowledge

We describe zero-knowledge simulator $\mathcal{S}_\Sigma$ as follows:

$\mathcal{S}_\Sigma(\mathsf{crs}, \mathbb{x}, c)$:

- On input $(\mathsf{crs}, \mathbb{x}, c)$, where c is uniformly distributed over $\mathbb{Z}_q$, parse $\mathsf{ek} = \mathsf{crs}$ and $(\boldsymbol{Y} \in \mathbb{G}^{n \times m}, \boldsymbol{U} \in \mathbb{G}^m) = \mathbb{x}$.
- Sample $\boldsymbol{z} \xleftarrow{\$} \mathbb{Z}_q^n$.
- Compute the element wise inverse $\boldsymbol{U}^{-1}$.
- Compute $\boldsymbol{S} = \boldsymbol{Y}^{\boldsymbol{z}} \bullet (\boldsymbol{U}^{-1})^c$.
- Sample $\boldsymbol{r_s}, \boldsymbol{r_w} \xleftarrow{\$} \mathbb{Z}_q^n$.
- Compute $\boldsymbol{r_z} = \boldsymbol{r_s} + c \cdot \boldsymbol{r_w}$.
- Compute encryptions $\boldsymbol{C_z} := \mathsf{MatEnc}(\mathsf{ek}, \boldsymbol{z}; \boldsymbol{r_z})$ and $\boldsymbol{C_w} := \mathsf{MatEnc}(\mathsf{ek}, 0^n; \boldsymbol{r_w})$.
- Compute homomorphically $\boldsymbol{C_s} := \mathsf{Add}(\boldsymbol{C_z}, -\mathsf{ScMult}(c, \boldsymbol{C_w}))$.

- Set $a := (\boldsymbol{S}, \boldsymbol{C_s}, \boldsymbol{C_w})$ and $z := (\boldsymbol{z}, \boldsymbol{r_z}))$.
- Output (a, c, z).

We argue that the simulated transcript is computationally indistinguishable from the real transcript of Fig. 1, as long as the semantic security and the homomorphic property of the underlying encryption scheme hold.

Observe that all values are distributed identically, except for the ciphertext $\boldsymbol{C_w}$. In the real execution $\boldsymbol{C_w} := \mathsf{MatEnc}(\mathsf{ek}, \boldsymbol{w}; \boldsymbol{r_w})$, whereas Sim sets $\boldsymbol{C_w} := \mathsf{MatEnc}(\mathsf{ek}, 0^n; \boldsymbol{r_w})$. Hence, the transcripts are indistinguishable, except when the adversary breaks the semantic security of AHE. We give the full reduction to the semantic security of AHE in the full version.   □

5   Universally Composable NIZK Protocol

We present our UC-NIZK protocol for relation $\mathcal{R}_{\mathsf{GenLin}}$. We perform this by applying the Fiat-Shamir transform over our straight-line extractable Sigma protocol and proving that it is UC-secure. Before presenting our protocol, we present the general UC-NIZK functionality [GOS12, CSW22] in Fig. 2.[7]

$\mathcal{F}_{\mathsf{NIZK}}$ is parameterized by an NP Relation $\mathcal{R}$ and runs with a prover P, a verifier $\mathcal{V}$ and an ideal simulator Sim which stores proof transcripts in a list Q.

- **Proof** On input $(prove, \mathsf{sid}, \mathrm{x}, \mathrm{w})$ from P, if $\mathcal{R}(\mathrm{x}, \mathrm{w}) = 1$, send $(prove, \mathsf{sid}, P, \mathrm{x})$ to Sim. On receiving $(proof, \mathsf{sid}, \pi)$ from Sim, store $(\mathsf{sid}, \mathrm{x}, \pi)$ in Q and respond to P with $(proof, \mathsf{sid}, \pi)$.
- **Verify** On input $(\mathsf{sid}, \mathrm{x}, \pi)$ from $\mathcal{V}$, if $(\mathrm{x}, \pi) \notin Q$ then send $(verify, \mathsf{sid}, \mathrm{x}, \pi)$ to Sim. Upon receiving a witness $(witness, \mathrm{w})$ from Sim, if $\mathcal{R}(\mathrm{x}, \mathrm{w}) = 1$, store $(\mathsf{sid}, \mathrm{x}, \pi)$ in Q. Return $(verification, \mathsf{sid}, \mathrm{x}, \pi, \mathcal{R}(\mathrm{x}, \mathrm{w}))$ to $\mathcal{V}$.

Fig. 2. Ideal functionality $\mathcal{F}_{\mathsf{NIZK}}$

Next, we present our NIZK protocol Π_{GenLin} and show that it UC-securely implements $\mathcal{F}_{\mathsf{NIZK}}$ for relation $\mathcal{R}_{\mathsf{GenLin}}$.

In Fig. 3, we present our UC-NIZK protocol Π_{GenLin} for $\mathcal{R}_{\mathsf{GenLin}}$ (Eq. 1). It is obtained by applying the standard Fiat-Shamir transformation [FS87] to our interactive straight-line-extractable Sigma protocol (from Fig. 1) using the hash function $\mathcal{H}_{\mathcal{V}}$. We note that our Sigma protocol was in the URS model where the encryption key ek was part of the URS. But in our NIZK we use the public sampleability property of the underlying AHE scheme and generate the ek using

---

[7] We do not require sub-session IDs, denoted ssid's, in $\mathcal{F}_{\mathsf{NIZK}}$; in the UC framework, ssid's are used for modelling multi-instance functionalities that have a local/internal shared resource such as a common reference string. The simulation-extractability and non-malleability properties are required for UC, independently of whether the NIZK functionality has access to a shared local resource.

a separate hash function $\mathcal{H}_{ek}$. As a result, we do not require additional URS and prove security of our protocol in the random oracle model by modeling $\mathcal{H}_{ek}$ and $\mathcal{H}_{\mathcal{V}}$ as random oracles. Before presenting our UC proof we show that our NIZK satisfies the standard property based definitions. We summarize it in Theorem 2.

Π_{GenLin}

Ingredients and Settings:

- **Input:** Both prover and verifier know the public instance $\mathbb{x} := (\boldsymbol{Y} \in \mathbb{G}^{n \times m}, \boldsymbol{U} \in \mathbb{G}^m)$, and the prover exclusively has witness $\mathbb{w} := \boldsymbol{w} \in \mathbb{Z}_q^n$.
- **Primitives:** The interactive Sigma protocol from Fig. 1 (Setup, $\mathcal{P} = (\mathcal{P}_1, \mathcal{P}_2), \mathcal{V} = (\mathcal{V}_1, \mathcal{V}_2))$ based on an AHE scheme (Gen, Enc, Dec) with oblivious sampleability enabled by a hash function $\mathcal{H}_{ek} : \{0,1\}^* \to \mathcal{K}_{ek}$. Another hash function, $\mathcal{H}_{\mathcal{V}} : \{0,1\}^* \to \mathbb{Z}_q$. Both together are modeled as random oracle RO $= (\mathcal{H}_{ek}, \mathcal{H}_{\mathcal{V}})$

Protocol Description:

- $\mathcal{P}^{\mathrm{RO}}(prove, \mathsf{sid}, \mathbb{x}, \mathbb{w}) \to \pi$.
  - Parse RO as $(\mathcal{H}_{ek}, \mathcal{H}_{\mathcal{V}})$.
  - Compute $\mathsf{ek} := \mathcal{H}_{ek}(\mathsf{sid}, \mathbb{x})$ and set $\mathsf{crs} := \mathsf{ek}$.
  - Run $(\boldsymbol{S}, \boldsymbol{C_s}, \boldsymbol{C_w}) := \mathcal{P}_1(\mathsf{crs}, \mathbb{x}, \mathbb{w}; \rho)$ where $\rho := (\boldsymbol{s}, \boldsymbol{r_w}, \boldsymbol{r_s})$.
  - Define $a := (\boldsymbol{S}, \boldsymbol{C_s}, \boldsymbol{C_w})$.
  - Compute $c := \mathcal{H}_{\mathcal{V}}(\mathsf{sid}, \mathbb{x}, a)$.
  - Run $(\boldsymbol{z}, \boldsymbol{r_z}) := \mathcal{P}_2(\mathsf{crs}, \mathbb{x}, \mathbb{w}, a, c, \rho)$.
  - Define $z := (\boldsymbol{z}, \boldsymbol{r_z})$.
  - Output $\pi := (a, c, z)$.
- $\mathcal{V}^{\mathrm{RO}}(\mathsf{sid}, \mathbb{x}, \pi) \to 1/0$.
  - Parse $(a, c, z) := \pi$.
  - Parse RO as $(\mathcal{H}_{ek}, \mathcal{H}_{\mathcal{V}})$.
  - Compute $\mathsf{ek} := \mathcal{H}_{ek}(\mathsf{sid}, \mathbb{x})$.
  - Output $(c = \mathcal{H}_{\mathcal{V}}(\mathsf{sid}, \mathbb{x}, a) \land \mathcal{V}_2(\mathsf{crs}, \mathbb{x}, a, c, z))$.

Fig. 3. Our UC-NIZK protocol for $\mathcal{R}_{\mathsf{GenLin}}$.

We formalize the security analysis of Π_{GenLin} via the following thoerem.

Theorem 2. *Suppose that:*

- *the underlying Sigma protocol satisfies perfect completeness, computational honest verifier zero-knowledge and statistical straight-line knowledge soundness;*
- *the underlying AHE scheme is obliviously sampleable; and*
- *RO $= (\mathcal{H}_{ek}, \mathcal{H}_{\mathcal{V}})$ are programmable random oracles.*

Then Π_{GenLin} *of Fig. 3 satisfies the following:*

- **Perfect completeness** *based on the perfect completeness of the Sigma protocol;*
- **Computational zero-knowledge** *based on the honest verifier zero-knowledge of the underlying Sigma protocol, assuming $\mathcal{H}_{\mathcal{V}}$ to be a programmable random oracle and AHE satisfies oblivious sampling;*
- **Computational straight-line knowledge soundness** *based on the oblivious sampleability of the underlying encryption scheme, programmability of the random oracle $\mathcal{H}_{\mathsf{ek}}$ and the statistical straight-line knowledge soundness of the underlying Sigma protocol.*

Proof Sketch. The perfect completeness is immediate from the perfect completeness of the underlying Sigma protocol.

Computational zero-knowledge follows in a standard Fiat-Shamir argument by sampling a random challenge c, invoking the HVZK simulator $\mathcal{S}_{\Sigma}$ of Sigma protocol on $(\mathbb{x}, c)$ and then programming $\mathcal{H}_{\mathcal{V}}$ on $(\mathsf{sid}, \mathbb{x}, a)$ s.t. it returns c. We formally demonstrate this by explicitly defining the $\mathcal{S}_1$ and $\mathcal{S}_2$ algorithms below.

$\mathcal{S}_1(\cdots)$:

- *Answering $\mathcal{H}_{\mathsf{ek}}(\mathsf{sid}, \mathbb{x})$ queries:* Return $\mathcal{H}_{\mathsf{ek}}(\mathsf{sid}, \mathbb{x})$.
- *Answering $\mathcal{H}_{\mathcal{V}}(\mathsf{sid}, \mathbb{x}, a)$ queries made by $\mathcal{A}$:* Return $\mathcal{H}_{\mathcal{V}}(\mathsf{sid}, \mathbb{x}, a)$.
- *Answering $\mathcal{H}_{\mathcal{V}}(\mathsf{sid}, \mathbb{x}, a)$ queries made by $\mathcal{S}_2$:* Read $(\mathsf{sid}, \mathbb{x}, a, c, z)$ from st. Program $\mathcal{H}_{\mathcal{V}}$ s.t. it return $\mathcal{H}_{\mathcal{V}}(\mathsf{sid}, \mathbb{x}, a) = c$. If the query is repeated in the future then return c.

$\mathcal{S}_2(\mathsf{sid}, \mathbb{x})$:

- On input $(\mathsf{sid}, \mathbb{x})$ compute $\mathsf{ek} \leftarrow \mathcal{H}_{\mathsf{ek}}(\mathsf{sid}, \mathbb{x})$.
- Sample $c \leftarrow \mathbb{Z}_q$ and obtain simulated transcript $(a, c, z) \leftarrow \mathcal{S}_{\Sigma}(\mathsf{ek}, \mathbb{x}, c)$ by the invoking the HVZK simulator $\mathcal{S}$ of the Sigma protocol.
- Update st as $st := st \cup (\mathsf{sid}, \mathbb{x}, a, c, z)$. Store simulated transcript as $\mathcal{T} = \mathcal{T} \cup (\mathsf{sid}, \mathbb{x}, a, c, z)$
- Query $\mathcal{H}_{\mathcal{V}}(\mathsf{sid}, \mathbb{x}, a)$ to obtain c.
- Return $\pi = (a, c, z)$.

The only way an adversarial verifier can prevent zero-knowledge is if it queries the random oracle on $(\mathsf{sid}, \mathbb{x}, a)$ before the simulator programs it to output c. However, this is not possible since the first message a is determined by $s \in \mathbb{Z}_q^n$ in the Sigma protocol. Concretely, the probability that an adversarial verifier prevents the ZK simulator from programming $\mathcal{H}_{\mathcal{V}}$ on a particular a is $\frac{Q_{\mathcal{H}_{\mathcal{V}}}}{\min(q^n, |\mathbb{G}|^m)}$, where $Q_{\mathcal{H}_{\mathcal{V}}}$ is the number of queries made by the adversarial verifier to the hash function $\mathcal{H}_{\mathcal{V}}$, a is computed by sampling $s \leftarrow \mathbb{Z}_q^n$ and computing $a := \boldsymbol{S} := \boldsymbol{Y}^s \in \mathbb{G}^m$.

Next, we focus on straight-line knowledge soundness. According to the definition (Sect. 3.3) the stateful extractor $\mathcal{E}$ has two modes $\mathcal{E}(1, \cdots)$ which programs and simulates the random oracle and $\mathcal{E}(2, \cdots)$ which extracts the witness. We define them as follows for Π_{GenLin}.

$\mathcal{E}(1, \cdots)$:

- *Answering* $\mathcal{H}_{\text{ek}}(\text{sid}, x)$ *queries:* Sample $(\text{ek}, \text{dk}) \leftarrow \text{AHE.Gen}(1^\kappa)$ and program $\mathcal{H}_{\text{ek}}$ to return ek and store (ek, dk) in st. If the query is repeated in the future then return ek.
- *Answering* $\mathcal{H}_{\mathcal{V}}(\text{sid}, x, a)$ *queries:* Sample $c \leftarrow \mathbb{Z}_q$ and program $\mathcal{H}_{\mathcal{V}}$ to return c. If the query is repeated in the future then return c.

$\mathcal{E}(2, \text{sid}, x, \pi)$:

- On input (sid, x, π) parse $(a, c, z) := \pi$ and compute $\text{ek} = \mathcal{H}_{\mathcal{V}}(\text{sid}, x)$.
- Abort if $\mathcal{H}_{\text{ek}}(\text{sid}, x, a) \neq c$. Otherwise, retrieve dk corresponding to (sid, ek) from st and set $\text{crs} = \text{ek}$ and $\text{td} = \text{dk}$.
- Output $\mathcal{E}_\Sigma(\text{crs}, \text{td}, x, \pi)$.

Now we argue why the extraction works. First, due to oblivious sampleability of the underlying encryption scheme, the public key ek is computationally indistinguishable with the ek in the actual protocol Π_{GenLin}. Then, we note that with probability $1/Q_{\mathcal{H}_{\text{ek}}}$, $\mathcal{E}(2, \dots)$ does not abort in the first step, where $Q_{\mathcal{H}_{\text{ek}}}$ denotes the total number of random oracle queries asked by $\mathcal{A}$ to $\mathcal{H}_{\text{ek}}$. Next, if $\mathcal{A}$ can predict the output of $\mathcal{H}_{\mathcal{V}}(\text{sid}, x, a)$ without querying, then only the second abort condition is triggered, but this happens only with $\frac{Q_{\mathcal{H}_{\mathcal{V}}}}{q}$ probability where a can have q possibilities. Assuming no abort is triggered, $\mathcal{E}_\Sigma$ returns a correct witness except with negligible probability $\text{negl}(\lambda)$. So, if we bound both $Q_{\mathcal{H}_{\text{ek}}}$ and $Q_{\mathcal{H}_{\mathcal{V}}}$ to be at most sub-exponential in λ the extractor $\mathcal{E}$ outputs a correct witness except with negligible probability in λ as well. □

Next, we show that Π_{GenLin} UC-securely realizes $\mathcal{F}_{\text{NIZK}}$ for relation $\mathcal{R}_{\text{GenLin}}$. This requires constructing a simulator against a corrupt verifier and a simulator against a corrupt prover. For the former, we simply use the NIZK simulator against a corrupt verifier from the previous subsection. For the latter, we need straight-line blackbox simulation-extractability [KZM+15] where the environment $\mathcal{Z}$ corrupts (via dummy adversary $\mathcal{A}$) the prover in session sid and sees simulated proofs from sessions where the verifier is corrupt. We need to argue that the environment $\mathcal{Z}$ still cannot distinguish the ideal world execution of sid from a real-world execution of the same session. To argue simulation-extractability, we need to show that the protocol satisfies weak-unique response property [FKMV12]. We refer to Definition 3.3 for the formal definitions of simulation-extractability and weak unique response. The formal UC-proof is more involved and we refer to the full version for the full proof.

6   Concrete Instantiation of AHE Using Class Groups

We instantiate our additive homomorphic encryption scheme with the class-group based PKE scheme of [CL15]. However, we need to additionally show that it satisfies our newly introduced *oblivious sampleability* and *homomorphic well-formedness* properties. All other required properties were already shown to hold in prior works, and hence we omit the details for them.

Background and Notation. We provide a brief background (which is mostly borrowed from [KMM+23,CCL+19,BDO23]) on class-groups before recalling the encryption scheme. The class-group setting considers a finite abelian group $\widehat{\mathbb{G}}_{\mathsf{CL}}$ of unknown order $q \cdot \widehat{s}$, where q is known and $\widehat{s}$ is unknown and hard to compute. Consider a cyclic subgroup $\mathbb{F}_{\mathsf{CL}} = \langle f \rangle$ of $\widehat{\mathbb{G}}_{\mathsf{CL}}$ of order q, where q is prime. The set $\widehat{\mathbb{G}}_{\mathsf{CL}}^q = \{g^q : g \in \widehat{\mathbb{G}}_{\mathsf{CL}}\}$ is a subgroup of $\widehat{\mathbb{G}}_{\mathsf{CL}}$ of order $\widehat{s}$. Therefore, $\widehat{\mathbb{G}}_{\mathsf{CL}}$ is factored as $\widehat{\mathbb{G}}_{\mathsf{CL}} \simeq \mathbb{F}_{\mathsf{CL}} \times \widehat{\mathbb{G}}_{\mathsf{CL}}^q$. Let $U \in \mathbb{Z}$ be an upper bound of $\widehat{s}$, which is known. Although $\widehat{\mathbb{G}}_{\mathsf{CL}}$ is the base group, we are focusing on a cyclic subgroup $\mathbb{G}_{\mathsf{CL}}$ of $\widehat{\mathbb{G}}_{\mathsf{CL}}$, such that $\mathbb{G}_{\mathsf{CL}}$ has order $q \cdot s$ and s divides $\widehat{s}$. So, $\mathbb{F}_{\mathsf{CL}}$ is also a cyclic subgroup of $\mathbb{G}_{\mathsf{CL}}$. Consider $\mathbb{G}_{\mathsf{CL}}^q = \{g^q : g \in \mathbb{G}_{\mathsf{CL}}\}$ which is a cyclic subgroup of $\mathbb{G}_{\mathsf{CL}}$ of order s. Now, q and s are also co-prime. Therefore, $\mathbb{G}_{\mathsf{CL}}$ can be factored as $\mathbb{G}_{\mathsf{CL}} \simeq \mathbb{F}_{\mathsf{CL}} \times \mathbb{G}_{\mathsf{CL}}^q$. Both $s, \widehat{s}$ are odd and all $s, \widehat{s}, q$ are exponential in λ. While discrete log is hard in groups $\widehat{\mathbb{G}}_{\mathsf{CL}}, \mathbb{G}_{\mathsf{CL}}, \widehat{\mathbb{G}}_{\mathsf{CL}}^q, \mathbb{G}_{\mathsf{CL}}^q$, it is easy in $\mathbb{F}_{\mathsf{CL}}$. Precisely, there are two efficient algorithms:

- $(U, \widehat{\mathbb{G}}_{\mathsf{CL}}, \mathbb{F}_{\mathsf{CL}}, f, g_q, \mathcal{D}, \mathcal{D}_q, \rho) \leftarrow \mathbf{Gen}(1^\lambda, 1^{\lambda_{\mathsf{st}}}, q)$. This algorithm, on input the computational security parameter λ, the statistical security parameter λ_{st}, and a prime q, outputs the class group parameters and the randomness ρ used to generate them. For convenience, we include the descriptions of the distributions $\mathcal{D}$ and $\mathcal{D}_q$ as well, which we define below.
- $x \leftarrow \mathbf{Solve}(X = f^x, U, q, \widehat{\mathbb{G}}_{\mathsf{CL}}, \mathbb{F}_{\mathsf{CL}}, g_q, f)$. This algorithm solves the discrete log problem deterministically and efficiently in the group $\mathbb{F}_{\mathsf{CL}}$.

We also consider two distributions $\mathcal{D}$ and $\mathcal{D}_q$ over $\mathbb{Z}$ such that $\{g^x \mid x \leftarrow \mathcal{D}\}$ and $\{g_q^x \mid x \leftarrow \mathcal{D}_q\}$ produce almost uniform distributions over $\mathbb{G}_{\mathsf{CL}}$ and $\mathbb{G}_{\mathsf{CL}}^q$ respectively, which are statistically close (within distance $2^{-\lambda_{\mathsf{st}}}$, for a statistical security parameter λ_{st}, typically set to 40 in practice) to uniform distributions over $\mathbb{G}_{\mathsf{CL}}$ and $\mathbb{G}_{\mathsf{CL}}^q$ respectively.

Hardness Assumptions. We use the following hardness assumptions over class groups. All assumptions below use a common setup: for the security parameters $\lambda, \lambda_{\mathsf{st}} \in \mathbb{N}$, modulus $2^\lambda \leq q \in \mathbb{Z}$ consider a set of public parameters $(U, \widehat{\mathbb{G}}_{\mathsf{CL}}, \mathbb{F}_{\mathsf{CL}}, f, g_q, \mathcal{D}, \mathcal{D}_q, \rho) \leftarrow \mathbf{Gen}(1^\lambda, 1^{\lambda_{\mathsf{st}}}, q)$ generated using a random ρ and the oracle **Solve**. We recall the following assumptions from prior works.

Definition 1 (Hard Subgroup Membership Assumption [CLT22]). *Sample* $x \xleftarrow{\$} \mathcal{D}_q$ *and* $u \xleftarrow{\$} \mathbb{Z}_q$. *Sample a bit* $b \xleftarrow{\$} \{0, 1\}$ *uniformly at random. If* $b = 0$, *define* $h^* \leftarrow g_q^x$, *otherwise if* $b = 1$ *define* $h^* \leftarrow f^u \cdot g_q^x$. *Then we say that the hard subgroup membership assumption holds over the class group framework, if for any PPT adversary* $\mathcal{A}$, *the following probability is negligible in* λ.

$$\left| \Pr\left[b = b^* \mid b^* \leftarrow \mathcal{A}(\mathsf{pp}_{\mathsf{CG}}, h^*)^{\mathsf{CG.Solve}(\cdot)} \right] - \frac{1}{2} \right| .$$

Definition 2 (C-Rough Order Assumption [BDO23]). *Let* $C \in \mathbb{N}$ *be a natural number. Define* $\mathcal{D}_C^{\mathsf{rough}}$ *to be the uniform distribution over the set* $\{\rho \in$

$\{0,1\}^\lambda \mid (U, \widehat{\mathbb{G}}_{\mathsf{CL}}, \mathbb{F}_{\mathsf{CL}}, f, g_q, \mathcal{D}, \mathcal{D}_q, \rho) \leftarrow \mathbf{Gen}(1^\lambda, 1^{\lambda_{\mathsf{st}}}, q; \rho) \wedge \forall \ prime\ p < C\ :\ p \nmid ord(\widehat{\mathbb{G}}_{\mathsf{CL}})\}$. *Then we say that C-rough order assumption holds over the class group framework, if for any PPT adversary $\mathcal{A}$, the following probability (distinguishing advantage) is negligible in λ:*

$$\left| \Pr\left[b = b^* \mid b^* \leftarrow \mathcal{A}(\mathsf{pp}_{\mathsf{CG}}, \rho^*) \right] - \frac{1}{2} \right|$$

for a uniform random b such that if $b = 0$, the ρ^* is uniform random in $\{0,1\}^\lambda$, and when $b = 1$, then ρ^* is sampled from $\mathcal{D}_C^{\mathsf{rough}}$.

We now present a variant of hard sub-group membership assumption, which is a new assumption we use in this paper.

Definition 3 (Hard Cyclic Subgroup Membership Assumption). *Sample $x_0 \xleftarrow{\$} \widehat{\mathbb{G}}_{\mathsf{CL}}$, and $x_1 \xleftarrow{\$} \mathbb{G}_{\mathsf{CL}}$. Then we say that the hard cyclic subgroup membership assumption holds over the class group framework, if for any PPT adversary $\mathcal{A}$, the following probability is negligible in λ.*

$$\left| \Pr\left[b = b^* \mid b^* \leftarrow \mathcal{A}(\mathsf{pp}_{\mathsf{CG}}, x_b)^{\mathsf{Solve}(\cdot)} \right] - \frac{1}{2} \right|$$

for a uniform random bit b.

Discussion. We note that, this assumption (Definition 3) was mentioned informally in many earlier works [Tuc20, BDO23]: it is hard to identify elements from $\mathbb{G}_{\mathsf{CL}}$. Also, we note that the hash functions constructed in [SBK24, CLR24] map to $\widehat{\mathbb{G}}_{\mathsf{CL}}$. So, we need to rely on this assumption to ensure that an oblivious sampling procedure works without providing any leverage to the adversary.

Construction. Now we are ready to describe the encryption scheme $\mathsf{CG\text{-}AHE} := (\mathsf{CG.Gen}, \mathsf{CG.Enc}, \mathsf{CG.Dec})$ for message space $\mathcal{M} = \mathbb{Z}_q$, and encryption key-space $\mathcal{K}_{\mathsf{ek}} = \mathbb{G}_{\mathsf{CL}}^q$.

Let $\mathsf{pp}_{\mathsf{CG}} := (U, q, \widehat{\mathbb{G}}_{\mathsf{CL}}, \mathbb{F}_{\mathsf{CL}}, \mathbb{G}_{\mathsf{CL}}^q, g_q, f, \mathcal{D}, \mathcal{D}_q, \rho) \leftarrow \mathbf{Gen}(1^\lambda, 1^{\lambda_{\mathsf{st}}}, q)$ for some computational security parameter λ and for some statistical security parameter λ_{st} and a prime q. The scheme $\mathsf{CG\text{-}AHE}$ works as follows:

$\mathsf{CG.Gen}(\mathsf{pp}_{\mathsf{CG}})$
$\to (\mathsf{dk}, \mathsf{ek})$:
- $\mathsf{dk} \xleftarrow{\$} \mathcal{D}_q$
- $\mathsf{ek} := g_q^{\mathsf{dk}}$

$\mathsf{CG.Enc}(\mathsf{pp}_{\mathsf{CG}}, \mathsf{ek}, m) \to c$:
- $r \xleftarrow{\$} \mathcal{D}_q$
- $R := g_q^r$
- $E := f^m \cdot \mathsf{ek}^r$
- Set $c := (R, E)$

$\mathsf{CG.Dec}(\mathsf{pp}_{\mathsf{CG}}, \mathsf{dk}, c) \to m$:
- Parse $c = (R, E)$
- $M := \frac{E}{R^{\mathsf{dk}}}$
- $m := \mathbf{Solve}(\mathsf{pp}_{\mathsf{CG}}, M)$

We show that $\mathsf{CG\text{-}AHE}$ encryption satisfies all properties required, including *homomorphic well-formedness* and *oblivious sampleability of the encryption key*, as defined in Sect. 3.1. We note that the perfect correctness, semantic security and additive homomorphism are already shown in [CL15, BDO23, KMM+23,

CLT18, CCL+19, CCL+20] based on computational assumptions, such as hard subgroup membership (Definition 1).

Homomorphic Well-formedness of CG-AHE**.** We first recall the specifications of Add and ScMult:

- Add(c_1, c_2) : Parse $c_1 = (R_1, E_1)$ and $c_2 = (R_2, E_2)$. Then compute $R_{(+)} := R_1 \cdot R_2$ and $E_{(+)} := E_1 \cdot E_2$. Output $c_{(+)} = (R_{(+)}, E_{(+)})$.
- ScMult(s, c) : Parse $c = (R, E)$, $s \in \mathbb{Z}_q$ and compute $R_{(\cdot)} := R^s$ and $E_{(\cdot)} := E^s$. Output $c_{(\cdot)} = (R_{(\cdot)}, E_{(\cdot)})$. Note that, s can just be parsed as an integer for R^s operation, since this is in a cyclic group.

Now note that, unlike ElGamal encryption, CG-AHE does not have *dense ciphertexts*, which is the property that for any element $c \in \mathcal{C}$, we can get $m \leftarrow$ CG.Dec$(\mathsf{pp}_{\mathsf{CG}}, \mathsf{dk}, c)$. We call such successfully decryptable ciphertexts, *valid ciphertexts*. However, for CG-AHE, not all ciphertexts are valid. For example, choose a random ciphertext $(R, E) \xleftarrow{\$} \mathcal{C}$. Then, $R = g_q^r$ and $E = g^e$. The operation E/R^{dk} yields g^δ which, with overwhelming probability, is not in the easy group $\mathbb{F}_{\mathsf{CL}}$. Hence **Solve** will fail in CG.Dec. It is easy to see that, for any valid ciphertext (R, E) it holds that $R/E^{\mathsf{dk}} \in \mathbb{F}_{\mathsf{CL}}$.

Now, consider the following lemma:

Lemma 1. *As long as the C-rough order assumption holds with distinguishing advantage δ_{rough} (Definition 2), CG-AHE has the homomorphic well-formedness property except with probability $\delta_{\mathsf{st-ks}} \leq \delta_{\mathsf{rough}} + \delta$ where $\delta = \max(1/q, 2/C)$. This is negligible whenever C is super-polynomial and δ_{rough} is negligible.*

Proof. Fix two arbitrary elements $c_1, c_2 \in \widehat{\mathbb{G}}_{\mathsf{CL}}^2$. Then sample a uniform random $s \xleftarrow{\$} \mathbb{Z}_q$, and compute $c_3 := $ Add$(c_1, \mathsf{ScMult}(s, c_2))$. Now, if c_3 is valid, that implies $E_3/R_3^{\mathsf{dk}} = (E_1/R_1^{\mathsf{dk}}) \cdot (E_2/R_2^{\mathsf{dk}})^s$ is in $\mathbb{F}_{\mathsf{CL}}$, where $c_i = (R_i, E_i)$ for $i \in \{1, 2, 3\}$. Now, using the claim below, setting $G := \widehat{\mathbb{G}}_{\mathsf{CL}}$ and $H := \mathbb{F}_{\mathsf{CL}}$, we have that individually each E_i/r_i^{dk} for $i \in \{1, 2\}$ is in $\mathbb{F}_{\mathsf{CL}}$ except with probability $\delta = \max(1/q, 2/p)$ where p is the smallest prime dividing the order of $\widehat{\mathbb{G}}_{\mathsf{CL}}$. Writing $E_i/R_i^{\mathsf{dk}} = f^{m_i}$, for $i \in \{1, 2, 3\}$ we obtain that $m_3 = m_1 + sm_2 \bmod q$. Using C-rough order assumption we obtain $\delta = \max(1/q, 2/C)$. So, accounting for the distinguishing advantage of the rough order assumption, the total error probability can be bounded by $\leq \delta_{\mathsf{rough}} + \delta$.

Claim. Let G be any commutative group with unknown order, and let H be a subgroup of G. For any two elements $g, h \in G$, and a uniformly random $s \xleftarrow{\$} \mathbb{Z}_q$ for some integer q, if $g \cdot h^s \in H$, then we have that both $g, h \in H$, where p is the smallest prime factor of the order of G, except with probability $\max(1/q, 2/p)$.

Proof. Consider the factor group $G' := G/H$. Let $g', h' \in G'$ correspond to g and h respectively. Observe that $g \cdot h^s \in H$ implies $g' \cdot h'^s = 1 \in G'$. Clearly, the only non-trivial case is when at least h' is a non-identity element ($\neq 1$) in G' – in that case the equivalent condition is $h'^{-s} = g'$.

We compute the probability of the bad event, i.e. that $g' = h'^{-s} \in G'$ and $(h' \neq 1 \in G')$. Now, let p be the smallest prime factor of the order of G. Then consider two cases: (i) $p \geq q$; and (ii) $p < q$.

In Case (i), since $h' \neq 1$, h'^{-s} maps to exactly q distinct elements in G' since s takes q distinct values (in $\mathbb{Z}_q$). If g' is one of them, then the probability that $h'^{-s} = g'$ holds over uniform choice of $s \xleftarrow{\$} \mathbb{Z}_q$ is at most $1/q$.

For Case (ii), since p does not divide q, the distribution of h'^{-s} may not be uniform for uniform random $s \xleftarrow{\$} \mathbb{Z}_q$, which is of size at least p. However, since s is uniform at random, the distribution of h'^{-s} would be such that, any element would be at most twice probable than any other element. Since the support is at least of size p, the probability with which $h'^{-s} = g'$ holds over uniform random $s \leftarrow \mathbb{Z}_q$ is at most $2/p$.

This concludes the proof.   □

Oblivious Sampleability of Encryption Key. Recall that, oblivious sampleability requires existence of a hash function mapping to $\widehat{\mathbb{G}}_{\mathsf{CL}}^q$ such that a random sample from the co-domain of the hash function is indistinguishable from the public key of the class group encryption. Using any hash function constructed in [SBK24, CLR24] we get a point in $\widehat{\mathbb{G}}_{\mathsf{CL}}$, which is statistically close to a random point in $\widehat{\mathbb{G}}_{\mathsf{CL}}$, as shown in those works. subsequently, computing the q-th power we obtain a close of random point in $\widehat{\mathbb{G}}_{\mathsf{CL}}^q$. Then, relying on the hard cyclic sub-group membership Assumption 3, we can argue that this is computationally indistinguishable from a random point in the cyclic subgroup $\mathbb{G}_{\mathsf{CL}}^q$, which is actually the public key space for the class group encryption. Finally, since the class group encryption has dense public key space (each point in the space is equally likely), we can conclude oblivious sampleability. For details we refer to the full version [CDG+24].

Discussion on Our Choice. We elaborate on our choice of class-group based AHE. First we note that, among existing AHE candidates, exponentiated ElGamal does not support large message space $\mathbb{Z}_q$ efficiently. The Paillier encryption scheme falls short as it does not satisfy the crucial oblivious sampleability property. Other prominent AHE candidates come form lattice-based cryptography, such as Regev's [Reg04] encryption, GPV [GPV08] etc. While their basic versions only support bit-encryption, there are complex optimization techniques to pack large plaintext. In contrast, the class-group based encryption satisfies all our requirements in a fairly straightforward manner.

7   Application of Our UC-NIZK

We demonstrate concrete applications of our compiler by applying to the well-known Chaum-Pedersen Protocol [CP93]. We make it UC-secure at the cost of two additional encryptions without performing any repetition of the original

Chaum-Pedersen protocol. It can be used in the works of [TGL+19, BGJP23]. Our UC-NIZK for Chaum-Pedersen is as follows:

- **Input:** Prover and verifier have input statement $\mathbb{x} = (g, h, W_1, W_2)$. Prover has secret witness $\mathbb{w} = w$ s.t. $W_1 = g^w$ and $W_2 = h^w$.
- **Primitives:** $\mathcal{H}_{\mathcal{V}}$ and $\mathcal{H}_{\mathsf{ek}}$ are random oracles. AHE is the additively homomorphic encryption scheme.
- **Setup:** A key pair $(\mathsf{ek}, \mathsf{dk})$ for AHE.
- **Prover Algorithm:** $\mathcal{P}(\mathsf{ek}, \mathbb{x}, \mathbb{w}) \to a$:
    1. Compute $\mathsf{ek} := \mathcal{H}_{\mathsf{ek}}(\mathsf{sid}, \mathbb{x})$.
    2. Sample $s \leftarrow \mathbb{Z}_q$. Compute $S_1 := g^s$ and $S_2 := h^s$.
    3. Sample encryption randomnesses r_s, r_w.
    4. Compute $C_s := \mathsf{Enc}(\mathsf{ek}, s, r_s)$ and $C_w := \mathsf{Enc}(\mathsf{ek}, w, r_w)$.
    5. Set $a := (S, C_s, C_w)$ to $\mathcal{V}$.
    6. Compute $c := \mathcal{H}_{\mathcal{V}}(\mathsf{sid}, \mathbb{x}, a)$.
    7. Compute $z := s + c \cdot w \in \mathbb{Z}_q$, and send z to $\mathcal{V}$.
    8. Compute $r_z := r_s + c \cdot r_w \in \mathbb{Z}_q$, and send (a, c, z, r_z) to $\mathcal{V}$.
- **Verifier Algorithm:** $\mathcal{V}(\mathsf{ek}, \mathbb{x}, (a, c, (z, r_z))) \to b$:
    1. Compute $\mathsf{ek} := \mathcal{H}_{\mathsf{ek}}(\mathsf{sid}, \mathbb{x})$.
    2. Check that:
        - $g^z = S_1 \cdot W_1^c \in \mathbb{G}$; and
        - $h^z = S_2 \cdot W_2^c \in \mathbb{G}$; and
        - C_s, C_w are valid AHE ciphertexts; and
        - $\mathsf{Enc}(\mathsf{ek}, z, r_z) = C_s + c \cdot C_z$.
    3. If all checks pass, output 1. Otherwise, output 0.

It can be observed that the above protocol is a specific instantiation of Π_{GenLin} for $n = 1$ and $m = 2$ and we incurred the cost of two additional encryptions. A generalized version of Chaum-Pedersen where the same witness is used to prove m statements can be similarly considered as $\mathbb{x} = (g_i, g_i^w)$ for secret witness $\mathbb{w} = w$. In that case, our compiler still incurs two encryptions as overhead for UC security for those m statements. That would amortize the cost of those two encryptions over m statements since the entire Chaum-Pedersen Proof would be dominated by the cost of $2m$ exponentiations over group $\mathbb{G}$. This also captures AND composition using our compiler. The Schnorr's protocol can be found in Sect. 2 where $n = 1$ and $m = 1$. We refer to the *Applications* paragraph in Sect. 1.1 for the concrete applications of Schnorr's and Chaum-Pedersen's proof of knowledge. We provide the OR composition using our compiler in the full version [CDG+24]. This will improve existing works like [TGL+19] where both OR composition and Chaum-Pedersen is used.

Acknowledgements. We are grateful to Lennart Braun and Ivan Damgård for pointing out two separate subtle issues (and respective fixes) in the class group instantiation in a prior version of this work. We also thank Ran Canetti for helpful discussions in the preliminary phases of this project.

References

[ABK+21] Abdalla, M., Barbosa, M., Katz, J., Loss, J., Jiayu, X.: Algebraic adversaries in the universal composability framework. In: Tibouchi, M., Wang, H. (eds.) ASIACRYPT 2021. LNCS, vol. 13092, pp. 311–341. Springer, Cham (2021). https://doi.org/10.1007/978-3-030-92078-4_11

[AF07] Abe, M., Fehr, S.: Perfect NIZK with adaptive soundness. In: Vadhan, S.P. (ed.) TCC 2007. LNCS, vol. 4392, pp. 118–136. Springer, Heidelberg (2007). https://doi.org/10.1007/978-3-540-70936-7_7

[Ano] Anonymous. Private communication

[BCS16] Ben-Sasson, E., Chiesa, A., Spooner, N.: Interactive oracle proofs. In: Hirt, M., Smith, A. (eds.) TCC 2016. LNCS, vol. 9986, pp. 31–60. Springer, Heidelberg (2016). https://doi.org/10.1007/978-3-662-53644-5_2

[BDO23] Braun, L., Damgård, I., Orlandi, C.: Secure multiparty computation from threshold encryption based on class groups. In: Handschuh, H., Lysyanskaya, A. (eds.) CRYPTO 2023. LNCS, vol. 14081, pp. 613–645. Springer, Cham (2023). https://doi.org/10.1007/978-3-031-38557-5_20

[BFKT24] Bobolz, J., Farshim, P., Kohlweiss, M., Takahashi, A.: The brave new world of global generic groups and uc-secure zero-overhead snarks. In: Boyle, E., Mahmoody, M. (eds.) TCC 24, vol. 15364, pp. 90–124. Springer, Heidelberg (2024). https://doi.org/10.1007/978-3-031-78011-0_4

[BFM90] Blum, M., Feldman, P., Micali, S.: Proving security against chosen ciphertext attacks. In: Goldwasser, S. (ed.) CRYPTO 1988. LNCS, vol. 403, pp. 256–268. Springer, New York (1990). https://doi.org/10.1007/0-387-34799-2_20

[BGJP23] Bartusek, J., Garg, S., Jain, A., Policharla, G.-V.: End-to-end secure messaging with traceability only for illegal content. In: Hazay, C., Stam, M. (eds.) EUROCRYPT 2023. LNCS, vol. 14008, pp. 35–66. Springer, Cham (2023). https://doi.org/10.1007/978-3-031-30589-4_2

[BKM20] Brakerski, Z., Koppula, V., Mour, T.: NIZK from LPN and trapdoor hash via correlation intractability for approximable relations. In: Micciancio, D., Ristenpart, T. (eds.) CRYPTO 2020. LNCS, vol. 12172, pp. 738–767. Springer, Cham (2020). https://doi.org/10.1007/978-3-030-56877-1_26

[BLS01] Boneh, D., Lynn, B., Shacham, H.: Short signatures from the weil pairing. In: Boyd, C. (ed.) ASIACRYPT 2001. LNCS, vol. 2248, pp. 514–532. Springer, Heidelberg (2001). https://doi.org/10.1007/3-540-45682-1_30

[BSMP91] Blum, M., De Santis, A., Micali, S., Persiano, G.: Noninteractive zero-knowledge. SIAM J. Comput. **20**(6), 1084–1118 (1991)

[Can01] Canetti, R.: Universally composable security: a new paradigm for cryptographic protocols. In: 42nd FOCS, pp. 136–145. IEEE Computer Society Press (2001)

[CCH+19] Canetti, R., et al.: Fiat-shamir: from practice to theory. In: Charikar, M., Cohen, E. (eds.) Proceedings of the 51st Annual ACM SIGACT Symposium on Theory of Computing, STOC 2019, Phoenix, AZ, USA, 23–26 June 2019, pp. 1082–1090. ACM (2019)

[CCL+19] Castagnos, G., Catalano, D., Laguillaumie, F., Savasta, F., Tucker, I.: Two-Party ECDSA from hash proof systems and efficient instantiations. In: Boldyreva, A., Micciancio, D. (eds.) CRYPTO 2019. LNCS, vol. 11694, pp. 191–221. Springer, Cham (2019). https://doi.org/10.1007/978-3-030-26954-8_7

[CCL+20] Castagnos, G., Catalano, D., Laguillaumie, F., Savasta, F., Tucker, I.: Bandwidth-efficient threshold EC-DSA. In: Kiayias, A., Kohlweiss, M., Wallden, P., Zikas, V. (eds.) PKC 2020. LNCS, vol. 12111, pp. 266–296. Springer, Cham (2020). https://doi.org/10.1007/978-3-030-45388-6_10

[CD24] Cascudo, I., David, B.: Publicly verifiable secret sharing over class groups and applications to DKG and YOSO. In: Joye, M., Leander, G. (eds.) EUROCRYPT 2024. LNCS, vol. 14655, pp. 216–248. Springer, Heidelberg (2024). https://doi.org/10.1007/978-3-031-58740-5_8

[CDG+24] Chen, M., Dey, P., Ganesh, C., Mukherjee, P., Sarkar, P., Sasmal, S.: Universally composable non-interactive zero-knowledge from sigma protocols via a new straight-line compiler. Cryptology ePrint Archive, Paper 2024/1713 (2024)

[CDS94] Cramer, R., Damgård, I., Schoenmakers, B.: Proofs of partial knowledge and simplified design of witness hiding protocols. In: Desmedt, Y.G. (ed.) CRYPTO 1994. LNCS, vol. 839, pp. 174–187. Springer, Heidelberg (1994). https://doi.org/10.1007/3-540-48658-5_19

[CF24] Chiesa, A., Fenzi, G.: zksnarks in the rom with unconditional uc-security. In: Boyle, E., Mahmoody, M. (eds.) TCC 24. LNCS, vol. 15364, pp. 67–89. Springer, Heidelberg (2024). https://doi.org/10.1007/978-3-031-78011-0_3

[CGH98] Canetti, R., Goldreich, O., Halevi, S.: The random oracle methodology, revisited (preliminary version). In: 30th ACM STOC, pp. 209–218. ACM Press (1998)

[CGKN21] Chalkias, K., Garillot, F., Kondi, Y., Nikolaenko, V.: Non-interactive half-aggregation of EdDSA and variants of Schnorr signatures. In: Paterson, K.G. (ed.) CT-RSA 2021. LNCS, vol. 12704, pp. 577–608. Springer, Cham (2021). https://doi.org/10.1007/978-3-030-75539-3_24

[CJS14] Canetti, R., Jain, A., Scafuro, A.: Practical UC security with a global random oracle. In: Ahn, G.J., Yung, M., Li, N. (eds.) ACM CCS 2014, pp. 597–608. ACM Press (2014)

[CL15] Castagnos, G., Laguillaumie, F.: Linearly homomorphic encryption from DDH. In: Nyberg, K. (ed.) CT-RSA 2015. LNCS, vol. 9048, pp. 487–505. Springer, Cham (2015). https://doi.org/10.1007/978-3-319-16715-2_26

[CL24] Chen, Y.H., Lindell, Y.: Optimizing and implementing fischlin's transform for uc-secure zero-knowledge. IACR Cryptol. ePrint Arch., 526 (2024)

[CLR24] Chalkias, K.K., Lindstrøm, J., Roy, A.: An efficient hash function for imaginary class groups. Cryptology ePrint Archive, Paper 2024/295 (2024). https://eprint.iacr.org/2024/295

[CLT18] Castagnos, G., Laguillaumie, F., Tucker, I.: Practical fully secure unrestricted inner product functional encryption modulo p. In: Peyrin, T., Galbraith, S. (eds.) ASIACRYPT 2018. LNCS, vol. 11273, pp. 733–764. Springer, Cham (2018). https://doi.org/10.1007/978-3-030-03329-3_25

[CLT22] Castagnos, G., Laguillaumie, F., Tucker, I.: Threshold linearly homomorphic encryption on $\mathbf{Z}/2^k\mathbf{Z}$. In: Agrawal, S., Lin, D. (eds.) ASIACRYPT 2022. LNCS, vol. 13792, pp. 99–129. Springer, Cham (2022). https://doi.org/10.1007/978-3-031-22966-4_4

[CP93] Chaum, D., Pedersen, T.P.: Wallet databases with observers. In: Brickell, E.F. (ed.) CRYPTO'92. LNCS, vol. 740, pp. 89–105. Springer, Heidelberg (1993). https://doi.org/10.1007/3-540-48071-4_7

[CPSV16] Ciampi, M., Persiano, G., Siniscalchi, L., Visconti, I.: A transform for NIZK almost as efficient and general as the fiat-shamir transform without programmable random oracles. In: Kushilevitz, E., Malkin, T. (eds.) TCC 2016. LNCS, vol. 9563, pp. 83–111. Springer, Heidelberg (2016). https://doi.org/10.1007/978-3-662-49099-0_4

[CPV20] Ciampi, M., Parisella, R., Venturi, D.: On adaptive security of delayed-input sigma protocols and fiat-shamir NIZKs. In: Galdi, C., Kolesnikov, V. (eds.) SCN 2020. LNCS, vol. 12238, pp. 670–690. Springer, Cham (2020). https://doi.org/10.1007/978-3-030-57990-6_33

[CS04] Canny, J., Sorkin, S.: Practical large-scale distributed key generation. In: Cachin, C., Camenisch, J.L. (eds.) EUROCRYPT 2004. LNCS, vol. 3027, pp. 138–152. Springer, Heidelberg (2004). https://doi.org/10.1007/978-3-540-24676-3_9

[CSW22] Canetti, R., Sarkar, P., Wang, X.: Triply adaptive UC NIZK. In: Agrawal, S., Lin, D. (eds.) ASIACRYPT 2022. LNCS, vol. 13792, pp. 466–495. Springer, Cham (2022). https://doi.org/10.1007/978-3-031-22966-4_16

[Dam91] Damgård, I.: Towards practical public key systems secure against chosen ciphertext attacks. In: Feigenbaum, J. (ed.) CRYPTO 1991. LNCS, vol. 576, pp. 445–456. Springer, Heidelberg (1992). https://doi.org/10.1007/3-540-46766-1_36

[DDN91] Dolev, D., Dwork, C., Naor, M.: Non-malleable cryptography (extended abstract). In: 23rd ACM STOC, pp. 542–552. ACM Press (1991)

[DDO+01] De Santis, A., Di Crescenzo, G., Ostrovsky, R., Persiano, G., Sahai, A.: Robust non-interactive zero knowledge. In: Kilian, J. (ed.) CRYPTO 2001. LNCS, vol. 2139, pp. 566–598. Springer, Heidelberg (2001). https://doi.org/10.1007/3-540-44647-8_33

[DG03] Damgård, I., Groth, J.: Non-interactive and reusable non-malleable commitment schemes. In: 35th ACM STOC, pp. 426–437. ACM Press (2003)

[DSW08] Dodis, Y., Shoup, V., Walfish, S.: Efficient constructions of composable commitments and zero-knowledge proofs. In: Wagner, D. (ed.) CRYPTO 2008. LNCS, vol. 5157, pp. 515–535. Springer, Heidelberg (2008). https://doi.org/10.1007/978-3-540-85174-5_29

[FHJ20] Fischlin, M., Harasser, P., Janson, C.: Signatures from sequential-OR proofs. In: Canteaut, A., Ishai, Y. (eds.) EUROCRYPT 2020. LNCS, vol. 12107, pp. 212–244. Springer, Cham (2020). https://doi.org/10.1007/978-3-030-45727-3_8

[Fis05] Fischlin, M.: Communication-efficient non-interactive proofs of knowledge with online extractors. In: Shoup, V. (ed.) CRYPTO 2005. LNCS, vol. 3621, pp. 152–168. Springer, Heidelberg (2005). https://doi.org/10.1007/11535218_10

[FKL18] Fuchsbauer, G., Kiltz, E., Loss, J.: The algebraic group model and its applications. In: Shacham, H., Boldyreva, A. (eds.) CRYPTO 2018. LNCS, vol. 10992, pp. 33–62. Springer, Cham (2018). https://doi.org/10.1007/978-3-319-96881-0_2

[FKMV12] Faust, S., Kohlweiss, M., Marson, G.A., Venturi, D.: On the non-malleability of the fiat-shamir transform. In: Galbraith, S., Nandi, M. (eds.) INDOCRYPT 2012. LNCS, vol. 7668, pp. 60–79. Springer, Heidelberg (2012). https://doi.org/10.1007/978-3-642-34931-7_5

[FLS99] Feige, U., Lapidot, D., Shamir, A.: Multiple noninteractive zero knowledge proofs under general assumptions. SIAM J. Comput. **29**(1), 1–28 (1999)

[FS87]   Fiat, A., Shamir, A.: How to prove yourself: practical solutions to identi-
           fication and signature problems. In: Odlyzko, A.M. (ed.) CRYPTO 1986.
           LNCS, vol. 263, pp. 186–194. Springer, Heidelberg (1987). https://doi.
           org/10.1007/3-540-47721-7_12

[GJKR99]   Gennaro, R., Jarecki, S., Krawczyk, H., Rabin, T.: Secure distributed
           key generation for discrete-log based cryptosystems. In: Stern, J. (ed.)
           EUROCRYPT'99. LNCS, vol. 1592, pp. 295–310. Springer, Heidelberg
           (1999). https://doi.org/10.1007/3-540-48910-x_21

[GKO+23]   Ganesh, C., Kondi, Y., Orlandi, C., Pancholi, M., Takahashi, A., Tschudi,
           D.: Witness-succinct universally-composable SNARKs. In: Hazay, C.,
           Stam, M. (eds.) EUROCRYPT 2023. LNCS, vol. 14005, pp. 315–346.
           Springer, Cham (2023). https://doi.org/10.1007/978-3-031-30617-4_11

[GLOW21]   Galindo, D., Liu, J., Ordean, M., Wong, J.M.: Fully distributed verifiable
           random functions and their application to decentralised random beacons.
           In: IEEE European Symposium on Security and Privacy, EuroS&P 2021,
           Vienna, Austria, 6–10 September 2021, pp. 88–102. IEEE (2021)

[GMY03]   Garay, J.A., MacKenzie, P., Yang, K.: Strengthening zero-knowledge pro-
           tocols using signatures. In: Biham, E. (ed.) EUROCRYPT 2003. LNCS,
           vol. 2656, pp. 177–194. Springer, Heidelberg (2003). https://doi.org/10.
           1007/3-540-39200-9_11

[GMY06]   Garay, J.A., MacKenzie, P.D., Yang, K.: Strengthening zero-knowledge
           protocols using signatures. J. Cryptol. 19(2), 169–209 (2006)

[GOP+22]   Ganesh, C., Orlandi, C., Pancholi, M., Takahashi, A., Tschudi. D.: Fiat-
           shamir bulletproofs are non-malleable (in the algebraic group model).
           In: Dunkelman, O., Dziembowski, S. (eds.) EUROCRYPT 2022, Part II.
           LNCS, vol. 13276, pp. 397–426. Springer, Heidelberg (2022). https://doi.
           org/10.1007/978-3-031-07085-3_14

[GOP+23]   Ganesh, C., Orlandi, C., Pancholi, M., Takahashi, A., Tschudi, D.: Fiat-
           shamir bulletproofs are non-malleable (in the random oracle model). Cryp-
           tology ePrint Archive, Paper 2023/147 (2023). https://eprint.iacr.org/
           2023/147

[GOS06]   Groth, J., Ostrovsky, R., Sahai, A.: Perfect non-interactive zero knowl-
           edge for NP. In: Vaudenay, S. (ed.) EUROCRYPT 2006. LNCS, vol.
           4004, pp. 339–358. Springer, Heidelberg (2006). https://doi.org/10.1007/
           11761679_21

[GOS12]   Groth, J., Ostrovsky, R., Sahai, A.: New techniques for noninteractive
           zero-knowledge. J. ACM 59(3), 11:1–11:35 (2012)

[GPV08]   Gentry, C., Peikert, C., Vaikuntanathan, V.: Trapdoors for hard lattices
           and new cryptographic constructions. In: Proceedings of the Fortieth
           Annual ACM Symposium on Theory of Computing, STOC 2008, pp. 197–
           206. Association for Computing Machinery, New York (2008)

[Gro06]   Groth, J.: Simulation-sound NIZK proofs for a practical language and
           constant size group signatures. In: Lai, X., Chen, K. (eds.) ASIACRYPT
           2006. LNCS, vol. 4284, pp. 444–459. Springer, Heidelberg (2006). https://
           doi.org/10.1007/11935230_29

[Gro16]   Groth, J.: On the size of pairing-based non-interactive arguments. In:
           Fischlin, M., Coron, J.-S. (eds.) EUROCRYPT 2016. LNCS, vol. 9666,
           pp. 305–326. Springer, Heidelberg (2016). https://doi.org/10.1007/978-3-
           662-49896-5_11

[JJ21]   Jain, A., Jin, Z.: Non-interactive zero knowledge from sub-exponential DDH. In: Canteaut, A., Standaert, F.-X. (eds.) EUROCRYPT 2021. LNCS, vol. 12696, pp. 3–32. Springer, Cham (2021). https://doi.org/10.1007/978-3-030-77870-5_1

[JP14]   Jain, A., Pandey, O.: Non-malleable zero knowledge: black-box constructions and definitional relationships. In: Abdalla, M., De Prisco, R. (eds.) SCN 14. LNCS, vol. 8642, pp. 435–454. Springer, Cham (2014). https://doi.org/10.1007/978-3-319-10879-7_25

[JT20]   Jaeger, J., Tessaro, S.: Expected-time cryptography: generic techniques and applications to concrete soundness. In: Pass, R., Pietrzak, K. (eds.) TCC 2020. LNCS, vol. 12552, pp. 414–443. Springer, Cham (2020). https://doi.org/10.1007/978-3-030-64381-2_15

[Kat21]   Katsumata, S.: A new simple technique to bootstrap various lattice zero-knowledge proofs to QROM secure NIZKs. In: Malkin, T., Peikert, C. (eds.) CRYPTO 2021. LNCS, vol. 12826, pp. 580–610. Springer, Cham (2021). https://doi.org/10.1007/978-3-030-84245-1_20

[KG20]   Komlo, C., Goldberg, I.: FROST: flexible round-optimized schnorr threshold signatures. In: Dunkelman, O., Jacobson, Jr., M.J., O'Flynn, C. (eds.) SAC 2020. LNCS, vol. 12804, pp. 34–65. Springer, Cham (2021). https://doi.org/10.1007/978-3-030-81652-0_2

[Kil92]   Kilian, J.: A note on efficient zero-knowledge proofs and arguments (extended abstract). In: 24th ACM STOC, pp. 723–732. ACM Press (1992)

[KKK21]   Kerber, T., Kiayias, A., Kohlweiss, M.: Composition with knowledge assumptions. In: Malkin, T., Peikert, C. (eds.) CRYPTO 2021. LNCS, vol. 12828, pp. 364–393. Springer, Cham (2021). https://doi.org/10.1007/978-3-030-84259-8_13

[KMM+23] Kate, A., Mangipudi, E.V., Mukherjee, P., Saleem, H., Thyagarajan, S.A.K.: Non-interactive VSS using class groups and application to DKG. Cryptology ePrint Archive, Report 2023/451 (2023)

[KMMM23] Kate, A., Mangipudi, E.V., Maradana, S., Mukherjee, P.: FlexiRand: output private (distributed) VRFs and application to blockchains. In: Meng, W., Jensen, C.D., Cremers, C., Kirda, E. (eds.) ACM CCS 2023, pp. 1776–1790. ACM Press (2023)

[KNYY19] Katsumata, S., Nishimaki, R., Yamada, S., Yamakawa, T.: Exploring constructions of compact NIZKs from various assumptions. In: Boldyreva, A., Micciancio, D. (eds.) CRYPTO 2019. LNCS, vol. 11694, pp. 639–669. Springer, Cham (2019). https://doi.org/10.1007/978-3-030-26954-8_21

[KNYY20] Katsumata, S., Nishimaki, R., Yamada, S., Yamakawa, T.: Compact NIZKs from standard assumptions on bilinear maps. In: Canteaut, A., Ishai, Y. (eds.) EUROCRYPT 2020. LNCS, vol. 12107, pp. 379–409. Springer, Cham (2020). https://doi.org/10.1007/978-3-030-45727-3_13

[KS22]   Kondi, Y., Shelat, A.: Improved straight-line extraction in the random oracle model with applications to signature aggregation. In: Agrawal, S., Lin, D. (eds.) ASIACRYPT 2022, vol. 13792, pp. 279–309. Springer, Heidelberg (2022). https://doi.org/10.1007/978-3-031-22966-4_10

[KZM+15] Kosba, A.E., et al.: How to use snarks in universally composable protocols. IACR Cryptol. ePrint Arch., 1093 (2015)

[Lin15] Lindell, Y.: An efficient transform from sigma protocols to NIZK with a CRS and non-programmable random oracle. In: Dodis, Y., Nielsen, J.B. (eds.) TCC 2015. LNCS, vol. 9014, pp. 93–109. Springer, Heidelberg (2015). https://doi.org/10.1007/978-3-662-46494-6_5

[Lin22] Lindell, Y.: Simple three-round multiparty schnorr signing with full simulatability. Cryptology ePrint Archive, Report 2022/374 (2022)

[LR22a] Lysyanskaya, A., Rosenbloom, L.N.: Efficient and universally composable non-interactive zero-knowledge proofs of knowledge with security against adaptive corruptions. IACR Cryptol. ePrint Arch., 1484 (2022)

[LR22b] Lysyanskaya, A., Rosenbloom, L.N.: Universally composable Σ-protocols in the global random-oracle model. In: Kiltz, E., Vaikuntanathan, V. (eds.) TCC 2022. LNCS, vol. 13747, pp. 203–233. Springer, Cham (2022). https://doi.org/10.1007/978-3-031-22318-1_8

[Lyu12] Lyubashevsky, V.: Lattice signatures without trapdoors. In: Pointcheval, D., Johansson, T. (eds.) EUROCRYPT 2012. LNCS, vol. 7237, pp. 738–755. Springer, Heidelberg (2012). https://doi.org/10.1007/978-3-642-29011-4_43

[Mau09] Maurer, U.: Unifying zero-knowledge proofs of knowledge. In: Preneel, B. (ed.) AFRICACRYPT 2009. LNCS, vol. 5580, pp. 272–286. Springer, Heidelberg (2009). https://doi.org/10.1007/978-3-642-02384-2_17

[Mau11] Maurer, U.: Constructive cryptography – a new paradigm for security definitions and proofs. In: Mödersheim, S., Palamidessi, C. (eds.) TOSCA 2011. LNCS, vol. 6993, pp. 33–56. Springer, Heidelberg (2012). https://doi.org/10.1007/978-3-642-27375-9_3

[Mic00] Micali, S.: Computationally sound proofs. SIAM J. Comput. **30**(4), 1253–1298 (2000)

[Oka93] Okamoto, T.: Provably secure and practical identification schemes and corresponding signature schemes. In: Brickell, E.F. (ed.) CRYPTO'92. LNCS, vol. 740, pp. 31–53. Springer, Berlin, Heidelberg (1993). https://doi.org/10.1007/3-540-48071-4_3

[ORV14] Ostrovsky, R., Rao, V., Visconti, I.: On selective-opening attacks against encryption schemes. In: Abdalla, M., De Prisco, R. (eds.) SCN 14. LNCS, vol. 8642, pp. 578–597. Springer, Cham (2014). https://doi.org/10.1007/978-3-319-10879-7_33

[Pas03] Pass, R.: On deniability in the common reference string and random oracle model. In: Boneh, D. (ed.) CRYPTO 2003. LNCS, vol. 2729, pp. 316–337. Springer, Heidelberg (2003). https://doi.org/10.1007/978-3-540-45146-4_19

[PR05] Pass, R., Rosen, A.: New and improved constructions of non-malleable cryptographic protocols. In: Gabow, H.N., Fagin, R. (eds.) 37th ACM STOC, pp. 533–542. ACM Press (2005)

[PS96] Pointcheval, D., Stern, J.: Security proofs for signature schemes. In: Maurer, U. (ed.) EUROCRYPT 1996. LNCS, vol. 1070, pp. 387–398. Springer, Heidelberg (1996). https://doi.org/10.1007/3-540-68339-9_33

[PS19] Peikert, C., Shiehian, S.: Noninteractive zero knowledge for np from (plain) learning with errors. In: Boldyreva, A., Micciancio, D. (eds.) CRYPTO 2019. LNCS, vol. 11692, pp. 89–114. Springer, Cham (2019). https://doi.org/10.1007/978-3-030-26948-7_4

[Reg04] Regev, O.: A subexponential time algorithm for the dihedral hidden subgroup problem with polynomial space. arXiv:quant-ph/0406151 (2004)

[RWGM23] Rosenberg, M., White, J.D., Garman, C., Miers, I.: zk-creds: flexible anonymous credentials from zkSNARKs and existing identity infrastructure. In: 2023 IEEE Symposium on Security and Privacy, pp. 790–808. IEEE Computer Society Press (2023)

[Sah99] Sahai, A.: Non-malleable non-interactive zero knowledge and adaptive chosen-ciphertext security. In: 40th FOCS, pp. 543–553. IEEE Computer Society Press (1999)

[SBK24] Seres, I.A., Burcsi, P., Kutas, P.: How (not) to hash into class groups of imaginary quadratic fields? Cryptology ePrint Archive, Paper 2024/034 (2024). https://eprint.iacr.org/2024/034

[Sch91] Schnorr, C.-P.: Efficient signature generation by smart cards. J. Cryptol. 4(3), 161–174 (1991)

[Sho97] Shoup, V.: Lower bounds for discrete logarithms and related problems. In: Fumy, W. (ed.) EUROCRYPT 1997. LNCS, vol. 1233, pp. 256–266. Springer, Heidelberg (1997). https://doi.org/10.1007/3-540-69053-0_18

[SV12] Scafuro, A., Visconti, I.: On round-optimal zero knowledge in the bare public-key model. In: Pointcheval, D., Johansson, T. (eds.) EUROCRYPT 2012. LNCS, vol. 7237, pp. 153–171. Springer, Heidelberg (2012). https://doi.org/10.1007/978-3-642-29011-4_11

[TGL+19] Tyagi, N., Grubbs, P., Len, J., Miers, I., Ristenpart, T.: Asymmetric message franking: content moderation for metadata-private end-to-end encryption. In: Boldyreva, A., Micciancio, D. (eds.) CRYPTO 2019. LNCS, vol. 11694, pp. 222–250. Springer, Cham (2019). https://doi.org/10.1007/978-3-030-26954-8_8

[Tuc20] Tucker, I.: Functional encryption and distributed signatures based on projective hash functions, the benefit of class groups. PhD thesis, ENS DE LYON (2020)

Transparent SNARKs over Galois Rings

Yuanju Wei[1,2] (iD), Xinxuan Zhang[1,2(✉)] (iD), and Yi Deng[1,2(✉)] (iD)

[1] State Key Laboratory of Information Security, Institute of Information
Engineering, Chinese Academy of Sciences, Beijing, China
{weiyuanju,zhangxinxuan,deng}@iie.ac.cn
[2] School of Cyber Security, University of Chinese Academy of Sciences, Beijing,
China

Abstract. Recently, there is a growing need for SNARKs to operate
over a broader range of algebraic structures, and one important structure
is Galois ring. We present transparent SNARK schemes over arbitrary
Galois rings. Compared with Rinocchio scheme in Ganesh et al. (J Cryptol 2023), our SNARK schemes do not require a trusted third party to
establish a structured reference string (SRS).

In this paper, we present the expander code over arbitrary Galois
rings, which can be encoded in $O(n)$ time. Using this expander code,
we then extend the Brakedown commitment scheme in Golovnev et al.
(CRYPTO 2023) to Galois rings. By combining the Libra framework in
Xie et al. (CRYPTO 2019), we present a transparent SNARK for logspace uniform circuits over Galois rings, achieving $O(n)$ prover time,
$O(\sqrt{n})$ proof size, and $O(\sqrt{n})$ verifier time. And by combining HyperPlonk in Chen et al. (EUROCRYPT 2023), we present a transparent
SNARK for NP circuits over Galois rings, with $O(n \log^2 n)$ prover time,
$O(\sqrt{n})$ proof size, and $O(\sqrt{n})$ verifier time.

Keywords: SNARKs · Galois rings · Polynomial commitment

1 Introduction

Succinct Non-interactive Arguments of Knowledge (SNARK) are cryptographic
protocols that allow a verifier to efficiently check the validity of any NP statement without interacting with the prover [7,19,23,25]. One of the most important security properties of SNARKs is soundness. Soundness demands that for
any incorrect NP statement, it is infeasible for any prover to generate a proof
that will pass verification. To ensure the soundness property, SNARK protocols are typically designed for arithmetic circuits over a large prime field $\mathbb{F}_p$.
Recently, there is a growing demand to deploy them over more general algebraic
structures. While arithmetic circuits over large prime fields $\mathbb{F}_p$ can simulate various algebraic structures, such simulation often comes at an expensive efficiency
cost. It is more practical to design SNARKs directly for arithmetic circuits tailored to specific algebraic structures. Arithmetic circuits over rings are both a
natural extension of field-based arithmetic circuits and hold significant value in

© International Association for Cryptologic Research 2025
T. Jager and J. Pan (Eds.): PKC 2025, LNCS 15674, pp. 418–451, 2025.
https://doi.org/10.1007/978-3-031-91820-9_14

various applications. One important use case is in Fully Homomorphic Encryption (FHE), where computations are performed over rings, and the need for SNARKs to prove correctness in these settings has gained attention. In particular, second-generation FHE schemes like BGV and (B)FV [10,11] are defined over large integer rings. In this paper, we focus on Galois rings. Galois rings are a type of finite commutative rings which generalize both the finite fields and the rings of integers modulo a prime power. According to the Chinese Remainder Theorem, any integer ring (extension) can be mapped one-to-one to several Galois rings.

SNARKs for arithmetic circuits over rings have garnered significant attention, but there are relatively few solutions specifically tailored for such settings. The Rinocchio protocol, proposed by Ganesh et al. [18], is the first complete SNARK designed for ring-based arithmetic circuits. Rinocchio is a ring version of the Pinocchio protocol [26] and the Groth16 protocol [21]. These SNARKs are based on Linear PCP constructions, and they require a trusted setup to generate a structured reference string (SRS). In recent years, newer SNARK schemes have moved away from Linear PCP-based constructions, instead adopting a combination of PIOP and polynomial commitment schemes. Examples include Libra [32], Plonk [17], Spartan [27], Marlin [15], STARK [2–4], Brakedown [20], and Orion [33]. Many of these schemes do not require a trusted third party to set up an SRS. However, none of these SNARK schemes can be directly applied to arithmetic circuits over rings because, to date, there are no known polynomial commitment schemes for ring arithmetic.

Current polynomial commitment schemes over finite fields can generally be classified into three categories. The first category is the KZG commitment scheme based on pairing structures, proposed by Kate et al. [22]. And it also relies on an SRS. The second category is based on the hardness of the discrete logarithm problem, such as Bulletproofs proposed by Bünz et al. [12] and Dory proposed by Lee [24]. The third category is based on encoding techniques, such as FRI (Fast Reed-Solomon Interactive Oracle Proof of Proximity) proposed by Ben-Sasson et al. [2,4], Brakedown proposed by Golovnev et al. [20], and Basefold proposed by Zeilberger et al. [34]. These polynomial commitment schemes rely on algebraic structures applicable to finite fields, such as pairing structures, which are difficult to satisfy over Galois rings. Thus, this naturally leads to the following question:

Is it possible to construct polynomial commitments over Galois rings, and furthermore, is there a transparent SNARK scheme over Galois rings?

We found that the Brakedown scheme only relies on linear codes with fixed relative distance. Since linear codes are typically designed for finite fields, and given the "similarity" between Galois rings and finite fields, the Brakedown scheme appears to be the most feasible scheme to implement over Galois rings, and it does not require a trusted setup for generating an SRS. Therefore, we present the Brakedown commitment scheme over Galois rings and proposes a SNARK scheme over arbitrary Galois rings without the need for an SRS.

1.1   Our Contribution

We present a polynomial commitment and transparent SNARK schemes over arbitrary Galois rings in this paper.

We extend expander codes to arbitrary Galois rings, enabling linear-time encoding with a fixed relative distance that is a constant depending on the Galois ring. Then, using this encoding, we present the Brakedown polynomial commitment scheme over Galois rings. Combining this construction with Libra, we present a transparent SNARK for log-space uniform circuits over Galois rings, achieving $O(n)$ prover time, $O(\sqrt{n})$ proof size, and $O(\sqrt{n})$ verifier time. And by combining HyperPlonk, we present a transparent SNARK for NP circuits over Galois rings with $O(n \log^2 n)$ prover time, $O(\sqrt{n})$ proof size, and $O(\sqrt{n})$ verifier time.

1.2   Technique Overview

We revisit the Brakedown polynomial commitment. A multilinear polynomial f with l variables can be written as

$$f(x_1, \cdots, x_l) = \sum_{\mathbf{b} \in \{0,1\}^l} \prod_{i \in [1,l]} ((1 - x_i)(1 - b_i) + x_i b_i) \, f(\mathbf{b})$$

The values of f over the hypercube can be viewed as the basis of the polynomial, resulting in 2^l basis elements. These 2^l elements can be arranged into a $2^{l/2} \times 2^{l/2}$ matrix S:

$$\begin{bmatrix} f(0, \cdots, 0, 0, \cdots, 0) \, f(0, \cdots, 0, 0, \cdots, 1) \, \cdots \, f(0, \cdots, 0, 1, \cdots, 1) \\ f(0, \cdots, 1, 0, \cdots, 0) \, f(0, \cdots, 1, 0, \cdots, 1) \, \cdots \, f(0, \cdots, 1, 1, \cdots, 1) \\ \vdots \qquad\qquad \vdots \qquad\qquad \vdots \qquad\qquad \vdots \\ f(1, \cdots, 1, 0, \cdots, 0) \, f(1, \cdots, 1, 0, \cdots, 1) \, \cdots \, f(1, \cdots, 1, 1, \cdots, 1) \end{bmatrix}$$

To evaluate f at a point $\mathbf{r}$, one computes

$$f(r_1, \cdots, r_l) = \sum_{\mathbf{b} \in \{0,1\}^l} \prod_{i \in [1,l]} ((1 - r_i)(1 - b_i) + r_i b_i) \, f(\mathbf{b})$$

Using matrix S, this calculation involves two vectors, $\mathbf{s}_1$ and $\mathbf{s}_2$, each of length $2^{l/2}$. Specifically,

$$\mathbf{s}_1 = ((1 - r_1, r_1) \otimes \cdots \otimes (1 - r_{l/2}, r_{l/2}))$$

and

$$\mathbf{s}_2 = ((1 - r_{l/2+1}, r_{l/2+1}) \otimes \cdots \otimes (1 - r_l, r_l))$$

Therefore, $f(\mathbf{r}) = \mathbf{s}_1^\top S \mathbf{s}_2$.

The core of the Brakedown commitment is to ensure that the prover can correctly compute $s_1^\top S$ using encoding techniques and then send the result to the verifier, who completes the remaining computation. By employing encoding methods as described in Ligero (AHIV17) [1], proposed by Ames et al., the verifier can ensure that the prover correctly forms the linear combination of the encoded vectors.

Linear Codes over Galois Rings. During the encoding process of expander codes over large prime fields $\mathbb{F}_q$, a crucial step is performing linear combinations on k non-zero elements. The linear combinations are performed $b(k)$ times, where $b(k)$ is a function of k and $b(k) = \max(k+4, 1.28k)$. Let z is the probability that a single linear combination is zero. According to the union bound, the probability that all $b(k)$ linear combinations of any k non-zero elements are zero is bounded by:

$$\Pr[b(k) \text{ all zeros}] \le q^k z^{b(k)}$$

To ensure codeword distance, this probability must be negligible. While this is easily achievable in large prime fields, however, in Galois rings $\mathrm{GR}(p^s, r)$, zero divisors significantly increases this probability, braking the code distance.

A key observation to solve this problem is that in a Galois ring $\mathrm{GR}(p^s, r)$ all zero divisors reside in the ideal (p), meaning the proportion of zero divisors is $\frac{1}{p^r}$. If p^r is exponentially large relative to the security parameter λ, then the proportion of zero divisors becomes negligible. However, the total number of elements in the Galois ring is p^{sr}, and as p^r increases, the total number of elements in the Galois ring grows accordingly. We need that any k non-zero elements satisfy the distance condition. At this time, $z = \frac{1}{p^r}$, so we have

$$\Pr[b(k) \text{ all zeros}] \le p^{ksr} \left(\frac{1}{p^r}\right)^{b(k)} = \frac{p^{ksr}}{p^{b(k)r}}$$

In this case, as long as $s \ge 2$, the probability will not be negligible.

We solve this problem by performing a more refined parameter analysis. By analyzing the distribution of zero divisors in the Galois ring, we categorize the zero divisors into s classes based on their membership in the ideals $(p^{s-1}), \ldots, (p^2), (p)$. Each element is classified according to the smallest ideal it belongs to. For instance, if an element is in the ideal (p^i), it is also contained in (p^{i-1}), but it is classified as being in the i-th class rather than the $(i-1)$-th class. We then analyze the impact of the zero divisors from each of these s classes on the code distance. As i increases, the probability that a random linear combination of elements from the ideal (p^i) results in zero increases, thus having a greater impact on the code's distance. However, the proportion of such zero divisors in the entire Galois ring decreases. Through this more detailed parameter analysis, we prove that expander codes can maintain a constant relative code distance with $1 -$ negligible probability in Galois rings $\mathrm{GR}(p^s, r)$, provided that p^r is sufficiently large (exponential scale relative to the security parameter λ).

If the Galois ring $\mathrm{GR}(p^s, r)$ does not satisfy the large condition, we draw inspiration from the block-level encoding approach introduced in [16] and adapt it from binary fields to arbitrary Galois rings. Specifically, if a Galois ring $GR(p^s, r)$ requires an expansion by a factor of k to meet the necessary conditions, we treat k elements from $GR(p^s, r)$ as a single element in $GR(p^s, kr)$ during the encoding process. We further demonstrate that this encoding method maintains linearity over $GR(p^s, r)$. This construction thus results in a linear code defined over any Galois ring $GR(p^s, r)$.

Polynomial Commitments over Galois Rings. Using the linear codes defined over Galois rings, we apply the Brakedown construction framework to present a polynomial commitment scheme over Galois rings. Since Brakedown commitments rely on the linear code detection lemma from AHIV17 [1], we must first discuss this lemma for arbitrary Galois rings. If a Galois ring $GR(p^s, r)$ does not satisfy the condition that p^r is sufficiently large, we can say this ring is a "small ring". We need to account for cases where the polynomial to be committed is defined over a small ring.

Reviewing the construction of the Brakedown polynomial commitment, the verifier must ensure that the prover correctly performs a linear combination on each row of the coefficient matrix. In the encoding step, we mentioned that adjacent k elements in the small ring are treated as a single element in the extension ring for encoding. If the verifier directly selects a challenge e from the extension ring, then e will multiply with the larger element formed by the k elements from the small ring. This results in the "mixing" of the original k coefficients of the polynomial, meaning the operation is no longer within the small ring. In such scenarios, it is preferable for the verifier's challenge to be selected from $GR(p^s, r)$ to ensure that the coefficients used in the linear combination of the codewords are drawn from $GR(p^s, r)$. However, if the verifier selects challenges only from the small ring, it cannot guarantee the soundness of the polynomial commitment.

We employed Interleaved codes and Block-wise relative distance [8] to discuss the "repetition" version of the lemma over Galois rings to solve this problem: the verifier can ensure soundness by repeatedly selecting challenges multiple times. This approach, to some extent, avoids the need for field expansion operations, leading to an improvement in computational efficiency.

In practical applications of polynomial commitment, it is often encountered that polynomial coefficients come from a smaller ring $GR(p^s, r)$, but for security reasons, the challenges are drawn from $GR(p^s, kr)$, such as sumcheck. In [16], this issue is solved by using a two-dimensional extension. In this work, we explain the problem from the perspective of "repetition", using a more intuitive expression. When the prover computes $s_1^\top S$, only s_1 comes from $GR(p^s, kr)$. Therefore, each element of s_1 can be broken down into k-dimensional vectors, with each dimension being computed separately. This allows for a more efficient polynomial commitment process by avoiding the need to pad each element in $GR(p^s, r)$ to the larger ring $GR(p^s, kr)$ during the commitment phase.

SNARKs over Galois Rings. We combine polynomial commitments over Galois rings with PIOP (Polynomial Interactive Oracle Proof) to obtain SNARKs schemes over Galois rings. While sumcheck protocols over rings have been widely discussed, such as the extension to infinite non-commutative rings in [28], some PIOP frameworks those involving set consistency checks, cannot be directly extended from fields to Galois rings. This issue arises from the presence of zero divisors in Galois rings, which complicates set consistency checks.

In a field, to determine whether two sets S_1 and S_2 are identical, we encode them as polynomials, $p_1(x) = \prod_{a \in S_1}(x - a)$ and $p_2(x) = \prod_{a \in S_2}(x - a)$, and compare the polynomials. However, in Galois rings, zero divisors can result in different sets being encoded as identical polynomials. For example, under modulo 8, we have $(x - 1)(x - 7) = (x - 5)(x - 3) \pmod 8$.

So we selected an IOP framework that avoids set consistency checks: Libra and HyperPlonk. Using Libra, we constructed a transparent SNARK scheme for log-space uniform circuits over Galois rings, with $O(n)$ prover time, $O(\sqrt{n})$ proof size, and $O(\sqrt{n})$ verifier time. Similarly, using HyperPlonk, we constructed a transparent SNARK for NP circuits over Galois rings, achieving $O(n \log^2 n)$ prover time, $O(\sqrt{n})$ proof size, and $O(\sqrt{n})$ verifier time.

1.3 Related Work

Proof Systems over Rings. Due to the widespread application of proof systems, some efforts have been made to extend these systems to broader algebraic structures. Several works aim to migrate proof systems to arithmetic circuits over rings. In [14], Chen et al. presented the sumcheck and GKR protocols to finite commutative rings, where the verifier's challenges are required to come from an exceptional set within the ring. In [9], Bootle et al. constructed a sumcheck protocol over rings and used it to solve the Rank-1 Constraint System (R1CS) problem over rings. Furthermore, Soria-Vazquez extended the sumcheck protocol to infinite non-commutative rings in [28]. These protocols are rooted in the information-theoretic framework. However, due to the absence of a polynomial commitment scheme, none of these protocols are complete SNARK schemes.

Ganesh et al. [18] proposed the Rinocchio protocol, the first SNARK scheme for arithmetic circuits over rings. This protocol is based on the Linear PCP framework and does not require a polynomial commitment, but it does rely on a trusted third party to generate a structured reference string (SRS), which can raise concerns in practical applications. In recent years, new SNARK schemes have been introduced that eliminate the need for an SRS but instead depend on polynomial commitments. However, there is no polynomial commitment schemes over rings. In this paper, we present the Brakedown polynomial commitment scheme over Galois rings and present a SNARK based on an PIOP + polynomial commitment framework, differing from Rinocchio. Unlike Rinocchio, the new SNARKs do not require an SRS.

Code Based Polynomial Commitment. Some of the latest polynomial commitment schemes are code-based. Compared to previous approaches, these commitment schemes only rely on collision-resistant hash functions cryptographic primitive, and they are transparent.

The first representative scheme in this category is the FRI (Fast Reed-Solomon Interactive Oracle Proof of Proximity) scheme, proposed by Ben-Sasson et al. [2,4]. FRI-based polynomial commitments exploit the efficient detection of Reed-Solomon codes to commit to polynomials. However, this scheme requires an "FFT-friendly" field and uses an iterative structure similar to FFT, resulting in a prover time complexity of $O(n \log n)$.

Another key scheme based on encoding is the Brakedown scheme, proposed by Golovnev et al. [20]. The construction of Brakedown is based on linear codes with fixed relative distances and the only cryptographic primitive used is a collision-resistant hash function. Brakedown provides linear-time prover efficiency but with larger proof sizes and slower verifier time.

Additionally, the recently proposed Basefold protocol by Zeilberger et al. [34] is also based on encoding techniques and serves as a trade-off between FRI and Brakedown. Although Basefold retains the same asymptotic complexity of $O(n \log n)$, it offers faster prover times compared to FRI and an improved verifier time of $O(\log n)$, whereas Brakedown has a verifier time of $O(\sqrt{n})$. The Basefold construction depends on foldable linear codes.

Given these comparisons, Brakedown has the minimum coding requirement and is the most "friendly" for Galois rings, which is why we choose the Brakedown framework.

2   Preliminaries

We denote a finite field by $\mathbb{F}$, a security parameter by λ, and a negligible function with respect to λ by $\mathrm{negl}(\lambda)$. We use PPT to denote probabilistic polynomial time. For any integer n, we define $\mathrm{Poly}(\mathbb{F}, n)$ as the set of polynomials with n variables and coefficients in the field $\mathbb{F}$.

2.1   Galois Rings

In this part, we will focus on discussing certain properties of Galois rings that will be used later. These properties are fundamental to establishing codes over Galois rings.

A Galois ring is constructed from the ring $\mathbb{Z}/p^s\mathbb{Z}$ similar to how a finite field $\mathbb{F}_{p^m}$ is constructed from $\mathbb{F}_p$ [30]. It is a Glaois extension of $\mathbb{Z}/p^s\mathbb{Z}$, when the concept of Galois extension is generalized beyond the context of fields.

Definition 1. *A Galois ring is a commutative ring of characteristic p^s which has p^{rs} elements, where p is a prime and s and r are positive integers. It is usually denoted $GR(p^s, r)$. It can be defined as a quotient ring*

$$GR(p^s, r) \cong \mathbb{Z}[x]/(p^s, f(x))$$

where $f(x) \in \mathbb{Z}[x]$ is monic polynomial of degree r which is irreducible modulo p. Up to isomorphism, the ring depends only on p, n, and r and not on the choice of f used in the construction.

Every Galois ring is a local ring. The unique maximal ideal is the principal ideal $(p) = pGR(p^s, r)$, consisting of all elements which are multiples of p. Furthermore, $(0), (p^{s-1}), \cdots, (p), (1)$ are all the ideals.

If a Galois ring $GR(p^s, r)$ does not satisfy the condition that p^r is exponential scale relative to the security parameter λ, we can say this ring is a "small ring".

Fact 1. *All zero divisors in the Galois ring $GR(p^s, r)$ are in the ideal (p).*

We define a ring homomorphism ϕ

$$
\begin{aligned}
\mathbb{Z}_{p^s} & \to \mathbb{F}_p \\
c_0 + c_1 p + \cdots + c_{p-1} p^{s-1} & \mapsto c_0
\end{aligned}
$$

where $0 \le c_i \le p - 1$ and its kernel is the ideal (p) of the ring $\mathbb{Z}_{p^s}$. And the ring homomorphism can be extended to ψ

$$
\begin{aligned}
\mathbb{Z}_{p^s}[x] & \to \mathbb{F}_p[x] \\
a_0 + a_1 x + \cdots + a_n x^n & \mapsto \bar{a}_0 + \bar{a}_1 x + \cdots + \bar{a}_n x^n
\end{aligned}
$$

where $\bar{a}_i = \phi(a_i)$ and the kernel of ψ is the ideal (p) of the ring $\mathbb{Z}_{p^s}[x]$. So the ideal $(h(x))$ is the ideal $(\bar{h}(x))$. So we induce a ring homomorphism Φ

$$
\begin{aligned}
\mathbb{Z}_{p^s}[x]/(h(x)) & \to \mathbb{F}_p[x]/(\bar{h}(x)) \\
a_0 + a_1 x + \cdots + a_{r-1} x^{r-1} + (h(x)) & \mapsto \bar{a}_0 + \bar{a}_1 x + \cdots + \bar{a}_{r-1} x^{r-1} + (\bar{h}(x))
\end{aligned}
$$

The kernel of the ring homomorphism Φ is the ideal $(p + (h(x)))$ generated by $p + (h(x))$ in $(\mathbb{Z}_{p^s}[x]/h(x))$. By the fundamental theorem of homomoprphisms of rings

$$
(\mathbb{Z}_{p^s}[x]/(h(x)))/(p + h(x)) \simeq \mathbb{F}_p/(\bar{h}(x))
$$

Definition 2. *a is an element of ring $GR(p^s, r)$ and n is an integer. We define $gcd(a, n)$ as $gcd(a_0, \cdots, a_{r-1}, n)$. Where a is represented by $a_0 + a_1 x + \cdots + a_{r-1} x^{r-1}$.*

Fact 2. *Consider elements a and b in the Galois ring $GR(p^s, r)$. Let $d = gcd(a, p^s)$. The linear equation $ax = b$ has at most d^r solutions within $GR(p^s, r)$.*

Proof. If $gcd(a, p^s) = 1$, then a is not in the ideal (p). According to the properties of the Galois ring, a is not a zero divisor in $GR(p^s, r)$, implying that a has an inverse. Therefore, $x = b \cdot a^{-1}$ has a unique solution.

If $gcd(a, p^s) = d$, then we have

$$
ax = b \pmod{(p^s, f)}
$$

The condition for this equation to have a solution is $d \mid b_i$ for all i, $0 \le i \le r - 1$, where b_i is the coefficient in b. Thus, we have

$$
\frac{a}{d} x = \frac{b}{d} \pmod{(p^s/d, f)}
$$

where $\frac{a}{d}$ and $\frac{b}{d}$ mean each coefficient in a and b is divided by d. Let $\frac{a}{d} = a'$ and $\frac{b}{d} = b'$. Then a' and b' are elements of the Galois ring $\mathrm{GR}(p^s/d, r)$. Since $\gcd(a', p^s/d) = 1$, a' is not a zero divisor in the ring $\mathrm{GR}(p^s/d, r)$, so a' has an inverse. Therefore, x has a unique solution in the ring $\mathrm{GR}(p^s/d, r)$. This solution is obtained by determining each coefficient of x.

$$x_0 \equiv c_0 \pmod{p^s/d}$$
$$x_1 \equiv c_1 \pmod{p^s/d}$$
$$\cdots$$
$$x_{r-1} \equiv c_{r-1} \pmod{p^s/d}$$

So

$$x_0 \equiv c_0 + r_0 \frac{p^s}{d} \pmod{p^s}, r_0 \in [0, d-1]$$
$$x_1 \equiv c_1 + r_1 \frac{p^s}{d} \pmod{p^s}, r_1 \in [0, d-1]$$
$$\cdots$$
$$x_{r-1} \equiv c_{r-1} + r_{r-1} \frac{p^s}{d} \pmod{p^s}, r_{d-1} \in [0, d-1]$$

Obviously $r_i, i \in [0, d-1]$ has d values, so each coefficient x_i of x has at most d values, and x has at most d^r values.   □

Fact 3. *In the Galois ring $\mathrm{GR}(p^s, r)$, the probability that a degree-d polynomial f evaluates to zero at a randomly chosen point is at most $\frac{d}{p^r}$.*

Fact 4. *If a monic polynomial f is irreducible in the field $\mathrm{GF}(p, r)$, then f is also irreducible in the Galois ring $\mathrm{GR}(p^s, r)$.*

In the full version of this paper [31], we provide detailed proofs for 3 and 4.

Definition 3 (Exceptional Set [18]). *Let $A = \{a_1, \cdots, a_n\} \subset R$. We say that A is an exceptional set if $\forall i \neq j$, $a_i - a_j \in R^*$, where R^* is the set of all invertible elements in the ring R.*

Lemma 1 (Genralized Schwartz-Zippel Lemma [6,18]). *Let $f : R^n \to R$ be an n-variate nonzero polynomial. Let $A \subseteq R$ be an finite exceptional set. Let $\deg(f)$ denote the total degree of f. Then:*

$$\Pr_{\mathbf{a} \leftarrow A^n}[f(\mathbf{a}) = 0] \leq \frac{\deg(f)}{|A|}$$

2.2 SNARKs

We adapt the definition from Rinocchio [18]. Let $\mathcal{R}$ be an efficiently computable binary relation which consists of pairs of the form (x, w) where x is a statement and w is a witness. Let $\mathbf{L}$ be the language associated with the relation $\mathcal{R}$, i.e. $\mathcal{L} = \{x | \exists w, \text{s.t.} \mathcal{R}(x, w) = 1\}$.

A proof or argument system for R consists in a triple of PPT algorithms $\Pi = (\mathbf{Setup}, \mathbf{Prove}, \mathbf{Verify})$ defined as follows:

– Setup$(1^\lambda) \rightarrow (\sigma, \text{vk})$: take a security parameter λ and outputs a common (structured) reference string σ together with private verification information vk.
– Prove$(\sigma, x, w) \rightarrow \pi$: on input σ, a statement x and witness w, outputs an argument π.
– Verify$(\sigma, \text{vk}, x, \pi) \rightarrow 1/0$: on input σ, the private verification key vk, a statement x and a proof π, it outputs either 1 indicating accepting the argument or 0 for rejecting it.

Definition 4 (SNARK). *A triple of polynomial time algorithms* (Setup, Prove, Verify) *is a SNARK for an NP relation $\mathcal{R}$, if the following properties are satisfied:*

- *Completeness. For all $(x, w) \in \mathcal{R}$, the following holds:*

$$Pr\left[\begin{array}{c} (\sigma, vk) \leftarrow \mathbf{Setup}(1^\lambda); \pi \leftarrow \mathbf{Prove}(\sigma, x, w) : \\ \mathbf{Verify}(\sigma, vk, x, \pi) = 1 \end{array}\right] = 1.$$

- *Knowledge Soundness. For any PPT adversary $\mathcal{A}$, there exists a PPT algorithm $\mathcal{E}_\mathcal{A}$ such that the following probability is negligible in λ:*

$$Pr\left[\begin{array}{c} (\sigma, vk) \leftarrow \mathbf{Setup}(1^\lambda); ((\tilde{x}, \tilde{\pi}); w') \leftarrow \mathcal{A} | \mathcal{E}_\mathcal{A}(\sigma) : \\ \mathbf{Verify}(\sigma, vk, \tilde{x}, \tilde{\pi}) = 1 \wedge \mathcal{R}(\tilde{x}, w') = 0 \end{array}\right]$$

- *A non-interactive argument of knowledge satisfies knowledge is succinct if the size of proof π and the time to* **Verify** *are sublinear in the size of the statement proven.*

If a SNARK does not require a private verification key vk, then the SNARK scheme is referred to as a public-key SNARK. If a SNARK does not require a CRS σ, then the SNARK scheme is referred to as transparent.

2.3 Polynomial Commitment Scheme

We adapt the definition from Brakedown [20].

Definition 5 (Polynomial Commitment Scheme). *A polynomial commitment scheme for multilinear polynomial over Galois Ring $GR(p^s, r)$ is a tuple of four protocols $PC = (Gen, Commit, Open, Eval)$:*

- $pp \leftarrow Gen(1^\lambda, \mu)$ *takes as input* μ *(the number of variables in a multilinear polynomial); produces public parameters pp.*
- $\mathcal{C} \leftarrow Commit(pp, \mathcal{G}, \gamma)$: *takes any input a* $\mu-variate$ *multilinear polynomial over a Galois Ring* $\mathcal{G} \in \text{Poly}(GR(p^s, r), \mu)$ *and a random string* γ *produces a commitment* $\mathcal{C}$.
- $b \leftarrow Open(pp, \mathcal{C}, \mathcal{G}, \gamma)$: *verifies the opening of commitment* $\mathcal{C}$ *to the* $\mu-variate$ *multilinear polynomial* $\mathcal{G} \in \text{Poly}(GR(p^s, r), \mu)$; *outputs* $b \in \{0, 1\}$.
- $b \leftarrow Eval(pp, \mathcal{C}, z, v, \mu, \mathcal{G})$ *is a protocol between a PPT prover* $\mathcal{P}$ *and verifier* $\mathcal{V}$. *Both* $\mathcal{V}$ *and* $\mathcal{P}$ *hold a commitment* $\mathcal{C}$, *the number of variables* μ, *a scalar* $v \in GR(p^s, r)$ *and* $z \in GR(p^s, r)^\mu$. $\mathcal{P}$ *additionally knows a* $\mu-variate$ *multilinear polynomial* $\mathcal{G} \in \text{Poly}(GR(p^s, r), \mu)$. $\mathcal{P}$ *attempts to convince* $\mathcal{V}$ *that* $\mathcal{G}(z) = v$. *At the end of the protocol,* $\mathcal{V}$ *outputs* $b \in \{0, 1\}$.

A tuple of four protocol (Gen, Commit, Open, Eval) is an extractable polynomial commitment scheme for multilinear polynomials over Galois Ring $GR(p^s, r)$ *if the following conditions hold.*

- **Completeness.** *For any multilinear polynomial* $\mathcal{G} \in \text{Poly}(GR(p^s, r), \mu)$,

$$\Pr \left[\begin{array}{c} pp \rightarrow Gen(1^\lambda, \mu); \mathcal{C} \leftarrow Commit(pp, \mathcal{G}, \gamma) : \\ Eval(pp, \mathcal{C}, r, v, \mu, \mathcal{G}) = 1 \wedge v = \mathcal{G}(r) \end{array} \right] \geq 1 - negl(\lambda)$$

- **Binding.** *For any PPT adversary* $\mathcal{A}$, *size parameter* $\mu \geq 1$,

$$\Pr \left[\begin{array}{c} pp \leftarrow Gen(1^\lambda, \mu); \mathcal{C}, \mathcal{G}_0, \mathcal{G}_1 \leftarrow \mathcal{A}(pp); \\ b_0 \leftarrow Open(pp, \mathcal{C}, \mathcal{G}_0, \gamma); b_1 \leftarrow Open(pp, \mathcal{C}, \mathcal{G}_1, \gamma); \\ b_0 = b_1 \neq 0 \wedge \mathcal{G}_0 \neq \mathcal{G}_1 \end{array} \right] \leq negl(\lambda)$$

- **Knowledge soundness.** *Eval is a succinct argument of knowledge for the following NP relation given* $pp \leftarrow Gen(1^\lambda, \mu)$.

$$\mathcal{R}_{Eval}(pp) = \{\langle (\mathcal{C}, z, v), (\mathcal{G}) \rangle : \mathcal{G} \in GR(p^s, r)[\mu] \wedge \mathcal{G}(z) = v \wedge Open(pp, \mathcal{C}, \mathcal{G}, \gamma) = 1\}$$

3   Linear Codes over Galois Rings

In SNARKs, the encoding is typically defined over a large prime field $\mathbb{F}_q$, as this ensures a large codeword distance and provides the verifier with a large challenge space. However, in the case of Galois rings, zero divisors can disrupt the code distance. In this section, we solve this problem and show expander codes over arbitrary Galois rings.

3.1   Linear Codes over Partial Galois Rings

We utilized the construction framework of expander codes from Brakedown [20] and use a similar approach when proving the code distance. When analyzing codeword distances, for lemmas (Lemma 2 and Lemma 3) that are applicable to large prime fields but not to Galois rings, we provide versions of these lemmas for Galois rings $\mathrm{GR}(p^s, r)$ and their proofs. We use the same encoding parameters as in Brakedown. While the failure probability in Brakedown does not exceed 2^{-100}, we proved that in Galois rings $\mathrm{GR}(p^s, r)$, the error probability does not exceed $s \cdot 2^{-100}$. In practical applications, s typically does not exceed 2^8, so our scheme remains secure.

Firstly, we need to define some parameters related to expander codes in Brakedown: $0 < \alpha < 1$, $0 < \beta < 1$, and $t > \frac{1+2\beta}{1-\alpha}$, with $c_n, d_n \geq 3$. Let $\mathcal{M}_{n,m,d} \subset \mathrm{GR}(p^s, r)^{n \times m}$ be a matrix distribution where each row has exactly d non-zero entries, with these d entries randomly selected from the non-zero elements of $\mathrm{GR}(p^s, r)$. For $x \in [0,1]$, $H(x) = -x\log_2(x) - (1-x)\log_2(1-x)$.

$$
c_n = \left\lceil \min\left(\max\left(1.28\beta n, \beta n + 4\right), \right.\right.
$$

$$
\left.\left. \frac{1}{\beta \log_2\left(\frac{\alpha}{1.28\beta}\right)} \left(\frac{100}{n} + H(\beta) + \alpha H\left(\frac{1.28\beta}{\alpha}\right) \right) \right) \right\rceil
$$

$$
d_n = \left\lceil \min\left(\left(2\beta + \frac{(t-1)+100/n}{\log_2(p^r)} \right) n, D \right) \right\rceil
$$

$$
D = \max \left(\frac{t\alpha H\left(\frac{\beta}{t}\right) + \mu H\left(\frac{\nu}{\mu}\right) + \frac{100}{n}}{\alpha\beta \log_2\left(\frac{\mu}{\nu}\right)}, \right.
$$

$$
\frac{t\alpha H\left(\frac{\beta}{t}\right) + \mu H\left(\frac{2\beta+0.03}{\mu}\right) + \frac{100}{n}}{\beta \log_2\left(\frac{\mu}{2\beta+0.03}\right)},
$$

$$
\left. (2\beta + 0.03)\left(\frac{1}{\alpha t - \beta} + \frac{1}{\alpha\beta} + \frac{1}{\mu - 2\beta - 0.03} \right) + 1 \right)
$$

where $\mu = t - 1 - t\alpha$, $\nu = \beta + \alpha\beta + 0.03$.

Algorithm 1: Enc Algorithm: $\mathrm{GR}(p^s, r)^n \rightarrow \mathrm{GR}(p^s, r)^{tn}$

Input: $\mathbf{x} \in \mathrm{GR}(p^s, r)^n$
parameter: $\alpha, \beta, t, c_n, d_n$
Output: $\mathbf{w} \in \mathrm{GR}(p^s, r)^{tn}$

1 **if** $n < n_0$ **then**
2 | $\mathbf{w} = M\mathbf{x}$ and return $\mathbf{w}$;
3 Matrices $A^{(n)} \leftarrow \mathcal{M}_{n, \alpha n, c_n}$ and $B^{(n)} \leftarrow \mathcal{M}_{\alpha tn, (t-1-t\alpha)n, d_n}$ for are choosen in pre-processing;
4 $\mathbf{y}^\top = \mathbf{x}^\top \cdot A^{(n)} \in \mathrm{GR}(p^s, r)^{\alpha n}$;
5 $\mathbf{z} = \mathrm{Enc}(\mathbf{y}) \in \mathrm{GR}(p^s, r)^{t\alpha n}$;
6 $\mathbf{v}^\top = \mathbf{z}^\top \cdot B^{(n)} \in R^{(t-1-t\alpha)n}$;

7 $\mathbf{w} = \begin{pmatrix} \mathbf{x} \\ \mathbf{z} \\ \mathbf{v} \end{pmatrix} \in \mathrm{GR}(p^s, r)^{tn}$;

8 return $\mathbf{w}$

Here, n_0 is a small constant and M can be any generator matrix that meets the code rate and distance parameters, such as selecting an Reed-Solomon code and using padding zeros to meet the requirements. The Algorithm 1 is the encoding algorithm over Galois rings. We prove that by choosing α, β, t, c_n, and d_n with the same parameters as in the Brakedown scheme, it can still ensure the relative code distance over Galois rings with a probability of $1 - \mathrm{negl}(\lambda)$.

Since the proof framework for the relative code distance of expander codes over Galois rings is similar to that in Brakedown [20], we only highlight the differences specific to Galois rings here. The complete proof is provided in the full version of this paper [31].

Define the four events $E_{n,k}^{(1)}$, $E_{n,k}^{(2)}$, $E_{n,k}^{(3)}$, and $E_{n,k}^{(4)}$.

As explained in Brakedown [20], as long as the probability of these four events occurring does not exceed $s \cdot 2^{-100}$, Then, the relative code distance holds with a probability of $1 - s \cdot 2^{-100}$.

- $E_{n,k}^{(1)}$: There exists a set of k coordinates of $\mathbf{x} \in \mathrm{GR}(p^s, r)^n$ that doesn't "expend" into $b(k) = max(k + 4, 1.28k)$ coordinates of $\mathbf{x}^\top \cdot A$.
- $E_{n,k}^{(2)}$: Given the event that, given that every set of size k expands into a set of size at least $b(k)$ (that is, conditioned on the complement of $E_{n,k}^{(1)}$), there exists an $\mathbf{x}$ of Hamming weight $\|\mathbf{x}\|_0 = h$ such that $\mathbf{y}^\top = \mathbf{x}^\top \cdot A = \mathbf{0}$.
- $E_{n,k}^{(3)}$: There exists a set of k coordinates of $\mathbf{z} \in \mathrm{GR}(p^s, r)^{\alpha rn}$ that doesn't expand into $b'(k) = \left(\beta + k/n + \frac{(r-1)+110/n}{\log_2 q} \right) n$ coordinates of $\mathbf{v}^\top = \mathbf{z}^\top \cdot B$.
- $E_{n,k}^{(4)}$: Given that all sets of size k expand into at least $b'(k)$ coordinates, there exists a $\mathbf{z} \in \mathrm{GR}(p^s, r)^{\alpha rn}$ of Hamming weight $\|\mathbf{z}\|_0 = k$ which is mapped to $\mathbf{v}^\top = \mathbf{z}^\top \cdot B$ of Hamming weight $\|\mathbf{v}\|_0 < \beta n$.

Next, we demonstrate that by selecting an appropriate parameter r, the probability of the event $E_{n,k}^{(2)}$ occurring remains below $s \cdot 2^{-100}$.

Lemma 2. *For every* $n \leq 2^{30}$ *and every Galois Ring* $GR(p^s, r)$ *satisfying* $p^r \geq 2^{127}$, *for every* n *and* $k \leq n$, $Pr[E_{n,k}^{(2)}] \leq s \cdot 2^{-100}$.

Proof. Let $\mathbf{x}$ be an element in $GR(p^s, r)^n$ with $\|\mathbf{x}\|_0 = k$, and let $K \subseteq [n]$ represent the indices of the nonzero elements in $\mathbf{x}$. Let T_K be a random variable denoting the number of columns of $A \leftarrow \mathcal{M}_{n, \alpha n, c_n}$ with at least one non-zero element in the rows with indices from K.

The occurrence of the event $E_{n,k}^{(2)}$ depends on the non-occurrence of the event $E_{n,k}^{(1)}$, we have that $T_k \geq b(k) = max(k + 4, 1.28k)$. We have at least T_k coordinates of $A\mathbf{x}$ are non-zero linear combinations of the non-zero coordinates of $\mathbf{x}$ with indices form $K_{\mathbf{x}}$.

Here, a more complicated analysis than that used in the Brakedown scheme is necessary. Drawing from the Fact 2, we know that for any two elements a and b in the Galois ring $GR(p^s, r)$, if $d = gcd(p^s, a)$, then the linear equation $ax = b$ has at most d^r solutions. If we treat the coefficients of the randomly selected linear combination as a variable x, and one of the k non-zero elements as a, then the condition that the random linear combination equals zero means that for some b, the equation $ax = b$ hold. According to Fact 2, the proportion of x values that satisfy this condition is $\frac{d^r}{p^{sr}}$, which implies that the probability of the random linear combination being zero does not exceed $\frac{d^r}{p^{sr}}$. It is noted that the likelihood of a random linear combination being zero is influenced by the element with the smallest greatest common divisor with p^s. Therefore, we can categorize and discuss based on the smallest greatest common divisor of k elements. Assuming that the k nonzero elements in $\mathbf{x}$ have the smallest greatest common divisor with p^s as d, the probability that a random linear combination is zero is $\frac{d^r}{p^{sr}}$. There are $b(k)$ positions in $\mathbf{x}^\top \cdot A$ that are nonzero elements for the linear combination, thus the probability that all are zero is $\left(\frac{d^r}{p^{sr}}\right)^{b(k)}$.
Given that $\mathbf{x}$ has k nonzero elements, and the greatest common divisor of these nonzero elements with p^s does not exceed d, the number of potential selections is $\binom{k}{n} \cdot \left(\left(\frac{p^s}{d}\right)^r\right)^k$. Consequently, when the k nonzero elements in x have the smallest common factor with p^s as d, the probability of event $E_{n,k}^{(2),d}$ occurring does not exceed:

$$\left(\frac{d^r}{p^{sr}}\right)^{b(k)} \cdot \left(\left(\frac{p^s}{d}\right)^r\right)^k \cdot \binom{k}{n} = \binom{k}{n} \left(\frac{d^{b(k)-k}}{p^{s(b(k)-k)}}\right)^r.$$

It is evident that the larger the value of d, the greater the probability of error. When d reaches its maximum at p^{s-1}, the error probability attains its highest value of:

$$\binom{k}{n} \left(\frac{1}{p^{b(k)-k}}\right)^r = \binom{k}{n} \left(\frac{1}{p^r}\right)^{b(k)-k}.$$

for $k \geq 15$, $n \leq 2^{30}$, and $p^r > 2^{127}$,

$$\Pr[E_{n,k}^{(2),d}] \leq \binom{k}{n}\left(\frac{1}{p^r}\right)^{b(k)-k} \leq \binom{k}{n}(p^r)^{-0.28k} \leq \left(\frac{en}{k}\right)^k \cdot (p^r)^{-0.28k}$$

$$= \left(\frac{en}{k(p^r)^{0.28}}\right)^k \leq 2^{-120}.$$

for $k \leq 14$, $n \leq 2^{30}$, and $p^r > 2^{127}$,

$$\Pr[E_{n,k}^{(2),d}] \leq \binom{k}{n}\left(\frac{1}{p^r}\right)^{b(k)-k} \leq \binom{k}{n}(p^r)^{-4} \leq \left(\frac{en}{k}\right)^k \cdot (p^r)^{-4}$$

$$= \left(\frac{en}{14}\right)^{14} \leq 2^{-120}.$$

Of course, this scenario pertains to when d attains its largest value. The maximum number of possible values for d is s, which includes $1, p, \cdots, p^{s-1}$. According to the union bound, the soundness error can increase by at most s times. In this case, the error probability remains below $\frac{s}{2^{100}}$, a value which is still negligible. □

Lemma 3. *For every n and $\alpha\beta n \leq k \leq \beta n$, if $2\beta + \frac{(t-1)+110/n}{\log_2(p^r)} \leq t - 1 - t\alpha$,* $\Pr[E_{n,k}^{(4)}] \leq s \cdot 2^{-100}$.

Proof. Assuming that every set of size k expands to at least

$$b'(k) = \left(\beta + \frac{k}{n} + \frac{(t-1) + \frac{110}{n}}{\log_2(p^r)}\right)n$$

we need to demonstrate that, with overwhelming probability, every element z in $GR(p^s, r)^{\alpha t n}$ with a Hamming weight of $\|z\|_0 = k$ can be mapped to a vector $\mathbf{v} = B \cdot \mathbf{z}$ in $GR(p^s, r)^{(t-1-t\alpha)n}$ with a Hamming weight $\|\mathbf{v}\|_0 \geq \beta n$.

Fix an element $\mathbf{z}$ in $GR(p^s, r)$ with a Hamming weight $\|\mathbf{z}\|_0 = k$. Given that the non-zero coordinates of $\mathbf{z}$ will expand to at least $b'(k)$ coordinates, there are at least $b'(k)$ positions in the vector v comprising random linear combinations of non-zero vectors. As in the previous proof, if the k non-zero elements in x have the smallest greatest common divisor with p^s as d, then the probability of a random linear combination resulting in zero is $\frac{d^r}{p^{sr}}$. Consequently, with $\mathbf{z}$ fixed, the probability that $\|\mathbf{v}\|_0 \leq \beta n$ is bounded by:

$$\binom{b'(k)}{\geq b'(k) - \beta n}\left(\frac{d^r}{p^{sr}}\right)^{b'(k)-\beta n} \leq \binom{(t-1-t\alpha)n}{\geq (t-1-t\alpha)n - \beta n}\left(\frac{d^r}{p^{sr}}\right)^{b'(k)-\beta n}$$

$$\leq 2^{(t-1-t\alpha)n}\left(\frac{d^r}{p^{sr}}\right)^{b'(k)-\beta n}.$$

assuming $b'(k) \leq \left(2\beta + \frac{(t-1)+\frac{110}{n}}{\log_2(p^r))}\right) n$. For all $\mathbf{z}$ in $GR(p^s, r)^{\alpha t n}$ that satisfy $\|\mathbf{z}\|_0 = k$ and whose greatest common divisor with p^s is d, the upper bound is given by:

$$Pr[E_{n,k}^{(4),d}] \leq \binom{t\alpha n}{k} \left(\left(\frac{p^s}{d}\right)^r\right)^k \cdot 2^{(t-1-t\alpha)n} \cdot \left(\frac{d^r}{p^{sr}}\right)^{b'(k)-\beta n}$$

$$= \binom{t\alpha n}{k} \cdot 2^{(t-1-t\alpha)n} \cdot \left(\frac{d^r}{p^{sr}}\right)^{b'(k)-\beta n-k}.$$

It is evident that the larger the value of d, the greater the probability of error. When d reaches its maximum at p^{s-1}, the error probability attains its highest value of:

$$\binom{t\alpha n}{k} \cdot 2^{(t-1-t\alpha)n} \cdot \left(\frac{1}{p^r}\right)^{b'(k)-\beta n-k}$$

$$Pr[E_{n,k}^{(4),d}] \leq \binom{t\alpha n}{k} \cdot 2^{(t-1-t\alpha)n} \cdot \left(\frac{1}{p^r}\right)^{b'(k)-\beta n-k} \leq \frac{2^{t\alpha n+(t-1-t\alpha)n}}{(p^r)^{b'(k)-\beta n-k}}$$

$$\leq \frac{2^{(r-1)n}}{(p^r)^{\left(\frac{(t-1+100/n)}{\log_2(p^r)}\right)n}} << 2^{-100}.$$

Of course, this scenario pertains to when d attains its largest value. The maximum number of possible values for d is s, which includes $1, p, \cdots, p^{s-1}$. According to the union bound, the soundness error can increase by at most s times. In this case, the error probability remains below $\frac{s}{2^{100}}$, a value which is still negligible.   □

3.2   Linear Codes over Extensions of Small Galois Rings

In the first part of this section, the encoding was designed for rings $GR(p^s, r)$ where p^r is sufficiently large. However, if p^r is not exponentially large relative to the security parameter λ, what can be done? If the parameter p^r in a Galois ring requires a k-fold extension such that p^{kr} becomes exponentially large with respect to λ, a trivial solution is to perform a k-fold expansion by padding each element of $GR(p^s, r)$ into $GR(p^s, kr)$. However, this padding method is inefficient.

Inspired by the block-level coding approach from the Binius scheme [16], we treat k consecutive elements from $GR(p^s, r)$ as a single element in $GR(p^s, kr)$ for encoding, resulting in higher encoding efficiency.

In [30], Theorem 14.23 proves that the extension of any Galois ring is still a Galois ring.

Claim 1 ([30] Theorem 14.23). *For any Galois ring $R = GR(p^s, r)$, $h(x)$ is a monic irreducible polynomial of degree k over R. Then the residue class ring*

$R[x]/(h(x))$ *is a Galois ring of characteristic* p^s *and it has* p^{skr} *elements and contains* R *as a subring. Thus*

$$R[x]/(h(x)) = GR(p^s, kr)$$

Through this claim, we can conclude that the extension of a Galois ring remains a Galois ring.

In this paper, if the Galois ring $G_1 = GR(p^s, r)$ does not satisfy the requirement that p^r is large enough, and an extension $G_2 = GR(p^s, kr)$ is needed. At this time, G_2 is obtained as an extension of G_1 by a degree-k irreducible polynomial. Elements of G_2 can be viewed as polynomials of degree $k - 1$ with coefficients in G_1. Therefore, an element of G_2 can be represented as a vector consisting of k elements from G_1. The multiplication of an element a from G_1 with an element b from G_2 can be interpreted as performing the multiplication of a with each entry of the length-k vector corresponding to b. In this paper, the relationship holds for the corresponding Galois rings $GR(p^s, r)$ and $GR(p^s, kr)$.

From Fact 4, we conclude that if a monic polynomial is irreducible over $GF(p, r)$, then it remains irreducible over $GF(p^s, r)$. Therefore, we can search for irreducible polynomials over the Galois field corresponding to the Galois ring. The method for finding irreducible polynomials of degree d over a general Galois field has already been provided in [5].

For small Galois rings, the encoding involves two Galois rings. Below is the definition of the $[l, n, d]$-k-$GR(p^s, r)$ code.

Definition 6. *($[l, n, d]$-k-$GR(p^s, r)$ Code) For a vector of length kn over Galois Ring $GR(p^s, r)$, treat each k consecutive elements as a single element in $GR(p^s, kr)$ (we treat the adjacent k elements of $GR(p^s, r)$ as a k-dimensional vector.), where the parameters p, k, and r satisfy the condition that $\frac{1}{p^{kr}}$ is negligible relative to the security parameter λ. The generator matrix G is an $n \times l$ matrix defined over $GR(p^s, kr)$. After encoding, the result is a vector of length l over $GR(p^s, kr)$. Furthermore, for any two distinct vectors of length kn over $GR(p^s, r)$, at least d elements in $GR(p^s, kr)$ are different after encoding.*

Algorithm 2: Enc$'$ Algorithm: $GR(p^s, r)^{kn} \rightarrow GR(p^s, kr)^{tn}$

Input: $\mathbf{x} \in GR(p^s, r)^{kn}$
parameter: $\alpha, \beta, t, c_n, d_n$
Output: $\mathbf{w} \in GR(p^s, kr)^{tn}$ ($GR(p^s, kr)$ is obtained as an extension of $GR(p^s, r)$ by a degree-k irreducible polynomial.)
1 Treat the adjacent k elements of $GR(p^s, r)$ as a k-dimensional vector. According to Claim 1, a k-length $GR(p^s, r)$ vector is considered an element of $GR(p^s, kr)$. This leads to treating the vector $\mathbf{x}$ of length kn into a vector $\mathbf{x}'$ of length n over $GR(p^s, kr)$;
2 Call Enc$(\mathbf{x}')$ to obtain $\mathbf{w}$ and output $\mathbf{w}$;

It can be observed that the encoding over $GR(p^s, r)$ is essentially an encoding over $GR(p^s, kr)$. However, we must demonstrate that Enc$'$ supports linear combinations over $\mathrm{GR}(p^s, r)$; otherwise, it cannot be considered a linear code over $\mathrm{GR}(p^s, r)$.

Lemma 4. *Enc$'$ supports linear combinations over $\mathrm{GR}(p^s, r)$.*

Proof. One important point to note is that an element of $\mathrm{GR}(p^s, kr)$ can be viewed as a vector of k elements over $\mathrm{GR}(p^s, r)$. Let $a \in \mathrm{GR}(p^s, r)$ and $b \in \mathrm{GR}(p^s, kr)$. At the same time, a can be considered as an element in $\mathrm{GR}(p^s, kr)$.

The multiplication $a \cdot b$ in $\mathrm{GR}(p^s, kr)$ can be understood as the component-wise multiplication of a with each element of b. Therefore, the dot product of an element $a \in \mathrm{GR}(p^s, r)$ with a vector of length l over $\mathrm{GR}(p^s, kr)$ can be viewed as the dot product of a with a vector of length lk over $\mathrm{GR}(p^s, r)$.

Let $a_1, a_2 \in \mathrm{GR}(p^s, r)$, and let $\mathbf{b}_1, \mathbf{b}_2 \in \mathrm{GR}(p^s, r)^{kn}$, with $\mathbf{b}'_1$ and $\mathbf{b}'_2$ being the vectors padded to length n over $\mathrm{GR}(p^s, kr)$. Then we have:

$$
\begin{aligned}
a_1 \cdot \mathrm{Enc}'(\mathbf{b_2}) + a_2 \cdot \mathrm{Enc}'(\mathbf{b_2}) &= a_1 \cdot \mathrm{Enc}(\mathbf{b}'_1) + a_2 \cdot \mathrm{Enc}(\mathbf{b}'_2) \\
&= \mathrm{Enc}(a_1 \cdot \mathbf{b}'_1 + a_2 \cdot \mathbf{b}'_2) \\
&= \mathrm{Enc}(a_1 \cdot \mathbf{b_1} + a_2 \cdot \mathbf{b_2})
\end{aligned}
$$

The second equality holds because Enc is a linear code defined over $\mathrm{GR}(p^s, kr)$, and $a \in \mathrm{GR}(p^s, kr)$. Therefore, it can be concluded that Enc$'$ supports linear combinations over $\mathrm{GR}(p^s, r)$. □

3.3 Costs

Table 1 is the performance comparison for different parameters. While Brakedown applies its operations over a large 127-bit prime, our approach utilizes a Galois ring $\mathrm{GR}(p^s, r)$. Additionally, in Brakedown, the probability of encoding failure does not exceed 2^{-100}, while in the Galois ring $\mathrm{GR}(p^s, r)$, the failure probability does not exceed $s \cdot 2^{-100}$. In practical applications, s is almost never greater than 2^8, so the scheme remains secure over Galois rings.

Beyond those, the parameters α, β, t, c_n, and d_n can be selected in a manner consistent with those in the Brakedown scheme. If the encoding length is n, data from Brakedown suggest that, depending on the selected parameters, encoding a vector of length n will require between $13.2n$ to $25.5n$ multiplications on $\mathrm{GR}(p^s, r)$. We denote this constant as c_0, with c_0 approximately ranging from 13.2 to 25.5. The cost of the expander code in this work is consistent with that in Brakedown, except for the difference in the basic computational unit.

4 Linear Time Polynomial Commitment

The Brakedown polynomial commitment relies on the lemma from AHIV17 [1], so our first step is to prove that this lemma holds over arbitrary Galois rings. So we must consider the case where polynomial coefficients lie in a small ring. Recall that during encoding, we treat k elements from the small ring as a single element from the extension ring. If the verifier directly selects a challenge e from

Table 1. Linear Code over Galois rings $GR(p^s, r)$ performance according to Brakedown [20].

n	p^r	Pr[failure]	Run-time	Distance	Rate	α	β	t	c_n	d_n
$\leq 2^{30}$	$\geq 2^{127}$	$< s \cdot 2^{-100}$	$13.2n$	0.02		0.704	0.1195	0.0284	1.42	6	33
$\leq 2^{30}$	$\geq 2^{127}$	$< s \cdot 2^{-100}$	$14.3n$	0.03		0.68	0.138	0.0444	1.47	7	26
$\leq 2^{30}$	$\geq 2^{127}$	$< s \cdot 2^{-100}$	$15.8n$	0.04		0.65	0.178	0.061	1.521	7	22
$\leq 2^{30}$	$\geq 2^{127}$	$< s \cdot 2^{-100}$	$17.8n$	0.05		0.60	0.2	0.082	1.64	8	19
$\leq 2^{30}$	$\geq 2^{127}$	$< s \cdot 2^{-100}$	$20.5n$	0.06		0.61	0.211	0.097	1.616	9	21
$\leq 2^{30}$	$\geq 2^{127}$	$< s \cdot 2^{-100}$	$25.5n$	0.07		0.58	0.238	0.1205	1.72	10	23

the extension ring, then e will multiply with the larger element formed by the k elements from the small ring. So the adjacent k coefficients will be mixed together. However, if the verifier selects challenges only from the small ring, the soundness cannot be guaranteed.

To solve this issue, we prove a "repetition" version of the AHIV17 [1] lemma over arbitrary Galois rings. In the "repetition" version lemma, the verifier ensures soundness by selecting multiple challenges from the small ring, while also preventing the mixing of the k coefficients. To prove the "repetition" version lemma, it is necessary to utilize the definitions of Interleaved Codes and Block-wise Relative Distance.

Definition 7 (Interleaved code and Block-wise relative distance [8]).
Let $C \subset \mathbb{F}^n$ be an $[n, k, d]$ linear code over $\mathbb{F}$. We let C^m denote the $[mn, mk, d]$ (interleaved) code over $\mathbb{F}^m$ whose codewords are all $m \times n$ matrices A such that every row A_i of A satisfies $A_i \in C$. For $A \in C^m$ and $j \in [n]$, we denote by $A[j]$ the jth symbol of A.

Moreover, we introduce the definition of block-wise distance of (A, C^m):

$$d(A, L^m) := \frac{|\{j \in [n] | \exists i \text{ s.t. } A_i[j] \neq c_i[j]\}|}{n}$$

where c_i denote the closest codeword with A_i in C.

Definition 8 (Interleaved code and Block-wise relative distance over Galois Rings). *Let $C \subset GR(p^s, kr)^n$ be an $[n, k, d]$ linear code over $GR(p^s, kr)$. We let C^m denote the $[mn, mk, d]$ (interleaved) code over $GR(p^s, kr)^m$ whose codewords are all $m \times n$ matrices A such that every row A_i of A satisfies $A_i \in C$. For $A \in C^m$ and $j \in [n]$, we denote by $A[j]$ the jth symbol of A.*

Moreover, we give the definition of the block-wise distance of (A, C^m):

$$d(A, L^m) := \frac{|\{j \in [n] | \exists i \text{ s.t. } A_i[j] \neq c_i[j]\}|}{n}$$

where c_i denote the closest codeword with U_i in C.

Claim 2 (Ames, Hazay, Ishai, and Venkitasubramaniam [1], Roth and Zémor) *Fix an arbitrary $[n, k, d]$-code $L \subset \mathbb{F}_q^n$, and a proximity parameter $e \in \{0, \cdots, \lfloor \frac{d-1}{3} \rfloor\}$. Supposed $d(U, C^m) > e$. Then for a random w^* in the row-span of U, we have*

$$\Pr[d(w^*, L) \leq e] \leq (e+1)/|\mathbb{F}|$$

The presence of zero divisors in the Galois ring $GR(p^s, r)$ increases the possibility $\frac{e+1}{q}$. To maintain this probability at a negligible level, we repeatedly select challenges to reduce it.

Claim 3 (AHIV17 Repetition Version). *Fix any k-$[l, n, d]$ code $C \subset GR(p^s, kr)^l$ over the Galois ring $GR(p^s, r)$, and a proximity parameter $e \in \{0, \cdots, \lfloor \frac{d-1}{3} \rfloor\}$. For a matrix $U \in GR(p^s, kr)^{m \times l}$ with $d(U, C^m) > e$, and a matrix $R \in GR(p^s, r)^{k \times m}$ where each element of R is randomly chosen from $GR(p^s, r)$, let $W = RU$. Then we have:*

$$\Pr[d(W, C^k) \leq e] \leq \frac{e+1}{p^{rk}}.$$

We provide the proof of this claim in the full version of this paper [31].

With the verification lemma established above, we can now give a polynomial commitment over the Galois ring $GR(p^s, r)$.

This polynomial commitment is designed to compute a multilinear polynomial $f(x_1, \cdots, x_l)$ defined over $GR(p^s, r)$, where polynomial coefficient $x_i \in GR(p^s, r)$. Assume that the encoding over $GR(p^s, r)$ uses a k-$[l, n, d]$ code, where $k \geq 1$.

Polynomial Commitment for $GR(p^s, r)$:

- **Commit Phase**
  - The prover splits the multilinear polynomial with l variables into a matrix U of size $2^{l/2} \times 2^{l/2}$. Let $m = 2^{l/2}$. Each row of the matrix is encoded using a k-$[tm, m, d]$ code to obtain a matrix $\hat{U}$ with m rows, $\hat{U}_1, \cdots, \hat{U}_m$, where $\hat{U}_i \in GR(p^s, kr)^{tm/k}$, and $\hat{U}_i[j]$ represents the element in the i-th row and j-th column of the matrix $\hat{U}$. The prover constructs a Merkle Tree to commit to $\hat{U}$.
- **Testing Phase**
  - **Verifier → Prover**: A random matrix $R \in (GR(p^s, r))^{k \times m}$, where each element of R is randomly chosen from $GR(p^s, r)$.
  - **Prover → Verifier**: Treat every k adjacent elements in each row of matrix U as an element in $GR(p^s, r)$, and compute $V = RU \in GR(p^s, kr)^{k \times (m/k)}$ and calims that $V = RU$. Then, send V to the verifier.
  - **Verifier**: Choose a random set Q of size $l_Q = \Theta(\lambda)$, with $Q \subseteq [tm/k]$. For each $j \in Q$:
    - Verifier queries all m entries of the corresponding "column" of $\hat{U}$: $\hat{U}_1[j], \cdots, \hat{U}_m[j]$. The verifier receives these values and the associated Merkle Tree paths from the prover. If one of the paths is invalid, reject.

- For each row V_i of matrix V, the verifier confirms that $\mathrm{Enc}(V_i)[j] = \sum_{s=1}^{m} R_i[s] \cdot \hat{U}_s[j]$, rejecting if the condition is not satisfied.

– **Evaluation Phase**
  - To compute $f(r_1, \cdots, r_l)$, calculate $\mathbf{q_1} = (1-r_1, r_1) \otimes \cdots \otimes (1-r_{l/2}, r_{l/2}) \in \mathrm{GR}(p^s, r)^m$ and $\mathbf{q_2} = (1 - r_{l/2+1}, r_{l/2+1}) \otimes \cdots \otimes (1 - r_l, r_l) \in \mathrm{GR}(p^s, r)^m$.
  - The evaluation phase is similar to the testing phase, but with R replaced by $\mathbf{q_1}$ to obtain $\mathbf{v}$.
  - If all previous checks pass, the verifier treats $\mathbf{v}$ as a vector of length m over $\mathrm{GR}(p^s, r)$, and computes $f(r_1, \cdots, r_l) = \langle \mathbf{v}, \mathbf{q_2} \rangle$.

The Proof of Completeness

Proof. To demonstrate completeness, we first express the matrix U as:

$$U = \begin{bmatrix} f(0, \cdots, 0, 0, \cdots, 0) & f(0, \cdots, 0, 0, \cdots, 1) & \cdots & f(0, \cdots, 0, 1, \cdots, 1) \\ f(0, \cdots, 1, 0, \cdots, 0) & f(0, \cdots, 1, 0, \cdots, 1) & \cdots & f(0, \cdots, 1, 1, \cdots, 1) \\ \vdots & \vdots & \vdots & \vdots \\ f(1, \cdots, 1, 0, \cdots, 0) & f(1, \cdots, 1, 0, \cdots, 1) & \cdots & f(1, \cdots, 1, 1, \cdots, 1) \end{bmatrix}$$

To compute $f(r_1, \cdots, r_l)$, we use the formula:

$$f(r_1, \cdots, r_l) = \sum_{\mathbf{b} \in \{0,1\}} \prod_{i \in [1,l]} ((1 - r_i)(1 - b_i) + r_i b_i)\, f(\mathbf{b}),$$

which can be rewritten as:

$$f(r_1, \cdots, r_l) = \mathbf{q_1}^\top U \mathbf{q_2}.$$

An important observation is that if we treat the i-th row of the matrix U, denoted U_i, as m/k elements $w_1, \cdots, w_{m/k}$ in $\mathrm{GR}(p^s, kr)$, then for $a \in \mathrm{GR}(p^s, r)$, we have:

$$a \cdot (w_1, \cdots, w_{m/k})$$
$$= (a \cdot w_1, \cdots, a \cdot w_{m/k})$$
$$= (a(w_{1,1}, \cdots, w_{1,k}), \cdots, a(w_{(m/k),1}, \cdots, w_{(m/k),k}))$$
$$= (aw_{1,1}, \cdots, aw_{1,k}, \cdots, aw_{(m/k),1}, \cdots, aw_{(m/k),k})$$
$$= a \cdot (U_i[1], \cdots, U_i[m]).$$

Since each w_i can be viewed as k elements from $\mathrm{GR}(p^s, r)$, the computation is the same whether we treat U as a matrix in $\mathrm{GR}(p^s, r)^{m \times m}$ or in $\mathrm{GR}(p^s, kr)^{m \times (m/k)}$. Thus, the result of $\mathbf{q_1}^\top U$ remains the same in "form" regardless of the interpretation. Therefore, the linear combination of the matrix can be seen as a linear combination over $\mathrm{GR}(p^s, r)$, ensuring the completeness of the polynomial commitment. $\qquad\square$

The Proof of Soundness

Proof. The encoded coefficient matrix $\hat{U} \in \mathrm{GR}(p^s, kr)^{m \times (m/k)}$, where $N = m/k$, has a code distance of d and a relative distance of $\gamma = d/N$. First, we show that if the prover can pass the testing phase with a probability greater than $\frac{1}{p^{kr}} + \left(1 - \frac{\gamma}{3}\right)^{l_Q}$, then there must exist a codeword $[c_1, \cdots, c_m] \in C^m$ such that:

$$E := |\{j \in [N] : \exists i \in [m], \text{ such that } c_{i,j} \neq \hat{U}_{i,j}\}| \leq \left(\frac{\gamma}{3}\right) N.$$

Let $e = \left\lfloor \frac{\gamma N}{3} \right\rfloor$. If no such codeword $[c_1, \cdots, c_m]$ exists, then we have $d(\hat{U}, C^m) > e$. According to claim 3, since $V = R \cdot \hat{U}$, the probability that $d(V, C^k)$ is greater than e is at least $1 - \frac{e+1}{p^{kr}}$.

Thus, during the testing phase, the probability that the verifier randomly selects l columns without hitting any columns in $\Delta(V, C^k)$ is at most $\left(1 - \frac{e}{3}\right)^{l_Q} = \left(1 - \frac{\gamma}{3}\right)^{l_Q}$. Define the event E_1 as $d(V, C^k) > e$, and the event E_2 as the verifier selecting l columns without hitting any in $\Delta(V, C^k)$. Then, we have:

$$\Pr[P^* \text{wins}] \leq \Pr[P^* \text{wins} | \bar{E}_1] \Pr[\bar{E}_1] + \Pr[P^* \text{wins} | E_1] \Pr[E_1]$$
$$\leq \Pr[\bar{E}_1] + \Pr[E_2 | E_1] \Pr[E_1]$$
$$< \frac{1}{p^{kr}} + \Pr[E_2 | E_1] = \frac{1}{p^{kr}} + \left(1 - \frac{\gamma}{3}\right)^{l_Q}$$

This contradicts the fact that the prover could pass the testing phase, so there must exist such a codeword $c_1, \cdots, c_m$.

We can observe that each c_i is the closest codeword to each row U_i of $\hat{U}$; otherwise, the distance between two codewords would be less than d. Define $w := \sum_{i=1}^{m} q_{1,i} \cdot c_i$. Next, we show that if the prover can pass the testing phase with a probability greater than $\frac{e+1}{p^k} + \left(1 - \frac{d}{3}\right)^{l_Q}$, and pass the evaluation phase with a probability greater than $\left(1 - \frac{2\gamma}{3}\right)^{l_Q}$, then let $u := \sum_{i=1}^{m} q_{1,i} \cdot U_i$ and $w = \mathrm{Enc}(u)$.

If $w \neq \mathrm{Enc}(u)$, then w and $\mathrm{Enc}(v)$ are two distinct codewords in C, meaning that the number of positions where they are identical will not exceed $(1 - \gamma)N$. Let the set of positions where the two codewords are identical be denoted as A. If the verifier selects a column $j \notin A \cup E$, then the test will fail because w and $\mathrm{Enc}(u)$ can only match within $A \cup E$. We have $|A \cup E| \leq |A| + |E| \leq (1 - \gamma)N + \left(\frac{\gamma}{3}\right) N = \left(1 - \frac{2\gamma}{3}\right) N$. Since the verifier selects the set of columns Q randomly, if the prover is cheating, the probability of passing the evaluation phase will not exceed $\left(1 - \frac{2\gamma}{3}\right)^{l_Q}$.

Thus, if the prover can pass the testing phase with a probability greater than $\frac{e+1}{p^k} + \left(1 - \frac{d}{3}\right)^{l_Q}$, and the evaluation phase with a probability greater than $\left(1 - \frac{2\gamma}{3}\right)^{l_Q}$, the binding property of the scheme is ensured. □

4.1   Extractability

If the committed polynomial has l variables, let $m = 2^{l/2}$, so the matrix U being committed is an $m \times (m/k)$ matrix over $\mathrm{GR}(p^s, kr)$. Let $N = m/k$. The key to extraction lies in finding an invertible $N \times N$ matrix over the Galois ring. In a finite field, a matrix formed by selecting N linearly independent non-zero vectors of length N is invertible. Randomly selecting N vectors of length N results in a non-negligible probability of the matrix being invertible. However, in a Galois ring, due to the presence of zero divisors, a set of linearly independent vectors does not necessarily form an invertible matrix.

We prove that a randomly chosen $N \times N$ matrix over the Galois ring $\mathrm{GR}(p^s, r)$ is invertible with high probability. First, we consider the case where $p^r > N$ and $1 - \frac{N}{p^r}$ is non-negligible.

Lemma 5. *Assuming that $1 - \frac{N}{p^r} > 0$ and is non-negligible, then by randomly selecting an $N \times N$ matrix R from $\mathrm{GR}(p^s, r)$, there is a probability of $1 - \frac{N}{p^r}$ that R is invertible.*

Proof. Using the adjugate matrix method for matrix inversion,

$$R^{-1} = \frac{A^*}{\det(A)} = \frac{1}{\det(A)} \begin{bmatrix} R_{11}^* & \cdots & R_{1N}^* \\ \vdots & \ddots & \vdots \\ R_{N1}^* & \cdots & R_{NN}^* \end{bmatrix}^{\top}$$

Let R_{ij}^* represent the algebraic cofactor of matrix R with respect to the (i,j) entry. We observe that if $\det(R)$ is non-zero and not a zero divisor, then R^{-1} exists. Now, we calculate the probability that $\det(R)$ is non-zero and not a zero divisor.

$$\det(R) = \sum_{\sigma \in S_N} \mathrm{sgn}(\sigma) \prod_{i=1}^{N} A_{i,\sigma(i)}$$

where S_N is the set of all permutations on $\{1, 2, \cdots, N\}$, and $\mathrm{sgn}(\sigma)$ denotes the sign of permutation σ. If σ has an even number of inversions, then $\mathrm{sgn}(\sigma) = 1$; otherwise, $\mathrm{sgn}(\sigma) = -1$. In fact, $\det(R)$ can be viewed as a multilinear polynomial in the N^2 variables R_{ij}, and the degree of the polynomial is at most N. Let us define this polynomial as f_R.

By a known fact about Galois rings, all zero divisors in $\mathrm{GR}(p^s, r)$ lie in the ideal (p). Therefore, we only need to show that f_R is non-zero modulo p with a non-negligible probability. Consider the isomorphism map ψ

$$\begin{aligned} \mathbb{Z}_{p^s} &\to \mathbb{F}_p \\ c_0 + c_1 p + \cdots + c_{p-1} p^{s-1} &\mapsto c_0 \end{aligned}$$

For a polynomial f of degree at most d with coefficients in $\mathrm{GR}(p^s, r)$, we define a mapping Ψ, where $\Psi(f)$ is derived by applying ψ to each coefficient of f, resulting in a polynomial f'. Clearly, Ψ is a homomorphism. If at some point $\mathbf{x}$, we have $f(\mathbf{x}) = 0 \pmod{p}$, then it follows that $\Psi(f)(\psi(\mathbf{x})) = 0$.

Let $\Psi(f_R) = f'_R$. If f'_R evaluates to a non-zero value, then f_R will not be a zero divisor in $\mathrm{GR}(p^s, r)$. Since the variables R_{ij} are randomly chosen from $\mathrm{GR}(p^s, r)$, so $\psi(R_{ij})$ are randomly chosen from $\mathrm{GF}(p, r)$. By the Schwartz-Zippel lemma for fields, the degree of f'_R is at most N, so the probability that a randomly chosen point evaluates to 0 is at most $\frac{N}{p^r}$. Therefore, the probability that f'_R is non-zero is at least $1 - \frac{N}{p^r}$, which is non-negligible. This completes the proof. $\square$

If the ring $\mathrm{GR}(p^s, r)$ does not satisfy $p^r > N$, then the $\mathrm{GR}(p^s, r)$ code used in encoding must be a $[l, n, d] - k - \mathrm{GR}(p^s, r)$ code, where $p^{kr} \gg N$. Choose a k' such that k' is a divisor of k and $p^{k'r} > N$. At this point, the extractor can send k' challenges from $\mathrm{GR}(p^s, r)$ to simulate a challenge from $\mathrm{GR}(p^s, k'r)$. Then, using Lemma 5, we can obtain an invertible $N \times N$ matrix with non-negligible probability.

If the probability that the matrix is invertible is p_i, by repeating the process $\mathrm{poly}(\frac{1}{p_i})$ times, we can ensure that with probability $1 - \mathrm{negl}(\lambda)$, the matrix U can be successfully extracted.

4.2   More Efficient

When using polynomial commitment schemes in SNARKs, it is typically required that the challenge space for the verifier is exponential in size relative to the security parameter λ, while the polynomial coefficients may come from a smaller Galois ring. Suppose the coefficients come from $\mathrm{GR}(p^s, r)$, while the challenges come from $\mathrm{GR}(p^s, kr)$. In this case, when committing to the coefficients, each coefficient element needs to be treated as an element in $\mathrm{GR}(p^s, kr)$. This increases the cost of encoding and hashing by a factor of k.

In Binius [16], a two-dimensional expansion was used to address this issue. In this work, we explain the problem from the perspective of "repetition": using the observations that even though elements are treated as being in $\mathrm{GR}(p^s, kr)$ during the encoding phase, the commitment still supports linear combinations over $\mathrm{GR}(p^s, r)$. This allows the algebraic structures used during the commitment and evaluation phases to differ. Below, we present a polynomial commitment scheme where the coefficients come from $\mathrm{GR}(p^s, r)$, but the challenges come from $\mathrm{GR}(p^s, kr)$.

The polynomial commitment scheme is designed to compute a multilinear polynomial $f(x_1, \cdots, x_l)$ over $\mathrm{GR}(p^s, r)$, where the coefficients come from $\mathrm{GR}(p^s, r)$ and each $x_i \in \mathrm{GR}(p^s, kr)$. Assume that the encoding over $\mathrm{GR}(p^s, r)$ uses a k-$[l, n, d]$ code, where $k \geq 1$.

More Efficient Polynomial Commitment for Small Rings

– **Commit Phase**
  - The prover splits the multilinear polynomial with l variables into a matrix U of size $2^{l/2} \times 2^{l/2}$. Let $m = 2^{l/2}$. Each row of the matrix is encoded

using a k-$[tm, m, d]$ code to obtain a matrix $\hat{U}$ with m rows, $\hat{U}_1, \cdots, \hat{U}_m$, where $\hat{U}_i \in \mathrm{GR}(p^s, kr)^{tm/k}$, and $\hat{U}_i[j]$ represents the element in the i-th row and j-th column of the matrix $\hat{U}$. The prover constructs a Merkle Tree to commit to $\hat{U}$.

- **Testing Phase**
  - **Verifier** $\rightarrow$ **Prover**: A random matrix $R \in (\mathrm{GR}(p^s, r))^{k \times m}$, where each element of R is randomly chosen from $\mathrm{GR}(p^s, r)$.
  - **Prover** $\rightarrow$ **Verifier**: Treat every k adjacent elements in each row of matrix U as an element in $\mathrm{GR}(p^s, r)$, and compute $V = RU \in \mathrm{GR}(p^s, kr)^{k \times (m/k)}$ and calims that $V = RU$. Then, send V to the verifier.
  - **Verifier**: Choose a random set Q of size $l_Q = \Theta(\lambda)$, with $Q \subseteq [tm/k]$. For each $j \in Q$:
    - Verifier queries all m entries of the corresponding "column" of $\hat{U}$: $\hat{U}_1[j], \cdots, \hat{U}_m[j]$. The verifier receives these values and the associated Merkle Tree paths from the prover. If one of the paths is invalid, reject.
    - For each row V_i of matrix V, the verifier confirms that $\mathrm{Enc}(V_i) = \sum_{s=1}^{m} R_i[s] \cdot \hat{U}_s[j]$, rejecting if the condition is not satisfied.
- **Evaluation Phase**
  - To compute $f(r_1, \cdots, r_l)$, calculate $\mathbf{q_1} = (1 - r_1, r_1) \otimes \cdots \otimes (1 - r_{l/2}, r_{l/2}) \in \mathrm{GR}(p^s, kr)^m$ and $\mathbf{q_2} = (1 - r_{l/2+1}, r_{l/2+1}) \otimes \cdots \otimes (1 - r_l, r_l) \in \mathrm{GR}(p^s, kr)^m$.
  - Split each element of $\mathbf{q_1}$ into a k-length vector over $\mathrm{GR}(p^s, r)$. Let $\mathbf{q}_{1,i}$ represent the i-th position of each element. Then, for each $\mathbf{q}_{1,i}$, perform the evaluation phase to get k vectors $\mathbf{v}_1, \cdots, \mathbf{v}_k$.
  - Combine the k vectors into one m-length element $\mathbf{v}$ over $\mathrm{GR}(p^s, kr)$, where $\mathbf{v}_i[j]$ represents the i-th coefficient at the j-th position. The verifier then computes $\mathbf{v}^\top \mathbf{q_2}$ to obtain $f(r_1, \cdots, r_l)$.

To demonstrate the completeness of this scheme, we express $f(r_1, \cdots, r_l)$ as a matrix multiplication: $\mathbf{q_1}^\top U \mathbf{q_2}$. When computing $\mathbf{q_1}^\top$, note that only the elements of $\mathbf{q_1}$ come from $\mathrm{GR}(p^s, kr)$. Thus, when multiplying the elements of $\mathbf{q_1}$ with the elements of U, it can be viewed as multiplying each component of the elements in U with each component of the elements in $\mathbf{q_1}$.

$$\mathbf{q_1}^\top U = \begin{bmatrix} \mathbf{q}_{11}^\top \\ \vdots \\ \mathbf{q}_{1k}^\top \end{bmatrix} U$$

Thus, the verifier can correctly compute $f(r_1, \cdots, r_l)$. The binding and extractability properties of this protocol remain consistent with the previous proof. We now focus on analyzing the prover's computational cost. The prover needs to construct a Merkle Tree over $\frac{2^l}{k}$ elements from $\mathrm{GR}(p^s, r)$, which takes time $t_1 = O\left(\frac{2^l}{k}\right)$. Additionally, the prover needs to perform linear encoding on $\frac{2^{l/2}}{k}$ elements from $\mathrm{GR}(p^s, r)$, requiring $\frac{c_0 2^l}{k}$ multiplications in $\mathrm{GR}(p^s, kr)$. In the testing phase and evaluation phase, $t2^l k$ multiplications in $\mathrm{GR}(p^s, \ \mathrm{kr}) \cdot \mathrm{GR}(p^s, r)$ are needed, where $\frac{1}{t}$ is the code rate. Moreover, the prover must open $|Q|2^{l/2}$ Merkle Tree nodes, taking time t_2.

Let ee represent the time required for one multiplication in $\mathrm{GR}(p^s, kr)$, and be represent the time for one multiplication in $\mathrm{GR}(p^s, kr) \cdot \mathrm{GR}(p^s, r)$. The prover's total cost is $t_1 + t_2 + \frac{c_0 2^l}{k} ee + t2^{l+1} kbe$.

Without this commitment scheme, if the prover commits to elements from $\mathrm{GR}(p^s, r)$ by directly calculating over $\mathrm{GR}(p^s, kr)$ in the commitment phase, they would need to construct a Merkle Tree over 2^l elements from $\mathrm{GR}(p^s, r)$, taking time $kt_1 = O\left(\frac{2^l}{k}\right)$. Then, the prover would perform linear encoding on $2^{l/2}$ elements from $\mathrm{GR}(p^s, r)$, requiring $c_0 2^l$ multiplications in $\mathrm{GR}(p^s, kr)$. In the testing phase and evaluation phase, $t2^l$ multiplications in $\mathrm{GR}(p^s, kr)$ are needed. Additionally, $|Q|2^{l/2}$ Merkle Tree nodes must be opened, taking time t_2. Thus, the total prover cost is $kt_1 + t_2 + (c_0 + \ 2t)2^l ee$.

It is clear that using this approach results in approximately k times more ee computations. And the ee operations are significantly more time-consuming than be and bb operations.

5   Proof Toolboxes over Galois Rings

The sumcheck protocol over rings has been widely discussed, and in [28], the sumcheck protocol was extended to infinite non-commutative rings. However, [28] did not propose a corresponding polynomial commitment scheme. In this section, we explore the sumcheck protocol over Galois rings.

5.1   Sumcheck Over Galois Rings

To ensure the soundness of the sumcheck protocol, the verifier's challenges can be selected from the exceptional set of the ring. Therefore, to ensure a sufficiently large challenge space, the exceptional set must be large enough. An extension method is typically used to expand the size of the exceptional set. In fact, if a ring has a sufficiently large exceptional set, it indicates that the proportion of zero divisors is very small, and in this case, according to Fact 3, the verifier's challenge can be selected from the entire Galois ring.

Below, we introduce the sumcheck protocol where the challenges are selected from the entire Galois ring $\mathrm{GR}(p^s, r)$, assuming that p^r is sufficiently large and the degree of the polynomial p does not exceed d. As long as the verifier's challenges are selected from the ring $\mathrm{GR}(p^s, r)$, where p^r is exponentially large in relation to the security parameter λ, security can be ensured. Meanwhile, the coefficients of the polynomial being proven can still come from a "smaller ring" G_1, as long as $\mathrm{GR}(p^s, r)$ is an extension of G_1. This allows arithmetic circuits defined over a "small ring" to be encoded into polynomials with coefficients that remain in the smaller ring. This aligns with the scenario mentioned at the end of the previous section and it can reduce the prover's time complexity.

Our sumcheck protocol is adapted from the protocol presented in Chapter 4 of the [29]. We use $\deg_i(g)$ to denote the highest degree of the i-th variable of the polynomial g.

Sumcheck Over Galois Rings Construction

- The prover sends a value H to the verifier, which is equal to

$$\sum_{x_1 \in \{0,1\}} \sum_{x_2 \in \{0,1\}} \cdots \sum_{x_l \in \{0,1\}} g(x_1, ..., x_l)$$

- In the first round, the prover sends a univariate polynomial $g_1(X_1)$ claim to equal

$$\sum_{(x_2,...,x_l) \in \{0,1\}^{n-1}} g(X_1, x_2, ..., x_l)$$

  Then verifier checks
  $$H = g_1(0) + g_1(1)$$

  and g_1 is a univarite polynomial of degree at most $\deg_1(g)$. If not, the verifier terminates and returns reject.
- The verifier randomly selects a challenge r_1 from the $GR(p^s, r)$ and sends r_1 to the prover.
- In the ith round, $1 < i < n$, the prover sends a univariate polynomial $p_i(X_i)$ and claim it is equal to

$$\sum_{(x_{i+1},...,x_l) \in \{0,1\}^{l-i}} g(r_1, ..., r_{i-1}, X_i, x_{i+1}, ..., x_l)$$

  verifier checks whether g_i is a univariate polynomial with degree at most $\deg_i(g)$, and checks $g_{i-1}(r_{i-1}) = g_i(0) + g_i(1)$. If the check does not hold, then terminates and rejects.
- The verifier randomly selects a challenge r_i from $GR(p^s, r)$ and sends r_i to the prover.
- In the last round, the prover sends a univariate polynomial $g_n(X_n)$ to the verifier and claims equal $g(r_1, ..., r_{l-1}, X_l)$ verifier checks whether g_l is a univariate polynomial whose degree does not exceed $deg_l(g)$ and checks $g_{l-1}(r_{l-1}) = g_l(0) + g_l(1)$. If not, terminate and rejects.
- Verifier chooses a random challenge r_l from $GR(p^s, r)$ and evaluates $g(r_1, ..., r_l)$ with a single oracle query to g. Verifier checks $g_l(r_l) = g(r_1, ..., r_l)$, if not, terminate and rejects.
- If all the above checks pass, then the verifier accepts.

Lemma 6. *The soundness error of the sumcheck protocol over Galois rings will not exceed* $\frac{ld}{p^r}$.

In the full version of this paper [31], we provide the proof for this lemma.

In addition to the sumcheck protocol, constructing SNARKs often requires a ZeroCheck protocol to prove that a polynomial p evaluates to zero on $\{0, 1\}^l$. We now present a scheme over the Galois ring $GR(p^s, r)$, where p^r is exponentially large with respect to the security parameter λ. Define

$$eq(\mathbf{x}, \mathbf{y}) = \prod_{i \in [l]} ((1 - x_i)(1 - y_i) + x_i y_i).$$

ZeroCheck Over Galois Rings Construction

- Statement: For a polynomial f of degree d, we want to assert that $f(\mathbf{x}) = 0$ for all $\mathbf{x} \in \{0, 1\}^l$.
- Input: The prover has the polynomial p, and the verifier has an oracle for evaluating f at any point.
- Procedure:
    - The verifier randomly selects an l-length vector $\mathbf{a}$ from $GR(p^s, r)$ and sends it to the prover.
    - Upon receiving $\mathbf{a}$, the prover and verifier execute the sumcheck protocol to prove that

$$\sum_{\mathbf{x} \in \{0,1\}^l} eq(\mathbf{a}, \mathbf{x}) f(\mathbf{x}) = 0,$$

Lemma 7. *The soundness error of the zero-check protocol over the Galois ring does not exceed $\frac{l(d+2)}{p^r}$.*

In the full version of this paper [31], we provide the proof for this lemma.

6   SNARKs over Galois Rings

With the polynomial commitment scheme, sumcheck protocol, and ZeroCheck protocol over Galois rings, we can construct transparent SNARK schemes over Galois rings. In this section, we primarily discuss two SNARK schemes: Libra and HyperPlonk. Libra is designed for log-space uniform circuits but achieves a prover runtime of $O(n)$. While HyperPlonk is applicable to arbitrary proof circuits but has a prover runtime of $O(n \log^2 n)$.

6.1   Libra Over Galois Rings

In Galois rings, the presence of zero divisors can affect set consistency checks. In fields, to determine whether two sets S_1 and S_2 are identical, we encode them as polynomials: $p_1(x) = \prod_{a \in S_1} (x - a)$ and $p_2(x) = \prod_{a \in S_2} (x - a)$. We then check if the polynomials are equal to verify the sets' equality. However, in Galois rings, due to the influence of zero divisors, it is possible for different sets S_1 and S_2 to produce the same polynomial encoding. For example, under modulo 8, $(x - 1)(x - 7) = (x - 5)(x - 3) \pmod 8$, making it impossible to distinguish between the sets $(1, 7)$ and $(5, 3)$. Libra targets log-space uniform circuits, avoiding the need for set consistency checks.

Libra [32] provides a linear IOP construction specifically for log-space uniform circuits. According to the discussion in Sect. 5, the challenge must come from the Galois ring $\mathrm{GR}(p^s, r)$ that p^r is exponential with respect to the security parameter λ, and the performance over Galois rings is similar to that over the Galois field $\mathrm{GF}(p, r)$. By using Libra's IOP framework combining with the Brakedown polynomial commitment scheme over Galois rings, we can construct a transparent SNARK with linear prover time for log-space uniform circuits. This SNARK has $O(n)$ prover time, $O(\sqrt{n})$ proof size, and $O(\sqrt{n})$ verifier time.

If the circuit to be proven is defined over the ring $G_1 = \mathrm{GR}(p^s, r)$, the challenge needs to be selected from $G_2 = \mathrm{GR}(p^s, kr)$. Let ee denote the cost of performing a multiplication over the ring G_2, be represent the cost of multiplying an element from G_1 with an element from G_2, and bb signify the cost of multiplication within G_1. Additionally, t_1 is the time required for constructing a Merkle tree, t_2 is the time needed to open $|Q|$ positions of the Merkle tree. Taking parameters that maximize the encoding distance, $c_0 = 25.5$, $t = 1.72$, the cost for polynomial commitment is $t_1 + t_2 + \frac{25.5n}{k} ee + 3.44nkbe$. Then the total prover time required for the entire protocol is:

$$t_1 + t_2 + \frac{25.5 + 19k}{k} nee + (3.44k + 11)nbe$$

The details of the protocol and analysis of prover's time is provided in the full version of this paper [31].

6.2 HyperPlonk over Galois Rings

HyperPlonk [13] is capable of handling all NP arithmetic circuits. It has a constraint system that is divided into two parts: gate constraints and permutation constraints. For each gate in the circuit, there are three parts: left input, right input, and output. Each output wires can become the input wires of another gates. We encode the wires according to each circuit gate, using a multilinear polynomial to represent the circuit to be proved. If the circuit has q public input gates, one output gate, and s remaining circuit gates (including secret input gates and intermediate calculation gates), let L_i represent the left input of the i-th gate, R_i represent the right input of the i-th gate, and O_i represent the output of the i-th gate. Define $\langle i \rangle$ as the binary representation of i. Let the multilinear polynomial M be defined such that $M(0, 0, \langle i \rangle) = L_i$, $M(0, 1, \langle i \rangle) = R_i$, and $M(1, 0, \langle i \rangle) = O_i$. Assume $q + s + 1 = 2^v$, where M is a multilinear polynomial with $v + 2$ variables. The multilinear polynomial M serves as the witness for the SNARK.

Gate Constraints. Let $S_1(x)$, $S_2(x)$ be multilinear polynomials with v variables. To prove the gate constraint, we need to show that the following polynomial holds for all $\mathbf{x} \in \{0, 1\}^v$:

$$0 = S_1(\mathbf{x}) \cdot (M(0, 0, \mathbf{x}) + M(0, 1, \mathbf{x})) + S_2(\mathbf{x}) \cdot M(0, 0, \mathbf{x}) \cdot M(0, 1, \mathbf{x}) - \\ M(1, 0, \mathbf{x}) + I(\mathbf{x}) \tag{1}$$

For different multiplication, addition, and input-output gates, the multilinear polynomials S_1, S_2 take on different values.

- for an addition gate: $S_1(\langle i \rangle) = 1$, $S_2(\langle i \rangle) = 0$, so $L_i + R_i = O_i$.
- for an multiplication gate: $S_1(\langle i \rangle) = 0$, $S_2(\langle i \rangle) = 1$, so $L_i \cdot R_i = O_i$.
- when $i < q$ or $i = q + s$, $S_1(\langle i \rangle) = 0$, $S_2(\langle i \rangle) = 0$, this applies to input-output gates, so $O_i = I(\langle i \rangle)$.

By invoking the ZeroCheck protocol over the Galois ring, we can prove that Eq. 1 holds.

Permutation Constraints. We adopted the second permutation constraint from HyperPlonk. Due to the presence of zero divisors in Galois rings, set consistency check is affected. HyperPlonk's [13] first approach to prove permutation constraint needs set consistency check. Similarly, when using the Spartan IOP framework [27], sparse polynomial processing requires the Sparse technique, which also involves set consistency checks. Therefore, we ultimately used the approach in HyperPlonk to express permutation constraints directly in the form of a sumcheck, thereby avoiding this problem.

Given a permutation $\sigma : \{0, 1\}^l \to \{0, 1\}^l$, the permutation is to demonstrate that for any $\mathbf{x} \in \{0, 1\}^l$, the equation $f(\mathbf{x}) = f(\sigma(\mathbf{x}))$ holds. The permutation σ can be decomposed into l bits, resulting in $\tilde{\sigma} = (\sigma_1(\mathbf{x}), \ldots, \sigma_l(\mathbf{x})) : \mathrm{GR}(p^s, r)^l \to \mathrm{GR}(p^s, r)^l$, where σ_i signifies the position of the i-th bit following the permutation. Notably, for all $\mathbf{x} \in \{0, 1\}^l$, each $\sigma_i(\mathbf{x})$ falls within $\{0, 1\}$. Consequently, the expression to be verified is:

$$f(\tilde{\sigma}(\mathbf{x})) - g(\mathbf{x}) = 0, \text{ for all } \mathbf{x} \in \{0, 1\}^l.$$

Since $f(\tilde{\sigma}(\mathbf{x}))$ cannot be easily described using a multilinear polynomial, it is represented in multilinear form through an equivalence polynomial, denoted as:

$$\sum_{\mathbf{y} \in \{0,1\}^l} (f(\mathbf{y}) \cdot eq(\tilde{\sigma}(\mathbf{x}), \mathbf{y}) - g(\mathbf{y}) \cdot eq(\mathbf{x}, \mathbf{y})) = 0, \text{ for all } \mathbf{x} \in \{0, 1\}^l.$$

Then use ZeroCheck to introduce eq and random numbers to turn it into a sumcheck protocol.

$$\sum_{\mathbf{x} \in \{0,1\}^l} eq(\mathbf{a}, \mathbf{x}) \cdot \sum_{\mathbf{y} \in \{0,1\}^l} (f(\mathbf{y}) eq(\tilde{\sigma}(\mathbf{x}), \mathbf{y}) - g(\mathbf{y}) eq(\mathbf{x}, \mathbf{y})) = 0$$

To facilitate better computation, the above expression can be rewritten as

$$\sum_{\mathbf{x} \in \{0,1\}^l} eq(\mathbf{r}, \mathbf{x}) \cdot \sum_{\mathbf{y} \in \{0,1\}^l} (f(\mathbf{y}) eq(\mathbf{x}, \tilde{\sigma}^{-1}(\mathbf{y})) - g(\mathbf{y}) eq(\mathbf{x}, \mathbf{y})) = 0$$

$\tilde{\sigma}^{-1}$ is the inverse of $\tilde{\sigma}$, and we can split every bit just like $\tilde{\sigma}$.

If the circuit to be proven has a size of n, in HyperPlonk, the permutation constraints apply to the polynomial M, where the size of the coefficients of M

is $4n$, with $2^l = 4n$. The definitions of ee, be, bb, t_1, and t_2 are identical to those provided in the last paragraph of Sect. 6.1.

The total prover time cost of the protocol is:

$$\frac{39k + 2(\log n + 3)^2 k + 204}{k} nee + (13.76k + 2\log n + 25)nbe$$
$$+ (2(\log n + 4)(\log n + 2) + 7)nbb + 4t_1 + 4t_2$$

The details of the protocol and analysis of prover's time is provided in the full version of this paper [31].

7   Comparison with Rinocchio

For a circuit with ℓ wires, t addition gates, m multiplication gates and public input and output x, we provide the following comparison (Table 2).

Table 2. Comparison with Rinocchio

	Rinocchio [18]	This work (Libra)	This work (HyperPlonk)
circuit type	NP circuit	log-space uniform circuit	NP circuit
prover time	$O(\ell + m\log m)$	$O(t + m)$	$O((t + m)\log^2(t + m)))$
proof size	$O(1)$	$O(\sqrt{t + m})$	$O(\sqrt{t + m})$
verifier time	$O(|x|)$	$O(\sqrt{t + m})$	$O(\sqrt{t + m})$
SRS length	$O(\ell + m)$	$-$	$-$

The Rinocchio and our system primarily provide proofs for two-input circuits. Beyond the initial input gates, each circuit gate corresponds to both a left and right input wire, hence ℓ is approximately twice $(t+m)$. More details are provided in the full version of this paper [31].

Acknowledgments. We would like to thank the anonymous reviewers for their valuable suggestions, and we also thank Sihuang Hu, Chong Shangguan, Kaijie Jiang, Hexiang Huang, Yuanting Shen and others for their valuable discussions on this work. We are supported by the National Key Research and Development Project of China (Grant No. 2023YFB4503203), the Strategic Priority Research Program of Chinese Academy of Sciences (Grant No. XDB0690200) and the National Natural Science Foundation of China (Grant No. 62372447 and No. 61932019).

References

1. Ames, S., Hazay, C., Ishai, Y., Venkitasubramaniam, M.: Ligero: lightweight sublinear arguments without a trusted setup. In: Thuraisingham, B., Evans, D., Malkin, T., Xu, D. (eds.) Proceedings of the 2017 ACM SIGSAC Conference on Computer and Communications Security, CCS 2017, Dallas, TX, USA, 30 October–03 November 2017, pp. 2087–2104. ACM (2017). https://doi.org/10.1145/3133956.3134104

2. Ben-Sasson, E., Bentov, I., Horesh, Y., Riabzev, M.: Fast reed-solomon interactive oracle proofs of proximity. In: Chatzigiannakis, I., Kaklamanis, C., Marx, D., Sannella, D. (eds.) 45th International Colloquium on Automata, Languages, and Programming, ICALP 2018, 9–13 July 2018, Prague, Czech Republic. LIPIcs, vol. 107, pp. 14:1–14:17. Schloss Dagstuhl - Leibniz-Zentrum für Informatik (2018). https://doi.org/10.4230/LIPIcs.ICALP.2018.14

3. Ben-Sasson, E., Bentov, I., Horesh, Y., Riabzev, M.: Scalable, transparent, and post-quantum secure computational integrity. IACR Cryptol. ePrint Arch. 46 (2018). http://eprint.iacr.org/2018/046

4. Ben-Sasson, E., Carmon, D., Ishai, Y., Kopparty, S., Saraf, S.: Proximity gaps for reed-solomon codes. In: Irani, S. (ed.) 61st IEEE Annual Symposium on Foundations of Computer Science, FOCS 2020, Durham, NC, USA, 16–19 November 2020, pp. 900–909. IEEE (2020). https://doi.org/10.1109/FOCS46700.2020.00088

5. Benger, N., Scott, M.: Constructing tower extensions of finite fields for implementation of pairing-based cryptography. In: Hasan, M.A., Helleseth, T. (eds.) WAIFI 2010. LNCS, vol. 6087, pp. 180–195. Springer, Heidelberg (2010). https://doi.org/10.1007/978-3-642-13797-6_13

6. Bishnoi, A., Clark, P.L., Potukuchi, A., Schmitt, J.R.: On zeros of a polynomial in a finite grid. Comb. Probab. Comput. **27**(3), 310–333 (2018). https://doi.org/10.1017/S0963548317000566

7. Bitansky, N., Canetti, R., Chiesa, A., Tromer, E.: From extractable collision resistance to succinct non-interactive arguments of knowledge, and back again. In: Goldwasser, S. (ed.) Innovations in Theoretical Computer Science 2012, Cambridge, MA, USA, 8–10 January 2012, pp. 326–349. ACM (2012). https://doi.org/10.1145/2090236.2090263

8. Bootle, J., Chiesa, A., Groth, J.: Linear-time arguments with sublinear verification from tensor codes. In: Pass, R., Pietrzak, K. (eds.) TCC 2020, Part II. LNCS, vol. 12551, pp. 19–46. Springer, Cham (2020). https://doi.org/10.1007/978-3-030-64378-2_2

9. Bootle, J., Chiesa, A., Sotiraki, K.: Sumcheck arguments and their applications. In: Malkin, T., Peikert, C. (eds.) CRYPTO 2021, Part I. LNCS, vol. 12825, pp. 742–773. Springer, Cham (2021). https://doi.org/10.1007/978-3-030-84242-0_26

10. Brakerski, Z.: Fully homomorphic encryption without modulus switching from classical GapSVP. In: Safavi-Naini, R., Canetti, R. (eds.) CRYPTO 2012. LNCS, vol. 7417, pp. 868–886. Springer, Heidelberg (2012). https://doi.org/10.1007/978-3-642-32009-5_50

11. Brakerski, Z., Gentry, C., Vaikuntanathan, V.: (leveled) fully homomorphic encryption without bootstrapping. ACM Trans. Comput. Theory **6**(3), 13:1–13:36 (2014). https://doi.org/10.1145/2633600

12. Bünz, B., Bootle, J., Boneh, D., Poelstra, A., Wuille, P., Maxwell, G.: Bulletproofs: short proofs for confidential transactions and more. In: 2018 IEEE Symposium on Security and Privacy, SP 2018, Proceedings, 21–23 May 2018, San Francisco, California, USA, pp. 315–334. IEEE Computer Society (2018). https://doi.org/10.1109/SP.2018.00020

13. Chen, B., Bünz, B., Boneh, D., Zhang, Z.: Hyperplonk: plonk with linear-time prover and high-degree custom gates. In: Hazay, C., Stam, M. (eds.) Advances in Cryptology - EUROCRYPT 2023, Part II. LNCS, vol. 14005, pp. 499–530. Springer, Cham (2023). https://doi.org/10.1007/978-3-031-30617-4_17

14. Chen, S., Cheon, J.H., Kim, D., Park, D.: Verifiable computing for approximate computation. IACR Cryptol. ePrint Arch. 762 (2019). https://eprint.iacr.org/2019/762

15. Chiesa, A., Hu, Y., Maller, M., Mishra, P., Vesely, N., Ward, N.: Marlin: preprocessing zkSNARKs with universal and updatable SRS. In: Canteaut, A., Ishai, Y. (eds.) EUROCRYPT 2020, Part I. LNCS, vol. 12105, pp. 738–768. Springer, Cham (2020). https://doi.org/10.1007/978-3-030-45721-1_26

16. Diamond, B.E., Posen, J.: Succinct arguments over towers of binary fields. IACR Cryptol. ePrint Arch. 1784 (2023). https://eprint.iacr.org/2023/1784

17. Gabizon, A., Williamson, Z.J., Ciobotaru, O.: PLONK: permutations over lagrange-bases for oecumenical noninteractive arguments of knowledge. IACR Cryptol. ePrint Arch. 953 (2019). https://eprint.iacr.org/2019/953

18. Ganesh, C., Nitulescu, A., Soria-Vazquez, E.: Rinocchio: snarks for ring arithmetic. J. Cryptol. **36**(4), 41 (2023). https://doi.org/10.1007/s00145-023-09481-3

19. Gentry, C., Wichs, D.: Separating succinct non-interactive arguments from all falsifiable assumptions. In: Fortnow, L., Vadhan, S.P. (eds.) Proceedings of the 43rd ACM Symposium on Theory of Computing, STOC 2011, San Jose, CA, USA, 6–8 June 2011, pp. 99–108. ACM (2011). https://doi.org/10.1145/1993636.1993651

20. Golovnev, A., Lee, J., Setty, S.T.V., Thaler, J., Wahby, R.S.: Brakedown: linear-time and field-agnostic snarks for R1CS. In: Handschuh, H., Lysyanskaya, A. (eds.) Advances in Cryptology - CRYPTO 2023, Part II. LNCS, vol. 14082, pp. 193–226. Springer, Cham (2023). https://doi.org/10.1007/978-3-031-38545-2_7

21. Groth, J.: On the size of pairing-based non-interactive arguments. In: Fischlin, M., Coron, J.-S. (eds.) EUROCRYPT 2016, Part II. LNCS, vol. 9666, pp. 305–326. Springer, Heidelberg (2016). https://doi.org/10.1007/978-3-662-49896-5_11

22. Kate, A., Zaverucha, G.M., Goldberg, I.: Constant-size commitments to polynomials and their applications. In: Abe, M. (ed.) ASIACRYPT 2010. LNCS, vol. 6477, pp. 177–194. Springer, Heidelberg (2010). https://doi.org/10.1007/978-3-642-17373-8_11

23. Kilian, J.: A note on efficient zero-knowledge proofs and arguments (extended abstract). In: Kosaraju, S.R., Fellows, M., Wigderson, A., Ellis, J.A. (eds.) Proceedings of the 24th Annual ACM Symposium on Theory of Computing, 4–6 May 1992, Victoria, British Columbia, Canada, pp. 723–732. ACM (1992). https://doi.org/10.1145/129712.129782

24. Lee, J.: Dory: efficient, transparent arguments for generalised inner products and polynomial commitments. In: Nissim, K., Waters, B. (eds.) TCC 2021, Part II. LNCS, vol. 13043, pp. 1–34. Springer, Cham (2021). https://doi.org/10.1007/978-3-030-90453-1_1

25. Micali, S.: CS proofs (extended abstracts). In: 35th Annual Symposium on Foundations of Computer Science, Santa Fe, New Mexico, USA, 20–22 November 1994, pp. 436–453. IEEE Computer Society (1994). https://doi.org/10.1109/SFCS.1994.365746

26. Parno, B., Howell, J., Gentry, C., Raykova, M.: Pinocchio: nearly practical verifiable computation. In: 2013 IEEE Symposium on Security and Privacy, SP 2013, Berkeley, CA, USA, 19–22 May 2013, pp. 238–252. IEEE Computer Society (2013). https://doi.org/10.1109/SP.2013.47

27. Setty, S.: Spartan: efficient and general-purpose zkSNARKs without trusted setup. In: Micciancio, D., Ristenpart, T. (eds.) CRYPTO 2020, Part III. LNCS, vol. 12172, pp. 704–737. Springer, Cham (2020). https://doi.org/10.1007/978-3-030-56877-1_25

28. Soria-Vazquez, E.: Doubly efficient interactive proofs over infinite and non-commutative rings. In: Kiltz, E., Vaikuntanathan, V. (eds.) Theory of Cryptography - TCC 2022, Part I. LNCS, vol. 13747, pp. 497–525. Springer, Cham (2022). https://doi.org/10.1007/978-3-031-22318-1_18

29. Thaler, J.: Proofs, arguments, and zero-knowledge. Found. Trends Priv. Secur. **4**(2–4), 117–660 (2022). https://doi.org/10.1561/3300000030

30. Wan, Z.X.: Finite fields and Galois rings. World Scientific Publishing Company (2011)

31. Wei, Y., Zhang, X., Deng, Y.: Transparent SNARKs over galois rings. Cryptology ePrint Archive, Paper 2025/263 (2025). https://eprint.iacr.org/2025/263

32. Xie, T., Zhang, J., Zhang, Y., Papamanthou, C., Song, D.: Libra: succinct zero-knowledge proofs with optimal prover computation. In: Boldyreva, A., Micciancio, D. (eds.) CRYPTO 2019, Part III. LNCS, vol. 11694, pp. 733–764. Springer, Cham (2019). https://doi.org/10.1007/978-3-030-26954-8_24

33. Xie, T., Zhang, Y., Song, D.: Orion: zero knowledge proof with linear prover time. In: Dodis, Y., Shrimpton, T. (eds.) Advances in Cryptology - CRYPTO 2022, Part IV. LNCS, vol. 13510, pp. 299–328. Springer, Cham (2022). https://doi.org/10.1007/978-3-031-15985-5_11

34. Zeilberger, H., Chen, B., Fisch, B.: Basefold: efficient field-agnostic polynomial commitment schemes from foldable codes. In: Reyzin, L., Stebila, D. (eds.) Advances in Cryptology - CRYPTO 2024, Part X. LNCS, vol. 14929, pp. 138–169. Springer, Cham (2024). https://doi.org/10.1007/978-3-031-68403-6_5

Lattice-Based Proof-Friendly Signatures from Vanishing Short Integer Solutions

Adrien Dubois[1(✉)] , Michael Klooß[2] , Russell W. F. Lai[3] ,
and Ivy K. Y. Woo[3]

[1] ENS de Lyon, Lyon, France
adrien.dubois@ens-lyon.fr
[2] Karlsruhe Institute of Technology, Karlsruhe, Germany
[3] Aalto University, Espoo, Finland

Abstract. Efficient anonymous credentials are typically constructed by combining proof-friendly signature schemes with compatible zero-knowledge proof systems. Inspired by pairing-based proof-friendly signatures such as Boneh- Boyen (BB) and Boneh-Boyen-Shacham (BBS), we propose a wide family of lattice-based proof-friendly signatures based on variants of the vanishing short integer solution (vSIS) assumption [Cini-Lai-Malavolta, Crypto'23]. In particular, we obtain natural lattice-based adaptions of BB and BBS which, similar to their pairing-based counterparts, admit nice algebraic properties.

[Bootle-Lyubashevsky-Nguyen-Sorniotti, Crypto'23] (BLNS) recently proposed a framework for constructing lattice-based proof-friendly signatures and anonymous credentials, based on another new lattice assumption called ISIS_f parametrised by a fixed function f, with focus on f being the binary decomposition. We introduce a generalised ISIS_f framework, called $\mathsf{GenISIS}_f$, with a keyed and probabilistic function f. For example, picking $f_b(\mu) = 1/(b-\mu)$ with key b for short ring element μ leads to algebraic and thus proof-friendly signatures. To better gauge the robustness and proof-friendliness of $(\mathsf{Gen})\mathsf{ISIS}_f$, we consider what happens when the inputs to f are chosen selectively (or even adaptively) by the adversary, and the behaviour under relaxed norm checks. While bit decomposition quickly becomes insecure, our proposed function families seem robust.

Keywords: Lattice cryptography · Proof-friendly signatures · BBS signature · Vanishing SIS · ISIS_f assumption

1 Introduction

Constructing secure and concretely efficient lattice-based signature schemes is by now a well solved problem. Indeed, schemes following both of the main construction paradigms, Hash-and-Sign [28] and Fiat-Shamir-with-abort (FSwA) [38], have been standardised [39,46] with signature size in single-digit kilobytes and with security connected to the hardness of worst-case lattice problems[1]

---

[1] We say connected because parameters chosen for the schemes differ from those which admit worst-case to average-case reductions.

© International Association for Cryptologic Research 2025
T. Jager and J. Pan (Eds.): PKC 2025, LNCS 15674, pp. 452–486, 2025.
https://doi.org/10.1007/978-3-031-91820-9_15

in the random oracle model. However, the verification relations of most efficient schemes in either paradigm, including standardised ones, inherently require evaluating a hash function on the signed message and additionally on part of the signature in the case of FSwA. Since this hash function needs to be modelled as a random oracle for security proofs to go through, it is typically instantiated with a *non-algebraic* (hence not proof-friendly) hash function. While signatures based on non-algebraic hashes suffice for standalone uses, they may not be well suited as building blocks for efficient constructions of privacy-preserving authentication primitives, such as anonymous credentials, blind signatures and group signatures.

Constructing efficient privacy-preserving authentication primitives is of high practical interest, e.g. in the context of the European Digital Identity framework. Concretely efficient constructions typically require a user to prove knowledge of a message-signature pair which satisfies the verification relation of a signature scheme, in zero-knowledge. For example, the message could be the secret attributes of the user, and the signature could be issued by an authority who asserts that the attributes are genuine. For such a proof to be computed efficiently, a common approach is to instantiate the constructions with "proof-friendly" signatures and zero-knowledge proofs (ZKP), such that the verification relations of the signatures are "natively" supported by the proof system.[2]

Lattice-Based Proof-Friendly Signatures. In the context of lattice-based signatures, we regard a signature scheme as *proof-friendly* if 1) it natively supports signing committed messages (via a hiding and binding commitment), and 2) its verification relation can be expressed as the bounded-norm satisfiability of a system of low-degree polynomial equations. Combined with efficient lattice-based ZKPs for proving well-formedness of commitments and bounded-norm relations (e.g. [41]), a signature scheme with the above properties can be efficiently turned into constructions of privacy-preserving authentication primitives, as demonstrated in [18]. In this area, two competing approaches represent the state of the art:

1. Jeudy, Roux-Langlois and Sanders [33], building upon [36], considered signature schemes of the following form: A signature of a short message vector $\mathbf{m}$ is a tuple $(x, \mathbf{s}, \mathbf{r})$, where x is an invertible element, and $\mathbf{s}, \mathbf{r}$ are short vectors satisfying

$$[\mathbf{A}|\mathbf{B} + x\mathbf{G}] \cdot \mathbf{s} = \mathbf{v} + \mathbf{C}[\begin{smallmatrix} \mathbf{m} \\ \mathbf{r} \end{smallmatrix}] \bmod q,$$

where $\mathbf{A}, \mathbf{B}, \mathbf{C}$ are public random matrices, $\mathbf{v}$ is a public random vector, and $\mathbf{G}$ is the so-called gadget matrix [43]. This type of signatures relies on the gadget lattice trapdoor machinery [43], which tends to be concretely less efficient than GPV trapdoors [28]. Indeed, [33] reported signature sizes in the hundreds of kilobytes.

---

[2] Such a combination of signatures and ZKPs is sometimes called "signatures with efficient protocols" [21]. In the pairing-based setting, a typical choice is to combine the BBS signatures [16] with the Groth-Sahai proof system [30].

2. Bootle, Lyubashevsky, Nguyen and Sorniotti [18] considered signature schemes of the following form: A signature of a short message vector $\mathbf{m}$ is a tuple $(x, \mathbf{s}, \mathbf{r})$, where x is chosen uniformly at random from an appropriate domain, and $\mathbf{s}$, $\mathbf{r}$ are short vectors satisfying

$$\mathbf{A} \cdot \mathbf{s} = f(x) + \mathbf{C}[\begin{smallmatrix} \mathbf{m} \\ \mathbf{r} \end{smallmatrix}] \bmod q,$$

where $\mathbf{A}, \mathbf{C}$ are public random matrices and f is a function. This signature scheme can be instantiated efficiently, with [18] reporting signature sizes as low as dozens of kilobytes. However, the security of such scheme is based on a new lattice assumption, called ISIS_f, introduced in the same work, whose hardness crucially depends on the choice of f. Indeed, it is very easy to come up with (linear) functions f for which the assumption and the scheme are completely broken. The authors advocated picking f to be the binary decomposition function, but were light on the evidence supporting the hardness of ISIS_f for this f. In Sect. 5.4, we illustrate that this choice of f is not very robust. Security breaks down under the (relatively benign) relaxation to one selective f-query and norm relaxation by a factor of $\sqrt{2}$.

Translating BB(S) Signatures. In view of the scarcity of lattice-based proof-friendly signatures, a natural strategy is to translate proof-friendly pairing-based signatures to the lattice setting, for example, using the general translation strategy proposed in [3]. Signature schemes which utilise only generic pairing group operations are abundant. Of particular importance are the related signature schemes of Boneh and Boyen (BB) [15], whose signature consists of a single group element, and Boneh, Boyen and Shacham (BBS) [8,16,50], which allows to sign messages committed via Pedersen's commitment. (More discussion in Sect. 1.2.) Below, we outline a translation attempt of the simpler BB signatures and highlight the difficulty behind.

To recall, using implicit notation for group elements, a public key in the BB signature scheme is a tuple of group elements $([1], [b]) \in \mathbb{G}^2$, the secret key is $b \in \mathbb{Z}_q$, and a signature of $\mu \in \mathbb{Z}_q \setminus \{b\}$ is $[u] = [1/(b - \mu)]$. Signature verification simply checks if $([b] - [1] \cdot \mu) \cdot [u] \overset{?}{=} [1]$, where $\cdot$ denotes the pairing operation.

Adopting the translation strategy of [3], a natural lattice-analogue of BB signatures would be as follows: The public key consists of a random matrix $\mathbf{A}$ and a random vector $\mathbf{b}$, the secret key is a trapdoor $\mathsf{td}_{\mathbf{A}}$, and a signature of μ is a short vector $\mathbf{s}$ satisfying $\mathbf{As} = \mathbf{1}_n \oslash (\mathbf{b} - \mathbf{1}_n \cdot \mu) \bmod q$, where $\oslash$ denotes component-wise division. Equivalently, the verification equation is $(\mathbf{As}) \odot (\mathbf{b} - \mathbf{1}_n \cdot \mu) \overset{?}{=} \mathbf{1}_n \bmod q$, where $\odot$ denotes the component-wise product, which apparently shares structural similarities with that of the BB signatures.

Despite the above natural translation of the BB signature scheme, its original security proof, based on the Q-strong Diffie-Hellman assumption (Q-SDH), unfortunately fails to translate to the lattice setting. In brief, a core argument in the security proof of BB signatures relies on constructing a polynomial

$$f(\tilde{b}) := \prod_{i=1}^{Q} (\tilde{b} - \mu_i)$$

where $\mu_1, \ldots, \mu_Q$ are selective signing oracle queries, and using properties of the quotients $f(\tilde{b})/(\tilde{b} - \mu)$ for $\mu \in \{\mu_1, \ldots, \mu_Q, \mu^*\}$, where μ^* is the target message of a forgery, to answer signing oracle queries and extract a Q-SDH solution. A major difficulty in carrying this argument over to the lattice setting, among others, lies in the inability to control the norm of the coefficients of both the quotient and remainder of $f(\tilde{b})/(\tilde{b} - \mu)$. This suggests that, rather than proving security of the lattice-BB signatures based on a lattice-analogue of Q-SDH, an alternative strategy is needed.

1.1   Our Contributions

In this work, we present a wide family of lattice-based proof-friendly signatures, including those obtained by translating the pairing-based BB and BBS signatures. We prove security of these signature schemes under new but natural extensions of existing lattice-based assumption, specifically, the (strong) hinted variants of the vanishing short integer solution (vSIS) assumption [24] family, which can also be seen as variants of the kRISIS assumption [3] family with slightly more flexible adversaries. Our results are summarised in Fig. 1.

(Strong) Hinted vSIS Assumptions, Plausibility Criteria, Reduction. We propose the hinted vSIS assumption and its strong variant in Sect. 3. The original vSIS assumption, introduced by [24] and parametrised by a set of rational functions $\mathcal{F}$, asserts hardness of the following task:

> Given a random matrix $\mathbf{A}$, find a short linear combination of $(f(\mathbf{A}))_{f \in \mathcal{F}}$ vanishing to $\mathbf{0}$ modulo q.

The hinted vSIS assumption, further parametrised by two (possibly intersecting) sets of rational functions $\mathcal{G}, \mathcal{H}$, asserts hardness of the following task:

> Pick a Q-subset $\mathcal{Q} = (h_1, \ldots, h_Q)$ of $\mathcal{H}$ and some g^* in $\mathcal{G} \setminus \mathcal{Q}$, receive a random matrix $\mathbf{A}$ and short linear combinations of $(f(\mathbf{A}))_{f \in \mathcal{F}}$ which evaluate to $h_i(\mathbf{A})$ modulo q for each $i \in [Q]$, and find a short linear combination of $(f(\mathbf{A}))_{f \in \mathcal{F}}$ which evaluates to $g^*(\mathbf{A})$ modulo q.

The strong variant, which is strong in the same sense as in Q-SDH, asks to perform the above task with the flexibility that g^* can be picked after seeing $\mathbf{A}$.

We suggest general criteria for the hinted vSIS assumptions[3] to be plausible. Further, under the Evasive SIS assumption envisioned by [51] (but which was not formalised nor used), we show that the (non-strong) hinted vSIS assumption is implied by the (plain) vSIS assumption for certain parameter choices (Theorem 2). Similar to the gaps between strong and non-strong assumptions in the group setting, e.g. (strong) Diffie-Hellman and (strong) RSA, formal reductions from non-strong to strong hinted vSIS are out of reach except in trivial cases.

---

[3] Apply also to the (plain) vSIS and kRISIS assumptions upon appropriate adaption.

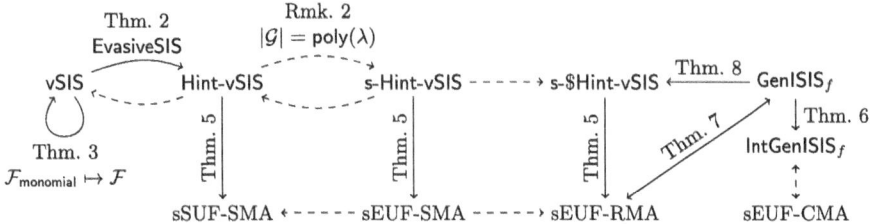

Fig. 1. Overview of results. An arrow from A to B means "Assumption/Security A implies Assumption/Security B". Dashed arrows denote trivial reductions.

Lattice-Based Adaption of the BB(S) Signatures. We construct a family of lattice-based signatures in Sect. 4, capturing the lattice-BB signatures sketched above as a special case. In brief, suppose $\mathcal{H} = \{h_{\mu,\chi}\}_{\mu,\chi}$ is a set of rational functions indexed by messages μ and signing randomness χ. For a public key $(\mathbf{A}, \mathbf{b})$, a signature is simply a tuple $(\chi, \mathbf{s})$, where $\mathbf{s}$ is a short vector satisfying $\mathbf{A}\mathbf{s} = h_{\mu,\chi}(\mathbf{b}^{\mathsf{T}}) \bmod q$. Assuming strong hinted vSIS holds for $\mathcal{G}$, then the signature scheme has strong selective-query security (Theorem 5). By instantiating $\mathcal{G}$ appropriately, we obtain natural lattice-analogues of the BB and the BBS signature schemes, elaborated in Sect. 4.2.

Generalised ISIS$_f$. We generalise the ISIS$_f$ assumption of [18] to allow the function f inputting additional randomness, which we call the GenISIS$_f$ assumption, presented in Sect. 5. Analogous to ISIS$_f$ of [18], the GenISIS$_f$ assumption can be generically lifted to an interactive GenISIS$_f$ assumption without additional overhead (Theorem 6). Applying the transformation to our strongly selective-query-secure signature scheme yields a fully strongly secure one. Moreover, we show that the GenISIS$_f$ assumption implies a weakened version of the strong hinted vSIS assumption, where the set of hints $\mathcal{Q}$ is sampled uniformly randomly.

1.2 Related Work

The BBS signature scheme was implicit in their group signature construction [16] and can be seen as an extension of another signature scheme by Boneh and Boyen (BB) [15]. The BBS scheme was later explicitly cast as a standalone signature scheme [22]. The BBS+ signature scheme [8] is a slightly modified and provably secure version of BBS, under the q-strong Diffie Hellman (q-SDH) assumption. For almost two decades since its introduction, the BBS+ signature scheme is a de facto standard building block for pairing-based anonymous credentials. Only until recently [50] it is shown that the original BBS signature scheme is also provably secure under the same assumption.

The combination of (lattice-based) proof-friendly signatures with a tailored zero-knowledge proof system is a general template for privacy-preserving authentication primitives (see e.g. [23]). Anonymous credentials tend to be the hardest to construct, as typically both the signature and parts of the signed message should remain hidden when the credential is shown. Thus, efficient proof-friendly signatures [1, 18, 26, 43] along with suitable proof systems [19, 41, 53] had to be devised first, and still much optimisation was (and is) required [14, 18, 33, 36].

For group and blind signatures, using a random oracle to hash the message provides some leverage. Indeed, in the lattice setting, we have seen earlier and steady development with group signatures [12, 20, 29, 35, 37, 42, 45]. The situation with blind signatures is less fortunate, where all prior works based on the blind Schnorr-type template [5–7, 47] have been found gaps in their proofs [31], and later broken by the so-called ROS attacks [10, 11, 34]. Schemes that remain standing [2, 13, 40, 44] follow Fischlin's two-move template [27]. From the efficiency perspective, the most competitive blind signatures to-date are based on either the ISIS_f assumption [18] which our work extends, the one-more-ISIS assumption [2], or heuristic assumptions [13], namely succinct arguments proving about random oracles, which is concretely expensive but achieves small signature size.

2 Preliminaries

Let $\lambda \in \mathbb{N}$ denote the security parameter. For two (ensembles of) distributions $\mathcal{D}_0, \mathcal{D}_1$, we write $\mathcal{D}_0 \approx_c \mathcal{D}_1$ if they are computationally indistinguishable. We write poly and negl for the sets of functions polynomial and negligible in λ, respectively. We write matrices and vectors in bold upper and lower case letters, e.g. $\mathbf{A}$ and $\mathbf{x}$, respectively. For matrices and vectors of compatible dimensions, we write $\odot$ and $\oslash$ for the Hadamard (i.e. component-wise) product and division, respectively. We write $\mathbf{1}_n$ for the all-1 vector of dimension n over whichever ring within context. For real vectors $\mathbf{x} \in \mathbb{R}^n$, we write $\|\mathbf{x}\| := \|\mathbf{x}\|_2$ for its Euclidean norm. If S is a finite set, we write $\mathcal{U}(S)$ for the uniform distribution over S and $x \leftarrow_\$ S$ for the sampling of a uniformly random element x from S.

For a sequence of k formal variables $\tilde{\mathbf{x}}$ and a ring $\mathcal{X}$, we write $\mathcal{X}[\tilde{\mathbf{x}}^\mathsf{T}]$ and $\mathcal{X}(\tilde{\mathbf{x}}^\mathsf{T}) = \{f/g : f, g \in \mathcal{X}[\tilde{\mathbf{x}}^\mathsf{T}]\}$ for the set of k-variate polynomial and rational functions over $\mathcal{X}$ respectively.[4] We use $\tilde{}$ to denote formal variables using the same letter as the intended input. For example, we write $f(\tilde{x})$ for a function f with variable $\tilde{x}$, which is intended to be evaluated at a point x. We will use the following shorthand for vectors consisting of evaluations of one or multiple functions at multiple points. For $f : \mathcal{X}^k \to \mathcal{X}$ a k-variate function, $\mathcal{F} = (f_j : \mathcal{X}^k \to \mathcal{X})_{j=1}^m$ a sequence of k-variate functions, and $\mathbf{A} \in \mathcal{X}^{n \times k}$ a $\mathcal{X}$-matrix with the i-th row given by $\mathbf{a}_i^\mathsf{T} \in \mathcal{X}^k$, we write

$$f(\mathbf{A}) := \left(f(\mathbf{a}_1^\mathsf{T}) \ \ldots \ f(\mathbf{a}_n^\mathsf{T}) \right)^\mathsf{T} \in \mathcal{X}^n,$$

$$\mathcal{F}(\mathbf{A}) := \left(f_1(\mathbf{A}) \ \ldots \ f_m(\mathbf{A}) \right) = \begin{pmatrix} f_1(\mathbf{a}_1^\mathsf{T}) & \ldots & f_m(\mathbf{a}_1^\mathsf{T}) \\ \vdots & \ddots & \vdots \\ f_1(\mathbf{a}_n^\mathsf{T}) & \ldots & f_m(\mathbf{a}_n^\mathsf{T}) \end{pmatrix} \in \mathcal{X}^{n \times m}.$$

---

[4] The transposes in $\mathcal{X}[\tilde{\mathbf{x}}^\mathsf{T}]$ and $\mathcal{X}(\tilde{\mathbf{x}}^\mathsf{T})$ matter due to the notation of evaluating functions at matrices defined below.

2.1   Algebraic Number Theory

We state our results over the cyclotomic field $\mathbb{Q}(\zeta)$, where $\zeta = \zeta_{\mathfrak{f}}$, with conductor $\mathfrak{f}$ and degree $\varphi := \varphi(\mathfrak{f})$, and its ring of integers $\mathcal{R} = \mathbb{Z}[\zeta]$. All results can be specialised to the integer setting, i.e. $\mathcal{R} = \mathbb{Z}$. For $q \in \mathbb{N}$, we write $\mathcal{R}_q := \mathcal{R}/q\mathcal{R}$. Let $\sigma = (\sigma_i)_{i \in \mathbb{Z}_{\mathfrak{f}}^{\times}} : \mathbb{Q}(\zeta) \to \mathbb{C}^{\varphi}$ denote the canonical embedding of $\mathbb{Q}(\zeta)$, with its definition naturally extended to $\mathbb{Q}(\zeta)$-vectors by concatenation. We norm a $\mathbb{Q}(\zeta)$-vector $\mathbf{x}$ geometrically by the ℓ_p-norm of its canonical embedding, i.e. $\|\mathbf{x}\|_p := \|\sigma(\mathbf{x})\|_p$. For any $a, b \in \mathbb{Q}(\zeta)$, it holds that $\|a \cdot b\|_p \leq \|a\|_p \cdot \|b\|_\infty$. We omit the subscript p when $p = 2$.

Any $\mathcal{R}$-module $\mathcal{M} \subseteq \mathcal{R}^m$ can be viewed as a lattice via $\sigma(\mathcal{M})$. In particular, for $\mathbf{A} \in \mathcal{R}_q^{n \times m}$ and $\mathbf{v} \in \mathcal{R}_q^n$, we consider the following lattice (cosets):

$$\Lambda_q^{\perp}(\mathbf{A}) := \{\mathbf{x} \in \mathcal{R}^m : \mathbf{A}\mathbf{x} = \mathbf{0} \bmod q\}, \quad \Lambda_q^{\mathbf{v}}(\mathbf{A}) := \{\mathbf{x} \in \mathcal{R}^m : \mathbf{A}\mathbf{x} = \mathbf{v} \bmod q\}.$$

2.2   Discrete Gaussians, Lattice Trapdoors

The Gaussian function with parameter $s > 0$ is $\rho_s(\mathbf{x}) := \exp(-\pi \|\mathbf{x}\|^2 / s^2)$ for all $\mathbf{x} \in \mathbb{R}^n$. For a discrete set $A \subseteq \mathbb{R}^n$, the discrete Gaussian distribution with parameter s is $\mathcal{D}_{A,s}(\mathbf{x}) := \rho_s(\mathbf{x})/\rho_s(A)$ for any $\mathbf{x} \in A$, where $\rho_s(A) := \sum_{\mathbf{x} \in A} \rho_s(\mathbf{x})$.

Lemma 1 ([9, Lemma 1.5]). *For any lattice $\Lambda \subseteq \mathbb{R}^n$ and $s > 0$, it holds $\Pr[\|\mathcal{D}_{\Lambda,s}\| > s\sqrt{n}] \leq 2^{-n}$.*

We summarise the properties of lattice trapdoors as a "lattice trapdoor scheme".

Definition 1 (Lattice Trapdoors [28]). *Let $\mathcal{R}$ be parametrised by λ. A lattice trapdoor scheme over $\mathcal{R}$ consists of PPT algorithms (TrapGen, SampPre):*

> *$(\mathbf{A}, \mathsf{td}_{\mathbf{A}}) \leftarrow \mathsf{TrapGen}(1^\lambda, 1^n, 1^m, q)$: Sample a matrix $\mathbf{A} \in \mathcal{R}_q^{n \times m}$ together with a trapdoor $\mathsf{td}_{\mathbf{A}}$.*
> *$\mathbf{u} \leftarrow \mathsf{SampPre}(\mathsf{td}_{\mathbf{A}}, \mathbf{v}, s)$: Given the trapdoor $\mathsf{td}_{\mathbf{A}}$, a target image vector $\mathbf{v} \in \mathcal{R}_q^n$ and a Gaussian parameter s, sample a preimage vector $\mathbf{u} \in \mathcal{R}^m$.*

A tuple of parameters $\mathsf{params}_{\mathsf{td}} = (\mathcal{R}, n, m, q, s)$ is said to be admissible if they satisfy the following properties:

1. *It holds that $\{\mathbf{A} : (\mathbf{A}, \mathsf{td}_{\mathbf{A}}) \leftarrow \mathsf{TrapGen}(1^\lambda, 1^n, 1^m, q)\} \approx_c \mathcal{U}(\mathcal{R}_q^{n \times m})$.*
2. *For any $s' \geq s$ and for all but a negl-fraction of $(\mathbf{A}, \mathsf{td}_{\mathbf{A}})$ in the support of $\mathsf{TrapGen}(1^\lambda, 1^n, 1^m, q)$, the following hold:*
   - *For any $\mathbf{v} \in \mathcal{R}_q^n$, it holds that $\mathsf{SampPre}(\mathsf{td}_{\mathbf{A}}, \mathbf{v}, s') \approx_c \mathcal{D}_{\Lambda_q^{\mathbf{v}}(\mathbf{A}), s'}$.*
   - *It holds that $\left\{(\mathbf{u}, \mathbf{v}) \,\middle|\, \begin{matrix} \mathbf{v} \leftarrow_{\$} \mathcal{R}_q^n \\ \mathbf{u} \leftarrow \mathcal{D}_{\Lambda_q^{\mathbf{v}}(\mathbf{A}), s'} \end{matrix} \right\} \approx_c \left\{(\mathbf{u}, \mathbf{v}) \,\middle|\, \begin{matrix} \mathbf{u} \leftarrow_{\$} \mathcal{D}_{\mathcal{R}^m, s'} \\ \mathbf{v} := \mathbf{A}\mathbf{u} \bmod q \end{matrix} \right\}.$*

We refer, for example, to [28,43] for how to instantiate a lattice trapdoor scheme with admissible parameters.

$\mathrm{Pre}_{\mathcal{A}}(1^\lambda)$	$\mathrm{Post}_{\mathcal{B}}(1^\lambda)$
$(\tilde{\mathbf{P}}, \tilde{\mathbf{A}}, \mathsf{aux}) \leftarrow \mathsf{Samp}(1^\lambda)$	$(\tilde{\mathbf{P}}, \tilde{\mathbf{A}}, \mathsf{aux}) \leftarrow \mathsf{Samp}(1^\lambda)$
$\mathbf{B} \leftarrow_\$ \mathcal{R}_q^{n \times m}$	$\mathbf{B} \leftarrow_\$ \mathcal{R}_q^{n \times m}$
	$\mathbf{U} \leftarrow_\$ \mathcal{D}_{\mathcal{R},s}^{m \times m_P}$ conditioned on $\mathbf{BU} = \tilde{\mathbf{P}} \bmod q$
$\mathbf{u}^* \leftarrow \mathcal{A}(\mathbf{B}, \tilde{\mathbf{P}}, \tilde{\mathbf{A}}, \mathsf{aux})$	$\mathbf{u}^* \leftarrow \mathcal{B}(\mathbf{B}, \tilde{\mathbf{P}}, \tilde{\mathbf{A}}, \mathbf{U}, \mathsf{aux})$
$b_0 := ((\mathbf{B}|\tilde{\mathbf{P}}|\tilde{\mathbf{A}})\mathbf{u}^* = \mathbf{0} \bmod q)$	$b_0 := ((\mathbf{B}|\tilde{\mathbf{A}})\mathbf{u}^* = \mathbf{0} \bmod q)$
$b_1 := (0 < \|\mathbf{u}^*\| \leq \beta_1)$	$b_1 := (0 < \|\mathbf{u}^*\| \leq \beta_0)$
return $b_0 \wedge b_1$	**return** $b_0 \wedge b_1$

Fig. 2. Experiments Pre and Post for evasive SIS assumption.

2.3 Lattice Assumptions

The vanishing SIS (vSIS) assumption [24] is parametrised by, among others, a set of rational functions $\mathcal{F}$. It states that, given a random matrix $\mathbf{A}$, it is hard to find a short linear combination of $\{f(\mathbf{A})\}_{f \in \mathcal{F}}$ which vanishes modulo q.

Definition 2 (Vanishing-SIS ([24])). *Let* $\mathsf{params} = (\mathcal{R}, n, k, q, \beta, \mathcal{F})$ *be parametrised by* λ, *where* n, k, q *are positive integers,* $\beta \in \mathbb{R}^+$ *and* $\mathcal{F}$ *is a set of k-variate functions over* $\mathcal{R}$. *The* $\mathsf{vSIS}_{\mathsf{params}}$ *assumption states that, for any PPT adversary* $\mathcal{A}$, *it holds that*

$$\Pr\left[\begin{array}{c} \mathcal{F}(\mathbf{A}) \cdot \mathbf{u}^* = \mathbf{0} \bmod q \\ \wedge\; 0 < \|\mathbf{u}\|^* \leq \beta \end{array} \;\middle|\; \begin{array}{c} \mathbf{A} \leftarrow_\$ \mathcal{R}_q^{n \times k} \\ \mathbf{u}^* \leftarrow \mathcal{A}(\mathbf{A}) \end{array} \right] \leq \mathsf{negl}.$$

In this work, we consider also settings where $|\mathcal{F}|$ could be super-polynomial in λ, as long as $\mathcal{F}$ and the answer $\mathbf{u}^*$ by the adversary admits a succinct description.

The evasive SIS assumption was informally introduced by Wee [51] (in conjunction with the public-coin evasive LWE assumption) and envisioned as a tool for analysing the plausibility of SIS-based hinted lattice assumptions.

Definition 3 (EvasiveSIS). *Let* $\mathsf{params} = (\mathcal{R}, q, n, m, m_P, m_A, s, \beta_0, \beta_1)$ *be parametrised by* λ, *where* $\mathcal{R}$ *is a ring admitting an embedding as a lattice in* $\mathbb{R}^\varphi$ *for some* $\varphi \in \mathbb{N}$, *and* $s, \beta_0, \beta_1 > 0$. *Let* Samp *be a PPT algorithm which, on input* 1^λ, *outputs*

$$\left(\tilde{\mathbf{P}} \in \mathcal{R}_q^{n \times m_P}, \;\; \tilde{\mathbf{A}} \in \mathcal{R}_q^{n \times m_A}, \;\; \mathsf{aux} \in \{0,1\}^* \right)$$

where aux *contains all coin tosses used by* Samp. *The* $\mathsf{EvasiveSIS}_{\mathsf{params}}$ *assumption states that, for any PPT* Samp *and* $\mathcal{B}$ *there exists a PPT* $\mathcal{A}$ *such that*

$$\Pr\left[\mathrm{Pre}_{\mathcal{A}}(1^\lambda) = 1 \right] \geq \Pr\left[\mathrm{Post}_{\mathcal{B}}(1^\lambda) = 1 \right] / \mathsf{poly} - \mathsf{negl},$$

where the experiments Pre *and* Post *are defined in Fig. 2.*

Analogous to the evasive LWE assumption [51], the evasive SIS assumption says that "if SIS is hard for the matrix $(\mathbf{B}, \tilde{\mathbf{P}}, \tilde{\mathbf{A}})$, then SIS is also hard for

$(\mathbf{B}, \tilde{\mathbf{A}})$ even when given short preimages $\mathbf{U}$ of $\tilde{\mathbf{P}}$ w.r.t. $\mathbf{B}$". This stems from the intuition that, there seems no alternative meaningful use of $\mathbf{U}$, other than multiplying which to $\mathbf{B}$ to obtain $\tilde{\mathbf{P}}$ and solve (the potentially easier) SIS problem for $(\mathbf{B}, \tilde{\mathbf{P}}, \tilde{\mathbf{A}})$ jointly. Following [51], Definition 3 is "public-coin" in that we insist Samp to output all its random coins, which avoids obfuscation-based counterexamples.

We note that Definition 3 is heuristically no stronger than the evasive LWE assumption of [51], in the following sense: Suppose there exists a PPT solver $\mathcal{B}$ for Post in Fig. 2, then immediately $\mathcal{B}$ is also a successful distinguisher for the analgous LWE problem – distinguish $\mathbf{s}^{\mathsf{T}}(\mathbf{B}, \tilde{\mathbf{A}}) + \mathbf{e}^{\mathsf{T}} \bmod q$ from random given $\mathbf{U}$. Assuming evasive LWE, there exists a PPT $\mathcal{A}$ distinguishing $\mathbf{s}^{\mathsf{T}}(\mathbf{B}, \tilde{\mathbf{P}}, \tilde{\mathbf{A}}) + \mathbf{e}^{\mathsf{T}} \bmod q$ from random. At this point, under the common heuristic that solving decision-LWE is no easier than solving SIS (which is quantumly true at least for uniformly random matrices [49]), we arrive at a solver for Pre in Fig. 2.

2.4 Signatures

Definition 4 (Signature Scheme) . *A signature scheme for a message space $\mathcal{M}$ is a tuple of PPT algorithms $\Sigma = (\mathsf{Setup}, \mathsf{KGen}, \mathsf{Sign}, \mathsf{Verify})$:*

pp $\leftarrow$ Setup(1^{λ}): *Generate the public parameters* pp.
(pk, sk) $\leftarrow$ KGen(pp): *Generate a public key* pk *and a secret key* sk.
sig $\leftarrow$ Sign(sk, msg): *Sign a message* msg $\in \mathcal{M}$ *with a signature* sig.
$b \leftarrow$ Verify(pk, msg, sig): *Decide if* sig *is a valid signature of* msg *under* pk.

A signature scheme Σ is said to be correct if, for any message msg $\in \mathcal{M}$,

$$\Pr\left[\mathsf{Verify}(\mathsf{pp}, \mathsf{pk}, \mathsf{msg}, \mathsf{sig}) = 1 \;\middle|\; \begin{array}{l} \mathsf{pp} \leftarrow \mathsf{Setup}(1^{\lambda}) \\ (\mathsf{pk}, \mathsf{sk}) \leftarrow \mathsf{KGen}(\mathsf{pp}) \\ \mathsf{sig} \leftarrow \mathsf{Sign}(\mathsf{sk}, \mathsf{msg}) \end{array}\right] \geq 1 - \mathsf{negl}.$$

A signature scheme Σ is said to have strong existential unforgeability under chosen message attack (sEUF-CMA) if, for any PPT $\mathcal{A}$, it holds

$$\mathsf{Adv}_{\Sigma, \mathcal{A}}^{\mathsf{sEUF\text{-}CMA}}(\lambda) := \Pr\left[\mathsf{sEUF\text{-}CMA}_{\Sigma, \mathcal{A}}(1^{\lambda}) = 1\right] \leq \mathsf{negl},$$

where $\mathsf{sEUF\text{-}CMA}_{\Sigma, \mathcal{A}}$ is defined in Fig. 3. It is said to have strong existential unforgeability under selective message attack (sEUF-SMA) and strong selective unforgeability under selective message attack (sSUF-SMA) respectively, if for any $Q \leq \mathsf{poly}$, the above holds for $\mathsf{sEUF\text{-}SMA}_{\Sigma, \mathcal{A}, Q}$ and $\mathsf{sSUF\text{-}SMA}_{\Sigma, \mathcal{A}, Q}$ defined in Fig. 3 respectively. Strong existential unforgeability under random message attack (sEUF-RMA) is similarly defined in Fig. 3.

Remark 1 (Key-dependent message space.) . *We also consider a relaxed definition of signature schemes where the public parameters specify a subspace of the message space. In this case, we say that the signature scheme is correct if for all but a negl-fraction of* pp $\in$ Setup(1^{λ}) *and for any message* msg *in the message*

$$\underline{\text{sEUF-CMA}_{\Sigma,\mathcal{A}}(1^\lambda)}$$

$S := \emptyset; \ \ \mathsf{pp} \leftarrow \mathsf{Setup}(1^\lambda)$

$(\mathsf{pk}, \mathsf{sk}) \leftarrow \mathsf{KGen}(\mathsf{pp})$

$(\mathsf{msg}^*, \mathsf{sig}^*) \leftarrow \mathcal{A}^{\mathsf{SignO}(\cdot)}(\mathsf{pp}, \mathsf{pk})$

$b_0 := \mathsf{Verify}(\mathsf{pp}, \mathsf{pk}, \mathsf{msg}^*, \mathsf{sig}^*)$

$b_1 := ((\mathsf{msg}^*, \mathsf{sig}^*) \notin S)$

return $b_0 \wedge b_1$

$$\underline{\mathsf{SignO}(\mathsf{msg})}$$

$\mathsf{sig} \leftarrow \mathsf{Sign}(\mathsf{pp}, \mathsf{sk}, \mathsf{msg})$

$S := S \cup \{(\mathsf{msg}, \mathsf{sig})\}$

return sig

| $\underline{\text{sEUF-SMA}_{\Sigma,\mathcal{A},Q}(1^\lambda)}$ | $\underline{\text{sSUF-SMA}_{\Sigma,\mathcal{A},Q}(1^\lambda)}$ |

$(\mathsf{msg}_1, \dots, \mathsf{msg}_Q, \mathsf{msg}^*) \leftarrow \mathcal{A}(1^\lambda)$

$\mathsf{pp} \leftarrow \mathsf{Setup}(1^\lambda)$

$(\mathsf{pk}, \mathsf{sk}) \leftarrow \mathsf{KGen}(\mathsf{pp})$

$\mathsf{sig}_i := \mathsf{Sign}(\mathsf{pp}, \mathsf{sk}, \mathsf{msg}_i) \ \ \forall i \in [Q]$

$(\boxed{\mathsf{msg}^*}, \mathsf{sig}^*) \leftarrow \mathcal{A}(\mathsf{pp}, \mathsf{pk}, \mathsf{sig}_1, \dots, \mathsf{sig}_Q)$

$b_0 := \mathsf{Verify}(\mathsf{pp}, \mathsf{pk}, \mathsf{msg}^*, \mathsf{sig}^*)$

$b_1 := ((\mathsf{msg}^*, \mathsf{sig}^*) \notin \{(\mathsf{msg}_i, \mathsf{sig}_i)_{i=1}^Q\})$

return $b_0 \wedge b_1$

Fig. 3. Security experiments for sEUF-CMA, sEUF-SMA and sSUF-SMA. For sEUF-RMA, modify the sEUF-SMA experiment to have $\mathsf{msg}_1, \dots, \mathsf{msg}_Q \leftarrow_\$ \mathcal{M}$.

subspace defined by pp, it holds that $\mathsf{Verify}(\mathsf{pp}, \mathsf{pk}, \mathsf{msg}, \mathsf{Sign}(\mathsf{pp}, \mathsf{sk}, \mathsf{msg})) = 1$ except with negl probability. Corresponding, we modify the security experiments so that the Sign algorithm aborts whenever it is called on messages outside the message subspace defined by pp.

3   (Strong) Hinted vSIS Assumptions

Aiming to construct algebraic lattice signatures akin to pairing-based ones based on assumptions such as strong Diffie Hellman (SDH), we introduce hinted variants of the vanishing short integer solution (vSIS) assumption.

We define in Sect. 3.1 general families of two vSIS assumption variants – hinted, and strong hinted – which extend the existing vSIS assumption. The strong hinted variant is strong in the same sense as in the SDH (and others such as strong RSA) assumption – the adversary is allowed to choose its "target" freely. More discussions on the relations to existing assumptions follow.

Since the hinted vSIS assumptions have numerous parameters, we discuss in Sect. 3.2 what we believe to be plausible choices of them. To install confidence in the new assumptions, we show in Sect. 3.3 that some of them admit reductions from the plain vSIS assumption of [24].

3.1   Assumptions Statements

We define extended variants of the vSIS assumption. These variants aim to capture natural lattice-analogues of group-based assumptions such as the strong Diffie-Hellman (SDH) assumption.

Definition 5 ((Strong) Hinted vSIS Assumptions) . *Let*

$$\mathsf{params} = (\mathcal{R}, n, k, q, Q, \beta, s, \mathcal{F}, \mathcal{G}, \mathcal{H}, \mathcal{P})$$

be parametrised by λ, *where* n, k, q *are positive integers,* Q *is a non-negative integer,* $\beta, s \in \mathbb{R}^+$, $\mathcal{F}, \mathcal{G}, \mathcal{H}$ *are* k-*variate rational functions over* $\mathcal{R}_q$ *such that* $Q \leq |\mathcal{H}|$, *and* $\mathcal{P}$ *is a predicate over sets of* k-*variate rational functions. We define the following hinted variants of the vSIS assumption.*

Hinted. *The* $\mathsf{Hint\text{-}vSIS}_{\mathsf{params}}$ *assumption states that, for any PPT stateful adversary* $\mathcal{A}$, *it holds that*

$$\Pr\left[\begin{array}{l} \mathcal{F}(\mathbf{A}) \cdot \mathbf{u}^* = g^*(\mathbf{A}) \bmod q \\ \wedge\ 0 < \|\mathbf{u}^*\| \leq \beta \\ \wedge\ \mathcal{Q} \subseteq_Q \mathcal{H} \\ \wedge\ g^* \in \mathcal{G} \setminus \mathcal{Q} \\ \wedge\ \mathcal{P}(\mathcal{F} \cup \mathcal{Q} \cup (\{g^*\} \setminus \{0\})) = 1 \end{array} \middle|\ \begin{array}{l} (\mathcal{Q}, g^*) \leftarrow \mathcal{A}(1^\lambda) \\ \mathbf{A} \leftarrow_\$ \mathcal{R}_q^{n \times k} \\ \mathbf{V} := \mathcal{Q}(\mathbf{A}) \bmod q \\ \mathbf{u}_i \leftarrow_\$ \mathcal{D}_{\Lambda_q^{\mathbf{v}_i}(\mathcal{F}(\mathbf{A})), s}\ \ \forall i \in [Q] \\ \mathbf{u}^* \leftarrow \mathcal{A}(\mathbf{A}, \mathbf{u}_1, \ldots, \mathbf{u}_Q) \end{array}\right] \leq \mathsf{negl}.$$

Strong Hinted. *The* $\mathsf{s\text{-}Hint\text{-}vSIS}_{\mathsf{params}}$ *assumption states that, for any PPT stateful adversary* $\mathcal{A}$,

$$\Pr\left[\begin{array}{l} \mathcal{F}(\mathbf{A}) \cdot \mathbf{u}^* = g^*(\mathbf{A}) \bmod q \\ \wedge\ 0 < \|\mathbf{u}^*\| \leq \beta \\ \wedge\ \mathcal{Q} \subseteq_Q \mathcal{H} \\ \wedge\ g^* \in \mathcal{G} \setminus \mathcal{Q} \\ \wedge\ \mathcal{P}(\mathcal{F} \cup \mathcal{Q} \cup (\{g^*\} \setminus \{0\})) = 1 \end{array} \middle|\ \begin{array}{l} \mathcal{Q} \leftarrow \mathcal{A}(1^\lambda) \\ \mathbf{A} \leftarrow_\$ \mathcal{R}_q^{n \times k} \\ \mathbf{V} := \mathcal{Q}(\mathbf{A}) \bmod q \\ \mathbf{u}_i \leftarrow_\$ \mathcal{D}_{\Lambda_q^{\mathbf{v}_i}(\mathcal{F}(\mathbf{A})), s}\ \ \forall i \in [Q] \\ (g^*, \mathbf{u}^*) \leftarrow \mathcal{A}(\mathbf{A}, \mathbf{u}_1, \ldots, \mathbf{u}_Q) \end{array}\right] \leq \mathsf{negl}.$$

Strong Random-Hinted. *The* $\mathsf{s\text{-}\$Hint\text{-}vSIS}_{\mathsf{params}}$ *assumption is almost identical to the* $\mathsf{s\text{-}Hint\text{-}vSIS}_{\mathsf{params}}$ *assumption, except that* $\mathcal{Q}$ *is sampled as a uniformly random* Q-*subset of* $\mathcal{H}$, *not chosen by* $\mathcal{A}$.

Compared to the plain vSIS assumption (Definition 5, [24]), the (strong) hinted vSIS assumption is further parametrised by an integer Q, two sets of rational functions $\mathcal{G}, \mathcal{H}$, and a predicate $\mathcal{P}$. The sets $\mathcal{G}$ and $\mathcal{H}$ are where the adversary could choose the target g^* and the Q queries $\mathcal{Q}$ respectively. The adversary is considered successful if $g^* \notin \mathcal{Q}$ i.e. not queried and $\mathcal{F} \cup \mathcal{Q} \cup \{g^*\}$ (or $\mathcal{F} \cup \mathcal{Q}$ if g^* is the all zero function) satisfies the predicate $\mathcal{P}$. The non-strong and strong variants differ by whether g^* is chosen before or after seeing $\mathbf{A}$.

Analogous to the discussion below Definition 2, we allow the sets $\mathcal{F}, \mathcal{G}, \mathcal{H}$ of rational functions to have cardinalities super-polynomial in λ, as long as they and the answer $\mathbf{u}^*$ output by $\mathcal{A}$ admit succinct representations. We note, however, that the number Q of queries $\mathcal{Q}$ output by $\mathcal{A}$ must be polynomial in λ, for otherwise $\mathcal{A}$ could not input all preimages $\mathbf{u}_1, \ldots, \mathbf{u}_Q$ while still being PPT.

Remark 2 (Hint-vSIS ⇒ *s-Hint-vSIS).* If $|\mathcal{G}| \leq$ poly, then the Hint-vSIS$_{\text{params}}$ assumption implies the s-Hint-vSIS$_{\text{params}}$ assumption (for the same params), where a trivial reduction simply guesses g^* upfront.

Beyond obvious connections to the vSIS assumption, we discuss further connections of Definition 5 to other existing assumptions.

Relation to SDH. The vSIS assumption variants are defined in a way intended to translate certain group-based assumptions such as SDH. Recall that the $(Q-1)$-SDH problem asks to find, given $[1], [b], \ldots, [b^{Q-1}]$, a tuple $(\mu, [1/(b+\mu)])$. To translate this to a strong hinted vSIS problem, let $\tilde{\mathbf{x}}^{\mathsf{T}} = (\tilde{\mathbf{a}}^{\mathsf{T}}, \tilde{b})$ denote a sequence of formal variables, $\gamma > 0$ and $B_\gamma = \{\mu \in \mathcal{R} : \|\mu\| \leq \gamma\}$. For suitably selected parameters, in particular

$$\mathcal{F}(\tilde{\mathbf{x}}^{\mathsf{T}}) = \tilde{\mathbf{a}}^{\mathsf{T}}, \quad \mathcal{H} = \left\{1, \tilde{b}, \ldots, \tilde{b}^{Q-1}\right\}, \quad \mathcal{G} = \left\{1/(\tilde{b} + \mu) : \mu \in B_\gamma\right\},$$

the s-Hint-vSIS assumption can be seen as a natural lattice-analogue of the $(Q-1)$-SDH assumption.

Relation to kRISIS. The kRISIS assumption family is introduced in [3], stronger than the (plain) vSIS assumption family, but weaker than the BASIS assumption family introduced by [52].[5] We observe that certain members of the (strong) hinted vSIS family are in between (plain) vSIS (obviously) and kRISIS. More precisely, for suitably selected parameters, in particular $\mathcal{H} \cap \mathcal{G} = \emptyset$, $|\mathcal{H}| = Q$ (so $\mathcal{Q} = \mathcal{H}$) and $|\mathcal{G}| = 1$ (so there is only one choice for g^*), the s-Hint-vSIS assumption is essentially a kRISIS assumption.[6] Note also that, since $|\mathcal{G}| = 1$, the strong and non-strong variants are equivalent.

3.2 Criteria for Plausible vSIS Assumptions

In Definition 5, the vSIS assumption variants are parametrised by a predicate $\mathcal{P}$ which dictates which combinations of functions are admissible. We discuss criteria for $\mathcal{P}$ for the vSIS assumption variants to plausibly hold.

One uninteresting way to violate a vSIS assumption is to consider ill-formed sets of functions $\mathcal{F}, \mathcal{G}$. For example, if $\mathcal{F}$ contains the all-zero function, then it is trivial to find short $\mathbf{u}^*$ satisfying $\mathcal{F}(\mathbf{A}) \cdot \mathbf{u}^* = \mathbf{0} \bmod q$. Similarly, if $\mathcal{F} \cap \mathcal{G}$ is not empty and contains some g^*, then it is trivial to find short $\mathbf{u}^*$ satisfying $\mathcal{F}(\mathbf{A}) \cdot \mathbf{u}^* = g^*(\mathbf{A}) \bmod q$. A more sophisticated example is where $\mathcal{F} \supseteq \{1, \tilde{x}^q\}$

---

[5] By an assumption family A being stronger than another family B, we mean that for any member in family B there exists a member in family A which implies the former.

[6] In the kRISIS assumption definition stated in [3], the images for which preimages are given to an adversary take the form $\mathbf{t} \cdot h_i(\mathbf{v}^{\mathsf{T}})$. We believe this is an oversight, since it would mean that solving kRISIS by solving the vSIS instance $(h_i(\mathbf{v}^{\mathsf{T}}))_{i=1}^{Q}$ is significantly easier (due to lower lattice dimension) than solving SIS w.r.t. $\mathbf{A}$.

and $\mathcal{R}_q$ fully splits into a product of fields. In this case, we have $1 - x^q = 0 \bmod q$ for any $x \in \mathcal{R}_q$. To rule out this type of counterexamples which exploits linear dependency between the chosen functions, we suggest to restrict $\mathcal{P}$ so that it only accepts tuples satisfying a "strong linear independence" property defined below.

Definition 6 (Strong Linear Independence) . *Let $\mathcal{F} \subseteq \mathcal{R}_q(\tilde{\mathbf{x}}^{\mathsf{T}})$ be a set of k-variate rational functions where $1 \in \mathcal{R}_q$-span$(\mathcal{F})$. For $\epsilon > 0$, we say that $\mathcal{F}$ is ϵ-strong linear independent if, for any not-all-zero coefficients $(c_f)_{f \in \mathcal{F}}$ over $\mathcal{R}_q$,*

$$Pr\left[\sum\nolimits_{f \in \mathcal{F}} c_f \cdot f(\mathbf{a}^{\mathsf{T}}) = 0 \bmod q \,\middle|\, \mathbf{a} \leftarrow_\$ \mathcal{R}_q^k\right] \le \epsilon.$$

If $1 \notin \mathcal{R}_q$-span$(\mathcal{F})$, then we say $\mathcal{F}$ is ϵ-strong linear independent if $\mathcal{F} \cup \{1\}$ is.

Remark 3. In case the denominator of f vanishes at $\mathbf{a}$, we let $f(\mathbf{a}) = \mathsf{undef}$. We take "$a \times \mathsf{undef} = a + \mathsf{undef} = \mathsf{undef}$" for any value a, meaning that if one of the terms is undefined then the whole sum is (which does not equal zero).

Remark 4 (Implicit guaranteed min-entropy). . In Definition 6, we distinguish between $1 \in \mathcal{R}_q$-span$(\mathcal{F})$ or $1 \notin \mathcal{R}_q$-span$(\mathcal{F})$ for technical reasons: We actually want that for any fixed $d \in \mathcal{R}_q$ and $(c_f)_{f \in \mathcal{F}}$, we have $\Pr\left[\sum_{f \in \mathcal{F}} c_f \cdot f(\mathbf{a}^{\mathsf{T}}) = d \bmod q\right] \le \epsilon$. That is, we want that the min-entropy (over $\mathbf{a}$) is at least $\log_2(\epsilon)$. However, if $1 \in \mathcal{R}_q$-span$(\mathcal{F})$, this is trivially false (for $\epsilon < 1$), e.g. if $1 \in \mathcal{F}$ then simply set $c_1 = d$ and all other $c_f = 0$. In fact, if $1 \in \mathcal{R}_q$-span$(\mathcal{F})$, then the min-entropy guarantee is already implied (by an analogous reasoning). Hence, if $1 \notin \mathcal{R}_q$-span$(\mathcal{F})$, we consider $\mathcal{F} \cup \{1\}$ (instead of introducing d explicitly).

The strong linear independence property could be unwieldy to work with. We show that for certain sets of rational functions, strong linear independence is equivalent to linear independence.

Theorem 1. *Let $q \in \mathbb{N}$ prime and $\mathcal{R}_q \cong \mathbb{F}^e$ split into e fields.[7] Let $\mathcal{F} \subseteq \mathcal{R}_q(\tilde{\mathbf{x}}^{\mathsf{T}})$ be a set of k-variate rational functions. Suppose $m \in \mathcal{R}_q[\tilde{\mathbf{x}}]$ is such that, for each rational function in $\mathcal{F}$ represented as $f/g \in \mathcal{F}$ where $f, g \in \mathcal{R}_q[\tilde{\mathbf{x}}]$, it holds that $m \in \langle g \rangle_{\mathcal{R}_q[\tilde{\mathbf{x}}]}$, i.e. m is a common multiple of $(g)_{f/g \in \mathcal{F}}$. Let $d := \deg(m) + \max_{f/g \in \mathcal{F}} \deg(f)$ and $\epsilon := d/|\mathbb{F}|$. If $\mathcal{F}$ is linearly independent, then it is ϵ-strong linearly independent.*

The proof is deferred to the full version.

Next, we show that the property of being strongly linearly independent is closed under "proper" set union.

Lemma 2. *Suppose $\mathcal{F}, \mathcal{G} \subseteq \mathcal{R}_q(\tilde{\mathbf{x}}^{\mathsf{T}})$ are $\epsilon_{\mathcal{F}}$- and $\epsilon_{\mathcal{G}}$-strong linearly independent respectively, and $\mathsf{span}_{\mathcal{R}_q}(\mathcal{F}) \cap \mathsf{span}_{\mathcal{R}_q}(\mathcal{G}) = \{0\}$. Then $\mathcal{F} \cup \mathcal{G}$ is $\max(\epsilon_{\mathcal{F}}, \epsilon_{\mathcal{G}})$-strong linearly independent.*

---

[7] This happens when q has multiplicative order φ/e modulo $\mathfrak{f}$.

The proof is deferred to the full version.

Finally, we highlight a counterexample against the strong-hinted-vSIS assumption, which exploits the denominators of rational functions and the adaptivity to specify g^* after seeing $a \leftarrow_\$ \mathcal{R}_q$. Specifically, let

$$1 \in \mathcal{F} \qquad \text{and} \qquad \mathcal{G} = \mathcal{H} = \{1/(\tilde{a} - b) : b \in \mathcal{R}_q\}.$$

Consider this choice of $\mathcal{F}, \mathcal{G}, \mathcal{H}$, and an adversary $\mathcal{A}$ whose set of queries $\mathcal{Q}$ contains $1/(\tilde{a} - b)$ for some $b \in \mathcal{R}_q$. Upon receiving $a \leftarrow_\$ \mathcal{R}_q$, $\mathcal{A}$ specifies $g^*(\tilde{a}) := 1/(\tilde{a} - a + 1)$. Note that $1 - g^*(a) = 0 \bmod q$, where the coefficients 1 and -1 for the functions 1 and g^* respectively are both short. One way to avoid this kind of counterexamples is to let $\mathcal{P}$ accept only rational functions represented as f/g where the denominator g has short coefficients.

To summarise, for a norm bound γ and probability ϵ, we propose the following "natural" predicate $\mathcal{P}_{\gamma,\epsilon}$.

Definition 7 (Natural vSIS Predicates) . *For a ring $\mathcal{R}$, a modulus $q \in \mathbb{N}$, a norm bound $\gamma > 0$, and a probability $\epsilon \in [0,1]$, the predicate $\mathcal{P}_{\gamma,\epsilon}$ inputs a set $\mathcal{F}$ of rational functions over $\mathcal{R}_q$ and outputs 1 if and only if the following hold:*

  - *$\mathcal{F}$ is ϵ-strongly linearly independent.*
  - *For any rational function represented as $f/g \in \mathcal{F}$, where f, g are polynomials over $\mathcal{R}_q$ written in expanded form, each coefficient of g is of norm at most γ.*

Heuristically, we think of γ to be as small as the norm bound for the plain SIS assumption to hold and $\epsilon \le \mathsf{negl}$.

We remark that although the plain vSIS assumption (Definition 2, [24]) is not parametrised by a predicate, it is advisable to only rely on a vSIS assumption for $\mathcal{F}$ satisfying $\mathcal{P}_{\gamma,\epsilon}(\mathcal{F}) = 1$. Similar could be recommended for the kRISIS assumption [3].

3.3   Reductions from vSIS

To gain confidence in the hinted vSIS assumptions, we give two hardness reductions. Theorem 2 says that under certain parameters, the (non-strong) hinted vSIS assumption is implied by the vSIS and evasive SIS assumptions together.

Theorem 2 (EvasiveSIS + vSIS ⇒ Hint-vSIS). *Let $k_f, k_g \in \mathbb{N}$ and $k = k_f + k_g$. Let $\mathcal{F}, \mathcal{G}, \mathcal{H}$ be sequences of k-variate functions, such that for any $\mathbf{A} = [\mathbf{A}_f, \mathbf{A}_g] \in \mathcal{R}_q^{n \times (k_f + k_g)}$, it holds $\mathcal{F}(\mathbf{A}) = \mathbf{A}_f$, $\mathcal{G}(\mathbf{A}) = \hat{\mathcal{G}}(\mathbf{A}_g)$ and $\mathcal{H}(\mathbf{A}) = \hat{\mathcal{H}}(\mathbf{A}_g)$ for some $\hat{\mathcal{G}}, \hat{\mathcal{H}}$ independent of $\mathbf{A}_f$.*

Let $\beta, \beta_1 > 0$, $\beta_0 = \sqrt{\beta^2 + 1}$. Let $\mathsf{params}_0 = (\mathcal{R}, q, n, k_f, Q, 1, s, \beta_0, \beta_1)$, $\mathsf{params}_1 = (\mathcal{R}, n, k, q, \beta_1, \mathcal{F} \cup \hat{\mathcal{G}} \cup \hat{\mathcal{H}})$, and $\mathsf{params}_2 = (\mathcal{R}, n, k, q, Q, \beta, s, \mathcal{F}, \mathcal{G}, \mathcal{H}, \mathcal{P})$. If the $\mathsf{EvasiveSIS}_{\mathsf{params}_0}$ and $\mathsf{vSIS}_{\mathsf{params}_1}$ assumptions hold, then the $\mathsf{Hint\text{-}vSIS}_{\mathsf{params}_2}$ assumption holds.

Proof. Suppose there exists a PPT solver against $\mathsf{Hint\text{-}vSIS_{params_2}}$. Below we show that under $\mathsf{EvasiveSIS_{params_0}}$, there exists a PPT solver against $\mathsf{vSIS_{params_1}}$, hence a contradiction and the theorem follows.

To begin, we observe that a successful PPT solver against $\mathsf{Hint\text{-}vSIS_{params_2}}$ implies a PPT $\mathcal{A} = (\mathcal{A}_1, \mathcal{A}_2)$ such that

$$\Pr\left[\begin{array}{l} (\mathbf{A}_f | \hat{g}^*(\mathbf{A}_g))\mathbf{u}^* = \mathbf{0} \bmod q \\ \wedge\ 0 < \|\mathbf{u}^*\| \leq \beta_0 \\ \wedge\ \mathcal{Q} \cup \{\hat{g}^*\} \subseteq_{Q+1} \hat{\mathcal{G}} \cup \hat{\mathcal{H}} \\ \wedge\ \mathcal{P}(\mathcal{F} \cup \mathcal{Q} \cup (\{g^*\} \setminus \{0\})) = 1 \end{array} \middle| \begin{array}{l} (\mathcal{Q}, \hat{g}^*, \mathsf{st}) \leftarrow \mathcal{A}_1(1^\lambda) \\ [\mathbf{A}_f, \mathbf{A}_g] \leftarrow_\$ \mathcal{R}_q^{n \times k_f} \times \mathcal{R}_q^{n \times k_g} \\ \mathbf{V} := \mathcal{Q}(\mathbf{A}_g) \bmod q \\ \mathbf{u}_i \leftarrow_\$ \mathcal{D}_{\Lambda_q^{v_i}(\mathbf{A}_f), s} \quad \forall i \in [Q] \\ \mathbf{u}^* \leftarrow \mathcal{A}_2(\mathbf{A}_f, \mathbf{A}_g, \mathbf{u}_1, \ldots, \mathbf{u}_Q, \mathsf{st}) \end{array}\right] > \mathrm{negl},$$

where for all $i \in [Q]$, $\hat{h}_i \in \mathcal{Q} \subset \hat{\mathcal{H}}$ is independent of $\mathbf{A}_f$, similarly for $\hat{g}^*$, and st is arbitrary internal state of $\mathcal{A}$ which we assume w.l.o.g. to contain $(\mathcal{Q}, \hat{g}^*)$. Indeed, given a valid solution $\mathbf{u}'$ to $\mathsf{Hint\text{-}vSIS_{params_2}}$, we have

$$\mathcal{F}(\mathbf{A}) \cdot \mathbf{u}' = g^*(\mathbf{A}) \bmod q \iff (\mathbf{A}_f | \hat{g}^*(\mathbf{A}_g)) \cdot \begin{pmatrix} \mathbf{u}' \\ -1 \end{pmatrix} = \mathbf{0} \bmod q,$$

where we make use of that $\mathcal{F}(\mathbf{A}) = \mathbf{A}_f$ and $g^*(\mathbf{A}) = \hat{g}^*(\mathbf{A}_g)$. Similarly, the distribution of each preimage $\mathbf{u}_i$ in the above is identical to that in a $\mathsf{Hint\text{-}vSIS_{params_2}}$ instance, as $h_i(\mathbf{A}) = \hat{h}_i(\mathbf{A}_g)$. Therefore $\mathcal{A}$ succeeds by outputting $\mathbf{u}^* = \begin{pmatrix} \mathbf{u}' \\ -1 \end{pmatrix}$, whose norm satisfies $\|\mathbf{u}^*\|^2 \leq \|\mathbf{u}'\|^2 + 1 \leq \beta^2 + 1 = \beta_0$.

Next, consider a PPT Samp which runs $(\mathcal{Q}, \hat{g}^*, \mathsf{st}) \leftarrow \mathcal{A}_1(1^\lambda)$ and outputs

$$\tilde{\mathbf{P}} := \mathcal{Q}(\mathbf{A}_g) \bmod q, \qquad \tilde{\mathbf{A}} := \hat{g}^*(\mathbf{A}_g) \bmod q$$

where $\mathbf{A}_g \leftarrow_\$ \mathcal{R}_q^{n \times k_g}$ is sampled uniformly randomly, together with aux containing $\mathbf{A}_g$, $\mathcal{Q}$, $\hat{g}^*$, st, and all random coins used. From above, we have that $\mathcal{A}_2$ is a successful solver for the Post experiment in Fig. 2 w.r.t. Samp. Invoking the $\mathsf{EvasiveSIS_{params_0}}$ assumption, there exists a PPT solver $\mathcal{B}_2$ such that

$$\Pr\left[\begin{array}{l} (\mathbf{A}_f | \mathcal{Q}(\mathbf{A}_g) | \hat{g}^*(\mathbf{A}_g))\mathbf{u}^* = \mathbf{0} \bmod q \\ \wedge\ 0 < \|\mathbf{u}^*\| \leq \beta_1 \\ \wedge\ \mathcal{Q} \cup \{\hat{g}^*\} \subseteq_{Q+1} \hat{\mathcal{G}} \cup \hat{\mathcal{H}} \\ \wedge\ \mathcal{P}(\mathcal{F} \cup \mathcal{Q} \cup (\{g^*\} \setminus \{0\})) = 1 \end{array} \middle| \begin{array}{l} (\mathcal{Q}(\mathbf{A}_g), \hat{g}^*(\mathbf{A}_g), \mathsf{aux}) \leftarrow \mathsf{Samp}(1^\lambda) \\ \mathbf{A}_f \leftarrow_\$ \mathcal{R}_q^{n \times k_f} \\ \mathbf{u}^* \leftarrow \mathcal{B}_2(\mathbf{A}_f, \mathcal{Q}(\mathbf{A}_g), \hat{g}^*(\mathbf{A}_g), \mathsf{aux}) \end{array}\right]$$

is $> \mathrm{negl}$. We note that to invoke $\mathsf{EvasiveSIS_{params}}$, we rely on that $\mathbf{A}_f$ is uniformly random over $\mathcal{R}_q^{n \times k_f}$, and that $\tilde{\mathbf{P}}, \tilde{\mathbf{A}}$ in above are independent of $\mathbf{A}_f$.

Expressing the code of Samp inline and rewriting, the above is equivalent to

$$\Pr\left[\begin{array}{l} (\mathbf{A}_f | \mathcal{Q}'(\mathbf{A}_g))\mathbf{u}^* = \mathbf{0} \bmod q \\ \wedge\ 0 < \|\mathbf{u}^*\| \leq \beta_1 \\ \wedge\ \mathcal{Q}' \subseteq_{Q+1} \hat{\mathcal{G}} \cup \hat{\mathcal{H}} \\ \wedge\ \mathcal{P}(\mathcal{F} \cup \mathcal{Q} \cup (\{g^*\} \setminus \{0\})) = 1 \end{array} \middle| \begin{array}{l} (\mathcal{Q}' = \mathcal{Q} \cup \{g^*\}, \mathsf{st}) \leftarrow \mathcal{A}_1(1^\lambda) \\ [\mathbf{A}_f, \mathbf{A}_g] \leftarrow_\$ \mathcal{R}_q^{n \times k_f} \times \mathcal{R}_q^{n \times k_g} \\ \mathbf{u}^* \leftarrow \mathcal{B}_2(\mathbf{A}_f, \mathbf{A}_g, \mathsf{st}) \end{array}\right] \geq \mathrm{negl}.$$

Finally, given the above $(\mathcal{A}_1, \mathcal{B}_2)$, we construct a PPT solver $\mathcal{B}^*$ against $\mathsf{vSIS}_{\mathsf{params}_1}$:

- Obtain $\mathbf{A} \in \mathcal{R}_q^{n \times k}$ from the $\mathsf{vSIS}_{\mathsf{params}_1}$ challenger.
- Run $\mathcal{A}_1$ to obtain $(\mathcal{Q}', \mathsf{st})$, pass $[\mathbf{A}_f, \mathbf{A}_g] = \mathbf{A}$ and st to $\mathcal{B}_2$ to obtain $\mathbf{u}^*$. Write $\mathbf{u}^* = \begin{pmatrix} \mathbf{u}_{\mathcal{F}} \\ \mathbf{u}_{\mathcal{Q}'} \end{pmatrix}$, where $\mathbf{u}_{\mathcal{F}} \in \mathcal{R}^{|\mathcal{F}|}$ and $\mathbf{u}_{\mathcal{Q}'} \in \mathcal{R}^{Q+1}$.
- Let π be the permutation mapping $(\mathcal{Q}', (\hat{\mathcal{G}} \cup \hat{\mathcal{H}}) \setminus \mathcal{Q}') \mapsto \hat{\mathcal{G}} \cup \hat{\mathcal{H}}$, where the order of $(\hat{\mathcal{G}} \cup \hat{\mathcal{H}}) \setminus \mathcal{Q}'$ is arbitrary. Return $\tilde{\mathbf{u}}^* = (\mathbf{u}_{\mathcal{F}}^{\mathsf{T}}, \pi(\mathbf{u}_{\mathcal{Q}'}^{\mathsf{T}}, \mathbf{0}^{\mathsf{T}}))^{\mathsf{T}}$.[8]

Whenever $(\mathcal{A}_1, \mathcal{B}_2)$ succeeds, we have $0 < \|\mathbf{u}^*\| = \|\tilde{\mathbf{u}}^*\| \leq \beta_1$ and

$$(\mathcal{F} \cup \hat{\mathcal{G}} \cup \hat{\mathcal{H}})(\mathbf{A}) \cdot \tilde{\mathbf{u}}^* = (\mathcal{F} \cup \mathcal{Q}')(\mathbf{A}) \cdot \begin{pmatrix} \mathbf{u}_{\mathcal{F}} \\ \mathbf{u}_{\mathcal{Q}'} \end{pmatrix} + ((\hat{\mathcal{G}} \cup \hat{\mathcal{H}}) \setminus \mathcal{Q}')(\mathbf{A}) \cdot \mathbf{0} = \mathbf{0} \bmod q$$

so that $\mathcal{B}^*$ has the same advantage against $\mathsf{vSIS}_{\mathsf{params}_1}$, non-negligible.

The second reduction, summarised by Theorem 3 below, says that the (plain) vSIS assumption family over sets of rational functions is implied by its much smaller subclass which restricts to monomials, up to an exponential blow up in norm bound in the worst case.

Theorem 3 (Monomial-vSIS $\Rightarrow$ vSIS). *Let $d, \beta, \beta_f > 0$. Let $\mathcal{F} \subseteq \mathcal{R}_q(\tilde{\mathbf{x}}^{\mathsf{T}})$ be a set of k-variate rational functions, such that for each rational function in $\mathcal{F}$ represented as $f/g \in \mathcal{F}$ where $f, g \in \mathcal{R}_q[\tilde{\mathbf{x}}]$, it holds $\deg(f), \deg(g) \leq d$ and $\|f\| \leq \beta_f$. Define the following:*

- $\mathcal{F}_{\mathsf{monomial}} := \left\{ \tilde{\mathbf{b}}^{\mathbf{i}} : \mathbf{i} \in \mathbb{N}_0^k,\ 0 \leq \|\mathbf{i}\|_1 \leq 2d \right\}$, *the set of all k-variate monomials of degree at most $2d$ (independent of $\mathcal{F}$),*
- h *an arbitrary common multiple of the denominators $\{g : f/g \in \mathcal{F}\}$ of $\mathcal{F}$,*
- $\beta' = \sqrt{n} \cdot \|h\| \cdot \beta_f \cdot \beta \cdot \min(|\mathcal{F}|, \mathsf{poly})$.

Let $\mathsf{params}_0 = (\mathcal{R}, n, k, q, \beta', \mathcal{F}_{\mathsf{monomial}})$ and $\mathsf{params}_1 = (\mathcal{R}, n, k, q, \beta, \mathcal{F})$. If the $\mathsf{vSIS}_{\mathsf{params}_0}$ assumption holds, then the $\mathsf{vSIS}_{\mathsf{params}_1}$ assumption holds.

Proof. The idea is to clear the denominators of $\mathcal{F}$ by multiplying with their common multiple. Concretely, assume that $\mathcal{A}$ is a PPT solver against $\mathsf{vSIS}_{\mathsf{params}_1}$, we construct a PPT solver against $\mathsf{vSIS}_{\mathsf{params}_0}$ as follows:

- Receive $\mathbf{A}$ from the $\mathsf{vSIS}_{\mathsf{params}_1}$ challenger, pass which to $\mathcal{A}$, and receive $\mathbf{u}^* = (u_1^*, \ldots, u_{|\mathcal{F}|}^*)^{\mathsf{T}}$.
- Let $I \subseteq \mathcal{F}$ be the index set of the non-zero entries of $\mathbf{u}^*$, i.e. $u_i^* \neq 0$ if and only if $i \in I$. Note that $|I| = \min(|\mathcal{F}|, \mathsf{poly})$ since $\mathcal{A}$ is PPT.
- For each $f \in I$, write $h \cdot f$ as $\mathcal{F}_{\mathsf{monomial}} \cdot \mathbf{c}_f$ for some $\mathbf{c}_f \in \mathcal{R}^{|\mathcal{F}_{\mathsf{monomial}}|}$, i.e. a linear combination of monomials in $\mathcal{F}_{\mathsf{monomial}}$ with coefficient vector $\mathbf{c}_f$.
- For each $f \in \mathcal{F} \setminus I$, let $\mathbf{c}_f = \mathbf{0}$ be all-zero. Let $\mathbf{C} := (\mathbf{c}_f)_{f \in \mathcal{F}} \in \mathcal{R}^{|\mathcal{F}_{\mathsf{monomial}}| \times |\mathcal{F}|}$ (whose description size $\leq \mathsf{poly}$). Return $(\mathbf{1}_n \otimes \mathbf{C}) \cdot \mathbf{u}^*$.

---

[8] $\tilde{\mathbf{u}}^*$ has $\leq \min(|\mathcal{F}|, \mathsf{poly}) + Q + 1$ non-zero entries, although of dimension $|\mathcal{F} \cup \hat{\mathcal{G}} \cup \hat{\mathcal{H}}|$. Both π and $\tilde{\mathbf{u}}^*$ admit representation of size $\leq \mathsf{poly}$ since $\mathcal{F}, \hat{\mathcal{G}}, \hat{\mathcal{H}}$ do.

First we note that Step 3 in the above is possible, since for any $f \in I \subseteq \mathcal{F}$, it holds $h \cdot f$ is a k-variate polynomial of degree at most $2d$, so that $h \cdot f$ can always be written as a linear combination of the monomials in $\mathcal{F}_{\mathsf{monomial}}$. Further, $\|\mathbf{c}_{f.}\| = \|h \cdot f\| \leq \|h\| \cdot \beta_f$. Suppose $\mathcal{A}$ is successful, then

$$\mathcal{F}(\mathbf{A}) \cdot \mathbf{u}^* = \mathbf{0} \bmod q,$$
$$(h \cdot \mathcal{F})(\mathbf{A}) \cdot \mathbf{u}^* = (\mathcal{F}_{\mathsf{monomial}})(\mathbf{A}) \cdot (\mathbf{1}_n \otimes \mathbf{C}) \cdot \mathbf{u}^* = \mathbf{0} \bmod q,$$

where $\mathbf{1}_n$ is the all-one vector. Also, we have $\|(\mathbf{1}_n \otimes \mathbf{C})\mathbf{u}^*\| \leq \sqrt{n} \|\mathbf{C}\| \|\mathbf{u}^*\| \leq \sqrt{n} \cdot \|h\| \cdot \beta_f \cdot \beta \cdot \min(|\mathcal{F}|, \mathsf{poly}) = \beta'.$

Remark 5 (Norm of common multiple.) . For Theorem 3, suppose for any $f/g \in \mathcal{F}$ it holds $\|g\| \leq \beta_g$ and there are at most $\ell \leq |\mathcal{F}|$ distinct denominators, then $\|h\| \leq \beta_g^\ell$. For specially chosen $\mathcal{F}$ a tighter bound is possible.

4 Proof-Friendly Signatures from Strong Hinted vSIS

We present a general family of algebraic lattice-based signature schemes inspired by the ISIS_f framework and pairing-based signatures such as that of Boneh and Boyen (BB) [15] and of Boneh, Boyen and Shacham (BBS) [8,16,50]. The sEUF-SMA security of the construction is tightly connected to the s-Hint-vSIS assumption, which we defined and analysed in Sect. 3. We then suggest concrete instantiations of the general construction, which can be seen as translations of BB and BBS to the lattice setting.

4.1 General Construction

Our general construction is parametrised by a ring $\mathcal{R}$, dimensions $n, m, \ell \in \mathbb{N}$, a modulus $q \in \mathbb{N}$, a Gaussian parameter $s > 0$, a norm bound $\beta > 0$, a failure probability $\delta \geq 0$, a message space $\mathcal{M}$, a randomness space[9] $\mathcal{X}$, and a set $\mathcal{H} = \{h_{\mu,\chi} : \mu \in \mathcal{M}, \chi \in \mathcal{X}\} \subseteq \mathcal{R}(\tilde{\mathbf{b}}^{\mathsf{T}})$ of ℓ-variate rational functions over $\mathcal{R}$ indexed by the set $\mathcal{M} \times \mathcal{X}$. The public parameter space is $\mathcal{R}_q^{n \times \ell}$. For any public parameter $\mathbf{B} \in \mathcal{R}_q^{n \times \ell}$, define the message subspace

$$\mathcal{M}_{\mathcal{X},\mathcal{H},\mathbf{B}} := \{\mu \in \mathcal{M} : \Pr[h_{\mu,\chi}(\mathbf{B}) = \bot \mid \chi \leftarrow_{\$} \mathcal{X}] \leq \delta\}.$$

That is, a valid message $\mu \in \mathcal{M}$ w.r.t. the sets $\mathcal{X}$ and $\mathcal{H}$ and public parameter $\mathbf{B}$ is such that, over the randomness of $\chi \leftarrow_{\$} \mathcal{X}$, the probability of $h_{\mu,\chi}(\mathbf{B})$ being undefined is at most δ. The full construction Σ_{vSIS} is presented in Fig. 4.

To explain, the public parameters consists of a random matrix $\mathbf{B} \leftarrow_{\$} \mathcal{R}_q^{n \times \ell}$. A public key is a trapdoored matrix $\mathbf{A} \in \mathcal{R}_q^{n \times m}$ and the corresponding secret key is the trapdoor $\mathsf{td}_{\mathbf{A}}$. To sign a message μ, sample randomness χ, and evaluate

---

[9] We assume for simplicity that the randomness space is a finite set and randomness are drawn from the uniform distribution over this set. In general, $\mathcal{X}$ could be a distribution over a possibly infinite set.

Setup(1^λ)	KGen(pp)
$\mathbf{B} \leftarrow_{\$} \mathcal{R}_q^{n \times \ell}$	$(\mathbf{A}, \mathsf{td_A}) \leftarrow \mathsf{TrapGen}(\mathcal{R}, 1^n, 1^m, q)$
pp $:= \mathbf{B}$	return (pk, sk) $:= (\mathbf{A}, \mathsf{td_A})$
Sign(pp, sk, msg)	Verify(pp, pk, msg, sig)
$\chi \leftarrow_{\$} \mathcal{X}$	$\mathbf{t} := h_{\mu,\chi}(\mathbf{B}) \bmod q$
$\mathbf{t} := h_{\mu,\chi}(\mathbf{B}) \bmod q$	$b_0 := (\mu \in \mathcal{M}_{\mathcal{X},\mathcal{G},\mathbf{B}}) \wedge (\chi \in \mathcal{X})$
$\mathbf{s} \leftarrow \mathsf{SampPre}(\mathsf{td_A}, \mathbf{t}, s)$	$b_1 := (\mathbf{As} = \mathbf{t} \bmod q) \wedge (0 < \|\mathbf{s}\| \leq \beta)$
return sig $:= (\chi, \mathbf{s})$	return $b_0 \wedge b_1$

Fig. 4. vSIS-based Signatures Σ_{vSIS}.

the function $h_{\mu,\chi}$ at $\mathbf{B}$ to obtain an image $\mathbf{t}$. The signature of μ then consists of the randomness χ and a short preimage $\mathbf{s}$ of $\mathbf{t}$ with respect to $\mathbf{A}$, sampled using $\mathsf{td_A}$. To verify a signature, check that μ belongs to the message subspace $\mathcal{M}_{\mathcal{X},\mathcal{H},\mathbf{B}}$ and χ belongs to the randomness space $\mathcal{X}$. Also check that $\mathbf{s}$ is of norm bounded by β and satisfies $\mathbf{As} = h_{\mu,\chi}(\mathbf{B}) \bmod q$.

Theorem 4 (Correctness) *If $(\mathcal{R}, n, m, q, s)$ are admissible parameters for $(\mathsf{TrapGen}, \mathsf{SampPre})$, $\beta \geq s\sqrt{\varphi m}$ and $\delta \leq$ negl, then the signature scheme in Fig. 4 is correct in the sense of Remark 1.*

Proof By Definition 1, for all but a negligible fraction of $(\mathbf{A}, \mathsf{td_A})$, it holds that $\mathsf{SampPre}(\mathsf{td_A}, \mathbf{t}, s) \approx_c \mathcal{D}_{\Lambda_q^\mathbf{t}(\mathbf{A}), s}$. Combining with Lemma 1, for any $\mathbf{t} \in \mathcal{R}_q^n$, $(\mathbf{A}, \mathsf{td_A}) \leftarrow \mathsf{TrapGen}(\mathcal{R}, 1^n, 1^m, q)$ and $\mathbf{s} \leftarrow \mathsf{SampPre}(\mathsf{td_A}, \mathbf{t}, s)$, it holds that $\mathbf{As} = \mathbf{t} \bmod q$ and $\|\mathsf{SampPre}(\mathsf{td_A}, \mathbf{t}, s)\| \leq s\sqrt{\varphi m} \leq \beta$ with overwhelming probability in λ.

Theorem 5 (Security) *Let* params $= (\mathcal{R}, n, k, q, \beta, \mathcal{F}, \mathcal{G}, \mathcal{H}, \mathcal{P}, Q)$, m, ℓ, s, δ, $\delta', \mathcal{M}, \mathcal{X}$ *be parametrised by λ and satisfy the following constraints:*

- *$(\mathcal{R}, n, m, q, s)$ are admissible parameters for $(\mathsf{TrapGen}, \mathsf{SampPre})$, $\beta > 0$, $0 \leq \delta, \delta' \leq$ negl, and $k = m + \ell$.*
- *For formal variables $(\tilde{\mathbf{a}}^\mathsf{T}, \tilde{\mathbf{b}}^\mathsf{T})$ of dimension $m + \ell$, $\mathcal{F}(\tilde{\mathbf{a}}^\mathsf{T}, \tilde{\mathbf{b}}^\mathsf{T}) = \tilde{\mathbf{a}}^\mathsf{T}$.*
- *$\mathcal{H} = \{h_{\mu,\chi} : \mu \in \mathcal{M}, \chi \in \mathcal{X}\} \subseteq \mathcal{R}(\tilde{\mathbf{b}}^\mathsf{T})$ is a set of ℓ-variate rational functions over $\mathcal{R}$, as defined above.*
- *$\mathcal{G} = \mathcal{H} \cup \{0\}$ extends the set $\mathcal{H}$ with the all zero function.*
- *For random $\chi_1, \ldots, \chi_Q \leftarrow_{\$} \mathcal{X}$ and arbitrarily chosen $\mu_1, \ldots, \mu_Q, \mu' \in \mathcal{M}$ where $\mu' \notin \{\mu_1, \ldots, \mu_Q\}$, and $\chi' \in \mathcal{X}$ possibly dependent on $(\chi_1, \ldots, \chi_Q)$, it holds except with probability δ' that*

$$\mathcal{P}(\mathcal{F} \cup \{h_{\mu_i, \chi_i}\}_{i=1}^Q \cup \{h_{\mu', \chi'}\}) = 1.$$

1. *If the $\mathsf{s\text{-}Hint\text{-}vSIS}_{\mathsf{params}}$ (resp. $\mathsf{s\text{-}\$Hint\text{-}vSIS}_{\mathsf{params}}$) assumption holds for every polynomial $Q(\lambda)$, then Σ_{vSIS} is sEUF-SMA (resp. sEUF-RMA) secure.*

2. *If $\mathcal{X}$ is a singleton set (so that an image $\mathbf{t}$ is deterministic in μ), and the*
   Hint-vSIS$_{\mathsf{params}}$ assumption holds for every polynomial $Q(\lambda)$, then Σ_{vSIS} satis-
   fies a relaxed sSUF-SMA security with the restriction that all signing queries
   are distinct.[10]

Proof We prove the implication from s-Hint-vSIS$_{\mathsf{params}}$ to sEUF-SMA security,
and then highlight differences of the proofs for the other implications. Define the
following hybrid security experiments:

Hyb$_0$: Identical to sEUF-SMA$_{\Sigma_{\mathsf{vSIS}},\mathcal{A},Q}$, the sEUF-SMA security experiment.
Hyb$_1$: Recall that, in Hyb$_0$, the step Sign(sk, msg$_i$) for msg$_i$ = μ_i is
computed as follows: Sample $\chi_i \leftarrow_\$ \mathcal{X}$, compute $\mathbf{t}_i := h_{\mu_i,\chi_i}(\mathbf{B})$, compute
$\mathbf{s}_i \leftarrow$ SampPre($\mathsf{td}_{\mathbf{A}}, \mathbf{t}_i, s$) and return $(\chi_i, \mathbf{s}_i)$. In Hyb$_1$, we change to sample
$\mathbf{s}_i \leftarrow_\$ \mathcal{D}_{\Lambda_q^{\mathbf{t}_i}(\mathbf{A}),s}$ directly from the Gaussian distribution (inefficiently).
Hyb$_2$: We change how the public key $\mathbf{A}$ is sampled. In Hyb$_2$, we sample
$\mathbf{A} \leftarrow_\$ \mathcal{R}_q^{n \times m}$ uniformly at random.

By the properties of lattice trapdoors (Definition 1), the above hybrids are clearly
computationally indistinguishable.

Next, we show that if $\mathcal{A}$ is such that Hyb$_2$ outputs 1 with a non-negligible
probability $\epsilon > \mathsf{negl}$, then there exists a PPT algorithm $\mathcal{B}$ for s-Hint-vSIS$_{\mathsf{params}}$.
Our reduction $\mathcal{B}$ simulates Hyb$_2$ for $\mathcal{A}$ as follows:

- Run $\mathcal{A}$ to obtain Q messages $\mu_1, \ldots, \mu_Q$.
- Sample $\chi_i \leftarrow_\$ \mathcal{X}$ for $i \in [Q]$.
- Return the subset $\mathcal{Q} := \{h_{\mu_i,\chi_i} : i \in [Q]\} \subseteq \mathcal{G}$. Except with probability at
  most $Q\delta$, for a random $\mathbf{B} \leftarrow_\$ \mathcal{R}_q^{n \times \ell}$, it holds that $h_{\mu_i,\chi_i}(\mathbf{B}) \neq \perp$ for all $i \in [Q]$.
  In the following, we assume that this is the case.
- Receive in return $([\mathbf{A}, \mathbf{B}], \mathbf{s}_1, \ldots, \mathbf{s}_Q)$ where $[\mathbf{A}, \mathbf{B}] \leftarrow_\$ \mathcal{R}_q^{n \times m} \times \mathcal{R}_q^{n \times \ell}$,
  $\mathbf{s}_i \leftarrow_\$ \mathcal{D}_{\Lambda_q^{\mathbf{t}_i}(\mathbf{A}),s}$ and $\mathbf{t}_i = h_{\mu_i,\chi_i}(\mathbf{B})$ for all $i \in [Q]$.
- Set pp = $\mathbf{B}$, pk = $\mathbf{A}$ and sig$_i$ = $(\chi_i, \mathbf{s}_i)$ for all $i \in [Q]$, and run $(\mu^*, \mathsf{sig}^*) \leftarrow$
  $\mathcal{A}(\mathsf{pp}, \mathsf{pk}, \mathsf{sig}_1, \ldots \mathsf{sig}_Q)$ where $\mathsf{sig}^* = (\chi^*, \mathbf{s}^*)$. Assuming that $\mathcal{A}$ is successful,
  we have $\mu^* \in \mathcal{M}_{\mathcal{X},\mathcal{G},\mathbf{B}}$, $\chi^* \in \mathcal{X}$, $(\mu^*, \chi^*, \mathbf{s}^*) \notin \{(\mu_1, \chi_1, \mathbf{s}_1), \ldots, (\mu_Q, \chi_Q, \mathbf{s}_Q)\}$,
  $\mathbf{As}^* = h_{\mu^*,\chi^*}(\mathbf{B}) \bmod q$, and $0 < \|\mathbf{s}^*\| \leq \beta$.
- If $(\mu^*, \chi^*) \notin \{(\mu_1, \chi_1), \ldots, (\mu_Q, \chi_Q)\}$, set $g^* := h_{\mu^*,\chi^*}$ and return $(g^*, \mathbf{s}^*)$.
- Otherwise, let i^* be such that $(\mu^*, \chi^*) = (\mu_{i^*}, \chi_{i^*})$. Set g^* to be the zero
  function and return $(g^*, \mathbf{s}^* - \mathbf{s}_{i^*})$.

Clearly, the reduction $\mathcal{B}$ runs in PPT and the failure event of $h_{\mu_i,\chi_i}(\mathbf{B}) = \perp$
for some $i \in [Q]$ happens with probability at most $Q\delta$. Moreover, by the con-
straint on $\mathcal{P}$, we have $\mathcal{P}(\mathcal{F} \cup \mathcal{Q} \cup (\{g^*\} \setminus \{0\})) = 1$ except with probability δ'. If
$(\mu^*, \chi^*) \notin \{(\mu_1, \chi_1), \ldots, (\mu_Q, \chi_Q)\}$, then clearly $g^* \in \mathcal{G} \setminus \mathcal{Q}$. Otherwise, we have
$(\mu^*, \chi^*) = (\mu_{i^*}, \chi_{i^*})$ and thus

$$\mathbf{A} \cdot \mathbf{s} = h_{\mu^*,\chi^*}(\mathbf{B}) = h_{\mu_{i^*},\chi_{i^*}}(\mathbf{B}) = \mathbf{A} \cdot \mathbf{s}_{i^*} \bmod q,$$
$$\mathbf{A} \cdot (\mathbf{s} - \mathbf{s}_{i^*}) = \mathbf{0} = g^*(\mathbf{B}) \bmod q,$$

---

[10] The restriction can be lifted by derandomising the signing algorithm with a pseudorandom function.

Table 1. Instantiations to obtain lattice-analogues of BB and BBS signatures.

	Message μ	Randomness χ	Function $h_{\mu,\chi}(\tilde{\mathbf{b}}^{\mathsf{T}})$
BB-lite	u	$-$	$1/(\tilde{b} - u)$
BB-full	$\mathbf{u}$	$\mathbf{x}$	$1/((1, \mathbf{u}^{\mathsf{T}}, \mathbf{x}^{\mathsf{T}}) \cdot \tilde{\mathbf{b}})$
BB-tran	$\mathbf{u}$	$(\mathbf{x}_0, x_1)$	$(\mathbf{u}^{\mathsf{T}}, \mathbf{x}_0^{\mathsf{T}}) \cdot \tilde{\mathbf{b}}_0 + 1/(\tilde{b}_1 - x_1)$
BBS	$\mathbf{u}$	$(\mathbf{x}_0, x_1)$	$((1, \mathbf{u}^{\mathsf{T}}, \mathbf{x}_0^{\mathsf{T}}) \cdot \tilde{\mathbf{b}}_0)/(\tilde{b}_1 - x_1)$

where $\mathbf{s}^* - \mathbf{s}_{i^*} \neq \mathbf{0}$ since $\mathbf{s}^*$ is a valid forgery. In either case, $\mathcal{B}$ solves the s-Hint-vSIS$_{\mathsf{params}}$ instance with probability at least $\epsilon - Q\delta - \delta' > \mathsf{negl}$.

For the implication from s-\$Hint-vSIS$_{\mathsf{params}}$ to sSUF-RMA security, the argument is identical except that $\mathcal{B}$ samples $\mathcal{Q}$ as a uniformly random Q-subset of $\mathcal{H}$. For the implication from Hint-vSIS$_{\mathsf{params}}$ to sSUF-SMA security, we make the following modifications. First, we define Hyb_0 to be identical to sSUF-SMA$_{\Sigma_{\mathsf{vSIS}}, \mathcal{A}, Q}$, and propagate this change to Hyb_1 and Hyb_2. Then, the reduction $\mathcal{B}$ changes as follows. At the beginning, $\mathcal{B}$ receives from $\mathcal{A}$ in addition to $\mu_1, \ldots, \mu_Q$ the target message μ^*. Since $\mathcal{X} = \emptyset$, $\mathcal{B}$ no longer needs to sample $\chi_1, \ldots, \chi_Q$. If $\mu^* \notin \{\mu_1, \ldots, \mu_Q\}$, it sets $g^* := h_{\mu^*}$. Otherwise, say $\mu^* = \mu_{i^*}$, it sets g^* to be the all zero function. It outputs the set $\mathcal{Q} = \{h_{\mu_i} : i \in [Q]\}$ and g^*. Towards the end, upon receiving $\mathbf{s}^*$ from $\mathcal{A}$, $\mathcal{B}$ simply returns $\mathbf{s}^*$ if $\mu^* \notin \{\mu_1, \ldots, \mu_Q\}$, and $\mathbf{s} - \mathbf{s}_{i^*}$ if $\mu^* = \mu_{i^*}$. Clearly, the reduction $\mathcal{B}$ runs in PPT and solves the Hint-vSIS$_{\mathsf{params}}$ instance with probability at least $\epsilon - Q\delta - \delta' > \mathsf{negl}$.

Remark 6 (Constraint on $\mathcal{P}$). In Theorem 5, we require that $\mathcal{P}(\mathcal{F} \cup \{h_{\mu_i, \chi_i}\}_{i=1}^{Q} \cup \{h_{\mu', \chi'}\}) = 1$ with high probability. We remark that this indeed captures both cases – whether the adversary chooses to forge a signature on μ^* belonging to $\{\mu_1, \ldots, \mu_Q\}$ or not. If $\mu^* \notin \{\mu_1, \ldots, \mu_Q\}$, by setting $(\mu', \chi') = (\mu^*, \chi^*)$ we directly recover the constraint $\mathcal{P}(\mathcal{F} \cup \{h_{\mu_i, \chi_i}\}_{i=1}^{Q} \cup (\{g^*\} \setminus \{0\})) = 1$ where $g^* = h_{\mu^*, \chi^*}$. If $\mu^* \in \{\mu_1, \ldots, \mu_Q\}$, then for any $\mu' \notin \{\mu_1, \ldots, \mu_Q\}$, the condition $\mathcal{P}(\mathcal{F} \cup \{h_{\mu_i, \chi_i}\}_{i=1}^{Q} \cup \{h_{\mu', \chi'}\}) = 1$ implies that $\mathcal{P}(\mathcal{F} \cup \{h_{\mu_i, \chi_i}\}_{i=1}^{Q}) = 1$, equivalent to $\mathcal{P}(\mathcal{F} \cup \{h_{\mu_i, \chi_i}\}_{i=1}^{Q} \cup (\{g^*\} \setminus \{0\})) = 1$ with $g^* = 0$ the all-zero function.

4.2   Candidate Instantiations

In Table 1, we suggest a few natural candidate instantiations of the parameters, as inspired by the BB [15] and BBS [8,16,50] signatures. The first two rows are attempts to translate the selective-query secure (BB-lite) and fully secure versions of the BB signatures. The third row is obtained by interpreting the BB-lite instantiation as a (generalised) ISIS$_f$ instance, and then applying the transformation from ISIS$_f$ to interactive ISIS$_f$ presented in [18] and generalised in Sect. 5.2. The last row is an attempt to translate the BBS signatures which, after adapting notation, take the following form:

$$[((1, \mathbf{u}^{\mathsf{T}}) \cdot \mathbf{b}_0)/(b_1 - x)]$$

where $([1], [b_0], [b_1])$ is the public key, $\mathbf{u}$ a message, and x the signing randomness.

We remark that, for all instantiated signature schemes suggested in Table 1, we are not aware of any efficient attacks against the sEUF-CMA (i.e. adaptive query) security of the schemes, although Theorem 5 only guarantees their sEUF-SMA (i.e. selective-query) security. Furthermore, in Sect. 5.2, we show that the BB-tran scheme indeed provably achieves sEUF-CMA security under the same strong hinted vSIS assumption along with other mild parameter constraints.

Satisfiability of Natural vSIS Predicates. Recall that, for Theorem 5 to apply, we require the following constraint:

> For random $\chi_1, \ldots, \chi_Q \leftarrow_\$ \mathcal{X}$ and arbitrarily chosen $\mu_1, \ldots, \mu_Q, \mu' \in \mathcal{M}$, with $\mu' \notin \{\mu_1, \ldots, \mu_Q\}$, and $\chi' \in \mathcal{X}$ possibly dependent on $(\chi_1, \ldots, \chi_Q)$, it holds except with negligible probability that
>
> $$\mathcal{P}(\mathcal{F} \cup \{h_{\mu_i, \chi_i}\}_{i=1}^Q \cup \{h_{\mu', \chi'}\}) = 1.$$

As discussed in Remark 6, such a constraint on $\mathcal{P}$ captures both cases – where the adversary chooses to forge a signature of a previously queried message or a new message. Let $\mathcal{P} = \mathcal{P}_{\gamma, \epsilon}$ for some $0 < \gamma \ll q$ and $\epsilon \leq \mathsf{negl}$ as defined in Definition 7, and let $\mathcal{X}$ contain vectors of norm at most γ. We sketch below an argument for why the predicate would be satisfied for all candidates listed in Table 1. We observe the following:

- The denominators of all choices of $h_{\mu, \chi}(\tilde{\mathbf{b}}^\mathsf{T})$ mentioned in Table 1 clearly satisfy the norm bound constraint of $\mathcal{P}_{\gamma, \epsilon}$.
- For χ with sufficient entropy and for $\mathcal{R}_q \cong \mathbb{F}^e$ splitting into large enough copies of $\mathbb{F}$, it is clear that $\{h_{\mu_i, \chi_i}\}_{i=1}^Q$ for all choices in Table 1 is linearly independent with overwhelming probability, and thus ϵ-strongly linearly independent by Theorem 1.
- The intersection between the span of $\mathcal{F}$ and that of $\{h_{\mu_i, \chi_i}\}_{i=1}^Q$ (or $\{h_{\mu', \chi'}\}$) is clearly zero, since $\mathcal{F}$ depends only on $\tilde{\mathbf{a}}$ but not on $\tilde{\mathbf{b}}$.

To show that $\mathcal{F} \cup \{h_{\mu_i, \chi_i}\}_{i=1}^Q \cup \{h_{\mu', \chi'}\}$ is ϵ-strongly linearly independent with overwhelming probability, by Lemma 2, it suffices to show that the intersection of the spans of $\{h_{\mu_i, \chi_i}\}_{i=1}^Q$ and $h_{\mu', \chi'}$ is trivial with overwhelming probability.

By assumption, we have that $\mu' \notin \{\mu_1, \ldots, \mu_Q\}$, but (μ', χ') may arbitrarily depend on $(\mu_i, \chi_i)_{i=1}^Q$. From the constraint $\mu' \notin \{\mu_1, \ldots, \mu_Q\}$, the (strong) linear independence between $\{h_{\mu_i, \chi_i}\}_{i=1}^Q$ and $h_{\mu', \chi'}$ is clear for the BB-lite and BB-full cases, since they consist of distinct denominator polynomials. For the BB-tran and BBS cases, write $\chi = (\chi_0, \chi_1) = (\mathbf{x}_0, x_1)$. If $x_1' \notin \{x_{1,i}\}_{i=1}^Q$, then again the denominator polynomials are distinct and therefore the claim holds. Now, suppose $x_1' = x_{1,i'}$ for some $i' \in [Q]$. Then clearly the sets $\{h_{\mu_i, \chi_i}\}_{i \neq i'}$ and $\{h_{\mu_{i'}, \chi'}, h_{\mu', \chi'}\}$ are (strong) linearly independent because denominator polynomials are distinct.

To finish the claim, we must show that $\{h_{\mu_{i'},\chi'}, h_{\mu',\chi'}\}$ is (strongly) linearly independent. We first handle the BB-tran case which is clearer. We have

$$h_{\mu_{i'},\chi'} = (\mathbf{u}_{i'}^{\mathsf{T}}, \mathbf{x}_{0,i'}^{\mathsf{T}}) \cdot \tilde{\mathbf{b}}_0 + 1/(\tilde{b}_1 - x_1') \quad \text{and}$$

$$h_{\mu_{i'},\chi'} = ((\mathbf{u}')^{\mathsf{T}}, (\mathbf{x}_0')^{\mathsf{T}}) \cdot \tilde{\mathbf{b}}_0 + 1/(\tilde{b}_1 - x_1'),$$

to cancel out the second term, the only way is to take the difference. However, since $\mu_{i'} = \mathbf{u}_{i'}$ and $\mu' = \mathbf{u}'$ are distinct, taking difference does not make the first term vanish, thus proving the claim. For the BBS case, any linear combination of

$$((1, \mathbf{u}_{i'}^{\mathsf{T}}, \mathbf{x}_{0,i'}^{\mathsf{T}}) \cdot \tilde{\mathbf{b}}_0)/(\tilde{b}_1 - x_1') \quad \text{and} \quad ((1, (\mathbf{u}')^{\mathsf{T}}, (\mathbf{x}_0')^{\mathsf{T}}) \cdot \tilde{\mathbf{b}}_0)/(\tilde{b}_1 - x_1')$$

to zero would also be a linear combination of

$$(1, \mathbf{u}_{i'}^{\mathsf{T}}, \mathbf{x}_{0,i'}^{\mathsf{T}}) \cdot \tilde{\mathbf{b}}_0 \quad \text{and} \quad (1, (\mathbf{u}')^{\mathsf{T}}, (\mathbf{x}_0')^{\mathsf{T}}) \cdot \tilde{\mathbf{b}}_0$$

to zero. However, since $\mu_{i'} = \mathbf{u}_{i'}$ and $\mu' = \mathbf{u}'$ are distinct, the two coefficients of such a linear combination must either be zero or have different magnitudes. In the latter case, the coefficient of the first variable in $\tilde{\mathbf{b}}_0$ in the linear combination would not be zero. We thus conclude that the only possible linear combination to make zero is the one with zero coefficients.

Proof-Friendliness of Suggested Candidates. We briefly comment on the proof-friendliness on the BB-tran and BBS instantiations suggested in Table 1, since we believe they are of the most practical relevance. Essentially, the verification relation of both schemes are simple bounded-norm satisfiability relations of quadratic equations, which can be handled concretely efficiently by state-of-the-art lattice-based proof systems such as [41].

For simplicity, for signature verification we collect all supposedly bounded-norm components as a vector and check the norm of such a vector.[11] The verification relation of the BB-tran instantiation then takes the form:

$$\mathbf{A} \cdot \mathbf{s} = \mathbf{B}_0 \cdot \begin{pmatrix} \mathbf{u} \\ \mathbf{x}_0 \end{pmatrix} + \mathbf{1}_n \oslash (\mathbf{b}_1 - \mathbf{1}_n \cdot x_1) \bmod q \quad \text{and} \quad \|(\mathbf{s}^{\mathsf{T}}, \mathbf{u}^{\mathsf{T}}, \mathbf{x}_0^{\mathsf{T}}, x_1)\| \le \beta$$

which can be rearranged to the form

$$(\mathbf{b}_1 \boxdot (\mathbf{A} \, -\mathbf{B})) \cdot \begin{pmatrix} \mathbf{s} \\ \mathbf{u} \\ \mathbf{x}_0 \end{pmatrix} - (\mathbf{A} \, -\mathbf{B}) \cdot \begin{pmatrix} \mathbf{s} \\ \mathbf{u} \\ \mathbf{x}_0 \end{pmatrix} \cdot x_1 = \mathbf{1}_n \bmod q,$$

$$\|(\mathbf{s}^{\mathsf{T}}, \mathbf{u}^{\mathsf{T}}, \mathbf{x}_0^{\mathsf{T}}, x_1)\| \le \beta$$

where $\mathbf{b}_1 \boxdot (\mathbf{A} \, -\mathbf{B})$ denotes the matrix obtained by taking the Hadamard products between $\mathbf{b}_1$ and every column of $(\mathbf{A} \, -\mathbf{B})$. To produce a zero-knowledge proof of such a relation, one strategy is to commit to the expanded witnesses

---

[11] We note that, depending on the application, the norm bounds for the signature vector $\mathbf{s}$ and the message $\mathbf{u}$, for example, could differ.

$$\mathbf{w}_1 = \begin{pmatrix} \mathbf{s} \\ \mathbf{u} \\ \mathbf{x}_0 \end{pmatrix}, \qquad w_2 = x_1, \qquad \mathbf{w}_3 = \begin{pmatrix} \mathbf{s} \\ \mathbf{u} \\ \mathbf{x}_0 \end{pmatrix} \cdot x_1,$$

prove that $\mathbf{w}_1$ and w_2 are of bounded norm and satisfy the linear relation, and prove that $\mathbf{w}_3 = \mathbf{w}_1 \cdot w_2$.

Similarly, the verification relation of the BBS instantiation takes the form:

$$\mathbf{A} \cdot \mathbf{s} = \left(\mathbf{B}_0 \begin{pmatrix} 1 \\ \mathbf{u} \\ \mathbf{x}_0 \end{pmatrix} \right) \oslash (\mathbf{b}_1 - \mathbf{1}_n \cdot x_1) \bmod q \quad \text{and} \quad \left\| (\mathbf{s}^{\mathsf{T}}, \mathbf{u}^{\mathsf{T}}, \mathbf{x}_0^{\mathsf{T}}, x_1) \right\| \leq \beta$$

which can be rearranged to the proof-friendly form

$$(\mathbf{b}_1 \boxdot \mathbf{A}) \cdot \mathbf{s} - \mathbf{A} \cdot \mathbf{s} \cdot x_1 - \mathbf{B}_0 \cdot \begin{pmatrix} 1 \\ \mathbf{u} \\ \mathbf{x}_0 \end{pmatrix} = \mathbf{0}_n \bmod q, \qquad \left\| (\mathbf{s}^{\mathsf{T}}, \mathbf{u}^{\mathsf{T}}, \mathbf{x}_0^{\mathsf{T}}, x_1) \right\| \leq \beta.$$

We expect proving knowledge of a signature for the BBS instantiation is slightly more efficient, since the quadratic part $\mathbf{s} \cdot x_1$ is of lower dimension (independent of the message $\mathbf{u}$) than $\begin{pmatrix} \mathbf{s} \\ \mathbf{u} \\ \mathbf{x}_0 \end{pmatrix} \cdot x_1$ in the BB-tran instantiation.

We further note that proving knowledge of a signature for either instantiation suggested above only requires proving that the witness is norm-bounded. In contrast, the concrete scheme suggested in [18] requires proving that the witness has a binary component, on top of the witness being norm-bounded.

Concrete Parameters. To estimate performance, we heuristically assume that breaking the sEUF-CMA security of the BB-tran and BBS instantiations are both as hard as solving SIS with dimension φn. As in [18], we consider instantiations based on NTRU trapdoors [25] for power-of-2 cyclotomic rings, meaning that $n = 1$, $m = 2$, and φ is a power of 2. NTRU trapdoors [25] allow sampling preimages statistically close to Gaussian with parameter $s \geq 1.17 \cdot \sqrt{q} \cdot \eta_\epsilon(\mathbb{Z}^{2\varphi})$ where $\eta_\epsilon(\mathbb{Z}^{2\varphi}) \leq \sqrt{\log(4\varphi(1 + 2^\lambda))/\pi}$. Recall that a message-signature tuple is $(\mathbf{s}^{\mathsf{T}}, \mathbf{u}^{\mathsf{T}}, \mathbf{x}_0^{\mathsf{T}}, x_1) \in \mathcal{R}^{2 + \ell_m + \ell_r + 1}$. We hence set the norm bound β to be such that $s\sqrt{(3 + \ell_m + \ell_r) \cdot \varphi} \leq \beta < q$. We adopt the standard optimisation of omitting one ring element from the signature (which can be derived from the verification equation), and thus a signature is of size $(2 + \ell_r) \cdot \varphi \cdot \log \beta$ bits. Since the signature schemes' security anyway rely on the hardness of vSIS, we also adopt the optimisation of deriving the entire public key from a single $\mathcal{R}_q$ element (given by the NTRU trapdoor algorithm), hence the public key size is $\varphi \cdot \log q$ bits. Following [18], we set $\ell_r = 2$ and $\ell_m = 1$, and additionally consider $\ell_m = 128$. We run the Lattice Estimator [4][12] with these parameter constraints and obtain the parameters and sizes presented in Table 2.

---

[12] Commit 162c5053 of https://github.com/malb/lattice-estimator/.

Table 2. Estimated parameters for BB-tran and BBS. Sizes are in KB.

Security Level	φ	q	β	s	ℓ_m	ℓ_r	$|\mathsf{pk}|$	$|\mathsf{sig}|$
193	1024	2^{20}	$2^{18.99}$	2^{13}	1	2	2.5	9.5
150	1024	2^{25}	$2^{23.73}$	2^{16}	128	2	3.1	11.9
399	2048	2^{22}	$2^{20.77}$	2^{14}	1	2	5.5	20.8
312	2048	2^{27}	$2^{25.50}$	2^{17}	128	2	6.8	25.5

5 Generalised ISIS$_f$

We define a generalised version of the ISIS$_f$ assumption [18] and relate it to the security of the signature scheme Σ_{vSIS} in Sect. 4, therefore also the hinted vSIS assumptions. We provide cryptanalytic discussions around these assumptions.

5.1 ISIS$_f$ and Interactive ISIS$_f$

We first recall the ISIS$_f$ assumption and its interactive variant IntISIS$_f$ defined in [18], both parametrised by some fixed public function $f : [N] \to \mathcal{R}_q^n$.

In the ISIS$_f$ experiment, the adversary receives a random matrix $\mathbf{A}$ over $\mathcal{R}_q$ and polynomially many tuples $(\mathbf{s}_i, \mu_i)$, where $\mu_i \leftarrow_\$ [N]$ and $\mathbf{s}_i$ is a short preimage $\mathbf{A} \cdot \mathbf{s}_i = f(\mu_i) \bmod q$. Its goal is to find a new tuple $(\mathbf{s}^*, \mu^*)$ which satisfies $\mathbf{A}\mathbf{s}^* = f(\mu^*) \bmod q$, where $\mathbf{s}^*$ is short and $\mu^* \in [N]$.

Note that an ISIS$_f$ instance immediately yields a signature scheme which is sEUF-RMA secure. However, instead of building cryptographic primitives directly from the ISIS$_f$ assumption, [18] introduced an intermediate assumption which they call *interactive* ISIS$_f$.

In the interactive ISIS$_f$ experiment, the adversary receives random matrices $\mathbf{A}, \mathbf{C}$ over $\mathcal{R}_q$ and is given access to an oracle which, on the i-th (adaptive) query short vectors $(\mathbf{m}_i, \mathbf{r}_i)$, returns a short preimage $\mathbf{s}_i$ and a value μ_i satisfying

$$\mathbf{A} \cdot \mathbf{s}_i = f(\mu_i) + \mathbf{C} \begin{bmatrix} \mathbf{m}_i \\ \mathbf{r}_i \end{bmatrix} \bmod q, \text{ where } \mu_i \leftarrow_\$ [N]. \text{ Its goal is to find new tuple}$$

$(\mathbf{s}^*, \mu^*, \mathbf{m}^*, \mathbf{r}^*)$ which satisfies $\mathbf{A}\mathbf{s}^* = f(\mu^*) + \mathbf{C} \begin{bmatrix} \mathbf{m}^* \\ \mathbf{r}^* \end{bmatrix} \bmod q$, where $\mathbf{s}^*, \mathbf{m}^*, \mathbf{r}^*$ are short, $\mu^* \in [N]$, and $\mathbf{m}^* \notin \{\mathbf{m}_1, \ldots, \mathbf{m}_Q\}$.

An important step in [18] is to show that the interactive ISIS$_f$ assumption is implied by the (non-interactive) ISIS$_f$ assumption, hence providing a convenient interface for yielding simple constructions of ordinary, group and blind signatures. Furthermore, [18] showed how it can be turned into an efficient anonymous credential system when combined with compatible zero-knowledge proof systems.

5.2 Generalised Assumptions

Recall that the ISIS$_f$ assumption is parametrised by a fixed (deterministic) function f. Below, we generalise the ISIS$_f$ assumption and its interactive variant by

$\mathsf{ExpGenISIS}^{+}_{\mathrm{params},\mathcal{A}}(1^{\lambda})$	$\mathsf{ExpIntGenISIS}_{\mathrm{params},\mathcal{A}}(1^{\lambda})$
$S := \emptyset$	$S := \emptyset$
$\kappa \leftarrow_\$ \mathcal{K};\quad \mathbf{A} \leftarrow_\$ \mathcal{R}_q^{n\times m}$	$\kappa \leftarrow_\$ \mathcal{K};\quad \mathbf{A} \leftarrow_\$ \mathcal{R}_q^{n\times m};\quad \mathbf{C} \leftarrow_\$ \mathcal{R}^{n\times(\ell_{\mathrm{msg}}+\ell_{\mathrm{tag}})}$
$(\mathbf{s}^*,\mu^*,\chi^*) \leftarrow \mathcal{A}^{\mathsf{OPre}}(\kappa,\mathbf{A})$	$(\mathbf{s}^*,\mu^*,\chi^*,\mathbf{m}^*,\mathbf{r}^*) \leftarrow \mathcal{A}^{\mathsf{OSign}}(\kappa,\mathbf{A},\mathbf{C})$
$\mathbf{t}^* := f(\kappa,\mu^*,\chi^*)$	$\mathbf{t}^* = f(\kappa,\mu^*,\chi^*) + \mathbf{C}\begin{bmatrix}\mathbf{m}^*\\\mathbf{r}^*\end{bmatrix}$
$b_0 := (\mathbf{A}\cdot\mathbf{s}^* = \mathbf{t}^* \bmod q)$	$b_0 := (\mathbf{A}\cdot\mathbf{s}^* = \mathbf{t}^* \bmod q)$
$b_1 := (0 < \|\mathbf{s}^*\| \le \beta)$	$b_1 := (0 < \|\mathbf{s}^*\| \le \beta)$
$b_2 := ((\mathbf{s}^*,\mu^*,\chi^*) \notin S)$	$b_2 := ((\mathbf{s}^*,\mu^*,\chi^*,\mathbf{m}^*,\mathbf{r}^*) \notin S)$
$\mathbf{return}\ b_0 \wedge b_1 \wedge b_2$	$b_3 := (\|(\mathbf{m}^*,\mathbf{r}^*)\| \le \gamma)$
	$\mathbf{return}\ b_0 \wedge b_1 \wedge b_2 \wedge b_3$
$\mathsf{OPre}(\mu')$	
$\mathbf{assert}\ |S| < Q$	$\mathsf{OSign}(\mathbf{m},\mathbf{r})$
$\mu \leftarrow_\$ \mathcal{M};\quad \chi \leftarrow_\$ \mathcal{X}$	$\mathbf{assert}\ (\|(\mathbf{m},\mathbf{r})\| \le \gamma) \wedge (|S| < Q)$
$\mu := \mu'\quad /\!\!/\ \text{Overwrite with input}$	$\mu \leftarrow_\$ \mathcal{M};\quad \chi \leftarrow_\$ \mathcal{X}$
$\mathbf{t} = f(\kappa,\mu,\chi)$	$\mathbf{t} = f(\kappa,\mu,\chi) + \mathbf{C}\begin{bmatrix}\mathbf{m}\\\mathbf{r}\end{bmatrix}$
$\mathbf{s} \leftarrow_\$ \mathcal{D}_{\Lambda_q^{\mathbf{t}}(\mathbf{A}),s}$	$\mathbf{s} \leftarrow_\$ \mathcal{D}_{\Lambda_q^{\mathbf{t}}(\mathbf{A}),s}$
$S := S \cup \{(\mathbf{s},\mu,\chi)\}$	$S := S \cup \{(\mathbf{s},\mu,\chi,\mathbf{m},\mathbf{r})\}$
$\mathbf{return}\ (\mathbf{s},\mu,\chi)$	$\mathbf{return}\ (\mathbf{s},\mu,\chi)$

Fig. 5. The GenISIS, GenISIS$^+$ and IntGenISIS experiments.

extending the input space of f as follows: 1) It additionally inputs a function key $\kappa \in \mathcal{K}$ which is sampled from a distribution at the beginning of the security experiment. 2) It additionally inputs a randomness χ chosen from $\mathcal{X}$. We denote the non-interactive and interactive variants of the generalised assumptions GenISIS$_f$ and IntGenISIS$_f$ respectively. Unlike [18], we consider a "strong unforgeability" flavour for IntGenISIS (i.e., the set S contains full "signatures", not just $\mathbf{m}$). Further, in contrast to [18] where the input μ to f in the ISIS$_f$ experiment is always random, we additionally consider an adaptive variant GenISIS^+_f, where the adversary can freely choose μ.

Definition 8 (Generalised ISIS$_f$ Assumptions (GenISIS$_f$)). *Let* $\mathcal{R}, n, m,$ *$\ell_{\mathrm{msg}}, \ell_{\mathrm{tag}}, q, Q, \beta, \gamma, s, f$ be parametrised by λ, where $n, m, \ell_{\mathrm{msg}}, \ell_{\mathrm{tag}}, q$ are positive integers, Q is a non-negative integer, $\beta, \gamma, s \in \mathbb{R}^+$, and $f \colon \mathcal{K} \times \mathcal{M} \times \mathcal{X} \to \mathcal{R}_q^n$ is a function where the domain is efficiently sampleable[13]. Let* $\mathrm{params} = (\mathcal{R}, n, m, q, Q, \beta, s, f)$. *The* GenISIS$_{\mathrm{params}}$ *(resp.* GenISIS$^+_{\mathrm{params}}$*) assumption states that, for any PPT adversary $\mathcal{A}$,*

$$\mathsf{AdvGenISISf}^{\mathrm{params}'}_{\mathcal{A}'}(\lambda) := \Pr\left[\mathsf{ExpGenISIS}_{\mathrm{params},\mathcal{A}}(\lambda) = 1\right] \le \mathsf{negl},$$

$$(resp.\quad \mathsf{AdvGenISISf}^{+,\mathrm{params}'}_{\mathcal{A}'}(\lambda) := \Pr\left[\mathsf{ExpGenISIS}^+_{\mathrm{params},\mathcal{A}}(\lambda) = 1\right] \le \mathsf{negl})$$

---

[13] I.e. there are efficient algorithms for uniformly sampling from $\mathcal{K}, \mathcal{M}, \mathcal{X}$, respectively.

where the experiments are defined in Fig. 5. Similarly, for params $= (\mathcal{R}, n, m,$ $\ell_{\mathrm{msg}}, \ell_{\mathrm{tag}}, q, Q, \beta, \gamma, s, f)$, *the* IntGenISIS$_{\mathrm{params}}$ *assumption states that, for any PPT adversary* $\mathcal{A}$, AdvIntGenISISf$_{\mathcal{A}'}^{\mathrm{params}'}(\lambda):=\Pr\left[\mathrm{ExpIntGenISIS}_{\mathrm{params},\mathcal{A}}(\lambda) = 1\right]$ $\leq$ negl. *When the parameters are clear from the context, we drop most of them and simply write* GenISIS$_f$, GenISIS$_f^+$ *and* IntGenISIS$_f$.

The GenISIS$_f$ and IntGenISIS$_f$ experiments (and hence assumptions) essentially coincide with the ISIS$_f$ and IntISIS$_f$ assumptions from [18] respectively if f is a trivial family of deterministic functions, i.e. if $\mathcal{K} = \mathcal{X} = \{0\}$ are sets with a single element.[14] A minor change is the *"strong unforgeability"* flavour in our definition of IntGenISIS$_f$ where, compared to [18], S contains $(\mathbf{s}, \mu, \chi, \mathbf{m}, \mathbf{r})$ instead of just $\mathbf{m}$.

Theorem 6 (Adapted from [18, Theorem 3.3]). *Let the parameters* params $= (\mathcal{R}, q, n, m, \ell_{\mathrm{msg}}, \ell_{\mathrm{tag}}, s, \beta, \gamma, f)$ *be such that* $\mathcal{R}$ *is a power-of-two cyclotomic ring,* $q/2 > \gamma \geq 1$, $m = n \log q + \omega(\log \lambda)$. *Let* $\epsilon \leq$ negl. *Suppose that* $s \geq \max\left(\eta_{\min}(\epsilon), \sqrt{\lambda}\gamma\varphi\sqrt{(\ell_{\mathrm{msg}} + \ell_{\mathrm{tag}})m}\right)$, *where* $\eta_{\min}(\epsilon)$ *is such that* $\eta_\epsilon(\Lambda_q^\perp(\mathbf{A})) \geq \eta_{\min}(\epsilon)$ *with probability at most* $2^{-\varphi}$ *over the randomness of* $\mathbf{A} \leftarrow_\$ \mathcal{R}_q^{n \times m}$, *and that* $\varphi \in \omega(\log \lambda)$. *Then for every PPT adversary* $\mathcal{A}$ *in* ExpIntGenISIS$_{\mathrm{params},\mathcal{A}}$, *there is a PPT adversary* $\mathcal{A}'$ *in* ExpGenISIS$_{\mathrm{params}',\mathcal{A}'}$ *such that*

$$\mathrm{AdvGenISISf}_{\mathcal{A}'}^{\mathrm{params}'}(\lambda) \geq \mathrm{AdvIntGenISISf}_{\mathcal{A}}^{\mathrm{params}}(\lambda)/\mathrm{poly} - \mathrm{negl}$$

where params$' = \left(\mathcal{R}, q, n, m, \mathrm{poly} \cdot Q, s, \beta' = \beta + \gamma, \varphi\sqrt{(\ell_{\mathrm{msg}} + \ell_{\mathrm{tag}})m}\right)$.

The proof of Theorem 6 is almost identical to that of [18, Theorem 3.3] (despite the *"strong unforgeability"* of IntGenISIS$_f$). We make the following translations:

- (From probabilistic to deterministic f.) The function f in [18] is *deterministic*, i.e. there is no randomness space $\mathcal{X}$. However, since we sample both $\mu \in \mathcal{M}$ and $\chi \in \mathcal{X}$ uniformly (in the non-adaptive setting), we could as well consider $f': \mathcal{K} \times \mathcal{M}' \to \mathcal{R}_q^n$ where $\mathcal{M}' = \mathcal{M} \times \mathcal{X}$. Thus, for the sake of proving Theorem 6, we can w.l.o.g. assume f is deterministic.
- (Function families.) The (deterministic) function f in [18, Theorem 3.3] is used in a completely black-box way. Thus, as long as f is specified and fixed at the beginning of the experiment (so that it can be used in the proof), the proof applies verbatim to any choice (of distributions) of f, in particular any function sampled from a function a function family over $\mathcal{K}$.

For the *"strong unforgeability"* of IntGenISIS$_f$, first suppose (as above) w.l.o.g. that $\mathcal{X} = \{0\}$, so that GenISIS$_f$ coincides with ISIS$_f$ (up to being a function family). Given a forgery $(\mathbf{s}^*, \mu^*, 0, \mathbf{m}^*, \mathbf{r}^*)$, the proof of [18, Theorem 3.3] proceeds through indistinguishable game hops to prepare for the reduction to ISIS$_f$ that

---

[14] The mostly syntactical difference is that we give $\mathcal{A}$ access to a sampling *oracle*, whereas [18] chose to produce Q samples up front and give them to $\mathcal{A}$.

is explained after [18, Lemma 3.12]. There, it is asserted that $(\mathbf{s}^*, \mu^*)$ must be fresh for the adversary to win, which means the reduction wins its ISIS_f instance. This assertion holds even if $(\mathbf{m}^*, \mathbf{r}^*)$ were reused.

Remark 7. We expect that Theorem 6 generalises to any ring $\mathcal{R}$ for which there is a suitable regularity lemma.

5.3   Generalised ISIS and Strong Hinted vSIS

We establish connection between $\mathsf{GenISIS}_f$ and the sEUF-RMA security of the vSIS-based signature scheme Σ_{vSIS} (Fig. 4). In essence, we show that these two are equivalent experiments by simple renaming of variables. Chaining with Theorem 5 yields a reduction from s-\$Hint-vSIS to $\mathsf{GenISIS}_f$. The reverse reduction, provided by Theorem 8, establish the equivalence of s-\$Hint-vSIS and $\mathsf{GenISIS}_f$ for given parameters. Note that it is the parameters of $\mathsf{GenISIS}_f$ that are restricted, as it corresponds to a more general assumption. In particular, the equivalence holds only when the set of functions f consists of ℓ-variate rational functions.

Theorem 7 ($\mathsf{GenISIS}_f \Leftrightarrow$ sEUF-RMA$_{\Sigma_{\mathsf{vSIS}}}$). *Let* $\mathcal{R}, n, m, \ell, q, s, \beta, \delta, \mathcal{M}, \mathcal{X}, \mathcal{H}$ *be parameters of the signature scheme* Σ_{vSIS} *in Fig. 4, in particular* $\mathcal{H} := \{h_{\mu,\chi} \mid \mu \in \mathcal{M}, \chi \in \mathcal{X}\}$ *is a set of ℓ-variate rational functions. Let* $\mathsf{params}_1 := (\mathcal{R}, n, m, q, Q, \beta, s, f)$ *with* $f : \mathcal{R}_q^{n \times \ell} \times \mathcal{M} \times \mathcal{X} \to \mathcal{R}_q^n$ *such that* $f(\mathbf{B}, \mu, \chi) = h_{\mu,\chi}(\mathbf{B})$ *for any* $\mathbf{B} \in \mathcal{R}_q^{n \times \ell}$, *and* $Q \leq \mathsf{poly}$. *Suppose* $(\mathcal{R}, n, m, q, s)$ *are admissible parameters for* (TrapGen, SampPre). *There is a PPT adversary* $\mathcal{B}$ *winning the* $\mathsf{ExpGenISIS}_{\mathsf{params}_1, \mathcal{B}}$ *experiment with non-negligible probability if and only if there is a PPT adversary* $\mathcal{A}$ *winning the* sEUF-RMA$_{\Sigma_{\mathsf{vSIS}}, \mathcal{A}, Q}$ *experiment with non-negligible probability.*

Theorem 8 ($\mathsf{GenISIS}_f \Rightarrow$ s-\$Hint-vSIS). *Let* $\mathsf{params}_1 := (\mathcal{R}, n, m, q, Q, \beta, s, f)$, $\mathcal{H} := \{h_{\mu,\chi} \mid \mu \in \mathcal{M}, \chi \in \mathcal{X}\}$ *a set of ℓ-variate rational function,* $\mathcal{G} := \mathcal{H} \cup \{0\}$, *and* $\mathcal{P}$ *a predicate on sets of rational functions with* $f : \mathcal{R}_q^{n \times \ell} \times \mathcal{M} \times \mathcal{X} \to \mathcal{R}_q^n$ *such that* $f(\mathbf{B}, \mu, \chi) = h_{\mu,\chi}(\mathbf{B})$. *Let* $\mathsf{params}_0 := (\mathcal{R}, n, k, q, Q, \beta, s, \mathcal{F}, \mathcal{G}, \mathcal{H}, \mathcal{P})$, *where* $k = m + \ell$ *and* $\mathcal{F}$ *is such that for formal variables* $(\tilde{\mathbf{a}}^\mathsf{T}, \tilde{\mathbf{b}}^\mathsf{T})$ *of dimension k,* $\mathcal{F}(\tilde{\mathbf{a}}^\mathsf{T}, \tilde{\mathbf{b}}^\mathsf{T}) = \tilde{\mathbf{a}}^\mathsf{T}$. *Suppose also that for all* $\mathcal{Q} \subseteq \mathcal{H}$, *all* $g^* \in \mathcal{G} \setminus \mathcal{Q}$, *it holds* $\mathcal{P}(\mathcal{F} \cup \mathcal{Q} \cup (\{g^*\} \setminus \{0\})) = 1$. *If the* $\mathsf{GenISIS}_{\mathsf{params}_1}$ *assumption holds, then the* s-\$Hint-vSIS$_{\mathsf{params}_0}$ *assumption holds.*

The proofs of Theorems 7 and 8 are deferred to the full version. Applying Theorems 5 and 7, we have the following immediate corollary.

Corollary 1 (s-\$Hint-vSIS $\Rightarrow \mathsf{GenISIS}_f$). *Let* $\mathsf{params}_0 = (\mathcal{R}, n, k, q, \beta, \mathcal{F}, \mathcal{G}, \mathcal{H}, \mathcal{P}, Q)$ *and* $m, \ell, s, \delta, \delta', \mathcal{M}, \mathcal{X}$ *be such that the constraints in Theorem 5 are satisfied. Let* $\mathsf{params}_1 := (\mathcal{R}, n, m, Q, q, \beta, s, f)$ *with* $f : \mathcal{R}_q^{n \times \ell} \times \mathcal{M} \times \mathcal{X} \to \mathcal{R}_q^n$ *such that* $f(\mathbf{B}, \mu, \chi) = h_{\mu,\chi}(\mathbf{B})$ *for any* $\mathbf{B} \in \mathcal{R}_q^{n \times \ell}$. *If the* s-\$Hint-vSIS$_{\mathsf{params}_0}$ *assumption holds for every polynomial* $Q(\lambda)$, *then so does the* $\mathsf{GenISIS}_{\mathsf{params}_1}$ *assumption.*

5.4   Robustness and Linear Combination Attacks Against (Gen)ISISf

We study the robustness of (generalised) ISIS_f assumptions, in particular in relation to a natural attack that was also discussed in [18] for the special case where the function f was binary decomposition.[15] We extend this discussion to our setting, and connect it to the (strong) hinted vSIS assumption (Definition 5). For simplicity, we omit the function key κ for f and the randomness $\mathcal{X}$ in the first discussion, and consider a fixed $f\colon \mathcal{M} \to \mathcal{R}_q^n$ as in the original ISIS_f assumption.

Preimage Resistance. A necessary requirement on $f\colon \mathcal{M} \to \mathcal{R}_q^n$ is that it is hard to invert on random elements in the codomain. Otherwise, the hash-then-sign paradigm is clearly broken, and $\mu^* = f^{-1}(\mathbf{A}\mathbf{s}^*)$ for a random short $\mathbf{s}^*$ breaks the assumption. Note here that "hard-to-invert" can be statistically satisfied, if $|\mathcal{M}| / |\mathcal{R}_q|^n$ is negligible. For example, this is the case in [18] and our BB-lite instantiation. Examples for computational hardness include the non-BB-lite instantiations in Table 1, and f being a collision-resistant hash or random oracle.

Linear Combination Attacks (LCA). The attack idea of an LCA is quite simple: Given tuples $(\mathbf{s}_i, \mu_i)$ with $\mathbf{A}\mathbf{s}_i = f(\mu_i)$, somehow compute short coefficients c_i together with μ^* such that

$$\sum_i c_i f(\mu_i) = f(\mu^*) \tag{1}$$

holds. Then, for $\mathbf{s}^* = \sum_i c_i \mathbf{s}_i$, we get

$$\mathbf{A}\mathbf{s}^* = \sum_i c_i \mathbf{A}\mathbf{s}_i = \sum_i c_i f(\mu_i) = f(\mu^*). \tag{2}$$

Intuitively, the attack exploits (approximate) linearity of f, or rather, within the image $\mathrm{im}(f)$. For example, in [18], the binary decomposition function $f\colon [N] \to \mathcal{R}_q^n$ appears to be highly non-linear at first glance. However, the required linearity for the attack is present in the image $\mathrm{im}(f) = \mathcal{R}_2^n \subseteq \mathcal{R}_q^n$. Indeed, since f is far from one-way over its image, for the purpose of analysing LCA against f, we can equivalently replace f by $g\colon \mathcal{R}_2^n \to \mathcal{R}_q^n$, where g is simply the identity embedding.

LCAs Against Binary Decomposition. We first discuss how and why linear combination attacks do (not) break the ISIS_f assumption, when instantiated with $f(x) = \mathsf{bindecomp}(x) \in \mathcal{R}_2^n$ as in [18]. As noted earlier, we consider $g\colon \mathcal{R}_2^n \to \mathcal{R}_q^n$ where $g(\mathbf{m}) = \mathbf{m}$ and $\mathcal{M} = \mathcal{R}_2^n$, instead of the function f.

The presumed security of $g\colon \mathcal{R}_2^n \to \mathcal{R}_q^n$ against linear combination attacks crucially relies on two properties. On the one hand, the domain $\mathcal{R}_2^n \subseteq \mathcal{R}_q^n$ should

---

[15] More precisely, in [18], f is a function which first binary decomposes the input, linear-maps it to the domain of the coefficient embedding, then outputs the corresponding ring vector.

be high dimensional. This makes it unlikely that for two random $\mathbf{m}_1, \mathbf{m}_2 \in \mathcal{R}_2^n$, their sum or difference $\pm \mathbf{m}_1 \pm \mathbf{m}_2$ is again in $\mathcal{R}_2^n$, i.e. again a bitstring; indeed, the probability is precisely $2 \cdot (3/4)^{\varphi n} - 2^{-\varphi n}$ as is easily checked.[16] Hence, we can hope that finding a *sufficiently short* linear combination of $\mathbf{m}_i = f(\mu_i)$ with

$$\sum_i c_i \mathbf{m}_i = \mathbf{m}^* \in \mathcal{R}_2^n$$

for any choice of $\mathbf{m}^*$ remains difficult, given sufficiently high dimensions (at the very least $\varphi n \geq \lambda / \log_2(4/3) \approx 2.41\lambda$). Moreover, one should account for attacks which use integer linear programming (ILP) to tackle similar problems [17,32], see [18, Section 3.1.2]. On the other hand, the dimension φm of preimages should be high and the norm bound β very strict, so that even if we have two ISIS_f pairs $(\mathbf{s}_1, \mathbf{m}_1), (\mathbf{s}_2, \mathbf{m}_2)$ where $\mathbf{m}_1 \pm \mathbf{m}_2$ is again binary, we get $\|\mathbf{s}_1 \pm \mathbf{s}_2\| > \beta$ almost certainly. To thwart the attacks, [18] exploits the high dimension φm and sets the bound β close to $\sqrt{\varphi m}s$.

Limited Robustness of Binary Decomposition. To investigate the security-efficiency tradeoff, we strengthen the $\mathsf{GenISIS}_f$ assumption slightly: (1) we consider *selective* $\mathsf{GenISIS}_f^+$ where the adversary chooses $(\mu_1', \ldots, \mu_Q')$, receives $\mathsf{OPre}(\mu_i')$ for $i \in [1, \ldots, Q]$, and has no further access to OPre; (2) we allow a relaxed norm bound, namely $\sqrt{2}\beta$ instead of β, for forgeries. While this seems like a mild strengthening, security completely breaks down for $f = \mathsf{bindecomp}$, even with a single selective query: By selectively querying a standard unit vector $\mathbf{e}$ (in coefficient embedding), say $\mathbf{e}_1 = (1, 0, \ldots) \in \{0, 1\}^{\varphi n}$ (or even $\mathbf{0}$), and one (random) query $\mathbf{m}_1$, the naive linear combination $\mathbf{e}_1 + \mathbf{m}_1$ breaks with probability $1/2$. Of course, this attack generalises: Any $\mathbf{e}$ of low Hamming weight is beneficial for linear combination attacks, and success can be amplified by trying many $\mathbf{m}_i$'s. The above total break with just a single selective query suggests, that one should consider other (presumably) more robust functions f, which perhaps allows a better security-efficiency tradeoff and gives higher confidence in the hardness of the problem.

LCA Against Candidate Rational Functions. We elaborate on why we believe our candidate instantiations of $\mathsf{GenISIS}_f$ (cf. Section 4.2) offer better security than the binary decomposition function. First, by Theorem 8, to break $\mathsf{GenISIS}_f$ it suffices to break the corresponding s-$Hint-vSIS assumption. For concreteness, we focus on the function $h_{\mu, \chi}(\tilde{b}_0, \tilde{b}_1) = \frac{\tilde{b}_0 - \mu}{\tilde{b}_1 - \chi}$ which captures all important structures of the examples in Table 1. For simplicity, we consider module rank $n = 1$.

To begin, we observe that, for $\beta_\mu \geq \sqrt{q}$, the distribution $1/\mu \pmod{q}$ of inverses of short elements $\mu \leftarrow \mathcal{M} = \{|\mu| \leq \beta_\mu \mid \mu \in \mathbb{Z}\}$ is "close to uniformly" [48] for some non-cryptographic measure of closeness. Nevertheless,

---

[16] We just need to count strings which are pointwise $\leq$ or $\geq$. Perhaps surprisingly, for $\varphi n = 256$, this happens with probability roughly $2^{-105.25} \gg 2^{-128}$.

let us adopt the heuristic that $(b_0 - \mu)/(b_1 - \chi) \bmod q$ for short (μ, χ) is "uniformly random enough" for the purpose of attaining SIS hardness. Given many short samples $(\mathbf{s}_i, \mu_i, \chi_i)$ satisfying $\langle \mathbf{a}, \mathbf{s}_i \rangle = (b_0 - \mu_i)/(b_1 - \chi_i) \bmod q$, there are two natural strategies to find a new short solution $(\mathbf{s}^*, \mu^*, \chi^*)$.

The first is to ignore the hints and attempt to solve the problem directly. Towards this, an idea is to sample a random short $\mathbf{s}^*$, compute $t^* := \langle \mathbf{a}, \mathbf{s}^* \rangle \bmod q$, and try to find (μ^*, χ^*) such that $h_{\mu^*, \chi^*}(b_0, b_1) = t^* \bmod q$. In our example, this means solving $t^* \chi^* - \mu^* = t^* b_1 - b_0 \bmod q$ for a short solution (μ^*, χ^*). However, if we sampled $\mathbf{s}^*$ from a sufficiently entropic distribution, then t^* would be close to uniformly random, and thus we essentially need to solve a random ISIS instance.

Another strategy is to somehow make use of the hints. The idea is essentially that of the LCA – to find a short linear combination of $h_{\mu_i, \chi_i}(b_0, b_1)$ which yields $h_{\mu^*, \chi^*}(b_0, b_1)$ for some (μ^*, χ^*). As before, if we pick the linear combination blindly and then attempt to solve the equation for (μ^*, χ^*), then we will face an ISIS instance. Since $h_{\mu_1, \chi_1}, \ldots, h_{\mu_Q, \chi_Q}, h_{\mu^*, \chi^*}$ are strongly linearly independent, choosing the linear combination without taking (b_0, b_1) into account is unlikely to succeed. We are thus left with the option of picking the short linear combination by somehow exploiting our knowledge on (b_0, b_1), which appears difficult.

We remark that the difficulty of the above attacks crucially rely on the restriction that μ, χ are short. Indeed, if the shortness condition is dropped, then there are simple attacks by simple arithmetic. Also note that all attack strategies discussed are non-adaptive. At present, we are unaware of meaningful ways to exploit adaptivity. This holds true even when additionally considering a relaxed norm bound $\beta' \gg \beta$ on forgeries. As long as the related problems (such as SIS, inverting f) remain hard, we do not know how to exploit a norm check for $\beta' \gg \beta$, even if β' is much larger than the expected norm $\sqrt{\varphi m} s$ of preimages $\mathbf{s}$ which are obtained by an (adaptive) OPre. Intuitively, the non-linearity of f obstructs the LCA attack, which is the only way we know how to take advantage of the short preimages $\mathbf{s}$ to obtain a slightly longer preimage (e.g. as for $f = \mathsf{bindecomp}$).

To summarise: The $\mathsf{GenISIS}_f^{(+)}$ assumption(s) for our families f seems quite robust, but better cryptanalysis is crucial to gauge its hardness and robustness.

$\mathsf{GenISIS}_f$ vs. One-More ISIS. The one-more ISIS (OM-ISIS) assumption was introduced in [2] for building lattice-based blind signatures. There, an adversary is given a *preimage oracle* $\mathsf{O}_{\mathsf{Pre}}$ which produces preimages of images *freely chosen* by the adversary. It also has oracle access to (an arbitrary number of) random challenge vectors (that is, ISIS syndromes). To win the game, the adversary must produce preimages of $\ell + 1$ challenge vectors, if it has made ℓ queries to $\mathsf{O}_{\mathsf{Pre}}$.

OM-ISIS does not seem directly comparable to any variant (generalised, adaptive, interactive, etc.) of $(\mathsf{Gen})\mathsf{ISIS}_f$. We focus our discussion on $\mathsf{GenISIS}_f$. For OM-ISIS, the images for which $\mathsf{O}_{\mathsf{Pre}}$ provides preimages are chosen freely, but the challenge images are truly random. For $\mathsf{GenISIS}_f$, the preimages are for random images $y = f(\kappa, \mu, \chi)$ and there is no specified challenge, i.e. the adversary chooses freely (μ^*, χ^*). Interestingly, the selective and adaptive variants of $\mathsf{GenISIS}_f^+$ are closer to OM-ISIS because O_{Pre} now works on adversarial inputs, but the choice is still not free as the inputs are "hashed" by f.

As a qualitative difference, we note that in OM-ISIS it is possible to learn a trapdoor of $\mathbf{A}$, e.g. by requesting sufficiently many preimages of $\mathbf{0}$. Under a relaxed norm check $\beta' > \beta$, the above implies that β' cannot be too large, e.g. OM-ISIS with $\beta' > \sqrt{m} \cdot \sqrt{\varphi m}s$ is broken, cf. [2]. Thus, similar to ISIS_f, there is a close tie between admissible $\beta' > \beta$ and the expected norm $\sqrt{\varphi m}s$ of the sampled preimages. In contrast, for (adaptive) $\mathsf{GenISIS}_f$, we are not aware of how to obtain a short basis, or even take advantage of relaxed norm checks.

Overall, we can hope that our $\mathsf{GenISIS}$ assumptions are as secure (or more so) than OM-ISIS, while leading to smaller round-optimal blind signatures than [2].

Acknowledgement. The research of Russell W. F. Lai and Ivy K. Y. Woo are supported by Research Council of Finland grants 358951 and 358950 respectively.

References

1. Agrawal, S., Boneh, D., Boyen, X.: Lattice basis delegation in fixed dimension and shorter-ciphertext hierarchical IBE. In: Rabin, T. (ed.) CRYPTO 2010. LNCS, vol. 6223, pp. 98–115. Springer, Berlin, Heidelberg (2010). https://doi.org/10.1007/978-3-642-14623-7_6

2. Agrawal, S., Kirshanova, E., Stehlé, D., Yadav, A.: Practical, round-optimal lattice-based blind signatures. In: Yin, H., Stavrou, A., Cremers, C., Shi, E. (eds.) ACM CCS 2022, pp. 39–53. ACM Press (2022). https://doi.org/10.1145/3548606.3560650

3. Albrecht, M.R., Cini, V., Lai, R.W.F., Malavolta, G., Thyagarajan, S.A.K.: Lattice-based SNARKs: Publicly verifiable, preprocessing, and recursively composable - (extended abstract). In: Dodis, Y., Shrimpton, T. (eds.) CRYPTO 2022, Part II. LNCS, vol. 13508, pp. 102–132. Springer, Cham (2022). https://doi.org/10.1007/978-3-031-15979-4_4

4. Albrecht, M.R., Player, R., Scott, S.: On the concrete hardness of learning with errors. J. Math. Cryptology **9**(3), 169–203 (2015). https://doi.org/10.1515/jmc-2015-0016

5. Alkeilani Alkadri, N., El Bansarkhani, R., Buchmann, J.: BLAZE: practical lattice-based blind signatures for privacy-preserving applications. In: Bonneau, J., Heninger, N. (eds.) FC 2020. LNCS, vol. 12059, pp. 484–502. Springer, Cham (2020). https://doi.org/10.1007/978-3-030-51280-4_26

6. Alkeilani Alkadri, N., El Bansarkhani, R., Buchmann, J.: On lattice-based interactive protocols: An approach with less or no aborts. In: Liu, J.K., Cui, H. (eds.) ACISP 20. LNCS, vol. 12248, pp. 41–61. Springer, Cham (2020). https://doi.org/10.1007/978-3-030-55304-3_3

7. Alkeilani Alkadri, N., Harasser, P., Janson, C.: BlindOR: an efficient lattice-based blind signature scheme from OR-proofs. In: Conti, M., Stevens, M., Krenn, S. (eds.) CANS 21. LNCS, vol. 13099, pp. 95–115. Springer, Cham (2021). https://doi.org/10.1007/978-3-030-92548-2_6

8. Au, M.H., Susilo, W., Mu, Y.: Constant-size dynamic k-TAA. In: De Prisco, R., Yung, M. (eds.) SCN 06. LNCS, vol. 4116, pp. 111–125. Springer, Berlin, Heidelberg (2006). https://doi.org/10.1007/11832072_8

9. Banaszczyk, W.: New bounds in some transference theorems in the geometry of numbers. Math. Ann. **296**, 625–635 (1993)

10. Benhamouda, F., Lepoint, T., Loss, J., Orrù, M., Raykova, M.: On the (in)security of ROS. In: Canteaut, A., Standaert, F.X. (eds.) EUROCRYPT 2021, Part I. LNCS, vol. 12696, pp. 33–53. Springer, Cham (2021). https://doi.org/10.1007/978-3-030-77870-5_2

11. Benhamouda, F., Lepoint, T., Loss, J., Orrù, M., Raykova, M.: On the (in)security of ROS. J. Cryptol. **35**(4), 25 (2022). https://doi.org/10.1007/s00145-022-09436-0

12. Beullens, W., Dobson, S., Katsumata, S., Lai, Y.F., Pintore, F.: Group signatures and more from isogenies and lattices: generic, simple, and efficient. In: Dunkelman, O., Dziembowski, S. (eds.) EUROCRYPT 2022, Part II. LNCS, vol. 13276, pp. 95–126. Springer, Cham (2022). https://doi.org/10.1007/978-3-031-07085-3_4

13. Beullens, W., Lyubashevsky, V., Nguyen, N.K., Seiler, G.: Lattice-based blind signatures: short, efficient, and round-optimal. In: Meng, W., Jensen, C.D., Cremers, C., Kirda, E. (eds.) ACM CCS 2023, pp. 16–29. ACM Press (2023). https://doi.org/10.1145/3576915.3616613

14. Blömer, J., Bobolz, J., Porzenheim, L.: A generic construction of an anonymous reputation system and instantiations from lattices. In: Guo, J., Steinfeld, R. (eds.) ASIACRYPT 2023, Part II. LNCS, vol. 14439, pp. 418–452. Springer, Singapore (2023). https://doi.org/10.1007/978-981-99-8724-5_13

15. Boneh, D., Boyen, X.: Short signatures without random oracles and the SDH assumption in bilinear groups. J. Cryptol. **21**(2), 149–177 (2007). https://doi.org/10.1007/s00145-007-9005-7

16. Boneh, D., Boyen, X., Shacham, H.: Short group signatures. In: Franklin, M. (ed.) CRYPTO 2004. LNCS, vol. 3152, pp. 41–55. Springer, Berlin, Heidelberg (2004). https://doi.org/10.1007/978-3-540-28628-8_3

17. Bootle, J., Delaplace, C., Espitau, T., Fouque, P.A., Tibouchi, M.: LWE without modular reduction and improved side-channel attacks against BLISS. In: Peyrin, T., Galbraith, S. (eds.) ASIACRYPT 2018, Part I. LNCS, vol. 11272, pp. 494–524. Springer, Cham (2018). https://doi.org/10.1007/978-3-030-03326-2_17

18. Bootle, J., Lyubashevsky, V., Nguyen, N.K., Sorniotti, A.: A framework for practical anonymous credentials from lattices. In: Handschuh, H., Lysyanskaya, A. (eds.) CRYPTO 2023, Part II. LNCS, vol. 14082, pp. 384–417. Springer, Cham (2023). https://doi.org/10.1007/978-3-031-38545-2_13

19. Bootle, J., Lyubashevsky, V., Seiler, G.: Algebraic techniques for short(er) exact lattice-based zero-knowledge proofs. In: Boldyreva, A., Micciancio, D. (eds.) CRYPTO 2019, Part I. LNCS, vol. 11692, pp. 176–202. Springer, Cham (2019). https://doi.org/10.1007/978-3-030-26948-7_7

20. Boschini, C., Camenisch, J., Neven, G.: Floppy-sized group signatures from lattices. In: Preneel, B., Vercauteren, F. (eds.) ACNS 18International Conference on Applied Cryptography and Network Security. LNCS, vol. 10892, pp. 163–182. Springer, Cham (2018). https://doi.org/10.1007/978-3-319-93387-0_9

21. Camenisch, J., Lysyanskaya, A.: A signature scheme with efficient protocols. In: Cimato, S., Galdi, C., Persiano, G. (eds.) SCN 02. LNCS, vol. 2576, pp. 268–289. Springer, Berlin, Heidelberg (2003). https://doi.org/10.1007/3-540-36413-7_20

22. Camenisch, J., Lysyanskaya, A.: Signature schemes and anonymous credentials from bilinear maps. In: Franklin, M. (ed.) CRYPTO 2004. LNCS, vol. 3152, pp. 56–72. Springer, Berlin, Heidelberg (2004). https://doi.org/10.1007/978-3-540-28628-8_4

23. Chator, A., Green, M., Tiwari, P.R.: SoK: Privacy-preserving signatures. Cryptology ePrint Archive, Report 2023/1039 (2023). https://eprint.iacr.org/2023/1039

24. Cini, V., Lai, R.W.F., Malavolta, G.: Lattice-based succinct arguments from vanishing polynomials - (extended abstract). In: Handschuh, H., Lysyanskaya, A. (eds.) CRYPTO 2023, Part II. LNCS, vol. 14082, pp. 72–105. Springer, Cham (2023). https://doi.org/10.1007/978-3-031-38545-2_3

25. Ducas, L., Lyubashevsky, V., Prest, T.: Efficient identity-based encryption over NTRU lattices. In: Sarkar, P., Iwata, T. (eds.) ASIACRYPT 2014, Part II. LNCS, vol. 8874, pp. 22–41. Springer, Berlin, Heidelberg (2014). https://doi.org/10.1007/978-3-662-45608-8_2

26. Ducas, L., Micciancio, D.: Improved short lattice signatures in the standard model. In: Garay, J.A., Gennaro, R. (eds.) CRYPTO 2014, Part I. LNCS, vol. 8616, pp. 335–352. Springer, Berlin, Heidelberg (2014). https://doi.org/10.1007/978-3-662-44371-2_19

27. Fischlin, M.: Round-optimal composable blind signatures in the common reference string model. In: Dwork, C. (ed.) CRYPTO 2006. LNCS, vol. 4117, pp. 60–77. Springer, Berlin, Heidelberg (2006). https://doi.org/10.1007/11818175_4

28. Gentry, C., Peikert, C., Vaikuntanathan, V.: Trapdoors for hard lattices and new cryptographic constructions. In: Ladner, R.E., Dwork, C. (eds.) 40th ACM STOC, pp. 197–206. ACM Press (2008). https://doi.org/10.1145/1374376.1374407

29. Gordon, S.D., Katz, J., Vaikuntanathan, V.: A group signature scheme from lattice assumptions. In: Abe, M. (ed.) ASIACRYPT 2010. LNCS, vol. 6477, pp. 395–412. Springer, Berlin, Heidelberg (2010). https://doi.org/10.1007/978-3-642-17373-8_23

30. Groth, J., Sahai, A.: Efficient non-interactive proof systems for bilinear groups. In: Smart, N.P. (ed.) EUROCRYPT 2008. LNCS, vol. 4965, pp. 415–432. Springer, Berlin, Heidelberg (2008). https://doi.org/10.1007/978-3-540-78967-3_24

31. Hauck, E., Kiltz, E., Loss, J., Nguyen, N.K.: Lattice-based blind signatures, revisited. In: Micciancio, D., Ristenpart, T. (eds.) CRYPTO 2020, Part II. LNCS, vol. 12171, pp. 500–529. Springer, Cham (2020). https://doi.org/10.1007/978-3-030-56880-1_18

32. Herold, G., May, A.: LP solutions of vectorial integer subset sums — cryptanalysis of Galbraith's binary matrix LWE. In: Fehr, S. (ed.) PKC 2017, Part I. LNCS, vol. 10174, pp. 3–15. Springer, Berlin, Heidelberg (2017). https://doi.org/10.1007/978-3-662-54365-8_1

33. Jeudy, C., Roux-Langlois, A., Sanders, O.: Lattice signature with efficient protocols, application to anonymous credentials. In: Handschuh, H., Lysyanskaya, A. (eds.) CRYPTO 2023, Part II. LNCS, vol. 14082, pp. 351–383. Springer, Cham (2023). https://doi.org/10.1007/978-3-031-38545-2_12

34. Katsumata, S., Lai, Y.F., Reichle, M.: Breaking parallel ROS: implication for isogeny and lattice-based blind signatures. In: Tang, Q., Teague, V. (eds.) PKC 2024, Part I. LNCS, vol. 14601, pp. 319–351. Springer, Cham (2024). https://doi.org/10.1007/978-3-031-57718-5_11

35. Laguillaumie, F., Langlois, A., Libert, B., Stehlé, D.: Lattice-based group signatures with logarithmic signature size. In: Sako, K., Sarkar, P. (eds.) ASIACRYPT 2013, Part II. LNCS, vol. 8270, pp. 41–61. Springer, Berlin, Heidelberg (2013). https://doi.org/10.1007/978-3-642-42045-0_3

36. Libert, B., Ling, S., Mouhartem, F., Nguyen, K., Wang, H.: Signature schemes with efficient protocols and dynamic group signatures from lattice assumptions. In: Cheon, J.H., Takagi, T. (eds.) ASIACRYPT 2016, Part II. LNCS, vol. 10032, pp. 373–403. Springer, Berlin, Heidelberg (2016). https://doi.org/10.1007/978-3-662-53890-6_13

37. Libert, B., Ling, S., Nguyen, K., Wang, H.: Zero-knowledge arguments for lattice-based accumulators: Logarithmic-size ring signatures and group signatures without trapdoors. In: Fischlin, M., Coron, J.S. (eds.) EUROCRYPT 2016, Part II. LNCS, vol. 9666, pp. 1–31. Springer, Berlin, Heidelberg (2016). https://doi.org/10.1007/978-3-662-49896-5_1

38. Lyubashevsky, V.: Lattice signatures without trapdoors. In: Pointcheval, D., Johansson, T. (eds.) EUROCRYPT 2012. LNCS, vol. 7237, pp. 738–755. Springer, Berlin, Heidelberg (2012). https://doi.org/10.1007/978-3-642-29011-4_43

39. Lyubashevsky, V., et al.: CRYSTALS-DILITHIUM. Tech. rep., National Institute of Standards and Technology (2022). https://csrc.nist.gov/Projects/post-quantum-cryptography/selected-algorithms-2022

40. Lyubashevsky, V., Nguyen, N.K., Plançon, M.: Efficient lattice-based blind signatures via gaussian one-time signatures. In: Hanaoka, G., Shikata, J., Watanabe, Y. (eds.) PKC 2022, Part II. LNCS, vol. 13178, pp. 498–527. Springer, Cham (2022). https://doi.org/10.1007/978-3-030-97131-1_17

41. Lyubashevsky, V., Nguyen, N.K., Plançon, M.: Lattice-based zero-knowledge proofs and applications: shorter, simpler, and more general. In: Dodis, Y., Shrimpton, T. (eds.) CRYPTO 2022, Part II. LNCS, vol. 13508, pp. 71–101. Springer, Cham (2022). https://doi.org/10.1007/978-3-031-15979-4_3

42. Lyubashevsky, V., Nguyen, N.K., Plançon, M., Seiler, G.: Shorter lattice-based group signatures via "almost free" encryption and other optimizations. In: Tibouchi, M., Wang, H. (eds.) ASIACRYPT 2021, Part IV. LNCS, vol. 13093, pp. 218–248. Springer, Cham (2021). https://doi.org/10.1007/978-3-030-92068-5_8

43. Micciancio, D., Peikert, C.: Trapdoors for lattices: simpler, tighter, faster, smaller. In: Pointcheval, D., Johansson, T. (eds.) EUROCRYPT 2012. LNCS, vol. 7237, pp. 700–718. Springer, Berlin, Heidelberg (2012). https://doi.org/10.1007/978-3-642-29011-4_41

44. del Pino, R., Katsumata, S.: A new framework for more efficient round-optimal lattice-based (partially) blind signature via trapdoor sampling. In: Dodis, Y., Shrimpton, T. (eds.) CRYPTO 2022, Part II. LNCS, vol. 13508, pp. 306–336. Springer, Cham (2022). https://doi.org/10.1007/978-3-031-15979-4_11

45. del Pino, R., Lyubashevsky, V., Seiler, G.: Lattice-based group signatures and zero-knowledge proofs of automorphism stability. In: Lie, D., Mannan, M., Backes, M., Wang, X. (eds.) ACM CCS 2018, pp. 574–591. ACM Press (2018). https://doi.org/10.1145/3243734.3243852

46. Prest, T., et al.: FALCON. Tech. rep., National Institute of Standards and Technology (2022). https://csrc.nist.gov/Projects/post-quantum-cryptography/selected-algorithms-2022

47. Rückert, M.: Lattice-based blind signatures. In: Abe, M. (ed.) ASIACRYPT 2010. LNCS, vol. 6477, pp. 413–430. Springer, Berlin, Heidelberg (2010). https://doi.org/10.1007/978-3-642-17373-8_24

48. Shparlinski, I.E.: Modular hyperbolas. Japan. J. Math. **7**(2), 235–294 (2012)

49. Stehlé, D., Steinfeld, R., Tanaka, K., Xagawa, K.: Efficient public key encryption based on ideal lattices. In: Matsui, M. (ed.) ASIACRYPT 2009. LNCS, vol. 5912, pp. 617–635. Springer, Berlin, Heidelberg (2009). https://doi.org/10.1007/978-3-642-10366-7_36

50. Tessaro, S., Zhu, C.: Revisiting BBS signatures. In: Hazay, C., Stam, M. (eds.) EUROCRYPT 2023, Part V. LNCS, vol. 14008, pp. 691–721. Springer, Cham (2023). https://doi.org/10.1007/978-3-031-30589-4_24

51. Wee, H.: Optimal broadcast encryption and CP-ABE from evasive lattice assumptions. In: Dunkelman, O., Dziembowski, S. (eds.) EUROCRYPT 2022, Part II. LNCS, vol. 13276, pp. 217–241. Springer, Cham (2022). https://doi.org/10.1007/978-3-031-07085-3_8

52. Wee, H., Wu, D.J.: Succinct vector, polynomial, and functional commitments from lattices. In: Hazay, C., Stam, M. (eds.) EUROCRYPT 2023, Part III. LNCS, vol. 14006, pp. 385–416. Springer, Cham (2023). https://doi.org/10.1007/978-3-031-30620-4_13

53. Yang, R., Au, M.H., Zhang, Z., Xu, Q., Yu, Z., Whyte, W.: Efficient lattice-based zero-knowledge arguments with standard soundness: construction and applications. In: Boldyreva, A., Micciancio, D. (eds.) CRYPTO 2019, Part I. LNCS, vol. 11692, pp. 147–175. Springer, Cham (2019). https://doi.org/10.1007/978-3-030-26948-7_6

Author Index

© International Association for Cryptologic Research 2025
T. Jager and J. Pan (Eds.): PKC 2025, LNCS 15674, pp. 487–488, 2025.
https://doi.org/10.1007/978-3-031-91820-9

The manufacturer's authorised representative in the EU is Springer
Nature Customer Service Centre GmbH, Europaplatz 3, 69115 Heidelberg,
Germany. If you have any concerns regarding our products, please
contact ProductSafety@springernature.com

Printed and bound by CPI Group (UK) Ltd, Croydon, CR0 4YY

28/04/2026
02098518-0010